MANUFACTURING POLICY

A Casebook of Major Production Problems in Six Selected Industries

By STANLEY S. MILLER, D.C.S.
Associate Professor

and DAVID C. D. ROGERS, D.B.A.
Assistant Professor

From Basic Material Developed by
JOHN G. McLEAN, D.C.S.
Formerly Professor

With Principal Contributions by
ROBERT WM. HAIGH, D.C.S.
Formerly Assistant Professor

RICHARD S. ROSENBLOOM, D.B.A.
Assistant Professor

and CURTIS H. JONES, D.B.A.
Assistant Professor

ALL OF THE GRADUATE SCHOOL OF BUSINESS ADMINISTRATION
HARVARD UNIVERSITY

Revised Edition · 1964
RICHARD D. IRWIN, INC.
Homewood, Illinois

Revised Edition

First Printing, January, 1964

Library of Congress Catalogue Card No. 63–14229

PRINTED IN THE UNITED STATES OF AMERICA

Preface

The industry approach to manufacturing policy, which forms the basis of this book, was conceived and developed by John G. McLean, formerly Professor of Business Administration at the Harvard Business School and now Vice President of the Continental Oil Company. Professor McLean presented the approach in 1948 in his doctoral thesis, "The Development of Teaching Methods and Materials for a Course in Manufacturing Policy." He started teaching the course in 1947 as an elective in the second year of the two-year graduate program leading to the degree of Master of Business Administration.

Until Professor McLean's departure for business in 1954, he was responsible for the continued development of the course material, with Professor A. Zaleznik, who collaborated in the research and teaching from 1949–52. During the period 1947 to 1954 the framework of the background industry data was established and the first new group of cases was researched and tested in the classroom. During the later part of this period, John McLean and Robert Wm. Haigh undertook the extended research for their study, "The Growth of Integrated Oil Companies," which was the source of the Wood River case, the Ohio Oil (A) and (B) cases, and some of the oil reference exhibits. From 1954 Robert Wm. Haigh taught the course until 1956 when he left to become vice president of Helmerich and Payne and later of the Standard Oil Company of Ohio. Stanley Miller has been involved with the course since 1954, and David Rogers since 1962, with James R. Bright and Richard S. Rosenbloom teaching during the 1957–59 period.

Thus, the material in this book represents fifteen years of discussion in the classroom with several thousand students. It also represents a collaboration of many instructors, case research workers, library workers, and draftsmen. In addition to the principal authors listed on the title page, the undersigned wish to acknowledge the cases contributed by Abe Zaleznik and Arnold R. Saitow. Industry research was done by William W. Sihler, Ruth Hetherston, and Priscilla Hildum, and typing and drafting by Mrs. Jean S. Burleson and Mrs. Madelyn B. Wisnia.

We wish to thank Dean George P. Baker for providing the opportunity to write the book. We should like particularly to thank the many business executives who gave so freely of their time and information in order to provide students of business administration with material specific enough to learn from their experiences. These men are the real authors of the book.

Finally, we should like to express our thanks to the President and Fellows of Harvard College, by whom the cases have been individually copyrighted.

STANLEY S. MILLER
DAVID C. D. ROGERS

Harvard University
July, 1963

NOTE

The cases included in this book have been selected on the basis of their interest and educational value as raw material for discussion. They are not necessarily intended to illustrate either correct or incorrect, desirable or undesirable, management policies or procedures.

Table of Contents

CONTENTS

Introduction to the Revised Edition

The material in this boook constitutes an industry approach to case analysis. It focuses attention on decisions directed at operating programs and manufacturing policies at the level of the vice-president of manufacturing in six selected industries.

The purpose of the industry approach is to provide the student with an understanding of the way products are manufactured and marketed in an industry before attempting to deal with top-level manufacturing decisions in particular companies in that industry. The intention is to place the student as far as feasible into the industrial climate so that he can draw upon his own knowledge during the decision-making process rather than rely solely upon data selected for him by the case writer. The hope is that by spending some introductory sessions on each industry and by moving from company to company in the same industry he can go deeper into case analysis.

THE NEW INDUSTRY APPROACH

In the introduction to the first edition of the book in 1957, it was felt necessary to discuss the problem of decision-making in the classroom as a way of justifying the case method in general and an industry approach in particular. By 1963, this should no longer be necessary. It is generally recognized that the approach has a value in strengthening a student's feel for the industrial environment with which a manufacturing company interacts. The real problem has rather been at another level: to define the *rationale*—the specific objective for which this understanding of the environment is developed.

It is a curious fact that the industry approach does not of itself tend to reveal any special educational objective other than the general one of responding to change in the environment. This is a laudable goal, but rather broad for the rigorous requirements of modern management education. Our own course at the Harvard Business School is still entitled "Advanced Production Problems," indicating the original objective of emphasizing the operating problems of production managers, largely in industries in which the process technology was important. In fact, however, the industry approach naturally generated material that lifted the course into the business policy area. For example, the process and reference notes tended to deal with the broad sweep of economics in the industry, and at least some of the cases to deal with broad problems of diversification and vertical integration. The approach was full of new insight, but in order to make better use of the technical information, the last five years have been devoted to developing a more specific focus in manufacturing strategy.

The new approach is pitched between the operating level of "Advanced Production Problems" and the general management level of "Business Policy" to the viewpoint of the vice-president of manufacturing, and thus could be called "Manufacturing Policy" or "Manufacturing Strategy." The aim has been to select pertinent background data and pinpoint the case material to a level that combines the operating analysis with a large policy issue. In other words, we focus on operating problems that raise basic questions of corporate strategy before they can finally be resolved, or broad policy issues that must be tested out by the analysis of detailed operating plans. The present material can be viewed as a valiant attempt in this direction, rather than a definitive solution.

In general, the course development effort in recent years has been directed along three lines that aim to make maximum use of the industry approach and to sharpen the focus of the course: greater selectivity in the use of technical and economic data; application of such data to a concept of "normal" standards for a particular company; and application of the standards to define the manufacturing task for a company operating under the stress of change and competition.

Technical and Economic Factors

In recent years, the process notes have taken on additional importance, as industries have moved into more advanced technological areas. The problem of understanding the business implications of technological change appears to be of general and increasing importance. It was relatively easy a decade ago for nontechnical minded students to discuss the business problems of a company making radio sets or gasoline. But when the same company today makes instrumentation for space capsules or cyclohexane, the technical aspects of the company's operations can no longer be "delegated" to the engineers; they become embedded in the heart of the company's product line. How can we even think of discussing a company's strategy until we understand the function of its product, the nature of alternate ways of accomplishing that function, or the possible changes that can obsolete the function? The task is no longer to segregate the nontechnical aspects, but to train nontechnical students to understand the technical aspects without entering into the province of engineering judgments. This is a task not only for the classroom, but for the increasing number of executives who find themselves responsible for managing product lines in which they have had little contemporary technical training.

The process notes have been rewritten with certain basic concepts of process and product technology in mind. We wish to consider the scale, operating range, capital cost, method of control, and degree of mechanization at each successive stage in the process. We wish to know whether the processes can be coupled or should be separated. We wish to define product quality in terms of tensile strength, conductivity, percentage of impurities, to evaluate alternative materials or designs in some kind of cost-quality relationship.

The reference notes have also been rewritten to emphasize certain basic economic factors that determine the environmental pressures on the system as well as the internal cost structure of the business unit. Externally, this deals with the growth and decline of markets, price pressures, product mix changes, seasonality of different regions, and so on. It also deals with the nature and scale of competing companies, their structure, objectives, and entry into or exit from the market.

Internally, what we wish to know about the cost structure is the way it responds to external pressures. Holding constant the manufacturing process, materials specifications, and product design, what is the mix of costs from materials, capital facilities, labor, overhead, outward freight? How does this mix respond to changes in volume? What kinds of controls are needed to ensure adequate response?

A Concept of Normal

In a coherent industry, the restraints brought about by economic pressures and process technology necessarily emphasize a certain kind of thinking. An executive in an oil company makes a different kind of judgment than his counterpart in a clothing concern, not because business management is not a common skill, but because the restraints in his industry impose a different range of emphasis. One interesting by-product of the industry approach is the light it can shed on these judgment issues. Proper determination of industry conditions should bring about a concept of what is normal to the production management in that industry.

We can postulate three statements on this observation of the industry restraints.

1. Under stable conditions, management structure and standards of judgment will adapt to the restraints of economic pressures and technical requirements. These will help determine a standard of normal effective operation in the industry.
2. Under changing economic conditions, a determination of the external pressures should help indicate the nature of the stress on the company's operating system.
3. Under dynamic technological conditions, evaluation of the resources of the new process should help indicate areas in which the company can make a breakthrough into new markets.

Industry-wide balance sheets and income statements, comparative cost breakdowns over a period of years, and selected conversion factors indicate the contrasts between industries. For example, the ratio of net plant to total assets is about 62 percent in the oil industry, but only 26 percent for television set assembly; the value of the product is one cent per pound in cement, two cents for gasoline, five cents for petrochemicals, twenty-five cents for plastics; the ratio of materials to labor cost is 10 to 1 in an oil refinery, and about 2 to 1 in a steel mill; a typical oil refinery might require an investment of at least $30 million, while a plastics fabricator can operate on less than $1 million. These factors imply considerable differences in the nature of the manufacturing task, and similar differences may well occur between stages of the process in the same industry, as for example between the manufacture of picture tubes and the assembly of television sets.

Defining the Manufacturing Task

Once a concept of the normal range of operation within an industry is established, it can be used to highlight differences between companies in the same market, or to evaluate the stress on a company when it enters a new market or simply undergoes technical or economic changes that impose a new manufacturing task.

The problem of determing "normals" and applying them to new conditions has turned out to be challenging enough to keep the six industries of the old casebook rather than change them for new ones. Despite the attractions of the automotive or the space industries, so many things seemed to have happened to the old industries since 1957 that the historical perspective seemed well worth keeping. For this reason, a number of cases in the 1946 to 1952 period have been retained, though in a condensed version, to enable the student to compare "normals" for that period with the more recent data, or to permit him to follow the same company through to later periods. Thus, the Catalin series and the Ohio Oil series cover about 15-year spans, and others, like Lunn, Armco, Mengel, and Textron are designed to use the later cases as a means of defining changes in industry conditions from one period to the next. Since most of the cases are not disguised, the student can follow up these cases from press releases, magazine articles, annual reports, and investment studies, past the publication date of the casebook.

TEACHING METHODS

The cases in this book are intended to accomplish two kinds of analysis that are interdependent: first, a detailed quantitative analysis of a production program, and second, a qualitative analysis dealing with the implications of the program to the company's overall growth. The figure analysis is necessary to push the student to work his way through the actual facts of an important decision in the production area. The policy discussion is necessary to allow the student to swing the program into alignment with the other considerations necessary for the company's growth.

Teaching experience with these cases seems to indicate that general discussion arises more readily than figure analysis. It is evidently easier for a student to sit back and comment about the growth of a company than to determine the degree to which fixed and variable costs will change at a higher level of output. It is the objective of the program analysis to orient the student squarely with the facts of a problem in order to "ground" his policy discussion into the reality of the case. To attain the heavy work load required by quantitative analysis, it has proved helpful for the professor to direct the students in their assignments and make use of supplementary aids such as written reports to keep the analyses specific.

Assignments

If the cases in this book are assigned without specific questions to direct the student, he tends to lapse into discussion of the issues based on his common sense alone. For example, in one of the television cases a situation is described in which a price decline in the industry threatens the market of a small manufacturer. If no assignment is given, the student tends to discuss the general problem of a small company with higher production costs than its competitors. Suppose we ask the student to decide whether or not the company should reduce its prices to meet its major competitors. The student then tends to discuss the difficulties of a small company in reducing costs, in obtaining sufficient volume to gain mass production economies, and of the alternative of maintaining high prices and lower volume to compete in the quality market. But suppose we ask the student to determine whether the company should reduce its prices 10 percent or cut back its volume 20 percent. Now the student has to go down the line to determine how each type of cost varies with output, what effect a lower production volume would have on the labor force, market position, production cost, and so on. By the time he starts to discuss the policy implications of the decision, the figure analysis has given him a more thorough understanding of the company's operations than he otherwise might have. Appendix A contains suggested assignment questions. Appendix B outlines some of the considerations useful for figure analysis of a business.

A second aspect of the careful direction of assignments is the use of the process and reference notes to solve a case. Consider the problem of executives in a steel company deciding whether or not to expand plant facilities. If the assignment is specific enough to require the student to estimate a return on investment or payback period for the new facilities, he is obliged to make use of every scrap of evidence he can find. Will the new equipment be threatened with obsolescence soon? Will it break a bottleneck in the production flow? Is there an alternative way of handling the bottleneck? The process notes should give the answers. Will the company be able to operate the new facilities at capacity? Are there seasonal fluctuations in demand? Are price and cost increases apt to change the profitability? The industry reference notes should provide clues.

In order for the student to have a meaningful learning experience from these cases, he should be required to do a considerable amount of figure analysis—but not so much figure analysis that he becomes bogged down in the details of a problem. He must be required to take a problem apart, but the assignment must not be so intricate that he has no energy left to put it back together again in the framework of top company policy considerations. He must not only *work:* he must also have time to *think.* For this reason, it has been found advisable to provide supplementary data with some of the assignments so that the student can start his analysis one stage further along. The data provide him with some of the tedious groundwork so that his analysis can progress further. Appendix A contains several assignments in which such supplementary material is provided.

Written Reports

Thus far, it has been the intention of the instructors working with these cases to direct the student's effort toward case analysis. For this reason, it has not seemed wise to allow the students to spend outside time writing a long report on some subject of their choosing for this course. Rather, the student has been assigned a short report on the final case in each industry, covering exactly the same assignment he would ordinarily have prepared for class discussion. Thus, the reports have been intended to support class discussion by periodic written case analysis.

Classroom Techniques

In cases such as these, which require quantitative analysis, it is sometimes useful to conduct a class in four stages: first, general comments from as many students as possible concerning the varied aspects of the problem and approaches to a solution; second, detailed presentation of a set of figures analyzing the quantitative aspects of the problem; third, discussion and disagreement over the validity of the figures, the range of reliability in estimates of future circumstances; and fourth, a judgment of the course of action most consistent with all aspects of a company's strengths and weaknesses. The difficulty of moving from stage two to stage three is that the set of figures presented by one student may be very different from those devised by others. Furthermore, if there are any errors of addition or multiplication, the details begin to consume excessive class time. How do all the students arrive at a common quantitative framework from which to launch their judgments about a company's policy?

To begin with, of course, a common framework of figures may not be necessary. But some explanation of each other's figures in class is often important to a recognition of the different ways of attacking a problem. Generally speaking, it seems to be more difficult to explain a set of figures in class discussion than to explain an idea. But there are ways of presenting figures with a minimum of delay.

One method that has been found helpful is to ask a team of students to prepare a group presentation for the subsequent class. The students on the team then have the blackboards filled by the time class starts and everyone has some common meeting ground with which to agree or disagree.

Another method is to prepare key figures on a hidden blackboard or vu-graph machine. When the class discussion has progressed to the point where the argument is lost in detail, the instructor can review certain known facts from the board and move the discussion toward important issues.

RESULTS SECURED FROM THE INDUSTRY APPROACH

With fifteen years of classroom experience in the industry approach, the following observations[1] can be made about the results to be expected from the material in this book:

1. The industry approach provides a powerful vehicle for training students in the handling of advanced management cases in the industrial field. In the judgment of the instructors, there is an unmistakable difference in the level, range, and depth of case analysis work which the student can be trained to do with the industry approach and that which he can be trained to do in the conventional industrial management course developed along topical or functional lines. As the work progresses through the various industry sections, there is a slow, but clearly perceptible, growth in the student's capacity to relate the problems of a particular company to the pertinent aspects of the industrial environment and to the technological characteristics of the process with which the company is working.
2. The industry approach provides a framework in which the student may be given some training in the viewpoints and capacities of industrial leadership. The industry approach, and particularly the work it involves on the analysis of industry conditions, offers an opportunity to develop in the students some of the viewpoints and habits of thinking which must be added to those of the company leader if he is also to become an industry leader.
3. The greatest single hazard involved in using the industry approach is that the student will become so absorbed in gaining an understanding of processes and industries that he will regard such work as the primary mission of the course and view the case problems merely as a source of further information about the industries or as a device for analyzing further the forces at work in the industries.
4. The primary sacrifice made in using the industry approach is that of foregoing the opportunity to develop particular topical subjects on a systematic basis. The teaching of topical subject matter or skills in functional areas is not, however, the primary responsibility of a course using the industry approach, and is not necessary when most of the students' other work is in courses organized on a topical or functional basis.
5. The simple logic of the industry approach appeals to the students. To them it seems eminently reasonable that they should first study the manufacturing process used by an industry and the competitive and economic conditions prevailing in that industry before attempting to tackle the major problems in the formulation of management programs and policies. There is, in fact, considerable reason to believe that the industry approach supplies a "missing link" in the training which a student receives from case courses taught on a topical basis. It appears that the handling of isolated cases in other courses leaves the student with a slight feeling of insecurity because he is frequently called upon to make decisions without any real understanding of the production processes involved or of the industrial situations in which the companies operate. From his sense of insecurity, the student gradually develops a desire to orient the administrative skills he has acquired to the total situation in which a company operates. In providing an experience of this type, the industry approach gives the student a sense of fulfillment and lends new meaning to many things he has learned in other courses.

[1] John G. McLean, "The Industry Approach to the Teaching of Business Administration by the Case Method," from Malcolm P. McNair and Anita C. Hersum, *The Case Method at the Harvard Business School* (New York: McGraw-Hill Book Co., Inc., 1954).

Profitability of Six Industries

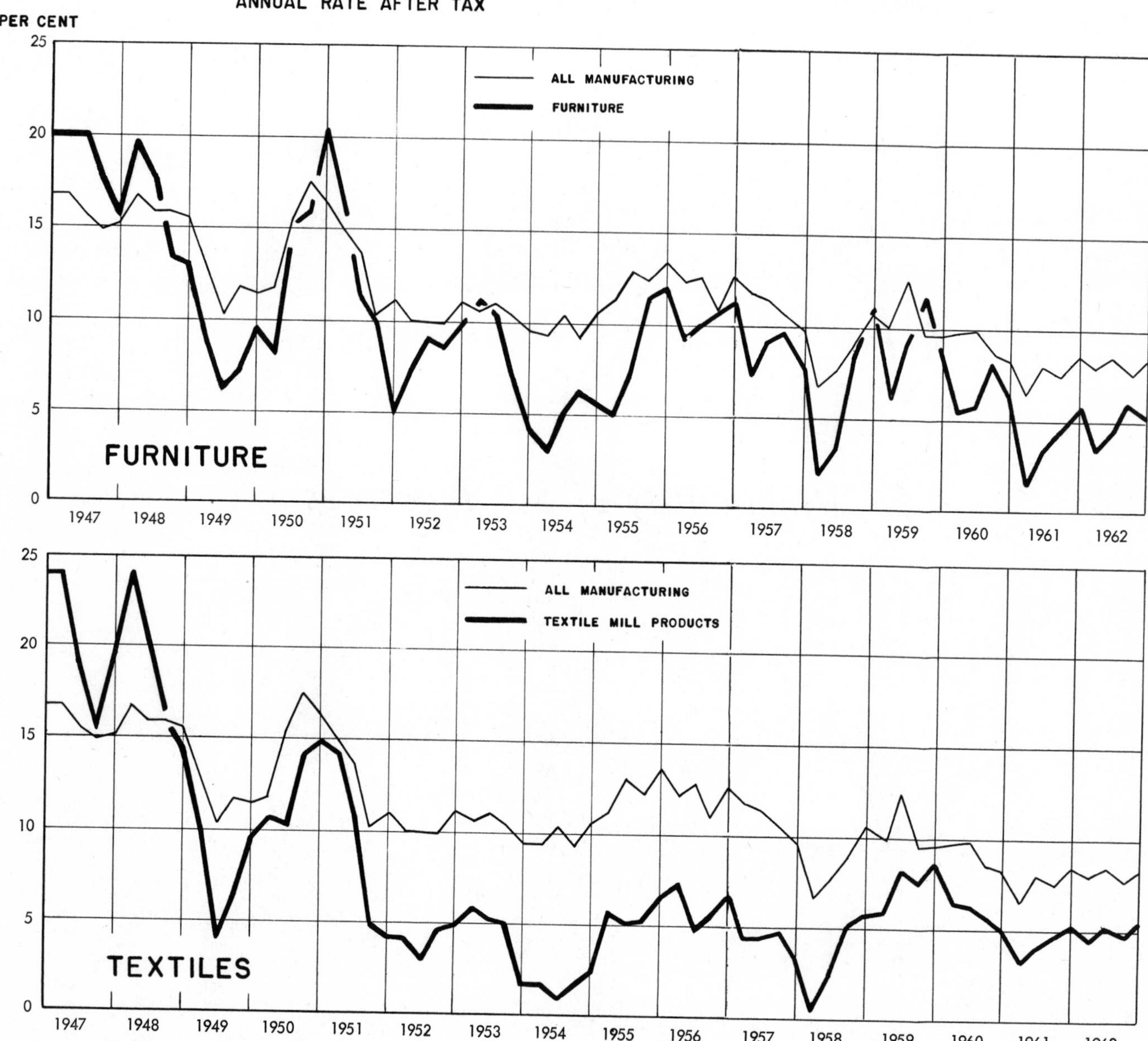

Source: Federal Trade Commission, Securities and Exchange Commission, Quarterly Financial Reports.

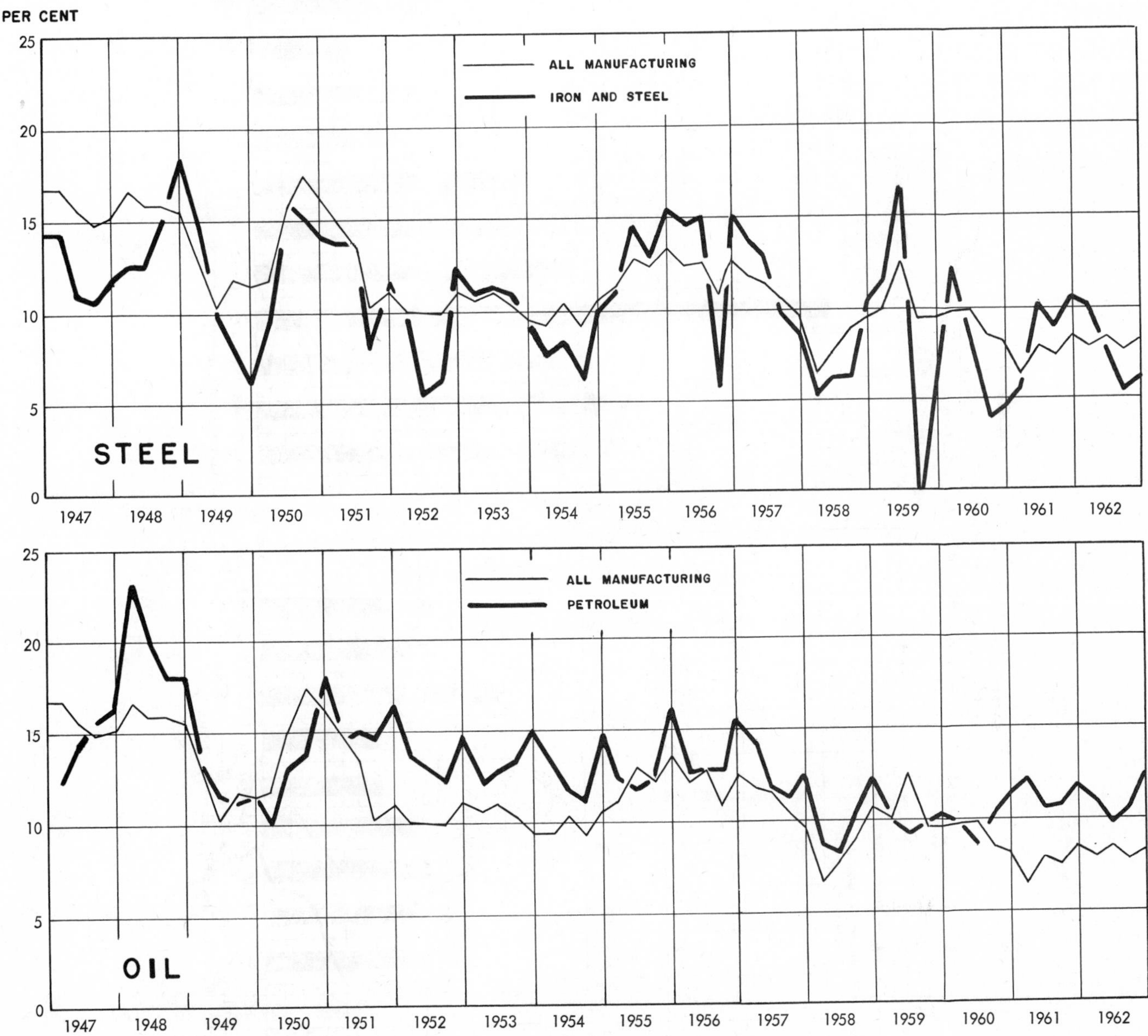

Source: Federal Trade Commission, Securities and Exchange Commission, Quarterly Financial Reports.

RETURN ON STOCKHOLDERS' EQUITY
ANNUAL RATE AFTER TAX

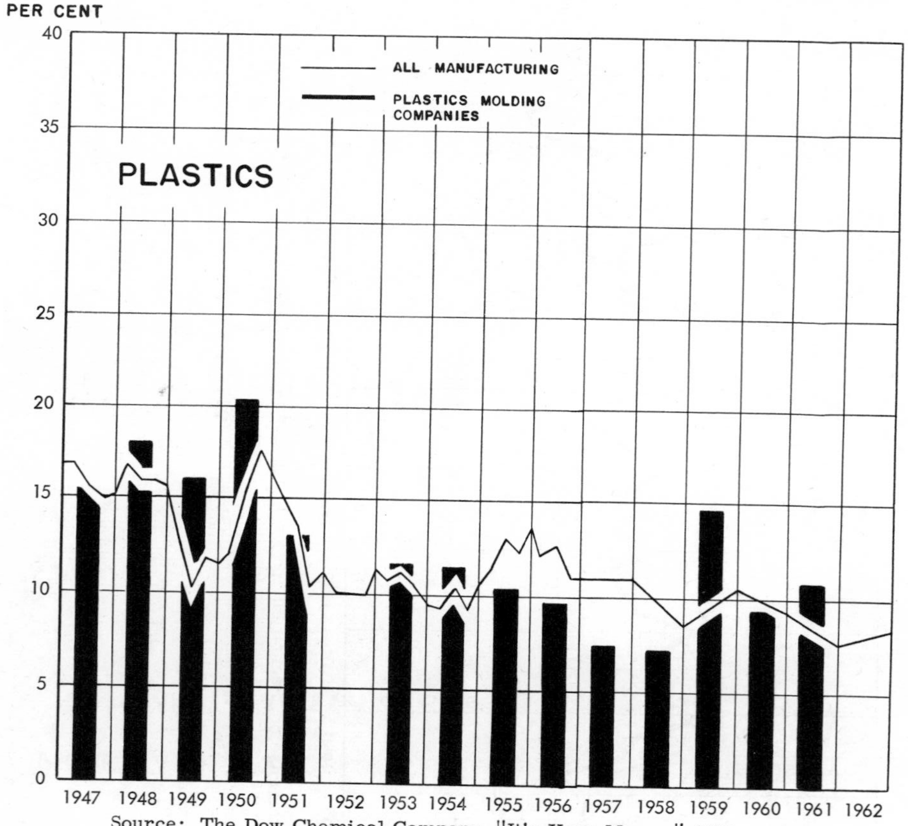

Source: The Dow Chemical Company, "It's Your Money," 1952;
Tarnell Company, Inc., "The Plastics Molding Industry," 1956.

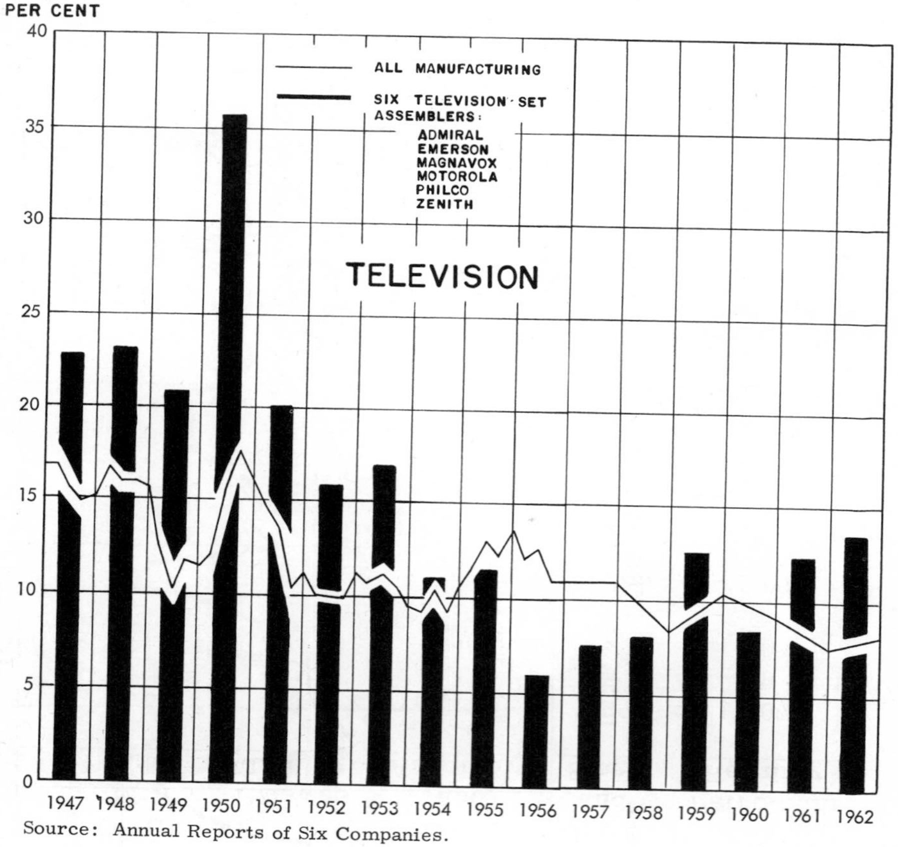

Source: Annual Reports of Six Companies.

OPERATING RATIOS OF SIX INDUSTRIES IN 1955

	All Industry	Furni- ture	Textile Mill Products	Plastics Molding	Television and Assembly	Iron and Steel	Petroleum Refining
PROFITABILITY							
Net Profit (after Tax) on Sales	5.4%	2.8%	2.6%	2.9%	3.3%	7.2%	11.0%
Ratio of Sales to Total Assets	1.5	2.2	1.5	2.3	2.0	1.3	0.9
Net Profit on Total Assets	8.1	6.2	3.9	6.2	6.6	9.4	9.9
Net Profit (after Tax) on Sales	5.4%	2.8%	2.6%	2.9%	3.3%	7.2%	11.0%
Depreciation and Depletion	2.8	1.2	2.0	3.0	1.1	4.6	7.1
Total	8.2%	4.0%	4.6%	5.9%	4.4%	11.8%	18.1%
Profit (after Tax) on Equity	12.5%	9.1%	5.7%	10.7%	12.1%	13.5%	13.3%
Ratio of Equity to Debt	4.7x	6.9x	4.5x	4.9x	5.8x	4.8x	5.2x
Profit on Total Invested Capital	10.3%	7.9%	4.7%	8.9%	10.3%	11.2%	11.2%
PER CENT OF TOTAL ASSETS							
Cash	15.8%	14.7%	10.1%	10.6%	17.6%	21.4%	12.5%
Receivables	14.7	25.0	17.1	22.0	29.3	10.5	8.6
Inventory	24.4	29.8	30.2	24.9	28.8	16.8	10.3
Net Plant	37.1	25.0	36.4	38.0	18.2	46.0	57.5
Current Liabilities	22.4	25.7	21.0	30.7	34.3	19.0	12.2
Long-Term Debt and Other Noncurrent	11.7	6.3	9.3	11.7	9.9	13.4	15.7
Equity	65.8	67.9	69.9	57.6	55.9	67.6	72.1

Sources: Federal Trade Commission, Securities and Exchange Commission, Quarterly Financial Reports.
Plastics molding data is from the Tarnell Co., "The Plastics Molding Industry," 1956.
Television set assembly data was derived from analysis of the annual reports of the Admiral, Emerson, Magnavox, Motorola, and Zenith companies.

Furniture Industry Process Notes

In the manufacture of wood household furniture, the entire process from treatment of the raw lumber stock through the manufacture of components and the assembly of the finished product is ordinarily carried out in the same plant. Here the lumber is dried, cut to rough shape, milled to finish shape, and then assembled and finished with protective coatings. This note will describe operations at Plant 2 of the Drexel Furniture Company, one of ten company plants located in the South.

Drexel Plant 2, in Morganton, North Carolina, contained 291,000 square feet of floor space and produced traditional dining room and living room furniture. It ordinarily had about 480 employees, of which the largest groups were assigned as follows:

Lumber yard	15	Finishing	90
Rough mill	45	Rubbing	45
Finish mill	55	Shipping	40
Machine sanding	35	Maintenance	20
Cabinet assembly	85	Inspection and other	15

About 20 percent of the plant work force was classed as indirect labor, and there were about fifteen in the supervisory staff.

The Morganton plant contained three kilns which were used to reduce the natural moisture in the lumber from about 60 or 70 percent to about 5 to 8 percent in order to prevent excess moisture from warping or shrinking the furniture. The incoming lumber was sorted and stored directly on kiln trucks which ran on railroad tracks in the lumber storage sheds. From the sheds, the trucks were moved into the kilns, which could hold a total of about 180,000 board feet. The cure, or drying cycle, required from two days to more than a week, depending upon the type of lumber and the moisture content.

After removal from the dry kilns, the material was moved successively upward through the four floors of the Morganton plant. On the ground floor, the rough milling operations were carried out; the second floor housed machines for the finish mill and sanding operations; the third floor was for cabinet assembly and another part of the third floor, together with the fourth floor, was conveyorized for the final finishing operations.

Ground Floor: Rough Mill

Furniture was ordered into production in lot sizes ranging from about 100 to 600 pieces or more. Each type of machine in the rough and finish mill was given a code number and the process sheet that accompanied each lot of component parts indicated the allowed process time for a particular machine. The following sequence for an oak drawer slide used in a chest-on-chest can be related to the machine numbers on the floor layout:

Machine	*Operation*	*Time per 100 Pieces*
1	Cut	10.5 Minutes
3	Rip	12.0
5	Size	9.3
6	Glue	19.0
4	Rip	6.0
3	Plane	5.4
7	Trim	3.1
4	Mold	17.4
24	Sand two sides	5.7
23	Dovetail	27.3
10	Bevel one edge	12.3

The purpose of the rough milling was to cut raw lumber to approximate width and length and to remove the natural defects in the raw wood. The east section of the rough mill in the Morganton plant contained three conveyorized cutting lines. Each line consisted of one lumber lift, two cut-off saw positions, one surfacer, one planer, and four ripsaws. The dried lumber was taken from the kilns and placed on one of the three lumber lifts which automatically maintained the lumber pile at a predetermined height for easy handling.

DREXEL FURNITURE: MORGANTON PLANT

Ground Floor: Rough Mill

LIST OF ROUGH END MACHINES

L	LIFT	1	CUT-OFF SAW	6	GLUE REEL	20	TURNING LATHE	26	DRAWER FRONT SIZER
C	CONVEYOR	2	PLANER	7	TRIM SAW	21	NASH SANDER		
S	SURFACER	3	RIP SAW	8	TENON MACHINE	23	DOVE TAILERS	31	HAND SANDER
		4	MOULDER	10	VARIETY SAW	24	DRUM SANDER	37	ELECTRONIC GLUE PRESS
		5	SIZE SAW	11	BAND SAW	25	HAND JOINTER		

Photo, Courtesy Mattison Machine Works

1. Cut-Off Saw

1. Cut-Off Saw. The radial cut-off saw was mounted on an overhead arm that could be pulled across the board. A guide strip helped position the lumber, and stops were used to permit adjustment to specified lengths. The operator determined the position of the cut and, therefore, the amount of usable lumber obtained from any given piece of lumber stock. The average cut-off saw cost about $2,500 and could handle lumber up to about four inches in thickness and twenty-two inches in width.

The stock from the cut-off saw was fed to a powered roller conveyor which carried the wood back to the main belt conveyor. It then moved through the surfacer or facer. To offset the warping caused by the dry kiln, at least one flat face was necessary to produce a rectangular piece of stock.

The stock was fed into the facer and grasped by steel spikes affixed to an endless belt conveyor above the cutting head. Each spike was spring-loaded to allow for variations in the thickness of the lumber and staggered to accommodate stock of any width. For other adjustments, the feeding mechanism could be raised or lowered. The spikes carried the lumber over the rotating cutter head which extended across the surface of the cutting table. The cutting head rotated at about 3,600 rpm while the feed rate could be adjusted between 40 and 125 lineal feet per minute.

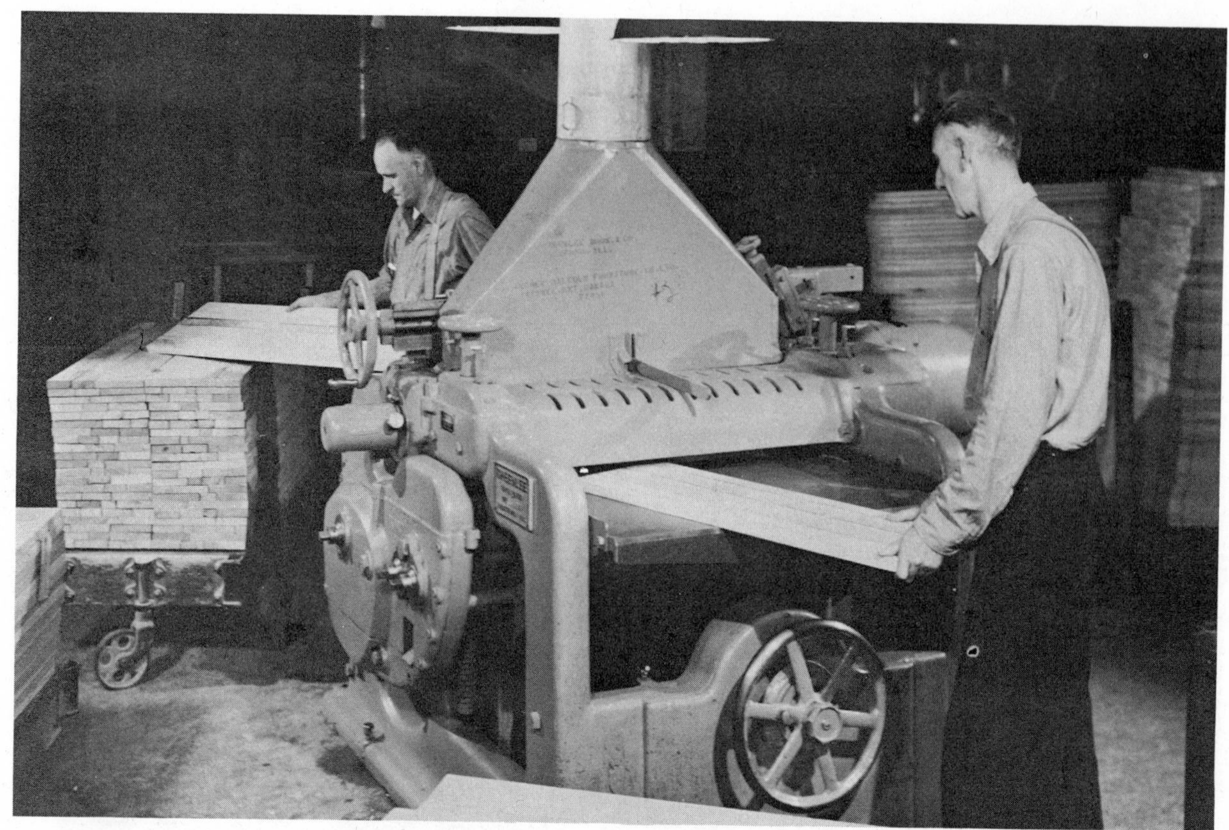

Photo, Courtesy Greenlee Bros. & Co.

2. Double Planer

2. *Planer*. The wood was then carried to a rough planer, which was used to cut stock to a specified uniform thickness. In the planer the direction of feed was opposite to the direction of the knife motion. A chip-breaker was used to hold the stock in place and reduce the amount of torn grain. A pressure bar held the stock in place immediately behind the cutter head. The single planer had one cutting head which dressed the upper surface of the board. A double planer had two cutting heads for upper and lower surfaces. A double planer cost about $16,000 and could handle stock up to 8 inches in thickness and 48 inches in width. Standard feeds usually ranged from about 25 to 100 lineal feet per minute.

The conveyor then took the wood to the ripsaws, which cut parallel to the grain. Each saw on the line was set up for wood of a certain thickness. The lumber was carried under a circular saw by a chain-feed mechanism set in a surface of the table. Adjustable rollers in the head of the machine held the lumber firmly against the chain feed. Guide strips parallel to the length of the piece were used to control the width of the cut. The ripsaw cost about $3,500 and could be operated at feeds from about 62 to 186 feet per minute.

The judgment of the sawyers at the cut-off and ripsaw in deciding where to make a cut was a prime factor in the amount of avoidable lumber waste. A 10 percent slower rate of productivity could be offset by a gain of less than one half of 1 percent in material usage.

3. *Molder*. As the wood emerged from the ripsaw it was stacked in handcarts and moved to one of the four molders located in the center of the floor. Molders cut to finished width, thickness, and cross-sections, but not length. The boards were carried through the machine by a chain feed, past four cutter heads, each mounted on its own spindle. There was a cutter head for the top face, outside edge, inside edge, and bottom face. On any one cutter head the knives could be straight or curved to cut a groove or pattern. A medium-sized molder could accommodate stock up to 8 inches in width and 4 inches in thickness. Operating speeds usually ranged from about 20 feet to 160 feet per minute for an $18,000 molder.

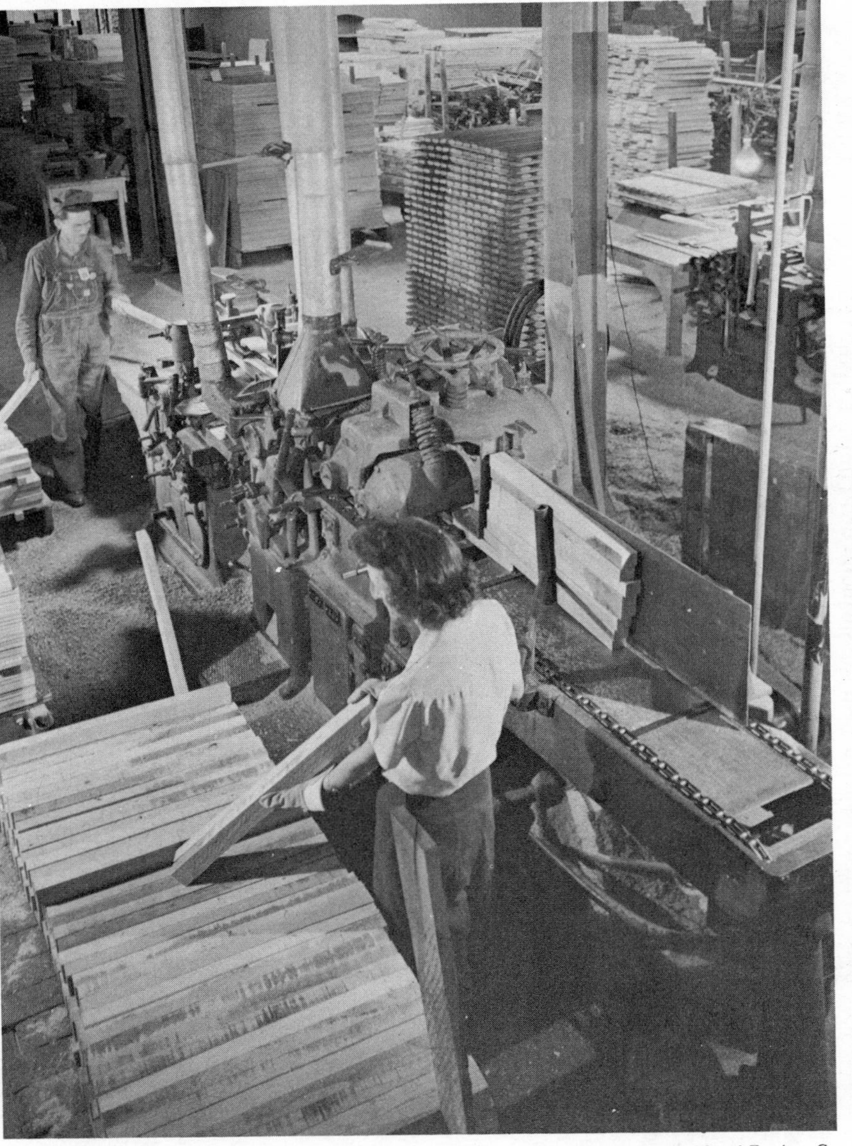

Photo, Courtesy Mengel Furniture Co.

3A. Molder

Photo, Courtesy Mattison Machine Works

3B. Molder, Cutterheads, and Workpieces

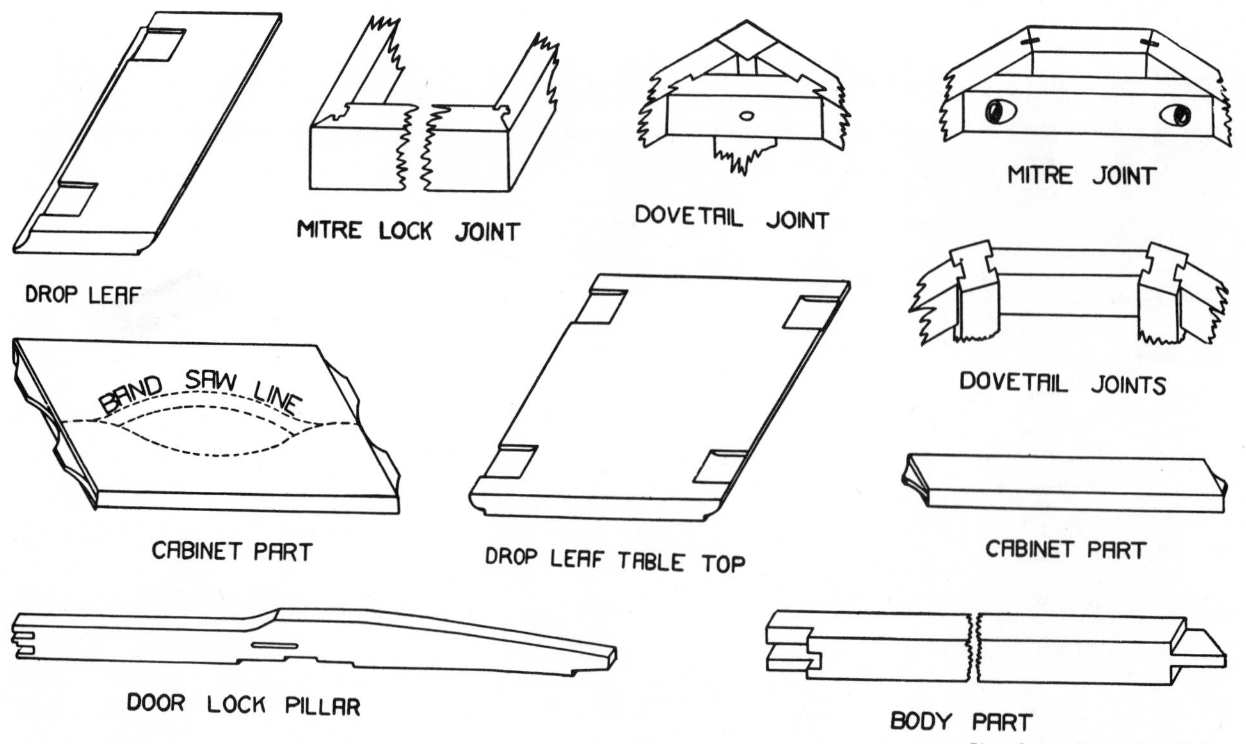

Photo, Courtesy Greenlee Bros. & Co.

4A. Typical Cuts and Joints Made on the Double-End Tenoner

4. Tenoner. The double-end tenoner was similar to the molder, but designed to cut at right angles to the grain of the wood. Stock was loaded on a chain-feed mechanism which carried the lumber past a series of rotating cutter heads. A pressure beam, located above each feed chain, held the stock firm. The first cutters were a pair of circular trim saws which cut to finish length. Next, a pair of top cutting heads, capable of lateral and vertical adjustment, could cut a variety of shapes on the upper ends of the stock. Another set of heads then cut from below.

Scoring saws could be added to the tenoner to avoid tearing the grain. Cope spindles, which were highly adjustable, could make patterned cuts, while heads mounted on a dado arbor set on a shaft above the machine, could make a uniform cut across the entire width of the stock.

A medium-sized tenoner cost about $25,000 and could handle boards ranging up to 8 feet in length. Feed rates ranged between 17 and 60 lineal feet per minute. Setup time on the tenoner ranged from a few minutes for minor adjustments to several hours for a new size or type of cut.

Miscellaneous sawing operations were usually performed on variety or band saws. Variety saws were used for cross-cutting, ripping, mitering, beveling, grooving, and other operations. They consisted of a flat table through which projected a circular saw that could be tilted at angles up to about 45 degrees. The spindle could also be adjusted to vary the distance above the table top. Guides on the table top could be set in various positions to control the angle which the stock was fed into the saw blade. They cost about $4,200 and the blades were usually run at about 3,600 rpm.

Band saws were used for either straight cutting or accurate contour cutting. They consisted of an endless, saw-toothed, steel band running on two pulley wheels. The wood was usually hand-fed against the saw blade with the operator guiding the work piece along a predetermined pattern cut in the work piece itself.

Gluing operations at Drexel were done either by hand or by electronic glue press. Hand-gluing involved coating the parts to be joined and placing them on one of six large glue reels, each fitted with a number of radial spokes. At the end of each spoke was a series of individually hand-operated presses. The glue reel was used to clamp together individual pieces and hold them in a fixed position until the glue set sufficiently to allow the pressure to be released. As the cured piece was removed from the press, the wheel was rotated and a new piece was inserted. It took about 40 minutes for the work piece to complete the drying cycle in the glue reel.

Drexel engineers had also designed an electronic glue press. The individual work pieces were placed on a moving belt which carried the edges over a glue wheel. Pressure was applied to hold the pieces together while electrodes cured the glue in less than one minute. Drexel executives estimated the replacement cost of this press at about $25,000.

Photo, Courtesy Greenlee Bros. & Co.

4B. Work Platform of Double-End Tenoner

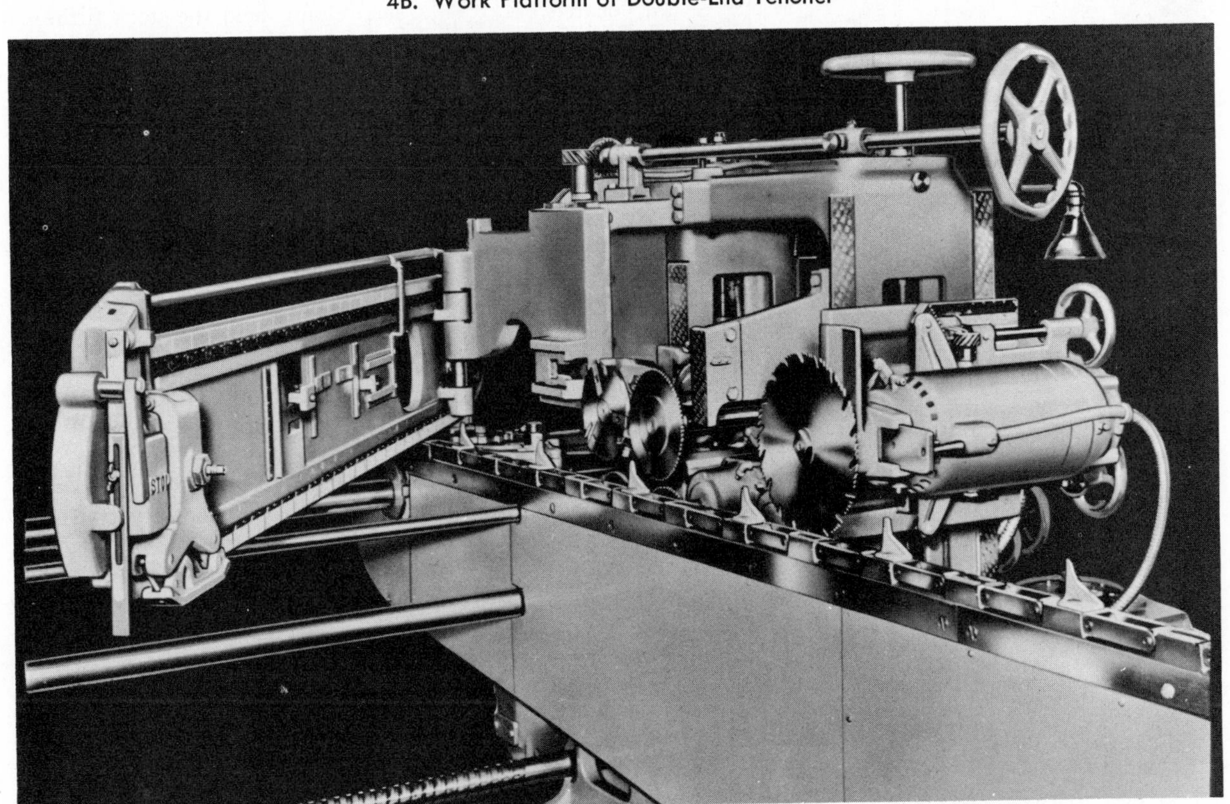

Photo, Courtesy Greenlee Bros. & Co.

4C. Tenoner with Pressure Beam Swung Away to Facilitate Head Changes and Adjustments

DREXEL FURNITURE: MORGANTON PLANT

Second Floor: Finish Mill and Sanding

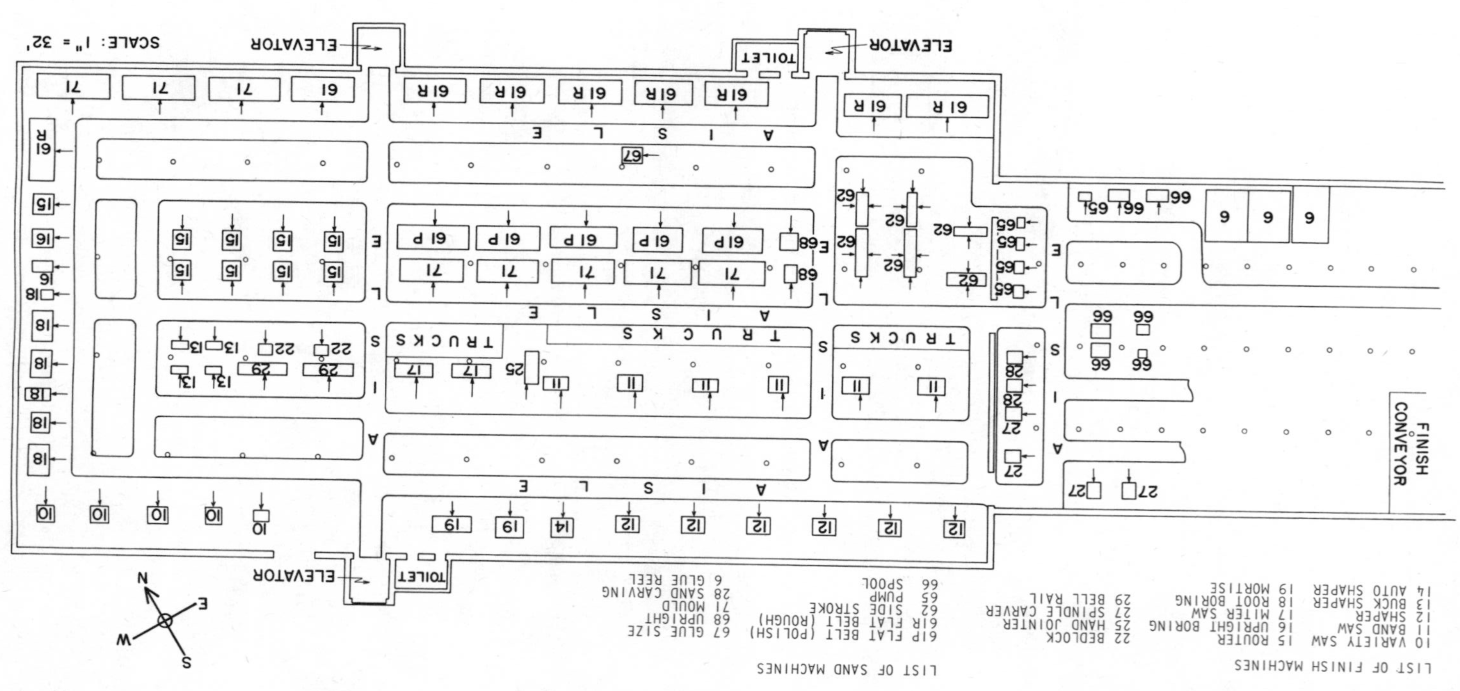

Second Floor: Finish Mill and Sanding

The second floor of the Morganton plant contained the finish mill and sanding department. Work pieces were brought up from the first floor by one of the three elevators and moved by handcart to the machine or sander specified by the process sheet. Each handcart measured about 3 by 5 feet and with corner uprights or enclosed sides it could stack parts to a height of about four feet. Machines in the finish mill were spaced so as to allow room for at least two handcarts to each machine. The usual practice was for the machine operator to remove the part from one cart, machine it, and place it on the second cart for removal to the next operation. Operations in the finish machine shop included additional saw work, shaping, lathe work, boring, mortising, and routing.

Photo, Courtesy Greenlee Bros. & Co.

5A. Shaper

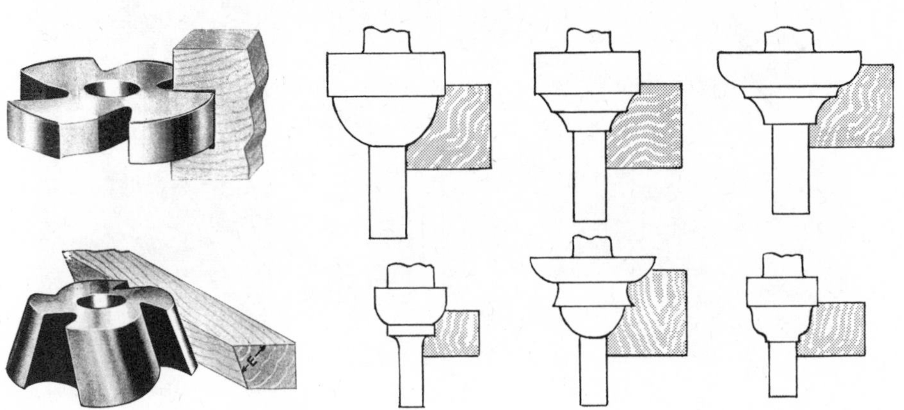

Photo, Courtesy Onsrud Machine Works, Inc.

5B. Shaper: Cutters and Workpieces

5. *Shaper.* The six shapers, located against the south wall, were used to cut irregular designs on or near the edges of straight or curved pieces. The shaper consisted of a flat table through which a vertical, adjustable spindle projected that carried the cutter knives. The operator forced the work against the cutter blades, turning it as required to follow the outline and grain of the wood. In some cases templates could be used to guide the work piece and control the cutting. A double spindle shaper, with one spindle running clockwise, the other running counterclockwise, permitted the operator to maintain a constant rate of feed when cutting against the grain of the wood. Shaper spindles generally ran between 7,200 and 10,000 rpm and their exposure required great care by the operator.

Photo, Courtesy Onsrud Machine Works, Inc.

6A. Large Automatic Shaper

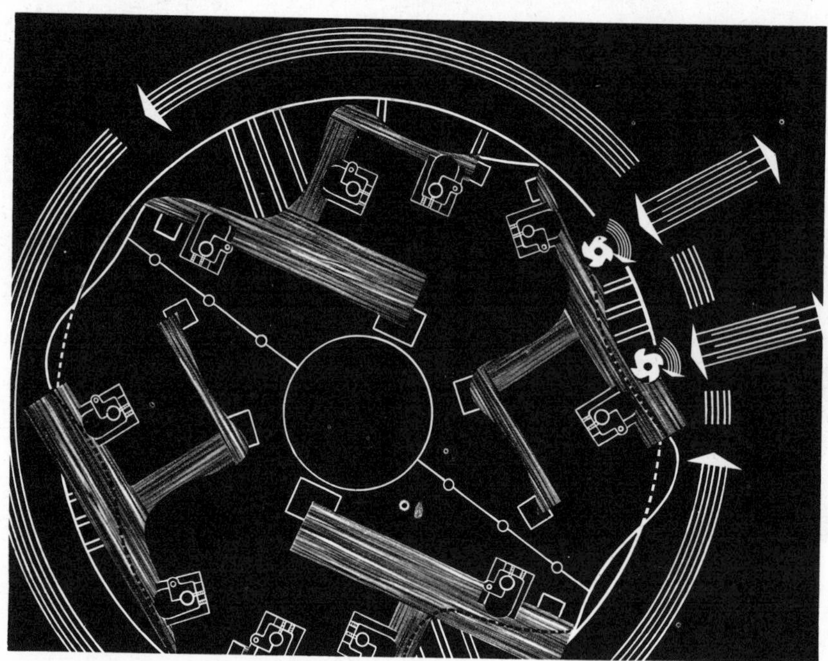

Photo, Courtesy Onsrud Machine Works, Inc.

6B. Diagram of Shaper Table

6. Automatic Shaper. An operator copied pieces on the automatic shaper by placing a wood pattern on the circular table and allowing the cutters to revolve against work pieces as the table turned. Pneumatic clamps held the pattern and the work pieces on the table. When the table rotated, the cutters were guided by the contour of the pattern to reproduce the shape in the piece.

Table speeds of 1½ to 7 rpm were possible, with slower speeds available with a variable speed transmission. Cams provided automatic speed changes and double cutter heads enabled a finished cut to follow a rough cut so that the work could be completed in one pass through the machine. Tables were available in sizes ranging from 18 inches to 85 inches in turning capacity. An automatic shaper cost about $12,000 compared to $6,000 for the manual model.

Photo, Courtesy Mattison Machine Works

7A. Automatic Lathe

7. *Automatic Lathe.* The four automatic lathes or spindle carvers were used to turn the sides of stock for producing table legs and other complex shapes. The work piece was mounted between a headstock and tailstock and driven at speeds ranging from 2 to 30 rpm. The cutting knives were mounted on an arbor running parallel to the work piece and turning at a speed of about 2,700 rpm. The headstock and tailstock were mounted on a carriage so that the work pieces could be moved up to and away from the rotating knives. A number of cutting knives could be mounted on the arbor at one time and the entire length of the piece, except for an inch at each end, could be turned in one operation. The machine operated very rapidly and pieces could be completed in a matter of seconds.

Automatic lathes could be fitted with polygonal dies which moved the carriage in and out automatically in accordance with the shape of the die. This arrangement made it possible for the lathe to turn square, oval, or hexagonal cross-sections. The lathes could also be fitted with automatic stock-handling devices which could chuck the piece after the operator laid it on the centering jaws and unloaded the finished trimmings automatically.

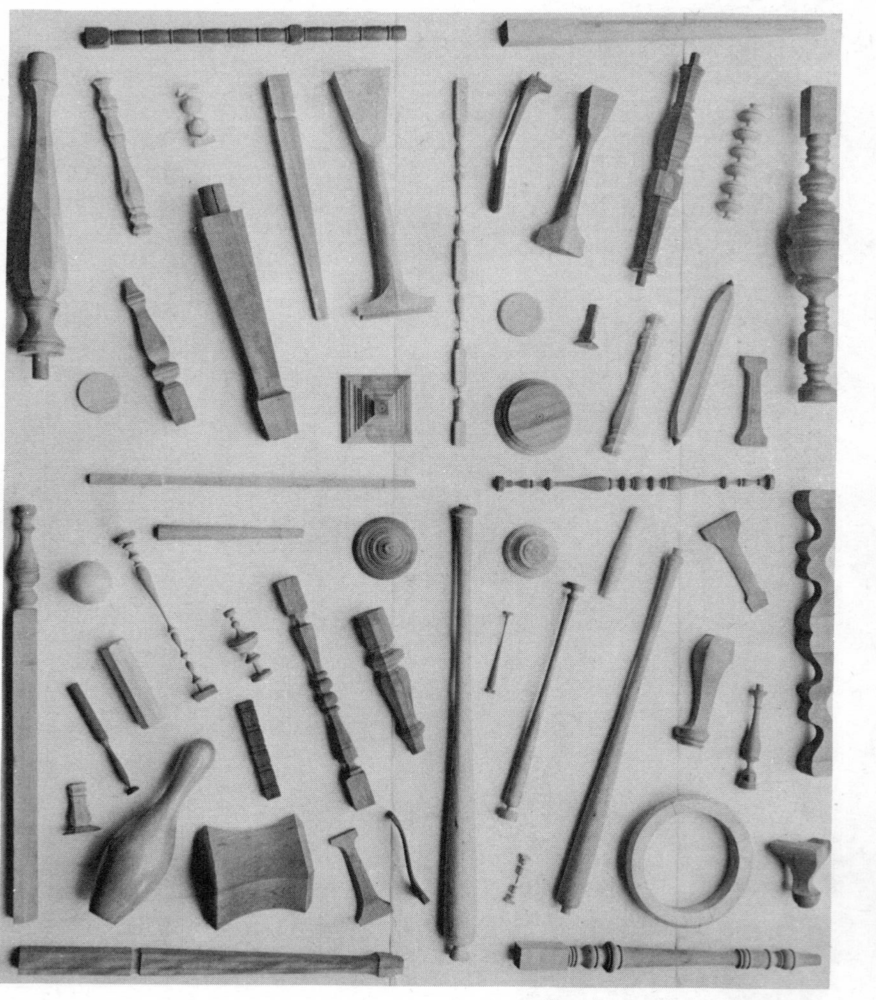

Photo, Courtesy Mattison Machine Works

7B. Automatic Lathe Workpieces

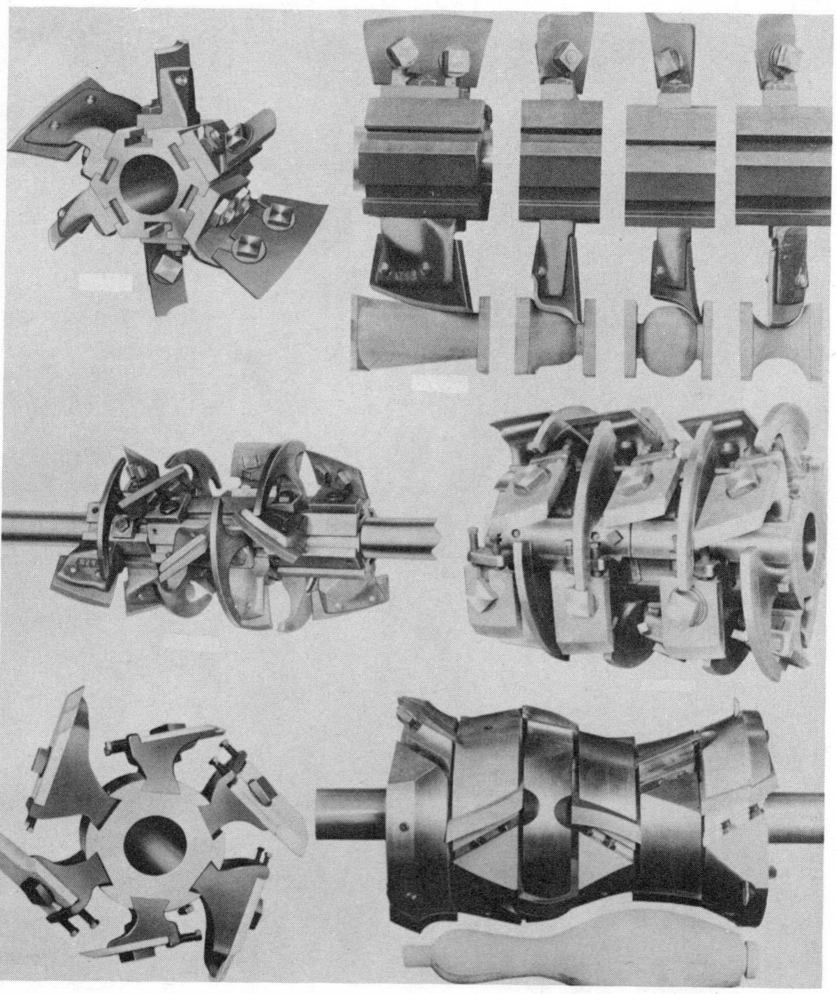

Photo, Courtesy Mattison Machine Works

7C. Automatic Lathe: Cutterheads

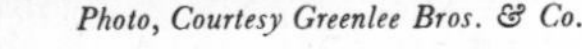

Photo, Courtesy Greenlee Bros. & Co.

8. Gang Borer

Photo, Courtesy Greenlee Bros. & Co.

9. Hollow-Chisel Mortiser

8. Gang Borer. The multiple spindle borer was used on production jobs for drilling a number of holes simultaneously in a work piece. The spindles were fitted with Universal joints and telescoping shafts so that they could be located at any point over the entire length and width of the table. The feed on the machine, which cost about $8,000, was obtained by a vertical movement of the table.

9. Hollow Chisel Mortiser. The hollow chisel mortiser was a machine for cutting square or rectangular holes in wood. The holes or mortises were designed to receive projections or tenons on mating pieces when two parts were joined together. The cutting tool on the mortiser consisted of a hollow chisel inside of which was a rotating cutter bit. In operation, the chisel remained fixed while the cutter hollowed out the interior space.

For sanding flat surfaces, belt sanders and drum sanders were the most common machines in use.

Photo, Courtesy Mattison Machine Works

10. Automatic Stroke Sander

10. Stroke Belt Sander. The stroke belt sander consisted of an endless loop of sandpaper running on two pulley wheels, a shoe for pressing the paper against the work, and a table which could be moved back and forth under the belt. In operation, the shoe was moved back and forth along the belt and the table in and out at right angles to the path of the belt. The sanding pressure could thus be applied to all surface of the work piece. A pressure control handle regulated stroke length and a dial controlled the shoe speed.

In the drum sander, the drums were wrapped with different grades of sandpaper, ranging from coarse to fine. The stock was placed on an endless belt conveyor and carried under the rotating drums.

In the rough and finish mill, the percent of setup time for a lot of 100 parts out of the total production time for the lot was estimated as follows for selective machines:

Tenoner	40.4%	Hand shaper	23.0%
Variety saw	11.7	Mortiser	24.3
Band saw	7.3	Turning lathe	14.3
Boring machine	22.7	Drum sander	0.0

The importance of large lot sizes to reduce setup time per piece is indicated in the following survey of selected parts:

Lot Size	*Minutes per 100 Pieces*
25	.640
50	.494
100	.291
150	.267
200	.253
600	.225

DREXEL FURNITURE: MORGANTON PLANT

Third Floor: Cabinet Assembly

LIST OF EQUIPMENT

T	TABLE	BC	BED CLAMP	B	BENCH
L	LIFT	CC	CASE CLAMP	S	HAND SANDER
AC	ASSEMBLY CLAMP	DC	DRAWER CLAMP	BS	BELT SANDER
				25	JOINTER

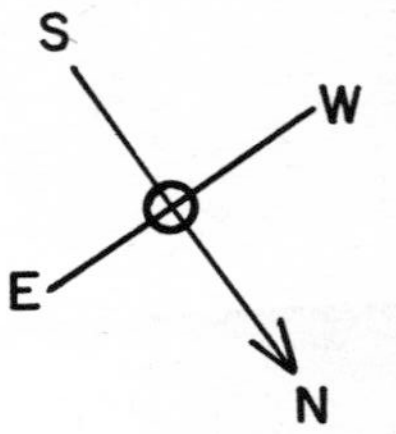

S W E N

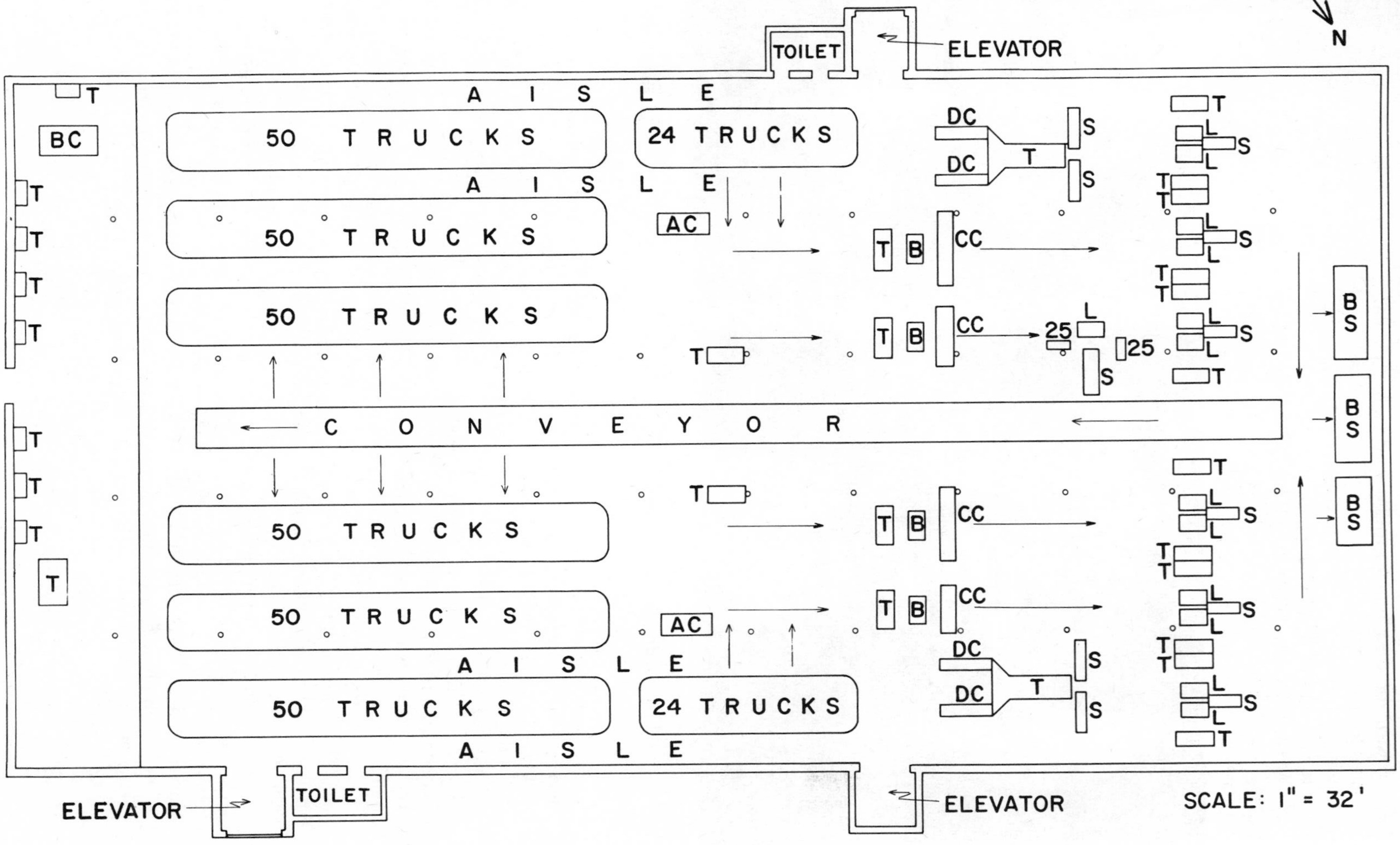

TOILET ELEVATOR

AISLE

50 TRUCKS 24 TRUCKS

CONVEYOR

SCALE: 1" = 32'

C. *Third Floor: Cabinet Assembly*

When the operations on the first two floors were completed, all the component parts for a run of one furniture lot were brought to the third floor. The large storage area was necessary to bring together the parts for one item, which were held in handcarts in the eastern half of the Drexel plant.

The assembly of a chest took place on two separate lines, with the cabinet assembly on one and the drawers on the other. Component parts were moved from the storage area to one of the two assembly clamps located in the center of the floor. Each clamp marked the beginning of an assembly line.

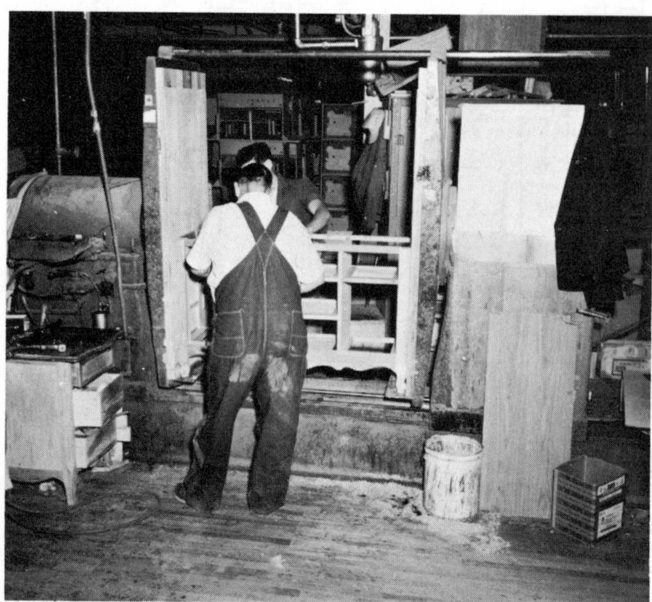

Photo, Courtesy Drexel Furniture Co.

11A. Hydraulic Case Clamp

Photo, Courtesy Drexel Furniture Co.

11B. Hydraulic Case Clamp

11. Hydraulic Case Clamp. The first step required hand-gluing the basic frame of the chest, including the legs and sides and the cross-members that held the sides together. The frame was then placed in the assembly clamp and pressure was applied to fit the parts securely. Staples were inserted with air guns into all of the glue joints to keep the parts together while the glue set. The frame was then removed from the clamp and moved to the next stations where the top, side panels, backs, and interior panels were added. A wooden skid or pallet was then secured to the bottom of the unit to prevent damage to it while being pushed to and from subsequent operations.

The assembled cabinet and drawers met at one of the six case-fitting stations at the end of each assembly line. Each of these stations was equipped with a workbench and lift. The workbench contained a number of small air-driven tools, such as a staple gun, hammer, screwdriver, and tacker. The cabinet was placed on the lift, a circular metal platform about three feet in diameter, which was free to rotate 360 degrees. The platform was operated by a foot treadle and could be raised or lowered hydraulically while the operator ensured a proper fit between drawers, doors, and cabinet.

The cabinet was then pushed to a line of sanders for additional sanding of the interior and exterior of both the drawers and the chest. Sanding operations in the cabinet room were primarily done by hand, as contrasted with the machine sanding on the second floor. The cabinet was inspected for defects, nicks, or improper fit. If necessary, it was routed to a three-man repair department in the back of the sanding station. Assembly and inspection could take 45 to 80 minutes, depending on the complexity of the cabinet. Daily output figures were maintained by units assembled.

DREXEL FURNITURE: MORGANTON PLANT

Third and Fourth Floors: Finishing Conveyor

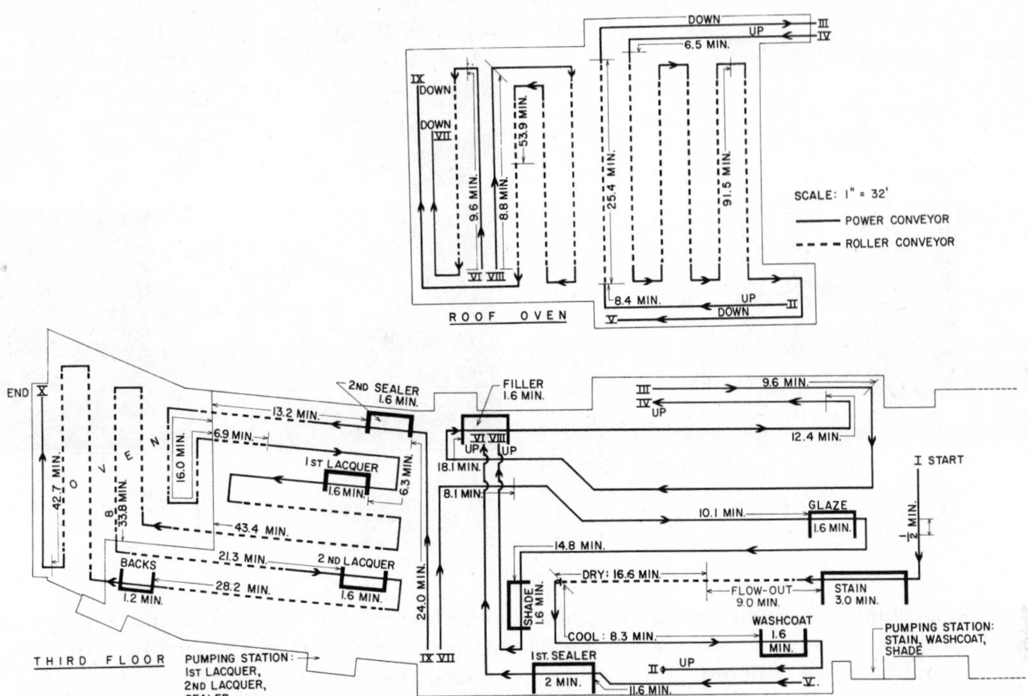

D. Third and Fourth Floors: Finishing Conveyor

The finishing operation was entirely conveyorized, with each piece mounted on pallets and moved through a series of spray booths under a controlled timing system to permit proper drying periods between each operation. The 4,900-foot conveyor, including spray booths, ovens, fans, drying lamps, and sprinklers would cost between \$30 and \$90 per foot, depending on whether new or used equipment was obtained, and on how much work was done by the plant engineers.

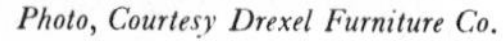

Photo, Courtesy Drexel Furniture Co.

12. Spray Booth

Photo, Courtesy Drexel Furniture Co.

13. Hand Wiping

The basic finishing operations were on the third floor, while most of the oven drying was done on the fourth. Two types of conveyors were used. Powered belt conveyors, as represented by a single line on the floor layout, alternated with unpowered roller conveyors, as represented by a dotted line. The use of roller conveyors saved floor space. For example, the powered conveyor moved at a rate of 10 feet per minute, so that for the stain flow-out, 9.0 minutes were required, which would mean 90 feet of powered conveyor. However, only 38 feet of roller conveyor were needed because the chests could be held on the rollers without moving until the stain dried.

In the finishing operations, the cabinet was moved through staining, shellac, oven dry, filler, another oven dry, sealer, glaze, oven dry, second sealer coat, and again oven dry. These operations required considerable care and continual movement by conveyor between the third and fourth floors. At certain points great care was taken to ensure the quality of the finish. For example, after the filler had been applied to close the pores of the wood, there was a precise moment at which excess filler had to be wiped off, using a special technique. The sealer formed a film that could be sanded to a surface with a "tooth" to which top coats could adhere. Final operations included several coats of lacquer, with oven drying after each coat. At the completion of the finishing, the cabinet was allowed to dry for 24 hours and then brought to the basement for rubbing, inspection, installation of hardware, and crating and shipping.

For each piece in the product line, a standard cost card was maintained, such as the following breakdown for a typical chest-on-chest:

	Material	*Labor*	*Overhead Expense*
Rough mill	$19.20	$ 4.94	$ 5.13
Veneer	5.33	.62	.61
Finish mill	3.94	1.45	1.43
Cabinet assembly	4.94	5.82	4.79
Finishing	2.50	2.23	2.13
Rubbing	—	1.26	1.08
Trim	3.56	.59	.99
Packing and shipping	2.09	.48	.54
	$41.56	$17.39	$16.70

Throughout the finishing operations, different parts of a suite of furniture, as well as different suites of furniture were often mixed together on the conveyor. Production control was established through the speed of the powered sections of the conveyor, while the roller sections were used to save floor space and to act as process inventory surge points covering any slack in the process.

Furniture Industry Reference Notes

In 1959, the furniture and fixtures industry ranked 17th in the 20 industry groups listed by the U.S. Census of Manufactures, with 368,000 employees, and 18th in value added by manufacture, with $2.61 billion. In 1954, the comparable rankings had been 16th and 17th. Of the total industry, which included furniture for offices and public buildings and partitions and fixtures, the household furniture segment accounted for 74 percent of the employees and 69 percent of the value added. Of the household furniture segment, which included metal furniture, mattresses, and springs, this note will be principally concerned with the wood and upholstered furniture. This group totaled between $2.2 and $2.3 billion annually in total manufacturers' shipments between 1956 and 1958, and about $2.5 billion during 1959 and 1960. Since materials have typically accounted for about 42 percent of manufacturers' sales, the value added was about $1.3 billion before 1959 and under $1.5 billion after 1959.

The fluctuations in demand for furniture have often been related to changes in disposable personal income and residential construction. Exhibit 1 shows how the decline in these factors during the 1930's depression and the control over residential construction during World War II affected furniture sales. Exhibit 2 shows the value of shipments in various categories of furniture since 1947. Exhibit 3 shows how changes in various manufacturing cost factors since 1947 related to general economic indexes and how they affected the profitability of furniture manufacturers.

CHARACTERISTICS OF FURNITURE MANUFACTURERS

The furniture industry is a highly competitive, nonintegrated industry, composed largely of small- and middle-sized family-controlled companies. In 1960, 20 of the largest companies accounted for only 20 percent of total industry shipments.

As noted in Exhibits 4 and 5, the profits of furniture manufacturing never equalled their high levels of 1947–1948 after the end of this postwar boom period. However, certain of the larger plants located in the Southeast have been particularly successful in achieving the operating ratios that enable a manufacturer to attain a high level of activity from its investment. Exhibit 6 defines some of these characteristics, while Exhibits 7 and 8 demonstrate the degree to which regional wage differences might account for such success.

In 1958 there were 627 metal furniture plants, 1,761 upholstered furniture plants and 2,816 wood furniture plants. The great majority of these plants were small, with very few employing as many as 500 workers. In 1958, the average furniture factory employed 161 people.[1]

Although furniture manufacturing plants are scattered throughout nearly all sections of the country, the Southeast, the Middle Atlantic, and the Great Lakes regions contain about two thirds of the plant and employees in the industry. In 1958, North Carolina was the largest household furniture-producing state in the nation (see Exhibit 9), while New York had the greatest number of furniture manufacturing establishments.

While the industry at the present time is divided among producing centers of the South, the Middle Atlantic states, and the Middle West, there have been gradual shifts in the area of concentration. The industry was originally located in the New England and Middle Atlantic states, but spread to the Middle West as the population moved in that direction. The development of the industry in the Middle West was encouraged not only by the bulky nature of furniture and consequent high transportation costs involved in shipping it from plants in the East, but also by the presence of an excellent supply of hardwood in Michigan and other midwestern states.

Furniture manufacturing began to develop in the South shortly after 1900. It was encouraged there by an abundance of lumber, cheap labor, and a wide market for low-priced furniture. Moreover, veneered furniture began to take the place of solid furniture soon after 1900, and the

[1] National Association of Furniture Manufacturers, *1961 Study of Comparative Operating Ratios*, p. 40.

most common corewood for the veneer stock was southern gum. As a result of these circumstances, the industry developed very rapidly in the South. The southern plants concentrated, at first, on low-priced, low-quality lines. At the present time, however, they produce their share of the better grades and compete with most northern producers.

The most recent development of furniture manufacturing has been on the Pacific Coast. Manufacturers in this area have an ample supply of lumber and can reach their regional customers with lower freight costs than can producers shipping from the eastern and southern plants. At the present time, the Pacific Coast is very nearly self-sufficient in many types of furniture.

The furniture manufacturer typically buys rough lumber from the sawmill, dries it in his own kilns, and cuts it into furniture parts. He then assembles the parts into pieces of furniture and performs the necessary finishing operations. With the exception of a few plants on the West Coast and certain large manufacturers, few furniture companies have undertaken their own logging or sawmill operations. Furniture manufacturers do not generally perform these operations because the resulting species and grades of lumber are nearly always more than any one firm would require.

The practice with regard to the manufacture of plywood varies. Many manufacturers, particularly those in the Southeast, buy veneer from veneer mills and manufacture all their own plywood. A few companies, mainly in the northeast section of the country, buy all their own plywood from the plywood mills. Very few furniture manufacturers undertake to cut veneer from the rough logs.

In recent years a number of furniture manufacturers have developed the practice of buying furniture parts (dimension stock) cut to their specifications from dimension stock plants which are located close to the sources of lumber supply. This practice has had increasing usage, particularly by manufacturers located in or near the metropolitan centers of the Northeast.

Manufacturing equipment and processes vary considerably in the furniture industry depending on the type and quality being made. Some of the finer grades of furniture are produced almost entirely by the hand labor of highly skilled artisans. In contrast, some of the cheaper grades are produced by highly mechanized, mass production methods. In between these two extremes there are innumerable gradations, depending largely upon the manufacturer's product policies.

Characteristically, the furniture industry operates on a one-shift basis. The great majority of the plants have dry kiln, lumber conditioning, and storage capacity to accommodate one-shift operations in the manufacturing departments. The establishment of a second shift thus usually requires substantial new investment in capital equipment. Moreover, the seasonal variations in sales and competitive conditions in the industry are such that few manufacturers have been able to secure sufficient volume to warrant changing over to a two-shift basis of operation.

Overtime operation is quite commonly used in furniture plants as a means of adjusting production to the seasonal variations and demand which occur. It has, for the most part, been found impractical to build inventories of finished furniture during a slack period for shipment in the later peak periods because of the possibility of style changes, the bulky nature of furniture, and the fact that warehouse handling usually results in a certain amount of damage to the highly polished surfaces.

Labor costs represent a substantial part of the total cost of manufacturing furniture. The relatively high proportion of direct labor cost to sales is the result of the manufacturing methods existing in the industry. Although the use of machinery has advanced, considerable hand labor is required, particularly in the assembling and finishing of furniture and in moving work from one operation to the next. The U.S. Department of Labor, in 1954, reported that "significant strides had been made by furniture manufacturers in the adoption of scientific plant layouts, specialized machinery and devices, and assembly-line methods of production."[2]

In the upholstered furniture industry, the increased use of foam rubber, replacing hand-tying of springs and padding, has also cut labor costs.

Before World War II, the labor force in the industry was made up almost entirely of male workers; in 1941, only 6 percent of the workers were women. During the war years, however, the number of women employees increased sub-

[2] Bureau of Labor Statistics, *Monthly Labor Review*, January, 1955, pp. 68–75.

stantially. In 1945, women constituted about 20 percent of the industry's labor force; in 1956 they constituted 17 percent; in 1959 the percentage had dropped further to 11 percent. In the wood furniture plants the women are used primarily in the finishing department and as hand sanders. In upholstered furniture plants they are used primarily in the cutting and sewing of covers.

Average hourly earnings in the furniture industry have for many years been lower than the hourly earnings in durable goods industries as a whole. Similarly, average weekly earnings have been lower in the furniture industry, even during those years when average weekly hours of employment in furniture manufacturing have exceeded the average weekly hours of employment in durable goods manufacturing (see Exhibit 7).

Hourly earnings in the southern branch of the industry are generally lower than in other geographic regions (see Exhibit 8). For example, cut-off saw operators, who are among the most highly skilled workers in furniture manufacturing, average $1.74 in the Great Lakes and $2.12 an hour in the Pacific region, but in the Winston-Salem High Point Furniture Center in North Carolina, they receive $1.30 an hour.

As for methods of wage payment, the Bureau of Labor Statistics in 1959 reported as follows:

> Earnings of approximately a fifth of the production workers were based on incentive plans. Regionally, these proportions ranged from two-fifths in the Middle Atlantic and Great Lakes regions and three-tenths in New England and the Southwest, to about one-tenth or less in the remaining regions.

The same report went on to add that:

> Establishments with collective bargaining agreements covering a majority of the workers employed approximately one-third of the industry's production workers in 1959. Regionally, the proportion of workers employed in the establishments with which contract coverage ranged from about four-fifths in the Pacific states to less than three-tenths in the border states, and less than one-tenth in the Southeast. In the remaining regions for which wage data are shown, the proportion varied from about one-half to three-fifths. Approximately one-half of the production workers in Standard Metropolitan Areas were employed in establishments in which the majority of the workers were covered by union contracts, as contrasted with about one-quarter in nonmetropolitan areas. The major unions in the industry are the United Furniture Workers of America, and the United Brotherhood of Carpenters and Joiners of America, although a sizeable number of the establishments in the survey sample have contracts with the Upholsterers International Union of North America.[3]

Union membership is much more extensive in the upholstery branch of the industry than it is in the case goods, novelty, and kitchen furniture branches. This condition results from the fact that upholstery plants are located primarily in the metropolitan areas of the North, Midwest, and West where the union movement is the strongest.

Furniture manufacturers usually concentrate their activities upon a particular group of furniture articles, with only the larger firms attempting to make all types of furniture. Some manufacturers have chosen to specialize in one or another of the following major groups: Case goods (bedroom and dining room furniture), upholstered furniture, solid wood furniture (breakfast sets and wood seat chairs), porch and outdoor furniture, juvenile furniture, and occasional tables and chairs. Specialization in upholstered furniture is particularly common, and there are many small producers in the field because the plants can be set up and operated with a very small capital investment. Specialization in wooden seats, chairs and other solid wood furniture is likewise common because the equipment required for these articles is somewhat specialized and different from that used for the manufacture of case goods and upholstered furniture.

The above major categories are, however, frequently bridged in all sorts of combinations. Manufacturers of case goods, for example, may undertake to manufacture other upholstered furniture in order to round out their lines for selling purposes and to ease the problem of

[3] Bureau of Labor Statistics, Report No. 152, *Wage Structure, Wood Household Furniture, Except Upholstered,* April, May, 1959, pp. 5–6.

making up carload lots for shipment to their customers. Case good manufacturers also frequently produce occasional tables and novelty furniture. The smaller case goods manufacturers usually buy the wood seat chairs required for their suites from manufacturers. The larger firms often manufacture their own chairs but usually set up a separate plant or department for the different type production equipment required for chairs as opposed to case goods. As a general rule, the practice of producing a wide range of furniture articles in one plant is more common among high-quality than among low-quality producers. In recent years there has been a definite trend among the larger producers in the South to undertake to manufacture several different types of furniture, with separate plants for the production of each line.

A manufacturer usually concentrates on a fairly narrow quality range within the particular group of products he has selected to produce. It is common practice to specialize on high- or medium-quality furniture. The northern producers have tended to follow the former policy and the southern producers the latter, although as noted above, there are a substantial number of high-quality producers in the southern states. Manufacturers who have attempted to span a wide quality range have usually encountered difficulties in getting their labor force to operate economically and efficiently on the grades at both the upper and lower ends of the scale.

Since 1956, however, several corporate mergers were undertaken, with the result of creating larger multiplant companies carrying wider product lines.

The Kroehler Company acquired the Mengel Furniture Company, a case goods manufacturing organization with $11 million in sales. Again, the Drexel Furniture Company with sales of $29 million in medium- to high-priced case goods, acquired the Heritage Furniture Company, with sales of $7½ million in high-style upholstery, and the Morganton Furniture Company, with $2.7 million in medium-priced case goods. In 1961, Drexel acquired Southern Desk Company, a manufacturer of tables and chairs for church, school, and auditorium use. As a result of these moves, common manufacturing facilities could be used to produce both upholstery and case goods in all three priced lines. The president of the Drexel company stated, "You might say that we are applying the General Motors' concept to furniture for the first time. The Heritage line will be our equivalent of Cadillac, Drexel will be our Buick-Oldsmobile, and Morganton our Pontiac."[4]

It has been common practice with furniture manufacturers to produce a wide range of different styles, patterns, and suites in the lines they have chosen to manufacture. A case goods manufacturer, for example, will often have as many as 25 to 50 different dining room and bedroom suites in his line. Moreover, the makeup of the line undergoes continual change; new suites are added at frequent intervals and old suites are redesigned or discontinued.

This situation, which greatly complicates the manufacturing job, has developed for a number of reasons. For each of the furniture markets, the manufacturer must have "something new" to offer if he is to attract the retail buyers to his exhibit. For their part, the retailers are anxious to obtain new styles to feature in their sales talks and in their advertising programs. The retailers also exert pressure on the manufacturers to carry a number of different suites and patterns. Individual tastes with regard to furniture vary widely, and the retailer feels that he must, therefore, keep a fairly broad selection on the floor of his showroom.

The furniture manufacturer is also under compulsion to carry a large number of suites and patterns as a result of the market variations in consumer preferences in different sections of the country. Furniture which sells well in Hollywood or Brooklyn may be entirely unsuitable for Philadelphia or Boston.

Once a suite has been introduced to the trade, the manufacturer frequently has trouble in discontinuing it. Each salesman tends to insist that the particular pattern which is selling well in his area be kept, regardless of what it is doing in the rest of the country. Moreover, the individual customer often buys furniture with the intention of adding pieces to the suite at a later date.

All of these influences combined usually lead the manufacturer to increase the number of patterns carried in his line. Long manufacturing runs on any one suite are difficult to obtain. The smaller manufacturers usually consider

[4] Norris Willatt, "New Look in Furniture," *Barrons'*, March 11, 1957.

themselves fortunate if they cut as many as 50 suites in any one pattern. In an effort to control the number of styles in their lines and to satisfy a need in the small postwar home, many manufacturers have been featuring groupings of furniture in styles that can be used in several rooms of a house. Many of the pieces serve a dual purpose. Chests of drawers, for instance, are designed for use in bedroom or dining and living room areas.

Despite the number of suites which they carried and the frequency with which they attempted to restyle their lines prior to the war, the furniture manufacturers as a group were not very progressive in the development of furniture designs until after World War II. Prior to this time, most of the advances in design were originated by a small minority of manufacturers and the better designers. The promotion of the new designs was accomplished primarily by the women's and home magazines. The majority of the manufacturers fitted their design programs to what the market required, and the market got its education from the home magazines. The lack of interest in design showed by manufacturers was attributed to the belief that furniture buyers in the markets bought on the basis of price alone without regard for style.

The shift to modern design, which became strikingly apparent after 1950, had a major impact on the industry. It signaled the sudden increased importance of the younger American designers and newer companies as well as increasing Scandinavian imports; it removed much of the traditional intricate carving and curved surfaces; it caused a decline in some woods such as mahogany in favor of walnut and cherry; it almost eliminated the dark shiny stains in favor of oil finishes, lighter woods, or painted surfaces; it greatly strengthened the trend to modern informal architecture in residential construction; and it opened the way to new production methods and materials such as prefabrication, molded plywood, fiber glass molded plastics, and so on.

In 1962, walnut and cherry were still the most important furniture woods. Maple and butternut were increasing in popularity and there were indications of renewed interest in dark-stained mahogany.[5] In early 1962, walnut was selling for $310 to $370 per thousand feet, depending on quality, and cherry for $210 to $290. Prime mahogany was selling for $280 to $320, and gum for $110 to $170, maple for about $155 and birch about $175. In 1950, similar quality maple had been $120 and birch $140.

[5] J. A. Hager, President of Grand Rapids Varnish Co., in a press release through the National Association of Furniture Manufacturers, February, 1962.

FURNITURE MARKETS

The furniture markets are a dominant factor in the industry, particularly in the distribution of furniture. They consist of manufacturers' exhibits held periodically in the major manufacturing retail centers. At the markets the manufacturers set up displays of their products. Furniture retailers come to these markets from all over the country to select stock for their stores. The markets, which usually last about two weeks, are held from two to four times each year. They are closed to the public and sales are made only to retail stores and wholesale buyers.

1. Present Markets

Chicago is the most important market center for the furniture industry at the present time. Semiannual markets are held at the American Furniture Mart and the Merchandise Mart. The American Furniture Mart is reputedly the largest commercial building in the world devoted to a single industry.

The Merchandise Mart, built in 1930, contains 93 acres of floor space. It is used for showing a wide line of consumer goods, ranging from apparel to appliances, as well as furniture. Over 200 furniture lines are displayed on more than two full floors.

Prior to the war, four furniture markets were held each year in Chicago. The major markets were in January and July and the midseason markets in April and October. The midseason markets were originally developed to accommodate the department stores which insisted on buying at different times than the regular furniture stores. Gradually, however, the midseason markets have been visited by buyers from all types of outlets. In recent years only two markets (January and June) have been scheduled in Chicago.

The number of manufacturers exhibiting at the Chicago market runs between 500 and 1,000. In terms of dollar volume, probably 75 percent of the industry is represented at one or more of the Chicago markets. In addition, a number of manufacturers maintain very elaborate permanent exhibits throughout the year at the American Furniture Mart and the Merchandise Mart.

The other major furniture markets in approximate order of importance are as follows: New York, High Point, Dallas, Grand Rapids, Los Angeles, Jamestown, San Francisco, and Boston. Prior to the war two markets a year were held at all of these centers with the exception of Boston.

Over a period of years several markets have taken on individual characteristics. The New York and Chicago markets, for example, give a picture of the entire industry; the Grand Rapids markets emphasize quality furniture; and the High Point markets are particularly important in the case goods field. A manufacturer may, of course, display his products at as many of these markets as he pleases. Likewise, retail buyers will go to as many markets as necessary to meet their individual requirements.

A recent trend noted by executives of the Drexel Furniture Company was the increasing tendency of many of the large furniture manufacturers, especially in the South, to hold shows at their own plants instead of displaying at the various markets throughout the country.

2. *Participation by Retailers*

The furniture markets have always been strongly supported by the furniture retailers. Furniture buyers generally attend two markets a year. The number of retail stores sending representatives to more than two markets a year is relatively small.

The furniture buyer secures a number of advantages from attending the furniture market. The market gives him an opportunity to inspect the products of a large number of manufacturers and to make detailed comparisons of the prices on competitive items. From observing other buyers he can obtain an idea of the particular designs in suites that are likely to prove popular. He also can obtain helpful ideas with regard to advertising and merchandising through informal discussions with retailers from other cities who are not in competition with him.

The cost of attending a market is relatively low for the retail buyer. The major items of expense are railroad fares and hotel accomodations. Entertainment during the markets is often provided by the manufacturers. Moreover, it is seldom necessary for a retailer to attend more than two markets a year because similar merchandise is displayed at all the markets in any one buying season.

Some manufacturers obtain almost all their business from orders placed at the markets, while others display their products at the markets and later send salesmen out to the retail stores to write up the orders. It has been estimated, however, that on the average, manufacturers exhibiting at the markets obtain perhaps 40 percent of their total sales from orders written during the market periods. Shipments on these orders are usually made 60 to 120 days after the close of the market.

The efficiency of the furniture markets as a method of distribution has long been a bone of contention among furniture manufacturers. Moreover, it is almost universally agreed that the number of markets is excessive. Due to the multiplicity of markets, a move was started in 1957 to reestablish the midseason markets in Chicago in order to bypass the showings in High Point. The undesirable aspects of the markets, from the viewpoint of the manufacturer, include the following:

(*a*) *National Competition:* The markets provide the manufacturer an opportunity to gain national disribution for his products at a relatively low cost of perhaps $1,000 to $5,000. At the same time, however, they bring him into direct competition with manufacturers of all types and sizes from all sections of the country.

(*b*) *Price Cutting:* As noted previously, price competition in the furniture industry is very severe, and the pricing policies of the manufacturers have been notoriously loose. In years when the market is slack, many manufacturers wait to see what their competitors will do and then attempt to set their own prices a shade lower. The markets thus provide the buyers with an opportunity to instigate price competition among the manufacturers. Unscrupulous buyers sometimes circulate from one manufacturer to another telling each that his prices are out of line with those of his competitors.

(*c*) *Use of Price Leaders:* It is a common practice for each manufacturer to include in his exhibit at the markets one or two items which are price leaders. Rarely, however, do the manufacturers select the same articles as leaders. It is thus possible for a careful buyer at a large market to select almost his entire stock from the leader category.

(*d*) *Copying of Designs:* It is almost impossible to patent furniture designs because nearly all of them with the exception of a few modern designs, are modified copies of museum pieces. Since nearly all designs can be proven to be reproductions of some old master's craftsmanship, unscrupulous firms can steal designs from their competitors almost at will. When a particular design is found to be selling well at a market, these firms send their salesmen around to inspect it. The specifications are then sent to the factory, and within a few days the "pirate" has an almost identical article in his own exhibit, usually at a lower price. During recent years, the practice of design copying has been curtailed and has presented less of a problem than it did in earlier years. In 1956, a federal court upheld a complaint of design infringement and ordered the copier to pay $180,000 in damages.

(*e*) *Pressure for Frequent Restyling:* The manufacturer who participates actively in the markets usually feels compelled to restyle or "brighten up" a major portion of his line about four times a year. The "new" designs are used by the manufacturer as a means of attracting the retail buyers to his exhibits.

(*f*) *Encouragement of Undesirable Competition:* The furniture markets encourage the development of many small, fly-by-night concerns, particularly upholstery firms, which otherwise would not be able to exist. These firms obtain nearly all their business by attending one or two markets and employing destructive price tactics. They also avoid design costs by using the markets as a source of their new patterns and styles.

DISTRIBUTION OF FURNITURE

The procedures used in the distribution of furniture are fairly simple and are quite uniform for nearly all branches of the industry. Four major agencies are involved: manufacturers, wholesalers, retailers, and interior decorators.

1. Manufacturers

Manufacturers of other than upholstered furniture usually distribute their products over a fairly wide geographic area. This practice has developed for several reasons. First, the manufacturers tend to concentrate on particular groups of products so that they have to seek a fairly wide market if they are to secure an adequate sales volume. Second, the demand for furniture is very sensitive to business conditions. Adverse developments, such as a failure of the citrus crop in Florida, or a decline in the stock market in New York, may temporarily destroy the market in any one region. Finally, the furniture markets tend to encourage widespread distribution because they bring together retailers and manufacturers from all sections of the country. It should be noted, however, that no manufacturer in the industry has national distribution in the same sense that it has been obtained by manufacturers of chewing gum, electrical appliances, soap, and certain other consumer products. The largest firms in the industry do not have their products in more than about one third of the furniture stores in the country.

One method of widening distribution involves the manufacture and partial assembly of furniture components at large plants, followed by shipment to smaller assembly and finishing plants scattered about the country near large local markets. It was hoped that this process would reduce labor and delivery costs; a carload can take 75 percent more furniture unassembled than it can assembled.

Upholstered furniture, unlike other furniture, is usually sold in the vicinity of the plant in which it is manufactured. Upholstered furniture is very bulky and expensive to ship. Moreover, it is usually necessary for the customer to see samples of the fabric before a piece can be finished.

Sales representatives usually carry the products of several different noncompeting manufacturers and are paid commissions of about 5 to 10 percent of the value of the furniture they sell. In a 1961 survey, The National Association of Furniture Manufacturers reported that 64 percent of the 216 manufacturers reporting hired independent contractor salesmen only. Thirty percent hired both employee and independent contractor salesmen, and only 6 percent restricted their sales force to employee salesmen exclusively.[6]

In selling to the retail trade, very few furniture manufacturers make use of exclusive distributorships or attempt to give their retailers protection on the lines they are handling. It is generally contended that if a line of furniture is limited to a single store, it immediately becomes a target for abuse by all the other stores in the same vicinity.

The practice of a furniture manufacturer attempting to set up his own retail outlets on any extensive scale is practically nonexistent, although a company recently set up a chain of shops selling its contour chairs exclusively.

(*a*) *Brand Policies:* While brand name promotion began on a small scale in the 1930's, it has received its greatest impetus since 1947. Prior to the war, furniture manufacturers generally did very little to develop brand names or to advertise their products to consumers. It was estimated that in 1941 expenditures for advertising by furniture manufacturers did not exceed $900,000. The average expenditure for the prewar years is estimated at about one tenth of 1 percent of the product value. In 1949, advertising expenditures on household furniture were $5.8 million. The amount increased to $11.0 million in 1957, then declined gradually to $9.0 million in 1961.[7]

For their part, many retailers tended to discourage the development of manufacturers' brands. Some stores make it a regular policy to conceal the identity of the manufacturer. When a customer inquired as to the manufacturer of a particular piece, he was given an erroneous or evasive answer or frankly told that the store preferred not to reveal the name of the supplier. When furniture was received bearing labels, trademarks, or brand names, the marks were often removed before the pieces were placed on the retailer's showroom floor. This practice was so prevalent, in fact, that some manufacturers went to the extent of burning their marks into the wood before shipping the furniture from the plant.

In the years since the close of World War II, several prominent furniture manufacturers have initiated programs to establish their brand names as a basis for consumer purchases of furniture. The advertising of a brand name is sometimes combined with the establishment of exclusive dealership arrangements and the development of merchandising and training programs to sell furniture on a brand name basis.

2. *Wholesalers*

Wholesalers sell about 22 percent of the manufacturers' production. There are two kinds of furniture wholesalers: service wholesalers and drop-shipment wholesalers. The service wholesalers buy merchandise on their own accounts, carry stock in their places of business, and resell to furniture retailers. The drop-shipment wholesalers perform most of the same functions but do not carry stocks; shipments to their customers are made from the furniture factories. Actually, many service wholesalers sell by both of the methods, making part of their sales by drop shipment. Normally, about 60 percent of the wholesale business is done by service wholesalers and 40 percent by the drop-shipment method.[8]

Wholesalers render a service to manufacturers selling in remote sections of the country. Freight costs on furniture are so high that it is difficult for manufacturers to ship their products great distances unless they use wholesalers or find some other means of making their shipments in carload lots. The freight costs are particularly important on the cheaper grades of furniture where they may constitute 10 to 20 percent of delivered value, depending on whether carload or L.C.L. rates were applied. In addition, the wholesaler performs a warehousing service for the manufacturer and the retail outlets. This is a very useful service since most furniture manufacturers do not have their own warehouses, and retailers often have limited storage space. Most manufacturers converted warehouse space to production space during World War II, and others lost their warehouses during the depression.

In selling to retailers, the furniture wholesalers use practically the same methods as do the furniture manufacturers, maintaining showrooms and salesmen. They render a particular service to the small retailer who cannot afford

[6] NAFM, *Salesmen's Compensation Survey*, 1961.

[7] Publishers Information Bureau, "Leading National Advertisers."

[8] National Wholesale Furniture Association, *The Facts of Life About Furniture Wholesaling*, 1946.

to go to the markets, by carrying complete catalogues from which the retailer may choose his stock. In 1962, much of the higher quality furniture was carried by wholesalers. Individual retailers often did not have the space to display higher quality lines regularly nor could they afford the inventory cost of offering much variety in them. The retailer who aimed at the middle-income family could offer his customers this higher priced, quality furniture through the use of the wholesaler.

Complaints have often been made that some service wholesalers maintained showrooms which were purportedly for the trade but which were actually open to the public. Retailers would send or bring their customers to get special bargains "at wholesale prices." These so-called "open showrooms" are the subject of much controversy in the industry with much opposition to them coming from better retail outlets and wholesalers who sell to the trade.

Common operating ratios for furniture wholesalers are shown in Exhibit 10.

3. Retailers

Furniture manufacturers sell about 80 percent of their output directly to retailers. These approximately 29,000 retail outlets sell an estimated 70 percent of all furniture and home furnishings to the consumer. The remaining 30 percent moves through department stores, mail-order houses, and other retail outlets.

In purchasing furniture from manufacturers, the retailers make extensive use of the furniture markets as outlined previously. It is usually necessary for the retail stores to buy from several different manufacturers in order to obtain types, styles, and quality grades required. A typical store, for example, might buy from six or eight different manufacturers. The retail store does, however, limit its purchase to as few manufacturers as possible in order that inward freight costs may be kept to a minimum.

Since the retailer does purchase direct from the manufacturer, he must also undertake the functions of a wholesaler or jobber, such as warehousing, servicing, and delivery of the furniture to the customer.

In selling furniture, the retailer, like the manufacturer, has always placed a great deal of emphasis on price: fire sales, clearance sales, and phony markdowns are common promotional devices. In contrast to the manufacturer, however, the retailer spends a very substantial amount for advertising.

Statistics concerning the operations of retail furniture stores are shown in Exhibits 11 to 14.

Installment and open account business constitutes about 85 percent of the total sales. Installment volume declined with the imposition of credit controls during World War II, between September, 1948 and June, 1949, and again from September, 1950 to May, 1952. Subsequently, the total amount of consumer installment credit outstanding continued to mount. Recently, however, furniture sales have had a much closer relationship to consumer confidence in the economy than to the level of installment credit.[9]

[9] Standard & Poor's *Industry Survey of Home Furnishings*, p. 817.

1. FURNITURE INDUSTRY

Comparison of Income, Residential Construction, and Household Furniture Expenditures

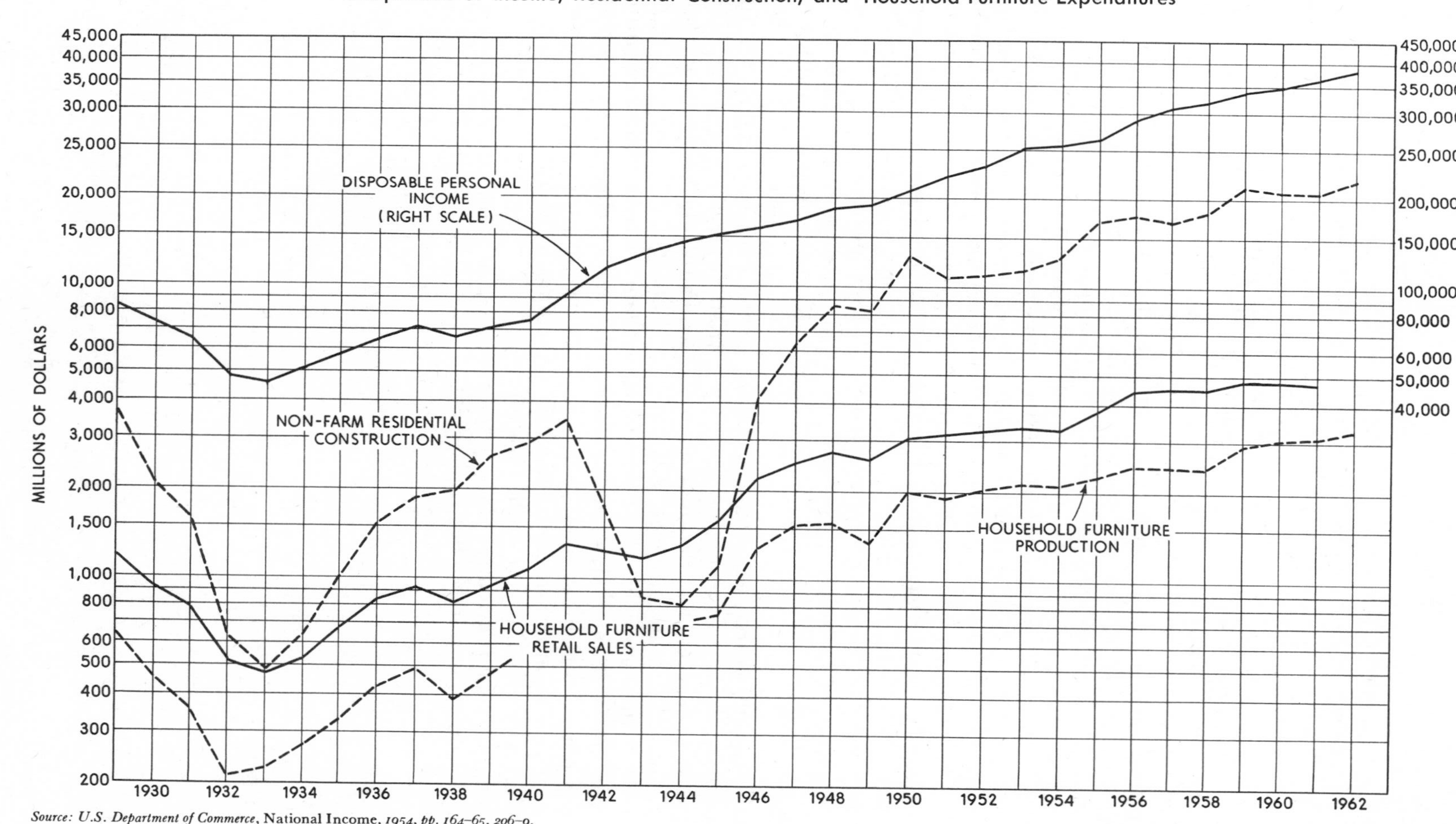

Source: U.S. Department of Commerce, National Income, *1954, pp. 164–65, 206–9.*

2. FURNITURE INDUSTRY

Value of Manufacturers' Shipments, 1947-1961

	1947	1948	1949	1950	1951	1952	1953	1954	1955	1956	1957	1958	1959	1960	1961
1. Total Furniture Shipments*	$1,538	$1,551	$1,355	$2,078	$1,971	$2,043	$2,123	$2,219	$2,553	$2,705	$2,699	$2,590	$2,913**	$2,835**	$2,738
2. Wood Furniture	901	867	727	1,092	1,009	1,039	1,075	1,113	1,244	1,306	1,266	1,340	1,525	1,486	1,449
a. Living Room	226	241	223	200	205	220	219	212	225	237	253	222	260	267	264
b. TV Cabinets	---	---	---	232	144	134	142	103	103	100	101	114	120	107	105
c. Bedroom	353	361	288	388	379	411	439	391	465	490	444	457	533	512	497
d. Dining Room	119	129	119	152	159	142	152	145	160	172	161	167**	200**	204**	188**
e. Kitchen	54	40	31	41	47	50	43	126	145	154	155	190**	(211**	199**	201**
f. Porch & Lawn	6	6	6	7	7	10	10	13	(NA	(NA	(NA	53	61	61	61
g. Juvenile and Other	143	90	60	72	68	72	70	123	(146	(153	(152	137	141	136	133
3. Upholstered Furniture***	419	454	409	595	598	638	693	690	814	882	920	765	854**	843**	813
4. Metal Furniture	218	230	219	361	346	335	355	416	495	517	513	485	533	506	476
5. Other Furniture#		---	---	30	18	31	---	---	---	---	---		---	---	

*Excludes bedding.
**Not strictly comparable with prior years.
***Excludes frames shipped separately.
#Rattan, wicker, plastic, etc.

Sources: U.S. Department of Commerce, Bureau of the Census, Facts for Industry, Series M25D (1947-1961).
U.S. Department of Commerce, 1959 Census of Manufactures (1958-1959).

3. FURNITURE INDUSTRY

Indexes of Cost and Profit Factors
(1947-1949 = 100)

	Economic Factors			Furniture Manufacturing Factors					Furniture Manufacturing Results	
	1. All Wholesale Commodity Prices*	2. Disposable Personal Income**	3. Nonfarm Residential Construction**	4. Lumber Price*	5. Hourly Earnings*	6. Number of Employees**	7. Product Price*	8. Value of Shipments[1]	9. Net Profits on Sales[2]	10. Net Profits on Equity***
1947	96.4	92.9	82.8	94.5	94.0	101.6	95.6	103.8	114.0	124.2
1948	104.4	103.4	111.3	107.3	101.7	104.3	102.8	104.7	115.1	114.1
1949	99.2	103.7	106.0	98.3	105.1	94.1	101.5	91.5	70.9	61.7
1950	103.1	113.5	154.8	114.5	109.4	108.7	105.2	140.0	100.2	90.6
1951	114.8	124.3	137.6	123.6	118.8	105.3	116.4	133.1	73.4	94.0
1952	111.6	130.4	141.0	120.5	125.6	104.6	113.0	137.9	59.1	48.3
1953	110.1	138.0	151.3	119.3	131.6	108.4	113.9	143.3	59.1	61.7
1954	110.3	140.4	168.9	117.3	134.2	98.5	113.3	149.8	55.8	30.2
1955	110.7	149.9	205.5	124.4	138.5	105.3	114.0	172.3	76.6	57.0
1956	114.3	160.1	194.2	127.2	144.4	108.0	119.0	182.7	82.6	70.5
1957	117.6	168.7	186.9	119.7	149.6	106.3	122.5	182.3	64.8	60.4
1958	119.2	173.7	198.3	118.0	152.1	100.6	123.0	175.2	43.3	41.6
1959	119.5	184.3	274.2#	127.1	155.6	108.7	124.1	196.7	56.7	59.1
1960	119.6	192.2	247.7#	121.4	160.4	108.0	125.1	191.5	52.0	43.6
1961	119.2	200.0	241.8#	114.5	163.2	102.9	126.4	185.2	55.8	25.2
1962	119.5	216.2	269.9#	116.5	167.7	107.0	127.9	NA	NA	32.8

Sources:
*U.S. Department of Commerce, Survey of Current Business, Monthly Labor Review.
**U.S. Department of Commerce, Office of Business Economics, Business Statistics, 1961.
***FTC, SEC, Quarterly Financial Reports.
#Not strictly comparable with prior years.
[1]Exhibit 2.
[2]Exhibit 4.

4. FURNITURE INDUSTRY

Operating Costs of Furniture Manufacturers, 1948-1961
(In Cents per Sales Dollar)

A. CASE GOODS

	1948	1949	1950	1951	1952	1953	1954	1955	1956	1957	1958	1959	1960	1961
1. Material Cost	41.25	38.40	39.28	39.55	39.43	40.03	41.21	41.50	41.56	41.35	43.95			
2. Direct Labor	19.78	21.31	20.01	20.82	20.10	19.80	20.37	18.71	19.43	20.38	20.61			
3. Factory Overhead	15.65	18.87	17.51	16.56	18.18	17.45	16.14	15.34	14.46	15.65	15.96			
4. Selling Expense	7.38	9.58	8.77	9.19	9.29	9.37	9.14	9.16	8.35	8.43	8.47			
5. Administrative	4.74	5.27	4.37	4.94	4.99	5.27	5.19	4.60	4.64	4.95	4.58			
6. Income Taxes	4.33	2.85	4.69	4.85	4.37	4.55	4.31	5.59	6.01	5.01	3.65			
7. Net Profit	6.87	3.72	5.37	4.09	3.64	3.53	3.64	5.10	5.55	4.23	2.78	4.13	3.64	4.34

B. CHAIRS

	1948	1949	1950	1951	1952	1953	1954	1955	1956	1957	1958	1959	1960	1961
1. Material Cost	44.33	39.41	44.09	45.86	44.37	41.26	36.37	36.53	35.10	41.18	38.59			
2. Direct Labor	20.80	21.32	20.30	20.63	21.20	23.19	23.98	23.63	23.37	20.86	20.76			
3. Factory Overhead	15.77	19.49	15.45	12.98	15.98	15.48	19.52	19.45	18.47	15.55	16.84			
4. Selling Expense	9.13	9.03	8.53	8.99	8.69	9.74	8.85	8.88	9.12	10.68	11.72			
5. Administrative	4.77	6.43	5.81	5.10	5.74	5.49	6.91	7.05	7.42	5.77	5.84			
6. Income Taxes	2.08	1.83	2.50	3.62	2.31	2.73	2.32	2.23	3.22	2.89	3.10			
7. Net Profit	3.12	2.49	3.32	2.82	1.71	2.11	2.05	2.23	3.30	3.07	3.15			

C. UPHOLSTERED

	1948	1949	1950	1951	1952	1953	1954	1955	1956	1957	1958	1959	1960	1961
1. Material Cost	46.80	46.17	46.34	48.06	48.16	46.40	45.75	48.69	45.59	46.54	46.59			
2. Direct Labor	15.17	16.68	15.40	14.86	15.75	15.64	15.69	15.11	16.17	16.44	17.21			
3. Factory Overhead	14.98	16.12	14.60	15.28	16.61	17.48	17.94	13.85	15.09	15.26	15.75			
4. Selling Expense	7.95	9.02	7.87	8.99	8.39	8.60	8.90	8.51	8.52	8.86	9.71			
5. Administrative	4.98	5.41	4.68	5.07	5.08	5.82	5.95	5.88	5.85	5.84	5.89			
6. Income Taxes	3.69	2.32	4.93	3.56	2.99	2.97	2.73	3.95	4.47	3.49	2.53			
7. Net Profit	6.43	4.28	6.18	4.18	3.02	3.09	3.04	4.01	4.31	3.57	2.32	2.27	1.87	1.23

D. ALL FURNITURE

	1948	1949	1950	1951	1952	1953	1954	1955	1956	1957	1958	1959	1960	1961
1. Material Cost	42.86	41.60	42.15	42.97	43.20	42.31	42.28	43.32	42.59	42.41	43.59	42.30	42.28	42.01
2. Direct Labor	18.32	19.47	18.16	18.72	18.56	18.81	18.95	18.01	18.27	18.77	19.28	18.73	19.07	19.34
3. Factory Overhead	15.78	18.12	16.53	16.20	17.47	17.80	17.97	16.12	15.87	16.66	17.10	17.59	17.44	16.98
4. Selling Expense	7.98	9.14	8.33	8.83	8.73	8.56	8.97	8.63	8.64	9.19	9.32	9.30	9.40	9.60
5. Administrative	4.92	5.36	4.85	5.07	5.22	5.58	5.56	5.38	5.31	5.48	5.46	5.20	5.50	5.20
6. Income Taxes	3.87	2.45	4.52	4.21	3.60	3.72	3.23	4.37	4.82	3.96	2.89	3.50	3.26	3.58
7. Net Profit	6.27	3.86	5.46	4.00	3.22	3.22	3.04	4.17	4.50	3.53	2.36	3.09	2.83	3.04

Sources: Frank E. Seidman, *Furniture Age*, July, 1949-1953; *Home Furnishings Daily*, June, 1954-1960; July, 1961, 1962.

5. FURNITURE INDUSTRY

Profit Levels and Size of Company

A. Profit Margin per Dollar of Sales by Percent of Total Plants Reporting

	1948	1949	1950	1951	1952	1953	1954	1955	1956	1957	1958	1959	1960	1961
Over 10¢ Profit	9	2	4	1.5	1	0	0	0.5	2.0	---	---	---	---	---
5.1¢ to 10¢ Profit	37	32	36	21.5	9	10	10	13.0	13.9	15.3	10.1	15.5	11.9	14.6
1.1¢ to 5¢ Profit	(45	(43	(46	57	61	69	55	60.5	59.2	51.3	45.7	58.9	49.7	39.5
Less than 1¢ Profit	(	(	(	6.5	12	11	8	10.8	10.5	12.8	17.8	9.6	14.1	16.6
0.0¢ to 5¢ Loss	(	(	10	8.5	11	7	21	9.9	12.0	11.1	16.2	9.6	16.7	22.3
5.1¢ to 10¢ Loss	(9	(23	(	2.5	4	2	5	4.5	1.0	6.3	5.6	3.2	5.4	3.8
Over 10¢ Loss	(	(	(	2.5	2	1	1	0.8	1.4	3.2	4.6	3.2	2.2	3.2

B. Profit Margin by Plant Sales Volume (In Cents per Sales Dollar)

	1948	1949	1950	1951	1952	1953	1954	1955	1956	1957	1958	1959	1960	1961
$ 250,000 or less	.9	(3.4)	(.1)	1.87	(	(	(	(.09	(	(	(	(	(	
Over $ 250,000 up to $ 500,000	2.9	1.2	2.4	2.00	(.71	(.57	(.38	(	(.06	((.34)	((.93)	(.29	((1.83)	(
Over $ 500,000 up to $1,000,000	5.2	3.0	3.8	2.45	2.28	2.65	1.52	2.17	1.81	1.07	.25	.76	1.43	(3.11
Over $ 1,000,000 up to $2,500,000	5.2	2.5	4.1	3.59	2.47	2.77	1.71	2.29	2.72	2.35	1.10	3.03	2.09	0.22
Over $ 2,500,000 up to $5,000,000	5.0	3.1	5.8	3.76	2.38	2.76	2.11	3.20	3.28	2.58	1.19	2.44	1.48	(
Over $ 5,000,000	8.0	6.0	7.1	5.03	4.59	4.00	4.99							(1.78
$ 5,000,000-$10,000,000								2.82	2.79	3.19	2.28	1.31	2.02	2.93
$10,000,000-$25,000,000								6.34	7.14	5.54	3.62	4.98	4.70	3.98
Over $25,000,000								6.98	7.50	6.02	4.77	4.46	4.18	4.39

Source: Frank E. Seidman, Furniture Age, July, 1949-1953; Home Furnishings Daily, June, 1954-1960; July, 1961, 1962.

C. Furniture Manufacturers Employing 500 or More[1]

	No. of Employees	$ Sales
Kroehler Mfg. (Ill.)	6,000	91
Drexel Ent. (N.C.)	5,000	50
Bassett Furniture Inc. (Va.)	2,500	48
Heywood-Wakefield (Mass.)	2,500	24
Baumritter Corp. (N.Y.)	2,200	--
American Furniture (Va.)	1,600	22
Lane Co. Inc. (Va.)	1,500	--
Lenoir Chair Co. (N.C.)	1,225	10
Dixie Furniture Co. (N.C.)	1,000	10
Williams Furniture Corp. (S.C.)	1,000	--

	No. of Employees	$ Sales
Basic-Witz Furniture Ind. (Va.)	900	--
Stanley Furniture Co. (Va.)	900	11
Memphis Furniture Mfg. (Tenn.)	800	--
Mersman Bros. Corp. (Ohio)	600	9
Ward Furniture Mfg. (Ark.)	600	8
Eisen Bros. Inc. (N.J.)	500	12
White Furniture Co. (N.C.)	500	7
Tell City Chair Co. (Ind.)	500	--
Rway Furniture Co. Inc. (Wis.)	500	--
Lewisburg Chair & Furniture (Pa.)	500	--

[1]Standard Industrial Classification 2511 is primary product.
Source: Dun & Bradstreet, "Million Dollar Directory," 1962.

6. FURNITURE INDUSTRY

Cost Factors of Manufacture, 1950 and 1960

A. Case Goods Manufacturing Costs, 1950
(In Cents per Sales Dollar)

		North	South
1.	Materials	39.5	50.1
	Direct Labor	17.2	12.0
	Indirect Labor	11.8	6.0
	Repairs, Maint., Deprec'n	3.7	2.2
	Tools & Supplies	2.5	2.0
	Light, Power, Fuel, Water	2.1	0.9
	Local Taxes & Insurance	2.8	0.5
	Selling Salaries & Commissions	5.8	6.1
	Advertising & Other Selling	3.7	3.3
	Officers' & Office Salaries	3.3	2.9
	Other General Expense	1.7	1.0
	Interest	0.2	0.2
	Federal Taxes	2.3	5.5
	Net Profits	3.4	7.3
2.	Ratios:		
	Net Profit to Real Capital	7.4%	23.4%
	Sales to Real Capital	2.1 to 1	3.2 to 1
	Current Assets to Current Liabilities	3.4 to 1	2.0 to 1
	Value of Plant to Productive Wages	1.0 to 1	1.5 to 1
	Direct to Indirect Workers	3.0 to 1	11.0 to 1
3.	Other Factors:		
	Rate of Stock Turnover	2.7 mos.	1.0 month
	Floor Space per Direct Worker	708 sq. ft.	380 sq. ft.
	Wood Waste	68%	45%
	Average Manufacturing Cycle	6 weeks	10 days
	Average Delivery from Date of Order	7 weeks	4 weeks

Source: Anglo-American Council on Productivity, Productivity Team Report on Furniture, April, 1962, p. 60.

B. Furniture Manufacturing Costs, 1960
(In Cents per Sales Dollar)

		Drexel	Plants over $25 mm Sales	Southern States	All Manufacturers
1.	Materials	37.72	42.99	43.95	42.28
	Direct Labor	16.94	17.65	18.66	19.07
	Indirect Labor	9.84	11.08	6.88	8.71
	Depreciation	1.49	1.76	1.64	1.63
	Local Taxes	1.61	1.71	1.51	1.90
	Other Overhead	6.00	3.76	3.88	5.20
	Selling Expense	8.49	7.10	9.00	9.42
	General & Administrative	4.17	5.26	4.70	5.51
	Other Income	0.13	0.19	(0.06)	(0.19)
	Income Taxes	7.43	4.70	5.19	3.26
	Net Profits	6.44	4.18	4.53	2.83
2.	Other Factors:				
	Operating Profit per Employee	$1,655	$1,134	$1,209	$ 833
	Net Worth per Employee	6,083	6,784	4,884	5,169
	Manufacturing Overhead to Del.	112%	104%	75%	91%
	Inventory Turnover	3.9	5.5	5.5	4.9
	Capital Investment to Shipments	50.47%	51.87%	39.46%	38.99%
	Capital Investment to Profit	3.11%	8.20%	11.88%	7.46%

Source: Seidman and Seidman, Cost Survey of the Furniture Industry, 1961.

7. FURNITURE INDUSTRY

Wage Rates in Furniture Plants

A. Earnings in Furniture Industry and All Durable Goods

Year	Furniture Industry: Average Weekly Earnings	Furniture Industry: Average Weekly Hours	Furniture Industry: Average Hourly Earnings	All Durable Goods Manufacturing: Average Weekly Earnings	All Durable Goods Manufacturing: Average Weekly Hours	All Durable Goods Manufacturing: Average Hourly Earnings
1946	$39.97	41.6	$0.962	$46.49	40.2	$1.156
1947	45.45	41.7	1.090	52.45	40.6	1.292
1948	46.76	40.8	1.146	57.11	40.5	1.410
1949	47.04	39.8	1.182	58.03	39.5	1.469
1950	51.91	41.9	1.239	63.32	41.2	1.537
1951	55.08	40.8	1.344	69.97	41.7	1.678
1952	58.93	41.5	1.42	73.46	41.5	1.77
1953	60.38	40.8	1.48	77.23	41.3	1.87
1954	60.25	39.9	1.51	77.18	40.2	1.92
1955	63.76	41.4	1.54	83.21	41.4	2.01
1956	68.95	40.8	1.69	86.31	41.1	2.10
1957	70.00	40.0	1.75	88.66	40.3	2.20
1958	70.31	39.5	1.78	90.06	39.5	2.28
1959	74.44	40.9	1.82	97.10	40.8	2.38
1960	75.20	40.0	1.88	97.44	40.1	2.43
1961	76.21	39.9	1.91	100.10	40.2	2.49
1962	79.37	40.7	1.95	105.11	40.9	2.57

B. Earnings by Payment Method, 1959

Men	Time Workers: Number of Workers	Time Workers: Average Hourly Earnings	Incentive Workers: Number of Workers	Incentive Workers: Average Hourly Earnings
Assemblers, case goods	5,127	$1.49	2,296	$1.86
Assemblers, chairs	695	1.35	197	1.71
Cut-off saw operators	1,351	1.54	341	1.69
Gluers, rough stock	1,627	1.28	470	1.67
Off-bearers, machine	4,835	1.20	901	1.52
Packers, furniture	2,161	1.29	513	1.65
Rubbers, hand	1,738	1.30	489	1.77
Sanders, belt	3,003	1.43	914	1.69
Sanders, hand	3,077	1.30	670	1.68
Shaper operators	991	1.62	333	1.81
Sprayers	3,251	1.48	926	1.85

C. Earnings under Selected Conditions, 1959

	Number of Workers	Average Hourly Earnings
1. All Production Workers:	101,310	$1.46
Men	90,371	1.47
Women	10,939	1.34
2. Size of Community:		
Metropolitan areas	39,161	1.61
Nonmetropolitan areas	62,149	1.36
3. Size of Establishment:		
20-99 Workers	27,708	1.53
100 or more Workers	73,602	1.43
4. Labor-Management Contracts:		
Majority of workers covered	35,739	1.70
None or minority of workers covered	65,571	1.32

Sources: U.S. Department of Commerce, Office of Business Economics, Business Statistics, 1961; Bureau of Labor Statistics Report #152, "Wage Structure, Wood Household Furniture, Except Upholstered," April-May, 1959.

8. FURNITURE INDUSTRY

Earnings by Region, 1959

	New England		Middle Atlantic		Great Lakes		Pacific	
	Number of Workers	Average Hourly Earnings	Number of Workers	Average Hourly Earnings	Number of Workers	Average Hourly Earnings	Number of Workers	Average Hourly Earnings
Assemblers, case goods	273	$1.59	1,142	$1.90	1,624	$1.86	630	$2.27
Assemblers, chairs	106	1.66	193	1.66	132	1.45	46	1.93
Cut-off saw operators	143	1.49	278	1.82	298	1.74	159	2.12
Gluers, rough stock	76	1.60	230	1.75	302	1.54	96	2.04
Maintenance men, general utility	68	1.82	165	1.82	255	1.79	37	2.52
Off-bearers, machine	279	1.36	333	1.50	608	1.47	394	1.79
Packers, furniture	119	1.46	283	1.68	522	1.62	58	2.03
Rubbers, hand	101	1.77	184	1.96	387	1.71	78	1.92
Sanders, belt	209	1.64	429	1.78	717	1.72	224	2.12
Sanders, hand	92	1.60	591	1.66	505	1.64	242	1.79
Shaper operators, hand, setup, and operate	120	1.71	201	1.75	298	1.79	144	2.24
Sprayers	176	1.71	659	1.92	852	1.82	143	2.08

	Southeast		Border States		Southwest		United States	
	Number of Workers	Average Hourly Earnings	Number of Workers	Average Hourly Earnings	Number of Workers	Average Hourly Earnings	Number of Workers	Average Hourly Earnings
Assemblers, case goods	2,160	$1.27	964	$1.39	567	$1.25	7,423	$1.61
Assemblers, chairs	381	1.19	68	1.32	---	---	892	1.43
Cut-off saw operators	551	1.30	162	1.49	82	1.24	1,692	1.57
Gluers, rough stock	893	1.19	407	1.26	88	1.21	2,097	1.37
Maintenance men, general utility	422	1.44	182	1.58	91	1.39	1,224	1.63
Off-bearers, machine	2,823	1.11	1,037	1.21	209	1.15	5,736	1.25
Packers, furniture	1,136	1.16	372	1.26	167	1.18	2,674	1.36
Rubbers, hand	1,024	1.17	333	1.27	120	1.22	2,227	1.40
Sanders, belt	1,665	1.27	517	1.39	156	1.29	3,917	1.49
Sanders, hand	1,731	1.16	432	1.25	138	1.19	3,747	1.37
Shaper operators, hand, setup, and operate	398	1.38	101	1.54	58	1.39	1,324	1.67
Sprayers	1,491	1.29	636	1.41	188	1.36	4,177	1.57

Source: Bureau of Labor Statistics Report #152, "Wage Structure, Wood Household Furniture, Except Upholstered," April-May, 1959.

9. FURNITURE INDUSTRY

Value of Furniture Shipped by State, 1954, 1958, and 1961
(Dollars in Thousands)

State	Wood (Not Upholstered)			Upholstered			Metal			Total		
	1954	1958	1961	1954	1958	1961	1954	1958	1961	1954	1958	1961
1. North Carolina	$ 187,891	$ 235,784	$ 263,783	$ 66,368	$120,097	$155,523	NLS	NLS	NLS	$ 256,553	$ 355,881	$ 419,306
2. Virginia	141,374	175,962	47,381	NLS	21,357	24,304	NLS	$ 3,266	NLS	157,374	200,585	71,685
3. California	NLS	102,750	92,837	56,126	81,122	92,903	$ 20,015	41,720	$ 22,681	126,088	225,412	208,421
4. Indiana	108,901	100,449	131,090	31,581	38,273	32,672	44,831	46,426	39,059	185,317	185,148	202,821
5. New York	76,975	96,914	73,512	82,247	75,559	50,304	NLS	62,624	33,635	205,161	235,097	157,451
6. Pennsylvania	62,987	74,036	44,024	27,370	NLS	36,335	38,044	61,258	23,527	129,148	135,294	103,886
7. Illinois	65,502	69,464	46,328	58,127	53,703	35,782	65,237	87,004	59,211	201,865	210,171	141,321
8. Tennessee	33,730	50,376	35,825	29,943	42,575	49,115	5,711	6,310	8,637	33,730	99,261	93,577
9. Michigan	51,352	49,173	22,309	NLS	21,881	20,635	16,280	NLS	13,872	103,504	71,054	56,816
10. Arkansas	25,829	43,443	45,114	9,923	16,714	11,101	NLS	4,469	NLS	25,829	64,626	56,215
11. Massachusetts	39,007	39,861	18,388	31,937	31,257	27,814	12,254	NLS	13,062	85,917	71,118	59,264
12. Kentucky	27,737	29,533	25,151	5,633	10,795	NLS	6,281	12,979	NLS	27,737	53,307	25,131
13. Wisconsin	31,725	28,514	17,580	19,486	10,751	12,872	8,479	NLS	NLS	81,006	39,265	30,452
14. Ohio	14,927	25,886	20,393	33,353	32,031	25,303	39,286	37,668	12,527	90,426	95,585	58,223
15. Texas	9,909	18,406	17,116	24,985	30,991	24,712	5,117	NLS	5,757	60,452	49,397	47,585
16. All Others	197,469	237,989	466,204	189,277	195,994	133,607	93,792	137,423	224,853	356,929	571,406	824,664
Total	$1,075,135	$1,378,360	$1,367,015	$666,356	$783,100	$732,982	$355,327	$501,147	$456,821	$2,127,036	$2,662,607	$2,556,818

Note: 1961 figures may not be exactly comparable.
NLS: Not listed separately.
Sources: Bureau of the Census, Facts for Industry, November 12, 1954; 1958 Census of Manufactures. 1961 U.S. Department of Commerce, Current Industrial Reports (Series M25D) 1961-1 ("Household Furniture and Bedding Products").

10. FURNITURE INDUSTRY

Selected Statistics for Furniture Wholesalers

	1955	1958	1959	1960	1961
Sales	100	100	100	100	100
Cost of Sales	78.6	78.1	77.5	78.5	76.55
Gross Profit	21.4	21.9	22.6	21.6	23.45
Expenses	19.1	20.2	19.7	20.0	21.72
Profit before Tax	2.4	1.7	2.8	1.6	1.73
Taxes	1.0	0.9	1.4	0.7	0.81
Profit after Tax	1.4	0.9	1.4	0.9	0.92
Net Worth/Fixed Assets	5.3	7.2	6.6	8.8	8.4
Net Worth/Debt	1.9	1.9	2.0	2.2	1.7
Sales/Receivables	8.7	7.4	7.5	7.9	5.4
Cost of Sales/Inventory	5.4	5.2	4.9	4.9	4.7
Stockturn (Days)	67	69	74	73	77
Sales/Fixed Assets	22.3	26.6	24.0	32.4	28.9
Sales/Net Worth	4.2	3.7	3.7	3.7	3.2
% Profits/Net Worth	5.7	3.2	5.4	3.2	2.0
Sales/Total Assets	2.8	2.4	2.4	2.5	2.2
Sales (Millions $)	3.17	5.11	6.19	5.58	6.95
Total Assets (Millions $)	1.15	2.09	2.55	2.22	3.22
Number of Companies	24	33	34	30	41

Source: Robert Morris Associates, Statement Studies.

11. FURNITURE INDUSTRY

Operating Ratios of Large Furniture Retailers
(In Percent of Net Sales)

	1947	1948	1949	1950	1951	1952	1953	1954
Gross margin on sales	39.72%	38.91%	38.50%	39.78%	38.93%	38.84%	39.12%	39.02%
Operating expenses:								
Administrative (incl. buying)	9.54	9.72	10.27	10.15	10.93	11.13	11.53	11.09
Occupancy	4.79	5.00	5.80	5.24	5.45	6.12	6.44	5.85
Advertising and publicity	3.84	4.40	4.57	4.57	4.71	5.49	5.38	5.52
Selling	5.87	5.92	5.92	6.30	6.51	6.50	6.79	7.22
Handling	3.76	3.66	4.06	3.87	4.03	4.22	4.51	4.50
Delivery	2.50	2.46	2.82	2.82	2.90	3.02	3.29	3.26
Total operating expenses	30.30%	31.16%	33.44%	32.95%	34.53%	36.49%	37.94%	37.44%
Net profit before income tax*	10.87	8.75	6.48	8.07	5.64	4.54	4.18	3.73
Net profit after income tax	6.86	5.72	4.09	5.05	2.98	2.65	2.23	1.96

	1955	1956	1957**	1958	1959	1960	1961	1962
Gross margin on sales	38.52%	38.75%	38.66%	37.74%	38.77%	38.11%	38.40%	38.32%
Operating expenses:								
Administrative (incl. buying)	11.00	11.10	11.42	10.86	12.15	13.28	12.88	12.10
Occupancy	5.67	5.83	6.60	6.41	6.65	6.88	6.62	6.62
Advertising and publicity	5.11	5.32	5.97	5.24	6.44	5.97	6.56	5.77
Selling	7.21	7.24	7.12	7.00	6.58	6.59	6.68	7.15
Handling	4.43	4.19	4.63	4.17	3.96	4.45	4.16	4.64
Delivery	3.18	3.34	3.14	3.36	3.03	3.60	3.51	3.76
Total operating expenses	36.60%	37.02%	38.88%	37.04%	38.81%	40.77%	40.41%	40.04%
Net operating profit	1.92	1.73	(.22)	.70	(.04)	(2.66)	(2.01)	(1.62)
Other income	3.35	3.01	3.67	2.14	3.85	4.65	5.54	4.48
Net profit before income tax	5.27	4.74	3.45	2.84	3.81	1.99	3.53	2.76
Net profit after income tax	2.88	2.59	1.79	1.48	2.50	.95	2.00	1.82

*Net operating profit plus net other income or less net other charges.
**Classified as over $350,000 until 1956; over $1,000,000 from 1957.

Sources: Professor Ira D. Anderson, National Furniture Review, July, 1949; May, 1950-1957; June, 1959-1963.

12. FURNITURE INDUSTRY

Department Data of Retail Furniture Stores

	1954				1956			
	Net Sales	Inventories*	Turnover**	Gross Margin***	Net Sales	Inventories	Turnover	Gross Margin
1. Furniture								
Living Room--Uphol.	18.4%	14.9%	2.6	44.8%	18.5%	16.8%	3.0	44.5%
Living Room--Wood	4.9	6.3	1.6	43.4	5.4	7.8	1.9	43.6
Dining Room	4.1	6.6	1.6	46.2	4.7	6.6	1.8	44.7
Bedroom	10.7	12.6	2.1	44.4	12.2	13.8	2.3	44.4
Bedding	12.1	8.9	3.3	42.2	11.5	7.4	4.6	43.0
Kitchen	3.7	3.5	3.1	39.7	3.8	3.2	3.0	41.2
Sunroom	1.5	1.9	2.3	36.0	1.6	1.6	3.0	36.7
Juvenile	1.4	1.4	2.2	38.7	0.8	1.2	2.2	39.4
2. Appliances								
Television	3.9	2.7	5.3	28.9	3.4	2.4	5.4	28.3
Refrigerators	3.4	3.2	3.7	32.6	3.6	3.2	4.0	31.3
Stoves & Ranges	3.4	3:5	2.5	36.2	2.5	2.8	3.0	36.5
Washers & Ironers	3.2	3.3	4.0	34.5	3.8	3.0	4.1	32.9
3. Store-Wide	100	100	24	38.0	100	100	3.0	38.8

	1958				1960			
	Net Sales	Inventories	Turnover	Gross Margin	Net Sales	Inventories	Turnover	Gross Margin
1. Furniture								
Living Room--Uphol.	18.3%	15.3%	3.2	43.1%	19.8%	17.5%	2.9	44.2%
Living Room--Wood	5.0	7.9	1.9	42.2	5.0	7.9	1.7	43.9
Dining Room	3.9	5.9	1.9	42.6	4.2	6.6	1.7	44.0
Bedroom	10.7	11.6	2.6	43.3	11.1	12.2	2.3	43.9
Bedding	11.1	8.1	4.4	41.2	12.1	7.6	4.3	42.8
Kitchen	3.5	3.4	3.2	39.5	3.0	2.8	3.2	39.2
Sunroom	1.5	1.8	3.1	32.5	1.8	1.5	2.7	33.6
Juvenile	0.7	1.1	2.2	36.9	0.8	0.9	2.3	38.7
2. Appliances								
Television	4.3	3.4	5.0	29.0	4.6	3.1	4.1	28.7
Refrigerators	4.1	3.4	4.7	28.9	2.8	2.7	4.2	28.7
Stoves & Ranges	2.5	2.3	3.2	33.0	2.3	2.0	3.4	34.9
Washers & Ironers	3.7	3.2	4.2	31.2	3.8	3.3	4.0	29.6
3. Store-Wide	100	100	3.0	37.7	100	100	30	38.1

*Average Inventory of Each Department Divided by Total Average Inventory.
**Cost of Sales for Each Department Divided by the Average Inventory of That Department.
***Gross Margin of Each Department Divided by Net Sales of That Department.

Sources: Professor Ira D. Anderson, National Furniture Review, June, 1955, p. 64; June, 1957, p. 59; June, 1959, p. 76; July, 1961, p. 44.

13. FURNITURE INDUSTRY

Retail Market Factors

A. Volume of Sales by Furniture Stores, 1948 and 1958

Annual Sales	1948 Number of Stores	1948 Sales (In Millions)	1958 Number of Stores	1958 Sales (In Millions)
Under $20,000	5,622	$ 55.9	6,627	$ 65
$ 20,000 to $ 29,000	2,517	61.8	2,875	69
$ 30,000 to $ 49,000	4,320	168.8	4,300	169
$ 50,000 to $ 99,000	6,992	504.9	7,202	521
$100,000 to $299,000	7,425	1,238.8	9,669	1,634
$300,000 to $499,000	1,259	476.6	1,915	727
$500,000 to $999,000	646	434.2	1,055	698
Over $1,000,000	250	486.1	366	690
	29,031	$3,427.1	34,009	$4,573

B. Share of Market by Single Store and Chain Stores, 1948 and 1958

	1948 Number of Stores	1948 Sales (In Millions)	1958 Number of Stores	1958 Sales (In Millions)
One-store firms	24,612	$2,447	30,747	$3,424
One-store operated by nonfurniture chain	714	115	1,085	164
2 or 3 stores	2,654	466	2,947	589
4 or 5 stores	425	158	425	146
6 to 10 stores	361	112	295	181
11 to 25 stores	166	91	308	98
Over 26 stores	99	37	289	180
	29,031	$3,427	36,096	$4,782

C. Monthly Sales of Furniture Stores

	1953	1954	1961
January	7.3%	6.9%	6.8%
February	6.9	6.8	6.6
March	7.6	7.5	7.4
April	7.7	7.7	7.5
May	8.9	8.4	8.4
June	8.8	8.3	8.6
July	8.0	8.0	8.1
August	8.5	8.2	8.9
September	7.6	8.2	8.4
October	9.2	9.2	9.0
November	9.0	9.5	9.4
December	10.5	11.5	10.9

D. Style Changes in Furniture

	Modern	English	American	French, Italian, and Others
1935	25%	22%	13%	40%
1940	27	36	11	26
1945	35	27	6	32
1950	44	22	8	26
1955	61	8	11	20
1960	50	2	14	34
1962	40	3	13	44

Sources: U.S. Census of Business, Retail Trade General Statistics Vol. II, 1948, 1958; Burdett Green, "The Fight for Style Supremacy," National Furniture Review, December, 1951, p. 59; and American Walnut Association.

14. FURNITURE INDUSTRY
Consumer Market Factors

A. Pattern of Consumer Spending for the Home, 1950-1959
(As a Percent of Disposable Personal Income)

	1950	1951	1952	1953	1954	1955	1956	1957	1958	1959
1. Share of Home Spending										
Construction	7.2	5.9	5.8	5.8	6.3	7.1	6.3	5.8	5.9	6.8
Household Goods	10.7	10.0	9.4	9.2	9.1	9.4	9.2	8.9	8.7	8.8
Household Services	4.6	4.6	4.7	4.8	4.9	5.1	5.3	5.3	5.6	5.3
Rent	10.2	10.2	10.6	10.9	11.3	11.3	11.2	11.5	12.0	12.0
2. Share of Household Goods										
Furniture	1.5	1.4	1.4	1.4	1.4	1.5	1.5	1.5	1.4	N.A.
Rugs and China	3.5	3.4	3.0	2.8	2.6	2.7	2.7	2.6	2.6	
Appliances	1.9	1.7	1.6	1.6	1.6	1.7	1.7	1.5	1.4	
Radio and TV	1.2	1.0	1.0	1.0	1.1	1.0	1.0	1.0	1.0	
Fuel	1.6	1.5	1.4	1.3	1.3	1.3	1.2	1.2	1.1	
Cleaning and Other	1.1	1.1	1.0	1.1	1.1	1.1	1.2	1.2	1.2	
3. Disposable Income (In Billions of Dollars)	$207.7	$227.5	$238.7	$252.5	$256.9	$274.4	$292.9	$308.8	$317.9	$337.3

Source: Fortune, "Markets of the Sixties," 1960, p. 235.

B. Purchase Rates of Furniture, 1950
(Average Income Families)

	Purchase Interval	Purchase Amount
Living Room	16 years	$250
Bedroom	18	235
Dining Room	35	158
Bedding	10	40
Kitchen	10	35

Source: U.S. Chamber of Commerce, Domestic Distribution Department, Distribution News Letter #14, January 6, 1950.

C. Median Expenditures

	1951	1953	1955	1957
Furniture	$200	$200	$255	$230
TV Set	300	300	250	210
Refrigerator	255	280	260	245
Washing Machine	180	200	205	210

Source: U.S. Board of Governors, Federal Reserve Bulletin, June, 1954; May, 1955; Federal Reserve Survey, 1958.

White Furniture Company

The White Furniture Company, one of the oldest manufacturers of fine furniture in the South, produced bedroom, dining room, and upholstered furniture. The company was located in Mebane, a small town in North Carolina with a population of approximately 3,500. The nearest large metropolitan centers were Greensboro and Raleigh at distances of about 30 and 50 miles, respectively. The company's sales volume for the year ending November 1, 1946, totaled about $2,500,000; for the year ending November 1, 1947, it was estimated that sales would exceed $3,000,000.

In January, 1947, the company was considering an extensive program for the modernization of its plant equipment and production processes. This program involved a total expenditure of about $275,000. The executives were also reviewing all of their policies and procedures in order that the company might be put in the best possible shape for the intense competitive struggle which they believed was very likely to develop in the furniture industry in the near future.

COMPANY HISTORY

The White Furniture Company had a very humble beginning. It was founded in 1881 by two brothers, Will and Dave White. The two young men had been working as telegraph operators and were able to save up a few hundred dollars from their wages. With this money and a loan from a family friend, they purchased a carload of lumber and a secondhand planer and set up a plant to manufacture wood products. Within a short time they began to make bedroom furniture, and it was not long before dining room furniture was added to the line. One of the first products on which the company secured a substantial sales volume was a solid oak bedroom suite consisting of a bed, dresser, and wash stand. This suite was sold at a price of $9 to hotels, hospitals, and other institutions.

The White brothers were conservative and wished to guard against "expansion for expansion's sake." Mr. Will White insisted throughout his lifetime that under no circumstances should the company cheapen the quality of its products. In 1946, the White family still held about 85 percent of the common stock.

In the latter part of 1939, the White Furniture Company purchased the Orange Furniture Craftsmen Company. This concern which was located in Hillsboro about nine miles from Mebane, was a small manufacturer of inexpensive, upholstered furniture.

Shortly after the purchase of the Orange Furniture Company, the White Furniture Company set aside two floors in one of its warehouses at Mebane for the manufacture of a line of upholstered furniture comparable in quality to its case goods products.

PRODUCT POLICIES

The products of the White Furniture Company were divided into three major groups: The case goods, the White line of upholstered furniture, and the Orange line of upholstered furniture.

Case Goods: For many years the company had styled and designed its case goods line of bedroom and dining room suites to fill one specific "niche" in the industry. The entire line consisted of fine quality, mahogany veneer suites. The designs were "commercialized 18th Century"; that is, they were variations of Hepplewhite, Chippendale, Sheraton, and other 18th century patterns. Over a period of years, the company had identified itself rather closely with its product line. As the executives expressed it: "When people think of fine quality, mahogany veneer furniture in traditional 18th century patterns, they think of Whites'."

In normal times the company manufactured three or four different dining room suites and 15 or 20 different bedroom suites. During the war years the number of patterns was greatly reduced to compensate for the rising costs of materials and labor; without simplification of the line the company would not have been able to operate profitably under the wartime price ceilings. In

January, 1947, the company was producing one dining room suite and two bedroom suites. It was anticipated, however, that the number of suites would increase substantially in the near future. An illustration of one of the suites is shown in Exhibit 1A.

White Upholstered Furniture: The White line of upholstered furniture was styled in much the same manner as was the case goods line, but was somewhat less highly specialized. The quality of the upholstered furniture was comparable to that of the case goods. In normal times the company manufactured about 25 different sofas and about 50 different chairs; in January, 1947 it was producing about five sofas and five chairs.

The executives of the company believed that the upholstered furniture constituted a useful supplement to the case goods line because it gave customers a greater opportunity to make their purchases from the White Furniture Company in carload lots.

Orange Upholstered Furniture: The Orange line of upholstered furniture consisted primarily of platform rockers (see Exhibit 1B). The executives of the company described the products of the Orange plant as being of "good quality, reasonably priced." These products were sold under the name Orange Furniture Craftsmen. The stationery, shipping invoices, and bills sent to customers included also in fine type the phrase "Division of the White Furniture Company."

The products of the Orange plant were suitable for sale in many stores which were not able to carry the higher priced White line. It had been found, however, that occasionally stores started out handling the Orange line and later became interested in and able to handle a small volume of the White products.

Division of Sales Volume and Profits: In January, 1947, the weekly volume of production was divided among the three product groups approximately as follows: case goods $27,000, White upholstered furniture $8,000, and Orange upholstered furniture $9,000.[1] If proper machinery and additional employees could be secured, it would be possible to raise the output of case goods to about $40,000 per week. In its operating reports the company usually grouped together the case goods and the White upholstered furniture, but the basic records were such that the results for the two product lines could be determined separately whenever necessary. The executives of the company were of the opinion that the case goods and the White upholstered furniture yielded about the same profit margins. The Orange line was somewhat more profitable than the other two lines because of the circumstances under which the plant facilities at Hillsboro had been acquired.

[1] The production figures do not coincide exactly with the sales figures because the company purchased its benches and chairs from outside sources.

DISTRIBUTION POLICIES

In the years following 1930, the White Furniture Company made a number of changes in its distribution policies in the interests of obtaining a greater diversification in its sales outlets. The marketing program which had been developed By January, 1947, may be outlined as follows:

Sales Organization: The sales organization consisted of about 15 factory representatives, each of whom was assigned a particular geographic territory. These agents sold the products of the White Furniture Company along with noncompetitive products of other furniture manufacturers to the retail furniture stores in their respective areas. The representatives usually employed from one to six salesmen. The White Furniture Company paid the representatives a commission of 7 percent on sales of the White furniture and a commission of 9 percent on sales of the Orange furniture.

Retail Sales: By 1947 the company had secured distribution for its products in nearly all sections of the country with the exception of a strip of territory a few hundred miles wide just east of the Rocky Mountains. The volume of sales was divided among over 3,000 customers, with no one account responsible for more than one half of 1 percent of the total. The major market was in the New York, Philadelphia, Baltimore area; the second largest market was on the West Coast.

In selling to the retail outlets, it had not been the policy of the company to grant exclusive agencies. The executives believed that a larger and more stable sales volume could be secured if sales were scattered among a large number of

Production of White Upholstered Furniture: The first and second floors of the No. 11 Warehouse (see Exhibit 2) were used for the manufacture of the White upholstered furniture. The company purchased the wood frames for the upholstered pieces from outside contractors. Other components purchased from outside sources included springs for sofas and chairs, coil spring units for upholstered cushions, upholstery fabric, cotton batting, and sea moss.

The wood frames were purchased in the white and the exposed parts thus required finishing. This work was done in the finishing department of the case goods plant. The frames were then moved across the bridge (see Exhibit 2) to the upholstery departments.

There were about 21 people employed in the upholstery division, and their output was about $8,000 of finished furniture per week.[4] Wage payment was on a piece rate basis. The company was very careful not to operate this division more than 40 hours a week because the wage rates were high; upholsterers, for example, averaged $2.50 per hour and outsiders averaged about $1.25 per hour. The total manufacturing cost on upholstered pieces was divided approximately as follows: labor 10 percent, materials 75 percent, and burden 15 percent.

Orange Upholstered Furniture: The Hillsboro plant was used exclusively for the production of the Orange upholstered furniture. The production operations were basically the same as those for the upholstery division at Mebane. The difference in quality standards, however, made possible a faster rate of operation than could be secured at Mebane. Nearly all operations at the Hillsboro plant were paid on a piece rate basis, the operations were further broken down than at the Mebane plant, and the workers specialized more on particular jobs than they did at the Mebane plant. The Hillsboro plant also differed from the Mebane plant in that the former made its own frames for upholstered pieces.

The Hillsboro plant employed about 90 people, and the output was about $9,000 of finished furniture per week.

Labor Force: The company employed 230 people at the Mebane plant and 80 people at the Hillsboro plant. In January, 1947, the minimum wage was $.68 per hour as compared with $.30 in 1940. In February, 1947, there was a general wage increase of 10 percent which raised the minimum wage to $.75 per hour. A wage increase of $.19 per hour had been granted during the year 1946, and the executives intended to make further increases as soon as it was possible to do so. A Christmas bonus equal to 2 percent of the employee's annual earnings was a regular part of the company's wage program. All wages were paid on a straight hourly basis with the exception of the upholstery work which was paid on piece rates. The executives had not attempted the installation of piece rates in the case goods division because of the diversity of products and operations.

[4] Individual pieces varied widely in construction and cost, but this volume represented roughly 100 finished pieces per week.

PLANT MODERNIZATION PROGRAM

Immediately after the close of the war, the White Furniture Company considered an extensive program for the modernization and improvement of its production facilities. It was estimated that the entire program would involve a capital expenditure of about $275,000. This amount was a relatively large one for the company; the entire plant had cost only $480,000 in 1924 and since that time less than $75,000 had been spent for new equipment.

During the year 1946 the company bought a number of new woodworking machines. In addition, air actuated presses, power driven hand tools, and other automatic devices were installed wherever they could be used effectively. Other changes which were contemplated for future installation included the following:

Handling of Green Lumber: Under existing procedures, incoming green lumber was handled three times before it went into the dry kilns. The lumber was delivered to the plant in railroad cars on the siding next to the plant. The cars were unloaded, and the lumber stacked in piles along the tracks. When the lumber was needed in the production process, it was loaded onto a transfer truck and moved to the charging end of the dry kilns. It was then loaded onto the kiln truck on which it moved through the dry kilns. The work of handling the lumber was usually done by a team of three or four men and an inspector or supervisor. It was estimated that each handling involved a direct labor cost of about $2.50 per 1,000 board feet of lumber. As noted above, the plant used about 60,000 feet of lumber per week.

The new facilities being considered in January, 1947, consisted of a system of storage tracks placed along one side of the railroad track. The tracks were to be so arranged that the incoming lumber could be unloaded directly from the box cars onto kiln trucks. These trucks were to be left standing on the storage tracks until the lumber they carried was required for production operations. They were then to be moved directly into the dry kilns by means of transfer trucks and a turntable arrangement. By this means the lumber would be handled only once instead of three times.

Conveyors in the Machine Department: A large proportion of the rough lumber consumed by the plant was used for core wood in the veneered pieces.

For many years it had been the practice of the company to move the stock from one machine to another through this sequence of operations by means of pallets and lift trucks. During 1946 a system of belt conveyors was considered which operated in the following manner: The cut boards were moved automatically from the cross-cut saws to a conveyor belt by means of a trip mechanism which was actuated on the return stroke of the saws. This conveyor carried the lumber to the feed tracks of the first planer. Upon coming out of the first planer the stock fell onto another conveyor which carried it to the feed tracks of the second planer. As the boards came through the second planer, they were caught by a workman and fed into the jointer. After passing through the jointer the boards were flipped over automatically and fed back along the other side of the machine. They then fell onto a conveyor which carried them to the ripsaw operators. From the ripsaws, the same conveyor carried the pieces to the head of the gluewheel line. At this point a workman either set the pieces aside for the resaw machine or placed them on another conveyor to be carried down past the gluewheel operators.

Without the conveyor system, the sequence of operations required 27 men; output was about 46,000 board feet per week. With the new equipment 22 men would be able to cut 60,000 board feet per week. The conveyor equipment would be built in the company's plant and the cost would be small.

Frame Plant: It had been the practice of the company to purchase the wood frames for the White upholstered furniture from contractors in New York and Philadelphia. In January, 1947, however, the executives of the company were considering facilities for the manufacture of wood frames. The necessary boring mills, mortisers, sanders and other tools, the cost of which was estimated at about $20,000, were to be installed in a vacant building adjacent to Warehouse No. 11 (see Exhibit 2). This building the company already owned. The cross-cut and ripsaw work was to be done in the machine department of the case goods plant.

The company was currently paying about $26.50 for the frames it used in sofas which were manufactured and sold at a price of about $100. Inward freight on the frames was about $.75 each; the amount of breakage and damage in transit was considerable. The production executives of the company estimated that the new plant would make it possible to produce frames at a cost of about $17 or $18. It was believed that the White Furniture Company could manufacture the frames at a lower cost because it could obtain labor at slightly lower wages and could make use of various labor saving devices which the unions had kept out of the Northern plants.

Conveyorized Finishing System: The largest single item in the $275,000 plant modernization program was an expenditure of $100,000 for a conveyorized finishing system. The proposed finishing system is outlined in Exhibits 5B and 4.

The proposed system involved the use of an overhead, monorail conveyor to move the furniture through the sequence of finishing operations. The pieces of furniture were to be carried on pallets suspended at 88-inch intervals along the length of the conveyor. Each pallet was to be large enough to accommodate one major piece of furniture such as a chest, dresser, table, or bed headboard. At appropriate points along the path of the conveyor, spray booths were to be installed for the application of the various finishing materials. Force drying ovens were also to be installed in suitable positions to speed the drying of the furniture between operations.

It was intended to operate the new conveyor on only one suite of furniture at a time. As in the past, the furniture would be held in the cabinet room until the entire production lot of one suite had accumulated. The old spray booths were to be kept in operation after the new system was installed to handle special work and repair finishing.

The production executives of the company believed that the new system would reduce finishing costs, increase output, and improve quality. The improvement in quality was expected to come from better handling and greater uniformity in drying conditions. Under existing procedures, the furniture was frequently bumped and scratched as it was shoved along from one operation to another. Moreover, when the pieces were stood aside to dry, it was difficult to get good air circulation past all surfaces and to avoid the formation of air pockets between the pieces.

In trying to determine whether or not the White company should invest $100,000 for the finishing conveyor, the executives noted that they might be able to break a production bottleneck in the plant. Exhibits 5A and 5B specify the difference in operation between the existing and the proposed conveyors. By means of the conveyor, the weekly production of case goods might be increased to $40,000 without substantial increase in burden charges. It was also believed that the in-process inventory would be reduced under the new system. In addition to a study of the cost aspects, executives of the White company wished to examine the layout of the proposed conveyor to make sure it would operate effectively. They were also considering the advisability of extending the conveyor through the Dulux drying operation rather than leaving the units at rest in the Dulux oven for six hours.

1A. WHITE FURNITURE COMPANY
Chippendale Dining Room Suite—China Cabinet

1B. WHITE FURNITURE COMPANY
Platform Rocker, Orange Division

2. WHITE FURNITURE COMPANY
Plant View

CUTTING, SHAPING, GLUEING MACHINE SHOP
NO. 1
FINISHING
ASSEMBLING (CABINET DEPT.)
GLUEING & VENEERING
STGE. VENEER & GLUE
NO. 2
ENAMELING & FURNITURE STGE.
STGE. FINISHED FURNITURE
NO. 3
SHOW ROOM
OFFICE
NO. 8
NO. 1
MACHINE ROOM
280 x 100
FIREWALL
NO. 2
FINISHING BLDG.
238 x 83
NO. 3
WAREHOUSE
128 x 84
NO. 8
OFFICE
NO. 3-A
SHOWROOM & STORE HOUSE
87 x 28
SPRAY BOOTHS
NO. 5
ENGINE AND BOILER HO.
NO. 10 PUMP HOUSE
NO. 9
BRIDGE
NO. 4
WAREHOUSE & SHIPPING BLDG.
87 x 79
103 x 57
NO. 7
COOLING BLDG.
111 x 53
NO. 6
DRY KILNS
154 x 54
LUMBER PILE 4-12 ft. high
LUMBER PILE 4-12 ft high
COAL STORAGE
CLAY STREET
MEBANE LUMBER CO.
NO. 11
WAREHOUSE
140 x 50
PROPOSED FRAME PLANT
FINISHING
ASSEMBLING (CABINET DEPT.)
STGE. VENEER & GLUE
NO. 2
STGE. FIN. FURN.
ENAMELING
FURN. STGE.
STORAGE OF FINISHED FURNITURE
SHOOK STGE.
NO. 3
STGE. FIN. FURN.
STGE. FIN. FURN.
STGE. CRATED FURN.
STGE. CRATING LUMBER
NO. 4
STGE. FINISHED FURNITURE
STGE. FINISHED FURNITURE
STGE. FINISHED FURNITURE
NO. 11

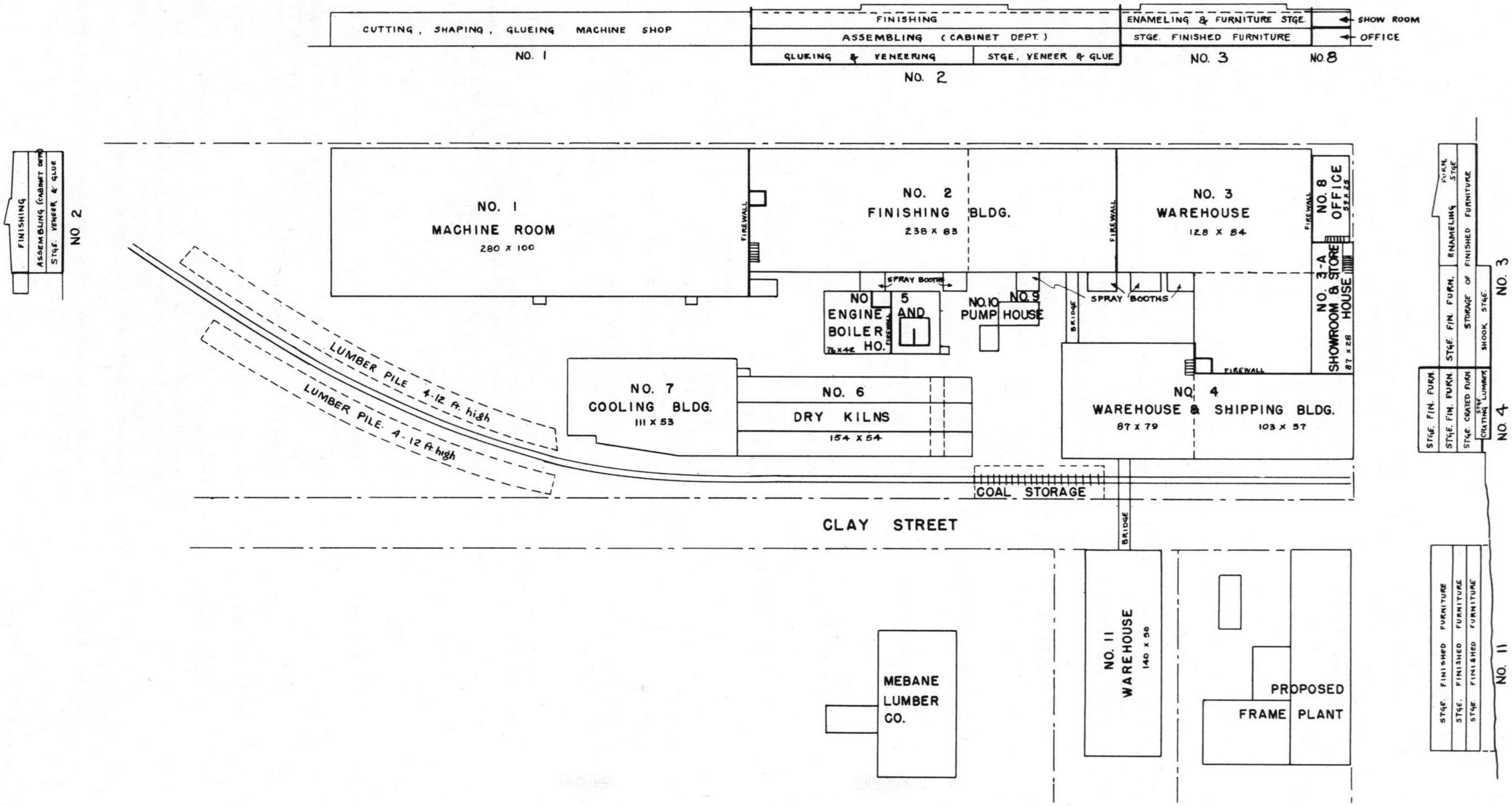

3. WHITE FURNITURE COMPANY
Description of Existing Finishing Procedure

Operation	Men	Description
1. Elevator	1	Furniture was brought up from the cabinet room by elevator. It was then unloaded and moved 25 feet to the first operation.
2. Stain Edges	1	An operator applied stain with a brush to the edges of the drawers and doors, and then shoved the pieces 50 feet to spray booth.
3. Apply Stain	2	At the first spray booth stain was applied by an operator and his helper. The two men lifted the furniture onto a turntable, and the operator applied the stain with a spray gun. The two men then lifted the piece off the turntable, and the helper moved it 50 feet with the hand truck to a drying area.
4. Dry Stain	-	Approximately 30 minutes was allowed for drying the stain.
5. Sand Stain	4	Four men moved the pieces 25 feet to their work area, sanded them, and shoved them 20 feet to the filler area.
6. Apply Filler	2	Two men working with brushes applied filler to the pieces. One man shoved the pieces 15 feet along the floor to the wiping area.
7. Pad and Wipe	5	The excess filler was wiped off by 5 men. One or more of these men then moved the pieces 15 feet to another wiping area.
8. Wipe and Pick	5	Five men continued the wiping, using brushes and picks to clean out the corners and beaded moldings, then shoved the pieces 25 feet to a drying area.
9. Dry Filler	-	The furniture was allowed to stand overnight for drying of the filler.
10. Apply Sealer	2	A helper from the sealer spray booth brought the furniture to the booth (50 feet) and helped lift it onto turntable. The operator applied sealer with a spray gun. The two men lifted the piece off the turntable, and the helper moved it 50 feet with hand truck to a drying area.
11. Dry Sealer	-	About 30 minutes was allowed for drying the sealer coat.
12. Sand Sealer	5	Five sanders moved the furniture about 25 feet to their work space. After the sanding was completed, they pushed the pieces 50 feet to the glazing area.
13. Apply and Wipe Glaze	6	The glaze was applied by a group of six men working in pairs. Two men placed a piece on a low work bench. One man applied the glaze with a brush; the second man followed immediately behind him and wiped off the excess glaze until the exact color blend desired was obtained. The two men then shoved the piece 50 feet to a drying area.
14. Dry Glaze	-	The glaze was allowed to dry overnight.
15. Apply Shade	2	A helper hauled the piece 50 feet with a hand truck to the booth. Operator and helper placed the piece on a turntable. The operator then used a spray gun to even out any dark and light places resulting from glazing. The two men lifted the piece off the turntable, and the helper moved it about 25 feet to a drying area.
16. Dry Shade	-	About 30 minutes was allowed for drying the shade coat.
17. Apply Dulux	2	A helper from the Dulux booth hauled the furniture 50 feet with a hand truck to the booth. Operator and helper placed the piece on a turntable. The operator applied the Dulux finish coat with a spray gun. The two men lifted the piece and the helper moved it about 75 feet to the Dulux drying room.
18. Dry Dulux	-	The Dulux was dried for a minimum of 6 hours at a temperature of 125°F.

4. WHITE FURNITURE COMPANY

Description of Proposed Finishing Conveyor

Operation	Men	Equipment Required	Total Time
1. Spray Stain	1	Spray Booth	2.8 min.
2. Stain Air Dry			6.4
3. Stain Oven		Oven at 115°-125°F.	12.0
4. Stain Cooling			24.0
5. Stain Sanding	2		22.0
6. Spray Filler	2	Spray Booth	2.8
7. Filler Pad, Wipe, Pick, and Inspect	6		58.0
8. Filler Oven		Oven at 140°-150°F., Humidity 25% to 35%	98.4
9. Filler Cooling			46.0
10. Spray Sealer	1	Spray Booth	2.8
11. Sealer Air Dry			6.0
12. Sealer Oven		Oven at 115°-125°F.	25.0
13. Sealer Cooling			11.2
14. Sealer Sanding	2		24.0
15. Spray Glaze	1	Spray Booth	2.8
16. Glaze Wiping	3		30.0
17. Glaze Oven		Oven at 140°-150°F., Humidity 25% to 35%	97.4
18. Glaze Cooling			50.0
19. Spray Shade	1	Spray Booth	2.8
20. Shade Air Drying			10.0
21. Spray Dulux	1	Spray Booth	2.8
22. Dulux Air Drying			15.0
23. Dulux Oven		Oven at 125°F.	6 hours

Miscellaneous Data

The space available for the new finishing conveyor was to include the existing finishing department plus the adjacent warehouse room. The spray booths were to be 14 feet long, 9 feet high, and 12 feet in over-all depth. The hanging pallets were to project about 24 inches from the center line of the monorail conveyor on the loaded side and about 12 inches from the center line on the back side. The minimum turning diameter in which the monorail conveyor could reverse its direction was estimated to be about 48 inches. Bedrails were to be finished separately and not run on the conveyor. Mirror frames were to be hung on hooks between the pallets. The edge staining was to be done in the cabinet room before the pieces were placed on the conveyor.

The new conveyor was to run at a maximum speed of 5 feet per minute. The ceiling height in the finishing department was about 10 feet. The wing of the building in the upper left corner contained space in which the Dulux drying oven could be located. In the case of the cooling and drying operations, the times given represent the minimum times required for these operations in order to secure the desired surface finishes. In the case of all other operations, the times represent the number of minutes the engineers believed each piece <u>should be available</u> in the work areas allotted to the opertions. The number of men to be assigned to the several work areas is given in the second column. These times <u>do not in all cases</u> represent the number of man-minutes of work to be done on each piece.

5A. WHITE FURNITURE COMPANY
Path Followed in Existing Finishing Procedure

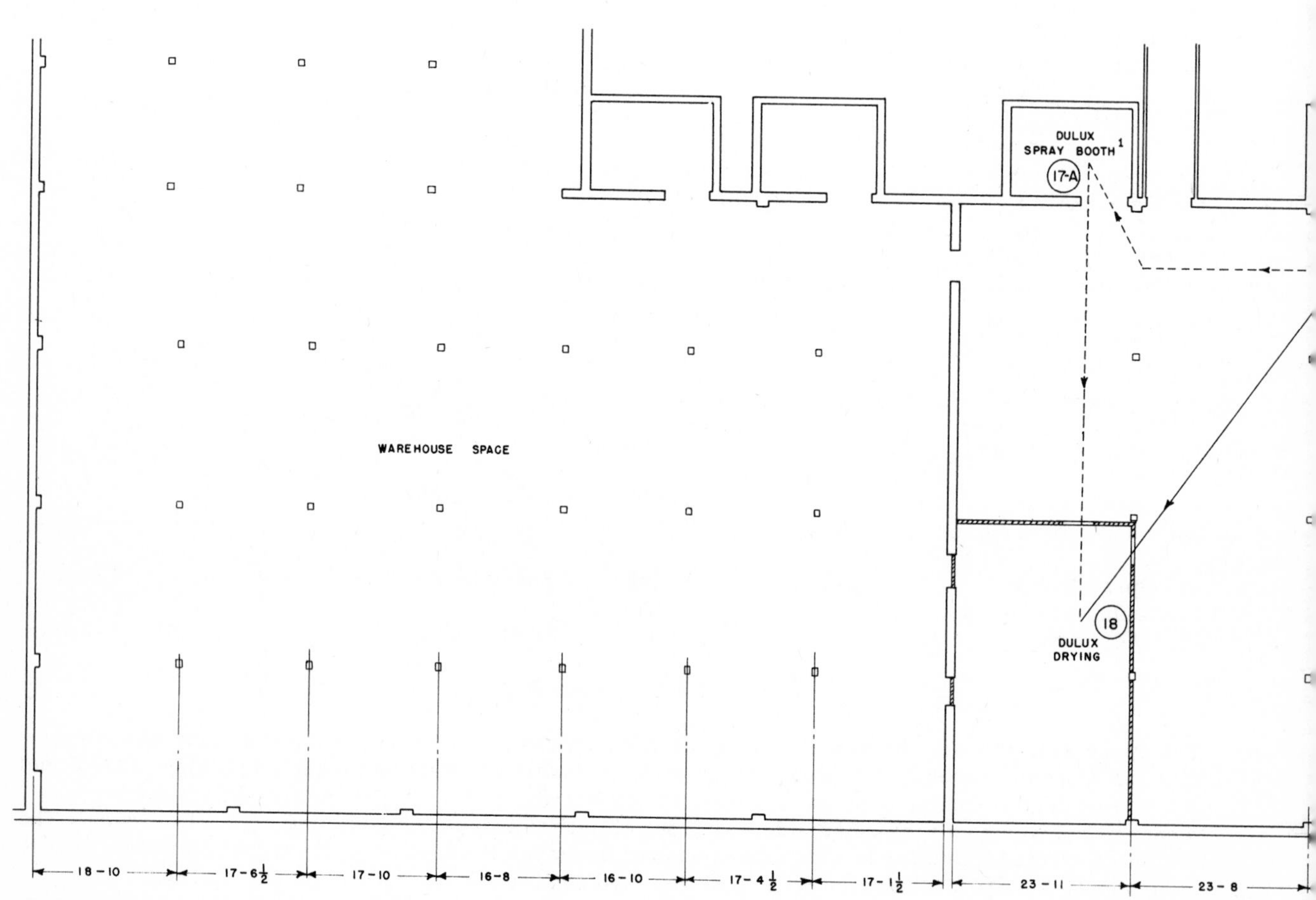

1. THE TWO DULUX SPRAY BOOTHS WERE USED INTERCHANGEA
TWO FINISH COATS WERE APPLIED.

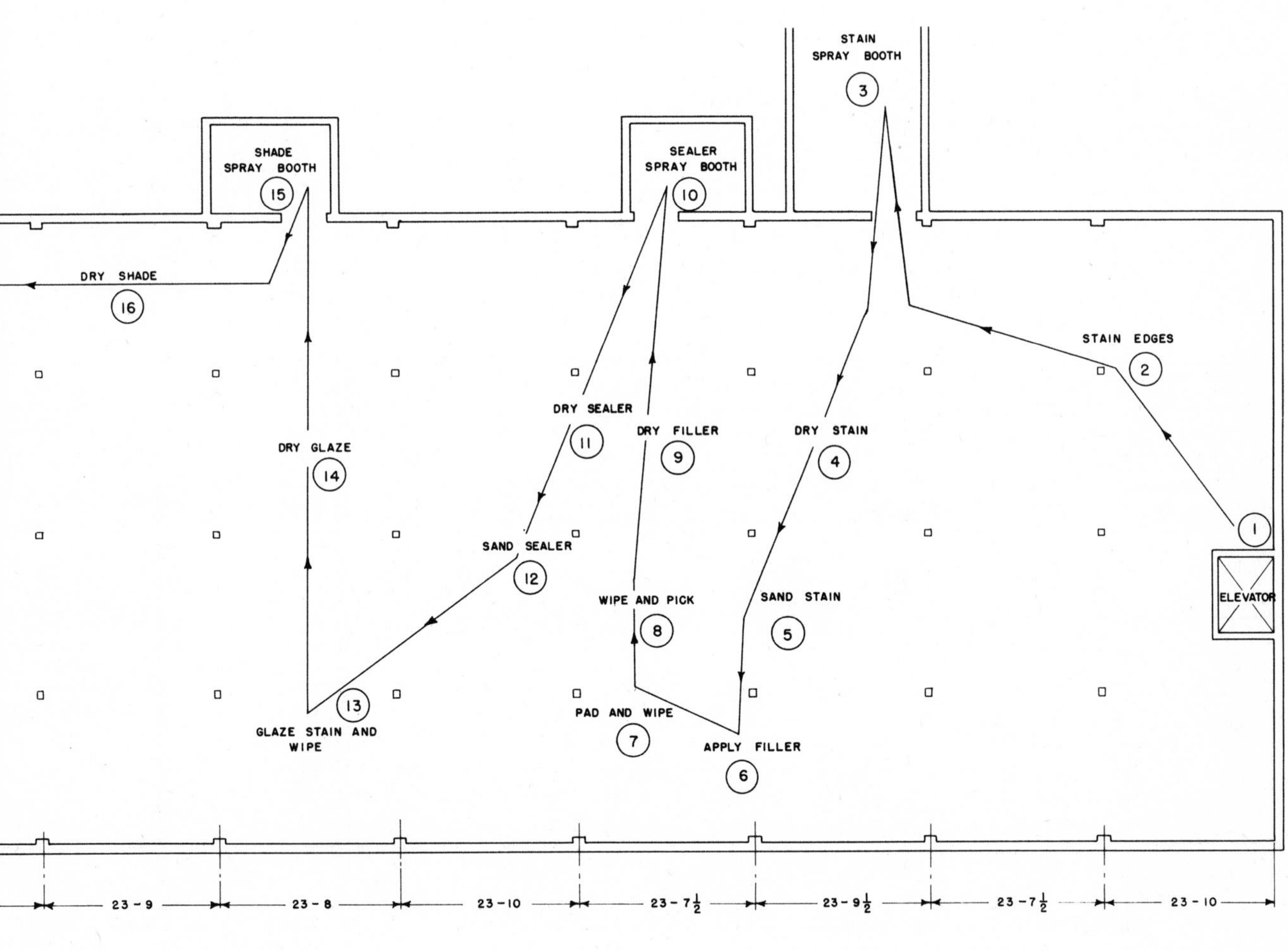
STAIN
SPRAY BOOTH
3
SHADE
SPRAY BOOTH
15
SEALER
SPRAY BOOTH
10
DRY SHADE
16
STAIN EDGES
2
DRY SEALER
11
DRY FILLER
9
DRY STAIN
4
DRY GLAZE
14
1
SAND SEALER
12
ELEVATOR
WIPE AND PICK
8
SAND STAIN
5
13
GLAZE STAIN AND
WIPE
PAD AND WIPE
7
APPLY FILLER
6
23 - 9
23 - 8
23 - 10
23 - 7½
23 - 9½
23 - 7½
23 - 10
CASES

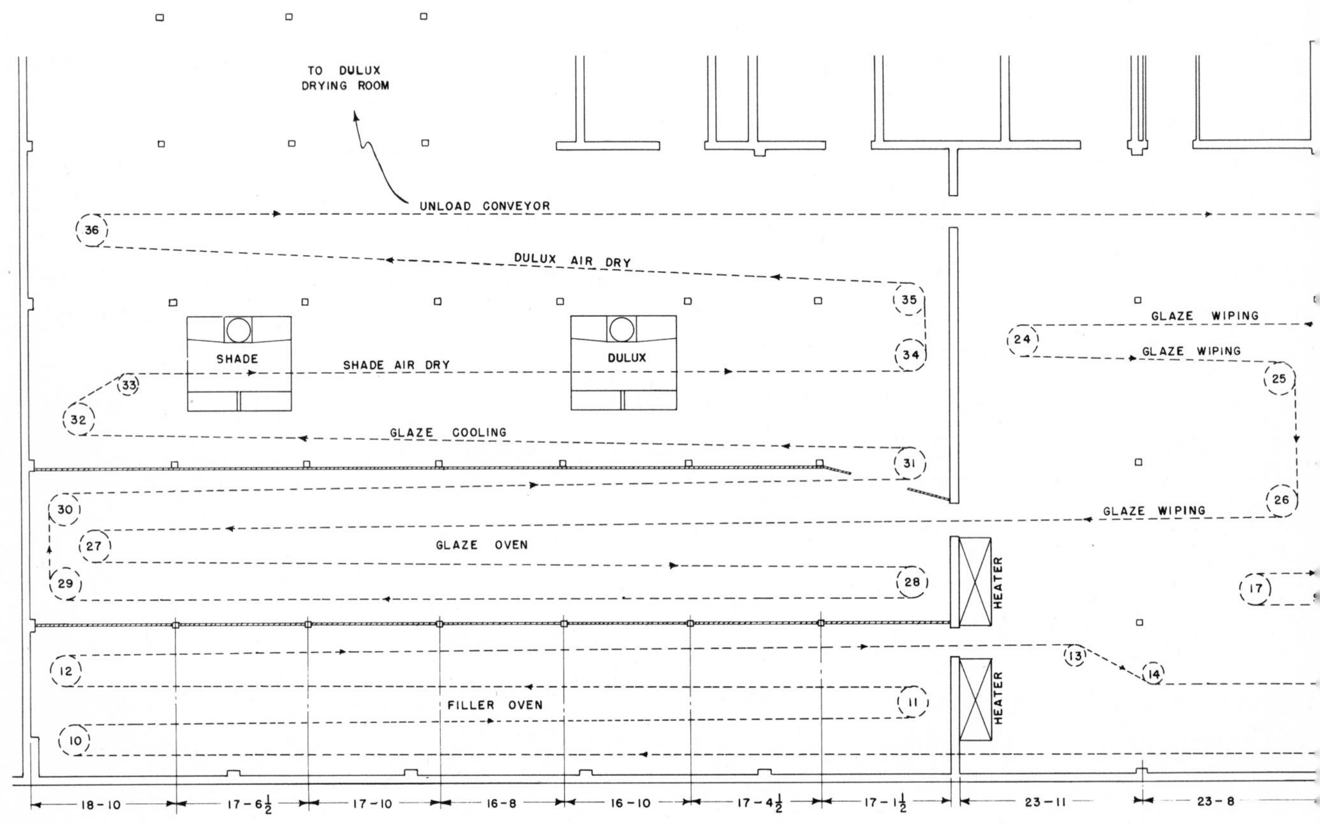

TO DULUX DRYING ROOM
UNLOAD CONVEYOR
36
DULUX AIR DRY
35
34
SHADE
DULUX
SHADE AIR DRY
33
32
GLAZE COOLING
31
30
27
GLAZE OVEN
29
28
HEATER
12
FILLER OVEN
11
10
HEATER
24
GLAZE WIPING
GLAZE WIPING
25
26
GLAZE WIPING
17
13
14
18-10
17-6½
17-10
16-8
16-10
17-4½
17-1½
23-11
23-8

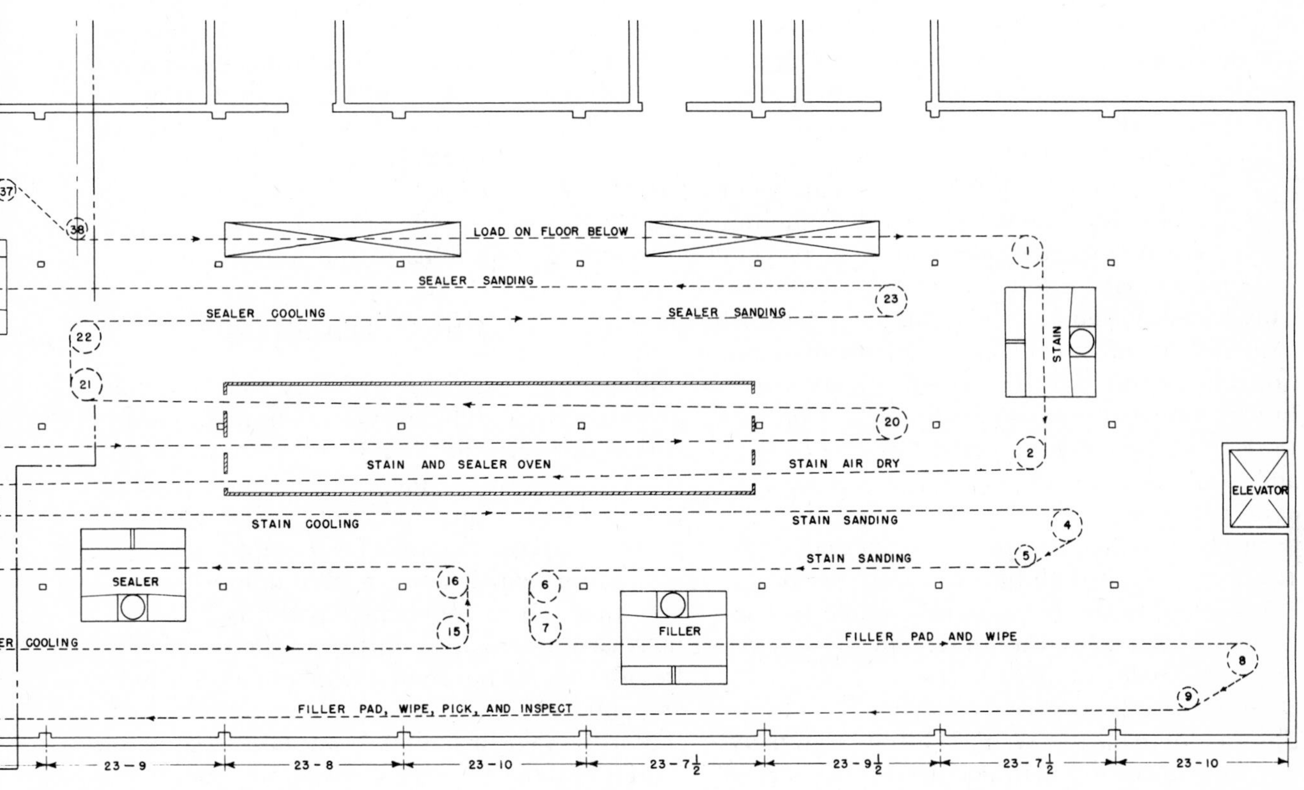

LOAD ON FLOOR BELOW
SEALER SANDING
SEALER COOLING
SEALER SANDING
STAIN
STAIN AND SEALER OVEN
STAIN AIR DRY
ELEVATOR
STAIN COOLING
STAIN SANDING
STAIN SANDING
SEALER
FILLER
ER COOLING
FILLER PAD AND WIPE
FILLER PAD, WIPE, PICK, AND INSPECT
23 - 9
23 - 8
23 - 10
23 - 7½
23 - 9½
23 - 7½
23 - 10

W. F. Whitney Company

The W. F. Whitney Company, Inc., manufactured birch and maple furniture of colonial design. Its plant was located in South Ashburnham, Massachusetts. South Ashburnham was a small town about five miles from Gardner, Massachusetts, a long-established furniture manufacturing center. The company produced living room, dining room, bedroom, and upholstered furniture. Its products were branded as "Whitney Birch" or "Whitney Maple" and were sold through a select group of retail furniture and department stores. Whitney furniture had long enjoyed a reputation for excellent quality and good design. Its prices were among the highest in birch and maple furniture.

Total sales of the W. F. Whitney Company in 1948 amounted to $1,007,841. Of this amount, case goods comprised approximately 81 percent and upholstered furniture 7 percent. The company also did some woodworking on a contract basis and manufactured a woven plastic material, called plasticane, which was used as a seat covering in trains, buses, and subways. Contract work comprised about 2 percent of sales in 1948 and plasticane about 10 percent. A consolidated balance sheet and a breakdown of sales by major product groups for the period 1936–1948 are given in Exhibits 1 and 2. Net profits after taxes for the business as a whole had increased from 1.46 percent of sales in 1940 to 3.25 percent of sales in 1947.

In the three-year period following the close of the war in 1945, the W. F. Whitney Company, like most furniture manufacturers, experienced a very high demand for its products. During this period and throughout most of 1948, the demand for the company's furniture exceeded the capacity of the plant, and it was necessary to allocate the output to the retail accounts.

In January, 1949, Mr. W. D. Miller, president of the company, was of the opinion that a return to the highly competitive selling conditions which had characterized all branches of the furniture industry in the prewar years was imminent. During 1947 and 1948 there had been a noticeable slackening in the demand for the low and medium quality grades of furniture. The demand for high quality furniture, such as that made by the W. F. Whitney Company, had continued to be strong, but the retail stores were becoming more selective in their purchases and were ordering fewer pieces at a time than they had in the past.

In studying the company's immediate situation, Mr. Miller found that the volume of shipments from the factory was running at fully as high a level as in previous months, but that the backlog of orders was decreasing. He also observed that the company was falling behind on its delivery schedules and yet accumulating excessive inventories of certain items. Mr. Miller was considering what steps should be taken to meet these immediate problems and what plans should be made to meet the return of competitive selling conditions to the industry.

PRODUCT POLICIES

In January, 1949, the company was producing 43 patterns (or different pieces) in maple furniture, 43 patterns in birch furniture, and 18 patterns in upholstered pieces. The wood parts of the upholstered pieces were of birch. The total of 104 patterns compared with approximately 50 patterns which were in production in January, 1948. The number of patterns had been increased to anticipate buyers in their demands. Before the war the company manufactured over 300 patterns of furniture. The executives were convinced that this number was far too large for economical operations. They pointed out, however, that the company was not as well known before the war as in 1949, and that competitive conditions had seemed to require the larger number of patterns. They did not believe that it would be necessary to have as many patterns again in the future.

In the years prior to the war, about 30 new patterns were added to the line each year. In addition to the new designs which were added to the line, a few simple pattern changes were usually made for the furniture shows in January and July. Once a pattern was in production, it was the policy of the company to continue it as long as it was acceptable to the customers. From 15 to 20 patterns in the company's line had been in production for well over ten years. Many more patterns had been altered only slightly over the years by minor changes in such things as drawer pulls and trim. The effect of the design changes on manufacturing costs could not be precisely determined, but the changes, even though slight, were known to be expensive. The executives believed, however, that the continual shifting and changing of patterns was necessary to obtain an adequate sales volume.

The company's case goods patterns were divided into several rather loose groups. All of the patterns in any one group had the same general proportions and the same basic design. It was therefore possible to assemble several different suites[1] from each of the groups, according to the desires of the customer. In January, 1949, there were three groups of patterns in bedroom furniture and two in dining room furniture. For the living room, the company manufactured a series of occasional pieces.

The company employed one designer on a retainer basis. He maintained his office in Grand Rapids and visited the factory about twice a year. He also designed for manufacturers of noncompeting lines of furniture, such as mahogany and walnut, but had agreed not to work on any other maple furniture.

The reputation of the company had been built in maple furniture, but during the war when maple was virtually unobtainable the company had switched to birch. The manufacture of maple was resumed on a small scale in 1948. Maple was generally regarded in the trade as a better furniture wood than birch. By using a light finish it was possible to bring out the grain in maple which was impossible in birch. Maple was, however, the more expensive wood to use. Its initial cost was higher, the percentage of waste was greater, and it was harder to work; knives had to be sharpened more often, more sanding was required, and a greater amount of hand work was necessary to remove defects which became apparent only after the stain was applied. About 70 percent of the maple pieces required repair work after finishing whereas such work was necessary on only 15 percent of the birch pieces. It was estimated that the total cost of producing a piece of maple furniture averaged roughly 15 percent more than for a similar piece in birch. Prices were therefore higher for maple furniture than for birch.

In the few months since the company had resumed the manufacture of maple, the executives believed that it had been somewhat less profitable than the birch line.

In maple furniture the executives had found that there were four or five concerns in direct competition with the company. One of these was located in New England, one in the Midwest, and the rest along the Eastern seaboard. One and possibly two had as large a sales volume in maple furniture as the W. F. Whitney Company. In birch furniture the executives had found that there were about 20 direct competitors. Five or six of these were New England concerns and the rest were located largely in the East. Most of these were smaller in sales volume than the W. F. Whitney Company, but one was about the same size and one was considerably larger. In the lower quality birch furniture there were a large number of companies, mostly small in size.

MARKETING PROGRAM

The company exhibited its furniture at the furniture shows in Grand Rapids in January and July of each year. A permanent show room was maintained in Grand Rapids for this purpose. In 1947 and 1948 the company sold a larger portion of its total sales volume at the furniture shows than had been the case in the past. It was estimated that in 1948 orders were received for 10 to 20 percent of the company's annual sales volume at the shows. Ordinarily, delivery of complete suites or groups of furniture was promised about three months after the show. The various pieces were stored at the factory until the suites could be shipped all at one time. The policy of shipping complete suites or groups of furniture had been followed by the company for a number of years as a service to the retail stores. The retailers normally displayed suites or groups of furniture which could be sold as a unit. For example, a table and six chairs was considered a

[1] The word "suite" indicates the several pieces from a group used to furnish a single room. A "group" is a loose collection of pieces or patterns all having the same general proportions and basic design. A "piece" or "pattern" is an individual unit of furniture such as a chair or chest. A "production lot" consists of a certain number of pieces, such as 250 chairs.

unit. The company tried to ship the orders in the groups in which they were sold.

Sales Organization: The company's salesforce consisted of eight men in addition to Mr. Kerr, the sales manager. These men were assigned territories throughout the country and were paid a commission of 7 percent. With the exception of the New England representative, each of the men also sold other noncompeting lines of furniture. All accounts were handled by these representatives. The company made no direct sales and credit for orders taken at the furniture shows was given to the sales representatives in whose territories the customers were located.

Retail Outlets: The company distributed its furniture through a group of about 270 carefully selected retail furniture and department stores located throughout the country. It was the policy of the company to sell to the best store available in each community. In Boston, Whitney furniture was handled by Paine's, and in Chicago by Marshall Field's. Ordinarily, sales were made to only one retail store in a community, but in New York City there were three retail outlets and the company was attempting to obtain a fourth.

The company protected its retail outlets by exclusive sales franchises and expected its outlets to protect the company in return. It was anticipated that retail stores would push the Whitney line and would not place too many other birch and maple lines in competition with it. The number of competing lines which the executives thought was permissible depended upon and size and location of the store. Such matters were usually negotiated and were handled with a good deal of caution. Considerable emphasis was placed upon inducing the stores to push the Whitney line, because the executives believed that furniture was "sold" to people. It was relatively easy, they had found, for a retail store salesman to switch sales to similar but cheaper lines. The company burned its brand name into each piece of furniture and had experienced few instances of its brand being removed. The executives believed that most stores considered it an advantage to advertise the Whitney name.

Some 50 or 60 of the retail stores were large and were classed as key accounts; the rest were smaller and more scattered. The larger stores usually accounted for somewhat over 50 percent of the company's annual sales volume. A few of the smaller stores ordered as little as one suite or less of furniture at a time, but orders were normally larger. Some stores ordered as many as 24 suites at a time. The largest concentration of sales was on the East Coast, but West Coast sales were substantial. Sales in the postwar period had been distributed fairly well throughout the year. In more normal times the company usually had a slump in the spring.

Advertising: The company advertised its furniture in such magazines as *House and Garden, House Beautiful, Living,* and *Bride's Magazine.* The advertisements usually emphasized the company's maple furniture. Advertising expenditures were normally concentrated during the last months of the year, from September through December. During 1947, about $12,000 was spent for advertising and during 1948 approximately $15,000.

MANUFACTURING OPERATIONS

The plant of the W. F. Whitney Company consisted of a group of wood frame buildings most of which were erected after the fire in 1903. Two main buildings were erected at that time on the theory that if one burned production could be continued in the other. The two parts were subsequently joined together by a double ramp. A picture of the plant is shown in Exhibit 3A.

The factory was divided into ten departments as follows: yard, mill, machining, sanding, cabinet or assembly room, finishing, upholstery, shipping and receiving, plasticane, and maintenance. Each department was supervised by a foreman.

A layout drawing of the yard, buildings, and factory departments is shown in Exhibit 3B.

Lumber Procurement: Approximately 15 percent of the cost of the company's case goods consisted of lumber. In January, 1949, the company was using an average of about 5,000 board feet of lumber a day. Only the better grades of birch and maple were used. In normal periods, the lumber was usually purchased from four to six months ahead of requirements. During the postwar period, however, when lumber was difficult to obtain, purchases were made whenever the lumber was available.

Production Scheduling: Production was scheduled through the plant by lots or cuttings for each single piece of furniture. During 1948 the cuttings or lot sizes for each piece of furniture manufactured by the company usually averaged from 250 to 300 pieces and were never less than 100 pieces. Before the war cuttings had been as low as 20 pieces and had averaged about 50 pieces. The larger cuttings had been an important factor in enabling the company to hold its prices within reason during the war and postwar period when the costs of labor and materials were rising. It had been found that 250 to 300 pieces was the most economical sized cutting for the company's plant. The amount of storage space available and the size of the plant placed an upper limit on the size of the cuttings. It had been found by experience that if the cuttings were reduced below 100 pieces, unit costs increased very rapidly. The increase in unit costs on the small cuttings resulted primarily from decreased labor efficiency; the output per man was lower on the small cuttings because the men were shifted too often from one pattern to another.

The number of cuttings in process in the plant at any one time usually averaged from 20 to 25. Cutting schedules were planned at irregular intervals as needed. All of the executives participated in the planning. The schedule on which the company intended to start cutting during January, 1949, had been set up in October. Many months of planning had gone into design changes and additions to the line before that time. Enough cuttings were included in the schedule to keep the plant busy until about the middle of April. There was frequently some overlapping of schedules, and it had often been necessary in the past to start in process supplementary cuttings of fast moving items which had not originally been included in the schedule.

In line with the company's policy of shipping complete suites or groups of furniture, production was scheduled so that the pieces of a group would be finished at about the same time. This required very careful planning and necessitated a certain amount of in-process and finished storage space so that operations in the plant could be performed economically.

The amount of time required for a cutting to go through the plant usually averaged about three months. An additional month was required to prepare the lumber.

Production Processes: The incoming lumber was loaded onto kiln trucks and placed in the lumber storage shed until needed. The storage sheds had a capacity of approximately 1,500,000 board feet. From the storage shed the lumber was moved through the dry kilns to the dry storage shed. The company had three kilns in 1949, each with a capacity of 25,000 board feet. About 100,000 board feet could be stored in the dry storage shed.

From the dry storage shed the lumber moved to the mill room which was on the first floor of one of the company's two main buildings. The lumber was cut, planed, glued up to rough dimensions, inspected, and placed in storage. From the mill room onward, case goods, chairs, and upholstered pieces followed different routings through the plant.

The parts for each cutting were kept together and moved by truck from one operation to the next. Each lot of a piece of furniture was put together separately. After assembly the pieces were placed in white stock storage where they received their third inspection.

During the postwar period, approximately $75,000 had been spent in improving the company's equipment and facilities. A new dry kiln was installed and the company's two older dry kilns, which were made of wood, were completely rebuilt of brick. Belt drives in the factory were replaced with individual electric motors and a generator was installed to provide electric power; the company had previously used steam power. The task of electrifying the plant was completed in the fall of 1948. Some new woodworking equipment was purchased to replace older equipment, and some machines were rebuilt and improved or adapted to new uses. Fluorescent lighting was installed throughout the plant, and a new blower system for dust collection was acquired.

Wage Payment Methods: About half of the employees in the plant were paid on piece rates. The piece rate system was installed by a firm of management consultants in 1943. Base rates, ranging from 55 cents per hour for unskilled work to 80 cents per hour for skilled work, were guaranteed. The incentive wage scale was so set that a man would earn about 25 percent more than the base wage if he did his work in standard time. Actually, the earnings of most of the men averaged considerably more than 25 percent above the base wage.

COST CONTROL AND PRICING

Cost records were maintained by the company for each cutting of each piece of furniture produced. These records provided a basis for comparing current costs with those in the past for the same or a similar piece of furniture. They were also used as a basis for setting prices on new patterns and for adjusting the prices of furniture already in production. A cost sheet for one piece of furniture manufactured by the company is shown in Exhibit 4. Cost records were built up in the following manner.

Lumber and other materials were charged directly to each cutting. Lumber requirements were determined by adding to the actual net board footage required for the finished pieces a percentage for lumber waste calculated on the experience of the previous year. The actual percentage of lumber waste was figured every six months when inventories were taken, but unless the change was radical the same percentage was used throughout the year. The company's lumber waste usually ran in the neighborhood of 45 percent. Some of the waste lumber was recovered and used for such things as dowels, but the majority of it was burned in the furnaces.

Direct labor costs were broken down by departments in the factory and charged to each cutting on the basis of piece work records. For those operations not on piece rates, such as the cut-off saws, direct labor costs were charged to the cuttings on the basis of timecard records.

Factory overhead was assigned to cuttings on the basis of direct labor costs. The overhead rates were determined annually for each department in the factory and were based on the actual costs of the previous year. Indirect labor costs were charged directly to the departments in which the men worked. Design expenditures and social security and unemployment taxes were allocated to departments in proportion to the total labor costs (direct and indirect) in each department. Local and excise taxes, depreciation of buildings, maintenance supplies, and all types of insurance were allocated according to the percentage of total floor space occupied by each department. Depreciation of machinery was charged to each department at the rates allowed for tax purposes. Sandpaper and glue were charged according to their actual use by departments. The rent for a railroad siding was divided between the lumber yard and shipping and receiving. Electricity purchased outside was charged to departments according to the horsepower of the motors used.

The overhead percentages thus derived were used to allocate indirect labor and indirect expense to each cutting. Overhead rates in use in past years are shown in Exhibit 2.

Administrative overhead costs included executives' salaries, office expense, federal taxes, cost of bad debts, collection fees, interest, legal fees, postage, telephone and telegraph costs, cash discounts, donations, and all selling expenditures. To cover these expenditures, 31 percent was added to the cost of each cutting.

CURRENT PROBLEMS

In January, 1949, Mr. Miller was concerned because the company was falling behind in meeting its promised delivery dates. The problem had developed during the latter months of 1948 and had become acute by December. Ordinarily, the company promised delivery about three months after an order was received. In January, 1949, Mr. Miller found that shipments on many items in the company's line were overdue by as much as two to four months. Meanwhile, excessive inventories were accumulating on other items. All of the available storage space at the plant was filled to capacity, and as a result the company had been forced in many instances to depart from its usual practice of holding individual pieces in stock until complete suites could be shipped to customers.

Shipments from the factory were currently running at a level of about $85,000 per month. The backlog of orders, however, had decreased during 1948 from about three months' production at the first of the year to about one month's production at the end of the year. Mr. Miller expected that sales at the January furniture show would be light, and that more highly competitive selling conditions would develop in the quality furniture market in 1949 than had existed in 1948.

Mr. Miller believed that the ability to make prompt deliveries of complete suites would have an important bearing on the company's competitive strength in the coming months. He was, therefore, anxious to correct the existing delivery and inventory situation as promptly as possible.

1. W. F. WHITNEY COMPANY

Balance Sheets, 1941-1947

	1941	1942	1943	1944	1945	1946	1947
ASSETS							
Cash	$ 9,026	$ 10,186	$ 21,802	$ 29,239	$ 35,307	$ 34,795	$ 23,272
Accounts Receivable--Net	83,631	69,593	41,274	34,549	40,833	78,387	73,182
Inventories	187,448	247,466	183,509	147,324	136,632	178,664	238,608
Total Current Assets	$280,105	$327,245	$246,585	$211,112	$212,772	$291,846	$335,062
Land, Buildings, and Machinery	177,306	181,830	182,015	178,351	187,604	204,238	243,375
Investments	2	2	20,002	60,002	60,002	2	1,302
Deferred and Other Assets	5,330	10,278	5,478	2,291	4,861	7,671	4,893
Total Assets	$462,743	$519,355	$454,080	$451,756	$465,239	$503,757	$584,632
LIABILITIES							
Accounts Payable	$ 11,098	$ 16,121	$ 12,535	$ 18,386	$ 11,767	$ 9,970	$ 77,973
Notes Payable	34,000	74,000	19,000	19,000	19,000	19,000	15,000
Accrued Expense	32,133	22,483	11,166	13,901	15,040	29,380	17,023
Total Current Liabilities	$ 77,231	$112,604	$ 42,701	$ 51,287	$ 45,807	$ 58,350	$109,996
Mortgage on Land, Buildings, and Machinery	23,500	23,500	23,500	23,500	23,000	23,000	21,000
Reserve for Depreciation	73,205	85,905	95,160	104,181	113,814	122,455	132,672
Capital Stock*	133,415	133,415	133,415	133,415	133,415	133,415	133,415
Less: Treasury Stock	-	-	-	21,330	21,330	21,330	21,330
Net Capital Stock	$133,415	$133,415	$133,415	$112,085	$112,085	$112,085	$112,085
Earned Surplus	78,495	87,034	82,407	83,806	93,636	187,867	208,879
Capital Surplus	76,897	76,897	76,897	76,897	76,897		
Total Liabilities	$462,743	$519,355	$454,080	$451,756	$465,239	$503,757	$584,632

*Capital Stock:

First Preferred--1,000 shares, no par, authorized. 600 shares issued and outstanding	$ 60,000
Second Preferred--750 shares, no par, authorized. 540 shares issued and outstanding	54,000
Common--3,250 shares, no par, authorized. 1,223 shares issued and outstanding	19,415
	$133,415

2. W. F. WHITNEY COMPANY

Sales by Major Product Groups, 1937-1948

Year	Case Goods and Chairs	Upholstered Furniture	Plasticane	Contract and Other Sales	Total Sales	Discounts and Returns	Net Sales
1936	$551,000	$ 93,000	-	$ 7,000	$ 651,000	$15,000	$ 636,000
1937	553,000	109,000	-	4,000	666,000	15,000	651,000
1938	418,000	75,000	-	3,000	496,000	20,000	476,000
1939	455,000	78,000	-	2,000	535,000	29,000	506,000
1940	451,000	85,000	-	4,000	540,000	31,000	509,000
1941	572,000	94,000	-	5,000	671,000	12,000	659,000
1942	500,000	97,000	-	38,000	635,000	22,000	613,000
1943	390,000	40,000	-	153,000	583,000	17,000	566,000
1944	394,000	56,000	-	61,000	511,000	13,000	498,000
1945	396,000	67,000	$ 39,000	57,000	559,000	13,000	546,000
1946	526,000	111,000	70,000	22,000	729,000	20,000	709,000
1947	792,000	73,000	112,000	27,000	1,004,000	27,000	977,000
1948	836,000	69,000	103,000	20,000	1,028,000	20,000	1,008,000

Percentages Used in Allocating Factory Overhead, 1938-1947

	Milling	Machining	Sanding	Cabinet	Shipping	Finishing	Upholstery
1938	126	78	103	112	170	67	104
1940	109	123	122.5	135.4	124.5	137.5	95.7
1945	117.5	104.8	99.6	107.1	321.7	137.0	70.6
1946	114.2	150.6	101.8	136.2	357.4	132.0	91.6
1947	139.6	170.2	103.8	157.5	357.6	147.5	115.8

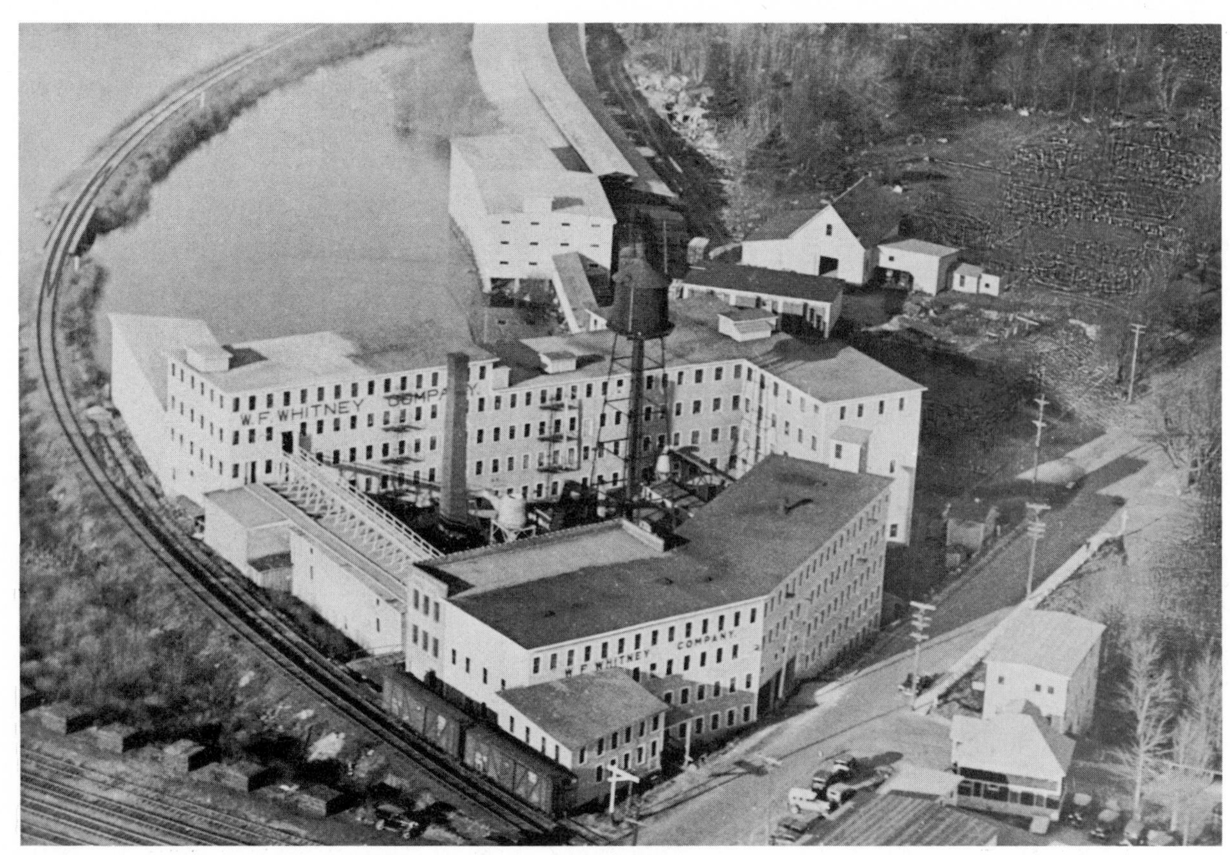

3A. W. F. WHITNEY COMPANY
Plant Photograph

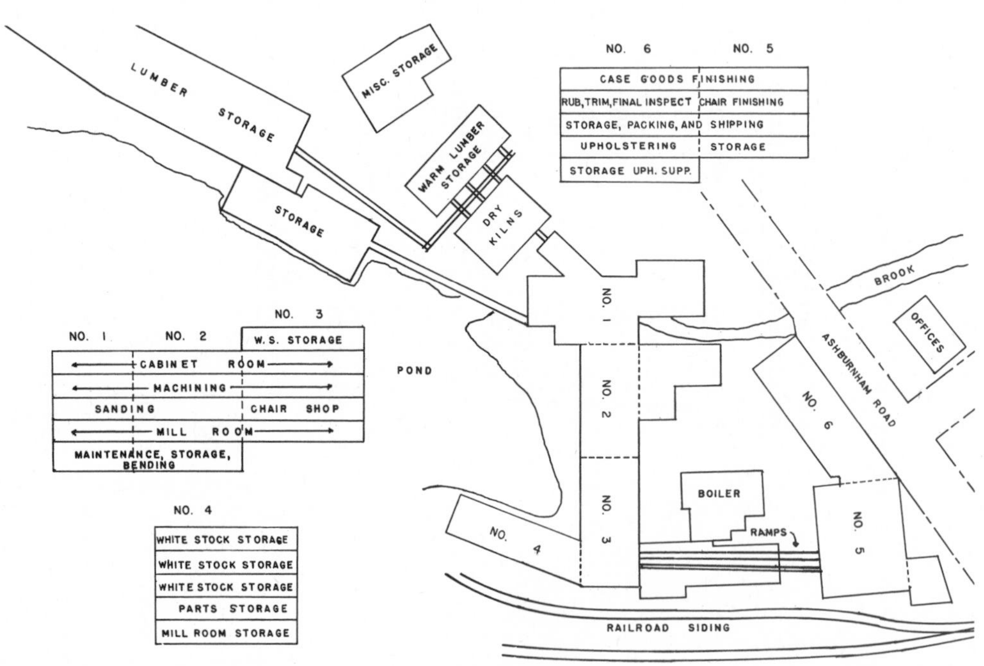

3B. W. F. WHITNEY COMPANY
Plant Layout

4. W. F. WHITNEY COMPANY

Cost Record of a Night Table, 1945-1948 (Cost per 100 Pieces)

	Quantity	Est. Cost	10-16-45 to 12-24-45 Cut 400 Act. Cost	12-14-45 to 6-5-46 Cut 450 Act. Cost	7-8-46 to 12-6-46 Cut 500 Act. Cost	12-23-46 to 3-31-47 Cut 650 Act. Cost	2-19-47 to 8-1-47 Cut 200 Act. Cost	10-22-47 to 12-12-47 Cut 200 Act. Cost	11-12-47 to 5-1-48 Cut 350 Act. Cost[1]	11-13-47 to 6-3-48 Cut 300 Act. Cost[1]
Lumber	780 bd. ft.	127.84	127.84	127.84	152.22	152.22	175.62	175.62	175.62	175.62
Veneer		7.31	7.31	7.31	9.03	9.03	9.03	9.03	9.03	9.03
Dowels		2.50	2.50	2.50	3.00	3.00	3.00	3.00	3.00	3.00
Screws	12	2.31	2.31	2.31	2.98	2.98	2.98	2.98	2.98	2.98
Nails	2(1 1/4");4(1")	.31	.31	.31	.37	.37	.40	.40	.40	.40
Glides (5/8 single)	4	.74	.74	.80	1.19	1.19	1.19	1.19	1.19	1.19
Drawer Pulls	1	4.00	4.00	4.00	3.15	3.15	3.15	3.15	6.20	6.20
Screw Eyes #410	4	.86	.86	.86	1.03	1.03	1.03	1.03	1.03	1.03
Bullet Catch										
Thumb Tacks	2	.15	.15	.20	.20	.20	.20	.20	.20	.20
TOTAL		146.02	146.02	146.13	173.17	173.17	196.60	196.60	199.65	199.65
Mill		28.08	28.08	28.08	31.20	35.10	35.10	36.86	42.28	42.28
Machine		21.80	30.37	22.77	25.22	26.42	31.46	38.85	34.02	33.47
Sand		28.77	26.46	26.46	26.46	29.56	28.29	31.25	30.58	30.58
Assemble		69.01	54.46	56.65	56.65	57.38	57.38	60.25	63.57	63.57
Overhead		186.66	174.59	143.87	150.11	188.11	194.41	214.47	248.78	247.85
TOTAL		334.32	313.96	277.83	289.64	336.57	346.64	381.68	419.23	417.75
PAINT SHOP										
Material		32.00	32.00	32.00	35.20	35.20	35.20	35.20	35.20	35.20
Labor		45.78	45.78	43.56	46.98	47.42	47.89	54.33	56.32	56.32
Overhead		63.18	63.18	59.68	64.36	62.59	63.21	71.72	83.07	83.07
TOTAL		140.96	140.96	135.24	146.54	145.21	146.30	161.25	174.59	174.59
TRIM										
Labor		1.50	1.50	1.61	1.72	1.72	1.72	1.81	1.86	1.86
Overhead		1.10	1.10	1.19	1.28	1.56	1.56	1.64	2.21	2.21
TOTAL		2.60	2.60	2.80	3.00	3.28	3.28	3.45	4.07	4.07
SHIPPING ROOM										
Material		24.87	24.87	28.01	31.30	31.46	41.90	43.97	43.97	43.97
Labor		5.79	5.79	5.78	5.78	6.06	6.06	6.36	6.57	6.57
Overhead		7.24	7.24	18.59	18.59	21.66	21.66	22.73	23.49	23.49
TOTAL		37.90	37.90	52.38	55.67	59.18	69.62	73.06	74.03	74.03
TOTAL (Cost per Piece)[2]		6.62	6.41	6.14	6.68	7.17	7.62	8.16	8.72	8.70
Administration[3]		8.67	8.40	8.04	8.75	9.39	9.98	10.69	11.42	11.40
List Price				10.51	11.60	11.60	11.60	12.00	12.00	12.00

[1]Used 1947 factory overhead rates.

[2]Total cost divided by 100 to get unit costs.

[3]Thirty-one per cent added to unit cost to cover administrative overhead.

Mengel Company (A)

On June 1, 1946, an article in *Business Week* described the activities of the Mengel Company as follows:

"This month the Mengel Company of Louisville, largest manufacturer of hardwood products in the United States, will make one of the very few attempts on record to market furniture under a brand name on a national scale.

The nation's 3,500 household furniture makers usually sell their product locally or regionally to 20,000 retailers. This restricted pattern of production and distribution results from (1) the manufacturer's original desire to stay close to a lumber supply, (2) the dealer's inclination to buy as near home as possible to cut down freight costs, and (3) the great variety of products in the furniture field.

A result is that brand names in furniture usually are a secondary consideration with the consumer. Price and dealer reputation come first. . . . Mengel will try to buck this situation by spending $500,000 in national advertising in 1946 to plug its brand name "Permanized" and to make the average consumer style-conscious. . . .

Mengel's profits are expected to come from volume production and complete integration. In addition to cutting its own oak, maple, and other American woods, and importing its own mahogany from Africa, the firm also makes plywoods, and veneers and follows through every step in the manufacturing operation, even to doing its packaging in containers made in Mengel factories. . . . The final assembly line is a 2-mile system pattern after assembly lines in the automotive industry."

ORIGIN OF POLICIES

The history of the Mengel Company was characterized by periods of extreme contraction and expansion in sales volume and by radical changes in the product lines which the company manufactured. These developments were caused by technological changes occurring in the industries which the company served. Exhibit 1 presents financial data that characterize these changes.

The Mengel Administration, 1877–1934

At the outset the company concentrated primarily on the manufacture of cigar boxes and chewing tobacco boxes, but also produced a wide variety of wooden containers for other purposes.

In the early 1920's, the Mengel Company began the conversion of its main box plant at 12th Street in Louisville to the manufacture of wooden parts for automobile bodies. The equipment required for this business was quite different from that used in the manufacture of wooden boxes. As a result, a substantial portion of the box making machinery was either sold or moved to other plants. The automobile parts business increased rapidly in volume, and in 1923 the company constructed a second automobile parts plant at 4th Street in Louisville.

By 1928 the automotive parts business had become the largest single factor in the company's operations, and an addition to the 4th Street plant was constructed. Shortly thereafter, however, the all steel body began to gain general acceptance in the automotive industry, and the company was thus doubly vulnerable to the general business depression which struck in 1929. The number of employees required in the automotive parts business declined in the space of a few months after 1929 from 3,500 to 70, and in 1932 the company closed the 12th Street plant and removed or sold most of the equipment which it contained. In order to keep the 4th Street plant in operation, the company began in 1931 to manufacture a small volume of dimension stock for furniture manufacturers. This work involved the cutting and machining of lumber into parts which were then shipped to the furniture manufacturers for assembly and finishing.

The Hoge Administration, 1934–1939

After Colonel Mengel's death in 1934, Mr. William L. Hoge, who had formerly been vice-president and manager of the automotive parts division, became president of the company.

In 1933 and 1934 the company had begun to manufacture novelty furniture on a contract basis for several drop shipment jobbers. Many of the executives were of the opinion that any further attempt to manufacture finished furniture would have a disastrous effect upon the company's sales of dimension stock and other products to furniture manufacturers. However, furniture sales increased.

The Voit Administration from 1939

Once a decision was made to make finished furniture, orders flowed into the company in a steadily increasing volume. In later years the executives of the company came to view the decision to manufacture finished furniture as "just like an opening of the door" to a large influx of new business.

Net sales of finished furniture amounted to approximately $955,000 in 1939, $1,780,000 in 1940, $3,161,000 in 1941, $2,458,000 in 1942, $572,000 in 1943, and $812,000 in 1944. The company was thus able to reopen in 1939 its plant at 12th Street which had been shut down for most of the period since 1932.

The finished furniture business in the period 1939 to 1945, except for novelties made for jobbers, consisted primarily of bedroom furniture manufactured under contract for two large mail-order houses. The designs and brand names, if any, were those of the mail-order houses, and the furniture was in no way identified as a product of the Mengel Company. For the most part it was inexpensive furniture, intended to sell in large volume at low prices to a mass market.

In 1943 Mr. Voit interested executives of the United States Plywood Corporation in a joint marketing program for plywood and plywood products. Subsequently, in accordance with a contract, dated July 1, 1943, the two companies jointly formed a sales corporation, U.S.-Mengel Plywoods, Inc., in which the Mengel Company owns 51 percent of the outstanding voting stock and 40 percent of the non-voting stock. The agreement affected only the plywood division of the Mengel Company; was for manufacturing and marketing purposes only; and involved no financial alliance between the two companies.

In 1944 the executives of the company drew up the broad outlines of the policy the company would follow in its furniture business. This policy provided that approximately one third of the company's furniture business would consist of contract furniture for the mail-order houses and certain other large customers and of dimension stock. The remaining two thirds was to consist of a branded, trademarked line of Mengel furniture which was to be produced by mass production methods for distribution on a national scale. The designs of the Mengel furniture were to be distinct from those sold to contract customers, and the contract furniture was to be in no way identified as a Mengel product.

The branded line of furniture was to be advertised nationally to both the trade and consumers and was to be sold direct to retail stores by Mengel salesmen. The retail dealers were to be carefully selected, and the company planned to do everything possible to aid them in promoting and selling the Mengel line.

In the summer of 1944 Marschalk & Pratt conducted, through a fact finding agency, three surveys for the Mengel Company. The first was a consumer survey involving 6,081 interviews in 49 cities from coast to coast. The purpose of this survey was to learn something about the nature of the consumer demand for bedroom and dinette furniture and about the consumer's reaction to manufacturer's and dealer's brands. Some of the findings of this survey are shown in Exhibit 2. The second survey was a dealer survey covering 505 dealers in 53 cities from coast to coast. The purpose of this survey was to determine dealer opinions as to the popularity of various styles, finishes, and price ranges, dealer attitudes toward manufacturer's brands and minimum retail prices, and dealer interest in advertising and sales help. Extracts from the survey are shown in Exhibit 3. The third survey was a manufacturers' survey in which 25 manufacturers were visited by the vice-president of the research company instead of by field workers.

Many of the executives were of the opinion that the company should produce an inexpensive line of furniture similar to that which the company had manufactured for the mail-order houses. This furniture was easy to produce by mass production methods, and the production organization was already familiar with the required manufacturing techniques. However, it was decided that the inexpensive furniture was sold primarily to low-income population groups which had little interest in anything other than price. It was therefore decided that the Mengel furniture should be constructed and priced to sell in the low to medium end of the middle price range and consist of bedroom furniture.

In the closing months of 1945 and the early part of 1946 a total of about $1,500,000 was spent on production equipment and installations at the furniture division plants. The 12th Street plant was tooled up to run almost exclusively on the branded line of bedroom furniture. Included in the new equipment for this plant was an assembly and finishing conveyor, approximately 2½ miles in length, which was installed at a cost of about $250,000. The 4th Street plant was tooled up to handle the contract, novelty, and specialty furniture and most of the dimension stock business. A somewhat simpler assembly and finishing conveyor for case goods was installed at this plant at a cost of $75,000.

SCOPE OF OPERATIONS IN 1946

When the new furniture program was in the initial stages of development, the operations of the company consisted of three major divisions: the container division, the plywood division, and furniture division.

Container Division

The container division operated plants in Kentucky, New Jersey, North Carolina, and New York. These plants purchased paperboard in rolls, manufactured it into corrugated board, and converted the corrugated board into corrugated shipping containers. The containers were sold to large manufacturers of tobacco, food, soap, beverages, and miscellaneous other products. The container division also supplied the furniture division of the Mengel Company with shipping containers for its products.

Plywood Division

The plywood division operated a plywood and lumber mill in Louisiana, a plywood mill in North Carolina, a veneer and door mill in Kentucky, and two smaller plants for the manufacture of Flexwood, Flexglass, and certain other specialty items. The chief products of the plywood division were plywood and Mengel doors. These products were nationally advertised and sold through the United States Plywood Corporation and the jointly owned sales corporation, U.S.-Mengel Plywoods, Inc. In addition, the plywood division sold one third to one half of its plywood output to the furniture division.

The plywood division of the Mengel Company was the largest single producer of southern hardwood plywood in the United States. Mr. Voit estimated that it manufactured perhaps 10 percent of the total volume of hardwoods sold by the industry.

Furniture Division

The furniture division operated seven plants; four of these manufactured furniture or furniture parts and three manufactured industrial products.

In August, 1946, the 12th Street plant was running almost exclusively on the branded line of Mengel bedroom furniture. Five different suites were manufactured: two colonial suites, one in gum with a maple finish and one in solid maple; two modern suites, one in oak and one in beech with a maple finish; and a mahogany veneer suite of fuctional modern design.

The 4th Street plant manufactured one modern oak suite of the branded Mengel bedroom furniture, two bedroom suites for sale on a contract basis to the mail-order houses, a substantial volume of dimension stock, some novelty furniture for sale to large jobbers, and a line of specialty furniture called "Module."

MANUFACTURING

By 1946 the research activities had resulted in two major developments: a carefully controlled method of construction called "permanizing" and a patented drawer design called "permaslide."

The permanizing process was described in the company's advertising as follows: "Permanizing is Mengel's exclusive scientific method of prolonging the charm and life of its furniture. It keeps the joints and veneered surfaces from coming apart in any climate, no matter how damp or dry, or how hot or cold." In developing this process the research laboratory worked with 20 different types of adhesives, 300 glue formulas, 400 glued dowel joints, 3,000 glue block joints, 300 test panels, and 30 different pieces of furniture for tests and comparison. Tests were made for the tensile shear strength of adhesives, the acidity, viscosity, and gap filling characteristics of adhesives, and the resistance of adhesives to crazing or cracking and to long exposure to excessive heat and moisture.

A second feature developed by the research laboratory was the permaslide drawer. This drawer had a rounded plywood bottom and was hung on side slides cut in heavy pieces of wood in such a manner that swelling and sticking was made impossible.

In 1946 the research laboratory employed four people and had responsibility for research and development as well as quality and process control. The laboratory had approximately $10,000 worth of equipment which included ovens, accelerated weathering units, autoclaves, potentiometers, facilities for testing tensile, shear, and compression strength, and facilities for testing nail, screw, and glue holding power.

The annual appropriation for maintenance of the research and quality control department was approximately $30,000.

Furniture Design

Furniture designs were developed by three procedures. First, the company employed one full-time designer. Second, it made use at various times of three contract designers who were employed on a retainer basis. In 1946 it retained one such designer. Also the company purchased designs outright from three independent designers.

One design advance had been the development of a line of interchangeable furniture called "Module." It consisted of six basic cases or units; five bases; drawers, doors, and shelves; and a number of accessories such as beds, tables, chairs, and mirrors. The six basic units were so proportioned that they could be used either horizontally or vertically and could be combined at the will of the owner into innumerable furniture arrangements. The units were connected to one another by a simple locking device which could be operated with a coin.

The executives of the furniture division did not anticipate that they would be making frequent and extensive revisions in their furniture designs. They intended that the Mengel permanized line would not exceed seven or eight basic suites in addition to the Module group with perhaps two suites being replaced each year with new designs. During the first six months of 1946 expenditures for design development, the construction of samples, and the testing of designs with consumer groups ran about $4,000 per month. It was expected that these expenses would average less than 1 percent of sales. Exhibit 4 shows the Modern and the Module suites.

Production Lot Size

Bedroom furniture was scheduled into production in lots of 500 to 1,000 suites. A suite design contained eight or nine different pieces such as a chest, vanity, dresser, chest-on-chest, 4-foot 6-inch bed, 3-foot 3-inch bed, bench, and night stand. Selling prices for a suite were quoted to cover any three major units which the customer wished to select; for additional pieces the price was increased. From past experience the Mengel Company was able to estimate the approximate ratio in which the various units in a suite would be sold. Since customers nearly always included a chest in their selection, the chest was used as the base unit for production and sales schedules. A production order for 1,000 suites of a particular design would thus mean 1,000 chests and perhaps 800 3-foot 3-inch beds, 500 4-foot 6-inch beds, 700 dressers, 300 vanities, 500 benches, and 700 night stands; probably 200 chest-on-chests would be included in the 1,000 "chests."

Each piece in a suite contained on the average about 30 different parts. From one to eight of each part might be required per assembly. As a result, a production lot of 1,000 suites might involve runs of anywhere from a few hundred to several thousand pieces or individual parts. The lot sizes of 500 to 1,000 suites had been selected because they reduced setup costs to a relatively small amount per piece and because they enabled the workmen to make their piece rates on individual operations without too much difficulty. It had also been found that production lots of 2,000 suites resulted in no significant cost savings as compared to lots about 1,000 suites.

The executives of the furniture division had given considerable attention to the problem of reducing inventories and were trying to obtain an average inventory turnover of five times a year. To obtain this objective they were trying to hold the stock of finished furniture to not more than two weeks' supply, work-in-process to six weeks' supply, lumber to four months' supply, plywood and veneer to six weeks' supply, packing material to two months' supply, and finishing materials to one month supply.

Manufacturing Costs

The plant operated on a standard cost system, and periodic analyses were made for control purposes of the variances between standard and actual costs by types of accounts. The division of costs between material, labor, and overhead varied depending upon the volume of production. At normal rates of operation, however, it was estimated that the factory costs, exclusive of selling and administrative expense and profit, would consist of about 55 percent material, 20 percent direct labor, and 25 percent manufacturing burden.

MARKETING PROGRAM

The marketing program of the furniture division was based upon an earnest conviction held by the executives of the company that furniture could be sold on a national scale with a manufacturer's brand like radios, carpets, automobiles, and similar products. The basic objective of the program was, therefore, not so much to sell furniture to retail stores but rather to sell through the stores to consumers.

Selection of Market Territories

Before deciding on the sales territories to be used in the United States, the director of sales and his staff made careful studies of market statistics, trading centers, trading areas, and buying power. The United States was divided into 31 sales territories. Each territory was assigned a percentage of the national quota and grouped under one of the five sales districts.

Sales Organization

In September, 1946, the sales organization was composed of five district sales managers and eleven salesmen. Two or three of the 31 territories were assigned to each of the eleven salesmen. It was intended that five or six additional men might be added to the sales force if it developed that the existing group could not render proper service to the dealers as the volume of production and the number of stores increased. The salesmen were employed on a full time basis by the Mengel Company, sold only to retail stores, and handled Mengel furniture exclusively.

Distribution Policies

In determining the sequence of the various steps in the distribution program, consideration was given to the circulation of the magazines in which the company carried advertising, trading area buying power, and the size and importance of different stores. Instead of beginning with cities and towns near Louisville, it was decided to secure distribution first in the ten largest cities, then the next ten, and so on until dealers had been selected in the first one hundred cities. Retail outlets were then secured in the second hundred cities. In November, 1946, the company had 236 stores in 191 cities. The company sold to these stores only through its own salesmen, and these men did not, as is usually the case, carry other furniture lines.

1. *Selection of Dealers:* The first step in securing distribution in a city was for the territory salesman, and frequently his district manager, to visit a number of the leading department and furniture stores in the city. In selecting the particular stores to be used primary stress was laid upon the personal appraisal made by the Mengel representatives.

It was the policy of the company to sell through a relatively small number of carefully selected stores and to work very closely with them in order to sell a fairly large volume per store. The number of stores selected in a city depended upon the buying power of the trading area. In metropolitan markets like New York and Chicago, the company had five or six stores; but in most cities of 300,000 and over, two or three stores were franchised. In the smaller cities, the company franchised only one store.

In view of the company's program of selective selling, the executives of the furniture division decided to delay for the time being participation in any of the periodic furniture shows which were used extensively by other furniture manufacturers as a means of selling their products to retailers.

2. *Sales Franchise:* The arrangements between the Mengel Company and its retail stores were embodied in a written franchise. The company was the first in the furniture field to sell under a written franchise, and the executives hoped that it would help to avoid future misunderstandings concerning the representations made by the company and the dealers. The franchise required that the store feature Mengel merchandise, accept a minimum quota, and maintain the minimum resale prices established by the Mengel Company.

The stores were encouraged but not obligated to use the Mengel name and trademark in their advertising. The minimum quota for a store was set at about one third the amount of furniture it was believed the store would like to have in normal times. Stores were permitted to sell above but not below the minimum resale prices established under the Federal and State Fair Trade laws. It was believed that this arrangement would give the stores ample flexibility in their pricing policies and yet prevent them from "footballing" the company's nationally advertised merchandise by cutting prices. The minimum resale prices established by the company carried a gross margin of about 40 percent of the minimum retail price which was equivalent to 67 percent of the furniture cost, f.o.b. factory. The actual selling prices established by the stores frequently included 50 percent gross margin on the retail price, or 100 percent on the f.o.b. factory cost.

The suites sold by the company in November, 1946, together with their cost prices to the stores for a three-piece suite (chest, dresser, and bed, f.o.b. factory) and the required minimum resale prices were as follows:

Suite No.	*Description*	*Cost f.o.b. Factory*	*Minimum Resale Price*
#500	Maple finish colonial	$ 75.00	$125.50
#503	Oak veneer—modern[1]	130.00	217.00
#504	Solid maple—colonial	125.00	208.50
#506	Solid oak—modern[1]	90.00	150.00
#509	Solid beech, maple finish—modern	135.00	225.25
#510	Mahogany veneer—functional modern	120.00	200.25

[1] The modern oak suite was produced in a solid and veneered construction.

Advertising and Sales Promotion Program

The executives of the furniture division decided to spend 500,000 per year to establish consumer and trade recognition of the Mengel brand and the qualities for which it stood. Of this amount, approximately $280,000 per year was to be spent for advertisements in consumer magazines. Studies made by the company indicated that all of the furniture manufacturers combined had spent less than $900,000 for consumer advertising in 1941, with no one firm spending more than $106,000.

The Mengel Company planned to spend about $23,000 per year for advertising in trade papers and about $200,000 for sales promotion work. The latter included booklets, displays, newspaper mats, and aids for the training of retail furniture salesmen. The company supplied each of its stores with an advertising kit which contained a letter of explanation, the specifications of each suite of furniture, copy suggestions for retail advertisements, glossy prints of art work for use in retail advertisements, a schedule of the company's magazine advertising, and reprints in color of forthcoming full-page advertisements.

The consumer advertising program for 1946 involved the use of full-page, four-color advertisements in accordance with the following schedule:

	May	*June*	*July*	*August*	*Sept.*	*Oct.*	*Nov.*	*Dec.*
Saturday Evening Post	May 18			Aug. 24	Sept. 28		Nov. 23	
Ladies Home Journal		X				X		X
Better Homes & Gardens		X	X		X		X	
American Home				X	X	X		X
House Beautiful		X				X	X	

All of the Mengel line was identified by a trademark identical to that used in the advertisements. The trademark was made up in the form of a small metal and plastic button which was sunk into the edge of the top drawer of each case unit. The trademark was also stamped on the inside of the drawer walls. This procedure of marking had been developed in order to make certain that the trademark would not be removed or covered up by the dealers.

The executives of the Mengel Company stated that their objective was to attain an annual sales volume of $12 million from the Louisville furniture plants. They believed that it was necessary to turn out furniture in great volume with comparatively few patterns and infrequent design changes in order to make low unit costs possible in spite of high hourly wage rates. In view of these objectives, the vice-president of manufacturing was considering ways to establish production facilities capable of meeting the requirements of the marketing program.

1. MENGEL COMPANY (A)

Sales of Furniture Division, 1936-1946

(In Thousands)

Year	Novelty Furniture and Misc.	Radio Cabinets	Bedroom Furniture	Furn. Dim. Stk. Semi-Finished	Furniture Dim. Stk. Fully Machined	Indus. and Radio Dim. Stk.	Auto-motive	Boxes and Crates	Misc.	Total Excl'g Aircraft	Aircraft Sales
1936	$ 802	$446		$ 55	$ 371	$196	$1,104		$ 24	$2,998	
1937	752	529		81	548	212	539		27	2,688	
1938	602			205	545	126	110		53	1,641	
1939	911		$ 84	150	939	147	152	$ 81	164	2,628	
1940	1,099		764	143	951		104	375	158	3,594	
1941	1,799		1,631	347	1,357		186	647	47	6,014	
1942	1,397		1,334	239	956		2,331	1,861	289	8,407	$1,399
1943	1,038		43	229	966		2,749	2,911	432	8,368	4,636
1944	675		466	76	1,107		2,424	3,765	895(a)	9,408	7
1945	481		1,190	95	962		1,426	1,933	1,660(b)	7,745	
(c) 1946	1,000		4,750(d)	65	1,600		5			7,420	

(a) Includes $810,980 of army cots.
(b) Includes $1,603,280 war products (fully machined).
(c) Estimated for October, November, and December—rest actual.
(d) Includes Module Furniture.

2. MENGEL COMPANY (A)

Selected Excerpts from the Consumer Survey

(6,081 Homes, Coast to Coast)

Furniture Features Considered Most Important

This question was divided into general features and specific features. In the general features, a good finish is the dominant leader with 44.2% mentions, the next highest being style with 17.7%, and the third being waterproof glue construction with 14.7%. This applies, of course, only to those features which were in our list, and there was no request for mention of any other features.

In terms of specific construction features, cedar-lined drawers are the dominant leader as most important, with 46.2% mentions, among the features listed, and it is only when we get to second in importance that we find an important second feature which is dresser with 4 drawers instead of 3.

Life Expectancy of Furniture

About one-third of all ages of people expect furniture to last indefinitely or for a life time, but this ranges from 26% in ages under 25 progressively upward with age to about 50% of people over 50 years old expecting furniture to last for the rest of their lives.

The bulk of the replies, however, amounting to over 40%, fall in the brackets between 10 and 25 years, this being true of all ages up to 50, the folks beyond 50 thinking in terms of life time.

Attitude towards a Brand Name on Furniture

Asked whether they would prefer a brand name on furniture, we find the vote divides into three nearly equal parts:

36.0%	do not care
32.6%	do not prefer a brand name
31.4%	do prefer a brand name
100.0%	

Indicating that up to this time, at least, no one has made the brand name on furniture seem outstandingly important.

Among the 1,907 who prefer a brand name on furniture:

78.2%	prefer it to be the manufacturer's brand
6.6%	prefer the store brand
15.5%	do not care whose brand name
100.3%	

Type of Store at Which People Prefer to Buy Furniture

Furniture stores lead with 57.3% of mentions, followed by

Department stores	20.4
No preference	16.2
Interior Decorator	3.3
Mail Order Stores	2.3
Roadside store	.3
Mail Order Catalog	.2
	100.0%

(Note: The above quotations represent only a very small portion of the consumer survey. The entire survey covered many other points such as the particular styles, designs, woods, and finishes preferred by customers, the relative demand for bedroom as opposed to living room and other types of furniture, and the amount which customers expected to spend for furniture. The summary statements above were, of course, supported by detailed statistical tabulations of the results of the survey.)

3. MENGEL COMPANY (A)

Selected Excerpts from the Dealer Survey (505 Dealers in 53 Cities, Coast to Coast)

Question 9. What features of bedroom furniture do you consider most important?

In the general classification the three items named as being of first importance are style—179 mentions; good finish--135 mentions; dust proofing—96 mentions.

In specific features, the leaders in first importance are shirt partition--151 mentions; dresser with 4 drawers instead of 3—115 mentions; cedar-lined drawers—101 mentions.

Question 13. In any one year, from how many manufacturers do you buy?

Most dealers buy their bedroom furniture from 6 to 35 manufacturers in any one year. Most of them buy their dining room furniture from 3 to 20 manufacturers, and most respondents indicated that they buy their dinette and breakfast furniture from 2 to 20 manufacturers in any one year.

Question 15 (a). Do you prefer the manufacturer's brand on the furniture you sell?

52.1% say yes   37.0% say no   10.9% say don't know

If the manufacturer's brand is on, only 16.4% say they would add their own, plus 3% who say they would under certain conditions.

Only 10.5% say they would remove it and replace it with their own; plus 4.5% who say they would, under certain conditions.

Question 15 (b). Do you expect manufacturers to give you any protection?

78.8% say yes   12.1% say no   9.4% undecided

The protection they would expect falls into four principal groups:

133 want adjustments, such as replacement of defective parts, faulty constructions, fading colors, breakage, mistakes.
87 want protection from nearby competitors.
51 want price protection.
43 expect the manufacturer to back up their merchandise and all statements made by them.

Question 15 (d). What do you consider yourself obligated to do in return for this protection?

298 of the 398 who expect protection say they would reciprocate in every way, such as concentrating on the line, creating volume, buying regularly, etc.

Question 15 (e). Who do you think should set the retail price?

455 of the 505 dealers think that the retail price of furniture should be set by the dealer.
25 think it should be set by the manufacturer.
The rest are not sure of their choice.

Question 15 (f). Do you think the manufacturer should set a minimum but not a fixed retail sale price?

27.7% say yes   54.7% say no   17.6% don't know

Question 16 (b). What do you like about markets?

The three answers given with greatest frequency are: 135 say concentrated exhibits simplify buying; see large, varied exhibits. 131 say it gives them an opportunity to examine the actual merchandise. 108 say it gives them an opportunity to see new styles and get acquainted with new trends and new features in furniture.

4A. MENGEL COMPANY (A)
Module Furniture

4B. MENGEL COMPANY (A)
Suite #503—Oak Veneer—Modern Design

Mengel Company (B)

During the period April, 1946, to March, 1948, the furniture sales of the Mengel furniture increased markedly and consumer interest in the brand was stimulated. The Mengel line was carried by 500 furniture and department stores. Over 425,000 requests were received for the company's booklet "Let's Plan a Bedroom Around You," which won the 1947 Best of Industry award of the Direct Mail Advertising Association. A series of sound slide films were made to help Mengel salesmen describe the product line to retail furniture salesmen. A survey of retailers indicated that 94 percent of those who replied to the survey had experienced having customers come into the store and ask for Mengel furniture by name. A survey of consumers who had requested a Mengel booklet revealed that 50 percent said they had visited a store to see the furniture. The Module line was advertised in *House Beautiful* and *Living* and received much editorial comment, including prominent mention in an article on furniture in *Fortune* magazine for January, 1947.

Beginning in the second quarter of 1948, however, what Mr. Voit called "the greatest market of scarcity on record in recent times" ended and a buyers' market appeared. An "avalanche of troubles" befell the company, described as follows in the Annual Report for 1949:

> . . . What might be termed a "quickie depression" occurred in most wood industries, but I believe it had a more than average bad effect on this company mainly because of our being rather a newcomer in the finished product markets in which we now operate in the wood end of our business (bedroom furniture, flush doors, kitchen cabinets). Sales of the wood end dropped about 60% from the peak first quarter of 1948 to the low second quarter of 1949, and the difference between the years as a whole was a drop of approximately 35%. . . .
>
> . . . The circumstances which prevailed in 1949 were not only difficult to cope with from a strictly management standpoint but they have been extremely trying in their effect on all people associated with the business, including the men in our plants. In many cases, drastic changes have been made both in personnel and in methods."

Although the advent of the Korean War in June, 1950, signaled an increase in consumer furniture purchases, the buying programs of the retail stores caused production planning difficulties for the Mengel Company. Scare buying ceased about March, 1951, and the retail stores cut back orders precipitously in order to reduce their inventories.

The executives of the Mengel Company dealt with the buyers' markets of 1949 and 1951, by concentrating on a program involving the following elements: (1) reorganizing certain product divisions, (2) broadening the furniture line, (3) developing new construction features, (4) concentrating on production control, and (5) widening the distribution of the furniture.

Reorganizing Certain Product Divisions: The kitchen cabinet operations were separated from household furniture in order to leave management free to concentrate on production and distribution problems unique to furniture. The new kitchen cabinet division had its own plants in Indiana, Missouri, and North Carolina.

Broadening the Furniture Line: In order to satisfy changing tastes and enter a wider market, the company began making nonbedroom furniture, produced lines in different styles, many woods, and other price ranges than were originally offered in 1946. As a result of changes in the postwar period, the Mengel line included: case goods for dining rooms and living rooms; lines in modern, traditional, and contemporary (a blend of the two); lines of mahogany veneer, solid maple, solid mahogany, and walnut; a line scaled to smaller size for use in smaller apartment houses; two lower priced lines.

New Construction Features: Beginning in 1949, the company announced several new features: steel drawer "kickers" to prevent drawers from sticking or from sagging when pulled out —achieved by fitting curved metal rods to the sides of the drawer and resting the rods along a crack; flexible drawer partitions to divide up the space in drawers according to the individual requirements of the consumer; a "vanity organizer" or removable plastic tray divided into 11 small compartments designed to hold women's make-up accessories; and a "hosiery compartment," a sliding drawer under the seat of the vanity bench, designed to hold women's stockings.

Distribution: The selective distribution plan, which resulted in 500 furniture and department store outlets was revised in a campaign to attract 2,000 outlets by 1950. The Mengel Company opened its first sales showroom in July, 1948, at the major summer furniture market in Chicago. The advertising program was continued and extended by space in *Life* magazine. By 1950 it was estimated that the company had spent more than $1.5 million in advertising "Mengel Permanized Furniture" since World War II and that retail outlets had spent more than double that amount. The Mengel Company printed a new booklet "Make Your Own Design for Living" and launched a retail training course with a monthly newsletter entitled "Merchandise with Mengel."

In 1952 the Mengel Company discontinued the manufacture of furniture for other manufacturers and concentrated entirely on furniture sold under the company's name and brand. This action was said to result in economies and to enable the company to extend its own product line. Mengel furniture was broadened to include higher and lower priced numbers and add many dining room and living room pieces. The company introduced the "American Bounty" line, a chest constructed without cross pieces between the drawers so as to provide 40 percent more storage area with the same space and to reduce manufacturing costs. In addition, an entire line was designed for the Mengel Company by Raymond Loewy, the famous industrial designer, and attracted much editorial comment.

In 1953 and 1954 the company experienced difficulty maintaining its profit margin as sales increased and then declined suddenly without a concurrent reduction in costs. In 1953, the Annual Report contained the following statement:

> The company was originally a box company and its experience in the box field runs back many, many years. In its other fields, the company is a relative newcomer, its experience with the present products running back only to about the end of the Second World War. Partly because of its newness in these fields, but mainly in an attempt to reduce the sharpness of cyclical peaks and valleys, the company has adopted merchandising methods which we consider more aggressive and which we know to be more costly than those of many companies in the industries.
>
> While we are not yet in position to evaluate the decline in our business in the consumer durable goods fields in comparison with that experienced by others in the same businesses, nevertheless we know that the decline is too great for comfort. Therefore, we are moving quickly to re-examine the products, production costs and merchandising costs of this part of our business. . . .

In view of the changed marketing program, the vice-president of manufacturing was considering means of adapting his production facilities to smaller lots and more frequent design changes. Exhibits 1 to 5 indicate the extent to which the finishing system had been set up for mass production of large lots.

Production

The production process consisted of five major steps.

1. *Kiln Drying:* As the lumber was unloaded from the box cars it was sorted and loaded directly onto kiln trucks. It remained on these trucks during the time it was held in green storage. The kiln trucks ran on parallel tracks which led to a row of 21 dry kilns. The lumber was moved from storage into the kilns for a drying period which ranged from one to three weeks. During this time the moisture content of the lumber was reduced to 5 or 6 percent. Upon coming out of the dry kilns the lumber was placed in "dry storage" in a closed warehouse where the temperature and humidity could be controlled.

MENGEL COMPANY (B)

Results of Operations

	1946	1947	1948	1949	1950	1951	1952	1953	1954
Net sales	$25,342	$35,292	$35,630	$26,431	$42,478	$42,418	$36,486	$41,870	$38,632
Taxes on income	1,075	1,300	910	(140)	2,730	1,905	805	1,190	800
Net earnings (loss)	1,619	2,296	1,829	(169)	2,744	1,576	1,094	1,420	1,062
Per share of common stock*	2.91	3.95	3.12	(.44)	4.38	2.49	1.70	2.23	1.65
Dividends to stockholders									
Total amount	639	779	781	221	680	1,092	654	654	651
Per share of preferred stock	2.50	2.50	2.50	2.50	2.50	2.50	2.50	2.50	2.50
Per share of common stock	1.00	1.25	1.25	.25	1.05	1.75	1.00	1.00	1.00
Earnings retained	na	na	na	na	2,074	484	440	766	411
Depreciation	na	na	na	na	670	608	631	676	835
Plant additions--net	na	na	na	na	656	855	894	1,001	825

Financial Condition December 31

	1946	1947	1948	1949	1950	1951	1952	1953	1954
Cash and government securities	$ 1,675	$ 1,586	$ 1,287	$ 1,469	$ 3,732	$ 1,862	$ 1,426	$ 1,289	$ 1,730
Receivables	2,485	2,584	1,580	2,276	3,732	2,699	3,336	3,126	3,200
Inventories	5,016	5,693	7,032	4,563	6,344	7,195	6,017	6,955	5,888
Total current assets	9,176	9,863	9,899	8,308	13,808	11,756	10,779	11,370	10,818
Total current liabilities	3,937	3,861	3,197	1,530	4,989	3,523	3,142	3,612	2,619
Net working capital	5,239	6,002	6,702	6,788	8,819	8,233	7,637	7,757	8,199
Plant, timber, other assets	8,244	8,827	9,026	8,499	8,372	9,278	10,134	10,608	11,102
Long-term debt	2,200	2,050	1,900	1,750	1,600	1,522	1,342	1,170	1,502
Total capital	11,283	12,780	13,828	13,526	15,591	15,990	16,429	17,196	17,798
Book value per share of common stock*	17.27	19.93	21.80	20.89	24.49	24.57	25.28	26.52	27.49

*Earnings and book value per share for years 1950-54 are stated on basis of shares outstanding at end of 1954.

2. *Rough Milling:* From the crane lift the lumber was transferred to hydraulic lifts or "lowerators" which kept the top of the pile at a convenient height for handling. When the cross-cut operators received a "cutting order" to cut the pieces for a production lot of, say, 500 suites, they began by first cutting out the longer pieces such as the bed headboards. A cutting for 500 headboards might yield, for example, 200 pieces suitable for chests, 100 pieces suitable for dressers, and 50 pieces suitable for night stands. The cross-cut saws worked at high rates of speed and the seven of them together might cut all of the pieces required for a lot of 500 suites in a few days.

In August, 1946, the rough mill was operating two shifts and employed a total of about 75 men. Neither shift was fully manned, and the mill was running at about 40 percent of two-shift capacity. In nearly all cases the men were paid individual or group piece rates. It was estimated that the minimum production cycle in the rough mill for a lot of 1,000 suites would be about four days. In August, 1946, a lot of 500 suites required about 8 to 10 days to work its way from one end of the rough mill to the other. The amount of waste and scrap lumber in the rough and finish mill together ran between 30 and 40 percent, depending on the skill of the cross-cut and ripsaw operators.

3. *Finish Milling:* In the finish mill the parts were cut to final shape and dimension. A floor plan of the finish mill is shown in Exhibit 1. Each part passed through whatever sequence of operations was indicated on the operation routing (see Exhibit 2), but, in general, the parts followed a U-shaped path, down through the mill and back up through inspection and repair. Usually the parts were moved from one machine to another in truck-load lots.

The finish mill operated on a two-shift basis and employed a total of 57 men. As in the rough mill, neither shift was fully manned and the department was running at about 40 percent of two-shift capacity. Individual or group piece rates were used on nearly all operations. The time required for a production lot of 500 suites to work its way through the finish mill was about the same as in the rough mill.

Upon leaving the finish mill the parts were carried down the elevator either into the assembly department or into white storage. The inventory in white storage was used as a "buffer" between the parts producing department and the assembly department. This inventory was kept very small in order to hold down investment costs and because the finished parts were subject to some deterioration and might require additional sanding or refinishing if carried in stock too long. As a general rule, parts seldom remained in white storage for more than a few days.

4. *Assembling:* Separate assembly lines or floor areas were used for the different pieces of furniture.

Cases (chests, vanities, dressers, and chest-on-chests) were built up from subassemblies. Parts were taken from the flats (trucks) and fitted together on the assembly tables. Presses, clamps, jigs, and various other pieces of simple equipment were used. The operation usually involved nailing or gluing the parts together and the use of some device to hold or press them into a squared position for a moment while the glue was setting. The finished subassemblies were loaded on flats ready to be moved to the presses for final case assembly.

In the final case assembly, the subassemblies and other parts were coated with glue and fitted together in an assembly press. Four presses were for chests, vanities, dressers, and chest-on-chests, respectively. The press was closed, often by air pressure, to square up the parts in the correct position for a moment while the glue dried. The cases were then loaded onto the case assembly conveyor.

On the assembly conveyor four operations were performed: drawers were fitted, the cases were sanded and cleaned, backs were nailed on, and the finished cases were inspectd. To fit the drawers the men worked in teams of two. The case was pulled to the side of the conveyor and the two men fitted the drawers using hand planers and sand paper. The case was then returned to the conveyor which carried it through a group of eight men, each of whom did a portion of the sanding and cleaning on each case. The case was then removed from the conveyor by teams of two men who nailed on the backs.

The assembly department operated at about 50 percent of capacity on a one-shift basis and employed a total of 68 men. Nearly all of these men were paid an individual or group piece rate. On the conveyor lines each team or individual was paid for the number of units which he completed satisfactorily, irrespective of what might be done by others further down the line.

5. *Finishing:* The furniture was carried through the sequence of finishing operations by means of a monorail conveyor approximately 10,000 feet in length. At 6-foot intervals along the conveyor were hung "hanging pallets." The furniture was placed on these pallets at the loading areas on the second floor and remained on them throughout the sequence of operations. The layout and arrangement of the finishing system and the photographs which accompany it are included in Exhibits 3 to 5.

The finishing system consisted of eight major spray booths or stations through which the furniture was carried by means of the conveyor. At each station, finishing coats were applied by means of spray guns in accordance with the sequence shown in Exhibit 4. In between several of the stations were forced-drying ovens, in which the temperature and the humidity were controlled. These operations were done by groups of workers who walked along slowly with the conveyor. Each worker did part of the work on each case. The worker assigned to the lower portions of the pieces followed the work by means of a small scooter on which he kneeled or sat. An operation such as wiping and cleaning might require as much as 20 minutes per case, but by dividing the work between enough workers it could be done easily while the pieces were moving between stations.

The various pieces of a suite, such as beds, dressers, chests, night stands, and vanities were loaded onto the conveyor on the second floor in random order. The conveyor often carried pieces from two or three different suites at the same time. This could be done by having two or three spray guns at the booths, each loaded with a different finishing material. As the pieces from the different suites came along the line, the workers could then shift from one gun to another.

The time schedule for the finishing operations is shown in Exhibit 4. A conveyor speed of 10 f.p.m. has been used in this table in order to permit easy conversion to other rates of operation. The conveyor had a maximum capacity of about 50 three-piece suites an hour. In August, 1946, it operated on a one-shift basis and was running at a speed of about 12 to 14 feet per minute or about 50 percent of capacity. There were about 57 workers used at various points along the finishing conveyor. All of these workers were paid piece rates, depending on the total output delivered by the conveyor. The warehouse was not very large, and the executives of the furniture division anticipated that they would never carry more than about two weeks' supply in stock.

All of the suites went through about the same sequence of finishing operations. Depending on the wood and particular finish desired, however, particular operations were sometimes added or omitted. In addition, the different woods in the several suites required variations in the way the spraying, wiping, sanding, and rubbing operations were performed.

The total time required in process for a 500 suite lot for assembly, finishing, packing, and shipping operations was about 6 to 8 days in August, 1946. The minimum production cycle for these operations was estimated to be about 3½ days.

1. MENGEL COMPANY (B)
Layout of Finish Mill

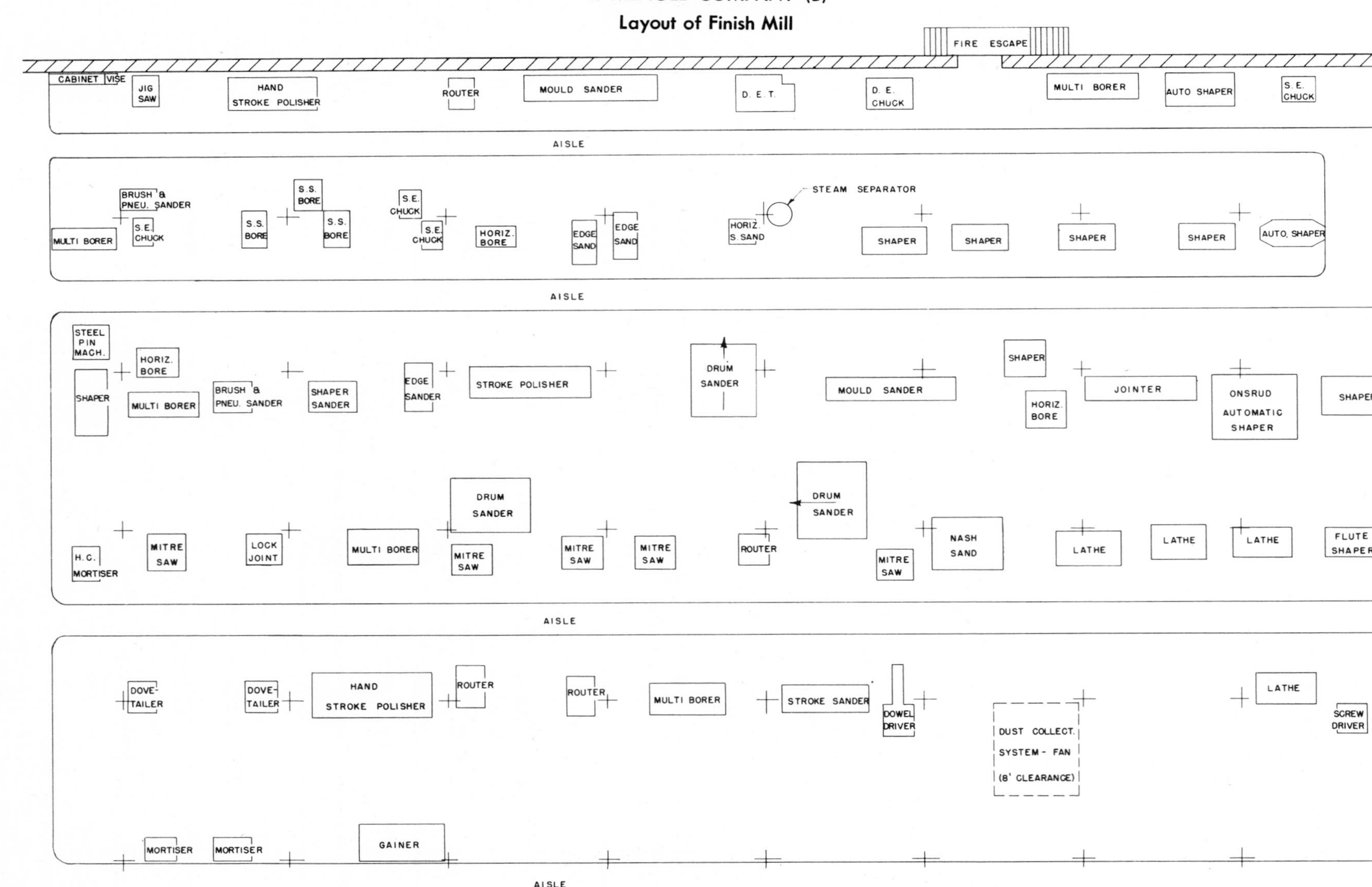

2. MENGEL COMPANY (B)

SPECIFICATION AND ROUTING SHEET

CUSTOMER Mengel PART NAME Top Drawer Front PART NUMBER 509 | 03 | 301

CUSTOMERS' NO. ______ NET FT. .597 GRADE OF CUTTING C2S1E PCS. PER JOB 2

DEPT. 12th St. GLUE Resin WOOD Beech ROUGH SIZE L. 17 W. 5 1/16 T. 4/4 MAKES ______

AVG. LOAD 900 PCS. REMARKS ______ FINISH SIZE 16 5/16 x 4 13/16 x 3/4

SEQ.	OPR. NO.	OPERATIONS	PCS. PER OPR.	SET UP	MAN HRS. @ BASE	MEN REQ.	PCS. PER HR. @ 120%	STD. LABOR	STD. BURDEN	DATE
1	1	Plane						.109		
2	2	X Cut						.237		
3	5	Rip						.275 .249		
4	26	Glue wheel						.553		
5	20	Face and finish plane						.064 .063 .063		
6										
7	23	Stick to patt. after D.E.T.--37'		.383 .347		2	1,270	.068 .061		
8										
9								1.742	2.178	
10	33	D.E. Shape ends B4--		.466 .422		2	650	.134 .120		
11	33	D.E. Tenon ends		.108 .098		2	1,000	.086 .078		
12	49	Bore 4 holes in jig for grinder		.380		1	360	.223		
13	49	Bore 2 holes for drawer pull		.210		1	500	.161		
14	93	Rout groove for bottom and sides	1	.260	1.25	1	96 1/2	.835		
15	51	Bore 1 hole top edge 50%		.130				.130		
16	96	Drum sand 2 sides (1o)				2	689	.116 .114		
17										
18	98	Mould sand 4 sides and 4 corners (On Pin)	1		.85	1	142	.609		
19										
20	107	Stroke polish face						.280		
21				2.804				2.886	4.329	
22		(500)		.561				4.628	6.507	
23		To assemble 509 | 03 | 300								

3. MENGEL COMPANY (B)
Layout of Finishing Room

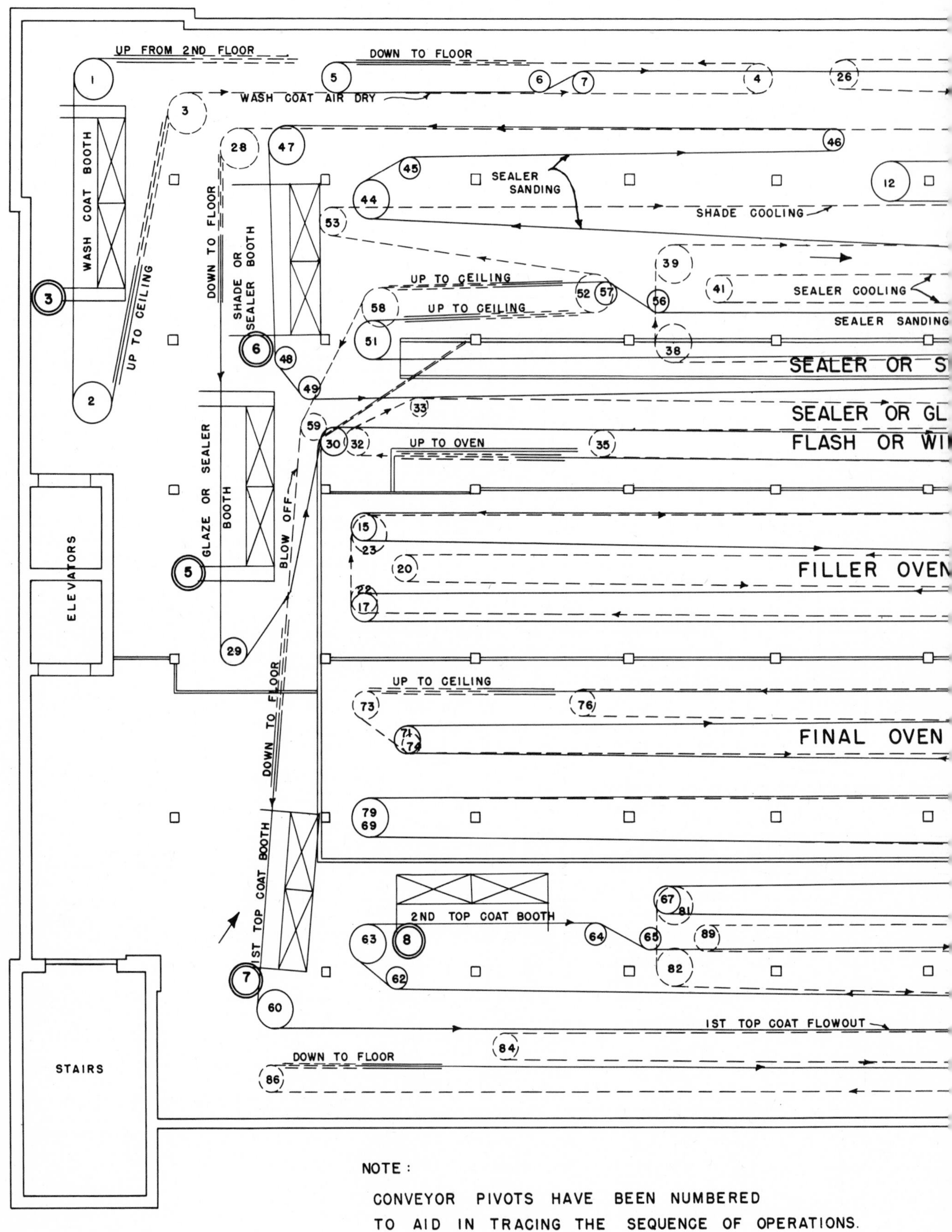

NOTE:

CONVEYOR PIVOTS HAVE BEEN NUMBERED TO AID IN TRACING THE SEQUENCE OF OPERATIONS.

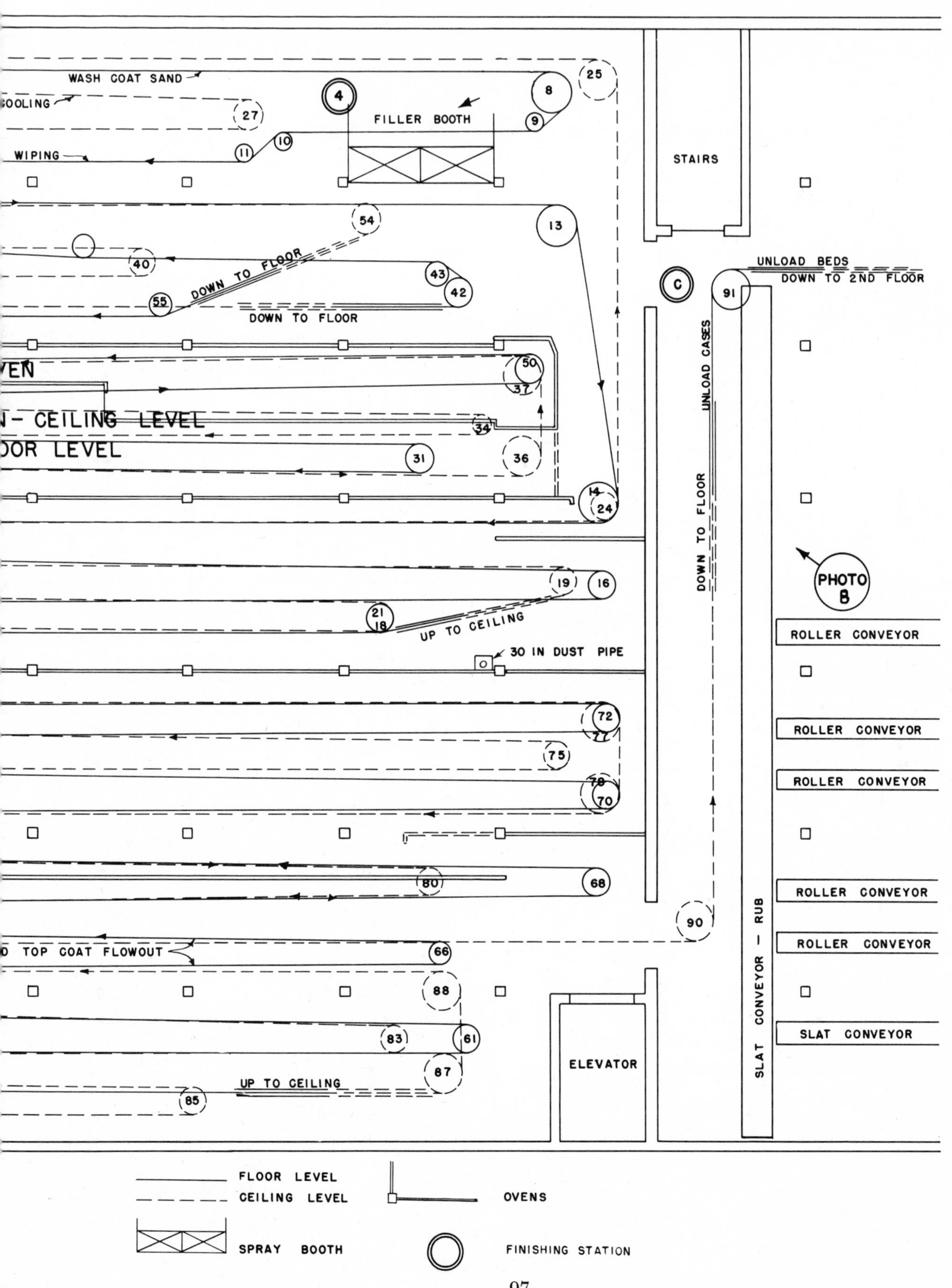

WASH COAT SAND
FILLER BOOTH
WIPING
STAIRS
DOWN TO FLOOR
DOWN TO FLOOR
UNLOAD BEDS
DOWN TO 2ND FLOOR
UNLOAD CASES
DOWN TO FLOOR
UP TO CEILING
30 IN DUST PIPE
PHOTO B
ROLLER CONVEYOR
ROLLER CONVEYOR
ROLLER CONVEYOR
ROLLER CONVEYOR
ROLLER CONVEYOR
SLAT CONVEYOR
SLAT CONVEYOR - RUB
TOP COAT FLOWOUT
ELEVATOR
UP TO CEILING
FLOOR LEVEL
CEILING LEVEL
OVENS
SPRAY BOOTH
FINISHING STATION

4. MENGEL COMPANY (B)

Start of Finishing Operations on Second Floor and Description of Finishing Procedure

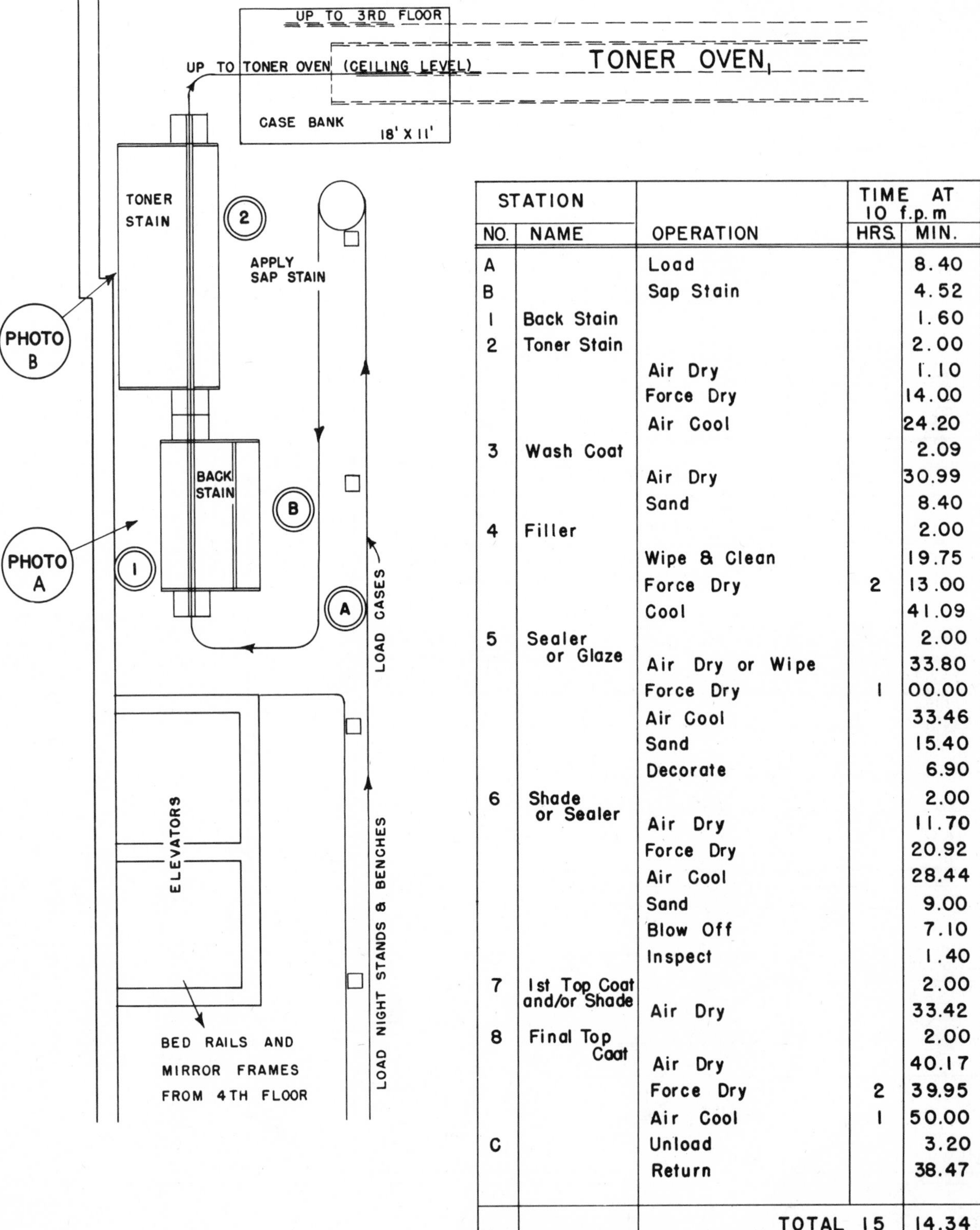

STATION		OPERATION	TIME AT 10 f.p.m	
NO.	NAME		HRS.	MIN.
A		Load		8.40
B		Sap Stain		4.52
1	Back Stain			1.60
2	Toner Stain			2.00
		Air Dry		1.10
		Force Dry		14.00
		Air Cool		24.20
3	Wash Coat			2.09
		Air Dry		30.99
		Sand		8.40
4	Filler			2.00
		Wipe & Clean		19.75
		Force Dry	2	13.00
		Cool		41.09
5	Sealer or Glaze			2.00
		Air Dry or Wipe		33.80
		Force Dry	1	00.00
		Air Cool		33.46
		Sand		15.40
		Decorate		6.90
6	Shade or Sealer			2.00
		Air Dry		11.70
		Force Dry		20.92
		Air Cool		28.44
		Sand		9.00
		Blow Off		7.10
		Inspect		1.40
7	1st Top Coat and/or Shade			2.00
		Air Dry		33.42
8	Final Top Coat			2.00
		Air Dry		40.17
		Force Dry	2	39.95
		Air Cool	1	50.00
C		Unload		3.20
		Return		38.47
		TOTAL	15	14.34

Minimum Speed 4 f.p.m.
Maximum Speed 28 f.p.m

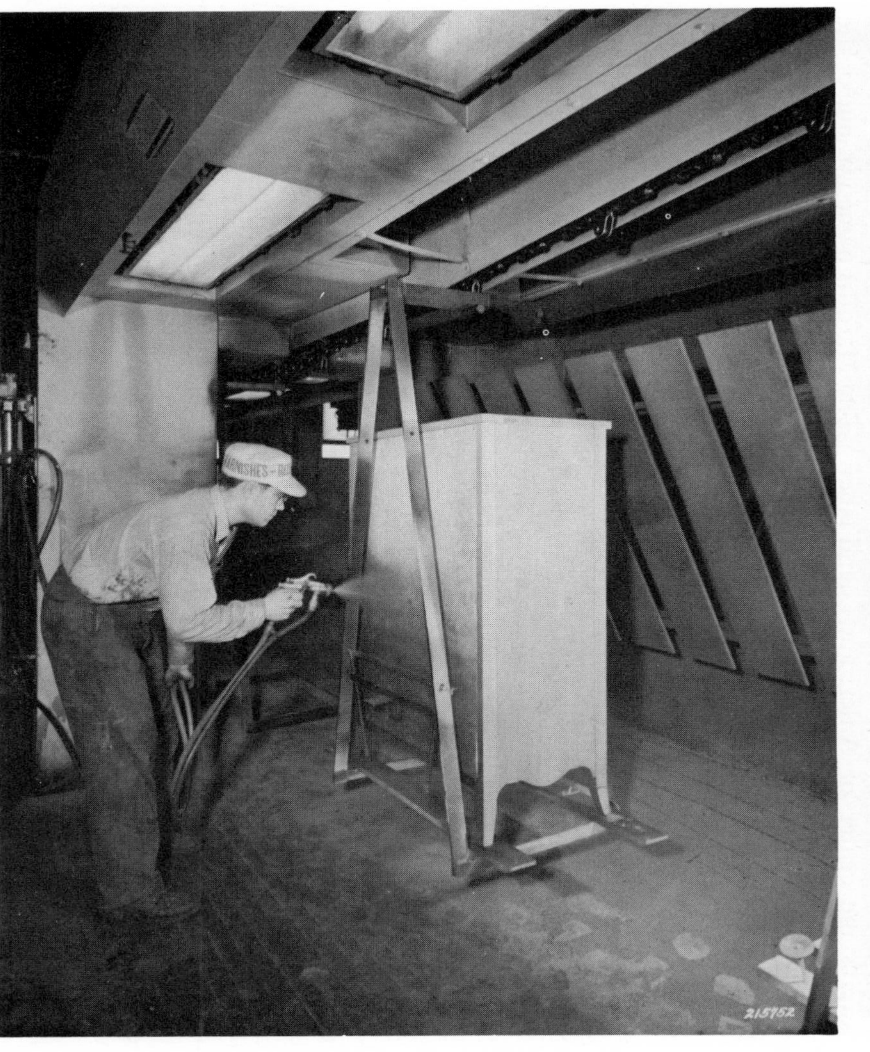

5A. MENGEL COMPANY (B)
Station No. 1 on Finishing Conveyor

5B. MENGEL COMPANY (B)
Final Mathine and Hand Rubbing

Devon Furniture Company

The Devon Furniture Company, of Grand Rapids, Michigan, was one of the two largest manufacturers of high quality furniture in the United States. The company had succeeded in establishing a reputation for selling furniture of intricate design, mellow finish, and excellent construction with a wide catalogue of items to choose from. The plant was organized to make use of mechanization, work specialization, production machinery, and cost saving work methods wherever possible. Financial figures of the Devon Furniture Company between 1947 and 1955 are contained in Exhibit 1. Balance sheets are contained in Exhibit 2 and Profit and Loss Statements are included in Exhibit 3.

COMPANY HISTORY

The Devon family name was closely associated with the early development of the industry which made Grand Rapids the center of American furniture manufacture by 1900.

The Devon Furniture Company prospered through the period of World War I, though Mr. William Devon, Sr., died in 1910, leaving the management to his son and other members of his immediate family. By 1917 the plant contained 50,000 square feet of floor space. In 1924 the company began the large scale manufacture of French provincial furniture. Using largely imported beech and walnut from France and domestic cherry wood, the Devon Furniture Company pioneered the introduction of French provincial styles to the United States. For the next thirty years, the Devon design and name was associated with French provincial reproductions of the highest quality, primarily in cherry wood. At one time, the company was the largest user of cherry in the United States although it also used fruitwood and rare veneered inlays such as yew. Photographs of items in the French provincial line are included in Exhibits 4A, 4B, and 4C.

In 1929, the ownership of the Devon Furniture Company changed hands. At that time, Mr. Franklin Price became sales manager and principal stockholder.

During the 1930's, the Devon Furniture Company operated as a job shop, with a wide line of pieces in its catalogue and very limited production runs of each item. At that time there were over fifty complete suites in the line, with as many as ten different pieces in each suite and a wide range of custom finishes.

During the boom of 1947 and 1948, the line was reduced to ten loose groupings and the amount of special finishing was substantially reduced. At this time, production runs were quite large. Many methods changes were developed and special jigs and fixtures were made to enable the workers to handle large volumes of work.

In 1950, the Devon Furniture Company bought out two other high quality furniture manufacturers, the Bradford Marquis Company and the President Furniture Company.

The Marquis company had a very high quality line of 18th century mahogany and yew veneered furniture, carefully made with much hand labor. The Marquis name was one of the oldest in Grand Rapids and was associated in the trade with distinguished reproductions of English furniture.

Although the initiative for the purchase came from the owner of the Marquis Company, who wished to retire, Mr. Price believed that the Marquis line would complement the Devon Furniture Company furniture effectively. In 1950, the Devon Furniture line of French provincial was largely made up of bedroom groupings. The Marquis line consisted for the most part of dining room and living pieces, including breakfronts and occasional tables. The Marquis plant was recognized to be a good piece of real estate, and the Marquis workers were very skilled. Since Mr. Price wished to retain the Marquis name, the integration of the new company into Devon Furniture operations presented problems as well as opportunities. Due to franchise agreements, dealers sometimes handled both lines, sometimes one or the other. Also, the Marquis plant was located in a different part of Grand Rapids and its workers, who were largely of Dutch descent, were older and perhaps more individualistic than the unionized workers at the Devon Furniture plant. In 1952,

Marquis accounted for about 15 percent and in 1955 about 20 percent of the combined company sales.

The President line consisted entirely of fine Victorian furniture, all of it in solid mahogany and requiring a considerable amount of hand carving. Many of the President pieces were upholstered sofas and chairs and it was this aspect that particularly interested Mr. Price. Prior to 1950, the Devon Furniture Company had done little upholstery work except for dining room chairs. With the broadened line resulting from the acquisition of dining and living room tables through Marquis, Mr. Price wished to obtain skilled upholsterers who could work with sofas and chairs in all types and styles of furniture. By the acquisition of President, the services of about a dozen skilled upholsterers were acquired by the company. In 1952, President accounted for about 7.5 percent and in 1955 about 1.8 percent of the combined company sales.

After the immediate postwar demand for furniture was satisfied in 1949, there was a lull in the market and customers became increasingly style conscious. When furniture purchases resumed volume after 1950, new designs were demanded and many old favorites dropped completely out of favor. These changes occurred so rapidly that many furniture companies were badly upset with inventories that could not be sold. Perhaps the most important shifts in consumer taste included the change from dark mahogany finishes to a preference for lighter woods, a change from English to French traditional, and a markedly increased interest in modern furniture of various types.

The shift from English mahogany to French cherry created much enthusiasm in the market for the Devon Furniture line, which had pioneered fine French provincial for over a generation. To meet this demand, the company brought out new French pieces and introduced a new grouping of fine Italian provincial furniture. At one time, the company had over $100,000 worth of original antique furniture in the plant, to serve as models for those pieces which were reproduced authentically.

The shift in interest to modern furniture, however, was more difficult for the company to follow. In 1950, when the Devon Furniture Company first brought out a line of modern furniture, the market response was considered disappointing because the line was too different from the fine provincial cherry with which the company's name had so long been associated. In revising their approach, the company's designers decided to concentrate on conservative "contemporary" furniture, rather than the more extreme "modern" in order to establish a blend between traditional and modern styles. As a result, the "New World" grouping was produced, which had a highly successful response in the market and equaled the sales of French provincial by 1955.

New furniture designs were somewhat difficult to fit into the Devon Furniture line because the company's name as well as the Marquis name had been built on the elegant curving lines and carved or inlaid surfaces that are associated with fine traditional furniture. Much of the modern design, however, was simple and straight, with flat surfaces, sharp edges, and rectangular shapes almost devoid of decoration. Furniture with such simplicity could be manufactured by almost any plant; it did not draw upon the skills of the Devon Furniture Company in doing intricate work. The Devon Furniture designers therefore wished to establish "a contemporary spirit of elegance" rather than entering the arena of modern designs which could more easily be copied. The executives believed that it was necessary not only to produce furniture that pleased the consumers, but also furniture that competing manufacturers in lower price brackets could not easily duplicate.

PRODUCTION

Most of the traditional furniture in the Devon Furniture line was considered to be very difficult to make. There was a great deal of carving, many curved surfaces, much inlay work and a considerable amount of custom finishing. For example, most of the provincial bureaus had drawer fronts that curved in and out lengthwise, and some also curved along the surface from top to bottom. Most tables and chairs contained legs or other pieces with much carving and no straight lines. The yew wood veneer used in some tables was so difficult to work that 80 percent scrap was not uncommon, and the workman was even obliged to fit individual knots and edges into the wood to achieve the proper appearance. In order to obtain an antique finish, the provincial furniture was worked over many times with different types and colors of finishing coats to bring out the grain of the wood. Much of the furniture was spotted with brush points and distressed with steel chains to give the appearance of age.

Plant Equipment

The company had a battery of eight dry kilns which were more than sufficient to dry its own lumber. Four of the kilns had been converted to forced draft operation, which reduced the drying time from weeks to days for an equivalent load of lumber. Since the kilns were lined up directly opposite the milling room, no double handling was required to transport dried lumber to the cut-off saws.

Subsequent to World War II, the rough milling room had been converted to an intermediate milling room containing certain types of finish milling machines to eliminate excessive moving of the work pieces. The cut-off saw was conveyorized and modernized so as to provide steady flow from the kiln trucks through cut-off to the planers. A special gluing machine had been obtained to supplant the old-fashioned gluewheel for the construction of large surfaces and core stock. An automatic shaper had been purchased, at a cost of about $12,000, largely to eliminate hand work in the cutting of intricate edges for table tops. Two automatic lathes had been installed to cut entire curved surfaces in solid drawer fronts at a single pass of the machine.

Finish milling equipment had also been automated to a large degree during the postwar period. For example, a double mitre boring machine had been purchased for about $11,000. The boring machine, as shown in Exhibit 5A, was able to grasp a stick of wood, mitre both ends simultaneously by cross sawing at an angle, and bore two holes simultaneously in each end. The finished pieces could then be used as cross pieces to reinforce corners in the assembly of chests, chairs, and tables.

Other examples of highly automatic equipment were the three 24-head master carvers, which the Devon Furniture Company had purchased at an approximate cost of $14,000 each. A master carver, as shown in Exhibit 5B, was a machine with a bed about twenty feet in length and about six feet deep, provided with a great superstructure containing twelve cutting heads on each side of a center guide. The operator placed a hand-carved model in the center and guided the superstructure back and forth to follow the outline of the center piece. Individual motors turned cutting heads at great speeds along the superstructure and simultaneously cut twenty-four pieces of wood into identical carved shapes. Due to the force of the cutting operation, it was necessary to position the pieces very carefully in the machine and to assure absolute accuracy of alignment throughout the operation.

A conveyor ran through the finishing room past all spraying operations and through the drying ovens. Although the conveyor was unpowered in those sections which passed the rubbers and sprayers, it moved at one and a half feet per minute through the ovens. Pieces were spaced to move at a rate of less than two feet per minute through most of the hand operations. Work was specialized to allow as continual a flow of pieces as possible. The line was under the general supervision of a production specialist who had put into operation the finishing conveyor at the Mengel Company, which was believed to be the most highly mechanized conveyor in the furniture industry for both speed and volume.

Production Costs

When the Marquis and the President companies were purchased in 1950, they were operated as independent plants. The two new operations increased the Devon Furniture payroll from 236 workers to 316 workers. Consolidated net sales in 1952 were about 30 percent higher than they would have been without the two new lines. During the period from May, 1946 to May, 1954, wage rates increased from 88 cents per hour to $1.82 per hour. In the same period, materials prices increased 110 percent and selling prices increased 50 percent.

In 1954, it was decided to consolidate all Marquis and President operations in the Devon Furniture plant. The number of workers had been reduced from 316 in 1951 to 269 in 1955 despite an increase of approximately 13 percent in net sales. It was estimated that output had increased from $5,600 per man and $3.40 per square foot of floor space in May, 1946 to $11,500 per man and $13.20 per square foot of floor space in May, 1954.

Much of the cost of raw materials was due to the purchase of solid cherry in prime grades.

Until the outbreak of World War II, the Devon Furniture Company had used French furniture woods. Subsequent to 1939, however, almost all its cherry came from western Pennsylvania and New York. The price of green cherry per thousand board feet (undried lumber in two inch thicknesses containing 48 to 65 percent water) varied about as follows from year to year:

1946	$130	1951	$260
1947	210	1952	265
1948	255	1953	260
1949	220	1954	270
1950	240	1955	280

In December, 1955, however, the extreme popularity of cherry furniture caused a severe shortage of cherry lumber and drove the price as high as $325 per thousand board feet for the best grades. The southern manufacturers were taking such large quantities of cherry off the market that certain Devon Furniture executives were considering the feasibility of purchasing lumber tracts and building a sawmill in western Pennsylvania.

SALES

The Devon Furniture Company distributed its furniture through its factory showroom in Grand Rapids, a large showroom in New York, five distributors in major cities, and 600 dealers throughout the United States and Canada.

Showroom

A permanent showroom was maintained in downtown Grand Rapids at the Exhibitors Building, where most of the major furniture manufacturers had display space. The company had 16,000 feet of space, including half the first floor of the building for the Devon Furniture line and half of an upper floor for the Marquis and President lines.

The Grand Rapids showroom served as a central display for all the company's retailers as well as a regional display for customers in western Michigan. Devon Furniture Company maintained a large showroom in New York serving dealers and decorators throughout the East who used the facilities to supplement their own inventory.

Independent Distributors

There were five distributors, located in Chicago, Indianapolis, Cleveland, Minneapolis, and Los Angeles, who were completely independent. The independent distributors carried no stock but maintained samples of the Devon Furniture line on display. These outlets accounted for somewhat more than 10 percent of the company's sales. The Chicago distributor displayed the Devon Furniture line at the Chicago furniture shows.

Dealers

There were 600 dealers in major cities throughout the country. Some of them, such as those in New York and Boston maintained substantial floor space to display the Devon Furniture line. Others had only a few samples and relied on photographs and on the regional showroom to display the line. Only accredited stores and decorators were ever sold as customers. Consumers could enter the distributors' showrooms only through introduction by a dealer or distributor. All sales were made for the account of the dealer or distributor who first introduced the consumer.

The retail dealers were serviced by six salesmen who reported directly to the sales manager at the factory. Three salesmen were on salary, one was on commission and the other two were independent sales representatives who also sold on commission. The two independent contractors carried noncompeting lines and covered outlying areas which the company's staff could not easily deal with.

Advertising

The company's executives wished consumers to take the initiative in searching out Devon furniture by locating a dealer or a regional showroom. The high price of the line restricted advertising media to those magazines which connoted high quality and were read by higher income families. The magazines used were *House Beautiful* and the *New Yorker* as well as *Town and Country, Interiors, Interior Designs,* and *Architectural Record.* Less attention was devoted to newspaper advertisements as the company wished to avoid special promotions and price cutting sales. Although the furniture was designed for families with $20,000 per year income or higher, it was often purchased for newlyweds as a combined gift from an entire family of relatives. For this reason, a bedroom suite costing $2,000 might often be delivered to a middle-class apartment house.

CONSULTANTS' REPORT

In August, 1955, a firm of management engineers was invited to make a study of the Devon Furniture Company. In their report to the company, the consultants stated their belief that the difference in operating results between the two periods 1948–1949 and 1951–1954 could be attributed to an increase in the number of patterns in the line. There were 552 different patterns in the line in 1955, of which 215 were in the Marquis and 337 in the Devon Furniture line.

The consultants recommended that the company review each pattern in the line to determine which patterns should be eliminated, which ones maintained, and which ones marked for a change in selling price. A plan was developed to make use of the company's standard cost data in evaluating the profitability of each item in the line. The consultant's report might be paraphrased as follows:

> When profits are based on selling prices calculated upon both materials and manufacturing cost, the varying proportion of materials will distort the profit return on these products. It is therefore necessary to eliminate the materials cost in order to evaluate manufacturing profits.

Sales Factor

To determine the product profitability of each pattern, we have established a Sales Factor, which is the expression in one figure, of the profit value of a pattern at its current selling price in relation to its cost of production. The Sales Factor eliminates any distortion caused by excessively high or low materials costs. Let us cite an example.[1]

Pattern #987 has a present selling price of	$90.00
Its materials cost is	22.98
The conversion revenue is	$67.02

The standard direct labor in pattern #987 is $23.06. The Sales Factor is the conversion revenue, $67.02, divided by the standard direct labor, $23.06, or 2.90.

Cost Factors for Entire Plant

For the plant as a whole, overhead charges per unit of production increase as the company drops below its full production capacity. For the plant as a whole, then, all expenses other than materials (including direct labor, variable and fixed manufacturing overhead, and selling and administrative costs) can be related to direct labor charges at different levels of capacity. The ratios of all expenses (other than materials) to direct labor have been determined plantwide at different levels of capacity. These ratios, which we can call the Cost Factors, are as follows:

at 60% capacity	3.67
at 70 "	3.39
at 80 "	3.28
at 90 "	3.05
at 100 "	2.97

Cost Factors of Individual Patterns

The company has developed a standard overhead cost for every pattern in the line. The standard overhead cost includes an allowance for manufacturing burden and an allowance for selling and administrative expenses.

The total standard manufacturing burden set for each pattern depends upon the amount of each particular labor operation, such as milling and waxing, performed on that pattern. Separate burden rates have been established for each direct labor operation. Thus, on any one pattern, $1.17 of standard manufacturing burden is included for each labor dollar paid for milling operations and $0.77 of manufacturing burden is added for each labor dollar paid for waxing. Standard selling and administrative costs are allocated to patterns based upon a standard rate per labor dollar. All manufacturing, selling, and administrative overhead absorption rates are figured upon operations at 100 percent of capacity.

The standard overhead cost of pattern #987 (including manufacturing burden and selling and administrative costs) is $43.50. By adding $23.06 for direct labor, we find that the total cost (less materials) is $66.56.

[1] Pattern numbers and figures have been somewhat disguised to maintain the confidential nature of the company's costs.

Based upon the plantwide cost factors cited above, it is possible to approximate the costs (less materials) of pattern #987 at different levels of capacity. This can be done by setting $66.56 equal to the overall plant factor of 2.97 at 100 percent capacity, and increasing the cost in proportion to the increases in the plant cost factors:

at 60% capacity	3.67	$82.25
at 70 "	3.39	75.97
at 80 "	3.28	73.51
at 90 "	3.05	68.35
at 100 "	2.97	66.56

Having derived the total costs (less materials) for pattern #987, we can now determine the cost factors of that pattern at different levels of capacity by dividing costs by direct labor of $23.06:

at 60% capacity	$82.25	3.57
at 70 "	75.97	3.29
at 80 "	73.51	3.19
at 90 "	68.35	2.96
at 100 "	66.56	2.89

Profitability

The pertinent figures developed for pattern #987 are as follows:

Capacity	*Conversion Revenue*	*Full Cost Less Materials*	*Profit*	*Sales Factor*	*Cost Factor*
60%	$67.02	$82.25	$(15.23)	2.90	3.57
70	67.02	75.97	(8.95)	2.90	3.29
80	67.02	73.51	(6.49)	2.90	3.19
90	67.02	68.35	(1.33)	2.90	2.96
100	67.02	66.56	.46	2.90	2.89

Based on the current selling price, pattern #987 reaches a break-even point with operations slightly below 100 percent. If the selling price of pattern #987 were raised 10 percent, the conversion revenue would become $76.02. The Sales Factor of pattern #987 would then become $76.02 divided by $23.06, or approximately 3.29. At a Sales Factor of 3.29, this particular pattern would show a break-even point of about 70 percent capacity and a profit at 100 percent of $9.46.

Analysis shows that the entire line has an overall average sales factor of 3.26 and a break-even point at about 81 percent.

We suggest that the company review the product profitability of each pattern in the light of a desirable sales factor as determined by the earnings potential, and eliminate the unprofitable patterns.

Executives of the Devon Furniture Company were anxious to distinguish between materials costs and production costs in their evaluation of the company's ability to earn money. They believed that the addition of the Marquis line greatly increased the cost of materials due to the expense of the precious veneers used in its construction and the necessarily high scrap rate. They were concerned at the sudden increase in the price of cherry in the autumn of 1955. For these reasons, they were interested in reviewing the product line with both materials and production factors in mind.

In proceeding to carry out the recommendations of the consultants, executives of the Devon Furniture Company assembled cost, sales, and production data for different patterns in the line. Exhibit 6 contains cost data for the first ten patterns to be evaluated. Exhibit 7 shows sales rates and inventory figures for the same patterns during 1954 and 1955 and actual production lot sizes. The sales manager provided the following description of each of the ten patterns from the point of view of its importance to the line:

914 Eighteenth century drop leaf extension table. Old history in the line—but not part of a group. Known for this since 1935. Have several others in the line in different styles of this general type.

917 One of first provincial beds made in U.S. Dates from 1920's. Part of a large group with a long history. Cannot easily raise the price as it is high now. Several alternate beds but none as heavy in design, that fit with case pieces. Larger production lots would reduce cost but could not sell more at lower price.

922 Provincial mirror. Catalogue contains some alternate mirrors that are lighter, though same size. Could not sell more at lower price.

923 Provincial bedside table. In line 10 years. Excellent selling table. Sales dropped during 1954. Not essential, but desirable to the line. Other tables could be used. Could not sell substantially more at lower price.

926 "New World" modern mirror. Only one of this size in the line. Other mirrors are twice the area. Helps round out the line, but not a determining factor. Could not sell substantially more at lower price.

927 Modern chair. Very important. Best selling chair we ever made. Helps sell other pieces in the line. Could not sell substantially more at lower price.

951 Eighteenth century. Good selling table. A novelty. Yew wood top. Marquis. Relatively inexpensive to the rest of the line. Not part of a group, but helps get the line into outlets that could not handle the most expensive items. Good eye value. But yew wood very hard to work.

952 Provincial writing desk. Desirable in the line but not essential. Fits into the line. Could fit into the Marquis group to give it depth.

959 Thin console with marble top. Novelty piece. Relatively excellent sales record, for Marquis. No recent fall-off in sales. Few other manufacturers make this.

960 Triangular modern table. A better seller in the line. Constantly good sales record, relative to other tables in the line. Few sales fluctuations. Good eye value.

Sales Factor and Cost Factors of Ten Selected Patterns

Pattern	*Sales*	*Cost Factors*				
Number	*Factor*	*100%*	*90%*	*80%*	*70%*	*60%*
914	4.07	3.14	3.22	3.46	3.58	3.88
917	3.26	2.96	3.04	3.27	3.38	3.66
922	2.54	2.93	3.01	3.24	3.34	3.62
923	3.54	3.03	3.11	3.34	3.46	3.74
926	5.08	2.98	3.06	3.29	3.40	3.68
927	3.22	2.97	3.05	3.28	3.39	3.67
951	4.26	2.99	3.07	3.30	3.41	3.69
952	3.39	3.00	3.08	3.31	3.42	3.71
959	3.71	3.05	3.13	3.36	3.48	3.77
960	3.99	3.08	3.16	3.39	3.52	3.81

1. DEVON FURNITURE COMPANY
Financial Figures, 1947-1955
(In Thousands)

	Net Sales	Borrowed & Inv. Capital	Total Assets	Materials	Labor	Mfg. Expenses	Selling Expense	Admin. Expense	Net Profit after Taxes	Net Plant
1947	$1,248							$ 57	$ 39	
1948	2,001	$ 608	$ 877	$424	$644	$411	$101	69	220	$254
1949	2,091	806	1,170	429	605	478	122	87	229	300
1950	1,730	850	1,068	400	549	446	138	107	56	314
1951	2,814	1,090	1,711	675	787	662	401	136	132	486
1952	3,285	1,275	1,699	821	856	764	477	177	87	473
1953	3,219	1,305	1,691	779	790	699	546	144	124	494
1954	3,309	1,284	1,655	739	812	793	610	148	103	513
1955	3,422	1,459	1,875	731	819	789	622	204	122*	445

*Plus 70 for sale of Marquis plant.

2. DEVON FURNITURE COMPANY
Balance Sheets, 1948 to 1955
(May 31)

Assets	1948	1949	1950	1951	1952	1953	1954	1955
Cash	$ 43,125	$ 214,648	$ 80,037	$ 52,120	$ 70,559	$ 58,764	$ 110,932	$ 256,294
U.S. Government Notes	40,218	85,667	15,053		70,351	30,000	5,086	117,258
Accounts Receivable	110,392	118,175	129,300	196,696	183,240	247,278	214,265	231,231
Inventories	403,379	427,072	504,156	940,796	867,547	837,199	789,279	795,751
Current Assets	$597,114	$ 845,562	$ 728,546	$1,189,612	$1,191,697	$1,173,241	$1,119,562	$1,400,534
Other Assets	10,429	10,558	8,222	14,068	13,948	10,251	2,060	6,539
Property:								
Land (Cost)		$ 56,421	$ 56,421	$ 76,421	$ 76,421	$ 76,421	$ 76,421	
Machinery & Buildings		451,098	488,802	668,149	681,560	704,914	749,041	
Depreciation		207,740	231,619	258,104	285,205	287,766	312,115	
Net Plant	$254,438	$ 299,779	$ 313,604	$ 486,466	$ 472,776	$ 493,569	$ 513,347	$ 445,121
Prepaid Expenses	$ 15,324	$ 14,555	$ 17,366	$ 21,121	$ 20,773	$ 13,665	$ 19,605	$ 22,735
Total Assets	$877,305	$1,170,454	$1,067,738	$1,711,267	$1,699,194	$1,690,726	$1,654,574	$1,874,929
Liabilities								
Notes Payable	$ 22,040	$ 18,800	$ 42,090	$ 192,375	$ 45,000			
Accounts Payable	111,682	203,061	113,348	257,145	155,614	$ 201,990	$ 203,035	$ 208,023
Deferred Profit			25,000	40,000	40,000	40,000	40,000	40,000
Federal Taxes	135,269	143,000	37,120	106,095	132,314	134,061	117,585	168,421
Current Liabilities	$268,991	$ 364,861	$ 217,558	$ 595,615	$ 372,928	$ 376,051	$ 360,620	$ 416,444
Long-Term Debt:								
To Bank				$ 103,000	$ 234,000	$ 108,000		
To Individual	$ 52,262	$ 25,350	$ 13,500	54,333	47,333	37,333	$ 27,334	
Stock and Surplus:								
Common Stock	191,850	193,350	193,350	188,350	188,350	188,350	186,100	$ 186,100
Capital Surplus	194,040	187,652	187,652	182,652	182,652	182,652	179,502	179,502
Earned Surplus	170,162	399,241	455,678	587,317	673,931	798,340	901,018	1,092,883
	$556,052	$ 780,243	$ 836,680	$ 958,319	$1,044,933	$1,169,342	$1,266,620	$1,458,485
Total Liabilities	$877,305	$1,170,454	$1,067,738	$1,711,267	$1,699,194	$1,690,726	$1,654,574	$1,874,929

3. DEVON FURNITURE COMPANY
Income Statements, 1948 to 1955
(Year End May 31)

	1948	1949	1950	1951	1952	1953	1954	1955
Net sales	$2,001,384	$2,090,596	$1,729,944	$2,814,057	$3,285,241	$3,218,893	$3,308,772	$3,421,715
Cost of Sales*	$1,478,366	$1,512,045	$1,395,473	$2,034,308	$2,441,177	$2,268,274	$2,344,086	$2,339,453
Selling and admin. exp.	170,204	209,443	245,472	536,892	653,764	689,751	758,165	825,501
	$ 352,814	$ 369,108	$ 88,999	$ 242,857	$ 190,300	$ 260,868	$ 206,521	$ 256,761
Other Income:								
Rent	3,900	2,277	2,026	278	100		192	
Gain on sale of assets	1,188	665	760			552	7,145	87,652
Miscellaneous	1,124	2,211	3,059	2,621	1,092	1,498	1,338	1,216
	$ 359,026	$ 374,261	$ 94,844	$ 245,756	$ 191,492	$ 262,918	$ 215,196	$ 345,629
Other Deductions:								
Interest	4,456	2,817	2,408	7,642	16,779	10,509	3,612	798
Loss on sale of assets	100			2,595	99			
	$ 354,470	$ 371,444	$ 92,436	$ 235,519	$ 174,614	$ 252,409	$ 211,584	$ 344,831
Federal taxes	134,624	142,366	36,000	103,879	88,000	128,000	108,906	152,966
	$ 219,846	$ 229,078	$ 56,436	$ 131,640	$ 86,614	$ 124,409	$ 102,678	$ 191,865

*Includes depreciation:

1948 = $16,547	1952 = $38,093
1949 = 21,910	1953 = 37,933
1950 = 25,680	1954 = 38,129
1951 = 32,313	1955 = 38,978

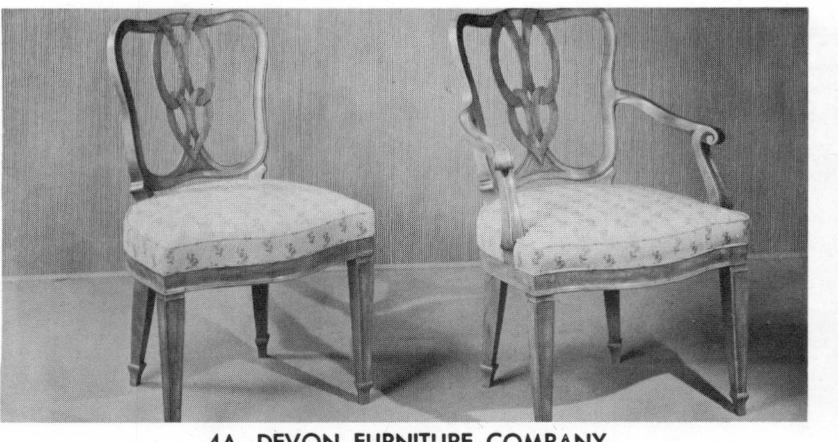

4A. DEVON FURNITURE COMPANY

Photograph of Provincial Chair

The curved sections of arms and backs required special jigs and fixtures to be shaped on production machinery.

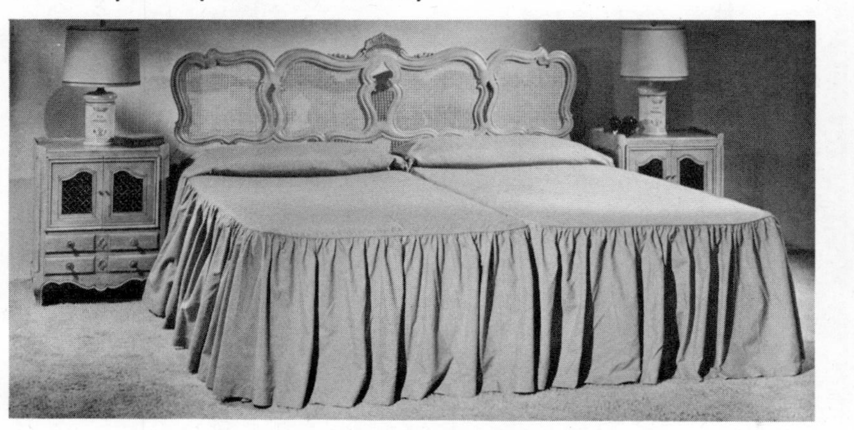

4B. DEVON FURNITURE COMPANY

Photograph of Provincial Bed

The back panel of the bed required careful hand carving in certain sections to supplement the production machinery.

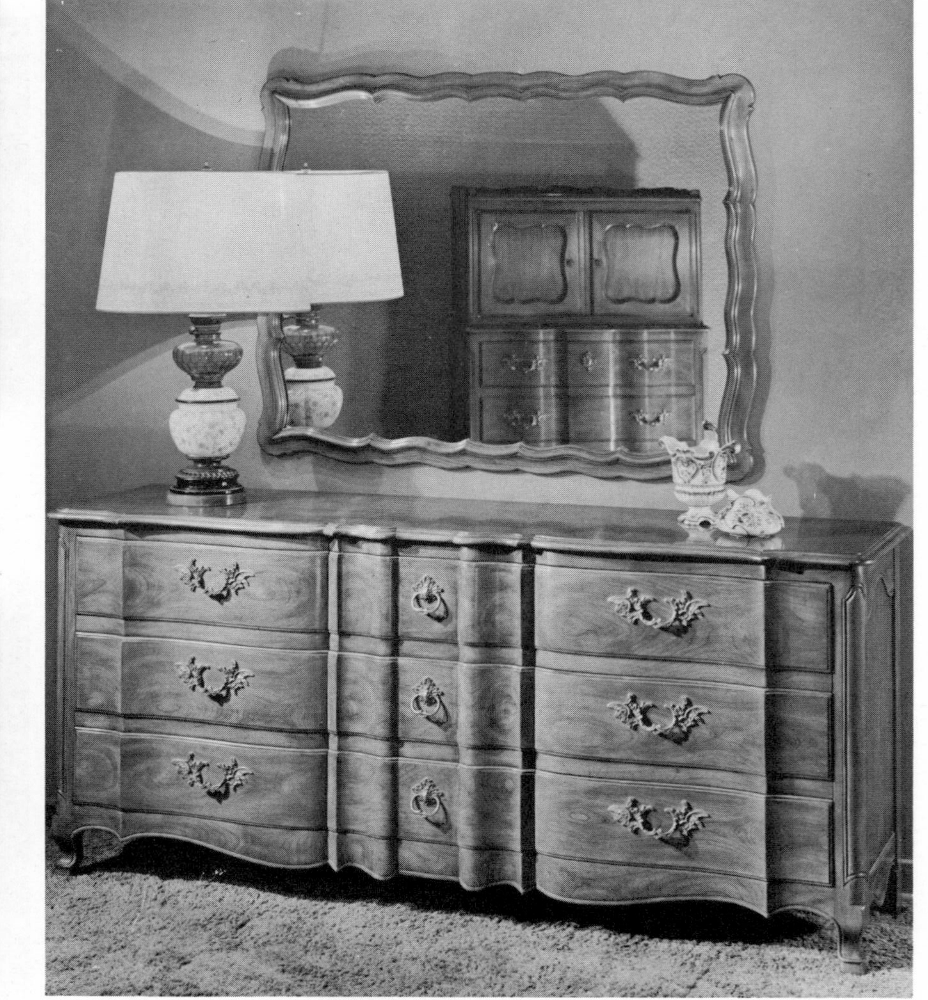

4C. DEVON FURNITURE COMPANY

Photograph of Provincial Dresser

The drawer fronts of solid cherry were shaped in an automatic lathe fitted with a cam attachment. It was then necessary to chisel out the deepest indentations by hand.

5B. DEVON FURNITURE COMPANY

Photograph of Master Carver

There are 12 cutting heads on each side of the central lever guide. The operator carves out an intricate shape on the center piece and the machine cuts duplicate shapes on the other 24 pieces set in the frame.

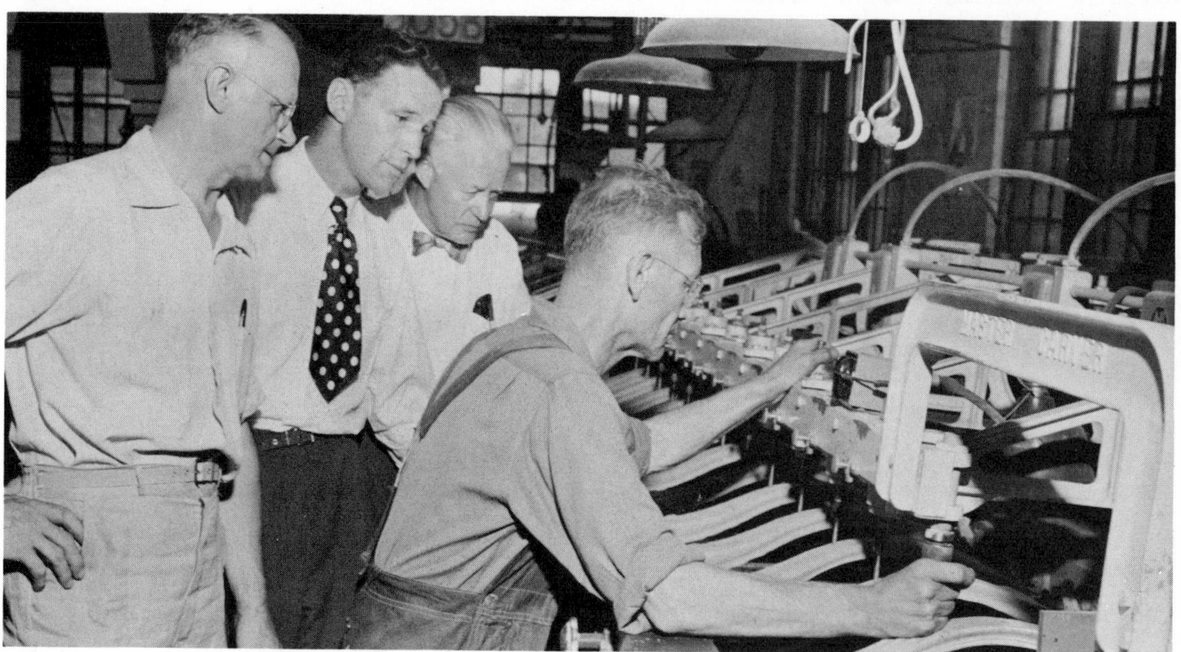

5A. DEVON FURNITURE COMPANY

Photograph of Boring Machine

The boring machine mitred both ends of a length of wood and bored two holes at each end in a two-stage automatic operation.

6. DEVON FURNITURE COMPANY

Unit Production Costs of Ten Selected Patterns

Pattern Number	Unit of Production	Cost in White: Labor Hours	Labor Cost	Mfg. Burden	Materials	Total	Uncrated Cost: Labor Hours	Labor Cost	Overhead*	Materials	Total	Selling Price
914	120	6.86	$13.19	$16.00	$24.28	$ 53.47	12.67	$24.36	$ 52.14	$30.88	$107.38	$130.00
917	36	14.31	28.43	29.56	16.70	74.69	23.14	45.91	90.16	21.16	157.23	171.00
922	24	13.09	27.11	26.67	3.31	57.09	24.63	49.22	95.09	14.86	159.17	140.00
923	144	5.09	10.20	10.61	6.37	27.18	8.49	16.57	33.57	9.27	59.41	68.00
926	48	1.40	2.68	2.60	2.70	7.98	2.97	5.63	11.12	16.38	33.13	45.00
927	300	3.96	7.91	8.07	4.58	20.56	7.02	13.87	27.39	13.02	54.28	58.00
951	60	3.02	5.71	6.32	10.41	22.44	5.52	10.29	20.45	21.21	51.95	65.00
952	36	22.27	44.14	44.87	28.76	117.77	31.54	61.28	122.71	34.52	218.51	242.00
959	72	10.65	21.54	22.83	9.29	53.66	15.68	31.06	63.61	34.69	129.36	150.00
960	72	3.58	7.04	7.82	4.84	19.70	6.15	11.84	24.65	6.75	43.24	54.00

*At 100% capacity (includes manufacturing burden and selling and administrative costs).

7. DEVON FURNITURE COMPANY

Orders for Selected Patterns, in Units*

Pattern Number	Inventory Jan. 1, 1954	1954 1st Qtr.	2d	3d	4th	1955 Jan.	Feb.	Mar.	Apr.	May	June	July	Aug.	Sept.	Oct.	Nov.	Inventory Dec. 1, 1955
914	5	40 (120)	39	24	42 (96)	17	31	15	9	18	14 (96)	7	9	8	11	4	29
917	3	9 (30)	6	8	13	1	4 (30)	2	1	1	1	2	6	4	3	2	0
922	16	3	6	4	1	2	8 (20)	1	1	0	0	1	2	1	0	0	6
923	7	63 (96)	56	80 (120)	43	9	19	14 (96)	17	19	11	22 (96)	5	6	11	17	23
926	7	9	15 (36)	6	14	5	5	8	4	4 (36)	5	5	8	5	2	4	0
927	0	148 (240)	213 (240)	182 (240)	174	59 (240)	144	47	71	47 (240)	50	99	37 (240)	86	119	50	0
951	0	43 (60)	28	31 (60)	52 (60)	28	22	19	11 (60)	15	9	17	9 (60)	7	18	14	0
952	14	11	7	9 (36)	8	4	4	4	4	1	2 (36)	2	3	1	0	1	25
959	48	34	28 (96)	23	36	20 (96)	21	12	12	15	10	6	8	11	9	8	0
960	27	16	74 (90)	32	43 (90)	15	17	14	2	16	22 (90)	13	15	10	11	21	0

*Numbers in parentheses show the lot size of cuttings produced during the period indicated.

Drexel Furniture Company

On May 27, 1957, Mr. G. M. Hill, Vice-President and Director of Manufacturing of the Drexel Furniture Company, presided over an urgent meeting of the company's management committee on production scheduling. A decline in orders for Drexel products during the months of April and May had caused a sudden increase in inventories of finished goods. The value of inventory on hand increased by $500,000 during the month of May and, by the 27th of the month, the physical volume of furniture to be stored was equal to the company's economic warehousing capacity. Furthermore, the latest company estimate of sales volume for the remainder of the year indicated a rate of sale 5 percent below the planned rate of production. Hence the objective of the committee meeting was to draft a plan of action which could be implemented immediately to relieve the current inventory problem while providing a suitable operating program for the remainder of 1957.

The Drexel Furniture Company manufactured and sold dining room, bedroom, and living room furniture of traditional and contemporary design and style. More than 90 percent of the company's products were sold to the consumer market under the registered brand name "by Drexel" and the remainder of output was sold under contract to government and industrial customers. Branded Drexel furniture was sold in the middle- and upper-priced brackets and the company was the largest manufacturer of bedroom and dining room pieces in those price lines. The Drexel company achieved a record volume of sales in 1955 and surpassed this volume in 1956. Its six furniture manufacturing plants had been operating at capacity from the end of 1954 through May of 1957. Net sales grew from $19 million in 1954 to $29 million in 1956, while profits were increased from $1.2 million to $2.1 million during the same period. Balance sheets and income statements are given in Exhibits 1 and 2.

HISTORY

The Drexel Furniture Company was founded in 1903 with an original investment of $35,000 by Mr. Samuel Huffman, the first president of the firm. The first plant was built in Drexel, North Carolina and additional manufacturing property was purchased in nearby Marion in 1921 and in Morganton in 1923. In the company's 25th year, 1928, sales exceeded $2 million and total assets were approximately $1.7 million. Subsequently, the depression of the 1930's seriously affected the company's operations as its sales volume fell and losses were incurred. The Drexel company substantially enlarged its sales volume, profits, and share of the market during the early postwar years. Mr. Huffman believed that four basic policies had been instrumental in this achievement. First, the company had moved contrary to industry practice in 1947 by starting to spend substantial amounts for national brand advertising. However, as Mr. Huffman pointed out, "brand advertising carries obligations as well as advantages." Thus, the second key policy was to properly merchandise the line and sell it to "honest" accounts—avoiding stores that would use the Drexel brand and product for "bait" and would otherwise trade down the company name. A third factor was the emphasis on good design and quality construction for all Drexel furniture. Finally, beginning in 1950, Drexel began to move counter to another industry tradition by developing a force of salaried salesmen to supplant the independent commission agents representing the company.

Plant Expansion

Increased production to keep pace with wartime and early postwar growth in sales was accomplished entirely through additions and improvements in the existing plants at Drexel, Morganton, and Marion. The gross value of fixed assets increased by $1.2 million from 1947 to 1950. Then an additional plant was acquired in early 1951 when the Drexel company acquired the assets of the Table Rock Furniture Company. The Table Rock company's 140,000 square foot plant was located adjacent to the Drexel company's Morganton plants and after modernization in 1951 was felt to be an important addition to Drexel's manufacturing facilities.

The level sales plateau of the years 1950 through 1954 was followed by another sharp upsurge in business in 1955 and 1956. Plant expansion continued, but at the end of 1956 the manufacturing facilities were again being used to their capacity. Then in January, 1957, through an exchange of common stock, the Drexel company acquired control of the Morganton Furniture Company, a producer of case goods, and Heritage Furniture, Inc., which manufactured upholstered furniture. The Drexel company had never produced upholstered furniture but, in 1955 and 1956, had found it desirable to purchase some upholstered pieces on contract from outside sources to complement its coordinated furniture groupings. The acquisition of the Heritage company provided the Drexel company with what was, in the management's opinion, a dependable supply of high-grade upholstered furniture.

Following the merger, plans were being formulated for the presentation of a correlated line of bedroom, dining room, and living room furniture to be offered under the Heritage brand name. Bedroom and dining room pieces would be manufactured in the Morganton, North Carolina plant of the Morganton Furniture Company. At the same time, the Morganton company would continue to produce and sell its regular branded line. Upholstered pieces would be produced by Heritage in High Point, North Carolina, about 100 miles from Morganton.

MERCHANDISING

In 1957, the Drexel product line included 1,200 different furniture pieces. The cornerstone of the product policy was the sale of related pieces in open stock groups from which individual suites might be selected. A group generally contained 50 to 80 pieces of living room, dining room, and bedroom furniture styled on a basic design theme. Pieces from correlated groups provided 80 percent of Drexel dollar sales in 1956. In addition to groups, the Drexel company also produced a few suites of approximately 10 pieces each as "promotional" items for retailers.

Price

Drexel furniture was sold at retail in the medium to medium-high price brackets and was sold by the company direct to retailers at 50 percent off list price. A typical dining room suite of nine pieces would carry a retail price between $800 and $1,000, while a typical three-piece bedroom suite would be priced between $400 and $500. Factory prices had been increased by approximately 12 percent in the past two years with individual increases as follows: 20 percent in June, 1955 and 3 percent in October, 1955; 2 percent in April, 1956 and 3 percent in October, 1956.

Style

The Drexel company, according to Mr. Brunn, the Merchandising Vice-President, tried "to cover every fast-selling style field in the country." In 1957 the product line covered the following important styles: contemporary; traditional (18th century mahogany); French provincial; Italian provincial (a contemporized provincial); Early American and colonial; and casual (includes "ranch type" styles). In recent years, changing consumer tastes and competitive pressures in the industry had led to frequent introduction of new styles by furniture manufacturers. As a result, the Drexel company was faced with an increasingly rapid turnover of items in the product line, a steady increase in the number of items in the line, and changes in the relative importance of different styles and types of furniture being sold.

The postwar years had brought a steady decline in the sales of dining room furniture relative to sales of bedroom furniture. In 1946, 60 percent of the Drexel company's dollar volume had come from dining room furniture sales. In 1954, however, only 37 percent of sales were in dining room furniture, while 57 percent came from bedroom pieces and 6 percent from living room pieces. This trend was especially significant for Drexel because, in 1950, the company had an estimated 7 percent share of the market for dining room furniture, but only 1.5 percent of the market for bedroom furniture.

Shifts in consumer style preference had also led to changes in the importance of various Drexel "groups." Only five groups accounted for 80 percent of dollar sales in the year 1950. In 1953, five groups accounted for 57 percent of total sales and included four of the five groups that had been the largest sellers in 1950. By 1956, however, only two of the first five groups of 1953 were still of importance. Those two groups represented 17 percent of total sales, while three groups of contemporary style which had been introduced in 1955 and 1956 accounted for one third of sales.

New Designs

Mr. Brunn and his marketing executives kept a close watch on the rate of incoming orders on every group of the line. Production was based on a 90-day cycle and was not economic for lots of fewer than 150 units of a major piece, such as a china cabinet or dresser. Thus when the rate of sales for key pieces fell below 50 units per month, serious consideration was given to dropping the group from the line or redesigning it.

The Drexel company employed a full-time staff of four designers, plus several free-lance designers, of which three were under contract in 1957. Mr. Brunn actively participated in the creative work and closely supervised the execution of new designs. Mr. Brunn felt that after 1950, the Drexel company had, at first, been unable to keep pace with the growing consumer demand for contemporary styles. This lost ground, he said, was regained, however, in 1955 and 1956 following the introduction of the *Profile* group, a collection of 80 contemporary pieces for living, dining, and bedrooms designed by a well-known free-lance designer. The group represented the company's first major introduction of fully upholstered furniture.

Markets

The Drexel company participated in four major furniture markets annually, and, like most southern furniture manufacturers, introduced important new designs at the April and October markets in High Point, North Carolina. The company also attended the January and June national markets in Chicago. The Drexel company usually introduced from one to three new groups at each major market and acceptance of these groups was closely watched. Every new design was shown at a major market before production was started. For that reason items shown at an April market would not be available to retailers until the following fall. In the past some new designs had been abandoned before production as a result of an unfavorable market reaction.

Advertising

The Drexel national advertising served to create and sustain consumer awareness of the "by Drexel" brand and what it represented, to create consumer demand for new groups as they were introduced, and to sustain demand for existing groups in the product line. The budget for advertising and sales promotion was set annually according to a percentage of expected sales for the coming year. Expenses in 1957 would exceed $900,000, of which approximately one half was allocated for space and production costs in national magazine ads. An independent research organization had made annual consumer surveys to determine the consumer brand consciousness for furniture. The results of the 1955 survey are given below:

	Type of Furniture		
	Bedroom	*Dining Room*	*Living Room*
Percent knowing any brand	45.2	33.8	54.9
Drexel rank	First	First	Third
Percent knowing Drexel brand	18.2	16.3	7.1
Percent knowing second-ranking company	5.7	4.8	11.6
Percent knowing first-ranking company	—	—	37.3

SALES AND DISTRIBUTION

Prior to 1951 all Drexel selling had been done by independent commission salesmen. On the basis of a detailed study the company decided in 1952 to develop a force of salaried salesmen. In 1957 the sales department was still in a period of transition toward the ultimate objective of having all sales channeled through salaried men. At that time, the vice-president of sales was assisted by a general sales manager in the home office and salesmen in the field reported to one of three regional managers. Eastern, central, and western regional offices supervised the company salesmen through most of the country, while three commission sales offices still handled sales in the southeastern and some of the central plains states. The company employed 35 salaried salesmen in 1957.

Salesmen's compensations were intended to limit selling expenses to approximately 3.5 percent of sales. Company salesmen were paid a salary based on the size of quota and a bonus for sales over quota. The company's experience in 1956 was that salaried salesmen sold more than 40 percent of total sales while representing about 35 percent of total selling costs. In addition, their performance with respect to quota was 3 percent better than that of the commission salesmen.

Dealers

Drexel products were sold to approximately 2,500 retail stores from coast to coast. These retailers were franchised selectively by the field salesmen. The franchise agreement provided that the dealer would show a representative part of the Drexel line, display it properly, maintain a basic stock of goods and locally promote and advertise the Drexel line. The company tried to franchise only those local stores with an established reputation for quality merchandise. Usually a dealer would carry only part of the Drexel line. In most localities, there would be only one dealer franchised to carry any given group of Drexel furniture.

Using shipment by pool cars and pool trucks and by carload shipments the Drexel company was able to compete with manufacturers in all parts of the country. In 1956 the sales of Drexel products by region closely approximated the percentage of sales of all United States home furnishing sales by regions. Although each year 10 of the top 12 or 15 Drexel dealers according to dollar volume of sales were department stores, the department store group as a whole accounted for only 25 to 30 percent of total Drexel sales. In recent years, the 500 largest Drexel dealers had accounted for approximately two thirds of Drexel sales and about one half of the dealers accounted for over 90 percent of total sales.

MANUFACTURING

Mr. G. Maurice Hill, Vice-President and Director of Manufacturing, was responsible for the operation of the 10 manufacturing plants of the company. Mr. Hill came to the company when Mr. Huffman assumed active control and, although his title had changed, had been in charge of manufacturing for the 13 years since.

Policy Changes

The first big change made during the postwar period was to establish a "model" factory that made only samples. In this way scale models, jigs, and fixtures could be produced and methods worked out without disrupting the flow of production in the larger plants. By improvements such as this, Mr. Hill felt the company could gain a competitive edge in the face of constant style change. The new administration's second objective had been to improve the central control over the production process. A standard cost system was installed, wages reset and job specifications prepared on the basis of a thorough job evaluation, a central production planning and control system established, and a central engineering department set up to handle research, plant engineering, machine design, and the like.

Organization

Prior to 1945 the plant managers had been responsible for all phases of production; they were "given a drawing only." Mr. Hill, however, adhered to the basic concept of decentralized production under central control, giving the plant manager the maximum autonomy within certain limits. Basic production schedules were developed centrally, giving lot sizes and required delivery dates along with suggested starting dates. Parts requirements, methods, and routing specifications were also furnished for the plant manager. A central engineering staff served for setting standards, breaking bottlenecks, and the like. Getting the production out was still the plant manager's job, however.

The manufacturing staff at the central office in Drexel worked closely as a team. Weekly meetings were held with Mr. Hill to review the rates of sales and production, stock position, and status of operations in each plant. Important problems in any plant or in any of the staff departments were also reviewed at these conferences.

Production Facilities

The 10 manufacturing units included six end-product plants and four others for sample, veneer, and panel production and for overflow storage. The end-product plants were located within 30 miles of each other in northwestern North Carolina. Pictures of selected plants are shown in Exhibit 3. The organization of the 10 plants in 1957 was as follows:

Plant Number	*Location*	*Area (Square Feet)*	*Principal Product*
1	Drexel, N.C.	280,000	Traditional and provincial bedroom furniture
2	Morganton, N.C.	291,000	Traditional dining room and bedroom furniture
3	Morganton, N.C.	120,000	Chairs
4	Morganton, N.C.	140,000	Traditional bedroom furniture
5	Marion, N.C.	220,000	Contemporary bedroom furniture
6	Marion, N.C.	153,000	Contemporary dining room furniture
7	Marion, N.C.	41,000	Parts for Plants #5 and #6
8	Morganton, N.C.	66,000	Storage
9	Morganton, N.C.	18,000	Samples, jigs, and fixtures
10	Kingstree, S.C.	45,000	Commercial veneers and gumwood panels

The Drexel plant was located next to the company's main offices and adjacent to a tract of 52 acres of land available for expansion. All of the Morganton plants (#2, 3, 4, 8, and 9) were located on adjoining tracts of land totaling 120 acres. Plants #2 and #3 were contiguous buildings served by the same lumberyard and dry kiln, while Plant #4 was an independent unit. The latter plant was acquired in the purchase of the Table Rock company in 1951. Plant #8 consisted of a series of four warehouse buildings purchased from a cotton mill in 1949. The buildings were used to store overflow from the primary warehouses located at most end-product plants as well as "odds and ends" and slow-moving items. The warehouses also served as principal storage space for the Table Rock plant (#4) which contained no storage space. Plant #9, although administratively a separate unit, occupied an area within the building of Plant #3. The three plants in Marion were separate buildings served by the same heating units, lumberyard, and dry kiln and located on a site of 10 acres. The Kingstree plant (#10) was operated to supply materials for use in the other Drexel manufacturing units.

Plant Specialization

All six end-product plants were specialized to produce furniture of particular type and style. Dining room furniture was considered to be more complex to produce than bedroom furniture, and required a different balance of machinery. While a plant producing dining room pieces could be used to manufacture bedroom pieces, a bedroom furniture plant could not easily produce dining room pieces such as "chinas" and tables. Chairs for all groups and styles were produced in one plant (#3).

The balance of plant machinery depended on the basic style of the furniture. Cabinets of traditional design utilized posts as principal supporting members; the end panels were generally thin wood. Contemporary cabinet designs, however, were structurally more similar to a box placed on legs or a base. For these contemporary pieces, thick end panels provided support. Hence lathes and carvers were vital to production of traditional pieces, but might be superfluous in a plant designed for contemporary styles.

Labor

The Drexel company employed approximately 2,300 hourly workers. Although several efforts had been made to unionize different plants of the company, none had succeeded. In the most recent election in 1956, the union lost by a margin of five to two. Production workers were paid an hourly rate with no piece rate or similar direct incentive pay. The average hourly wage in the southern furniture industry had been $1.23 in October, 1955 and rose to $1.28 in March, 1956 and to $1.32 in October, 1956. All hourly rated employees received an annual bonus under the company's profit-sharing plan. Since the plan's inception in 1951, employee bonuses each year had been in amounts representing from five to eight and one-half weeks' pay.

Since the company's plants were located in rural communities, almost 75 percent of the employees were drawn from outside the limits of the towns where the plants were situated. Mr. Hill felt that furniture manufacture had traditionally been a "craft" industry, with one man to each machine. Usually the operator paced the machine. The men knew their machines and were responsible for their performance. Among other reasons, this had tended to discourage multiple-shift operations.

MANUFACTURING COSTS

Raw materials represented the most important cost factor in manufacturing, accounting for one half the factory cost of products. The important materials purchased and their share of total material costs were:

Core lumber	35%
Veneer and panels	25
Hardware, glass and mirrors	15
Finishing materials	10
Miscellaneous	15

The remaining portion of factory cost was divided equally between labor and manufacturing expense. Typically, about 50 percent of overhead was fixed and 50 percent variable. Direct labor accounted for three fourths of all labor cost. Departmental direct labor costs, as a percentage of total direct labor for a plant, were approximately as follows:

Cabinet assembly	35%
Finish machine	16
Rub, pack, and ship	15
Rough machine	12
Veneer	5
Carving	2
Finishing	15

PLANNING AND CONTROL

Production scheduling required the close cooperation of executives in both the manufacturing and selling organizations. The basic work was done jointly by members of the production and home office sales staffs. Inventory position, rate of sale, and rate of production were reviewed weekly by the production staff and were also examined in regular meetings of the scheduling subcommittee of the management committee. Biweekly reports of unsold merchandise in stock (in dollar value, by suites), weekly reports of orders received by suites, and daily reports on the status of production at each plant were available for use in scheduling.

The Sales Forecast

Scheduling began with a forecast of expected weekly dollar sales by group. Since the factory production cycle stretched over three months, forecasts and plans were prepared quarterly for six-month periods. By organizing the sales forecast according to the plant in which each item would be produced, it was possible to determine the probable weekly value of shipments for each plant. On the basis of this forecast, the management scheduling subcommittee would establish the daily rate of production to be used as the basis for detailed plant schedules. This rate was always expressed in terms of the dollar value of production at Drexel's *selling* prices.

The seasonal factor in furniture sales was an important consideration in planning. One index of the monthly volume of orders received, with 100 equal to 1/12 the annual sales, was:

Jan.	103	April	77	July	93	Oct.	96
Feb.	134	May	72	Aug.	112	Nov.	108
March	111	June	79	Sept.	114	Dec.	102

This index was an average of the experience in 1951 through 1954, when sales averaged $19.5 million. One executive commented, however, that this pattern was not true in 1955 and 1956 when the company had had great success in the April markets and thus had sustained volume throughout the springtime.

Planning Lot Sizes

Production was planned in lots or "cuts" of pieces from one group or suite. At least one cut of most suites was planned for each three-month period, but the size of the cut varied according to the inventory position and expected rate of sale. A basic objective in scheduling was to see that on average, no unsold items in a group were in stock during the 30 days before the next cut of that group would be ready for shipment. For example, for an item selling at the rate of $10,000 per week, lots worth $130,000 might be scheduled every three months. If $80,000 worth of unsold goods were in inventory on January 1, the inventory would be expected to sell out by March 1, and a new lot worth $130,000 would be scheduled for completion at the end of March. By that time, a backlog of $50,000 in unfilled orders should have accumulated. While the level of unsold inventory usually followed this "ideal" pattern, the physical inventory almost always contained some items in every group. Shipping delays and other factors tended to maintain the gap between order receipt and shipment date.

The Cutting Schedule

Cutting schedules for each plant were prepared regularly in accordance with the basic inventory policy and on the basis of the planned rate of production and forecast rates of sale. The cutting schedule indicated the lot size and starting date for each cut planned for the next six months. For each lot the schedule also showed the dates for preparation of the detailed cutting order, expected start of cabinet assembly, and predicted shipping date. For purposes of the schedule the size of the cut was expressed in terms of the number of days' production it represented. This was derived by dividing the total sales value of the pieces to be produced by the daily production rate for the plant. The cutting schedules in effect May 20, 1957 are shown in Exhibit 5.

Cutting Order

The cutting order was the basis for operations within the plants. The orders were prepared jointly by the production planning manager and general sales manager after lumber for the cut had reached the kilns but before the scheduled cut-off date. The cutting order specified the pieces to be produced and the number of each in the lot.

Cutting orders were planned to maintain production in lots greater than 100 units for each piece. The preferred lot size was from 300 to 500 units, but typical lots were in the range of 100 to 300 units. For pieces where only a small quantity was needed the parts might be produced in minimum lot size and the overrun of parts held for future assembly. The lot size was most important in the rough and finish machine shops where setup time might represent 15 percent of direct labor time on a lot of 200 pieces. Experience had shown that unit cost would rise sharply if the lot size were cut below 100 units, although costs changed relatively little as lot size increased from 200 to 500 units.

Situation in May, 1957

When the management scheduling subcommittee met on May 27, 1957, it faced an urgent problem in planning production for the last half of the fiscal year. The company's six plants were producing a total of $563,000 worth of furniture weekly, but new orders since April 1 had averaged only $245,000 weekly. Inventories had reached a maximum level. A careful forecast of expected sales for the next six months indicated probable average weekly sales of $533,000, or 5½ percent less than current production rates.

Mr. Hill presided over the meeting which included Mr. Brunn, the general sales manager, and all the members of the production staff group. Data presented to the group included:

Exhibit 4—The existing cutting schedules for all furniture plants except the chair plant.
Exhibit 5—Monthly records of production and employment by plant for 1957.
Exhibit 6—Sales forecasts by suite and by plant for the next six months.

The meeting's objective was to develop guide lines for revision of the current cutting schedule. In discussing the schedule, it was noted that the average lot size for key pieces would be about 200 units for the size of cut indicated in each plant's current schedule. The schedule allowed for a full week of vacation during the week of July 4, plus a one-day shutdown on Labor Day, September 2. The last column on the cutting schedule indicated the revised prediction of out-of-stock dates, based on the latest sales forecast.

Order backlogs on May 1 had totaled $2.4 million, of which $400,000 was for new items introduced at the April furniture market. One new industrial contract and a government contract nearing completion accounted for $1 million of the backlog and the remaining $1 million was for branded items already in the line. Shipments for the month of May were expected to total $1.75 million but a drop to $1.5 million monthly was forecast for June and July. Unsold merchandise in stock on May 9, 1957 was worth $2.7 million, valued at the Drexel sales price.

The personnel manager commented that short-time work with a full labor force was a reasonable possibility, but only for the short run. In the past, employees had seemed to prefer that to a layoff, but after a while there was a tendency to slow down and the best workers would leave for other jobs. He estimated one month as the maximum period for short time. Layoffs, on the other hand, usually meant that the better men got other jobs and this created a hiring and training job for Drexel when production was to be accelerated again.

While it was hard to place a figure on the cost of inventory, Mr. Hill felt that a fair charge would be 15 percent per annum for the out-of-pocket costs of carrying inventory in excess of the normal level. This cost would include rent, handling, taxes, insurance, and damage to goods, but not the capital cost or obsolescence of inventory. All of the company's end-product plants were at the limits of their storage capacity and future additions to inventory would have to be shipped to the overflow warehouses.

The company's six main plants were operating in May at budgeted volume on a 40-hour work week. Mr. Hill felt that a decision to reduce the budgeted rate of production would have to consider the minimum economic rates which applied to these plants. Past experience had indicated that overhead costs became excessive when production fell below $20,000 per day at Plants #1, #2, and #5 and below $13,000 per day at Plants #3, #4, and #6.

1. DREXEL FURNITURE COMPANY

Comparative Balance Sheets
In Thousands

(November 30)

ASSETS	1947	1948	1949	1950	1951	1952	1953	1954	1955	1956
Current Assets:										
Cash	$ 653	$1,151	$ 816	$ 1,471	$ 1,777	$ 1,458	$ 2,006	$ 1,796	$ 1,995	$ 4,271
U.S. Government securities	241	241	242	453	506	395	1,211	854	571	-
Accounts receivable	733	1,182	1,232	2,037	1,487	2,348	2,129	2,339	3,727	3,300
Inventories	2,413	2,859	3,205	3,588	5,705	4,483	4,476	4,855	4,728	4,708
Prepaid expense	170	163	171	161	188	297	164	236	189	181
Total	$4,210	$5,596	$5,666	$ 7,710	$ 9,663	$ 8,981	$ 9,986	$10,080	$11,210	$12,460
Investments	191	192	160	176	154	112	152	99	104	92
Property:										
Land, buildings, equipment	2,838	3,472	3,905	4,079	5,000	5,330	5,470	5,809	6,101	6,393
Less depreciation	872	1,004	1,178	1,312	1,630	1,841	2,014	2,086	2,181	2,302
Net property	$1,966	$2,468	$2,727	$ 2,767	$ 3,370	$ 3,489	$ 3,456	$ 3,723	$ 3,920	$ 4,091
Total Assets	$6,367	$8,256	$8,553	$10,653	$13,187	$12,582	$13,594	$13,902	$15,234	$16,643
LIABILITIES										
Current Liabilities:										
Accounts payable	$ 555	$1,335	$ 841	$ 1,153	$ 2,410	$ 1,440	$ 1,448	$ 1,439	$ 1,945	$ 2,263
Federal taxes	558	997	810	1,177	1,766	549	836	662	738	723
Installments on note	-	-	-	-	-	100	125	100	175	425
Total	$1,113	$2,332	$1,651	$ 2,330	$ 4,176	$ 2,089	$ 2,409	$ 2,201	$ 2,858	$ 3,411
Long-Term Debt:										
5% debentures	164	164	164	164	164	164	164	164	164	-
Note	-	-	-	-	-	825	700	600	425	-
Total	$ 164	$ 164	$ 164	$ 164	$ 164	$ 989	$ 864	$ 764	$ 589	-
Stockholders' Equity:										
Common stock	1,137	1,132	1,132	1,133	1,137	1,137	1,137	1,137	1,137	1,137
Capital surplus	-	696	696	698	720	720	720	720	720	720
Earnings	3,953	3,932	4,910	6,328	6,990	7,647	8,464	9,080	9,930	11,375
Total	$5,090	$5,760	$6,738	$ 8,159	$ 8,847	$ 9,504	$10,321	$10,937	$11,787	$13,232
Total Liabilities	$6,367	$8,256	$8,553	$10,653	$13,187	$12,582	$13,594	$13,902	$15,234	$16,643

2. DREXEL FURNITURE COMPANY

Comparative Income Statements
In Thousands

(Year Ending November 30)

	1947	1948	1949	1950	1951	1952	1953	1954	1955	1956
Net sales	$11,145	$14,483	$13,158	$18,313	$20,140	$19,265	$20,797	$18,906	$24,244	$28,895
Cost of goods sold	8,201	10,004	9,469	12,344	13,992	14,197	15,100	13,565	18,033	20,780
	$ 2,944	$ 4,479	$ 3,689	$ 5,969	$ 6,148	$ 5,068	$ 5,697	$ 5,341	$ 6,211	$ 8,115
Selling, administration and general	1,574	1,954	1,901	2,338	2,883	2,860	2,892	2,779	3,082	3,561
	$ 1,370	$ 2,525	$ 1,788	$ 3,631	$ 3,265	$ 2,208	$ 2,805	$ 2,562	$ 3,129	$ 4,554
Other income	58	47	23	65	31	34	57	95	72	89
	$ 1,428	$ 2,572	$ 1,811	$ 3,696	$ 3,296	$ 2,242	$ 2,862	$ 2,657	$ 3,201	$ 4,643
Other deductions	4	24	26	51	49	76	90	110	64	80
Earnings before taxes	$ 1,424	$ 2,548	$ 1,785	$ 3,645	$ 3,247	$ 2,166	$ 2,772	$ 2,547	$ 3,137	$ 4,563
Taxes on income	498	1,067	639	1,774	1,981	1,054	1,500	1,363	1,719	2,504
Net earnings	$ 926	$ 1,481	$ 1,146	$ 1,871	$ 1,266	$ 1,112	$ 1,272	$ 1,184	$ 1,418	$ 2,059
Cash dividends paid	$ 273	$ 387	$ 453	$ 453	$ 544	$ 455	$ 455	$ 568	$ 568	$ 614

3A. DREXEL FURNITURE COMPANY
Manufacturing Plant No. 1, Drexel

3B. DREXEL FURNITURE COMPANY
Manufacturing Plants No. 2 and 3, Morganton

4. DREXEL FURNITURE COMPANY

Production and Employment by Plant--1957

Plant #1 - Drexel

	January	February	March	April
Monthly Production	$540,346	$423,728	$479,512	$508,509
Average Production per Day	$ 23,493	$ 21,186	$ 22,834	$ 24,215
No. Days Worked Month	23	20	21	21
No. Employees	402	399	395	406

Plant #2 - Morganton

	January	February	March	April
Monthly Production	$461,090	$400,700	$420,923	$393,196
Average Production per Day	$ 20,047	$ 20,035	$ 20,044	$ 18,724
No. Days Worked Month	23	20	21	21
No. Employees	476	474	475	485

Plant #3 - Morganton

	January	February	March	April
Monthly Production	$374,780	$327,052	$337,257	$347,324
Average Production per Day	$ 16,294	$ 16,353	$ 16,060	$ 16,539
No. Days Worked Month	23	20	21	21
No. Employees	341	332	353	358

Plant #4 - Table Rock

	January	February	March	April
Monthly Production	$335,824	$301,546	$299,700	$291,174
Average Production per Day	$ 14,601	$ 15,077	$ 14,271	$ 13,865
No. Days Worked Month	23	20	21	21
No. Employees	286	287	290	293

Plant #5 - Marion

	January	February	March	April
Monthly Production	$584,234	$474,166	$500,008	$486,848
Average Production per Day	$ 25,401	$ 23,708	$ 23,810	$ 23,183
No. Days Worked Month	23	20	21	21
No. Employees	445	443	440	434

Plant #6 - Marion

	January	February	March	April
Monthly Production	$346,423	$304,001	$327,013	$327,000
Average Production per Day	$ 15,061	$ 15,200	$ 15,572	$ 15,571
No. Days Worked Month	23	20	21	21
No. Employees	297	295	293	293

5. DREXEL FURNITURE COMPANY

Cutting Schedules

Date: May 17, 1957

Production Planning Memo No. 57

Subject: Proposed Cutting Schedule

Drexel Plant #1--Budget $22,500/Day

Suite	No. of Days' Production	Kiln Date	Cutting Order Required	Start Cabinet Assembly	Ready for Shipping	Stock Position* May 27
Y	9				5/13	
K	6				5/21	70%
B (Contract)	2				5/23	100%
F1	15			5/16	6/13	41%
G 1st Cut	6			6/6	6/21	62%
100 1st Cut	5			6/14	6/28	71%
J2	6			6/21	7/15	29%
R	7	5/2	5/20	7/8	7/24	7/4
J1	13	5/13	5/29	7/17	8/12	7/1
K	6	5/30	6/17	8/5	8/20	7/11
B	10	6/7	6/25	8/13	9/4	9/26
J2	6	6/16	7/16	8/27	9/12	8/29
G 2nd Cut	5	7/8	7/24	9/5	9/19	-
100 2nd Cut	5	7/3	7/31	9/12	9/26	-
F1	10	7/22	8/7	9/19	10/10	9/5
K	6	8/5	8/21	10/3	10/18	9/19
J1	12	7/24	8/28	10/11	11/5	9/26

Morganton Plant #2--Budget $20,000/Day

Suite	No. of Days' Production	Kiln Date	Cutting Order Required	Start Cabinet Assembly	Ready for Shipping	Stock Position* May 27
N	6				5/8	
F1	14			5/1	5/28	10%
E 1st Cut	8			5/21	6/7	27%
400 1st Cut	4			5/31	6/13	26%
F1 (Fill-In)	3			6/6	6/18	-
G 1st Cut	5			6/11	6/25	53%
V Tables	2			6/18	6/27	-
P	5			6/20	7/11	8/8
B	9			6/27	7/24	8/1
J2	4	5/16	5/29	7/17	7/30	7/25
F1	20	5/22	6/4	7/23	8/27	9/5
U	7	6/19	7/9	8/20	9/6	-
E 2nd Cut	7	6/28	7/18	8/29	9/17	-
V	5	7/16	7/29	9/10	9/24	-
G 2nd Cut	5	7/23	8/5	9/17	10/1	-

*Indicates percentage of scheduled cut already sold or date when present finished goods inventory of suite will be sold out.

Exhibit 5 (continued)

Table Rock Plant #4--Budget $15,000/Day

Suite	Days	Kiln	Cutting	Cabinet	Shipping	May 27
Y	5				5/9	100%
N (Contract)	5				5/16	-
X 4th	4			5/9	5/22	100%
P	11			5/15	6/6	7/25
E 1st Cut	11			5/30	6/21	35%
X 5th	4			6/14	6/27	100%
N	11			6/20	7/19	8/8
X 6th	4	5/9	5/24	7/12	7/25	100%
D1 2nd Cut	8	5/15	5/30	7/18	8/6	8/8
X 7th	4	5/27	6/11	7/30	8/12	100%
300	6	5/31	6/17	8/5	8/20	8/22
U	10	6/10	6/25	8/13	9/4	-
X 8th	4	6/24	7/16	8/27	9/10	100%
E 2nd Cut	10	6/28	7/22	9/3	9/24	-
X 9th	4	7/19	8/5	9/17	9/30	100%
?	5	7/25	8/9	9/23	10/7	-
X 10th	4	8/1	8/16	9/30	10/11	100%

Marion Plant #5--Budget $23,000/Day

Suite	Days	Kiln	Cutting	Cabinet	Shipping	May 27
S	8				5/21	24%
Q	5			5/14	5/28	10%
T	10			5/21	6/11	7/11
H1 (Contract)	1			6/4	6/12	100%
C	12			6/5	6/28	7/18
W 1st Cut	8			6/21	7/17	36%
200 1st Cut	4			7/10	7/23	37%
H2	6	5/6	5/21	7/16	7/31	8/15
S	7	5/14	5/29	7/24	8/9	8/29
Q	6	5/23	6/7	8/2	8/19	9/5
C	11	5/31	6/17	8/12	9/4	9/19
L	4	6/17	7/9	8/27	9/10	7/18
W 2nd Cut	10	6/21	7/15	9/3	9/24	-
M1	5	7/12	7/29	9/17	10/1	8/22

Marion Plant #6--Budget $15,000/Day

Suite	Days	Kiln	Cutting	Cabinet	Shipping	May 27
L	6				5/2	27%
H2	7				5/13	42%
M1	2				5/15	21%
C	13			5/8	6/3	16%
S 2nd Cut	8			5/27	6/13	9%
T	7			6/6	6/24	7/18
W 1st Cut	11			6/17	7/16	36%
C	12			7/9	8/1	8/29
H2	8	5/14	5/30	7/25	8/13	9/12
S 3rd Cut	8	5/24	6/11	8/6	8/23	-
W 2nd Cut	10	6/5	6/21	8/16	9/9	-
M1	5	6/19	7/12	8/30	9/16	10/24
C	12	6/26	7/19	9/9	10/2	10/31

6. DREXEL FURNITURE COMPANY

Analysis of Orders Forecast and Received

Sales Forecast June 1 - November 30, 1957 (Sales in Dollars per Week)									Analysis of Orders by Group						
Group #										Orders Received		Ratio Orders to Budget			
Style	Finish	Plant #1	Plant #2	Plant #3	Plant #4	Plant #5	Plant #6	All Plants	1957 Weekly Budget##	Week Ending May 16	24 Wks. to Date (000)	Current	24 Weeks	Style	Finish
A		-	-	-	-	-	-	-	$ 7,000	$ 2,600	$ 156	37	93	A	
B		$ 13,000	$ 9,400	$ 3,600	-	-	-	$ 26,000	48,000	11,737	632	24	55	B	
C		-	-	18,000	-	$ 30,000	$17,000	65,000	72,000	35,145	1,481	49	86	C	
D	1	-	2,000	-	$ 5,000	-	-	7,000	11,000	2,198	116	20	44	D	1
D	2	-	4,500	-	3,500	-	-	8,000	11,000	3,348	129	30	49	D	2
E*		-	10,000	5,000	15,000	-	-	30,000	-	10,130	10	-	-	E	
100*		12,000	-	-	-	-	-	12,000	-	29,065	29	-	-	100	
F	1	12,000	26,000	9,000	-	-	-	47,000	53,000	20,762	1,025	39	81	F	1
F	2	5,000	5,000	2,000	-	-	-	12,000	10,000	7,665	299	77	125	F	2
G*		15,000	10,000	5,000	-	-	-	30,000	-	13,617	14	-	-	G	
200*		-	-	-	-	6,000	-	6,000	-	4,702	5	-	-	200	
H	1	-	-	1,700	-	3,200	2,100	7,000	12,000	4,040	169	34	59	H	1
H	2	-	-	3,300	-	5,800	3,900	13,000	17,000	5,363	302	32	74	H	2
J	1	20,000	-	1,000	-	-	-	21,000	21,000	13,554	474	65	94	J	1
J	2	9,500	3,500	2,000	-	-	-	15,000	14,000	12,536	360	90	107	J	2
K		10,000	-	-	-	-	-	10,000	16,000	5,801	414	36	108	K	
L		-	-	-	-	7,000	-	7,000	20,000	20,805	302	104	63	L	
300		-	-	-	4,000	-	-	4,000	4,000	1,794	89	45	93	300	
M	1	-	-	600	-	2,200	1,200	4,000	14,000	2,153	111	15	33	M	1
M	2	-	-	700	-	2,800	1,500	5,000	19,000	3,839	167	20	37	M	2
N		-	7,000	3,500	14,500	-	-	25,000	38,000	13,866	523	36	57	N	
P		-	5,200	3,300	8,500	-	-	17,000	29,000	5,569	423	19	61	P	
Q		-	-	-	-	10,000	-	10,000	8,000	4,623	200	58	104	Q	
R		9,000	-	-	-	-	-	9,000	17,000	6,230	266	37	65	R	
S		-	-	1,800	-	15,000	4,200	21,000	21,000	10,212	637	49	126	S	
T		-	-	5,000	-	16,000	7,000	28,000	38,000	10,591	622	28	68	T	
U**		-	10,000	5,000	15,000	-	-	30,000	-	-	-	-	-	U	
V**		-	3,500	500	-	-	-	4,000	-	-	-	-	-	V	
W*		-	2,000	7,200	-	16,800	14,000	40,000	-	-	-	-	-	W	
X***		-	-	-	12,500	-	-	12,500	-	-	-	-	-	X	
Y***		-	7,300	-	-	-	-	7,300	-	-	-	-	-	Y	
400*		-	-	-	-	-	-	-	-	5,416	5	-	-	400	
BB		-	-	-	-	-	-	-	8,000	2,508	144	31	75	BB	
CC		-	-	-	-	-	-	-	4,000	3,481	49	87	51	CC	
Misc.###		-	-	-	-	-	-	-	25,000	10,280	1,752	-	-	Misc.	
Totals		$105,500	$105,400	$78,200	$78,000	$114,800	$50,900	$532,800	$596,000+	$283,628	$10,905	48	76	Total	

*Introduced in April 1957 market.
**To be introduced in June 1957 market.
***Government and industrial contracts.

#Letters indicate "Groups." Numbers (100, etc.) indicate "Promotional Suites."
##Established November 1956.
###Styles no longer in the line.
+Total includes budget for items not included in this column, which adds to only $537,000.

Cotton Textile Industry Process Notes

The following Note is based upon the Columbia Weaving Company, a modern Southern mill producing 659,000 yards of "80 square" print cloth in a 144-hour week. An understanding of the amount and type of fixed assets used to produce this unfinished or "greige" cloth may be gleaned from the first three exhibits. A layout of the 316,000 square foot mill is shown in Exhibit 1, examples of textile machinery and improvements made during 1945–1962 are described in Exhibit 2, and a list of fixed assets in the Columbia mill is given in Exhibit 3. The current mill operating schedule is presented in Exhibit 4 and labor costs for each operation are detailed in Exhibit 5.

Each stage of the production process—from the time bales of raw cotton arrive until the unfinished cloth is shipped to the finishing plant—will be described in detail.

1. Raw Cotton. Cotton is sold commercially in compressed bales weighing about 500 pounds. There are many different kinds of cotton, and each mill buys the particular kinds best suited for the end use of the products it is making. The selection and blending of raw cottons to secure the best mixture for a particular mill is one of the most important operations in cotton textile manufacturing.

Raw cottons differ from one another in three major respects: staple length, color and grade, and growth.

(*a*) Staple length is the length of the cotton fiber. Domestic cottons vary in stable length from ¾ to 1¾ inch. In general, the longer staple lengths are used for making the finer cotton fabrics.

(*b*) Color and Grade: Color refers to the degree of whiteness of cotton. There are six major color groups: extra white, white, spotted, tinged, yellow stained, and grey. Each color group is divided up into grades to cover variations in the amount of leaf, trash, and other foreign matter, variations in the quality of the ginning preparation, and minor differences in color. For the white cotton, nine full grades are recognized in the cotton markets. Standards for each grade are kept in a vault in the Department of Agriculture. Samples are available to anyone in the industry and constitute the basis for commercial transactions in cotton.

(*c*) Growth: Growth refers to the geographic area in which the cotton was grown. Cotton from different areas will have certain physical characteristics which distinguish it from cotton grown in other areas.

In ordering raw cotton, a mill specifies the staple, grade, and growth desired: for example, 1,000 bales of 1 1/16 staple, middling grade, California growth. (Assumed white unless otherwise specified.)

When the raw cotton bales arrive at the Columbia mill, the cotton classer takes samples from the top and bottom of each bale and compares them against the government standards. If the samples do not come up to the standards for the grade ordered by the mill, they are sent to the broker, and the defective bales may subsequently be returned to the shipper. Disputes between buyers and sellers are submitted to cotton arbitration boards.

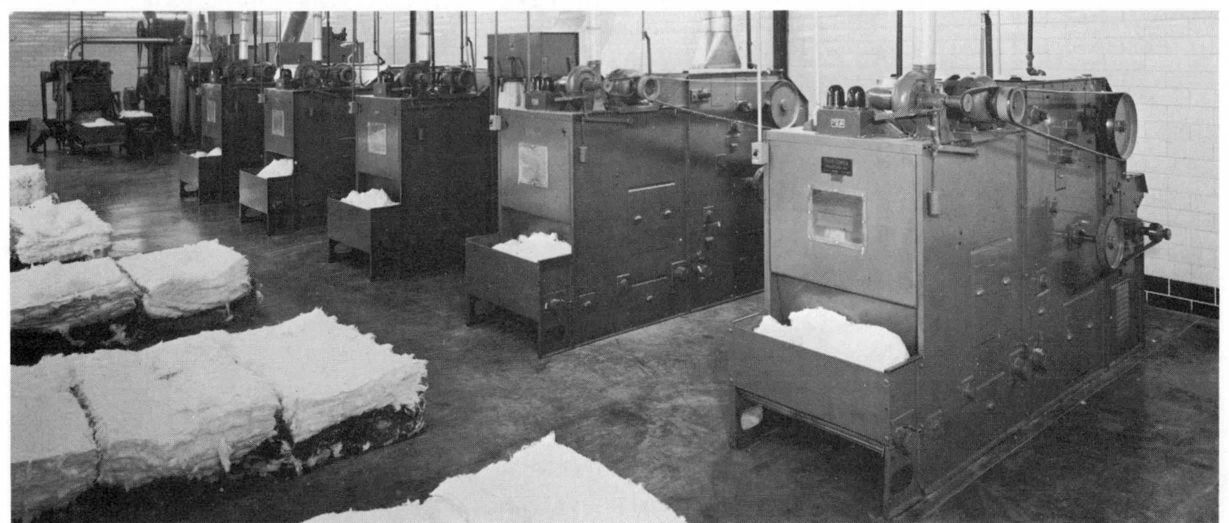

Photo, Courtesy Saco-Lowell Shops

2. Blender Feeders: Cotton is Loaded into Hopper in Foreground

Selected Flow Chart of the Cotton Textile Industry

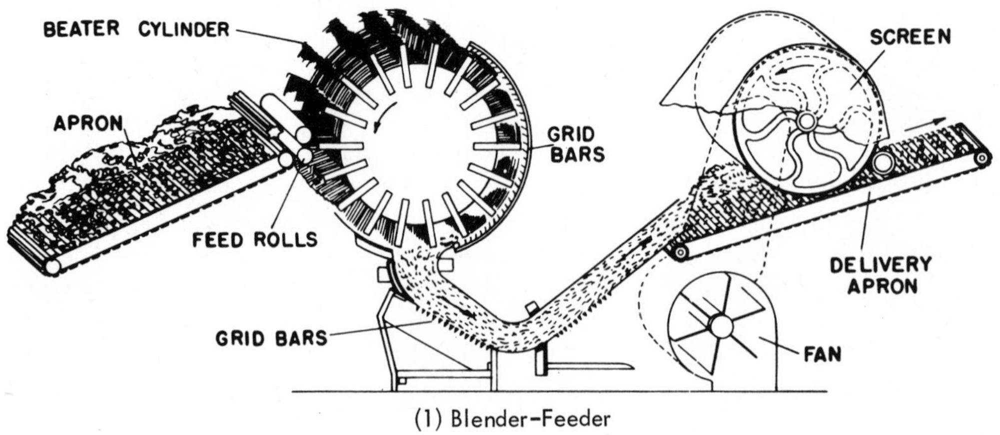

(1) Blender-Feeder

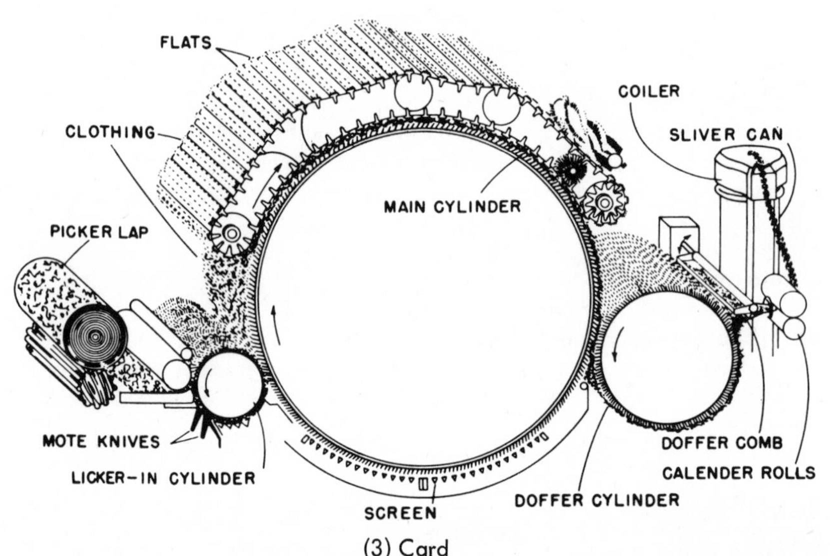

(3) Card

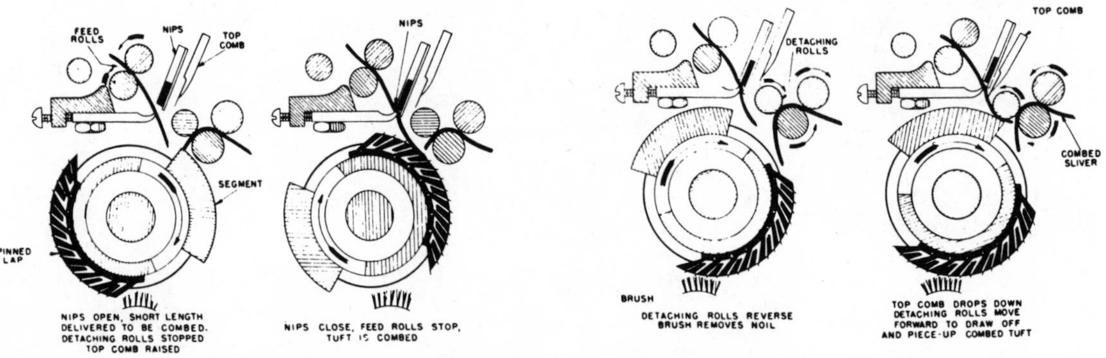

(5) Comb

Source: General Electric Company, *An Outline of the Textile Manufacturing Processes* (1948), pp. 3, 4, 5, 7, 8, 19.

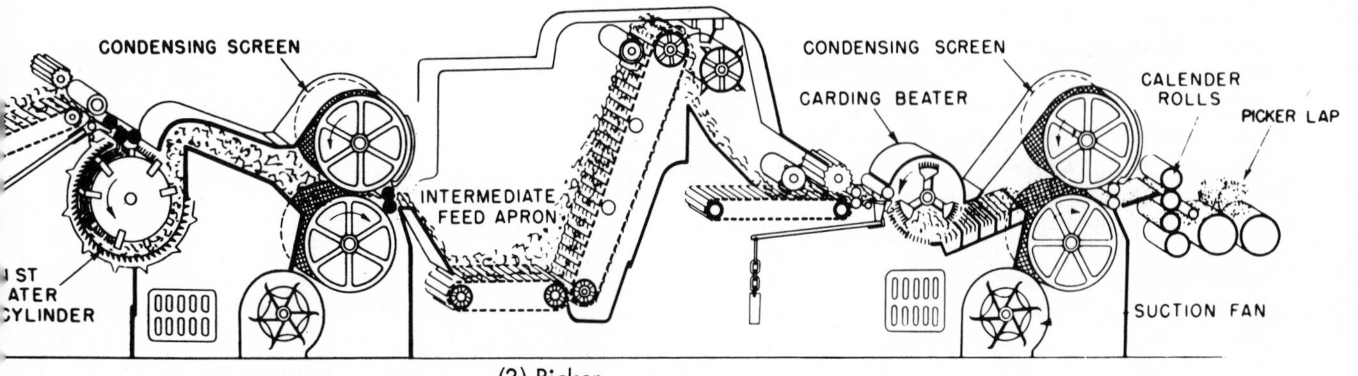

(2) Picker

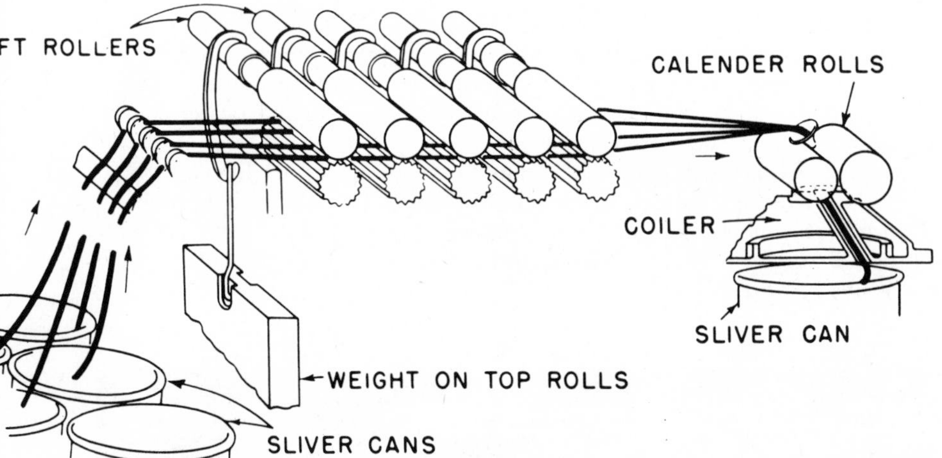

(4) Draw Frame (same drafting principle used in lapping, roving, spinning)

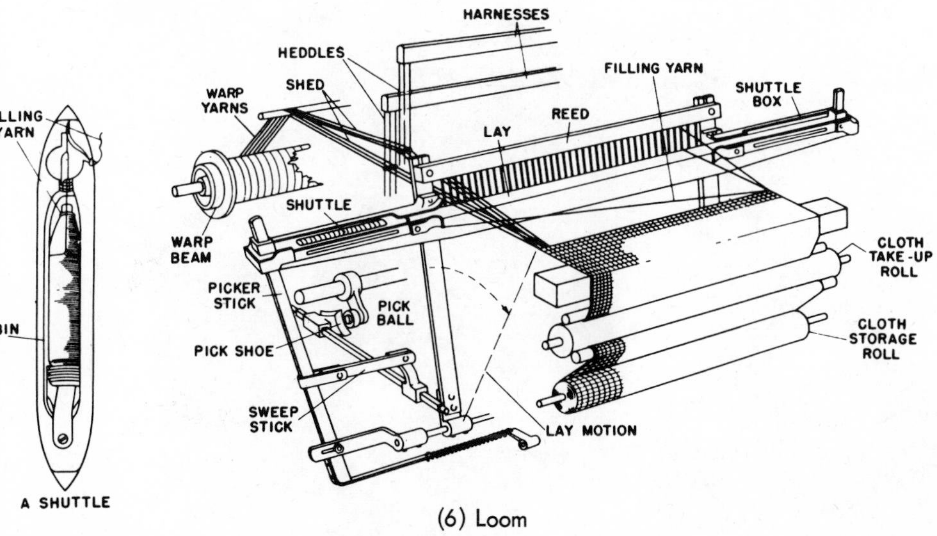

(6) Loom

2. *Opening and Cleaning Machines.* The first operation, opening and cleaning, is designed to: (1) blend the contents of several bales, and (2) loosen and separate the matted bunches of cotton fibers into small tufts. While many different arrangements of equipment may be used, Columbia has eight blender-feeders and one cleaner (see Exhibit 3).

The machines are tended by an opening-room man. He takes four-inch layers of cotton from 20–30 bales in a prearranged sequence and places them in the blender hoppers. The blender feeders (see flow chart on preceding page) tear apart, loosen, and fluff the fiber bunches; dirt and trash fall through grids to floor-level receptacles. The cotton fibres are carried forward and deposited on a conveyor in a fairly uniform and continuous volume. The conveyor carries the cotton from the eight blender-feeders to a cleaner for further separation of foreign matter from the cotton. The cotton is drawn through the cleaner by air suction created by a fan. The further cleaning and reduction of the size of the cotton tufts is accomplished by passing the stock between two spike-studded cylinders. These cylinders are mounted in a parallel position lengthwise of the cleaner. As the large tufts drop on to these rotating cylinders and reduced in size, they are thrown upward by a centrifugal force and exhausted from the cleaner by the suction created by the fan. Heavier impurities and some short fibers are deposited in a receptacle under the machine. The air current from the fan draws the cotton on to a cylindrical cage known as a cage section or condenser. The cotton is then drawn through a pipe by air suction, to the pickers. Once started in operation, the opening and cleaning equipment requires few adjustments other than frequent scourings.

3. *One Process Picking Machines.* The pickers form the cotton into a uniform, continuous sheet or lap while continuing the cleaning. Cotton from the opening room falls into a hopper from which a feed apron delivers a fairly even amount to a beater. After passing through the first beater section the mass of cotton is drawn onto condensing cylindrical cages and then repeated through a second beater-condenser combination before being delivered to calender rolls and wound on an arbor in lap form.

The laps are 40 inches wide, about ½ inch thick, and weigh from 12 to 16 ounces per linear yard. As delivered from the picker, the cylindrical laps are about 18 inches in diameter and weigh between 40 and 50 pounds. A given lap, say 12¾ ounces per yard, can produce a variety of different yarns. Adjustments are fairly easy to produce laps of different weights, to handle cottons of different staple lengths, or to compensate for humidity variations.

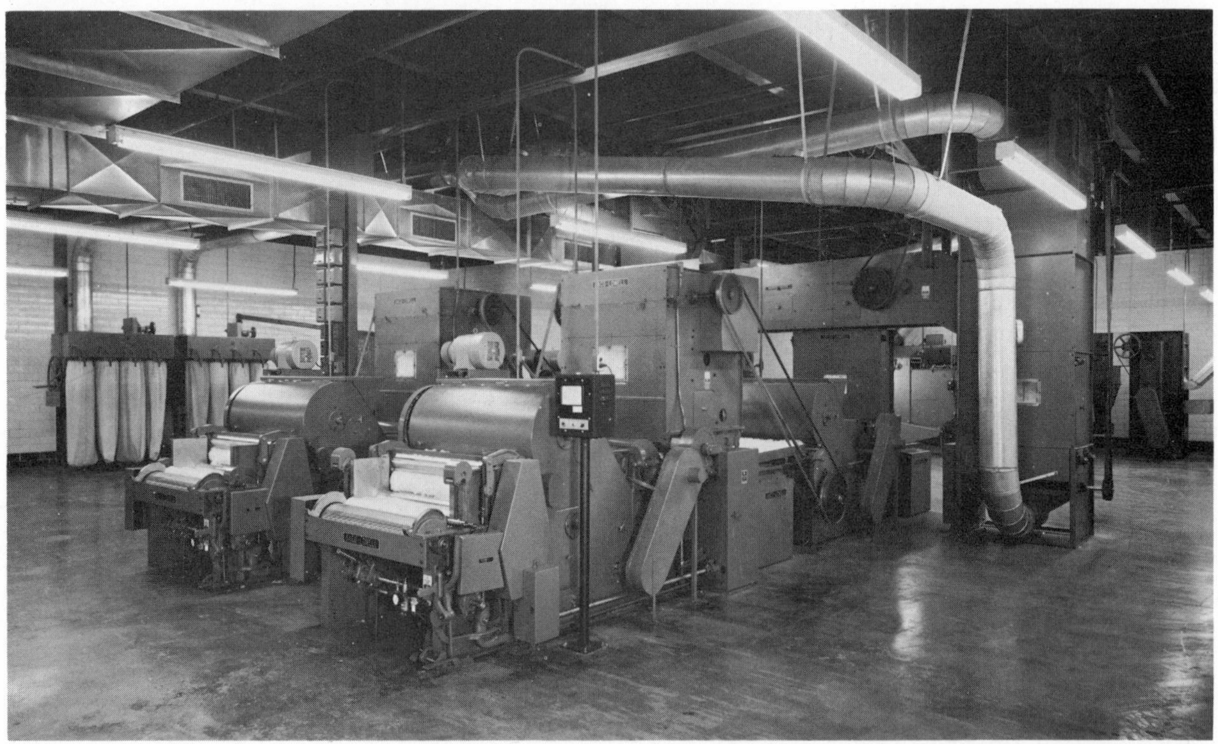

Photo, Courtesy Saco-Lowell Shops

3. Picker: Cotton from the Cleaner Is Loaded at the Back and Emerges as a Roll of Picker Lap in Front

Photo, Courtesy Saco-Lowell Shops

4. Card: Picker Lap Is Fed at One End and the Sliver Is Produced at the Other

Photo, Courtesy Saco-Lowell Shops

4. Card: Picker Lap Being Licked in; Note Card Flats at Top of Picture

4. Cards. Carding is designed to continue opening and cleaning the cotton, separating the fibers too short for spinning, straightening the other fibers and producing a continuous untwisted strand called a sliver. The picker lap is fed to the licker-in, a saw-toothed cylinder that bites off tufts of cotton. These are picked up by the faster moving card cylinder which is 50 inches in diameter and covered with bent-toothed clothing averaging 65,000 points per square foot. These points meet similar clothing mounted on an endless chain of card "flats" with the points inclined in the opposite direction with a clearance of .009 inches to .012 inches.

The interaction of these wire points is the key to the process. *Carding action* is accomplished when the wires of two surfaces are inclined in opposite directions and the faster moving cylinder (26,000 inches per minute) passes the slower moving flats (two to three inches per minute), point against point. (The flats move to enable a revolving brush to comb the dirt and waste fibers or "neps" from the flats upon leaving the cylinder.) The cotton is removed from the cylinder by a point against point *carding action* with a slower moving doffer cylinder, 27 inches in diameter (865 inches per minute) picking up fibers from the cylinder due to centrifugal force and the better gripping power of finer count clothing. The fibers are removed by a reciprocating doffer comb (16 teeth per inch) vibrating some 1,500 times a minute. The comb points are in the same direction as the doffer points, producing a *stripping action*. The fine web of intertwined fibers that falls away from the doffer is condensed into a loose rope (sliver) and coiled in a can.

Card clothing has gone through considerable evolution. Originally bent metal wires were pressed through a leather foundation. Lower costs and better control saw the substitution of a plied textile base. Since 1928 some cards have had metallic clothing consisting of a narrow steel band punched with points and coiled around the cylinder. All these points required some three hours of grinding per 142 hours of running time. In 1960, a hard wire clothing that reduced grinding to buffing two hours per 4,000 of operation was marketed for $820 a card.

A sliver may weigh between 40 and 70 grains per yard (1,000 grains equals one seventh of a pound), but there is sufficient flexibility in the succeeding processes to use one sliver weight for all yarn weights or "counts" from 2's count to 41's count on carded yarns.

Photo, Courtesy Saco-Lowell Shops

4. Card: Doffer Comb Stripping and Forming a Sliver

Photo, Courtesy Saco-Lowell Shops

5. Draw-Frame: Ends from Ten Sliver Cans Being Fed to Each of Two Deliveries

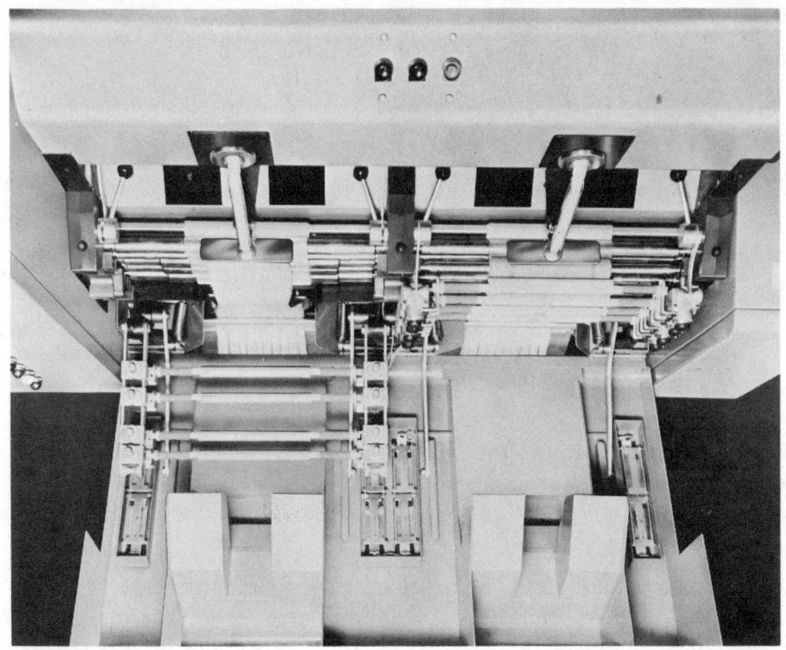

Photo, Courtesy Saco-Lowell Shops

5. Draw-Frame: Close-up of Deliveries Showing Drafting Rollers

5. Draw Frames. Drawing is the process of progressively sliding fibers by each other, causing a reduction in the mass per unit of length, and further fiber paralleling. These results are accomplished by feeding slivers through a series of rollers rotating at increasing rates of speed. The reduction in mass, or "draft," is measured by the weight per yard fed divided by the weight per yard delivered; usually it is between six and eight. In addition, increased uniformity is obtained by feeding the ends from six sliver cans through the rollers and condensing the result through a hole into a single sliver. For better yarns, six cans of sliver are taken from the delivery side of a frame and fed into a second frame. The two processes are called breaker and finisher drawing.

Drawing frames are built in multiple units called deliveries. Most frames now are built with two deliveries, each fed by from 6 to 10 cans of sliver.

There are two major types of spinning mills: carded yarn mills and combed yarn ones. In carded mills, such as Columbia, which produce coarse grades of cloth, the sliver goes directly from carding, to drawing, to spinning. In the combed mills, three additional processes—precomber drawing, lapping, and combing—are added, usually between breaker and finisher drawing. These processes parallel the fibers and eliminate those of short staple length. The resulting combed sliver has increased strength and uniformity and thus may be spun into a smooth, lustrous fine yarn.

Photo, Courtesy Whitin Machine Work

6. Lapper

6. Lapping. Similar to a draw frame, the lapper takes some 16 breaker drawing slivers, drafts them about 2.5, and combines them into a ribbon-like sheet about 11¾ inches in width. Until 1959 two machines, a sliver and a ribbon lapper, were required. Besides paralleling the fibers, lappers put cotton in the form necessary for combing.

7. Combing. The purpose of combing is (1) to separate the short cotton fibers ("noils") from the longer ones, thus producing a sliver of very uniform staple length; (2) to continue the paralleling and cleaning processes; and (3) to remove neps which are tightly tangled fibers about the size of the head of a common pin.

Combing consists of a series of intermittent and at times overlapping actions. (1) The lap is mounted on one of a comber's 8 to 12 heads. (2) Feeding rolls introduce the lap about one sixth of an inch at a time. (3) Nippers grip the fibers between two parallel jaws to retain the longer fibers while the noils, neps, and dirt are removed. (4) A cylinder consisting of a comb on one side and a raised segment on the other does the combing. When the comb part is finished combing, three detaching rolls move the previously combed web *backwards* 1⅜ inches to overlap the succeeding tuft just combed. The nippers open and, with the help of the segment, the detaching rolls move *forward* 2⅜ inches for a net gain of one inch. The result is that those fibers farthest from the nippers have been reformed into a continuous web and separated from those at the mouth of the nippers. (5) Meanwhile, a metal top comb straightens and cleans the detached fibers and ensures no noils are carried along. (6) The noils are brushed off the needles of the half-lap by a rotating brush while the segment is detaching. These noils are drawn onto the aspirator roll by air suction created by a fan. As the aspirator rotates, the noils are deposited into large box-shaped cans at the back of the comber. The combed cotton is delivered at the front of the comber. (7) The combed lap is condensed through a tapered hole, drafted, and combined with those from the other heads into a single comber sliver. Combing speed is gauged by the number of times the nippers close or "nip."

Noils average 10 to 18 percent of input pounds and are sold to mills producing low-grade yarn for about 70 percent of the raw cotton price. This wastage reduces the actual average draft per head of about 9 to 7.5.

Photo, Courtesy Saco-Lowell Shops

7. Comber: Twelve Heads Feeding Two Comber Sliver Cans

8. Long-Draft Roving. The purpose of roving is to reduce the sliver to a size suitable for spinning. The carded or combed sliver is passed through some three pairs of rollers that impart a draft ranging between 6 and 20. The roving yarn is threaded through a metal arm or "flyer" and wound onto a bobbin. Both flyers and bobbins have independent drives; the rotating flyer imparts a slight twist to the roving for strength.

Roving frames, together with spinning and to a lesser extent drawing frames, have a problem of fiber control. Increases in draft have been obtained by speeding up the front rolls and widening the distance between rolls. Clearly, if the rolls are closer than the fiber staple length, the fiber will break, but if the rolls are too far apart the sliver sags and goes out of control. In so-called "long-draft" frames the roll separation is increased and the sliver supported by stationary guide plates, aprons, or condensing trumpets. Although long-draft spinning appeared in 1920, long-draft roving was introduced in 1946. In the early days of long-draft, the maximum draft recommended to produce yarn of satisfactory quality was 16 to 18. Improvements were gradually made during the period from the early thirties to the early fifties resulting in yarn of satisfactory quality with drafts up to 40.

Photo, Courtesy Whitin Machine Works

8. Long-Draft Roving Frame: Yarn from 36 Sliver Cans Being Drafted and Wound on Bobbins

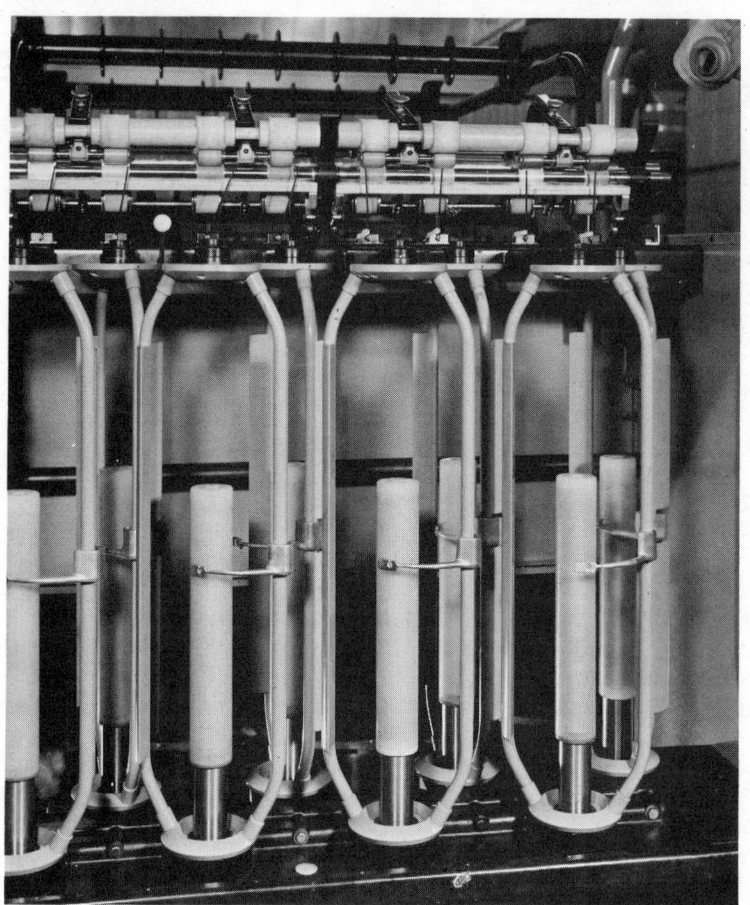

Photo, Courtesy Saco-Lowell Shops

8. Long-Draft Roving Frame: Close-up of Bobbins Showing Metal "Flyer" Arm with Hole for Yarn and Drafting Rolls at Top

Photo, Courtesy Whitin Machine Works

9. Long-Draft Spinning: Roving Bobbins Are Mounted on Top and Threaded through Drafting Rolls

Photo, Courtesy Saco-Lowell Shops

9. Long-Draft Spinning: Close-up of Drafting Rolls; Note Continuous Belt Supporting Strand between Rolls

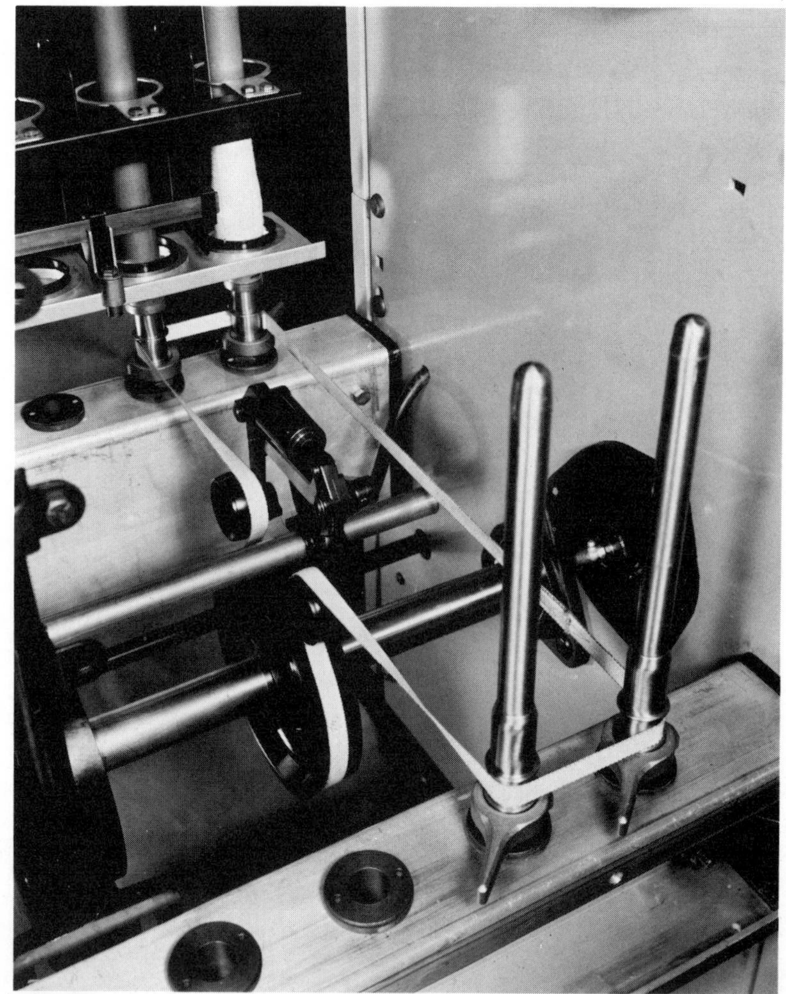

Photo, Courtesy Saco-Lowell Shops

9. Long-Draft Spinning: Close-up of Spindle Drive; Note Traveler Ring Rail around Rear Bobbins

9. Long-Draft Spinning. The purpose of the long-draft spinning operation is to reduce the cotton roving to the required yarn size and impart the right amount of twist. The operation is similar to roving: a single unit roving strand (or two in the case of fine yarns) is given drafts up to 40, depending upon the grade and staple of cotton and the counts of yarn to be spun, and then wound on a bobbin. Drafting is done with three pairs of rolls. As the drafted roving leaves the delivery roll, twist is inserted and the yarn is wound on a bobbin or peger tube. Twist is obtained by threading the yarn through a tiny c-shaped metal ring, called a "traveler," that can rotate on a track or "ring rail" around the whirling bobbin. The twist gives the strand emerging from the front roller needed strength. Warp yarns (the longitudinal strands of woven fabrics) have a relatively high twist for maximum strength, while filling yarns (the crosswise interlacing) have less twist to avoid kinking.

The fineness of yarn is called count. There are 840 yards of yarn in a hank. When it takes just one hank to make a pound, the yarn is number 1 count. If it takes 10 840-yard hanks to make a pound, the yarn is number 10 count; if 60 hanks, it is 60 count, or 60's. Yarns are seldom spun finer than 140's in the United States. Occasionally two or more yarns are plied on a twisting machine to make a plied yarn. A 60 count, 2-ply yarn would be designated 60/2.

Spinning frames are built with varying numbers of spindles per frame and in different sizes depending on the size of yarn and whether they are to be used for warp or filling. Frames for filling yarn have much smaller bobbins, suitable for use in a loom shuttle.

The frames are tended by spinners and doffers. The spinners load new roving bobbins onto the frame, piece yarn strands together when they break, and shut down frames when bobbins are full. The number of strands or ends it is necessary to piece per hour per 1,000 spindles is called ends "down." Doffers remove the full bobbins from the frames and replace them with empty ones. A skilled operator can doff 36,000 to 50,000 bobbins per 40 hours, but many mills are installing automatic doffers.

10. Automatic Spooler. Warp yarn bobbins contain too little yarn for a loom; therefore, the contents of several must be combined into cylindrical packages, appropriately called cheeses, containing about 60,000 yards each. An automatic spooler can wind yarn at 1,200 yards per minute, tie knots, eject empty bobbins and automatically disengage the cheese when full. The operator places full bobbins in a slot, leads the ends through a guide, and removes full cheeses.

11. High-Speed Warper. The purpose of warping is to wind the yarn from about 350 to 600 cheeses side by side onto a large spool, four to six feet in length, called a section beam. The cheeses are placed in racks or "creels," threaded through "drop wires" which stop the loom if a strand breaks, and wound on the beam between 250 and 900 yards per minute depending upon the count. Lengths of 40,000 yards are obtained by joining the end of one cheese to the beginning of an adjacent one.

12. Slasher. This operation performs a dual job: coating the yarn with starch to prevent chafing in the loom and combining the contents of several section beams onto a loom beam to obtain the number of warp ends needed in the fabric. Several section beams (a "set") are placed in racks and the yarn immersed in boiling starch and other compounds for a few seconds before being dried on a heated cylinder and rewound at 18 to 75 yards per minute.

12a. Filling Yarn Conditioner. Bobbins of filling are passed through a steam chamber or a wetting agent bath to counteract the tendency of the yarn to kink and snarl when the tension is released.

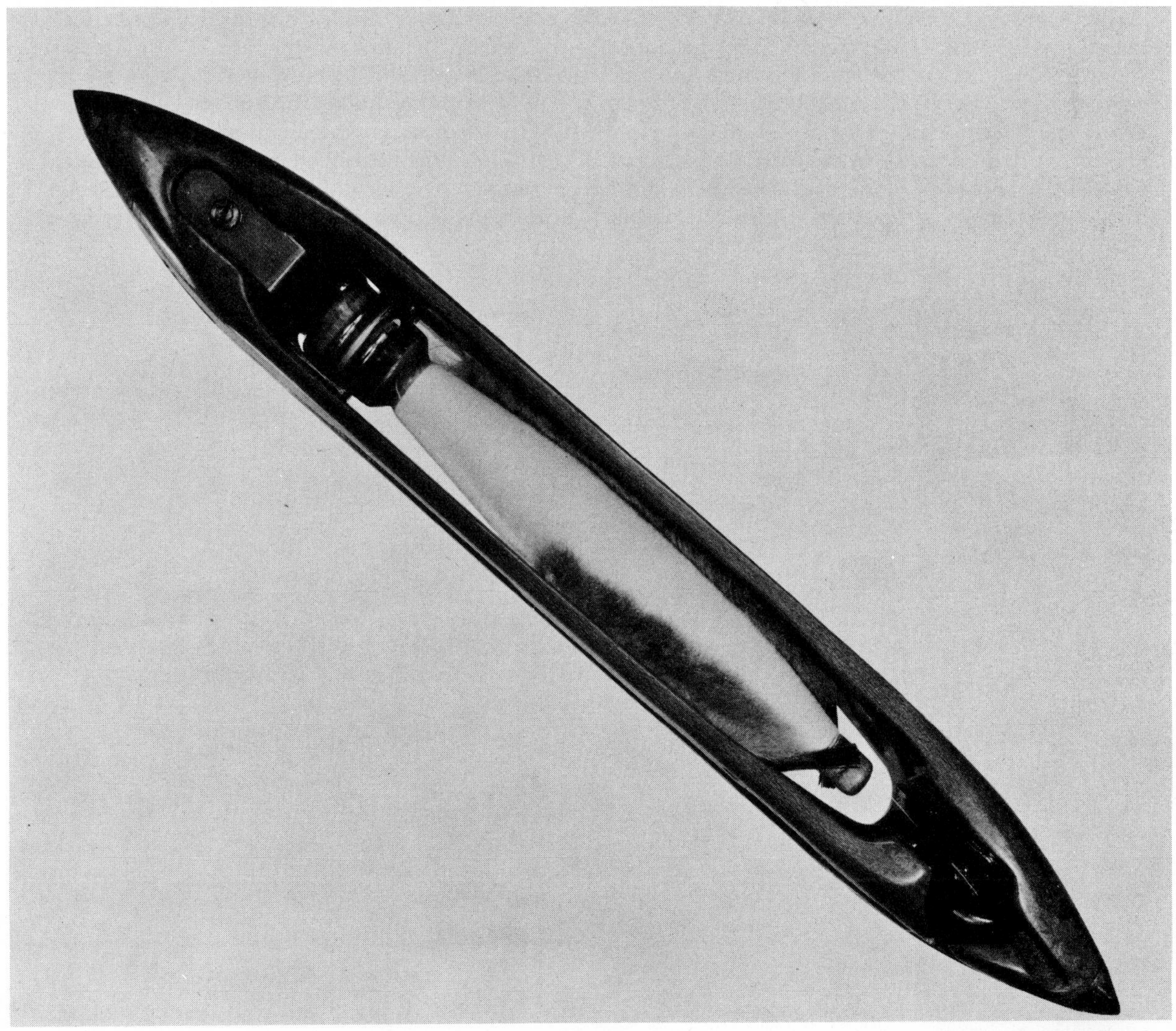

Photo, Courtesy Draper Corporation

13. Loom: A Wooden Shuttle Containing a Filling Bobbin

13. Looms. Weaving consists of interlacing two systems of threads crosswise, at right angles to each other to form a fabric. The lengthwise system of threads is made up of the warp yarns drawn from the loom beam. The number of warp threads per inch is called the "sley." The crosswise system of threads comes from the filling yarn on the bobbins. The number of filling threads per inch in the fabric is refered to as "picks."

There are three primary motions on cotton looms: "shedding," "picking," and "beating-up." Shedding is the raising of certain warp threads to form a v-shaped opening through which the shuttle containing the filling bobbin is passed. (The shuttle resembles an oblong wooden box which tapered wooden ends and weighs about two pounds.) The passing of the shuttle is picking, while the subsequent pushing of the loose filling thread (pick) up to the rest of the cloth is beating-up.

Warp yarns are first threaded through drop wires and then through 2 to 25 wooden frames (harnesses) supporting a number of wire strips (heddles). Each warp thread is drawn through the eye of a heddle and raised for shedding when that harness is raised. The threads next pass through a comb-like wire reed mounted on an oscillating narrow platform called the lay. Finally the warp threads are wound on the cloth take-up roll at the front of the loom.

With this background, the loom operation may be described. (1) Shedding is performed by cams that raise straps to operate the harnesses. The selvage or edges of the cloth are usually of heavier warp for strength and may be controlled separately. (2) Picking is also performed by cams actuating a picker stick at either side of the loom. These throw the shuttle across the lay from one open shuttle box to another during the shedding. The shuttle can travel between 100 and 225 picks per minute. A loom running at 160 picks weaves cloth having a construction of 80 picks to the inch at two inches per minute. (3) Beating-up is accomplished by the oscillating motion of the crankshaft-operated lay. It is back during picking, moves forward to beat-up, and back for shedding and picking again.

Four auxiliary motions facilitate these processes: (1) The let-off and take-up motions regulate the warp tension. (2) The shuttle box change motion permits changing filling threads for color fabrics. Boxes on either side of the loom are raised or lowered by risers on a moving chain actuating levers to present the desired shuttle in the path of a picker stick. (3) The filling bobbin change motion is operated when filling thread in the shuttle is nearly exhausted as detected by a feeler. This causes a full bobbin from a magazine to be forced into the shuttle, displacing the empty bobbin with no delay in weaving cycle.

Photo, Courtesy Draper Corporation

13. Loom: A Plain Loom from the Rear Showing Drop Wires and Harnesses

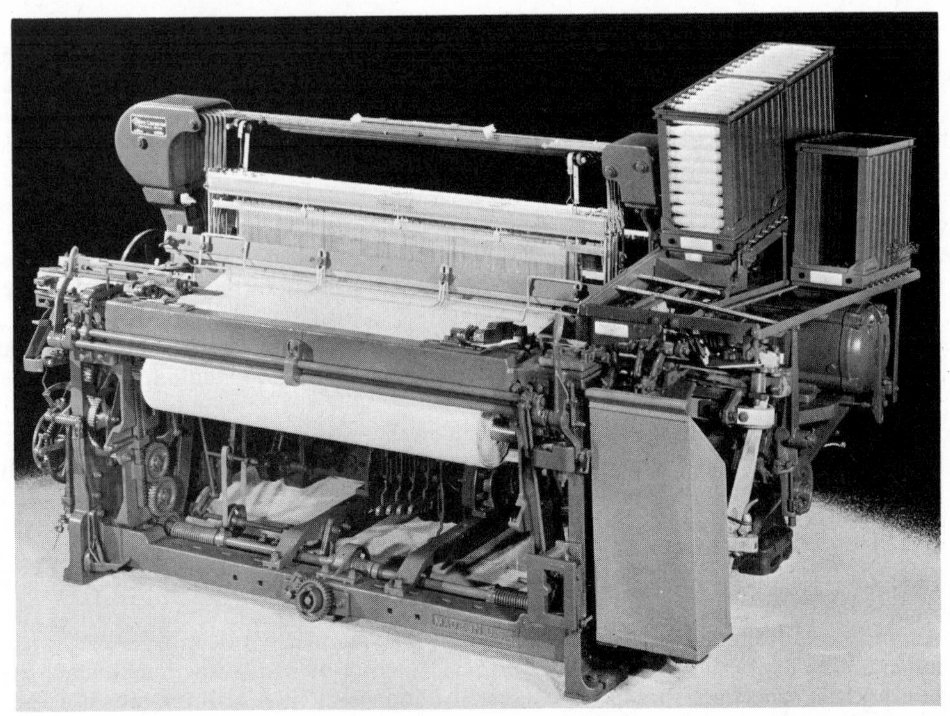

Photo, Courtesy Draper Corporation

13. Loom: Draper X-3 Loom; Note Supply of Filling Bobbins at Top Right

Photo, Courtesy Crompton and Knowles Corp.

13. Loom: A C&K C-5 Box Loom; Note the Dobby Head Attachment, the Four Shuttle Boxes, and the Picker Stick to the Left

The time consumed in changing fabrics depends on the warp threads. If the number is the same, an automatic tie-in machine can join the new warp ends to the old ones before they pass through the harness; the job takes 1 to 1½ hours. If the number of ends changes, the threading has to be redone, usually on an automatic machine; this process can consume a full day or more, depending upon the fabric complexity. It is usually done in a special room and the completed loom beam, drop wires, harnesses, and reed carried to the loom as a package

Looms vary principally by the type of fabric they can weave. There are four basic weave patterns: plain weaves, twill weaves, satin weaves, and figured.

In the plain weaves, the filling thread passes alternately over and under every other warp thread. This weave requires but two harnesses, with every other warp thread passing through an alternate harness. In operation, one harness is raised and the other lowered, thus separating the warp threads for the passage of the shuttle containing the filling threads. For the next passage of the shuttle the action of the harnesses is reversed. Plain weaves are woven on plain or cam looms built to accommodate from two to seven harnesses.

Twill weaves give the effect of diagonal lines running on the face of the fabric. This effect is produced by raising two or more warp threads and depressing one as the shuttle passes across the loom. The simpler twills can be woven on the plain or cam looms. The more complicated twills need a "dobby head" attachment that consists of a perforated plastic tape (like the old player piano) actuating up to 25 harnesses.

Satin weaves have a smooth surface with a predominance of either warp or filling threads showing, but without noticeable twill lines. These weaves require five or more harnesses and can be produced on a plain or dobby loom.

Figured patterns require large numbers of harnesses. The simpler ones can be woven with a dobby head attachment. The more complicated ones require a "Jacquard head" attachment which permits the raising and lowering of each warp thread to be controlled independently of all the others. The action of the head is controlled by a series of cardboard cards with holes punched into them in accordance with the design desired.

For weaving plaids, checked ginghams or other fabrics with *colored* filling yarn, a box loom is needed. The left-hand battery of this loom will accommodate as many as four different colors of filling yarn and the colors may be changed automatically after a minimum of two picks (over and back). Such a loom is considerably more expensive than the plain loom. For example, a cotton dobby box loom cost $1,300 in 1945; it cost $4,500 in 1962 although there were several improvements that affected cloth quality.

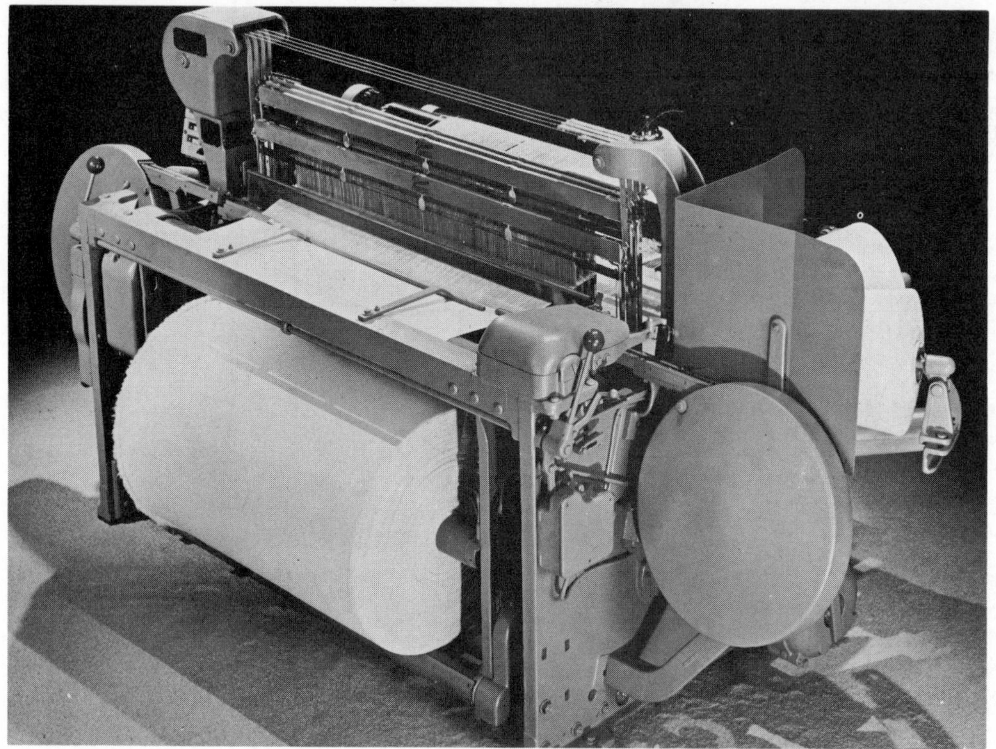

Photo, Courtesy Draper Corporation

14. Shuttleless Loom: The DSL Loom with Yarn Supply at Right

14. Shuttleless Looms. In 1959 the Draper Corporation announced a shuttleless loom to produce fabrics 36–64 inches wide at speeds between 200 and 250 picks per minute. In 1962 speed for a 50-inch fabric was 247 picks per minute with 40 stops per hour. The loom was to (1) increase speed 40 percent, weaver productivity 40 percent, and fixer productivity 100 percent; (2) decrease the cost of maintenance and operating supplies 70 percent; (3) eliminate battery hands; and (4) reduce materials handling, filling preparation costs, power consumption, waste, noise level. Cost was $2,800 plus about $200 in harnesses, loom beams, and other necessary equipment.

The prime difference between the DSL and the conventional plain loom is the way filling is placed in the warp. Filling yarn supply consists of two eight- to nine-pound packages creeled together and mounted at the right-hand end of the machine. Two carriers, which place the pick, are mounted on the ends of flexible steel tapes that go in and out of the shed from opposite sides of loom like two rapiers. Each tape is fastened to an oscillating aluminum wheel. As the aluminum wheels turn, the carriers enter the open shed from each side, mate in the center, and the filling is transferred from the right-hand carrier to the left-hand one. As the tapes withdraw, the left-hand carrier pulls the loose end of filling across the shed. A filling control mechanism positions, measures and cuts the thread for the right-hand carrier.

Filling is laid in cycles of two picks (one to a shed). These picks are laid like a hairpin with the open end at the left-hand side and the bend at the right, which results in a conventional selvage on the right-hand side of the cloth and a trimmed selvage on the left. The outside warp ends (known as binder cords) in the left-hand selvage are on separate spools. As these revolve, a full leno locks each pick in place.

The looms had been tested since 1957, but the first public report on commercial operating results was made by Carolina Mills in the July, 1961, issue of *Textile World*. Weaving 35- and 37-inch flannels for three shifts, 200 DSL's at 240 picks per minute and 92 percent efficiency wove 317,952,000 picks per week and replaced 240 updated prewar E model looms that ran 170 ppm, 93 percent efficiency and wove 273,-196,800 ppw. Employee jobloads increased from 80 to 100 looms per fixer and 48 to 50 looms per weaver with the elimination of 3 fixers, 3 weavers, 24 battery hands, 7.5 maintenance men, 1.5 cloth doffers, 6 filling-winding operators, 6 bobbin stripper operators, 3 filling haulers and the addition of 3 selvage clippers and 3 filling yarn creelers. In addition to looms, Carolina paid for: a new 21,000 square foot air-conditioned building ($223,000); electrical work ($7,500); selvage trimmer ($5,000); loom lubrication system ($6,900); mechanical loom cleaner equipment ($24,000); and a new winder and modifying two old ones ($20,500).

COTTON TEXTILE FINISHING OPERATIONS

The grey cloth which comes from the looms of the weaving mills is brown or grey in color, harsh to the feel, and has a rough, unfinished appearance. Except for a few industrial uses, the majority of the cloth is finished. The following paragraphs will briefly describe some of the finishing operations in Georgia Print Works, a mill processing six to seven million yards per month of cotton and blended fabrics, employing 900 people operating 48 hours a week, and using 100 gallons of water per pound of cotton.

Some of the processes are mechanical, but most are dependent upon carefully controlled chemical reactions. The steps may be divided into three major groups: preparatory, color, and finishing. The preparatory processes include such operations as laying out, singeing, desizing, kier boiling, bleaching, and drying. The color processes include printing and dyeing. The finishing processes include starching, sanforizing, tentering, calendering, napping, water repelling, and a number of other operations.

1. Laying Out. Grey goods arrive in 400- to 800-pound bales or rolls consisting of 100- to 200-yard lengths. The first step is sewing together a continuous strip up to the length of the customer's order or the kier boiler capacity.

2. Singeing. This operation burns off lint, fuzz and loose threads by passing the cloth through 1,500°F. gas flames at 6,000 to 9,000 yards per hour. A water quench box follows.

3. Desizing. Still in rope form, the cloth is run through a tank containing about ½ percent sulphuric acid solution or other starch solvent and then put in wooden bins to steep for several hours. After the starch is dissolved, the cloth goes through wash tanks at 220 yards per minute (y.p.m.). These tanks have several rollers so that the cloth may be run up and down in the tank 16 or 18 times before emerging.

4. Kier Boiling. This step completes the dissolution of the sizing and removes any grease, oil, or natural impurities. About 2,000 to 10,000 pounds of cloth are placed in cylindrical steel tanks and boiled 6 to 18 hours in a weak alkaline solution under vacuum and 10 to 15 pounds of steam pressure. A 5-ton kier would be about 6 feet in diameter and 10 feet deep.

5. Bleaching. One of many methods is to run the cloth at about 20 yards a minute through a chlorinated soda solution, steep it 2 to 6 hours in a pit, and then pull it through wash tanks.

Photo, Courtesy Burlington Industries, Inc.

6. Dryers: Can Dryer

Photo, Courtesy J. P. Stevens & Co., Inc.

6. Dryers: Tenter Frame

6. Drying. Next comes can dryers or tenter frames, or both. Can drying consists of running the cloth at 220 y.p.m. around up to 60 steam-heated cylinders about 12 to 18 inches in diameter. In tenter dryers, the cloth is held taut by a traveling set of clips and passed under a heated oven. Print cloths are often tenter dried in order to pull the threads into their natural square position before printing.

7. Mercerizing. This process is designed to improve the luster of the cloth and increase its affinity for dye stuffs. At 10 to 30 y.p.m., the steps include a bath of sodium hydroxide solution, tentering, cold water, weak acid solution, warm water, and can drying.

8. Printing. Quantity printing is usually done on a printing machine consisting of a large steel drum 6 to 8 feet in diameter, around which are arranged 2 to 16 engraved copper rollers. The cloth passes around the drum and between it and the copper rollers. The pattern is applied by the rollers, each of which is engraved with that portion of the design relating to a particular color. Near each roller is a shallow color pan containing dyestuff which is fed to the roller by a revolving furnisher brush. A steel doctor blade scrapes excess color off the roller in order that only the engraved portions carry color when they make contact with the cloth. Upon emerging from the machine at some 300 y.p.m., the cloth is run to a can dryer to set the color.

Several skilled jobs are involved in printing. First there is the engraver of the rolls, then the adjuster of rollers for proper color registration (set-up for 10 to 12 colors, runs 4 to 8 hours), third the colorist responsible for the dye color and viscosity, and finally the printers supervising a two-man crew per machine.

9. Ageing. The colors are developed and set in varying ageing processes. One is 5 to 15 minutes in a steam chamber, followed by a series of washing solutions and a can dryer.

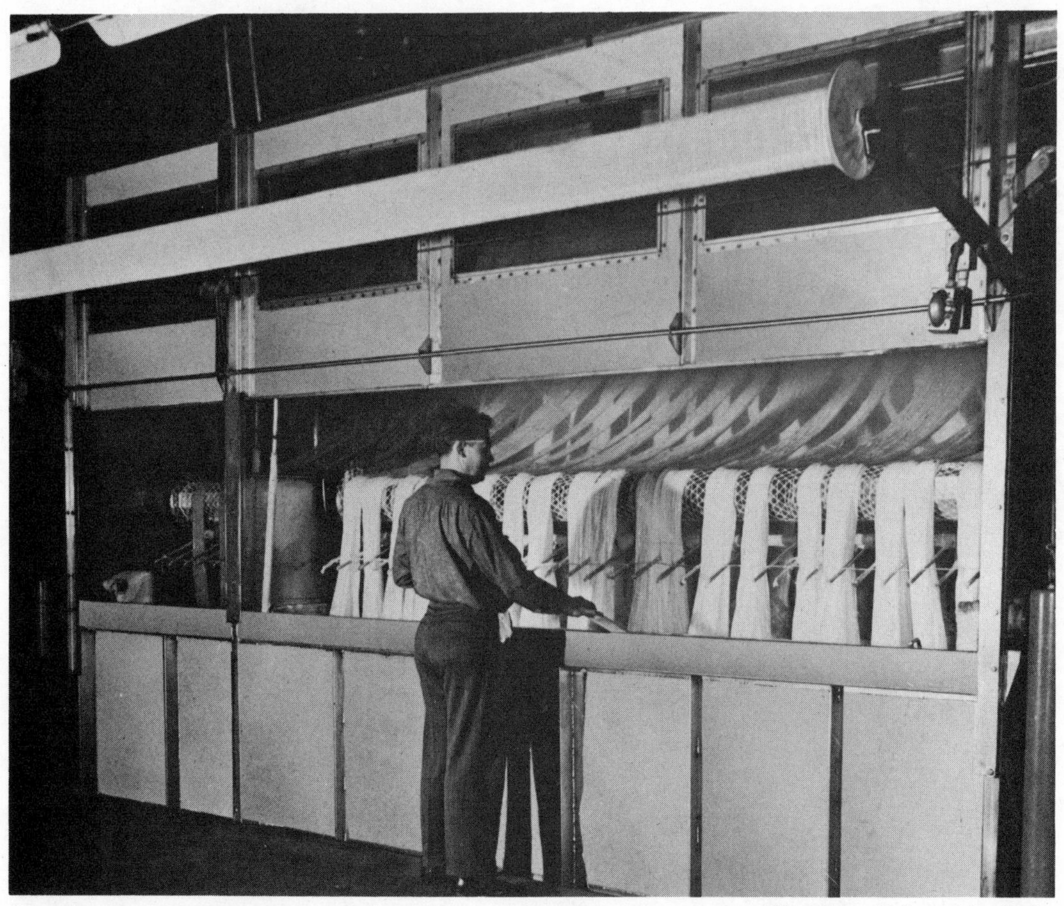

Photo, Courtesy Burlington Industries, Inc.

8A–9A. Dyeing: A Dye Vat; Note the Loops of Cloth Rotating on the Spindle

8A–9A. Dyeing. An alternative to printing is dyeing, usually done in a rotating stainless steel vat followed by a dryer.

10. Starching. The first finishing process is starching, where the cloth is run through a starch solution which sometimes contains bluing, oils, waxes, synthetic resins, or water-repelling, fire-proofing, or mildew-proofing substances, depending upon the finish desired. Can drying and tentering follow, all at some 2,000 yards per hour.

11. Calendering. In the finisher's version of the flat iron, the cloth is run through 3 to 11 hot or cold rollers to obtain the required texture and "hand" ("feel"). Embossed rollers are used for special effects.

12. Sanforizing. This is a patented controlled shrinking process to reduce potential shrinkage upon subsequent washing and ironing to 1 percent instead of the normal 10 percent. In a Sanforizing range, the cloth goes through a cold water spray, over a short tenter frame, runs between a heavy cloth blanket and a series of electrically heated shoes, and finally is pressed against a large steam-heated drum by a cloth blanket. The action of the drum and blanket shrinks the cloth a precise amount.

13. Inspection, Putting-Up, Shading. The final operations are inspecting the cloth, cutting, binding it into 20- to 100-yard lengths, and grouping the lot into one to four color shades.

COTTON TEXTILE CUTTING

After finishing, the cloth is sent to stores for sale as piece goods or to the cutting up trade to be made into apparel or home furnishings. The following paragraphs describe the manufacture of work pants at Salant & Salant, Inc., a producer or men's and boys' work shirts, sport shirts, work pants and slacks. Exhibits 6 and 7 show layouts of a pants factory and a shirt factory.

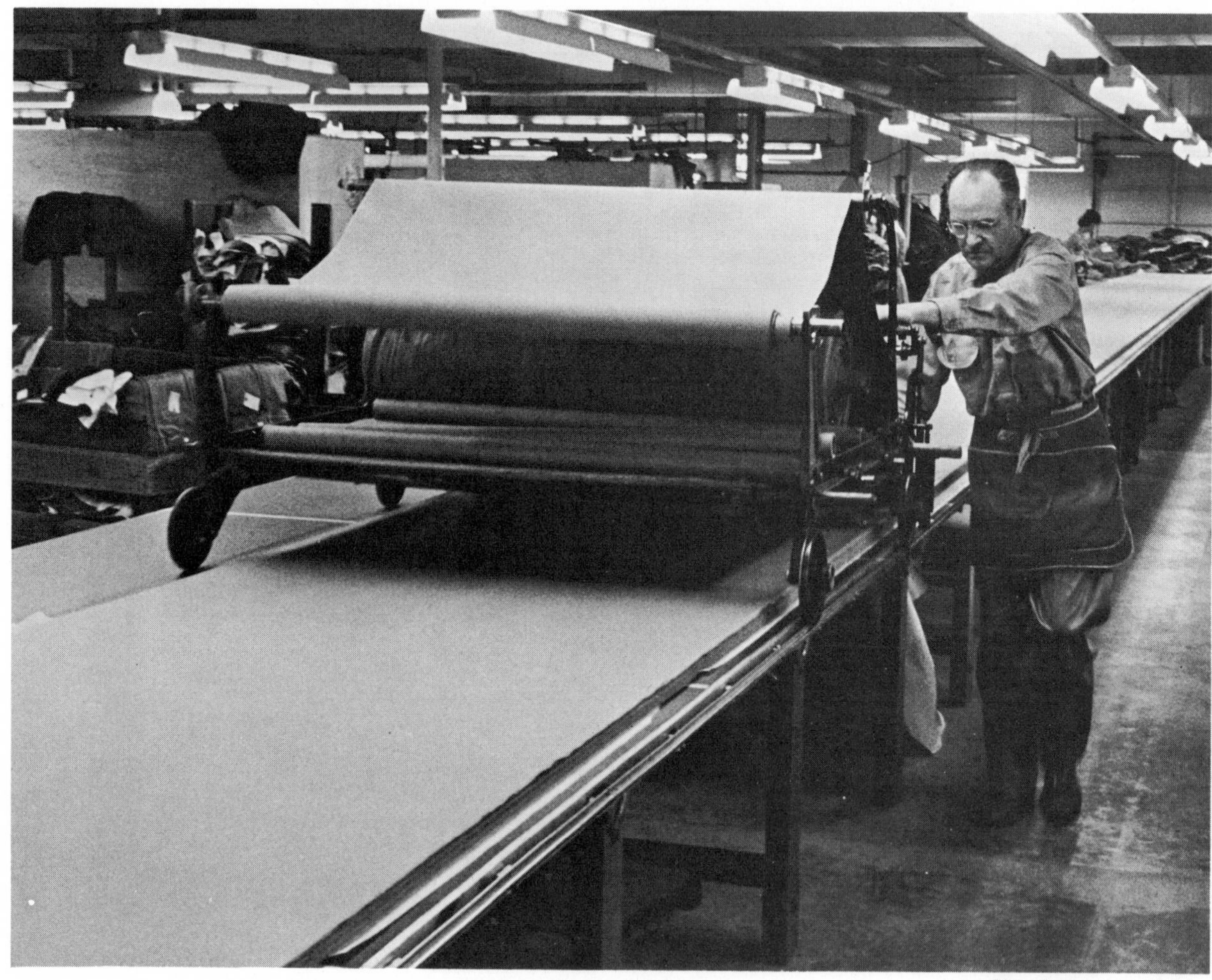

Photo, Courtesy Salant & Salant

1A. Laying out Cloth

1. Cutting. After shading, the rolls of cloth are placed on a buggy that moves on a track down the 60-foot cutting table spreading the cloth behind it. At the end, the cloth is cut and the cycle repeated about 72 times. Meanwhile, the cutter prepares a marker or template on a long roll of paper outlining what is to be cut. The cutters follow the pattern lines with power tools, tie the pieces in bundles, and mark them to ensure pieces will be matched from the same layer.

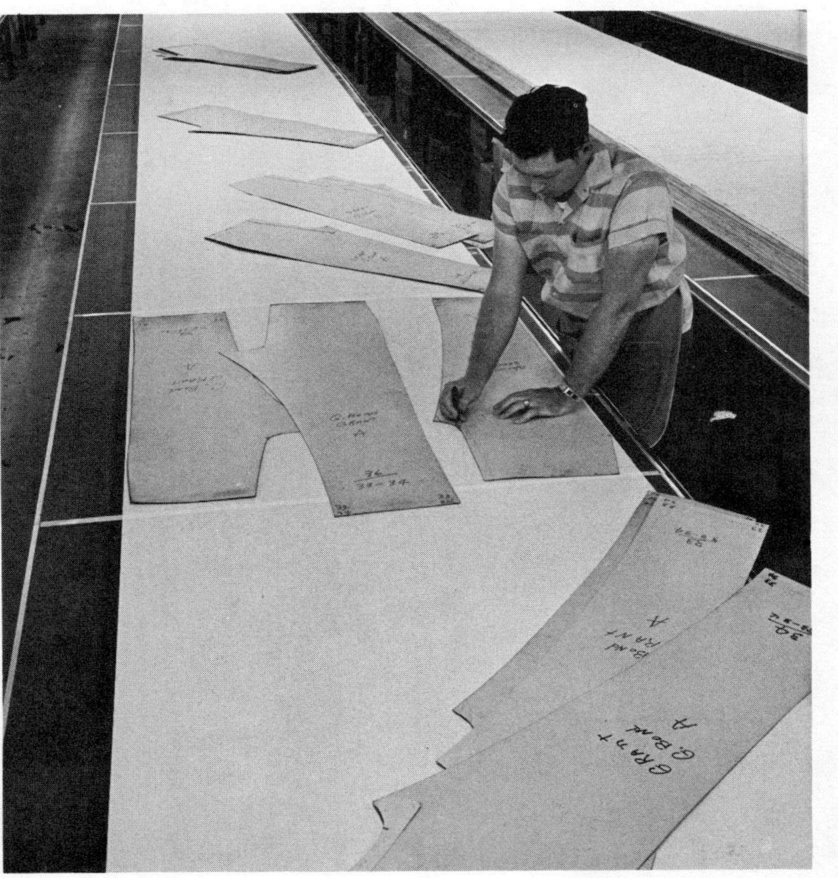

Photo, Courtesy Salant & Salant

1B. Laying out and Marking Pattern

Photo, Courtesy Salant & Salant

1C. Cutting

Photo, Courtesy Salant & Salant

2. General Sewing

2. Sewing Parts. Preparing parts entails a variety of operations of differing skills. One girl cuts zippers from a long roll, while others make belt loops and still others serge the front and back leg pieces to prevent unraveling. About a third of the pants need a crotch piece sewn onto the back leg to decrease the width required. Another group folds, sews, and turns pockets while still another turns, sews, and buttonholes back flaps. White flies are attached to the front pant leg, zippers sewn first to the white fly and then to the left (or black) fly. Finally, a cardboard ticket showing size and style is sewn to the waistband and the hook and eye for the front closure attached. The completed parts are placed in hand carts.

3. Assembly. In this area, carts are moved from girl to girl with each performing only one operation. The front pockets are attached to the front leg piece. The back pockets are attached and the welt and a top reinforcing strip added. The front legs are matched and tacked together. The front and back legs are joined on the side and on the inseam. The seat seam is sewn. The waistband is attached to the legs (a particularly demanding job because the two parts must be fed in evenly to match at the end). The waistband lining, or curtain, is attached with rokap stitching. The bottom of this curtain and the bottom of the belt loops are sewed in by the top stitching operation. The crotch is tacked and a metallic wire strip placed on the bottom of the zipper. The cuffs are turned and hemmed. Finally, the seam bursting operation flattens the inseam and side seams.

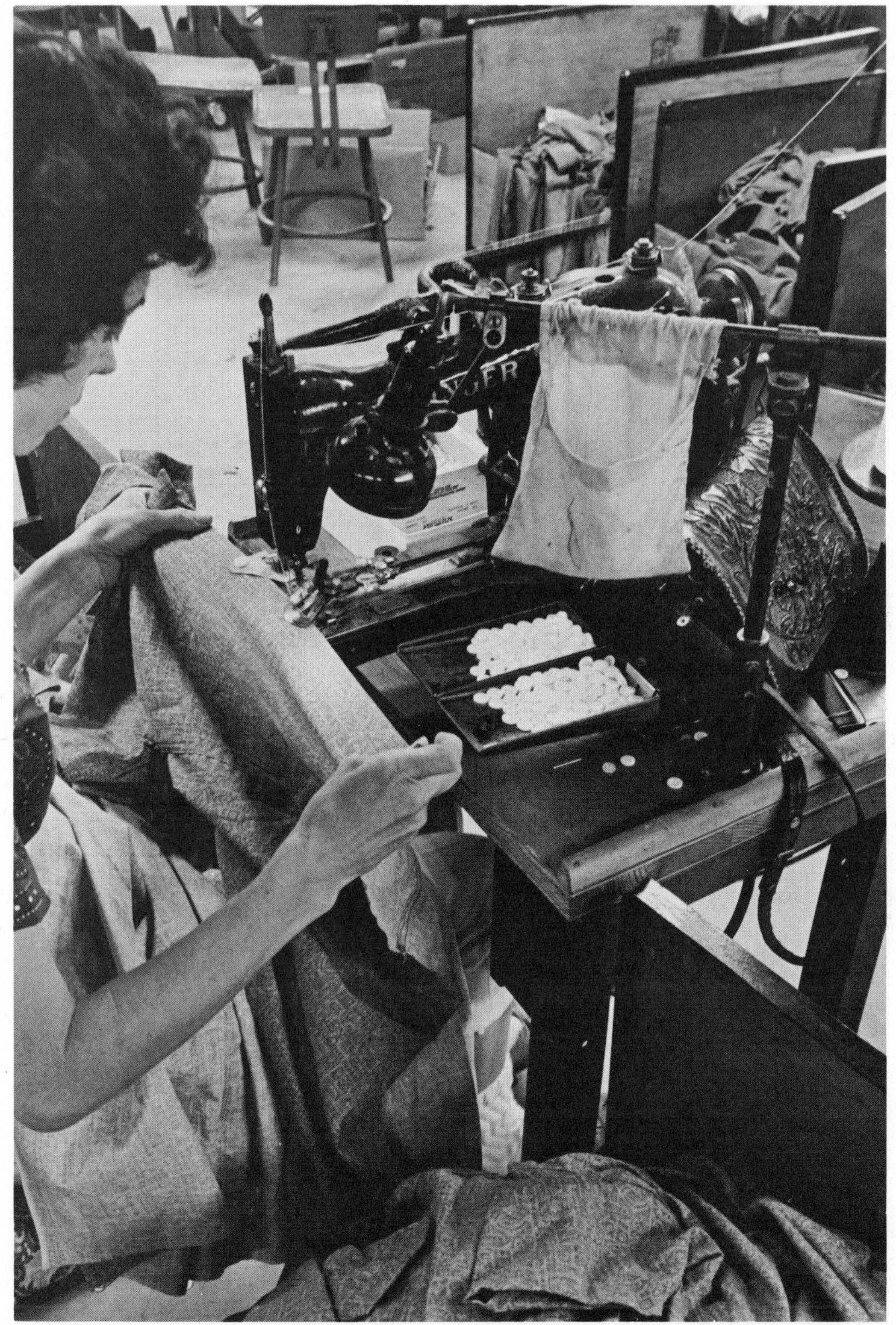

Photo, Courtesy Salant & Salant

4. A Finishing Operation: Sewing Buttons

4. Finishing. The remaining operations are checking size, removing loose threads, inspecting, pressing (one operator does the top part, another the legs), cuff tacking, and final inspection.

EXHIBIT 1
Layout of Columbia Weaving Mill, 1962

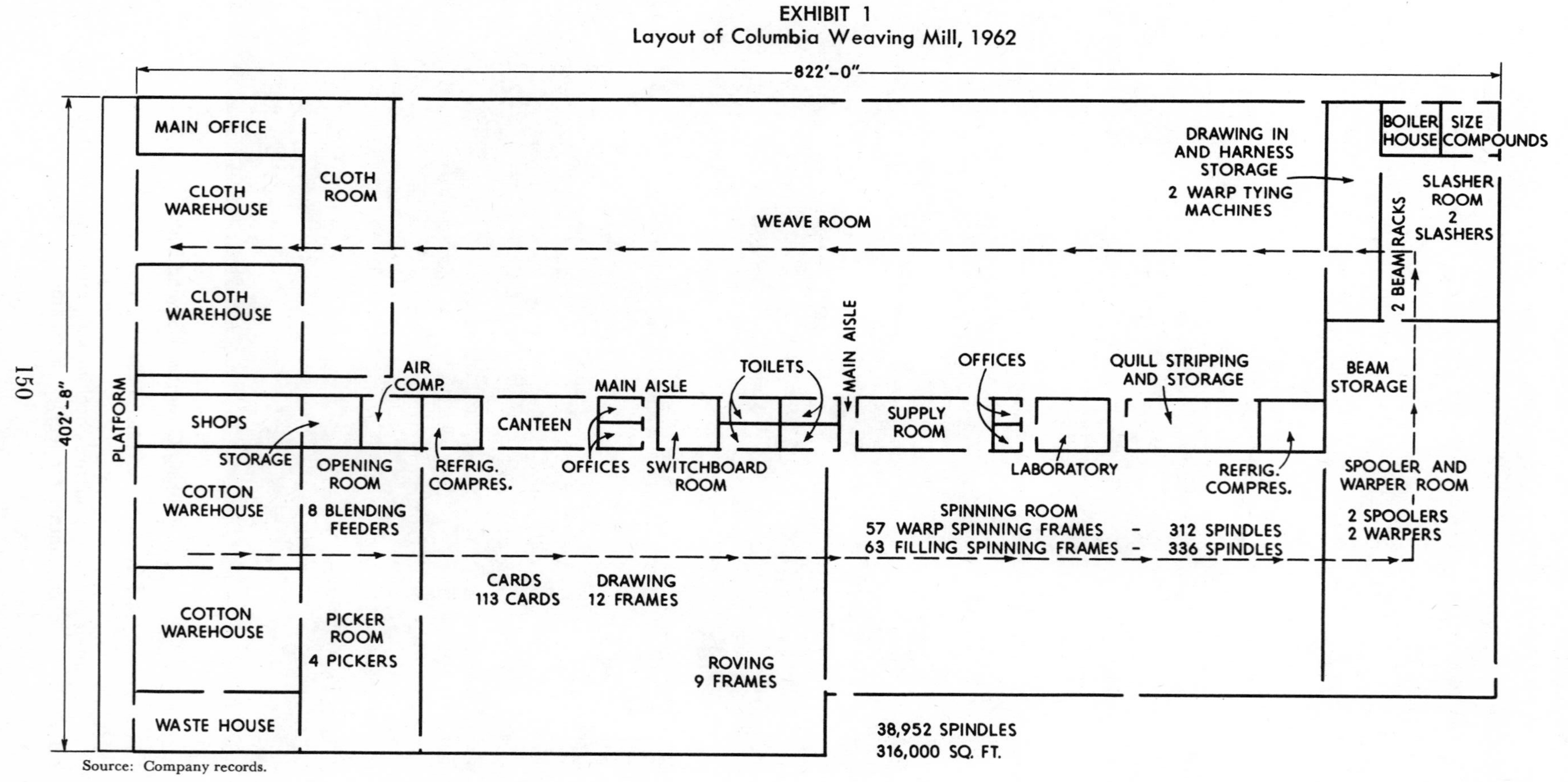

Source: Company records.

EXHIBIT 2

Description of Selected Textile Machinery and Improvements, 1945-1962

	1945	1950	1955	1962
A. YARN MILL				
1) Blender Feeder				
Output*	200 lbs./hr.	200 lbs./hr.	200 lbs./hr.	200 lbs./hr.
Cost	$1,369	$1,775	$2,069	$3,872
Workload	10/operator	10/operator	10/operator	10/operator

Advantages: Speed and workloads same, but new equipment should reduce breakdowns and improve quality by more careful handling.

	1945	1950	1955	1962
2) Pickers				
Output	382 lbs./hr.	382 lbs./hr.	382 lbs./hr.	382 lbs./hr.
Cost	$7,711	$12,457	$14,061	$16,501
Workload	6/operator	6/operator	6/operator	6/operator

Advantages: The change from three to two beaters in 1950 made a simpler system that damaged the fibers less.

	1945	1950	1955	1962
3) Cards				
Output	7 lbs./hr.			10 lbs./hr.
Cost	$2,211	$3,950	$3,950	$5,091
Workload:				
Average	36/operator	48/operator	64/operator	88/operator

Advantages: Assignments permissible with increased weight of picker laps and larger sliver cans lengthening the creeling and doff cycle.

	1945	1950	1955	1962
4) Drawing (per delivery)				
Speed	100 ft./min.			800 ft./min.
Cost	288	$829	$1,500	$2,800
Draft	8	8	8	8
Workload	40 del./opr.	44 del./opr.	32 del./opr.	28 del./opr.
Can size	12" x 36"	12" x 36"	12" x 36"	18" x 42"
Can load	12 lbs.	12 lbs.	12 lbs.	40 lbs.
Can price	$12	$12	$12	$14

Advantages: Major changes in 1955 and 1959 increased speed and improved drafting. Note the materials handling advantages of larger cans.

	1945	1950	1955	1962
5) Lapping				
Output	150 lbs./hr.	150 lbs./hr.	150-190 lbs./hr.	500 lbs./hr.
Draft	1.09	1.09	1.09	2.4
Lap weight	10 lbs.	10 lbs.	10 lbs.	30 lbs.
Cost	$4,956	$7,804	$9,610	$11,500

Advantages: The 1959 lapper eliminated the sliver and ribbon lappers with the result of greatly increased output, more draft, and a smoother, evener yarn.

*Outputs are for an 80-square print cloth [39" $\frac{80 \text{ x } 80}{31\text{'sw x } 41\text{'s F}}$] although the yarn mill poundage approximate the amounts from counts five higher or lower than a 31 or a 41.

Exhibit 2 (continued)

	1945	1950	1955	1962
6) Combing (8 head frames)				
Output	28 lbs./hr.	30 lbs./hr.	33 lbs./hr.	45 lbs./hr.
Speed	100 nips/min.	150 nips/min.	150 nips/min.	150 nips/min.
Lap weight	700 grains/yd.	750 grains/yd.	850 grains/yd.	1,000 grains/yd.
Yield	82-85%	90-95%	90-95%	90-95%
Cost	$3,775	$7,800	$9,882	$13,335
Workload	36 heads/oper.	48 heads/oper.	64 heads/oper.	64-80 heads/oper.

Advantages: The major advance came in 1958 with a unit that combined better quality with increased production and yield.

	1945	1950	1955	1962
7) Roving (96 spindles)				
Output-warp	1.01 lbs./spdle./hr.	1.01 lbs./spdle./hr.	1.15 lbs./spdle./hr.	1.53 lbs./spdle./hr.
Output-filling	.696 lbs./spdle./hr.	.696 lbs./spdle./hr.	.795 lbs./spdle./hr.	1.06 lbs./spdle./hr.
Speed	660 rpm	660 rpm	750 rpm	1,200 rpm
Package size	46 oz.	64 oz.	80 oz.	90 oz.
Cost	$8,450	$9,727	$12,227	$20,193
Workload	240 spin/oper.	288 spin/oper.	384 spin/oper.	480 spin/oper.

Advantages: Major change between 1950-1960 was increasing package size; the 1962 model was a redesigned version with new flyers and other components.

	1945	1950	1955	1962
8) Spinning (288 spindles)				
Output-warp	.0219 lbs./spin/hr.	.0232 lbs./spin/hr.	.0258 lbs./spin/hr.	.0347 lbs./spin/hr.
Output-filling	.0154 lbs./spin/hr.	.0163 lbs./spin/hr.	.0192 lbs./spin/hr.	.0222 lbs./spin/hr.
Spindle Speed				
-warp	8,500 rpm	9,000 rpm	10,000 rpm	11,000 rpm
-filling	8,000 rpm	8,500 rpm	9,000 rpm	11,500 rpm
Cost	$4,895	$10,025	$11,576	($18,642-"K" frames ($11,356-"N" frames
Workload				
-warp	2,000 spin/oper.	2,400 spin/oper.	2,600 spin/oper.	6,000 spin/oper.
-filling	3,000 spin/oper.	3,500 spin/oper.	4,000 spin/oper.	5,000 spin/oper.

B. WEAVING MILL

1) Looms	X-2	X-2	X-2	X-3
Speed	185 picks/min.	185 picks/min.	195 picks/min.	212 picks/min.
Cloth width	39"	39"	45"	47.5"
Cost	$700	$700	$1,500	$2,000
Workload	60 looms/weaver	60 looms/weaver	80 looms/weaver	100 looms/weaver
	60 looms/fixer	60 looms/fixer	80 looms/fixer	100 looms/fixer

Advantages: The X-3 increases quality with a center fork filling motion that stops the loom on the pick that the thread breaks rather than run over a pick. The automatic let-off increases fabric uniformity, while the improved drive allows greater fixer loads. Yarn beam diameter increased from 26" to 28".

EXHIBIT 3

Cost of Fixed Assets at Date of Acquisition (Shown in Parentheses)

1. Land (1962)	$ 20,000
2. Grading and Yard Improvements (1962)	130,000
3. Building (1962)	3,690,000
4. Opening Equipment	
a. Eight blenders @ $1,369 each (1945)	10,700
b. Cleaner (1962)	4,400
c. Auxiliary equipment and supplies (1945)	5,600
5. Picking	
a. Four pickers @ $7,711 each (1945)	30,850
b. Auxiliary equipment and supplies (1945)	15,000
c. Overhead conveyor (1962)	10,000
6. Carding	
a. 113 cards @ $2,211 each (1945)	249,850
b. 113 motors, drives (1945)	28,250
c. 113 metallic clothing @ $820 each (1962)	90,400
d. Auxiliary equipment and supplies (1945)	2,000
7. Drawing	
a. 12 draw frames (24 deliv. total) @ $2,800 each (1962)	67,200
b. 2,000 cans @ $18.40 each (1962)	38,000
8. Roving	
a. Nine frames @ $20,193 each (1962)	181,737
b. Auxiliary equipment (1962)	15,000
c. 97,400 bobbins @ $700/1,000 (1962)	68,000
9. Spinning	
a. 57 warp frames of 312 spindles each @ $13,619 each (1962) filling frames of 366 spindles each @ $13,828 each (1962)	1,647,500
b. Automatic doffing (1962)	195,000
c. Warp tubes and 60,000 filling bobbins (inc. 30,000 reserve bobbins) (1962)	26,300
10. Spooling and Warping	
a. Two spoolers, two warpers (1962)	225,000
b. Warp beams and auxiliary equipment (1962)	17,500
11. Slashing	
a. Two slashers (1962)	56,600
b. Size preparation equipment and exhaust system (1962)	8,500
12. Weaving	
a. 1,205, 39.4" Draper x-2 looms @ $700 (1945)	843,500
b. Extra harnesses, reeds, etc. (1945)	40,000
c. Auxiliary equipment (1945)	6,000
13. Tying-in	
a. 2 tie-in machines (1945)	7,500

Exhibit 3 (continued)

14.	Cloth Room	
	a. Three shearing machines @$4,000 each (1945)	$ 12,000
	b. 13 inspection machines @ $1,000 each (1945)	13,000
	c. Folders, balers, brushers, etc. (1945)	20,000
	d. Overhead conveyor (1962)	5,500
15.	Machine Shop	
	a. Two lathes, one plain miller (1962)	53,000
	b. Welder, gear hobber, drills, etc. (1945)	15,000
16.	Warehouse and Yard	
	a. Truck, scale (1962)	12,600
17.	Office (1962)	12,000
18.	Laboratory (1962)	25,000

Source: Company records.

EXHIBIT 4

Estimated Production and Waste Losses at Capacity on 80-Square Print Cloth

	31's	Pounds per 144 Hours	41's
Baled Cotton			
Baled Cotton		180,000	
Bagging, ties, etc., Waste @ 3.33%		6,000	
Open Cotton		174,000	
Opening and Picking Waste @ 3.0%		5,220	
Picker Production		168,780	
Card Waste, Strips @ 1.5% (metallic wire)		2,532	
Fly 2.0%		3,376	
Card Production		162,872	
Drawing Waste @ .25%		407	
Drawing Production		162,465	
Roving Waste @ 1.5%		2,437	
Roving Production		160,028	
	91,216		68,812
Spinning Waste @ 2.5%		4,001	
Spinning Production		156,027	
	88,935		67,092
Spooling, Warping and Slashing Waste @ 2.0%		1,779	
Production before Regain for Sizing		154,248	
	87,156		67,092
Size Regain @ 13% on Warp		11,330	
Production entering Weave Room		165,578	
Weaving and Cloth Room Waste @ .5%		828	
Weaving Production		164,750	

Source: Company records.

EXHIBIT 5

Labor Costs for Each Operation, 1962

A. Operation: Opening, Picking, Carding, Drawing, Roving

Employees	Hourly Rate Shift 1-2	Hourly Rate Shift 3	Employees Shift 1	Employees Shift 2	Employees Shift 3	Amount
Overseer	Salaried		One for 3 Shifts			
Second Hand	2.25	2.30	1	1	1	$ 353.60
Opener Tenders) Picker Tenders)	1.30	1.35	1	1	1	205.40
Card Tenders	1.36	1.41	1	1	1	214.76
Man to tend 25 cards, strip every 60 hours, remove waste, clean cards and sweep, etc.	1.36	1.41	1	1	1	214.76
Section man to make settings and maintain cards	1.80	1.85	1	1	1	283.40
Drawing Tenders	1.48	1.53	1	1	1	233.48
Roving Tenders	1.60	1.65	2	2	2	504.40
Overhauler	1.65		1	0	0	85.80
Overhauler Helper	1.30		1	0	0	67.60
Total			10	8	8	$2,163.20

B. Operation: Spinning

Employees	Hourly Rate Shift 1-2	Hourly Rate Shift 3	Employees Shift 1	Employees Shift 2	Employees Shift 3	Amount
Overseer	Salaried					
Second Hand	2.25	2.30	1	1	1	$ 353.60
Spinners:						
Warp	1.42	1.47	3	3	3	672.36
Filling	1.42	1.47	4	4	4	896.48
Roll Pickers	1.25	-	2	0	0	100.0 5 days only - 40 Hours
Doffers:						
Warp	1.56	1.61	2	2	2	491.92)AUDO-MAC
Filling	1.56	1.61	2	2	2	491.92)Automatic Doffer
Section Man	1.80	1.85	1	1	1	283.40
Roving Man	1.25	1.30	1	1	1	197.60
Overhaulers	1.60		2	0	0	166.40 (8 Hrs. Downtime per Frame)
Overhauler Helper	1.25		2	0	0	130.00
Steel Roll Cleaner	1.25		3			195.00
Yarn Hauler	1.25	1.30	1	1	1	197.60
Sweepers	1.25		0	0	0	000.00 (Not required with AUDOMAC)
Traveler Changer	1.25		1	0	0	65.00
Total			25	15	15	$4,241.28

Exhibit 5 (continued)

C. Operation: Spooling and Warping

Employees	Hourly Rate Shift 1-2	Hourly Rate Shift 3	Employees Shift 1	Employees Shift 2	Employees Shift 3	Amount
Second Hand	Combined with spinning or weaving.					
Section Hand	1.80	1.85	1	1	1	$ 283.40
Spooler Girls	1.43		4	4		594.88
Warper Tenders	1.44		1	1		149.76
Assistant Warper Tenders	1.25		1	1		130.00
Yarn Distributors	1.25	1.30	1	1	1	197.60
Total			8	8	2	$1,355.64

D. Operation: Slashing and Tying-In

Employees	Hourly Rate Shift 1-2	Hourly Rate Shift 3	Employees Shift 1	Employees Shift 2	Employees Shift 3	Amount
Slasher Man	1.50		1	1		$ 156.00
Slasher Helper	1.35		1	1		140.40
Drawing-In-Hands	1.60		1	0	0	83.20
Tying-In-Hands	1.73	1.78	1	1	1	272.48
Total			4	3	1	$ 652.08

E. Operation: Weaving

Employees	Hourly Rate Shift 1-2	Hourly Rate Shift 3	Employees Shift 1	Employees Shift 2	Employees Shift 3	Amount
Second Hand	2.25	2.30	1	1	1	$ 353.60
Weavers	1.71	1.76	15	15	15	4,040.40
Loom Fixers	1.89	1.94	15	15	15	4,461.60
Battery Hands	1.33	1.38	10	10	10	2,100.80
Smash Hands	1.40	1.45	2	2	2	442.00
Cloth Doffers	1.25	1.30	1	1	1	197.60
Warp Hanger (Lease out man)	1.50	1.55	2	2	2	473.20
Greaser	1.25	1.30	1	1	1	197.60
Sweeper	1.25	1.30	1	1	1	197.60
Blow Off Men	1.25	1.30	1	1	1	197.60
Harness Cleaners	1.25		1			65.00
Quill Stripper	1.25	1.30	1	1	1	197.60
Filling Grate Cleaner	1.25	1.30	1	1	1	197.60
Overhauler	1.89		1	0	0	99.28
Total			53	51	51	$13,221.48

F. Operation: Cloth Room

Employees	Hourly Rate Shift 1-2	Hourly Rate Shift 3	Employees Shift 1	Employees Shift 2	Employees Shift 3	Amount
Overseer	Salaried					
Second Hand			0			
Shear, brush, rolling range operator (130 yds. min.)	1.45		3			$ 226.20
Inspectors	1.45		12			904.80
Folder Operators	1.45		3			226.20
Cloth Graders	1.45		4			301.60
Baler	1.45		2			150.80
Cloth Man, utility helper, etc.	1.45		1			75.40
Total			25			$1,885.00

Exhibit 5 (continued)

G. Operation: Warehouse, Yard

Employees	Hourly Rate Shift		Employees Shift			Amount
	1-2	3	1	2	3	
Foreman	2.25		One for 3 shifts			$ 117.00
Supply Clerks	1.54	1.59	1	1	1	242.84
Laborers	1.25	1.30	3	2	2	460.20
Total			4	3	3	$ 820.04

H. Operation: Machine Shop

Employees	Hourly Rate Shift		Employees Shift			Amount
	1-2	3	1	2	3	
Master Mechanic-Electrician	Salaried					
Machinists	1.81		2	0	0	$ 188.24
Millwright	1.81		1	0	0	94.12
Mechanics	1.81	1.86	0	1	1	190.84
Electrician and Utility	1.81	1.86	0	1	1	190.84
Total			3	2	2	$ 664.04

I. Operation: Laboratory

Employees	Hourly Rate Shift		Employees Shift			Amount
	1-2	3	1	2	3	
4 Employees	1.50		4	0	0	$ 312.00

EXHIBIT 6

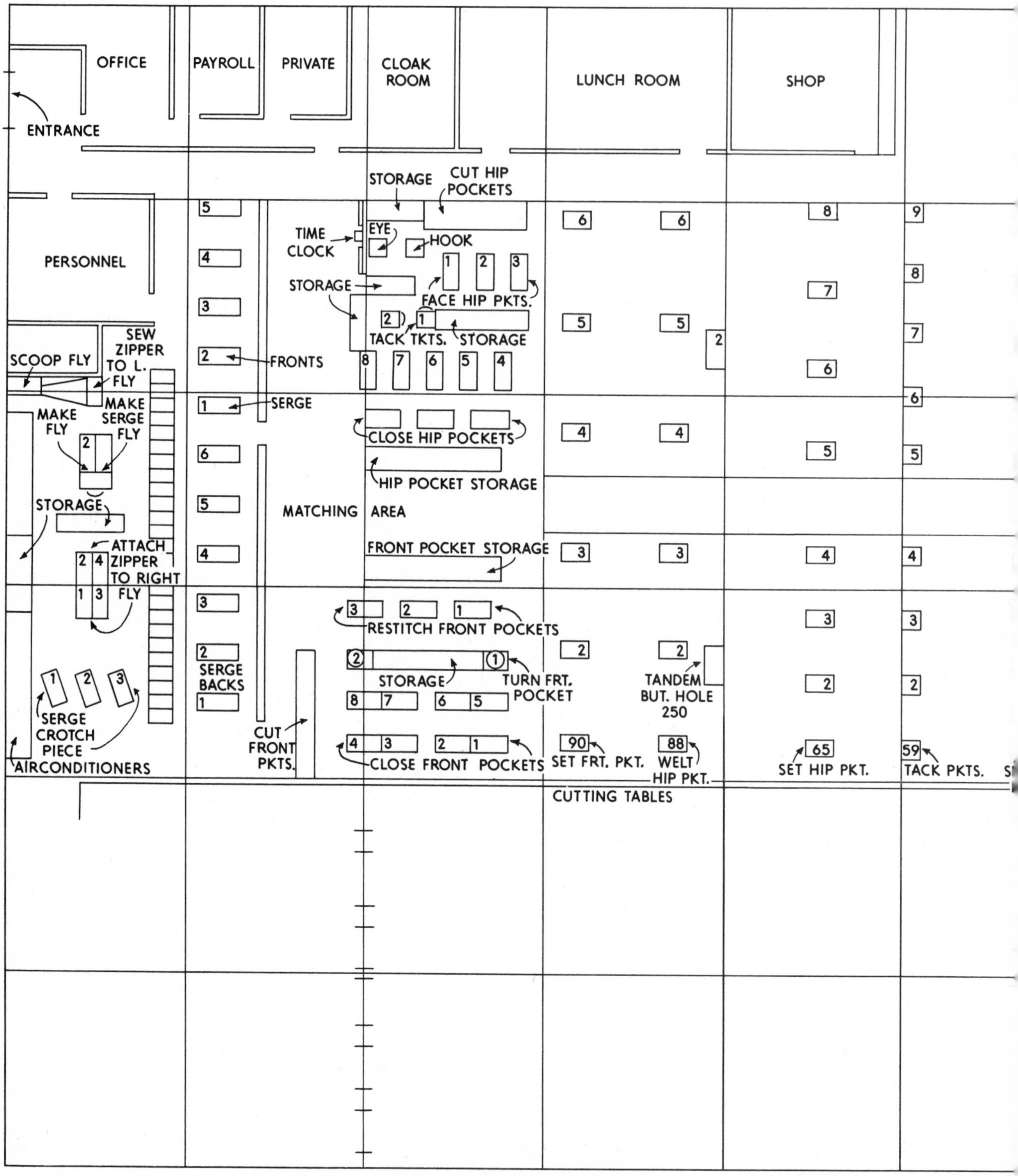

SALANT & SALANT INC. LEXINGTON TENN.
500 DOZEN MEN'S UNIVERSITY
SCALE: 1/16 IN. = 1 FT.

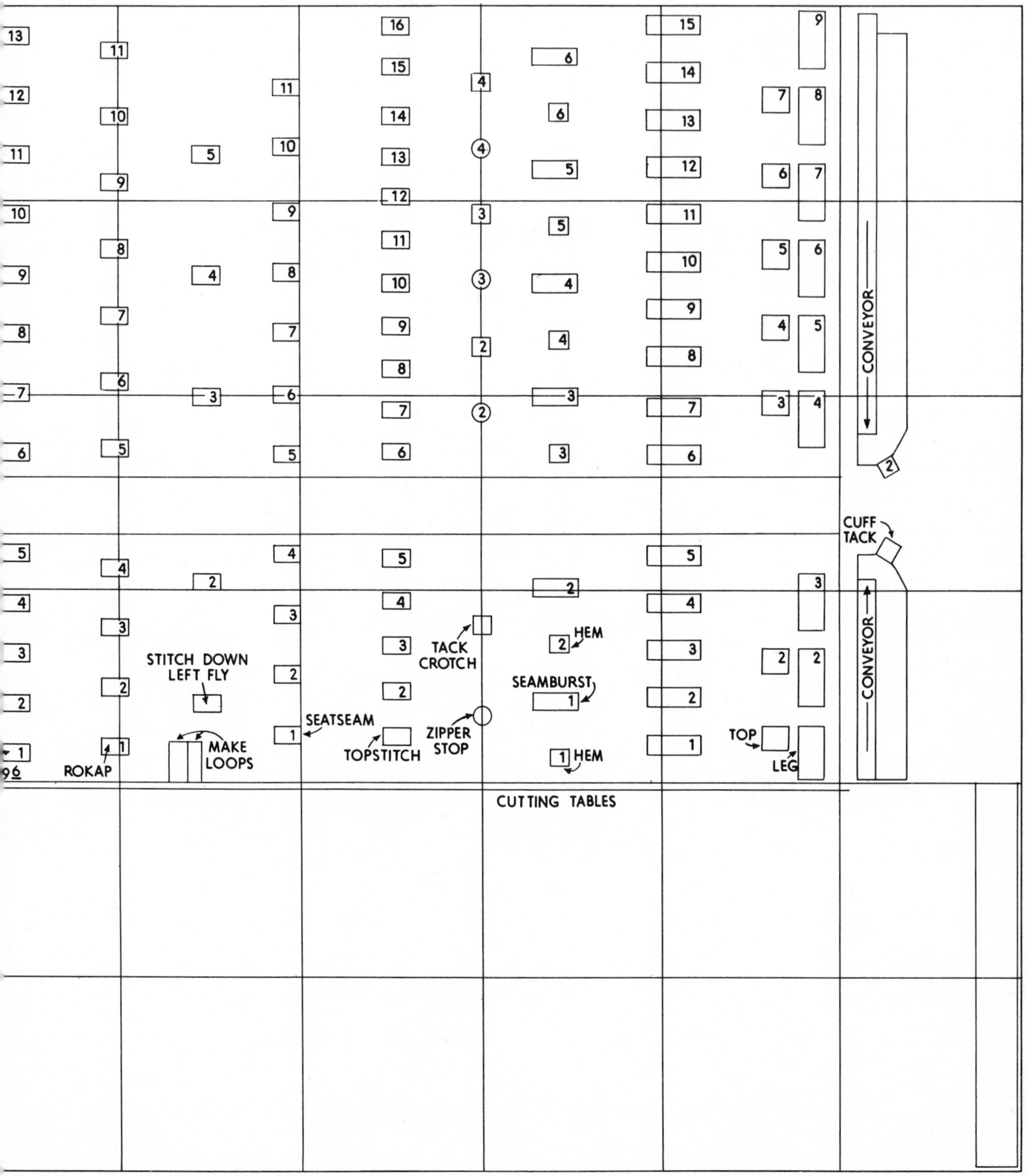

CONVEYOR
CUFF TACK
CONVEYOR
STITCH DOWN LEFT FLY
MAKE LOOPS
ROKAP
SEATSEAM
TOPSTITCH
TACK CROTCH
ZIPPER STOP
HEM
SEAMBURST
HEM
TOP
LEG
CUTTING TABLES

EXHIBIT 7

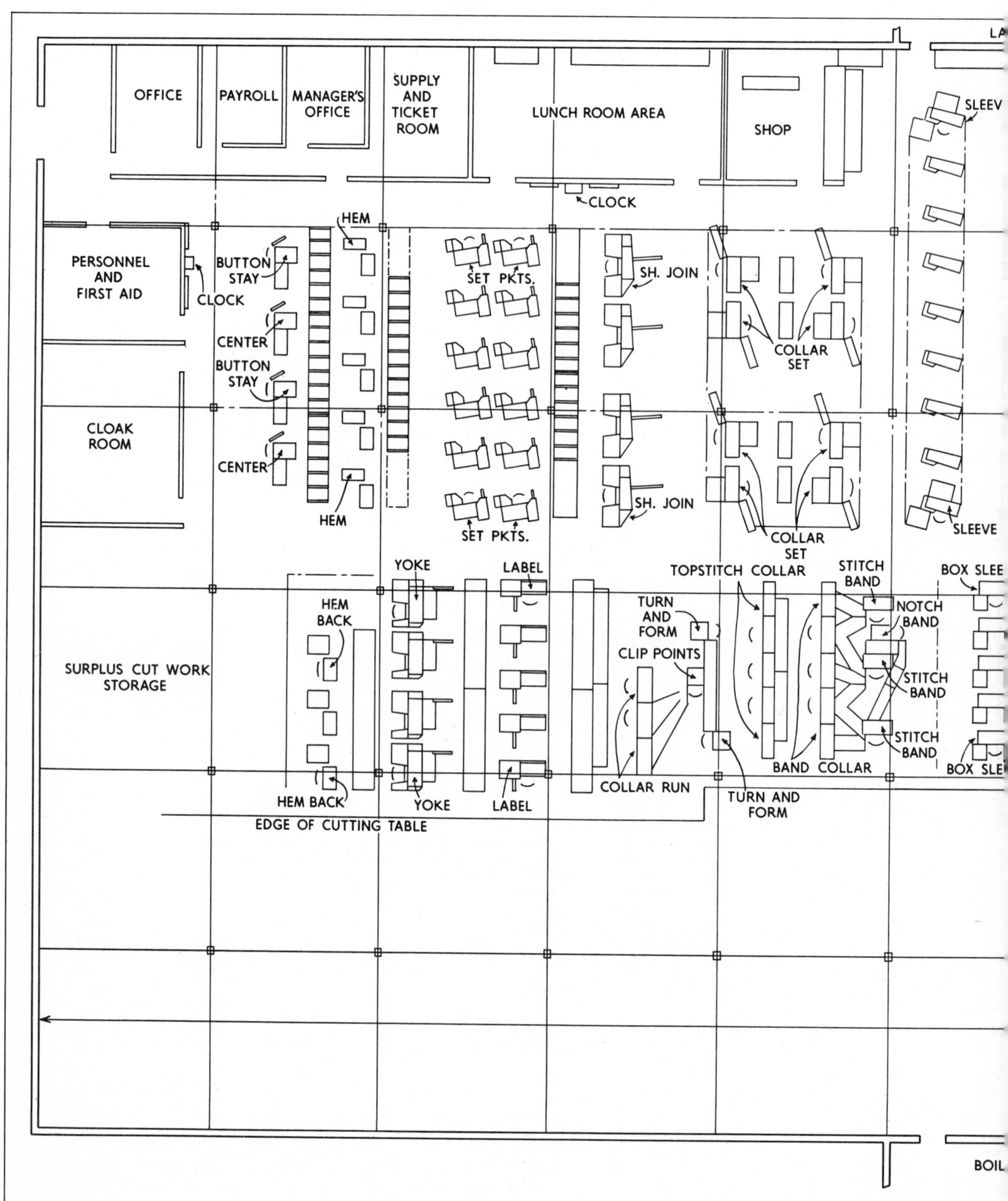

OFFICE
PAYROLL
MANAGER'S OFFICE
SUPPLY AND TICKET ROOM
LUNCH ROOM AREA
SHOP
CLOCK
PERSONNEL AND FIRST AID
CLOCK
BUTTON STAY
CENTER
BUTTON STAY
CENTER
HEM
HEM
CLOAK ROOM
SET PKTS.
SET PKTS.
SH. JOIN
SH. JOIN
COLLAR SET
COLLAR SET
SLEEVE
SURPLUS CUT WORK STORAGE
HEM BACK
HEM BACK
YOKE
YOKE
LABEL
LABEL
TOPSTITCH COLLAR
TURN AND FORM
CLIP POINTS
COLLAR RUN
TURN AND FORM
STITCH BAND
NOTCH BAND
STITCH BAND
STITCH BAND
BAND COLLAR
BOX SLEE
BOX SLE
EDGE OF CUTTING TABLE
BOIL

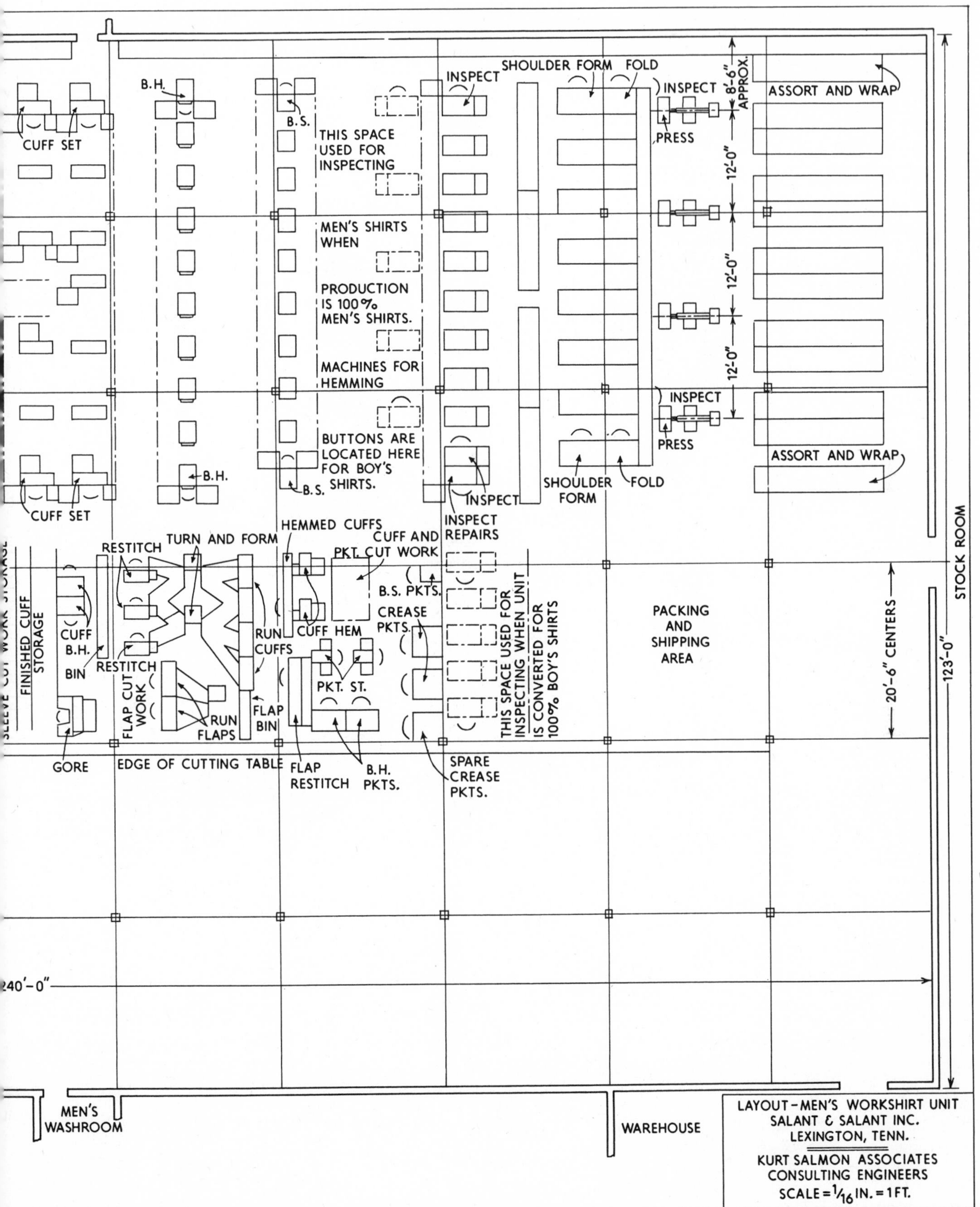
B.H.
CUFF SET
B.S.
THIS SPACE USED FOR INSPECTING MEN'S SHIRTS WHEN PRODUCTION IS 100% MEN'S SHIRTS. MACHINES FOR HEMMING BUTTONS ARE LOCATED HERE FOR BOY'S SHIRTS.
INSPECT
SHOULDER FORM
FOLD
INSPECT
8'-6" APPROX.
ASSORT AND WRAP
PRESS
12'-0"
12'-0"
12'-0"
INSPECT
PRESS
ASSORT AND WRAP
B.H.
B.S.
CUFF SET
INSPECT
SHOULDER FORM
FOLD
INSPECT REPAIRS
HEMMED CUFFS
CUFF AND PKT. CUT WORK
TURN AND FORM
RESTITCH
SLEEVE CUT WORK STORAGE
FINISHED CUFF STORAGE
CUFF B.H. BIN
RESTITCH
FLAP CUT WORK
RUN FLAPS
RUN CUFFS
FLAP BIN
CUFF HEM
B.S. PKTS.
CREASE PKTS.
PKT. ST.
THIS SPACE USED FOR INSPECTING WHEN UNIT IS CONVERTED FOR 100% BOY'S SHIRTS
PACKING AND SHIPPING AREA
20'-6" CENTERS
123'-0"
STOCK ROOM
GORE
EDGE OF CUTTING TABLE
FLAP RESTITCH
B.H. PKTS.
SPARE CREASE PKTS.
240'-0"
MEN'S WASHROOM
WAREHOUSE
LAYOUT-MEN'S WORKSHIRT UNIT
SALANT & SALANT INC.
LEXINGTON, TENN.
KURT SALMON ASSOCIATES
CONSULTING ENGINEERS
SCALE = 1/16 IN. = 1 FT.

Cotton Textile Industry Reference Notes

The textile industry represents one of the largest and most important manufacturing activities in the United States. In 1961 textile mill products (spinning, weaving, dyeing, and finishing) accounted for 5.7 percent of all manufacturing employees (916 thousand out of 15,878 thousand) and 3.6 percent of manufacturing national income ($4,346 million out of $121,704 million). The apparel, or cutting-up trade, had 7.5 percent (1,198 thousand) of manufacturing employees and 4.05 percent ($4,940 million) of manufacturing national income.[1]

The 1958 Census of Manufacturers presented a more complete picture. Textile mill products and apparel combined ranked (*a*) first in the number of plants having 20 or more employees; (*b*) first in the number of employees on the payroll; (*c*) fourth in dollar volume of the payroll; (*d*) first in the number of production workers; (*e*) first in the number of production man-hours; (*f*) third in total wages paid production workers; (*g*) sixth in value added by manufacturing; and (*h*) eleventh in capital expenditures for new equipment. Comparative figures for 1958 given in Exhibit 1 indicate the relative size of segments of the industry.

Since 1947 the textile industry has failed to keep pace with the enormous growth of the U.S. economy, as is indicated in Exhibit 2. The reasons for the static output shown in Exhibit 3 were many and included:

1. The proportion of personal consumption expenditures allocated to clothing and accessories[2] fell steadily from 9.4 percent in 1947 to 7.1 percent in 1961.
2. The shift in consumer demand from natural to lighter weight synthetic fibers resulted in lower per capita consumption[3] (see Exhibit 3-A).
3. Chronic overcapacity that had plagued the industry since 1932 continued (see Exhibit 3-B).
4. While the wholesale price index for nonfarm products rose from 95.3 in 1947 to 127.2 in 1962, the textile products and apparel index declined from 100.1 to 95.1 (see Exhibit 4).
5. As shown in Exhibit 4-A, fiber and labor were the most important costs and for the most part they continued to rise. The fluctuating trend for fiber and yarn prices is shown in Exhibit 6, while selected hourly earnings are shown in Exhibit 4-B. The rise in labor cost was to some extent offset by increased worker productivity. For example, in the basic textile industry (spinning and weaving), hourly earnings rose from $1.07 to $1.34 or 34 percent between 1947 and 1957, but over the same period yards per man-hour increased from 7.8 to 11.6 or almost 49 percent.[4]
6. Competition from foreign countries and from nontextile products, especially plastics and paper, increased. Both these topics are discussed at the end of this note.

Despite stiff competition from man-mades, cotton is still the major textile fiber, with 58.7 percent of mill consumption poundage in 1962, and the most important division of both the textile products and apparel groups. This note will summarize the cotton textile segment of the industry under the following headings: (1) manufacture of cotton textiles; (2) marketing of cotton textiles; (3) problems of the cotton textile industry; and (4) current trends and developments.

Exhibit 7 presents summary statistics on cotton equipment, operation, and market during the period 1946–1960.

MANUFACTURE OF COTTON TEXTILES

The manufacture of cotton textiles usually involves four major operations: (*a*) the spin-

[1] U.S. Department of Commerce, *Survey of Current Business*, July, 1962.

[2] According to the annual surveys of textile end uses made by *Textile Organon*, apparel accounted for about 40 percent of fiber consumption in pounds. With the addition of apparel linings, piece goods and narrow fabrics (substantial amounts of which were used in clothing), this percentage rose to approximately 50 percent, 1957–1960.

[3] Textile consumption = mill fiber consumption, plus imports minus exports of manufactured and semimanufactured textile products.

[4] *Problems of the Domestic Textile Industry*, Hearings . . . Pursuant to S. Res. 287, Part 2, p. 949.

ning of cotton into yarn, (*b*) the weaving of yarn into cloth, (*c*) the dyeing, printing, or finishing of the cloth, and (*d*) the cutting and sewing of the cloth to produce garments or other finished products. The relationship of processes to products is indicated in Exhibit 8 and selected statistics are given in Exhibit 1.

1. *Spinning and Weaving Mills:* Spinning and weaving operations are carried out in three types of mills: specialized spinning mills which limit their activities to the spinning of yarn, specialized weaving mills which engage only in weaving, and combined mills which do both spinning and weaving. In number of mills and volume of output, the combined mills are by far the most important.

Since the mid-1920's the majority of the spindles and looms have been in the South; by 1958 this preponderance was over 88 percent of the spindles and over 76 percent of the looms. South Carolina led with 30 percent and 32 percent, respectively. The combined spinning and weaving mills, that produced an estimated 80 percent in pounds of cotton spun and woven, were almost all in the South. Likewise the specialized spinners, that concentrated on a narrow range of yarns for fabric or tire cord, were Southern. The specialized weavers, on the other hand, were grouped mostly in Pennsylvania. They tended to concentrate on one or two products such as drapes, towels, or rugs.

The size of individual mills varies a great deal. A mill with less than 25,000 spindles would be regarded as small, a mill with 25,000 to 60,000 spindles as medium size, and a mill with over 60,000 spindles as large. Moreover, a 1953 analysis of the size of individual spinning mills indicated that more than half the plants still had less than 60,000 spindles, two thirds less than 70,000, and 90 percent less than 120,000 spindles. The number of looms in a particular mill depends upon the type of goods woven. For mills weaving fine goods the spindle-loom ratio is about 50 to 1, for mills weaving prints and narrow sheeting about 40 to 1, and for mills weaving osnaburgs and similar fabrics about 30 to 1.

In both spinning and weaving, the individual unit is small in terms of the total market. In 1958, the four largest companies shipped 26 percent of the dollar value of cotton yarn, the eight largest 40 percent, and the twenty largest 56 percent. For weaving, the four largest shipped 18 percent of the total value, the eight largest 29 percent, and the twenty largest 49 percent.

The output of the combined and most of the specialized weaving mills is broad woven cotton or cotton blend fabrics. The most important of these cloths are shown in Exhibit 9-A; each may be produced in a variety of different constructions. Prices for one construction, the "80 square" print cloth, are given in Exhibit 10. Textile merchants regard this cloth as the "bellwether" of the cotton broadcloth business and follow the price and volume trends closely.

Despite this fairly high degree of specialization, roughly 75 percent of the production in the cotton goods industry consists of fabrics that can be produced on the equipment found in any standard cotton mill. Of course, as the yarn count changes, the equipment balance shifts; however, as an old rule of thumb a mill can stray with a range of five counts either side of its "balance fabric" without carrying idle equipment.

The various fabrics produced by the combined mills are sold for three major purposes: for manufacture into clothing, for manufacture into household goods, and for industrial use. The distribution between 1949–1961 is given in Exhibits 13 and 8. There are no hard and fast distinctions between the fabrics used in one market as opposed to those used in the other markets; frequently a single fabric will find applications in all three fields.

2. *Finishing Plants:* About 84 percent of the output of the weaving mills consists of grey goods; the remaining 16 percent consists of colored yarn fabrics. The colored yarn fabrics (woven from dyed yarns) are in finished form when they leave the looms and may be sold without further processing. Of the grey goods, about 10 percent find applications in the grey form. The remainder, however, must be dyed, bleached, printed, or otherwise finished before it can be put to use.

Finishing plants, the majority of which are located in the Middle Atlantic States, are of three types: bleacheries which bleach and finish; dye works which bleach, dye, and finish; and print works which usually bleach, dye, finish, and print. In number of plants, the dye works represent the largest category. The finishing plants tend to specialize on certain types of fabrics, a certain range of finishes, and a particular quality of work. The extent of the specialization, however, is much less than in the case of the spinning and weaving mills.

Concentration resembled that of the spinners and weavers. In 1958 the four largest companies accounted for 24 percent of the total dollar shipments, the eight largest 32 percent, and the twenty largest 48 percent.

Finishing plants, and print works in particular, require a relatively larger volume of output to operate economically than do spinning and weaving mills. It has been estimated that a print works requires a capital investment of at least $700,000 and the yarn output from about 250,000 spindles to operate economically.

The majority of a finishing plant's output is on a commission basis. For example, about 60 percent of the 7.4 billion linear yards processed in finishing plants in 1954 were produced on commission for goods owned by textile converters. For the cotton goods owned by the finishing plants themselves, 67 percent were bleached, 27 percent were plain dyed, and 5 percent were printed. For the cotton goods finished on commission, however, 26 percent were bleached, 33 percent were plain dyed, and 40 percent were printed. The difference between owned and commission finishing was also striking for synthetic broad woven goods. There were 2.2 billion linear yards of broad woven synthetics processed in 1954, of which 95 percent was on commission. For the synthetic goods finished on commission, 8 percent were bleached, 77 percent plain dyed, and 15 percent were printed.

3. *Cutters:* The work of cutting and sewing cloth to manufacture wearing apparel, household articles, and other finished products is done by cutters. Although there were almost four times as many cutting-up plants as there were textile plants in the United States, their average size was considerably smaller than a typical weaving plant. In 1954, there were 8,082 plants in the textile mill products group, 28 percent of which had more than 100 employees. There were 31,334 plants in the apparel products group, only 8 percent of which had more than 100 employees.

The cotton garment cutters are the largest single factor in the apparel industry. It is estimated that they account for about one third of the total apparel plants. The principal products of the cotton garment plants, in order of number of workers employed, are: men's shirts, women's cotton dresses, overalls, work pants, work shirts, semidress pants, and pajamas. As a general rule, cutters tend to specialize on particular products and on particular grades of work.

Unlike the other apparel plants, the cotton-garment plants are not concentrated in New York, Chicago, or Philadelphia, but are scattered all over the country and are most frequently located in small towns. The production of certain garments is, however, sometimes concentrated in particular areas. For example, the production of men's dress shirts is concentrated in Pennsylvania and New York while the production of work shirts is concentrated in the South. The cotton-garment plants are usually quite small in size, employing on the average between 60 and 100 workers. Where large units exist, they are usually engaged in the manufacture of dress shirts, work shirts, or overalls for which the style factor is of minor importance.

Most cutters, like finishing plants, are independent concerns, but about half operate on a contract basis. The manufacturer owns the material, assigns it to the cutter for fabrication, and then merchandises the finished product. A few cutting plants, mostly in household articles, are owned and operated by weavers.

MARKETING OF COTTON TEXTILES

Textile products usually are bought and sold several times before reaching the ultimate consumer. The chief agencies involved are described below.

1. *Selling Houses and Selling Agents:* The products of a weaving mill first are sold through selling houses or agents. The former is owned fully or partially by the mill and the latter is an independent agent operating on 2–5 percent commission for 5–75 mills. During World War II many stronger sales agents (such as J. P. Stevens), integrated backwards and in 1962 few major ones were left.

Whether there is an intermediary between the sales house and buyer depends mainly on the amount of finishing required and the susceptibility of the product to fashion changes. Industrial fabrics, requiring little finishing and not being subject to fashion, are sold direct. Most of the household fabrics are finished and sold by the mill to large retailers and wholesalers; however, highly styled household fabrics (piece goods) are sold to converters for finishing and reselling. Apparel fabrics, except those carefully branded or destined for the carriage trade, are sold in the greige (unfinished) to converters.

2. *Converters:* Converters assume much of the risk-taking function in the styled cotton and man-made woven fabric fields. They buy grey goods from the mill, have them finished to order on a commission basis, and sell them to two main customer groups: (*a*) manufacturers of clothing and household articles (cutters), and (*b*) wholesalers, chains, department stores, and retailers, for sale by the yard as piece goods. Although converters usually do no physical handling of the goods, they often own large inventories; their buying commitments to a grey goods mill are firm, while selling arrangements with customers are subject to cancellation.

Besides the converting departments of vertically integrated mills, there were in 1962 approximately 300 cotton converters in the United States (mostly located in New York City). Converters claim the advantages over integrated mills of (1) gauging style trends more effectively through close (often blood) relationships with cutters and buyers, and of (2) making faster deliveries of larger quantities of goods through using multiple sources of supply.

3. *Intermediaries:* There are two main intermediaries in these distribution channels. The first are brokers, now active on only a small fraction of transactions, who bring together buyers and sellers in a so-called "secondary market" where prices are, however, closely watched as guides to what the market will be. The second intermediaries are factors who extend credit to mills and converters, and sometimes introduce converter clients to mill clients in the hopes of promoting business. In addition, by refusing to increase credit the factor can limit the scope of the borrower's activities.

PROBLEMS OF THE COTTON TEXTILE INDUSTRY

Since the end of the textile boom in 1948 and with the exception of a brief period during the speculation surrounding the Korean War, cotton textiles have constituted a depressed industry. Some of the problems are of long standing:

1. *Instability of Prices and Margins:* Cotton and cloth prices have always fluctuated greatly to result in unstable mill margins (see Exhibits 6 and 11).

2. *Susceptibility to Fashion Changes:* About 50 percent of the cotton textile products are affected by style and fashion. This problem is compounded for cotton clothing by the lead time requirements: the spring season reaches a peak in April–June and the fall season in October–December. Planning and designing fabrics begins at the close of the corresponding season of the preceding year.

3. *Seasonality of Demand:* Other factors—weather and the extra-industry shifts such as automobile production—combine with fashion to make even industrial fabrics seasonal.

4. *Excess Capacity:* The effects of excess capacity may be gleaned from Exhibit 7.

CURRENT DEVELOPMENTS

Some of the old trends, such as the movement south and the change to the third shift for looms and spindles, have pretty well run their course but most remain with some new additions.

1. *Movement South:* Following a long established trend, textile mill activity continued shifting southward after World War II, as illustrated by the following figures:

Cotton Spindles in Place by Region

	1947		*1962*	
	Thousands	*Percent*	*Thousands*	*Percent*
North	5,012	21.1%	1,200	6.1%
South	18,164	76.5	18,236	93.4
Other	551	2.4		0.5
Total	23,727	100.0%	18,436	100.0%

Source: U.S. Department of Commerce and Association of Cotton Textile Merchants, New York.

An important aspect of this shift was the hardship caused to workers by the industry's decline in New England. For example, from 1947 through 1957, textile mill employment in New England fell from 298,800 to 134,600, for a fall of 54.3 percent as compared with 24.2 percent for the industry as a whole. With so much of the outward movement accomplished and the wage differential between North and South closing, the movement of the textile mill industry was expected to be less disruptive in the future than in the past.

2. *Industry Shrinkage:* Liquidations, declining employment, and fewer spindles and looms in place spell out the shrinkage of the textile industry:

Decline of the Textile Mill Industry to 1957

	Number	*Percent Decline*
Mills involved in liquidation (1946–1957)	717	—
Decline in employment (1947–1957)	331,000	24%
Decline in production workers (1947–March '58)	326,300	28
Decline in equipment in place (1947–1957)		
Cotton mills:		
Spindles	2,655,000	11
Looms	44,000	11
Silk and synthetic mills: Looms	13,000	12
Woolen and worsted mills (except carpet):		
Worsted combs	1,092,000	41
Woolen spindles	664,000	51
Worsted spindles	1,212,000	63

Source: Textile Workers Union of America and Bureau of the Census.

Partially offsetting the decline of equipment in place was the increased incidence of three-shift operation. In the cotton broadwoven fabrics industry, for example, the percentage of first-shift looms active on the third shift ranged between 30.1 and 55.2 percent a month in 1947, and between 96.5 and 97.8 percent in 1960. For cotton spindles, hours run per average spindle per year increased from 5,731 to 6,360 over the same period.

3. *Integration:* Statistics on mergers and acquisitions in the textile industry have been called "grossly inadequate." For textile mills alone, union sources compiled a list of 38 "leading mergers or acquisitions" December, 1957–November, 1958. For textiles and apparel combined, the *Statistical Abstract of the United States* reported 264 cases, 1948–1959. Mill integration has aimed not only at familiar objectives, such as assuring sources of supply or outlets, stability through diversification, and economies of size, but also at reaping tax advantages through the operation of the loss carry-forward provision of the Internal Revenue Act. Integrations have been both vertical and horizontal, although vertically integrated firms do not necessarily behave as such:

> . . . unlike the result in many other industries, in which vertical integration has led to an increasing degree of centralized control, in textiles the managers of each stage of the production process retain a great deal of autonomy, even under single corporate ownership.
>
> . . . .
>
> For example, the finishing plant of an integrated concern does not limit its dyeing and finishing to cloth woven by mills of the parent company, and at times, the company's mills may send their cloth to outside finishing plants. Similarly, the company's converting establishment deals not only in the gray goods produced by that company's mills but will also buy gray goods from other mills. Thus instead of a linear flow from the mill through the selling house, fabrics cross corporate boundaries as they move from mills to their end uses.[5]

4. *Increasing Size:* Often as a consequence of integration, some units of the industry have increased their relative size. An indication of this trend is given by sales data for 12 of the largest firms: whereas in 1938 these companies accounted for 8.7 percent of total industry sales, in 1948 they accounted for 12.6 percent and in 1958 for 20.9 percent. Over the entire 20-year period, their sales expanded 648 percent as compared with 210 percent for the industry as a whole.

According to a study published in 1958, the 15 largest cotton cloth producers (seven of which also wove man-made fiber fabrics) accounted for some 30–35 percent of total employment and sales. According to labor testimony, 38 "basic textile" companies had over 3,000 workers as of November, 1958. These operated 483 plants, had more than half the equipment in the industry, 70 percent of the spindles, 60 percent of the looms, 53 percent of the employees, and all the large selling agencies.

There was also evidence (based on a study of

[5] Business and Defense Services Administration, *Textile Outlook for the Sixties,* p. 18.

revenue returns for the year starting July 1, 1955) that the larger companies accounted for a higher than proportionate share of textile mill industry profits and assets:

Size in Relation to Assets and Profits, Textile Mill Industry Fiscal 1956

Company Asset Size (millions)	*Percent of Industry*	*Percent of Industry Net Profit*	*Percent of Industry Assets*
$0–$1	78%	6%	11%
$1–$10	19	28	32
$10–$50	2	25	23
$50 and over	1	41	34

Source: *Report . . . Pursuant to S. Res. 287*, Part 4, p. 1665.

5. *Fiber Diversification:* Whereas historically most textile companies concentrated on either cotton, wool, or man-made fibers, several factors have recently contributed to a progressive blurring of these distinctions. These factors include integration, or the common ownership of mills using different fibers; the increasing popularity of blends or cloth composed of more than one fiber; and the development of machines capable of switching from one fiber to another. Indicative of the recent trend toward blends are the following figures for broad woven fabrics:

Broad Woven Goods Production Mixtures and Blends (Millions of Linear Yards)

	1958	*1959*	*1960*	*1961*
Man-made fabrics:				
Rayon and/or acetate	214	283	218	223
Noncellulosic	158	234	303	338
Total, man-made fabrics	372	517	521	561
Natural fibre fabrics:				
Cotton	46	75	128	140
Silk	6	7	4	4
Total, natural fibre fabrics	52	82	132	144
Total, blends and mixtures	424	599	653	705
Percentage increase from previous year:				
Man-made fabrics		39.0%	0.7%	7.7%
Natural fibre fabrics		57.7	61.0	6.1
Total blends and mixtures		41.3	9.0	8.0

Source: U.S. Census Bureau and *Textile Organon*, November, 1962.

Assisting synthetics to capture a larger share of the market were some relatively deep product-price declines:

Annual Average Wholesale Price Index (1947–1949 = 100)

	1947	*1962*
Textile products and apparel	100.1	94.4
Cotton products	103.1	90.6
Wool products	90.6	101.0
Man-made fiber products	96.6	75.8
Silk products	117.2	133.9

Source: Bureau of Labor Statistics.

The newer synthetics effected not only a *shift* in fiber demand but also contributed to a net *decrease,* inasmuch as their strength gave wearing properties to lighter weight fabric; their durability minimized need for replacements; and their easy care reduced consumers' inventory needs. In interpreting statistics of the textile industry, it should be held in mind that all the synthetics, including rayons, replace more than their own weight in natural fibers. For example, in 1960 the total per capita consumption of all man-made fibers was 9.88 pounds, but this was equivalent to 15.66 pounds of cotton.

6. *Low Investment:* Following World War II, when heavy demands were placed on the industry and when profits were relatively high, expenditures for textile mill plant and equipment were substantial; between 1946 and 1952 they totaled an estimated $2.9 billion, or $.2 billion more than the estimated gross capital assets of the industry at the end of 1945. After 1951, however, expenditures were generally "off" until 1960, as illustrated by Exhibit 14 and by the following figures:

Textile Mill Industry Expenditures on New Plant and Equipment

Years	*Expenditures in Millions*
Average, 1947–1951	$516
Average, 1952–1959	348
1960	530
1961	500
1962	620[est.]

Source: Office of Business Economics, *Survey of Current Business*, 1961 and 1962 figures from *Textile Highlights* (Winter, 1963).

Although most of the industry's capital expenditures have been for new equipment rather than for plant, the textile industry in 1957, according to a McGraw-Hill Survey, had more "outmoded" capacity than any other United States industry and more than the all-manufacturing average:

Age of Manufacturing Capacity

	Prior to Dec. '45	*Dec. '45 to Dec. '50*	*Dec. '50 to Dec. '57*
Texiles	59%	21%	20%
All manufacturing	48	19	33

Source: McGraw-Hill Publications.

7. *Nontextile Competition:* Former textile markets have also been invaded by nontextiles, mainly plastic and paper. This trend has been particularly important in the case of disposable

household items and in certain industrial end uses. For example, since 1950 substantial decreases have occurred in the pounds of textile fiber used in the following applications:

Percent Decline in Pounds of Fiber Used

	1950–1955	*1955–1960*
Transportation upholstery	16%	31%
Automobile seat covers	22	21
Electrical applications	21	11
Bags and bagging	40	15

Source: *Textile Organon* annual end-use surveys.

Commenting on nontextile competition, a Senate Subcommittee report on problems of the industry stated in 1959:

The decline in the industrial consumption of textile mill products has contributed even more than the fall in per capita consumption of apparel and other textile products to the overall reduction in the demand for domestically produced fabrics and fibers.[6]

8. *Foreign Competition:* In addition to its problems with sluggish and fluctuating demand, the United States textile industry—being "labor intensive"—has recently suffered at a fast increasing rate from invasion of its home and foreign markets by textiles made abroad where labor costs are lower:

Imports and Exports of Manufactured and Semimanufactured Textile Products

	1947	*1957*	*1960*	*1962*
Exports (millions of pounds)	915.8	380.3	360.9	367.3
Imports (millions of pounds)	24.9	190.3	415.7	485.6
Exports as a percent of mill fiber consumption	14.3%	6.3%	5.5%	5.1%
Imports as a percent of domestic fiber consumption	0.5%	3.1%	6.4%	6.8%

Source: Agricultural Marketing Service and *Textile Organon*, March, 1963.

In terms of value, 1960 imports of finished and semifinished textile manufactures were $931.5 million, or equivalent to 7.2 percent of sales ($13,254 million) for the textile industry as a whole. While increasingly impressive, neither the dollar nor the poundage figures indicate the total impact of imports:

. . . in judging the importance of textile imports, pound for pound, or dollar for dollar comparison between imported and domestically produced items tends to give a false picture. In many cases, the imported item is equal in value to domestically produced items selling at a higher price, and allowance should be made for this fact in any value comparisons. Import statistics show foreign value, which is much lower than value in the United States. Secondly, many imported items are staple in character, and compete not so much with all items produced in this country as with items of a similar character. Since many domestic manufacturers make a small margin on their staple items, and use these items to even out production and employment schedules in seasonal off-periods, this aspect of imports has very serious potential effects on domestic producers.

Even at a time when textile imports had a smaller share than now of United States consumption, it was argued that, according to well-known principles of marginal analysis, imports were sufficient to set cloth prices in domestic markets. Also, being unevenly distributed among fibers and categories of cloth, imports have affected some segments of the United States textile industry (especially wool) more than the overall totals would suggest:

Imports as a Percent of Domestic Consumption by Fiber, 1962
Millions of Pounds

Fiber	*Imports of Manufactured and Semimanufactured Products*	*Domestic Fiber Consumption*	*Imports as a Percent of Consumption*
Cotton	309.4	4,278.1	7.2%
Wool	145.7	568.7	25.8
Man-made	30.5	2,313.1	1.3

Source: Agricultural Marketing Service and *Textile Organon.*

9. *Political Aspects:* According to management and labor spokesmen, the textile industry has seen its problems compounded by various government programs and policies.

Agricultural price support and quota policies have been under the most fire. Cotton textile

[6] Report of the Committee on Interstate and Foreign Commerce, made by a Special Subcommittee, United States Senate, pursuant to S. Res. 287, *Problems of the Domestic Textile Industry,* Senate Report No. 42 (85th Cong., 1st sess.) (Washington, D.C.: U.S. Government Printing Office, 1959), p. 8.

interests have stressed the inequity of the "two-price system," under which United States cotton has been made available to foreign competitors at prices approximately 20 percent lower (up to 8.5 cents per pound) than that paid by domestic users. All textile interests have cited unfavorable export-import trends and the failure so far to obtain relief under the "Escape Clause"[7] provision of the Reciprocal Trade Agreement Extension Act of 1951. What many have demanded is a supplementary system of import quotas on manufactured and semimanufactured goods. Partly to forestall such a move, Japan adopted a voluntary export quota system in 1956 and 1957, first on woolens and then on cottons. The principle of export quotas was also the solution proposed by an international conference of 16 cotton trading nations, including the United States, which in July, 1961, negotiated a pact calling for a one-year standstill in the level of textile exports to unrestricted markets. In February, 1962, the agreement was extended for five years with the understanding that the United States industry's proposal for an "8.5 cent equalization duty" on cotton content of imported textiles be shelved.

In respect to foreign aid, domestic textile interests point to the fact that the International Cooperation Administration (ICA) has financed expenditures for textile machinery ($141 million, April 3, 1943–June 30, 1958) to build up competing capacity abroad. Also, of total ECA-financed textile expenditures, the percentage devoted to buying basic textiles fabricated in the United States steadily declined for several years (from 64 percent of $15.5 million to 7 percent of $96.3 million in 1957).

Under industry pressure, textile depreciation rates were revised in October, 1961. The 30-year-old Bulletin F based rates (ranging from 15–40 years for textile machinery) on the assumption of 2,000 hours per year operation. The new rates were 14 years on preparatory, spinning and weaving machines, and 12 years on finishing equipment. With a reduction in life from 25 to 14 years, the lower depreciation rate was stepped up about two thirds.

Textile labor unions have supported management views on price supports, quotas, foreign aid, and depreciation rates and, in addition, urged revisions of the loss carry-forward provisions of the Internal Revenue Code and the allowability of state and local tax inducements to attract new plants. These tax provisions are seen as speeding the movement South and, together with the Taft-Hartley Law, helping prevent unions from organizing more than 30 percent of the industry.[8]

[7] This clause provided that an industry claiming to be threatened with "serious injury" as a result of rising imports could bring its case before the U.S. Tariff Commission, which in turn could advise the President to grant relief in the form of higher import duties.

[8] *Report . . . Pursuant to S. Res 287*, p. 22; *Hearings . . . Pursuant to S. Res 287*, p. 377.

1. COTTON TEXTILE INDUSTRY

Selected Statistics, 1958

Type of Manufacturer	Companies	Plants: Total	Plants: Over 20 Employees	Plants: Over 100 Employees	All Employees: Number (Thousands)	All Employees: Payroll (Millions)
Total Textile Mill Products	*	-	4,683	-	919	3,016
Yarn mills (except wool)	268	355	309	233	67	179
Thread mills	70	86	49	23	11	35
Throwing and winding	182	195	119	33	12	38
Woolen yarn mills	142	150	122	58	16	54
Cotton weaving mills	325	495	394	342	243	722
Synthetic weaving mills	324	401	310	182	82	277
Woolen weaving and finishing	411	469	311	159	56	206
Cotton finishing plants	426	446	174	85	49	190
Synthetic finishing plants	185	197	132	52	16	74
Apparel Products	*	-	12,914	-	1,168	3,538
Men's suits and coats	1,286	1,365	763	291	122	408
Separate trousers	719	748	367	161	52	134
Work clothing	376	500	396	124	65	155
Men's dress shirts, nightwear	737	879	605	315	103	254
Women's blouses	1,246	1,260	735	85	47	125
Women's dresses	4,502	4,653	2,899	305	185	588

*Omitted because of excessive duplication.

Source: U.S. Bureau of the Census, Census of Manufactures, 1958.

Type of Manufacturer	Value Added by Manufacturer (Millions)	Cost of Materials (Millions)	Value of Shipments (Millions)	New Capital Expenditures (Millions)
Total Textile Mill Products	5,019	*	*	220
Yarn mills (except wool)	290	557	848	15
Thread mills	63	106	168	2
Throwing and winding	68	106	175	3
Woolen yarn mills	91	181	274	5
Cotton weaving mills	1,075	1,618	2,740	48
Synthetic weaving mills	468	750	1,226	15
Woolen weaving and finishing	337	577	929	10
Cotton finishing plants	289	399	686	16
Synthetic finishing plants	115	95	210	4
Apparel Products	5,962	*	*	107
Men's suits and coats	643	651	1,295	5
Separate trousers	209	243	452	4
Work clothing	255	435	690	3
Men's dress shirts, nightwear	421	543	965	6
Women's blouses	200	253	454	2
Women's dresses	971	1,073	2,043	9

*Omitted because of excessive duplication.

Exhibit 1 (continued)

Type of Manufacturer	Production Workers		
	Number (Thousands)	Man-Hours (Thousands)	Wages (Millions)
Total Textile Mill Products	826	1,601	2,472
Yarn mills (except wool)	64	117	157
Thread mills	10	18	27
Throwing and winding	10	20	29
Woolen yarn mills	15	29	45
Cotton weaving mills	228	442	645
Synthetic weaving mills	74	151	234
Woolen weaving and finishing	49	99	166
Cotton finishing plants	42	86	149
Synthetic finishing plants	14	29	58
Apparel Products	1,020	1,837	2,736
Men's suits and coats	107	185	322
Separate trousers	47	85	110
Work clothing	59	104	132
Men's dress shirts, nightwear	94	168	210
Women's blouses	42	72	98
Women's dresses	161	280	452

1-A. COTTON TEXTILE INDUSTRY

Financial Data for Selected Types
of Textile and Apparel Firms

(A) Combined Balance Sheets for Year Ending on or about December 31, 1961

	Men's and Boys' Suits and Coats	Broad Woven*	Dyeing and Finishing*	Yarn Mills*
Assets (Number of Firms)	(95)	(83)	(31)	(42)
Cash	9.08	5.82	4.10	8.84
Accounts Receivable	38.87	16.94	21.15	19.84
Inventory	34.06	34.25	24.49	28.49
Securities	2.03	0.66	1.67	1.70
Other	1.25	1.58	.16	1.23
Total Current	85.28	59.26	51.56	60.10
Fixed Assets	8.63	35.07	44.09	35.48
Other Assets	6.09	5.67	4.35	4.42
Total Assets	100.00	100.00	100.00	100.00
Liabilities				
Banks	13.93	6.69	9.48	11.00
Trade	11.29	8.28	11.40	6.58
Taxes	3.62	2.59	1.69	3.97
Other	7.14	5.89	3.97	3.95
Total	35.98	23.45	26.54	25.51
Long-Term Debt	3.90	5.59	3.72	3.56
Total Debt	39.88	29.04	30.26	29.06
Net Worth	60.12	70.96	69.74	70.94
Total	100.00	100.00	100.00	100.00
Sales ($000)	287,431	358,411	112,719	222,725
Total Assets ($000)	151,805	195,084	61,449	129,588

(B) Combined Income Statements

	Men's and Boys' Suits and Coats	Broad Woven*	Dyeing and Finishing*	Yarn Mills*
Net Sales	100.00	100.00	100.00	100.00
C.G.S.	81.93	87.60	86.60	87.99
Gross Profit	18.07	12.40	13.40	12.01
Other Expense	14.60	9.48	12.00	6.60
Profit (BT)	3.47	2.92	1.41	5.40
Tax	1.80	1.56	.87	2.84
Net Profit	1.67	1.36	.54	2.56
Current Ratio	2.37	2.53	1.94	2.36
N.W./Fixed	6.98	2.02	1.58	2.20
N.W./Debt	1.51	2.44	2.30	2.44
A.R. Turnover**	.74	.33	.41	.41
Inv. Turnover**	.79	.76	.55	.68
Sales/Fixed	21.95	5.36	4.16	4.48
Percent Profit N.W.	5.26	3.59	1.42	6.20
Sales/Total/Assets	1.82	1.84	1.83	1.72

*Cotton, silk, and synthetics.
**Days.
Source: Robert Morris Associates, Statement Studies, 1961.

2. COTTON TEXTILE INDUSTRY

Indexes of Production for Textile Mill Products and All Manufactures, 1947-1962
(1947-1949 = 100)

Year	Textile Mill Products	All Manufactures
1947	101	100
1948	105	103
1949	94	97
1950	111	113
1951	107	121
1952	103	125
1953	104	136
1954	95	127
1955	107	140
1956	104	144
1957	98	145
1958	96	133
1959	111	152
1960	107	157
1961	109	158
1962*	118	172

Source: Board of Governors, Federal Reserve System.
*Preliminary.

3. COTTON TEXTILE INDUSTRY

Total Broadwoven Fabric Production and Mill Consumption of Fiber 1947-1962

Year	Broadwoven Fabric Production (Millions of Linear Yards)	Mill Fiber Consumption (Millions of Pounds)
1947	12,371	6,424.9
1948	12,405	6,403.7
1949	10,923	5,445.4
1950	13,091	6,846.4
1951	12,887	6,838.5
1952	12,160	6,440.1
1953	12,944	6,481.5
1954	12,518	6,028.2
1955	13,119	6,709.7
1956	12,931	6,543.5
1957	12,118	6,230.1
1958	11,627	5,967.5
1959	12,409	6,839.1
1960	12,022	6,491.3
1961	11,841	6,533.2
1962	12,325 (est.)	7,159.9

Source: Bureau of the Census and Agricultural Marketing Service.

3-A. COTTON TEXTILE INDUSTRY

Mill Consumption, Selected Years, 1935-1962

	Millions of Pounds						Percent of Total					
Year	Cotton	Wool	Rayon and Acetate	Other Man-Made	Silk	Total	Cotton	Wool	Rayon and Acetate	Other Man-Made	Silk	Total
1935	2,754.7	417.5	259.2	--	62.3	3,493.7	78.8	12.0	7.4	--	1.8	100
1940	3,953.6	407.9	482.1	4.4	35.8	4,883.8	81.0	8.3	9.9	.1	.7	100
1945	4,511.3	645.1	769.1	49.8	.5	5,976.6	75.5	10.8	12.9	.8	--	100
1947	4,668.1	708.3	987.9	51.4	2.0	6,417.7	72.8	11.0	15.4	.8	--	100
1949	3,838.2	511.0	993.5	92.8	4.4	5,439.9	70.5	9.4	18.3	1.7	.1	100
1951	4,846.8	495.0	1,276.6	195.5	5.6	6,819.5	71.1	7.2	18.7	2.9	.1	100
1953	4,521.0	503.8	1,223.0	279.6	5.4	6,532.8	69.2	7.7	18.7	4.3	.1	100
1955	4,384.2	428.2	1,419.2	432.1	7.2	6,670.9	65.7	6.4	21.3	6.5	.1	100
1857	4,043.5	380.6	1,177.5	561.3	5.9	6,168.8	65.5	6.2	19.1	9.1	.1	100
1958	3,867.0	331.1	1,127.2	636.9	5.3	5,967.5	64.8	5.5	19.0	10.6	.1	100
1959	4,337.1	429.2	1,252.5	812.3	8.0	6,839.1	63.4	6.3	18.4	11.8	.1	100
1960	4,203.2	404.2	1,005.4	871.6	6.9	6,491.3	64.8	6.2	15.4	13.5	.1	100
1961	4,107.7	409.9	1,076.7	932.2	6.7	6,533.2	62.9	6.3	16.5	14.2	.1	100
1962	4,203.3	427.4	1,319.3	1,204.0	5.9	7,159.9	58.7	6.0	18.4	16.8	.1	100

Civilian per Capita Consumption, Selected Years, 1935-1962
(Pounds per Person)

Year	Total	Man-Made	Wool	Cotton	Year	Total	Man-Made	Wool	Cotton
1935	26.8	2.2	3.4	21.2	1953	38.8	9.0	3.4	26.4
1940	35.8	3.7	3.2	28.9	1954	35.3	8.7	2.7	23.9
1945	40.5	5.8	4.3	30.4	1955	39.3	11.0	3.0	25.3
1947	38.4	6.6	4.6	27.2	1956	37.8	9.7	3.1	25.0
1948	40.2	7.8	4.9	27.5	1957	35.1	9.9	2.6	22.6
1949	33.5	6.7	3.5	23.3	1958	33.3	9.6	2.4	21.3
1950	43.5	9.5	4.6	29.4	1959	38.4	11.3	3.1	24.0
1951	41.7	9.0	3.5	29.2	1960	36.2	9.9	3.0	23.3
1952	38.9	8.9	3.5	26.5	1961	35.6	10.7	2.9	21.9
					1962	38.4	12.4	3.1	22.9

Source: Textile Organon, January, 1962, and following issues.

3-B. COTTON TEXTILE INDUSTRY

Supply and Requirements Assuming Full Mobilization, 1960

	Wool and Worsted Woven Fabric*	Cotton and Man-Made Broadwoven Goods	Nylon Fiber**
	(Millions of Linear Yards)		(Millions of Pounds)
Supply	365.8	14,763	857
Requirements	295.7	14,180	529
Surplus or deficit.	+70.1	+583	+328
Surplus as a percent of supply	18.9%***	1.3%	38.3%
Actual 1960 production	284.0	11,721	#

*Assumes imports of 3.2 million yards and exports of 31.3 million.

**Based on an estimate in Textile Organon. This source makes continuing reviews of actual and projected capacity in relation to use in the man-made fiber field.

***Assumes 1960 was the second war year. For the first, surplus would be lower--only 14.3%.

#Total noncellulosic fiber production, including nylon, was 856.4 million pounds in 1960.

Source: Hearings . . . Pursuant to S. Res. 287, Part 5, pp. 1835-39; Textile Organon; "Textile Hi-Lights."

4. COTTON TEXTILE INDUSTRY

Wholesale Price Indexes (1947–1949 = 100)

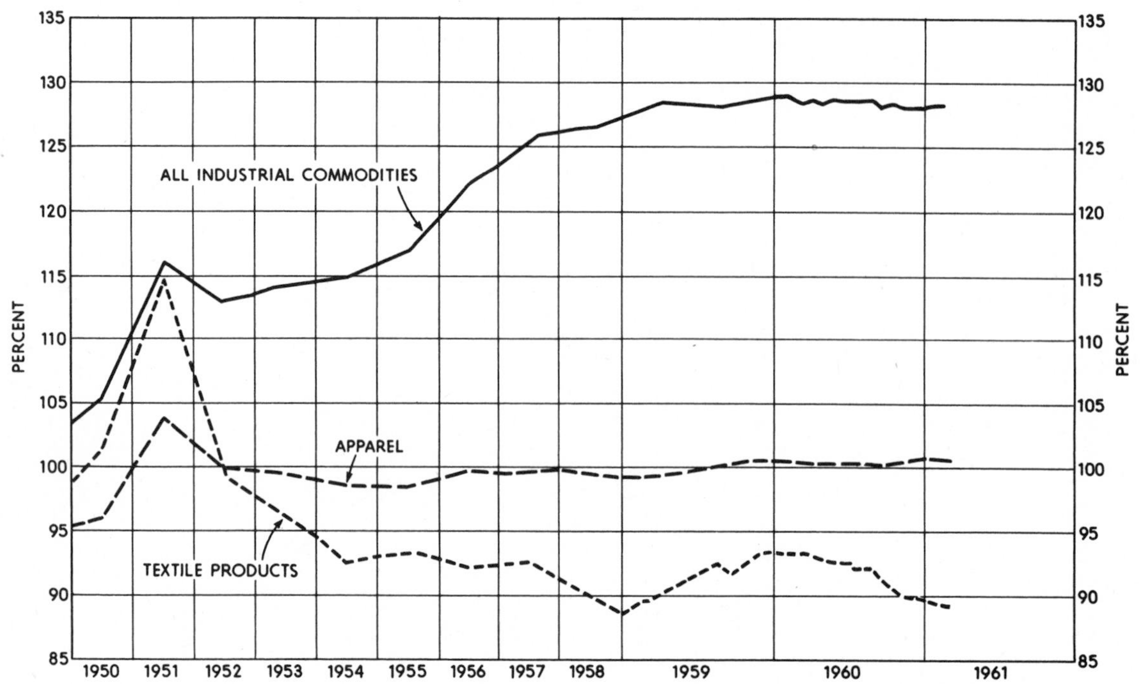

COMMODITY	YEARLY INDEXES											1962			
	1950	1951	1952	1953	1954	1955	1956	1957	1958	1959	1960	1961	Jan.	Apr.	July	Oct.
ALL INDUSTRIAL COMMODITIES	107.0	115.9	113.2	114.0	114.5	117.0	122.2	125.6	126.0	128.2	128.3	127.5	127.9	127.7	127.5	127.4
TEXTILE PRODUCTS & APPAREL	99.2	110.6	99.8	97.3	95.2	95.3	95.3	95.4	93.5	95.0	96.1	94.4	94.9	95.2	95.6	95.2
TEXTILE PRODUCTS, Excl. Hard Fiber*	n.a.	n.a.	n.a.	n.a.	92.8	93.3	92.3	92.3	91.4	91.4	92.2	88.8	89.5	90.0	90.1	85.8
COTTON PRODUCTS	99.5	111.5	98.5	93.5	89.2	91.5	93.0	90.7	88.4	91.7	94.2	90.6	92.0	92.5	91.9	91.1
Yarns	101.0	120.4	104.0	94.1	88.6	93.6	95.8	92.6	92.1	93.9	93.8	91.8	95.0	94.3	92.7	91.6
Broad Woven Goods	99.4	110.3	96.4	92.1	87.0	89.3	90.7	87.6	85.0	89.3	92.4	87.3	88.6	88.9	88.7	88.8
Narrow Fabrics	90.7	111.9	93.6	86.3	76.3	76.1	79.0	77.8	76.7	77.0	77.5	70.6	66.6	72.4	72.4	68.2
Thread	94.2	108.3	105.0	102.5	100.4	100.4	100.4	102.1	104.2	108.7	115.3	115.9	116.8	116.8	116.7	116.7
Housefurnishings	100.4	110.4	100.3	96.0	94.1	94.5	95.6	96.3	92.5	93.7	96.0	96.4	98.4	98.7	98.1	98.1
WOOL PRODUCTS	112.9	114.6	113.0	111.8	109.1	104.7	103.7	109.5	100.8	101.6	102.1	101.0	101.7	102.6	103.2	103.6
Tops	126.8	171.2	113.0	114.7	112.5	99.9	95.9	108.8	88.5	92.5	85.8	92.6	94.4	96.6	97.7	98.2
Yarns	115.4	151.9	107.5	112.2	108.8	98.1	98.4	107.6	92.2	97.0	95.2	93.4	94.4	96.3	97.2	98.8
Blankets, Incl. Part Wool	116.2	158.0	136.3	130.5	122.2	124.8	123.5	123.4	120.6	119.9	121.6	121.8	121.8	121.8	121.8	121.8
Broad Woven Fabrics	109.1	136.0	113.0	109.7	107.5	106.3	105.6	109.1	104.4	103.3	105.5	103.7	104.2	104.6	104.8	105.1
Knit Outerwear Fabrics	106.1	144.2	121.2	121.1	119.1	114.3	110.0	122.6	113.9	112.9	117.2	113.0	114.5	115.1	115.1	114.5
MAN-MADE FIBER PRODUCTS	95.3	97.0	88.9	87.1	85.7	86.6	81.4	82.0	80.2	81.1	79.1	75.8	75.7	76.0	76.9	75.9
Filament Yarns & Fibers	103.9	109.7	107.2	104.6	104.3	105.6	100.0	101.6	100.6	100.9	94.6	93.1	92.9	92.9	92.7	92.6
Spun Rayon	82.5	94.2	90.6	83.7	79.2	80.9	81.4	77.3	74.4	77.9	77.4	69.8	70.6	70.6	71.2	70.6
Broad Woven Goods	89.2	87.5	74.9	72.7	70.8	72.2	67.2	66.9	64.9	65.9	66.1	62.0	61.6	62.2	63.4	62.1
Knit Goods	95.9	100.7	89.8	89.3	86.4	83.5	75.9	73.9	71.0	72.0	70.3	66.4	68.0	68.2	68.2	67.8
Narrow Fabrics	104.6	104.6	104.6	114.2	114.5	114.5	114.5	128.1	128.0	128.0	128.0	140.5	140.5	140.5	140.5	140.5
SILK PRODUCTS	99.7	128.8	133.7	136.6	129.8	123.8	121.9	122.1	113.5	113.5	122.9	113.9	131.8	143.7	154.4	154.1
APPAREL	96.3	103.8	100.0	99.3	98.5	98.5	99.6	99.6	99.3	100.0	100.9	100.5	100.8	100.9	101.3	101.3
Women's, Misses', Juniors'	95.8	100.8	97.3	97.0	97.6	98.9	99.8	99.5	99.2	100.4	100.6	101.0	100.8	100.8	99.7	100.2
Men's and Boys'	98.2	108.1	103.4	102.8	101.5	100.3	102.5	103.2	102.9	103.0	105.0	105.8	106.6	106.8	106.9	107.3
Hosiery	87.7	92.3	87.0	84.8	82.3	81.2	80.6	79.4	76.9	76.3	76.2	76.1	76.2	76.2	75.8	75.8
Infants' and Children's	92.7	104.6	112.1	110.1	108.5	108.6	109.2	109.5	109.6	111.3	111.5	111.1	111.1	111.1	111.5	111.5
Underwear and Nightwear	100.0	108.9	103.7	102.3	100.6	99.6	101.1	101.1	101.4	102.1	102.9	103.1	103.7	103.7	104.7	104.7
Knit Outerwear	101.5	116.1	110.0	107.4	100.8	99.6	99.6	99.6	101.1	102.1	104.8	101.1	101.4	101.6	101.6	101.6

Sources: (1950–1958) Bureau of Labor Statistics, Wholesale Price Index. American Cotton Manufacturers' Institute

*Textile Hi-Lights (1959–62). 1961 and 1962 figures recalculated at the Harvard Business School from 1957 - 59 base to 1947 - 59 base.

4-A. COTTON TEXTILE INDUSTRY

Production Cost Breakdown of Selected Fabrics for the U.S. and Foreign Countries, 1960

A. Total Costs of Four Cotton Fabrics (cents per linear yard):

	Print Cloth				Sheeting			
	United States			Japan	United States			Japan
	Spinning	Weaving	Total	Total	Spinning	Weaving	Total	Total
Basic labor	2.22	2.87	5.09	1.54	1.75	1.78	3.53	1.01
Fringe benefits	.21	.28	.49	.92	.19	.20	.39	.71
Total	2.43	3.15	5.58	2.46	1.94	1.98	3.92	1.72
Materials, dyes	--	.26	.26	.82	--	.22	.22	.15
Overhead	1.57	1.59	3.16	1.81	.70	.84	1.54	1.05
Total manufacturing . .	4.00	5.00	9.00	5.09	2.64	3.04	5.68	2.92
General expenses			.19	1.05			.20	.31
Seconds			.15	*			.07	.04
Sales			.35	.18			.25	.31
Total			9.69	6.32			6.20	3.58
Cotton			8.71	8.23			8.40	7.81
Total			18.40	14.55			14.60	11.39

*Included in fiber costs.

	Broadcloth				Gingham			
Basic labor	3.76	4.57	8.33	2.01	3.73	6.99	10.72	2.85
Fringe benefits	.34	.42	.76	1.17	.45	.82	1.27	1.72
Total	4.10	4.99	9.09	3.18	4.18	7.81	11.99	4.57
Materials, dyes	--	.33	.33	*	--	2.01	2.01	2.78
Overhead	2.31	1.47	3.78	3.73	3.05	4.43	7.98	4.38
Total manufacturing . .	6.41	6.79	13.20	6.91	7.23	14.25	21.48	11.73
General expenses			.68	.74			.80	.91
Seconds			.10	.08			.27	.10
Sales			.37	.33			.67	.34
Total			14.35	8.06			23.22	13.08
Cotton			11.80	10.29			10.33	9.05
Total			26.15	18.35			33.55	22.13

*In overhead.

Note: Fabric constructions are carded print cloth,

$39'' \frac{80 \times 80}{31'sw \times 41's}$ 4.00 yards/lb.; carded sheeting,

$40' \frac{44 \times 40}{40'sw \times 18's}$ 4.25 yards/lb.; combed broadcloth $40'' \frac{136 \times 60}{40'sw \times 40's}$

3.65 yards/lb.; combed two-color gingham, $47'' \frac{90 \times 60}{40'sw \times 40's}$ 4.25 yards/lb.

All in gray.

Exhibit 4-A (continued)

B. Selected other Fabric Costs (cents per linear yard):

	Worsted Sharkskin			Woolen Flannel*		Woolen Flannel**		Spun Rayon Challis	
	U.S.	Japan	U.K.	U.S.	U.K.	U.S.	Italy	U.S.	Italy
Labor	110	55	107	66	61	47	33	5.16**	4.28***
Materials, dyes	8	31	17	8	16	07	03	.20	.95
Overhead	74	42	89	46	63	45	15	8.17	11.19
Sales expense	28	13	13	29	10	14	04	-	-
Fiber	142	123	105	128	98	85	22	8.35	7.39
Total	362	264	331	277	248	191	77	21.88	23.81

*Higher grade.
**Lower grade.
***Labor in weaving only.

NOTE: Fabric Constructions are worsted sharkskin, 60" 85 x 64, 11 to 11.5 oz./yd. finished; higher grade woolen flannel, 60" 55 x 42, 11 to 11.5 oz./yd. finished; lower grade woolen flannel, 60" 34 x 34, 11 to 11.5 oz./yd. finished; gray spun rayon challis 45" $\frac{54 \times 54}{30'sw \times 20's}$, 3.8 yds./lb.

C. Man-Hours per 100 Yards Produced for Selected Fabrics:

	Print Cloth		Sheeting		Broadcloth		Gingham	
	U.S.	Japan	U.S.	Japan	U.S.	Japan	U.S.	Japan
By stage of manufacturing								
Spinning	1.52	4.99	1.17	1.73	2.42	3.90	2.43	4.40
Weaving	1.88	5.40	1.16	3.01	2.90	5.40	4.48	13.60
Total	3.40	10.39	2.33	4.74	5.32	9.30	6.91	18.00
By category of labor								
Direct	1.91	8.78	1.61	3.32	2.98	6.50	4.02	14.50
Indirect, maintenance	1.49	1.61	.72	1.42	2.34	2.80	2.89	3.50
Total	3.40	10.39	2.33	4.74	5.32	9.30	6.91	18.00

	Worsted Sharkskin			Woolen Flannel*	
	U.S.	Japan	U.K.	U.S.	Italy
By stage of manufacturing					
Spinning	27	58.0	N.A.	12.76	10.47
Weaving	33	65.7	54.6	15.62	40.88
Finishing	5.2	31.3	29.8		
Total	65.2	155.0	N.A.	28.38	51.35

*Lower grade.

C. Hourly Labor Costs for Selected Fabrics (U.S. Dollars):

	Sheeting		Print Cloth		Broadcloth		Gingham	
	U.S.	Japan	U.S.	Japan	U.S.	Japan	U.S.	Japan
Spinning	1.66	.36	1.60	.27	1.69	.34	1.72	.37
Weaving	1.71	.36	1.67	.21	1.72	.34	1.74	.22
All	1.68	.36	1.64	.24	1.71	.34	1.73	.25
Direct	1.68	.29	1.64	.21	1.70	.25	1.70	.20
Indirect	1.69	.51	1.64	.43	1.71	.53	1.77	.41

	U.S.	U.K.	Japan	Italy
Sharkskin	1.70	.72	.35	-
Flannel, higher grade	1.75	.75	-	-
Flannel, lower grade	1.67	-	-	.64

Source: Surveys and Research Corporation, for the Business and Defense Services Administration, Comparative Fabric Production Costs in the United States and Four Other Countries (Washington: U.S. Government Printing Office, 1961). As stated in the summary of findings, p. 5, "The United States plants studies were all highly modern and efficient."

4-B. COTTON TEXTILE INDUSTRY

Hours and Gross Earnings of Production Workers, 1950-1960

	Average Weekly Earnings			Average Weekly Hours			Average Hourly Earnings		
	1950	1955	1960	1950	1955	1960	1950	1955	1960
Nondurable Manufacturing	57.41	68.06	81.33	39.7	39.8	39.1	1.38	1.71	2.08
Textile mill products	48.95	55.74	63.99	39.6	40.1	39.5	1.24	1.39	1.62
Yarn and thread mills	45.01	50.04	58.44	38.9	39.4	38.7	1.16	1.27	1.51
Broadwoven fabric mills	49.28	54.27	64.48	40.1	40.5	40.3	1.23	1.34	1.60
Dyeing and finishing	53.87	65.14	71.10	40.9	42.3	40.4	1.32	1.54	1.76
Apparel	43.68	49.41	55.69	36.4	36.6	35.7	1.20	1.35	1.56
Men's and boys' suits and coats	50.22	59.86	68.64	36.9	36.5	37.1	1.36	1.64	1.85
Men's and boys' work clothing	36.43	41.92	48.05	36.8	37.1	36.4	.99	1.13	1.32
Women's outer wear	49.41	52.90	57.96	34.7	35.5	33.5	1.42	1.49	1.73

Source: Bureau of Labor Statistics.

5. COTTON TEXTILE INDUSTRY

U.S. Fiber Consumption, 1920–1962

(Monthly Figures Averaged Quarterly)

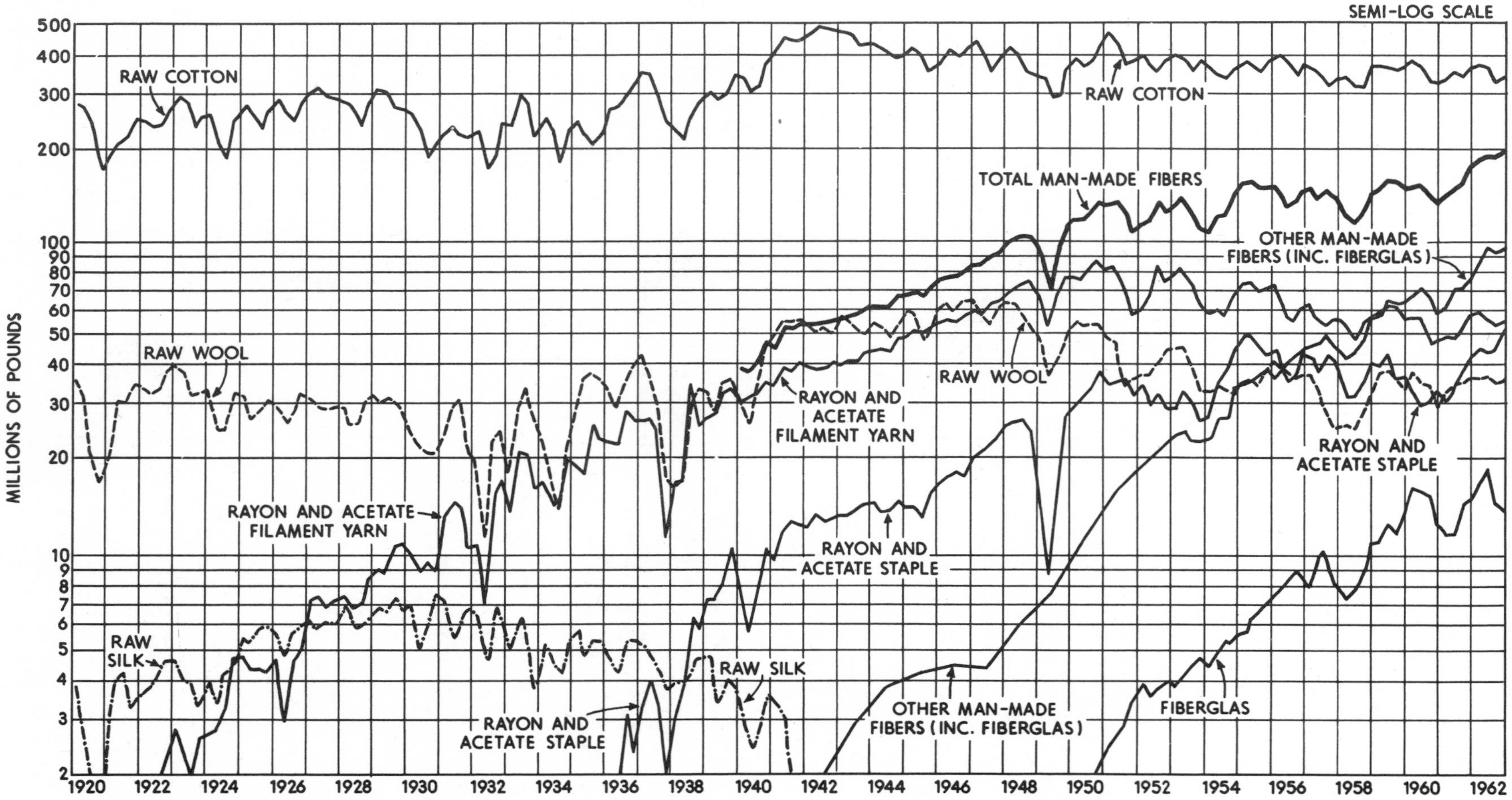
SEMI-LOG SCALE
MILLIONS OF POUNDS
500
400
300
200
100
90
80
70
60
50
40
30
20
10
9
8
7
6
5
4
3
2
1920
1922
1924
1926
1928
1930
1932
1934
1936
1938
1940
1942
1944
1946
1948
1950
1952
1954
1956
1958
1960
1962
RAW COTTON
RAW COTTON
TOTAL MAN-MADE FIBERS
OTHER MAN-MADE FIBERS (INC. FIBERGLAS)
RAW WOOL
RAW WOOL
RAYON AND ACETATE FILAMENT YARN
RAYON AND ACETATE FILAMENT YARN
RAYON AND ACETATE STAPLE
RAYON AND ACETATE STAPLE
RAYON AND ACETATE STAPLE
RAW SILK
RAW SILK
OTHER MAN-MADE FIBERS (INC. FIBERGLAS)
FIBERGLAS

Note: This graph is plotted on a semi-log or ratio scale; equal vertical distances on the chart mean equal percentage changes. While such a graph shows clearly the relative fluctuations of fiber consumption, it can obscure the magnitude of the quantities involved.

The lines represent average monthly consumption during each quarter of the natural fibers and deliveries to the mills of man-made fibers and yarns, except fiberglas which represents production figures. Part of the larger fluctuations in the man-made fiber series may be due to changes in fabricators' inventories.

Source: *Textile Organon*, March, 1963.

6. COTTON TEXTILE INDUSTRY

U.S. Fiber and Yarn Prices, 1920–1962

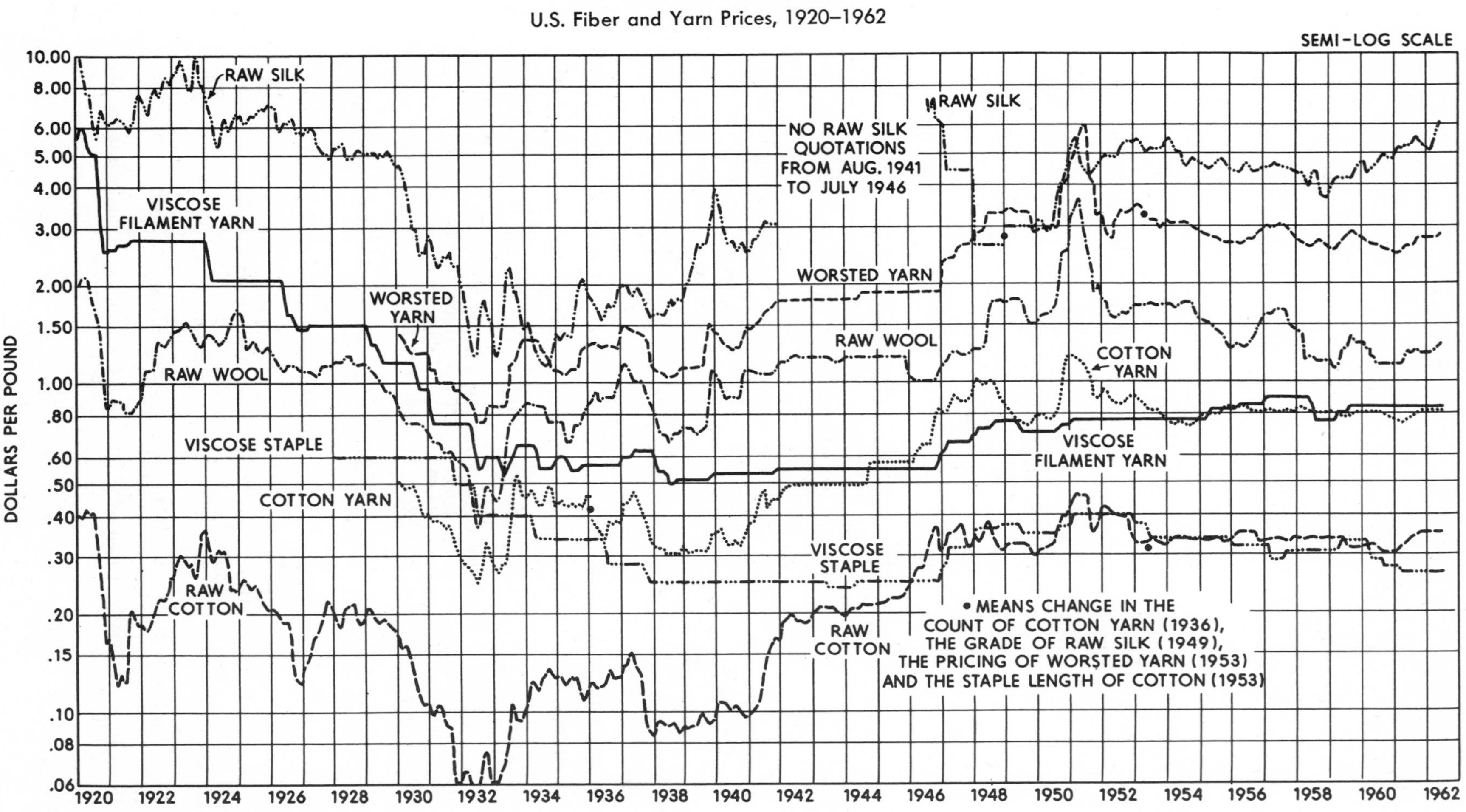

Note: This graph is plotted on a semi-log or ratio scale.

Source: *Textile Organon*, July, 1962.

7. COTTON TEXTILE INDUSTRY

Summary Statistics of Cotton Equipment, Operations, and Market, 1946-1963

	1946	1947	1948	1949	'1950	1951	1952	1953	1954
COTTON SYSTEM EQUIPMENT (IN THOUSANDS)									
Spindles in place (start of year)	23,787	23,928	23,727	23,751	23,341	23,113	23,178	23,131	22.906
Increase (decrease) from preceding year	681	141	(201)	24	(410)	(228)	65	(47)	(225)
New installation and replacements	323	417	607	859	650	771	296	267	219
OPERATIONS (IN THOUSANDS)									
Cotton Only									
Average number of active spindles	21,475	21,588	21,391	20,063	20,449	20,662	19,944	20,051	19,383
Other than Cotton									
Average number of active spindles	1,172	1,198	1,337	1,174	1,295	1,261	1,337	1,323	1,327
All Cotton System									
Average number of idle spindles	1,212	1,066	1,050	2,334	1,372	1,264	1,887	1,572	2,015
Spindle hours run: (millions)									
On 100% cotton	109,474	116,040	115,846	97,874	117,753	118,163	109,986	118,647	108,930
On other fibers, blends	5,875	6,346	7,432	5,816	7,502	7,563	7,583	7,487	7,560
Hours run per average active spindle	5,094	5,371	5,424	4,882	5,760	5,735	5,524	5,901	5,625
Raw cotton processed (millions of pounds)	4,803	4,668	4,461	3,838	4,680	4,908	4,479	4,456.1	4,127.3
Cotton processed per spindle per hour (pounds)	.0439	.0402	.0385	.0392	.0397	.0415	.0407	.0376	.0379
MARKET (IN MILLIONS OF SQUARE YARDS)									
Cotton Textiles									
Production in square yards	10,171	11,083	10,863	9,391	11,207	11,415	10,593	11,333	10,892
Exports in square yards	775	1,480	939	880	559	802	761	621	605
Imports in square yards	44	16	32	20	48	45	36	64	73
Domestic consumption	9,440	9,619	9,956	8,531	10,696	10,659	9,868	10,776	10,361
Population at midyear (millions)	141	144	147	149	152	154	157	160	162
Per capita consumption in square yards	66.77	66.74	67.90	57.18	70.52	69.05	62.84	67.50	63.79
Spindles in place (start of year)	22,560	22,226	21,553	21,075	20,689	20,111	19,931	19,561	19,518
Increase (decrease) from preceding year	(346)	(334)	(673)	(478)	(386)	(578)	(180)	(370)	(43)
New installation and replacements	322	404	190	73	279	1,557*	1,214*	N.A.	
OPERATIONS (IN THOUSANDS)									
Cotton Only									
Average number of active spindles	19,137	19,064	18,278	17,671	17,638	17,589	17,308	16,754	
Other than Cotton									
Average number of active spindles	1,541	1,534	1,582	1,647	1,636	1,677	1,712	2,043	
All Cotton System									
Average number of idle spindles	1,628	1,234	1,443	1,539	1,036	710	656	706	
Spindle hours run: (millions)									
On 100% cotton	116,809	115,210	107,099	103,494	112,185	110,303	106,444	105,617	
On other fibers, blends	9,613	8,550	9,008	9,120	10,396	10,205	10,641	13,314	
Hours run per average active spindle	6,114	6,008	5,847	5,829	6,360	6,255	6,156	6,327	
Raw cotton processed (millions of pounds)	4,382.4	4,362.6	4,060.4	3,867.0	4,337.1	4,198.6	4,107.7		
Cotton processed per spindle per hour (pounds)	.0375	.0379	.0379	.0374	.0387	.0381	.0385		
MARKET (IN MILLIONS OF SQUARE YARDS)									
Cotton Textiles									
Production in square yards	11,319	12,048	11,105	10,470	11,238	10,927	10,824	10,969**	
Exports in square yards	537	507	548	501	472	437	466	415	
Imports in square yards	133	188	122	143	241	455	255	464	
Domestic consumption	10,915	11,729	10,679	10,111	11,006	10,945	10,613	11,018**	
Population at midyear (millions)	166	169	172	175	178	181	184	187	
Per capita consumption in square yards	65.78	69.45	62.09	57.82	62.24	61.33	57.76	59.05**	

*This total includes: New - 457, Rebuilt - 1,100 in 1960 and New - 382, and Rebuilt - 832 in 1961.
**Preliminary figures.
Source: The Association of Cotton Textile Merchants of New York from Bureau of the Census Reports.

8. COTTON TEXTILE INDUSTRY

Manufacturing Processes in Relation to Products (1954)

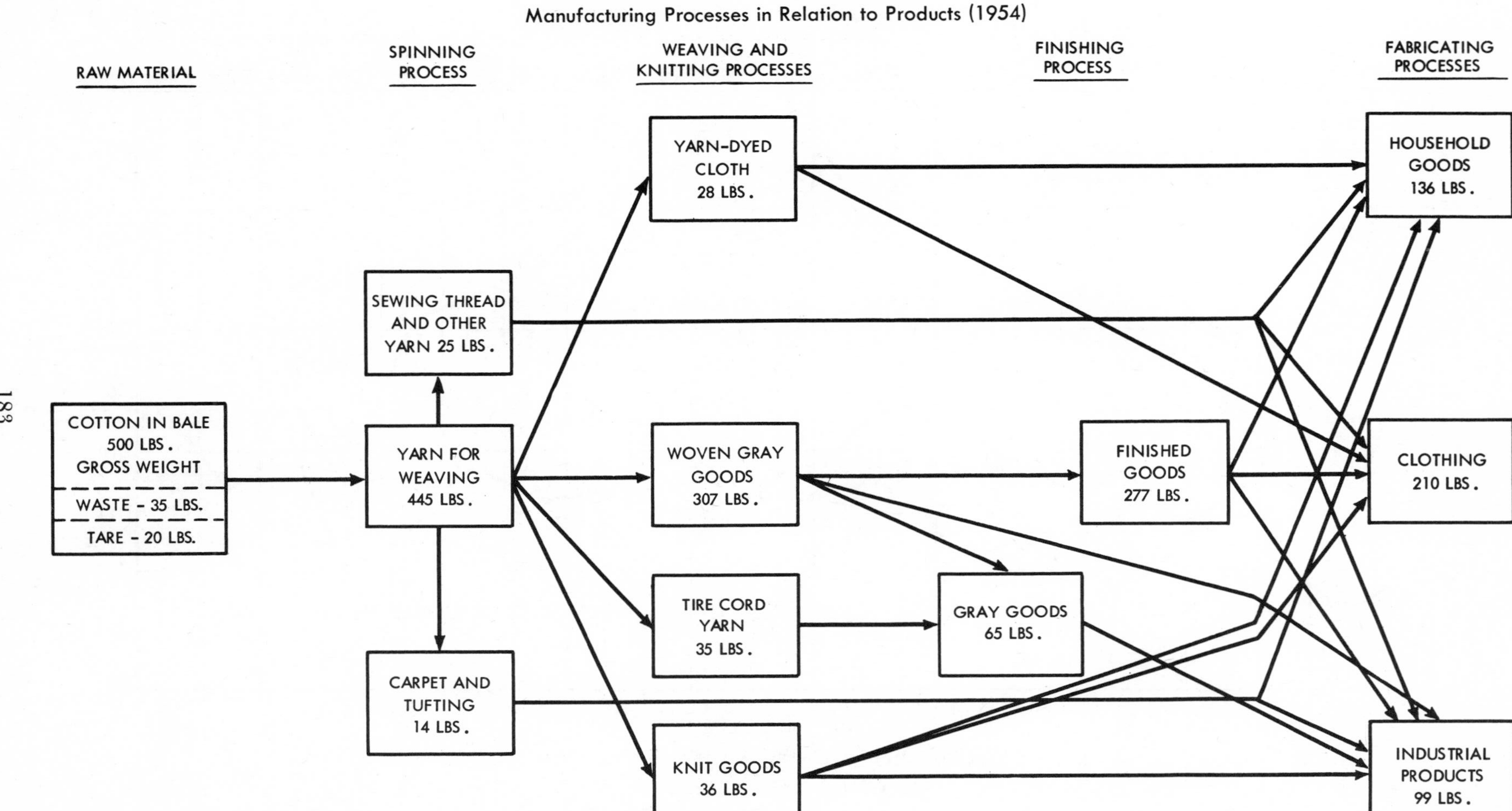

Source: L. D. Howell, *Changes in American Textile Industry*, U.S. Department of Agriculture, Technical Bulletin No. 1210, November, 1959, p. 16.

9. COTTON TEXTILE INDUSTRY

Broad Woven Goods Production by Fiber, 1947–1962

(1947–1949 = 100)*

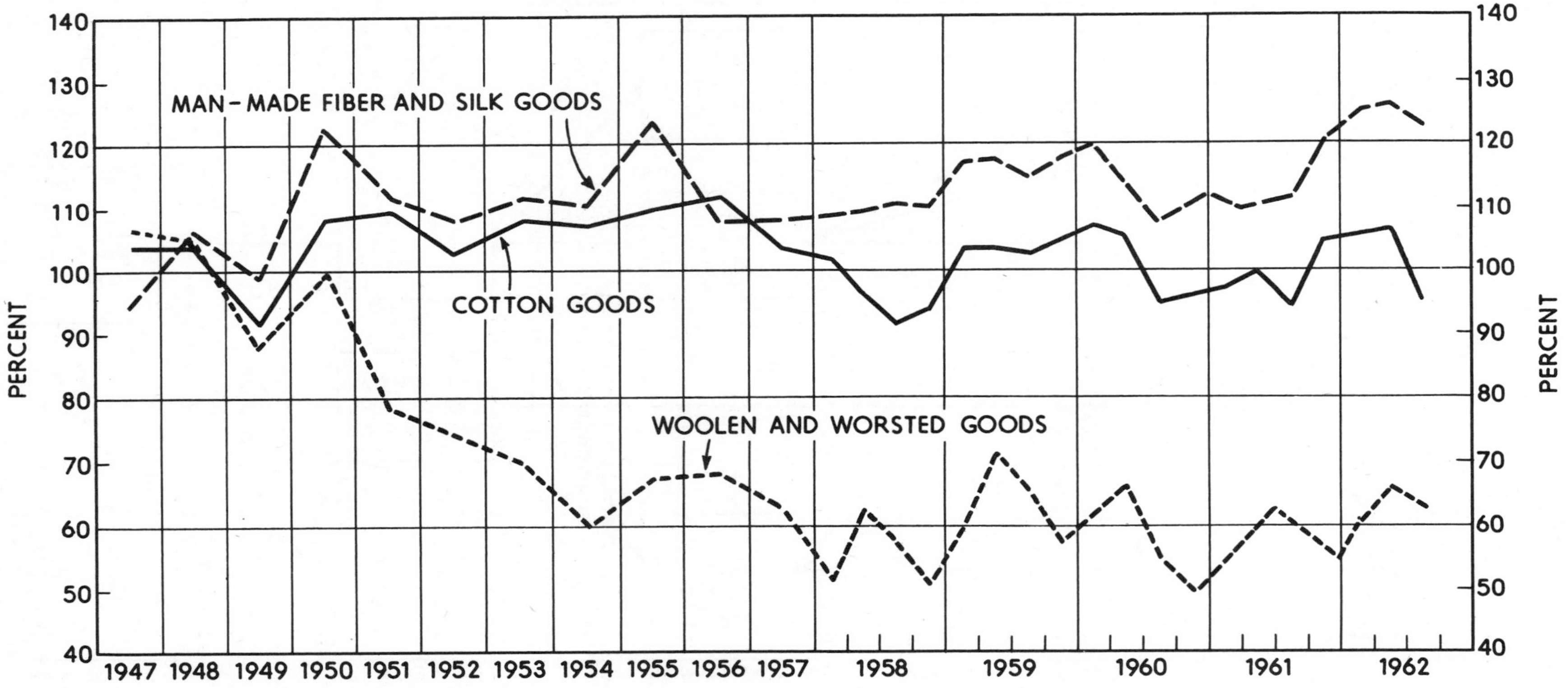

Indexes are based on Average Weekly Production for each year or quarter as computed by ACMI Economic Information Division from Census Bureau data.

Source: Bureau of the Census figures (reprinted from *Textile Hi-Lights*, Winter, 1963).

9-A. COTTON TEXTILE INDUSTRY

Broad Woven Goods Production by Fiber, 1947-1962

	1947	1948	1949	1950	1951	1952	1953	1954	1955	1956	1957	1958	1959	1960	1961	1962**
	(Million of Linear Yards)															
Cotton Broad Woven	9,817	9,640	8,406	10,013	10,136	9,515	10,203	9,891	10,171	10,317	9,534	8,974	9,605	9,366	9,168	9,274
Cotton Duck	2.1%	2.1%	2.6%	1.9%	2.4%	2.2%	2 6%	2.4%	2.4%	2.5%	2.3%	2.2%	2.3%	2.3%	2.4%	2.5%
Sheetings and Coarse Fabrics	30.9	27.9	28.0	27.5	28.4	25.8	25.0	25.2	25.4	25.9	26.3	25.7	27.1	26.5	26.5	27.6
Print Cloth	32.8	35.9	37.6	36.8	37.0	38.9	38.7	40.8	39.0	37.7	39.2	37.2	35.2	35.4	35.2	34.5
Colored Yarn	7.7	8.3	7.8	8.7	7.8	8.8	8.4	7.5	6.9	6.1	5.6	5.4	5.4	4.8	4.5	4.8
Fine Cotton	13.4	13.4	12.0	12.2	12.3	11.9	12.8	12.6	13.5	14.7	14.2	16.2	16.8	18.2	18.2	17.4
Napped Fabrics	5.1	5.0	3.9	4.0	4.1	3.2	2.8	2.4	2.4	2.3	2.2	2.2	2.1	2.2	2.0	1.9
Towelings	4.2	3.8	4.1	4.6	4.2	4.6	4.7	4.6	4.9	5.4	5.7	6.0	6.0	5.9	6.3	6.6
Specialties, Other	3.7	3.6	4.0	4.3	3.8	4.6	4.8	4.5	5.5	5.4	4.5	5.1	5.1	4.8	4.9	4.7
Total	100.0%	100.0%	100.0%	100.0%	100.0%	100.0%	100.0%	100.0%	100.0%	100.0%	100.0%	100.0%	100.0%	100.0%	100.0%	100.0%
Rayon Broad Woven	1,977	2,187	1,957	2,406	2,084	1,852	1,903	1,731	1,928	1,626	1,464	1,654	1,618	1,434	1,465	1,562
Filament Rayon	62.6%	62.0%	66.3%	66.6%	62.2%	54.2%	55.3%	49.0%	46.0%	48.6%	47.2%	42.2%	41.2%	46.0%	47.5%	43.7%
Spun Rayon	16.8	17.4	17.4	18.0	19.6	21.7	23.2	25.7	27.4	21.6	19.3	25.4	19.1	15.7	16.2	18.4
Combination Filament and Spun	9.0	11.6	9.4	8.4	9.1	12.1	7.3	6.9	5.7	6.6	7.3	7.3	7.5	5.7	5.7	6.4
Upholstery, Drapery, Tie Fabrics.	2.9	1.8	1.5	1.6	1.8	2.7	3.3	5.1	6.1	7.1	9.9	9.5	11.7	13.7	12.0	13.2
All Other Rayon	8.7	7.2	5.4	5.4	7.3	9.3	10.9	13.3	14.8	16.1	16.3	15.6	20.5	18.9	18.6	18.3
Total	100.0%	100.0%	100.0%	100.0%	100.0%	100.0%	100.0%	100.0%	100.0%	100.0%	100.0%	100.0%	100.0%	100.0%	100.0%	100.0%
Other Man-Made Broad Woven*	51	61	129	172	266	401	464	559	629	602	783	694	836	928	908	1,085
Woolen, Worsted Broad Woven	516	498	414	471	375	351	336	284	318	324	294	271	310	286	287	306
Silk, Part Silk Broad Woven	10	19	16	29	26	42	38	43	43	41	28	21	29	27	23	25
Paper Yarn and Miscellaneous	--	--	--	--	--	--	--	11	27	20	14	13	15	15	12	13
Total Broad Woven	12,371	12,405	10,923	13,091	12,887	12,160	12,944	12,518	13,116	12,931	12,118	11,628	12,414	12,056	11,863	12,265
	Percentage Analysis															
Cotton Broad Woven	79.3%	77.7%	77.0%	76.5%	78.6%	78.3%	78.8%	79.0%	77.6%	79.8%	78.7%	77.2%	77.4%	77.6%	77.3%	75.7%
Rayon Broad Woven	16.0	17.6	17.9	18.4	16.2	15.2	14.7	13.8	14.7	12.6	12.1	14.2	13.1	11.9	12.3	12.8
Other Man-Made Broad Woven	.4	.5	1.2	1.3	2.1	3.3	3.6	4.5	4.8	4.7	6.5	6.0	6.7	7.8	7.7	8.9
Woolen, Worsted Broad Woven	4.2	4.0	3.8	3.6	2.9	2.9	2.6	2.3	2.4	2.5	2.4	2.3	2.5	2.4	2.4	2.5
Silk, Part Silk Broad Woven	.1	.2	.1	.2	.2	.3	.3	.3	.3	.3	.2	.2	.2	.2	.2	.2
Paper Yarn and Miscellaneous	--	--	--	--	--	--	--	.1	.2	.1	.1	.1	.1	.1	.1	.1
Total Broad Woven	100.0%	100.0%	100.0%	100.0%	100.0%	100.0%	100.0%	100.0%	100.0%	100.0%	100.0%	100.0%	100.0%	100.0%	100.0%	100.0%
	Millions of Pounds															
Tire Cord and Fabric	565	536	435	523	604	531	521	418	524	449	449	387	470	417	391	427
Cotton	62.0%	53.2%	35.8%	43.2%	47.9%	26.2%	14.1%	14.3%	13.0%	11.4%	9.4%	9.7%	8.4%	7.2%	4.7%	4.4%
Rayon and Nylon	38.0	46.8	64.2	56.8	52.1	73.8	85.9	85.7	87.0	88.6	90.6	90.3	91.6	92.8	95.3	95.6
Total	100.0%	100.0%	100.0%	100.0%	100.0%	100.0%	100.0%	100.0%	100.0%	100.0%	100.0%	100.0%	100.0%	100.0%	100.0%	100.0%

*Includes Nylon, acrylic, polyester, Saran and polyethylene, and textile glass fiber fabrics and mixtures.

Source: "Ten Years of Broad Woven Fabrics" assembled by the Association of Cotton Textile Merchants of New York. Figures, Bureau of the Census, Annual Survey of Manufacturers. Percentages prepared by Harvard Business School, Bureau of Business Research.

10. COTTON TEXTILE INDUSTRY

Print Cloth Prices, 1947–1961

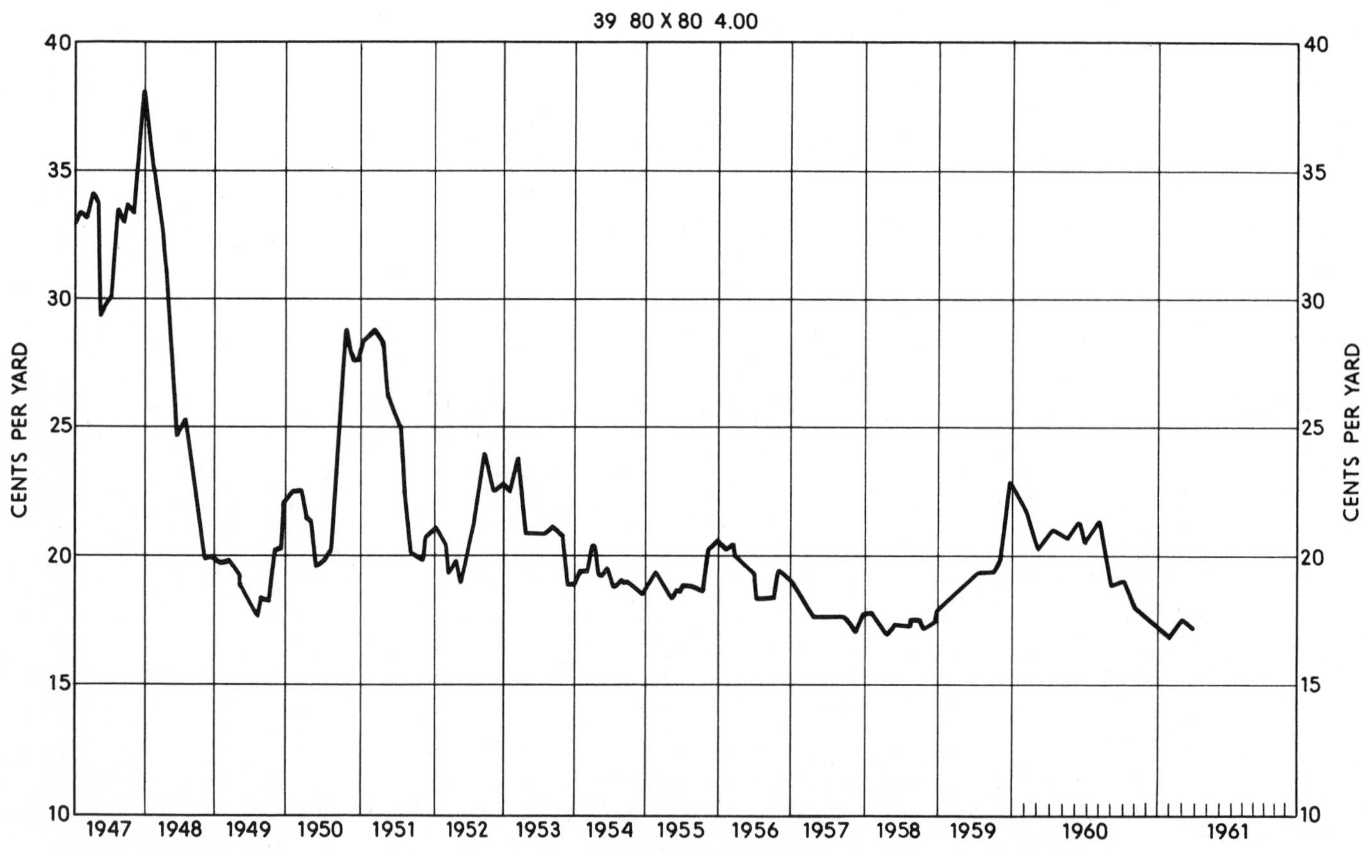

PRINT CLOTH PRICES (39",80x80,4.00)													
MONTH / YEAR	JAN	FEB	MAR	APR	MAY	JUN	JUL	AUG	SEP	OCT	NOV	DEC	MONTHLY AVERAGE
1947	.326	.333	.330	.340	.290	.301	.334	.329	.337	.355	.373	.380	.335
1948	.360	.343	.324	.293	.272	.250	.252	.250	.232	.210	.202	.201	.266
1949	.198	.197	.199	.195	.186	.181	.179	.186	.202	.208	.222	.220	.198
1950	.226	.226	.215	.197	.198	.203	.233	.260	.285	.276	.280	.283	.240
1951	.286	.288	.285	.260	.258	.250	.214	.204	.201	.200	.207	.214	.239
1952	.210	.205	.195	.197	.190	.198	.205	.213	.225	.233	.225	.226	.210
1953	.225	.238	.210	.210	.210	.210	.210	.211	.210	.205	.190	.190	.210
1954	.194	.195	.203	.195	.193	.193	.191	.189	.190	.190	.187	.186	.192
1955	.193	.190	.188	.186	.187	.188	.190	.190	.189	.195	.205	.208	.192
1956	.205	.206	.200	.194	.192	.190	.186	.186	.186	.194	.193	.190	.194
1957	.186	.181	.180	.179	.178	.179	.179	.179	.178	.176	.174	.178	.179
1958	.178	.175	.174	.172	.173	.174	.174	.177	.177	.176	.177	.183	.176
1959	.183	.185	.186	.187	.188	.195	.195	.195	.195	.198	.218	.230	.196
1960	.229	.223	.211	.205	.208	.213	.210	.203	.191	.185	.180	.178	.203
1961	.175	.173	.175	.175	.174	.175	.175	.178	.178	.178	.178	.178	.176
1962	.178	.178	.175	.175	.176	.176	.178	.178	.176	.175	.175	.178	.176
1963	.180	.180											

Source: 1947-1961 (April) U.S. Department of Labor (reprinted from Textile Hi-Lights, spring 1961.) 1961 (May, 1963) U.S. Department of Labor, Bureau of Labor Statistics, Wholesale Prices and Price Indices.

11. COTTON TEXTILE INDUSTRY

Cotton Prices versus Cloth Prices,
Monthly Averages, 1947-1962 and Monthly 1961
(Cents per Pound)

Year		Raw Cotton Price	Cotton Cloth Price*	Cotton Mill Margins**	Percent
1947		34.15	88.99	54.84	61.62
1948		33.43	81.01	47.58	58.73
1949		31.37	63.89	32.52	50.90
1950		36.23	76.64	40.41	52.73
1951		37.97	73.64	35.67	48.44
1952		38.73	68.16	29.43	43.18
1953		34.60	66.77	32.17	48.18
1954		35.80	62.55	26.75	42.77
1955		36.04	62.62	26.58	42.45
1956		35.60	63.51	27.91	43.95
1957		34.76	59.63	24.87	41.71
1958		34.81	57.56	22.75	39.52
1959		34.03	63.23	29.20	46.18
1960		32.36	64.61	32.25	49.91
1961		34.17	58.65	24.48	41.73
1962		35.72	60.96	25.24	41.41
1961:	January	35.78	60.63	24.85	40.99
	February	35.82	60.76	24.94	41.05
	March	35.98	61.07	25.09	41.08
	April	35.85	61.23	25.38	41.45
	May	36.13	61.19	25.06	40.95
	June	36.34	61.24	24.90	40.66
	July	36.19	61.29	25.10	40.95
	August	35.89	61.12	25.23	41.28
	September	35.23	60.93	25.70	42.18
	October	35.08	60.71	25.63	42.24
	November	35.10	60.68	25.58	42.16
	December	35.30	60.67	25.37	41.82
1962:	January	35.45	60.55	25.10	41.45
	February	35.66	60.47	24.81	41.03

*Based on 20 constructions 1955 on; constructions 1954 and previous years.

**Mill margins are the difference between the price of the approximate quantity of grey cotton goods obtainable from a pound of cotton and the average "landed" price of four territory growth assumed to be used in each kind of cloth.

Source: Agricultural Marketing Service figures, adjusted from a crop year basis 1947-1959 by Standard and Poor's Textiles, Basic Analysis, June, 1962. 1962 monthly figures from Cotton Situation, Economic Research Service, U.S. Department of Agriculture, March, 1963. Percentage figures prepared by the Bureau of Business Research, Harvard Graduate School of Business Administration.

12. COTTON TEXTILE INDUSTRY
Ratio of Inventories to Unfilled Orders
Cotton Broadwoven Goods, 1951–1962

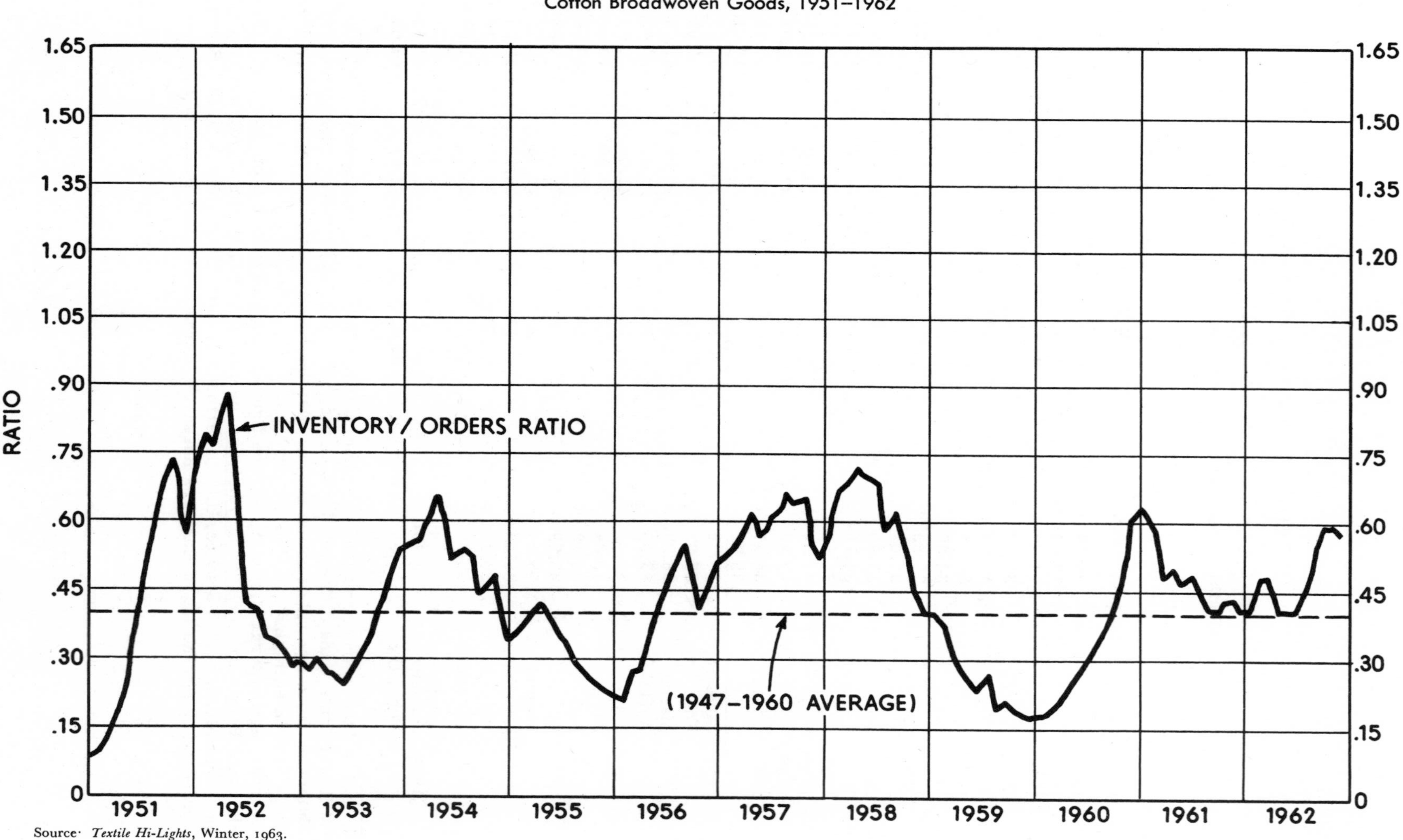

Source: *Textile Hi-Lights*, Winter, 1963.

13. COTTON TEXTILE INDUSTRY

Major End Use Consumption Summary, 1949-1961

	Apparel	Home Furnish-ings	Other Consumer Type Products	Indus-trial Uses	Exports	Total Percent	Total Million Pounds
1949-52 average	39.8%	19.9%	10.1%	24.1%	6.1%	100%	5,837
1953-56 average	41.9	22.6	9.9	20.8	4.8	100	6,167
1956	42.3	23.4	9.8	19.7	4.8	100	6,384
1957	42.3	23.2	9.8	19.2	5.5	100	6,287
1958	42.8	23.8	10.1	18.1	5.2	100	6,156
1959	42.3	24.1	10.0	19.0	4.6	100	6,788
1960	42.5	24.6	10.0	18.2	4.7	100	6,596
1961	43.5	24.4	10.3	17.3	4.5	100	6,651

*Comprises fibers used in 101 items.
Source: Textile Organon, November, 1962.

14. COTTON TEXTILE INDUSTRY

Textile Industry Capital Spending, 1956-1960
(In Millions of Dollars)

	1956	1957	1958	1959	1960
Retained earnings	$139	$ 77	$ 74	$288	$189
Depreciation charges	304	321	320	293	306
Total: retained earnings and depreciation charges	443	398	394	581	495
Total: capital spending	465	408	288	412	530
Spent for modernization	442	302	236	346	408
Percent of total spent for modernization	95%	74%	82%	84%	77%
Modernization spending: percent of retained earnings and depreciation charges	100%	76%	60%	60%	82%
Total capital spending: percent of retained earnings and depreciation charges	105%	103%	73%	71%	107%

Source: McGraw-Hill Department of Economics (Textile World, November, 1961).

Textron Incorporated (A)

During the postwar years 1946 and 1947, the activities of Textron Incorporated[1] were a subject of much interest and discussion in the textile industry. Comments in the press included the following:

> Textron, high stepping newcomer to the country's aged and often ailing textile-industry, has branched out again. With some fanfare, Royal Little, president, announced last week that a new subsidiary, Textron Southern, Inc., has just bought the controlling interest in Gossett Mills of Anderson, S. C., which owns 12 cotton and rayon mills in the Carolinas.
>
> This move adds 200,000 spindles and 4,600 looms to the sizeable total already controlled by Textron. By the same token, it will take a large slice of their product (2,000,000 yards of cloth and 250,000 pounds of yarn a week) out of the dwindling pool of goods available to independent textile converters.
>
> The publicity that went with Textron's purchase set many a mill owner pondering the familiar arguments for and against vertical integration of the textile industry. Textron is probably the most enthusiastic and certainly the most dramatic proponent of integration all the way from the original yarn to the final garment. Older mill owners, trying to figure which way the postwar tide will be running, would give a lot to know what its income statement will look like 10 years from now.[2]

The purchase just described represented one of the concluding steps in a swift, bold program of expansion and integration of manufacturing facilities which Textron initiated in the concluding years of the war. The management believed that if the program could be brought to a successful conclusion the company would be able to guarantee a higher standard of quality to the consumer and would gain some freedom from the instability, price cutting, extreme competition, and other ills which were characteristic of the prewar textile industry. The venture was viewed by the industry with mixed opinions, but it was generally agreed that if the structure created by the company proved sound, Textron would be assured of a dominant and profitable position in the postwar textile market for some years to come.

EARLY HISTORY

Two jobs provided Mr. Royal Little the background to enter the infant rayon industry. Mr. Little had left Harvard College during World War I to serve in the Army in France. After his return he spent 6 months working in a textile mill to learn the silk operations upon which many of the rayon processes were eventually to be patterned. He then worked for a company which held some of the basic patents on the acetate process for the manufacture of rayon yarn.

In 1923, Mr. Little formed the Special Yarns Corporation, the predecessor of Textron, with $10,000 borrowed from the First National Bank of Boston. The company started in operation with three employees and a small rented space in the Old King Terminal in South Boston. Its business consisted of the processing of rayon yarn, or artificial silk, as it was then called, for the growing New England rayon weaving industry. Up until then, the dyeing, throwing,[3] and other service industries had been located largely in Pennsylvania, New Jersey, and New York State. There was a need for these service operations to be performed in New England, and the new company's operations expanded rapidly.

In 1928, a merger was effected with a subsidiary of the Franklin Process Company in order to enter the package dyeing of yarn as opposed to skein dyeing. The Franklin Process Company had been trying for some time to adapt its cot-

[1] "Textron Incorporated" was the official name of the entire corporation, while "Textron Inc." designated a single subsidiary operating most of the New England mills together with the consumer product sales. For the purposes of the case, the term "Textron" will refer to the corporation as a whole. Subsidiaries will be referred to by their full names, such as "Textron Inc." or "Textron Southern, Inc."

[2] *Business Week,* May 18, 1946.

[3] Throwing is the trade name of treating silk or rayon filament yarns with soaking solutions and twisting to customer specifications. Depending on the use to which the yarn is put, 5 to 70 turns per inch may be required. Most filament yarn is woven without going through the throwing process.

ton package dyeing technique to rayon, but there seemed to be so many technological obstacles that the executives of the Franklin Process Company eventually withdrew and sold their interests in the merged company to Mr. Little's group. The merged company was moved to Providence, Rhode Island where it eventually became known as the Atlantic Rayon Corporation. In 1943, the name was changed to "Textron Incorporated."

In the period following 1928, the company purchased raw rayon filament yarn from rayon manufacturers and resold it, with or without further processing, to hosiery, knitting, and weaving mills. The growth of the company from 1928 to 1939 was in three general directions: (1) A substantial business was developed as a wholesale distributor of rayon yarns to small users whom the rayon manufacturers were not equipped to supply directly. (2) The package dyeing of rayon was finally achieved on a commercial basis to customer specifications. (3) Increased investment in rayon throwing machinery enabled the company to service many New England mills which had been buying thrown yarn from Pennsylvania, New York, and New Jersey. In 1939, the company tripled its throwing capacity by establishing a yarn throwing plant in Lowell, Massachusetts.

By December, 1941, the plants in Providence and Lowell employed a total of about 800 people. No yarn dyeing or other processing was performed until firm orders with detailed specifications had been received from customers and no woven, knitted, or other fabrics were manufactured. The company's customers included about 600 firms in many different branches of the rayon industry.

In January, 1942, the company formed the Atlantic Parachute Corporation to manufacture parachutes for the United States Government in the surplus floor space of the company's Lowell plant. A procurement division subcontracted to about 30 of the smaller New England textile mills government orders for the component parts of parachutes made of nylon. Physical testing and control laboratories were built at its Lowell plant to maintain quality and supervise the subcontractors' manufacturing operations. By the end of 1942, the Lowell plant was turning out parachutes at the rate of 3,600 a week, having expanded to one of the largest parachute operations of any single plant in the United States.

In early 1943 a second large sewing plant to manufacture military products was established in Manchester, New Hampshire. During the war years, the Lowell and Manchester plants produced human escape, bomb fragmentation, and other types of parachutes as well as tents, hammocks, and various items of protective clothing.

In December, 1942, the corporation began to withdraw from yarn dyeing by selling the real estate of its Providence plant for $66,500 and renting back the property on a 6-year lease. In June, 1944, the corporation sold for $640,000 its yarn dyeing business, which had accounted for 14 percent of the Textron sales in 1943. The throwing operations at Providence were transferred to the plant at Lowell.

EXPANSION 1943–1947

During the summer of 1943 Army and Navy stockpiles of certain textile items reached their goals, and the government began contract cancellations which soon totaled $4,500,000 for Textron alone. The cancellations, for the most part, contained "please stand by" provisions suggesting that the cancelled orders might be revived at any time.

The executives of Textron were very reluctant under these circumstances to release the 3,500 people whom they had employed in their sewing plants. Hence, they began the diversion of production facilities to such consumer goods as shower curtains and draperies made from water repellent fabrics and women's lingerie. In late March, 1944, a men's wear sewing plant was leased in Easthampton, Massachusetts. After the war, a series of satellite plants was set up in Maine, New Hampshire, and Massachusetts. In March, 1947, the corporation had six such small sewing plants in Lowell, Manchester, and Easthampton. During the early period of expansion, the Textron company leased sewing equipment.

As the number of consumer products increased, company executives began the advertising and promotion of the Textron brand name. In the expansion of sewing facilities, it seemed less dangerous to expand in several lines rather than to build up any one line to too large a percentage of the potential market. In the period 1943–1945, therefore, negligees, men's wear, and blouses were added to the group of consumer products. It was in connection with the new product line that the "Textron" company name was selected, as an indication of the broad line of cotton and synthetic products manufactured.

At this period of growth during the summer of 1943, Mr. Royal Little saw in the existing market and financial situation an opportunity to create an integrated textile operation. During the war, it was impossible for a new user to buy either grey or finished cloth. However, since OPA price ceilings and excess profits taxes limited earnings, it was possible to provide the cloth by purchasing mills for approximately the value of their net working capital. Mr. Little also believed that as a postwar market developed, grey cloth would continue to be difficult to obtain for his sewing plants from outside suppliers. He therefore decided to integrate backward into spinning and weaving facilities as opportunities presented themselves for the acquisition of mills.

Acquisition of the Suncook Mills

The first major step toward integration was the acquisition of the Suncook Mills at Suncook, New Hampshire in September, 1943, for the sum of $1,754,000 in cash, of which $1,454,000 was for inventories. The Suncook plant, which had been built in 1870, contained 1,400 looms, of which approximately 70 percent were of recent design installed subsequent to 1936. The plant contained no spinning equipment, but had for many years operated weaving facilities for cotton and rayon grey cloth. Its principal product, a cotton fabric for military uses called "Flightex," was closed out together with its inventory for $1,062,000 in June, 1944, in order for the weaving capacity to be integrated with the Textron product line.

Acquisition of Nemasket Mill

In order to provide a supply of yarn for the weaving facilities at Suncook, Textron obtained the Nemasket Mill in Taunton, Massachusetts in November, 1944. The Nemasket Mill, which was built in 1890, contained 30,000 spindles and 77 cards for the preparation of spun rayon yarn and rayon-cotton-wool yarn blends. The cost of plant and inventories amounted to $280,000, of which $180,000 was for inventories alone.

Withdrawal from the Yarn Throwing Business

In December, 1944, the corporation sold its yarn throwing machinery and equipment at Lowell and leased back the property from the purchaser. The sewing facilities at Lowell, however, were maintained. The disposal of the job throwing facilities was undertaken because it was felt that the business had no place in the integrated program. Certain throwing machinery was retained at a small leased plant (the Pembroke Mill) located at Suncook, New Hampshire, in order to supply all of the twisted yarns needed at the Suncook weaving plant.

Acquisition of the Manville Jenckes Corporation

In March, 1945, the corporation acquired the Manville Jenckes Corporation, one of the oldest and largest textile mills in New England, with an initial purchase of $5,550,000 in preferred and common stock. In addition to the financial opportunities involved, the corporation's interest in the company was to acquire its wide loom production of high-grade spun rayon and wool blended fabrics as well as to augment its supply of other types of filament rayon goods.

The Manville plants, which were built in the 19th century, contained 83,000 spinning spindles, 13,000 twisting spindles, and 2,540 looms. Its cotton fabrics were largely sheer goods such as marquisettes and plaids, while the rayon fabrics were fancy weaves for drapery and upholstery material. Since all Manville cloth had been sold in the grey, its line increased the yardage available to the Textron sewing plants and made possible active participation in the War Production Board's essential clothing program. In addition, certain of the Manville spun rayon blends were believed capable of supplementing the Suncook Mills' filament rayon fabrics in order to increase Textron sewing operations in slacks, robes, and other apparel items. A large converting operation was established to distribute the finished wide blend fabrics to the men's and women's wear trade. The Manville Jenckes product line also permitted the corporation to increase its sales of finished piece goods to department stores for over-the-counter distribution.

The method used to obtain control of the Manville Jenckes Corporation, which was similar to that employed in the acquisition of the Lonsdale and other companies, is explained in the Appendix.

Acquisition of the Lonsdale Company

In October, 1945, the corporation acquired the stock of the Lonsdale Company from a charitable trust for less than $1,700,000. The Lonsdale Company, which operated two spinning and weaving mills and a bleachery, had acquired a reputation for producing high quality cotton fabrics used by better dress and shirt manufacturers under the Lonsdale name. The two mills contained 99,660 spindles and 2,190 looms, of which 360 were of the latest model. The entire output of the company was sold as finished cloth, only a portion of which was used by Textron sewing plants as constituted in 1946 and 1947. Following its acquisition, the Lonsdale Company contributed over $2,600,000 in dividends to the Textron system during the subsequent two years.

Acquisition of the Nashua Manufacturing Company

In December, 1945, the corporation undertook the purchase of the common stock of the Nashua Manufacturing Company of Nashua, New Hampshire for a total sum of more than $10,000,000. The Nashua company had been engaged in the manufacture of textiles since 1823. Its principal products consisted of cotton-, wool- and rayon-mixture blankets, cotton sheets, pillowcases, sheetings and other cotton fabrics in the grey, napped, bleached, or piece-dyed condition, and spun rayon blends. Its facilities enabled it to perform all the processing operations from the raw cotton, wool, or rayon fiber to the finished product ready for consumption or use. The two groups of mill buildings at Nashua, New Hampshire, contained 170,900 spindles and 3,700 looms approximately 30 years old. Many of the company's products were sold under well-recognized brand names which had been established in the textile trade for many years, such as Indian Head cotton fabric and Nashua blankets. Although Textron contracted a bank loan of almost $8,000,000 for the purchase of Nashua stock, financial measures involving the use of the company's working capital were able to reduce the loan to $2 million within 18 months.

Formation of Textron Southern, Inc.

In May, 1946, a new subsidiary, Textron Southern, Inc., was formed to acquire the properties of the Gossett Mills, which operated 12 mills and a bleachery in the Carolinas. These properties were acquired in part because they provided in the grey state certain types of cotton print cloth, rayon fabrics and fine lawns which were of value to the Textron sewing plants in New England. After certain of the plants which did not fit the integrated program were sold, the 4 mills in Anderson and the plant in Williamston, South Carolina, together with 4 mills in Charlotte, North Carolina, added 184,000 spindles and 4,280 looms to the Textron spinning and weaving capacity. Most of the plants were built subsequent to 1900 and modernized after World War I.

The purchase cost of the southern mills was $12,000,000, furnished in part by a $5,800,000 bank loan and a $4,000,000 issue of new stock. Within a year, the bank loan was reduced to $300,000 through funds obtained from earnings, excess working capital, and the sale of surplus plants.

Formation of Textron Puerto Rico

In 1947, Textron invested $500,000 to build a modern cotton mill in Puerto Rico with a capitalization of $3,500,000. The new plant was granted complete tax exemption for 12 years by the Puerto Rican government. It was believed that tax exemptions and low labor costs would combine to enable the new organization to produce cotton print cloth at a substantial competitive advantage for shipment to Textron finishing and sewing plants in New England.

Formation of Textron Inc.

During 1947 all of the New England mills except those of the old Lonsdale Company were grouped together in a single subsidiary named "Textron Inc." and the entire group of finishing and sewing plants were brought under its supervision. Textron Inc. thereupon assumed the problems of consumer product manufacture for the Textron, Nashua, and Manville lines while the southern subsidiary concentrated on grey cloth production. Meanwhile, top executive planning was centralized in New York City where Textron purchased stock in a seven-story building on Fifth Avenue.

By the steps outline above, the Textron system expanded in 6 years from a company with assets of $2,500,000 and net sales of $8,000,000 in 1941 to a corporation with assets of $57,000,000 and sales of $125,000,000 in 1947. In the same period, the company changed from a processor of rayon yarns to a manufacturer of consumer products, performing all operations from the spinning of the yarn and the weaving of the cloth, to the sewing and marketing of finished garments. The bank loans incurred to purchase the various plants had reached a peak of more than $17,000,000 in September, 1946. By April, 1947, these obligations were reduced to $3,500,000 through reduction of excess working capital in the new subsidiaries and through extensive use of sale and lease-back arrangements such as that described in the Manville case in the Appendix. Exhibits 1 and 2 provide financial data relative to the growth of Textron between 1941 and 1947.

PRODUCTS IN 1947

During 1946 and 1947, Textron made a number of rearrangements in the business operations of its subsidiaries. Properties not essential to the program of integration were sold or leased; cetain functions and operations were transferred from one subsidiary to another; new companies were formed and old ones dissolved. In general, the purpose of these changes was to consolidate the corporation's holdings, coordinate the activities of the various divisions, and improve the balance of manufacturing operations. The products which the corporation sold were divided into four major groups:

Textron Line: The Textron line of consumer goods consisted of four subgroups:

(*a*) Women's Wear
- Woven lingerie (slips and nightgowns)
- Negligees (housecoats, plain and quilted robes, and bedjackets)
- Blouses
- Tricot knit underwear (slips, nightgowns, and panties)

(*b*) Men's Wear
- Pajamas, shorts, sport shirts

(*c*) Home Fashions
- Shower curtains and draperies
- Bedroom ensembles (bedspreads, curtains)

(*d*) Drapery and upholstery fabrics
- Over-the-counter piece goods

These products were advertised nationally and sold under the brand name "Textron"; they were distributed on a nation-wide scale to the better department stores and men's and women's specialty shops. For the most part, the Textron products were priced to sell in the upper middle price range.

Nashua Line: The Nashua Manufacturing Company continued to produce approximately the same products as it had prior to the acquisition. This line, which was priced to sell in the medium and low price brackets, consisted of the following:

(*a*) Blankets
- The Nashua Purrey—88 percent rayon, 12 percent wool
- Wool blends with cotton and rayon sold under various names
- Cotton blankets and warm sheets sold under various names

(*b*) Sheets and pillowcases
- Type 180 carded percale—Indian Maiden
- Type 140 carded or muslin—Dwight Anchor and other names

The above products were sold by the Nashua sales organization to retail, chain, mail-order, wholesale, and special outlets.

(*c*) Indian Head Fabric: Sold to uniform and some garment cutters and to wholesale and retail outlets for over-the-counter sale as piece goods.

(*d*) Industrial and General Purpose Fabrics:
- Sold as grey goods
- Shoe linings
- Table canton—laundry trade
- Mitten flannel—work gloves
- Sheeting
- Other special items

The above products were sold by the Nashua sales organization to the outlets indicated.

(*e*) Rayon and Wool Wide Blends: Sold in the grey, through a selling agent, to the better class of women's and men's wear converters.

Lonsdale Line: The Lonsdale Company continued to manufacture the same line of fine cotton goods for the shirt and dress trade which it had produced prior to its acquisition. These products were finished and sold by the company's own converting division, and only a small part of the output went to the sewing plants of Textron Inc. The Lonsdale Company was well-known in the textile industry for the high quality fabrics which it produced.

Manville Line: The Manville mills produced a general line of finished fabrics, including wide blends for men's and women's outerwear, cottons, and filament rayons. These materials were sold for the most part to cutters.

OPERATIONS IN 1947

The operating divisions and subsidiaries of the corporation were grouped into six major units.

Textron Southern, Inc.: This subsidiary operated eight spinning and weaving mills in the Carolinas and Alabama. These mills produced cotton and rayon cloth and different blended fabrics. The company also operated a finishing plant in South Carolina and had facilities for bleaching and dyeing a certain portion of its output. Almost all of the output of Textron Southern, Inc. was either used by Textron Inc. in finished products or was sold as finished goods by one of the subsidiaries.

Nashua Manufacturing Company: The Nashua company operated two mills in Nashua, New Hampshire, which were used to produce the Nashua line of fabrics and products described above. These products were sold in substantially the same manner as prior to the acquisition and only a small portion of the output went to the sewing plants of Textron Inc.

In February, 1947, the Nashua Manufacturing Company was also operating the Pembroke, Nemasket, Suncook, and Manville mills. Most of the output from these mills was converted and used in the corporation's sewing operations or sold to outside customers.

A third activity of the Nashua Manufacturing Company was the operation of a large converting division (Manville Fabrics). This division took grey goods from the various subsidiaries and had them converted in the corporation's own plants or by outside finishers for use in the corporation's sewing plants or for outside sale.

Finally, the Nashua Manufacturing Company operated the fabric development laboratories for Textron Inc. These laboratories created new fabrics and fabric constructions, consulted with the operating divisions on matters concerning the processing and finishing of fabrics, checked and analyzed competitive items for weave formation, quality, finish, and workmanship, and experimented with new yarns and fibers such as nylon, glass, and other synthetics. The laboratories also worked with the merchandise managers on new fabrics and merchandising plans.

Lonsdale Company: The Lonsdale Company operated two spinning and weaving mills and a bleachery. The properties of the Lonsdale Company were such that they could be easily adapted to the processing of spun rayon without major expense for additional machinery.

Sewn Products Division: The sewn products division operated the sewing plants used in the manufacture of the Textron line of consumer goods. In general, these plants were organized in groups by products. The Lowell group of plants was used primarily for home fashions, the Easthampton group for men's wear, and the Manchester group for lingerie. Negligees and blouses were fabricated by groups of subcontractors in the New York area.

In some cases, the groups of sewing plants consisted of a "mother" plant and a number of "feeder" plants. The mother plant did all of the cutting, packing, and shipping and some of the stitching. The feeder plants received cut parts from the mother plant, performed the stitching operations, and then returned the finished garments to the mother plant for packing and shipping.

Tricot[4] *Division:* This division consisted of a small plant and office at East Greenwich, Rhode Island, which had been established for the manufacture of knitted lingerie.

Research and Development Division: From the time the Textron line was first offered to the public, the corporation had attached a great deal of importance to research and quality control. The research and development laboratories had been established as a separate operating division to make certain that their functions were properly developed.

The division did basic textile and chemical research on such things as new textile fibers, dyestuffs, printing inks, water repellents, mildewcides, wash fastness, light fastness, and the union dyeing of mixed fibre fabrics. The division also kept abreast of developments in the plastics field.

A second major function of the research and development division was that of quality control. The activities of the quality control departments were roughly parallel to the vertical structure of the corporation. The control program provided for the establishment of uniform quality standards and inspection procedures at each of the various levels in the production process. The ultimate purpose of this program was to see that the necessary tests were made and steps taken throughout the entire organization to obtain the quality standards required in the merchandising programs.

Flow of Products

The flow of products and materials between the different operating divisions and subsidiaries of the corporation was adjusted constantly in accordance with changes in market conditions at the various levels and the merchandising plans for the several lines of consumer goods. The general plan for operations during the first quarter of 1947 as shown in Exhibit 3, is based on a total volume of output of 4,500,000 yards of cloth a week. The diagram does not indicate the flow of yarn from spinning to weaving mills. The spinning and weaving capacities of most of the mills were in balance, and the corporation purchased very little yarn from outside sources.

[4] Tricot (pronounced tree'co) is a knitted runproof fabric.

MARKETING PROGRAM

In February, 1947, Textron had three major marketing programs, each with a separate sales organization. The program conducted by the parent company included the sale of the Textron branded line of consumer goods and a small volume of finished fabrics for export to foreign markets. The program of the Nashua Manufacturing Company included the sale of the Nashua consumer products; the sale of finished fabrics to cutters, industrial customers, retailers, and wholesalers; and the sale of grey goods to converters and industrial customers. The third program, that of the Lonsdale Company, involved the sale of finished fabrics to cutters and of grey goods to converters. The output of Textron Southern, Inc. was distributed in one or another of these three programs. The relative volume of goods handled in the various programs and the amount moving into the several markets may be seen from Exhibit 3.

The following discussion will be confined to the program used for the sale of the Textron branded line.

Merchandise Managers

The task of merchandising the Textron consumer products was divided among the six merchandise managers indicated in Exhibit 4. Each manager decided on the type and variety of items to appear in his line, supervised the designing and styling of the items, selected fabrics and finishes, worked out patterns, and decided on prices.

Sale Organization

A staff of about 65 salesmen operated from the regional offices shown in Exhibit 4. Each salesman handled the entire line of Textron products and covered a particular geographic territory.[5] The salesmen called on a selected group of the better department stores and specialty shops in each city. The policy of selective selling had been adopted because the executives believed that it would involve the company in less severe competition than would a policy of selling to all types of outlets. Moreover, Mr. Royal Little had contended from the outset that the acceptance and promotion of the company's

[5] The typical practice in the industry was for the salesmen to specialize by product lines.

products by the quality retailers would hasten consumer acceptance of the unknown "Textron" label.

Public Relations Group

In addition to its sales organization, Textron Inc. maintained a public relations staff of about 15 highly trained young women. This group operated under the direction of the vice-president in charge of advertising. One or more of the women was assigned to each sales region. These women called on the retail stores, not for the purpose of selling merchandise, but rather to inform the stores about the promotion and advertising plans of Textron Inc., and to give them every possible assistance in merchandising the Textron products.

Advertising Program

In the period 1937 to 1947, Textron Inc. conducted an extensive advertising program designed to make the public aware of the Textron name and the standards of quality for which it stood. Selling, advertising, and administrative expenses, which had averaged less than 3 percent of sales prior to the expansion program, rose to 8 percent in 1946. Approximately one third of this amount was for advertising alone.

All of the advertising was designed to emphasize in some way or another the integrated structure of Textron and its unique facilities for quality control. The individual advertisements were never used to sell a specific item such as a blouse, but were rather designed to convey the idea that Textron Inc. manufactured a broad line of products such as blouses, slips, housecoats, and shower curtains.

The corporation's advertising developed some very distinctive characteristics. In describing the advertising copy Mr. Spooner, vice-president in charge of advertising, spoke as follows:

> You've seen it in the magazines, no doubt . . . and maybe it's made you gasp. If you haven't seen it, the best way I know to describe it is to say it's out of this world.
>
> For instance, it may picture a lovely lady floating through the heavens with the greatest of ease in a wine-colored hostess coat. Fleecy clouds and a cluster of tiny parachutes provide a tender background.
>
> Or you may see a pleasant-faced gentleman in smartly striped pajamas making a two-point landing in his bed with the aid of a parachute.
>
> Screwball? Maybe. I wouldn't argue that. It isn't like any slip or housecoat or pajama advertising that you or I ever saw before. But here's what it's done. It's made every major retailer ask questions. It's impelled people to go into stores in a fine frenzy of curiosity. It's made the Textron name known.

Coordination of Sales and Production

From the time the integrated program was undertaken, a good deal of attention was devoted to the problem of coordinating sales and production to the different levels in the structure and to controlling the flow of materials between the different divisions and subsidiaries of the company. In February, 1947, a new group was being set up consisting of three divisions: a production control branch, a price and cost analysis branch, and a fabric allocation control branch (see Exhibit 4). It was intended that after this group was established, the procedures for coordinating merchandising and production programs would be somewhat as follows:

The merchandise managers would develop plans for their lines at periodic intervals in accordance with the traditional selling seasons in the industry. Plans for the men's wear and home fashions lines would be drawn up semiannually while plans for blouses, negligees, and lingerie would be prepared quarterly. The plans prepared by the merchandise managers were to include decisions as to the items and styles in the line, the fabrics and finishes to be used, prices, and the probable volume which would be sold during the next selling season. In deciding on the estimated volume, the merchandise managers were to be aided by the sales department; in deciding on the prices, they were to be aided by the price and cost analysis branch of the production control group.

After the plans for a particular selling season were completed, the production control group would schedule production. If because of the weave construction, the size of the run, the existing volume of production, or other reasons, it appeared impractical for any of the mills to undertake the manufacture of a particular fabric, the production control group was to investigate the possibility of purchasing the material from outside sources. The executives anticipated that the corporation might always purchase a small volume of finished fabrics in order to secure for novelty items fabrics which it was not economical to make in the mills.

In cases where a particular fabric required in the merchandising plans could not be fitted into the mill schedule or secured from outside sources at a reasonable cost, the production control group was to review the situation with the merchandise manager. If the merchandise manager still felt that the fabric was essential to his program, the production control group would then present the entire situation to Mr. Rawle, executive vice-president, and other top executives for decision.

A continuing production control problem was developing merchandising plans and fabric requirements far enough in advance of the selling seasons to allow for the required spinning, weaving, finishing, and fabricating operations. In February, 1947, the production cycle was about 3 months; that is, fabrics scheduled for production in one quarter were usually available as finished garments in the next quarter.

GENERAL PLANS AND OBJECTIVES

By February, 1947, the executives of Textron had gone about as far as they expected to go, in the immediate future, in the acquisition of new properties and facilities. The immediate problem was rather one of consolidating, coordinating, and balancing the activities of the existing holdings. A map of the holdings in 1947 is given in Exhibit 5.

No final decision had been made as to the balance of production capacity to be established at the different levels in the integrated structure. Currently, the executives preferred to remain in a flexible position and to shift and change operations as circumstances seemed to warrant. It was intended, however, that as soon as proper yarns became available from the spinning mills, the relative volume of fabrics going into the corporation's sewing operations would be increased. It was anticipated that in the long run the corporation might sell only a very small volume of grey goods. On the other hand, it was believed that the corporation might continue to sell a substantial volume of fabrics in order to make use of the well-established reputations which the Nashua and Lonsdale mills had in the finished fabric markets. For finishing operations, it was believed that the corporation would continue to rely heavily on outside concerns.

A preliminary decision was made in February, 1947, to keep the sales and merchandising organization of the Nashua Manufacturing Company intact within Textron Inc., and to continue the sale and promotion of the Nashua products. It was believed possible that consumer goods such as men's wear, blouses, negligees, and home fashions might eventually be added to the Nashua line. These items, if adopted, would sell in a somewhat lower price range than did the Textron products. The Nashua brands were well-established in the trade and sold to a large number of retail and wholesale outlets which did not handle the Textron line. No final decision had been made as to the range of consumer products which might eventually be included in either of the two lines.

APPENDIX

Acquisition of the Manville Jenckes Corporation[6]

Though numerous companies have been converted into charitable trusts in recent years, Textron Incorporated has been the only company, to our knowledge, in which sale and lease-back arrangements with charitable trusts have been utilized to effect acquisition of the business of other concerns. This form of transaction played a major role in Textron's expansion which was largely responsible for the increase in the company's sales from $8 million in 1941 to $110 million in 1946. From 1943 through 1948 Textron acquired the business of seven other companies; in five of these instances the acquisition involved charitable trusts in one fashion or another.

An Example—Manville. A good illustration of Textron's use of this technique is furnished by its acquisition of the Manville Jenckes Corporation, followed by the subsequent sale and lease-back of Manville's principal plant to the Rhode Island Charities Trust and the sale of a second plant to other interests. This was a relatively large acquisition for Textron. In the year prior to the transaction (1944) Manville's sales had totaled $14 million compared with Textron's $26.5 million. Also, 3 months before the acquisition, in January, 1945, Textron had about 3,000 employees, while after the acquisition the Manville mill alone (excluding the plant resold to another company) employed 1,960 persons.

As the first step, in March, 1945, Textron bought Manville's capital stock—common plus preferred—for a total of $5,550,000, borrowing $4,500,000 from the banks to help finance the purchase. The purchase price was somewhat less than the net worth of Manville as shown by its December 30, 1944, balance sheet, tabulated below in Table A.

Prior to December 31, 1945, however, Manville's two plant properties, one in Woonsocket, R.I., and the other in Manville, R.I., were sold, the Manville plant to the Rhode Island Charities Trust and the Woonsocket plant to a non-affiliated company. The total sale price of these properties was $2,200,000; since their aggregate basis, after depreciation, was about $4,000,000 Manville thereby realized a loss of about $1,800,000. This loss, by virtue of Section 117 (j) of the Internal Revenue Code could be offset against Manville's 1945 operating profit of $2,700,000 (before Federal Taxes), thereby reducing Manville's Federal taxes by some $1,300,000 and freeing that much more of Manville's generous cash balances, already in excess of the normal needs of the business at the time of its acquisition by Textron.

The plant at Manville, R.I., which had been sold to the Rhode Island Charities Trust for a $1,200,000 installment promissory note was immediately leased back to Textron. The lease provided for an annual rental of $210,000 (net of taxes, insurance and repairs, all paid by Textron), plus a sliding scale varying with the activity of the mill, up to a possible maximum of $270,000 annually. As far as the charitable trust was concerned, the minimum rentals would fully amortize its investment in something less than 6 years.

On the other hand, as far as Manville Jenckes (now wholly operated by Textron) was concerned, the annual costs of renting compared favorably with costs of ownership; eliminating taxes, insurance, and repairs, since under the lease, as well as under outright ownership, Manville was required to pay all such charges, the net rental of $210,000 to $270,000 can be compared with annual depreciation charges of $262,000 on this property actually absorbed by Manville in the immediately preceding year. Other terms of the lease provided for a term of 10 years and an option to renew for an additional 10 years at a substantial reduction in rent —$60,000 a year minimum, plus an additional amount based upon percentage of operation in the mill up to an additional $60,000. The lease

[6] This material has been taken directly from a doctoral thesis by Powell Niland entitled *Considerations Determining the Form of Transaction by Which One Company Acquires Another,* Harvard Graduate School of Business Administration, 1953, pp. 255–61, 267, 270–71, 277.

could be terminated by Textron on 90 days' notice, if desired.

While the sales of both plant properties were for promissory notes and provided Textron with no cash immediately, Manville's cash was nevertheless sufficient to retire its issue of preferred stock at a cost of $4,300,000 on December 24, 1945. This preferred, as previously noted, had been purchased along with the common by Textron and, while the stock was retired at the same figure as it had cost Textron, the case thereby returned to Textron provided practically all the funds required to pay off the $4,500,000 bank loan which Textron had obtained to help acquire Manville originally. Furthermore, by March, 1946, the $1 million promissory note of a non-Textron company, accepted in payment for the Woonsocket Mill, had been paid off in full.

Within about 12 months after the Manville purchase, therefore, Textron had recouped substantially all of its $5,550,000 cash outlay. It still owned directly or through a subsidiary, all of Manville's assets except the two plant properties, the largest of which, however, was operating as part of the Textron organization under a long-term lease. Table A shows Manville Jenckes' balance sheet at December 29, 1945, after Textron had liquidated the company, transferring inventories and furniture and fixtures to a new subsidiary, Manville Fabrics, Inc., which continued the business.

* * *

The following is a summary of the steps in the Manville Jenckes acquisitions:

Manville Jenckes

(1) Textron bought capital stock borrowing from bank $4.5 million of $5.6 million needed.

(2) Manville sold its plants to charitable trust, receiving little cash, mainly purchase money mortgages, one of which was paid up 12 months later and the other was cleared off 20 months later. In the meantime, however, the operating company (Manville) realized tax savings of approximately $1.3 million dollars.

(3) Textron caused Manville to retire its preferred stock, all held by Textron, about a year later, and Textron thus obtained sufficient funds to pay off its bank loan.

(4) Rhode Island Charities Trust, which purchased the larger property for a mortgage (no cash down) realized a profit, all in cash, of about $185,000 for the 12 months it owned the Manville Mill.

* * *

The tax benefits from the sale and lease-back transaction are based upon the deductibility of losses on the disposal of "property used in the trade or business"—a term used to include depreciable assets and real estate—as provided in Section 117 (j) of the Internal Revenue Code, which allows such losses to be offset against ordinary income rather than subject to the operation of the capital gains provisions. Such a loss, according to Mr. Little's understanding of the Treasury's interpretation, cannot be taken into account in computing carry-backs and carry-overs, and thus the tax benefit of the loss is confined to the year in which the fixed assets are sold. The amount of the tax benefit obtained is therefore a function of the loss on the sale of the fixed assets, the current year's taxable net income before consideration of such loss, and the effective marginal tax rate.

The size of the loss, both as an absolute dollar sum and relative to the dollar value of the assets sold, is of course an important consideration. The transaction becomes less and less attractive, as far as the tax benefits are concerned, as the sale price increases towards the adjusted tax basis (cost less accrued depreciation) of the property involved—in other words, as the loss on the sale becomes smaller, the benefits become less worthwhile. The tax benefits from a $200,000 loss on the sale of a $5,000,000 plant would not, of itself, furnish much incentive to undertake a sale and lease-back of the property; other objectives accomplished by such a sale, however, may motivate such a transaction even though the tax benefits from the loss are small.

* * *

Another advantage of the sale and lease-back is its effect similar to accelerated depreciation charges. Since the lease, with option to renew, usually covers a period of from 15 to 20 years, the period of the lease plus options can cover the same number of years as the estimated life of the property used in calculation of deprecia-tion charges. The leases, however, typically contain terms allowing the purchaser sufficient rental payments initially to return the total cost of the purchase over the first 5 years, together with a profit. Thereafter, the rental charges are greatly reduced.

TABLE A

BALANCE SHEETS OF MANVILLE JENCKES CORPORATION
(Rounded to Nearest Thousands)

December 30, 1944

Cash and Govts.	$2,210,000	Fed. Inc. Taxes Pay.	$1,120,000
Accounts Receivable	170,000	Other Curr. Liabs.	850,000
Inventories	1,902,000		
Total Current Assets	$4,282,000	Total Curr. Liabs.	$1,970,000
Plant (net)	4,149,000	Noncurrent Debt	463,000
Other Assets	415,000	Capital Stock and Surplus*	6,413,000
Total Assets	$8,846,000	Total Liabilities	$8,846,000

* Including 78,435⅔ shares of $50 par preferred stock, carried at $3,921,783.

December 29, 1945

Cash	$ 275,000	Fed. Inc. Taxes Pay.	$ 627,000
Accounts and Notes Receivable	479,000	Other Current Liabs.	1,449,000
Due from Aff. Companies	1,419,000		
Total Current Assets	$2,173,000	Total Curr. Liabs.	$2,076,000
Mtg. Notes Rec.	1,962,000		
Plant	42,000	Capital Stock and Surplus**	2,494,000
Cash Val. Life Ins.	314,000		
Other Assets	79,000		
Total Assets	$4,570,000	Total Liabilities	$4,570,000

** After retirement of all preferred stock at a cost of $4,300,000.

1. TEXTRON INCORPORATED (A)

Balance Sheets, 1941-1947
(In Thousands)

	1941	1942	1943	1944	1945	1946	1947
ASSETS							
Cash	$ 146	$ 458	$ 296	$ 447	$ 3,062	$ 4,120	$ 3,935
Accounts Receivable	310	586	398	628	2,258	9,755	7,746
Inventories	825	1,681	4,980	4,322	11,456	23,109	23,485
Other Current Assets	90	99	250	279	157	222	531
Total Current Assets	$1,371	$2,824	$5,924	$5,676	$16,933	$37,206	$35,697
Fixed Assets	$1,823	$1,526	$1,453	$ 842	$ 1,776	$28,772	$29,419
Reserve for Depreciation	(616)	(593)	(548)	(185)	(647)	(15,016)	(11,180)
Other Assets	76	268	611	764	9,316	4,492	3,074
TOTAL ASSETS	$2,654	$4,025	$7,440	$7,097	$27,378	$55,454	$57,010
LIABILITIES							
Accounts Payable	$ 630	$1,174	$1,800	$ 575	$ 5,052	$ 4,415	$ 5,632
Accrued Liabilities	112	771	2,760	1,350	4,486	14,123	11,498
Total Current Liabilities	$ 742	$1,945	$4,560	$1,925	$ 9,538	$18,538	$17,130
Other Liabilities and Reserves			225	2,165	3,098	8,318	5,292
Minority Interest					16	7,986	6,419
Capital Stock and Surplus							
Capital Stock	257	257	508	507	5,060	5,000	5,398
Common Stock	221	221	322	222	495	506	566
Earned Surplus	598	766	989	1,442	276	3,591	9,409
Capital Surplus	836	836	836	836	8,895	11,515	12,796
Total Stock and Surplus	$1,912	$2,080	$2,655	$ 3,007	$14,726	$20,612	$28,169
TOTAL LIABILITIES	$2,654	$4,025	$7,440	$7,097	$27,378	$55,454	$57,010

Source: Company records.

2. TEXTRON INCORPORATED (A)

Income Statements, 1941-1947
(In Thousands)

	1941	1942	1943	1944	1945	1946	1947
Net Sales	$8,203	$11,862	$24,125	$26,254	$46,853	$112,952	$124,776
Cost of Sales	7,762	10,574	21,144	21,669	37,798	87,526	101,011
Gross Profit	$ 441	$ 1,288	$ 2,981	$ 4,585	$ 9,055	$ 25,426	$ 23,765
General Expenses	177	237	879	2,157	4,217	8,767	9,592
Profit from operations	$ 264	$ 1,051	$ 2,102	$ 2,428	$ 4,838	$ 16,659	$ 14,173
Other Income							
Purchase discount	$ 88	$ 9	$ 46				
Disposal of Fixed Assets							$ 1,549
Miscellaneous Income	9	11	18	$ 51	$ 249	$ 384	393
	$ 97	$ 20	$ 64	$ 51	$ 249	$ 384	$ 1,942
	$ 361	$ 1,071	$ 2,166	$ 2,479	$ 5,087	$ 17,043	$ 16,115
Other Charges							
Sales discount	$ 84	$ 89	$ 129				
Interest	16	7	32	$ 69	$ 312	$ 824	$ 551
Separation payments						316	346
Bad debt	40	39	46	31			
Disposal of Property	1	246	245	13	1,788		
Miscellaneous charges			50	18	970	314	314
	$ 141	$ 381	$ 502	$ 131	$ 3,070	$ 1,454	$ 1,211
Net Profit	$ 220	$ 690	$ 1,664	$ 2,348	$ 2,017	$ 15,589	$ 14,904
Federal and State Income Tax	59	440	1,219	1,734	1,713	7,204	6,020
Net Profit after Tax	$ 161	$ 250	$ 445	$ 614	$ 304	$ 8,385	$ 8,884

Source: Company records.

3. TEXTRON INCORPORATED (A)
Consolidated Flow Chart, First Quarter, 1947
(In Yards per Week)

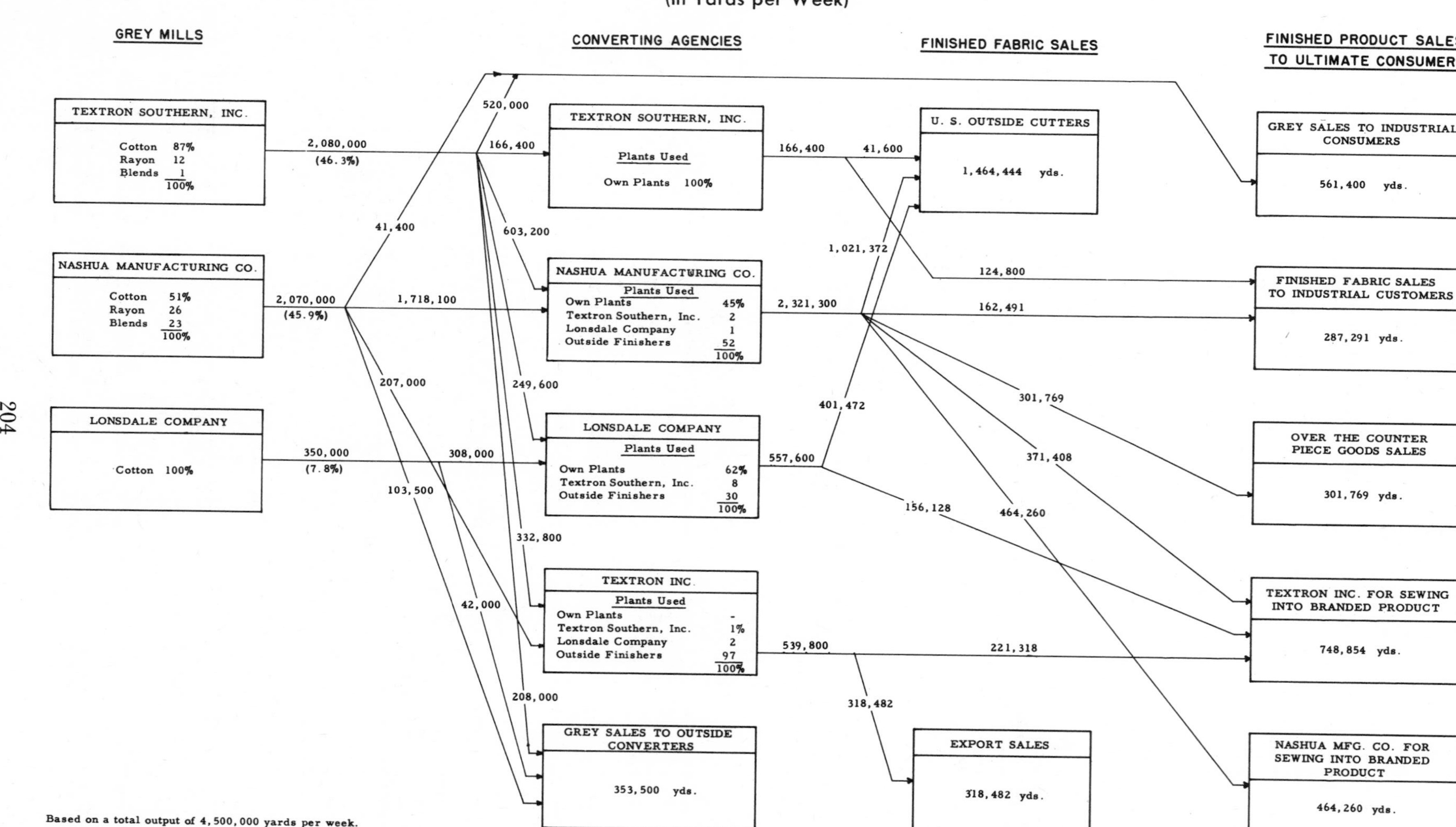

Based on a total output of 4,500,000 yards per week.
Source: Company records and interviews.

4. TEXTRON INCORPORATED (A)

Organization Chart—1947

BOARD OF DIRECTORS
PRESIDENT
ROYAL LITTLE
EXECUTIVE STAFF
EXEC. VICE PRESIDENT
MARSHALL RAWLE
DIRECTOR
CENTRAL PRODUCTION PLANNING
COORDINATION AND CONTROL
SEWN PRODUCTS
INDUSTRIAL REL.
MARKETING
MARSHALL RAWLE
VICE PRESIDENT
RESEARCH
PRODUCTION CONTROL BRANCH
PRICE AND COST ANALYSIS BRANCH
FABRIC ALLOCATION CONTROL BRANCH
MERCHANDISE GROUP MANAGERS
WOVEN LINGERIE
HOME FASHIONS
BLOUSE
TRICOT LINGERIE
NEGLIGEE
MENSWEAR
SALES
PUBLIC REL.
&
ADVERTISING
EXPORT
MARKETING
RESEARCH
TREASURER
CHARLES H. DYSON
ORG. & POLICY
FINANCE
CONTROLLER
SECRETARY
PURCHASING
OPERATING DIVISIONS AND SUBSIDIARIES
SEWN PRODUCTS
DIVISION
LOWELL, MASS.
LOWELL, MASS.
EASTHAMPTON, MASS
MANCHESTER, N.H.
LONSDALE
COMPANY
PROVIDENCE, R.I.
CUMBERLAND, R. I.
NO. SMITHFIELD, R.I.
LONSDALE, R. I.
NEW YORK, N.Y.
TRICOT
DIVISION
EAST GREENWICH, R.I.
EAST GREENWICH, R.I.
TEXTRON BLDG.
NEW YORK, N.Y.
RESEARCH &
DEVELOPMENT DIV.
LOWELL, MASS.
LOWELL, MASS.
MECHANICAL RESEARCH
& QUALITY CONTROL
LOWELL, MASS.
CHEMICAL RESEARCH
PROVIDENCE, R.I.
BRANCH RESEARCH LAB
NASHUA MFG. CO.
NASHUA, N.H.
NASHUA, N.H.
BOSTON, MASS.
NEW YORK, N.Y.
TEXTRON SOUTHERN
INC.
CHARLOTTE, N.C.
ANDERSON, S.C.
WILLIAMSTON, S.C.
CHARLOTTE, N.C.
CORDOVA, ALABAMA

Source: Company records.

5. TEXTRON INCORPORATED (A)

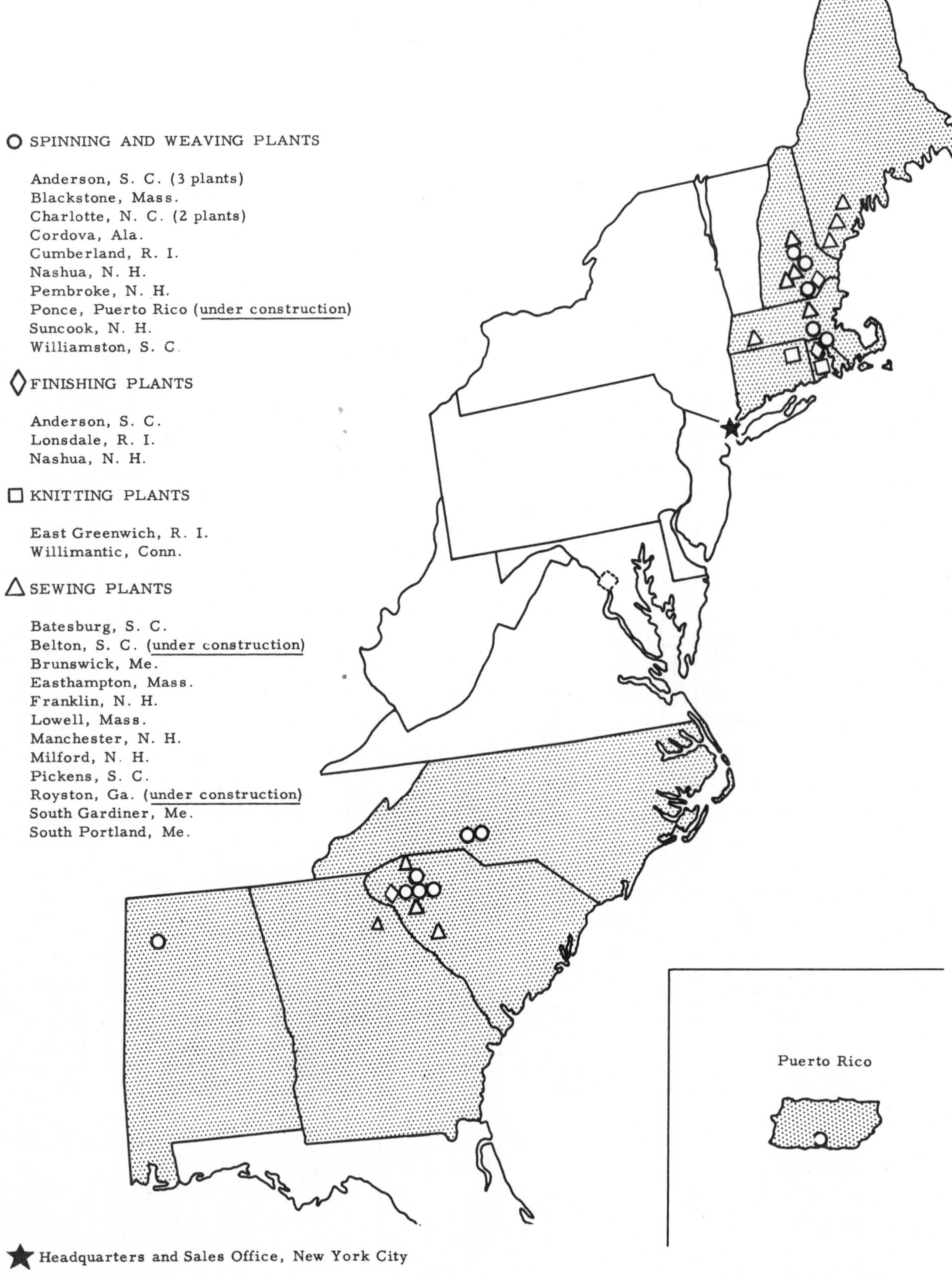

O SPINNING AND WEAVING PLANTS
Anderson, S. C. (3 plants)
Blackstone, Mass.
Charlotte, N. C. (2 plants)
Cordova, Ala.
Cumberland, R. I.
Nashua, N. H.
Pembroke, N. H.
Ponce, Puerto Rico (under construction)
Suncook, N. H.
Williamston, S. C.
◊ FINISHING PLANTS
Anderson, S. C.
Lonsdale, R. I.
Nashua, N. H.
□ KNITTING PLANTS
East Greenwich, R. I.
Willimantic, Conn.
△ SEWING PLANTS
Batesburg, S. C.
Belton, S. C. (under construction)
Brunswick, Me.
Easthampton, Mass.
Franklin, N. H.
Lowell, Mass.
Manchester, N. H.
Milford, N. H.
Pickens, S. C.
Royston, Ga. (under construction)
South Gardiner, Me.
South Portland, Me.
Puerto Rico
★ Headquarters and Sales Office, New York City

Source: Company records.

Textron Incorporated (B)

In the period 1941–1947, Textron Incorporated attracted considerable attention in the textile industry as a result of its bold moves to establish a fully integrated textile concern producing everything from yarn to apparel. The phenomenal growth of the corporation between 1941 and 1947 from total assets of $2,500,000 to $57,000,000 was accompanied by unorthodox financial, administrative, and merchandising policies. In 1947 the corporation earned $14,900,000 before taxes on net sales of $125,000,000.

Between 1948 and 1950, the operations of the Textron corporation experienced many changes and certain characteristics of the earlier organization were greatly altered. The company's New England mill properties, which had accounted for more than 50 percent of the spinning and weaving capacity in the integrated concern, were under careful scrutiny by the executives. The enthusiastic promotion of Textron branded products for the consumer market, which had been a significant feature of the company's marketing program in 1947, was reevaluated. Balance Sheets and Income Statements for 1948 and 1949 are contained in Exhibits 1 and 2.

DISPOSAL OF HIGH-COST MILLS

In the process of building Textron Incorporated, the management had acquired certain facilities to fill out the product line. Others were acquired for financial reasons or to assure the company of adequate supplies of yarn and fabrics in the war and postwar years when both products were often in short supply. When opportunities arose to purchase entire companies, it was sometimes necessary to absorb properties which did not fit too well into the integrated structure.

By 1947 it became apparent that certain of the older plants acquired in the expansion program would not be able to operate on an economical basis. In particular, the company became concerned by the operating costs of the New England mills, whose multistory buildings, old equipment, unionized labor force, and high tax charges made them more expensive to operate than the newer mills in the Carolinas. Textron executives released the following comparison of approximate cost figures between textile production in New England and the South:

	Nashua Mill	*Southern Mills*
Output	5.37 lbs./man-h.	9.62 lbs./man-h.
Earnings	$1.19 per hour	$1.10 per hour
"Fringe benefits"	8½¢ to 10¢ per hour	—
Taxes	$2.53 per spindle	58¢ per spindle
Power	1.2¢ K.W.H.	.8¢ K.W.H.

In addition to the costs cited above, construction costs were considered to be lower in the South and the cost of inward freight from the cotton areas was reduced. Southern workers were generally believed to be more willing to be transferred from plant to plant and to work on the night shift than those in New England.

Textron executives therefore began to reduce the operating costs of the older mills in New England or to dispose of them entirely. As a result, the number of employees in the corporation was reduced from 16,000 to 8,600 in 4 years and overhead expenses were cut almost 60 percent. The program eventually resulted in a radical change in the corporation's properties and thus influenced the nature of its products and its entire marketing and manufacturing program.

The Nashua Mills

The first target of the new cost reduction program was the Nashua group of plants, which was one of the largest and oldest properties acquired during the expansion program of 1944–1945.

The Nashua mills had been purchased in December, 1945, partly because the acquisition appeared attractive from a financial standpoint and partly because Textron needed additional supplies of fabrics for its sewing operations. Six months later, however, when the opportunity arose for Textron to purchase the large group of Gossett mills in the South, Mr. Royal Little indicated his willingness to sell the Nashua properties. The Nashua output consisted primarily of blankets, sheets, pillowcases, and piece goods which were sold under their own brand names and did not fit easily into the Textron marketing program. Moreover, it became apparent that in the long run the Gossett mills would provide a more economical source of supply for fabrics than would Nashua.

The sale of the Nashua properties did not materialize because of a decline in the securities market in early 1946. The Textron executives thereupon proceeded with the absorption of the company into the integrated operations. In order to repay the $7,800,000 bank loan incurred to buy Nashua, cash was secured by reducing the company's excess working capital and selling a portion of its raw cotton inventory. In addition, excess plant and machinery were sold and certain fabric weaving operations were removed to the Cordova Division of Nashua in Alabama. By 1947, the bank loan was almost completely repaid and Textron allocated $2,500,000 to advertise Nashua products and install new machinery in Nashua plants.

In July, 1947, Textron announced a drastic reorganization plan for Nashua to reduce its operating costs. The "New Nashua Plan" was designed to reduce labor, overhead, power, and tax costs by more than $2,000,000 during the first year and make the mill competitive with Southern ones.

The plan proposed that 50,000 spindles and 500,000 square feet of floor space in the main plant be sold and the best equipment, supervisors, and operating personnel concentrated in one unit of the plant, the Jackson Mill; that about $1,200,000 be spent in the modernization of the latter mill; and that the mill be operated on a three-shift basis with work loads comparable with those in other modern mills. It was anticipated that the changes would make possible a reduction in the workforce from 4,000 to 2,500 persons but that the dollar sales volume would continue to be approximately the same as in the past.

The plan called upon the union (Textile Workers Union of America CIO) to give the management freedom in the selection of supervisors and working personnel and in the adjustment of work loads. In August the union accepted a new contract and agreed to the general principles of the reorganization effort. At the same time a five cents per hour wage increase was granted. Textron Incorporated agreed to keep take-home pay on a par with that of its most efficient competitors, to provide small pension payments for workers over 65 years of age, and to make separation payments to all supervisors with over 10 years of service.

Despite the new plan, the Nashua mill lost $247,000 in the first six months of 1948. Textron executives became concerned by the inability of the plant to compete during a period when the postwar textile boom was ending. Rough estimates indicated that direct and indirect labor costs at Nashua were at least $1,000,000 per year higher than in similar Southern operations. In September, 1948, therefore, the Textron board of directors voted to run out all work in process at the Nashua Manufacturing Company prior to the end of that year and to dispose of all the corporation's physical properties in Nashua, New Hampshire. The action together with the events which followed were explained in a letter to the stockholders by Mr. Little dated December 31, 1948:

> The mill properties in Nashua were acquired in 1946 when substantially all of the common stock of Nashua Manufacturing Company was purchased by the company. Profits from such plants were satisfactory during the war and during the period of boom business which followed. It was known, however, that the mills were a high-cost operation. Consequently, in the summer of 1947 the management proposed and publicly announced the "New Nashua Plan" which was referred to in the last annual report to stockholders. Under this plan it was contemplated that the Nashua properties would be extensively modernized in equipment, competitive employee work loads would be established to increase production, and a three-shift operation would be introduced. It was believed that this plan would enable the mills to meet peacetime competition in a buyers' market.
>
> In accordance with this program the company carried out in substantial measure its plan for modernization. However, the arrangement for increasing work assignments to reduce costs to competitive levels did not develop as rapidly as expected and in the summer of 1948, when the market for the principal products of the Nashua mills, namely sheets, pillow cases and blankets, gave every indication of a return to traditional narrow profit margins, it became apparent that serious losses could no longer be postponed if production were continued on the same high cost operating basis. Ac-

cordingly, the closing of the mills was authorized by the directors early in September.

Thereafter the Textile Workers Union of the CIO brought about an investigation of the plant closing by a subcommittee of the Senate Committee on Interstate and Foreign Commerce, and a public hearing of three days duration was held in Nashua beginning September 22. At the outset the chairman of the subcommittee, Senator Tobey, announced that the hearing would be primarily fact-finding in character and that information was being sought as to why textile plants were moving from New England. The company welcomed this investigation and agreed to cooperate in supplying information and statistics.

Unfortunately there developed in the course of the hearing an entirely unfounded and irresponsible attack on the company and Royal Little, initiated by the president of the Textile Workers Union. Impassioned speeches stirred up the Nashua workers, who were present in substantial numbers. At the close of the second day of the hearings, feelings were running high. However, due to the intervention of a committee of Nashua citizens, the tone of the hearing turned for the better on the third day. The company, after receiving assurances of full cooperation from the workers, the Union, the Citizens Committee, and Senator Tobey, agreed to continue the operation of the more modern portion of the Nashua mills and to manufacture sheeting there until the end of 1949, and thereafter if a reasonable profit was realized, provided that the competitive work loads and work shift adjustments proposed in 1947 were established. This brought to a close the first phase of the hearing, which in October was reopened in Boston.

Toward the end of October a group of prominent New Hampshire citizens arranged to form a new charitable trust for the benefit of the New Hampshire Society for Crippled Children and Handicapped Persons for its Crotched Mountain Project. This trust has been named the Nashua-New Hampshire Foundation. With a view toward improving the general employment situation in Nashua and also to benefit this charity, the foundation entered into an agreement with the company to purchase all its real estate and mill buildings in Nashua, exclusive of all textile machinery and equipment. The company at the same time agreed to enter into ten-year lease of the sheeting mill referred to above and the bleachery facilities used therewith. The formation of the foundation and the arrangement of sale and lease back was publicly announced at the hearing in Boston.

Under the terms of the agreement with the Nashua-New Hampshire Foundation, Textron received $500,000 for its Nashua plants. Textron agreed to lease the Jackson Mill, containing 1,000,000 square feet of floor space, in order to continue the production of Nashua branded products on a trial basis. The remaining 2,000,000 square feet of floor space was offered for lease by the independent foundation.

Under the leadership of Mr. Lawrence Plowman, who later became a Textron executive, new industry was attracted to Nashua in order to protect the town from unemployment. Rather than bring in other textile business, Mr. Plowman sought companies in growth industries, such as electronics, plastics, and greeting cards. As a result of the program, 21 companies in different industries were located at the old mills. The town later suffered less unemployment than other cities in the area when conditions in the textile industry became more difficult. Mr. Little believed that the ability of the town to withstand a recession resulted from quick action in 1948. He was convinced that when conditions in an industry began to appear unfavorable, it was essential to take major action rapidly so as to avoid going under at a time when no alternatives were available.

Lonsdale Company

The earnings of the Lonsdale Company after taxes amounted to $1,560,000 in 1947 and $511,000 in the first quarter of 1948. In the 14 months subsequent to the acquisition on November 1, 1945, the profits of the company aggregated more than twice the purchase price paid by Textron Incorporated. In 1948, however, less than 10 percent of the output of the Lonsdale Company was being used in Textron branded products, and it was decided that the company should operate in the future as an independent concern.

Therefore, a new Lonsdale Company was organized in April, 1948, to acquire the business and operating properties of the existing Lonsdale Company from Textron Incorporated. The Textron stockholders were issued warrants to purchase one share of common stock in the new company at $3 per share for each share of stock which they held in Textron Incorporated. The total number of shares thus offered for sale was 1,133,000. An additional 100,000 shares were also offered to certain directors, officers, and employees of the Lonsdale Company at $3 per share.

Manville Mills

In July, 1948, Textron Incorporated cancelled its lease on the spinning and weaving plant in Manville, Rhode Island. Shortly after the Manville Jenckes Corporation was acquired in 1945, the mills were sold to and leased back from the Textron Pension Trust. In February, 1948, the mills and machinery were sold to an outside concern, the Crescent Corporation. Operation of the Manville mills had involved very high costs, and the Textron management decided that it would not be possible for the unit to compete effectively in the post-war markets. The mills employed about 2,000 people and contained approximately 80,000 spindles and 2,000 looms. The Crescent Corporation did not continue operation of the mills.

Nemasket Mill

The Nemasket Mill in Rhode Island had been purchased for $200,000 in 1944 in order to provide a temporary source of spun rayon for the Suncook Mills. Due to the character of its machinery, the Nemasket Mill proved difficult to operate on an efficient basis. Its 30,000 spindles were later sold to a foreign textile company for $900,000 and the plant disposed of for $176,000. The favorable selling price was obtained because certain textile corporations were short of equipment to meet the large post-war demand.

ADMINISTRATIVE REORGANIZATION

Under the plan of organization in effect in 1947 and 1948, senior executives in the New York office exercised central supervision over the production requirements and product lines of the various manufacturing plants. Although the details of factory management were left to local plant executives, production schedules were largely determined by merchandise managers in close touch with the style and volume demands of the retail market. Merchandise managers planned production schedules for a year in advance on the basis of sales budgets which were revised at six-month intervals. Furthermore, a planning and fabric allocation department was set up under the central supervision of the executive vice-president, Mr. Rawle, for the purpose of reviewing product lines and allocating fabric weaves to the various production units.

Since apparel styles in the consumer market were subject to rapid change, while cloth weaves had to be established far in advance in order to achieve the efficiencies of mass production, the integrated scheduling of textile products became particularly difficult in periods of shifting demand. An example of the problems may be found in the experience of the Jackson Mill at Nashua for the year 1949, discussed next.

Nashua Division Production Schedules for 1949

In the late spring of 1948, the various merchandise managers for the consumer products division began preparing sales estimates for 1949. These estimates, which were submitted to Mr. Rawle, predicted sales figures for each consumer division by major product grouping and by styles within each grouping. Mr. Rawle's staff prepared a cloth allocation program according to the production estimates for various types of fabrics. The final sales estimates and fabric allocations for the year 1949 were completed by October, 1948.

At that time, market indications for 1949 were contradictory. Mr. Little noted in November, 1948, that retail sales were running 10 percent below the previous year. He obtained inventory and sales statistics in order to follow the situation closely, and discovered that the retail buyers generally had a 10 percent higher textile inventory despite the lower rates of sales. He therefore warned the merchandise managers to take stringent action to reduce production; however, salesmen's reports indicated that the demand for textiles would increase.

Between 1945 and 1948, most of the consumer products divisions had been able to increase their sales each year both in absolute value and in terms of the company's share of the market. The retail buyers still believed that the lower rate of sales during November, 1948, was due to temporary conditions such as poor weather. The salesmen therefore brought back optimistic reports from the field and the merchandise managers were anxious to increase their sales for 1949. The director of the Jackson Mill of the Nashua Company reported his estimate for 1949 in part as follows:

> In considering general business conditions for 1949, I have made the same assumptions that we asked the salesmen to make in preparing their own forecasts; namely that general business conditions, particularly in the retail trades, will approximate the volume enjoyed in the year 1947. The recommended estimate for consumer goods for 1949 totals $33,000,000. I have assumed that at least $3,000,000 of blanket business would be in the crib blanket field, so that if this added line were removed from the recommended estimate, the total for consumers goods would stand at $30,000,000. Our 1947 actual billings amounted to $27,850,000. The total consumer goods figure for 1949, less the crib blankets, would yield a differential between 1947 and 1949 of approximately 8 percent. In reality, the increase percentage-wise would be larger if an adjustment were made for the decline in export business. Export business on consumer goods in 1947 approximated $2,380,000 and I have figured on no more than $750,000 for 1949. The table below gives a picture of the actual increase in domestic business over 1947 which the recommended 1949 plan calls for.
>
> | | *Actual 1947* | *Estimated 1949* |
> |---|---|---|
> | Total consumer goods | $27,850,000 | $33,000,000 |
> | Less export | 2,380,000 | 750,000 |
> | Domestic only | $25,470,000 | $32,250,000 |
> | Less crib blankets | — | 3,000,000 |
> | | $25,470,000 | $29,250,000 |
>
> Increase 1949 over 1947 = 14.8 percent
>
> It can be seen, therefore, that the recommended estimate for consumer goods for 1949 represents about 15 percent more domestic business than in 1947, the latter having been an extremely good business year.

Exhibit 3 contains the 1949 sales estimate for the Nashua division by product lines, which was accepted on the basis of the report submitted by the director of the Nashua Mills Division. Exhibit 3 also shows the actual sales during 1949 by product line, as well as the cost variances and profit margins of the Nashua Mills.

By the early spring of 1949, it became evident that actual sales were running below estimates due to a slump in the consumer demand for textile products. All Textron consumer products divisions were overcommitted in terms of the volume of cloth they had been scheduled to take from mills within the integrated system. As a result, the company found itself with an excessive inventory both of finished apparel and of cloth intended for cutting and sewing. Merchandise managers reported a return to highly competitive conditions in apparel lines and noted that competitors were reducing prices and broadening their lines with novelty items as a means of stimulating sales.

In March, 1949, the merchandise manager of the women's wear division submitted to Mr. Rawle the following memorandum describing market conditions similar to those in the Nashua division:

RÉSUMÉ—WOVEN LINGERIE

Current Market and Retail Conditions

1) Retailers are working present stocks down to bone level to be liquid if and when the market shows signs of downward pricing due to multifilament break (in price) the week of March 14.
2) Retailers buying on two week, or less, delivery.
3) Retailers picking hot "items" or lowest marginal profit items from every manufacturer. It is "dog-eat-dog" from now on.
4) Color and fussy styles are selling.
5) Woven nylon selling well, but stores are asking for lower prices in nylons.

Market Conditions—Manufacturers in an effort to sustain and build sagging volume are uncertain. (The memorandum then cited the case of five leading competitors in the lingerie business who had reduced prices.)

Textron's Position in this Market—Present and Future

There is a general opinion that our line is overpriced on certain items; that it is not "fussy" enough. Also, Cleary's[1] $2.50 competition in slips is a constant competitive hurdle. If Textron is integrated throughout, why can't we have a $3 slip?

It is generally agreed that Textron's quality, fabric, fit, wearability, consumer acceptance and service of orders is satisfactory. We are right in our thinking and price-lining in the volume brackets. But, in order for Textron to establish itself in the right competitive position in this market now and in the immediate future, certain definite, bold decisions must be made. These decisions will determine if we are to be in the volume woven lingerie business or not. And *volume* is the secret to our future success.

These are the recommendations of the merchandising divisions, prepared in a three-way pattern:

a) Price revisions on our current line to place ourselves in a competitive position with the market, and to liquidate current inventories.

b) Addition of new demand items now for May delivery to spice up the line.

c) Presentation of a long-range plan for the balance of 1949, based on the foregoing suggestions and changes.

1) Price-line coverage.
2) Number of items at each price line.
3) Per cent of planned production/sales of each price line.
4) Expansion of line into teen-age, 10 to 16; possible budget price slip and gown in pigment taffeta for "unbranded" sale; cottons, etc.
5) Increase of woven nylon availability to extend scope of items.
6) Inclusion of "hot" or fashion items, but with the understanding they will not be big volume items, but to satisfy seasonal trends, etc. These must be considered as *plus* business.

Similarly, the merchandise managers of other consumer product divisions revised their sales estimates in the spring of 1949, and broadened their product lines to include style, novelty items, and lower priced lines. The broadened product lines created difficult production problems for the sewing plants since they entailed smaller production runs. The sewing plants were unable to meet schedules and their actual costs of production exceeded standard costs. In the first six months of 1949, Textron lost $5½ million through inventory devaluation. Certain styled products which had been produced in excessive quantities had to be sold at a price discount.

[1] Disguised name.

Executive Reorganization

Mr. Little believed that the large size of the Textron company had been a factor in slowing down its response to the changing market situation in 1949. "In the textile industry," he said, "trends move like a tornado. The only way to save the situation is to make policy changes rapidly. But the bigger the company is, the more difficult it is for the chief executive to make sharp changes in policy based on an analysis of adverse trends. The people on the firing line [the merchandise managers] are influenced by enthusiastic reports from salesmen and are often anxious to maintain their own market position."

In order to obtain more flexibility of operations and to reduce the expense of administering an integrated market program, Mr. Little decided upon a policy of decentralization. Under the new program the New York headquarters was to be relieved of responsibility for the details of production scheduling. In June, 1949, Mr. Little released the following statement to the press:

> Textron in the past has had completely centralized control of all operations in its New York office. The directors have decided that this type of organization is too cumbersome and expensive for the fast going, traditionally decentralized textile industry. The directors have delegated to me authority to decentralize the business, appoint general managers for each division and eliminate all unnecessary staff functions. It is believed that the greater flexibility which will result from decentralization will be a special benefit to the further development for the Tex-

tron brand name, operation, and improved service for our customers.[2]

Mr. Little's announcement preceded a wave of resignations by top company executives. Mr. Rawle resigned, as did the treasurer, the vice-president in charge of finance, the vice-president in charge of advertising, and two directors of the board who were not operating executives.

Under the decentralization program which was executed during the last half of 1949, the merchandise managers of the various product divisions became general managers of these divisions. The managers were given full freedom to supervise the operation of their divisions within the limits of their sales estimates and cost budgets. Where formerly the manufacturing, sales, and merchandising of all the consumer product lines had been handled as staff functions at headquarters, these activities were now placed under the responsibility of the division general managers. The merchandise managers had complained previously that one of the problems resulting in operating losses was their dependency for sales on a group of salesmen who sold the company's entire product line and who for organizational purposes were beyond their management responsibility and control. Under the decentralization program each general manager was given an independent salesforce as well as the responsibility for advertising, which had formerly been centralized under a vice-president and with one agency. In several cases new agencies were selected.

In April, 1950, Mr. Little appointed Mr. James E. Robison general manager of all consumer products, with the individual divisional managers reporting to him. Mr. Robison's policy was stated as follows: "Because of the variety of different businesses involved, each divisional manager must have the maximum freedom of action and decision so that he can do whatever is necessary for his division to make a profit. Therefore, company-wide policies will be kept to an absolute minimum."

POLICY FOR CONSUMER PRODUCTS

A review of the accounting and statistical reports in May, 1950, revealed that the difficulties experienced in 1949 had continued during the first quarter of 1950. Sales billings had been below estimates due to the difficulty of delivering all the orders booked; standard gross profit had been reduced by mill variances; marketing expenses were high in relation to sales volume; excess inventories had led to markdowns. On the other hand, it was pointed out that the consumer products program had achieved certain objectives. The initial effort of selecting and training sales personnel had already been accomplished; the "Textron" brand name was well recognized; and the quality of Textron products was accepted in the large retail outlets through which they were distributed. Exhibit 4 includes the operating results for the first six months of 1950 for Textron Inc. and Textron Southern, Inc.

Considerable discussion was held in the spring of 1950 as to the future of the consumer products divisions. Examination of the comparative earnings ratios of selected textile companies in 1949, as shown in Exhibit 5, led some executives to oppose participation in sewing operations. It was generally agreed that the fundamental cause of the current problem at Textron had been the desire to "compete against all the giants of the industry on their own battlegrounds." As a result of the dispersion of effort, there had been a multiplicity of styles and stock-keeping units. In turn, the multiplicity of items had led to difficulties in the scheduling of cloth, and the choice of fabric finishes which resulted in short production runs and excessive inventories.

Suggested action included reduction of the product line by half, curtailment of delivery promises, and strict control of production plans; however, in June, 1950 Mr. Robison submitted the following recommendations:

> With the exception of Indian Head fabric, operating results for all consumer products divisions showed disastrous losses in 1949. Operating results for the first six months of 1950 will again show substantial losses for all consumer products except Indian Head. Estimated results for the last six months of 1950 show no hope of recouping losses for the first six months. Optimistic forecasts for 1950 show fair return on investment in certain lines, but these forecasts on consumer products have never been realized. Future

[2] *Women's Wear Daily,* for June 10, 1949.

prospects of realizing return on a large investment required commensurate with the risks involved appear to be poor. Recommendations: 1. That Textron withdraw from all consumer products operations by the end of the year 1950 with the exception of the following: Indian Head fabric blankets, lingerie, garments made in Puerto Rico. 2. That the men's wear division liquidate immediately. 3. That the lounge wear and drapery fabrics division be sold as a going concern as soon as possible or run out[3] through the fall season and be liquidated. 4. That the lingerie garment operation be run out through the fall season as presently planned. Garment operations should be transferred to Puerto Rico for chain distribution and domestic tricot fabric should be sold as cloth. 5. That the blouse division be run out through the fall season as presently planned, then sold as a going concern or liquidated. 6. That the sheet operation at Nashua be run out through the fall and liquidated.

[3] The term "run out" referred to the liquidation of process and finished stocks.

1. TEXTRON INCORPORATED (B)

Balance Sheets, 1948-1949

ASSETS	1948 Jan. 1, 1949	1949 Dec. 31, 1949
Cash	$ 4,528,422	$ 8,460,114
Accounts Receivable	5,545,076	5,812,892
Notes Receivable	686,993	789,655
Inventories	22,489,046	15,461,959
Estimated Tax Refund		600,000
Other Assets	897,357	517,619
Total Current Assets	$34,146,894	$31,642,239
Notes Receivable	807,500	657,923
Investments:		
Textron Puerto Rico	1,000,000	1,000,000
Other	290,466	7,755
Plant and Equipment	15,633,399	13,829,377
Depreciation	(6,103,815)	(6,090,037)
Intangible Assets	303,883	
Other Assets:		
Life Insurance	573,308	498,460
Deposits	279,697	211,605
Other Assets	306,552	77,564
Prepaid	817,721	378,764
Total Assets	$54,159,420	$48,303,687

LIABILITIES AND CAPITAL	1948 Jan. 1, 1949	1949 Dec. 31, 1949
Notes Payable		$ 364,807
Accounts Payable	$ 2,983,129	3,168,679
Accrued Liabilities	2,538,949	1,563,512
Provision for Taxes	5,235,822	78,158
Dividends Payable	285,116	406,975
Employees' Deposits	313,994	210,250
Other	430,736	144,223
Total Current Liabilities	$11,787,746	$ 5,936,604
Notes Payable	75,000	2,976,833
Long-Term Debt	1,976,500	1,725,000
Other Liabilities	526,863	374,471
Total Liabilities	$14,366,109	$11,012,908
Contingencies	3,000,000	2,500,000
Minority Interests:		
Common Stock of Subsidiaries	18,667	11,275
Preferred Stocks of Subsidiaries	1,093,961	945,449
Capital Stock:		
Cumulative Convertible Preferred	8,885,000	8,885,000
Common	566,316	566,316
Paid-In Surplus	8,265,613	8,265,613
Capital Surplus	4,358,901	4,367,396
Earned Surplus	13,604,853	11,749,730
Total Liabilities and Capital	$54,159,420	$48,303,687

Source: Company records.

2. TEXTRON INCORPORATED (B)

Income Statements, 1948-1949

	1948 Year Ending Jan. 1, 1949	1949 Year Ending Dec. 31, 1949
Net Sales	$98,847,174	$67,896,029
Cost of Sales*	79,668,835	63,476,526
Gross Profit on Sales	$19,178,339	$ 4,419,503
Selling, Advertising, and Administrative Expenses	8,212,759	5,807,828
Profit from Operations	$10,965,580	$ (1,388,325)
Other Income:		
Gain on Sale of Fixed Assets	$ 151,269	$ 69,019
Gain on Partial Liquidation of Nashua Mill	69,957	
Profit on Sale of Assets Acquired through Preferred Stock	500,360	134,100
Other Income	237,622	347,925
	$ 959,208	$ 551,044
	$11,924,788	$ (837,281)
Other Charges:		
Expenses of Decentralization		$ 1,197,039
Interest Expense	$ 509,356	307,847
Other Charges	264,796	373,729
	$ 774,152	$ 1,878,615
Profit or (Loss) before Taxes	$11,150,636	$ (2,715,896)
Income Taxes:		
Estimated Refund		(1,100,000)
Provision	4,045,000	25,000
Net Profit after Taxes	$ 7,105,636	$ (1,640,896)
Earnings Applicable to Minority Interests	168,913	53,026
Net Profit or (Loss)	$ 6,936,723	$ (1,693,922)

*Including depreciation: 1948, $1,012,422; 1949, $982,421.
Source: Company records.

3. TEXTRON INCORPORATED (B)
Nashua Division: Predicted and Actual Sales for 1949
(In Thousands)

	Blankets	Sheets	Indian Head	Drapery Fabrics	Other	Total Consumer
PREDICTED SALES:						
Merchandise Manager "A"	$ 5,873	$5,250	$ 8,594	$3,800	$1,275	$24,792
Merchandise Manager "B"	11,361	8,750	11,902	6,600	1,750	40,363
Field Estimates	5,934	7,180	10,520	4,070	1,408	29,112
Recommended Estimate	9,000	7,000	10,500	5,000	1,500	33,000
ACTUAL SALES	$ 2,560	$5,258	$ 6,824	$1,721	$1,800	$18,163
Standard cost of sales	2,637	5,491	5,387	1,517	2,118	17,150
Mat'ls., labor, o'head..variances	119	285	176	60	-	640
Overages and shortages	(46)	(40)	(67)	(11)	(37)	(201)
Changes in standards	(2)	(23)	82	233	(30)	260
Provision for write down	99	166	197	71	4	537
Write down absorbed in sales	(48)	(97)	(169)	(78)	(31)	(423)
Mill cost of sales	$ 2,759	$5,782	$ 5,606	$1,792	$2,024	$17,963
Mill door profit [or loss]	[199]	[524]	1,218	[71]	[224]	200
Merchandising expense	22	44	105	119		290
Field sales expense	74	120	243	172		609
Marketing overhead	20	29	54	22		125
Advertising	18	28	248	12		306
General and Administrative Expense	23	73	155	62		313
Total expenses	$ 157	$ 294	$ 805	$ 387		$ 1,643
Profit [or loss] from operations	[356]	[818]	413	[458]	[224]	[1,443]

( ) Denotes favorable variance.

[ ] Denotes loss.

Source: Company records.

4. TEXTRON INCORPORATED (B)

Comparative Income Statements, Textron Inc. and Textron Southern, Inc., for Selected Periods, 1949-1950
(In Thousands of Dollars)

	Textron Incorporated (Consumer Products Division)			Textron Southern, Inc.			Textron Incorporated* (All Divisions)		
	6 Months 7/2/49	12 Months 12/31/49	6 Months 7/1/50	6 Months 7/2/49	12 Months 12/31/49	6 Months 7/1/50	6 Months 7/2/49	12 Months 12/31/49	6 Months 7/1/50
Net sales:									
Trade	$22,268	$45,867	$21,033	$ 9,675	$21,979	$13,080	$31,943	$67,896	$34,128
Affiliated companies	549	1,416	45	2,600	4,497	3,700			
Total net sales	$22,817	$47,283	$21,078	$12,275	$26,476	$16,780	$31,943	$67,896	$34,128
Cost of sales	24,741	46,271	20,762	11,178	23,271	14,798	32,441	63,476	32,046
Sewing operations (loss) 1949		(206)			206				
Gross profit or (loss)	$ (1,924)	$ 1,218	$ 316	$ 1,097	$ 2,999	$ 1,982	$ (498)	$ 4,420	$ 2,082
Deduct:									
Advertising expenses	$ 1,037	$ 1,412	$ 599				$ 1,036	$ 1,415	$ 598
Selling expenses	1,436	2,639	1,139	$ 16			1,452	2,643	1,141
Service charges-selling	(96)	(220)	(131)	96	$ 220	$ 131			
Administrative expenses	998	1,636	763	23	(62)		1,078	1,750	800
Service charges-administrative	(205)	(454)	(262)	193	440	262			
	$ 3,170	$ 5,013	$ 2,108	$ 328	$ 598	$ 393	$ 3,566	$ 5,808	$ 2,539
Net profit or (loss)	$ (5,094)	$ (3,795)	$ (1,792)	$ 769	$ 2,401	$ 1,589	$ (4,064)	$ (1,388)	$ (457)
Other income:									
Profit or (loss) on sale of assets	$ (193)	$ 6	$ (98)	$ 3	$ 124	$ 19	$ (190)	$ 230	$ (80)
Southern loss (1948) transferred		473							
Miscellaneous	58	172	56	7	36	2	276	348	68
	$ (135)	$ 651	$ (42)	$ 10	$ 160	$ 21	$ 86	$ 551	$ (12)
	$ (5,229)	$ (3,144)	$ (1,834)	$ 779	$ 2,561	$ 1,610	$ (3,978)	$ (837)	$ (469)
Other expenses:									
Interest on bank loans			$ 5				$ 49	$ 96	$ 98
Interest on other loans	$ 29	$ 45	42						
Customers' anticipation	56			$ 2			58		
Expenses of decentralization	1,343	1,189					1,343	1,197	
Interest and anticipation		142	81		$ 65	$ 18		212	100
Southern loss (1948) transferred					472				
Miscellaneous	113	163	54	8	144		132	374	129
	$ 1,541	$ 1,539	$ 182	$ 10	$ 681	$ 18	$ 1,582	$ 1,879	$ 327
Net profit or (loss) before taxes	$ (6,770)	$ (4,683)	$ (2,016)	$ 769	$ 1,880	$ 1,592	$ (5,560)	$ (2,716)	$ (796)
Provision for taxes	(2,708)	(1,716)	(806)	330	594	685	2,246**	(1,075)**	(272)**
Net profit or (loss) after taxes	$ (4,062)	$ (2,967)	$ (1,210)	$ 439	$ 1,286	$ 907	$ (3,314)	$ (1,641)	$ (524)
Minority interests	22	44	20	4	8	4	26	53	24
Net profit or (loss)	$ (4,084)	$ (3,011)	$ (1,230)	$ 435	$ 1,278	$ 903	$ (3,340)	$ (1,694)	$ (548)

( ) Denotes red figures.
* Including certain additional subsidiaries.
** Represents estimated federal tax carry-back less estimated state income taxes.
Source: Company records.

5. TEXTRON INCORPORATED (B)

Comparative Earnings Ratios of Selected Companies in the Textile Industry

(Profits before Taxes as a Percent of Net Sales for 1949)

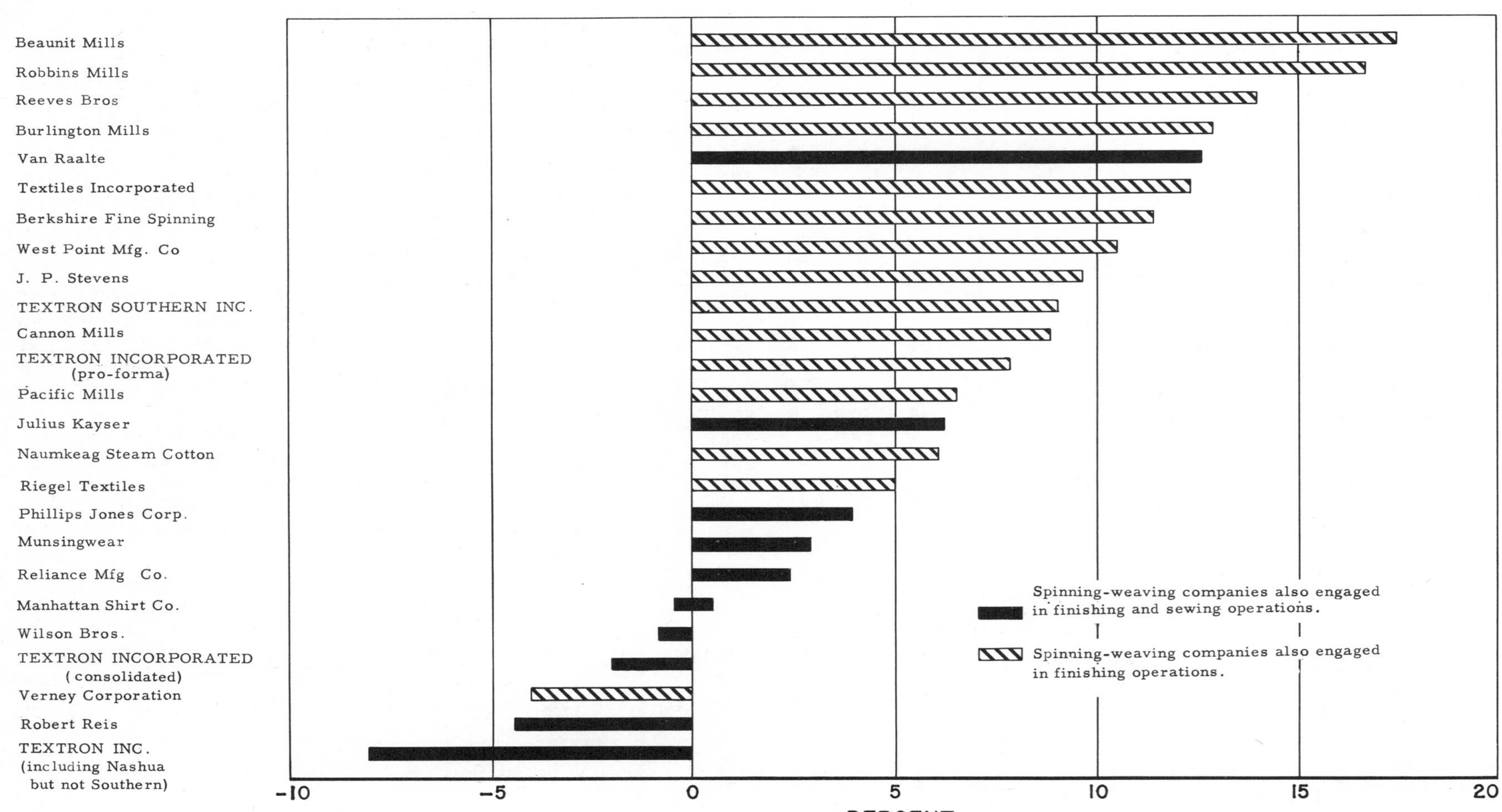

Source: Company records.

Textron Incorporated (C)

After reviewing the consumer production operations in 1949 and considering the earnings ratios of other textile companies involved in sewing operations, Mr. Little decided to eliminate cutting and sewing facilities.

Although Textron's consumer product line was not in the high style category of women's dresses, many items had been subject to serious style or seasonal changes. For example, women's blouses and negligees were subject to major style changes from year to year and negligees had to be designed separately for a winter as well as for a summer market. Such products were actually sold on eye-appeal, Mr. Little believed, and the Textron brand name was therefore of little value in convincing a customer to buy. Menswear constituted the only group of products in which the Textron name had been successful in creating a distinct brand preference.

CHANGE OF MANUFACTURING POLICY

Throughout the period while Textron disposed of its New England mills and withdrew from consumer marketing, the operation of Textron Southern, Inc. continued to be profitable. The market for greige (or cloth in the grey), which the Southern mills produced in large quantity, had been less affected than the consumer products by the retail slump of 1949. Mr. Little began to see in the Southern mills an opportunity to develop a modern corporation in a segment of the textile industry that was not subject to the difficulties of scheduling, the risks of inventory, and the vicissitudes of style that had marked the manufacture of consumer products.

In making the decision to concentrate on grey cloth, Mr. Little believed the new company should be completely opposite from the former diverse, integrated corporation. Whereas the former policy had relied on consumer preference for Textron branded merchandise to maintain the corporation's sales, the new company would produce a product that was indistinguishable from that of its competition.[1] The former Textron had also offered a wide line of fabrics, apparel, drapery materials, blankets, and other sewn products, but the new company would confine its facilities to a few standard weaves of print cloth, staple and filament rayons, and the finer knit goods. The former Textron continually shifted its products and varied its production runs to meet changing market conditions, but the new company would fix its machine settings for as long a period as possible and turn out the same weaves in large quantities. Finally, the former Textron had been able to rely on the higher margins of consumer marketing to cover its necessary selling and advertising costs, the new company would have to make its profit through operating efficiencies and the reduction of overhead costs.

In order to achieve the objectives of low-cost mass production, Textron executives conceived of a modern, fast-moving corporation with the latest cost-saving machinery, able to turn over its inventory with great rapidity. An objective of the new company was to achieve a higher level of sales for each dollar invested in assets than any major competitor. Mr. Little therefore believed that his primary goal should be the elimination of diverse or inefficient operations and the complete modernization of all plant facilities.

Changes in Production Facilities

Between December, 1947, and June, 1953, fixed assets approximating $37,000,000 at original cost before depreciation were disposed of by Textron, at a loss of $1,500,000 on the depreciated book value. The sale of the Nashua, Lonsdale, Manville, and Nemasket plants has already been discussed. In 1951, the Suncook mills, which constituted the first major purchase of the expansion program in 1943, finally were sold when the type of grey cloth they produced faced a declining demand. At the same time, the 960-loom mill at Manchester was moved south.

In 1953, the Indian Head fabric division, which had been maintained through the disposal of the Nashua plants, became a separate independent company under Mr. Robison, the former general manager of consumer products. Under the terms of the sale, the purchase price

[1] Although one or two of the grey cloth companies had established a reputation for quality that enabled them to achieve a slight preference among converters, grey cloth was generally considered to be a basic fungible product, such as steel or milled flour. Market prices of the most important types of print cloth were quoted each day in the *Daily Textile Reporter*. Print cloth was grey cloth scheduled to be printed during the finishing process.

of close to $5,000,000 was to be paid in monthly installments of $50,000 with discounts for prior payment. In addition, 94 percent of the Indian Head common stock was distributed to holders of Textron common on a proportional share basis, the remaining 6 percent of Indian Head common being held by Mr. Robison. Indian Head weaving facilities at Cordova, Alabama, were approximately in balance with its finishing operations at Nashua, New Hampshire, for a weekly output of 600,000 yards of cloth. In 1951, Indian Head earned $697,000 after taxes on net sales of $13,462,000 and in 1952, $462,000 on net sales of $12,721,000.[2] Under the sale agreement, no dividends would be paid and restrictions on executive compensation and capital expenditures would be maintained until the annual purchase installments of $600,000 paid the entire purchase price.

By June, 1953, the only sewing facilities remaining in the Textron corporation were those of the Atlantic Parachute Company, one of the original prewar units of Textron, which had remained on military contracts throughout the many product changes in the other divisions. Other than Atlantic Parachute, only two Textron plants still operated in the New England area.

During the six-year period between 1947 and 1953, in which so many of the older Textron plants were sold, approximately $43,000,000 was invested in new plant and equipment throughout the South and in Puerto Rico. Much of the new investment was allocated to the construction, expansion, and modernization of facilities to spin and weave standard constructions of cloth in the grey.

Modernization of the Williamston Mill: In 1947, the Williamston mill in South Carolina was a three-story building with 110,000 square feet of floor space, constructed in 1900. Its 26,000 spindles and 680 looms for cotton print cloth produced approximately 15 percent of the grey cloth made by Textron Southern, Incorporated. In 1951, 65,000 square feet of space were added, and additional machinery increased the print cloth facilities to 40,000 spindles and 1,100 looms.

In 1950, a new mill was built at Williamston for filament rayon and acetate fabrics. The new plant was a modern windowless, one-story building of brick and steel construction and was fully air conditioned. It originally contained 145,000 feet of space and 960 looms but was subsequently enlarged to 195,000 feet of space and 1,710 looms. Constructed at an ultimate cost of $4,400,000, the Williamston rayon plant was partially financed by a mortgage for $3,724,000. Under the terms of the mortgage, Textron agreed to pay, in addition to fixed annual payments of $750,000, an amount equal to 50 percent of the consolidated net earnings after taxes and after deduction of other fixed payments, preferred stock dividends, and dividends not in excess of $1.00 per share of common stock.

In 1952, a second modern one-story plant was constructed in Williamston for the throwing of filament rayon yarn. The throwing plant, built at a cost of $2,200,000 contained 230,000 feet of space and 34,000 throwing spindles.

Modernization of the Anderson Mills: In 1947, the property at Anderson, South Carolina, consisted of three multistory mills for cotton and rayon cloth and a bleachery. These plants were all built between 1901 and 1927 and contained an aggregate of 267,000 square feet of space, with 57,000 spindles and 1,500 looms.

In 1951, Textron added 90,000 feet of space in a separate plant near Anderson, bringing the area's production capacity up to 37,000 spindles and 990 looms. Meanwhile, the spun rayon plants were modernized, their machinery was reduced to 19,000 spindles and 685 looms, and the remaining equipment was moved to the new mills.

Purchase of New Plants near Anderson: In 1952, three new rayon weaving plants were purchased in the vicinity of Anderson, South Carolina. All of these plants were of the most modern windowless one-story construction and were fully air conditioned. The new plants added 305,000 square feet of space and 1,960 looms for the weaving of spun and filament rayon.

The total cost of the new weaving mills was $8,200,000. Although the new spun rayon plant in Anderson was fully owned as part of the main Anderson properties, the new filament plants

[2] Profit figures do not include allowance for interest or other nonoperating expenses, since Indian Head was not a separate company at this time.

nearby at Honea Path and Belton were subject to mortgage conditions.

By June, 1953, the total investment in plant modernization in the Anderson area, including Williamston, Honea Path, and Belton, amounted to $24,800,000.

Disposition of North Carolina Mills: In 1947, there were four Textron mills at Charlotte, North Carolina, containing over 400,000 square feet of space, 100,000 spindles, and 2,000 looms. Three of the plants were sold soon after acquisition. The Louise mill, however, built in 1897, of brick and frame construction, was retained due to its reputation for making fine quality combed cotton lawns. In 1950, the Louise mill was sold to Vanderbilt University for $2,700,000 and leased back for an annual rental of $330,000.

In 1952, a small 6,000 spindle spinning plant was purchased at Vass, North Carolina. Most of the $300,000 purchase price was paid by the issuance of 4 percent preferred stock.

Construction of Hartwell Plant: In 1949, a new modern rayon weaving plant was constructed at Hartwell, Georgia. The plant contained 134,000 square feet of space, 11,000 spindles and 770 looms for weaving filament rayon and nylon fabrics. The $1,200,000 cost of the building was recovered when Textron sold the property to an insurance company and leased it back for an annual rental of $260,000. Under the terms of the lease, the annual rental was to be reduced to $12,000 in June, 1954, at which time the cost of the plant would be fully amortized by the annual lease rentals.

Repurchase of the Lonsdale Mill: As noted above, Textron sold the Lonsdale Company for $3,500,000 in June, 1948. In July, 1952, Textron repurchased the Lonsdale Company through the issuance of 40,000 shares of 4 percent preferred stock. Two of the three Lonsdale plants were closed, but the Blackstone plant at North Smithfield, Rhode Island, was retained, and its production of fine shirtings continued.

Construction of New Plants in Puerto Rico: Textron Puerto Rico was organized in 1947 issuing $500,000 in common stock, a sum which was later doubled. The new company then entered into a contract under which the Puerto Rico Industrial Development Company, a semipublic agency, constructed and equipped a cotton print cloth plant at Ponce for a total expenditure of $4,000,000. Textron Puerto Rico was to repay the purchase price in installments, the investment being secured by a plant mortgage to the development company. By 1949, the new cotton mill had attained a capacity of 27,000 spindles and 620 looms.

In 1951, a new plant was built at Humacao for the knitting and finishing of acetate and nylon tricot fabrics. In the fall of 1952, Textron Puerto Rico sold both the Ponce and the Humacao plants to the development company for $6,000,000 and leased them back for an annual rental. Under the terms of the rental, Textron Puerto Rico paid each year 4 percent of the original cost if earnings exceeded $240,000 plus an annual fee of 50 percent of net earnings.

Affect of Facilities Changes on Operations

By 1953, most of the corporation's Southern mills were new, one-story air-conditioned buildings containing modern spinning and weaving equipment. Exhibit 1 shows the production capacity of all Textron plants in 1953. The spinning and weaving facilities were approximately in balance for the standard grey fabrics which the corporation produced, such as cotton print cloth and staple synthetic fabrics. Exhibit 2 contains selected operating figures which indicate the changes in the corporation between 1948 and 1952. Exhibit 2 also shows the character of the long-term debt in 1953.

During this period of change, considerable attention was devoted to the reduction of overhead burden made to keep grey goods costs on a competitive basis. Advertising was virtually eliminated and the public relations group was discontinued. Fabric research was curtailed in order to concentrate facilities on quality control and production methods. The selling organization was greatly reduced and detailed scheduling of mill production by a central group was avoided as much as possible. As a result of these measures, selling, advertising, and administrative expenses, which had averaged $8,900,000 per year in 1947 and 1948, were reduced to $3,400,000 by 1953. Sales per employee, which had been $7,700 in 1947 were doubled by 1951.

By June, 1953, Textron executives believed that the company's expenses in the production of cotton print cloth, which was then selling for approximately 20 cents per yard, were almost 2 cents per yard less than comparable operations would have been at its old mills. Balance sheets and Income Statements for 1951 and 1952 are contained in Exhibits 3 and 4. Exhibit 5 is a map on operating properties in June, 1953, while Exhibit 6 shows 1953 cost sheets for three staple fabrics and Exhibit 7 lists monthly yarn prices from 1951–1953.

RESULTS OF OPERATIONS

In 1952, Textron Incorporated achieved the highest ratio of net sales to gross investment of any major competitor in the textile industry. By attaining sales of more than $98,000,000 on an average gross investment of only $66,000,000, Textron was able to sell $1.50 of cloth for every $1.00 invested in inventory, plant, and equipment. Exhibit 8 indicates the relative position of Textron compared with other companies in the textile industry in 1952.

Despite its successs in achieving a large sales volume relative to its investment in assets, the efficiencies of the modernized plant did not result in a high net profit by the end of 1952. Textron executives attributed the lag in profitability to three general factors which influenced the company in 1952.

First, there were delays in achieving efficient production operations in certain of the new plants such as those in Puerto Rico. Because of the modern equipment, low wages, tax exemptions, and favorable freight costs, it was expected that the new Textron mills, which were the first textile plants to be established in Puerto Rico, would be highly profitable. Although sales trebled from $2,100,000 in 1950 to $5,600,000 in 1952, the mills lost $168,000 in 1950, $304,000 in 1951, and $254,000 in 1952. The principal difficulties were traced to high labor turnover, the relatively low productivity of the workers, and the costs involved in starting up a new plant. It was expected that as these problems became less important subsequent to 1953, future operations in the new Puerto Rico mills would be profitable.

A second factor affecting the cost of operations was the changing character of the corporation's production facilities. Although the basic facilities of the new Textron Incorporated were considered established by 1951, market pressures and financial opportunities caused a variety of equipment and facilities changes to be made between 1951 and 1953. For example, in 1951 an investment was made in specialized equipment to make a certain type of rayon cloth in order to take advantage of the market for spun rayon suitings, which had been highly profitable throughout the industry in 1950. However, the opportunities for rayon suitings lasted only a short time, due to an unexpected decline in the price of wool which competed for the suitings market. As a result, the rayon weaving operation was discontinued and the special equipment sold.

Textron executives believed that the revision of product lines to take advantage of market opportunities would strengthen the corporation's financial position. They recognized, however, that interruptions to production flow temporarily increased operating expenses. When it became evident in early 1952 that the changes in plant facilities would offset the profits from some of the modern mills, Mr. Little promptly filed a tax loss form indicating that the Textron company expected a deficit for the year 1952. Under the carry-back provisions of the Internal Revenue Department, this action relieved the company of the need to pay taxes accrued during 1951. If the tax action had been delayed, the company would have had to pay the 1951 tax and then carry the item on the books as an accrued asset until the Government returned the payment, rather than conserving working capital immediately.

A third factor affecting the corporation in 1952 was price movements. For example, consumer preference for nylon tricot caused the price of a certain type of rayon crepe to fall from 65 cents to 45 cents in three months. The price decline was largely responsible for the corporation's withdrawal from the Suncook Mills, which produced this type of rayon crepe in the grey.

Although its annual sales volume placed Textron fifteenth in the textile industry, it was fourth largest in the production of synthetic fabrics, which accounted for a large portion of the company's production. During 1951 and 1952, there was a style trend away from filament and acetate fabrics to cotton and nylon. Stocks of filament rayon in the hands of producers generally increased from a postwar average of 8 million pounds to a peak of 98 million pounds in April, 1952, and prices in certain rayon grey goods fell. In 1953, rayon demand appeared to be increasing, and favorable market indications in the second quarter caused many mills to overproduce for the third quarter.

ORGANIZATION PLANS

Due to the rapid changes in market conditions, the relationship between manufacturing and merchandising programs remained a difficult problem in the textile industry. Mr. Little believed that an ordinary administrator would fail in the textile industry unless he had the imagination to develop a feel for market changes. For example, he believed that due to the overcapacity in the industry, booms did not last long. Therefore, when customers first began to hesitate, it was necessary for the manufacturing company to cut back production rapidly in order to avoid inventory losses. When business did go on the downgrade, the company's salesmen were unwilling to push for sales because they did not wish to load inventory on the retailers. Mr. Little liked to keep strict working capital and inventory limits in order to force divisional managers to make quick production changes.

When modern plant facilities came into production and the Textron product lines diminished, a new system of organization was established to meet the needs of the company. A central sales organization in New York City handled the marketing of all Textron cloth, while the manufacturing organization left to about twenty plant managers the responsibility for efficient production.

An alternative system would have established several product divisions, such as cotton cloth, rayon cloth, and so on, with a single executive in charge of all management aspects of the division. Although certain other textile companies were organized in this manner, Mr. Little was concerned lest a divisional manager emphasize one function to the exclusion of another. If he selected a production executive to be manager of a product division there was the danger that the division might lose sales by running the mills on the same textile weaves in order to reduce operating costs. On the other hand, if he selected a merchandising executive to be a divisional manager, the operation might face increased costs as a result of excessive style changes.

The Textron sales organization in New York had five general managers under Mr. Huffines, the chief operating executive. The general managers scheduled production at the twenty mills based on their knowledge of changing market requirements. The local plant managers therefore acted in more of a staff than a line function in supervising manufacturing operations. There was some discussion in the Textron company as to the feasibility of placing a single executive in charge of production at all the mills and letting him work out scheduling problems with the general managers who were close to the market. Under this system, production-marketing disputes would be umpired by Mr. Huffines.

1. TEXTRON INCORPORATED (C)

Operating Capacity of Plants, June, 1953

Spinning

Filament rayon	
Hartwell, Georgia	11,400
Williamston, S.C.	35,600
Total throwing spindles	47,000

Spun rayon	
(Riverside) Anderson, S.C.	28,584
Vass, N.C.	5,760
Total spindles	34,344

Cotton	
N. Smithfield, R.I.	51,072
Williamston, S.C.	41,124
Charlotte, N.C.	35,744
(Toxaway) Anderson, S.C.	27,600
Ponce, P.R.	26,988
Total cotton spindles	182,528
Total Spindles	263,872

Weaving

Filament rayon	
Williamston, S.C.	1,710
Belton, S.C.	960
Hartwell, Ga.	768
Honea Path, S.C.	600
Total filament looms	4,038

Spun rayon	
(Southside) Anderson, S.C.	395
(Ladlassie) Anderson, S.C.	394
Total loams	789

Cotton	
Williamston, S.C.	1,100
N. Smithfield, R.I.	993
(Toxaway)Anderson, S.C.	880
Charlotte, N.C.	640
Ponce, P.R.	624
Total cotton looms	4,237
Total Looms	9,064

Nylon Tricot Knitting

E. Greenwich, R.I.	45
Humacao, P.R.	48
Total machines	93

Dyeing and Finishing

E. Greenwich, R.I.
Humacao, P.R.
Garnerville, N.Y
(Gossett) Anderson, S.C.

Sewing

Lowell, Mass.
parachutes

Total production of grey goods per week:

Cotton weaving	1,840,000 linear yards
Synthetic filament weaving	2,290,000 linear yards
Synthetic spun weaving	462,000 linear yards
Synthetic tricot knitting	596,000 linear yards

Source: Company records.

2. TEXTRON INCORPORATED (C)

Condensed Summary of Operating and Financial Data, 1948-1952

Year	Net Sales	Rental	Cost of Sales	Selling Expenses	Interest	Working Capital	Long-Term Debt	Taxes	Net Profit
1948	$98,847,174	$ 466,305	$79,668,835	$8,212,759	$509,356	$22,359,148	$ 2,051,500	$4,045,000	$6,934,435
1949	67,896,029	427,493	63,428,006	5,807,828	307,847	25,705,635	4,701,833	(1,075,000)*	(1,662,690)
1950	87,546,886	675,565	76,709,581	4,820,896	474,292	24,616,719	6,869,583	2,940,000	2,899,741
1951	98,290,016	990,146	87,298,665	3,576,762	605,695	21,774,042	5,972,472	3,725,000	4,417,151
1952	98,744,849	1,213,998	98,306,959	3,490,648	875,159	20,133,337	11,031,204	(2,933,000)	(3,543,360)

*Estimated refund under carry-back provisions of Internal Revenue Code, less provision for state taxes on income.

Repayment Schedule for Long-Term Debt Outstanding as of June, 1953

	Textron Incorporated		Subsidiaries		Textron Consolidated
Year	Debentures 4 1/2%	Mortgage Notes, Etc. 4 to 5%	Mortgage Note 4 1/2%	Unsecured Bank Loan 4%	Total
1953	$ 199,500.00	$ 193,333.32	$ 242,500.00	$ 50,000.00	$ 685,333.32
1954	232,500.00	1,895,066.40	242,500.00	50,000.00	2,420,066.40
1955	232,500.00	1,895,066.40	242,500.00	50,000.00	2,420,066.40
1956	232,500.00	1,867,503.62	242,500.00	50,000.00	2,392,503.62
1957 and later	306,500.00	2,797,067.21	682,500.00	12,500.00	3,798,567.21
Total Outstanding	$1,203,500.00	$8,648,036.95	$1,652,500.00	$212,500.00	$11,716,536.95

Source: Company records.

3. TEXTRON INCORPORATED (C)

Balance Sheets, 1951-1952

	1951 Dec. 29, 1951	1952 Jan. 3, 1953
ASSETS		
Cash	$ 6,451,345	$ 3,526,028
Accounts Receivable - Net	10,158,610	10,491,464
Inventories*	17,591,689	12,153,577
Other Current Assets	1,078,168	414,929
Total Current Assets	$35,279,812	$26,585,998
Notes Receivable Due After One Year	131,811	98,628
Investment in Textron Puerto Rico	1,000,000	-
Property, Plant and Equipment - Net**	21,379,485	28,374,268
Advances on Construction Contracts	635,501	-
Other Assets	615,782	666,161
Long-Term Rental Deposits	600,000	600,000
Prepaid Expenses and Deferred Charges	743,643	856,010
TOTAL ASSETS	$60,386,034	$57,181,065
LIABILITIES AND CAPITAL		
Notes Payable	$ 3,011,442	$ 485,833
Accounts Payable	3,488,920	3,494,446
Accrued Liabilities	1,806,139	1,938,075
Provision for Income Taxes	4,055,607	-
Dividends Payable	697,819	-
Other Current Liabilities	445,843	534,307
Total Current Liabilities	$13,505,770	$ 6,452,661
Notes Payable	4,731,472	10,027,204
Debentures, Due April 1, 1958	1,241,000	1,004,000
Other Liabilities	160,571	354,603
Total Liabilities	$19,638,813	$17,838,468
Reserve for Contingencies	2,500,000	2,157,000
Minority Interest	675,335	519,649
Capital Stock		
$1.25 Convert. Pfd. (291,000 sh)	7,290,975	7,287,400
4% Pfd., Par $100, (35,000 sh)	-	3,503,407
Common, Par $.50, (1,196,000 sh)	598,196	598,268
Paid-In Surplus	9,827,758	10,062,811
Capital Surplus	4,549,126	4,323,353
Earned Surplus	15,305,831	10,890,709
TOTAL LIABILITIES AND CAPITAL	$60,386,034	$57,181,065

*Inventories on December 30, 1950 were $15,595,351
Inventories on January 3, 1953 included: Raw Material $3,468,000
Work in Process 5,146,000
Grey Cloth 3,342,000

**Depreciation: $7,129,285 on Dec. 29, 1951 and $6,737,629 on Jan. 3, 1953.
Source: Company records.

4. TEXTRON INCORPORATED (C)

Income Statements for 1951 and 1952
(In Thousands)

	1951 (Year Ending Dec. 29, 1951)		1952 (Year Ending Jan. 3, 1953)	
Net Sales		$98,290		$98,745
Cost of Goods Sold:				
Maintenance	$ 3,992		$ 3,508	
Depreciation	1,287		1,844	
Social Security Taxes	847		798	
Real Estate Taxes, Etc.	263		389	
Rents	990		1,214	
Material, Labor, and Other	79,920		90,554	
Cost of Goods Sold (Total)		87,299		98,307
Gross Profit on Sales		$10,991		$ 438
Selling, General and Administrative Expenses	$ 3,344		$ 3,491	
Provision for Doubtful Accounts	232	3,576		3,491
Operating Profit (or Loss)		$ 7,415		$ (3,051)
Other Income		514		166
		$ 7,929		$ (2,887)
Income Deductions:				
Interest Expense	$ 606		$ 875	
Loss (or Gain) on Disposal of Property	(1,914)		1,882	
Other Deductions	1,056	(252)	780	3,537
Profit (or Loss) before Income Taxes		$ 8,181		$ (6,424)
Provision for Taxes:				
Federal Tax	$ 3,699		$ (2,944)	
Carry-Back Credit	-0-		-0-	
State Taxes	26	3,725	10	(2,934)
Profit (or Loss) after Taxes		$ 4,456		$ (3,490)
Applicable to Minority Interests		39		53
Net Profit (or Loss)		$ 4,417		$ (3,543)

Source: Company records.

5. TEXTRON INCORPORATED (C)
Map of Operating Properties, June, 1953

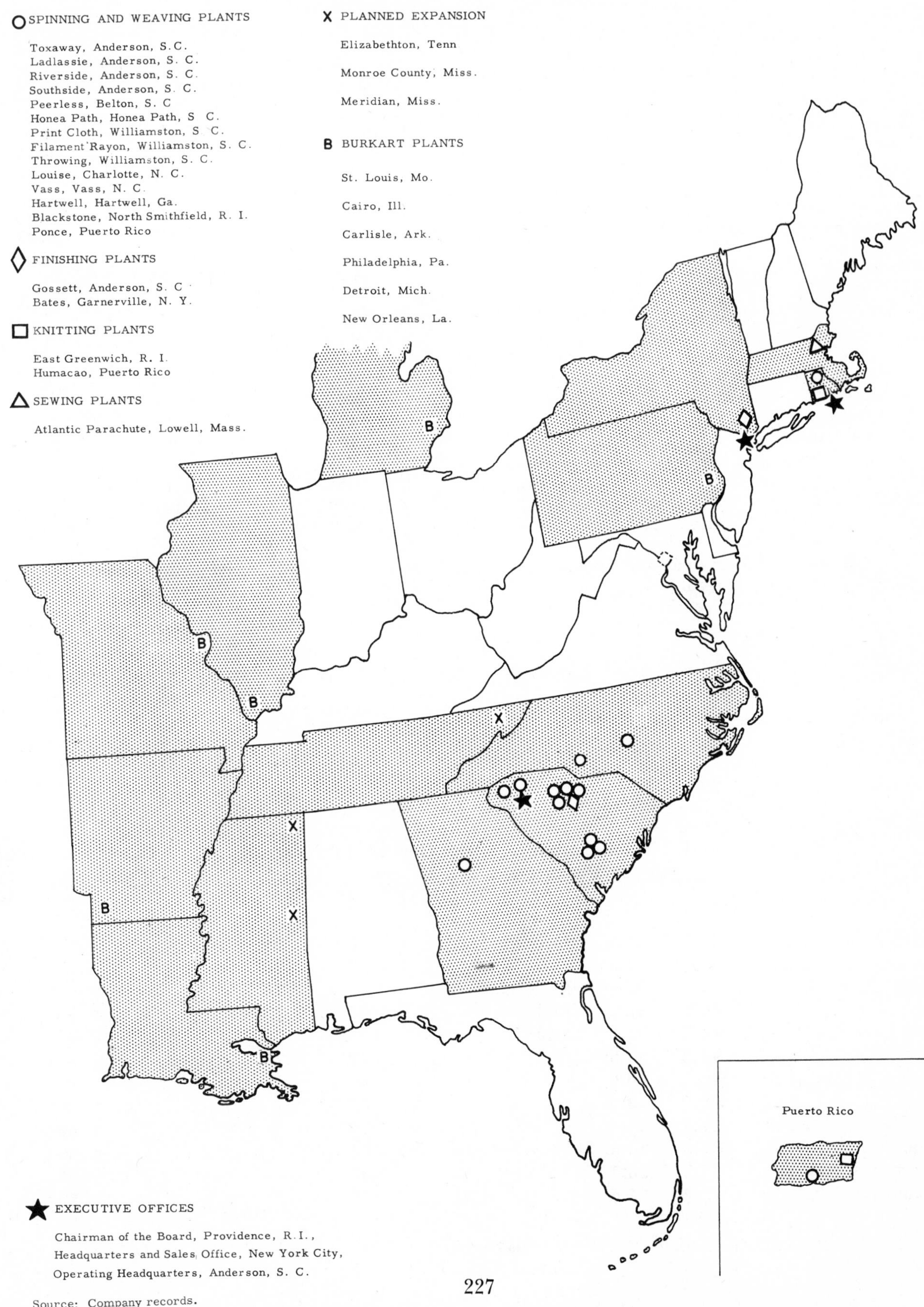

SPINNING AND WEAVING PLANTS
Toxaway, Anderson, S.C.
Ladlassie, Anderson, S. C.
Riverside, Anderson, S. C.
Southside, Anderson, S. C.
Peerless, Belton, S. C
Honea Path, Honea Path, S C.
Print Cloth, Williamston, S C.
Filament Rayon, Williamston, S. C.
Throwing, Williamston, S. C.
Louise, Charlotte, N. C.
Vass, Vass, N. C.
Hartwell, Hartwell, Ga.
Blackstone, North Smithfield, R. I.
Ponce, Puerto Rico
FINISHING PLANTS
Gossett, Anderson, S. C
Bates, Garnerville, N. Y.
KNITTING PLANTS
East Greenwich, R. I.
Humacao, Puerto Rico
SEWING PLANTS
Atlantic Parachute, Lowell, Mass.
X PLANNED EXPANSION
Elizabethton, Tenn
Monroe County, Miss.
Meridian, Miss.
B BURKART PLANTS
St. Louis, Mo.
Cairo, Ill.
Carlisle, Ark.
Philadelphia, Pa.
Detroit, Mich.
New Orleans, La.
Puerto Rico
EXECUTIVE OFFICES
Chairman of the Board, Providence, R.I.,
Headquarters and Sales Office, New York City,
Operating Headquarters, Anderson, S. C.

Source: Company records.

6. TEXTRON INCORPORATED (C)

Cost Sheets for Three Staple Fabrics, 1953

	Style A 100% Acetate Chromspun	Style B Cotton Print Cloth 80 x 90	Style C Acetate Suiting
Material Cost*	$.2282	$.13520	$.2072
Labor	.0414	.02383	.0375
Overhead	.0637	.01712	.0344
Mill Variance	.0131	.00589	.0172
Manufacturing Cost	.3464	.18204	.2963
Selling and Administrative	.0105	.00548	.0093
Allowance for Seconds	.0035	.00046	.0028
Total Cost	$.3604	$.18798	$.3084

Analysis of Labor Costs

	Style A	Style B	Style C
Warping	.0018		$.0023
Slashing	.0022	$.00069	.0036
Quilling	.0019		.0037
Weavers	.0060	.00678	.0058
Battery Hands	.0021	.00293	.0027
Loom Fixers	.0087		
Weaving Other Labor	.0156	.01156	.0121
Cloth Room	.0031	.00187	.0073
	$.0414	$.02383	$.0375

*The acetate chromspun and acetate were brought from yarn suppliers; the cotton yarn for print cloth was spun by Textron.

Source: Company records.

7. TEXTRON INCORPORATED (C)

Selected Monthly Cotton Yarn Prices, 1951-1953

	1 1/16-Inch Cotton (Cents per Pound)			Carded 30's Yarn (Cents per Pound)			Carded 40's Yarn (Cents per Pound)		
	1951	1952	1953	1951	1952	1953	1951	1952	1953
January	44.2	41.6	33.0		88.5	80		103	95
February	N.A.	41.9	33.1		87.5	78		102	92
March	45.1	N.A.	33.2		83.0	78		96	89
April	45.2	41.6	33.1		82	78		95	89
May	45.2	38.3	33.5		83	76		93	87
June	45.2	39.5	33.1		79	76		93	87
July	40.1	40.0			80			94	
August	35.0	39.9			83			97	
September	35.1	39.4			79			98	
October	36.9	38.5			84			99	
November	41.5	38.7			83			88	
December	42.2	34.5			80			95	

Source: Daily News Record, Annual Textile Issues, January, 1951-53.

8. TEXTRON INCORPORATED (C)

Detailed Comparison of Return on Investment of Selected Textile Companies, 1952

	Fiscal Year Ending	Average Gross Assets	Net Sales	Operating Profit	Gross Assets Turnover		Operating Profit as % of Sales		Operating Profit as % of Gross Assets	
					Times	Rank	Per Cent	Rank	Per Cent	Rank
Companies Pricing Inventory on First-In, First-Out Basis:										
American Woolen Co.	12/31	$145,916	$112,320	$(12,491)	.77	(7)	(11.12)	(7)	(8.56)	(7)
Bates Manufacturing Co.	12/31	43,360	55,372	875	1.28	(2)	1.58	(4)	2.02	(4)
Berkshire Fine Spinning Associates, Inc.	9/30	50,342	48,545	445	.96	(5)	.92	(5)	.88	(5)
Burlington Mills	9/30	300,315	320,261	18,276	1.07	(4)	5.71	(1)	6.11	(3)
Robbins Mills, Inc.	11/30	71,453	57,986	(1,054)	.81	(6)	(1.82)	(6)	(1.47)	(6)
J. P. Stevens & Co., Inc.	10/31	312,585	387,148	19,526	1.24	(3)	5.04	(2)	6.25	(2)
United Merchants & Manufacturers, Inc.	6/30	187,175	255,492	12,312	1.36	(1)	4.82	(3)	6.56	(1)
Companies Pricing Inventory on Last-In, First-Out Basis:										
Avondale Mills	8/31	41,658	61,655	2,435	1.48	(2)	3.95	(7)	5.85	(6)
Cone Mills Corp.	12/31	144,700	173,742	16,951	1.20	(7)	9.76	(3)	11.71	(4)
Erwin Mills	9/30	51,659	61,002	2,005	1.18	(8)	3.29	(8)	3.88	(8)
Kendall Company	12/31	67,977	94,223	8,223	1.39	(4)	8.73	(4)	12.13	(3)
Pacific Mills	12/31	107,462	111,070	4,756	1.03	(9)	4.28	(6)	4.41	(7)
Pepperell Mfg. Co.	6/30	62,350	80,101	6,849	1.28	(5)	8.55	(5)	10.94	(5)
Reeves Brothers, Inc.	6/30	56,225	71,357	7,215	1.27	(6)	10.11	(2)	12.84	(2)
Textron Incorporated	12/31	65,688	98,745	(3,053)	1.50	(1)	(3.09)	(9)	(4.64)	(9)
West Point Mfg. Co.	8/31	89,509	130,547	13,584	1.46	(3)	10.41	(1)	15.20	(1)

Note: Average gross assets represents average of beginning and ending gross assets less security investments.
Gross assets turnover represents net sales divided by average gross assets.
Operating profit (before taxes, interest, and other nonoperating income deductions) divided by net sales shows operating profit as a per cent of sales, which, when multiplied by gross assets turnover, gives operating profit as a per cent of gross assets.

Source: Annual Reports.

Algonquin Mills, Inc.

Algonquin Mills, Inc. was a small New England company engaged in the spinning and weaving of fine cotton textiles. In 1957, the Algonquin company, after more than 100 years of operation, still occupied its original mill building. In recent years, adverse conditions in the industry, supervisory problems within the company, and financial and sales difficulties had been contributing factors in a prolonged period of operating losses. The company had earned a profit only once during the previous eight years and by 1957 was in a precarious financial position. Balance Sheets and Income Statements are given in Exhibits 1 and 2.

In early February, 1957, Mr. Thomas Danforth was elected president and treasurer of the corporation. Mr. Herbert Pelham, who had been president for 25 years, became chairman of the board of directors and planned to restrict his activities to presiding at meetings and handling two important sales accounts. Mr. Danforth had been with the company since 1948 and represented the fourth generation of his family to be associated with the mill. Algonquin Mills' common stock was closely held but occasionally traded over-the-counter. The Pelham and Danforth families controlled about 75 percent of the common shares. After graduating from college, Mr. Danforth worked for a few years with a large textile concern before joining the Algonquin company. In 1957, he was concerned with reshaping the company's activities to permit profitable operations despite both the Algonquin company's severely restricted working capital and the generally adverse conditions throughout the cotton textile industry. He was also interested in establishing long-run operating policies to achieve greater stability of sales and profits and a sound capital base for future needs.

Three principal programs for adjustment of mill activities had been advanced. These similar programs were intended to reduce working capital requirements, eliminate products that could not be produced at a profit, retire the less efficient machinery, and concentrate sales activities on a smaller number of customers and products. The mill, which operated during 1956 on a two-shift basis, had 35,000 spindles and 705 looms in place; the proposals called for operations on a three-shift basis, using only 50 to 60 percent of spindle capacity and 282 looms. Instead of the 70 fabrics and 47 yarns then being produced, only 30 fabrics and 20 yarns would be in process at one time. The work force could then be cut from 650 to 315 men.

HISTORY

The company was founded shortly after 1850 by a group of investors from Boston, Massachusetts. The mill was constructed in Algonquin, Maine, and the original building, containing 10,000 spindles, was situated on the bank of the Derby River and powered by water from the river. The Algonquin Mill produced medium-fine cotton goods until 1931 when Mr. Herbert Pelham became treasurer and general manager in the midst of a financial crisis. Under Mr. Pelham's administration, emphasis was shifted to specialty products and "high-end" fine cotton goods. In the mid-1930's he established a New York City sales office which engaged in converting operations, selling Algonquin cloth in the finished state as well as contracting for grey goods sales. In 1941, the company converted to defense production and Mr. Pelham took advantage of a period of prosperity to reorganize both the physical plant and the capital structure of the corporation. During wartime the company produced goods exclusively for the military and a few selected civilian accounts. The New York office became inactive.

Postwar Operations

More than $500,000 was invested in 1946 to improve machinery and operating conditions. In converting to peacetime activities the management decided to concentrate on the development of specialized fabrics made of worsted,[1] rayon-worsted blends, and fine combed cotton. From 1946 to 1949 most of the Algonquin company's sales were in fabrics woven of rayon-wool or cotton-wool blends. These cloths were sold finished to the cutting-up trade by a New York commission agent. The remainder of the mill's volume was cotton grey goods which were sold direct from the mill to converters and cutters-up by an Algonquin salesman.

In 1949, the devaluation of the pound sterling permitted the importation of English Viyella cloth at prices below competitive domestic fab-

[1] Worsted is a combed woolen yarn spun from long-staple fiber. In the spinning it is given a twist greater than usual for woolens.

rics woven of cotton-wool blends. Problems concerning the company's manufacturing and sales personnel further complicated the situation and in March, 1949, a drop in orders caused the management to shut down the Algonquin mill in order to reduce inventory. Intermittent shut downs and losses on liquidation of inventories of rayon-wool blends caused an operating loss of $750,000 in 1949. Cotton sales showed a profit for the year.

Recovery in 1950

By the end of 1949, the mill's sales volume was entirely in cotton grey goods. At that time another New York commission house was taken on to handle cotton sales, in place of the mill's salaried salesman. Operating losses continued until June, 1950, when the Korean hostilities brought a sudden improvement in the entire textile industry. As a result, Algonquin's profits for July through December, 1950, exceeded $115,000.

Government contracts furnished a large share of the mill's sales volume from 1950 to 1953. When the order mix continued to be 60 percent for defense purposes in 1953, however, the relation with the commission agent was terminated and the management reestablished a New York sales office which took over all sales of cotton grey goods in the summer of 1953.

Polyester-Cotton Fabrics

In 1953, a new yarn development, a blend of polyester synthetic fiber and cotton, was brought to the stage where volume production could be achieved. Algonquin was the first mill to blend polyester and cotton fibers successfully. To handle sales and merchandising of cloth woven from polyester-cotton blends, the Algonquin company contracted with another New York commission house which was to sell the finished cloth to cutters-up for fine shirtings and dress goods. At the time, an annual sales volume of three to four million dollars was forecast for the blended fabric. Problems with the first large order for polyester-cotton cloth, however, led to another difficult financial problem in 1954 and delayed a return to profitable operations.

The company's most recent setback came in August, 1955, when the aftermath of a hurricane pushed the Derby River to a flood crest 10 feet higher than had ever been recorded in the mill's history. Everything on the first floor of the mill, including 40 percent of the spindle capacity and most of the power facilities had to be scrapped or rebuilt. Facilities lost had a replacement value of nearly one and one-half million dollars, and out-of-pocket cost to place the mill in operation totaled nearly $250,000. Emergency financial aid in the form of a $234,000 disaster loan kept the company solvent, and operations were resumed after a three-week shut-down.

At the time of the flood, an order backlog of one and one-half million dollars had given promise of renewed future earnings. The physical and financial damage resulting from the flood, however, was a serious handicap. The company's heavy indebtedness at a time of tight credit supply meant that financial requirements, as well as sales and manufacturing considerations, would dictate the level of mill activity in 1956.

MARKETING

In relating the mill's recent history, Mr. Danforth commented that a major problem was that there had been no continuity of merchandising since before World War II. During 1957 he hoped to effect a reorientation of the Algonquin company's merchandising and distribution policies that would lead the way for a reorganization of manufacturing activities and a subsequent return to profitable operations. "As a matter of corporate policy," he added, "a major change in mill balance must originate in sales."

Product Policies

During the postwar years the mill had sold cotton cloth only in the grey, with the exception of goods for the United States government and one important civilian customer. Rayon-wool blends, however, had been sold as finished cloth and this pattern was adopted for polyester-cotton blends in 1953. At the end of 1956, the Algonquin management decided to terminate their converting activities and offer only grey goods for sale. It was felt that equivalent profits could be realized while reducing financial requirements by eliminating the month's inventory-in-process at the contract bleachery. Since the agent for polyester-cotton sales had contacts primarily among cutters-up, the Algonquin company terminated its relationship with the commission house in December, 1956, and began to offer cotton-polyester greige to the converting trade through its New York sales office.

Algonquin was a "sheer goods" mill, spinning fine yarns of polyester staple and combed, long-staple cotton and weaving them into high quality cloth for dress goods, shirtings, and light-weight commercial cloths. Average yarn count was 68's and a high proportion of imported Egyptian cotton was employed. All production was on a job-order basis, thus no inventory goods were produced on company account.

Market

Algonquin's principal customers were converters selling to the dress goods and shirting trade. The most common cloth constructions sold were voiles, crepes, batistes, broadcloths, oxfords, and fancies for shirts, blouses, and dresses. Consumer demand for these fabrics was highest in spring and summer, therefore mill activity hit its peak in fall and winter. Because Algonquin produced "high-end" fabrics, its cloth was used in shirts priced at retail above $5.75 and dresses retailing above $18.75. Two customers that had been served steadily since before the war were both well-known producers of high quality men's shirts. Algonquin tried to avoid the competitive markets for "commodity" fabrics such as print cloths and duck. Instead the company concentrated on fine specialties.

A limited number of mills were equipped to compete with Algonquin in its field. Large mills found it uneconomical to compete for orders as small as 50,000 yards, and most mills could not readily spin fine yarns. The principal competition came from small weaving mills without yarn facilities and one or two mills similar in size to Algonquin's. Although there were a number of companies that competed with Algonquin in one way or another, there would be only one or two other mills in direct competition for any given fabric. However, despite the company's apparent separation from the major part of the industry, Algonquin's business seemed to be affected by the basic trends in the industry. The effects of a basic change in the market for textiles would be reflected in fluctuations in price and demand for something like 80-square print-cloth, a very competitive item produced in large volume at low cost. The same basic market condition would also be reflected in the demand and therefore the price for high-end goods such as those produced by Algonquin.

The textile industry underwent a recession of activity in 1956, and prospects for 1957 were not bright at the beginning of the year. Production of cotton broad woven goods during 1956 was about 2½ percent less than in 1955, but this decline occurred entirely in the second half of the year, after first-half production had been 5 percent ahead of 1955. The rate of output prevailing at the end of 1956 was expected to continue until late 1957. Prices were depressed also, despite industry-wide wage increases at the end of the year. One index of print-cloth prices fell 7 percent between November, 1955, and the end of 1956.

New York Sales Office

The company's selling office in Mahattan employed three salesmen, a stylist, and a secretary. Mr. Danforth supervised the operation, spending two days each week in New York. Considerable effort was devoted to the creative aspects of selling, such as originating designs for a customer, translating indefinite customer desires into fabric design and color, or modifying customer designs to permit more economical production. The salesmen worked on a salary and together served approximately 50 customers. Mr. Danforth tried to participate in sales activities at the opening and closing of negotiations with a customer, and also helped handle most "crisis" situations. The stylist participated in any work that involved questions of style or color, usually about 30 percent of the volume handled. Many fabrics developed by the sales office were "confined" patterns, offered only to one customer who was given exclusive access to it. Close liaison with mill production officials was required to establish approximate production cost and forecast delivery dates on any order. Sales of cotton cloth grew from $1.3 million in 1954 to $2.7 million in 1955, and then declined to $2.5 million in 1956. From 1950 through 1953 cotton goods had represented all of the Algonquin mill's sales volume; after 1954, the balance of sales was in cotton-polyester blends.

Competitive Factors

The competitive strength of the Algonquin company lay in its long history and established reputation as a quality producer of fine goods, plus its continuing ability to produce quality items in small lots at a competitive price. The company's personnel pioneered development of blends of rayon and wool and of polyester and cotton, enabling Algonquin to gain a leading position at the introduction of these new items. The management and facilities of the mill were geared to service orders involving low yardages but intricate constructions and high quality. Mr. Danforth felt that inspection of cloth at the Algonquin mill was far more careful than typical industry practice.

The company had also developed a reputation as a reliable producer of fabrics that were difficult to weave, in some cases turning out fabrics that could not have been produced at any other mill. During the war periods the mill had produced both coarse and fine fabrics for the Army, sometimes utilizing 72-inch wide looms that were not available in most mills. By careful production to establish a quality product, and careful inspection to maintain that quality, the management hoped to continue to enhance its reputation in the field.

MANUFACTURING

Mr. John Richards, vice-president and mill superintendent, had had more than thirty years of experience in the textile business. Starting as a card room hand in 1926, he had become spinning room second hand by 1933, a yarn mill superintendent in 1946, and superintendent of a combined yarn and weaving mill in 1948. He joined Algonquin Mills in June, 1950. In addition to extensive work experience in industry, he held a Bachelor's degree in Chemical Engineering from Northeastern University, a Bachelor of Law degree from Suffolk Law School (a night school), and had studied a course in textiles offered by the International Correspondence School. Mr. Richards remained active in developing new products and processes for textiles; during the 1930's he helped develop a novelty spinning frame, currently at Algonquin he was perfecting a process which he had developed for the improvement of the slashing operating through application of ultrasonic waves.

Mr. Richards emphasized the importance of correct mill balance for profitable operations. As an example he recalled the postwar operations at a mill in New Bedford, Massachusetts, where he had worked until joining Algonquin. By properly balancing the process flow in the New Bedford mill, profits were increased rapidly from $200,000 to more than $1 million. He explained that once the balance had been achieved it was maintained by accepting orders for only those fabrics that would be appropriate to the balanced flow.

Mill Facilities

There were five important mill departments: Carding, Spinning, Weaving, Cloth Inspection, and Mill Maintenance. Each of these departments was headed by an Overseer who reported to Mr. Richards. In addition, a small crew of workers maintained the outside facilities such as mill buildings, land, and other property. These outside costs were segregated from mill costs for accounting purposes. A process flow chart for the carding and spinning operations is given in Exhibit 3. The Carding and Spinning Departments together comprised the "yarn mill."

The Carding Department occupied approximately 39,000 square feet of floor space. Breakers were located in the cotton storeroom and fibers were blown through pipes into the main mill building where the pickers were located. The breakers and pickers were operated only one shift daily, all 94 cards were run three shifts, while the remaining equipment in the department was operated on a two-shift basis. Subsequent equipment included 138 drawing heads, 2 lap winders, and 12 combers. The polyester fiber was received in staple form and processed in a manner similar to cotton, although the rates of output were different. One of the five pickers was used solely for polyester staple which was then carded, drawn, and combed. At the breaker drawing frame after combing, the polyester comber slivers were blended with cotton slivers (usually to result in a blend containing 65 percent polyester and 35 percent cotton). Costs and comparative rates of output per 40-hour machine-week were as follows:

	Output[2] *(Pounds)*			*Costs*[2]	
	Domestic Cotton	*Imported Long-staple Cotton*	*Polyester*	*Labor*	*Overhead*
Pickers	11,255	9,417	9,787	$65.89	$63.98
Cards	200 to 300	126	194	4.52	4.24
Lap Winders	11,800	9,520	8,710	22.28	13.52
Combers	1,487	1,351	1,633	22.42	12.53

[2] All data for one machine operated 40 hours.

The 35,376 spindles in the Spinning Department occupied about 41,000 square feet of space. Additional equipment for winding, twisting, warping, and spooling occupied about 22,000 square feet, and the three slashers occupied another 8,000 square feet. The spinning frames were generally run on a three-shift basis, the other equipment operated one or two shifts, depending upon the mix of products. Only 15,000 spinning spindles were long draft; the remaining 20,000 were regular draft. The yarn mill was felt to be a relatively high-cost operation.

The Weaving Department had 705 looms in place, occupying a total of 62,000 square feet in several areas of the building. The types and numbers of the looms were as follows:

Loom	*Number*
Draper "E"	513
Box loom	80
Draper "XK"	42
Wide Draper	70

All the Draper looms were "plain looms," that is, only one color, usually natural, could be used for the fill yarn. The box looms, however, could handle as many as four different fill yarns and were used for "fancy" constructions such as checks, ginghams, and so forth; because of this they cost six to ten cents more per yard to operate. The Draper Model E looms wove 40- or 42-inch cloth. Some were cam looms, others were dobby[3] looms for more complicated twill weaves; the newer Draper XK's were all dobby looms. The Wide Drapers were looms which had been modified to produce 68-inch and 70-inch cloth, but were otherwise similar to the other Draper models; the Draper XK's were newer and more modern looms, and produced 50-inch cloth. After weaving, the cloth was taken to the Cloth Inspection Room, occupying 11,000 square feet of space, where it was carefully inspected, packed, and shipped to the customer.

Typical Order Process

Initial delivery on any cloth order would not come until two or three months after final confirmation of the order. Yarn production and preparation of the loom beams would take eight to ten weeks. If a color was required, two weeks had to be added for yarn dyeing, which was done by an outside firm on contract. A 40-inch loom beam might weigh over 300 pounds, and might hold yarn for 2,600 yards of a weave such as 96 × 100 batiste[4] or 1,200 yards for a 102 × 48 poplin. Although all the warp yarn had to be on the beam before any weaving could begin, the fill yarn was usually produced in quantities to march weekly weave requirements. Most orders were delivered 10 percent weekly, and thus ran out after ten weeks of weaving. The average loom speed was 156 picks. Loom output depended upon the cloth construction, loom speed, and loom efficiency rate.

Labor

The company's production workers were members of an International textile workers' union. The population of Algonquin was only a few thousand persons, and the mill was the principal source of employment. In the spring of 1957, however, a large corporation was scheduled to begin manufacturing in a new bathroom fixtures plant in Algonquin which would reportedly employ 300 workers.

Costs and Accounting

All the factory accounting was based on a system of standard costs. Each year, on the basis of machine loadings scheduled and forecast for the next twelve months, the controller prepared budgets for equipment, labor, and overhead. Overhead was split into fixed and variable portions, with fixed costs distributed to mill departments on the basis of plant area occupied, while variable overhead costs were allocated in proportion to direct labor. In 1956, about 60 percent of mill overhead was considered variable. Within each department, labor and overhead costs were apportioned to each machine, with separate rates for labor and overhead expressed in dollars per 40-hour machine-week.

To develop the standard cost for any cloth, the accounting group utilized the established machine cost rates and technical data on productivity. The yarn manufacturing cost was calculated first, using output rates for the type of fiber to be spun, and costs for the machines required. Once the manufacturing cost per pound of yarn had been calculated this way, it was converted to cost per woven yard, based on the yarn weight and cloth construction. Standard labor and overhead costs for slashing, warp

[3] A "dobby head" permitted use of as many as 25 harnesses for complicated weaves.

[4] A batiste was a plain weave of fine yarns of which 96 × 100 would be a typical construction.

drawing, and weaving were then added. Standard weave cost per yard of cloth included a direct charge for the weaver and battery hand based on the actual rates paid those workers, the number of looms they could tend, and the output per loom for the cloth. The weaving overhead expense included a charge for overhead allocated to the department plus department labor other than weavers and battery hands (such as fixers, changers, and cleaners).

Total manufacturing cost included yarn manufacturing, slashing, drawing-in, and weaving costs, plus the purchase cost of cotton or polyester, dyeing expense, and an allowance for loss on seconds. Purchase cost of fibers ranged from about 40 cents per pound for domestic cotton to approximately 75 cents for imported long-staple cotton, and $1.50 for polyester staple. There was an average loss of 20 percent in yarn production. Mr. Richards stated that a common "rule of thumb" in most cotton mills was that the cost of an average fabric was one-third for fiber, one-third labor, and one-third overhead.

Each week the standard cost of the week's output was computed and compared with actual expenditures. For each cloth the actual selling price per yard, less the standard cost per yard, multiplied by the yardage delivered, would indicate the standard profit or loss on sales. Each week the total standard profit or loss on sales, and the variances between actual and standard labor and overhead costs were reported to the top management. The standard profit was calculated before deductions for interest and selling expenses. Three other important operating figures were reported weekly: loom-weeks worked (loom-hours of operation divided by 40); weaving efficiency (the actual yardage produced divided by maximum potential yardage for the given loom speeds, cloth construction, and hours worked); and percentage of seconds to total yardage produced.

SITUATION IN 1957

A major objective of the management in February, 1957, was to alleviate the severe financial restrictions which had hampered mill operation for several years. Principal financial support was derived from three sources; a $375,000 mortgage note on all fixed assets payable over eight years; a factoring agreement under which accounts receivable were financed at a cost of 1 percent of face value; and a field warehousing arrangement under which the company was committed, in December, 1956, for 600,000 pounds of cotton worth $300,000 held in a nearby public warehouse. Additional funds could be borrowed at 6 percent interest under the factoring agreement by pledging inventories other than raw cotton. The company's inventories at the end of the last three years had been:

	Inventory Value (Thousands)		
	1954	*1955*	*1956*
Raw material	$ 22	$ 36	$ 10
Work in progress	309	416	396
Greige cloth	208	262	188
Finished cloth	147	153	69
Supplies	32	33	37

Cotton was withdrawn from the bonded field warehouse as needed. The company's lack of adequate cash resources, however, had limited fiber consumption to an average $20,000 weekly during January, 1957. The inventory loan from the factor was intended to be used as short-term financing primarily for seasonal needs. It was not intended to exceed peak balances of $150,000.

Analysis of 1956 Operations

The operating loss during 1956 had totalled $172,000, despite a $10,000 profit during the first six months. Analysis of variances from standard manufacturing costs showed the following:

	Average Weekly Variance from Standard	
	Overhead	*Labor*
January–March	$2,000	$(1,000)
April–June	2,000	(1,000)
July–September	(3,500)	(2,500)
October–December	(5,000)	(3,000)

( ) = Unfavorable Variance

Loom activity each week averaged 1,600 loom-weeks (40 hour basis) until June when it began to drop sharply; activity leveled off in September at a rate of 1,000 and soon rose to 1,100. Loom efficiency fluctuated little from an 80 percent average except in November and early December when it dropped briefly to 76 percent. Seconds averaged less than 5 percent each week throughout the year.

Proposals for 1957

In January, 1957, the Algonquin management decided that a complete revision of the company's product mix was necessary to achieve a balance of manufacturing operations and permit profitable operations. Feeling that mill balance was a very important factor in profitable operation, the mill manufacturing staff began a thorough study of more than a dozen alternative schedules for mill operations, estimating revenues and incomes from each proposal. The planned mix of products to be sold included a number of items previously produced plus one new fabric, a poplin cloth, for which sales efforts were then in progress. As of January 31, 527 looms were operating on a two-shift basis weaving 70 different fabrics. Orders being produced on 405 of those looms were scheduled to run out by mid-April, but the 42 Draper XK looms and the 80 Box looms were scheduled to be in production through August on orders already booked.

Planning at this point was based in large part upon the expectation that the company would book the order for a large volume of poplin cloth. Mr. Danforth himself was currently working with the expected customer for this cloth, a converter who specialized in cloth for uniforms and handled an estimated six million yards of poplin cloth annually. Algonquin had submitted a sample of its poplin for testing by the United States Testing Company and the sample was found to have better abrasion resistance than the cloth currently being used by the converter. Mr. Danforth expected that Algonquin could secure a contract calling for delivery of at least 35,250 yards per week at 39 cents per yard.

The poplin cloth would contain 50's two-ply combed cotton yarn in a 102 × 48 construction and therefore was a coarser cloth than that usually produced by Algonquin. On this basis, 35,250 yards of cloth would require 7,885 pounds of warp yarn and 3,671 pounds for fill. Although poplin was generally considered to be a "commodity" cloth, as distinguished from the specialty fabrics usually produced by Algonquin, the management felt that similar departures from the basic product policy had proven profitable during extraordinary situations in the past.

In preparing the proposals for future operations, the mill overseers estimated the poundage and yardage of material to be handled, and the number of machines, spindles, looms, and other equipment that would be required. Exhibit 4 presents the yarn mill and weave room schedules for three of the proposed operating programs. The overseers also prepared detailed schedules of machine operations and labor requirements for each proposal. These schedules were then translated into operating costs. Exhibits 5 and 6 present estimated revenues and expenses based on operation of facilities on a three-shift basis, five days per week.

Schedule #2 included a weave schedule identical to that of #1, except that an additional 20,700 yards of poplin would be produced. Yarn production in both instances would be scheduled to match the needs of the weaving department. Because both proposals #1 and #2 seemed to fall short of profitable operations, a new mix of products was set up as proposal #3. Specific differences in the weave schedules can be seen in Exhibit 4, but it should be noted that the major changes were in the volume of poplin cloth and the yardage of fancy cloth to be woven on box looms. Yarn mill output for this proposal also was planned to match weaving requirements. The pro forma income statement for proposal #3 indicated that a $3,600 weekly profit before taxes could be attained.

The schedule of operations set forth in proposal #3 was recommended to the management as a means of achieving a profitable mill balance. They planned to begin directing their efforts at achieving such a schedule, and hoped to reach that goal by late April, 1957, by which time the mill would have gone onto three-shift operation. The changes were expected to increase profits both through the more efficient utilization of machinery made possible by balanced mill operations and through the limitation of production to the more profitable present products on the most efficient mill machinery. Credit burdens would be eased by the reduction in inventory resulting from change to three-shift operations and the reduction in the volume of activity. Additional funds might also be obtained by selling excess machinery and renting unused mill space.

Mr. Danforth outlined some of the planned modifications in the marketing programs of the company. In the future, the objective of the sales department would be to maintain a balanced mix of profitable products in limited volume. Past efforts, on the other hand, had been directed at building a larger sales volume, with the resultant acceptance of many items only for their contribution to fixed costs. In line with the proposed policy changes, the staff of the New York sales office would be reduced to two salesmen and a secretary, while the stylist would be employed part-time on an "as used" basis.

The management felt confident that a reorientation of policies and operations to achieve a balance of mill operations would result in a reversal of the persistent operating losses. Pro forma income statements for the first three months of 1957, based on the transition to schedule #3, were as follows:

	(In Thousands)		
	January *5 weeks*	*February* *4 weeks*	*March* *4 weeks*
Sales	$310	$344	$291
Standard profit*	(15)	2.5	0.1
Variances			
Labor	(11)	(6)	(2)
Overhead	(10)	(6)	(2)

* Before interest charges and selling costs.

1. ALGONQUIN MILLS, INC.

Comparative Balance Sheets 1946 to 1956
December 31
(All Figures in Thousands)

	1946	1947	1948	1949	1950	1951	1952	1953	1954	1955	1956
ASSETS											
Current assets:											
Cash	$ 262	$ 64	$ 78	$ 40	$ 32	$ 50	$ 27	$ 8	$ 6	$ 12	$ 4
Government bonds	15	8	14	1	1	3	3	1	-	-	-
Accounts receivable	276	72	172	60	240	521	280	109	23	29	11
Inventories	652	1,604	1,640	893	750	910	1,452	822	740	912	710
Tax refund	-	-	-	204	-	-	-	-	-	-	-
Other	109	114	110	97	104	188	98	90	115	98	104
Total Current Assets	$1,314	$1,827	$1,978	$1,295	$1,127	$1,672	$1,860	$1,030	$ 884	$1,051	$ 829
Other assets	-	-	-	-	$ 7	$ 4	$ 6	$ 6	$ 1	$ 1	$ 1
Fixed assets--net	$ 538	$ 656	$ 621	$ 694	658	663	738	719	680	661	705
Total Assets	$1,852	$2,483	$2,599	$1,989	$1,792	$2,339	$2,604	$1,755	$1,565	$1,713	$1,535
LIABILITIES											
Current Liabilities:											
Secured notes--bank	-	$ 413	$ 194	$ 30	-	-	$ 283	-	$ 74	$ 78	$ 76
Due factor (secured)	-	-	148	297	$ 240	-	303	$ 23	55	185	197
Mortgage	$ 84	132	-	-	-	$ 282	46	-	44	34	45
Accounts payable	84	132	190	151	159	66	143	144	71	129	115
Miscellaneous	129	123	124	70	119	239	137	143	96	228	165
Total Current Liabilities	$ 213	$ 668	$ 656	$ 548	$ 518	$ 587	$ 912	$ 310	$ 340	$ 654	$ 598
Mortgage	-	-	-	-	-	$ 45	-	-	$ 166	$ 291	$ 332
Inventory reserve	$ 103	$ 80	$ 48	-	-	-	-	-	-	-	-
Preferred stock--6%*	669	669	669	$ 669	$ 669	669	$ 669	$ 669	669	669	669
Common stock	11	11	11	11	11	11	11	11	11	11	11
Capital surplus	334	334	334	334	334	334	334	334	334	334	334
Earned surplus	522	721	881	427	260	693	678	431	45	(246)	(409)
Total capital	$1,536	$1,735	$1,895	$1,441	$1,274	$1,707	$1,692	$1,445	$1,059	$ 768	$ 605
Total Liabilities	$1,852	$2,483	$2,599	$1,989	$1,792	$2,339	$2,604	$1,755	$1,565	$1,713	$1,535

*Cumulative only if earned.

2. ALGONQUIN MILLS, INC.

Comparative Income Statement: 1946 to 1956
Years Ending December 31

	1946	1947	1948	1949	1950	1951	1952	1953	1954	1955	1956
Sales	$3,742	$3,755	$4,139	$2,618	$3,013	$4,719	$3,861	$4,449	$2,104	$3,644	$4,284
Before tax oper. profit	785	382	304	(746)	(166)	517	(6)	(275)	(395)	(158)	(177)
Taxes	309	132	95	(277)	-	84	-	59	-	-	-

3. ALGONQUIN MILLS, INC.

Process Flow Chart for Yarn Production

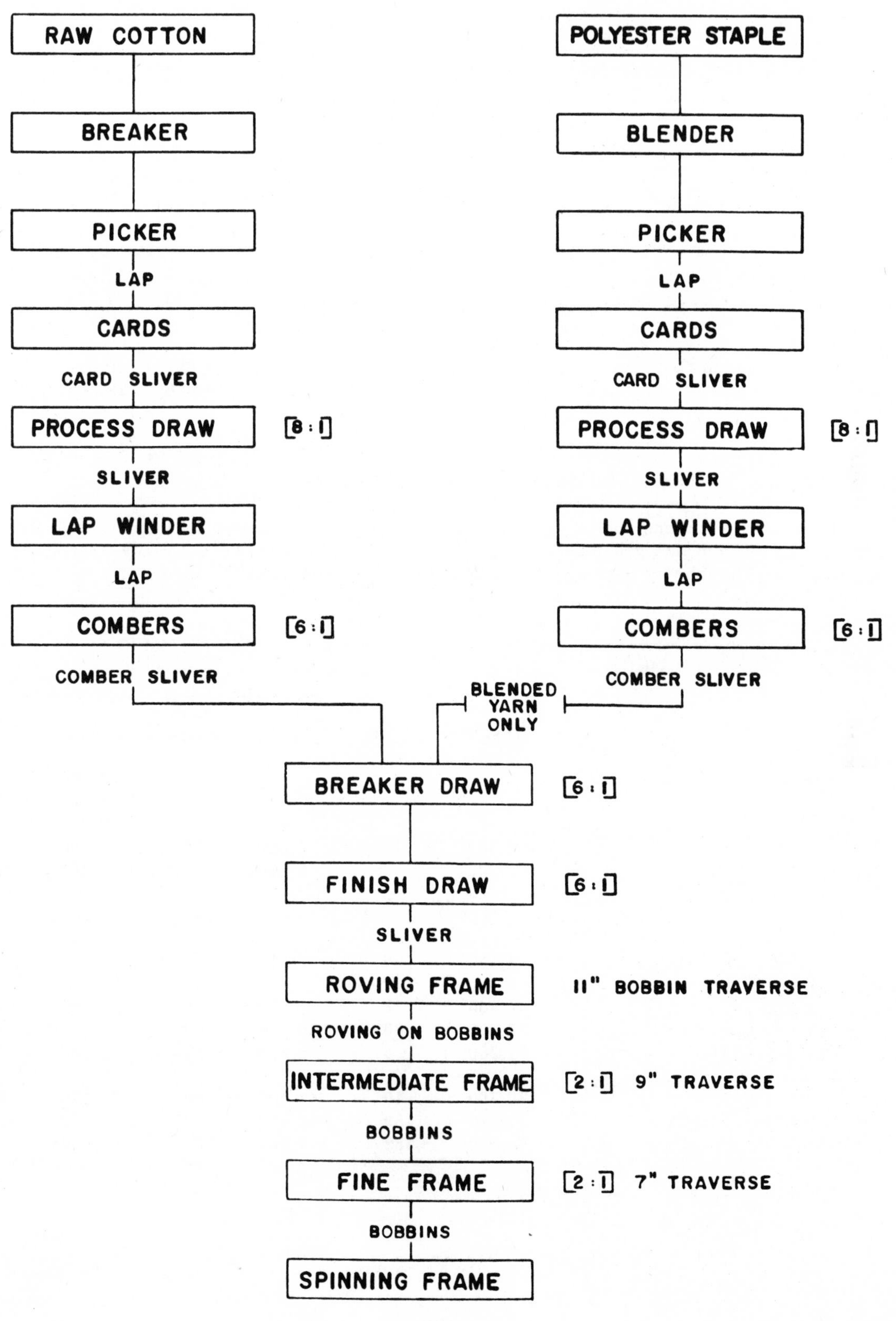

4. ALGONQUIN MILLS, INC.

Comparison of Proposed Weekly Schedules

A. Yarn Mill

	#1	#2	#3
Warp Yarn--Pounds	14,779	19,333	16,716
Spindles Used	10,940	12,888	12,042
No. Yarns	11	11	12
Fill Yarn --Pounds	9,112	11,268	10,627
Spindles Used	6,708	7,698	6,362
No. Yarns	11	11	8
Total pounds yarn spun	23,891	30,601	27,343
Total spindles used	17,648	29,586	18,404

B. Weave Room

Cloths Included in All Three Proposals

Fourteen fabrics totaling 36,350 yards per week, requiring 42 Draper XK looms and 74 Draper E looms. Fabrics from this group accounting for 21,700 yards weekly were already in production on January 31, 1957; the fabrics in production included 12,500 yards on 42 XK looms plus 9,200 yards on 27 Draper E looms.

Other Cloths Scheduled

	#1		#2		#3	
	Yds./wk.	No. Looms	Yds./wk.	No. Looms	Yds./wk.	No. Looms
Box Loom						
A. Pol. and Cot.	-	-	-	-	2,800	9
B. " " "	-	-	-	-	4,000	11
C. " " "	-	-	-	-	8,800	24
D. Cotton*	4,300	16	4,300	16	2,400	9
E. " *	2,200	8	2,200	8	3,300	12
F. " *	-	-	-	-	700	3
G. " *	-	-	-	-	1,400	5
H. " *	-	-	-	-	1,900	7
I. " *	3,400	16	3,400	16	-	-
Draper E Loom						
J. Cotton	400	2	400	2	-	-
K. Pol. and Cot. Bat.	20,000	80	20,000	80	-	-
L. Cot. Bd. Cl. Str.	1,200	4	1,200	4	2,800	9
M. Cotton	-	-	-	-	2,800	9
N. " Poplin	20,700	40	41,400	80	35,250	68
Subtotals	52,150	166	72,850	206	66,100	166
Totals	88,500	282	109,200	322	102,450	282

*In production January 31, 1957.

5. ALGONQUIN MILLS, INC.

Pro Forma Weekly Income Statements and Labor Budgets

A. Income Statements

Sales	Schedule 1	Schedule 2	Schedule 3
Cloth	$49,979	$58,052	$58,272
Waste	1,939	2,145	2,595
Remnant Store	946	946	946
Total Sales	$52,864	$61,143	$61,813
Expense			
Labor--direct and indirect	15,880	19,259	16,297
Raw material--fibers	24,238	27,674	23,465
Outside finishing	788	788	788
Yarn dyeing	1,297	1,297	3,199
Overhead	11,421	11,619	11,473
Interest	825	825	825
Factor--1% sales	499	581	583
Sample expense	550	550	450
Brokerage and selling	1,095	1,095	1,095
Profit or (Loss)	($ 3,729)	($ 2,545)	($ 3,638)

B. Labor Budgets

	1.		2.		3.	
	Men	Cost	Men	Cost	Men	Cost
Yarn Mill	152	$7,572	182	$9,577	142	$4,084
Weave Department	101	5,511	121	6,598	116	6,413
Cloth Inspection	28	1,337	34	1,624	30	1,440
Mill Maintenance	22	1,084	22	1,084	22	1,084
Outside	7	376	7	376	5	276

6. ALGONQUIN MILLS, INC.

Weekly Overhead Expense

	Average Actual 1956 Cost	1956 Budget	Project 3 Budget
MILL OVERHEAD			
Power purchased	$ 1,971	$ 1,154	$ 1,400
Fuel	540	500	540
General supplies	1,766	2,422	1,525
Repairs	780	1,058	600
Taxes and insurance	1,287	1,500	1,080
General expense	120	231	176
Depreciation	970	769	1,000
Starch and size	480	385	250
Salaries--superintendent and overseers	853	769	908
Salaries--laboratory and health	350	414	283
Payroll tax and benefits	2,893	2,884	1,423
Subtotal	$12,010	$12,086	$ 9,185
GENERAL AND ADMINISTRATIVE			
Salaries--executive	$ 320	$ 481	$ 350
Salaries--office	1,210	1,250	870
Legal and professional	340	288	350
Office supplies and expenses	190	231	150
Telephone and teletype	146	135	100
Travel and entertainment	241	192	100
General	200	172	208
Depreciation--furniture and fixtures	160	163	160
Subtotal	$ 2,807	$ 2,912	$ 2,288
Total	$14,817	$14,998	$11,473

Salant & Salant, Incorporated

Salant & Salant, Inc., was a major producer of men's and boys' work shirts, sport shirts, work pants, and slacks. In 1959, one half of the total sales of about $25 million reached the consumer through four major retail chains, but the company also sold under its own brand names through more than 2,000 retailers. In September, 1959, the production vice-presidents were under heavy pressure from the merchandising and sales vice-presidents to increase the production of plants to meet the demands of the market. On the first of September the merchandising vice-president emphasized this need by estimating the total lost sales at 100,000 dozen pairs of pants.[1]

PRODUCTS

Salant & Salant, Inc., sold popular priced men's, boys', and juvenile sports and utility shirts, work pants, slacks, and jackets.

Utility Shirts

The Salant company started out as a manufacturer of cotton work shirts in 1893. During the 1920's a Department of Commerce study showed that of 365 manufacturers reporting sales of work shirts, Salant & Salant, Inc., had 22 percent of the market. Work shirts were almost exclusively made of chambray and covert cloth until the late 1920's and early 1930's when men became interested in tan twill and cotton utility shirts to match their khaki pants. Salant & Salant, Inc., moved with this change and manufactured both types.

After World War II, the American working man changed his habits of dress and decreased his purchases of work shirts. The general decline in work shirts was particularly sharp on blue chambray shirts. Due to the low margins and declining volume, many manufacturers discontinued production of these shirts. The declining number of producers meant that the remaining producers had a larger share of the market. Despite this percentage increase, Salant & Salant sales of chambray shirts went from 1,000,000 dozen per year to 200,000 dozen over a 10-year period from 1948 to 1958. Sales continued to drop in 1959 but the executives thought the company was maintaining its share of the civilian market at about 50 percent.

Although the cloth was different, flannel utility shirts were cut and fabricated in approximately the same way as the work shirts. The flannel shirts were more styled and required the introduction of new patterns. They were, therefore, sold more like sport shirts.

Jackets

In an effort to use its idle work shirt production facilities, the company went into the production of outer jackets in 1954. Although some of the jackets were lined, they were cut like shirts. Salant & Salant, Inc., did not manufacture or sell coats or jackets cut in traditional outerwear patterns.

Pants

Salant & Salant, Inc., began production of utility pants in 1938. Workers had already started the trend away from the standard blue denim overalls toward tan twill cotton trousers. The immediate impetus for production was the desire of the chain stores to have matching pants and shirts. Work pants were made from twill, covert, corduroy, and whipcord. Wash and wear finishes were added in the late 1950's.

The shift from work pants to casual slacks in 1955 was an easy one from a manufacturing standpoint, but from the sales side it introduced the problem of style. One example of the style factor in pants was the sudden snowballing of demand for Ivy League slacks in 1957 and 1958. Retailers could not get enough of these slacks with the buckle in the back. Just as suddenly in late 1958, the retailers did not want the buckle. The result was large inventory losses throughout the industry as the manufacturers tried to liquidate the suddenly unwanted styles.

Slacks were made from lightweight twill, Bedford cord, corduroy, sateen, chino, combed cotton, and synthetic textiles. While men's

[1] In this case, the term "pants" is used to include work pants and slacks together.

shirts usually came in four (small, medium, large, and extra large) or seven (14, 14½, 15, 15½, 16, 16½, and 17) sizes, trousers came in twelve waist sizes and nine inseam lengths. As a result, an inventory of a given style and color of trousers required 66 different stockkeeping units. Pants were typically more expensive than shirts, so the inventory of pants was more expensive and also required more space than shirts.

Sport Shirts

Salant & Salant, Inc. entered the sport shirt business in 1949 due to a growing recognition of the increasing number of people who were wearing casual shirts instead of work shirts for both work and play. These items were highly styled and subject to massive shifts in style preference.

The production vice-president stated that the change from work or flannel utility shirts to sport shirts was as difficult as a change to pants. Although much of the equipment was the same for the various kinds of shirts, the work force required a completely different orientation. Standards of quality and cleanliness were much higher for sport shirts. A speck of dust or a loose piece of thread might make no difference on a work shirt, but would be unacceptable in a sport shirt. The collar, cuff, and shirt tail constructions required a different grouping of manpower and equipment. The finishing operations of inspecting, pressing, and folding had to be more carefully done on sport shirts. Packaging usually included tissue paper and cardboard supports in order to give the sport shirt a pressed look in the retail store while utility shirts were frequently just bundled together. There was more emphasis on novelty variations so the production facilities had to allow for more varieties. Sport shirts were typically made of gingham, broadcloth, oxford, and other unnapped fabrics as well as flannel.

ORGANIZATION

Robert Salant, the president, had six people reporting directly to him: S. J. Yaspan, treasurer; James Reynolds, first vice-president in charge of merchandising; John Rae, vice-president for sales; M. H. Gold, vice-president for production-planning; and Joseph Lipshie, vice-president for production-operations. Mr. Lipshie's office was in his home in Tennessee near the Salant & Salant manufacturing facilities. Mr. Rae had his office in the Empire State Building. Mr. Salant and the other four men had offices in the company's New York headquarters across the street from the Empire State Building.

Mr. Yaspan was in charge of all the financial and accounting functions.

Mr. Rae headed up the sales to all customers except the four major chains. A staff of 15 regional salesmen and 4 executive salesmen handled the more than 2,000 accounts of the King Kole division. The regional salesmen lived in their respective territories and usually visited New York only for the sales meetings kicking off each fall and spring line. These salesmen were paid on a commission basis and paid their own expenses out of their commissions. The four executive salesmen were based in New York and received a salary. They handled the sales to the regional chains and large customers of the King Kole division.

Mr. Lipshie supervised the Tennessee manufacturing operations. He spent his days visiting the various plants. He sent a schedule of these visits to the New York office so that the headquarters personnel would know where to contact him. He handled his correspondence either through dictating to a secretary in one of the plants or by dictaphone records sent to New York. In addition to supervising the plant managers, Mr. Lipshie was directly responsible for the technological development of the plants, the industrial engineering, and the labor relations. He had recently increased the number of rotating assistants helping him from two to four.

Mr. Gold handled manufacturing from the New York end. He decided which products should be made in which plants and oversaw the issuance of the cutting tickets directing the plants to begin production on the various items. He supplied the merchandising department with information on the feasibility and expense of suggested product changes. He was responsible for representing the manufacturing viewpoint in decisions involving immediate changes in level of production as well as longer range policies. Mr. Gold had worked closely with Mr. Lipshie over the last 25 years and had at one time handled the Tennessee job. This mutual experience enabled the two men to work very closely together despite the physical separation.

In recognition of the importance of the merchandising function, Mr. Reynolds was designated first vice-president. The merchandising department was responsible for determining what products were to be included in the line, designing them, pricing them, determining what quantities were to be produced of each item, purchasing the cloth, determining desired inventory levels, processing incoming orders, and deciding when items should be discontinued and sold at reduced prices. In addition, this department handled the sales to the four major customers. Mr. Reynolds had a staff of four salesmen and six other people to carry out these functions.

Messrs. Reynolds, Gold, and Lipshie were each backed up by one experienced younger man who shared a large part of the work load and helped supervise the personnel under them.

MERCHANDISING

The merchandising department took the first steps in the process of making a garment. This was particularly true on style items where the merchandisers made the basic decisions on which types were to be offered for sale for the coming season.

They began by examining the cloths and patterns being offered by the textile mills for the coming season. Many of the cloths were standard and were offered every year, but each sason the mills attempted to introduce the kinds of weaves, colors, and patterns that they thought would best meet consumer desires. Most of these designs were based on information and ideas developed in the continuous interchange between retail buyers, salesmen, merchandisers, and textile designers.

Based on this general information and also on specific information received directly from Salant & Salant customers or salesmen, the merchandisers decided what garment styles and cloth patterns should be offered and in what combinations.

The items for the chain stores were designed to meet specific requests from the chains. Salant & Salant, Inc., along with other firms, presented a number of suggestions to meet the various requirements of price, type of pattern, color, style, etc. Often these suggestions might be modified as a result of the discussions between the chain store and the Salant company. After the chain store chose the items to be purchased from Salant & Salant, Inc., it estimated its requirements and entered an order for (typically) 60 percent of the total. These items were not identical with the stock products and were not available to other customers. The cloth for these purchases was sometimes purchased and owned by the chain. The garments were manufactured at a rate to meet the requested delivery dates. Additional orders were placed through the season as the items were sold.

The items for sale to the other customers of Salant & Salant, Inc., were generally sold from an inventory whose size was determined by Salant & Salant estimates of sales, although some customers might have their orders specially made with their own labels. The merchandisers relied on their own judgment in deciding which items were to be made available. A lot number was assigned to each combination of pattern, color, and style. In 1959, the fall shirt line for general customer use included about 250 lot numbers.

On the basis of the chain store contracts and their estimates of the probable sales of each stock item, the merchandisers placed orders for the cloth. Patterned cloth was not purchased on general speculation but only to meet sales estimates of products in the line. Salant & Salant, Inc., did, however, make purchases of the more standard cloths used in work clothes in excess of their immediate requirements if the prices were relatively favorable. The merchandising department bought patterned cloth from many mills. A concentration in one or a few firms might have presented advantages in price and freight, but the company needed the widest possible choice of patterns for inclusion in its merchandise.

The primary raw material was cotton cloth although wool and various synthetics were also used. The textiles were purchased from Southern mills with the bulk of the material coming from the Carolinas.

One of the crucial factors in style items was the timing. New merchandise lines in the men's apparel industry were presented for two seasons, fall and spring. The textile mills presented their fall patterns in November and December of the preceding year. The textile designers liked to wait as long as possible in order to get the maximum reaction from the industry as to what types of cloth would be desired, but the apparel manufacturers were under pressure from their customers and salesmen for a fall offering and from their plants which needed production schedules to replace the completed spring line. Salant & Salant, Inc., usually had enough of the line developed to start ordering cloth early in January for its plants to fabricate in February. The merchandisers usually completed the line by the first of February, and it was presented to the salesmen in a meeting about the third week in February. Samples were shipped to the salesmen during the first part of March. The remaining items were sold from sample cards containing a drawing and a swatch of material. The New York office started receiving orders about the fifteenth of March for deliveries in June and subsequent months. Items for fall retail sales were usually delivered by the manufacturer in June, July, and August with decreasing quantities in September and October.

The spring line was of less importance to Salant & Salant, Inc. The textile patterns were shown in June and July. The designs were firmed up in July and August. The first cloth was ordered in August and production began in September. The salesmen reviewed the line in September and started selling for January through April or May delivery.

In the event orders did not develop in particular styles, Salant & Salant, Inc., might decide to drop certain lot numbers. The few customers who had requested the particular items were notified that the item had been dropped and asked to select another. Conversely, Salant & Salant, Inc., might add an item if the information feeding back to the New York office indicated a large gap in the line. However, such changes were relatively infrequent and the line did not change significantly after it was firmed up.

The utility and work clothes did not require the development of new lines at fixed intervals, but the merchandising department was continually responsible for changing styles, colors, or fabrics, adding or eliminating lot numbers, making price changes, and ordering cloth for their production.

All items were designed to sell at one of the standard prices. For example, Salant & Salant, Inc., manufactured sport shirts to be sold at retail prices of $1.98 and $2.98. If the customer wanted a shirt with a little more quality than a $1.98 shirt, he bought a $2.98 shirt. Conversely, if Salant & Salant, Inc., made erroneous estimates of the market and had an excessive inventory of $2.98 shirts, in order to move the merchandise, the price had to be reduced enough to allow the retailer to sell the shirt at $1.98. The cut in price to Salant & Salant, Inc., would, therefore, be on the order of from $23.50 per dozen to $16 per dozen. In other cases, it was necessary to take a 50 percent cut in the price in order to move the merchandise. This cut-price merchandise was sold both to regular customers and also to dealers who specialized in this type of merchandise.

MANUFACTURING

The production schedules were primarily based on weekly summaries of the order and inventory position of each stock lot number and on the contract status summaries showing production against the requested delivery schedules on the chain store contracts. Exhibit 8 summarizes the information on three of the weekly pants reports. The actual reports showed, on a line for each of the approximately 90 lot numbers, the previous year's sales, the amount ordered that week, the cumulative orders for the year to date, the balance on hand after allowing for all orders received to date, the quantity in process, the cloth style number, the inventory of cloth on hand in yards, and the amount of cloth on order. The production department was able to determine which inventories were low and which items could be supported by the cloth on hand. In the event that the total of contract requirements and low inventory items was not sufficient to maintain production at one or more of the plants at the agreed upon rates, the production department received assistance from the merchandising department in determining which items to schedule. Based on the production requirements, the production department prepared production requests listing specific lot numbers and quantities.

Although most of the purchasing and planning decisions were made on the basis of the total quantity of the lot number, the items were ordered by the retailer by size. The merchandising and production executives used a figure of 350 dozen as the minimum quantity which would cover all the sizes in a given men's pants lot number. Any quantity smaller than this would probably not cover all the sizes. The New York office maintained a perpetual inventory by size for each lot number. On the basis of these records a clerk broke the production requests into sizes and wrote up the cutting orders which were then mailed to the plants.

The work force was 85 percent female. The industry was not a high wage payer and had to be located in an area where labor was plentiful and relatively inexpensive. All operators were paid on a piece rate basis which brought the average hourly earnings to the $1.10–$1.15 range.

The skill of the workers in handling the garments was one of the primary factors in the determination of the output of one of these plants. Some of the machines such as tacking machines and buttonhole machines stitched at a fixed rate. The speed of the other machines could be varied by the operator but the machine was idle a major portion of the time while the operator picked up the item, placed it, and removed it.

Her skill was the result of learning the proper method of doing the job, continued attention to maintaining the proper method, and continuous practice. All jobs had been analyzed by Salant & Salant engineers to determine the correct method and the time it should take an operator to reach standard proficiency. These times ran from four weeks in running a pressing machine, to twenty-two weeks for inseam sewing on a pair of trousers. The Federal wage and hour laws recognized the time required to learn this work by granting an exception to the minimum wage law. Beginners on sewing machines could be paid as little as $.80 per hour for the first 480 hours. If an operator had not worked on these machines for two years, she could be classified as a beginner.

The skill was quite specialized. It involved picking up a particularly shaped piece of a particular type of cloth and performing a particular operation on that cloth. A girl who had performed a different operation had a head start of about four weeks over a girl who had never run a production sewing machine before. However, a girl with a great deal of experience in a number of different jobs was frequently able to find similar movements in a new job and thus have a much shorter learning period.

The United Garment Workers of America (CIO-AFL) represented the workers in six of the ten factories. The other plants were not unionized. The Salant & Salant executives felt that their company had enjoyed very good labor-management relations. A two-year contract had been signed in June of 1959 with the United Garment Workers.

The garment industry was not a high-capital industry. About $500 of equipment was used per worker. About 40 percent of the value lay in motors and frames which were interchangeable and could be used for a variety of operations. The remaining 60 percent was in specialized sewing machines and tables designed for the specific operation. Salant & Salant, Inc.'s largest investment in fixed assets was its approximately 2,700 sewing machines with their motors, tables, and related fixtures. This equipment was depreciated by the sum of the year's digit method over a 12-year period.

Most of the factory expenses of utilities, maintenance, and operating supplies were directly proportional to the level of operations. Similarly most of the direct labor costs varied with the volume of operations. The cutting room work force and the office, maintenance, and supervisory personnel were less flexible. Salant & Salant, Inc., had found that about 20 office, maintenance, and supervisory personnel were required for a plant employing 150 people up to a plant employing 250 people. The cutting room for any plant up to 250 employees required 9 people. The direct factory expenses including rent, utilities, taxes, upkeep, etc., but not payroll or depreciation, for a typical Salant & Salant factory that temporarily shut down for a week was estimated to be about $400 per week.

Since labor was the biggest cost item under the control of the plant manager, the criteria for evaluating the efficiency of the plant was the labor loss. This was the amount of wages paid in excess of the standard labor cost for the products produced. The Salant & Salant management expected a labor loss of about 6 or 7 percent.

In starting up a plant, Salant & Salant, Inc., had found through experience that it took about 22 weeks for a plant to attain capacity operations. However, the expected efficiency of a 7 percent labor loss was not reached for another six months. A new plant experienced higher than average labor turnover for the first four or five months so that by the end of the first twenty-two weeks a large portion of the work force had been at the plant for a shorter time. The production level was achieved through extra operators and overtime at the bottleneck operations. The labor loss might run around 20–25 percent at the point where full production was achieved. At this time point the quality level was expected to be acceptable but not up to the usual company standards. The volume level could only be maintained during this time if the production was standardized and there were no changes in style or cloth.

The Salant & Salant management had always avoided contracting out the production of garments if at all possible. They did not like the loss of control over quality and service as well as preferring to keep the manufacturer's profit to themselves.

Production could be expanded to meet increased sales requirements by about 15 percent beyond the point of maximum efficiency by putting extra machines in the aisles. Alternatively it could be expanded by working overtime. Legal limitations in Tennessee set a 50-hour maximum work week. Mr. Lipshie and Mr. Gold found their employees preferred working Saturday to working 10-hour days through the week. They also found that after about 8 weeks of working Saturdays, production efficiency started to drop off. The girls accumulated too many personal tasks and errands. The extra pay became less important, absenteeism rose, and morale lowered. Salant & Salant, Inc., had been unable to work any of the plants a second shift. There were insufficient additional workers in most of these communities to staff a second shift and in the rural environment, the girls did not like the night work.

Production could be decreased in a number of ways. The plant could be reengineered and rebalanced at a smaller production level with an almost corresponding reduction in work force. The workers could work a three or four day week. The plant could operate a week and shut down a week. The choice of method of reduction varied with the preferences of the workers, the level of inventory, and the importance of style changes in the product being manufactured.

In general terms the production processes for shirts, pants, and jackets were very similar. The manufacture of pants was described in the Cotton Textile Industry Process Note.

The propinquity of the plants to each other provided Salant & Salant, Inc., with a number of advantages. It allowed Mr. Lipshie and his staff to cover all the plants with minimal time spent traveling. The Savoy plant was considered an overnight trip, but the rest of the plants were less than 40 miles from Jackson, Mr. Lipshie's headquarters. Surplus sewing machines and other equipment could be easily transferred between plants. Key personnel could be sent to other plants for training. Finished products could be transferred to centralized shipping points.

Chester: Salant & Salant, Inc., manufactured its basic spring and fall sport shirts and the twill shirts to match the khaki work pants here.

Hanover: This plant manufactured flannel utility shirts. It was also used for the government contracts for utility shirts.

Jefferson: (Troy and Obion) Boys' and juveniles' shirts were cut at the Union City Airport. They were sewed at Obion and Troy and shipped from the Wilson warehouse at the Union City Airport. In addition to shipping the boys' and juvenile shirts produced in the Obion and Troy plants, Wilson also shipped the pants produced in Oxford for one of their large chain store customers.

Monroe: The work force at this plant was the most experienced. Salant & Salant, Inc., used it for all difficult shirt production: high-priced de luxe shirts, novelty items, miscellaneous short-run and rush requirements and samples. The company was currently experimenting with knitted sport shirts here.

Oxford: This plant was designed to produce 2,200 dozen pants weekly. In January of 1959 a reengineering was completed which raised the capacity to 2,400 dozen. Most of the production from this plant was work pants but some slacks were produced here.

Princeton: This plant filled a role in pants equivalent to that of Monroe for shirts. It was used for more complicated and shorter production runs and typically was making seven or eight different types of pants at once. It had the only work force experienced in handling synthetics and corduroy. It had extensive storage facilities in three warehouses and was used for the storage and shipment of all pants except those for one customer shipped from the Wilson warehouse in Union City. It also shipped the matching shirts produced in Chester.

Savoy: The entire production from this plant used to be blue chambray shirts. In 1956 the weekly production of work shirts was reduced from 6,000 dozen to 4,500 dozen and the production of 1,000 dozen jackets was introduced. Some of the government contracts for utility shirts were produced here. Physically this plant was somewhat removed from the other Salant & Salant factories.

SALES

Salant & Salant, Inc., had two basic sales channels. The first was under its own brands through about 2,000 retailers and wholesalers. The second was through four large chains: Sears Roebuck, Montgomery Ward, J. C. Penney, and W. T. Grant, under the chains' brands. In order to supply the specialized merchandising requirements, the four major chains were sold by the merchandising department. These salesmen were paid a salary.

Although the company sold some garments under its other brand names: Mansize, Grand Canyon, and Uncle Sam, its primary trade names were King Kole for utility wear and Kolesport for sportswear. Salant & Salant, Inc., used the term King Kole division to refer to sales to all customers except the four major chain and mail-order customers.

The King Kole division customers who were large enough to send their buyers to New York City to select merchandise were generally handled by the four executive salesmen. The remaining accounts were covered by the 15 regional salesmen.

The Salant & Salant management had considered setting up warehouses in areas away from the manufacturing plants, but the executives thought that industry experience had shown the additional handling costs and increased inventory levels more than made up for the bulk transportation savings and faster delivery. Salant & Salant, Inc., had consolidated its shipping point so that each customer order would be divided into fewer shipments than if each plant shipped its products separately. The cost of shipping pants to the West Coast in a typical order quantity was about $1 per dozen. The customer paid this freight expense.

In recent years, Salant & Salant, Inc., bid on and received a number of contracts for utility shirts for the armed forces. These contracts were not profitable but they were a means of maintaining operations and work forces. The sales to the government included 63,000 dozen shirts in 1958 and 80,000 in 1959. The company was an approved supplier of shirts and pants to the armed services and regularly received requests for bids on military contracts.

Salant & Salant, Inc., maintained a policy of no advertising. The management preferred to put the money into the quality of the merchandise. More than 50 percent of its merchandise was sold through brand names other than its own so these sales would not be helped by advertising. On its own products, Salant & Salant, Inc., used several different brand names. Mr. Robert Salant said that the variety of brands made it easier to sell competing outlets as well as providing an independent wholesaler with a bargaining advantage.

The primary competition came from other manufacturers similar to themselves. Two of the chain stores had manufacturing subsidiaries which made some of their requirements. Competition from the Far East, Japan and Hong Kong, was beginning to move into men's apparel from the women's clothing field where it had achieved greater significance. One of the large chains had just ordered some of its special promotional items from Hong Kong. Robert Salant expressed the opinion that this low-cost labor would be most important in the very lowest retail price ranges, such as 88-cent shirts, and in high quality merchandise involving much hand sewing. He felt, therefore, the Salant & Salant popular priced products would be less vulnerable to this competition.

RECENT HISTORY

In February of 1959 Salant & Salant, Inc., began to feel the pressure for increased production of pants. By means of putting machines in the aisles and adding extra girls, production was raised to 4,200 dozen in the Princeton plant and 2,800 dozen in the Oxford plant. In March, Mr. Gold, Mr. Spargo (Mr. Gold's assistant), Mr. Reynolds, and Mr. Herman (Mr. Reynolds' assistant) determined that requirements between the middle of March and the first week of July would be about 153,000 dozen pairs. Production was expected to stay at 7,000 dozen per week over the 19 intervening weeks. A deficit of 20,000 dozen was therefore anticipated. The inventory was down to 67,000 dozen. It was decided to start Saturday operations after the conclusion of the labor contract negotiations around the first of April. The overtime would increase the weekly output in the Princeton plant by 800 dozen and Oxford by 500 dozen. Over the 13-week period there would be an increase of 17,000 dozen.

Bedford cord pants enjoyed spectacular popularity during this season and the textile mills fell behind in their deliveries of this type of cloth. This caused most manufacturers to start missing their delivery promises. By virtue of its size and stability, Salant & Salant, Inc., received better than average service from its suppliers. Salant & Salant, Inc., kept a very close watch on its supplies and production schedules and was able to make more realistic delivery promises. This service was thought by the Salant & Salant executives to have been outstanding in the industry. The benefits of this policy were realized both through the development of goodwill for future orders and through the fact that competitors had their orders cancelled by stores who were hedging against the tight market by entering duplicate orders.

In June, business was still improving. Deliveries to King Kole customers were lengthened. Glowing reports from salesmen provided fantastic predictions of sales. Nobody added the promises of future business, but there was general agreement in the sales and merchandising departments that they could sell more than double the existing capacity. Substantial orders were being rejected because Salant & Salant, Inc., could not meet the requested delivery dates.

The Oxford plant was reengineered to 3,400 dozen pairs weekly production on a six-day week, and Mr. Lipshie thought the plant would be able to produce at a 2,900 dozen weekly rate when it returned to a five-day week.

Although historically, company policy was against contracting out, attempts now had to be made by Mr. Gold and Mr. Lipshie to find other manufacturers who would produce at least 10,000 to 20,000 dozen pairs of pants. Because business was booming for all manufacturers, no contractors were available to even ease the delivery pressures.

Mr. Lipshie heard of one pants factory in Northern Mississippi which was for sale. A brief inquiry established that this plant had a record of bitter labor-management strife. No serious consideration was given to this opportunity. Because of the high level of operations throughout the industry, Mr. Lipshie and Mr. Gold knew that the price of any going factory would be high.

The Town of Obion had recently approached Salant & Salant, Inc., to see if the company might be interested in taking over a recently vacated wooden heel factory. The past mutually satisfactory relationship with the town made this opportunity particularly attractive to Salant & Salant, Inc. Mr. Lipshie and one of his assistants arranged a labor survey to see if there were capable help available. Advertisements and word of mouth through local boosters asked people interested in working for the company to come in for interviews on a particular day. Through interviews and simple aptitude tests, Mr. Lipshie felt assured that the employment picture was very satisfactory. A contract was signed in mid-June committing Salant & Salant, Inc., to a 10-year lease of the Adams plant. In the following three months, equipment was purchased and installed. Operations were scheduled to begin on October 1 and the plant was expected to reach its capacity of 1,500 dozen pairs of pants per week by March 1, 1960. The plant was scheduled to produce King Kole twill work pants.

Mr. Reynolds and Mr. Herman were sure that Salant & Salant, Inc., could sell many more pants than they could produce during June, July, and August. Mr. Gold and Mr. Lipshie considered canceling the vacation shutdown scheduled for the week of July 6 for all plants. Partly because the company had made uncancelable arrangements for a special vacation in Biloxi for 86 long-service employees, Mr. Gold and Mr. Lipshie decided against this idea. They did, however, decide to maintain Saturday work through August, but no longer. The continuous overtime was working handicaps on both the workers and the supervising staff.

Although September and October shipments were expected to be high, Mr. Reynolds predicted a sharp drop in November and December. Salant & Salant, Inc., was dropping behind on its King Kole work pants so it was decided to rush production at the Adams plant. Mr. Lipshie hoped to produce at least 5,000 dozen pairs in that plant by the first of the year. Mr. Reynolds hoped this would allow Salant & Salant, Inc., to provide its usual good service to its customers.

By the first of September it was obvious that nothing more could be done to increase production to meet the 1959 demand. However, Mr. Reynolds and Mr. Herman felt that capacity would have to be increased for 1960. They made the following points to Mr. Gold:

(1) Mr. Reynolds estimated the total lost business during 1959 due to inadequate capacity at 100,000 dozen pairs of pants.

(2) Experience had shown that pants were the best entering wedge for new customers for the King Kole division. Almost all new customers started with Salant & Salant, Inc., by buying pants first. A lack of pants available for shipment would therefore effectively limit Salant & Salant's expansion possibilities.

(3) Large chain store "A" was discussing the purchase of 24,000 dozen pants for a spring promotion sale. This would be new business in addition to chain store "A" 's usual purchases from Salant & Salant, Inc.

(4) Chain Store "E," not now one of the big four customers was negotiating for the purchase of 15,000 dozen pants for early 1960.

(5) Chain store "B" was opening 10 percent new stores each year. The merchandising department expected to receive a share of this increase.

(6) On the basis of a customer-by-customer analysis, the King Kole division predicted a sharp increase in sales to 2,250 dozen work pants per week and 3,200 dozen slacks per week in 1960.

(7) The total pants business envisioned for 1960 is shown in Exhibit 7. Civilian shirt and jacket sales were expected to continue at about the 1959 levels.

Mr. Gold summarized the possibilities of obtaining new production facilities as follows:

(*a*) There was no land adjacent to the Oxford plant for plant expansion. There was some open space at the Princeton plant but the company had recently felt forced to convert this area into a parking lot for the employees. The Adams plant had land available but Mr. Lipshie had expressed considerable doubt as to whether local labor force could support much larger employment.

(*b*) The executives estimated that a new plant might be rented for about $.40 per square foot per annum. A suitable plant could be built in about six months and might cost about $5 per square foot.

(*c*) Additional new and used sewing machines were readily available.

(*d*) A new plant could be expected to produce the first finished garments one month after operations were started. Production should rise in a slightly convex curve to the capacity level three to four months later.

1. SALANT & SALANT, INC.

Summary of Earnings
(All Figures in Thousands of Dollars)

	Year Ending December 31								
	1950	1951	1952	1953	1954	1955	1956	1957	1958
Net sales	$15,079	$17,342	$18,905	$19,787	$18,617	$22,241	$20,121	$23,004	$21,361
Cost of goods sold	12,808	14,866	16,264	17,084	15,924	18,839	16,729	20,133	18,405
Gross profit	$ 2,271	$ 2,476	$ 2,641	$ 2,703	$ 2,693	$ 3,402	$ 3,392	$ 2,871	$ 2,956
Selling, administrative and general	822	978	1,068	1,212	1,137	1,235	1,251	1,367	1,387
Interest expense	19	45	46	76	79	104	156	164	111
Miscellaneous income	6	20	10	4	3	7	1	1	-
Earnings before federal income taxes	1,436	1,473	1,537	1,419	1,480	2,070	1,986	1,341	1,458
Federal income taxes	608	754	806	745	774	1,094	1,049	715	775
Earnings after taxes	828	719	731	674	706	976	937	626	683

	Six Months Ending June 30	
	1958	1959
Net sales	$7,528	$10,971
Cost of goods sold	6,486	9,331
Gross profit	$1,042	$ 1,640
Selling, administrative and general	640	752
Interest expense	62	39
Miscellaneous income	-	-
Earnings before federal income taxes	340	849
Federal income taxes	172	439
Earnings after taxes	168	410

2. SALANT & SALANT, INC.

Balance Sheets
(All Figures in Thousands of Dollars)

	Dec. 31, 1955	Dec. 31, 1956	Dec. 31. 1957	Dec. 31. 1958	June 30, 1959
ASSETS					
Cash	$1,050	$ 936	$ 1,496	$ 1,316	$ 1,019
Net accounts receivable	1,186	786	855	1,320	1,858
Finished goods inventory	2,837	5,289	3,741	3,475)	5,632
Work-in-process inventory	645	672	827	791)	
Raw materials inventory	3,367	2,591	1,776	2,025	2,962
Supplies inventory	159	167	139	139	481
Total inventory	$7,008	$ 8,719	$ 6,483	$ 6,430	$ 9,075
Prepaid expenses	25	36	45	36	75
Total current assets	$9,270	$10,477	$ 8,878	$ 9,102	$12,028
Loans to employees	19	17	21	18	28
Land	3	26	26	31	31
Buildings	34	85	85	127	127
Machinery and equipment	882	907	928	924	987
Office furniture and fixtures	88	105	145	153	155
Improvements on leased properties	167	190	737	724	725
Accumulated depreciation	478	563	684	778	858
Net property, machinery, equipment	696	749	1,237	1,181	1,167
	$9,985	$11,243	$10,136	$10,302	$13,222
LIABILITIES					
Notes payable	$ 900	$ 2,600	$ 1,500	$ 1,000	$ 3,595
Accounts payable	1,068	179	70	243	392
Accrued salaries	435	268	225	221	121
Federal income taxes	985	824	525	500	439
Other taxes	175	193	192	210	129
Total current liabilities	$3,563	$ 4,065	$ 2,512	$ 2,175	$ 4,776
Pension reserve	216	229	242	255	262
Capital stock	2,420	2,420	2,420	2,420	2,420
Accumulated earnings	3,786	4,530	4,963	5,452	5,766
Total net worth	6,206	6,950	7,382	7,872	8,185
	$9,985	$11,243	$10,136	$10,302	$13,222

3. SALANT & SALANT, INC.

Organization Chart

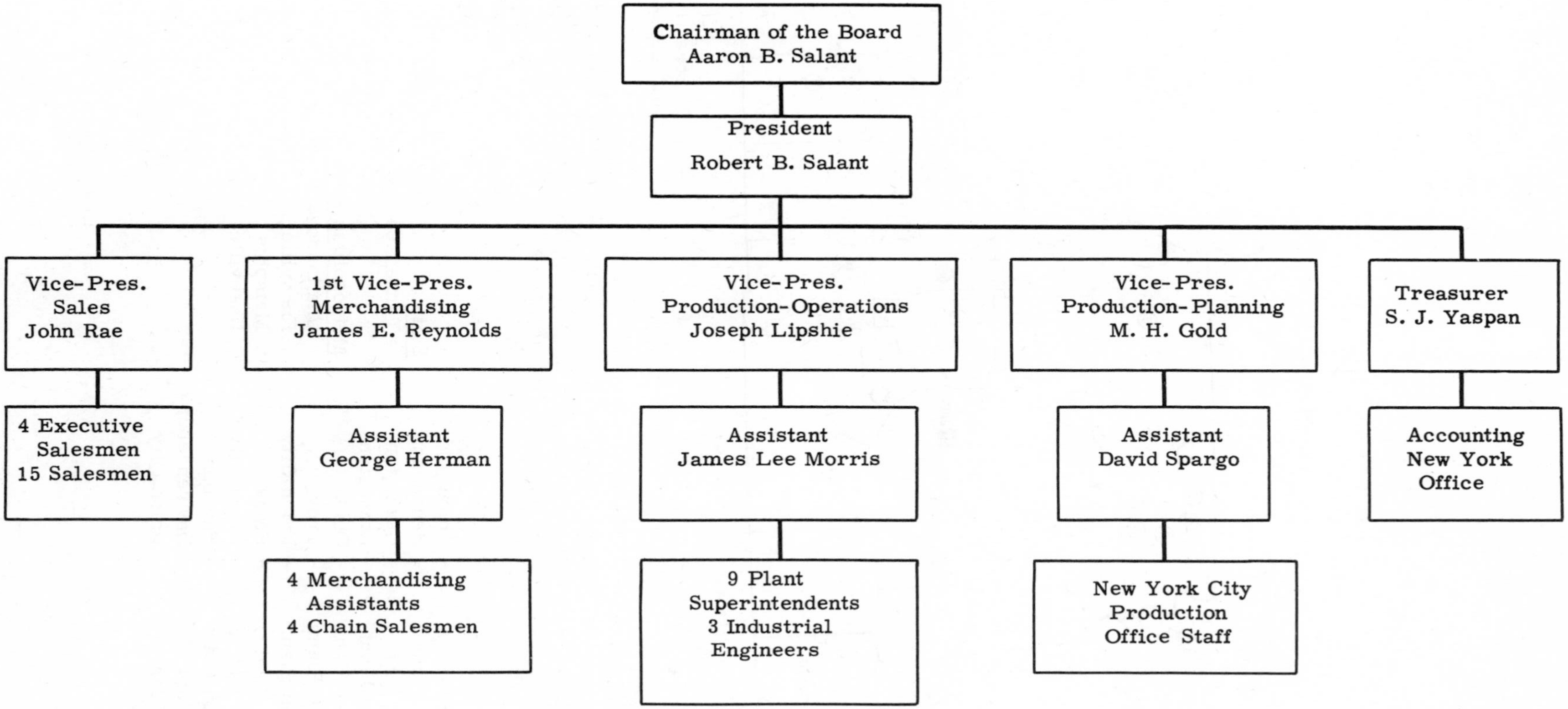

Chairman of the Board
Aaron B. Salant

President
Robert B. Salant

Vice-Pres.
Sales
John Rae

4 Executive
Salesmen
15 Salesmen

1st Vice-Pres.
Merchandising
James E. Reynolds

Assistant
George Herman

4 Merchandising
Assistants
4 Chain Salesmen

Vice-Pres.
Production-Operations
Joseph Lipshie

Assistant
James Lee Morris

9 Plant
Superintendents
3 Industrial
Engineers

Vice-Pres.
Production-Planning
M. H. Gold

Assistant
David Spargo

New York City
Production
Office Staff

Treasurer
S. J. Yaspan

Accounting
New York
Office

4. SALANT & SALANT, INC.

Location of Plants

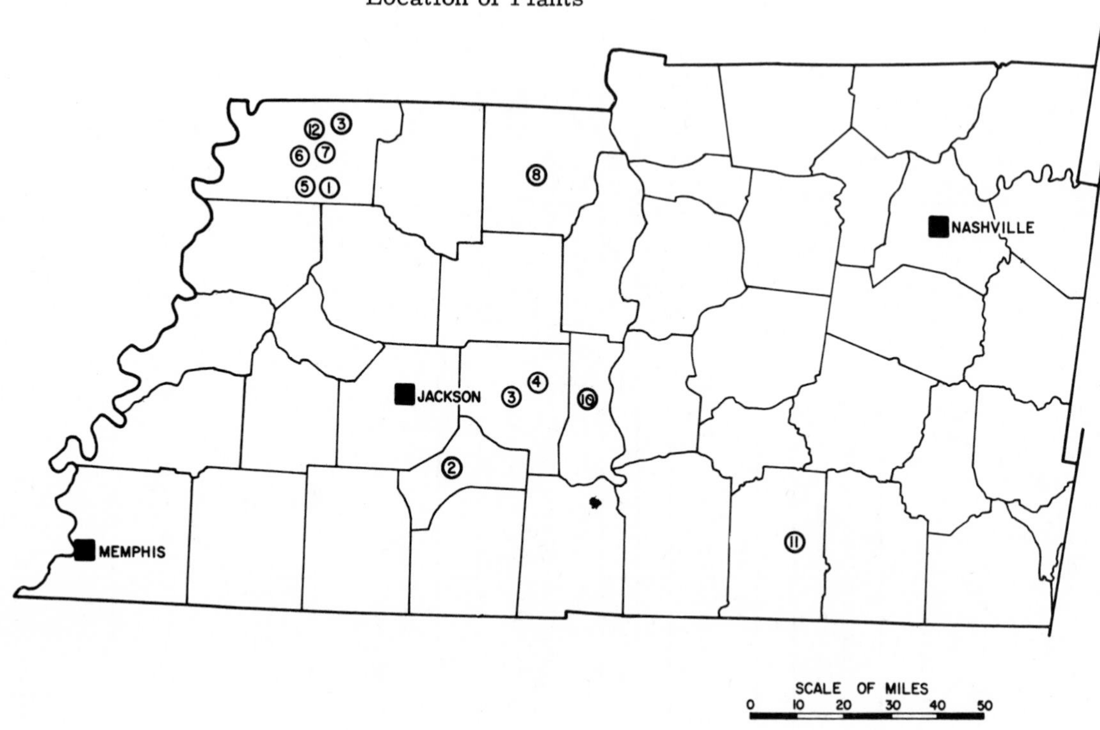

1	Adams Plant	- Obion
2	Chester Plant	- Henderson
3	Hanover Plant	- Lexington
4	Harrison Plant	- Lexington
5	Jefferson Plant	- Obion
6	Jefferson Plant	- Troy
7	Jefferson Plant	- Union City
8	Monroe Plant	- Paris
9	Oxford Plant	- Union City
10	Princeton Plant	- Parsons
11	Savoy Plant	- Lawrenceburg
12	Wilson Plant	- Union City

	No. of Workers in Mfg. (Thousands)	Avg. Hourly Earnings in Mfg.
State		
Tennessee	301	$1.76
Metropolitan Area		
Chattanooga	41	1.85
Knoxville	43	2.05
Memphis	44	1.94
Nashville	39	1.87

5. SALANT & SALANT, INC.

Government Statistics on United States Production of Selected Men's Apparel
(All Figures in Thousands of Dozens)

	1955	1956	1957	1958
Dress and sport trousers	8,244	9,054	9,569	9,363
Men's	5,613	6,027	5,972	5,949
Chiefly rayon	2,832	2,837	2,635	2,721
Chiefly cotton	1,161	1,542	1,785	1,715
Boys'	2,631	3,027	3,597	3,414
Other than wool	1,825	2,099	2,614	2,482
Work pants	6,415	6,533	6,406	6,443
Men's	5,812	5,871	5,702	5,820
Boys'	603	662	621	623
Woven sport shirts	14,327	15,137	13,967	13,733
Cotton	9,672	10,809	9,845	10,292
Rayon and acetate	3,766	3,471	3,360	2,926
Other including wool	889	857	762	515
Work shirts	4,557	4,800	4,120	3,687
Outerwear knit shirts	11,978	11,426	11,439	11,766

Source: Facts for Industry.

6. SALANT & SALANT, INC.

Sales
(All Figures in Thousands of Dozens)

	Sales by Product				
	1955	1956	1957	1958	1959 (est.)
Work pants			150	119	
Slacks			126	150	
Total pants	249	203	276	269	385
Matching twill shirts			53	44	
Sport collar work shirts			14	22	
Chambray and poplin work shirts			198	166	
Military work shirts			64	63	
Flannel utility shirts			69	36	
Fall line sport shirts			326	336	
Spring line sport shirts			218	178	
Total shirts	1,053	865	942	845	950
Jackets	16	20	41	52	50

	Sales by Type of Customer				
	1955	1956	1957	1958	1959
Pants--major chains	123	99	122	120	150
Pants--King Kole division	126	104	154	149	235
Shirts--major chains	830	659	731	654	725
Shirts--King Kole division	223	207	211	191	225
Jackets--major chains	11	15	39	49	44
Jackets--King Kole division	5	5	3	3	6

7. SALANT & SALANT, INC.

Sales and Inventories of Pants
(All Figures in Thousands of Dozens)

Year	Quarterly Sales History			
	Quarter	Work Pants	Slacks	Total
1957	1	38	26	64
	2	42	48	90
	3	44	32	76
	4	26	20	46
	Total	150	126	276
1958	1	25	24	49
	2	27	38	65
	3	41	62	103
	4	26	26	52
	Total	119	150	269
1959	1	32	90	122
	2	42	88	130
	3	29	53	82
	Total 9 Months	103	231	334

Customer	Prediction of 1960 Sales		
	Work Pants	Slacks	Total
King Kole Division.	117	167	284
Chain Store A.		45	45
Chain Store B--Men's Division	42	25	67
Chain Store B--Boys' Division.		25	25
Chain Store C.		68	68
Chain Store E.	15		15
Total	174	330	504

	Physical Inventory of Pants			
	1956	1957	1958	1959
January.	67	90	82	76
February.	65	82	84	82
March.	72	75	88	67
April.	83	75	90	72
May.	96	73	89	80
June	95	67	88	80
July	83	55	75	67
August.	79	54	64	61
September	74	51	56	56
October.	78	48	54	58
November	85	57	64	
December	94	68	77	
Annual Sales.	203	276	269	385

8. SALANT & SALANT, INC.

Summary of Weekly Report and Delivery Promises
King Kole Division Pants
(All Quantities in Thousands of Dozens of Pairs of Pants)

		March 2, 1959		June 29, 1959		August 31, 1959	
Type of Pants	1958 Sales	Cumulative Orders	Average Suggested Delivery on New Orders	Cumulative Orders	Average Suggested Delivery On New Orders	Cumulative Orders	Average Suggested Delivery on New Orders
Ivy League	36	5	Withdrawn	5	Withdrawn	5	Withdrawn
Continental	-		-	3	-	10	7 Weeks
Post-Grad	34	19	5 Weeks	81	7 Weeks	100	5 Weeks
Best Work Pants	37	8	1 Week	23	3 Weeks	29	5 Weeks
Better Work Pants	28	6	1 Week	21	3 Weeks	26	5 Weeks
Other Work Pants	16	3	2 Weeks	10	3 Weeks	13	5 Weeks
Total	151	41		143		183	

9. SALANT & SALANT, INC.

Description of Manufacturing Facilities

Name	Town	Area (Sq. Ft.)	Number of Employees	Primary Products	Optimum Volume (Weekly Production)
Chester	Henderson	72,000	312	Basic men's spring and fall sport shirts	4,000 dozen
				Twill shirts to match work pants	(inc. above)
Monroe	Paris	103,000	406	Men's and boys' novelty shirts	4,000 dozen
				High-price de luxe shirts	(inc. above)
Hanover	Lexington	85,000	250	Flannel utility shirts	2,500 dozen
Savoy	Lawrenceburg	107,500	452	Chambray and poplin work shirts	4,500 dozen
				Twill and poplin jackets	1,000 dozen
Harrison	Lexington	50,000	155	Juvenile and boys' western shirts	1,000 dozen
				Juvenile and boys' light-weight shirts	1,000 dozen
Jefferson	Union City	18,000)		Cuts shirts for Obion and Troy	
	Obion	6,000)	136	Juvenile and boys' flannel shirts	2,000 dozen
	Troy	9,000)		Juvenile and boys' flannel shirts	2,000 dozen
(Wilson)	Union City	32,000	19	Ships Obion and Troy shirts and some Oxford pants	
Adams	Obion	20,000	154	Work pants	1,500 dozen
Oxford	Union City	44,000	313	Work pants and slacks	2,900 dozen
Princeton	Parsons	113,000	569	Slacks	4,200 dozen
				Stores and ships all pants except for one customer	

10. SALANT & SALANT, INC.

Balance of Shirt Capacity and Requirements
(All Figures in Thousands of Dozens)

	Annual Capacity	Fall Line Requirements	Spring Line Requirements	Year-Round Items Requirements	Total Requirements
1958					
1. Chester and Monroe.	400	185	100	66	351
2. Savoy and Hanover. .	350	36		229	265
3. Harrison	100	50	28		78
4. Jefferson.	200	101	50		151
	1,050	372	178	295	845
1957					
1. Chester and Monroe.	400	180	113	67	360
2. Savoy and Hanover. .	350	69		262	331
3. Harrison	100	33	30		63
4. Jefferson.	200	113	74		187
	1,050	395	217	329	941

11. SALANT & SALANT, INC.

Illustrative Costs per Dozen Items

Description	Cloth	Trim	Piece-work	Time Work and Factory Expense	General Expense	Incoming Freight	Total Cost	Selling Price	Profit
Shirt	$ 7.96	$ .92	$2.48	$2.22	$ .97	$.13	$14.68	$15.75	$1.07
Pants A . . .	15.33	1.47	3.87	3.71	1.74	.33	26.45	29.50	3.05
Pants B . . .	16.20	1.14	4.59	3.54	1.82	.32	27.61	30.95	3.34

The costs shown for shirts were illustrative for both medium-price sport shirts and work shirts. Flannel utility shirts typically had the same labor costs but slightly higher material costs and profit margins.

The pants costs were typical of either work pants or slacks.

Plastics Industry Process Notes

The plastics process consists of four distinct stages which are dissimilar in process economics and technology and hence in the type of company that ordinarily participates in the business. The first stage is to obtain the basic chemical "building blocks," usually from petroleum refineries, chemical plants, or the coking ovens used by the steel industry. The second stage is to convert the building blocks into "monomer," the plastic raw material. The third stage is to combine or "polymerize" the monomer into long interlocking molecular chains which become gluey or resinous. The fourth stage is to mold or cast the plastic resin into final shape by any one of a variety of small machines.

---

1. The Building Blocks. The monomer for many plastics, such as phenolics, polystyrene, polyethylene, polyvinyl chloride, and others can be obtained from certain basic chemicals such as benzene, ethylene, and acetylene.

(*a*) *Benzene:* Benzene is an aromatic hydrocarbon, that is, a molecule in which the carbon atoms form a ring capable of forming additional linkages. It can be obtained as a by-product from the steel industry's coking ovens, where the destructive distillation of one ton of coal yields about fourteen pounds of benzene. It can also be obtained from the catalytic reforming units that most petroleum refineries used to upgrade their gasoline stocks.

Catalytic reformers were first installed during World War II to make toluene for explosives, such as TNT (trinitrotoluol). The reformer takes virgin naphtha from the distillation of crude oil and removes some of the hydrogen from its ring of carbon atoms to form aromatic rings. Since the aromatics have high antiknock ratings, many catalytic reformers were installed during the Korean War to make high-octane gasoline for aircraft. Later, the octane race brought about by the needs of the new high-compression automobile engines led to the installation of several hundred catalytic reformers throughout the country. Any of these reformers can be used to make toluene or benzene, simply by selecting the type of naphthas charged to the unit and installing special recovery units to retrieve the product. About 15 percent of the catalytic reformers in the United States have been converted to recover benzene.

Benzene can be alkylated with ethylene to make styrene monomer; it can be converted by various means to make phenol; it can be used to make cyclohexane, an intermediate used in the preparation of nylon; or it can be oxidized to form maleic anhydride, a source of one type of the polyester resins used in fiber glass reinforced plastics. About 35 percent of the benzene output is used to make styrene monomer, in a process that will be described more carefully later. About 21 percent is used in various processes to make phenol (carbolic acid). One process requires large quantities of sulfuric acid and caustic soda and generates sodium sulfite for paper mills as a by-product. Another process requires chlorine and caustic soda. A third process generates acetone as a by-product. A fourth yields few by-products, but requires large-volume continuous facilities to be economical, and a plant investment of $8 million yields about 40 million pounds of phenol annually.

(*b*) *Ethylene:* Ethylene is a light hydrocarbon that can be obtained from natural gas, from the lighter cuts of ethane in the distillation of crude oil, or from refinery waste gases. Mixed feed stocks are separated and cracked quickly at high temperatures and then purified in fractionating towers at low temperatures to yield ethylene or propylene. Such facilities require a large throughput to be economical, and an investment of $10 million might provide about 200 million pounds of ethylene annually. In order to reduce shipping costs, the product is usually transported by pipeline to nearby customer plants.

Ethylene is a very important petrochemical and forms the base for many large markets. About 30 percent is converted into ethylene oxide, to be used for making antifreeze and other products. About 26 percent is converted to ethyl alcohol, a major industrial chemical. About 9 percent is converted to ethyl chloride to make tetraethyl lead for antiknock gasoline. The remainder is used for three key plastics—with benzene to make styrene monomer, with chlorine as one means of making polyvinyl chloride, or it can be polymerized itself to make polyethylene.

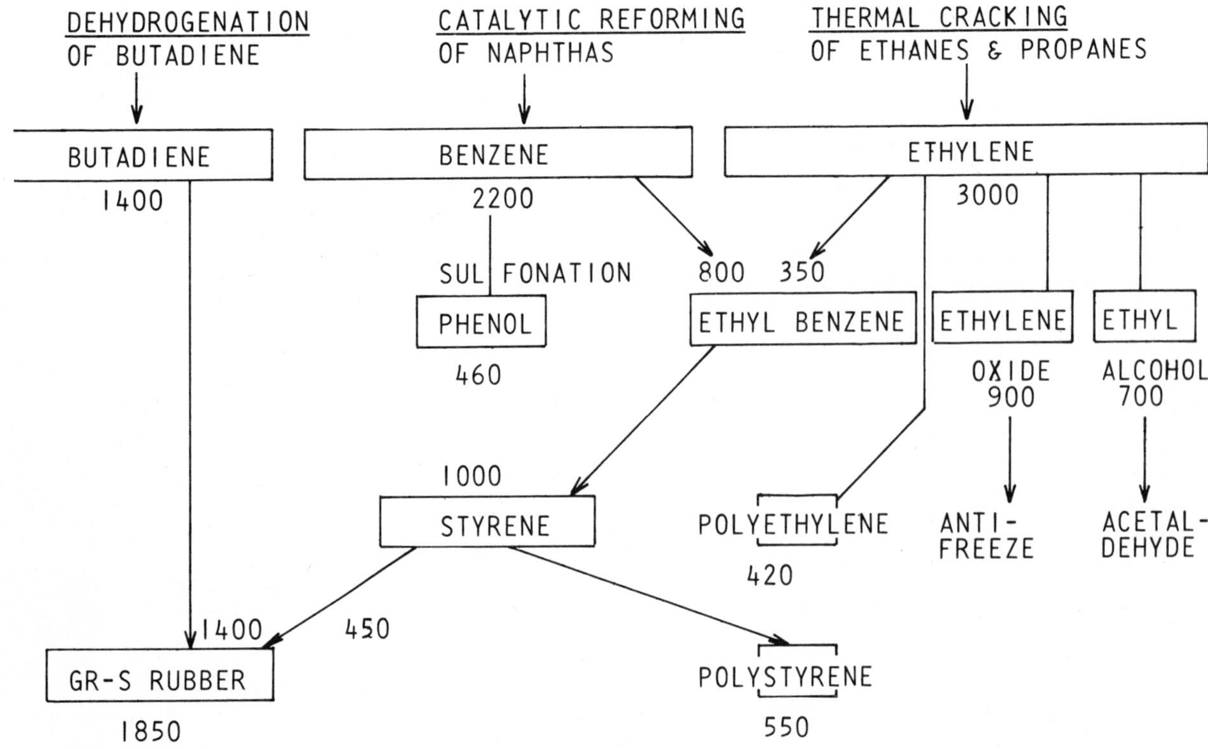

(*c*) *Acetylene:* Acetylene is a basic chemical that has long been used in large quantities in oxy-acetylene metal-cutting torches. It is derived from calcium carbide, which is manufactured in the electrie furnace from common lime and carbon. It can also be derived from natural gas or the light hydrocarbons in petroleum distillation. Acetylene can be treated with hydrochloric acid to make acrylonitrile, a source of synthetic fibers that is also used to improve the properties of polystyrene. The diagram above indicates how the three main building blocks are used in the plastic industry. The units are in millions of pounds of annual production.

2. *Styrene Monomer.* Styrene monomer is not only the source of polystyrene plastic resin but is also a component of GR-S, the most important synthetic rubber. To make 100 pounds of styrene monomer, 84 pounds of benzene are processed with 31 pounds of ethylene. To make 100 pounds of GR-S rubber, 22 pounds of styrene monomer are processed with 72 pounds of butadiene, a petrochemical derived from the distillation of crude oil. The styrene monomer that is polymerized to make polystyrene plastic must be purer than the rubber grade.

Styrene monomer is produced in large chemical plants from the treatment of benzene with ethylene, an alcohol type of hydrocarbon derived in large quantities from petroleum refining. Actually, the large-scale production of styrene was one of the major technological achievements of World War II, because styrene was an essential material in the manufacture of synthetic rubber. Synthetic rubber involving the manufacture of butadiene and styrene became a billion dollar industry within 18 months as the Government supported the construction of vast facilities of new design. After World War II, Government plants were auctioned to private industry, and styrene plants now operated by chemical corporations service both the rubber industry and the plastics industry.

Styrene is made in four major steps: the combination of ethylene and benzene to form ethyl benzene; the separation of ethyl benezene from the remaining chemicals; the "cracking" of ethyl benzene to form

Photo, Courtesy The Dow Chemical Co.

2. General View of Styrene Plant

At the right are three of the four units that combine and separate the ethyl benzene. In the center are the four cracking units which form styrene from ethylene benzene. At the left are the fractionating towers which separate the styrene under a vacuum by distillation.

styrene; and the separation of styrene from the remaining chemicals. As can be seen from the accompanying photographs, a styrene plant such as the Dow plant at Freeport, Texas consists of batteries of towers in which the chemical processes take place, connected by miles of piping to recycle the products in continuous flow, and serviced by facilities to generate heat, create vacuum, pump water, and so on.

The combination process, known as alkylation, operates at regular atmospheric pressure. The separation process, which takes place in high cooling towers, requires a large capacity pumping system to circulate water through the process.

The ethyl benzene is then pumped into huge heating furnaces which "crack" the material and form styrene. The ethyl benzene must be treated with steam at a temperature of 800° C. in the presence of a bauxite catalyst. The process, known as dehydrogenation, serves to crack down the more complex ethyl benzene molecule by removing hydrogen and forming styrene.

In the final step, fractionating towers are used to separate the styrene from the remaining chemicals. The separation process is very delicate, since there is only 9° C. difference in temperature between the styrene and the ethyl benzene still mixed with it, and because styrene has a tendency to polymerize into plastic resin at this stage of the process. The fractionating towers, which distill the chemicals by boiling each off at different temperatures, are very similar to the fractionating or bubble towers used for the same purpose in an oil refinery. Due to the particular problems in the styrene process, the separation is carried on under a high vacuum. Special chemicals are added to inhibit the styrene, that is, to prevent it from polymerizing until it arrives at the polymer plant.

Photo, Courtesy The Dow Chemical Co.

2B. Cracking Units to Transform Ethyl Benzene into Styrene

These units are furnaces which supply steam at 800° C. to crack ethyl benzene in the presence of a catalyst.

Photo, Courtesy The Dow Chemical Co.

2C. Fractionating Towers to Distill Styrene Monomer

The mixture of ethyl benzene and styrene is pumped from the cracking units at the right into the large bubble towers at center and left, where the styrene is distilled in a vacuum.

The economics of the styrene monomer are approximately as follows:

	Cents per Pound Styrene
Benzene cost @ 25.0¢ per gallon	2.93
Ethylene cost @ 5.0¢ per pound	1.60
Operating labor including associated costs	0.19
Maintenance labor	0.13
Other costs	1.67
Total plant costs:	
Research allocation	0.56
Selling and administrative	0.46
Average freight to customer	0.50
Total Costs	8.04

Utilities have been assumed to be purchased.

Operating labor would vary as follows with plants of differing capacity. Labor in a given plant at less than capacity operation would change very little in absolute dollars:

	Operating Labor	
Capacity—Pounds per Year	*Dollars per Year*	*Cents per Pound*
100,000,000	180,000	0.18
200,000,000	220,000	0.11
300,000,000	280,000	0.09

Plants smaller than 100,000,000 pounds per year would not be considered economical today.

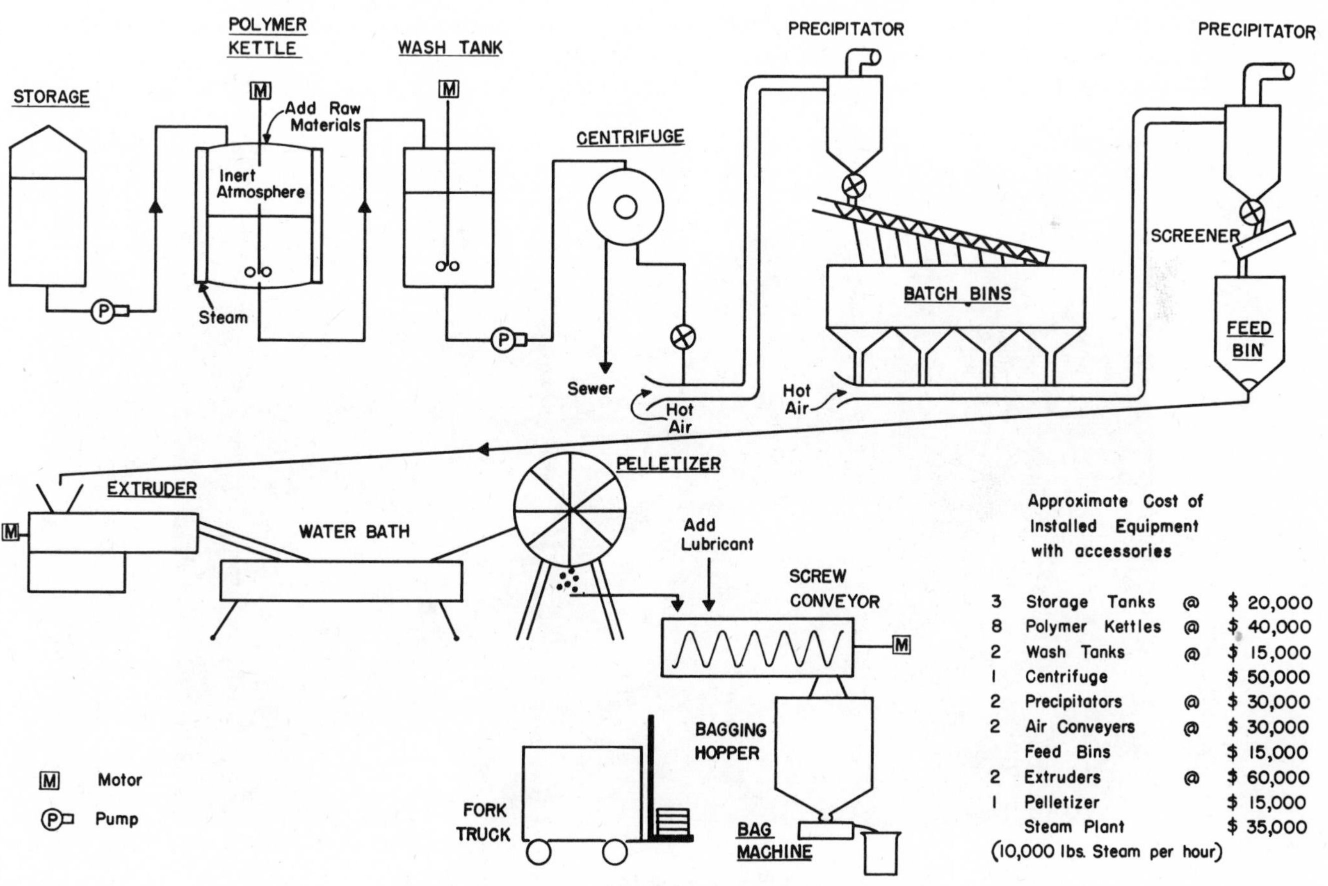

3A. Diagram of Polymerization Process

3. Polymerization of Styrene. Polymerization is a reaction by which single molecules, such as those of styrene monomer, are linked to form large molecules, such as those of polystyrene, without change in fundamental chemical composition. The polymerized plastic resin can then be extended with a filler or other materials to make the final molding compound.

Polymerization is a batch process conducted inside a resin kettle, rather than a continuous flow process conducted in processing towers. A fixed amount of monomer is pumped into the polymer kettle, certain other chemicals are added, and the kettle is closed to allow the reaction to take place. Ten or twelve hours later, the kettle is opened and the polymerized resin is drawn off. The cycle time, which is determined by the chemical characteristics of the reaction inside the kettle, is a fixed element around which the operations of the plant are geared.

As shown in the diagram of the polystyrene process, the resin kettle contains a motor-driven screw to rotate the liquid inside. To prevent oxygen or hydrogen from affecting the reaction, an inert gas can be pumped into the kettle. The double wall of the kettle is provided with piping to allow hot steam or cold water to be pumped in, thus heating or cooling the liquid inside the kettle. Steam is first introduced into the kettle walls to start the reaction, then water is introduced to draw off the heat generated by the reaction itself.

The remaining equipment in a polystyrene plant is used to purify and blend the resin and to form it into solid pellets that can be easily handled for molding purposes. The principal equipment used to form the pellets is the extruder, which pushes the resin through a screen by means of a screw action, similar to an ordinary kitchen meat grinder. The resin comes out of the extruder in long, hot, spaghetti-like lengths, which are cooled on the runoff table by water sprays. The hardened lengths are then chopped into pellets for molding.

Actually, a molding compound may contain as much filler as it does resin. The filler can be used to extend the quantity of the material, that is, to get more product for less money, in which case ordinary wood pulp in the form of fine wood flour is used. Fillers can also increase the heat resistance, impact strength, and insulating properties of a molding compound, in which case more expensive materials are used such as cotton fiber, asbestos, or glass. Plasticizers, made of high-boiling liquids, are also added to increase the ability of the compound to flow easily during the molding process. Color pigments can be added to those resins, such as crystal-clear polystyrene, which can be colored easily. Most molding compounds are offered in many grades and colors, depending upon whether low price, high heat resistance, good impact strength, easy flow properties, or bright color are desired. The matching of colors is often a difficult task since each batch may have slight differences of internal structure.

Photo, Courtesy Catalin Corporation of America

3B. Polystyrene Plant: View from the Control Window

The four polymerization kettles are nearest, with the two wash tanks beyond. The centrifuge is the small black equipment at the upper left, near the window.

Photo, Courtesy Catalin Corporation of America

3C. Polystyrene Plant: Polymer Kettles and Wash Tank

The workman is operating the hand control to charge material into the polymerization kettle. The bolts on the kettle rim and small door for charging additives serve to protect the inert gas inside from leakage. The apparatus on the kettle top include an electric motor which rotates the liquids in the kettle during the heating cycle. The large tank to the rear is a wash tank, with the centrifuge in the background. Both kettles and tanks extend below the platform to the floor below.

Photo, Courtesy Catalin Corporation of America

3D. Polystyrene Plant: Extrusion Room

The two extruders are located behind each control panel, with the runoff tables extending to the left. An air duct runs up to the ceiling from a position near the mouth of the extruder. The conveyor to the pelletizer can be seen at the front to the left of the runout table.

Photo, Courtesy Catalin Corporation of America

3E. Polystyrene Plant: Extruder, Close-Up

The polystyrene is extruded onto the runout table in long narrow strips. The control panel establishes the temperature, speed, humidity, and other physical conditions for the process. The air duct helps cool the extrusions and prevents dirt and foreign particles from settling into the soft, crystal-clear polystyrene strips.

4. Molding Plastic Resin. Once the molding resin has been prepared, there are many different methods to fabricate finished products or component parts: (1) thermosetting resins can be compression or transfer molded; (2) thermoplastic resins can be injection or extrusion molded; (3) liquid resins can be cast or rotation molded; (4) reinforced plastics can be molded by matched die or layed up by hand; (5) other processes can be used, such as thermoforming plastic sheets, blow molding bottles, foaming plastics, or using liquid resins for laminating, bonding, and adhesive applications.

(*a*) *Compression Molding:* Compression molding is the oldest process, using thermosetting resins, such as the phenolics, the ureas, and the melamines. When placed in a steel die under heat and pressure, these resins not only melt to fill the shape of the die, but also undergo a chemical change or "cure" which gives them improved properties of strength and heat resistance. Once they have undergone this cure in the die, the scrap cannot be melted for reuse.

Compression presses are fairly simple vertical machines capable of exerting about 1,500 pounds per square inch, usually applied through a hydraulic plunger. They are rated by tons of clamping pressure, an indication of size, and can range from about 50 to about 300 tons. Presses of this type cost about $7,000 for a 50-ton press, about $9,000 for a 100-ton press, and about $15,000 for a 350-ton press. Since the cure depends not only upon pressure but upon heat and time as well, the resin is usually preheated, and the dies are designed to take in steam or electricity in order to maintain a temperature between 280–350° F. The cure usually takes from one to four minutes, depending on the size of the part and the type of material. If the material is preheated for 15 minutes at 200° F., it can reduce the cure time and molding pressures about 15 to about 50 percent. Usually 3 to 10 percent excess material is placed in the die to ensure proper filling of the shape. This excess material "flashes" along the parting line where the two halves of the die join, and must later be removed from the cooled part by buffing or grinding. Tolerances between .003 and .025 inches can be obtained on parts smaller than 10 inches. It may take one to three man-hours to set up a machine to ensure proper placement of the die.

The molding procedure is as follows: (1) Measure the proper charge of molding powder required for the part. Often this is done by pressing powder in a "pill" maker, a simple machine that makes slugs or pellets called "pre-forms" of standard weight that are more easily handled than powder. (2) Heat the pre-forms in a small oven near the press, until they are ready to melt. (3) Place the proper number of measured pre-forms into the open die, close the die, and wait for the cure cycle to be completed. (4) When the die reopens after its preset cycle time, remove the hot piece and clean the mold cavity by an air blast. (5) Buff or grind the finished piece along the parting line to remove "flash."

Photo, Courtesy The Hydraulic Press Mfg. Co.

4A. Compression Molding Machine

Photo, Courtesy The Hydraulic Press Mfg. Co.

4B. Making the Pre-Forms, Single Cavity Die

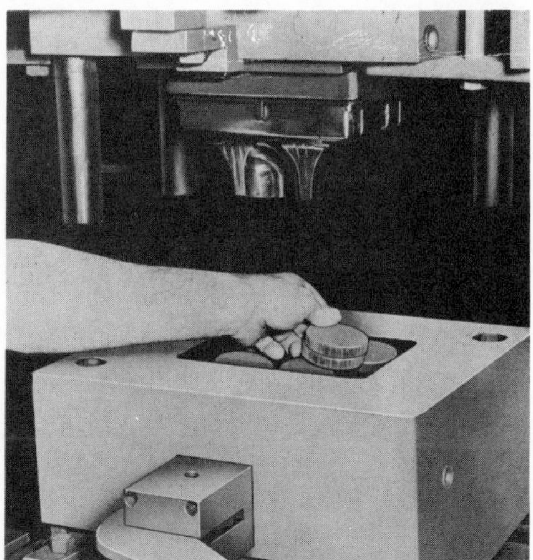

Photo, Courtesy The Hydraulic Press Mfg. Co.

4C. Loading the Mold, Single Cavity Die

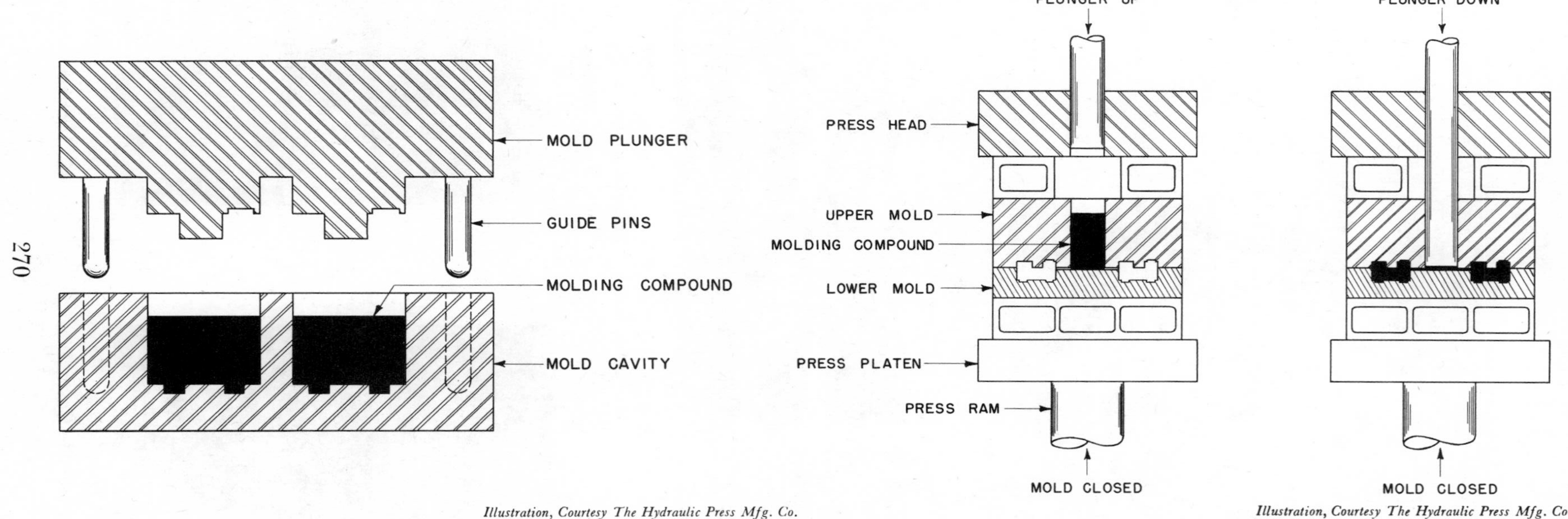

Illustration, Courtesy The Hydraulic Press Mfg. Co.

4D. Compression Molding

Illustration, Courtesy The Hydraulic Press Mfg. Co.

4E. Transfer Molding

If the piece to be molded has metal inserts, as do many electrical connection boards that are often made of phenolic resins, the direct closing of the die on the pre-forms may displace the inserts. In order to retain the alignment, the resin is squirted into the die in a liquid form by using a transfer press. This is simply a variation on compression molding, in which the press can close the die first and then actuate a hydraulic plunger which closes on the pre-forms located in the center of the die. The pre-form is melted by the plunger and squirts liquid resin into side cavities in the dies where the inserts are held in place. A transfer press may cost $1,000 or $2,000 more than a compression press of equal size, and can be used for compression molding.

For long runs, various special machine designs can be used to speed up compression molding. Five or more press units can be mounted as a rotary indexing machine so that when the die closes, the machine indexes to the next station around the circular mounting, and the die in the last press moves into position to be opened, cleaned, and new pre-forms inserted. The movement around the circle can be timed, of course, to equal the cure cycle. Other automation devices can be used for long runs of identical parts, such as phenolic bottle caps, multiple-cavity dies, automatic insertion devices for pre-forms, and automatic removal of finished parts. These devices, however, require machines of special design and thus limit the flexibility of the basic unit.

(*b*) *Injection Molding:* Injection molding was developed in the 1930's to take advantage of the faster molding cycles possible with thermoplastic resins such as polystyrene, polyethylene, rigid polyvinyl chloride, the cellulosics, nylon, and so on. Thermoplastic resins do not require a chemical cure, and can therefore be simply melted and squirted into a cool die to solidify to final shape. The machine can take over many of the functions of the compression molding worker, because it can preheat the material internally, inject the melted material into the die automatically, and then reopen the die and knock out the piece. The scrap material from thermoplastic resins can be reused by simply returning it to the hopper that feeds the machine, where it is remelted and combined with virgin material.

Injection molding machines are precision machine tools, capable of exerting 10,000 to 25,000 pounds per square inch along a horizontal axis against the clamping device that closes the die. They are rated by the weight of material that can be delivered in one shot. Ordinary commercial capacities range from about 2 to 60 ounces. The approximate base price of 2-, 6-, 12-, 24-, and 60-ounce machines is about $12,000, $25,000, $32,000, $49,000 and $62,000 respectively. The maximum size of injection moldings is about 6 pounds.

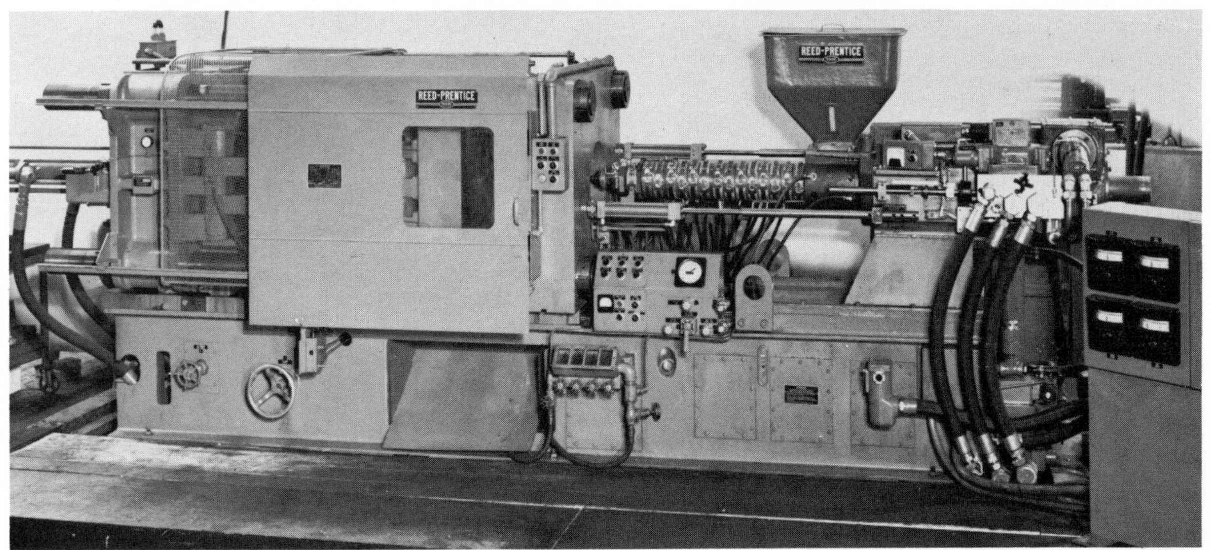

Photo, Courtesy Reed-Prentice Co.

4F. 1962 Model Screw Type Injection Molding Machine

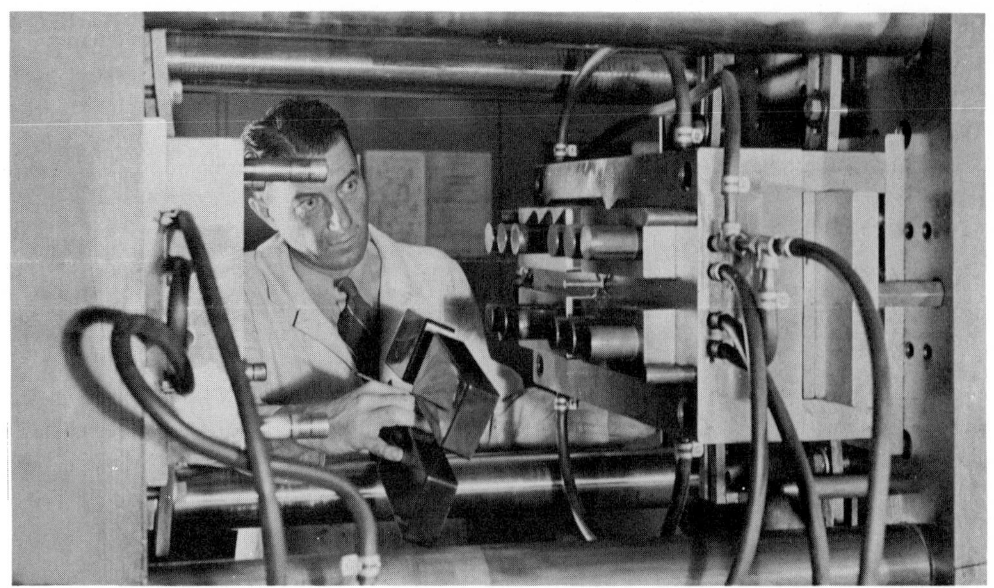

Photo, Courtesy The Hydraulic Press Mfg. Co.

4G. Action of Knock-Out Pins in a Large Injection Molding Machine

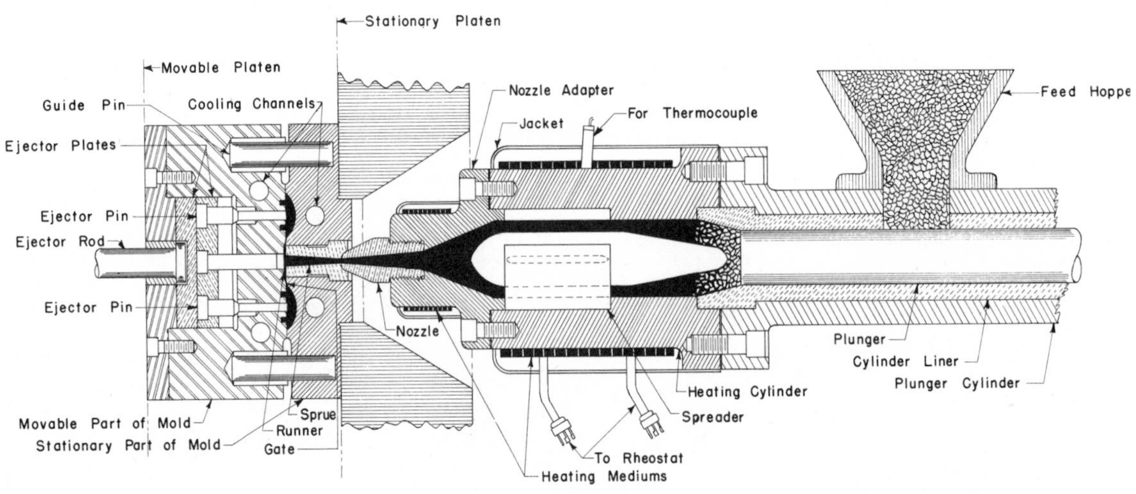

Illustration, Courtesy Tennessee Eastman and Chemaco Corp.

4H. Injection Machine

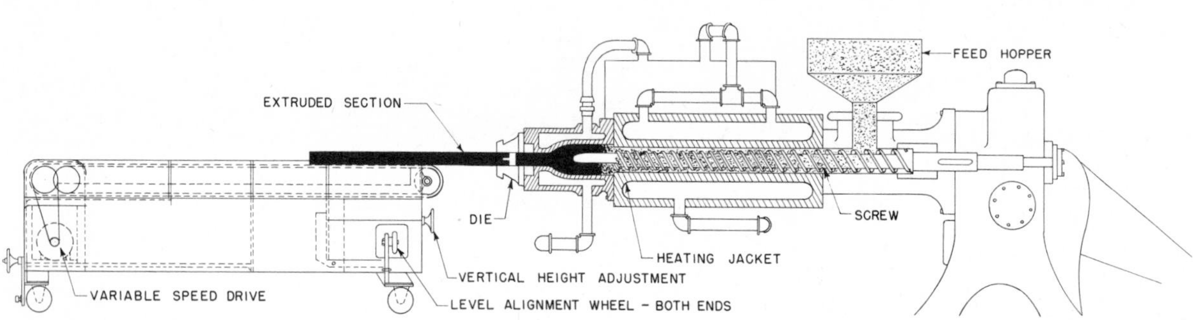

Illustration, Courtesy Tennessee Eastman and Chemaco Corp.

4I. Extrusion Machine

In operation, the machine is highly automatic. A girl can be trained to run one in less than an hour. The molding resin is fed into the press through a hopper. A plunger pushes it into a heating chamber where it is transformed into a plastic state through the application of heat and pressure. The heating chamber usually contains a "torpedo" or spreader which forces the molding compound along the walls of the chamber and thus facilitates uniform heating. Sometimes the torpedo contains a heating unit so that the material may be heated both inside and outside. The temperature in the chamber varies with the material but usually ranges between 265 to 500° F. The advance of the injection plunger serves to force the plastic from the chamber into the mold cavity. The injection pressures run from about 10,000 to 25,-000 pounds per square inch. The mold remains closed until the material has cooled enough to solidify. It is then opened and the piece ejected by hand, air blast, or knock-out pins. The molds for injection molding usually have chambers for the circulation of a cooling medium such as water, rather than steam as is used in compression molding.

Injection molding is a very fast and economical process, and it has greatly increased the use of plastic materials. The cycle time depends primarily on how fast the material can be plasticated in the machine and then cooled once it is in the mold. It is thus dependent on the plastic used and the thickness of the sections in the piece. The minimum cycle is less than three seconds and the maximum around a minute. The average is probably somewhere between 10 and 20 seconds. Multiple-cavity dies are frequently used, which makes it possible to produce a number of pieces per cycle. The cavities are interconnected in the die by sprues and runners. The sprues and runners are broken or clipped off after the piece is removed from the machine. The excess material can sometimes be salvaged and used over again. If the mold is correctly designed and the equipment properly operated, there should be no flash along the mold parting line. An 8-ounce machine, injecting 13 cubic inches of polystyrene per shot, can mold about 120 pounds of material per hour with tolerances between 0.009 and 0.046 inches on dimensions ranging from ¼ inch to 10 inches.

When an injection machine is shut down at the end of a day's run, a couple of shots are ejected into the air to clear the nozzle. When the machine is started again, about 45 minutes must be allowed to bring the heating chamber and the material in it up to operating temperature. It is also necessary to "purge" the machine by ejecting into the air the material which was in the chamber while the machine was cooling on the preceding day. This material would have cooked overly long and would not make satisfactory moldings. When the color of the plastic being run is changed, it is also necessary to purge the machine. In order to avoid color pollution, some molders have a number of different injection chambers, one for each color. The job of changing the injection chamber on a machine requires two or three hours. It is more difficult for certain materials, such as vinyl resins, which may decompose under the heat of the machine.

Although fairly automatic once it is set up for the operator, injection molding requires considerable skills to design the proper die and select the proper material to obtain a reliable part for the conditions of use.

Each plastic material has different properties which affect molding conditions. Nylon and the cellulosics tend to absorb moisture from the air and must be dried in an oven before being fed to the hopper, or the absorbed water will turn to steam during injection and cause streaks in the part. Polyvinyl chloride requires high-injection pressure up to 40,000 pounds per square inch to obtain adequate flow of the material into the die. Polyethylene shrinks in the die, and this has to be compensated by extra large die dimensions. Nylon requires temperatures above 500° F. to melt the material in the hopper, then when melted it tends to drip rapidly and must be controlled by special injection nozzles and very tight dies. On the other hand, if rigid polyvinyl chloride is subjected to temperatures much above 350° F. it tends to decompose in the machine. Polyethylene sticks to the walls of the machine cavities and must be flushed and scraped to obtain proper flow through to the die. Both polyethylene and polyvinyl chloride require a longer molding cycle than polystyrene. Polystyrene, however, tends to warp unless the flow into the mold is smooth, due to the development of internal stresses and strains. In general, nylon and polyvinyl chloride are the most difficult materials to control, and some molders have acquired special know-how in one or the other, to capitalize on the difficulties in order to improve their competitive position by being able to solve them.

The special problem in the case of molded vinyl is that the temperatures required in the molding machine are very close to the decomposition point of the material. Since the decomposed material is corrosive, it may be necessary to use chrome-plated injection cylinders. However, chrome-plated or corrosion-resistant alloys are expensive and cannot be used in the heating cylinder. It is therefore necessary to purge the hot material from the cylinder during a shutdown, to install close temperature controls on the machine, to train the workers to watch for danger signs, and to use higher pressures to inject the material, rather than relying upon heat to plasticate it fully.

The design of the die is also an important aspect of molding technology. Dies are usually quoted separately from piece prices in the bidding process, and dies are purchased by the customer but held and repaired by the injection molder. The die may be made by the machine shop of the molder or by an outside company specializing in die making. The die may be removed by the customer at any time and given to a different injection molder, but the molder often stipulates that there will be a 30 percent charge for such removal, in which case it is usually understood that the die price is close to actual cost and may not even cover some of the special engineering problems that may be encountered during its design.

Die design depends on the material, the size machine to be used, the length of run, and the design of the part. Polystyrene is difficult to release from the mold, and may require more taper than other materials. The size of the gate into the die and of the sprues and runners depends upon the melt characteristics of the material. Extra grooves must be located near the ends of the cavities to allow entrapped air to escape or it may burn the part. Also, the location and degree of water cooling through the dies may be critical in a large machine.

There are always alternative choices in die design to obtain the most economical overall operation. A small machine can be operated for a long time with a relatively inexpensive one- or two-cavity die; or several small dies can be run simultaneously on different machines; or a large machine can be used, with a large, multicavity die operating on a slower cycle, but producing more pieces per shot. Injection machines are usually operation-costed in terms of a burden charge per hour, which would include depreciation, maintenance, electricity, floor space charges, and so on. Such charges might vary between $5 and $15 per hour, as the machine size varies between 8 and 60 ounces.

The newer injection molding machines have attained faster shot cycles and more precise control of the plastic flow through certain design improvements that appeared about 1958 to reduce the melt time and improve the distribution of heat. A problem exists in the low thermal conductivity and high viscosity of plastic resins, which makes it difficult to transfer heat from the outside walls to the interior of the mass. The conventional torpedo acts as a spreader to thin out the material and bring it closer to the heated wall cylinder. Improved designs have changed the torpedo design into a melt extractor, which forces the resin inside a torpedo shape and out through spaces in the extractor, or a reverse flow cylinder, which forces the resin back and forth through channels. Another type removes the torpedo entirely and replaces the ram with an extruding-type screw which turns and mixes the material while it withdraws to ram it against the injection nozzle and thus complete the shot cycle. A different solution is to preplasticate the resin in a separate cylinder in the machine, allowing only melted material to be inserted into the main cylinder and rammed through the nozzle. Some machines obtain rapid overall cycles by using a two-speed system, for fast speeds to prepare for the molding cycle, and slower speeds during the actual molding itself.

To make film, sheeting, tubes, or profiles, an extruder is used instead of an injection machine. The design is similar, except that a continually turning screw forces the melted resin out through a die opening on to a moving belt conveyor which carries it away and cools it under water sprays. While the material is melted, it can be forced through a screen and die and emerge as a whole cylinder or be spread to a wide film. The take-off conveyor belt, some 40 feet in length, can be run as fast as 500 to 1,000 feet per hour for vinyls and styrenes, though polyethylene is slower. Dies are not expensive, but must be large enough to allow for substantial shrinkage. An extruder with a screw of 2½-inch diameter might cost $10,000 and extrude 180 pounds of polyvinyl chloride or 60 pounds of polyethylene per hour. A 4½-inch extruder costs $18,500 and extrudes 500 pounds of polyvinyl chloride. An 8-inch extruder costs $40,000 and extrudes 1,200 pounds of polyvinyl chloride.

(*c*) *Casting Methods:* While injection molding is more rapid and automatic than compression molding, the molding machines cost more and the dies are quite expensive, because the resin is in a solid form and has viscous and nonconducting properties that require steel alloy dies and high-injection pressures. If the resin can be used in a liquid form, however, and cast into shape, both the machines and the dies should be much less expensive. There are two basic means of accomplishing this: by casting certain resins in liquid form, and by making vinyl and polyethylene resins in such small particle size that they act as liquids when mixed with plasticizers, and can then be dip, slush, or rotational molded.

Phenolic, acrylic, and other resins can be cast in liquid form. Liquid phenolic resin for casting has very different properties from phenolic molding powder. As a liquid, it can be cast in brilliant colors or be made translucent, while compression molding limits its use to dark brown or black, and smaller sizes.

Acrylic resins are used for "potting" or "encapsulating," by holding in place some object, such as a lettered sign or a sample product or a butterfly, and then pouring the acrylic resin around it to create a clear block of plastic to display the object. Epoxy resins are cast to form large dies for metal-stamping purposes. The casting of phenolics requires a long cure time and is limited to certain shapes, but produces brilliant colors.

The use of liquid vinyls, called plastisols, requires somewhat different methods. There are several ways to polymerize vinyl chloride, and each method produces a different size particle. The emulsion process yields particles of only one micron. These fine particles can be suspended in a liquid plasticizer such as dioctyl phthalate without being dissolved by the phthlate. The plastisol is changed to a tough rubbery film by heating to about 350° F., at which temperature the phthlate dissolves and hardens the vinyl.

The simple process of heat-hardening the liquid permits various inexpensive fabricating processes for vinyl plastisols. They may be dip molded, as in making vinyl gloves, where a mold is made in the shape of a steel hand, heated, and merely dipped into a vat of plastisol which then hardens as a glove around the hand to a thickness depending upon the duration of the dip. They may be slush molded, as in making hollow dolls' heads, by first constructing a simple die through electro-deposition of copper on a plaster of Paris mold. The plastisol is then poured into the mold which is passed by conveyor through an oven to harden the vinyl, then the mold is turned upside down to pour out excess plastisol and the mold is carried to a second hardening oven and then a cooling chamber to permit removal of the piece by air blast.

Rotational casting is a development of the slush method to permit enclosed moldings for complete dolls or doll limbs and trunks. A hollow two-part mold is charged with plastisol and then rotated in two planes inside a heated chamber. After fusion, the mold is cooled and opened. The cycle takes from 10 to 30 minutes. It is used for automobile arm-rests, toys, and many complex shapes that would cost more using steel dies. Powdered polyethylene can also be used on rotational casting equipment. In vinyl plastisols, the degree of flexibility can be controlled by the amount of plasticizer that is used. A hard surface can be cast by using a minimum amount of plasticizer, thus making a "rigidisol."

(*d*) *Reinforced Plastics:* Reinforced plastics usually refer to the use of liquid polyester resin to bind glass fibers. The fiber may be in the form of chopped roving, matted fibers, or woven mats. Other plastic resins, such as phenolics or epoxies may be used, though most of the material used for commercial purposes is polyester with matted or chopped glass fiber. There are two economically quite different methods of

Photo, Courtesy General Motors and Society of Automotive Engineers

4J. Die Molding: Pre-Form in the Die

Photo, Courtesy General Motors and Society of Automotive Engineers

4K. Die Molding: Finished Piece

using the process: by investing in expensive presses and costly matched steel dies to form parts quickly and with little labor cost, or by employing much hand labor to construct the parts on cheap plaster, wood, plastic, or aluminum molds.

Matched die molding permits a rapid rate of production, low-unit cost, more uniform quality, and elimination of most trimming and finishing operations. Materials preparation for this process involves the production of a pre-form which has the approximate shape of the finished part. The photograph shows a pre-form being made by blowing chopped glass fibers onto a wire mesh form rotated in front of a large

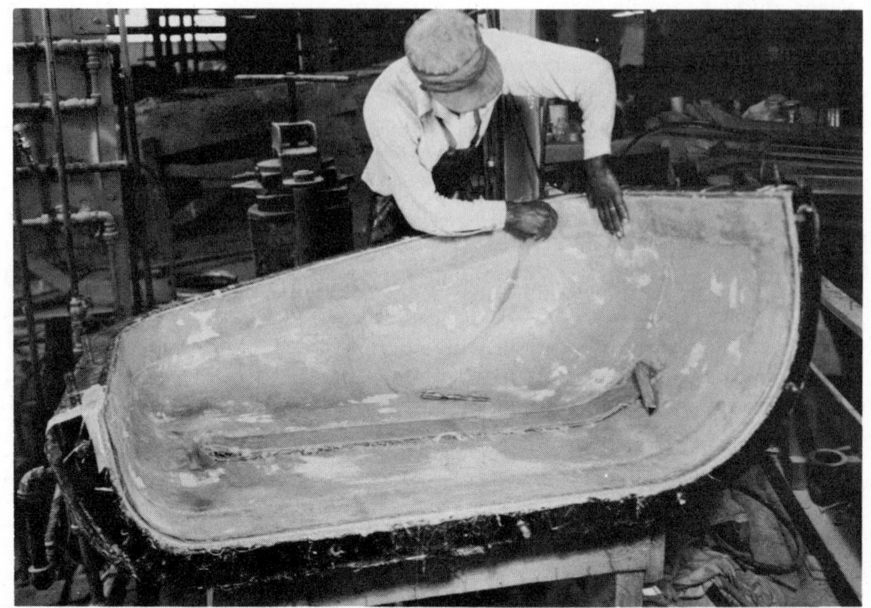

Photo, Courtesy Lunn Laminates, Inc.

4L. Laying Out Cloth for Bag Molding

Photo, Courtesy General Motors and Society of Automotive Engineers

4M. Making a Pre-Form for Die Molding

exhaust fan. Periodic application of a resin spray holds the fibers together, and the pre-form is cured for a few minutes in an oven before being placed in the molding die.

Accurately machined metal dies mounted in huge presses are used to mold the part. Dies and presses are similar to those used in compression molding, but shapes as large as 15 by 17 feet can be produced of reinforced plastics in presses as large as 500-ton capacity. When the pre-form is in the mold, the press closes, applying pressure and heat for a rapid cure. The photographs show a mold with pre-form and the finished part. Molding cycles usually are from 3 to 15 minutes, depending upon the part size. The finished part is accurately formed and finished on both surfaces by the mold.

Matched die molding requires a heavy investment, which can amount to more than $150,000 for a large press and die. Unlike bag molding, there is a practical limitation to the size of parts that can be molded. In addition, start-up costs may be heavy before the process and die are perfected for volume production of a new part.

Hand lay-up can be used to make very large complex shapes. For example, in 1961 a 65-foot yacht was made of reinforced polyester, with a displacement of 25 tons when afloat, using hand lay-up on plaster dies. In this process, the mold, which may be male or female, is first cleaned and then fiber glass mat is laid carefully over the mold and trimmed around the edges. The liquid polyester is then poured over the mat and the workers very carefully spread the resin smoothly over the mat and roll it down to prevent air spaces. Several layers of mat may be used, with careful rolling at each stage. When the mat is ready, a catalyst and actuator is applied to start the cure. The cure may proceed at room temperature with the proper accelerator, though it can be speeded up somewhat by a heat from infrared lamps or an oven. Once the gel stage is reached, the cure becomes rapid and exothermic, that is, it gives off heat which may carry the temperature to 500° F. In order to hold the mat securely against the mold, a transparent membrane made of a plastic film may be placed over the mat and then forced against it by vacuum pressure. However, careful rolling may do away with the need for such bag pressure. Complete cure may take an hour or more, before the mat can be released from the mold.

A variation of the hand lay-up to speed up the process is to use a twin-nozzle spray gun that simultaneously sprays resin and chopped fiber glass onto the mold. The main advantage of spray lay-up is that it reduces the scrap percentage since it can be sprayed to the form of the mold, while glass mat must be trimmed from standard sheets and the scrap is not reusable. Spray lay-up is said to be faster than hand lay-up, but this is controversial, since it requires special skills for the worker to spray an even coating, whereas the mat is already even and the worker merely rolls it tight against the mold.

A relatively recent development is filament winding, where glass filaments are passed through a resin bath and wound up on a rotating mold. Although such molds and fibers are more expensive, winding system produces structures of very high tensile strength—up to 150,000 pounds per square inch—and therefore suitable for pressure vessels or space probe vehicles.

(*e*) *Other Fabrication Processes:* Among the many other methods of fabricating plastics, thermoforming, blow molding, and foaming may be mentioned, as well as the use of liquid resins.

In thermoforming, plastic sheet is first heated by infrared lamps and then drawn over relatively inexpensive molds by vacuum pressure. The pressure comes from the normal atmosphere when the edges of the sheet are clamped against the edges of the mold to make a tight fit and the air inside is withdrawn. For long runs, thermoforming can be made into a continuous process by taking warm plastic sheet directly from the extruder.

In blow molding, a material like polyethylene is first extruded into a hollow mold to form a hollow bag called a "parison" and the bag is then blown up against the sides of the die to form hollow shapes such as plastic bottles. The flexibility of low-density polyethylene has permitted "squeeze" bottles to be designed to use this method.

In foaming, either a chemical reaction using urethanes or the release of carbon dioxide gas in regular resins such as polystyrene can expand the resin hollow cells. Such foamed plastics can be made either flexible, for use as seat cushions or rigid for use as insulation or boat flotation devices.

Liquid phenolics and other resins are very useful as bonding, laminating, and adhesive agents for industrial purposes. For example, plywood uses large quantities of such resins to bind the plies together, and the furniture industry uses special resin formulations extensively as adhesives. They are also used to bond friction materials such as brake linings and abrasive disks for grinding and polishing. As laminates, they form kitchen and bathroom counter tops, and table surfaces that are resistant to heat and moisture.

Plastics Industry Reference Notes

The plastics industry has been characterized by a remarkably high rate of growth and technological change. The growth rate in the unit volume of synthetic resins has been about 14.5 percent annually, from less than a billion pounds in 1946 to over six billion pounds in 1961. However, dollar volume of sales has lagged about 12 percent behind unit volume during this period, due to price decreases, and these have been particularly severe in the newer materials since about 1954. Data on output and price trends for the major raw materials and plastic resins are included in Exhibits 1 to 4.

Rapid growth has not only created opportunities for the chemical processors and plastics fabricators who were in the field before World War II, but has also attracted new companies from other fields. In the chemical industry, which has been expanding at an annual rate of 10 percent compared to 3 percent for the economy as a whole, payout periods for new ventures have usually been three to five years. A three-year payout means a return on investment after taxes of about 24 percent and a pretax profit margin on sales of about 47 percent, if a dollar in new plant generates one dollar in annual sales.

An example of the nature of competition among companies making plastics materials can be found in the history of styrene monomer. About 1,700 million pounds of styrene monomer were shipped in 1960, of which 835 million went to domestic polystyrene markets, 500 million to butadiene-styrene rubber, 95 million to water-based paints and paper coatings, 50 million to polyester resins for reinforced plastics, and 220 million to miscellaneous uses, including exported polystyrene. However, there was plant capacity in operation or under construction for over 2,400 million pounds by 1962–1963. Of this amount, Dow and Monsanto had 1,400 million pounds and Koppers and Union Carbide another 310 million. However, the oil companies had also entered the field. Shell, El Paso Gas, and Suntide had 350 million pounds of styrene capacity, and Cosden Oil (a subsidiary of Grace) and Sinclair Oil (associated with Koppers in this venture) had another 130 million between them. Moreover, two large users had integrated backward. Foster Grant, the largest injection molder of sunglasses had 150 million pounds and Borg-Warner's Marbon Division was constructing a 75-million pound plant.

As in many chemical fields, the economics of styrene supply and demand was closely interrelated with many other materials, such as benzene, ethylene, and butadiene. During the 1950's the oil companies had entered the benzene field in a large way through their catalytic reforming plants and even the Russians were offering benzene on the world market at discount prices. Similar price pressures on ethylene led to larger volume plant units to obtain processing efficiencies, and Dow expanded its large plants for this material in Texas, where several petrochemical empires were said to depend primarily on the great ethylene sources of supply, piped directly to customer plants. The butadiene field was almost entirely dominated by oil companies, using butane or butylene as their raw material, though Dow and Union Carbide had about 5 percent of the capacity using ethylene as their source. Moreover, by 1962 some promising new rubbers made of polybutadiene or other materials threatened to reduce the share of styrene taken by the rubber industry by about 15 percent.

The development of cross-industry competition was even more clear in other fields, such as the vinyls and polypropylene. In the vinyls, the tire companies had about one fourth the plant capacity, using acetylene as a source of material, while Dow, Monsanto, and Union Carbide had less than 40 percent, largely using ethylene. In the new field of polypropylene, Dow, Hercules, and Monsanto had only 35 percent of the capacity, while various oil companies had about 50 percent, and the remainder was accounted for by a tire company (Firestone), an Italian chemical company producing in West Virginia (Montecatini) and a large retail drug store chain (Rexall). Total polypropylene plant capacity for 1963 would be 585 million pounds, compared with expected demand in 1962 of 150 million.

The potential competition from oil companies can be noted by comparing their capital expenditures for refineries with their annual capital expenditures for petrochemical plants. In 1955, about $800 million was spent on refineries and about $500 million on petrochemicals. By 1960, the refinery expenditures had dropped to $500 million and petrochemical had increased to $700 million. By 1970, the figures were expected to be $800 million for refineries and $1,400 million for petrochemical plants.

In these notes we will first describe some of the major classes of plastics materials: phenolics, polystyrenes, polyolefins (polyethylene and polypropylene), polyvinyls, and polyesters. Then we will outline some of the ways of defining the properties of these materials. This will enable us to understand more of the methods by which properties are changed to enable plastics to compete with metals or with each other and to determine what companies at different stages in the process can do to improve these properties without major new capital investment.

MAJOR CLASSES OF PLASTICS MATERIALS

1. Phenolics

The phenolics are thermosetting resins made from phenol, a benzene derivative, and formaldehyde. It is the oldest synthetic plastic, developed in 1909 by Dr. Leo H. Baekeland, hence the trade name Bakelite used by the Union Carbide Plastics Company. As the dominant plastic for molding until the end of World War II, it has achieved a more stable position in the market than the faster growing newer postwar plastics. For example, phenolic prices increased slightly during the decade of the 1950's, a period in which many other plastics materials declined in price 40 percent or more.

As a compression or transfer molding material, the phenolics are low-cost (21 cents per pound for general purpose resin), dimensionally stable, (elongation less than 2 percent and a modulus of elasticity over 700,000 pounds per square inch) and resistant to chemicals and heat (distortion temperature about 250° F.). They have good dielectric strength for electrical insulation, even under humid conditions (dielectric constant of 5 at 60 cycles) and can be molded to close tolerance. However, they are attacked by caustics. They discolor or darken in sunlight, so are molded in dark colors only. Their electric qualities have led to uses in switch gear and wiring devices (39 million pounds in 1961), their heat insulation qualities to handles and knobs for appliance parts (30 million pounds), and their abrasion resistance to washing machine agitators and parts (12 million pounds). Although their use in automobiles, telephones, and bottle caps has been threatened by newer materials with more color range, their low cost has kept them strong in many markets. With fillers such as wood flour to reduce the cost, and compounds such as glass fibers, asbestos and other materials to increase heat resistance and impact strength, phenolic resins can be formulated to meet a very broad variety of different usage problems.

Phenolic resins can also be cast rather than molded. As castings, they can provide a very broad range of rich colors for decorative purposes. The casting process allows large-size parts to be made on low-cost dies, but the resin required for this purpose is relatively expensive and the curing time is long (from 6 to 48 hours).

More than two thirds of the phenolics are sold as liquid resins for industrial purposes such as adhesives for plywood and furniture, bonding material for abrasive particles and insulating material, laminates and protective coatings. Laminates used for printed circuits, terminal boards, and other electric parts have been affected by the miniaturization trend, which requires smaller parts with improved qualities of flame retardation and heat resistance. Decorative laminates for counter and table tops and wall surfacing took more than 60 million pounds in 1961. The plywood market depends largely on new housing starts. In 1961 the prices of fir plywood had reached a postwar low and there was overcapacity in the industry. Abrasives, used for grinding wheels, depend upon activity in the steel industry. Friction materials, used for brake linings, depend upon automotive sales and the automotive brake replacement market. Phenolics are used with fibrous glass insulation in the construction industry.

2. Polystyrenes

Between 1947 and 1961 polystyrene, a thermoplastic material derived from benzene and ethylene, increased its market from 100 million pounds per year to a million pounds. Since polystyrene resin is clear and colorless, it can be compounded in a broad range of bright colors and quickly injection molded or extruded. It is chemically resistant, but it is subject to heat distortion at temperatures of 170° F. and has low impact strength. During the decade of the 1950's, much effort was exerted to develop heat-resistant and high impact formulations which would more closely approach the qualities of thermosetting compounds. The most successful formulations were developed by polymerizing or compounding styrene together with butadiene rubber and/or acrylonitrile. Such formulations were able to increase impact strength from 0.3 to 6.0 (Izod test) and elevate the heat distortion temperature above 210 F., though at the loss of some other properties.

Molding and extrusion, which accounts for about 77 percent of the styrene market, is largely devoted to packaging (135 million pounds), refrigerators and air conditioners (90 million), other appliances (70 million), toys (90 million), and housewares (75 million). Packaging uses such as food containers have grown to 135 million pounds in 1961 and are largely disposable items that require continual production. Refrigerators may use 30 pounds of impact polystyrene per unit (240 ounces for component parts and 240 ounces for the inner liner). The food cabinet liner could also be made of polystyrene, but porcelain takes about 96 percent of the market. Freezers use 10 pounds of polystyrene per unit and air conditioners also take large quantities. Toys and houseware markets have been maintained by the use of the better grade of styrene compounds.

3. Polyolefins

The polyolefins attained in six years the market volume that the styrenes reached after fourteen, and in 1961 surpassed them by more than 400 million pounds. The polyolefins are thermoplastic compounds, consisting of low-density polyethylene (1100 million pounds in 1961), high-density linear polyethylene (300 million pounds), and polypropylene (100 million pounds).

A polyethylene molecule is made of thousands of carbon atoms, each with two hydrogen atoms attached. Conventional polyethylene is a material with low density (below 0.925) and a flexible structure resulting from the branching of carbon atoms along the main line. It is synthesized at high temperatures and very high pressures, up to 30,000 pounds per square inch. In the 1950's, Karl Ziegler developed a new process for polymerizing ethylene with catalysts at low pressures. The resulting molecule exhibits little branching, and the linear chains tend to crystallize in parallel and therefore are structurally rigid and more dense (about 0.941). Such crystallization provides an opportunity to polymerize other olefins stereospecifically. Polypropylene was developed commercially because low-cost propylene was available and the resulting resin had excellent properties of heat and chemical resistance, dimensional stability, light weight and flexural life.

Injection molding, largely housewares and toys, account for only 15 percent of the polyolefin market, but blow molding, largely for bottles, takes another 10 percent. The flexibility of low-density polyethylene enabled "squeeze" bottles to be designed, while the high-density polyethylene allowed rigid but "unbreakable" bottles for detergents and other household articles to replace glass. About three fourths of the film and sheeting uses are for packaging, such as wrapping bread and for laundry and dry cleaning bags. In wire coatings, pipe, and packaging, polyethylene competes with other plastics such as the vinyls as well as older materials such as rubber coating, copper and galvanized pipe, and waxed paper and cellophane wrapping.

4. Vinyls

The vinyls are thermoplastic resins derived from acetylene. Almost 80 percent of the 1,200 million pounds used in 1961 were polyvinyl chloride, the remaining materials being polyvinyl acetate, polyvinyl acetals, and polyvinylidene chloride ("saran").

Vinyl chloride can be polymerized by several methods, each process yielding a resin with different properties. Suspension polymerization, using high purity water, and a peroxide catalyst under pressure, can yield various types of general purpose resin. Emulsion polymerization yields resin particles that are less pure, but of very fine size (about one micron), which can be used as dispersion resins to make plastisols. Solution polymerization combines vinyl chloride and vinyl acetate to yield a pure and clear resin used in phonograph records, and for coating and flooring.

Vinyl resin is a brittle material and must, therefore, be compounded with large amounts of a plasticizer such as dioctyl phthalate to make the resin flexible. General purpose resins of medium particle size (about 100 microns) can be calendered with plasticizer at room temperature to produce film, sheeting, and coatings. The larger particles absorb plasticizer only when heated and are, therefore, heated and extruded to form materials with higher strength properties, such as for pipe uses. The small one-micron particles have a high surface to volume ratio and thus can be dispersed in plasticizer without being dissolved by the plasticizer at room temperature. These dispersion resins can be easily handled as liquids. They are, therefore, shaped in low-cost molds whose heated surfaces fuse the liquid plastisol without pressure, through slush, dip, or rotational molding. If little plasticizer is used with somewhat larger particles (50 microns), rigid plastisol can be made, a material with a hard, high-gloss surface.

Only one third of the polyvinyl chloride produced is molded or extruded. About 100 million pounds of it is used for wire coating, 55 million pounds for phonograph records, 55 million pounds for profiles such as automotive window edging, 55 million pounds as dispersion resins for plastisols and for injection molding, rigidisols, and 35 million for pipe and other shapes.

Polyvinyl acetate is used largely as an emulsion which mixes readily with water and is used in architectural paints, adhesives, sealers, fabric finishers, and paper coatings. As a paint vehicle, polyvinyl acetate requires very fine particle size (0.3 micron) to disperse the pigments. It is low-cost and quick drying. As adhesives, larger particles are needed for packaging uses. Polyvinyl acetate is also used to make polyvinyl butyral, the inside layer in safety glass "sandwiches."

5. *Polyesters*

The polyesters are thermosetting resins which are combined with glass fibers or other materials to form reinforced plastics. An ester is an organic salt, resulting from the combination of an acid and an alcohol. The polyesters used for reinforced plastics are unsaturated condensation products of such acids as maleic anhydride with alcohols such as ethylene glycol or propylene glycol. They are shipped as liquids containing styrene monomer, which can link with the unsaturated resin bonds when cured. An inhibitor such as hydroquinone is used to prevent premature curing. The cure is generally rapid and needs little or no heat. At first the material gels, then the final stage takes place rapidly, giving off heat above 400° F. Special types of anhydride can be used to permit larger molecules or polymer, with greater strength and chemical resistance. Also, glass fibers can be used in different forms to increase strength. For example, a glass mat with 65 percent resin content gives a tensile strength of 12,500 pounds per square inch, but strength can be increased to 47,500 p.s.i. using 12-ply glass cloth with 40 percent resin.

In 1961, the polyesters and the epoxies together had a market of about 260 million pounds, two thirds of which was due to polyester. The principal markets were in construction materials (52 million pounds), boats (48 million), transportation housings (48 million), and aircraft and missile parts (30 million).

Alkyd paint resins and polyurethane foams are different materials derived from saturated polyesters. The alkyds, polyesters produced from phthalic anhydride, accounted for 575 million pounds of resin in 1961, and they have taken an increased share of the paint market each year for over a decade. Although there are many means of foaming plastics, one widespread process combines saturated polyesters with isocyanates for form polymer linkages that give off carbon dioxide which makes the plastic into a foam. Flexible foams sold 100 million pounds in 1961, including 50 million pounds for furniture cushions, and 20 million for automotive and truck seatings. Rigid foams were being used in larger quantities for insulation in refrigerators and transportation housings and for flotation members in reinforced plastics boats.

6. *Other Plastics*

Although there are many other types of plastics, the principal ones are the ureas and the melamines (374 million pounds in 1961), the cellulosics (146 million pounds), the acrylics, and three "engineered" plastics—nylon, acetal, and polycarbonate.

The ureas and melamines are similar thermosetting resins, of which about 120 million pounds are compression molded, largely for dinner ware. They are also excellent industrial resins, sold as liquids for bonding and adhesive agents in making plywood and laminates, in textile treating to impart wrinkle resistance, and in paper treating to improve wet strength.

The cellulosics are thermoplastic resins derived from cotton linters. They are used largely for injection molding (90 million pounds) and for vacuum formed displays and transparent packaging.

The acrylics are thermoplastic resins with excellent light-transmission properties. They are used in large outdoor signs, in lighting fixtures, as school roof skylights, aircraft canopies, indoor lighting fixtures, automotive tail lights, and appliance trim and nameplates.

Nylon, acetal, and polycarbonate are high-cost thermoplastic resins with excellent mechanical and other properties. One type of nylon, for example, is resistant to heat up to 330° F., and can go to 400° with a glass fiber filler. Acetal has great dimensional stability, yet is springy and able to withstand high pressures and corrosion. Polycarbonates can be made transparent, yet have excellent mechanical and electrical properties.

PROPERTIES OF PLASTICS

It should be clear by now that plastics constitute a very wide variety of materials that can be processed and fabricated in a great many ways. In order, therefore, to determine the market potential of a particular material or process, it is necessary to define accurately the properties of the material, to understand its possibilities and limitations.

Test Procedures

In order to understand the value of different materials, we should study the engineering test procedures that have been developed to determine the mechanical, electrical, and other properties of materials under specified conditions.

Tensile Strength is the force in pounds per square inch of material perpendicular to the direction of pull, required to pull a material to its breaking or deformation point. The values range from under 3,000 p.s.i. for low-density polyethylene and some vinyls, to 11,000 p.s.i. for nylon 6, to more than 50,000 p.s.i. for glass-reinforced thermosets.

Elongation is the percent of stretch that a material will exhibit before break or deformation. Some materials, like the phenolics and styrenes, yield little before break, while others, like polypropylene, can be stretched many times their length before deformation.

Modulus of Elasticity is the force in pounds per square inch, required to stretch a material a specified unit of its length, usually taken as 0.1 percent elongation. Low-density polyethylene can be stretched by 25,000 p.s.i., while melamine requires 1,300,000 p.s.i., glass-filled phenolic 3,-300,000 p.s.i., fir wood 1,900,000 and steel 31,-000,000 p.s.i.

Compressive Strength is a measure of structural rigidity, in pounds per square inch.

Flexural Strength measures the force required to bend a material to rupture point, and is often higher than tensile strength because plastics have hard outer skins.

Impact Strength is measured in a special apparatus by the Izod test, in which a bar of the material is deliberately notched to reduce the force required to break the piece by concentrating the stress at the notches. The force, in foot pounds per inch of notch for a ½-inch square bar, ranges from less than 1 for low-impact materials, to more than 2 or 3 for higher impact materials.

Heat Distortion Temperature ranges from about 110° F. for low-density polyethylene to several hundred degrees for the thermosets or for nylon.

Specific Gravity is a measure of weight compared to an equal volume of water. The lightest weight plastic is polypropylene with a specific gravity of .905. The vinyls run about 1.4, and glass fibers can bring the figure for reinforced plastics up above 2.0. Since plastics resins are priced on a per pound basis, the specific gravity helps determine how much material a pound contains. It varies from less than 15 cubic inches per pound for some reinforced plastics to 30 cubic inches for polypropylene.

Volume Resistivity is the electrical resistance of the material, in ohms, measured as though the material were a conductor.

Dielectric Strength is the electric potential in volts per mil for a 1/8-inch thick material which would be necessary to cause failure of the dielectric material.

Dielectric Constant is the ratio of the capacity of a condenser made with the material to the capacity of a condenser with air as the dielectric.

Creep is the strength of a material kept under constant load for a long time.

Exhibits 5 and 6 summarize the properties of selected materials.

CONDITIONS OF USE

The mechanical and electrical properties described, and many others, have been determined for all of the common plastics materials in commercial use, and these test values have been increasingly used in descriptive sales data. For example, strength, weight, and price can be related for materials used in the structural walls of a component part. Thus, stainless steel, with compressive strength of 150,000 pounds per square inch and specific gravity of 7.85, can be compared to phenolic molded with wood flour, with compressive strength of 29,000 and specific gravity of 1.36:

	Comp. Strength	*Specific Gravity*	*Strength to Weight*	*S/W Ratio*
Phenolic	29,000	1.36	21,000	110.5
Stain. Steel	150,000	7.85	19,000	100.0

The specific gravity can be converted to pounds per 100 cubic inches through known conversion tables:

	Specific Gravity	*Lbs. per 100 Cu. Inches*	*Lbs. for Equal Strength*	*Cubic In. for Equal Strength*
Phenolic	1.36	4.91	25.38	517
Stain. Steel	7.85	28.35	28.35	100

The price per pound can be used to determine the cost per 100 cubic inches, and then the rough cost per required volume of material:

	Price per Cu. Inch	*Cost per 100 Cu. Inches*	*Cost for Equal Strength*
Phenolic	22¢	$ 1.08	$ 5.58
Stain. Steel	47¢	13.32	13.32

Since plastics generally cost *more* per pound than the metals they are trying to replace, their low specific gravities have been greatly emphasized in promotional campaigns to demonstrate the large volume that one pound can buy, often without equal emphasis on the lower strength properties which mean that more volume is usually required. For example, the phenolic described above would require 5.2 times the thickness of a sheet of steel to give equal strength for the same area, though it would still weigh about 11 percent less than the steel part.

The test properties of materials, however, are usually measured at room temperature and atmospheric pressure. They can only begin to describe the way the material will respond under actual conditions of use. For example, polystyrene liners used in refrigerators and freezers must be able to maintain their strength properties at continual exposure to low temperatures; parts used for toasters or motor housings must withstand high temperatures without loss of tensile strength or insulating protection. Films used for food packaging must be relatively impermeable to gases, flexible at refrigeration temperatures, and able to withstand the acids found in various foods. Parts used on boats must be able to withstand weathering, salt spray, exposure to ultraviolet light, and so on.

Often the test conditions do not duplicate certain conditions of use. For example, the Izod impact test is made by striking the material at a velocity of about 11 feet per second. However, a material that withstands 2-foot pounds of impact at that velocity might break down under the same impact delivered at a higher velocity. Plastic used in a football helmet may receive impact at 80 feet per second, and a batted baseball delivers its impact at several hundred feet per second. For these reasons, the plastics industry has had to develop an engineering knowledge of considerable detail in order to apply plastics to more varied products without putting in so much extra safety factor that the price becomes excessively high. In fact, such engineering knowledge is the key to reliable design at competitive cost, and therefore the daily business problem of the plastics fabricators, supplemented by whatever help the materials producers can give them. Exhibits 7 and 8 indicate the price, volume, and strength relationships of selected plastics and metals.

Exhibits 9 and 11 indicate trends in some of the fabrication methods and the competition between methods of forming metals and plastics.

METHODS OF IMPROVING MATERIALS PROPERTIES

At each stage of the plastics process, the manufacturer has an opportunity to improve his product in competition with other materials. The extent and nature of the improvement depends on the nature of the process, the size of the unit, and the needs of his customers. We will try to outline, from one stage to the next, what means are available to a plastics company to meet technological change and price competition by improving his product.

Basic Chemical Producers

At the stage of the basic chemicals, such as benzene or ethylene, much of the development in recent years has depended on the technology and economics of petroleum and natural gas refining. Plastics have generally required higher purity materials than rubber or chemicals and improved process controls, as the refineries have generally outpaced coke oven technology in the steel industry, to which these materials are only minor by-products. Furthermore, the rapid expansion of related fields, such as the extraordinary success of the synthetic rubber program during World War II and the development of synthetic detergents and new fertilizers, has helped provide the market base for investment.

Monomer Producers

New plastic monomers and the allied technology for their development has required large sums for research and development. In the case of nylon, the patents and licensing fees enabled the du Pont company to recover its investment in a few years. However, when du Pont introduced its new acetal resin "Delrin" in the late 1950's the Celanese company soon brought out a competing resin called "Celcon" which was claimed to use a somewhat different process and therefore not require a Delrin license. The matter was brought into the courts. Similarly, the uncertain patent status of polycarbonate resin tended to limit its production to General Electric and Mobay Chemical. However, there were several breakthroughs in the monomer field during the 1950's which resulted in major new markets, such as the Ziegler low-pressure method for rigid polyethylene and polypropylene and the variants on nylon made by different processes.

Polymerizers

At the polymer stage, there are various means of changing the resin properties. In the case of vinyls, the different polymerization processes yield different size particles and therefore quite different resins for extrusion and rotational casting. For other plastics, such as styrenes, new properties have been obtained by co-polymerizing the monomer with other materials, such as acrylonitrile and butadiene. In fact, the acrylonitrile-butadiene-styrene polymer has been so successful that it has been regarded as a new type of plastic, called ABS. Most companies offer a dozen or more formulations in basic molding resins, depending upon the properties required, such as heat, resistance, impact resistance, easy flow through the die, and corrosion resistance. For example, long playing phonograph records require easy flow during molding to obtain high fidelity in the microgrooves, so a co-polymer of polyvinyl acetate and polyvinyl chloride is used.

One important field for special formulations has been in the markets for liquid industrial resins. The companies that provide resins for textiles and paper treating, for bonding and adhesive agents, for laminates and so on, do a great deal of work to provide special formulations suited to the particular industrial customer. Such resins are usually sold on the basis of test samples and are made up in batches to special order.

Compounding and Treating

In turning the basic resin into a final material, various compounds and treating methods are used. The most obvious compound requirement is color, and a wide variety of pigments are available for a crystal material like polystyrene, though the compounding requires careful control to ensure color matching, particularly for appliances such as refrigerators or vacuum cleaners requiring interchangeable parts over long runs. The vinyl resins require plasticizers to make them less brittle, as we have seen, and different types and quantities of plasticizer are used for different properties. Wood flour can be used with phenolics to extend the material and obtain some strength improvement. Carbon black is used to prevent the discoloration of polystyrene in the sunlight.

One of the most useful resin additives is fibrous glass, which costs 37 cents per pound in roving form and 52 cents per pound as mat. Glass improves heat resistance, flexural strength, and impact strength, though it may interfere with some other properties. However, glass is heavy and increases the specific gravity of plastics, so one company (Sohio) has developed microglass balloons which provide many of the desired strength properties without sacrificing light weight.

After compounding, plastics materials can be treated externally, as by annealing or irradiation. One process is to orient film by heating and stretching it, and then allow it to shrink gradually as it cools. Such processes have improved the strength of film and sheeting, and also have permitted one company to make "shrink-tube," a product which can be used as tight jacket casing upon reheating in the customer's plant.

Problems of the Plastics Fabricator

The great variety of materials and processes has given the plastics fabricators considerable opportunities to enter many different kinds of end markets. Perhaps one of the most difficult problems facing the fabricator is to determine what kind of a business he should be in. Should he concentrate on his fabricating process and produce to custom order, or should he design proprietary products and enter the end markets himself? To what degree should he specialize in one type of fabrication process or product type? How flexible should he be to new markets and new processes?

Some of the most successful product applications have come about from combining imagination with a thorough knowledge of the materials properties. For example, nylon is self-lubricating, so it can be used to make gears in machines with difficult access conditions for oiling. Acetal is resilient, so it can be used for bottle cap liners forced past the internal threads without breaking. Propylene has a remarkably high flex life, so a box shape can be molded in one piece, with the thin wall between cover and holder providing a reliable integral hinge. Foams can be made in a range of densities. One use is to provide the proper shock protection as guards inside shipping containers. Reinforced plastics can be made into large complex shapes used for boat hulls or for rocket engine enclosures.

Two unusual properties of certain plastics, ablation and low atomic weight, illustrate some of the market opportunities available to an imaginative designer. Ablation is the process of decomposition under heat, in which certain reinforced plastics release gases that leave a char zone which provides a heat barrier for the virgin material underneath, until the char breaks off and the next layer decomposes. It is analogous to the chalking action of certain paints, which warp, but do not crack. As a result, certain phenolic-asbestos plastics can provide heat barriers of 2,000° F. for space vehicles. Another example is the observation that a high concentration of light-weight atoms blunts the energy of fast-moving neutrons. Since polyethylene has two light-weight hydrogen atoms for each carbon atom, it can act as a neutron barrier in places where its low weight offsets its higher cost. As a result, polyethylene, with 1 to 6 percent boron filler, can be used as radiation shielding for nuclear-powered ships.

As the custom fabrication business has become more competitive, the fabricators have tended to seek specialty markets where they can concentrate their skills and enter the end markets. For example, Foster Grant developed the resources necessary to integrate backward into styrene monomer by first entering the market for sunglasses and designing such a broad and highly styled line that it dominated this consumer market. Some companies develop specialties in industrial components or military products, some make parts for the shoe industry or the appliance field, others enter the final product field and make an entire line of assembled toys or boats. For most of them, however, there is the continual question to face as to whether they should concentrate on the fabrication process and let others design and market the products, or whether they should themselves design, assemble, and market the end product.

Exhibits 10, 12, and 13 indicate some of the operating and financial characteristics of the materials producers and the plastics fabricators.

1. PLASTICS INDUSTRY

1a. Annual Production of Major Plastics Chemicals

(Millions of Pounds)

	Benzene*	Ethylene	Styrene	Butadiene	GR-S Rubber	Phenol
1948	-	383	377	661		297
49	-	1,151	390	494		224
50	73	NA	539	610		312
1951	234	NA	707	1,222	1,561	388
52	255	1,809	700	1,106	1,394	338
53	462	2,136	798	1,152	1,415	382
54	674	2,345	703	809	973	417
55	723	3,048	1,014	1,411	1,635	516
1956	818	3,602	1,176	1,502	1,798	549
57	852	3,947	1,166	1,542	1,839	556
58	1,042	4,149	1,224	1,443	1,736	506
59	1,528	5,099	1,571	1,831	2,210	692
60	2,278	5,448	1,742	1,917	2,263	774
1961 est.			NA	1,866		768
62 est.			1,875	2,000		802

*Petroleum derived, Benzene does not include motor grade product.

1b. Raw Materials Prices

(Cents per Pound in Tank Car Lots)

	Benzene	Ethylene	Styrene Monomer Polymer Grade	Styrene Monomer Rubber Grade	Butadiene	Phenol 8-10% Cresol	Formaldehyde 12-15% Methanol	Vinyl Acetate Monomer
1947	2.3	5.0	9		8.0	10.5	4.0	14.0
48	2.9	6.0	10		8.0	12.0	3.7	15.0
49	3.0	6.0	15		9.0	13.5	3.7	15.0
50	5.1	NA	15		8.3	11.0	3.7	15.0
1951	6.5	NA	18		14.8	16.7	4.5	18.0
52	6.7	NA	21.0	NA	12.0	17.3	4.2	19.8
53	7.0	5.0	21.0	NA	14.0	17.0	4.2	19.8
54	6.5	4.7	21.0	18.0	15.0	16.0	4.2	16.5
55	5.9	4.7	21.0	18.0	15.0	15.0	4.0	16.5
1956	6.0	5.0	21.5	16.5	15.0	16.0	4.2	16.5
57	5.1	4.7	20.5	16.0	14.8	16.0	4.8	17.0
58	4.4	4.7	16.0	12.7	14.6	16.0	4.8	17.5
59	4.0	4.7	14.5	12.7	14.5	15.5	4.1	17.5
60	4.2	4.7	14.5	12.7	13.6	14.8	4.3	17.5
1961	4.2	4.7	14.5*	12.5*	12.8	14.8	4.3	15.6
62	4.1	5.0	12.8	10.8	12.8	13.0	4.3	15.6

*Prices escalated for each calendar year on the basis of the cost of benzene in the range of 31¢ to 34¢ per gallon and petroleum refining labor.

Source: Oil, Paint, and Drug Reporter.

2. PLASTICS INDUSTRY

Sales of Selected Resins, 1945 to 1962
(In Millions)

	Phenolics			Polystyrene			Polyethylene		
	Prod. Lbs.	Sales Lbs.	Value	Prod. Lbs.	Sales Lbs.	Value	Prod. Lbs.	Sales Lbs.	Value
1945	101	100	$ 36.2	22	21	$ 6.1			
1946	115	113	35.9	73	68	18.			
47	284	271	85.6	106	99	26.6			
48	377	327	77.3	165	155	43.0			
49	291	249	57.0	240	228	61.9			
50	451	390	90.5	355	355	100.9			
1951	474	408	110.5	394	356	118.0			
52	393	345	92.5	425	392	133.2			
53	485	426	114.3	508	468	159.2	NA	137	NA
54	434	392	100.8	481	458	151.2	NA	207	NA
55	563	483	127.0	619	572	180.7	402	350	$ 138.3
1956	563	497	129.5	680	603	191.4	566	514	187.7
57	532	473	128.8	680	653	193.8	708	662	214.6
58	488	440	116.6	763	724	201.2	865	845	270.1
59	625	555	154.2	977	906	254.7	1,195	1,116	354.9
60	651	531	146.6	1,062	980	271.7	1,337	1,195	342.5
61	665	544	149.4	1,145	1,079	281.8	1,606	1,582	387.8
1962 (Est.)	NA	670*	NA	NA	1,215	NA	NA	1,945	NA

	Vinyl			Urea-Melamine			All Synthetics		
1945	123	111	47.0	74	73	21.3	818	762	269.0
1946	156	148	57.7	91	90	27.0	1,025	966	339.2
47	177	161	68.1	112	105	35.1	1,252	1,135	431.3
48	218	195	80.1	150	140	43.1	1,486	1,244	372.5
49	268	253	106.7	134	129	38.5	1,491	1,261	384.5
50	381	361	144.1	219	211	59.0	2,151	1,876	570.9
1951	476	388	165.3	237	214	64.4	2,441	2,024	710.9
52	420	400	173.6	228	221	64.3	2,333	2,045	727.2
53	516	464	199.4	257	238	74.9	2,777	2,372	837.5
54	524	514	210.7	265	245	73.7	2,828	2,497	856.5
55	703	664	254.2	328	300	91.7	3,739	3,219	1,077.8
1956	760	722	248.4	342	311	92.0	3,977	3,465	1,142.4
57	887	797	266.7	349	322	98.3	4,340	3,789	1,234.1
58	869	829	266.6	349	326	96.9	4,518	4,057	1,274.9
59	1,166	1,102	340.2	424	387	115.7	5,865	5,170	1,640.1
60	1,203	1,130	329.1	399	363	105.5	6,143	5,347	1,653.0
61	1,260	1,212	306.7	440	384	107.4	6,710	5,989	1,710.9
							NA		
1962 (Est.)	NA	1,483	NA	NA	420	NA	NA	7,426	NA

*Figures for 1962 estimated by Modern Plastics Magazine, January, 1963. Volume for phenolics is higher than Tariff Commission figures, due to inclusion of captive plant production.
Source: U.S. Tariff Commission, "Synthetic Organic Chemicals."

3. PLASTICS INDUSTRY

Major Uses of Selected Plastics
(In Millions of Pounds)

Phenolics

	1957	1958	1959	1960	1961	1962
Mold	184	168	229	207	214	225
Laminate	74	63	76	72	79	88
Abrasive	17	12	17	15	17	17
Friction	16	13	17	22	20	24
Insulation	53	45	52	84	87	80
Plywood	47	52	62	71	64	70
Other bondings . .	51	40	64	71	82	80
Coating	50	34	36	33	33	35
Other.	40	42	51	50	49	51
Total.	532	469	604	625	645	670

Polystyrene

	1957	1958	1959	1960	1961	1962
Mold and Extrude	429	476	686	737	842	915
General purpose			286	300	313	815
Other			310	312	394	
Export			90	125	135	100
Coatings.	85	104	119	123	123	125
Other Resins. . . .	133	144	100	120	113	175
Total.	647	724	905	980	1,078	1,215

Polyethylene

	1957	1958	1959	1960	1961	1962
Injection mold. . .	80	120	175	180	255	310
Film and sheet . .	205	245	335	360	495	560
Blow mold bottles	20	28	30	65	130	170
Other blow mold	---	---	8	15	20	30
Wire and cable . .	75	87	105	112	125	145
Pipe, etc.	50	55	55	60	75	80
Coatings	35	40	51	52	95	145
Export.	190	242	305	330	358	380
Other.	7	38	52	21	29	125
Total.	652	855	1,116	1,195	1,582	1,945

Vinyl

	1957	1958	1959	1960	1961	1962
Mold or Extrude .	220	224	306	300	310	403
Film	78	74	90	98	90	85
Sheet.	80	74	95	112	147	165
Fabric.	55	55	77	67	62	75
Paper	10	9	11	12	10	12
Floor.	82	116	155	160	185	230
Coating	32	27	31	39	37	50
Other.	78	70	109	116	125	138
Total.	635	649	874	904	966	1,158

Source: U.S. Tariff Commission, as presented in Modern Plastics, January, 1963. Figures for phenolics include captive plant production.

4. PLASTICS INDUSTRY

Prices of Selected Plastics
(Cents per Pound)

	Phenolic	Polystyrene				Polyethylene		Poly-	Mela-			Poly-	Fiber Glass	
	G. P.	G. P.	Impact	Acrylo	ABS	Low	High	propyl	mine	Nylon	PVC	ester Epoxy	Roving	Chopped Mat
1946	15.5	26	-	-	-	52	-	-	-	-	33	-	-	-
1947	16.5	25	-	-	-	47	-	-	45	-	33	-	-	-
1948	17.2	27	-	-	-	43	-	-	48	-	34	-	-	-
1949	16.7	25.5	38.0	-	-	43	-	-	48	-	34	-	-	-
1950	19.7	30.5	39.5	-	-	45	-	-	45	-	36	-	-	-
1951	19.7	32.5	41.5	-	-	48	-	-	45	-	38	45	45	58
1952	19.7	32.5	41.0	-	-	47	-	-	45	-	38	42	40	57
1953	19.1	32.5	34.0	-	-	47	-	-	45	-	38	39	40	57
1954	18.7	30.5	33.0	-	70	41	-	-	45	-	37	36	40	57
1955	19.2	29.5	31.5	41.0	65	41	-	-	45	143.5	35	34	40	57
1956	20.2	27.5	32.0	41.0	65	41	-	-	45	133	32	34	40	57
1957	21.2	26.0	32.0	40.5	58	35	47	65	47	118	30	34	40	57
1958	19.2	24.3	32.0	40.5	58	35	43	49	47	118	23.5	34	40	57
1959	19.2	21.5	28.5	40.5	58	32.5	35	42	47	118	23.5	33	40	57
1960	21.0	17.5	28.5	40.5	49	26.0	35	42	37	98	18.5	33	40	52
1961	21.0	18.0	27.5	39.5	42	24.8	32	42	47	98	16.0	30	37	52
1962	20.5	18.0	27.5	25.0	38	22.5	35	38	NA	99	15.0	NA	NA	NA

Source: Modern Plastics, January, 1963 and preceding years.

5. PLASTICS INDUSTRY

5a. Properties of Selected Materials

Material	Price per Lb.	Spec. Grav.	Compress. Strength
Aluminum Sheet . .	46¢	2.70	40,000
Brass Sheet.	52	8.50	(NA)
Copper Sheet	46	8.90	(NA)
Glass Fibers	40	2.50	250,000
Grey Iron Castings	19	7.60	40,000
Leather Sole	58	0.94	(NA)
Gypsum Plaster . .	9	1.80	(NA)
Hard Rubber Sheets	27	1.50	10,000
Carbon Steel Strip.	7	7.70	60,000
Stainless Steel Strip	46	7.78	150,000
Fir Boards	3	0.45	(NA)

5b. Conversion Table for Specific Gravity

Spec. Grav.	Lbs. per 100 Cu. In.	Spec. Grav.	Lbs. per 100 Cu. In.
0.90	3.25	1.50	5.42
0.95	3.43	1.60	5.78
1.00	3.61	1.70	6.14
1.05	3.79	1.80	6.50
1.10	3.97	1.90	6.86
1.15	4.15	2.00	7.22
1.20	4.33	3.00	10.83
1.25	4.51	4.00	14.44
1.30	4.69	5.00	18.05
1.35	4.87	6.00	21.66
1.40	5.05	7.00	25.27

5c. Prices of Selected Grades of Phenolic Resins

Phenolic Resin Type	1950	1953	1956	1959	1962
Resin solution for making laminates	26¢	26¢	22¢	22¢	19 3/4¢
Liquid resin for various uses.	32¢	32¢	29 1/2¢	30 1/2¢	30 1/4¢
Liquid resin for use in grinding wheels	34¢	34¢	34¢	35¢	35 1/4¢
Liquid resin for use in adhesives	34¢	34¢	33¢	34¢	34 1/4¢
Liquid resin for use in brake linings.	31¢	31¢	32¢	32 1/2¢	32 1/4¢
Resin solution for making laminates	22 1/2¢	22 1/2¢	24 1/2¢	20 1/2¢	20 1/4¢
Water soluble resin for use in mineral wool batts	21¢	21¢	19 1/2¢	19 1/2¢	19 1/4¢
Resin solution for use in brake linings.	35 1/2¢	35 1/2¢	32 1/2¢	34¢	34 1/2¢
Resin solution for making laminates	23 1/2¢	23 1/2¢	24¢	23 1/2¢	23 1/4¢
Liquid resin for paper impregnation	22 1/2¢	22 1/2¢	22 1/2¢	22¢	21 3/4¢

Source: Durez Company.

6. PLASTICS INDUSTRY

Properties of Plastics

A. Properties of Selected Plactics

Plastic	Tensile Strength p.s.i.	Elongation %	Modular Elast. 10^5 p.s.i.	Compress Strength p.s.i.	Flexural Strength p.s.i.	Impact Strength ft. lb/in	Heat Distortion °F.	Specific Gravity	Price per Lb. $
Phenolic*	7,500	1.3	8.7	20,000	13,500	0.29	250	1.36	.21
Melamine	10,000	0.8	13.0	34,000	13,000	0.29	400	1.49	.47
Polyethylene:									
Low Density	1,600	250.	0.25	-	-	16.0	113	0.92	.25
High Density	4,300	55.	1.2	2,400	1,400	7.0	160	0.96	.32
Polypropylene	5,000	470.	1.6	9,200	-	1.3	220	0.90	.42
Polystyrene	7,000	1.7	4.5	13,700	11,300	0.32	172	1.05	.18
Vinyl Chloride	7,000	20.	4.7	10,500	13,000	10.0	147	1.30	.16
Nylon 6/6	9,500	85.	3.3	10,100	10,900	1.0	330	1.12	.98
Acetal	9,400	27.	3.9	18,000	13,000	2.5	327	1.43	.65

B. Properties of Phenolics with Various Fillers

Filler	Tensile	Elong.	Modular	Compress	Flexural	Impact	Heat	Gravity	Price
None	7,500	1.3	8.7	20,000	13,500	0.29	250	1.27	.21
Wood Flour	7,700	0.6	12.0	29,000	10,200	0.42	300	1.36	
Asbestos	6,500	0.3	20.0	25,000	11,000	1.85	450	1.76	
Mica	6,500	0.3	40.0	20,000	10,000	0.34	290	1.79	
Glass Fiber	7,500	0.2	33.0	21,500	35,000	30.0	600	1.85	

C. Properties of Polystyrenes of Various Types

Type	Tensile	Elong.	Modular	Compress	Flexural	Impact	Heat	Gravity	Price
General purpose	7,000	1.7	4.5	13,700	11,300	0.32	172	1.05	.18
Impact	4,400	40.	3.2	6,500	7,500	5.3	174	1.04	.27
Heat Resistant	9,200	1.9	5.0	13,700	13,500	0.47	207	1.08	
Glass Fibers	13,000	1.0	11.5	15,500	17,000	3.2	218	1.29	
Acrylonitrile	10,700	2.5	4.8	15,500	16,500	0.42	197	1.09	.39
ABS**	5,800	75.	2.5	6,700	8,600	6.0	195	1.10	.42

*With cellulose filler.
**Styrene with acrylonitrile and butadiene.
Source: Modern Plastics Encyclopedia, 1962.

7. PLASTICS INDUSTRY

Cost of Plastics in Comparison with Other Materials

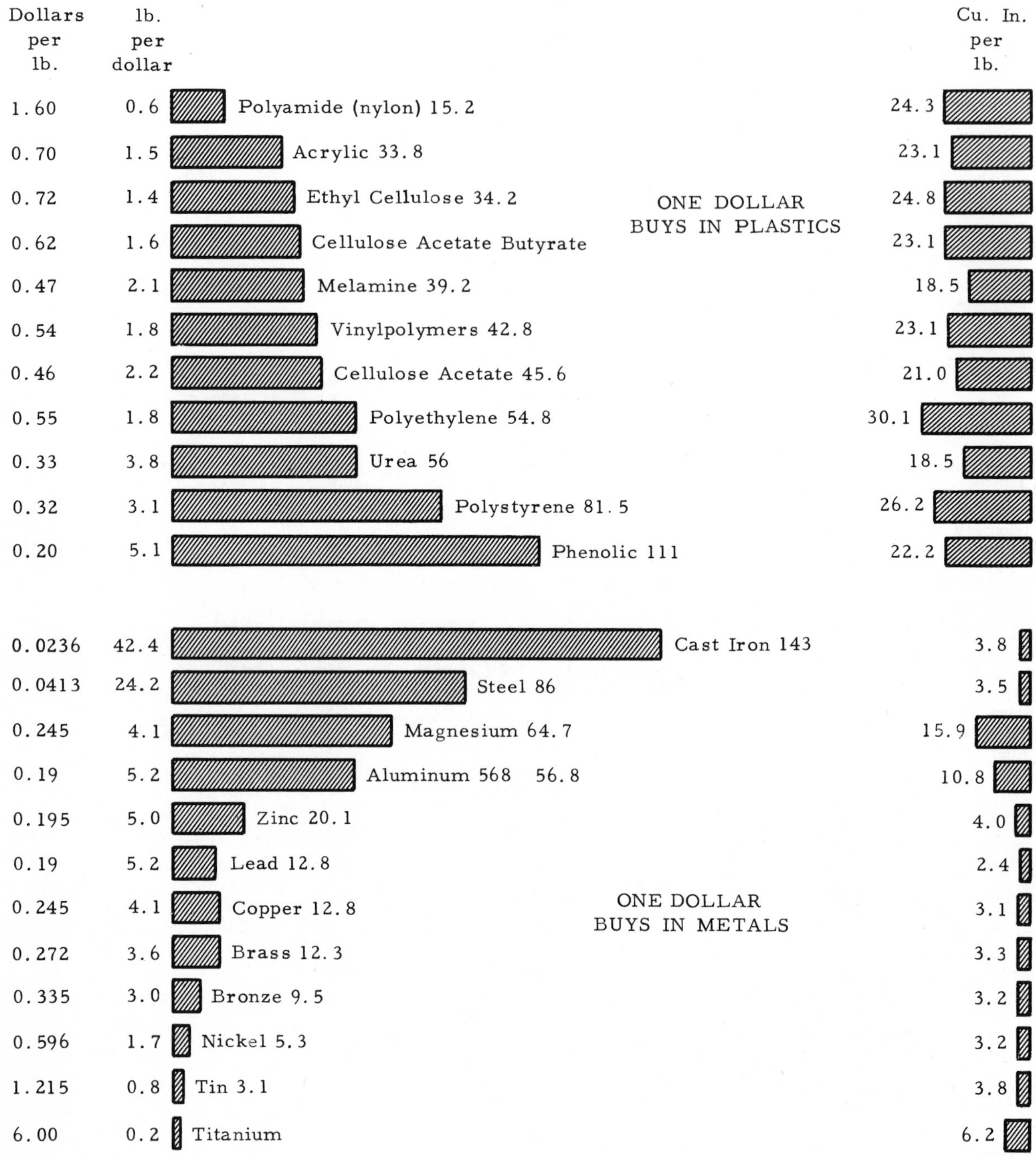

ONE DOLLAR BUYS IN PLASTICS

Dollars per lb.	lb. per dollar	Material	Cu. In. per lb.
1.60	0.6	Polyamide (nylon) 15.2	24.3
0.70	1.5	Acrylic 33.8	23.1
0.72	1.4	Ethyl Cellulose 34.2	24.8
0.62	1.6	Cellulose Acetate Butyrate	23.1
0.47	2.1	Melamine 39.2	18.5
0.54	1.8	Vinylpolymers 42.8	23.1
0.46	2.2	Cellulose Acetate 45.6	21.0
0.55	1.8	Polyethylene 54.8	30.1
0.33	3.8	Urea 56	18.5
0.32	3.1	Polystyrene 81.5	26.2
0.20	5.1	Phenolic 111	22.2

ONE DOLLAR BUYS IN METALS

Dollars per lb.	lb. per dollar	Material	Cu. In. per lb.
0.0236	42.4	Cast Iron 143	3.8
0.0413	24.2	Steel 86	3.5
0.245	4.1	Magnesium 64.7	15.9
0.19	5.2	Aluminum 568 56.8	10.8
0.195	5.0	Zinc 20.1	4.0
0.19	5.2	Lead 12.8	2.4
0.245	4.1	Copper 12.8	3.1
0.272	3.6	Brass 12.3	3.3
0.335	3.0	Bronze 9.5	3.2
0.596	1.7	Nickel 5.3	3.2
1.215	0.8	Tin 3.1	3.8
6.00	0.2	Titanium	6.2

Source: Theodore C. DuMond, *Fabricated Materials and Parts* (New York: Reinhold Publishing Corp., 1953), p. 11.

Properties and Costs of Reinforced Thermoplastics

Material	Properties					Cost of Achieving Equal Properties					
						Flexural Strength		Flexural Modulus		Tensile Strength	
	Flexural Strength p.s.i. x 10	Flexural Modulus p.s.i. x 10	Tensile Strength p.s.i. x 10	Price ¢/Lb.	Price ¢/Cu. In.	Thick-ness Needed In.	Cost ¢/100 In. Bar	Thick-ness Needed In.	Cost ¢/per In. Bar	Thick-ness Needed In.	Cost ¢/100 In. Bar
Nylon	13.8	0.41	11.8	98	4.02	0.148	59.5	0.365	147.0	0.008	3.41
40% glass-reinforced	37.0	1.80	30.0	165	9.06	0.090	81.6	0.223	202.0	0.003	3.02
30% glass-reinforced	22.0	0.985	19.1	146	7.60	0.117	88.5	0.273	208.0	0.005	3.98
Polystyrene, GP.	14.0	0.48	7.9	18	0.68	0.146	9.9	0.346	23.4	0.013	0.86
Polystyrene, high impact	10.0	0.39	6.5	28.5	1.11	0.174	19.3	0.372	41.3	0.015	1.71
30% glass-reinforced	17.5	1.21	14.0	54	2.48	0.132	32.6	0.254	63.1	0.007	1.77
20% glass-reinforced	15.0	1.16	11.0	49	2.30	0.142	32.6	0.258	59.4	0.009	2.09
Styrene-acrylonitrile. . . .	17.0	0.52	11.0	39.5	1.50	0.133	18.2	0.296	44.4	0.009	1.36
35% glass-reinforced	28.0	1.5	20.0	79	4.22	0.103	43.5	0.237	100.0	0.005	2.11
Polycarbonate	12.0	0.32	9.0	105	4.52	0.158	71.5	0.398	180.0	0.011	5.03
40% glass-reinforced	27.0	0.9	20.0	170	9.35	0.105	98.5	0.251	262.0	0.005	4.68
Acrylic.	17.0	0.45	11.0	55	2.36	0.133	31.4	0.354	83.5	0.009	2.14
ABS	13.5	0.40	9.0	50	1.85	0.149	27.6	0.368	68.1	0.011	2.05
Acetal.	14.1	0.41	10.0	65	3.34	0.146	48.7	0.365	122.0	0.010	3.34
Polypropylene	5.3	0.38	5.7	42	1.34	0.237	31.8	0.372	49.8	0.018	2.36
Aluminum, die cast.	8.0	10.0	8.0	21.5	2.15	0.194	41.5	0.126	27.1	0.013	2.86
Zinc, die cast.	-	-	24.0	13.8	3.27	-	-	-	-	0.004	1.36
Brass, yellow.	14.0	15.0	14.0	28	8.6	0.146	126.0	0.110	94.5	0.007	6.13
Magnesium, die cast	14.0	6.5	14.0	28.2	1.84	0.146	26.8	0.145	26.7	0.007	1.31

Source: Owens-Corning Fiberglas Corp., in Modern Plastics, March, 1962, p. 99.

9. PLASTICS INDUSTRY

Shipments of Thermoplastic Machines, 1952-1962

A. Injection Machines

Capacity in Ounces	1952	1953	1954	1955	1956	1957	1958	1959	1960	1961	1962
Less than 2.5	231	231	306	252	370	339	262	394	337	400	316
2.6 to 7	249	329	262	351	355	292	286	358	410	441	417
7.1 to 10	111	250	115	97	79	55	92	120	274	234	350
10.1 to 18	107	274	208	241	286	231	256	283	197	138	243
18.1 to 29	31	40	36	68	77	38	36	53	76	92	221
29.1 to 55	26	50	38	22	18	25	33	13	15	14	38
Over 55	9	15	12	21	23	15	35	31	22	21	36
Export	99	109	108	63	85	52	49	50	50	57	65
Total	863	1,298	1,085	1,115	1,293	1,044	1,049	1,302	1,381	1,397	1,686

B. Extrusion Machines

Screw Diameter (inches)	1952	1953	1954	1955	1956	1957	1958	1959	1960	1961	1962
Less than 1.7	90	101	81	106	102	99	123	128	208	261	253
1.7 to 3.2*	177	207	163	268	279	283	249	353	881	830	917
3.2 to 4.2	119	136	199	207	268	144	190	240	-	-	-
4.2 to 6.5	(101	(105	(154	160	206	181	178	273	238	334	301
Over 6.5	(	(	(	12	36	49	67	90	67	61	59
Export	137	91	90	75	128	181	148	117	92	107	161
Total	624	640	687	828	1,019	937	955	1,201	1,486	1,593	1,698

*Includes 3.5 inch machines in 1962.

C. Compression Presses

Nominal Size in Tons	1958	1959	1960	1961	1962
Less than 50	335	387	785	824	1,005
50 to 100	117	137	104	118	173
100 to 200	57	71	61	41	52
200 to 300	14	16	16	13	24
Over 300	33	45	24	17	57
Export	12	17	38	51	82
Total	568	673	1,028	1,064	1,393

D. Operable Machines in the United States

	1947	1950	1953	1956	1957	1958	1959	1960	1961	1962
Injection	3,395	5,272	6,570	9,096	9,818	9,309	10,331	10,947	NA	NA
Extruders	1,269	2,164	3,553	4,484	5,078	5,598	6,338	7,340	NA	NA
Sheet Thermoforming				970	1,285	1,618	2,107	2,694	NA	NA
Blow Molding						16	86	148	NA	NA

Source: Modern Plastics, January, 1960 and March, 1963.

10. PLASTICS INDUSTRY

a. Plastics Materials Producers

Year	Prod. Workers	All Workers	Hourly Wages	Cost of Materials	Prod. Wages	Value Added	Total Shipments	Capital Expend.
	(In Thousands)					(In Millions of Dollars)		
1947	21.8	28.6	$1.30	280.8	63.3	197.6	478.3	58.4
1948	(NA)	(NA)	(NA)	(NA)	(NA)	(NA)	(NA)	(NA)
1949	21.4	29.2	1.49	324.9	70.2	267.2	592.1	(NA)
1950	22.4	30.0	1.57	406.0	76.5	385.8	798.8	(NA)
1951	27.5	37.3	1.73	607.9	103.1	472.6	1,080.5	(NA)
1952	26.8	37.2	1.83	600.3	108.5	472.9	1,073.2	(NA)
1953	31.3	43.0	1.95	691.6	131.3	462.9	1,254.5	(NA)
1954	28.4	41.1	2.00	668.4	122.2	585.9	1,242.5	108.1
1955	31.1	44.0	2.09	789.5	144.0	723.4	1,498.5	(NA)
1956	35.6	50.4	2.23	918.8	171.7	759.8	1,651.3	166.4
1957	36.6	52.6	2.39	959.8	183.1	835.4	1,755.2	135.6
1958	35.3	51.0	2.50	973.0	189.3	871.6	1,846.7	138.6
1959	37.2	54.1	2.72	1,145.6	211.1	1,110.6	2,236.3	100.9
1960	37.8	55.3	2.79	1,167.3	216.9	1,041.4	2,183.0	140.0

b. Plastics Fabricators

Year	Prod. Workers	All Workers	Hourly Wages	Cost of Materials	Prod. Wages	Value Added	Total Shipments	Capital Expend.
1947	49.5	58.4	$1.15	214.0	119.5	258.9	473.0	27.0
1948	(NA)	(NA)	(NA)	(NA)	(NA)	(NA)	(NA)	(NA)
1949	47.8	59.1	1.28	248.9	120.9	303.8	553.7	(NA)
1950	64.0	75.6	1.34	400.8	179.6	473.4	874.1	36.2
1951	60.4	75.2	1.46	440.0	185.2	475.6	915.6	37.3
1952	60.5	74.6	1.55	449.9	191.2	514.3	964.1	34.7
1953	72.1	85.1	1.63	488.1	237.7	543.7	1,031.9	28.9
1954	75.7	92.0	1.68	633.0	249.0	598.4	1,227.1	45.3
1955	82.4	99.5	1.75	681.3	278.1	697.3	1,364.0	47.2
1956	87.8	106.8	1.82	730.3	303.2	742.6	1,459.1	67.3
1957	90.6	111.6	1.91	748.3	320.8	797.9	1,534.1	53.1
1958	89.9	113.1	1.95	935.1	337.5	894.4	1,822.1	75.2
1959	103.1	129.5	1.92	1,129.8	401.6	1,093.7	2,217.7	82.1
1960	106.2	134.0	1.96	1,172.1	424.0	1,147.9	2,303.2	104.5

Note: In 1954 there were 205 materials producers and 2,439 fabricators; in 1958 there were 349 materials producers and 3,208 fabricators.

Source: Census of Manufacturers, 1958, Series MC 58(2)-28B (Code 2821) and MC 58(2)-30A (3079); 1959 and 1960 figures from U.S. Bureau of the Census, Annual Survey of Manufactures, 1959 and 1960.

11. PLASTICS INDUSTRY

Cost Design and Production Factors in Selecting Fabricated Materials and Parts

	Molded Plastics	Sand Castings	Die Castings
RAW MATERIALS COST	Medium to high—on a per lb. basis 15¢ to $1.50 per lb.	Low to medium—depending upon metal	Medium—mostly zinc, aluminum and magnesium.
TOOL AND DIE COSTS	Medium to high—from $100 up usually	Low as compared to dies and molds	High—more than for other casting methods—$200 to $5,000 or more
OPTIMUM SIZED LOTS	Large—over 5,000 best	Wide range from a few pieces to 10,000	Large—1,000 to hundreds of thousands
DIRECT LABOR COSTS	Low—most operations automatic	High—men needed to mold, melt, clean, snag, etc.	Low to medium
FINISHING COSTS	Low—fins and flash removed by tumbling	High—require machining, cleaning and snagging	Low—little if any machining, only a simple trim
SCRAP LOSS	Medium to low—thermoplastics are reusable	Moderate—foundry scrap can be remelted	Low—gates sprues, etc. can be remelted
CHOICE OF MATERIALS	Wide range of plastics with many characteristics	Wide—ferrous, nonferrous, light and heavy alloys	Narrow—zinc, aluminum, magnesium and brass
COMPLEXITY OF PARTS	Limited by die, but some coring is possible	Considerable—holes, bosses, locating pads, complex shapes	Great—limited only by die, which can be complex
MAXIMUM SIZE	Moderate—under 2 lb. best in some materials; larger possible	High—as large or larger than any other method	Moderate—about 35 lb. for zinc, less for light metals
MINIMUM SIZE	Small—1/32 in. thick is common minimum	1/8 in. is the smallest practical section thickness	Tiny—from fractions of an ounce down to 0.012-inch sections
MECHANICAL PROPERTIES	Low as compared to metals	Fair to high, depending upon the material	Fair to good
PRECISION AND TOLERANCES	High—±0.005 in. common; can be closer	Low—±1/16 in. per in. of casting except for shell molding	High—±0.001 to ±0.003 in. common
SPECIAL STRUCTURAL CHARACTERISTICS	Inserts can be molded in	Good bearing structure	Inserts of other metals can be cast in
SURFACE SMOOTHNESS	Excellent	Poor	Good—often obviates finishing
SURFACE DETAIL	Good	Fair	Good
GETTING INTO PRODUCTION	Slow—molds require considerable time	Moderate—3 to 5 days for pattern to be made	Moderate to slow—from a week to several weeks
RATE OF OUTPUT	Moderate—20 to 300 shots per hour	25 to 600 or more pieces per hour by using modern methods	High—usual range from 100 to 1,000 per hour, up to 3,500
REMARKS	Can serve as alternates for metal parts at lower cost.	Most sand castings require some machining.	Among the most economical metal forms.

Source: Theodore C. DuMond, Fabricated Materials and Parts, 1953. Reinhold Publishing Corporation, New York.

Drop Forgings	Stamped and Formed Parts	Screw Machine Parts
Low to moderate—steels up to high alloys	Low to moderate—ranging from carbon steel to stainless	Low to medium—seldom on high alloys
High—great care needed in dies—$100 to $1,000 or more	High—$400 to $2,000 for small parts, more for large	Medium—from $50 to $200 common
Large—10,000 or more best, although used on smaller quantities	Large—over 10,000 best	Large—the larger the better, over 1,000
Medium—skilled labor needed for heating and hammer work	Medium—depending on size and shape	Low—one operator can handle several machines
Medium—ferrous need more than nonferrous due to scaling	Low—cleaning and trimming most frequent	Low—cleaning and deburring
Medium—depending on size, shape and machining needed	Low to moderate—some scrap in blanks can be reused	High—large quantities of chips generated
Medium—many alloys are forgeable	Wide—includes all workable sheet metals; plastics	Wide—although highly machinable materials best, including plastics
Moderate—limited by die restrictions	Limited—many restricted design rules	Limited to rotational shapes
Large—largest require steam hammers	Large—can be used on very large parts	Medium—most machines use stock up to 2 1/2 in. dia. and 6 in. long
Small—to fractions of an ounce on board hammers	Small—sections as thin as 0.003 to 0.005 in. possible	Small—often under 1/16 in. dia. and weighing fractions of an ounce
High	Fair to High	High
Medium—±0.010 to ±0.030 without coining	High—±0.001 in common, closer on small parts	High—±0.005 to 0.001 in. possible; ±0.001 to 0.003 in. common
Grain flow provides toughness	None	None
Fair	High	Excellent
Fair	Fair	Good—knurling and serrations readily made
Slow—one to several weeks to make dies	Slow—dies may require several weeks	Moderately fast—tooling and setup may take several days
Medium—120 per hour for small parts, less on large	High—up to several thousand pieces per hour	High—3,000 to 4,000 per hour on small parts
Used when high strength and high production are required. Preferred for large pieces.	Usually the cheapest when quantities are high enough; best for thin sections.	When shapes and materials agree, process is fastest, cheapest and most accurate.

12. PLASTICS INDUSTRY

Balance Sheet and Major Other Ratios
December 31, 1955, 1958, and 1961

	Industry			Injection: N.W. under $100M			Injection: N.W. over $100M			Compression			Extruders		
	12/55	12/58	12/61	12/55	12/58	12/61	12/55	12/58	12/61	12/55	12/58	12/61	12/55	12/58	12/61
Cash	10.6%	9.7%	8.6%	10.5%	10.6%	8.2%	9.0%	7.1%	9.1%	14.1%	15.2%	9.8%	10.7%	8.1%	6.7%
Accounts Receivable. . .	22.0	21.4	26.8	23.5	23.2	23.7	20.7	19.8	28.4	23.3	23.4	22.6	24.1	24.7	26.2
Inventory	24.9	23.1	22.5	17.9	19.5	16.7	24.9	24.1	21.4	25.3	20.1	24.8	25.8	28.3	25.2
Total Current Assets	57.5	54.2	57.9	51.9	53.3	48.6	54.6	51.0	58.9	62.7	58.7	57.2	60.6	61.1	58.1
Net Fixed Assets	38.0	37.3	33.2	43.8	43.1	46.3	40.5	40.3	30.0	33.9	32.4	37.2	34.6	28.9	35.7
Other Assets.	4.5	8.5	8.9	4.3	3.6	5.1	4.9	8.7	11.1	3.4	8.9	5.6	4.8	10.0	6.2
Total Assets	100.0%	100.0%	100.0%	100.0%	100.0%	100.0%	100.0%	100.0%	100.0%	100.0%	100.0%	100.0%	100.0%	100.0%	100.0%
Accounts Payable.	12.3%	14.2%	16.8%	17.2%	21.6%	22.4%	11.4%	12.9%	14.9%	9.9%	12.3%	10.8%	15.3%	25.8%	24.3%
Due Banks	3.5	5.0	5.3	2.3	2.3	3.5	4.2	5.4	6.2	0.9	3.1	3.7	5.6	9.9	4.3
Other Loans	3.3	3.1	3.0	7.7	10.4	8.1	2.4	3.2	2.8	4.8	2.3	1.8	2.3	1.1	3.1
Other Current Liabilities	11.6	9.6	13.3	7.0	11.8	9.9	11.5	10.1	15.6	13.9	8.4	10.9	10.7	9.4	9.5
Total Current Liabilities . . .	30.7	31.9	38.4	34.2	46.1	43.9	29.5	31.6	39.5	29.5	26.1	27.2	33.9	46.2	41.2
Term Debt	11.7	9.2	9.3	12.3	11.8	15.6	15.1	11.6	8.7	7.1	4.4	8.4	8.6	4.8	9.7
Net Worth	57.6	58.9	51.3	53.5	42.1	40.5	55.4	56.8	51.8	63.4	69.5	64.4	57.5	49.0	49.1
Total.	100.0%	100.0%	100.0%	100.0%	100.0%	100.0%	100.0%	100.0%	100.0%	100.0%	100.0%	100.0%	100.0%	100.0%	100.0%
Average Net Worth (000)	$ 319	$ 344	$ 298	$ 51	$ 45	$ 52	$ 443	$ 480	$ 481	$ 556	$ 646	$ 354	$ 300	$154	$ 293
Average Net Sales	1,180	1,238	1,162	184	171	224	1,510	1,584	1,828	2,115	1,873	1,310	1,560	601	1,143
Sales to Total Assets . .	2.16	2.12	2.00	2.47	1.60	1.74	2.01	1.87	1.97	2.34	2.19	2.38	2.46	1.91	1.92
Return on Investment . .	10.3%	7.2%	10.9%	11.5%	11.0%	18.1%	8.2%	6.6%	8.7%	10.6%	5.2%	10.0%	13.0%	7.8%	12.9%
% of Custom Sales	65	58	59	76	70	68	54	47	56	88	73	79	60	52	35

Source: Tarnell Co., Inc., The Plastics Processing Industry: Financial Ratios and Other Statistics (1959 and 1962 editions).

13. PLASTICS INDUSTRY

Combined Income Statements for Molding Companies, 1953 to 1961

	Industry									Sales under $250,000			Sales over $2,500,000		
	1953	1954	1955	1956	1957	1958	1959	1960	1961	1953	1958	1961	1953	1958	1961
% Sales Change	+20.3%	+7.0%	+12.7%	+12.7%	+5.8%	+6.0%	+25.6%	+19.4%	+10.8%						
Net Sales	100%	100%	100%	100%	100%	100%	100%	100%	100%	100%	100%	100%	100%	100%	100%
Materials	43.0	43.7	42.7	43.6	43.8	44.5	40.3	41.0	38.9	39.4	36.3	34.9	41.0	45.6	44.4
Direct Labor	19.8	19.8	19.0	20.8	18.9	18.7	19.1	18.7	19.1	20.2	22.4	20.9	19.5	18.5	17.7
Burden*	16.3	16.4	18.2	16.9	18.2	18.1	18.5	18.1	19.3	13.3	19.2	17.5	23.2	19.0	18.9
Cost of Goods Sold	79.1	79.9	79.9	81.3	80.9	81.3	81.6	81.4	81.0	72.9	77.9	77.7	83.7	83.1	83.1
Gross Profit	20.9	20.1	20.1	18.7	19.1	18.7	18.4	18.6	19.0	27.1	22.1	22.3	16.3	16.9	17.9
Selling Expense	6.2	6.1	6.1	5.2	6.4	5.9	5.5	6.1	5.9	5.6	5.1	5.2	7.4	6.4	7.2
Salaries and Commissions	3.0	2.9	2.6	2.8	3.1	3.2	2.6	3.2	3.2	2.4	2.3	3.0	4.3	3.2	3.9
Advertising	1.0	1.1	1.1	0.8	0.6	0.9	0.7	0.7	0.6	1.2	0.7	0.5	1.4	0.7	0.6
Travel and Entertainment	1.2	1.3	1.5	1.1	0.9	1.1	1.0	1.1	1.0	1.2	1.5	1.3	0.9	1.2	0.8
Other	1.0	0.8	0.9	0.5	1.8	0.7	1.2	1.1	1.1	0.8	0.6	0.4	0.8	1.3	1.9
General and Administrative Expense	8.9	9.1	9.1	8.9	9.4	9.3	10.4	11.4	11.9	8.9	11.4	14.2	5.6	6.7	7.8
Executive Salaries	4.1	4.0	3.9	4.3	4.3	4.1	5.3	6.0	6.4	8.0	8.0	8.7	2.2	1.5	1.7
Bad Debts	0.3	0.3	0.2	0.3	0.4	0.4	0.4	0.6	0.5	0.6	0.6	0.7	0.2	0.2	0.3
Other	4.5	4.8	5.0	4.3	4.7	4.8	4.7	4.8	5.0	2.8	2.8	4.8	3.2	5.0	5.8
Profit before Depreciation and Taxes	8.5	7.7	7.9	7.6	6.2	6.6	9.6	8.3	8.6	13.4	10.3	11.7	5.2	6.4	6.1
Depreciation	2.7	2.8	3.0	3.0	2.9	3.1	3.7	3.6	3.7	3.3	4.7	4.4	1.9	2.6	2.2
Taxes	2.5	2.0	2.0	2.2	1.4	1.5	2.5	1.9	2.1	3.6	1.5	2.5	1.8	1.8	2.1
Net Profit	3.3	2.9	2.9	2.4	1.9	2.0	3.4	2.8	2.8	6.5	4.1	4.8	1.5	2.0	1.9

*Includes depreciation.

Source: Tarnell Co., Inc., The Plastics Processing Industry: Financial Ratios and Other Statistics (1959 and 1962 editions).

Bell Plastics, Inc.

Bell Plastics, Inc., was a custom molder of thermoplastic and thermosetting plastic materials. The company used the injection, compression, and transfer processes. Total sales for the year ending March 31, 1947, amounted to approximately $1,537,000. The major part of the company's output consisted of industrial products which were complicated in design and often embodied inserts. These products were manufactured to close tolerances and their production required the use of carefully constructed, intricate molding dies. A relatively small percentage of the sales volume was secured from buttons of various kinds and three proprietary items which were distributed through chain stores.

The company employed approximately 250 people and was located in Trenton, New Jersey, a short distance from New York City. A comparative balance sheet and a comparative statement of income for the period 1942 to 1947 are presented in Exhibits 1 and 2.

In September, 1947, the management of the company was engaged in an aggressive, long-term program designed to establish Bell Plastics, Inc., as a custom molder of parts and products for the aircraft and business machines industries and for selected companies in other industries which had a good commercial standing and national distribution. As a part of this program and as a means of alleviating the difficulties arising from the current shortage of thermosetting molding powders, the management was seeking to establish a close and permanent relationship with one or two manufacturers of plastic materials. The management was also considering the development of from three to five additional, carefully selected and designed proprietary items.

COMPANY HISTORY

Bell Plastics, Inc., was organized as the Arthur Fisher Company, a partnership formed in 1936 to enter the new field of injection molding. The company was incorporated in 1938. During 1939 Mr. Fisher began searching for some one to enter the company with additional funds for expansion. At the same time, Mr. R. E. Bell, then vice-president of a large company engaged in heavy manufacturing, and his son, Mr. Edwin Bell, who had just graduated from the Harvard Business School, were seeking a small business in which Mr. Edwin Bell could be established. Through a mutual friend in the banking business, the Bells became acquainted with Mr. Fisher and subsequently purchased an interest in the company.

Mr. Fisher and Mr. Edwin Bell operated the small plastics company until the fall of 1942 when both entered the military service. In November, 1941, they erected a new and modern one-story factory and office building having a floor area of about 25,000 square feet. Molding equipment had increased by this time to four, 2- to 8-ounce injection presses and one angle press which was used for transfer molding. The company's products consisted of fancy buttons for ladies' dresses, thimbles, cosmetic containers, and dresser sets.

During 1941 and 1942 plans were formulated for making a fundamental change in the company's product policy. Mr. R. E. Bell realized that the current line of products was sold in a highly competitive field which was subject to invasion by a host of new small molding firms; any molder could produce products of this type. He felt that the company's products did not provide a sound basis for either war production or for the future growth of the company as a custom molder. He had also observed that the credit standing of the customers for these items was often poor. As a result, he decided to develop a line of products which required a good deal more engineering in their design and production. At the same time it was decided to confine the company's war work to molded plastic parts and products for the aviation and electronics industries. This policy was adhered to throughout the war years.

DEVELOPMENT PROGRAM

At the close of the war Bell Plastics, Inc., was faced with major reconversion problems in connection with its equipment, products, markets, and raw materials. At the start of the war the annual sales volume had totaled about $390,000 and had consisted primarily of buttons, novelties, and cosmetic items; by the end of the war the company had developed an annual volume of approximately $3,250,000 by producing, for the most part, specialized electrical equipment for the aviation and electronics industries.

As of June, 1945, the company's compression molding equipment consisted of five angle presses controlled by hand, four flat bed presses operated with either fixed or hand molds, and three other presses of from 75- to 500-ton capacity, one of which was hand operated. The injection equipment included ten 2- to 16-ounce presses. Between June, 1945, and November, 1946, a complete equipment modernization program was carried to completion. All of the companys' older presses were replaced with new equipment, and the total molding capacity of the plant was increased. Twenty-seven new presses were purchased at a cost of approximately $206,000. A public issue of capital stock financed the program. The total capacity of the new installation was based on an expected postwar sales volume of around $3,250,000 annually. Press capacity was divided between transfer-compression and injection in the ratio of 60 to 40. This ratio had been determined in accordance with figures released by the Society of the Plastics Industry on current sales of thermosetting and thermoplastic molding powders. When the installation was complete, Bell Plastics, Inc., had 16 injection presses and 23 transfer-compression presses. The latter could be used interchangeably for compression molding or transfer molding.

The new molding equipment displaced space in Plant #1 that had previously been used for the storage of raw materials. Therefore, a new storage addition was made to the factory early in 1947 at a cost of about $22,000. In September, 1947, Mr. Bell believed that Bell Plastics, Inc., had molding equipment and a physical plant which in efficiency was second to none in the industry.

Marketing Program: When it became apparent that the war would soon be over, the executives of Bell Plastics, Inc., began considering ways and means of maintaining the company's sales volume in the peacetime market. With the cessation of war orders it was evident that it would be necessary to develop new markets and new outlets for practically the entire capacity of the plant. To accomplish this purpose, the management decided to concentrate the company's sales efforts on certain selected industries and companies. The new marketing program was developed in conjunction with a firm of marketing consultants.

As a preliminary step, the types of industrial business open to Bell Plastics, Inc., as a custom molder were analyzed as follows:

(a) *"Competitive" Products*—This group of products included buttons, combs, thimbles, novelties and similar items. The manufacture of these products required very little engineering and presented few problems. The volume per order was high, price was extremely important, and margins were small. To compete successfully for this type of business required low overhead and operating costs.

(b) *"Less Competitive" Products*—This group of products included such things as clock cases, iron handles, and cutlery handles. The volume per order on these items was somewhat smaller, and price was less important than in the case of the previous group. The manufacture of these products required considerable designing and engineering work.

(c) *"Engineering and Assembled" Products*—The products in this category were industrial components, the manufacture of which required a high type of engineering skill. The use of plastics in these applications usually involved the displacement of other materials, such as metal or wood, after it had been established that the plastic would result in a better product and/or a reduction in costs. Obtaining orders for this type of business usually required a long and costly period of development work with customers. The profit margins were usually high and the volume per order small.

The company executives believed that Bell Plastics, Inc., was best equipped to manufacture the third group of products in view of the company's wartime experience with similar items. Moreover, they had observed that there were not over 18 molders in the country who were in a position to compete for business of this type. The executives decided that the company should seek to develop at least 50 percent of its sales volume from the "engineered and assembled" products.

After careful study, it was decided to concentrate the company's selling effort on the aircraft manufacturing and business machines industries. Companies in both industries were increasing their use of plastics as a means of improving the appearance and mechanical characteristics of their products. By establishing the company as a supplier of plastic parts and products for the aircraft and business machines industries, the management hoped to gain a unique position in the industry and to secure some freedom from the competition which was developing in the plastics molding business.

In addition to the program of concentrating selling effort on the two selected industries, the management decided to seek out as customers a group of selected companies in other industries which appeared to be desirable sources of repeat business. For the most part, it was intended that these customers would be concerns with national distribution. A preliminary list of potential customers of this type, located within the sales territories of Bell Plastics, Inc., was prepared and from this list particular companies were selected for further investigation. The investigation involved a complete analysis of the company's credit rating, present and potential usage of plastic parts, methods of buying, and prices. Consideration was also given to the permanence of the company's products and the competence of its management. The customers finally selected were approached slowly and carefully, a few at a time. It was anticipated that the work of developing these accounts would be a continuing process.

For 1947, the objective of the company was to attain $845,000 in sales to selected markets, $1,950,000 in sales to selected customers, $325,000 in specialty products, and $455,000 in buttons. Considerable progress had been made in establishing regular customers in the selected industries and among the selected companies. Sales to the aircraft industry, however, had failed to materialize to the extent anticipated as a result of cutbacks in production and a generally poor credit situation in the industry.

Sales Organization: The company had established four sales territories divided among six salesmen as follows: 2 men—New England; 1 man—New York City and New York State; 2 men—New Jersey, Eastern Pennsylvania, and Maryland; 1 man—Western Pennsylvania, Ohio, and Indiana. Manufacturer's representatives were used in other parts of the country. One additional salesman handled the development of new products. Out of the total of seven salesmen, four had been added after the new marketing program was undertaken. Mr. Edwin Bell, who was vice-president and sales manager, spent a good deal of his time traveling in the interests of the new marketing program.

ESTIMATING

The task of estimating prices on customers' orders was accomplished by means of a committee composed of the chief engineer, the factory manager, the chief chemist, and an estimating clerk. The group met twice each week to quote prices on orders received. The work of the committee included a study of such things as the method of molding required, the material to be used, the number of cavities per die, the cycle time, and the cost of inserts.

When the study of the order was completed, a price was quoted to the customer. If the price proved satisfactory and the order was closed, a physical data sheet was prepared covering all the information which would be necessary during production of the order. The necessary tools, dies, and materials were then ordered. It was usually eight to sixteen weeks before these arrived. The next step was the molding of samples by the foreman of the molding department under the supervision of the chief chemist, who was responsible for such things as the molding cycle, the correct pressure, and the proper heat. If the samples proved satisfactory to the customer, the article was placed in production. Usually, it was necessary to make several changes in the dies and prepare new samples; occasionally new die cavities had to be made. From the time an order was received until it was in full production generally required from four to six months.

The cost of making an estimate was high. Out of pocket expense, not including a charge for overhead, was approximately $60 per order. The average size of each order received was in the neighborhood of $13,000. Smaller orders were accepted, however, when they were from selected companies or selected industries. During the year ending March 31, 1947, Bell Plastics, Inc., received one out of eight orders on which it had submitted quotations. The management was attempting to raise the percentage of orders accepted. From the first of April through the end of June, 1947, 101 quotations were made.

Considerable screening took place during the estimating procedure. The proposed product was thoroughly studied with respect to its design, permanence in the market, and saleability. At the same time, the credit rating and potentialities of the customer as a source of repeat business were investigated. It was a firm policy of the company to accept orders only when the applications made proper use of plastics and involved products for which a fairly stable demand could be developed in the market. The executives were not interested in gadgets or novelties. Although this policy resulted in the loss of some short-term business, the executives believed that the policy would prove sound in the long run. For example, in the immediate postwar period the company had received many requests for quotations on molded plastic radio cabinets. Before the war there had been only about five major companies purchasing plastic radio cabinets, and it was believed that after the first rush of orders was over, the business would return to those concerns. Consequently, requests for estimates were accepted only from the five companies.

MANUFACTURING

The plant facilities of Bell Plastics, Inc., were clean, well lighted, well ventilated, and of modern construction. Molding was performed in Plant #1 which adjoined the executive offices while finishing and shipping activities were carried out in Plant #2. A floor layout plan of Plant #1 appears in Exhibit 3. Plant #1 had approximately 25,000 square feet of floor space devoted to manufacturing operations. Plant #2, which was leased, had about 20,000 square feet of floor space. Plant #2 was about one-half mile from the main factory and was located on the second floor of another company's factory.

During the summer of 1947 the company had from five to eight injection presses and from seven to nine transfer-compression presses in operation. The molding departments operated three 8-hour shifts a day. The purpose of three shift operations was to eliminate the daily heating up and adjustment period which usually occurred when the presses were not operated continuously.

Tools and Dies: The company maintained a small, well-equipped tool room, but manufactured only a minor part of its own tools and dies of the simpler designs. The shop was used mainly for adjusting and repairing dies, making changes requested by customers, and correcting defects resulting from faulty design or construction. The majority of the company's tool and die work was divided among five or six outside die-making concerns. The executives were not entirely satisfied with this arrangement, but did not want to increase overhead costs by purchasing die-making equipment and hiring additional manpower. During the year ending March 31, 1947, the company designed and had built a total of 82 dies. Twelve toolmakers were employed in the company's tool room.

Labor Forces: The employees of the company numbered approximately 250 in September, 1947. They were members of the United Gas, Coke and Chemical Workers of America, which was affiliated with the C.I.O. Wage payments were based on a guaranteed hourly rate plus a bonus which was expected to add around 25 percent to each employee's take home pay. There were no fixed limits to the amount of bonus which a man could earn. Guaranteed hourly rates were approximately as follows: transfer-compression department, $0.90–$1.35; injection department, $0.90–$1.25; finishing department, $0.75–$0.95.

CURRENT SITUATION AND FUTURE PLANS

Beginning early in 1947 and continuing through the summer, Bell Plastics, Inc., experienced a slump in its molding business. Sales, therefore, fell short of the goals which had originally been projected. For the first quarter, beginning April 1, 1947, total actual sales amounted to about 33 percent of the projected goals. Sales to the aviation and business machines industries were about 20 percent and sales to selected companies in other industries about 15 percent of the projected goals. Sales of proprietary or special products and buttons were about 35 percent and 15 percent, respectively, of estimated goals.

During September, 1947, executives of Bell Plastics, Inc., were considering the addition of from three to five carefully selected proprietary items to the company's line of products. By this means the management hoped to keep more of the molding presses busy between other orders and at the same time secure a reasonably high profit margin. Before a final decision was made on any one item, the management had formulated the following steps for investigation. The article would first be designed mechanically and styled to meet a given market price. Raw material manufacturers would be approached for quotations on the necessary molding powders. The possible channels of distribution would then be investigated and the advice of merchandising groups, such as chains stores, sought; perhaps the article would receive a trial sales run. On the basis of this information, a decision would be made as to the suitability of the product. On the items placed in production, the executives hoped that the company would be at least a year ahead of its competitors in the technical development of the design. The initial expense for developing the designs and securing the dies for three to five items was expected to be at least $65,000. No further estimates had been made as to costs or personnel requirements.

Other plans included the following:

(a) As soon as possible the executives hoped to be able to build an addition to Plant #1 to house the finishing operations. Adequate space was available for this purpose, but plans had been tabled until building costs were reduced.

(b) The executives intended to increase the size of the tool room and to reduce the amount of die work sent to outside concerns. On this project the executives were proceeding slowly, realizing that they would have the same problems in turning out good dies at a reasonable cost as did the outside concerns.

(c) In the development of the raw materials program, it was planned to approach a second producer of molding powders to assure the supply for a greater percentage of the company's requirements of thermosetting materials, provided that relations with the first manufacturer proved satisfactory.

(d) The maximum sales volume which the company would attempt to handle in its present plant had been set at around $6,500,000. If additional volume developed, other plants would be set up in other locations.

(e) Mr. R. E. Bell hoped to be able to retire from active participation in the company in the near future.

1. BELL PLASTICS, INC.

Balance Sheets, 1942-1947
(Year End Mar. 31)

	1942	1943	1944	1945	1946	1947
Assets						
Current						
Cash	$ 15,605	$ 203,891	$ 188,422	$ 281,923	$ 275,023	$ 97,747
U.S. Treasury Tax Notes		52,073	246,562	202,851	326,310	
Accounts Receivable--Net	102,974	281,698	294,986	263,949	252,946	258,612
Inventories	208,939	336,384	437,527	489,236	150,990	445,754
Claim for Refund of Federal Income Taxes					55,120	151,462
Other Current Assets		21,818	21,608	50,122		1,300
Total Current Assets	$327,518	$ 895,864	$1,189,105	$1,288,081	$1,060,389	$ 954,875
Land, Buildings, Machinery, Equipment, Etc.	$437,992	$ 545,883	$ 493,953	$ 566,377	$ 684,652	$ 928,161
Reserve for Depreciation	43,773	83,125	116,043	172,320	226,948	265,872
Net Property	$394,219	$ 462,758	$ 377,910	$ 394,057	$ 457,704	$ 662,289
Other Assets	$ 10,382	$ 10,845	$ 30,732	$ 47,134	$ 12,236	$ 8,330
Deferred Charges	8,798	15,692	16,843	13,963	8,525	7,567
Total Assets	$740,917	$1,385,159	$1,614,590	$1,743,235	$1,538,854	$1,633,061
Liabilities						
Current						
Notes Payable	$ 63,700	$ 530,811	$ 308,859	$ 386,118		$ 130,000
Accounts Payable and Accrued Accounts	191,781	214,014	240,335	274,477	$ 233,912	218,596
Mortgage Payable	7,800	7,800	7,800	7,800	7,800	
Income Tax Reserve		44,700	301,990	167,960		
Total Current Liabilities	$263,281	$ 797,325	$ 858,984	$ 836,355	$ 241,712	$ 348,596
Mortgage Payable	37,700	29,900	22,100	14,300	6,500	
Contingency Reserve			32,500	58,500		
Capital Stock (no-par value)	483,438	516,837	601,065	703,697	1,164,372	1,232,297
Earned Surplus	(53,502)	41,097	99,941	130,383	126,270	52,168
Total Liabilities	$730,917	$1,385,159	$1,614,590	$1,743,235	$1,538,854	$1,633,061

2. BELL PLASTICS, INC.

Income Statements, 1942-1947
(Year End Mar. 31)

	1942	1943	1944	1945	1946	1947
Net Sales	$618,254	$2,022,794	$3,204,265	$2,848,775	$2,470,398	$1,536,617
Cost of Goods Sold	516,645	1,656,987	2,451,881	2,177,802	2,075,710	1,475,457
Gross Profit	$101,609	$ 365,807	$ 752,384	$ 670,973	$ 394,688	$ 61,160
Selling, Administrative, and General Expense	116,424	196,264	340,193	427,349	392,639	307,806
Operating Profit	$(14,815)	$ 169,543	$ 412,191	$ 243,624	$ 2,049	$ (246,646)
Other Income	4,294	6,165	11,227	3,952	25,195	30,364
Total Income	$(10,521)	$ 175,708	$ 423,418	$ 247,576	$ 27,244	$ (216,282)
Other Deductions	10,565	36,409	56,580	30,945	31,144	6,221
Contingency Reserve			32,500	26,000		
Net Profit before Taxes	$(21,086)	$ 139,299	$ 334,338	$ 190,631	$ (3,900)	$ (222,503)
Federal and State Taxes on Income		44,700	275,494	160,189		
Claim for Refund of Federal Taxes on Income, less provision for additional prior year's taxes					40,457	148,401
Net Profit	$(21,086)	$ 94,599	$ 58,844	$ 30,442	$ 36,557	$ (74,102)

3. BELL PLASTICS, INC.

Floor Layout—Plant 1

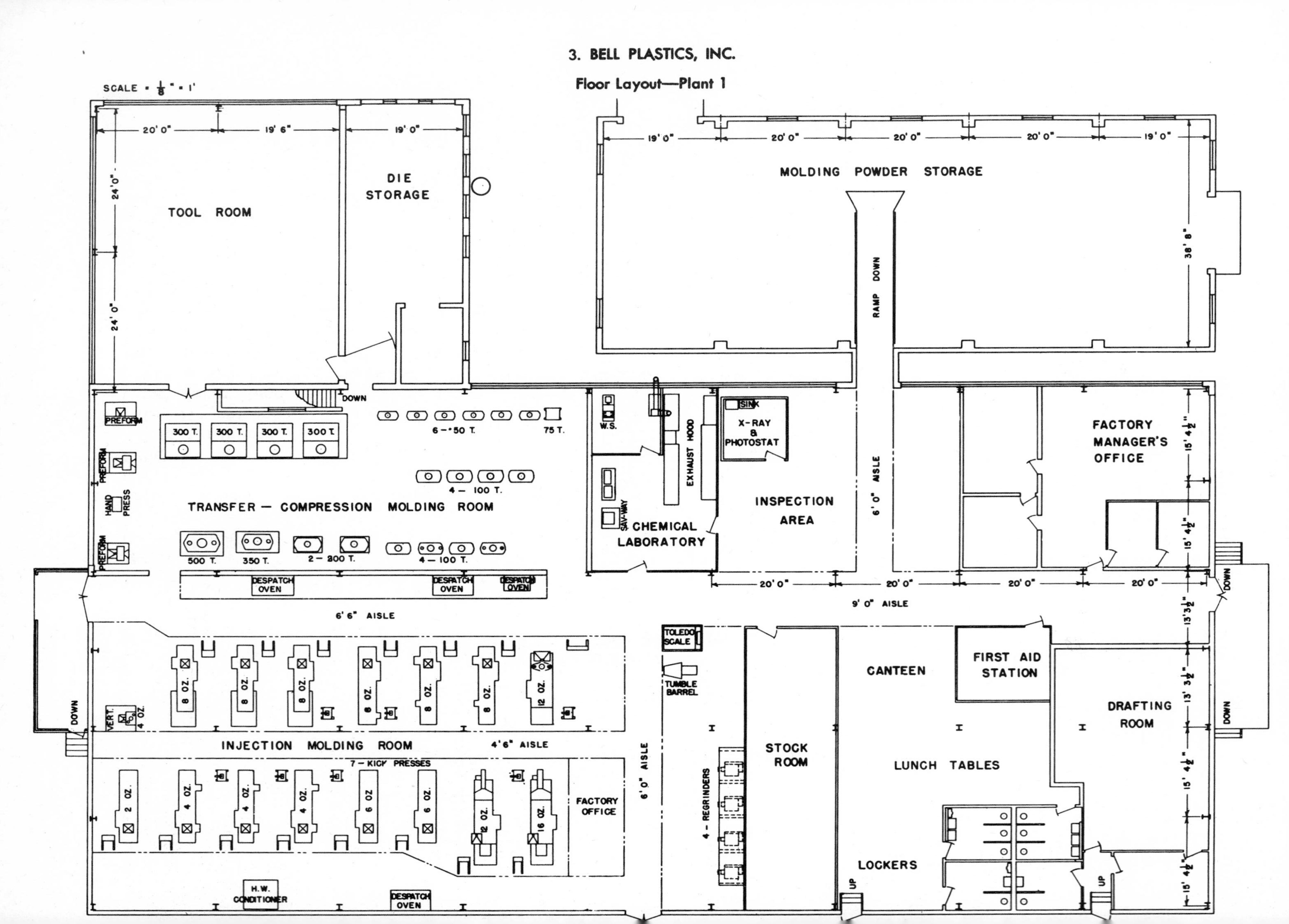

Hungerford Plastics Corporation

The Hungerford Plastics Corporation was established in 1946 to produce quality moldings of thermoplastics. Between 1947 and 1954, net worth increased from $282,000 to $491,000 and the company had become the leading molder of flexible vinyl products. Net sales increased from $436,000 in 1946 to $1,288,000 in 1954, and had risen to an annual rate in excess of $2 million by June, 1955. The Hungerford company was not only an established producer of injection moldings of flexible vinyl but was also developing new vinyl products involving extrusion and rotary plastisol molding. Balance sheets and income statements are provided in Exhibits 1 and 2.

In July, 1955, Mr. Daniel Hungerford, president of the company, was considering the construction of a new plant to provide greater manufacturing efficiency and expanded facilities for future growth. If the company were to construct the plant under consideration, the required investment of $450,000 for land and buildings and $150,000 for working capital would be raised by a 5 percent mortgage loan of $300,000 from an insurance company and by the sale of $300,000 of common and preferred stock.

COMPANY HISTORY

In 1942, Mr. Daniel C. Hungerford left his position as a vice-president and director of the Elastic Stop Nut Company in order to enter business for himself. He organized the Aircraft Parts Development Corporation to do research and development work in powder metallurgy and thermoplastics. The new company, the name of which was soon changed to the Hungerford Research Corporation, engaged in wartime development work under contract to the American Bosch Corporation, American Machine and Foundry Company, the Bofors Company of Sweden, and the Elastic Stop Nut Company.

In connection with its contract with the Elastic Stop Nut Company, the Hungerford Research Corporation had developed the "Plastimaker," a special process for preparing cellulose acetate molding compounds from purchased resins and chemicals. Mr. Hungerford decided that postwar activities should lie in the plastics industry and in mid-1945 the company began its first injection molding operations on a production basis. In 1946, the "Plastimaker" process was successfully adapted for use with vinyl materials.

The Hungerford Plastics Corporation was formed in February, 1946, to take over the operations of the Hungerford Research Corporation. At that time, assets totaled $220,000, and all of the common stock was owned by Mr. Hungerford and his wife. Following merger and recapitalization, the Hungerfords received 155,000 shares of $0.25 par common stock. An additional 74,000 shares were sold to the public at a price of $4 per share.

Molding operations were initially conducted in a 12,000 square foot, one-story plant in New Jersey constructed by the company in 1945 at a cost of $80,000. Molding, extruding, research, and tool room machinery and equipment were then valued at $78,000. The company soon leased an additional 10,000 square feet of space at another location which was used for finishing operations and storage. In early 1951, manufacturing operations were consolidated in 50,000 square feet of leased space in Rockaway, New Jersey.

In 1953, the company began development work in extrusion and rotary molding. Although the original rotary machines were never used in production, the Hungerford company in 1954 purchased the Walsamer Company, a pioneer in the plastisol field. The Walsamer Company was producing plastisol moldings in a leased plant of 6,000 square feet in Riverdale, New Jersey, and was purchased for $25,000 cash and 12,112 shares of Hungerford common stock. Mr. Wallace Quackenbush, president of Walsamer, was retained as vice-president and manager of the Hungerford Rotary Division.

PRODUCTS AND MARKETING

By 1955, the Hungerford corporation was divided into three operating divisions: injection molding, extrusion, and rotary molding. Sales volume for the year 1955 was expected to exceed $2,350,000, with the injection molding division accounting for $1,800,000 of that amount and the balance of sales divided between extrusion and rotary molding. The company did both custom and proprietary molding and tried to keep the sales volume in these two categories roughly equal. Contracts for custom molded industrial products were usually obtained as the result of competitive bidding, and the customer owned the molds. Proprietary items were sold to industrial and consumer markets, and the Hungerford company owned the molds. Exhibit 3 presents a comparison of the volume of custom and proprietary sales since 1947.

Flexible Vinyls

The Hungerford Plastics Corporation initially solicited injection molding orders for any thermoplastic material. However, because of the competitive advantage obtained through the "Plastimaker" compounding process, for which a patent application had been filed in 1946, and because of his belief in the potential applications of flexible vinyls, Mr. Hungerford set out to make his company a specialist in that field. Sales of flexible vinyl moldings as a percent of total sales for the early years were:

1948—11%
1949—66
1950—85
1951—93

The principal volume of the Hungerford company's custom molding sales had been in the replacement of rubber in component parts for automotive and home appliance manufacturers. In contrast to rubber, vinyl could be molded to closer tolerances, was not subject to oxidation, and could easily be molded in a variety of colors. In addition, special vinyl compounds could be formulated to provide physical characteristics for particular applications. Synthetic rubber was priced at 23 cents per pound in 1955. Although this price was lower than the price of the basic vinyl resin, the addition of low-cost filler could often make vinyl compounds competitive with rubber.

Mr. Hungerford estimated that his company obtained a greater sales volume from flexible vinyl moldings than all other competing companies combined.

The products of the Hungerford Plastics Corporation constituted a small segment of the vinyl market. The 1954 consumption of vinyl resin was estimated to be 386 million pounds. Only 127 million pounds were molded or extruded, of which extrusions accounted for 97 million pounds. The remaining 30 million pounds were used principally for phonograph records and for dolls or toys.[1]

Mr. Hungerford believed that "the people who produce the goods should sell them in this type of engineering product." For that reason, the closing of all custom molding contracts was handled by the senior operating executives.

Custom Products

In the late 1940's it proved difficult to convince manufacturers to specify flexible vinyl because of the large investment required for a mold and because the component usually had to be redesigned to fit the molding process. The first big contract, with a large vacuum cleaner manufacturer, was the result of two years of sales work during which the Hungerford company built the first mold at its own expense.

Despite the recent diversification, custom injection molding was still the core of the company's sales in 1955. Four large contracts negotiated by company executives with appliance manufacturers were expected to reach a volume of $890,000 for 1955, with one vacuum cleaner manufacturer accounting for about 55 percent of that amount. The Hungerford company was specialized to concentrate on the design and production of injection molded vinyl products and operations of this division were very profitable.

Although the extrusion division was returning a small profit in 1955, it was not fulfilling the original expectations of the management. The division manager felt that Hungerford Plastics could never be competitive with smaller shops on standard types of simple extrusions. Basement shops, with only one or two machines, could operate with practically no overhead and undercut any price that Hungerford could offer. The manager preferred to obtain contracts which had a profitable secondary operation, or those where a special vinyl compound would be needed.

The extruding department had developed "Shrinktube," a product that was of a semiproprietary nature. To produce this product, ordinary extruded vinyl tubing was pulled mechanically through a steam-jacketed pipe and expanded by air to about twice its initial diameter. From the steam pipe the tubing passed to an-

[1] Estimates prepared by *Modern Plastics* magazine, January, 1955, p. 80.

other pipe which cooled it at the expanded diameter. The Shrinktube could then be used to cover any tube, pipe, or cable with a diameter greater than the Shrinktube's initial diameter and less than its expanded diameter.

The acquisition of the Walsamer Company offered an entry into a new field of consumer sales. The output of the rotary division in early 1955 was devoted to a small volume of custom sales and to experimental work on proprietary items. About 60 percent of the 1955 dollar sales volume was due to one doll contract and almost all of the rotary contract work was the production of parts for four doll companies.

Proprietary Products

The company's early proprietary products included a bedside lamp and a coin bank which failed to develop a sustained sales volume. In June, 1948, development began on a line of vinyl hand grips and the first mold went into production in January, 1950. In 1955, these items, under the brand name "Flex-Grips" were available in a half-dozen designs, three sizes, and eight standard colors. Annual output of any one design, size, and color might range from 1,000 to 1,000,000 units. About 40 percent of the units sold were black; another 40 percent were red or white. There were 150 customers purchasing grips in April, 1953, when the first catalogue was issued, and over 400 in June, 1955. Unit sales increased 53 percent between 1950 and 1952, and 1955 sales were running at a rate three and one-half times the 1950 sales.

A line of dog leashes and dog collars accounted for a very small part of proprietary sales in 1955. These items were molded in one piece with metal inserts. The first shipments were made in June, 1949, and a modest volume was maintained after that date. They were sold nationally to wholesalers and distributors.

In 1955, various rotary molded proprietary items were in the development stage. The company had a license to produce Walt Disney character dolls and had designed several models for this line. In addition, a Heinz Baby Doll and a "Sweet Ann" model were being tried experimentally. Dolls were to be sold by manufacturers' agents working under the company consumer products sales manager and selling to chain stores, department stores, and wholesalers at from 5 percent to 10 percent commission. Exhibits 4A and 4B contain photographs of proprietary products.

The Ohio Rubber Company

The Ohio Rubber Company of Willoughby, Ohio was a large manufacturer of molded rubber products which had become an important outlet for both custom and proprietary products made by the Hungerford company. The association with Ohio Rubber began in 1950 when the Hungerford company first marketed its proprietary line of vinyl hand grips under the Flex-Grip brand. The grips were used for bicycle handles, lawn mowers, golf carts, and for some industrial purposes. The Ohio company, which had been the largest producer and seller of rubber grips, wanted to market the new vinyl line along with its own line of rubber grips. The Hungerford company, on the other hand, needed a distribution system for its grip line. An agreement was executed giving Ohio the exclusive sales franchise for the Hungerford Flex-Grip line, and nonexclusive rights to solicit custom molding accounts. The Ohio company maintained a field staff of 17 salesmen, and did a small amount of advertising. Sales were made under the Ohio name, shipped and invoiced from Rockaway. Hungerford billed Ohio twice monthly for the accumulated shipments at the billed price less 10 percent (for grips) or 7½ percent (for custom sales). Grip molds were built by the Hungerford toolroom and financed by Ohio Rubber. Ohio advanced the cost of the mold when built and was repaid by Hungerford at the rate of $2 per thousand units as the grips were produced from that mold. Molds remained the property of Hungerford and the repayment continued only until the full original investment had been returned. Mr. Hungerford was very pleased with the effectiveness of the Ohio company in producing sales leads. The Hungerford company received an average of one inquiry each day through the Ohio organization. Grip sales in 1955 were expected to reach $470,000, and Ohio custom sales were estimated to amount to an additional $500,000.

MANUFACTURING

In 1955, all injection and extrusion operations were located in the main plant at Rockaway while some plastisol work was undertaken at Riverdale.

Raw Material

A typical compound for injection molding flexible vinyl contained: (1) *Polyvinyl chloride resin,* usually 100 parts by weight; (2) *Plasticizer,* a high-boiling liquid ester, such as DiOctyl Phthalate, that imparted flexibility, usually 75 parts; (3) *Stabilizer,* made of basic lead salts or metallic soaps, such as Lead Sulfates, Phosphites, Phthalates, Stearates, added for greater heat stability, usually 2 to 10 parts; (4) *Lubricant,* less than one part; (5) *Extender,* an inexpensive material, such as wood flour or calcium carbonate, added as a modifier to improve certain characteristics or as an extender to lower the material cost, up to 50 parts; (6) *Color pigment,* included as desired.

Raw materials were available from a number of chemical suppliers and the Hungerford company attempted to maintain four sources for each important item. Polyvinyl chloride resin was obtained from the B. F. Goodrich Company, from the Bakelite Division of Union Carbide and Carbon Corporation, and from three other large concerns. The United States production capacity for the resin was in excess of 600 million pounds in 1955. The price of the best molding grade of PVC had been 39 cents per pound from 1950 until July, 1955, when it dropped to 31 cents per pound. There were two less-expensive grades priced two and four cents below the prime grade. Trade sources speculated that increased imports of resin from European countries, which had contributed to the July price decline, might push down prices even further in the future.

The primary suppliers of plasticizers were Union Carbide, Monsanto, and five other chemical companies. DiOctyl Phthalate prices, delivered, were 34 cents per pound in July, 1955. The price had dropped one cent since 1954 and had been as high as 43 cents in mid-1952.

It was a policy of the Hungerford company to purchase PVC resin and other component chemicals in order to mix the compound in its own plant. The "Plastimaker" process permitted uniform blending of the liquid plasticizer with the resin and other dry ingredients to produce a dry molding compound. The company also prepared its own plastisol solutions, utilizing a different procedure for this purpose.

Compounding

The compounding room at Rockaway was equipped with one 1,200-pound and four 150-pound Hungerford Plastimakers. Containers of dry materials were carried by conveyor to an upper platform from which they were loaded into the large drum. As the drum rotated, liquid plasticizer from a tank was sprayed into the mixture. In 1955, two men in the compounding room were working a 57-hour week.

Injection Molding

The injection molding department was equipped with 13 Reed-Prentice machines from 8 to 32 ounces in size. Six of these machines were less than one year old in 1955. Most of the machines had been modified by the company to adapt them to the molding of flexible vinyls. In 1955, the molding department was operating three shifts daily on a five-day week.

Molding pellets were accumulated in a small in-process inventory typically composed of about 25 compounds in quantities from 500 to 7,000 pounds. Two mechanics handled all setup and machine maintenance work in the injection molding department. Each mold change required about one and one-half hours of work. When a cylinder had to be purged for a change in material, the mechanics would remove the dirty one and install a spare. These spare cylinders were kept available in the toolroom to reduce the downtime on machines. The company tried to schedule all setups and cylinder changes for the day shift when the mechanics worked, but foremen were sometimes called upon to make changes during night shifts.

The finishing department had to be flexible enough to carry out complex assembly jobs, including reaming, gluing, and similar operations. The department also did final assembly work on the doll line and had a motorized conveyor on which seven women could assemble 2,000 dolls per day.

Rotary Molding of Plastisol

The Riverdale plant contained 6,000 square feet of space with two principal work areas of approximately equal size. One area was used for molding and as a toolroom; the other contained equipment for secondary operations and was used for parts storage. The molding room contained six rotary molding machines, all of which had been designed and four of them built by Mr. Quackenbush.

Rotary molding was an inexpensive method of producing items to rough tolerances in high volume with relatively small investment. Although a master die might cost several hundred dollars, many molds could be made from the die at a cost of five or six dollars per mold. Mr. Quackenbush believed that the Hungerford equipment gave the company a definite quality and cost advantage over competitors, and made it possible to produce some items that could not be made elsewhere.

Labor

In 1955, the company employed about 175 workers and expected to add another 100 at the summer peak of the doll season. The employees belonged to the International Chemical Worker's Union, A. F. of L. Mr. Hungerford felt that the local union, which had been elected in 1951, was a "good" union to work with and that union-management relations were excellent.

Workers in the injection molding department were paid under a group incentive plan based on standard hourly production rates for each job. A bonus was paid to each worker on the shift, except the foreman, for any week when shift efficiency was over 80 percent. In 1953, a weekly $1.00 bonus was paid for each 5 percent above 80 percent efficiency. Setup time was not included in the "productive hours" used to calculate standard production, and an allowance of 30 minutes was given for each color change. Exhibit 3 shows typical calculation of shift efficiency.

The group plan was the only incentive plan being used in the injection molding department during 1955. Other departments used group or individual incentives, or did not offer incentive pay, depending upon the nature of the job being done. Although the company did not maintain a regular time study department, some of the bonus systems were based on time studies, and the chief engineer intended to try some methods studies in the near future. The executives, from foreman level up, shared a bonus of about 12 percent of profit before taxes.

Estimating

Eight or nine requests for estimates were received by Mr. Sandler each week, but few became production jobs. In preparing an estimate, the physical volume of a piece (which could be computed from blueprint dimensions) was multiplied by the known density of each molding compound to give the weight per piece. For estimating purposes, the weight per 1,000 pieces was used and a material loss factor (usually around 10 percent) was added. A standard cost for each compound was used in calculating material cost, including raw material cost and compounding expense.

The critical part of the estimating procedure was in judging molding cost, which depended upon the number of mold cavities and the machine cycle time. Hourly production was computed and costed at a predetermined machine-hour rate which was established to be $8.75 per hour for injection molding in 1955. The machine rate was reviewed annually by the treasurer and the auditors in order to reflect the recent cost level of direct labor and overhead. The Hungerford company produced some molds and handled the purchase of all other molds as a service to customers. Blueprints were submitted to at least four toolmakers for bids and the company was able to get delivery in six to eight weeks. Mold costs ran from a few thousand to over ten thousand dollars and were charged separately to the customer.

A standard setup charge of $75 per production run was included in the estimating calculation to cover the direct cost of mechanics' time, the loss of profit contribution from machine time, and the molding material lost in purging the cylinder. Finishing cost was determined by the expected direct labor time, charged at a rate designed to cover direct and indirect factory costs. The total of these costs constituted the "shop cost." A percentage was added to the shop cost to cover general overhead which included administrative salaries, office and shipping expenses, and general selling expenses. Development or laboratory expenses were not included in the overhead rate, but were returned through profit. Prices were set to provide a profit margin and a percentage for selling expenses. When the bid was made the customer was notified only of mold cost and price per thousand units.

Production Scheduling

Injection molding work was scheduled weekly from daily orders submitted by the Ohio Rubber Company via teletype and from orders received directly by the company. The teletype in the Hungerford office produced an original order, the salesman's confirmation, and a ditto master used to reproduce internal scheduling forms and invoices. Although all molding production was done to order, many items were produced in advance of required delivery time and then kept in inventory in order to permit larger and more economical production runs. The company used 100 to 150 different compounds in its production. Since the process extruders and molding machines had to be purged for every color change, the company made a practice of always "stepping up" a change from a lighter to a darker color. Molding cylinders had to be cleaned intermittently to remove carbon deposits.

Cost control activities in the molding department centered around two important statistics: material consumption and production per machine hour. At the end of each shift the foreman submitted a report for each injection molding machine showing consumption, output, and reasons for downtime. Production and consumption figures were accumulated by product weekly and monthly, and results were compared with estimates. A typical record for a custom injection molded part is shown in Exhibit 5.

Toolroom

The toolroom maintained all molds and built special jigs and fixtures and experimental molds. Production molds for grips and for most proprietary products were also built in this toolroom. In 1955, four master toolmakers were employed on a 48-hour week and the shop was equipped with two milling machines, four lathes, a surface grinder, shaper, band saw, and miscellaneous smaller machines.

Laboratory

In 1955, the laboratory for research and quality control included a chemist and two lab assistants. The company received an average of five "reasonable" requests for new compound formulations from customers each month. Each development job typically required months of experimentation before the proper formulation could be determined, although customers were not charged directly for development work. On their own initiative, laboratory technicians had developed a vinyl dispersion compound known as a "rigidisol" that could be produced for one-third the cost of similar materials available for purchase from outsiders. Although similar in nature to the plastisol suspensions, the rigidisol produced a rigid, rather than flexible product when molded.

Mr. Hungerford described his company as "basically development minded." The work of the company's engineers and chemists, the toolroom and laboratory, was considered to be an important part of every sale made. The cost of development work was difficult to assess, but was estimated at about $26,000 for 1955, excluding technical personnel salaries and experimental time on productive machines. Development expense was charged, whenever possible, against operating income as part of general overhead.

EXPANSION PROGRAM

In 1952, the company began studying the capital requirements and profit possibilities of future expansion of sales volume. The company's auditors were retained to study these factors in injection molding operations.

Auditor's Report

The auditor's study estimated that, based on the product mix of 1952, each injection molding machine could produce sales of $175,000 annually if operated on a three-shift five-day-a-week basis, allowing for a two-week vacation shutdown. For each multiple of seven productive machines, one stand-by would be required to take care of downtime and the stand-by had to be installed when the third machine was placed in operation. Thus two stand-bys would be required for 10–16 productive machines and three for 17–21 machines. Each machine would cost $22,000 installed, including spare cylinder. An additional allowance of $3,000 was recommended for sundry machinery and equipment required to keep the rest of the plant in balance with the molding department. Injection molding machines had an estimated life of 10 years.

Working capital requirements were estimated as $19,000 for each productive machine. This sum included one month's sales for accounts receivable, and $11,000 added inventory, offset by increases of $6,000 in payables and $1,000 in accrued payroll.

A study was made of injection molding production based on data prepared during the first six months of 1954. From this data it was estimated that one hour's average output of an injection molding machine would consume 34 pounds of compound and require 24 minutes of work in the finishing department. The estimated costs of operating the injection molding and associated departments at various levels of capacity are shown in Exhibit 6.

Proposed New Plant

In mid-1955, plans were drawn for a new 80,000 square foot plant to be constructed in Hanover Township, New Jersey. The 10-acre site, adjacent to Morristown, was available for immediate purchase and construction. It was located in what Mr. Hungerford called a "high class industrial area," and he believed that the township's tax rate was stable and that the location was favorable in other respects.

The plant was to have two stories of 40,000 square feet each, according to a design prepared by company engineers. The architect's rendering as well as a proposed layout is given in Exhibits 7A and 7B. The space was large enough to permit consolidation of all manufacturing and storage in one building with area for future expansion to nearly double the 1955 capacity. The injection molding department, for example, was intended to have space for 24 molding machines.

The plant was to have a modern system of piping to bring water, gas, electricity, and drainage facilities to each machine location. Cooling water would be cleaned and recirculated. A special system of troughs would catch the hydraulic fluid which leaked from injection machines and collect it in a central basin for reclamation. The entire plant would be cooled by large roof fans.

Significant savings in material handling were expected to be realized from the consolidation of two plants and from the open layout and conveyor system of the new plant. One saving would be in the cost of the truck now used to carry goods between the Rockaway and Riverdale plants. The driver was paid $50 per week and the truck cost about $20 weekly to operate. At least an additional $2,000 in material handling expense was expected to be saved by the consolidation annually.

The executives did not know how much they might save as a result of more efficient production flow in the new plant. They felt, however, that movement of in-process materials was very expensive in the Rockaway building where ramps, stairways, and halls reduced the effective work space to 36,000 square feet.

Tangible savings would be realized in rent and other occupancy expenses. At present, rents on the two plants came to $30,150 annually, including heat and taxes. An additional $5,000 was expected to be needed each year for leasehold improvements if the Hungerford company remained in the Rockaway plant. Machinery, inventory, and occupancy insurance totaled $9,000 annually. Power was a $45,000 expense, with 80 percent incurred at the Rockaway plant. At the new plant, taxes would be $7,000, estimated building maintenance $1,000, and heat $6,500. Insurance at the new location would be only $2,000 for the building, machinery, and inventory because of the safer construction of the plant. Mr. Hungerford estimated that $10,000 could be saved annually on power, primarily by consolidating the small Riverdale consumption with a high-volume rate and the fact that the rate structure was more favorable in the new location.

Sources of Capital

Total cost of the land and building would be $450,000. Mr. Hungerford intended to have the company act as general contractor with the company's chief engineer in charge for the estimated eight months' construction period. The project, if started September 1, would be completed by May, 1956. The lease on the Rockaway plant would expire April 30, 1956, and the Riverdale lease, December 29, 1959. The Metropolitan Life Insurance Company was willing to purchase a 15-year $300,000 note, if an equal amount could be raised through equity financing. The funds in excess of the cost of the plant would be used for working capital.

The Metropolitan note would represent a first mortgage on all assets and bear interest at 5 percent from September 1, 1955 and require a sinking fund of $20,000 annually. Notes could not be redeemed as part of any refunding operation involving a debt bearing a lower interest rate and the company would be prohibited from having any active subsidiaries. Additional indebtedness would be prohibited except up to $100,000 in unsecured bank loans provided such loans were cleared up for 30 days in each year. Leases for more than $5,000 annually and for more than three years would also be prohibited. Mr. Hungerford would have to agree to remain active in the management and retain at least a one-third stock interest so long as his health permitted. In addition, dividends on common stock would be permitted only up to 50 percent of accumulated net earnings from June 30, 1955, and then only if net current assets after the dividend would equal 75 percent of the notes outstanding.

The required equity capital could be obtained through sale of stock to the Central Illinois Securities Corporation, an investment trust. The Central Illinois company proposed to buy 24,000 shares of $10 par value $0.60 cumulative preferred stock and 33,000 shares of unissued common stock. The preferred stock bore the usual rights and restrictions for cumulative preferred, including: (1) redemption at company's option at $11 per share; (2) sinking fund equal to 20 percent of net income after preferred dividends, or $12,000, whichever is larger; (3) common dividends restricted to a percentage of net income ranging from 20 percent the first year to 50 percent after six years; (4) consent of two thirds of the existing preferred stock required to issue additional preferred or to change existing management contracts. The market price of Hungerford corporation common stock on June 27, 1955 was 3⅛ bid, 4⅛ asked.

FUTURE PROSPECTS

In the summer of 1955, Mr. Hungerford and the board of directors were about to decide whether to build a new plant, look for an existing building to buy or lease, or remain in the present locations. Mr. Hungerford believed that sales would increase in the future, but was not sure which of the operating divisions would have the greatest growth.

Injection Molding

In 1955, most of the Hungerford company's custom production was for appliance manufacturing, especially for vacuum cleaners, while proprietary production was predominantly for Flex-Grips. The United States market for vacuum cleaners was dominated by two large companies which shared over 50 percent of the market. The Hungerford company's biggest customer was the larger of these two companies. A trade publication reported in July, 1955, that the other large manufacturer had switched from rubber to molded vinyl parts for its attachments and would include over two pounds of vinyl in its new model. The reasons for the change were said to be the superior aging qualities, lack of surface cracking, better color, high gloss finish, and better abrasion resistance of vinyl. The model described was a "tanktype" cleaner using an extruded vinyl hose (accounting for a large share of the two pounds) and molded nozzles, gaskets, and litter pickers. In 1954, production of vacuum cleaners, according to the U.S. Census of Manufactures, was 2,616,000 units with a factory value of $115,500,000. According to trade sources, 1955 production was 25 percent ahead of the 1954 rate. The percentage of wired homes containing vacuum cleaners was very low when compared to that of other household appliances.

Rotary Molding

Mr. Hungerford felt that the largest potential for rotary products was in the doll industry. However, despite the fact that $5,000 invested in rotary equipment could produce as much sales volume as $40,000 in injection facilities, the division was not profitable at first. The sudden expansion of production, heavy development expenditures, and an unforeseen materials problem caused the rotary division to show a deficit in 1955, which offset 40 percent of the before-tax profits of the other two divisions.

The Hungerford company's initial line of a dozen dolls was expected to be ready for the 1956 season. Estimating total sales, sales by item, or the seasonal pattern of sales was difficult because the doll industry was comprised of many companies with little brand loyalty on the part of consumers. The sale of character dolls seemed relatively uninfluenced by any manufacturer's brands, and depended rather upon the specific design of a particular doll. New companies in the field had scored overnight successes with a popular item and had lost their success equally rapidly.

Working capital requirements in doll production were expected to be relatively high. The business was decidedly seasonal with as much as 80 percent of retail sales originating in the Christmas selling season. Advance dating of invoices was a common trade practice, thus lengthening the collection period. Credit problems and bad debt losses were expected to increase as the company developed its doll business.

The first year's production and sales were expected to serve as a guide for future planning of doll operations. The executives hoped to sell 100,000 to 150,000 units in the doll line during 1956. About 60 percent of these sales were expected to be in the "Mouseketeer" doll, and perhaps 25 percent in the "Tinker Bell" line. Tentative plans called for an inventory of 50,000 Mouseketeers to be accumulated by mid-July, with no sizeable stock held for any other item.

Dolls were sold at the retail level in fixed "price lines," and had to be designed and produced to sell at a profit within that price. The Mouseketeer and Tinker Bell dolls were of a size and type customarily sold at $2.98 retail price or $17.10 per dozen factory price. A commercial artist was helping the company's engineers to develop new methods and designs to enable the company to become a volume producer of other proprietary dolls.

Market statistics were difficult to obtain since the toy industry included a large group of companies making a variety of products. The U.S. Census of Manufactures estimated that in 1947, 15,287,000 rubber dolls worth $18,526,000 and 17,154,000 dolls of all other varieties worth $21,271,000 were manufactured. The Hungerford dolls were designed primarily to compete in the market against rubber dolls.

1. HUNGERFORD PLASTICS CORPORATION
Comparative Balance Sheets, 1947-1955
(December 31, except 1955)

ASSETS	1947	1948	1949	1950	1951	1952	1953	1954	June 30, 1955
Current Assets:									
Cash	$ 20,038	$ 65,924	$ 16,338	$ 18,029	$ 15,446	$ 64,839	$ 41,851	$ 48,031	$ 86,010
Accts. receivable, net	41,950	71,367	51,538	117,676	99,223	101,611	52,635	79,293	168,362
Inventories	66,825	67,307	93,921	124,063	167,276	154,998	163,612	187,947	197,875
Est. refund of taxes	-0-	-0-	2,500	-0-	-0-	-0-	-0-	-0-	-0-
Total Current Assets	$128,813	$204,598	$164,297	$259,768	$281,945	$321,448	$258,098	$315,271	$452,247
Officer's life insurance	$ 2,230	$ 2,629	$ 3,038	$ 4,607	$ 6,084	$ 7,571	$ 9,117	$ 10,670	$ 11,820
Fixed Assets:									
Land	$ 13,524	$ 13,524	$ 13,524	$ 13,524	-0-	-0-	-0-	-0-	-0-
Buildings	88,654	88,654	88,929	88,929	-0-	-0-	-0-	-0-	-0-
Mach'y and equipment	156,701	173,920	180,668	233,457	$273,377	$297,799	$410,855	$508,224	$526,918
Less depreciation	(33,430)	(51,952)	(71,699)	(94,081)	(102,796)	(130,953)	(165,394)	(210,581)	(236,862)
Molds, less amortization	22,307	8,314	25,670	40,148	24,674	22,650	11,750	14,745	14,984
Own molds in process	-0-	-0-	3,775	15,630	10,297	12,210	4,111	9,042	15,178
Total Fixed Assets	$247,756	$232,460	$240,867	$297,607	$205,552	$201,706	$261,322	$321,430	$320,218
Deferred Charges:									
Leasehold improve.-net	-0-	-0-	-0-	-0-	$ 28,380	$ 36,567	$ 38,059	$ 28,831	$ 19,899
Leasehold sec. deposit	-0-	-0-	-0-	-0-	7,802	7,802	7,802	9,602	9,602
Prepaid expenses	$ 7,375	$ 4,397	$ 8,669	$ 9,056	11,620	9,816	10,166	12,478	35,689
Patents; other assets	8,402	11,176	10,903	10,246	9,588	8,931	8,271	29,614	27,086
Total Deferred Charges	$ 15,777	$ 15,573	$ 19,572	$ 19,302	$ 57,390	$ 63,116	$ 64,298	$ 80,525	$ 92,276
Total Assets	$394,576	$455,260	$427,774	$581,284	$550,971	$593,841	$592,835	$727,896	$876,561
LIABILITIES									
Current Liabilities:									
Note payable to bank	$ 30,000	$ 35,000	$ 25,000	-0-	$ 62,500	$ 45,000	$ 48,000	$ 60,000	$ 35,000
Accounts payable	46,802	70,535	65,313	$153,516	83,154	61,752	29,251	100,262	148,812
Accrued expenses					9,542	15,758	5,761	22,746	46,812
Payroll taxes accrued	-0-	-0-	-0-	-0-	12,467	3,754	4,186	20,440	15,322
Advance for molds	3,800	-0-	3,360	11,438	9,544	-0-	11,048	18,163	20,968
Fed. taxes on income	1,748	4,748	2,151	10,572	12,250	55,338	45,403	15,670	60,000
Mortgage pay.-current	3,750	3,750	3,750	55,550	-0-	-0-	-0-	-0-	-0,
Total Current Liab.	$ 86,100	$114,033	$ 99,574	$231,076	$189,457	$181,602	$143,649	$237,281	$326,914
Mort. on land and bldg.	$ 26,250	$ 22,500	$ 18,750	$ 15,000	-0-	-0-	-0-	-0-	-0-
Note payable (due 3/15/58)	-0-	-0-	-0-	-0-	-0-	-0-	-0-	-0-	$ 8,000
Stockholders' equity*	$ 57,250	$ 57,250	$ 57,250	$ 57,250	$ 57,250	$ 57,250	$ 57,250	$ 60,278	$ 60,278
Paid-in surplus	214,745	214,745	214,745	214,745	214,745	214,745	214,745	249,567	249,567
Retained earnings	10,231	46,732	37,455	63,213	89,519	145,244	182,191	190,770	241,802
Less stock held in treas.	-0-	-0-	-0-	-0-	-0-	(5,000)	(5,000)	(10,000)	(10,000)
Total Stockholders' Eq.	$282,226	$318,727	$309,450	$335,208	$361,514	$412,239	$449,186	$490,615	$541,647
Total Liabilities	$394,576	$455,260	$427,774	$581,284	$550,971	$593,841	$592,835	$727,896	$876,561

*Stock authorized: 350,000 shares
Outstanding (241,112 shares, 1954-1955)
(229,000 shares, 1947-1953)

2. HUNGERFORD PLASTICS CORPORATION

Income Statements and Selected Operating Data, 1945-1955

	1947	1948	1949	1950	1951	1952	1953	1954	Six Months Ended June 30, 1954	Six Months Ended June 30, 1955
Net sales	$403,329	$614,748	$466,346	$759,726	$896,804	$1,111,066	$1,291,604	$1,288,017	$596,723	$1,087,535
Cost of goods sold	394,279	536,457	414,639	656,171	819,289	895,252	1,055,097	1,133,092	513,325	843,289
Gross profit	$ 9,050	$ 78,291	$ 51,707	$103,555	$ 77,515	$ 215,814	$ 236,507	$ 154,925	$ 83,398	$ 244,246
Selling, general, and admin. expenses	87,555	105,355	104,091	106,922	106,535	111,663	137,736	126,593	52,479	120,685
Operating income (loss)	$(78,505)	$(27,064)	$(52,384)	$(3,367)	$(29,020)	$ 104,151	$ 98,771	$ 28,332	$ 30,919	$ 123,561
Other income:										
Royalty income	70,007	68,325	42,345	39,800	37,000	5,000	5,000	5,000	2,500	500
Gain on sale					25,367					
Loss on mold							(12,989)			
Interest	(2,194)	(1,759)	(1,738)	(2,634)	(2,287)	(2,659)	(1,452)	(1,553)	(616)	(1,223)
Gain on sale of machinery					14,222	1,233	(58)			
Moving expense					(7,976)					
Income before taxes	$(10,692)	$ 39,502	$(11,777)	$ 33,798	$ 37,306	$ 107,725	$ 89,272	$ 31,779	$ 32,803	$ 122,838
Federal taxes		3,000	(2,500)	8,040	11,000	52,000	41,000	12,000	11,558	60,000
Net income (loss)	$(10,692)	$ 36,502	$ (9,277)	$ 25,758	$ 26,306	$ 55,725	$ 48,272	$ 19,779	$ 21,245	$ 62,838
Dividends on capital stock							$ 11,325	$ 11,200	$ 11,200	$ 11,806
Common shares outstanding	229,000	229,000	229,000	229,000	229,000	226,500	226,500	236,112		
Common stock price—high	5 1/8	3 3/4	1 1/2	2 1/4	1 3/4	1 7/8	2 1/8	3 1/2		
—low	3	3/4	3/4	7/8	1 1/8	1 1/8	1 1/2	1 3/4		
Long-term debt, capital stock, surplus	$308,475	$341,227	$328,200	$350,208	$361,514	$ 412,239	$ 449,186	$ 490,614		
Maintenance and repairs:										
Machinery and equipment				$ 13,440	$ 11,498	$ 16,961	$ 22,491	$ 26,507		
Depreciation:										
Machinery and equipment				20,159	25,149	28,756	35,622	45,187		
Building				2,223	926					
Amortization:										
Molds*				12,680	19,620	24,423	22,076	5,974		
Leasehold improvements				341	2,950	7,942	13,640	18,967		
Intangible assets				657	657	868	797	657		
Rent				5,000	15,292	21,893	22,950	23,008		

*Amortized over three-year life.

3. HUNGERFORD PLASTICS CORPORATION
Sales of Proprietary and Custom Products
(Gross Sales, 1947-1950, Net Sales, 1951-1954)

	1947	1948	1949	1950	1951	1952	1953	1954
Proprietary Sales								
(1) First Half	$ 2,487	$ 55,193	$ 64,890	$115,000	$177,734	$ 144,361	$ 211,692	$ 235,840
(2) Second Half	2,708	96,665	115,050	239,652	195,580	173,677	213,987	216,244
(3) Full Year	5,175	151,858	179,940	354,652	373,314	318,038	425,679	452,084
Custom Sales								
(4) First Half	125,588	225,926	79,532	144,280	253,063	359,584	472,160	312,996
(5) Second Half	282,273	267,000	230,973	295,712	215,207	219,494	395,627	455,186
(6) Full Year	407,861	492,926	310,511	439,992	468,270	779,078	867,787	768,182
Total Sales								
(7) First Half	128,055	281,119	144,428	259,280	430,797	503,945	683,852	548,836
(8) Second Half	284,981	363,665	346,023	535,364	410,787	593,171	609,614	671,430
(9) Full Year	413,036	644,784	490,451	794,644	841,584	1,097,116	1,293,466	1,220,266

Typical Calculation of Shift Efficiency

Machine Number	Hours: Available	Hours: Productive	Product	Total Good Production	Av. Output/ Production Hour	Standard Output per Hour	Productive Efficiency	Productive Hours	Remarks
1	8	8	A	3,600	450	430	105.0	8.4	
2	8	7.5	B	2,400	320	350	91.5	6.9	1 Color Change
3	8	8	C	6,000	750	600	125.0	10.0	
4	8	0							No operator
5	8	4	D	1,500	377	375	100.5	4.0	Machine down 4 hours Mold Break
6	8	8	E	4,800	600	700	85.7	6.9	
Total	48	35.5						36.2	

Shift Efficiency - $\frac{36.2}{35.5}$ = 102%

4A. HUNGERFORD PLASTICS CORPORATION

Proprietary Products—"Flex-Grips"

4B. HUNGERFORD PLASTICS CORPORATION

Proprietary Product—Mouseketeer Doll

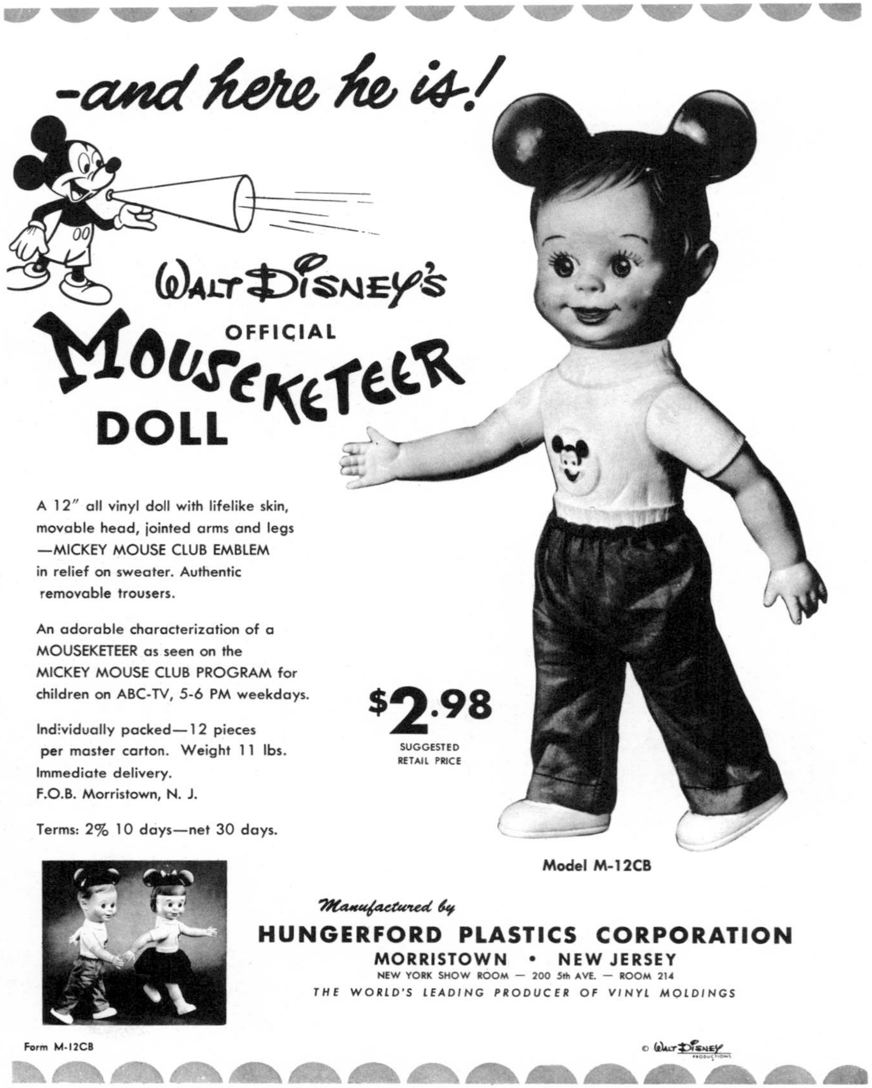

5. HUNGERFORD. PLASTICS CORPORATION

Production Record for Typical Custom Product

1955	Production	Wt. per 1,000	Material Consumed	Cost per Pound	Material Cost	Estimated per Hour	Estimated Hours	Actual Hours	Gain (Loss) Hours
Jan.	75,117	16.5	1,239.43	.37	$458.59	300	250.39	167.25	83.14
Feb.	96,926	16.5	1,599.28	.37	591.73	300	323.09	226.0	97.09
Mar.	84,304	16.5	1,391.02	.37	514.68	300	281.01	191.0	90.01
Apr.	27,149	16.5	447.96	.37	165.74	300	90.50	70.0	20.50
May	13,435	16.5	223.33	.37	82.63	300	44.78	35.0	9.78
June	99,207	16.5	1,636.92	.37	605.66	300	330.69	223.5	107.19

1955	Std. Molding Cost	Molding Variance	Total Cost	Estimated Cost/Unit	Actual Cost/Unit
Jan.	$2,190.91	$(389.93)	$2,259.57	$.03527	$.03008
Feb.	2,827.04	(455.35)	2,963.42	.03527	.03057
Mar.	2,458.84	(422.15)	2,551.37	.03527	.03026
Apr.	791.88	(96.15)	861.47	.03527	.03173
May	391.83	(45.87)	428.59	.03527	.03190
June	2,893.53	(502.72)	2,996.47	.03527	.03020

6. HUNGERFORD PLASTICS CORPORATION

Costs of Operation at Selected Capacity Levels

Number of Molding Machines Operating	Number of Molding Machines Stand-by	Net Annual Sales	Compounding Cost per Pound	Injection Molding Cost per Machine-Hour	Mold Amortization per Machine-Hour	Finishing Cost per Productive Man-Hour	Percentage of General Overhead to Cost of Sales
7	1	$1,225	$.085	$10.379	$.647	$2.991	19.02%
8	1	1,400	.075	9.626	.556	3.053	18.53
9	1	1,575	.072	9.461	.492	2.880	17.91
10	2	1,750	.066	9.167	.453	2.855	17.55
11	2	1,925	.062	8.874	.414	2.769	17.67
12	2	2,100	.065	8.645	.414	2.694	17.42
13	2	2,275	.062	9.129	.375	2.608	17.30
14	2	2,450	.064	8.976	.349	2.571	16.69
15	2	2,625	.062	8.798	.324	2.534	16.69
16	2	2,800	.059	8.619	.311	2.460	16.32
17	3	2,975	.066	8.619	.311	2.460	16.20
18	3	3,150	.066	8.632	.298	2.410	15.58
19	3	3,325	.064	8.823	.272	2.361	15.46
20	3	3,500	.061	8.657	.259	2.324	15.09
21	3	3,675	.057	8.504	.246	2.299	14.85

NOTE: This exhibit represents analyst's estimates of a projected cost structure for injection molding production only. Estimates based on operation of molding machines for 120 hours per week. Compounding, molding, and finishing rates include all labor, expense, and depreciation for those departments. Purchase cost of raw material is estimated to be one-third of sales. General overhead includes selling and administrative expenses and Cost of Sales represents compounding, molding, and finishing costs including cost of material but excluding mold amortization.

7A. HUNGERFORD PLASTICS CORPORATION

Architect's Rendering of Proposed Plant

7B. HUNGERFORD PLASTICS CORPORATION

First-Floor Layout of Proposed Plant

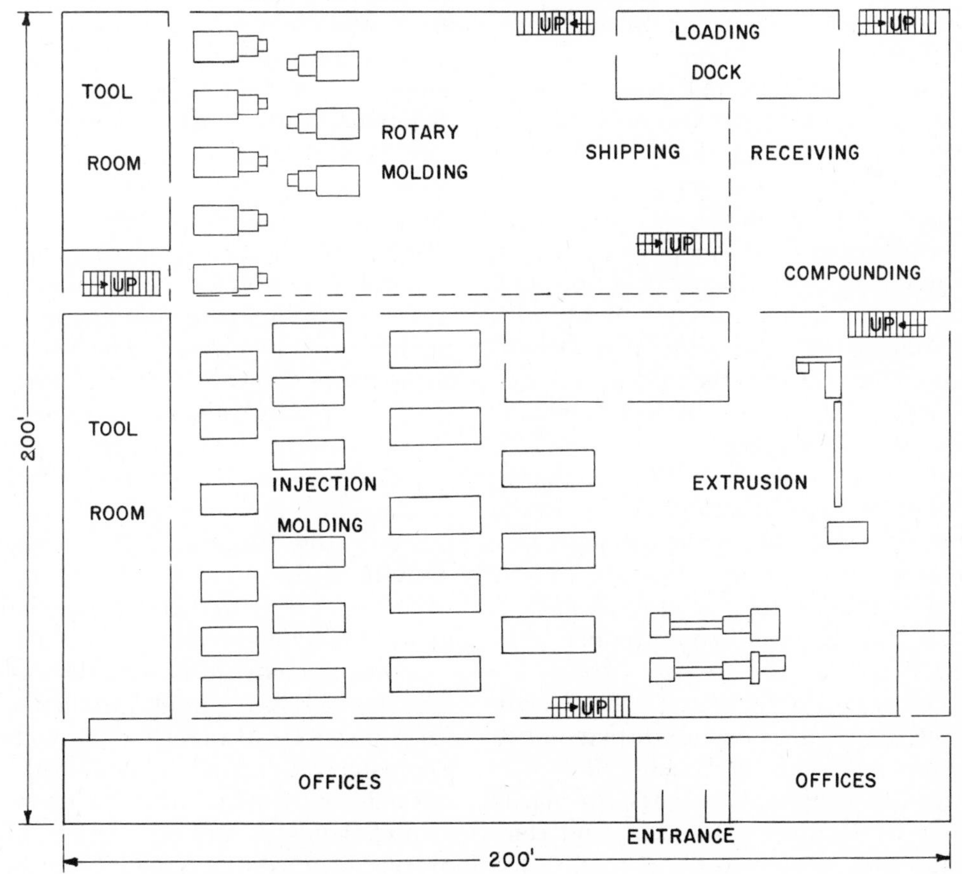

The Victory Plastics Company

The Victory Plastics Company was an independent manufacturer of injection, extrusion, and compression molded plastic items selling in both the military and civilian markets. In September, 1957, the president, Mr. Edwin Beckwith, was faced with the problem of adjusting his business to counterbalance the cancellation of several large military contracts.

HISTORY

The Victory Plastics Company, established in 1941 as a wholly owned subsidiary of the Beckwith-Arden Company with Mr. Edwin L. Beckwith as president and Mr. Charles P. MacIver as vice-president and general manager, was an offshoot of the Beckwith-Arden Company. The parent company had been started in the early twentieth century by Mr. H. H. Beckwith to take advantage of patented inventions for shoe stiffeners. Mr. Edwin Beckwith, the son of the founder, had been vice-president of the Felt Process Company (another Beckwith-Arden subsidiary) and prior to this, director of the laboratory for the Beckwith-Arden Company. In 1937, Mr. Edwin Beckwith and a laboratory associate of his, Mr. C. P. MacIver, started looking for opportunities to participate in the growing war effort. They learned that the United States Army was using an old and expensive bayonet scabbard made of wood, metal, and canvas. In 1938 they succeeded in developing a cheaper and improved bayonet scabbard made of laminated canvas and cellulose acetate butyrate with a modified metal top. After the War Department accepted the scabbard, the Beckwith-Arden Company set up the Victory Plastics Company to manufacture the scabbards.

In addition to supplying 14 million scabbards, (98 percent of the bayonet scabbards used by the Allies came from this plant), the company produced knife handles, knife scabbards, mortar fuses, vinyl envelopes for vacuum packaging, target cloth and other military products during World War II.

In September, 1957, the largest volume civilian products were a line of store display boxes, shelves, counter dividers, and racks. The Victory Plastics Company molded parts (primarily polystyrene) by extrusion, injection, and compression, and then assembled the parts into fixtures. The Victory company warehoused the fixtures in the Hudson plant for its customer, Atlantic Paulson, a retail store design firm. The other major civilian products were a line of custom-molded wheels for casters and juvenile furniture and a proprietary line of extruded table edging and luggage handles.

One example of their application of military experience to the civilian market was the development of the plastic raincoat. The process of dielectric sealing of plastic film was jointly developed by the Radio Corporation of America and The Victory Plastics Company durng World War II as a means of packaging military items. After the war Victory executives conceived the idea of making polyvinyl chloride raincoats by this sealing method. Arrangements were made with a New England raincoat manufacturer for that manufacturer to distribute under its own name plastic raincoats manufactured by the Victory company. The other firm found the business of selling plastic raincoats profitable, but apparently due to conflicts with the Victory sales manager, felt forced to develop an alternative source of raincoats, which subsequently replaced the Victory company as a supplier. A similar arrangement was then negotiated with a national raincoat firm. In this case also, the sales manager seemed to present a barrier to effective communications between the two firms. When the public taste changed to cheaper raincoats, the distributor found a new supplier without letting The Victory Plastics Company attempt to manufacture the less expensive coats. The Victory company then set up its own distribution system for selling high-quality raincoats. Experienced sales personnel were hired but the company failed to generate the sales volume necessary for efficient production. This attempt at direct distribution was very costly and forced the company to withdraw from the raincoat business in 1956.

During the entire postwar period, the Victory company maintained its contacts with military procurement authorities and endeavored to gain both research and production contracts when they were available. The Victory Plastics Company was relatively successful in gaining research contracts and usually had about a dozen projects going at any one time. The military procurement contracts had been an on-again, off-again business. In addition to increases or decreases in the defense budget as the cold war changed in character, they were subject to various open or hidden political pressures.

MANUFACTURING FACILITIES

The Victory Plastics Company had secured a multistory brick factory in Hudson, a small town 30 miles west of Boston, through the services of the Boston and Maine Railroad. The building, which included office space and 275,000 square feet of manufacturing space, had been purchased at the same time the company was started. The following facilities were included:

1. A press room containing The Victory Plastics Company's own molding equipment, described below:

Injection. The capacity and limitations of the company's 10 injection machines are shown in Exhibit 6. Two of the machines were purchased during the war for military products, but the rest were purchased later for civilian products. The latest, the 100-ounce, was received in July, 1957, primarily in response to requests from the store fixtures customer for large lucite boxes. Mr. Beckwith also hoped that some of the other products could be produced more cheaply on this machine by using molds with more cavities.

Compression. The company's 20 compression machines were purchased during the war for scabbard production. The presses had been ordered with greater size and weight than required to make scabbards in order to give the company some capacity in the postwar period that small competitors could not equal.

The value of the compression equipment for the civilian market looked less attractive in 1957 than it did in the early postwar years before The Victory Plastics Company lost the radio cabinet sales to Philco, Emerson, Crosley, and other firms. As a result of the development of thermoplastics and injection molding equipment, and the rise in transportation costs which decreased the market area, the compression machines had not been used for civilian business at a rate higher than 50 percent of capacity.

The Victory Plastics Company was currently making use of the compression presses in making Belleville springs for the mines. The springs, resembling dish-shaped washers, were extremely difficult to produce, and the Victory company supplied them to some of its competitors, due to the latter's inability to manufacture the spring properly.

The compression equipment included seven 800-ton presses, eight 200-ton, one 40-ton, and four small experimental presses. The Victory executives thought their line of seven 800-ton presses was unique. Other companies might have had one or two machines as large, but they knew of none with seven. All the machines could also be used as transfer presses and one of the large presses had been specially adapted for laminating.

Extrusion. Two 50-pound-per-hour extruders had been purchased during the war for the production of carrying straps, packaging straps, and other miscellaneous parts of plastic military items. The president felt that the company had not effectively utilized this equipment. In the fall of 1957, the main extruded products were table molding and base stock tracks for display partitions.

2. A government area containing the equipment owned by the United States Government and constituting a facility for the manufacture of various land mines and fuses. The molding equipment and machine tools in this area had been purchased by the government from outside sources, but most of the assembly tools and fixtures had been designed and built by the Victory company and were now owned by the government. The molding equipment, consisting of 26 injection molding machines, included four 32-ounce machines, seven 24-ounce, three 16-ounce, ten 12-ounce, one 6-ounce, and one 4-ounce machine. Even though the work was highly automated there was sufficient assembling and machining equipment to employ several times as many workers as the molding equipment in the room required. The government equipment could not presently be used by the Victory company for nondefense work, but in the absence of any defense work, Mr. Beckwith thought it might be possible to lease this government equipment on reasonable terms for other purposes.

3. A large area devoted to electronic sealing equipment, substantially unused in September of 1957. The older portion of the equipment

had been purchased during the war to handle military vaccum packaging, but most of it was installed in 1947–1949 to produce plastic raincoats. There were about 60 bonders and 40 bar sealers. Both types of machine joined two pieces of plastic film together, but the bonders were more expensive, slower, and made a better joint. After the Victory company's pioneering efforts in making raincoats, many other firms entered the business and developed cheaper production methods. Competing firms made low-cost coats with about 60 bar sealers and 3 or 4 bonders.

4. A civilian assembly area containing workbenches, a varied assortment of minor jigs and fixtures, and some larger pieces of equipment for grinding, polishing, dipping, baking, and packaging.

5. An area used for storing the store display fixtures warehoused by Victory for its customer.

6. A large first-floor area adjacent to the railroad siding and truck-loading facilities used for storing molding compounds.

7. A very extensive machine shop containing more machine tools of all types than were being used in 1957. For 15 years the Victory company made its own molds. Although delivery was much more satisfactory and the quality was far superior, the molds were more expensive than molds purchased from outside suppliers. In 1954 and 1955 the company decided it could no longer afford to make its own molds. Since then the machine shop's work with molds had been limited to repair and maintenance.

ORGANIZATION

The chief engineer headed up the engineering work which was divided into three sections: engineering, drafting, and toolroom and molds. The engineering section included 15 engineers to take care of product engineering for existing products, some research and development projects, and customer inquiries. It also handled process engineering, designing equipment and fixtures made on the premises, and making specifications for equipment purchased outside.

The largest part of the laboratory's work was research and development work for customers or for Victory's own products. By far the most significant customer in this respect was the United States Army. Among the outstanding successful developments in this laboratory were nonmetallic armor, and its resultant products: helmets, body armor, vision blocks for tanks, rocket blast mats, and flak curtains for troop carriers and for the protection of gun emplacements. Another portion of their time was devoted to process changes arising out of quality control problems in the mill. Because of the understanding of both the customer's requirements and the technical problems of production gained in the product development stage, engineers and chemists from this group formed the source of the project chiefs mentioned below.

In September, 1957, the laboratory was working on 17 different military contracts with a total unexpended balance of $200,000. They were providing about $25,000 of work each month on these fixed-price and cost-plus-fixed-fee contracts. These military laboratory contracts occupied about half the 25 engineers employed in the laboratory.

The raincoat department was almost completely shut down in 1957, but it still required a foreman to lead the workers in the raincoat room who were doing the limited amount of cutting, bonding, and packaging required to meet the remaining orders, handling experimental production related to laboratory contracts, and producing occasional body armor orders.

The military finishing was quite complicated and production was departmentalized by major contract. In early September, 1957, there was an M19 mine assembly department and an M606 fuse assembly department.

Because of the complexity and size of the large government jobs, the engineer who had worked with this product in the development stages was detached from the laboratory to act as a project chief and to coordinate the production and inspection of the item. On problems relating to the military product or its specifications, the foreman reported to this project chief. On all other problems the foreman went directly to Bob Wade, the assistant superintendent, or Frank Millea, the production superintendent.

In September, 1957, The Victory Plastics Company employed 710 people. The press room was operating on a three-shift basis, while the military finishing departments were working two shifts. About 110 of the workers were clerical, engineering, laboratory, or executive personnel. The 600 production workers were organized in the AFL-CIO Chemical Workers Union. The management believed that both parties were reasonably satisfied with the existing labor-management relations. On August 25, 1957, a new contract was signed calling for an across-the-board wage increase of 3½ percent, effective September 1, 1957.

SALES

The Victory Plastics Company employed three salesmen. Almost all sales were in the northeastern United States, and no effort was being made to solicit orders actively outside this area. The region was divided in a way that would allow all the salesmen to be based in the home office and still give each man some calls which would not be overnight trips (defined as greater than 80 miles). Mr. Crosby covered Maine, New Hampshire, Vermont, and northern Massachusetts. Mr. Johnson covered a strip of central Massachusetts running from Boston to the New York State line, western Connecticut, and all of New York State except New York City and Long Island. Mr. Stuart covered southeastern Massachusetts, Rhode Island, eastern Connecticut, Long Island, New York City, New Jersey, and Pennsylvania. All government contracts were handled through the northern New England salesman because he had the smallest territory.

The sales manager had been dismissed two years earlier and had not been replaced. Some help was received from the president, and the controller if the president was unavailable, but, for the most part, the salesmen supervised themselves. The salesmen were paid on a straight salary basis.

The government contracts involved much time maintaining contacts and preparing and negotiating bids, schedule changes, design changes, requests for overtime, contract extensions, specifications, and price revisions. For this reason, Mr. Crosby spent full time and Mr. Stuart spent most of his time working with the Pentagon, the various Ordnance Districts, and the Rock Island and Picatinny arsenals.

Although all the information required for bidding on ordnance contracts was supposed to be available in the various Ordnance District headquarters, including Boston, the Victory company had found it necessary to maintain contact with personnel in the Pentagon and at several arsenals in order to obtain notice of what contracts might be available.

Most civilian sales were left to the third salesman. He spent the majority of his time maintaining relationships with existing customers. He was able to find some new possibilities and continued to forward new inquiries to the mill. In view of the overwhelming dollar volume of the military business and the usual penalties for delays in these contracts, the engineering and production departments felt obliged to give the military products the highest priority. While most civilian inquiries were handled expeditiously, the occasional delays made life frustrating for Mr. Johnson. The prevalence of the military business with its relatively high overhead also made the estimators less willing to reduce their overhead burden rates in order to obtain civilian business.

Depending on the nature of the calls and the area, a salesman might make from 2 to 20 calls per day. The Victory salesmen tried to call on potential customers at two-month intervals. Calls to regular customers were made at more frequent intervals. A large customer like the Bassick Division of the Stewart-Warner Corporation, which purchased plastic wheels for use in casters, would probably be called upon once every week or 10 days. The conversion of a potential customer to an actual customer typically took six calls: the first to receive the invitation to bid, the second to clarify questions arising from the invitation, the third to present the bid personally, the fourth to confer on the terms of the agreement, the fifth to submit the final drawings and mold design, and the sixth to present the first sample.

In preparing this estimate Mr. Beckwith liked to have some idea of the price required to get the business. Furthermore, he knew that certain competitors could do particular jobs more cheaply than Victory. If these competitors were involved there was little point in spending a great deal of time refining the figures. In some cases the salesman was able to provide this information.

Sometimes the business was either gained or lost at the original price quoted. Frequently the customer wanted a lower price. This might be done by changing the raw material or by specifying a lower grade. It might be done by persuading the customer to buy a mold with a larger number of cavities, thus increasing the original cost but lowering the unit cost. Finally, the customer might agree to order in larger quantities.

If all these failed, the Victory company might try to adjust the bid. This was done by reconsidering the uncertainties so as to change the burden rates involved, the estimated downtime, or the estimated scrap rate. The management might revise their estimates if the business was particularly attractive and if they felt the company was close to receiving the contract. A sample quote calculation is shown in Exhibit 5.

TYPES OF PRODUCTS

The executives of The Victory Plastics Company had had different experiences with three major types of products.

Military

Victory Plastics company's approach to the military business placed great emphasis on the engineering and technical aspects of the field. They bid on as many R & D contracts and engineering development contracts as they could. In the past the company had spent as much as $15,000 preparing a bid for an engineering development contract. The vendor who had done the engineering work seemed to have an almost unsurpassable lead over his competitors in bidding and making a profit on production contracts.

In early September, 1957, the company had three production contracts for antitank mines totaling about $10 million. All three contracts included the same items: the M19 mine, the M606 fuse, and the M2 activator. Each mine required one fuse and one activator. Contract #2887 was virtually completed. The M19 mines and the M2 activators were completed on contract #3646, but the fuses on this contract were still in production. The company was currently producing the mines and activators on contract #4158, but had not yet started the fuses. There was over $2 million of work yet to be performed on contract #4158. Since the parts were used in a one-to-one ratio, and each contract was for a given number of finished mines, the United States Army possessed about 300,000 mines and activators without fuses.

The present production contracts were on a negotiated price basis with a clause permitting renegotiation downward. Contract #3646 had been profitable, but contract #4158 was negotiated in 1956 when it was known that the price on #3646 was too high, but it was not known how far The Victory Plastics Company would be able to bring the cost down. In looking at the situation in September, 1957, it appeared that the price on #4158 was too low, because the company had not yet been able to bring its costs down to the contract price.

In view of the long-term military requirements for antitank mines, the Victory management had been led to expect this work to continue for at least two or three years, unless there were major technological breakthroughs making this kind of weapon obsolete.

The management was aware that the Army was receiving a decreasing share of military appropriations, but the trend was thought to have been stabilized. However, the company had just received word that the #3646 and #4158 contracts were to be cancelled effective September 15, 1957. The explanation for this cutback was understood to be that the Air Force and Navy had overspent their budgets and the Army was being cut back to supply the funds.

Consumer Goods

In the past the company had tried to sell plastic housewares through jobbers to retailers, but the jobbers had not sold enough to make it profitable for The Victory Plastics Company. Mr. MacIver thought that the Victory company had failed to do enough missionary selling and advertising to make the products attractive for the jobbers. He had strong reservations about the desirability of selling housewares through this channel because the jobbers were not in a position to push aggressively any items and tended to sell on a purely price basis. This meant that even if the desired volume could be reached, margins would tend to be low.

Mr. Beckwith estimated that it cost about $15,000 to develop a proprietary consumer item: $3,000 in development costs, $7,000 in a mold, and $5,000 in inventory investment. He thought that a company like Victory Plastics might be able to develop one new item (wastepaper baskets, wall brackets, cups, coat hangers, etc.) a month, so that after a year and a half it might have a line sufficiently large to merit the buyers' attention.

Industrial Products

There was a strong tendency for manufacturers of products requiring plastic components to develop stable relationships with one or two vendors and to have these firms do most of their plastics molding. The business was usually a stop-and-go business with short runs. In some cases the buyer arranged to buy a carload of molding compound and store it at the vendor's plant so that quantity discount prices could be obtained even though the individual run might not merit them. Since other suppliers were constantly trying to enter the business, prices were very competitive and margins were not high.

PROPOSALS FOR ACTION

In analyzing the situation, Mr. Beckwith came to the conclusion that the main difficulty with increasing the volume of consumer and industrial sales was the lack of sales contacts. He was, therefore, considering increasing the number of salesmen with the following factors in mind:

1. The figures of the Tarnell Company indicated that large plastic molding companies paid about 4 percent of their net sales out in salesmen's salaries and commissions. Since Mr. Beckwith hoped to have at least $1,600,000 of sales this would allow $64,000 for salaries and commissions. If the salesmen earned $8,000 each, a comparable budget would allow eight men.

2. During the previous eight months, the Victory company had $617,000 of consumer and industrial business. Of this volume, $383,000 had been in store display fixtures sold to Atlantic Paulson, a customer handled without a salesman. The remaining sales of $234,000 would indicate an annual rate of $350,000, gained by approximately one and a half salesmen. On this basis, one salesman could presently bring in about $230,000 of business a year.

Since new salesmen would probably take some time to achieve this level, Mr. Beckwith decided to assume that a new salesman might bring in $80,000 worth of business the first year, $160,000 the second year, and $230,000 the third year.

3. He itemized his selling expenses for the first eight months of 1957 as follows:

3/5 of the telegram, telephone, and postage*	$ 8,100
3/4 of the administrative and selling travel expenses*	18,200
All of the sales engineering	7,400
All of the selling and adv't supplies and adv't space	1,600
All of the salesmen's salaries	14,500
All of the selling and adv't social security taxes	700
Total selling expenses 3 salesmen for 8 months	$50,500
Predicted expenses 3 salesmen for 1 year	75,700
Predicted expenses 1 salesman for 1 year	25,200

* Mr. Beckwith estimated that 40 percent of the travel and communications expense was incurred by himself, the controller, and other nonsales personnel.

He, therefore, anticipated that each additional salesman would cost $25,200 per year. There would be some additional clerical work in Hudson supporting additional salesmen, so he rounded the cost off upwards to $80,000 for three additional salesmen.

4. Mr. Beckwith then examined his cost sheets to find out how much of his costs were either fixed or did not vary greatly with sales. He charted his remaining general and administrative expenses on an item-by-item basis against his sales for the past few years and drew a trend line through these points. He decided to consider the value of these lines at zero sales as his fixed expenses.

Administrative and Selling

Executive salaries	$ 41,000
Clerical salaries	41,000
Subscriptions, dues, donations	2,400
Rent	1,500
Auto expense	3,200
Insurance	2,800
Depreciation	6,100
Telegram, telephone, and postage	2,200
Travel expense	11,000
Professional services	14,000
Social security taxes	3,200
	$128,400

5. He performed similar calculations on his manufacturing expenses.

Manufacturing Burden

Supervision	$ 63,000
Boiler room	20,000
Heat, light and power	68,000
Maintenance, land and buildings	18,000
Maintenance, machinery and equipment	14,000
Taxes, real estate, water and sewage	24,000
Insurance	11,000
Depreciation	54,000
Clerical	3,000
	$275,000

6. He then used this breakdown of fixed and variable costs to evaluate the company's experience in the first eight months of 1957. He decided to eliminate the sales commission and the overtime premium expense from these calcula-

tions because he did not expect either to occur again.

Net sales	$4,718,563	100.0%
Material	2,280,000	48.3
Direct labor	830,000	17.6
Variable manufacturing burden*	803,000	17.1
Variable nonselling administration**	126,000	2.7

* $1,006,000 [=8-month manufacturing burden] − $20,000 [=overtime] − ⅔ ($275,000) [=12-month fixed manufacturing burden].

** $264,000 [=8-month G & A] − $50,500 [=variable selling] − $2,000 [=salesmen's commission] − ⅔ ($128,400) [=12-month fixed G & A].

By a process of subtraction, the contribution towards fixed costs and selling expenses was 14.3 percent. On an expected sales increase of $690,000, achieved through the addition of three salesmen, there would be a contribution of $98,000 to meet the increased selling expenses of $80,000 or a net contribution of $18,000 per year. In the first year, expenses would exceed outgo by $46,000, and, in the second year, The Victory Plastics Company would lose $11,000 under this proposal.

7. Mr. Beckwith felt that this figure seriously underestimated the profitability for the following reasons:

(*a*) The military products constituted a low-profit business. The same physical volume of civilian products would have sold at a higher price. If the military business had the same gross margin as the civilian business, net sales would have been $5,100,000 and the contribution towards selling expenses and fixed costs would have been 20.9 percent. This would make the net contribution $64,000 per year.

(*b*) The military contracts required more expensive premium molding powders with guaranteed properties. As a result the variable cost percentage of military sales was significantly higher than that of civilian sales.

(*c*) At the same time the travel expenses of the salesmen were also overstated. The defense contracts required frequent trips to places outside the company's normal territory, such as Washington, Rock Island, and Detroit. Civilian salesmen would not have to make these trips. Furthermore, the addition of salesmen would cause more compact sales territories and further decrease the travel expense as a percentage of sales.

8. His analysis of the regional shares of the industry's sales and production (Exhibit 7) showed that the regional market was a competitive one: 49 percent of the national custom molding capacity was competing for 36 percent of the industrial injection molded business, 43 percent of the industrial compression molding business and about 50 percent of the wholesaling of plastic consumer items. However, he did not want to expand beyond the New England and Middle Atlantic areas. On a product such as that in Exhibit 5, the cost of shipping to Chicago would increase the price by about $1.50 per hundred pounds. Delivery time would be increased by four to five days. Victory's transportation and communications expenses would be much higher.

9. The total custom molding business in the New England and Middle Atlantic states was about $85 million, and there was another large amount of business available in proprietary products. In view of Victory's experience, equipment, financial position, and skilled personnel, an increase in the Victory share of this business from $900,000 to $1,600,000 did not seem unreasonable.

10. He noticed the large regional concentration of purchasing of industrial plastics in a few selected industries such as shoes, office equipment, industrial electrical apparatus, and electronic tubes. He wondered if it would help additional salesmen to gain the maximum amount of business sooner if he arranged for them to concentrate on a particular industry.

11. He was extremely pessimistic about the immediate chances of getting additional military business.

1. VICTORY PLASTICS COMPANY

Profit and Loss Statement
(All Figures in Thousands of Dollars)

	1953	1954	1955	1956	8 Mos. 1957	August 1957
Sales	$3,748	$2,763	$3,759	$4,954	$4,718	$751
Cost of sales	3,075	2,237	3,082	4,872	4,113	712
Gross profit	673	526	677	82	605	39
Unabsorbed burden	203	289	135	(497)	(1)	(15)
Administrative and selling	435	525	490	413	264	29
Operating profit	35	(288)	52	166	342	25
Other income	50	11	44	54	17	1
Total income	85	(277)	96	220	359	26
Interest expense	12	16	71	48	12	1
Termination of raincoat business	-	-	-	267	-	-
Government sales liability	-	-	-	-	62	-
Profit before taxes	73	(293)	25	(95)	285	25
Excise and income taxes	-	-	9	8	158	14
Net profit	73	(293)	16	(103)	127	11

Balance Sheet

	Dec. 31, 1953	Dec. 31, 1954	Dec. 31, 1955	Dec. 31, 1956	Aug. 31, 1957
Cash	$ 49	$ 17	$ 71	$ 112	$ 380
Accounts receivable	539	255	236	356	540
Special tooling and facilities	-	-	197	150	-
Inventories	684	916	837	985	710
Other current assets	6	33	1	2	12
Total current assets	$1,278	$1,221	$1,342	$1,605	$1,642
Land	$ 2	$ 2	$ 2	$ 2	$ 2
Buildings and building equipment	201	201	202	206	248
Machinery	792	755	585	594	684
Molds, tools, and dies	39	54	-	7	20
Automobiles	7	8	6	12	11
Furniture and fixtures	52	53	52	52	53
Gross fixed assets	$1,093	$1,073	$ 847	$ 873	$1,018
Depreciation	590	663	487	546	580
Net fixed assets	$ 503	$ 410	$ 360	$ 327	$ 438
Other assets	30	31	35	14	4
Total Assets	$1,811	$1,662	$1,737	$1,946	$2,084
Accounts payable	$ 154	$ 577	$ 399	$ 315	$ 447
Notes payable	240	197	605	390	54
Accrued expenses	169	91	144	162	321
Reserve for government price renegotiation	-	-	-	554	615
Current liabilities	$ 563	$ 865	$1,148	$1,421	$1,437
Notes payable	431	430	429	-	-
Capital stock and surplus	817	367	160	525	647
Total Liabilities and Net Worth	$1,811	$1,662	$1,737	$1,946	$2,084

2. VICTORY PLASTICS COMPANY

Breakdown of Expenses

General and Administrative

	Jan. 1-Aug. 31, 1957	Month of August 1957
Executive salaries	27.0	3.4
Clerical salaries	107.5	12.0
Administrative supplies and expenses	15.8	1.1
Subscriptions, dues, and donations	4.8	0.1
Social security taxes--administrative	5.9	0.5
Rent expense	1.0	0.1
Overtime premium	1.1	-
Automobile expense	3.1	0.5
Telegrams, postage, and telephone	13.5	1.8
Travel expense	30.4	3.3
Professional services	20.8	2.8
Insurance	2.6	0.5
Depreciation	4.1	0.5
Sales engineering expense	7.4	0.6
Selling and advertising supplies and space	1.6	-
Salesmen's salaries	14.5	1.7
Commissions	2.2	-
Social security taxes, selling and advertising	0.7	0.1

Manufacturing

	Jan. 1-Aug. 31, 1957	Month of August 1957
Supervision	148.2	20.3
Clerical and timekeepers	49.2	6.5
Services and material handling	108.2	15.9
Janitors, watchmen, guards	41.6	5.7
Waiting for work or material	2.3	.1
Machine breakdown	2.3	.2
Taking inventory	2.1	.5
Tool and cutter grinding	6.4	1.0
Boiler room	14.0	1.6
Shipping expense	7.0	1.2
Overtime premium	20.2	4.4
Nonproduct time (vacations, lunch, etc.)	147.7	21.9
General factory supplies	32.5	3.3
Maintenance supplies	14.9	.9
Experimental and development	3.8	1.0
Social security taxes	72.9	8.6
Heat, light, and power	105.8	15.0
Expendable tools	7.7	1.0
Freight and trucking in	5.4	.9
Travel expense	6.4	.7
Maintenance--repairs to machine and equipment	62.1	6.3
Maintenance--repairs to land and building	37.8	5.7
Taxes, real estate, water and sewerage	15.9	1.9
Insurance	56.0	7.9
Depreciation	35.3	4.3
Total manufacturing expense	1,005.7	136.8
Burden absorbed	1,006.7	151.2
Overabsorbed burden	1.0	14.4
Direct labor input	829.9	124.2
Over-all burden rate	121.17%	110.13%

All figures except percentages in thousands of dollars.

3. VICTORY PLASTICS COMPANY

Sales, Costs, and Profit and Loss by Product Line
January 1, 1957 - August 31, 1957

	Factory Cost	Over-absorbed Burden	G & A Other Income and Expense*	Total Cost	Selling Price	Profit or (Loss) before Tax
M19 Mines Cont. No. 2887	$ 14,408	$ (76)	$ 1,062	$ 16,546	$ 0	$ (16,546)
M2 Act. Cont. No. 2887	4,593	(5)	408	5,006	0	(5,006)
M606 Fuse Cont. No. 2887	1,707,620	(7,336)	105,918	1,820,874	2,218,348	397,474
M19 Mines Cont. No. 3646	434,382	(7,336)	33,060	474,777	398,845	(75,933)
M2 Act. Cont. No. 3646	40,655	(697)	3,107	44,459	37,859	(6,600)
M606 Fuse Cont. No. 3646	765,281	11,218	43,859	797,923	790,260	(7,663)
M14 Mine Cont. No. 4099	5,269	(58)	365	5,692	7,348	1,656
M19 Mine Cont. No. 4158	428,306	8,309	22,989	442,986	435,646	(7,339)
M2 Act. Cont. No. 4158	28,097	604	1,225	28,718	28,007	(711)
All CPFF Contracts	129,952	1,290	7,359	136,021	133,458	(2,563)
All Other FP Contracts	55,645	778	3,298	58,164	51,583	(6,582)
All Other Miscellaneous	(280)	(5)	2	(273)	0	273
Total Government	3,614,928	6,686	222,652	3,830,894	4,101,354	270,460
Special Tools and Commercial Shop Orders	7,280	(7)	475	7,763	6,245	(1,518)
Atlantic Paulson	312,405	(5,032)	25,006	342,443	383,500	41,058
Custom Molding	118,594	(255)	7,958	126,807	136,926	10,119
Proprietary Items	35,267	(85)	2,401	37,752	48,445	10,692
Raincoats	24,622	(280)	1,751	26,654	42,093	15,439
Total Commercial	498,168	(5,659)	37,591	541,419	617,209	75,790
Total Sales	4,113,096	1,207	260,423	4,372,132	4,718,563	346,431

*Allocated on basis of Factory Cost.

4. VICTORY PLASTICS COMPANY

1957 Monthly Trend of Sales and Profit by Product Line

Military Items	Sales	Cost	Profit or (Loss)
Jan.	1,430	195,484	(194,054)
Feb.	590,083	545,257	44,826
Mar.	746,521	531,820	214,701
Apr.	313,758	195,551	118,207
May	914,173	789,057	125,116
June	542,617	556,704	(14,087)
July	301,908	344,375	(42,467)
Aug.	690,877	672,651	18,226

Atlantic Paulson Display Fixtures	Sales	Cost	Profit or (Loss)
Jan.	56,811	51,624	5,187
Feb.	90,767	79,560	11,207
Mar.	49,826	49,318	8,508
Apr.	67,331	64,134	3.197
May	46,455	38,215	8,240
June	(16,194)	(10,077)	(6,117)
July	66,358	59,737	6,621
Aug.	22,146	17,931	4,215

Custom Molding	Sales	Cost	Profit or (Loss)
Jan.	19,355	14,537	4,818
Feb.	14,416	12,202	2,214
Mar.	16,108	15,321	787
Apr.	18,644	17,268	1,376
May	11,257	10,407	850
June	18,899	19,714	(815)
July	9,873	9,587	286
Aug.	28,374	27,771	603

Proprietary Items	Sales	Cost	Profit or (Loss)
Jan.	4,836	(5,344)	10,180
Feb.	8,938	8,183	755
Mar.	6,522	7,052	(530)
Apr.	5,451	6,018	(567)
May	6,208	5,974	234
June	6,996	6,895	101
July	4,492	3,983	509
Aug.	5,001	4,991	10

Raincoats	Sales	Cost	Profit or (Loss)
Jan.	3,400	1,324	2,076
Feb.	6,240	3,224	3,016
Mar.	15,549	13,877	1,672
Apr.	4,453	1,678	2,775
May	4,199	3,636	563
June	1,511	525	986
July	2,660	931	1,729
Aug.	4,079	1,458	2,621

Special Tools and Commercial Shop Orders	Sales	Cost	Profit or (Loss)
Jan.	0	1,283	(1,283)
Feb.	887	825	62
Mar.	2,115	2,280	(165)
Apr.	0	0	0
May	142	100	42
June	902	834	68
July	813	539	274
Aug.	1,386	1,901	(515)

5. VICTORY PLASTICS COMPANY

Sample Caluclations on Quote

Product: Dust Cover	One Cavity		Two Cavity Production	
99137 IBM Signal Decoder	Lots of 750	Lots of 1,500	Lots of 750	Lots of 1,500
Direct Material				
Thermaflow 400				
.231875 lbs. x $.79/lb.	$ .18328	$ .18328	$ .18328	$ .18328
Waste and Scrap @ 20%	.04635	.04635	.04635	.04635
Packaging Materials	.00750	.00750	.00750	.00750
Direct Labor				
1. Pill hand operator done on cycle	-	-	-	-
2. Mold--2-1/2 min. cycle 24 hrs. direct labor/22 hours prod.				
$40.32/528 for 1 cavity	.07636	.07636		
$40.32/1056 for 2 cavity			.03818	.03818
3. Complete, Finish, Flash Drill direct labor/8 hours production $10.80/540	.02000	.02000	.02000	.02000
4. Inspect and Pack 8 hrs. direct labor/8 hrs. production $10.80/1350	.00800	.00800	.00800	.00800
Total	.34149	.34149	.30331	.30331
Burden Press 197%.	.15044	.15044	.07522	.07522
Burden Other 110%.	.03080	.03080	.03080	.03080
Total	.52272	.52272	.40932	.40932
Other Direct Charges ($200 setup). . .	.26666	.13333	.26666	.13333
Total	.78939	.65606	.67599	.54266
G and A--10%	.07894	.06561	.06760	.05421
Total	.86833	.72166	.74359	.59692
Profit at 12-1/2%.	.10854	.09021	.09295	.07461
Total	.97687	.81187	.83654	.67154
Price per hundred	97.69	81.19	83.66	67.16
Mold Cost.	1735.00	1735.00	2680.00	2680.00
Special Tooling-shrink fixture	110.00	110.00	110.00	110.00
Mold Delivery	9-11 wks.	9-11 wks.	9-11 wks.	9-11 wks.

Note: By similar calculations, the prices on lots of 3,000 and 9,000 from a one cavity die were $67.85 and $59.47 per hundred. If a two cavity die was used, the prices were $53.82 and $45.44.

6. VICTORY PLASTICS COMPANY

Machine Load Charts, September, 1957

Day of the week	M	T	W	T	F	S	S	M	T	W	T	F	S	S
Date of the month	2	3	4	5	6	7	8	9	10	11	12	13	14	15
Injection Presses--Company Owned														
IMP-1	-	-	-	-	-	-	-	-	-	-	-	-	-	-
WS-3	-	9	15	15	15	15	15	15	15	15	15	15	15	15
WS-4	-	17	17	17	17	-	-	4	4	4	7	7	7	7
HPM-1	-	18	18	18	18	-	-	1	1	1	1	1	1	1
RP8-1	-	19	19	19	19	-	-	19	19	19	19	19	19	19
WS-2	-	14	14	14	14	-	-	-	-	-	-	-	-	-
HPM16-2	-	5	13	-	14	14	14	14	14	13	13	13	13	13
IMP-2	-	-	-	-	-	-	-	50	-	-	-	-	-	-
WS-1	-	-	-	-	-	-	-	-	-	-	-	-	-	-
IMPCO-3	-	12	12	12	12	-	-	8	8	8	8	8	8	8
Compression Presses--Company Owned														
2-1-X	-	-	-	-	-	-	-	-	-	-	-	-	-	-
2-2	-	51	51	51	51	-	-	51	51	51	51	51	-	-
2-3	-	53	53	53	53	-	-	53	53	53	53	53	-	-
2-4-5	-	-	-	-	-	-	-	-	-	-	-	-	-	-
2-5	-	-	-	-	20	-	-	20	-	-	-	-	-	-
2-6	-	16	16	16	16	-	-	16	16	16	-	-	-	-
2-7	-	16	16	16	16	-	-	16	16	16	-	-	-	-
2-8	-	51	51	51	51	-	-	51	51	51	51	51	-	-
46-T	-	-	-	-	-	-	-	-	-	-	-	-	-	-
8-1	-	-	-	-	-	-	-	-	-	-	-	-	-	-
8-2	-	-	-	-	-	-	-	-	-	-	-	-	-	-
8-3	-	-	-	-	3	-	-	3	3	3	3	3	-	-
8-4	-	52	52	52	52	52	52	52	52	52	52	52	-	-
8-5	-	52	52	52	52	52	52	52	52	52	52	52	-	-
8-6	-	52	52	52	52	52	52	52	52	52	52	52	-	-
8-7	-	-	-	-	-	-	-	-	-	-	-	-	-	-
Injection Presses--Government Owned														
RP 32-26	-	56	56	56	56	-	-	56	-	-	-	-	-	-
RP 32-25	-	60	60	60	60	-	-	60	60	60	60	60	60	60
RP 32-24	-	58	58	58	58	-	-	58	58	58	58	58	58	58
RP 32-23	-	61	-	-	-	-	-	-	-	59	59	59	59	59
RP 16-15	-	64	64	64	64	-	-	64	64	64	64	64	-	-
RP 16-14	-	65	65	65	65	-	-	65	65	65	65	65	-	-
RP 16-13	-	67	67	67	67	-	-	67	67	67	67	67	-	-
RP 24-18	-	74	74	74	74	-	-	74	74	74	74	74	-	-
RP 24-17	-	72	72	72	72	-	-	72	72	72	72	72	-	-
RP 24-16	-	66	66	66	66	-	-	66	66	66	66	66	-	-
RP 4- 2	-	62	-	-	62	-	-	62	-	-	63	63	-	-
RP 24-22	-	71	71	71	71	-	-	71	71	71	71	71	-	-
RP 24-20	-	73	73	73	73	-	-	73	73	73	73	73	-	-
RP 24-21	-	57	57	57	57	-	-	57	57	57	57	57	-	-
RP 24-19	-	54	54	54	54	-	-	54	-	-	-	-	-	-
RP 12- 7	-	68	68	68	68	-	-	68	68	68	68	68	-	-
RP 12-12	-	70	70	70	70	-	-	70	70	70	70	70	-	-
RP 12- 6	-	82	82	82	82	-	-	87	87	88	-	-	-	-
RP 12-11	-	69	69	69	69	-	-	76	76	76	76	76	76	76
RP 12-S5	-	85	85	85	-	-	-	85	-	85	85	85	-	-
RP 12-10	-	77	-	77	77	-	-	77	77	-	-	-	-	-
RP 12-S4	-	80	80	80	80	-	-	86	86	-	-	-	-	-
RP 12- 9	-	81	81	81	81	-	-	81	81	81	81	81	-	-
RP 12-S3	-	-	-	-	78	-	-	78	78	78	79	79	-	-
RP 12- 8	-	83	83	83	75	-	-	75	75	75	75	75	-	-
WS 6- 5	-	-	-	84	84	-	-	84	84	84	84	84	-	-

7. VICTORY PLASTICS COMPANY

Total Shipments of Plastics Molding Industry 1954

Industry Classification Number	Industry	U.S. Total Shipments	New England Total Shipments	New England Per Cent of National	Middle Atlantic Total Shipments	Middle Atlantic Per Cent of National	N.E. and M.A. Total Shipments	N.E. and M.A. Per Cent of National
39711	Molded plastics products	$529,674	$94,051	17.8%	$153,599	29.0%	$247,650	46.8%
3981111	Compression and transfer molded	138,749						
3971121	Cast molded	11,298						
3971131	Injection molded	304,751						
3971151	Cold molded	9,064						
3971171	Extrusion molded	43,570						
3971100	Molded not specified by process	22,242						
3971211	Laminated sheet rods and tubes	102,401	962	0.9	25,530	24.9	26,492	25.8
39713	Table and kitchen articles	$ 39,958	-	-	-	-	21,588	54.0
39714	Fabricated plastics products	$390,319	43,172	10.8	121,903	30.6	165,075	41.4
3971415	Products fabricated from laminates	56,554						
3971417	Formed plastics	17,746						
3971421	Articles and gaiters	8,258						
3971425	Battery boxes, jobs, parts	18,817						
3971441	Boats, pontoons, and life rafts	1,163						
3971453	Packing for sealing moving parts	1,495						
397146	Floor covering and wall covering	35,987						
3971471	Commercial closures except collapsible tubes	20,425						
3971475	Collapsible tube closures	2,046						
397148	Hose, pipe, and tubing	52,747						

Dollar figures in thousands of dollars.

Source: U.S. Census of Manufactures - 1954.

Note: In contrast to these figures for the total plastics molding industry, Modern Plastics estimated in 1956 that 13% of the custom plastics molding was in New England, 36% in the Middle Atlantic states, 28% in the East North Central states and 10% in California.

Lunn Laminates, Inc. (A)

Lunn Laminates, Inc. was organized in 1948 as a fabricator of glass fiber reinforced plastics. With operations devoted exclusively to this relatively new material, net sales grew from $135,000 in 1950 to $3,554,000 for the year ended April 30, 1954. During the same period total assets increased from $89,000 to $1,268,000 and earnings grew from a $4,000 loss in 1950 to a profit of $136,000 in fiscal 1954. Comparative balance sheets and income statements are given in Exhibits 1 and 3; the balance sheet and income statement at October 31, 1954, are given in Exhibits 2 and 4.

In December, 1954, the company's president, Mr. James S. Lunn, was considering a vigorous program of expansion and diversification to utilize the growing capital and facilities of Lunn Laminates, Inc. At that time the company was operating two plants on Long Island, New York, and one in Ashtabula, Ohio, and had a backlog of orders of over $700,000. The operations at Ashtabula, however, had declined so as to make it necessary to find new business or shut down the plant. Meanwhile, the Lunn company had invested $800,000 to acquire a Detroit company that manufactured tools and dies for the automotive industry. Finally, Mr. Lunn intended to plan for the introduction of proprietary products to give added volume to the Long Island operations of the company.

COMPANY HISTORY

The predecessor of Lunn Laminates, Inc., was the Low-Preston Company. The Low-Preston Company was founded in 1945 by an aeronautical engineer who expected to find a large postwar market for reinforced plastics. In 1946, when the prospective partners changed their minds before investing the required capital, Mr. James S. Lunn bought a half interest in the company. At that time the business was located in Port Washington, Long Island, and had a modest sales volume. High materials prices and fabrication costs restricted the potential commercial applications for glass fiber reinforced plastics, and most of the early business was, therefore, due to government contracts. In 1947, Mr. Lunn purchased the remaining interest in the firm, and in 1948 it was incorporated as Lunn Laminates, Inc. Some stock was sold to former classmates of Mr. Lunn and to company executives in 1948. In July, 1952, a public offering of 149,000 shares at $2 yielded $250,000 to the Lunn company.

In June, 1948, all operations were moved to a 6,000 square-foot leased plant in Glen Cove, Long Island. To provide for an increasing volume of sales in early 1952, the Lunn company purchased for $90,000 a 22,000 square-foot building in nearby Huntington, Long Island. The Glen Cove plant was retained for storage purposes. By 1954, the Huntington plant had been expanded to 32,500 square feet and 150 workers were employed there.

The principal production area in the Huntington plant, accounting for over 40 percent of the space there, was a large, open room, designed to offer flexibility in production. All low-pressure molding was done there, with operations on a "job shop" basis. Molds, materials, and tools for a job were confined to the area in which the job had been set up. When one job was completed the area would be cleared to make way for the mold to be used on the next job. From two to a dozen jobs might be in progress at one time.

A smaller section of the plant contained eight presses permanently installed to do molding at high pressures. The press specifications were:

Type	*Tonnage*	*Bed Dimensions*
Hydraulic	170	55 × 36
Air	10	46 × 46
Hydraulic	40	35 × 24
Hydraulic	10	24 × 20
Aero-draulic	6	n.a.
Mechanical-hydraulic	75	42 × 28
Hydraulic	119	55 × 49
Hydraulic	113	42 × 36

The Lunn company had always been exclusively a contract fabricator of plastics reinforced with glass fiber. The company produced a wide variety of products, including: radomes and other radar housings, tanks for gasoline and other purposes, helmets, tool handles, boats and buoys, bathtubs, and automobile and truck bodies. Until 1953, approximately 95 percent of sales volume was on military contract. At the beginning of 1953, however, the management decided to try to increase commercial sales and by April, 1953, commercial products accounted for 30 percent of the $1,100,000 backlog of orders. The order backlog at selected dates in 1954 is given in Exhibit 5A.

The largest single contract in the company's history was with the Chevrolet Division of General Motors Corporation for the production of body parts for a new model car, the Corvette. To produce auto bodies under this contract, which ran from April, 1953 to July, 1954, a separate plant was set up in Ashtabula, Ohio, and a corporate subsidiary established there.

PRODUCTS

The Lunn company produced products of glass fiber-reinforced plastics, a basic structural material that could be molded to special shapes and fabricated with standard metalworking tools.

By use of a learning curve similar to that in the airframe industry, the estimator would calculate the number of labor units required to produce the number of items in the contract. Because of learning inefficiency, for instance, it might take 115 labor units to produce the first 100 units of production. Materials for a 35 × 25 × 15-inch tank are shown below. The labor unit was 111 man-minutes. Material preparation required 13 minutes by one man; another man spent 42 minutes mixing resin, cleaning mold, applying resins and glass, and removing the part; trimming took 20 minutes and finishing 18 minutes; the inspection allowance was 5 minutes and supervision 13 minutes. One man could produce 6 units in one day (not allowing for material preparation, inspection, and supervision).

Item	*Net Lbs.*	*Waste Factor*	*Gross Lbs.*	*Price per Lb.*	*Cost*
74″ Glass Mat	8.01	2.19	17.54	$ .60	$10.52
Gel Coat Resin	1.6	1.148	1.84	.49	.90
PVA Sheet	—	—	(1.171)	1.70	1.99
Binding Resin	7.69	1.148	8.83	.345	3.05
Other Chemicals	—	—	—	—	.36
	17.3		28.2		$16.82

The majority of work in the Lunn plant at Huntington was done by vacuum bag as in the tank example above, although some production involved the use of matched metal dies in hydraulic presses. Exhibit 5B shows a floor plan of the plant.

In bag molding, the production process started with the preparation of a mold. Starting from a wood or metal model of the part, a plaster cast would be made and used to form a cast phenolic mold. The mold would be mounted on a metal frame and might contain pipes for heating.

An alternative method of molding involved the use of matched metal dies in hydraulic presses. Press molding methods were similar to those used for compression molding of thermosetting materials, although much larger items were produced of reinforced plastics than had yet been made in conventional compression molding.

The smaller hydraulic presses used in molding reinforced plastics had capacities of 20 to 100 tons and beds of a few feet in width, and cost under $10,000. By use of much larger presses, however, it was possible to produce items ten or fifteen feet in length from reinforced plastics. Such products required the use of presses of over 500-ton capacities, with beds as large as eight by fifteen feet, and cost over $50,000.

Whereas a mold for bag molding was easily produced and cost only a few hundred dollars, matched metal dies took several months to procure and a complex set might cost more than $20,000. A set of dies used to produce a laundry tub, measuring about three feet in each dimension, had recently cost $12,000 to produce. Bag molding was thought to be a higher quality fabricating method. Press molding, however, offered a higher rate of output with resultant savings in labor. Substantial material cost savings could be attained in press molding because the use of glass in the form of roving eliminated the material losses usually resulting from cutting mat or cloth to pattern shapes.

OHIO OPERATIONS

In mid-1953, the Chevrolet Division of General Motors Corporation had asked for bids for the production of press molded reinforced plastic bodies for a new type sports car, the Corvette. The Lunn company participated in the bidding, but the prime contract was awarded to another company, the Molded Fiber Glass Body Company.

Press Molding Plans

The Molded Fiber Glass Body Company constructed a 30,000 square-foot plant in Ashtabula, Ohio to mold parts for the 10,000 Corvettes scheduled to be produced in 1954. Their new plant was equipped with 25 hydraulic molding presses, as well as preform machines, conveyor systems, ovens, and a finishing department compatible with the press capacity. Fifteen of the presses ranged in capacity from 250 to 500 tons with beds ranging from 42 × 49 to 84 × 144 inches in size; the largest press being for the underbody part which measured 72 × 120 inches and was 26 inches deep. The other ten presses were 18-ton capacity with 20 × 20 beds.

The Chevrolet Division purchased the $800,000 worth of dies required to produce the 96 parts of the Corvette. Production of the dies was expected to take three months, but in the interim Chevrolet requested that 300 units be produced by bag molding so that they would have items for early promotion. The Molded Fiber Glass Body Company gave the subcontract for bag molding to Lunn Laminates Inc., which leased an empty 15,000 square-foot warehouse in Ashtabula for that purpose.

Lunn Bag Molding Plant

Establishment of the Lunn plant involved the construction of molds and installation of utilities, small tools, vacuum pumps, and so on. Mold construction started with wooden models which were used to produce plaster casts from which plaster models were made. The female production mold was cast phenolic, formed on a metal frame around the plaster model.

The Lunn subcontract was extended to include substantially more than 300 units because delivery of press dies to the prime contractor took longer than had been anticipated. Although dies for smaller parts were delivered in a short time, dies for the underbody, the largest part, were not delivered until June, 1954. At the peak of production, the Lunn company employed 212 workers who produced as many as 55 complete sets of parts per day on a three-shift basis. Because of the unexpected volume, some molding work was transferred to the Huntington plant, and four molds for the underbody were put into operation in Huntington, in addition to the two in Ashtabula. Each mold turned out four or five units per shift, and one crew alternated between two molds. A total of 2,800 underbodies was produced by the Lunn company before the prime contractor began press molding that part in June, 1954.

From July through September of 1954, the Lunn company operated its Ashtabula plant to do subassembly work on the Corvette. Although the lease had three years to run, there was an opportunity to dispose of it with a negligible loss. Alternatively, the Lunn company might have retained the plant and attempted to acquire other molding business. Company executives thought that production of auto and truck bodies offered one source of possible new business.

Experience with Corvette production had shown that reinforced plastics could be economically used in production of automobiles. Although material and fabricating costs for press molded reinforced plastics were roughly three times as great as comparable costs for production of metal parts, the lower tooling cost kept the unit cost for plastics below the cost for steel for any volume up to 15,000 units. An estimated $4,500,000 would have been required for dies to produce the Corvette in steel, as compared with the $800,000 actually spent for tooling.

UEBER TOOL AND MFG. COMPANY

The use of glass fiber reinforced plastic in place of steel in metal-working dies for the automotive industry was another application that Mr. Lunn felt offered a huge future potential for the fiber-glass-reinforced plastics industry. Plastic dies would be far less expensive to produce, and could offer a saving over steel for low-volume items despite the longer wear characteristic of steel. The Lunn company had done some development work in this field, but it was felt that closer contact with the auto industry would provide a stronger basis for future improvement. Mr. Lunn went to Detroit to consider the purchase of a company in the tool and die business, and became aware that the Ueber Tool and Mfg. Company was available for purchase. In early December, 1954, Lunn Laminates, Inc. bought the Ueber Company.

For an investment of $800,000, one half of which went to the owner, and the remainder to holders of various property mortgages, the Lunn company acquired all the assets of the Ueber company. The Ueber plant was a modern, single-story, 50,000 square-foot building of steel frame construction, located nine miles northeast of Detroit, Michigan. The nine acres of land offered ample room for future expansion. The plant was fully equipped for the manufacture of automotive tools and dies. Two independent firms which appraised the property for Mr. Lunn valued the land and building at $475,000 and the machinery and equipment at $465,000.

The fourteen-year-old company had originally been a metal stamping shop, but for the previous two years had operated exclusively as a tool and die manufacturer. Mr. Herman Ueber, sole owner, had successfully operated the business until recent years when he had encountered severe labor troubles. As his relationship with the United Auto Workers union deteriorated, the business became less profitable, and in the fall of 1954 he shut down the plant and decided to liquidate the company.

Lunn Appraisal

An executive of the Lunn company had visited the Ueber plant in November and reported favorably to Mr. Lunn on the proposal to purchase the Ueber company. At that time, the staff at the Ueber plant in Detroit consisted of eight or ten maintenance workers, plus the plant manager and salesman. These latter two were considered to be very valuable since they were experienced men whom investigation indicated were well thought of in the industry. Since an estimated 200 production workers would be employed at peak times, the union appeared eager to have the plant returned to production, although Lunn executives feared their attitude might change once a high level of operations was achieved. The Lunn report asserted that contracts with the Ford, Pontiac, and Fisher Body companies could probably be negotiated for production in early 1955. There seemed to be a potential market for plastic dies, but early production would have to be entirely in metal until further improvement of plastic wear characteristics could be accomplished. The report concluded that the "plant was apparently good mechanically and technically, but poor organizationally. . . . Terrific interest exists in plastic tools and dies. . . . The sales prospects, the condition of the facilities, and the morale of the staff all point to a very healthy situation."

Cost Analysis

Although the plant capacity was estimated to be close to $4,000,000 annually, it was hard to forecast a sales volume. Industry practice was to separate material cost from labor and expense in preparing estimates for a contract, and to take a profit only on labor and expense. Bids were based on a machine-hour rate, with $5.00 being the most common apparent price in November. Competition for jobs was usually quite severe, but a rise in the prevalent rate was expected to occur within two months when tooling for 1956 model cars was placed. Exhibit 6 presents a projection of profit or loss for the Ueber operations as prepared by a Lunn executive. The shop rate used was based on his forecast of future price, with overhead and general administrative cost estimates based on past Ueber experience. The projection considered metalworking operations only.

PROPRIETARY PRODUCT DEVELOPMENT

In mid-1954, the Lunn management had begun to take action aimed at the development and marketing of proprietary products. Among the items considered were traffic signs, chemical resistant and photographic trays, truck bodies, and boats. As part of this new effort, the company contracted to build 25 delivery truck bodies for the United Parcel Service in New York City. United Parcel Service maintained a fleet of 5,000 trucks and Mr. Lunn estimated that his company could receive additional contracts to build as many as 300 bodies per year if the initial 25 performed satisfactorily. It was felt that the attractive appearance, longer wear, and simpler maintenance of the $1,650 plastic bodies would justify the $300 added cost over aluminum bodies.

Proposed Boat Program

The major proprietary product under consideration was a nine-foot dinghy weighing about 50 pounds to be produced by matched metal dies in a hydraulic press. With an investment of $125,000 for facilities, half of which would be for the die, and the remainder of which would be for the purchase of a suitable hydraulic press, the Lunn management estimated that boats could be press molded by a two-man crew with cycle time of 12 to 15 minutes. One man would produce pre-forms, the other would operate the press, and trim and pack the boats. There would be no assembly work, since the boat would be shipped "knocked down"; meaning that seats, oarlocks, and flotation tank would be installed by the dealer. An estimated $250,000 was believed necessary for working capital and market development. The first units could be shipped within six months, allowing one month for design, three or four for tooling, and another for production lead time. The company intended to have the design prepared by a prominent naval architect. Since the factory cost of the boat would be less than $50, it could be sold at retail for as little as $100.

Market Research

Market research for the boat was organized in two phases. The first was concerned with collecting data on the nature of the boating industry. The study found that boats such as the one under consideration were used with outboard motors either as "tenders" for large boats or as "car top" boats to be taken on fishing and hunting trips. Among the eight-foot boats already on the market, the average price was $168 and the low was $114 for a 79-pound boat. The lowest priced nine-foot boat was a 53-pound aluminum model selling for $157. One half of the 35 boats studied were constructed of fiberglass-reinforced plastic, produced either by hand lay-up or bag molding. In the trade, manufacturers usually sold direct to boat dealers, using direct mail and trade magazine advertising as promotion. A survey covering half of the nation's 10,000 boat dealers indicated that 1953 sales had been almost 30 percent greater than the 1952 volume. Dealers commonly took mark-ups of 30 to 40 percent.

The second phase of the research study involved the use of a questionnaire which was mailed to 432 dealers. The questionnaire is shown here as Exhibit 7A. The dealers selected represented 50 percent of the dealers located east of the Mississippi appearing on a list of 1,249 dealers compiled by *Yachting* magazine. The 88 replies were tabulated with nonrespondents considered negative, and results multiplied by two to get a national projection. The conclusion drawn from these replies was that during the first year the Lunn company could expect to sell 1,250 units of a nine-foot boat. The survey results also indicated that eight- or ten-foot boats were commonly used as tenders while twelve-foot boats were used as car tops. A volume of 1,900 units was forecast for the first year if a twelve-foot model were marketed. According to the survey results the boat season began in April, reached a peak in June, and ended in September.

The Lunn company had once marketed an eighteen-foot sailboat, the "Challenger," having a six-foot beam, weighing 700 pounds, and priced at $1,900, complete with sails. Three units were sold locally and then the program was stopped. For those three bag molded prototype boats, the material cost had been $2,400 and labor plus factory overhead amounted to $1,900. More recently, another boat, smaller in size, had been built for $1,850 under a research and development contract from a boat manufacturing company.

FINANCE AND ACCOUNTING

To provide capital for the future expansion of its operations, the Lunn company borrowed $750,000 on September 1, 1954, through 5 percent notes sold to a New York investment firm. The indenture provisions called for retirement of 10 percent of the balance each year after 1959, with final payment in 1969. Approval of two thirds of the note holders would be required for issuance of any capital stock or subordinated debt. These notes were to be subordinated to any debt of greater than one year maturity. Associated with the notes were 112,500 stock warrants which could be exercised at $6.66 until August, 1957, when the price would start to rise by $1.25 each subsequent year until expiration in 1961. All cash received through the exercise of warrants was to be applied immediately to redemption of the notes. In addition to the newly issued warrants, there were 87,000 outstanding warrants expiring September 30, 1958, which entitled their holders to purchase common stock at $1.66 per share. The stock was traded over the counter, and quotations for recent years had been:

	High	*Low*
1952	$2.125	$1.625
1953	4.375	1.50
1954	8.50	3.75

SITUATION IN NOVEMBER, 1954

During 1954, the Lunn company had been doing development and prototype construction of 10 wing-tip floats for a seaplane being developed for the U.S. Navy by a large airframe company. The first units were to be shipped in July, 1954, at a price of $4,870 per float, plus $30,000 for design and engineering, and $36,000 for tooling, with all prices subject to renegotiation downward only. The plastic floats were expected to be 50 pounds lighter and $3,000 less expensive than comparable aluminum floats. Production of as many as 400 units was anticipated if the development was successful. The design and engineering work was done by a prominent aeronautical engineering firm, but by the fall of 1954, it appeared that the two specifications of low weight and high stress resistance would be hard to achieve simultaneously. The first float shipped in July was returned in October as overweight. By November, the company appeared to be in default on its contract. If the situation were not rectified there might be a liability for damages suffered by the Navy or the airframe company as a result of delays in a $100 million program. The equivalent of 5½ floats had been completed or were in process, with $69,000 estimated to complete the job as of November, 1954. The tooling cost had been billed to the airframe company in August, but payment was held up pending shipment of an acceptable float. The job costs absorbed into inventory each month for production, design, and tooling are specified in Exhibit 7B.

1. LUNN LAMINATES, INC. (A)

Comparative Balance Sheets (April 30)

ASSETS	1950	1951	1952	1953	1954
Current Assets:					
Cash	$ 2,109	$ 8,973	$ 6,960	$ 31,489	$ 90,549
Accts. Receivable	41,711	64,657	103,922	221,661	412,751
Inventories	8,714	88,820	146,178	164,592	363,230
Other Current Assets	-	-	379	1,255	9,904
Total Current Assets	$52,534	$162,450	$257,439	$418,997	$ 876,434
Net Fixed Assets	25,161	27,786	159,665	194,758	324,474
Deferred Charges	11,454	12,149	25,606	29,994	67,371
TOTAL ASSETS	$89,149	$202,385	$442,710	$643,749	$1,268,279

LIABILITIES	1950	1951	1952	1953	1954
Current Liabilities:					
Notes Payable - Banks	$46,888	$ 79,448	$ 50,788	$ 37,449	$ 39,699
Notes Payable - Other	3,026	3,168	15,073	-	-
Accounts Payable - Trade	14,567	64,630	98,801	117,439	341,962
Accrued Liabilities:					
Payrolls	-	4,481	4,374	6,736	36,874
Federal Income Taxes	(425)	5,345	51,475	9,333	126,502
Other Taxes	1,093	3,633	9,002	5,310	14,690
Payroll Deductions	3,069	4,402	5,356	5,895	18,558
Adv. Billings on Contracts	2,500	-	29,130	11,650	6,200
Mtg. Loan - Current Portion	-	-	-	15,960	28,000
Total Current Liabilities	$70,718	$165,107	$263,999	$209,772	$ 612,485
Long-Term Debt:					
Notes Payable - Banks	-	-	-	-	13,099
Mortgage Loan - net of current portion	-	-	-	-	118,667
RFC Loan - 10-yr. maturity	-	-	112,515	105,397	-
Stockholders' Equity:					
Common Stock[1]	18,300	20,000	20,000	83,075	100,387
Warrants	-	-	-	363	455
Capital Surplus	-	-	-	183,865	242,444
Retained Earnings	131	17,278	46,196	61,277	180,742
	$89,149	$202,385	$442,710	$643,749	$1,268,279

[1]Authorized: 200 shares $100 par to June 30, 1952
600,000 shares $.25 par June 30, 1952 to April 30, 1954.

2. LUNN LAMINATES, INC. (A)

Balance Sheet, October 31, 1954

ASSETS	Huntington	Ashtabula	Consolidated
Current Assets:			
Cash	$ 465,210	$ 25,907	$ 491,117
Accts. Receivable	195,219	3,416	198,635
Inventory	355,938	31,054	386,992
Other Current Assets	33,817	393	34,210
Notes Receivable	25,000	---	25,000
Total Current Assets	$1,075,184	$ 60,770	$1,135,954
Net Fixed Assets	311,533	72,879	384,412
Deferred Charges	68,820	1,664	70,484
Ashtabula - Advances & Investment	(100,014)	100,014	---
TOTAL ASSETS	$1,355,523	$235,327	$1,590,850

LIABILITIES	Huntington	Ashtabula	Consolidated
Current Liabilities:			
Notes Payable - Bank	$ 4,367	---	$ 4,367
Accts. Payable - Trade	93,188	$ 2,708	95,896
Accrued Liabilities:			
Payrolls	3,895	1,714	5,609
Federal Income Taxes	19,827	105,665	125,492
Other Taxes	7,524	5,326	12,850
Accrued Interest	6,250	---	6,250
Payroll Deductions	9,913	680	10,593
Advance Billing on Contract	600	---	600
Total Current Liabilities	$ 145,564	$116,093	$ 261,657
Long-Term Debt:			
Notes Payable - Bank	8,733	---	8,733
Long-Term Notes	750,000	---	750,000
Capital:			
Common Stock	106,139	---	106,139
Warrants	263	---	263
Capital Surplus	274,952	---	274,952
Retained Earnings	69,872	119,234	189,106
	$1,355,523	$235,327	$1,590,850

3. LUNN LAMINATES, INC. (A)

Comparative Income Statements
(Year End April 30)

	1950	1951	1952	1953	1954
Net Sales	$135,203	$307,648	$892,172	$1,393,088	$3,544,306
Cost of Goods Sold	119,918	242,789	699,663	1,198,181	3,004,249
Gross Profit	$ 15,285	$ 64,859	$192,509	$ 194,907	$ 540,057
Selling, General & Administrative Expenses	20,371	42,367	112,116	158,303	255,301
Operating Profit	$ (5,086)	$ 22,492	$ 80,393	$ 36,604	$ 284,756
Other Income	-	-	-	-	937
	$ (5,086)	$ 22,492	$ 80,393	$ 36,604	$ 285,693
Other Expense	-	-	-	8,665	13,465
Income before Taxes	$ (5,086)	$ 22,492	$ 80,393	$ 27,939	$ 272,228
Provision for Taxes	1,094	5,345	51,475	10,530	136,000
Net Income	$ (3,992)	$ 17,147	$ 28,918	$ 17,409	$ 136,228
Factory Overhead	$ 39,887	$ 59,039	$175,137	$ 340,977	$ 901,088
Direct Labor and Materials	80,031	183,750	524,526	852,203	2,083,273

4. LUNN LAMINATES, INC. (A)

Income Statements, May-October, 1953-1954

	Huntington Monthly Statements, 1954						Consolidated Operating Statement 6 Months to Oct. 31	
	4 Wks. May	4 Wks. June	5 Wks. July	4 Wks. Aug.	4 Wks. Sept.	5 Wks. Oct.	1954	1953
Net Sales	$193,176	$214,223	$185,632	$ 88,565	$ 89,565	$116,389	$1,539,524	$1,142,371
Cost of Sales	130,177	179,022	174,144	114,805	102,672	106,164	1,369,819	1,004,216
Gross Profit	$ 62,999	$ 35,201	$ 11,488	$ (26,240)	$ (13,107)	$ 10,225	$ 169,705	$ 138,155
Other Income					8,000		8,000	---
							$ 177,705	$ 138,155
General Overhead:								
Administrative	13,018	11,350	14,208	7,165	11,083	13,808	82,490	67,330
Selling	6,377	4,963	8,988	7,898	9,083	17,081	54,510	24,459
Financial	2,749	3,972	2,778	3,801	6,068	5,027	23,840	16,082
Intercompany - Admin.	(3,673)	(3,599)	(3,759)	(3,802)	(3,451)	(4,354)	---	---
Interest	334	416	479	543	571	567	---	---
Net Operating Income	$ 44,194	$ 18,099	$ (11,206)	$ (41,845)	$ (28,461)	$ (21,904)	$ 16,865	$ 30,284
Income Taxes	23,000	9,500	(6,000)	(21,500)	(15,000)	(9,075)	8,500	14,540
Net Income	$ 21,194	$ 8,599	$ (5,206)	$ (20,345)	$ (13,461)	$ (12,829)	$ 8,365	$ 15,744
Factory Overhead:								
Indirect Labor	$ 23,485	$ 25,494	$ 31,838	$ 22,866	$ 25,290	$ 28,367	$ 230,503	---
Operating Materials	12,389	14,773	12,710	17,202	13,300	14,889	122,036	---
Other*	10,453	10,025	5,713	9,792	13,280	13,730	88,848	---
Total	$ 46,327	$ 50.292	$ 50,261	$ 49,860	$ 51,870	$ 56,986	$ 441,387	---

	Ashtabula Monthly Statements, 1954					
	May	June	July	Aug.	Sept.	Oct.
Net Sales	$329,314	$193,036	$ 54,798	$ 36,079	$ 30,761	$ 7,988
Cost of Sales	252,400	188,686	48,732	40,707	16,339	15,971
Gross Profit	$ 76,914	$ 4,350	$ 6,066	$ (4,628)	$ 14,422	$ (7,983)
General Overhead:						
Administrative	$ 2,055	$ 3,313	$ 1,792	$ 1,025	$ 1,434	$ 2,239
Selling	68	-	-	-	-	53
Financial	(191)	(183)	(153)	(17)	(4)	(6)
Intercompany - Admin.	3,673	3,599	3,759	3,802	3,450	4,354
Interest	(334)	(416)	(479)	(543)	(571)	(567)
Net Operating Income	$ 71,643	$ (1,963)	$ 1,147	$ (8,895)	$ 10,113	$ (14,056)
Income Taxes	37,200	(1,000)	600	(6,400)	4,675	(7,500)
Net Income	$ 34,443	$ (963)	$ 547	$ (2,495)	$ 5,438	$ (6,556)
Factory Overhead:						
Indirect Labor	$ 28,385	$ 22,535	$ 8,852	$ 4,243	$ 5,230	$ 5,479
Operating Materials	22,067	8,615	2,932	287	1,201	1,461
Other *	4,416	5,120	4,094	4,192	3,812	2,657
Total	$ 54,868	$ 36,270	$ 15,878	$ 8,722	$ 10,243	$ 9,597

*Rent, insurance, depreciation, and utilities.

5A. LUNN LAMINATES, Inc. (A)

Order Backlog--Selected Dates--1954

Commercial	May	June	July	Aug.	Sept.	Oct.
Chevrolet-Huntington	$136,000	-	-	-	-	-
-Ashtabula	750,000	-	-	-	-	-
Company A	53,488	$157,654	-	-	-	-
Company B	1,500	-	-	-	$ 1,100	$ 1,100
Company C	13,745	12,573	-	-	-	-
Company D		2,572	-	-	-	-
Company E		1,860	-	-	-	-
Company F		1,700	$ 1,700	$ 1,700	-	-
Company G		425	425	425	425	-
United Parcel Service					59,475	59,475
Company H					5,250	1,808
Total Commercial	$954,733	$176,784	$ 2,125	$ 2,125	$ 66,250	$ 62,383
Total Military	$646,830	$883,392	$773,802	$732,375	$644,863	$632,310
including Job #740	$112,965	$110,899	$ 43,316	$ 43,316	$ 43,316	$ 34,447

5B. LUNN LAMINATES, INC. (A)

Plant Layout--Huntington, Long Island

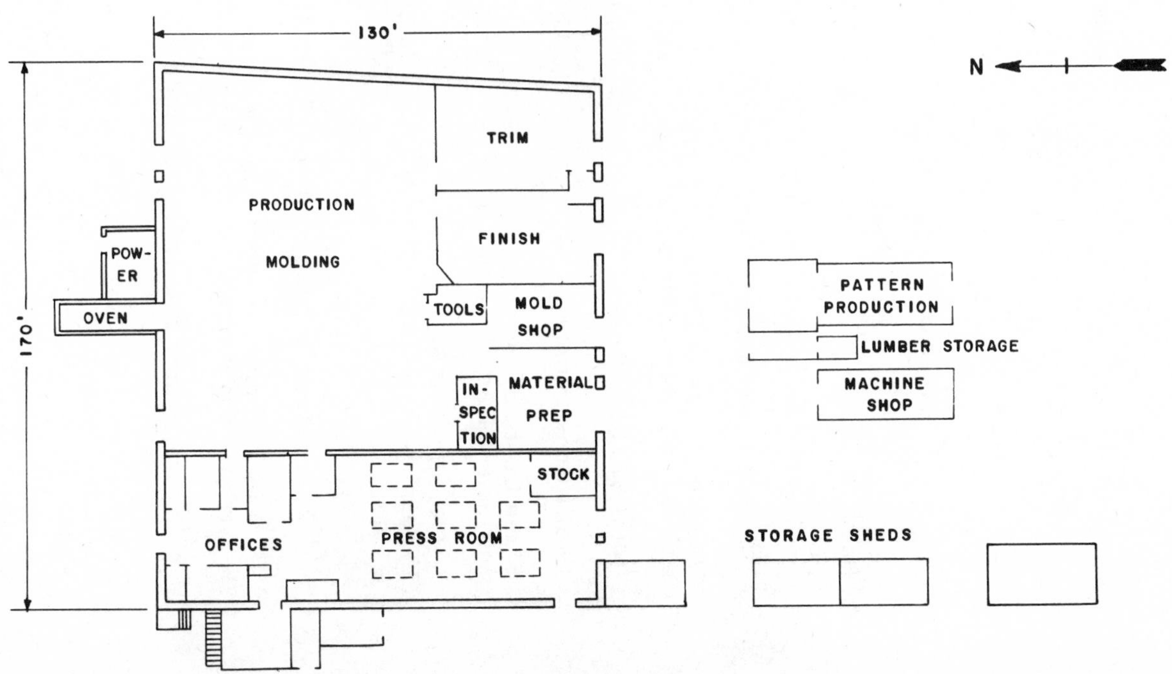

6. LUNN LAMINATES, INC. (A)

Ueber Tool Company
Break-Even Analysis
Based on Present Organization—Assuming Average Sales Price of $5.75 per Shop Hour[1]

Sales	$1,000,000	$1,500,000	$2,000,000	$2,500,000	$3,000,000	$3,500,000
[2]Material (25% of Sales)	$ 250,000	$ 375,000	$ 500,000	$ 625,000	$ 750,000	$ 875,000
[3]Labor Cost ($3.46 pr. hr.)	451,000	675,000	903,000	1,128,000	1,354,000	1,579,000
Variable Costs of Overhead and General Administration	117,000	176,000	235,000	294,000	352,000	411,000
Total Variable Cost	$ 818,000	$1,226,000	$1,638,000	$2,047,000	$2,456,000	$2,865,000
Profit Contribution	$ 182,000	$ 274,000	$ 362,000	$ 453,000	$ 544,000	$ 635,000
Fixed Costs of Overhead and General Administration	249,000	249,000	249,000	249,000	249,000	249,000
Net Profit or (Loss) before Federal Income Tax	$ (67,000)	$ 25,000	$ 113,000	$ 204,000	$ 295,000	$ 386,000

[1]This rate anticipates sale of 25% at $5.00, 25% at $5.50, 25% at $6.00 and 25% at $6.50.

[2]Material price or percentage does not affect profit since jobs are bid on the basis of material cost without regard for recovery of overhead or administrative cost.

[3]Average shop rate is approximately $3.00 per hour. $3.46 is used since union forces a 58 hour week.

7A. LUNN LAMINATES, INC. (A)

Huntington Station, N.Y.

FIBERGLAS BOAT QUESTIONNAIRE

(Estimated Weight of the Boat under 50 Lbs.)

1. Into what months falls the buying season for dinghies and/or car top boats in your locality? ________

2. In your opinion, what are the most popular dimensions of boats of that type? ________

   Length:

   Beam: ________

   Depth: ________

3. Without committing yourself in any way, how many Fiberglas boats would you estimate that you could sell a year at around $100? ________

4. If we marketed such a boat, would you be interested in adding it to your line?

   Yes ☐

   No ☐

5. This space is for your comments. Anything that you would care to let us know will be greatly appreciated. Use the back of this sheet for additional space.

Name: ________

Company: ________

Street: ________

City & State: ________

Please return this questionnaire in the enclosed stamped, addressed envelope.

Thank you!

7B. LUNN LAMINATES, INC. (A)

Job 740—Costs Absorbed into Inventory

Month	Labor	Overhead	Material & Subcontract	Total
1953 November	$ 25.15	$ 30.93	$ 81.00	$ 137.08
December	21.00	26.25	379.11	426.36
1954 January	-	-	3,008.20	3,008.20
February	559.74	933.37	4,433.56	5,926.67
March	860.43	1,577.17	5,137.09	7,574.69
April	1,986.79	3,989.48	4,977.83	10,954.10
May	3,855.08	5,397.12	5,843.35	15,095.55
June	6,716.21	9,584.04	2,454.22	18,754.47
July	13,403.03	20,466.43	9,118.20	42,987.66
August	4,399.91	8,285.04	7,603.93	20,288.88
September	8,409.12	14,766.42	10,084.00	33,259.54
October	9,849.78	20,300.40	7,760.83	37,911.01
November	4,250.11	11,662.30	4,047.91	19,960.32

8. LUNN LAMINATES, INC. (A)

Pictures of Corvette Facilities

1. Mahogany model used to produce mold to low-pressure molding.

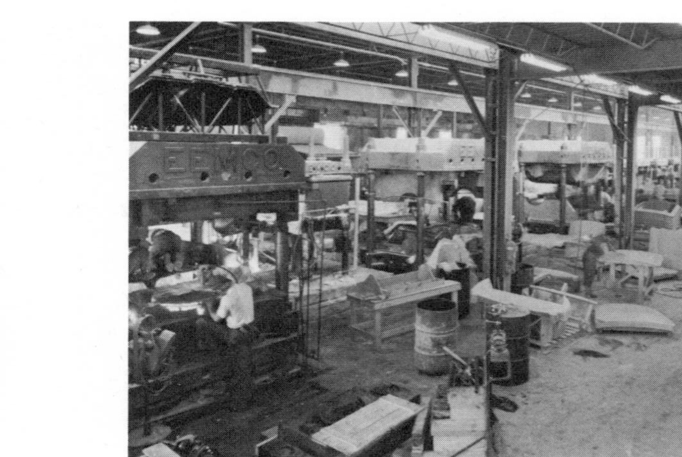

2. Cast phenolic mold for low-pressure molding.

3. Lunn workers sealing mold to cure bag molded part.

4. Large Molding Presses

Lunn Laminates, Inc. (B)

In January, 1962, Mr. James S. Lunn, President of Lunn Laminates, Inc., was considering a number of moves designed to improve his company's position as a producer of reinforced plastic products. The first of these was to review the company's experience with outboard motorboats and auxiliary motor sailboats for the commercial pleasure boat field. The second was the question of consolidating the company's operations in a single new location, about 10 miles from Lunn's present plants in Huntington, Long Island. Finally, in line with its announced policy of "keeping an ear-to-the-ground, open-minded attitude toward mergers," the company was considering the acquisition of another boat company with plants in Texas and Indiana.

Through moves such as these Mr. Lunn anticipated sales of $4.9 million by 1965, 50 percent of this volume to come from the sales of commercial products.

HISTORY: 1954–1961

A number of changes had occurred in the company's product line since 1954. The Ueber Tool Company, purchased in 1954 to produce reinforced plastic tools and dies for the automobile industry, suffered a $200,000 loss in 1955. Automobile makers were not willing to make the change from conventional metal tools and dies to reinforced plastic. Also in 1955, the Lunn company's Ashtabula Plant, which had produced parts for the Chevrolet Corvette bodies on a subcontract basis, was shut down. A new plant using matched dies built by the prime contractor, had made Lunn's facilities unnecessary. In 1956 both of the Lunn properties were sold, at a book loss of $120,000.

At about this time, the Lunn company was experiencing difficulties with a $115,000 contract for 10 wing-tip floats for the Navy. Lunn's total investment in the contract came to $265,-000 before the contract was closed out. An amicable settlement was reached with the Navy in 1956 at which time Lunn received $69,000 for work completed.

Contracts for some military products had been lost because of what Mr. Lunn termed a "get-the-job-at-any-cost type of competition." For example, in 1956 Lunn was underbid on contracts for 55-foot diameter Geodesic shelters for radar stations used by the Air Force in its DEW early warning system and for Tactical Air Navigation housings. Lunn had been the sole supplier of the TACAN equipment, and had also designed, engineered, and constructed the prototype for the Geodesic shelter.

Other products which had been produced and then discontinued included fiber-glass bath tubs, caskets, truck bodies, and deck panels for barges used by the Transportation Corps. Lunn also produced Monsanto Chemical's "House of Tomorrow," later put on display in Disneyland, and the fiber-glass building for the U.S. National Exhibit in Moscow.

In 1961, the product line included fairwaters and mast-fairings for submarine conning towers, radomes (housings for aircraft radar antennae), missile components, and a variety of small boats for the U.S. Navy. Navy boats and fairwaters accounted for 36 and 16 percent respectively of the 1961 sales volume with the balance coming from sales of missile components, mast-fairings, and other contract jobbing work. The Lunn company had conceived the idea of producing mast-fairings from reinforced plastic, and had designed and built a prototype which convinced the Navy of the practicality of the idea.

In 1959, the company underwent a capital reorganization at which time the New York investment firm that held the $750,000 worth of 5 percent notes agreed to convert these notes into common stock plus common stock warrants. After the reorganization, the New York firm controlled 375,000 shares of the outstanding common stock. Mr. Lunn's interest amounted to approximately 122,000 shares. Comparative balance sheets and income statements for the period 1954–1960 are presented in Exhibits 1 and 2.

BOAT PRODUCTION AT LUNN LAMINATES

Since 1954, Mr. Lunn had taken an increased interest in reinforced plastic boats. As demand for boats increased, boat production was set up in a 30,000 square-foot plant located about one mile from Lunn's main plant. Lunn leased this plant for $24,800. The lease was due to expire in November, 1962.

The boat plant housed office space, a stock room, and loading bay. The great bulk of the space, however, was used for the molding and assembly of reinforced plastic boats.

Aside from a few chain pulleys which were used to support hull molds and other heavy items, tooling in the plant consisted of ordinary workshop tools such as drills, disc sanders, knives, gauges and levels, and other basic hand tools.

Naval Work

Lunn's first experience with reinforced plastic boats had been in 1956. At that time Lunn was awarded a contract for the development and construction of 25 LCVP's (Landing Craft, Vehicle, Personnel) for the Navy. Completing this order significantly ahead of schedule, Lunn received a contract for 25 additional units. Since that time the company produced a wide variety of boats for the Navy including: 36-foot assault boats, 20-foot line handling boats, 26-foot motor whale boats, 40-foot utility boats, and 26-foot personnel boats. In 1960, Lunn expanded its Navy line by acquiring Mariner Laminates and the molds and tooling for 16-, 24-, and 30-foot life boats and rafts.

These boats were produced by a modification of the vacuum bag molding process called contact molding. This process was used for two reasons. First, boats did not require the high strength and quality obtained with bag molding. Second, contact molding resulted in a much lower cost product.

The process began with the construction of a wooden mock-up from which was prepared a female mold of 100 percent polyester plastic. The wood mock-up was not used directly because (1) wood had a tendency to expand and contract with the humidity; (2) wood imparted a rougher surface to the outside of the boat than would the smoother plastics. The polyester molds were expected to last indefinitely and minor design modifications could be made at small cost.

To make the 26-foot whale boat, the hull was mounted on wooden saw horses and supported by a chain pulley, and then sprayed with parting agent and gel coats to facilitate removal of the finished laminate. A precut piece of 10-ounce glass cloth was then applied for reinforcement. To make sure that no air bubbles formed between the cloth and the gel coat, the cloth was rolled down with 8-inch rollers mounted on long handles. After setting and checking for air bubbles the glass cloth was trimmed. Next came the application of 12 successive layers of 24-ounce roving and polyester resin until the desired thickness was reached. After each layer of roving, the laminate was rolled down to insure complete bonding. After the application of the final layer of roving and resin, which usually required 16 man-hours per hull, the hull was allowed to cure at room temperature and atmospheric pressure. After curing and before going to assembly, the hull was structurally reinforced with longitudinals made of wood and standard lengths of 10-foot cellulose acetate planks.

The normal work crew for the 26-foot whale boat was 19 men. Two men molded the hull while four to six men molded the other parts such as bulwarks and seats. The remaining 13 to 15 men performed the assembly operations, mounted the motor, and applied the final finish and trim. Next to the actual molding, the mounting of the motor (supplied by the Navy) was the most time-consuming process because of the necessity for perfect alignment of the drive shaft.

The 26-foot motor whale boats were very successful and Lunn received a congratulatory Navy certificate. Since 1959, Lunn had received three contracts calling for production of 163 whale boats at an average price of $7,800, less motor. Work on the final 39 units was scheduled for completion in June, 1962. On a fourth contract for 117 units, Lunn was underbid $2,000 per boat by a competitor.

In commenting upon this turn of events, Mr. Lunn stated that ". . . the low bidder in the fourth contract was a commercial boat builder. Most of the pleasure boat manufacturers are now going after government work to tide them over. I prefer to emphasize programs that make money, such as the submarine and missile components."

Outboard Motor Pleasure Boats

In late 1957, in line with his desire to develop proprietary items for the company's product line, Mr. Lunn negotiated an agreement with the S & M[1] Shipyards Company in Louisiana. Under this agreement Lunn Laminates would

[1] Name and location disguised.

have exclusive East Coast production and distribution rights to S & M's line of Ship Shape boats. Mr. Lunn projected 1958 sales of the line, which included a 15-foot, two 16-foot, and a 19-foot model, at $400,000.

Actual production of the Ship Shape line took place in April and May, 1958. The contact molding process was similar to that used in the production of the 26-foot whale boat except for the use of the wooden mock-up and the thickness of the completed laminate. Instead of building a wooden mock-up, Lunn had used completed Ship Shape boats to make the female polyester molds. Also, where the final laminate was about 12-ply thick for the whale boat, it ran about 6-ply for the Ship Shape.

Ship Shape hull sections were smaller than the whale boat, but they had three other large molds for the decks and cabins and seven smaller molds for other parts of the boats, in addition to the hull molds. The $70,000 tooling charge covered the initial construction of the polyester molds in 1958 and construction of small modifications to the hull and deck molds in 1959. Modifications were neither difficult nor costly to make in the appearance of the deck.

At peak efficiency one nine-man crew could mold one complete boat of each of the four types per shift. A total of 85 boats, in the four types, were produced. Of the 85, eight were rejected because of poor quality. List prices ranged from $995 for the 15-foot model to $2,665 for the 19-foot model. Optional accessories such as galvanized gas tanks, windshields, mattresses, and so on, were available at prices ranging from $10 to $165 each.

Although Mr. Lunn anticipated that the 43 dealers he had obtained to handle the Ship Shape line would build inventory as the boats were manufactured, it became necessary to supply them with samples and deliver from factory inventory as orders came in. Mr. Lunn explained, "There were three reasons why we had to carry the boats ourselves. First, since we were late in getting started in the business, we had to take whatever dealers we could get. Second, dealers usually made their purchases in December and January for the coming season. Consequently, they were reluctant to commit themselves further in the absence of firm orders. Lastly, S & M, which was primarily a shipyard, was unable to support dealer sales with very much promotional work." Sales of the Ship Shape amounted to $113,000 in 1958.

In 1959, 45 more boats, in the 16-foot and 19-foot lengths only, were produced to order from April through July. To maintain dealer effort with the shortened line, Lunn ordered 39 additional boats from S & M. Ship Shape sales were $179,000 in 1959.

At the end of the 1959 season, Mr. Lunn decided to dispose of the 30 boats left over from the 1958 model year. These were sold from the Lunn plant yard for between $600–700 per boat.

It was Mr. Lunn's belief that there was only one company in the country that used the matched die process in the manufacture of fiberglass boats. Furthermore, only one model in this company's line was produced on the dies, and this was a standard 14-foot lapstrake design outboard, of which more than 5,000 units were produced and sold annually.

According to Mr. Lunn the investment in matched dies for the 19-foot Ship Shape would be: dies, $80,000–90,000; press, $150,000; preform machine, $50,000 (optional). He stated, "We may never get our costs down to those associated with matched dies, but at least our molds can be made to last indefinitely and can be modified to meet style changes at no great expense."

The Sea Wind

In 1960, the Lunn company decided to make the large reinforced plastic sections for a 30-foot ketch, the Sea Wind, an auxiliary motor sailboat ordered by a private individual. Before the initial contract was completed, the customer ran short of the necessary funds to complete the ketch. Because of Mr. Lunn's great interest in sailing and sailboats, he purchased the parts and tooling as well as the design and engineering rights to the ketch for $16,000.

Mr. Lunn felt that with a boat such as the Sea Wind he could appeal to a smaller, more affluent part of the boating public to whom price was of less importance. The Sea Wind was priced at $13,850, less sails. Fully equipped, it was expected to sell for close to $20,000. Northrup and Johnson, a sales agent, was assigned exclusive distribution rights to the craft. In 1961, two prototypes of the Sea Wind were produced for display purposes. Further production would be against firm order only. By the end of 1961, orders for eight more units had been received by Lunn.

In late 1961, arrangements were completed for the formation of a separate company, the Allied Boat Company, to manufacture the Sea Wind. The new company was to be located in Catskill, New York, about 40 miles north of Albany on the Hudson River. The reasons for locating the new plant in upper New York State were: (1) labor costs were expected to run $1.60 (plus 21¢ for fringe benefits) in Catskill compared to the present $2.01 (plus 42¢ fringe benefits) in Huntington; and (2) delivery of the Sea Wind to the primary market areas of Long Island, Boston, Chesapeake Bay, and the Great Lakes would be facilitated by the new plant's location on the Hudson and close to the New York Thruway. The purchaser would pay for freight costs to his own mooring.

Three parties were involved in the formation of Allied. In return for its technical know-how, Lunn received 25 percent of Allied's stock; Northrup and Johnson received 25 percent; while a third party received 50 percent for supplying the necessary capital. Options were available on any additional common stock issued which would change the holdings to equal thirds.

PLANT RELOCATION

In early 1962, Mr. Lunn was considering the advisability of relocating in Wyandanch, New York, about 10 miles from Lunn's existing plants.

The new plant, housing some 90,000 square feet, was a U-shaped building available for lease by Lunn for $80,000 per year. The prime reasons for moving into the new plant would be: (1) to consolidate operations under one roof with resulting overhead economies; and (2) to provide more space for an expected increased volume of large reinforced plastic parts such as the fairwaters and mast-fairings. Since 17-foot masts could not be placed upright in the present plant, assembly had to be done with the fairing in a horizontal position, which interfered with the efficient use of space.

Mergers and Acquisition

Mr. Lunn first announced the new policy of open-mindedness toward merger or acquisition in August, 1960. In that year Lunn purchased Mariner Laminates for $20,000 and obtained the tooling, molds, and design of the line of lifeboats and life rafts mentioned above.

In 1961, at the initiative of the New York investment firm, negotiations for a merger between Lunn and the A & S Plastic Company[1] were opened. A & S was organized in 1955 to produce plastic boats. Wholly owned subsidiaries included A & S Chemical, producers of polyester resins used in the manufacture of the company's boats, and Daisy Manufacturing Company, manufacturers of wood, aluminum, and fiberglass boats. A & S Plastics manufactured boats ranging in length from 11 feet to 19 feet and retailing from $200 to $1,700. Boats were manufactured in plants in Texas and Indiana. Financial data are included in Exhibit 5.

[1] Name disguised. The A & S family held 88 percent of the outstanding common stock.

1. LUNN LAMINATES, INC. (B)

Balance Sheets, 1955-60

Assets	April 30 1955	April 30 1956	December 31 1956	December 31 1957	December 31 1958	December 31 1959	December 31 1960	October 1961
Cash	48	51	143	61	49	92	43	135
Accounts Receivable	170	237	138	222	162	159	212	394
Inventories	224	189	221	183	294	346	467	650
Other	28	11	6	15	5	13	14	10
Total Current Assets	469	488	508	481	510	610	737	1,189
Fixed Assets	1,058	308	269	225	200	176	166	158
Prepaid	48	12	14	11	16	12	27	20
Unamortized Debt Discount	10	9	9	7	6	5	---	3
Other	39	55	65	30	10	3	3	29*
Total Assets	1,625	873	864	754	741	807	933	1,399
Liabilities								
Notes Payable, Bank	300	29	---	---	---	---	---	150
Notes Payable, Other	303	12	---	---	---	---	---	---
Accounts Payable	103	68	59	61	89	102	190	362
Accrued Pay	12	12	15	16	12	15	22	5
Accrued Tax	15	16	16	15	14	15	17	24
Other	80	33	32	20	27	17	23	44
Total Current Liabilities	812	170	122	111	142	150	252	585
Long-Term Debt	750	750	750	750	750	---	---	138
Mortgage	---	---	---	---	68	62	56	51
Common Stock	108	109	109	109	109	203	203	203
Warrants	11	11	11	11	11	11	11	11
Surplus	293	304	304	304	304	381	383	383
Retained Earnings	(350)	(473)	(461)	(532)	(644)	---	28	28
Total Liabilities	1,625	873	864	754	741	807	933	1,399

*Includes seawind tools and molds of $16,000.

Source: Company records.

2. LUNN LAMINATES, INC. (B)

Income Statements, 1955-1960

	April 30		(8 Mos.)	Ending December 31				10 Mos. October
	1955	1956	1956	1957	1958	1959	1960	1961
Net sales	$2,190	$1,651	$934	$1,280	$1,419	$2,203	$2,203	$2,035
Cost of sales*	2,392	1,410	810	1,162	1,334	1,927	1,877	1,831
Gross profit	$ (202)	$ 241	$124	$ 118	$ 85	$ 276	$ 206	$ 204
Selling, G & A	423	206	150	143	150	196	180	215
Net profit	$ (625)	$ 36	$ (26)	$ (25)	$ (65)	$ 80	$ 26	$ (11)
Other income	18	7	1	2	1	21	7	12
	$ (607)	$ 42	$ (25)	$ (23)	$ (64)	$ 100	$ 33	$ 1
Other deductions:								
Interest	65	56	28	38	41	32	5	---
Loss on sale of fixed assets	---	36	2	1	---	4	---	---
Idle plant expense	---	72	3	9	6	---	---	---
	$ 65	$ 165	$ 33	$ 49	$ 48	$ 36	$ 36	---
Net income before taxes	$ (671)	$ (122)	$ (58)	$ (71)	$ (112)	$ 64	$ 28	$ 1
Taxes	(140)	---	---	---	---	---	---	---
Net income after taxes .	$ (531)	$ (122)	$ (58)	$ (71)	$ (112)	$ 64	$ 28	$ 1
Order backlog (12/31)								
Commercial	n.a.	n.a.	$176	$ 34	$ 390	$ ---	$ 5	$ 33
Military			664	778	1,010	1,500	997	872
Total			$841	$ 812	$1,400	$1,500	$1,002	$ 905

*Cost of sales:	1960	10 Mos. 1961
Direct labor	$ 402	$ 386
Materials	1,135	1,150
Factory overhead (65% variable)	455	451
Work-in-process inventory	(113)	(155)
	$1,879	$1,832

Analysis of Sales, 1961 and 1962

Product	1961	1962 (Est.)	Required Floor Space (New Plant)
Missile components	$ 296,000	$ 450,000	20,000 sq. ft.
Radomes (repairs)	6,000	105,000	---
Fairwaters	450,000	525,000	20,000
Mast fairings	254,000	1,150,000	10,000
Boats	972,000	432,000	8,000
Miscellaneous	745,000	685,000	7,000
Total	$2,723,000	$3,307,700	

3. LUNN LAMINATES, INC. (B)

Production Costs for Motor Whale Boat and Sea Wind

3A. Motor Whale Boat

Unit Cost of Glass and Resin

Material	Amount	Price	Cost
10 oz. glass cloth	72 yds.	$ .89	$ 64.00
24 oz. glass roving	1,300 yds.	.66	860.00
Polyester resin	1,532 lbs.	.45	690.00
Epoxy resin	155 lbs.	.37	57.50
Gel coat	120 lbs.	.48	57.50
Catalyst	18 lbs.	1.55	27.90
Hardener	10 lbs.	1.59	15.90
Styrene thinner	140 lbs.	.17	23.80
			$1,796.60

Manufacturing Costs (Month Ending 1-28-62)

	Phase	Materials Charged to Date: Raw Materials	Materials Charged to Date: Purchased Parts	Balance to Be Charged: Raw Materials	Balance to Be Charged: Purchased Parts
1	Production	$43,944	$122,275	$22,085	$16,550
2	Rework	---	---	---	---
3	Tooling	1,254	663	---	45
4	Engineering	---	6,191	---	---
5	Change order	32	6,568	---	1,168
6	Delivery*	---	678	---	9,344
7	Sea trials	---	292	---	7,258
8	Miscellaneous	---	1,244	---	---
	Totals	$45,230	$137,911	$22,085	$34,365

	Phase	Labor* Charged to Date	Balance to Be Charged
1	Production	$23,799	$17,220
2	Rework	---	---
3	Tooling	4,621	9
4	Engineering	1,580	659
5	Change order	1,135	1,924
6	Delivery**	148	---
7	Sea trials	77	---
	Totals	$31,360	$19,812

3B. Sea Wind Auxiliary Sailboat

Materials Cost

	First	Second
Glass and resin	$ 1,680	$ 1,601
Trim	2,933	1,080
Motor	530	530
Lead (for keel)	692	692
Mast/beam/rigging	1,366	1,297
Other purchased parts	289	690
Total	$ 7,490	$ 5,890

Unit Costs	First	Second
Materials	$ 7,490	$ 5,890
Labor***	6,040	3,870
Overhead	5,940	3,880
Total	$19,470	$13,640

Tooling
Engineering ($16,000
Publicity (440

*19-man crew working 150 hours on molding, 350 hours on assembly.

**Delivery costs were fixed within a given radius from the plant.

***Number of hours required was expected to decline to 600 at peak efficiency.

4. LUNN LAMINATES, INC. (B)

Ship Shape Outboard Motor Boat

4a. Production Costs (19' Express)

Material	Amount	Unit Price	Cost
8 1/2 oz. glass cloth	29 yds.	$ .89	$ 24.60
24 oz. glass roving	54 yds.	.66	35.40
Glass mat	71 yds.	.65	46.00
Polyester resin	340 lbs.	.45	153.00
Gel coat	50 lbs.	.70	35.00
Catalyst	5 lbs.	1.55	7.75
Miscellaneous	---	---	30.00
			$ 331.75
Trim materials			774.00
Labor			
Molding labor			$ 115.00
Trim and assembly labor			163.00
Direct Operating Costs			$ 1,384.00

4b. Tooling and Selling Costs (16' & 19' Models Combined)

Tooling	$73,500.00
Commissions	3,200.00
Publicity	4,500.00
Legal (nonrecurring)	2,000.00
Royalties	2,000.00
	$85,200.00

Note: 16' Runabout Unit Costs:

Raw materials	$283
Trim materials	245
Molding labor	100
Trim and assembly labor	55
Total direct costs	$683

4c. Sales Record, 1958-1959 (16' & 19' Models)

	1958	1959
Sold		
Boats	$ 74,500	$110,100
Accessories	38,500	57,000
Leftovers	---	11,900
Total	$113,000	$179,000
Units		
15'	10	--
16'	40	17
19'	18	53
Rejects	8	--
Leftover	9	--
Total	85	70

Exhibit 4 (continued)

	1958	1959
Materials	$ 78,600	$ 98,820
Labor	48,320	24,710
Overhead	53,060	29,380

4d. Production Process (19' Express)

			Man-Hours
(1)	Clean and prepare molds		4
(2)	Gel coat		3
(3)	Mold hull	5 1/2	
	Mold deck	6	
	Mold other small parts	4	15 1/2
(4)	Install wood reinforcements		3
(5)	Release, clean, trim		3 1/2
(6)	Assemble and install floors, flats, bulkheads		4
(7)	Assemble deck and hull		8
(8)	Install bathroom		5 1/2
(9)	Install trim		6 1/2
(10)	Install wood interiors		10
(11)	Electrical wiring		3 1/2
(12)	Install cabin, windows, windshield		5
(13)	Install hatch and motor mount		2 1/2
(14)	Install upholstery		3 1/2
(15)	Finish (resin coat, varnish, paint)		12
			89 1/2
	Fabrication of wooden parts		24

4e. Ship Shape Price Line

List Prices Effective April, 1958

15'	$ 995
16' Runabout	1,335
16' Express	1,695
19' Express	2,665

Note: There were three large and seven small molds for each boat type; fully amortized during 1958 and 1959 season. Process time given here was achieved at peak efficiency. Usual production time ran 10% more than the 113 1/2 man-hours noted here. Cure time usually ran 2 1/2 to 3 hours. By using faster reacting resin, cure time could be reduced to one-half hour. Dealers received discounts of 30% and 10% off list price. These prices were exclusive of optional equipment.

5. LUNN LAMINATES, INC. (B)

5a. Effect of Proposed Merger with A & S

	A & S	Lunn	% Lunn/A&S	Merged	% Lunn/Merged
Current assets	$2,239	$592	26.4%	$2,831	20.9%
Fixed assets	1,275	172	13.5	1,447	11.9
Other assets	5	27	540.0	32	118.0
Total Assets	$3,519	$791	22.5%	$4,310	18.4%
Current liabilities	$2,073	$ 65	31.5	$2,138	30.4
Funded debt	363	58	16.0	421	13.8
Total Liabilities	$2,436	$123	50.8%	$2,559	48.3%
Net worth	$1,090	$668	61.1%	$1,758	37.8%

	A & S	Lunn
Market price	1 1/2	1 3/8
Shares outstanding	2,500,000	814,000
Book value	44¢	82¢
Net profit/sales (%)	4	5
Profit/investment capital (%)	14	12
Working capital ($)	166,000	527,000
Current ratio (R)	1.1:1	9.1:1
Acid-test ratio (R)	.29:1	2.7:1

Terms: Each share of Lunn stock would be redeemed for 8/10 share of A & S Plastic stock. Of the 651,200 additional shares needed to complete the transaction, 1/2 are to be donated by the A & S family; 1/2 to be issued by A & S.

5b. Percentage Analysis of Income Statements of 25 Outboard Manufacturers

	1958	1959
Sales	100.00%	100.00%
Cost of goods sold:		
Materials	50.05	51.81
Subcontract work	0.33	0.53
Direct labor	12.88	13.18
Indirect labor	6.28	5.40
All other	9.75	10.55
Total cost of goods sold	79.29%	81.47%
Selling and administrative	13.56	12.95
Total operating costs	92.85	94.42
Net operating profit	7.15	5.58
Other income (net)	(0.51)	(0.48)
Tax	3.52	2.56
Net profit	3.12	2.54

Source: 1958-1959 Operating Report to the NAEBM compiled by Ernst and Ernst.

6. LUNN LAMINATES, INC. (B)

6a. Projected Costs in New Plant

	Actual 1961	Projected 1961
Materials	50.4%	44.5%*
Direct labor	18.0	16.5
Overhead	20.2	21.4
Gross profit	11.4	17.6
Gen. & admin.	10.1	11.9
Profit	1.3	5.7

*Savings from elimination of lines with high materials cost and from better estimating procedure.

6b. Projected New Plant Space Usage

	Sales Volume	Space Needed Sq. Ft.
Fairwaters	$ 500,000	20,000
Mast fairings	1,000,000	10,000
Missile components	200,000	2,500
Boats	317,000	8,000
Other	400,000	7,000

6b. Proposed New Plant Layout

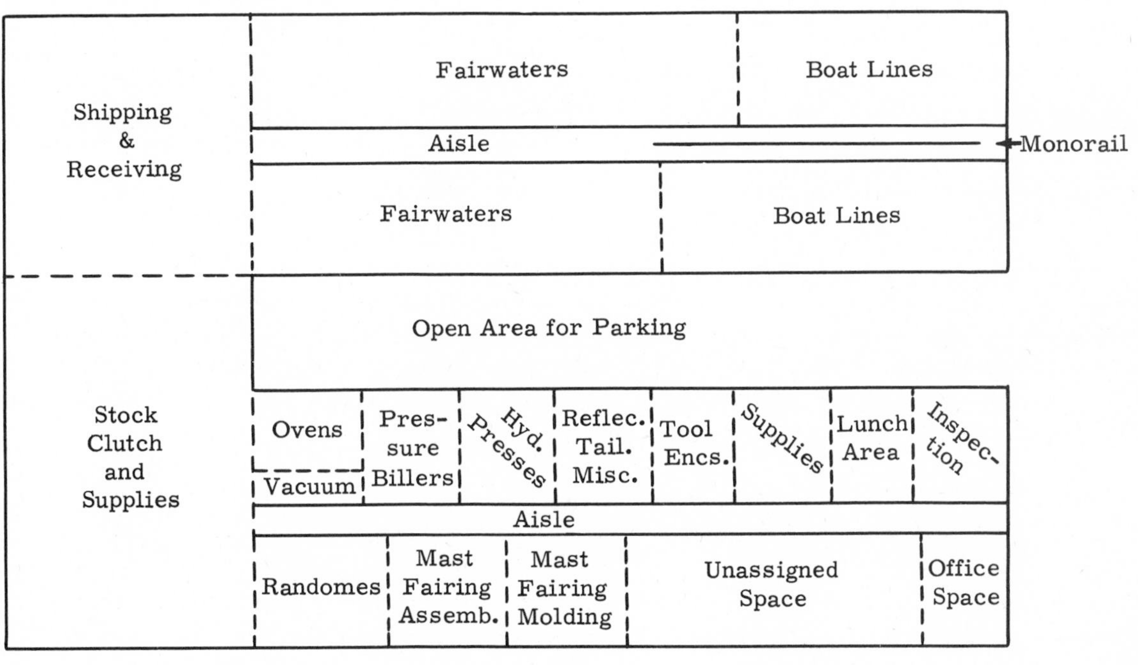

7. LUNN LAMINATES, INC. (B)

Monthly Boat Sales

Index Based on 1947-49 Monthly Shipments = 100

Shipments	Jan.	Feb.	Mar.	April	May	Jun.	July	Aug.	Sep.	Oct.	Nov.	Dec.	Monthly Average
1954	190	290	430	560	510	480	320	220	130	140	150	200	300
1955	230	360	600	770	750	690	510	360	210	270	280	320	450
1956	440	570	930	1,090	1,210	940	580	390	300	350	340	390	630
1957	530	750	1,270	1,290	1,360	1,210	880	530	360	450	430	520	800
1958	620	820	1,350	1,640	1,610	1,320	930	610	540	620	490	760	950
1959	810	1,200	1,860	2,240	2,230	2,080	1,390	700	660	700	660	750	1,270
1960	820	1,140	1,690	2,050	2,050								
Orders Received													
1958							750	660	720	950	800	1,030	
1959	1,330	1,740	2,620	2,370	1,980	1,480	1,010	750	1,000	1,250	1,010	930	1,450
1960	1,580	1,670	1,760	1,920	1,490								
Cancellations													
1958							20	20	10	20	30	20	
1959	50	50	90	130	200	250	140	160	50	50	30	50	100
1960	50	80	80	270	200								
Orders on Hand (End of Month)													
1958						470	270	300	470	780	960	1,210	
1959	1,680	2,170	2,830	2,830	2,380	1,530	1,020	900	1,190	1,690	2,010	2,130	
1960	2,840	3,290	3,280	2,870	2,160								

Source: National Association of Engine & Boat Manufacturers.

8. LUNN LAMINATES, INC. (B)

8a. Data on Boat Purchases for Selected States

State	$ of Motor Purchases	% of Boat Purchases	% of Trailer Purchases	% of Buying Power	% Estimated Population
New York	9.36	8.68	5.81	11.24	9.36
Indiana	2.47	2.39	2.59	2.62	2.62
New Jersey	2.93	3.04	2.12	4.04	3.31
Connecticut	1.58	1.60	1.15	1.83	1.36
Texas	5.35	5.61	6.96	4.71	5.49
Louisiana	2.34	2.26	2.43	1.37	1.76
Florida	5.30	6.04	6.38	2.48	2.70
Oregon	4.11	4.03	4.49	5.81	5.43

8b. Number of Companies Building Boats by Type of Boat

Pure Sailboats	108	Outboards & inboards	118
Outboard boats	392	Auxiliaries	53
Inboard boats	190	Custom yachts only	45
Above three types	12	Custom yachts and stock boats	35
Houseboats	46	Stock boats only	782

Total Spent on Recreational Boating at Retail, 1947-1961* (In Millions)

1947 -- $905	1952 -- $ 720	1957 -- $1,912
1948 -- 780	1953 -- 950	1958 -- 2,085
1949 -- 660	1954 -- 1,000	1959 -- 2,475
1950 -- 680	1955 -- 1,230	1960 -- 2,525
1951 -- 645	1956 -- 1,580	1961 -- 2,340

*Includes boats, fuel, equipment, marina fees, and so forth. Dollar sales of boats alone were approximately four times dollar sales of outboard motorboats (below).

8c. Outboard Motorboat Sales, 1947-1961

1947 -- 143,000 (Units)	1952 -- 164,000	1957 -- 320,000
1948 -- 198,000	1953 -- 231,000	1958 -- 316,000
1949 -- 171,000	1954 -- 223,000	1959 -- 329,000
1950 -- 131,000	1955 -- 258,000	1960 -- 294,000
1951 -- 154,000	1956 -- 302,000	1961 -- 237,000

8d. Dollar Sales (Millions) of Outboard Motorboats

1947 -- $ 30	1952 -- $ 43.8	1957 -- $144.0
1948 -- 43.6	1953 -- 63.5	1958 -- 170
1949 -- 39.4	1954 -- 72.2	1959 -- 204
1950 -- 31.2	1955 -- 84.4	1960 -- 185
1951 -- 38	1956 -- 112.6	1961 -- 154

Note: Sailboat sales were estimated at 20,000 units annually at an approximate cost of $2,000 without power, or $15,000 with power.

Source: National Association of Engine & Boat Manufacturers.

Catalin Corporation of America (A)

The Catalin Corporation of America was the largest manufacturer in the United States of cast phenolic resins. The company's products, which were sold under the trade name "Catalin," were distinguished by their unique color properties and were advertised as the "Gem of Plastics." The company also sold various types of liquid resins and molding compounds. The executive and sales offices were located at One Park Avenue, in New York, while the plant, which employed about 450 people, was located at Fords, New Jersey. The financial history of the company for the years 1940 to 1948 is shown in Exhibits 1 and 2.

In the spring of 1947, the company was engaged in adding a number of new plastic materials to its product line. The company had been founded originally to produce the cast phenolic resins and for many years these products had constituted the major part of the business. The patents on the formulas for the cast resins, however, were due to expire in 1949. Before the date of expiration, the company intended to be well established in the market with a general line of other plastic materials of a nonpatentable nature.

COMPANY HISTORY

In 1929, the original Catalin corporation was formed with an authorized capital of $120,000 of preferred stock and 13,000 shares of common stock. The organization was established to pioneer the production and sale of a new plastic material, about which the founders had obtained information from a German chemical corporation. The material was a cast phenolic resin which was superior in color range, transparency, and machineability to other plastics in the market. The process had been secret and the founders had purchased the services of a German chemist as well as the necessary technical information.

In 1933, a stronger capitalization of the company was authorized and complete patents were purchased to protect the process. The Catalin company was obliged to bring suit against several unlicensed competitors, but won its litigation by 1935. Thereafter the company licensed competitors to use the process. At one time during the 1930's the company's licensees included the DuPont, Monsanto, and Bakelite corporations. After a poor market during the war years, cast phenolic sales again expanded. The Catalin company sold more than $6.6 million of cast phenolics during 1945 and 1946.

The successful litigation and the company's increased profits affected the market appraisal of the company's stock. The stock went up from a low point of 25 cents a share in 1931 to over $16.00 a share in 1936. With this profit in sight, many of the original backers of the company disposed of their holdings, and the company's stock became widely scattered.

In order to broaden its product line, the Catalin company began making liquid resins in the late 1930's. Liquid resins were used in many industrial applications, to give a firm physical structure to rock wool or glass fiber insulation, to laminate paper and textiles, to bond veneers for furniture, and to impart crease resistance to textiles. Liquid resin production was of particular value to the company during World War II, when sales of cast phenolics fell off because their appeal as "appearance" products had few wartime applications.

Mr. William Theile, who had dominated the company since 1931 as president and principal stockholder, died suddenly in 1944. Mr. Alan Mann, the company's patent counsel, became chairman of the board. Mr. Harry Krehbiel, who had been in charge of sales since 1931 and executive vice-president since 1938, became president of the company. Mr. Leo Beck, who had been vice-president in charge of sales, became executive vice-president.

PRODUCTS AND MARKETS

The products sold by the Catalin Corporation were divided into three major groups: cast resins, liquid resins, and molding powders.

Cast Resins: Unlike other plastic materials, the cast phenolic resins were not supplied in powder form and could not be injection or compression molded. The resin was prepared as a liquid and cast in the company's plant. It was then furnished to the customer as a fully cured solid ready for machining and finishing operations. Although the production process was quite different, the Catalin Corporation served its customers in somewhat the same manner as does a foundry in the production of iron castings.

The cast resin business was of two types: special shapes and standard shapes. The special shapes accounted for the majority of the cast resin sales volume. Typical items in this category were radio cabinets, clock cases, cutlery handles, brush backs, jewelry boxes, and juke box parts. Customers gave the Catalin Corporation drawings and specifications for the objects they desired. The Catalin Corporation then had steel arbors or models prepared. These arbors were used in making the lead molds in which the resin was cast. The steel arbors were usually purchased and owned by the Catalin Corporation, but occasionally the sales agreement provided that they were to be owned by the customer.

The completed castings often went from the Catalin Corporation to a plastics fabricator for miscellaneous machining and finishing operations and thence to the manufacturer who was using the part in his product line. In some cases, however, the castings went directly to the manufacturer who performed the necessary machining operations himself. In a few instances, particularly in the case of large radio housings where the finishing required large grinding equipment, the Catalin Corporation performed the finishing operations before sending the castings the customer.

In addition to the special shapes, the cast resins were sold in a wide range of standard stock shapes, including round, square, octagonal, rectangular, hexagonal, scalloped, and oval rods, as well as cylinders and sheets. Over 3,300 different sizes and shapes were available, each of which could be ordered in about 200 different colors. These products were sold to manufacturers or plastic fabricators for machining into a wide range of articles such as buttons, costume jewelry, dice, poker chips, and various industrial parts. The Catalin Corporation itself was not in the fabricating business and produced no finished articles for sale to the trade.

The cast resins were distributed throughout the United States and in various foreign countries. The central sales office was at One Park Avenue in New York, and branch offices were maintained in Providence, Rhode Island, and Chicago. On the West Coast, the company was represented by a sales agent who handled other products in addition to the Catalin line. There were nine salesmen in the New York office who worked primarily with the cast resins. As will be noted later, some of these men also spent part of their time selling molding powders. There were two salesmen in each of the branch offices; these men handled the company's liquid resins and molding powders in addition to the cast resins.

The base price for the cast resins in simple shapes and plain colors was 61 cents per pound. The price for particular orders, however, sometimes ran as high as $1.10 per pound depending on the size of the order, the color, and the complexity of the part. The Catalin Corporation absorbed the freight costs on shipments made to customers within a radius of 300 miles of the plant. To customers outside the area, the company allowed up to 66 cents per hundred weight for freight charges.

The Catalin Corporation was the only major producer of cast phenolic resins in the United States. The other manufacturers produced only a relatively small volume, and most of them operated under licenses from the Catalin Corporation. The chief merchandising value of the cast resins lay in their extremely fine color properties. The range of colors and degree of translucency which could be secured in them was unquestionably superior to those obtainable in other phenolic plastics. The company also claimed that its materials had a depth and warmth of color which was superior to that obtainable with the various thermoplastic materials.

The cast resins had another competitive advantage in that the initial tooling cost was fairly low compared to that required for the steel dies used in compression and injection molding. Depending on their complexity, the steel arbors used in making the lead molds for the cast resins usually varied in cost from about $100 to $1,000. Dies for the injection or compression molding of comparable objects often ran from 2 to 10 times these amounts. As a result, manufacturers and plastic fabricators frequently turned to the cast resins for articles in which they anticipated a small total volume. Most of the radio manufacturers, for example, had a deluxe cabinet model made of cast resin while their other models, which they expected to sell in a larger volume at a lower price, were made from other plastics.

Finally, the cast resins had an advantage in relation to other plastics in that they could be used for large and bulky objects with little difficulty. Compression and injection molding techniques had not yet been developed to the point where large objects could be formed without an excessively long cure time in the molds and various other production difficulties.

Sales of the cast resins during 1946 amounted to about 6½ million pounds; they accounted for somewhat over half of the total dollar volume of business done by the company.

Liquid Resins: The liquid resins consisted primarily of three groups of materials, sold under the trade names "Catavar," "Catabond," and "Loabond." The Catavar resins, which accounted for the majority of the liquid resin sales volume, were phenolic resins and were used primarily in industrial and decorative laminates. These laminates ultimately found extensive usage in the refrigerator and building industries. The Catabond resins were likewise of the phenolic type and were used chiefly for bonding, impregnating, cementing, and gluing purposes. Among other things, these resins were employed in the preparation of glass fiber and rock wool insulating materials for use in refrigerators and various types of buildings. They were also used in the production of filters, electrical parts, and timing gears for the automotive industry and in the manufacture of sandpaper and grinding wheels. The Loabond resins were of the polystyrene type and had excellent electrical and water resistant properties. They were used for bonding glass fiber mats, protective coatings, leather treating, and similar purposes.

The liquid resin business had been started in the middle 1930's and substantially expanded during 1946. In the spring of 1947, the company was producing about 200 different resin formulations; of these, about 25 represented the bulk of the liquid resin sales volume.

The company had found that the number of potential customers in many of the markets for liquid resins was very small. The sales manager of the liquid resin division estimated, for example, that there were only 10 or 20 large laminating firms in the United States and that there were about an equal number of rock wool insulation manufacturers. Frequently, however, the requirements of these firms were very large. A laminator might use as much as 1,000,000 pounds of resin a month, and a rock wool manufacturer might use somewhat between 50,000 and 1,000,000 pounds a month.

In contrast to these large customers, the company also sold to a number of small firms who purchased only one or two 50-gallon drums a month. The company accepted orders for quantities as small as one to five gallons because these purchases were usually made for experimental purposes. In general, the company tried to avoid the preparation of special resin formulas unless the total sales volume was expected to be at least 5 drums or about 250 gallons a month.

The liquid resins were sold in direct competition with similar resins produced by other plastic material manufacturers. Raw materials made up a large part of the cost of the liquid resins, and the prices charged by the various producers were nearly identical. In April, 1947, prices ranged from about 15 cents to 55 cents a pound, depending on the particular resin formula. The Catalin Corporation had found that the best basis for securing new business was to offer the customer the maximum in the way of technical service and to convince him that the company's laboratory would give him the best possible help in keeping abreast of new developments in the plastics field.

During the year 1946, the company's sales of liquid resins amounted to about 10,000,000 pounds.

Molding Powders: The Company sold phenolic, cellulose acetate, and polystyrene molding powders.

(*a*) *Phenolic:* The phenolic molding powders were produced in the company's pilot plant at Matawan, New Jersey. During the spring of 1947 the output of the plant was limited by the current shortages of phenol and other raw materials.

These products were to be comparable in properties, applications, and prices to those produced by other plastic material manufacturers. Because of the high costs involved in the pilot plant operation, the company was currently selling the Catapak resin at about 19½ cents per pound as compared to a minimum price of 16½ cents per pound charged by other manufacturers for general purpose molding powders. The existing supply of phenolic molding powders was so short that the small price differential was of little significance to customers. In the future, however, the company anticipated that its costs and prices would have to be directly competitive with those of other manufacturers.

The capacity of the Matawan pilot plant was 80,000 to 100,000 pounds per month per shift. Shipments during the month of May, 1947, were approximately 40,000 pounds; for the month of June they were estimated at 70,000 to 80,000 pounds.

(*b*) *Polystyrene:* The company sold several different polystyrene molding powders, under the trade name "Loalin," at prices ranging from about 24½ cents to 80 cents per pound. The company had undertaken the manufacture of polystyrene molding compounds in 1940, but had been forced to abandon the project at the outbreak of the war because of the shortage of raw materials.

During the war, the government together with the large chemical companies had established extensive facilities for the production of an intermediate material used in the manufacture of polystyrene as a part of the synthetic rubber program. After the war, these facilities were diverted by the large chemical concerns to the production of polystyrene.

Rather than to attempt the production of polystyrene in competition with these firms, the Catalin Corporation made an arrangement to buy its requirements of the material from the Monsanto Chemical Company. The agreement provided that the Catalin Corporation would buy at the Monsanto Chemical Company's minimum selling prices, less 10 percent. In addition, the Monsanto Chemical Company absorbed freight charges to customers as far west as St. Louis. Customers beyond St. Louis paid the difference between the freight charges to their location and St. Louis. The polystyrene was shipped from the plants of the Monsanto Chemical Company to Easthampton, New Jersey, where it was warehoused for the Catalin Corporation. Shipments were made to customers from this warehouse. The Monsanto Chemical Company imposed no restrictions on the customers to which or the areas in which the Catalin Corporation might sell polystyrene.

The contract with the Monsanto Chemical Company was negotiated in the early part of 1946 and was to cover a period of five years.

During 1946, the company shipped approximately 6½ million pounds of molding powders. The shortage of raw materials limited shipments to about 50 percent of the orders received.

MANUFACTURING

The manufacturing activities of the Catalin Corporation, which were carried out at the plants in Fords and Matawan, involved the production of the cast resins, the liquid resins, and a small volume of phenolic molding powders. The principal raw materials purchased by the company were phenol and formaldehyde. Other raw materials included caustic soda, lactic acid, glycerin, pigments, plasticizers, lubricants, lignin fillers, and small amounts of miscellaneous chemicals.

Operations at Fords: The Fords plant housed the facilities for the manufacture of the cast resins and the liquid resins as well as the company's central research laboratories.

(*a*) *Cast Resins:* The production of the cast resins usually involved the preparation of steel arbors, the preparation of lead molds, the manufacture of the liquid resin, the pouring of the resin into the molds, the curing of the castings in ovens, the removal of the castings from the molds, and finishing, packing, and shipping operations.

Exhibits 3 to 5 present detailed information with regard to the work involved in the manufacture of the cast resins. The process was not an easy one to operate and extremely careful control was required at many points in order to secure perfect castings of the desired color and translucency or transparency. It was, for example, extremely important that contamination with iron be rigidly avoided. As a result, the raw materials had to be very pure, and the phenol-formaldehyde reaction had to be carried out in nickel kettles. The Catalin Corporation had observed that several companies had undertaken the process and abandoned it later because of the extensive experience and "know-how" required for successful operations.

As noted above, the company was currently carrying only a very small inventory of cast resin shapes which it planned to discontinue in the near future. The great bulk of the cast resin production was, therefore, to customer orders which were sent by teletype from the New York office. The production division held these orders and grouped them into full-size production batches in so far as it was possible to do so. There were 14 resin kettles in the cast resin division, 10 of which were designed to accommodate production batches of 2,000 pounds. The remaining four kettles could be used economically for somewhat smaller quantities.

In the spring of 1947, most of the departments in the cast resin division were operating on a three-shift basis. The pouring, shipping, and maintenance departments were, however, on a one-shift basis. Production costs were divided approximately as follows: raw materials 60 percent, labor 25 percent, and burden 15 percent.

(*b*) *Liquid Resins:* During the war years, when the production of the decorative cast resins was curtailed, the liquid resins were manufactured in the cast resin kettles. In 1946, after the production of the cast resins was resumed, three new resin kettles were installed for the manufacture of the liquid resins; it was planned to add two additional kettles in 1947. The problem of iron contamination was not critical in the case of the liquid resins because the colors were of minor importance. These kettles were, therefore, made of stainless steel rather than nickel.

RESEARCH

The various phases of the Catalin company's research program may be outlined as follows:

Main Laboratory: The main laboratory, which was located at Fords, employed about 23 research chemists and 13 laboratory technicians.

In 1947, the Catalin Corporation was spending somewhat over $100,000 a year for the operation of the main laboratory. The division of the total budget between the three departments was about as follows: general laboratory 58 percent, high polymer laboratory 24 percent, and physical testing and process development laboratory 18 percent. The largest item in the budget was for salaries, which accounted for about 85 percent of the total expenditures.

1. CATALIN CORPORATION OF AMERICA (A)
Balance Sheets, 1940-1948
(In Thousands)

ASSETS	1940	1941	1942	1943	1944	1945	1946	1947	1948
Cash	$ 115	$ 102	$ 120	$ 239	$ 230	$ 259	$ 835	$ 490	$ 455
Accounts Receivable	$ 290	$ 331	$ 246	$ 227	$ 368	$ 637	$1,235	$ 874	$ 622
Reserve for Doubtful Accounts	41	50	33	12	15	15	34	35	41
	$ 249	$ 281	$ 213	$ 215	$ 353	$ 622	$1,201	$ 839	$ 581
U.S. Government Notes	148	106	48	3	278	351			
Inventories	137	237	237	201	282	227	455	663	660
Current Assets	$ 649	$ 726	$ 618	$ 658	$1,143	$1,459	$2,491	$1,992	$1,696
Stock Subscription					$ 35		$ 39	$ 9	
Prepaid Expenses	$ 10	$ 20	$ 33	$ 30	31	$ 31	51	68	$ 58
Notes Receivable	51								
Fixed Assets	$ 991	$1,399	$1,312	$1,341	$1,220	$1,233	$1,440	$1,730	$1,739
Less Depreciation	476	563	513	634	632	550	523	565	642
	$ 515	$ 836	$ 799	$ 707	$ 588	$ 683	$ 917	$1,165	$1,097
Investments at Cost:									
Fords National Bank	$ 1	$ 1	$ 1	$ 1	$ 1				
Catalin, Limited	71	71	71	71	71	$ 71	$ 71	$ 12	$ 12
Total Investments	$ 72	$ 72	$ 72	$ 72	$ 72	$ 71	$ 71	$ 12	$ 12
U.S. Treasury Refunds					$ 13	$ 10			
Excess Profits Refund					16				
Processes, Patents	$ 344	$ 340	$ 337						
TOTAL ASSETS	$1,641	$1,994	$1,859	$1,467	$1,863	$2,289	$3,569	$3,246	$2,863
LIABILITIES AND CAPITAL									
Accounts Payable	$ 88	$ 115	$ 112	$ 123	$ 211	$ 372	$ 973	$ 627	$ 601
Notes Payable	75	315	143	63	280	436	493	192	91
Dividends Payable							111		
Bank Loan Payable								300	
Current Liabilities	$ 163	$ 430	$ 255	$ 186	$ 491	$ 808	$1,577	$1,119	$ 692
Mortgage		$ 20	$ 15						
Capital Reserve						$ 35	$ 39	$ 9	
Excess Profits Credit					$ 16				
Capital Stock	$ 537	$ 537	$ 537	$ 537	$ 537	$ 556	$ 565	$ 562	$ 561
Surplus, Earned	912	978	1,023	715	790	841	1,307	1,453	1,504
Surplus, Capital	29	29	29	29	29	49	81	103	106
Total Capital	$1,478	$1,544	$1,589	$1,281	$1,356	$1,446	$1,953	$2,118	$2,171
TOTAL LIABILITIES AND CAPITAL	$1,641	$1,994	$1,859	$1,467	$1,863	$2,289	$3,569	$3,246	$2,863

2. CATALIN CORPORATION OF AMERICA (A)

Income Statements, 1940-1948
(In Thousands)

	1940	1941	1942	1943	1944	1945	1946	1947	1948
Net Sales	$1,836	$2,345	$2,614	$2,459	$2,925	$4,387	$7,615	$7,386	$7,213
Cost of Sales	1,269	1,640	2,187	2,099	2,080	3,240	5,543	6,202	6,305
Gross Profit	$ 567	$ 705	$ 427	$ 360	$ 845	$1,147	$2,072	$1,184	$ 908
Selling and Administrative Expenses	214	228	195	143	283	338	493	538	525
Net Profit on Sales	$ 353	$ 477	$ 232	$ 217	$ 562	$ 809	$1,579	$ 646	$ 383
Other Income	30	42	35	30	21	18	40	30	33
Gross Income	$ 383	$ 519	$ 267	$ 247	$ 583	$ 827	$1,619	$ 676	$ 416
Other Expenses	139	158	107	114	66	215	333	280	197
	$ 244	$ 361	$ 160	$ 133	$ 517	$ 612	$1,286	$ 396	$ 219
Income Charges	3	9	4	4	78*	7	9	86	6
Income before Taxes	$ 241	$ 352	$ 156	$ 129	$ 439	$ 605	$1,277	$ 482	$ 213
Federal Taxes	67	149	59	50	246	407	479	170	79
Net Income after Taxes	$ 174	$ 203	$ 97	$ 79	$ 193	$ 198	$ 798	$ 312	$ 134
Earned Surplus, Beginning	872	912	978	1,023	715	790	841	1,307	1,453
Before Adjustments	$1,046	$1,115	$1,075	$1,102	$ 908	$ 988	$1,639	$1,619	$1,587
Adjustments		3		(333)	15	16			
Earned Surplus before Dividends	$1,046	$1,112	$1,075	$ 769	$ 923	$1,004	$1,639	$1,619	$1,587
Dividends Paid	134	134	53	54	134	163	331	166	84
Earned Surplus at End of Period	$ 912	$ 978	$1,022	$ 715	$ 789	$ 841	$1,308	$1,453	$1,503

*Includes loss on sale of Matawan Plant in 1944 of $75,731.73.

Sales by Product Lines, 1941-1948

	1941	1942	1943	1944	1945	1946	1947	1948
Liquid	$ 616,369	$ 639,840	$ 849,062	$ 824,471	$1,343,264	$1,365,025	$2,423,712	$2,678,139
Polystyrene	50,679	291,562	231,042	191,763	296,281	1,831,957	2,208,504	2,536,882
Cast Phenolic	1,676,603	1,311,929	449,316	1,458,990	2,444,705	4,219,338	2,370,315	1,119,196

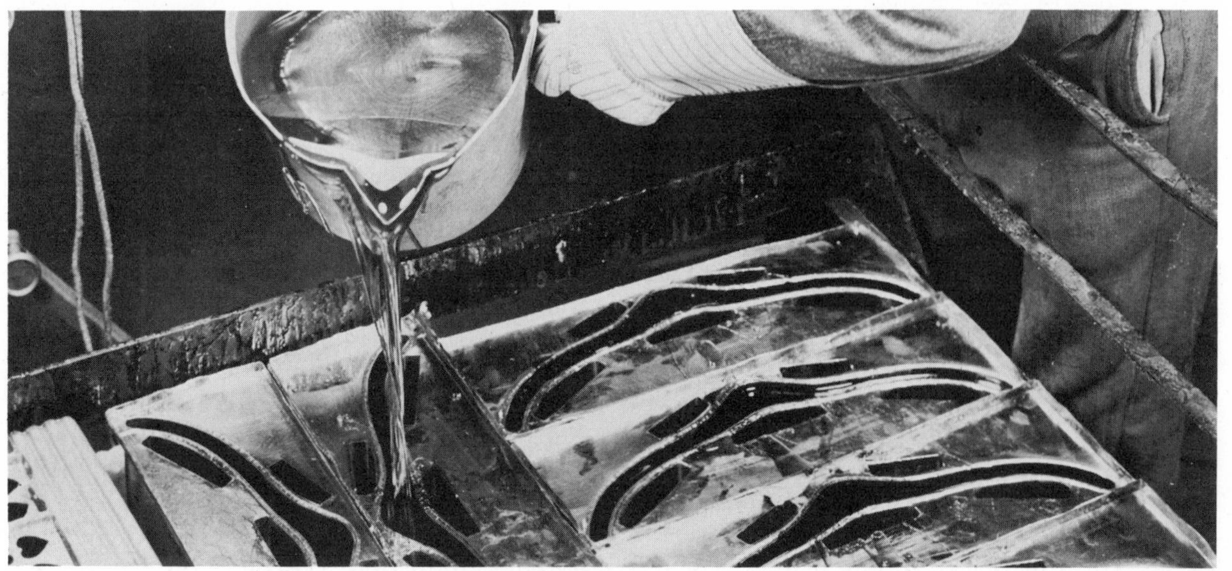

5A. CATALIN CORPORATION (A)
Pouring Lead Molds

5B. CATALIN CORPORATION (A)
Curing Ovens

Curing. After the pouring operation, the castings (still in the lead molds) were moved into steam-heated ovens for a curing period of 3 to 12 days. The oven temperatures during this period were maintained at 170° to 180° F. The ovens used by the Catalin Corporation were rectangular in shape, about 12 feet by 20 feet by 9 feet in height. Each oven had capacity for curing up to 8,000 pounds of resin during one operating cycle.

Finishing. A certain amount of finishing was done on radio cabinets because this work required large-size grinding equipment which most of the customers did not have. Round rods were also sometimes ground to remove the longitudinal taper which was necessary to permit their withdrawal from the molds.

For large radio cabinets, box castings, long tubes, plate castings, and similar items the minimum wall thickness was 3/16 inch. For small tubes, small boxes and other articles which could be removed readily from the molds, a wall thickness of 5/32 inch was possible. For very small castings, such as hollow bottle closures and finger rings, a wall thickness of 1/8 inch could be used. The maximum length of the cast rods was usually about 21 inches.

Catalin Corporation of America (B)

Between 1946 and 1954 the operations of the Catalin company changed substantially. Cast phenolics, which had accounted for 55 percent of sales in 1946, were eliminated completely from the product line by June, 1951. Liquid resins and oil additives, which together accounted for only 17 percent of sales in 1946, totaled 44 percent of sales in 1954. Polystyrene, which was only 24 percent of sales in 1946, accounted for more than 54 percent of sales in 1954, a growth of more than triple the dollar amount in eight years. Due to the importance of the polystyrene market and the intermediate position of the company between a resale and a manufacturing organization in this field, one of the most important problems faced by the senior executives in 1954 was to establish a long range policy with regard to polystyrene operations.

Summaries of the Catalin company's operations between 1949 and 1953 are contained in Exhibits 1 and 2. A breakdown of sales by product lines is included in Exhibit 2.

CHANGE OF PRODUCT LINE IN 1949

Between 1946 and 1949, the sales of cast phenolics decreased from $4,219,000 to $985,000. The sales decline was of the utmost significance to the Catalin company, which had pioneered the cast resin process, controlled its patents, and had become the largest factor in the cast resin market in the United States.

A major aspect of the change from cast phenolics to polystyrene was its effect on plant operations. In 1948, the Catalin company had a labor force of about 600 employees, many of whom were working directly on cast phenolics. Due to the decision at that time not to make the major capital investment necessary to manufacture polystyrene, there was no other place in the organization to absorb the surplus workers. In order to eliminate cast phenolics, therefore, the Catalin company had to lay off more than 400 workers and make large cash disbursements for termination pay. The effect on the company of the large scale lay-offs was such that it was found necessary to reorganize the executive staff as well, in order to bring up younger men who could work effectively with the new products.

As a result of the new product line, the Catalin company changed from a leader in the cast phenolics process to a direct competitor against large integrated polystyrene companies and to a specialist in the development of industrial resins. Under a long-term contract with a major chemical company, the Catalin company purchased polystyrene for 10 percent below market price, and sold the material to molders in "Catalin" branded bags. Although the new plan meant that the Catalin company was dependent upon its competitors for supply of its product, the contract was considered to be a reliable arrangement for the following two reasons. First, the Catalin sales contract enabled the chemical company to add a single large outlet for its polystyrene production. Second, the 10 percent margin did not have the nature of a special concession by the chemical company, but was rather generally available from any major polystyrene manufacturer to any selling organization with the volume of the Catalin company.

By 1954, the Catalin company had successfully offset the loss of its cast phenolics market through its sales of polystyrene and of industrial resins and additives. In that year, polystyrene accounted for 55 percent of sales, liquid resins 33 percent, powdered resins 1 percent and oil additives 11 percent.

Polystyrene

In 1954, the Catalin company had 407 active accounts among the molding companies. The five most important customers accounted for 18 percent of polystyrene sales; the remaining customers each averaged $11,000 sales from Catalin per year. The Catalin company had about 6 percent of the polystyrene market. Almost all the remainder of the market was shared by four large corporations ranking in the following order: Dow, Monsanto, Koppers, Bakelite. Although the Catalin company sold polystyrene tagged with the company's name, it was generally known in the trade that the material was manufactured by one of its competitors. The Catalin company's polystyrene contract authorized quality control problems to be referred by the Catalin salesmen back to the manufacturer. Responsibility for technical assistance and quality control was therefore borne by the contract manufacturer. Catalin company salesmen were free to develop sales contacts by providing delivery and other nontechnical services.

Liquid Resins

Although the Catalin company manufactured liquid resins prior to the post-war change in product line, 55 percent of sales in 1946 had been due to a single customer. When cast phenolics were dropped from the line, the Catalin sales force made a concerted drive to broaden the sales base by developing new customers in different industries. By 1951 there were 386 active accounts for liquid resins, of which the top five took 47 percent of the company's sales.

The market for liquid resins was very different from that of polystyrene. Although polystyrene molding powder came in several grades such as general purpose, heat-resistant, or high-impact, and in many colors, it was recognized to be a standard material acceptable to all molders according to the grade and color specified. Liquid resins, on the other hand, were used for a variety of purposes in many different industries, and most formulations had to be custom-developed specially for each use. In 1954, the Catalin company had over 1,000 liquid resin formulations, of which 47 formulations accounted for a large majority of the sales volume. The four resin categories sold by the company were phenolic, urea, resorcinol, and cresylic, of which phenolic was by far the largest type.

Oil Additives

In 1949, the Catalin company obtained a contract to produce a special additive for the lubricating oil refined by a large oil corporation. The contract was so successful that volume increased five times in the period from 1949 to 1951. In 1954 the Catalin company was installing new polymerization kettles to handle a larger volume of the additive.

MANUFACTURING FACILITIES

After its change in product line, the Catalin company maintained plant facilities at three locations. At Fords, New Jersey, the company was equipped to manufacture liquid and powdered resins and oil additives and to warehouse polystyrene. At Thomasville, North Carolina, the company produced resins for the furniture and textile industries located in the South. At Calumet City, Illinois, the company polymerized and warehoused polystyrene. Other storage points for polystyrene were located in East Hampton (Massachusetts), Chicago, Cleveland, Evansville (Indiana), Kansas City, and Los Angeles.

Fords Plant

In 1954, the largest plant building at Fords, which had originally been used for the production of cast phenolics, contained office and warehouse space, testing laboratories, and two polymerization kettles together with associated grinding equipment for producing powdered resins. A separate building contained six kettles for making liquid resins. A third building contained the equipment for producing oil additives. More than two dozen tanks were located outside the buildings to store raw materials and finished inventory. The engineering drafting rooms were located in a small wooden building near the main plant structure. The total space available was 128,000 square feet.

Liquid Resins: Six polymerization kettles were available to make liquid resins. The size of the kettles ranged from 2,000 pounds to 10,000 pounds and the average cycle was ten hours. The manufacturing process itself was quite simple. Large quantities of formaldehyde and phenol or urea were pumped into the kettle from storage tanks; special chemicals were added; heat controls were set and steam was piped into the outer lining of the kettle. When samples indicated that the final chemical stage had been reached, the liquid was drawn off into 55-gallon drums, to storage tanks, or directly to tank trucks.

Warehouse and Storage: Almost half the entire space of the former cast phenolic building was used for storing cardboard drums and 50-pound bags of polystyrene. Since the chemical company manufacturing the polystyrene had a supply of "Catalin" bags, the material was ordinarily shipped in by rail or truck with the Catalin name already on the bag. The bags were placed on wooden pallets and stacked two pallets high by fork trucks before being shipped to customer plants by truck. The Fords plant received approximately a million pounds of polystyrene per month, and also shipped about a million pounds out during the same period. Although there was little discernible seasonal change in orders for industrial resins, the demand for polystyrene for use in Christmas toys created a seasonal peak for that product during August, September, and October.

Large quantities of phenol and formaldehyde and other chemicals were used in the liquid resin process. To store raw materials for manufacture, the Fords plant had nine 20,000-gallon[1] tanks ordinarily used for phenol and one 200,000-gallon tank for formaldehyde. There were six 15,000-gallon tanks for other chemicals such as urea, resorcinol, and cresylic acid. There were also several tanks totaling approximately 30,000 gallons for finished liquid resin inventory. Separate tanks were available for the oil additive process. Many of the tanks were equipped to maintain raw materials within a narrow temperature range, either through protection of a small concrete-brick shed, through insulating covering, or by the use of individual heat exchangers fed by steam. The plant as a whole required large quantities of steam, which was supplied by an adjacent chemical corporation.

Laboratories: Since the purchase agreement made the contract supplier responsible for all quality control and product development, the Catalin company was not required to devote much effort to laboratory work with polystyrene. The Fords plant merely maintained an injection molding machine, principally to train salesmen and to make samples. Similarly, since oil additives were produced on an exclusive contract for one large oil corporation which had done its own development work, little laboratory effort was devoted to this product by the Catalin company. Almost the entire laboratory facilities were therefore devoted to quality control and technical development of liquid and powdered resins.

Thomasville, North Carolina

The North Carolina plant consisted of two buildings, constructed in 1950 and 1951, totaling 7,600 square feet. Originally, the plant served as a distributing warehouse, but in October, 1951, manufacturing facilities for certain liquid resins used by the furniture and textile industries were completed.

[1] A gallon of phenol or formaldehyde weighed approximately 9 pounds.

Calumet City, Illinois

The Chicago area plant was completed in 1951 and totaled 10,000 square feet of space. It contained polymerization kettles. Since it had not only a railroad spur but was located on the Calumet River, the plant was in a favorable position to make use of low-cost barge shipment rates as the inland waterway system expanded.

ORGANIZATION

The top management of the Catalin company included two groups. The older group consisted of the president and executive vice-president, who both had responsible positions in the 1930's. A newer group consisted of five senior executives who had either come to the company at the end of World War II or had been promoted to senior positions only after the war.

Executive Vice-President, Leo Beck:

Mr. Beck attemped to supervise the most important operating activities in the company.

One aspect of Mr. Beck's attention to negotiations was his interest in raw materials such as phenol and formaldehyde. The Catalin company as a whole used 12 million pounds of phenol and approximately 35 million pounds of formaldehyde annually, or a total account of about $3 million for the two chemicals. Mr. Beck believed that if these chemicals were purchased in small quantities on a continuing basis, they would not amount to a large enough order to justify special treatment on the part of suppliers. On the other hand, when several weeks' supply were ordered at one time, the order was important enough to justify price concessions.

Although it had enough storage capacity for only 8 days of finished liquid resin inventory, the Fords plant alone had storage for 82 working days of phenol and 79 working days of formaldehyde. By using the large storage capacity to increase the company's purchasing power, Mr. Beck was often able to take advantage of special situations. For example, when a large chemical company producing formaldehyde as a byproduct had a tanker of the chemical in New York harbor which it could not quite empty to its other customers, Mr. Beck could sometimes obtain 2 million pounds at a half cent under market price of 3½ cents. Similarly, he could often obtain phenol for 1½ cents or more under the market price of 16 cents per pound. Such extensive commitments to inventory naturally required careful attention to working capital requirements. Mr. Beck, therefore, kept close watch over cash disbursements and inventory levels at all three plants in order to avoid placing a strain on the financial requirements of the company by his own contract negotiations.

Secretary-Treasurer, Fred Martin:

As secretary-treasurer, Mr. Martin had primary responsibility for the financial stability of the company. The assurance of working capital had developed into a more important problem as a result of the change in product line. The very large amount of polystyrene handled on a resale basis required careful attention to the timing of payments for accounts receivable and accounts payable in order to maintain adequate cash flow. Since raw materials were a significant portion of the liquid resin costs, heavy inventory commitments had to be watched to prevent any burden on working capital. Mr. Martin, therefore, obtained complete operating and cash flow figures for all plants on a weekly basis through his comptroller. He maintained close contact between the Fords plant, where his office was, and the executive offices in New York City in order to keep Mr. Beck informed of the current financial status and to ensure proper control of receivables by the credit manager.

Vice-President of Manufacturing, Kendall Briggs:

Mr. Briggs had a long experience as industrial engineer before taking charge of plant operations in 1952. He had worked for a time with the Catalin company before the war, and then had become a consultant with an industrial management firm. Mr. Briggs considered that the company was much more sensitive to fluctuations in the price of raw materials than to labor costs, particularly since the product change had reduced the number of workers. There was a union at Fords, but not at Calumet City or North Carolina, where the productivity was a little higher. Wages were lower in North Carolina, but about five cents higher at Calumet City, due to the proximity of higher paid jobs at oil refineries. There were many fringe benefits except for a pension plan, which the union had turned down in favor of a cash increase.

Vice-President, Engineering, William Miller:

Mr. Miller had been with the Catalin company since the 1930's, though his vice-presidency was not attained until after World War II. The engineering department contained four engineers, two draftsmen and a secretary. Engineering work was about evenly divided between maintenance and new facilities. Mr. Miller was particularly interested in the optimum size and productivity of the key manufacturing units. For example, a study had been made to determine the proper kettle size for the liquid resin operation. There were six polymer kettles at Fords, ranging from 1,500 to 10,000 pounds in capacity. Many of the 47 active formulations were ordered in quantities larger than 10,000 pounds during a three-month period. There would be no increase in labor costs to run a larger batch and the problem of blending small batches to obtain uniform quality would be eliminated by larger size kettles. However, the sales department was unwilling to lose the flexibility which the small kettles afforded since special formulations in sample quantities were often necessary to develop new business.

Vice-President, Sales, Edward Bastian:

Mr. Bastian had started as a salesman for the Catalin company in 1945, became sales manager at Chicago in 1950, and was promoted to vice-president in 1953. In the sales organization, separate sales groups were required for polystyrene and for the resins, due to the difference between molding customers and industrial resin customers. There were 20 salesmen in 1954, earning an average of $8,400 per year of which 75 percent was base salary and the remainder commissions. Their assignments were as follows:

	Styrene	*Resin*	*Dual*
New York	4	2	1
Chicago	5	4	1
North Carolina	–	3	–

Selling polystyrene, Mr. Bastian believed, was more a problem of selling the company than selling technical know-how. The molders knew that polystyrene would work and had sufficient technical help from competing polystyrene suppliers, who ordinarily hired engineers to sell the product. Mr. Bastian considered that the use of sales engineers was often a disadvantage to competing companies because the men became so engrossed in technical details that they sometimes neglected methods of closing the sale. The Catalin personnel's sales sense was often a considerable advantage. For example, one Catalin salesman had called on a molder just when the prospect was setting up his plant. The harried plant manager had already turned away many salesmen because he was too busy to decide on a supplier at that time. Rather than trying to make a sale, the Catalin representative rolled up his sleeves and helped the plant workers move office furniture for a few hours, then mentioned that he would send around some polystyrene to help the manager test his molding machines.

Sales Promotion, William Brearley:

The advertising budget was approximately $130,000 in 1954. Mr. Brearley believed that samples and direct mail were the only effective means of promoting liquid resins due to the wide variety of customer applications. Molding powder, on the other hand, could be promoted by magazine advertisements since the molders constituted a more homogeneous customer group. Mr. Brearley spent $35,000 for monthly full color advertisements to promote Catalin styrene in *Modern Plastics* magazine. He spent about $20,000 in various other magazines such as *Chain Store Age, Housewares Review,* and *Playthings* in order to promote the use of Catalin styrene injection moldings for hardware, house utensils, and toys. Another $20,000 was used for trade shows and exhibits such as those made for the convention of the Society of the Plastics Industry. About $3,000 was used for direct mail solicitations. About $25,000 was spent for samples of specialty resins which were made by pilot plant facilities in small quantities and charged to the sales promotion budget.

Vice-President and Technical Director, Joseph Hyman:

Mr. Hyman had come to the Catalin company in 1945 and had taken charge of the laboratories in 1951. In 1954, the budget allowed $236,000 and 31 people for research and development as well as $43,000 and 11 people for production quality control. The quality control technicians at the three plant locations reported directly to the assistant production managers, who were ordinarily chemists. However, Mr. Hyman's department maintained the card file at Fords which recorded test specifications of all production batch samples at the three plants. The quality control system seemed to have attained its objective inasmuch as customer complaints were negligible and production losses due to poor quality had improved from one batch in about 20 to one batch in 200.

Mr. Hyman had 19 chemists and 8 technicians at the Fords laboratories. He assigned six group leaders to the major development areas—phenolics, adhesives, alkylated products, polystyrene, physical testing, and quality control. Once a development was assigned to a group leader and explained to him in full, Mr. Hyman delegated responsibility to him for having the work scheduled and completed by the chemists. He maintained supervision of the work status through informal meetings with group leaders twice a week, but did not interfere with their authority unless special problems required him to do so.

BACKWARD INTEGRATION INTO POLYSTYRENE MOLDING POWDER

By 1951, the sales of polystyrene were progressing favorably. The resale contract, allowing the Catalin company a 10 percent discount, afforded a satisfactory margin to cover selling and administrative costs. With the retail price of styrene polymer at 32½ cents per pound, and selling and administrative costs close to 1¾ cents per pound, the Catalin company considered the arrangement to be profitable. Moreover, although the original contract was only on a five-year basis, Catalin executives believed that the arrangement was a reliable one for the future since most plastics materials manufacturers allowed a 10 percent discount to reputable selling agents.

The majority of Catalin customers were small molders of toys and household articles. However there were a number of large molders of industrial items, such as makers of refrigerator and appliance parts in the Chicago area, who rejected Catalin because the company did not manufacture its own material. These molding companies were particularly anxious to ensure a steady supply of material since their sales depended on sure deliveries to meet the exacting production assembly schedules of their own customers. They wished to spread their polystyrene requirements among several suppliers so that if a strike or other accident cut off one company, the others could cover their needs. Since the Catalin company sold material manufactured by other companies, it did not qualify as an independent source of supply.

The executives of the Catalin company gave considerable thought to the construction of manufacturing facilities during the postwar period. In 1951, the company was selling 14 million pounds of polystyrene, but expected that it could increase this amount to 30 million pounds by 1953. Manufacture of the styrene monomer (the chemical from which molding powder was polymerized) was rejected because the smallest economical plant unit was for 45 million pounds per year and was believed to cost at least $6 million. Manufacture of polystyrene molding powder from the monomer, however, was a much less difficult process to enter. An economical plant unit to produce crystal polystyrene could handle 12 million pounds per year. On the basis of bids from chemical engineering and construction firms, it was believed that such a plant could be built inside the old cast resin plant at Fords for only $545,000. Exhibit 4A is an aerial view of the plant facilities at Fords. Since the additional equipment needed to color the polystyrene would cost about $250,000, the executives decided to investigate the manufacture of only the crystal. Particularly for the industrial product market which the company wished to develop, color matching was a very difficult and exacting requirement which could more easily be done by outside specialty firms who could color shipments of the company's own crystal powder.

The Catalin executives therefore asked a reputable consulting firm of management engineers to study the feasibility of a crystal styrene polymerization plant with capacity of 1,000,000 pounds per month. At the same time, it requested a well-known construction and engineering firm to make a detailed cost analysis to cover the construction of such a plant.

The consulting firm reported favorably on the plant project. A survey of Catalin customers revealed that the company could expect to sell about 2½ times the capacity of the plant, so that maximum operations would be ensured. Moreover, with the delivered price of styrene monomer at 19 cents per pound and the price of molding powder at 32½ cents, the company had a spread of 13½ cents to work with. Rather than purchasing the powder at 29¼ cents for resale, the company was informed that it could polymerize its own powder for 23¾ cents. The detailed estimate of operating costs figured by the consulting organization is included in Exhibit 5. The figures gave the plant an annual net profit after overhead, depreciation, and taxes, of $179,000.

In order to estimate the capital requirements, the consulting firm figured working capital requirements for the new plant at $575,000. This figure was made up of a 36-day period of accounts receivable, 30 days of finished inventory, 35 days' supply of styrene monomer in tanks and in process, and 10 days' supply of raw materials not due in accounts payable. Adding $545,000 for the construction of plant facilities, the firm estimated $1,120,000 of capital requirements. With the 562,000 shares of common stock then outstanding earning 90 cents per share in 1950, the consulting firm believed the Catalin company could raise the necessary funds by issuing an additional 200,000 shares of common stock at $6 per share.

As a result of further discussions about the plant, it was decided to locate the new facilities in Calumet City rather than at Fords. It was figured that inward freight costs from the various monomer plant locations would be about equal at either place. However, the Calumet City site would enable the Catalin company to be first with a molding plant in the Chicago market area itself. The Calumet site was also considered important in order to avoid the chlorine particles and dust that were in the air at Fords and could contaminate the delicate color clarity of the polystyrene beads. Unfortunately, a new building would have to be erected since the company could not then make use of the old cast resin space. The change increased the construction cost estimate from $545,000 to $900,000, but promised production efficiencies from a completely modern plant layout. The Board of Directors approved the new plant and a prospectus was printed offering 281,243 shares of common stock at $5 per share.[1] A three-year contract was concluded for the purchase of styrene monomer at market price, and the new plant was constructed, scheduled for completion in May, 1953.

OPERATION OF THE POLYSTYRENE PLANT

As the polystyrene plant took form, Catalin executives discovered that the start-up expenses were so large as to affect adversely the earning figures of the company as a whole. After several months of red figures, there was much talk about selling out or merging with larger or stronger companies. Mr. Krehbiel took great pains to convince the organization that a merger might be undertaken when a small company was in a strong position, but never at a time of weakness.

The following factors made the cost of polymerizing styrene far exceed original estimates: (1) the cost of installing accessory equipment, (2) the difficulty of obtaining economical production runs, and (3) the changing relationship between the prices of styrene monomer and of polystyrene molding powder. Exhibit 4B contains an aerial view of the new polystyrene plant.

Actual Construction Costs

Although a reliable and experienced chemical engineering firm had designed the polystyrene plant and estimated the total costs to be $900,000, it was found that actual construction costs exceeded the estimate by more than 50 percent. In large part, the additional costs could be traced to the installation of accessory items of equipment not included in the original plan, but which were later considered necessary or desirable to reduce operating costs. "It was like building a house," Mr. Martin remarked. "You think you have everything in the original estimate. Then the builder suggests a new electrical outlet here and your wife wants a cabinet there. By the time you're finished, the charges are well along." The Catalin executives became increasingly concerned by the effect of the cash drain on working capital. Mr. Krehbiel finally negotiated a fixed price of approximately $1,400,000 with the engineering-construction firm. Although the plant actually cost 20 percent more than this figure, the firm agreed to take the loss itself in view of its original low estimate for the Catalin company.

[1] Since the plant cost estimate had increased and the issue was not underwritten, the price per share was set at $5 rather than at the consulting firm's more optimistic estimate.

Actual Operating Costs

The plant was completed in September, 1953. However, due to the difficulty of getting the quality exactly right, the plant did not operate efficiently until the fall of 1954. In part, the difficulties were those which could ordinarily be expected from any unfamiliar new process. Although the company had experimented with a 50-pound pilot kettle, Mr. Briggs believed that the transition to four 8,000-pound kettles would have been easier if semiproduction runs on a 1,000-pound kettle had been tried. In part, the finished plant was not as automatic as had been hoped. For example, it was planned that one man could supervise the kettles from his position in the control room, overlooking the kettle platform through a large glass window. It was found, however, that the equipment was not sufficiently automatic to allow the control operator to make materials changes in the kettles from his post, and another man had to be used for this purpose on each shift. In order to obtain full labor efficiencies and to increase the capacity of the plant, an additional $700,000 would have had to be expended for materials handling equipment. Exhibit 6 shows the actual operating costs in the fall of 1954 when improved efficiency was obtained, using the additional workers in place of fully automatic equipment.

Materials Price Spread

By the time the polystyrene plant attained its practical operating efficiencies, the spread between styrene monomer and polystyrene powder had narrowed alarmingly. The price of monomer including freight had increased from 19 cents per pound to 22½ cents, while the price of polystyrene had decreased from 32½ cents to 31½ cents per pound.

The narrowing price spread could be traced, Catalin executives believed, to certain market considerations which encouraged integrated producers to maintain firm monomer prices as well as to the competitive strategy of one molding company which had entered the polystyrene market.

With the exception of the Catalin company, practically all producers of polystyrene also manufactured their own styrene monomer. Due to the fact that large monomer plants had been built to serve the synthetic rubber program during World War II, there was already considerable monomer capacity. Since the government had been instrumental in building these resources, standing contracts allowed the General Services Administration to purchase as much styrene monomer as it needed at 3 cents below the current market price. Catalin executives therefore believed that integrated chemical companies might be anxious to maintain monomer prices at a level which would allow them a profit on government sales as well as keeping the spread narrow enough to discourage molding companies from building their own polystyrene plants.

Meanwhile, the Foster Grant Company, a molding company, had announced the construction of its own monomer and polystyrene plants. Since the capacity of these plants was greater than its own requirements of molding powder, the company had entered the polystyrene market with its own brand of molding powder, "Fostarene." In order to obtain a share of the market sufficient to cover its excess capacity, Fostarene was sold at one cent below the market price of polystyrene. The major chemical companies later met this reduced price.

RESPONSE TO THE MARKET SITUATION OF NOVEMBER, 1954

In November, 1954, competitive moves again reduced by one cent the market price of polystyrene molding powder, to 30½ cents per pound. It was believed that the price of monomer would remain at 22½ cents and would be reduced only one cent at a time to match possible future reductions in the polystyrene price, thus continuing the unfavorable price spread. Catalin executives were considering the following three alternatives to respond to this situation: (1) Increase the production of the polystyrene plant to obtain further operating efficiencies, (2) Lease the plant to another company and rely entirely upon polystyrene purchased for resale, or (3) Decrease the production of the plant by operating with a nucleus crew.

By making an additional investment of $700,000 for more automatic materials handling equipment and to increase the capacity of certain bottleneck items such as the centrifuge, the extruders, and the supply tanks, Catalin executives believed they could expand production to 2,000,000 pounds of polystyrene per month. The expanded operations would require 40 workers rather than the present 32 workers. The executives were sure they could sell all the additional styrene. However, since all the styrene could not be absorbed by the Chicago market, the company would have to pay $1.29 per 100 pounds to ship the excess supply from Calumet City to warehouses in the New York area. In 1954, the midwest market area absorbed about 14 million pounds of Catalin styrene, while the eastern territory absorbed 10½ million pounds. The average monthly shipments by warehouse location were as follows:

Eastern Territory		888,000 pounds
Fords	650,000	
Easthampton	238,000	
Midwest Territory		1,161,000 pounds
Chicago	644,000	
Calumet (direct)	250,000	
Cleveland	219,000	
Kansas City	25,000	
Evansville	23,000	
Western Territory		96,000 pounds

Mr. Krehbiel had reason to believe that he could lease the polystyrene plant to a chemical company at a monthly rental which would cover the depreciation, expenses incidental to ownership, and give a small return on the investment. The loss of polystyrene capacity would then be offset by purchasing additional molding powder for resale at a 10 percent discount. Under such an arrangement, the materials supplier paid the freight on all shipments to Catalin warehouses. For this reason, the location of the supplying plants made little difference to the company. The Catalin company paid warehousing and shipping costs to its own customers, however. Warehousing charges totaled 18 cents per 100 pounds for handling, and 6 cents per 100 pounds per month for storage. The average freight costs from warehouses to molding company customers was 57 cents per 100 pounds. Selling expenses for polystyrene totaled about

$97,000 per year for salary, commissions, and travel expenses, or 38 cents per 100 pounds. Advertising cost was about 22 cents per 100 pounds. Administrative overhead was difficult to evaluate, since top executives expected to spend less than 25 percent of their time on polystyrene, though the billing and credit department was probably 70 percent on styrene accounts. Overhead allocated to styrene was estimated, however, to be less than 35 cents per 100 pounds. The total cost to handle polystyrene on a resale basis was therefore 1.76 cents per pound.

Mr. Briggs believed that by using a nucleus crew of only 11 men, the polystyrene plant could be operated so as to produce 240,000 pounds per month. Under this plan, ten men would work in two five-man shifts from eight A.M. to midnight and one man would take charge of the warehouse from nine A.M. to five P.M. On Monday and Tuesday, all the men would operate three of the polymer kettles starting them at two-hour intervals, at eight A.M., at ten A.M., and at noon. By the middle of the second shift on Monday the first batch of material would be through the kettle. The wash tanks and centrifuge could then be operated. On Wednesday a seventh batch could be started through one of the kettles, and the rest of the crew could start operating the extruders. On Thursday and Friday the crew would finish with the centrifuge and run the remainder of the seven batches through the extruders and bagging machines. Exhibit 7 contains a flow chart of the process.

1. CATALIN CORPORATION (B)

Balance Sheets, 1949-1953
(In Thousands)

ASSETS	1949	1950	1951	1952	1953
Cash	$ 668	$ 564	$ 807	$ 799	$ 538
U.S. Government Securities				300	
Accounts Receivable	798	1,361	975	1,541	1,489
Inventories	690	769	1,825	1,624	1,442
Total Current Assets	$2,156	$2,694	$3,607	$4,264	$3,469
Prepaid Expenses	37	75	103	133	91
Property	1,738	2,288	2,550	3,534	4,879
Depreciation	(707)	(700)	(656)	(742)	(895)
Long-Term			100	50	
Construction	350				
Total Assets	$3,574	$4,357	$5,704	$7,239	$7,544
LIABILITIES					
Accounts Payable	$ 808	$1,178	$1,696	$1,708	$1,780
Taxes Payable	130	262	409	198	116
Bank Notes		70	400		500
Mortgage Notes				59	59
Total Current Liabilities	$ 938	$1,510	$2,505	$1,965	$2,455
Long-Term Debt	$ 350	$ 280	$ 400	$1,009	$ 750
Capital Stock	$ 561	$ 561	$ 562	$ 844	$ 844
Earned Surplus	1,619	1,900	2,124	2,181	2,255
Capital Surplus	106	106	113	1,240	1,240
Total Capital	$2,286	$2,567	$2,799	$4,265	$4,339
Total Liabilities	$3,574	$4,357	$5,704	$7,239	$7,544

2. CATALIN CORPORATION (B)

Income Statements, 1949-June, 1954
(In Thousands)

	1949	1950	1951	1952	1953	1954 (1st 6 Mos.)
Net Sales	$7,172	$11,206	$13,412	$14,178	$15,397	$7,251
Cost of Sales	6,129	9,444	11,795	12,926	14,183	7,224
Gross Profit	$1,043	$ 1,762	$ 1,617	$ 1,252	$ 1,214	$ 27
General Expenses	484	487	541	616	706	
Net Profit	$ 559	$ 1,275	$ 1,076	$ 636	$ 508	
Other Income	8	6	10	16	18	
Gross Income	$ 567	$ 1,281	$ 1,086	$ 652	$ 526	
Other Expenses	247	329	326	302	317	
Nonrecurring Income			$ 198*			
Net Income before Taxes	$ 320	$ 952	760	$ 350	$ 209	(171)
Federal Taxes	122	447	509	124	92	(87)
Net Income after Taxes	$ 198	$ 505	$ 449	$ 226	$ 117	

*Net gain from sale of cast resin division.

Sales by Product Lines, 1941-1954

	1949	1950	1951	1952	1953	1954 (1st 6 Mos.)
Liquid	$2,553,655	$ 4,297,744	$ 6,295,947	$ 5,933,921	$ 5,911,404	$2,420,540
Polystyrene	3,198,293	4,703,381	4,376,360	6,034,077	7,749,195	3,958,493(b)
Oil Additive	433,386	1,051,100	2,158,400	2,199,480	1,632,354	795,970
Cast Phenolic	985,046	1,151,327	553,612(a)			
Other Resins	1,896	2,750	27,525	10,872	103,891	75,957
Total Net Sales	$7,172,276	$11,206,302	$13,411,844	$14,178,350	$15,396,844	$7,250,960

CATALIN *Styrene,* too, comes-up with the correct answers!

You are looking in on "home-work hour" and an action demonstration of the new Sterling ADDING MACHINE Pencil Box*. An amazing little wizard—it *simplifies* simple arithmetic. It adds . . . It subtracts . . . It's Fascinating.

This latest *addition* to Sterling's popular line of school supplies, comprises many coordinated plastic components; each precisely engineered, each requiring specification materials—and all calling for exacting mold control.

The exterior on-view parts, namely: the sealed adding machine housing (top cover) and the pencil box (bottom tray) are molded of dimensionally stable CATALIN STYRENE. Wizard though it be, this item couldn't have produced a more perfect answer . . . CATALIN STYRENE is light, strong, color-appealing and most favorable in cost. It should also be noted that the Sterling Ball Point Pen held in the little lady's fingers—and her near-at-hand school aids are also molded of CATALIN STYRENE . . . Looks like *the gem of plastics,* in more ways than one, is of *material* assistance!

**Product of Sterling Plastics Co., Union, N. J.*

CATALIN CORPORATION OF AMERICA
ONE PARK AVENUE • NEW YORK 16, N. Y.

3. CATALIN CORPORATION (B)

Sample of Magazine Advertising (*Modern Plastics* Magazine)

4A. CATALIN CORPORATION (B)
Aerial View of Plant Facilities at Fords

4B. CATALIN CORPORATION (B)
Aerial View of Polystyrene Plant at Calumet City

5. CATALIN CORPORATION (B)

Estimated Cost of Production, Crystal Styrene Molding Powder
Monthly Production 902,500 Pounds—3 Shifts

	Per Month		
Materials	Quantity	at	Amount
Styrene Monomer	950,000 lbs.	$ .18	$171,000
Styrene Monomer Freight	9,500 cwt.	.898	8,531
Chemical "A"	285 lbs.	.76	217
Chemical "B"	190 lbs.	.24	46
Chemical "C"	1,900 lbs.	.90	1,710
Chemical "D"	1,900 lbs.	1.00	1,900
Printed Bags--50 lb.	18.05 ms.*	131.40	2,372
			$185,776
Labor (25 men)			
Manufacturing--3 shifts			
1 Supervisor	520 hrs.	1.85	962
5 Operators	2,600 hrs.	1.70	4,420
Control--2 shifts (1 technician)	347 hrs.	1.50	521
Warehouse—1 shift (5 men)	867 hrs.	1.45	1,257
			$ 7,160
Utilities			
Steam	3,000 ms.	.83	2,490
Power	103,000 kws.	.011	1,133
City Water	900 m gals.	.216	194
Cooling Water	4,500 m gals.	.04	180
			$ 3,997
Expense			
Maintenance--5%			2,350
Insurance —1%			470
Taxes —1%			470
Factory Administrative and Miscellaneous			4,000
Research and Development			1,500
Depreciation			2,806
			$ 11,596
Ship and Warehouse			5,415
Total			$213,944
Cost per Pound (net yield 95% = 902,500 lbs.)			$.2371

*M = 1,000

6. CATALIN CORPORATION (B)

Actual Cost of Production, Crystal Styrene Molding Powder

Monthly Production 1,140,000 Pounds--7-Day Week 4 Shifts--32 Men
(Monthly Average Costs, Fall, 1954)

		Cost of Beads	Cost of Extruding & Bagging	Cost of Handling	Total
Manufacturing Expenses					
Productive and Nonproductive Labor		$ 5,500	$ 5,447	$ 715	$11,662
Maintenance and Repair Labor		1,264	1,264		2,528
Factory Supplies		621	400	40	1,061
Maintenance and Repair Material		1,636	1,636		3,272
Heat, Light, and Power		5,060	1,687	486	6,747
Administration and General (Out-of-Pocket Costs)		2,250	2,322	486	5,058
Research and Development (Out-of-Pocket Costs)		705	360		1,065
Insurance Compensation, Etc.		790	411	82	1,283
Social Security and Unemployment Insurance		125	105	27	257
Depreciation					
Bldg. Value $396,000 over 25 Years		} 5,077	} 1,590	} 227	1,320
Machinery and Equipment $1,000,000 over 15 Years					5,574
Office Bldg. Portion $50,000 over 25 Years		60	22	7	89
Control Laboratory		1,761	1,760		3,521
Shipping Bags $151 per M and Inward Freight			4,570		4,570
		$24,849	$21,574	$1,584	$48,007
Production 1,140,000 lbs. per month yield:					
Manufacturing or Handling Cost per Pound		$ .0218	$ .0189	$.0014	$ .0421
Raw Materials Including Freight: Monomer*	$.2363				
Other Materials	.0043	.2406			.2406
Manufacturing Cost to Make Beads		$ .2624	.2624		
Manufacturing Cost to Extrude and Bag			$ .2813	.2813	
Manufacturing Cost F.O.B. Calumet				$.2827	$ .2827
Shipping Cost (Calumet to Outside Warehouses)					.0030
Total Cost per Pound					$ .2857

*Allowing 5% extra on 22 1/2 cents per pound for loss on yield.

7. CATALIN CORPORATION (B)

Flow Chart of Styrene Plant Process

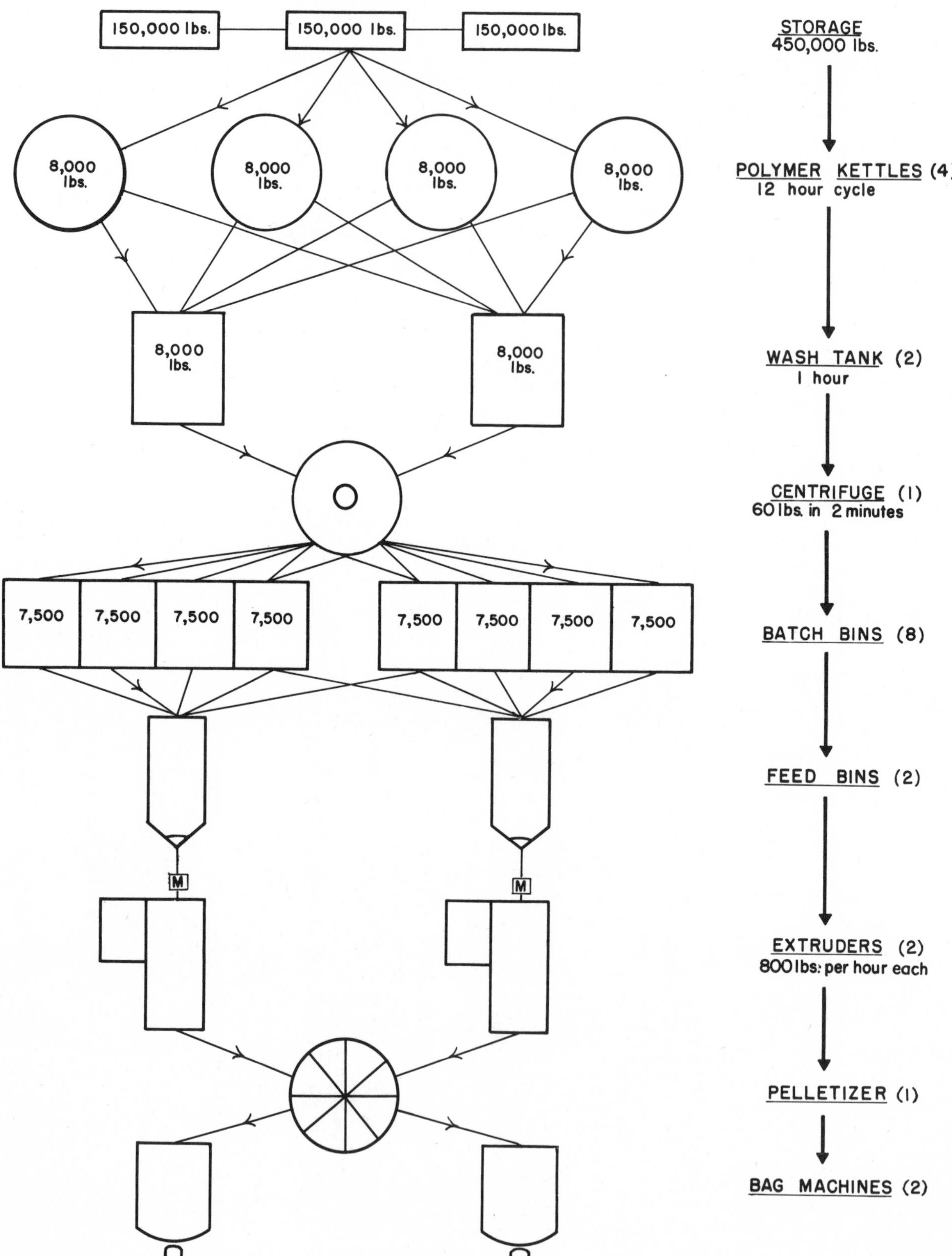

Catalin Corporation of America (C)

The Catalin Corporation of America was a plastics materials company selling its own products and products made by other companies. The products included molding compounds made by several large chemical companies, and various synthetic resins and chemicals made in its own plants. The company's sales had grown to about $22 million in 1959, of which a little over half were resale products (manufactured by others, but bearing the Catalin name). Most of the remaining $10 million was composed of synthetic resins.

In March, 1960, the Catalin executives reviewed their manufacturing facilities and plans in order to decide what to do with their Calumet City polystyrene plant. The plant had been leased to the Dow Chemical Company on a five-year lease which was to expire on April 1, 1960. The Dow company had indicated an interest in extending the lease.

In early 1955, the chances of achieving profitable operations in the Calumet City plant did not seem promising to the Catalin executives. The Dow Chemical Company offered to lease the polystyrene plant from the Catalin company for a five-year period for $255,000 per year.

Since 1955, the resale of molding compounds had continued to grow. In 1960, it amounted to about $12 million of which over 80 percent was polystyrene. The Catalin company included in its line several new plastics as they were introduced; polypropylene, nylon 6, high-density polyethylene, and styrene copolymers. It sold products made by Dow, Monsanto, Allied, W. R. Grace, Spencer, and U.S.I. and was thus able to select whichever company's formulation was best suited to the particular customer's requirements.

On the basis of its experience with liquid phenolic resins, the Catalin company expanded into a wide variety of synthetic resins. The Synthetic Resin Division became the company's most important manufacturing division. Products for the paint, paper, leather, rubber, textile, and building product industries were manufactured in the Catalin plants in Fords, New Jersey; Calumet City, Illinois; and Thomasville, North Carolina. These resins were used as a base for the preparation of latex and water emulsion paints. They added wet strength and various finishes to paper and were used also in glues for wood and to provide wash and wear finishes on textiles. They functioned as tackifiers and curatives in rubber processing and served as bonding agents for many insulation materials. Most of these resins were sold in liquid form, but some of the cresylic and phenolic resins used in abrasives, brake linings, and foundry molds were sold in powdered form.

During World War II, the Chemical Division had introduced production of an oil additive, which provided lubricating oils with self-cleansing properties. This business was discontinued immediately after the war, but in 1947 one oil company contracted with the Catalin company for its requirements of a special additive developed by the oil company. Sales of this product rose over $2 million per year, but in 1956 this customer discontinued its purchase of oil additives and began manufacturing the additive itself.

In the middle 1950's, the Catalin company began exploring the specialty chemical field. Particular effort was concentrated on the field of antioxidants and bacteriostats. The Catalin research laboratory developed several antioxidant compounds and bacteriostats which the company put into production. The antioxidants were used to prevent oxidation in jet fuels, lubricating oils, rubber, plastics, packaging, and many other products. The bacteriostats were designed to inhibit the growth of bacteria in cosmetic preparations. Sales of these chemicals were small, but the Catalin management felt they were very promising for the future.

MANUFACTURING FACILITIES

In 1960, the Catalin Corporation's primary manufacturing activities were devoted to synthetic liquid and powdered resins for use by manufacturers in many industries. These resins included urea, melamine, phenolic, cresylic, resorcinol and acrylic varieties, but the manufacturing processes were essentially similar. Phenol, formaldehyde, cresol, urea, acrylic acid, and other organic chemicals were mixed under controlled conditions of time, purity, temperature, and pressure with small quantities of other chemicals. The primary production facilities were the polymerizing kettles, but mixing, drying, grinding, and packaging equipment was also necessary. The diverse uses of the resins tended to be best achieved through variations in the exact formulation. The Catalin Corporation had thousands of formulations to meet various purposes and an engineering staff ready to develop additional formulations for its customers. Runs were generally short. Due to both the problems of storage and the variety of formulations, little or no production was made for stock. The problems of storage included not only the expense of double handling and the cost of storage facilities, but the fact that many of the products "set up" or solidified if stored too long or in too warm a location.

The manufacture of the antioxidants was very similar to the manufacture of the synthetic resins. Some of the same raw materials (phenol, cresol) were used and the chemical processes took place in similar vessels provided with an agitator, a heating or cooling jacket, and pressure controls. The chemicals were mixed in one vessel where alkylation took place. The addition of other chemicals in a second vessel caused crystallization to take place. The liquids and solids were then pumped into a storage tank. From there the material was placed in a centrifuge to remove the liquid. The crystals were then dried under heat and carried to a grinding machine where they were converted to a flour-like substance. The antioxidant was then blended with small additions such as lubricants to improve the handling properties. Finally, it went to a bagging or a drum-loading machine. The Catalin company had developed half-a-dozen antioxidants for use in different industries, but the products were all stock items. There was no problem of short shelf life for these products so the Catalin company maintained a stock of all its antioxidants.

The Catalin company's plant at Fords, New Jersey, had the largest production facilities. These facilities were divided into three parts. One part included eight polymerization kettles and a considerable quantity of auxiliary equipment used for the production of a wide variety of liquid and powdered synthetic resins. This section had a capacity of between 25 million and 30 million pounds a year depending on the product mix. The second part included six large kettles and was designed for the production of antioxidants. The antioxidant capacity was expanded in early 1960 to about six million pounds per year. The third part was the acrylic resin plant built in 1958–1959 for the production of 10 million pounds per year. The primary equipment in this part was three large kettles. The oil additive facilities had been dismantled since the cessation of that business. Some of the equipment was used in the antioxidant production, but the Catalin company took a $75,000 loss writing off the balance of the oil additive equipment in 1959. The Fords plants also had a fractionating tower used in the recovery of by-products from the basic processes. The bacteriostat production was currently carried out on a pilot plant basis.

The plant at Thomasville had been obtained originally as a storage warehouse for synthetic resin glues for the furniture industry. In 1951 it was expanded to three buildings totaling 13,000 square feet, and facilities for the production of urea and melamine resins for the furniture and textile industries were installed. This plant had three kettles averaging 5,000 pounds in size. Mr. Krehbiel, the Catalin president, estimated that this plant had an annual capacity of about 20 million pounds.

The synthetic liquid resin plant in Calumet City was built in 1950 and included 11,200 square feet of factory floor space and 2,400 square feet of office space. This plant had six kettles of varying size. The annual capacity of this plant was about 35 million pounds per year.

The polystyrene plant in Calumet City currently under lease to the Dow Chemical Company had an annual capacity of 25,000,000 pounds of polystyrene in a modern building completed in 1953.

After leasing the plant from the Catalin Corporation in early 1955, the Dow Chemical Company decided not to use the plant to produce polystyrene. Mr. Krehbiel thought this decision was probably due to the availability of polystyrene capacity elsewhere, the relatively small size of this plant, the distance from the managerial control in Midland, Michigan, and the possibility of labor relations problems in the Chicago area. He thought that Dow had spent several years in exploring first the possibility of using the plant to produce polystyrene and subsequently the possibility of producing other chemicals or plastics. The plant was idle for the entire lease period.

The treasurer, Mr. Martin, prepared a cost

sheet showing the costs of producing polystyrene in the Calumet City plant at a 1,087,500 pounds per month level (see Exhibit 3).

The primary facilities of the Calumet City plant, the polymerization kettles with the accompanying loading, mixing, and packaging equipment were suitable for a wide variety of chemical processes. The kettles could be used to produce many varieties of plastics (including polyesters, polyvinyl acetates, acrylic resins, urea and melamines, but not those plastics such as polyethylene requiring very high pressure conditions) and many other chemicals such as detergents. During 1958 and 1959, when it became generally known that the plant was idle, Mr. Krehbiel estimated that he received one letter every 60 days from a chemical, paint, drug, or oil company expressing an interest in purchasing the plant. Since Mr. Krehbiel had not encouraged this interest, none of these feelers turned into a concrete offer.

The Catalin company also explored the possibility of making other synthetic resins there. If the plant was used for a resin sold in a latex or liquid form, the capacity of the plant rose to 40 million pounds per year because the centrifuge and extruder bottlenecks were removed. For these products, the two wash tanks could easily be converted to polymerization kettles and there was space and auxiliary facilities to handle two additional kettles making a total of eight. This would raise the capacity to about 80 million pounds per year.

One of the easiest types of plastics to make was the polyester type. Intense competition among the many manufacturers had lowered profit margins. High transportation costs in relation to production costs severely limited the marketing area for each plant. In view of the general knowledge of the low profitability of this line, Mr. Krehbiel rejected the possibility of making polyesters.

Two products the Catalin company was considering were polyvinyl acetates and acrylic resins in latex form.

Polyvinyl acetate was sold in bead form for molding but the biggest market was in latex form for the paint industry. Because of its ability to form a strong thin film, polyvinyl acetate was receiving growth acceptance as a base in emulsion paints. Mr. Krehbiel asked his treasurer to prepare an estimate of the cost of producing polyvinyl acetate latex in the Calumet City polystyrene plant. Mr. Martin gathered figures from the technical personnel at Catalin as well as consulting with two engineering firms. The final estimate was that the fixed expenses of depreciation, insurance, interest and taxes, and an administrative and technical staff would run about $24,500 per month. The remaining costs would vary with the level of operations. At a volume of 375,000 pounds per month, labor, supplies, and utilities would cost about $3,000. At a volume of 2,800,000 pounds per month (capacity operations) these expenses would rise to $22,000. In the range of operations being considered, the raw materials would cost $.114 per pound and the labor and material expenses of putting the bulk product into drums would cost $.013 per pound. The above costs were the costs to be incurred in manufacturing the product F.O.B. Calumet City, and assumed an additional investment of $275,000 for storage, packaging, and other auxiliary facilities. Polyvinyl acetate in drums sold for 18½ cents per pound.

The Catalin Corporation already sold acrylic resins in latex form to the paint industry and a variety of other industries. The Calumet City plant could be used to expand the Catalin productive capacity for acrylic resins by about 30 million pounds. Acrylic resins in bulk for paint use sold for about 16½ cents per pound. The costs of operation were expected to be about the same as the costs in the Fords plant.

It was also possible to split the plant. The engineering staff had suggested that an investment of about $375,000 would enable the plant to produce 15 million pounds of acrylic resins and 20 million pounds of polyvinyl acetate. Both products would be latex types.

If the plant were used for the production of a latex, Mr. Krehbiel did not anticipate selling the unused blending and extruding equipment. So much of the cost lay in the installation that he did not think it would pay to remove the equipment.

SALES

The Catalin Corporation had recently reorganized its sales force from a product orientation to a regional one. The 25 salesmen were split into 5 regions: Northeastern United States,

Southeastern United States, Ohio-Michigan, Middle West and Great Plains, and the West Coast. Some of the salesmen split their time, but they were approximately divided up into 11 molding compound salesmen, 11 synthetic resin salesmen, and 3 antioxidant salesmen. Mr. Krehbiel thought this reorganization made more effective use of the salesmen's time and strengthened the ability of Catalin to concentrate on the most likely prospects.

The margin on the resale products varied on the different compounds from 12 to 15 percent. As a rule of thumb for analyzing new products, the management used a figure of 10 percent for selling costs including warehousing.

The Catalin company maintained 20 warehouses. Resale products were shipped to these warehouses at the manufacturer's expense. The Catalin company absorbed the freight from warehouse to final customer. Stocks of standard molding compounds were maintained at these points in order to provide fast service.

Due to both the expansion of Catalin's sales and the tendency of large users to integrate backwards, the Catalin company had decreased its dependence on a few customers. Only one customer had more than 4 or 5 percent of the Catalin sales volume and that customer was only slightly over that figure.

RESEARCH

The Catalin Corporation placed a great deal of emphasis on its research activities. A vice-president of research supervised a staff of about 40 engineers, scientists, and technicians working in the central research laboratory with a budget of almost $400,000 per year. In addition, each of the separate plants maintained small technical staffs to handle the quality control and process control functions in the individual plants.

The research vice-president was guided by a new products committee consisting of the president, the executive vice-president, the research vice-president, the production vice-president, the engineering vice-president, and the director of market research. This committee met at least once a month to discuss possible new products, to consider the reports of the research staff, and to decide where the research emphasis was to be placed. The research vice-president was responsible for the work assigned by this committee as well as the development tasks requested by salesmen to meet specialized customer requests.

While the number of personnel employed in research had not increased greatly over the preceding five years, the facilities at their disposal were much greater. The company had recently constructed a new laboratory building including many new types of equipment. The laboratory had a complete pilot plant so that new ideas could be tried out in small quantities without disrupting normal production. In addition, the company had an extensive collection of small process equipment for the paint, paper, rubber, and furniture industries so that the end use effect of the various resins or chemicals could be tried out. Finally, through an agreement with the Dow Chemical Company, the Catalin Corporation was able to take advantage of the testing facilities of the Dow company.

The research and development effort was primarily directed toward special chemicals and synthetic resins with the emphasis on research in the former and on development in the latter. In the molded compound field, the Catalin company relied almost entirely on the manufacturing firms both for the development of new products and for the solution of customer problems.

RECENT FINANCIAL HISTORY

In 1952, the Catalin Corporation of America required additional funds for the purchase of the land that had been leased in Fords, New Jersey, and for the construction of the powdered resin plant in Fords and the polystyrene plant in Chicago. This was financed through the assumption of $600,000 of long-term debt and the sale of 281,243 shares of common stock to the existing common stock owners at $5 per share. Each shareholder received rights for the purchase of one share for every two already owned.

In 1954, an additional 66,500 shares of common stock were sold at a price which netted the Catalin Corporation $4.92 after payment of underwriting expenses.

In 1955, the Catalin company issued 50,000 shares of a convertible preferred stock with a $20 par value. The stock had a $1.20 cumulative dividend and was convertible into two-and-one-half shares of common stock. It was callable at a price of $21. At the same time, the company consolidated its debt into a $1,500,000 loan shared between the Mutual Life Insurance Company of New York and the Chase Manhattan Bank.

In April of 1955, Mr. Henry Reichhold, the largest stockholder of Reichhold Chemicals Incorporated, informed the Catalin Corporation that he was by far the largest individual stockholder of the Catalin company.

Mr. Reichhold was then elected to the board of directors of the Catalin company and resigned from Reichhold Chemicals to avoid the possible legal implications of board membership in two competing companies. In October, the Catalin and Reichhold companies jointly announced that negotiations were authorized with respect to a possible merger, under the name of Reichhold-Catalin Chemicals, Inc., on the basis of approximately three Catalin shares to one Reichhold share. A substantial majority of this block of stock was to be placed in a voting trust.

The merger was thoroughly explored by both companies. Although the managerial and technical prospects were favorable, the two companies were unable to work out the financial details to the satisfaction of both, at this particular time. Following the termination of negotiations, Mr. Reichhold resigned from the Catalin board of directors.

In 1959, the company borrowed $2,300,000 from the Dow Chemical Company on a 30-year note bearing 5 percent interest. This loan was subordinated to all other financing and was convertible into common stock at $8.50 per share. This money was used to retire the preferred stock and to finance additions to the Fords plant including a new steam unit, fractionating equipment, and a building to produce annually 10 million pounds of acrylic resins.

The Catalin company bought annually approximately $10 million worth of basic chemicals and molding compounds from the Dow Chemical Company. The two companies had also signed an agreement whereby the Dow company would provide testing facilities and carry out physical and market testing on any new product ideas the Catalin Corporation might develop. In return, the Dow Chemical Company would receive the rights to use the ideas in certain noncompetitive fields such as agricultural chemicals. The Dow company had indicated a willingness to consider providing additional financing if the Catalin Corporation needed money for further expansion.

The Reichhold Chemical company had 18 plants in the United States producing a wide variety of chemical products. In 1959, the total sales of $94 million were divided as follows:

Surface coating resins and chemical colors: Acrylic emulsions, polyvinyl acetate, alkyd resins, epoxy resins, polyester resins, phenolic resins, and urea resins for paints and varnishes. Pigments for paints and inks.	38.9%
Materials for plastics: Melamines, polyesters, phenols	34.5%
Chemicals: Phthalic anhydride, formaldehyde, phenol, and other industrial chemicals	26.6%

The Reichhold company's research budget in 1958 was $1,750,000.

Reichhold Chemicals Inc., continued its policy of expansion through merger. In 1959, three companies were acquired.

In addition to cash dividends of $.15, $.50, $.90, and $.575 over the preceding four years, the Reichhold Chemical company issued stock dividends of 1 percent in 1956, 4 percent in 1957, 6 percent in 1958, and 2 percent in 1959. There was also a two for one split on April 16, 1959.

1. CATALIN CORPORATION OF AMERICA (C)

Balance Sheets

	1953	1954	1955	1956	1957	1958	1959
Cash and securities	$ 538	$ 633	$ 912	$ 575	$ 190	$ 711	$ 1,147
Accounts and notes receivable net	1,489	1,719	2,422	2,183	2,404	2,341	2,617
Inventories	1,442	1,531	2,550	2,709	2,739	2,557	2,914
Prepaid expenses	91	46	55	78	96	86	92
Total Current Assets	$3,560	$3,929	$ 5,940	$5,545	$5,429	$ 5,696	$ 6,771
Other assets		$ 25	$ 50	$ 10	$ 74	$ 47	$ 36
Land, buildings, machine and equipment	$4,879	5,031	5,436	5,759	6,350	6,702	7,223
Less reserve for depreciation	895	1,143	1,402	1,652	2,026	2,404	2,681
Net fixed assets	$3,984	$3,888	$ 4,034	$4,107	$4,325	$ 4,298	$ 4,542
Total Assets	$7,544	$7,842	$10,024	$9,662	$9,828	$10,042	$11,350
Accounts payable	$1,780	$1,720	$ 1,950	$1,535	$1,337	$ 2,219	$ 1,477
Taxes payable	116	36	587	343	346	156	91
Bank notes payable	500	350		250	500		500
Long-term debt due within one year	59	150	100	100	100	100	100
Total Current Liabilities	$2,455	$2,256	$ 2,637	$2,228	$2,283	$ 2,474	$ 2,169
Long-term debt due after one year	$ 750	$ 800	$ 1,400	$1,300	$1,200	$ 1,100	$ 3,300
Reserve for federal income tax deferred		41	85	130	175	219	207
Preferred stock $20 par value			828	813	813	813	
Common stock $1 par value	844	928	962	964	964	964	995
Capital in excess of par value	1,240	1,500	1,527	1,542	1,542	1,542	1,727
Earnings reinvested in the business	2,255	2,316	2,584	2,684	2,850	2,929	2,954
Stockholders' equity	$4,339	$4,745	$ 5,901	$6,004	$6,169	$ 6,249	$ 5,675
Total Liabilities	$7,544	$7,842	$10,024	$9,662	$9,828	$10,042	$11,350
Price range of common							
Low	4	4-1/8	6	6	4-7/8	4-7/8	6-5/8
High	6-5/8	7-1/2	14-1/8	12-1/2	8-3/8	8	14-7/8

All figures except common stock prices in thousands of dollars.
As of March 31, 1960, the common stock was selling for 8-5/8 per share.

2. CATALIN CORPORATION OF AMERICA (C)

Statement of Income and Retained Earnings
(In Thousands of Dollars)

	1953	1954	1955	1956	1957	1958	1959
Net sales	$15,397	$15,845	$20,493	$22,468	$23,752	$20,783	$22,261
Cost of sales	14,184	14,756	17,910	20,177	21,323	19,090	20,550
Gross profit on sales	$ 1,213	$ 1,089	$ 2,583	$ 2,291	$ 2,429	$ 1,693	$ 1,711
Selling and administrative expenses	706	967	1,363	1,557	1,504	1,401	1,521
Net profit on sales	$ 508	$ 121	$ 1,220	$ 734	$ 925	$ 292	$ 190
Other income including rent	18	51	98	177	192	197	227
Gross income	$ 525	$ 172	$ 1,318	$ 911	$ 1,118	$ 489	$ 416
Interest charges	55	56	55	70	72	65	169
Royalties paid	262			42	101	71	15
Net income before nonrecurring charge	$ 209	$ 116	$ 1,263	$ 798	$ 945	$ 353	$ 232
Sale or disposal of obsolete equipment							$ 79
Net income before taxes	$ 209	$ 116	$ 1,263	$ 798	$ 945	$ 353	153
Federal income taxes	92	55	669	408	490	176	72
Net income for the year	$ 117	$ 61	$ 594	$ 391	$ 455	$ 176	$ 82
Earnings retained beginning of period	$ 2,181	$ 2,255	$ 2,316	$ 2,584	$ 2,684	$ 2,850	$ 2,929
	$ 2,297	$ 2,316	$ 2,910	$ 2,975	$ 3,139	$ 3,026	$ 3,011
Less cash dividends paid	42		326	290	290	97	57
Earnings retained end of period	$ 2,255	$ 2,316	$ 2,584	$ 2,684	$ 2,850	$ 2,929	$ 2,954

	Liquid Resins	Oil Additives	Chemicals	Other	Polystyrene	Other	Total
1954	5,560,078	1,626,156		7,041	8,651,791*		15,845,066
1955	8,128,283	3,284,791		15,264	9,044,807	19,807	20,492,951
1956	8,295,549	1,329,284	605,101	15,711	11,887,902	334,060	22,467,607
1957	8,000,254	953,142	2,132,342	2,049	12,093,489	570,493	23,751,776
1958	7,102,240	213,770	2,388,562	7,528	9,832,722	1,238,306	20,783,128
1959	8,628,399	39,429	1,601,923	20,072	9,883,136	2,088,408	22,261,366

*This figure included polystyrene manufactured in the Catalin Calumet City Plant.

3. CATALIN CORPORATION OF AMERICA (C)

Monthly Expenses of Producing Polystyrene in the Calumet City Polystyrene Plant

	Actual Costs Fall 1954	Predicted in March 1960
Productive and nonproductive labor	$11,662	$13,995.50
Supplies	1,061	1,061.47
Maintenance and repair labor	2,528	3,033.66
Maintenance material	3,272	3,272.94
Heat, light, and power	6,747	7,201.30
Control laboratory	3,521	4,000.00
Administration--general	5,058	6,575.35
Research and development--polystyrene only	1,065	1,275.00
Insurance compensation, etc.	1,283	1,711.70
Social security and unemployment	257	342.76
Depreciation	6,983	7,256.00
Containers	4,570	5,500.00
Pension		300.00
Shipping labor and expense	(included above)	1,204.81
Total processing and shipping cost f.o.b. Calumet City	$48,007	$56,730.49
Output of polystyrene in pounds per month	1,140,000 pounds	1,087,500 pounds

Note: The expected product yield on the monomer is 95%.
At the time the lease was signed in 1955, the Catalin company estimated the cost of owning a leased plant at $108,000 per year including depreciation of $89,000.

Styrene Prices
(Cents per Pound)

	Monomer Range Low	Monomer Range High	Polymer Price
1952	21	21	32-1/2
1953	21	21	32-1/2
1954	21	21	31-1/2
1955	20-1/2	21	29-1/2
1956	20-1/2	21-1/2	27-1/2
1957	16	20	25-1/2
1958	14-1/2	16	24-1/4
early 1959	14-1/2	14-1/2	23

Prices include freight in tank car or tank truck prices. Prices are 2-1/2 cents higher for polymer in car load or truck loads in drums and 4-1/2 cents higher for less than car load lots in drums.

4. CATALIN CORPORATION OF AMERICA (C)

Reichhold Chemicals Inc.

	1955	1956	1957	1958	1959
Cash and marketable securities	$ 2.0	$ 1.2	$ 1.1	$ 2.5	$ 5.6
Receivables	7.2	9.1	8.2	11.6	13.8
Inventory	5.4	5.9	7.8	9.9	11.4
Prepaid	.7	.8	1.0	1.8	2.0
	$13.5	$17.0	$18.1	$25.7	$32.8
Other investments	5.1	5.5	5.8	5.2	8.4
Net plant	13.6	16.4	17.8	21.0	32.6
Total Assets	$32.2	$38.9	$41.7	$51.9	$73.8
Payables	$ 7.4	$ 7.2	$ 8.6	$12.6	$14.2
Long-term debt	9.4	8.8	8.1	8.2	14.1
Preferred stock	1.8	1.7	1.6	1.5	1.4
Common stock	1.0	1.2	1.3	1.5	3.6
Surplus	14.3	19.9	22.1	28.1	40.5
Equity	$17.1	$22.9	$25.0	$31.2	$45.5
Total Liabilities	$33.9	$38.9	$41.7	$51.9	$73.8
Sales	$53.6	$59.2	$65.3	$74.0	$93.6
Cost of goods sold	42.1	46.3	49.9	55.7	70.9
Gross profit	$11.5	$12.9	$15.4	$18.3	$22.7
Selling, general and administrative	8.0	10.1	11.5	14.0	17.7
Net before tax	$ 3.5	$ 2.9	$ 3.9	$ 4.3	$ 5.1
Other income	0.3	0.4	0.2	0.4	(.1)
	$ 3.8	$ 3.3	$ 4.1	$ 4.7	$ 5.0
Federal taxes	1.7	1.5	1.9	2.3	2.6
	$ 2.1	$ 1.8	$ 2.2	$ 2.4	$ 2.4
Gain from investments	-	0.1	0.7	1.0	1.2
Net Income	$ 2.1	$ 1.9	$ 2.9	$ 3.4	$ 3.6
Common stock price					
Low		22	20	21-3/8	25-5/8
High		24-3/4	26-1/2	59-3/8	40-1/4

As of March 30, 1960, the common stock price was 23-1/8.

All figures except common share prices in millions of dollars.

Electronics Industry Process Notes

The picture seen on the screen of a television receiver represents but one of the thousands of applications of electronics, the science dealing with the nature, flow, and control of electrons. All matter is made up of atoms which consist of negatively charged electrons revolving about a positively charged nucleus. The electrons are attracted to the nucleus but are repelled by other electrons. In the atoms of conducting materials the positive charge on the nucleus is not sufficient to hold in position all the electrons. Conductors, therefore, are said to contain "free electrons," which can be made to move from one atom to the next if a strong enough external positive charge is applied. The external positive charge overcomes the attraction of the nuclei for the "free electrons" and starts an electron flow known as an electric current. Electronic devices of all kinds are based on the principle of controlling electron flows to perform useful work.

Electrons can be made to flow in conducting metals, in gases, or through a vacuum. Under certain conditions, a source of heat or light can cause electrons to be separated from the conducting substance and emitted through a vacuum. The phenomenon of television, for example, is based on the fact that certain materials emit electrons when struck by a beam of light and that others release light when struck by a beam of electrons. This note will describe the manufacture of television receivers and of some representative electronic components.

The two basic production techniques used in electronic manufacturing are mechanical and electrical connecting. Mechanical connections are represented by rivets or the familiar nut and bolt, the affixing of a tube socket to a printed circuit board, or the plugging-in of components or cables (where the mechanical joining of the two parts also provides the necessary electrical connection). Electrical connections are usually made by "soldering" or by welding. A trained operator can hand solder four or five connections per minute.

The distinction between electrical and mechanical connections is not sharp. In most assembly operations, the component or components to be joined electrically are usually joined mechanically first. For example, the procedure for fixing a component such as a resistor or capacitor to a socket or terminal is as follows: first, the part is formed to the desired configuration, usually by bending the wire leads; second, it is inserted into position and "clinched" by wrapping the leads around the terminal to which they are to be joined; finally, the excess length of lead is trimmed off. A trained operator following the cycle of form, insert, clinch, and cut, can ordinarily complete some 120 cycles per hour. (This rate can be increased up to 180 cycles per hour if the component leads have been previously cut to length and preshaped.)

In the sections to follow, the widespread use of these basic connecting procedures will be evident as the manufacture of electron tubes, cathode ray picture tubes, a typical semiconductor (2N404 type transistor), and, finally, television receiving sets are described.

These products illustrate different production techniques and problems found in the industry: groups of girls performing hand operations (the 2N404 and the mounting of electron tubes); automatic equipment performing complex, repetitive tasks on often miniature parts (electron tubes); and conveyor-paced and operator-paced assembly lines (television sets). In addition, the material highlights some differences between components manufacturers and equipment assemblers and suggests some opportunities and pitfalls of vertical integration.

1. Basic Tube Types. There are thousands of types, sizes, and shapes of electron tubes, each requiring unique methods of parts preparation and manufacture. The two basic classes are "receiving type" and power and special purpose tubes. Receiving types are further. divided into: (1) "conventional types" used when high voltages and power-handling capability are required, and (2) low-cost miniature tubes, common in television and radio sets. Power tubes are used in television broadcast and other transmitters, while the TV cathode ray picture tube is an example of the special purpose tube.

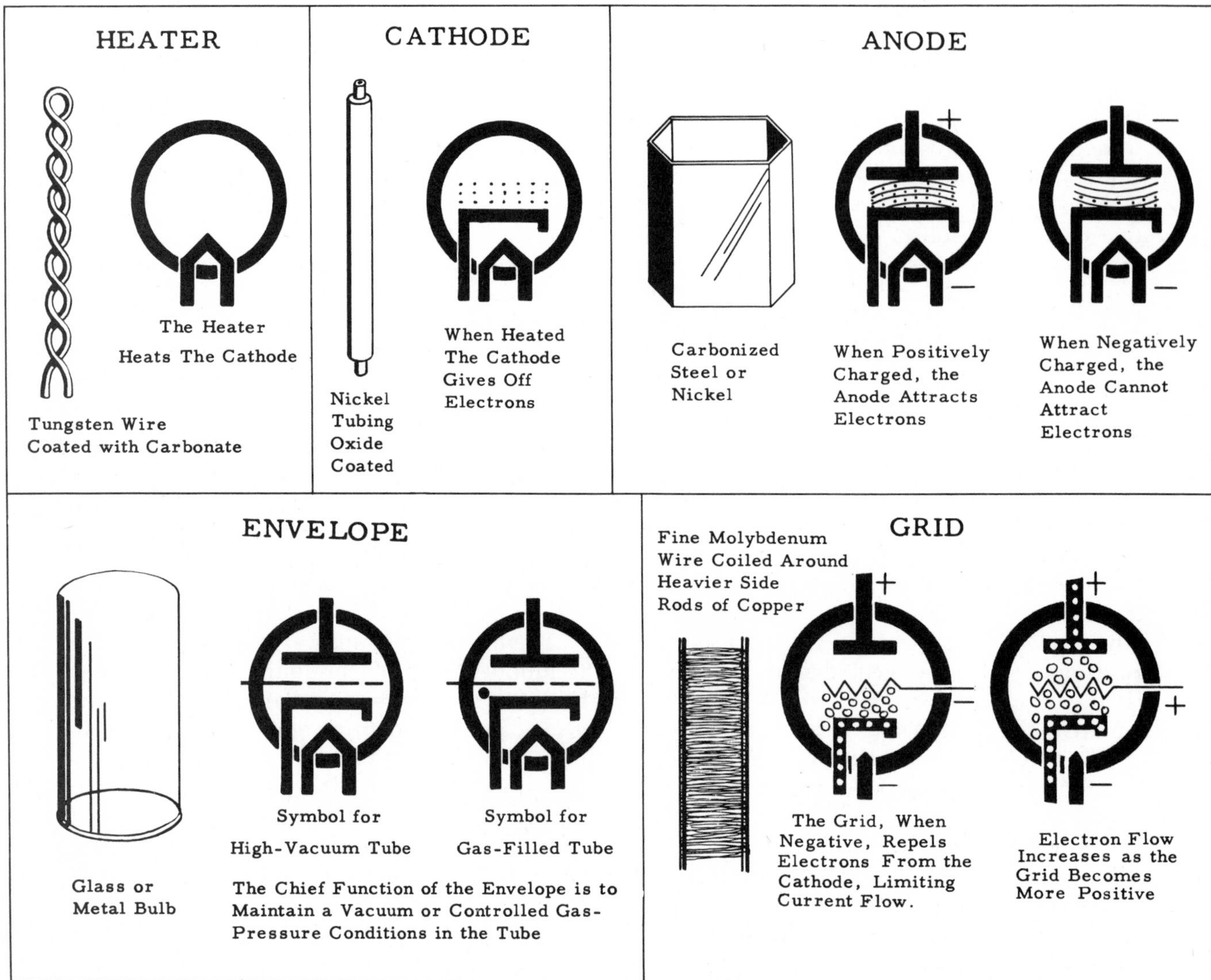

2. Receiving Tube: Basic Tube Parts

2. Basic Electron Tube Parts. In its simplest form an electron tube consists of the following parts: (*a*) a heating filament; (*b*) an incandescent surface called the cathode, which is heated by the filament; (*c*) a metal plate or anode; and (*d*) a glass envelope or bulb from which air has been evacuated. The cathode emits electrons which are drawn across the space in the tube to the plate. The plate, when it is positively charged, attracts the negatively charged electrons.

In addition, a wire grid is sometimes interposed between the cathode and plate to help control the flow of electrons. An electron tube may have none, one, or several grids, depending on its intended use.

Photo, Courtesy General Electric Co.

Photo, Courtesy Sylvania Electric Products, Inc.

3. Receiving Tube: An Automatic Stem Machine Producing 1,300 Stems per Hour

3. Receiving Tube Manufacture. As may be seen from the flow chart on pages 406–7, receiving tubes are made by a mixture of highly automatic machinery and precision hand labor; often the manufacturer has a choice of process. For example, cathode spraying or inserting the control heater wire into the cathode may be done by hand or on special purpose machines.

The balance of machines needed may be inferred from the differing outputs. For example, a grid winding machine can produce 175–200 close-wound grids and 750–800 loose-wound grids per hour. The output of a stem machine ranges from 1,200 to 1,300 stems per hour. The conventional tube base machine fills about 3,000 units per hour (miniature tubes have no separate bases). Mounting is a hand operation performed by five- to seven-girl teams; two to four teams feed a sealing machine. The sealex machine, manned by a single operator, seals and exhausts some 800 tubes per hour. Sometimes, the tubes are annealed on a preheating machine which has the same output rate. For the conventional tubes, one basing machine is required per sealex.

FLOW CHART OF THE ELEC

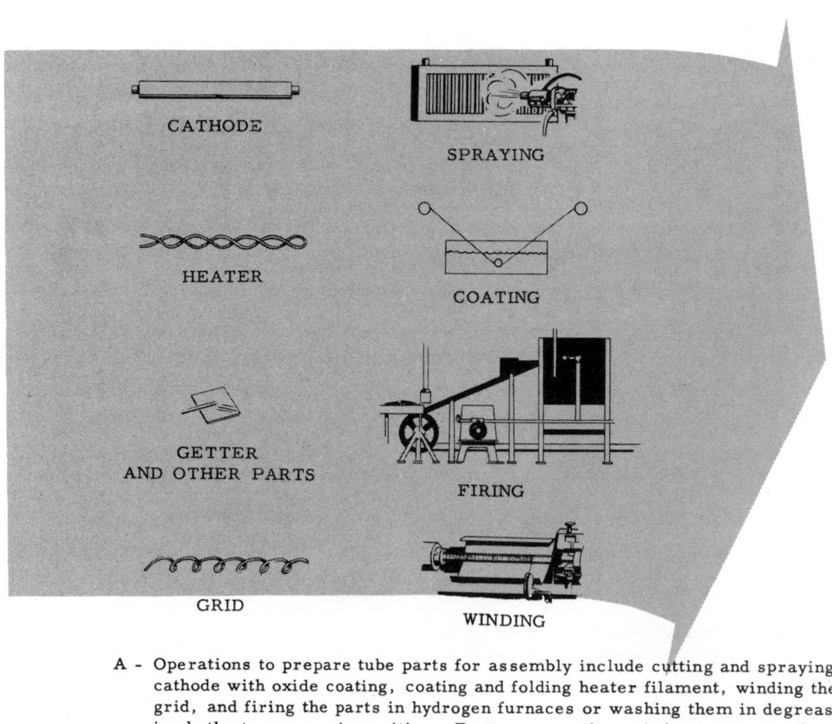

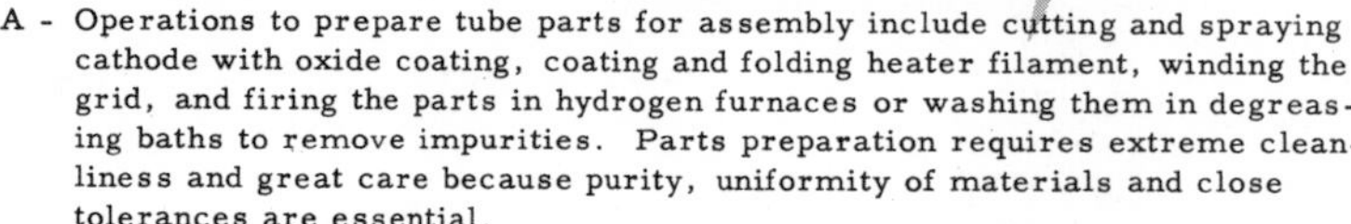

A - Operations to prepare tube parts for assembly include cutting and spraying cathode with oxide coating, coating and folding heater filament, winding the grid, and firing the parts in hydrogen furnaces or washing them in degreasing baths to remove impurities. Parts preparation requires extreme cleanliness and great care because purity, uniformity of materials and close tolerances are essential.

STEM MACHINE

PINS

HEADER

STEM

EXHAUST TUBE

B - The stem header or button, connecting pins and exhaust tube are sealed together by jets of flame on the stem machine.

C - MOUNTING TEAMS

C - The internal parts of the tube are assembled and attached to th stem by teams of girls using tweezers and small resistance ar spot welders. The completed subassembly is called the moun

E MANUFACTURING PROCESS

) - The assembled mount is annealed on a pre-heating wheel to reduce strain in the glass parts.

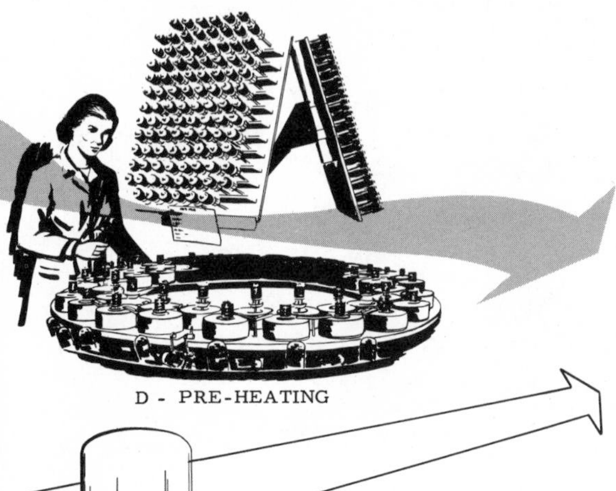

D - PRE-HEATING

E-SEALEX

BULB

E - The sealing and exhausting operation is performed by the rotary indexing sealex machine. The bulb and mount are sealed together by jets of flame. The tube elements are purified by induction heating while the air is being withdrawn from the bulb through the exhaust tube. The heating also vaporizes the barium getter, which condenses and combines with gaseous impurities in the tube. Finally, jets of flame seal or "tip off" the exhaust tube.

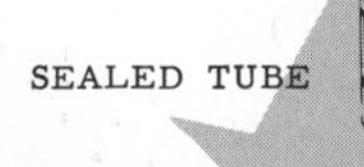

SEALED TUBE

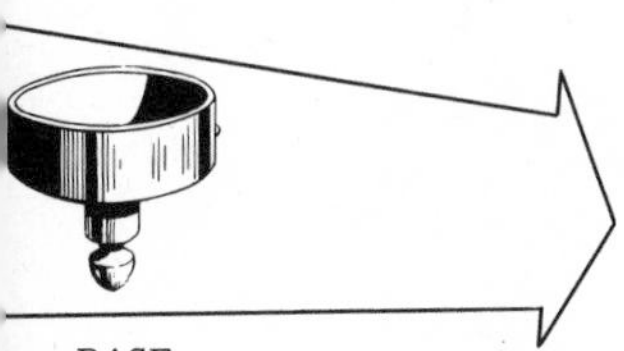

BASE

F - BASE FILLING

F - BASING

F - The tube and a metal or bakelite base which has been previously coated in the base filling machine with an insulating cement are clamped together in the basing machine and baked until the cement is hardened.

G - The tubes are placed on an aging conveyor which moves slowly through a number of electrical contacts. Various combinations of current and voltage are applied to the tube to stabilize its operating characteristics.

H - The completed tube receives its first 100% inspection. Tests to determine the tube's electrical characteristics and to locate defective tubes are performed. Life tests, percentage checks, and quality control checks are subsequently made on samples from each lot of tubes.

I - The tubes receive a final check and are branded and packed.

G - CONVEYOR AGER
H - INSPECTION

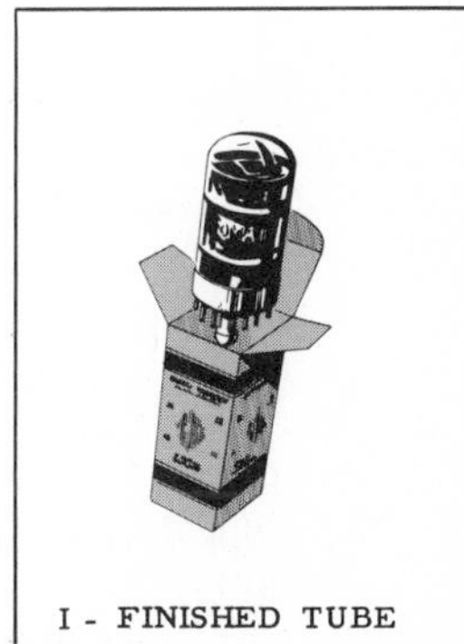

I - FINISHED TUBE

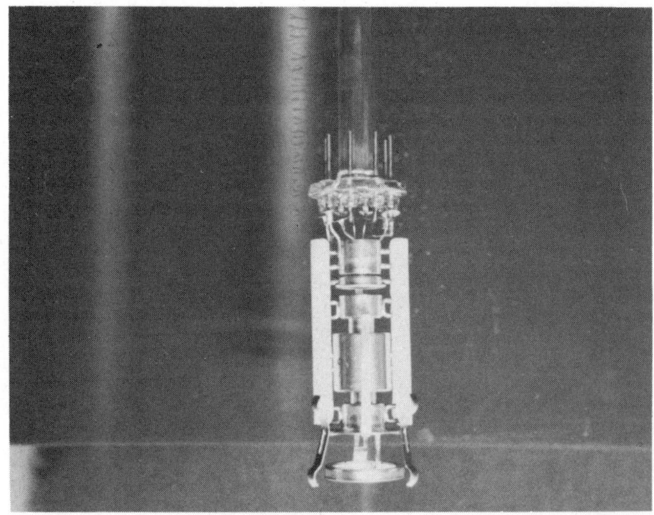

Photo, Courtesy National Video Corp.

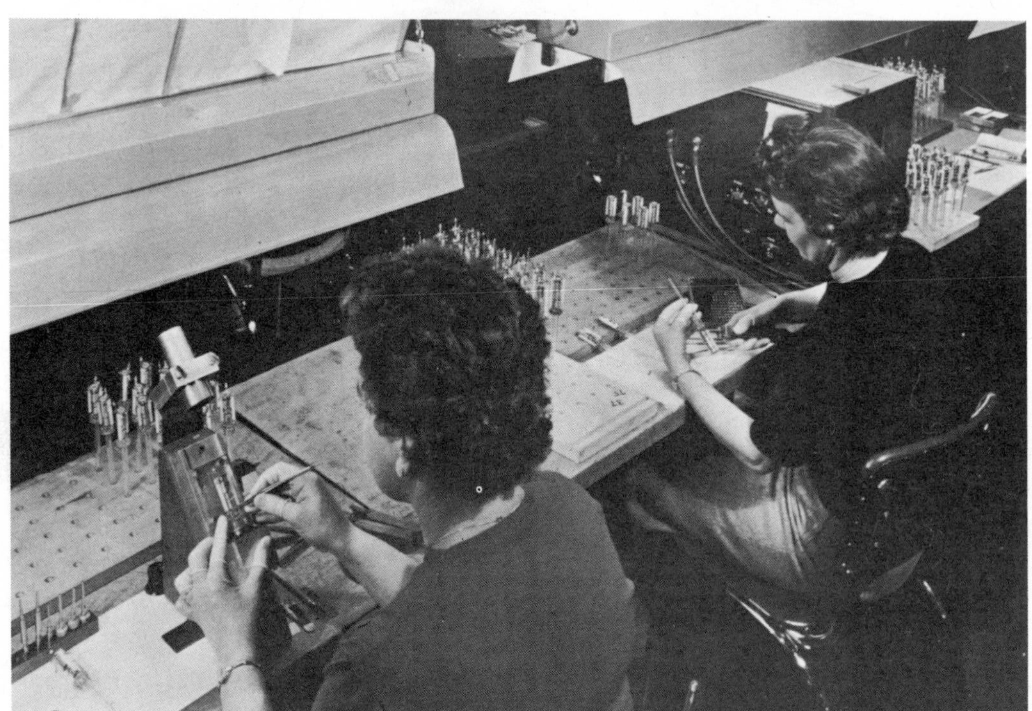

Photo, Courtesy National Video Corp.

4. Cathode Ray Tube: Electron Gun Assembly; Note Protective Finger Coverings

4. Basic Cathode Ray Tube Parts. The cathode ray picture tube has two main parts: (*a*) the mount or electron gun, and (*b*) the glass envelope or bulb.

The mount consists of a cathode, anode, and two grids. The anode and grids are hollow metal cylinders closed at one end except for a small central opening. When heated by a tungsten filament or heater, the cathode emits a stream of electrons which flow through the grids and anode toward the positively charged screen. The grids and anode control the flow of electrons which are attracted to the screen because of the speed at which they are emitted from the "gun." Screen sizes range from 10 to 30 inches, the most common sizes being 16- and 21-inch (diagonal measurement).

Deflecting coils and an external focusing coil are placed around the neck of the tube when the television receiver is assembled. The focusing coil focuses the electrons emitted by the cathode into a thin pencil-like beam. The deflecting coils move the beam horizontally and vertically, causing the beam to scan the tube face.

T-V PICTURE TUBE (ELECTRON GUN)

CATHODE
TAB
CATHODE
EYELET
CERAMIC SPACER
GRID 1
PINS
GRID
GRID 2
PINS
GRID
ANODE
PINS
RING
SHIELD
CATHODE ASSEMBLY
CATHODE SPACER
GRID 1 ASSEMBLY
GRID 2 ASSEMBLY
ANODE ASSEMBLY
SIDE RODS
GUN ASSEMBLY
TUBULATION
GLASS BUSHING
STEM ASSEMBLY
LEADS
FORMED STEM ASSEMBLY
HEATER
GUN ASSEMBLY
ANODE CAP
SPACERS
GETTERS
COMPLETED MOUNT ASSEMBLY

4. Cathode Ray Tube: The Parts of a Mount Assembly

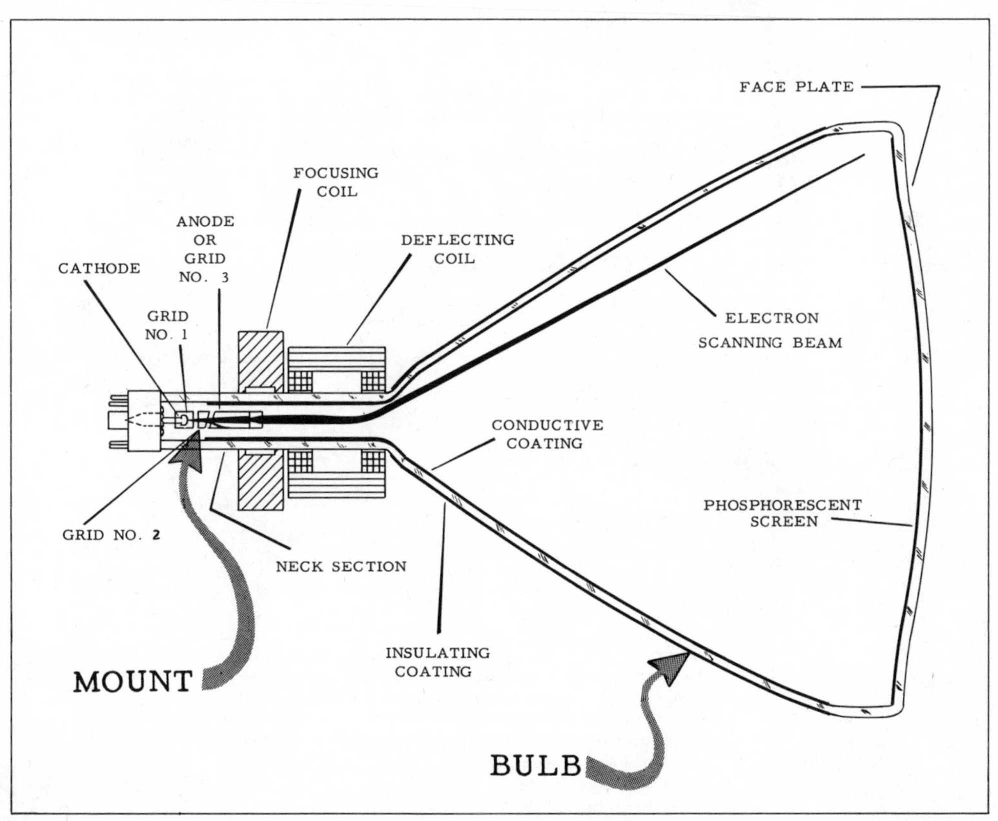

4. Cathode Ray Tube: Sectional View

FLOW CHART OF THE CATHODE

A - STAMPING

B - STEM MACHINE

B - STEM INSPECTION

B - Stem making: a glass bushing, eight to ten lead wires, and a short length of exhaust tubing are fused together by jets of flame on a rotary indexing stem machine; the completed stem is carried through an annealing oven; an operator then clips and forms the stem lead wires.

A - DEGREASING

A - PARTS FIRING

A - Preparation of the parts for mount assembly: stamping, punching, welding, deburring, degreasing, and parts firing to remove impurities.

C - MOUNTING TEAMS

C - Mount assembly: teams of worker the internal parts to the stem by form the mount or electron gun; th tweezers and welders requires de due to the close tolerances involve

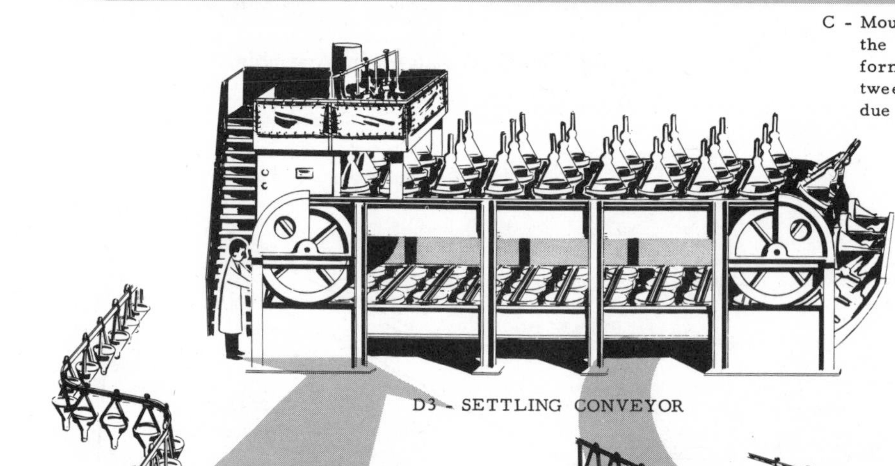

D3 - SETTLING CONVEYOR

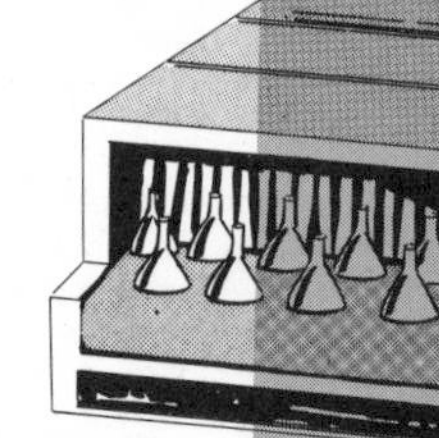

D6 - BAKE-OUT

D2 - BULB WASHING

D - Bulb preparation: (1) inspection of bulbs for scratches; (2) spraying with cleaning solution in automatic washing machine; (3) coating the inside face plate with phosphorescent material on the settling conveyor; and inspection for visual imperfections; (4) coating the inside surface of the cone and neck with graphite to form the high voltage anode; (5) aluminizing the bulb to increase brightness; (6) baking-out the bulb to dry the screen and the graphite coating.

D1 - BULB INSPECTION

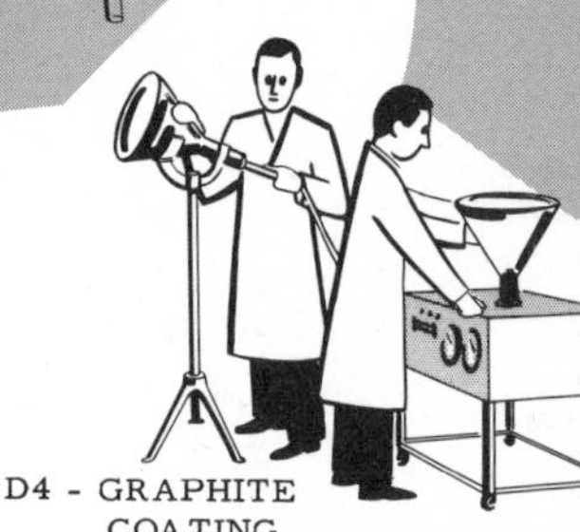

D4 - GRAPHITE COATING

D5 - ALUMINIZ

URE TUBE MANUFACTURING PROCESS

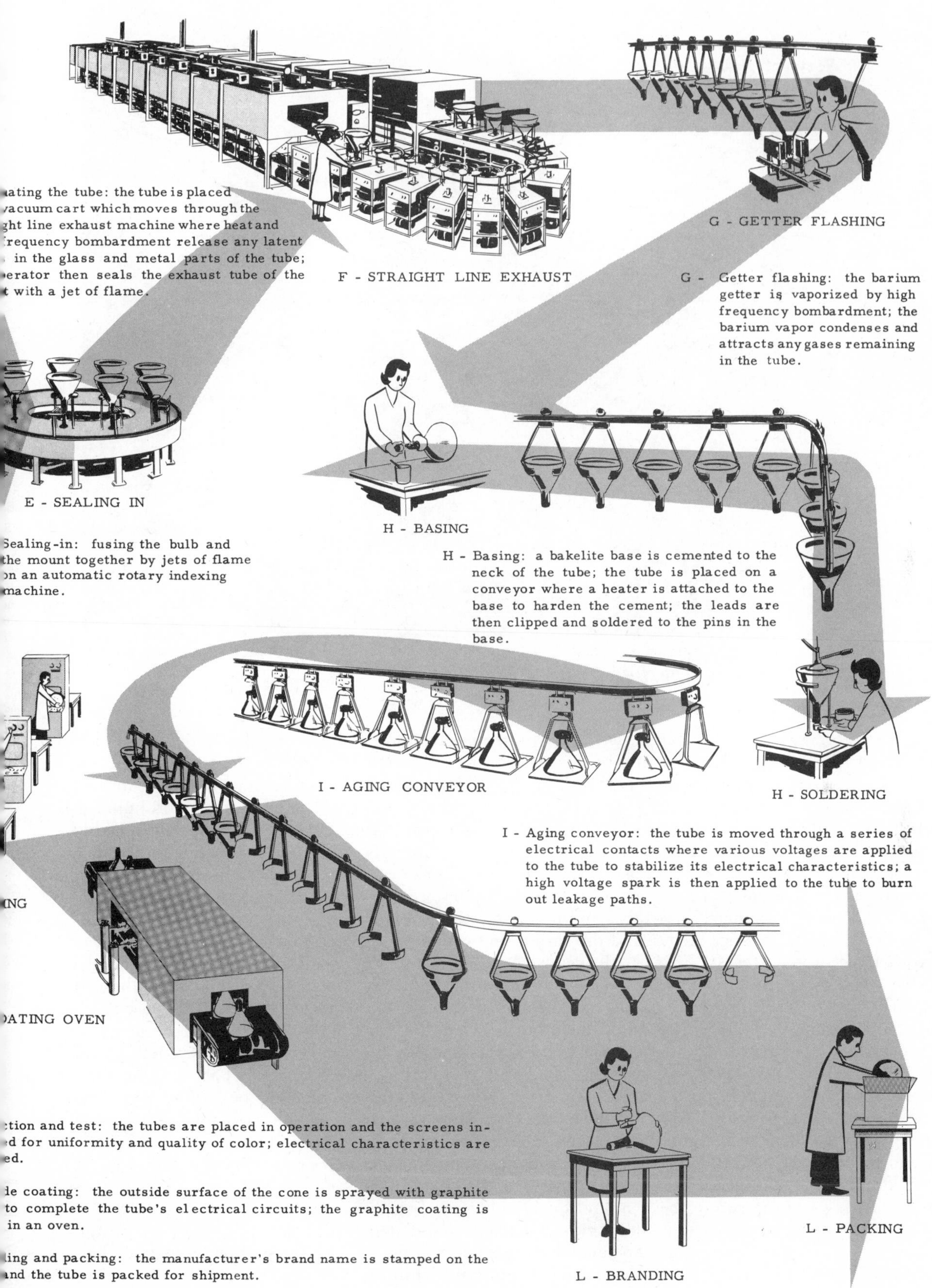

ating the tube: the tube is placed vacuum cart which moves through the ght line exhaust machine where heat and requency bombardment release any latent in the glass and metal parts of the tube; erator then seals the exhaust tube of the t with a jet of flame.

G - Getter flashing: the barium getter is vaporized by high frequency bombardment; the barium vapor condenses and attracts any gases remaining in the tube.

Sealing-in: fusing the bulb and the mount together by jets of flame on an automatic rotary indexing machine.

H - Basing: a bakelite base is cemented to the neck of the tube; the tube is placed on a conveyor where a heater is attached to the base to harden the cement; the leads are then clipped and soldered to the pins in the base.

I - Aging conveyor: the tube is moved through a series of electrical contacts where various voltages are applied to the tube to stabilize its electrical characteristics; a high voltage spark is then applied to the tube to burn out leakage paths.

ction and test: the tubes are placed in operation and the screens in- d for uniformity and quality of color; electrical characteristics are ed.

le coating: the outside surface of the cone is sprayed with graphite to complete the tube's electrical circuits; the graphite coating is in an oven.

ing and packing: the manufacturer's brand name is stamped on the and the tube is packed for shipment.

Photo, Courtesy National Video Corp.

5. Cathode Ray Tube: Ring Sealing the Electron Gun to the Bulb

5. Cathode Ray Picture Tube Manufacture. As with the electron tube, the various production rates indicate the machine balance for picture tubes (see chart, pages 410–11). To begin with, the output of the stem machine and continuous annealer is about 70 stems per hour. They feed mounting teams assembling some 100 units per hour. Meanwhile, two operators tend the machine washing 60 bulbs an hour. The settling conveyor requires two operators and the output is 250 bulbs per hour. The bake-out oven also has two operators and bakes 240 bulbs per hour. One operator tends the sealing-in machine that seals 90 units per hour. The $250,000 straight-line exhaust evacuates over 60 units per hour; alternatively, individual stationary exhaust pumps may be used at a cost of $1,000 each. The aging conveyor holds approximately 500 tubes and processes 200 per hour.

Besides graphite coating, basing, and the various inspections, the major hand operation is mounting. This is done in four stages. First, small metal glossing pins are spot welded to the grids and anode. In the second stage, two grids and the anode are held in alignment in a metal arbor and then joined together by two glass support beads that have been heated to a plastic state. After the glass has cooled, the completed gun assembly is slipped off the arbor. Third, the cathode is inserted under pressure in a circular piece of ceramic. The parts are placed in racks and the cylinder cap which protrudes beyond the ceramic spacer is sprayed with emitting chemicals in a carbonate suspension. The spraying must be carefully controlled to insure a coating of proper thickness. Finally, to complete the cathode assembly, a tab is spot welded to the cylinder. In the fourth stage, the completed cathodes are delivered to a table where girls join them to the gun assembly by inserting the cathode in the first grid. The cathode is carefully positioned, since the distance between the cathode and the upper surface of the grid must be held within very close tolerances.

The assembly of the gun to the stem and the attachment of small parts is done on an assembly line. To complete 100 mounts an hour, three girls join the gun and stem with lead wires, three attach the heater to the cathode, one puts on the anode cap, two add spacers and getters, and one inspects. The completed mount goes to the sealing-in machine for insertion into the bulb.

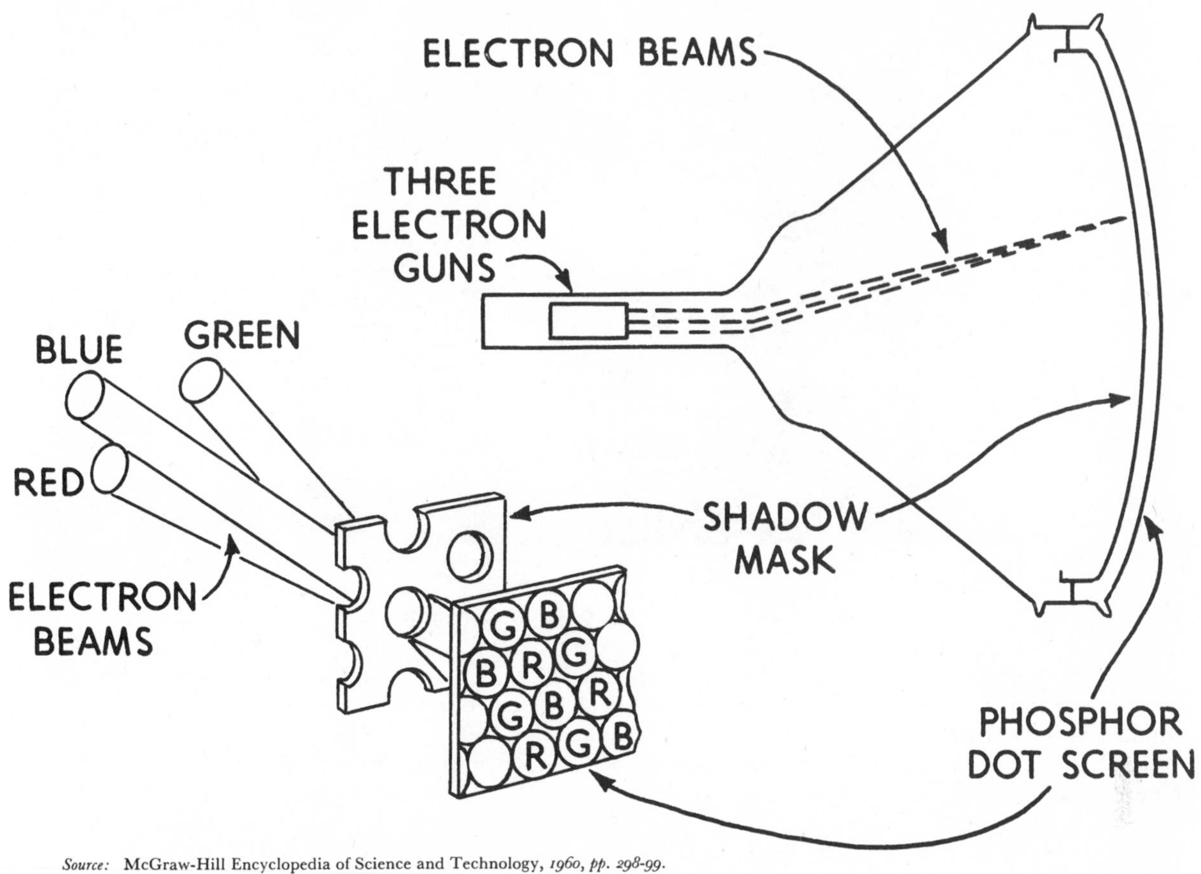

Source: McGraw-Hill Encyclopedia of Science and Technology, *1960, pp. 298-99.*

6A. Color Picture Tube

6. Color Television—Cathode Ray Picture Tube. The color picture tube is considerably more difficult to produce than the conventional black-and-white one. Whereas the face of the latter is covered with a phosphorescent coating from a settling solution, the color face plate must have over a third of a million accurately positioned dots of red, green, and blue phosphor. Instead of one gun, the color tube has three.

Mixing the primary colors of red, green, and blue produces the color picture. Balancing the mixture produces white, but changing the relative intensities of each color creates the chromatic components of the picture. The tube has a separate gun for red, green, and blue beams. The three guns, arranged in an equilateral triangle, move in synchronism and converge at a common point on a perforated metal plate (shadow mask) in front of the phosphor screen (faceplate). The beams then diverge and strike precisely located phosphor dots on the faceplate. The relative intensities of the beams, controlled by the electron gun voltage, determine the dominant color produced. The very rapid scanning of hundreds of thousands of these holes and dots produces the color picture image (see Figure 6A).

Placing the dots on the screen is done with a photographic technique similar to photoengraving. The entire screen is covered first with one of the three phosphors, then with a photosensitive material. A pinpoint of light, located where the color's electron gun will be, is shone through the shadow mask and exposes the photosensitive material in a pattern of dots all over the screen. Upon development, the exposed areas bind the phosphor beneath them to the faceplate; the remaining phosphor is washed away. The result is a phosphor dot array capable of producing one of the primary colors. The second and third dot arrays are added by moving the light source to coincide with the future positions of the other electron guns.[1]

[1] Milton S. Kiver, *Color Television Fundamentals* (New York: McGraw-Hill Book Co., Inc., 1955), p. 143.

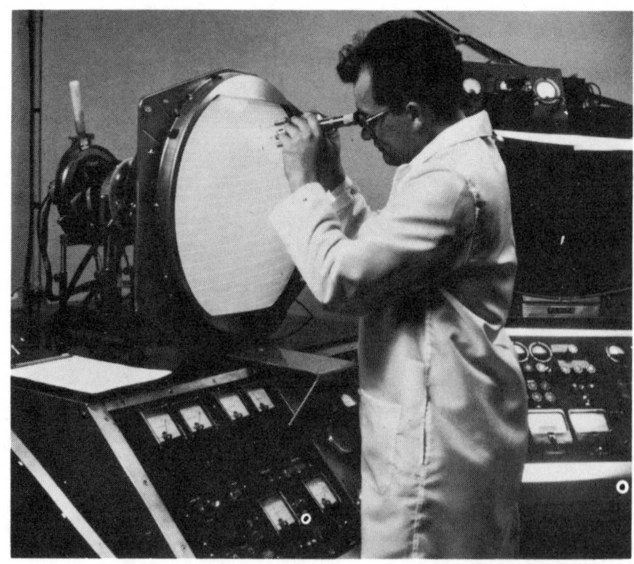

Photo, Courtesy Zenith Radio Corp.

6B. Color TV: Checking for Color Convergence

One of the major manufacturing problems is precisely aligning the shadow mask and phosphor dots on a mass production basis. The mask is to insure that each beam strikes one phosphor dot. Color contamination occurs when the holes allow an electron beam to hit the wrong dot or to overlap several dots. Examples of two 1955 attempts to overcome shadow mask placement problems are shown in Figure 6C.

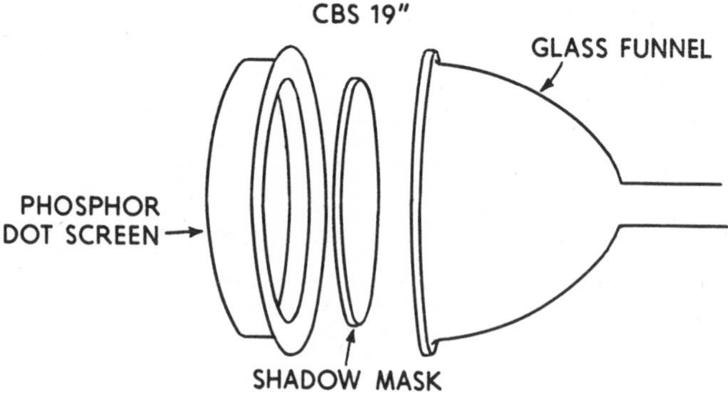

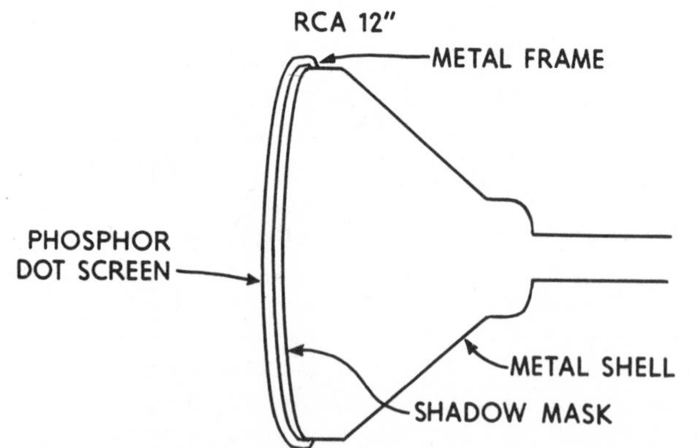

Source: Milton S. Kiver, Color Television Fundamentals *(New York: McGraw-Hill Book Co., Inc., 1955), p. 143.*

6C. Examples of 1955 Color Tubes

TRANSISTORS

Since the invention of the transistor in 1948, semiconductors have had an explosive impact on the electronics industry and undergone rapid changes in technology and manufacturing techniques. As the name suggests, semiconductors have controllable electrical properties that permit valence electrons to be dislodged and carry a current less easily than conductors.

1. Types of Semiconductors. Semiconductors are of two types: "N" and "P." An N-type contains a trace of impurity whose atoms carry one extra electron. For example, if the semiconductor germanium, with four valence electrons, is doped with five valence electron arsenic, only four electrons fit in the tight crystal structure and a free one is left as a "donor" to carry current. A P-type semiconductor contains an impurity with one *less* electron and is able to act as a positive charge and absorb an electron; in effect, there is a hole in the crystal lattice. Conventional current[2] can flow through an N-type from the positive to the negative terminals because the free valence electrons are attracted to the former terminal. Likewise, in a P-type, the application of an external battery supply makes valence electrons jump into the "holes"—and by so doing create new holes—on the way to the positive terminal. In effect, the holes move to the negative terminal. Most semiconductor devices are based on putting P- and N-type regions in the same crystal.

The semiconductor field may be split into three main segments: rectifiers, diodes, and transistors. Rectifiers and diodes (low-power rectifiers) act as a one-way electrical gate. Inside the crystal is a junction or area where the impurity changes from N-type to P-type. If a battery is connected across the P-N junction with the negative potential to the N-region, a current will flow from P to N as electrons are forced across the junction and combine with the electron deficient indium. Reversing the connections prevents a current flow. The P-type takes on a negative charge due to the "holes" moving towards the negative terminal and N-type takes on a positive charge because the free electrons go towards the positive terminal.

2. Transistors. Transistors look like a three-layer sandwich and behave like a valve. The two outer layers are either both P-type or both N-type; the much thinner center or base layer is the opposite type. In a PNP type, current flows from the emitter to the collector when a small current is injected into the base to increase the number of carriers or holes. The positive potential of one battery is connected to the emitter and the negative to the base, while the negative potential of another battery is connected to the collector and the positive to the base. The holes in the emitter region are repelled by the positive potential and most pass through the .0005-inch base-width to be filled by an electron emitted by the negative terminal. Depending upon the circuitry, the current or voltage may be greatly amplified.

Compared to an electron tube, the transistor has many basic superiorities. Transistors are generally housed in tiny cylinders less than an inch in length. They weigh just a fraction of an ounce, have no heaters or filaments, consume very little power, have long operating lives, are solid in construction and extremely rugged. Requiring no warm-up period, they begin to operate the instant power is applied. Transistors are hermetically sealed (against the atmosphere) and, in special applications, can even operate under water.

3. Fabrication Methods. Over the years, transistors have been designed and constructed in a multitude of ways; by 1963, they could be classified as combinations of five basic techniques: grown, alloy, electrochemical, diffusion, and epitaxial (see Figures 3A & B). Each will be described briefly below.

A. Grown Junction Types. These are offshoots of an early 1951 transistor. They consist of a germanium crystal to which P- and N-type impurities are added successively or simultaneously to the ends during the melt. The base region is usually in the middle.

B. Alloy Types. These consist of an N-type and P-type base with the opposite-type dots alloyed on each side. Alloy transistors may be mass-produced and permit a short electron transit time from emitter to collector; however, it is difficult to obtain and control the narrow base widths needed for high frequencies.

C. Diffused Types. In these transistors, one or more impurities are diffused into the semiconductors at high temperatures (such as 1,300°C.). The introduction of solid state diffusion techniques increases the control over impurity distribution and base width. For example, in a *drift* transistor the conductivity

[2] Conventional current in an external circuit flows from the positive to the negative terminals while electronic current represents the election flow from negative to positive. This note will use conventional current.

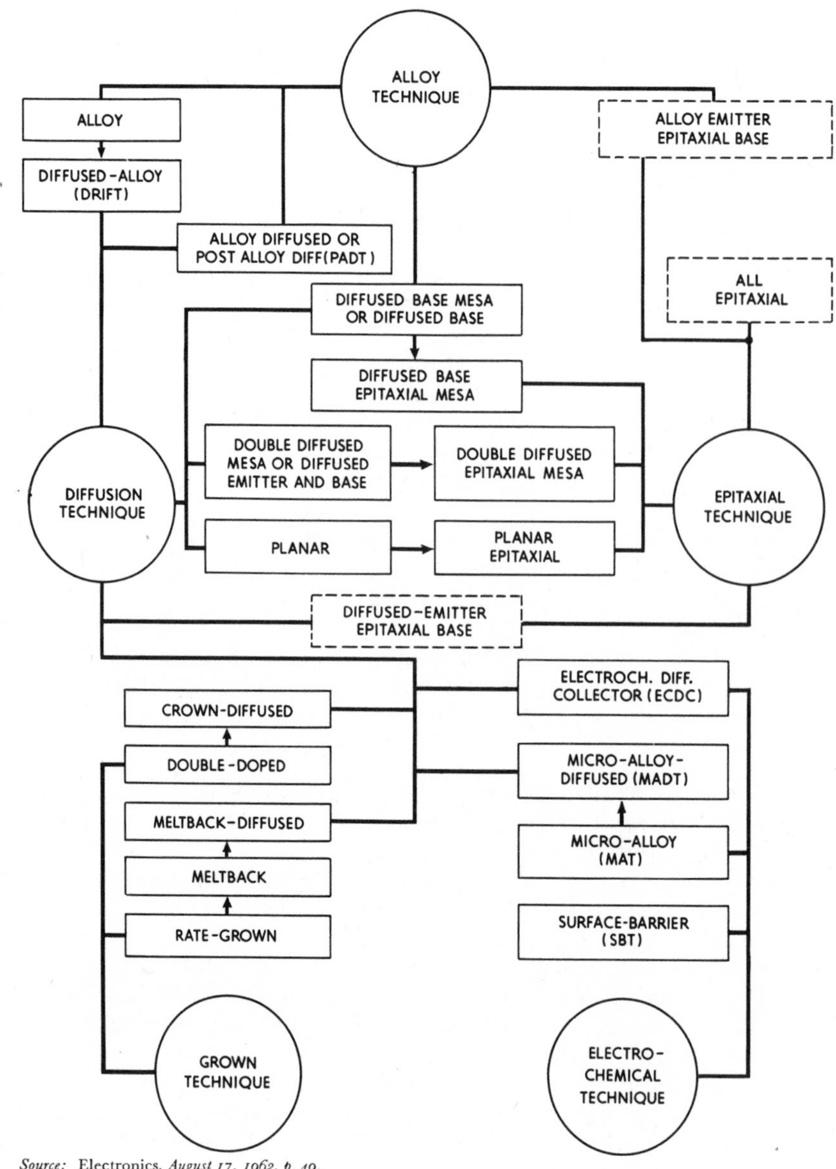

Source: Electronics, *August 17, 1962, p. 49.*

3A. A Classification of Transistor Types

of the base is varied so that it is high near the emitter and low near the collector; the result is accelerating carrier motion by a factor of 4. In manufacturing, an N-type impurity is diffused into a crystal. Then the resulting N-type skin is removed from the face, a P-type pellet alloyed to this surface, and a P-type emitter dot to the other; the N-skin serves as the base layer.

The *mesa* construction takes greater advantage of the dimensional control possible with diffusion and makes a distinct departure from the alloy approach. First, a base P-layer .00016 inches deep is diffused on an N-type silicon wafer. Next, the bottom layer is lapped off to expose a collector area and a photo-resist pattern is applied to protect the top surface, except .004 by .006-inch apertures which are to become emitter sites. Then an N-type material is diffused .0001 inches into the base region to form the emitter areas. Contact slits, .002 by .004 inches, are alloyed to the emitter and base layer. Finally, the junction between the base layer and the original N-type collector material is etched to reduce collector capacitance (hence the mesa appearance), and .001-inch gold emitter and base leads are attached. Lead attachment is done by thermo-compression bonding at 300° C. and 20,000 p.s.i. pressure under a microscope.

A variation is the *planar* transistor which has both P- and N-type impurities diffused into a wafer to produce two P-N junctions side-by-side in the original semiconductor material. The base diffusion is defined and controlled through a protective oxide mask.

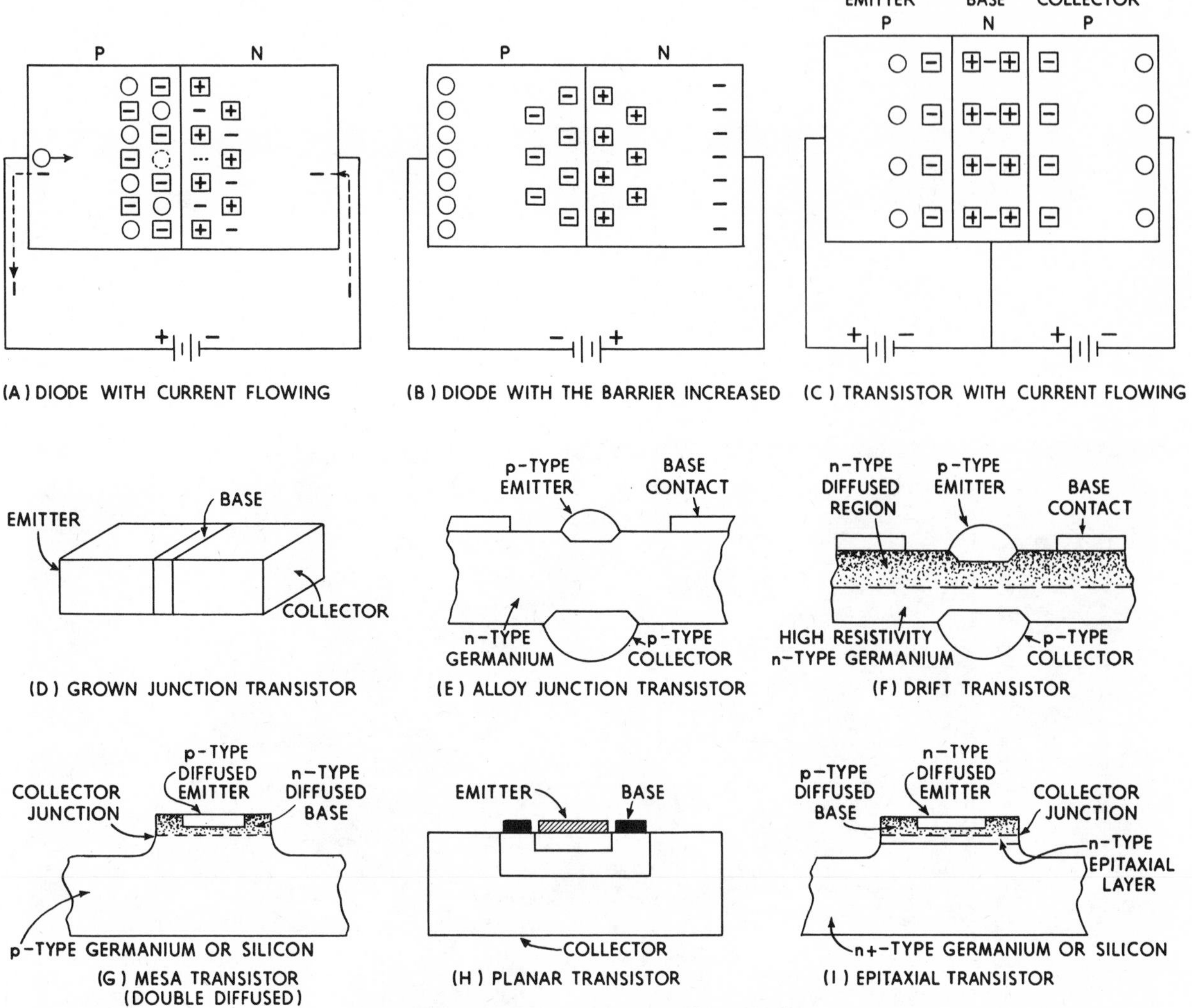

3B. Diagrams of Transistor Operation and Types

D. Electrochemical Types. The addition of electrochemical etching and plating reduces the alloy base widths still further. In the surface barrier transistor (SBT), emitter and collector junctions are electroplated in depressions etched on opposite sides of the wafer. The micro-alloy diffused transistor (MADT) adds a diffused nonuniform base to the surface barrier.

E. Epitaxial Types. The mesa technique has the disadvantage of higher collector saturation resistance and increased collector storage time; these are removed by epitaxial growth whereby vapor deposition builds up a single-crystal layer upon the original semiconductor crystal wafer. The result is a single crystal, but the layer and wafer may be doped with different types and densities of impurities. It has been used mainly to deposit a high-resistivity collector region on a low-resistivity substrate; however, it is theoretically possible to complete an all-epitaxial unit by epitaxially depositing collector, base, and emitter layers.

4. Transistor Manufacture. One transistor, which is quite representative with respect to design and manufacturing characteristics of many mass-produced semiconductors, is the alloy-junction-type 2N404 transistor. The following paragraphs describe in detail each of the nine basic steps involved in its manufacture at Consolidated Electric, Inc. Times, yields, and costs for each step are shown in Exhibit 1, selected job analyses in Exhibit 2, approximate equipment investments in Exhibit 3, the learning curve and selected job classifications in Exhibit 4, and a typical testing sequence in Exhibit 5.

A. Basic Crystal Manufacture. In the first basic step of transistor manufacture, 12 by 1 by 1-inch bars of pure germanium are transformed into several 2-inch long mounted segments of the desired crystal structure. Typically, two male machine attendants and two female operators are needed for these operations.

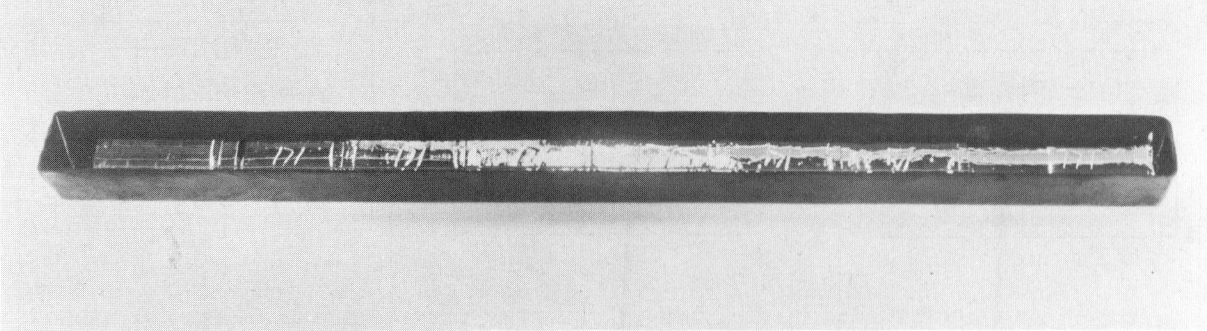

A3. Transistors: Quartz Boat with the Seed plus Cut Crystal Inside

Photo, Courtesy Radio Corporation of America

A3. Transistors: Crystal Growing Furnace

1) Schedule and Add Dope. Female operator A selects the bars to be run. Since a certain degree of impurity is required in the germanium, she checks the level of impurity required and chooses either pure bars or rejects those that have a lower level of impurity. Male operator A then checks the bars. After etching, girl A uses a small electric saw to cut a 3/16-inch notch in the front end of each bar and fills the hole with dope made of the desired impurity, in this case antimony. (Dope is a pulverized mixture of about two parts antimony to 600 parts germanium.)

2) Etch Bars. Male operator A puts up to a dozen bars in a teflon basket and dips them into a mixture of nitric, hydrofluoric, and acetic acids. The bars are immersed from 1 to 10 minutes, depending upon the temperature of the acids which are heated by the etching of the germanium bars. When the bars appear to be clean, the operator removes the basket and washes off the acid in deionized water.

3) Grow Crystals. The first girl carefully places each etched bar in an 18-inch quartz boat with a 2-inch "seed" in front and a 2-inch reject end in the rear. The seed serves as a model of the desired crystal structure; however, the resistivity (inverse of conductivity) is determined by the amount of doping. The boats are carbonized inside with candle flame to prevent the germanium from wetting the boat's walls and setting up little nucleation centers (one of the principal causes of imperfections called *lineage* [see below]). The boat is then placed in a quartz tube (5 feet long and 2.5 inches in diameter) within an electric coil furnace.

The furnace consists of the quartz tube, an insulated electric coil encircling the tube, and a motor to move the coil along the tube. A gas mixture (90 percent nitrogen and 10 percent hydrogen) is injected into the tube, the temperature within the tube is raised to between 950–1,000° C., and the coil is moved along at the rate of .8 millimeters per minute. The outside diameter of the furnace's electric coil is 12 inches, the inside, 3 inches.

The crystal structure of the 2-inch seed is duplicated throughout the bar being processed through the medium of "zone leveling." In zone leveling, a localized area of the ingot is melted and the antimony dope distributed evenly as the melted zone gradually moves from one end of the ingot to the other. The crystal seed sets up the desired molecular structure in the bar being processed, and it may be reused in later furnace runs.

The impurities in the germanium bar freeze out in proportion to the length of the melted zone. Since a certain precise level of impurity is required, the length of the melted zone must be controlled to insure the correct resistivity resulting from the impurity level. It is this resistivity factor which makes the transistor a semiconductor. For the 2N404, the operator varies the furnace's temperature to maintain an exact 2-inch molten zone of molten germanium (above 958° C.). The top of the bar is kept approximately 20 percent above the bottom of the furnace because otherwise the impurities tend to concentrate at the bottom of the bar, thereby causing uneven resistivity.

A4. Transistors: Two-Inch Mounted Uncut Segments

A9. Transistors: Two-Inch Cut Segment on Carbon Block

4) *Cut into Segments.* Girl B checks the orientation of the seed and then cuts the bar into 2-inch segments. A visual and, if needed, an X-ray check is made to insure that the axis of the crystal plane is within $\pm$ .5 degrees of the required standard.

Any small misalignment is corrected by varying the angle by which the bar is cut. A small cutting wheel cuts the seed off for later reuse, the impurity-filled end to be refined chemically, and the rest of the bar into 2-inch segments for further manufacture into transistors.

5) *Resistivity Check.* A four-point check (two for current and two for voltage) is performed to measure the resistivity of each segment in ohms-centimeters. (Resistivity is the resistance in ohms divided by the length of the bar and multiplied by the bar's diameter in centimeters.)

6) *Etch Ends.* The first male operator abrades the ends of the 2-inch segments with aluminum oxide paper, masks all but the ends of the segments with rubber sleeves, places the segments in a teflon basket and then immerses them into an acid wash solution. The basket is removed when the segments' ends are shiny.

7) *Lineage Check.* Girl B visually checks the ends of the segments for "lineage" against a 13-sample standard. Lineage is a measure of the number of imperfections or dislocations in the crystal lattice network per square centimeter. Dislocations may vary between 4,000 and 8,000 per square centimeter and in severe cases show up visually as scratches. Methods such as slowing the rate of temperature change by reducing the drag speed of the furnace, heating the rear of the coil hotter than the front, or adding an after heater are used to reduce lineage.

8) Face Etch. The first man places the bar segments in a teflon basket and dips them for one or two minutes without the protective rubber sleeves in a mixture of hydrofluoric acid, hydrogen peroxide acid, and water to "set" the crystal orientation. The bars are removed when the surface is glazed, not shiny.

9) Mounting. The second man mounts two segments with wax on a peaked carbon block. The job is done in a three-sided metal hot-box to allow the wax to cool slowly. The operator spreads wax over the block, aligns the two segments on top so that when cut the axis will be ±.5 degrees of specifications, and uses a jig clamp to secure the segments while the wax hardens. Finally a coating of wax is poured over the top of the segments.

10) Quality Checks. The quality control department sample-checks for specifications, resistivity, and for lineage between operations.

B. Wafer Fabrication. In this second basic stage, each 2-inch mounted bar segment is cut into approximately 96 wafers 9.5 mils thick. The wafers, which are approximately 5/8 inches by 3/4 inches high are then lapped. Typically, one male and two female operators are needed for these operations.

1) Cut Wafers. A converted milling machine with an inside diameter diamond cutter is used for cutting the mounted segments. The male operator visually, and with an X-ray probe, checks the orientation of the segments within the allowed tolerances of ±.5 degrees and mounts the block in the chuck. The cutting wheel, only .006 to .010 inches thick, slices 5/8 inches per minute. Spurts of water cover the cutting edge and wash away the sawed particles as sludge. The sludge is precipitated in polyethylene vats to recover 97 percent of the germanium.

2) Gauging. A female operator uses a hand micrometer gauge to determine on a sample basis how much should be lapped from each wafer to bring them within their required thickness tolerance, and to remove work surface damages. She grades the wafers into groups of approximately equal thickness for lapping.

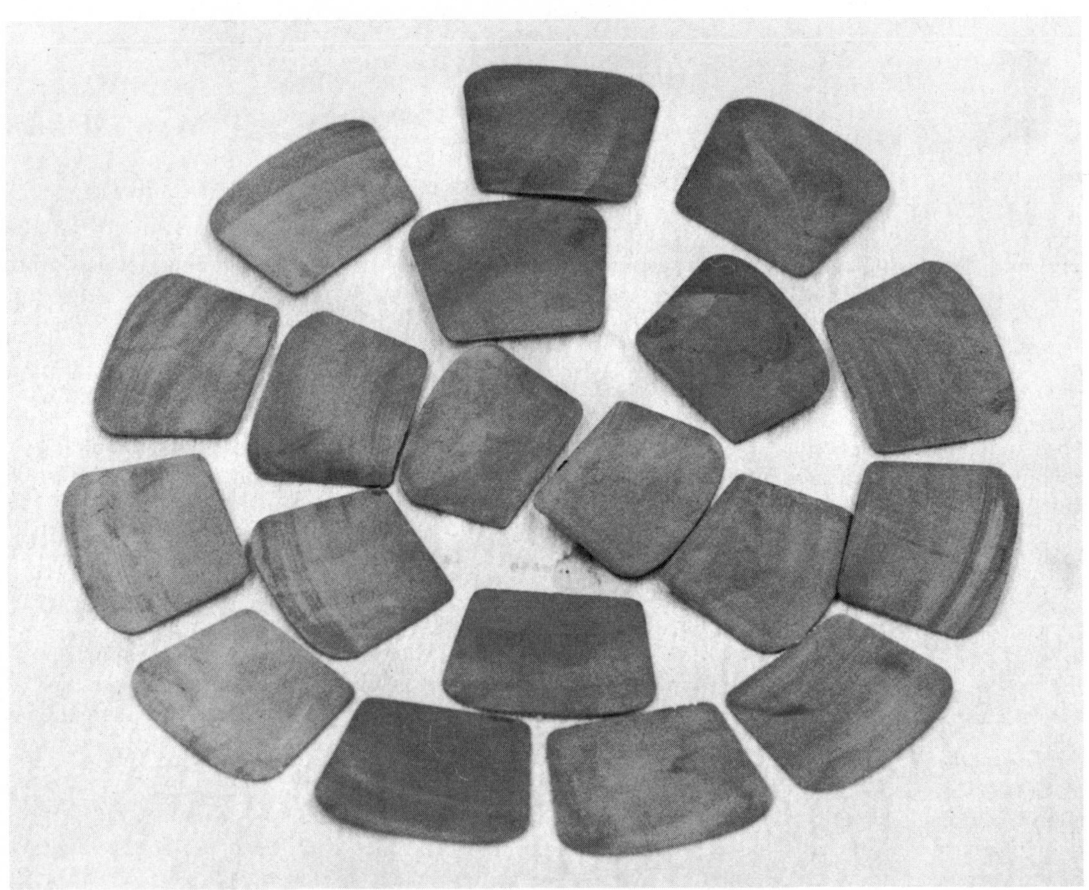

B3. Transistors: Circle of Wafers Ready for Lapping

3) Lapping. The same girl puts 18 wafers under each of the three 12-inch plates on a lapper and grinds first one side and then the other. The abrasive used in this operation consists of 80 grams of 14 micron size grit to a liter of lapping oil. A typical run might lap 1.5 mils from each side of a 9.5 mil wafer and take 15 minutes of process time.

After lapping, the excess abrasive is washed off. Here the operator puts the wafers into a sieve made from a plastic bottle and dips them into a low toxicity chlorinated solvent wash.

Photo, Courtesy Radio Corporation of America

B3. Transistors: Lapping Machine with Wafers in One of Three Rings

4) Sample-Check Gauging. During the lapping the operator sample-checks two or three wafers per 18-wafer batch to determine how much more to lap.

5) Sheffield Gauging. A second girl uses an air gauge to sort the wafers by thickness into .0001 of an inch categories and to reject those with nonparallel surfaces.

6) Quality Checks. The quality control department monitors each operation with sample-checks on crystals for outside dimensions, axis alignment, and resistivity.

C. Pellet Fabrication. In the third step, a wafer is cut into from 200 to 230 pellets, each 42 mils square. The pellets are then sorted into categories. Typically four female operators are needed.

1) Mount Wafers. In this operation, the metal wafers are treated as if they were glass. The first girl places 15 wafers on a glass plate covered with an adhesive, water-soluble wetting agent. Two plates are then placed in the vacuum chuck of an automatic scriber. The scriber consists of a motor and gear train which is designed to move a diamond stylus back and forth over the wafers and score them in pellet squares by turning the glass plate 90°.

Photo, Courtesy Radio Corporation of America

C1. Transistors: Scribing Machine for Dicing Wafers into Pellets

2) Ultrasonic Crack. While still attached to the glass, the scribed wafers are placed in a beaker of hot water. The beaker is then lowered into a water-and-detergent bath where ultrasonic waves separate the pellets from the glass and from each other. The production rate of this operation is 202,400 pellets per hour.

3) Wash. The second operator, who performs the ultrasonic crack operations, washes the pellets in water and then in an alcohol rinse to accelerate drying. The beaker of pellets is then placed in a dry box.

4) Sieve. The second girl uses a small paintbrush to remove the pellets from the beaker and place them into a sieve mounted on a vibrator. In this operation cracked or misshapen pellets fall through the sieve and are salvaged.

5) Etch. The pellets are etched in an automatic machine consisting essentially of four bell vessels. Each vessel includes two pumps and jets to circulate the etching liquid, and time and temperature regulators. Approximately 10,000 pellets are placed in each vessel and a 15 percent hydrogen peroxide solution circulated at a temperature of 70 degrees for about four hours. This process results in an almost perfectly uniform etch. The aim of this etching process is to remove about 1.5 mils per hour from N-type pellets and 1.2 mils from P-type. Periodically during the etch the operator uses a siphon to secure a few pellets for hand check gauging. When the etch is finally finished, the pellets are dried in an alcohol bath.

6) Loading, Unloading. This is a materials handling charge.

7) Gauging. An automatic gauge is used to measure the pellet thickness. In this machine, a vacuum pickup feeds pellets individually to a turret that drops a blunt transducer "drill" on each one. The drill measures the thickness at the point of contact within ±.00004 inches. Finally, the pellets are sorted into one of eight receptacles and the count automatically recorded.

8) Spot Check. A third girl uses a hand-operated gauge to sample-check pellets for overall width uniformity.

9) Count. The third girl uses scales to estimate pellet yield.

10) Re-etch. Some 30 percent of the pellets, by virtue of their being thicker than required standards, have to be re-etched.

11) Sort. The fourth girl separates the good pellets from the misshapen ones either by hand or by a simple machine consisting of a vibrating feeder, a bowl, and a converted table sander rotating a continuous paper belt. The vibrator jiggles pellets up a spiral path in the bowl from which they fall onto the

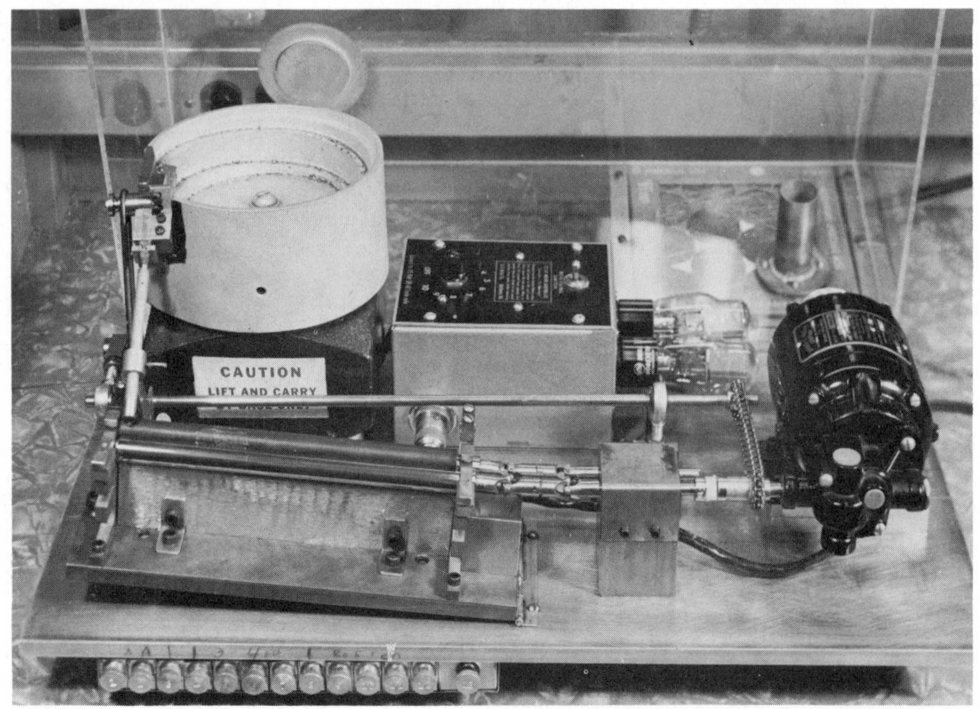

Photo, Courtesy Sylvania Electric Products

C11. Transistors: Sorting Pellets by Size; Note Vibrating Feeder in Back

moving belt. The operator removes rejects with a vacuum pencil and allows the others to fall into a receptacle.

12) Quality Checks. Two checks are made: one a gauge for pellet thickness and the other a thermal probe for P- or N-type characteristics.

Photo, Courtesy Radio Corporation of America

D1. Transistors: Tab Loading Machine

D. Alloy Process. In this fourth basic step, the pellet is soldered to a supporting tab, and emitter and collector dots are alloyed to the pellet. The finished pellet is between 1.7 and 1.9 mils thick, and after alloying, the base width is .064 mils. The diameter of the collector dot is 14 mils and the emitter dot, 10 mils. Typically, four girls are required to accomplish these tasks.

1) Load Tab. The supporting tabs come in double-rowed strips of 60 tabs each. The operator inserts a strip into a multipress. She then positions it underneath a 60-place ceramic jig, which is called a "boat." The boat is about 2½ inches long, 1 inch wide, and ⅛ of an inch thick. Five depressions of the press fill the boat with tabs, the strip of tabs and the boat automatically being indexed over each other each time.

After the second girl has loaded the pellets onto the tabs (see below), the first operator loads the alloying furnace in which the pellet is soldered to the indium-plated tab. The furnace, consisting of asbestos-covered electrical coils, is about 12 feet long and operates in a hydrogen atmosphere. It has several controlled heating zones to maintain a proscribed heating up and cooling cycle.

2) Load Pellets. The second girl uses a vacuum pickup to load pellets into the boat. The pickup consists of a jig with the same number of holes as an alloy boat, and a small rectangular box attached to the bottom of the jig. The box is filled with pellets. The operator turns the vacuum on, tilts the jig so that pellets slide from the box across the surface and fill all 60 holes. Excess pellets fall back into the box. The jig is lowered over a boat full of tabs, the vacuum turned off, and the pellets fall into place. Intermittently, the pellet loader operator also helps unload the furnace.

3) Transfer Collector Washer. A third girl unloads the alloy furnace. In addition, she uses a vacuum jig to pick up collector washers from boats that have gone through the alloy furnace, and deposits these washers on boats that are yet to receive dots and be alloyed. (See Job Motion Study, Exhibit 2-A.) This job used to be done with tweezers (see Job Motion Study, Exhibits 2-B and 2-C). The use of washers is merely a method of positioning the dots correctly for alloying.

4) Load Collector Dot. A "squeeze plate" box is used to load the "collector dots" into the holes in the washers. The squeeze plate device consists of a box with the width and length of a boat, a slanted top with five large slots, and two plates with holes drilled corresponding to the dot pattern on the boat. The second plate is spring-loaded so that when squeezed it will move parallel to the top plate. The operator pours "dots" into the large slots in the top, snaps on a plastic cover, and then tilts the box so that dots roll into each of the holes in the top plate, which is the same thickness as the dot and hence can receive only one dot at a time. Next, she positions the box horizontally over an alloy boat while the excess dots roll back against each of the slot bars. She then presses the spring of the second plate, making the rows of dots fall into place within the washers.

The dots are almost ready for the furnace. The second operator sprays the filled boats with a silicone grease to help maintain the surface tension of the dot and keep it from spreading while it is in a molten stage in the alloy furnace. The first operator places the filled boats in the furnace where they are heated to the proper alloying temperature. The temperature is varied 10° from its approximate temperature of 550° for each 1/10 mil in pellet thickness.

5) Transfer Emitter Washer. Same process as above for the collector washer except that the boats have to be flipped over to expose the emitter side. Since the emitter dot is smaller, the washer is, of course, smaller also.

6) Load Emitter Dot. Same process as above for the collector dot.

7) Inspect. A check is made under a microscope for missing components, spread diameters, surface faults, cracked pellets, misalignment, and the like. Units are periodically checked electrically after the alloy furnace for specifications.

8) Relief Operator. Charge for a furnace relief operator 25 percent of the time.

9) Tests. Charge for testing (furnace temperatures and adjustments).

10) Record. Production record keeping.

11) Salvage. Allowance of 4 percent.

12) Etch. A brief clean-up of etch bath, consisting of a hydrochloric acid and nitric acid solution, is the final step in the alloy process.

13) Quality Checks. Similar to the production inspections except that a toolmaker's micrometer is used to measure dot diameter.

E. Raw Stem Fabrication. In the fifth basic step, three wire "leads" and one dummy lead are inserted into a metal base or "header" and held in place by fused-glass pre-form beads to form a raw "stem."

Photo, Courtesy Radio Corporation of America

E1. Transistors: Loading Headers in Raw Stem Fabrication

1) Load Header. With the help of tweezers, operator loads headers into 20-hole ceramic jigs which are about ¼-inch high, 1½ inches wide and 3 inches long, and which cost $3.16 each.

2) Stamping. An identifying mark, such as 2N404, is stamped on the bottom of each header.

3) Load Pre-Forms. The glass pre-form beads are loaded automatically on a "jiggling" table. The ceramic jigs containing the headers are loaded into a frame about 15 inches square, glass pre-form beads are poured on top, and the table is jiggled while being tipped from one side to another. In this process the beads roll across the holes in the ceramic jigs and fall into places in holes in the headers. The operator then places another ceramic jig over the one which has just been loaded with glass pre-form beads and flips the two over so that the loaded headers are bottom-side-up.

4) Load Leads. At each header position, a girl inserts three wire leads through the first ceramic jig, the header, the glass pre-form and about half-way through the second jig where the holes end. The holes in the second jig are drilled to a depth such that the leads will protrude a predetermined amount from the jig assembly.

5) Load "Dummy" Lead. The operator drops a "dummy" lead through appropriate holes in the first jig at each header position so that now each header has three leads and a dummy lead.

6) Load Furnace. Two operators load the jig assemblies onto a conveyor belt leading to an electric furnace where the glass pre-forms are melted, thereby fusing the leads to the headers. The resulting fused assembly is called a raw stem.

7) Unload Furnace. One or two operators unload the furnace by jogging the jig to raise the stem units and then by using a metal comb to pull them out.

8) Quality Checks (2). Inspections are performed where the quality of the stem seal and the length of the stem leads are checked.

F. Mount Fabrication. In this sixth operation, an alloy assembly, a collector wire and an emitter wire are welded to a stem and the collector and emitter wires are soldered to their respective dots to form a mount assembly. The collector wire is 7 mils in diameter and the emitter wire, 5 mils. Both wires are of nickle-plated copper in order to achieve maximum heat dissipation at the welding and soldering junctures.

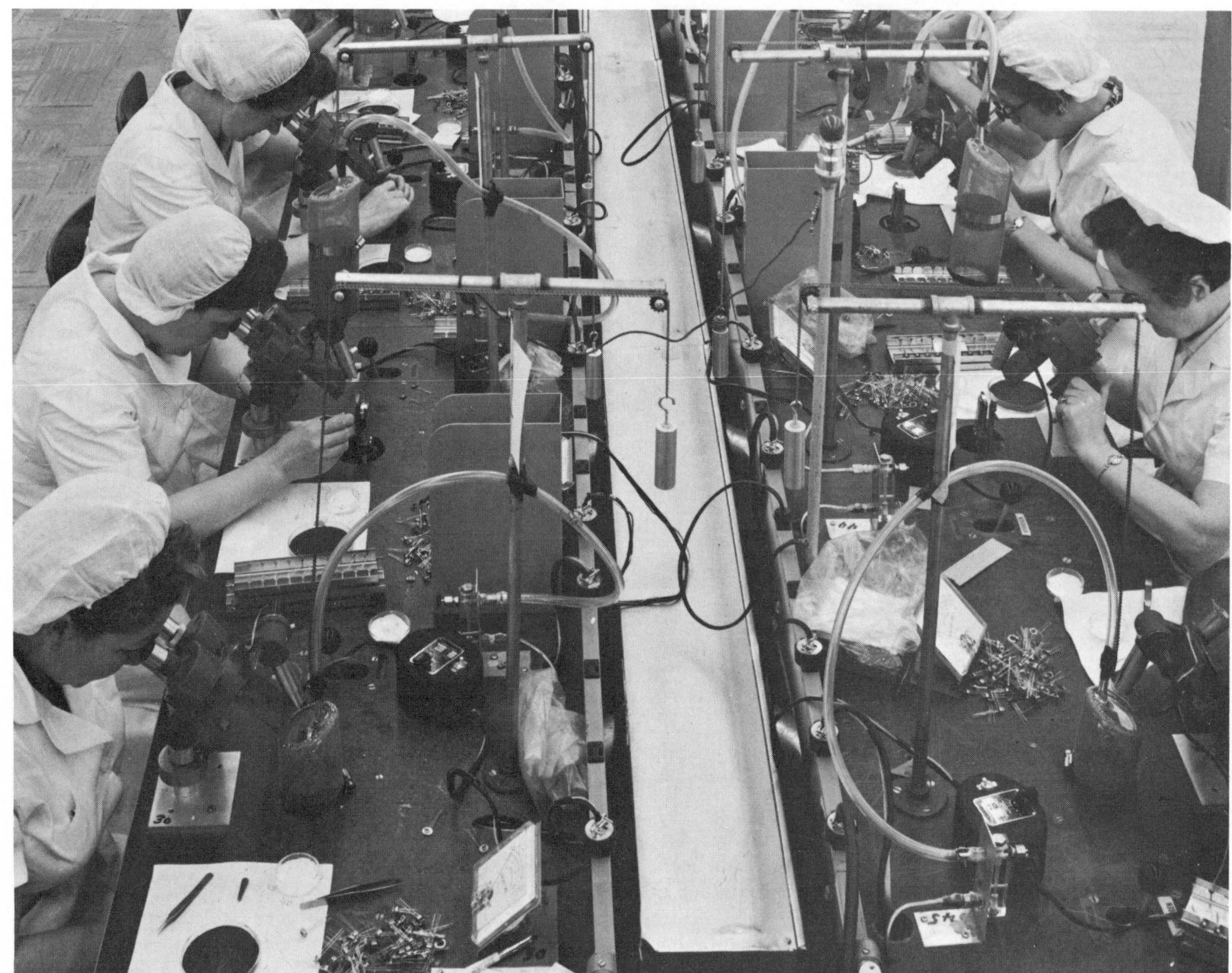

Photo, Courtesy General Electric Co.

F1. Transistors: Mounting; Note Etch Bar for Completed Units

1) Mount. An operator is seated in front of a 20-power microscope placed over a small spot welder. She picks up a stem from a pile with one hand, an alloy dot assembly with the other, and makes two welds to the stem. She then picks up a collector wire, welds one end to the stem and inserts the other into the collector dot. After doing the same operation for the emitter wire, she inserts the completed unit into a 12-position etch bar (see Mounting Job Analysis, Exhibit 2-D).

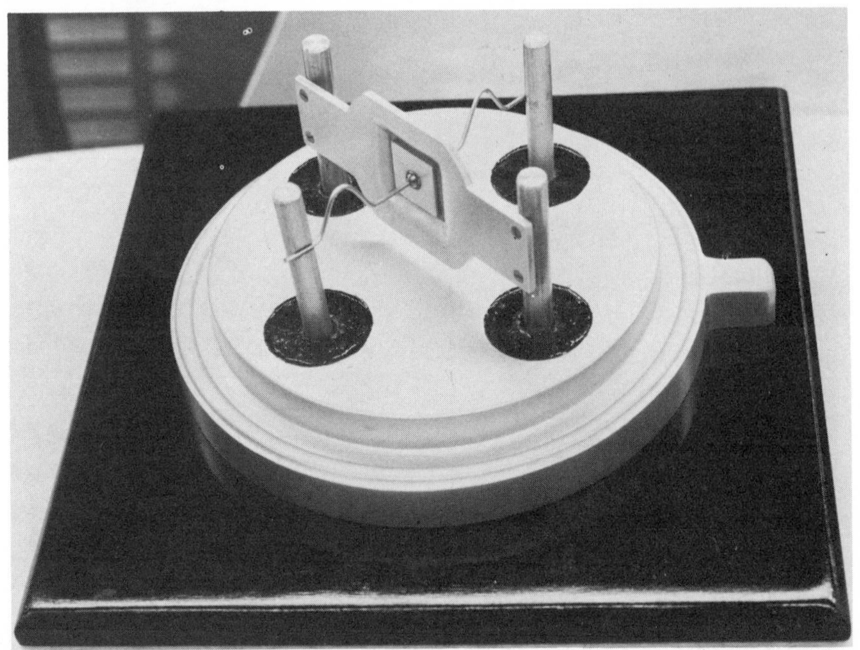

F1. Transistors: Close-up of Model of Mounted, but Uncapped, 2N404

F1. Transistors: Close-up of an Etch Bar with Twelve Mounted Units

Photo, Courtesy Radio Corporation of America

F2. Transistors: Hump-back Furnace to Solder Connector Wires to Dots

Photo, Courtesy Radio Corporation of America

G3. Transistors: Filling Cans with Molecular Sieve

2) Furnace. Six etch bars are loaded into a tray and placed on a conveyor belt leading to a "hump-back" gas solder furnace where the connector wires are soldered to the dots. The furnace has a reducing hydrogen atmosphere at 300° C.; the lighter-than-air hydrogen is contained in the raised heating section with the aid of a gas turnoff flame and an inert nitrogen curtain at each end. The etch bars are returned by conveyor to the loading operator cool enough to handle manually.

3) Etch. A third operator immerses five bars at a time in a 15 percent hydrogen peroxide bath solution at 70° for 14 minutes. The purpose here is to etch away a bit of the pellet surface and thereby form a clean bond between the pellet and the dot. After etching, the bars are rinsed in deionized water and placed in heated dryers.

4) Inspect. Welded samples from each mounting operator are checked hourly for strength of the weld joint. All units are also inspected for flaws or cracks which are revealed in the etching process.

5) Repair. An allowance of 4 percent is made for repairs.

6) Resolder. An allowance of 6 percent is made for resoldering.

7) Inspect Repairs. An allowance is made for inspecting repairs.

8) Etch Repairs. An allowance of 4 percent is made for two-minute re-etching of repairs.

9) Quality Checks (6). A check on each mounting operator is performed by selecting 10-unit random samples, expediting them through subsequent manufacturing processes, and then checking the ultimate quality of the welds. Other microscopic checks are also made on the tab weld acceptability and the quality of etching.

G. Hermetic Seal. In the seventh step, the mount assembly is hermetically sealed in a protective metal shell covering.

1) Dip. The mount assembly is dipped for three seconds in a highly concentrated peroxide dip to stabilize the surface. It is then dried immediately to stop any further etching. After this, it is baked in a 105° box furnace for 24 hours.

2) Load Cans. An operator loads cans into 100-unit trays (approximately 6 inches square) by dipping the tray into a bucket of metal cans or shells, skating off the excess, and seating those shells not in position.

3) Fill Sieve. Each tray is placed under a faucet dispensing a filler consisting of a special molecular sieve (grease-like mixture). This mixture serves to conduct potentially damaging heat from the mount to the shell during the transistor's operating life, and it also absorbs moisture prior to the unit's final hermetic seal. A gear pump automatically fills each shell to 95 percent full. The trays are then baked in another box furnace at 150° C. for four hours to dry out the sieve and shells of all moisture (which would disable the completed transistor).

Photo, Courtesy Radio Corporation of America

G4. Transistors: Dry Box for Can Sealing

4) Can Seal. The cans and mounted units are placed in a dry box where the humidity is no more than 50 parts water to a million parts air. The pressure in the box is maintained at about two pounds over the ambient atmospheric pressure in the plant in order to force any leakage outward rather than inward. The operator inserts her hands and arms into two long rubber gloves permanently attached to the front of the box. To her left are trays of shells, to her right are etch bars full of mounted units, and in front of her is a sealer. She places the can in the upper electrode of a can welder, the stem in the lower electrode, and then the machine automatically seals the two together under great pressure (see Can Sealing Job Analysis, Exhibit 2-E).

5) Inspect. The outside diameter of the sealed unit is checked on a go-no-go gauge to ensure that the shell doesn't protrude too far above the stem base.

6) Quality Checks (7). Periodic checks are made on the quality of the filler, the oven temperature, the dry box humidity, the seal welding operation, and the final sealed product. Finally, the completed unit is checked by way of a drop test (onto a metal block) and a centrifuge test.

H. Plating. In this eighth basic operation, the sealed units go through 18 different tank processes and finally emerge tin-plated. Each of the 18 process tanks costs about $1,200 and the necessary centrifuge dryers cost $800 each.

1) Finish. About 3,600 sealed units (16 square feet of surface area) are placed in a barrel (18 inches long and 8 inches in diameter). A 1-inch diameter solid copper contact bar goes through the center of the barrel and is connected to a melamine pinion drive gear at one end. The barrel is progressively lowered into the series of process tanks, each of which has a common worm gear designed to fit the barrel's pinion. Once in the tanks, the barrel is continuously rotated in the tanks' solution (the drive gear arrangement is used since fumes from the processes would corrode individual motors if they were mounted on the tanks). The units are finally dried in a 3-foot-high steam-heated centrifuge dryer.

Photo, Courtesy Radio Corporation of America

H1. Transistors: Plating Tanks

2) *Inspect.* The units are inspected for tin clinging to the leads, amount of tinplating, lead distortion, burnt marks, and leakage.

A "bomb test" is used for leakage. In this test, some 7,200 units are placed in a plastic basket, and lowered into a pressure unit containing water and a 1.6 percent detergent solution. They are then subjected to a pressure of 70 pounds per square inch for a period of 16 hours. The detergent works its way into any leaking units, rendering them inoperable.

3) *Replate.* Same as above for rejects.

4) *Reinspect.* For rejects only.

5) *Quality Check.* Final inspection.

I. Final Testing. The final operation consists of a series of tests, done mostly on automatic machines, to determine (*a*) the unacceptable or "fallout" units and (*b*) the classification of families by desired selections.

1) *Static Testing.* The transistors are loaded into an automatic machine that straightens the leads by hydraulic pressure, checks for mechanical aberrations, and then measures current leakage and saturation. The last check is done by noting the voltage at which breakdown occurs in current going from the collector to the base with the emitter open.

2) *Electrical Tests.* A sample is then run through an elevated temperature test and a pulse test set. The first checks the saturation current in an 80° oil bath while the second measures the switching time by hitting the transistor with a pulse, building up a charge on the base, and allowing it to dissipate.

3) *Detail Inspect.* A static testing machine checks a 22 percent sample.

Photo, Courtesy Sylvania Electric Products, Inc.

I. Transistors: Automatic Testing; This Unit Makes 8 Tests and Sorts into 16 Categories at a Rate of 5,000 per Hour

4) F α b. This is a frequency response check on a 4 percent sample basis.

5) Reruns. Charge for rerunning static test.

6) Relief Operator. Charge for relief operator 12 percent of the time.

The final step is to Quality Control for a life test up to 1,000 hours and any special checks specified and paid for by the customer. A sample is tested on a 1 percent cumulative basis—e.g., when the variations total 1 percent, the unit is rejected. It is then ready to be packaged and, hopefully, sold.

5. Mechanized Transistor Construction. The alternative to hand assembly is specialized automatic equipment. Most machinery is for the alloying-bonding-welding area or designed to perform a specific operation such as can welding.

One automatic line was developed by International Business Machines Corporation and Texas Instruments to alloy, bond, and weld NPN alloy junction transistors. The equipment consists of six multistation dial indexing units, with eight workspaces each, two temperature-controlled ovens, a welding machine, and belt conveyors. Each transistor is automatically tested after each step and rejected if defective; a total of 50 checks are performed.

Indexing turntables one through six assemble units for bonding. The steps by turntables are as follows: (1) the collector dot is loaded by a shuttle feed mechanism into a carbon boat, and the dot is positioned by vacuum applied to a hole in the boat bottom; (2) a germanium disk is dropped by vacuum probe and positioned by a funnel over the dot; (3) a funnel-shaped plug is inserted into the boat to guide and support the emitter dot which follows; (4) after alloying in a multizone oven, the plugs are removed and washer-shaped tabs are vacuum loaded onto the assembly; (5) a wire guide

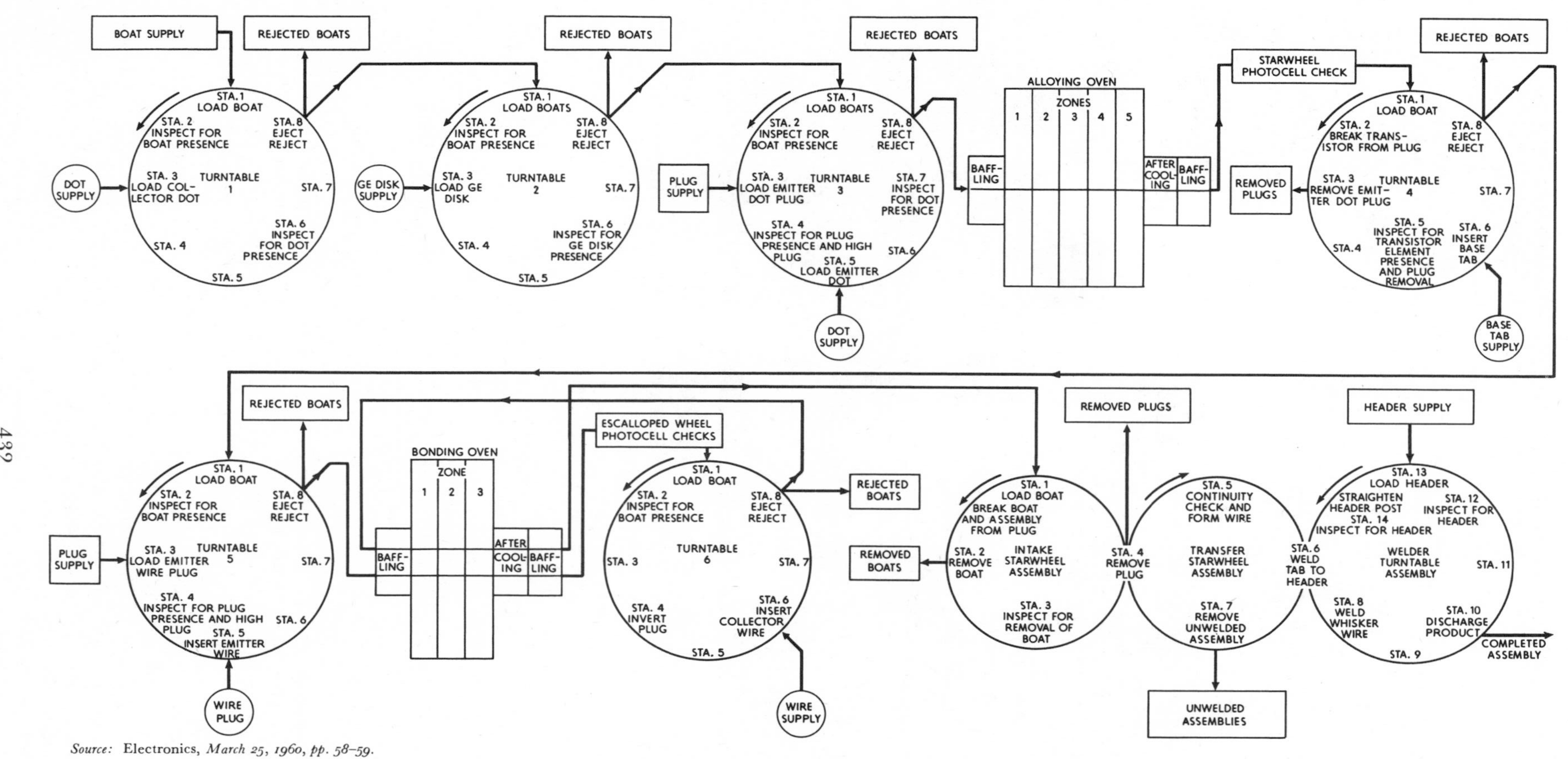

Source: Electronics, *March 25, 1960, pp. 58–59.*

5. Flow Diagram for the Automatic Assembly of an NPN Alloy Junction Transistor

Machine first assembles collector and emitter dots with the germanium disk and alloys them; it then assembles the base tab and the emitter leads and bonds them to the transistor; next, it bonds the collector lead; finally, it welds the base tab to the transistor mounting base and welds the emitter and collector wires to the mounting base posts. During these operations, machine performs 50 individual checking functions.

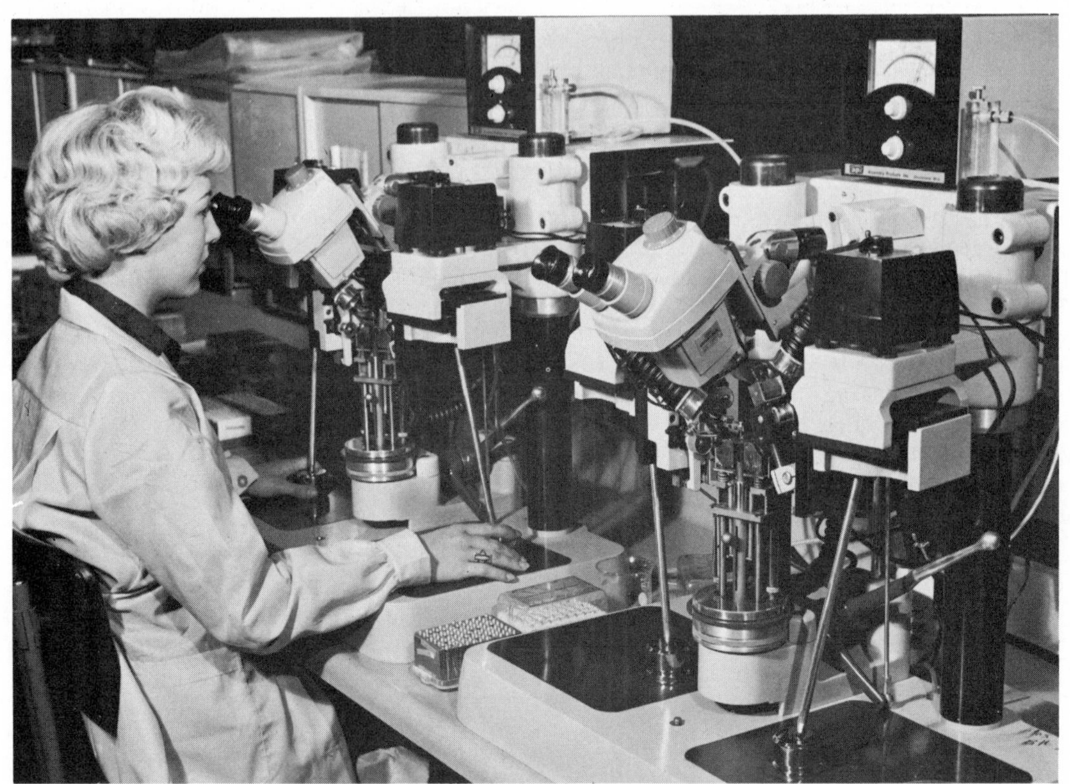

Photo, Courtesy Pacific Semiconductors, Inc.

5. Transistors: Bonding Machine for Silicon Transistors

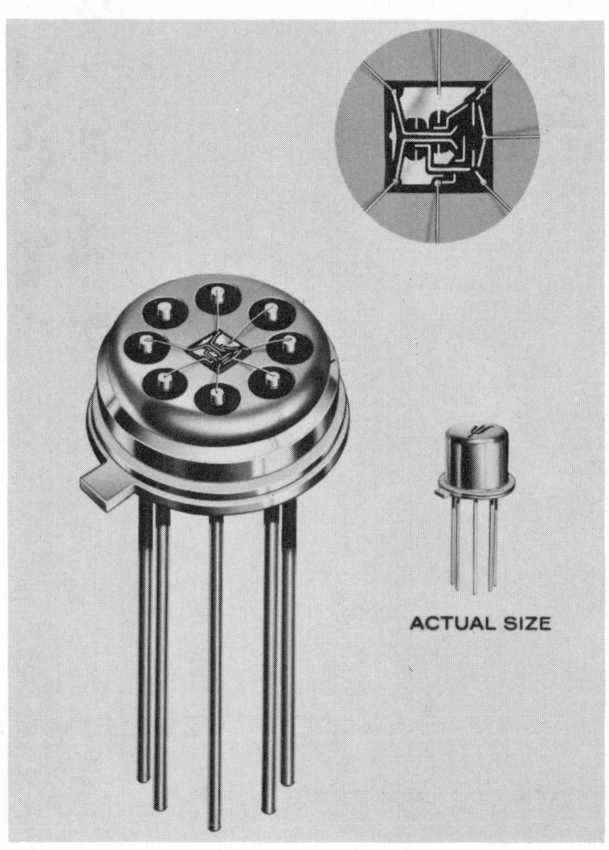

Photo, Courtesy Pacific Semiconductors, Inc.

5. Transistors: Integrated Circuit

plug is inserted and the emitter wire fed in; (6) after going through the bonding oven, the unit is inverted and a collector wire inserted. The unit is then recycled through the oven and ready for welding.

The welding machine has three dial indexing tables. At the first table, boats are removed and the assemblies lifted from the plugs. At the second, emitter and collector wires are formed, while at the third table the base is welded to the header, the emitter and collector wires welded to header leads, and the unit is discharged.

Output has steadily increased from 1,800 units per hour in early 1960 to 2,500 in January, 1961, and 3,600 in December, 1962. The yield is almost 90 percent.

About the same time, Philco developed a partly automated line to perform the same operation on the MADT. First an operator loads a tab onto the grip jaws of a stainless steel block "carrier." Then a germanium blank is manually soldered to the tab. Etching and plating of the emitter and collector areas are automatic as is attaching indium-dipped emitter and collector wires. After going through a rinsing machine, the units are ready for manual welding to stem leads and for manual capping in dry boxes. In 1959, the whole line required nine operators to produce 450 units per hour.

Many manufacturers have utilized the dial-indexing unit approach to mechanize one or two operations. For example, a manually loaded six-station machine has been developed to cap and seal 1,850 transistors per hour—the job done in Exhibit 2-E.

TELEVISION RECEIVING SETS

The manufacture of television receiving sets involves the assembly of approximately 1,000 components to a metal base and the insertion of the chassis and speaker into a cabinet. The chassis as-

Photo, Courtesy Westinghouse Electric Corp.

1. Television Sets: Tuner Subassembly Line

sembly consists of mechanical operations whereby large parts are attached to the chassis and hand operations whereby wire, resistors, and condensers are crimped and soldered to terminals. The equipment consists of simple hand tools such as crimping pliers, soldering irons, air gun nut runners and screwdrivers. Fixtures are used whenever possible, particularly in the mechanical operations.

Major components are frequently prepared on separate subassembly lines prior to delivery to the main lines for installation. Such operations generally include tuner assembly and the preparation of the chassis and small parts. The speaker, deflection and focus coils, the transformer and, in some cases, tuners are usually purchased from outside suppliers.

1. Tuner Assembly. The tuner is a subassembly unit which selects the signal to be passed through the receiver circuits depending upon the channel selected. The assembly of a tuner consists of positioning various components, tube sockets, and a rotary switch, on a small metal frame or chassis and making the necessary wire connections. Tubes are then inserted in the sockets and the tuner is tested and electrically aligned.

2. Chassis Preparation. The main chassis base, which is made of cadmium-plated steel, is often purchased already formed, punched, and plated from outside suppliers; however, some of the larger television manufacturers have their own chassis fabricating plants.

Fabrication requires expensive plating equipment as well as heavy presses and dies to punch the chassis from strip steel. Before being sent to the main chassis assembly line, the tube sockets, brackets, terminal boards, and other components to which wire connections are to be made are riveted or bolted to the base.

3. Wire, Resistor, and Capacitor Preparation. Wire is cut and stripped to size on automatic wire-cutting machines. Resistor and capacitor leads and "spaghetti," or insulating sleeving, are cut to length by hand with the aid of measuring jigs and cutting pliers.

On the main chassis assembly line all components necessary to complete the receivers' electrical circuits, with the exception of the speaker, are connected to the base chassis. The cathode ray picture tube, subassembly units, cut wire, resistors, capacitors, and other purchased parts such as the transformer and radio tubes are delivered to appropriate work positions.

4. Mechanical and Wiring Operations. The assembly operations on a chassis line are divided into two groups: (*a*) mechanical and (*b*) wiring. In the mechanical end the radio tubes are plugged into sockets, and parts such as transformers are bolted to the chassis with air gun nut runners and screwdrivers. Usually three to 10 mechanical positions start a line. In the wiring operations, wire, resistor leads, and capacitor leads are crimped to terminals and to tube socket lugs and then soldered. Above each girl's work position, there may be a schematic drawing showing the wire connections and/or solder joints she is supposed to complete.

There is considerable variation among receiver manufacturers as to the physical setup, number of workers, and work cycles. The line may be a moving conveyor staffed with 30 to over 100 workers, or it may be a "push-along" line with the chassis mounted on a dolly and pushed by hand from one operator to the next. A small-volume producer might have 35 or 40 operators and an output of 80 to 90 units per day. A large volume producer might have several assembly lines staffed with 80 to 100 workers and an output of 360 to 375 units a day from each.

Time Allowance for a Typical Crimping Operation in a Television Receiver Assembly Line

Part	*Operation*	*Time*
Resistor R109	Crimp to wire X102	.075
Capacitor C110	Crimp to wire X102	.075
	Crimp to lead G13	.075
Capacitor C185	Crimp to lead G13	.075
Black wire No. 83 / Red-Black } twisted	Crimp to power transformer	.150
Green wire No. 51	Crimp to lead TB17	.075
White wire No. 92	Crimp to lead R12	.075
Black wire No. 805	Crimp to lead R12	.075
Resistor R132	Crimp to lead R12	.075

The work cycle for each position on the assembly line varies between 1 minute on large lines staffed with 80 to 100 workers and 4 to 4½ minutes on small lines with 35 to 40 workers. The cycle is determined by adding the standard time allowances for each operation at a station. Usually, the shorter cycle is more efficient because each operator is required to memorize fewer work steps. The above table shows the time allowance for a single operation on an assembly line operating on a ¾-minute cycle.

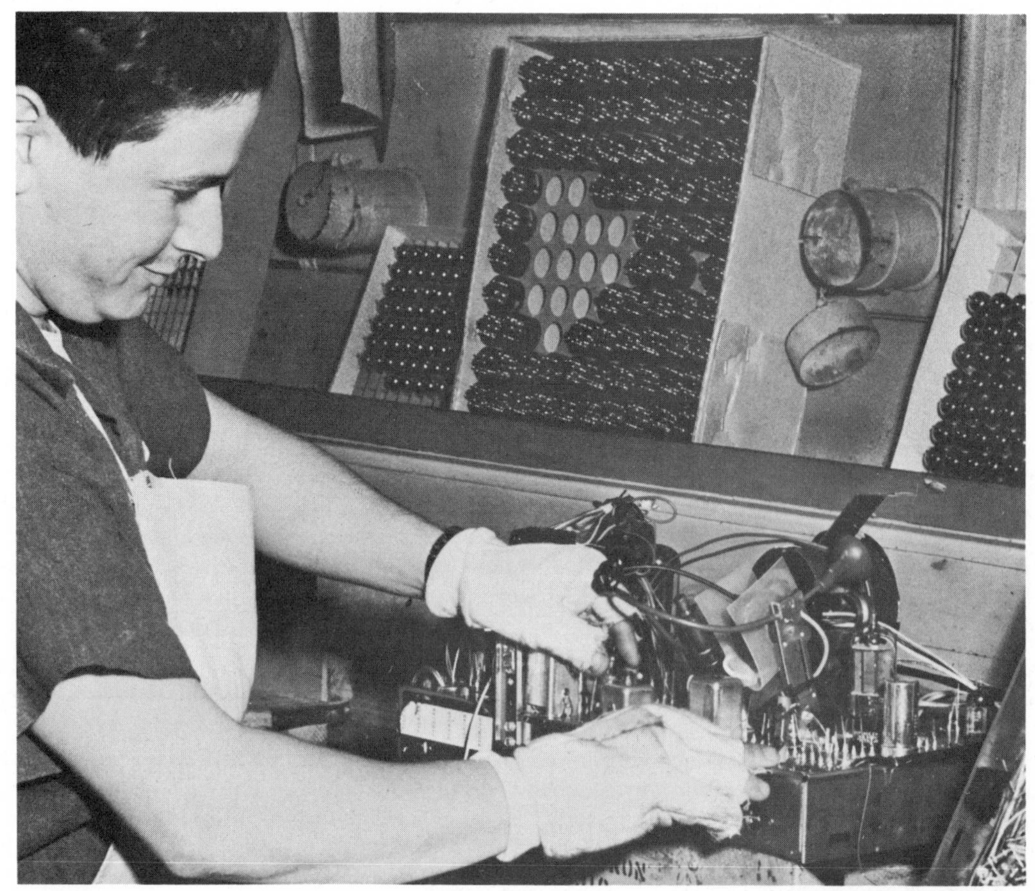

Photo, Courtesy Zenith Radio Corp.

4. Television Sets: Inserting Tubes

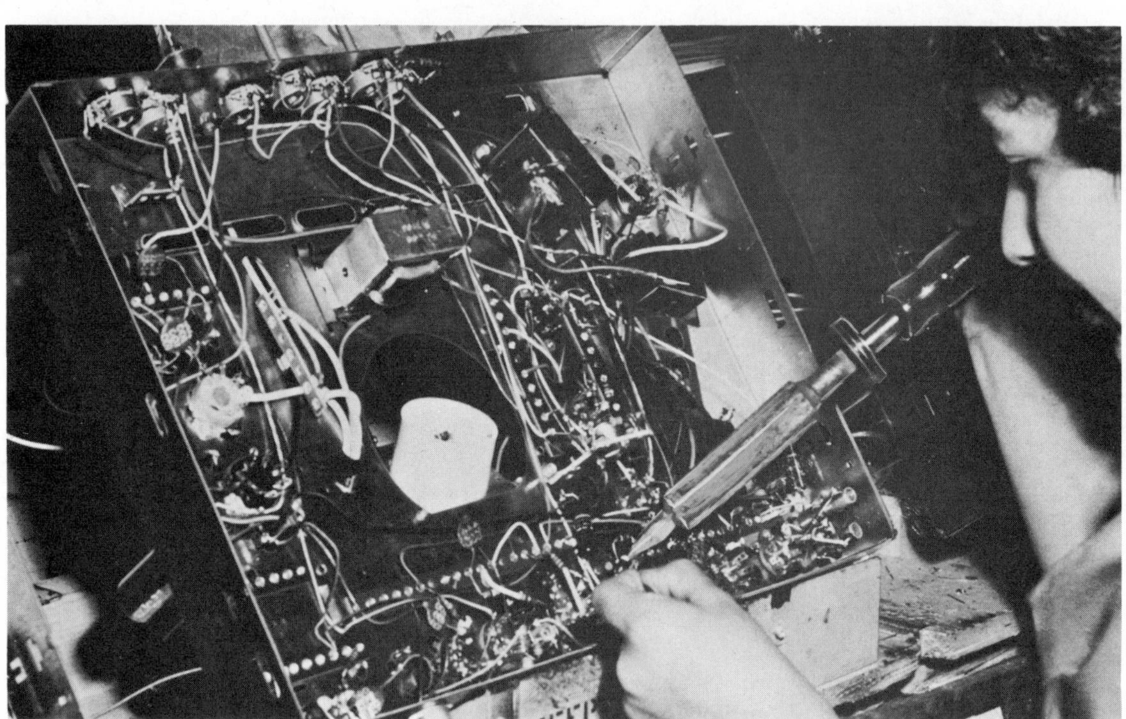

Photo, Courtesy Zenith Radio Corp.

4. Television Sets: Soldering Connections

Previous wiring experience greatly influences the length of the learning curve. An experienced girl can learn her cycle of operations and reach a standard production rate in under five days, but an inexperienced operator may require one to four weeks. Typically a group leader supervises every dozen operators.

Photo, Courtesy Westinghouse Electric Corp.

5. Television Sets: Final Chassis Inspection

5. Preliminary Inspection. Inspection is generally the last operation. A visual inspection determines if there are any broken parts, unsoldered connections, poor solder joints, or unconnected leads. Then a "hot check" is made using a voltmeter to determine whether the wires have been connected to the proper terminals or lugs and whether the proper components have been used. After inspection, the chassis is placed on a conveyor which carries it to the alignment and deflection test stations.

6. Alignment. Necessary circuit adjustments are made to assure proper receiver operation. An oscillation-generated signal is run through the receiver and appears as a curve on an oscilloscope. The operator adjusts the circuit until a predetermined pattern appears.

7. Deflection Test. This is the final test before set assembly. With the aid of an oscilloscope, the tester adjusts the set until a test picture is received with the desired clarity and contrast, horizontal and vertical linearity, and distortion. In addition, the operator strikes the tuner chassis with a rubber mallet; if the picture quivers or disappears, the set is rejected.

8. Set Assembly. In the set assembly area, television receiver chassis are placed in cabinets with the speaker and other units of the instrument (i.e., radio, phonograph). About 10 or 12 male operators can assemble approximately 400 table model sets in a day. Since cabinets are generally purchased from outside suppliers, the cabinets' original shipping cartons are used to ship completed television sets to customers.

9. Final Test. The set is given audio and video performance tests, and final tuning adjustments are made before the back plate is put on and the unit sent to the shipping area for polishing and packing.

TECHNOLOGICAL DEVELOPMENTS

By 1963, many of the conventional manual methods and procedures which had previously been used in the assembly of television receivers and other similar high-volume electronic equipments and devices were being mechanized and automated. The development of "printed circuit" techniques in the early 1950's served to introduce such mechanization as automatic component insertion, dip soldering, and automated circuit testing.

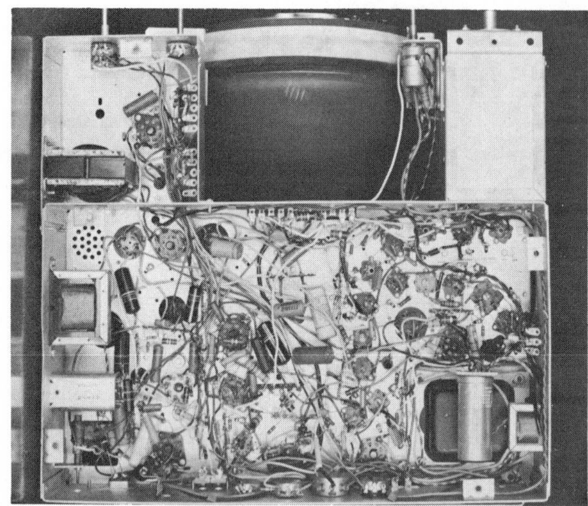

Photos, Courtesy Radio Corporation of America and Emerson Radio Company

1. Television Sets: Hand-wired Set (left); Printed Circuit (right)

1. Printed Circuits. In a printed circuit, the complex wiring portion of the circuit is "printed" (usually by photoetching) in silver or copper on an insulated base which is then pierced and the various circuit components are plugged or soldered in place. Such a circuit not only supplies the wiring and a component mounting structure, but also may eliminate passive components and wire crimping and soldering. Controlled amounts of resistance and capacitance may be "printed in" by varying the thickness and spacing of the conductor.

Automatic machines are available to drill the holes for leads, terminals, and plug-in components. One $10,000 machine can follow a paper tape program and punch 60 boards an hour. Tape preparation requires four hours and changing tapes six minutes.

2. Automatic Component Insertion. The next step is a machine to insert components into the holes in the boards. One $3,000 unit feeds, cuts, forms, inserts, and clinches some 800 components per hour including set-up, change-over and loading time. The machines may be hooked up in series with a conveyor if the components are numerous or require reindexing the boards.

3. Dip Soldering. Dip soldering is a mechanized technique for wiring printed circuit boards. In conventional chassis assembly, the wire and resistor and capacitor leads are crimped and soldered by hand to terminals or lugs on the metal chassis base. In dip solder assembly, the terminals or lugs are replaced by hollow metal rivets or printed wiring extending out from the bottom surface of the printed boards. The wire and resistor leads are placed into these rivets or holes from above. The bottom surface of the board is then dipped in a bath of solder, and all connections are made simultaneously. The operator's skill is extremely important in preventing "bridging" (making unwanted connections), and "icicling" (formation of solder icicles).

In continuous dip soldering, the bottom of the printed wiring board is carried through molten hot solder pumped upward through an orifice to form a hollow wave of molten metal whose motion opposes that of the circuit panel on the conveyor. Solder flow, volume, temperature, and contact time are precisely controlled to prevent "icicling" and "bridging"; little or no touch-up time is normally required.

4. *Automatic Testing.* Automatic testing of printed circuit boards involves two functions—electrical inspection and electrical evaluation. Electrical inspection is assuring that the assembly has the proper connection and that its components are within prescribed tolerances. Electrical evaluation is determining the compliance with design specifications by measuring, recording, and analyzing the effects of static and dynamic circuit operations.

One example is the automatic circuit tester that can perform up to 400 separate tests on up to 100 different boards at 3 minutes a board, compared to 45 minutes for a manual test series.

EXHIBIT 1

Times, Yields, and Costs for Each Step in Making a Typical Alloy Junction Transistor, 1962

The table below lists the approximate materials, labor, and overhead costs of one company making an alloy juntion transistor, type 2N404. The yield is based on 100 percent good units leaving each processing stage; any fallout are charged to the appropriate process areas. The total cost (materials, labor, and overhead) for one area becomes the gross materials cost of the next; dividing by the beginning yield and allowing for any scrap credits gives the net materials cost. Unless the process is denoted with an (m), all operators are female and paid straight time at $1.92 per hour. Male operators receive $2.42 an hour.

I. Basic Crystal Manufacture:

Pure refined germanium costs $314.48 per kilogram in 1962. There are five kilograms per 100 linear inches of bar, making the cost $15.72 per linear inch. With a 2 percent etching loss and a 56 percent yield the cost is $2,858.62 per 100 inches, less scrap credit of $1,090.30 for a net of $1,768.32.

Antimony dope is made for a cost of $565.80 per kilogram. Some 3.4 grams are used per 100 inches of germanium bar, so the cost is $1.92 per 100 inches. With a 2 percent scrap loss and a 56 percent yield the cost is $3.50 per 100 inches.

Process	Efficiency (Percent)	Time (Hours/100 Inches)	Yield (Percent)	Cost (Dollars)
Material:				
germanium.			56%	$1,768.32
antimony			56	3.50
				$1,771.82
A. Schedule, add dope.	70%	2.31	56	7.93
B. Etch bars (m).	70	2.30	56	9.99
C. Grow crystals.	70	2.31	56	7.93
D. Cut into segments	70	1.40	56	6.07
E. Resistivity check.	70	1.59	66	4.63
F. Etch ends (m).	70	.86	80	2.05
G. Lineage check.	70	.16	80	.38
H. Face etch.	70	1.00	100	1.92
I. Mounting (m)	70	1.11	100	2.69
J. Quality checks (2)	75	2.21	100	4.22
Total Labor		15.25		$ 47.81
Overhead (1760%)				841.45
Total crystal cost per 100 inches				$2,661.08

Exhibit 1 (continued)

II. Wafer Fabrication:

There are 2.08 inches of crystal per 100 wafers, or $26.61 x 2.08 = $55.35 material cost per 100 wafers. With an 83 percent yield the cost is $66.52 less a scrap credit of $12.52 for a net of $54.00.

Process	Efficiency (Percent)	Time (Hours/100 Wafers)	Yield (Percent)	Cost (Dollars)
Material:			83%	$ 54.00
A. Cut wafers (m)	85%	.75	83	2.18
B. Gauging	85	.16	89	.35
C. Lapping	85	1.40	90	2.98
D. Gauging	85	.16	96	.33
E. Sheffield gauging	85	.54	97	1.08
F. Quality checks (3)	75	.35	100	.67
Total Labor		$3.36		$ 7.59
Overhead (960%)				72.87
Total.				$134.46

III. Pellet Fabrication:

There are 4.35 wafers per 1,000 pellets or $1.3446 x 4.35 = $5.85, material cost per 1,000 pellets. With 2 percent scrap and an 82 percent yield, the cost is $7.30 per 1,000.

Process	Efficiency (Percent)	Time (Hours/100 Pellets)	Yield (Percent)	Cost (Dollars)
Material:			82%	$ 7.30
A. Load scriber	85%	.03	82	.06
B. Ultrasonic crack	85	-	-	-
C. Wash	85	.01	82	.02
D. Sieve	85	.01	82	.02
E. Etch	85	.09	82	.21
F. Loading, unloading	85	.04	85	.08
G. Gauging	85	.16	85	.36
H. Spot check	85	.05	85	.12
I. Count	85	.05	85	.12
J. Re-etch	90	.03	85	.08
K. Sort	90	.11	85	.25
L. Quality checks (2)	75	.13	100	.25
Total Labor		.71		$ 1.57
Overhead (629%)				9.86
Total				$18.73

Exhibit 1 (continued)

IV. Alloy Process:

In alloying, the pellets and dots are alloyed to the tabs; the dots and tabs are brought outside. The ingredient costs of alloying are (per thousand pellets):

	Raw Cost	Scrap/Loss	Yield	Net Cost
Pellet	$18.73	2%	89%	$21.53
Tab.	1.84	2	89	2.11
Collector Dot	2.11	16	89	2.81
Emitter Dot	.36	19	89	.50
				$26.95

With a $6.44 scrap allowance, the final material cost is $20.51.

Process	Efficiency (Percent)	Time (Hours/100 Pellets)	Yield (Percent)	Cost (Dollars)
Material:			89%	$20.51
A. Load tab	65%	.29	89	.63
B. Load pellets.	85	.34	89	.73
C. Transfer collector washer . . .	55	.34	89	.75
D. Load collector dot.	55	.34	89	.75
E. Trasfer emitter washer	55	.34	89	.75
F. Load emitter dot.	85	.34	89	.73
G. Inspect	85	.59	89	1.27
H. Relief operator.	65	.11	100	.21
I. Tests	100	.21	100	.38
J. Record	100	.06	100	.10
K. Salvage	100	.15	100	.27
L. Etch	100	.34	100	.63
M. Quality checks (2)	75	.07	100	.10
Total Labor				$ 7.32
Overhead (319%)				23.34
Total.				$57.61

V. Raw Stem Fabrication:

The making of the raw stems can be done previously or simultaneously with alloying. The "raw materials" are the header, four black glass preform beads, three long-stem leads, and one dummy lead to hold the tab in place and keep it from vibrating. The components and costs are as follows:

Exhibit 1 (continued)

	Raw Cost (Each)	Scrap Loss	Yield	Net Cost
Header	$7.05	3%	97%	$ 7.50
Preforms (4)	1.08	5	97	4.69
Stem leads (3)	1.04	5	97	3.39
Dummy leads	.35	5	97	.38
Amortization of rig	4.55	-	-	4.55
				$20.51

Process	Efficiency (Percent)	Time (Hours/1,000 Stems)	Yield (Percent)	Cost (Dollars)
A. Load header	90%	.47	97%	$ .92
B. Stamping	95	.65	97	1.29
C. Load preforms	90	.11	97	.21
D. Load leads.	85	2.51	97	4.99
E. Load dummy lead	90	1.04	97	2.07
F. Load furnace	85	.10	97	.21
G. Unload furnace	85	.23	97	.46
H. Quality checks	75	.08	100	.15
Total Labor		5.19		$10.30
Overhead (176%)				18.12
Total				$48.93

VI. Mount Fabrication:

Mounting is the most critical of all the operations. The "raw" material consists of the alloy pellet, the raw stem and emitter and collector wires. The components and costs are as follows:

	Raw Cost	Scrap Loss	Yield	Net Cost
Alloy Pellet	$57.61	1%	94	$61.94
Stem	48.93	1	94	52.61
Emitter Connector Wire.	.46	25	96	.64
Collector Connector Wire.	.93	25	96	.71
				$115.90

Exhibit 1 (continued)

Process	Efficiency (Percent)	Time (Hours/1,000 Stems)	Yield (Percent)	Cost (Dollars)
A. Mount	84%	7.99	94%	$ 16.30
B. Furnace.	87	.38	96	.75
C. Etch	85	.76	96	1.52
D. Inspect	90	2.22	96	4.47
E. Repair	84	.15	98	.31
F. Resolder	87	.02	99	.04
G. Inspect repairs.	90	.13	99	.25
H. Etch repairs.	85	.04	100	.08
I. Quality checks (6)	75	.50	100	.96
Total Labor		11.69		$ 24.68
Overhead (267%)				65.89
Total.				$206.47

VII. Hermetic Seal:

In this operation, mounted stems are sealed to a protective covering shell or can on a can welder located within a dry box (see picture, Exhibit ____). A molecular sieve (a grease-like mixture which is a poor electrical conductor) costing $7.42 a pound, is poured into the inside of the can to conduct heat from the connector wires and dots to the shell. The raw material costs are as follows:

	Raw Cost	Scrap Loss	Yield	Net Cost
Mounts	$206.47	-	99%	$208.55
Shell.	3.45	-	95	3.63
Sieve.	2.82	17%	95	3.55
				$215.73

Process	Efficiency (Percent)	Time (Hours/1,000 Units)	Yield (Percent)	Cost (Dollars)
A. Dip.	87%	.44	99%	$ .84
B. Load cans	90	.20	99	.38
C. Fill sieve.	87	.57	95	1.15
D. Can seal	78	5.21	99	10.09
E. Inspect	90	.20	100	.38
F. Quality checks (7)	75	.69	100	1.33
Total Labor		7.31		$ 14.17
Overhead (181%)				25.64
Total.				$255.54

Exhibit 1 (continued)

VIII. Plating:

The only raw material charged is the sealed units, which with a 99 percent yield cost $258.12.

Process	Efficiency (Percent)	Time (Hours/1,000 Units)	Yield (Percent)	Cost (Dollars)
A. Finish	65%	.18	99%	$ .46
B. Inspect.	85	.47	99	.92
C. Replate	85	.02	100	.05
D. Reinspect.	85	.09	100	.17
E. Quality check	75	.04	100	.08
Total		.80		$ 1.68
Overhead (317%)				5.23
Total.				$265.03

IX. Final Testing:

The yield on plated units reaching final test is 87 percent, making the unit cost $304.63.

Process	Efficiency (Percent)	Time (Hours/1,000 Units)	Yield (Percent)	Cost (Dollars)
A. Static testing.	65%	.43	87%	$ .94
B. Electrical tests.	90	.25	99	.50
C. Detail inspect	90	.10	100	.19
D. F & B	90	.02	100	.04
E. Re-runs.	90	.17	100	.33
F. Relief operator	90	.06	100	.11
Total		1.03		$ 2.11
Overhead (1200%)				25.32
Total.				$332.06

Source: Consolidated Electric, Inc.

EXHIBIT 2-A

Transfer Washers and Unloading Furnace Job Analysis--New Method

Left-Hand Analysis	Right-Hand Analysis	Time
1. Pick up boat and assemble to fixture.	1. Pick up boat and assemble to fixture.	.0238
	2. Pick up vacuum transfer tool, transfer washers, lay aside tool.	.0481
3. Inspect seat washers by tapping with tweezers. Correct as required, laying aside boat.		.0766 Insp. .1126 Corr. .0530 Insp. .0736 Corr.
4. Rotate stock of finished boats, removing units with missing dots and reassembling.		
	5. Pick up boats from furnace belt and place in supply stock.	3.00 Min./Hr. allowed in numerator minutes.

Workplace Layout

$$\frac{.3877}{60 \text{ units}}$$

Furnace Belt

Vacuum Transfer Tool

Finished Work

Supply of Work

Remarks: Relief operator for Furnace unloading. Rate applies to emitter a collector washers. 60 units/boat.

Select Time (min.) .0065

Tools and Equipment: Vacuum Transfer Tool, Tweezers.

Fatigue	5%
Delays	5%
Personal	-%
Total	10%

Base Time (min.)	
Numerator (min.)	50.75
Prod./Oper./Hr.	7800

Source: Consolidated Electric, Inc.

EXHIBIT 2-B

Washer Loading Job Analysis--Old Method

Left-Hand Analysis	Right-Hand Analysis	Time
	1. Shift tweezers and reach to fully reloaded boat.	
2. Reach to a new jig.	2. Grasp boat and place aside.	
3. Grasp jig and move to work area.	3. Unshift tweezers.	.0009
	4. Reach to washer with tweezers.	
	5. Preposition washer for correct side up.	
	6. Grasp washer and move to jig.	
	7. Align washer to hole in jig and insert.	
	8. Reseat washer in jig when necessary.	
	9. Continue filling 30 positions.	.0282

	Time
Select time (min.)	.0291
Dump net washers	.0005
2% select time material rejects.	.0006
Turnover jigs.	.0014
Straighten tabs in jigs.	.0028
Base Time (min.)	.0344
Numerator (min.)	51
Prod./Oper./Hr. 1480	

Tools and Equipment:
Dazor, Tweezers, rubber mat.

Fatigue	5%
Delays	5%
Personal	5%
Total	15%

Workplace Layout

Dazor Glass

Washers

Source: Consolidated Electric, Inc.

EXHIBIT 2-C

Unloading Washers and Furnace Job Analysis--Old Method

Left-Hand Analysis	Right-Hand Analysis	Time
	1. Lay aside tweezers, pick up stack of six finished boats and position aside. Pick up next six boats from furnace and move to work area. Pick up and position tweezers.	.0004
2. Pick up boat with washers in it; lay aside boat when empty.	2. Hold tweezers	.0010
3. Assist right hand.	3. Remove washers with tweezers.	.0204
	(Pick up one, move to second, grasp first and second; move to third; regrasp first, second, and third washer; and 3 washers aside.)	
	Select Time (min.)	.0218
	Place washers in box	.0001

Allowance	
Fatigue	5%
Delays	5%
Personal	5%
Total	15%

Base Time (min.)		.0219
Numerator (min.)		57
Prod./Oper./Hr.	2340	

Source: Consolidated Electric, Inc.

EXHIBIT 2-D

Mounting Job Analysis

	Left-Hand Analysis		Right-Hand Analysis	Time
1.	Pick up stem from random pile, grasp one unit and preposition it end for end. Move to electrode, rotate unit (use tab on unit to determine the right way).	1.	Take unit just completed, move to etch bar and insert into bar. After releasing unit, reach to tab tray while prepositioning tweezers.	.0273
2.	Hold stem.	2.	Move with tweezers to dot assemblies. Scatter units 50 percent of time, select one, grasp unit with tweezers.	
3.	Lower head to microscope and focus eyes in electrode.	3.	Move towards electrode.	
4.	Approach electrode with stem.	4.	Assemble tab to two little leads on stem.	
5.	Align stem and dot assembly to electrode. Rotate unit, align stem and dot assembly for the second weld. Make second weld and disassemble stem from electrode.	5.	Weld and disassemble unit from electrode.	.0952
6.	Move head away from microscope.	6.	Move to pick up one connector and select one unit. Approach and scatter connectors on a 10 percent basis, grasp one, lower head to microscope, approach electrode with a connector.	
7.	Approach and assemble stem to electrode.	7.	Approach and assemble connector to stem, weld connector.	
8.	Disassemble stem from electrode and reposition it.	8.	Disassemble tweezers from connector, approach and assemble tweezers to connector, grasp connector, push into dot.	

Exhibit 2-D (continued)

Left-Hand Analysis	Right-Hand Analysis	Time
9. Move head from microscope and reposition stem.	9. Release tweezers and disassemble from unit.	
Repeat for Second Connector (6-9)		
10. Release stem.	10. Move to grasp stem, grasp it.	.2022

Workplace Layout

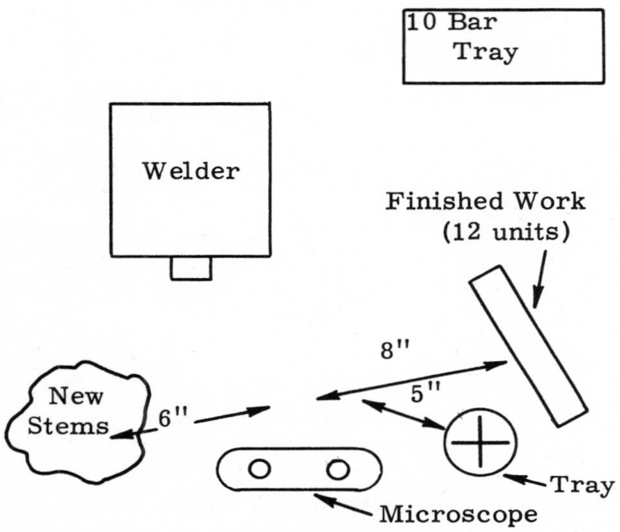

Source: Consolidated Electric, Inc.

Remarks: Single stage mounting
Double weld of tab

Tools and Equipment:
Microscope
Welder
Tweezers, Universal Bars
4 partition rubber parts tray

Fatigue	5%
Delays	5%
Personal	5%
Total	15%

Select Time (min.)		.3247
Mat'l Hand and Misc. Allow's		
Supply stems connectors, dots		.0029
Put aside and work in universal base		.0033
Welder maintenance		.0032
Paper work		.0010
2% material rejects		.0065
Base Time (min.)		3416
Numerator (min.)		51
Prod./Oper./Hr.	149	

EXHIBIT 2-E

Can Sealing Job Analysis

Left-Hand Analysis	Right-Hand Analysis	Time
1. Hold 10 units in etch bar in left hand.	1. Take out finished unit with tweezers from chuck. Lay aside by drop delivery. Move to grasp new unit from bar in left hand. Grasp unit, disassemble from bar and move to electrode.	
	2. Assemble stem into lower electrode. Release unit from electrode and move to grasp shell.	
	3. Grasp can from tray with tweezers, disassemble and move to upper electrode.	
	4. Assemble can to upper electrode, vacuum hold.	
5. Move to button and press.	5. Move to button and press.	
6. Machine cycle.	6. Machine cycle.	

Workplace Layout

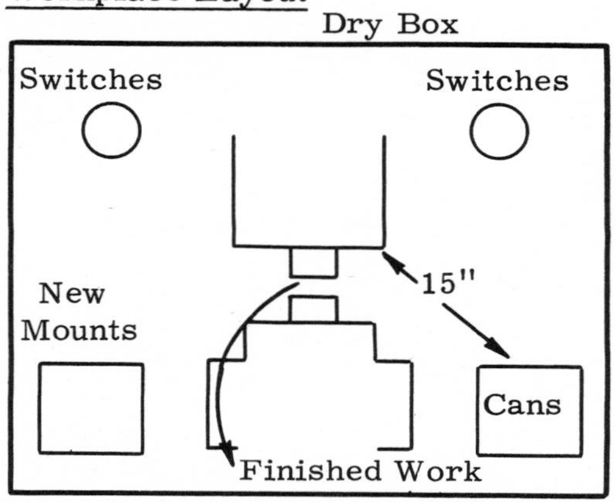

Tools and Equipment:
Can Welder

Fatigue	10%
Delays	5%
Personal	5%
Total	20%

Select time (min.)		.1879
Change cans		.0020
Finish work (morning)		.0020
Putting mounts in		.0020
Writing tickets		.0010
Base Time (min.)		1949
Numerator (min.)		48
Prod./Oper./Hr.	246	

Source: Consolidated Electric, Inc.

EXHIBIT 3

Selected Approximate Equipment Investments for Transistor Manufacture, 1962

I.	Basic Crystal Manufacture:	
	a) Double tube alloy furnace	$ 9,000
II.	Wafer Fabrication:	
	a) Wafer slicer	6,700
	b) Wafer lapper	2,000
	c) Wafer gauge	650
III.	Pellet Fabrication:	
	a) Wafer scriber	5,000
	b) Automatic wafer etcher	16,500
	c) Automatic pellet gauger	10,500
	d) Dust-free room for gauger	1,700
	e) Pellet scales (counting)	995
	f) Pellet vibrating feeder	520
IV.	Alloy Process:	
	a) Vacuum transfer tool	1,000
	b) Squeeze plate dot loader	950
	c) Furnace	11,000
V.	Raw Stem Fabrication:	
	a) Stem head loader and jigs	250
	b) Stem-making furnace	38,000
VI.	Mount fabrication:	
	a) Welder	650
	b) Microscope	345
	c) Gas solder furnace	11,200
	d) Etch bath	4,600
	e) Deionized water rinse	10,250
VII.	Hermetic Seal:	
	a) Peroxide dip	1,000
	b) Can baking oven	800
	c) Sieve mixing system	3,400
	d) Sieve dispenser	900
	e) Pre-seal bake oven	1,900
VIII.	Plating:	
	a) Each tank (18)	1,200
	b) Each dryer	800
	c) Bomb test	600
IX.	Final Testing:	
	a) Static tester	25,000
	b) Pulse and elevated temp.	5,700
	c) Detail inspect.	2,700
	d) F α B test	2,700

Source: Various equipment companies and Consolidated Electric, Inc.

EXHIBIT 4

A. Learning Curve for New and Experienced Operators

Weeks	Job Classification 2	3	4	5	6	8	10	12	14	16
1	78%	68%	63%	61%	58%	53%	48%	43%	38%	33%
2	100	87	76	72	68	63	57	51	45	40
3		100	90	84	77	71	65	59	53	47
4			100	94	86	78	73	66	60	54
5				100	94	85	79	73	67	60
6					100	91	84	79	73	66
7						96	89	84	78	72
8						100	94	89	93	77
9							98	93	87	81
10							100	96	91	85
11								99	94	89
12								100	97	92
13									99	95
14									100	97
15										99
16										100

If an experienced operator is shifted to another job, the number of learning curve weeks should be reduced by the following percentages:

FROM: \ TO:	A	B	C	D
A	50	40	30	20
B	40	30	20	10
C	30	20	10	0
D	20	10	0	0

The A-D categories represent degrees of transferrable manual dexterity. Going from a B job to one classed as 16-A means the curve is reduced to 9.6 or 10 weeks and starts at 85 percent.

Exhibit 4 (continued)

B. Selected Job Classifications

I. Basic Crystal:

Growing 8-D
Cut into segments 1-D
Testing 8-C
Etching 2-D
Mounting 1-D

II. Wafer Fabrication:

Slicing 5-D
Lapping 4-D

III. Pellet Fabrication:

Etching Wafer Pellets 6-C
Scribing 4-C
Clean, sieve 1-D
Sort 1-D
Gauge 10-B

IV. Alloy:

Load tabs 6-D
Pellet to tab 8-D
Multiple dot load 6-D
Misc. etch 4-D

V. Raw Stem Fabrication:

Load headers 4-D
Load leads 6-D
Load preforms 2-D
Furnace load 1-D
Unload 2-D

VI. Mount Fabrication:

Mount 16-A
Etch 2-D
Furnace 1-D

VII. Hermetic Seal:

Load cans 1-D
Fill sieve 4-D
Can seal 6-D

VIII. Plating:

Plating 4-D

IX. Final Testing:

Auto. static test 2-D
Others 4-D

Source: Consolidated Electric, Inc.

EXHIBIT 5

A Typical Testing Sequence

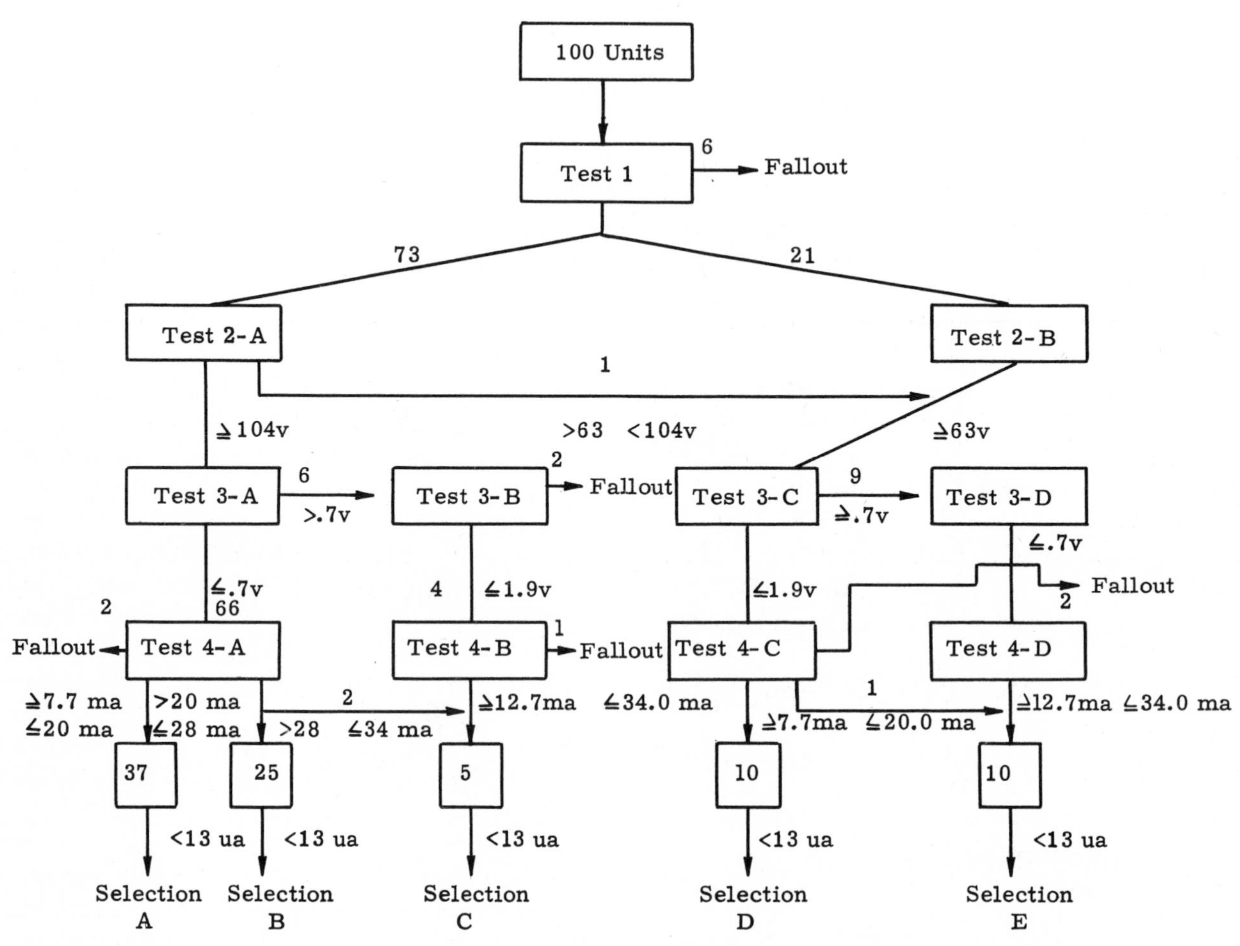

NOTE: This sequence is similar, although less complex, than that used for the 2N404.

Electronics Industry Reference Notes

In a span of less than 70 years, electronics has grown from Marconi's first experimental transmission to become the world's most dynamic and one of its largest industries. Within the United States, the industry has achieved a growth rate of almost 15 percent compounded annually—more than three and one-half times the average growth rate of all other U.S. industries combined. On the basis of value added by manufacture, the electronics industry grew from a position of 40th place in 1939 to 4th place by 1962. In terms of dollar volume of manufacturer's sales, this represents an increase from a volume of $340 million in 1939 to approximately $13 billion by 1962 (see Exhibit 1). Nearly three fourths of this sales volume is concentrated within the states of New York, Illinois, California, New Jersey, Pennsylvania, Massachusetts, and Indiana. About one third of the total output is located in the major metropolitan areas of New York City, Chicago, Boston, and Los Angeles (see Exhibit 2).

This dynamic sales growth has been dependent upon corresponding increases in the number of manufacturers and employees. From 305 in 1939, electronics companies proliferated to 4,000 (with 5,500 plants) in 1961, while the number of employees rose from about 200,000 to 850,000. Concentration is prevalent; according to *Fortune,* 20 manufacturers accounted for over half of the industry's $9.5 billion sales in 1959.[1]

Technological change has been the dominant force behind the electronic industry's growth since 1947. In addition to the commercial introduction of television, the past decade witnessed the invention of the transistor, the adaptation of the computer for business use, and the use of electronics for control of both industrial processes and military weapons. Three fourths of the value of current electronic production is represented by products that did not exist 10 years ago.

The scope of electronics makes definition and subclassification difficult. For purposes of this note, electronic equipment is defined as:

> A device or system of devices—usually containing electron tubes or semiconductors—employing a controlled variable flow of electrons for the processing of information.

[1] *Fortune,* "The Coming Shakeout in Electronics," August, 1960, p. 130.

Most of these devices may be classified as intended for one of three major market areas: *consumer, government,* and *industrial.* Each will be considered in turn.

HISTORICAL BACKGROUND

Most electronic products have a dual legacy: technical knowledge drawn from the physical sciences and business practices shaped by the first commercially important product, the home radio receiver.

In terms of a single product, the foundation of the electronics industry was the triode vacuum or electron tube invented by Dr. Lee DeForest in 1906. He built upon two pieces of research: (1) Thomas Edison's 1883 observation of the passage of an electric current from a hot filament (cathode) to a cold metallic plate (anode) in an evacuated enclosure and (2) J. A. Fleming's 1904 use of this unidirectional property to make a tube or diode for wireless signal detection. Dr. DeForest placed an electrode or grid between the anode and cathode to control the flow of electrons through the tube by the application of small voltage charges. Because the output voltage was greater than the grid voltage required to control it, the triode was an amplifier. The triode tube, which as the predecessor of the transistor became the heart of the modern radio, enabled a receiving set to provide much stronger signals and so ushered in commercial radio telegraphy and telephony.

Radio broadcasting developed over the period 1886 to 1927. One starting point was Heinrich Hertz' identification and measurement of electomagnetic (radio) waves in 1886. Ten years later Marçoni was transmitting wireless signals, and in 1901 the first trans-Atlantic signal sent by Marconi's assistants in England was received by him in Canada. Radio telephony, or speech broadcasting, was greatly facilitated by the DeForest tube and was technically feasible for commercial purposes after World War I but the secrecy of code seemed more desirable than speech. However, amateur radio telephony rapidly increased until, prompted by the popularity of an employee's broadcasts, the Westinghouse Electric Manufacturing Company established the first radio station, KDKA, in Pittsburgh on November 2, 1920.

Two years later the sale of home radio receiving sets was started by RCA. The initial sale of 100,000 units rose to 500,000 in 1923 and 1,520,000 in 1924, while the average manufacturer's price wavered from $50 to $27 to $33 (see Exhibit 4). New competitors were attracted: between 1923 and 1934, some 1,070 firms entered the radio set business and 960 failed.

Between 1922 and 1927, broadcasting became a new national medium with federal regulation and commercial sponsorship. Stations proliferated so fast that, at the suggestion of industry leaders, federal regulation of licenses, wave length allocation, and broadcasting was started in 1927. The first commercially sponsored program was the Dempsey-Carpentier fight on July 2, 1921, but the main influx of advertisements came with the establishment of the National Broadcasting System in 1926 and the Columbia Broadcasting System in 1927.

Although television remained relatively unknown until after World War II, research dated back to the beginnings of the vacuum tube in the 1880's. Mechanical scanning devices were conceived before the early 1900's when the first all-electronic systems using the cathode ray tube were developed. RCA jumped into the lead by obtaining the basic television patents on Dr. W. K. Zworykin's invention of the iconoscope (cathode ray camera tube) and his development of the kinescope (cathode ray receiving tube) in the 1920's. The corporation began experimental broadcasting in 1928. Commercial television started after the telecasting of the New York World's Fair in 1939, but further growth was delayed by the war until 1947.

Technological breakthroughs before, during, and after World War II added new products and companies to the electronics industry. Radar, navigational aids, control systems, data processing equipment and a host of other devices joined radio and television, while such companies as IBM, Motorola, Raytheon, Avco, Stromberg-Carlson, and thousands of smaller ones joined radio's pioneers, RCA, General Electric, Westinghouse, and AT&T.

THE CONSUMER MARKET

The most mature segment of the electronics business in 1962 was the $2 billion consumer or "entertainment" market. Principal products are radio and television receivers and music reproduction equipment sold for consumer use in the home (see Exhibits 3, 4, and 8).

Radios

Radio set sales were boosted by two trends: portable miniaturization and growing interest in FM. As noted in Exhibit 4, the number of portables with at least one transistor rose from 30 percent in 1956 to 95 percent in 1961. The number of FM receivers rose from 376,000 in 1958 to 541,000 in 1959, 905,000 in 1960, and 916,000 in 1961; meanwhile the number of FM stations went from 571 to 960. The net result was that households having radios in working order climbed from 44.0 to 47.7 million (although the percent of total households dropped from 92.5 to 89.9); however, the nonradio owners rose from 1.8 to 3.1 million, or from 3.7 to 5.3 percent. Radio households classified by sets working ranked as follows:

	1954	*1960*
One set	54.5%	54.7%
Two sets	29.6	26.8
Three sets	10.4	10.9
Four sets	3.5	4.9
Five sets	1.2	1.7
Six sets	.7	1.0

TV

From a production of 6,900 receivers in 1946, with a factory value just over one million dollars, the television manufacturing industry boomed to a dollar peak in 1950 and a unit top five years later before the shake-out began in 1956 (see Exhibit 4). Such trends as market saturation, changing consumer tastes, and discount selling were reflected in alarming profit declines. In 1950, six selected television assembly firms earned an average of 35 percent on investment; by 1956 they earned only 6 percent. The total number of assemblers went from the 1950 high of 140 to 51 in 1956 and 35 in 1961.

Some famous brand names disappeared. In 1956, International Tel. & Tel. Co. sold the inventories and name of its Capehart Division; the Raytheon Mfg. Co. sold its Belmont Radio Division operations to Admiral; the Sparks-Withington and Sentinel companies were acquired by Magnavox; and the Hallicrafters Company was acquired by Penn-Texas. Also, the Columbia Broadcasting System discontinued television set assembly in its CBS–Columbia Division and the Avco Mfg. Co. liquidated its Crosley Division. The shakeout slackened after 1956 with the latest concern to go being Hoffman Electronics.

In 1963 manufacturers were looking to featured thinness and/or portability (see Exhibits 4 and 14) as means of combatting such problems as fluctuating monthly sales, discounting, increasing market saturation, and decreasing scrappage rate. This strategy was initiated by the introduction of General Electric's 10- to 17-inch portables in 1955. The seasonality problem is documented in Exhibits 5 and 6. Discounting was fostered by the proliferation of nonexclusive dealers operating with a suggested 25–35 percent markup in retail price; only 34 percent of the 100,000 retail outlets even specialized in radio, television, and appliances. As for market saturation, the TV households rose from 67 percent in 1955 to 88 percent in 1960 and 90 percent in 1962, those with two or more sets increased from 2 to 12 percent, while the average set life moved from about 7 years to about 10. Sylvania Electric Products, Inc., summarized the trends as follows[2]

	Percent New TV Homes	*TV Sets / TV Home*	*Replace. Rate*	*Initial Instal.*	*Second Set*	*Replac. Set*	*Total (000)*
1950	15%	1.003	.7%	6,075	30	27	6,132
1953	18	1.025	4.2	5,155	305	911	6,371
1955	20	1.052	7.0	4,380	770	2,296	7,446
1957	19	1.085	6.4	2,790	1,090	2,745	6,625
1959	18	1.120	4.9	2,310	1,080	2,459	5,849
1960E	18	1.140	5.9	1,965	1,100	3,305	6,370
1961E	18	1.160	6.5	1,630	1,205	3,665	6,550
1965E	18	1.240	7.4	1,540	1,430	5,030	8,000

Another strategy pursued by an increasing number of firms was to make color sets. Between 1953 when the FCC approved the RCA system and 1962, some 20 manufacturers entered the color field. All the color tubes were produced by RCA, although National Video Corporation and a Zenith subsidiary planned to enter the field in 1963. The National Video version would be 20 percent thinner than RCA's.

One company estimated sales and sets in use as follows (all in thousands):[3]

Year	*Color*	*Black and White*	*Color Percent of Total*	*Color Sets in Use*
1961	160	6,050	2.6	575
1962	360	6,200	5.5	875
1963	625	6,000	9.4	1,490
1965	1,350	5,550	19.6	3,750
1967	2,350	5,000	32.0	8,000

In dollars, 1962 sales were about $200 million; however, half of the 1962 sets were reported to be in dealer inventories. Sales increases were ascribed to color programs jumping from 68 hours in 1954 to 486 in 1956 to 724 in 1959 and over 2,000 in 1962; to the increased drawing power of color (150 percent of the black-and-white audience), and to price reductions to meet the competition of Sears' $450 price leader. Major cost was the tube which ran $90 wholesale for the 21-inch version.

Phonographs

The impact of the decline of television after 1955 was alleviated somewhat by the increase in radio sales and the growing popularity of home phonographs (see Exhibit 8). The latter was boosted by the 33⅓ rpm "long-playing" record of 1948, the completely packaged "high fidelity" sets of 1956, and the stereophonic records and equipment of 1958.

In terms of receivers in use, the growth of the consumer market may be summarized as follows (in millions of units):

	Auto Radios	*Home Radios*	*TV*	*Phono.*
1950	18	31	10.6	16.8
1953	25	88	27.3	20.8
1955	29	91	37.4	24.0
1957	35	95	46.7	27.1
1959	39	97	52.1	32.0
1961	41	99	57.6	35.7

Other Consumer Products

The market for new and sometimes exotic consumer electronic items rose to $270 million in 1961. The largest segment is electronic organs ($150 million), followed by tape recorders ($60 million), electronic toy kits ($40 million),

[2] National Industrial Conference Board, *Forecasting Sales,* 1963, pp. 65–68.

[3] Sylvania Electric Products, Inc., news release, May 11, 1963.

and communication devices for pleasure boats ($15 million). The remainder includes electronic ovens, garage-door openers, saws, and radar speed detectors.

THE INDUSTRIAL MARKET

It is in the industrial market that the enormous breadth and versatility of the electronic technology and its potential are most clearly illustrated. It embraces the industry's earlier products—radio and television broadcast equipment, test instruments, navigational aids—and a myriad of other devices that measure, count, process, control, and diagnose problems. The expanse and rapid development make this area difficult to portray statistically (see Exhibit 9).

Computers and Data Processing Equipment

Since the Electronic Numerical Integration and Calculation System (ENIAC) was dedicated in 1945 at the Moore School in Philadelphia, the computing and data processing industry has grown impressively. There are about 13,000 computers in operation[4] (of which the federal government uses over 525); factory sales were $850 million in 1961 (with about two thirds of the manufacturing cost in components). IBM has an estimated 79 percent of this market in units and 77.8 percent in dollars, but newcomers still enter the fray. One type is the missile-based firm seeking to apply its electronic technology to business (e.g., General Electric, RCA, and Minneapolis-Honeywell), and another variety is the conventional business machine company (e.g., National Cash Register).

Industrial Control and Processing Devices

Some $180 million worth of electronic equipment was sold in 1961 to control complex industrial processes, such as an oil refinery or a steel rolling mill, or to direct with taped instructions a single machine, such as a lathe. The essentials for any automatic control system are: (1) a controllable condition (i.e., temperature); (2) a device for measuring the value of this condition (i.e., a measuring unit); (3) apparatus capable of affecting a change in the controlled condition (i.e., a regulating unit); and (4) means for operating the regulating unit in response to the measuring unit (i.e., a controlling unit). When the controlling unit acts as a link between the measuring and regulatory units this system is considered to be a "closed-loop" system.

Testing and Measuring Equipment

Concomitant with the growth of the electronics industry in general, and semiconductors in particular, has been the increased need to test and measure (see Exhibit 10). Such devices range from general purpose $20 voltmeters to special $40,000 automatic units for production line testing of circuitry or components.

Communications Equipment

This category embraces mobile radio transmitters, closed circuit television (CCTV), marine and aviation navigational aids, and broadcasting and sound equipment. In 1961, some 770,500 radio communication systems—ranging from police to taxicabs to amateurs—operated 2.7 million transmitters of which 85 percent were mobile; liberalized FCC regulations helped increase such systems 18 percent and transmitters 23 percent since 1960. Motorola and General Electric sell more than 90 percent of the $100 million land mobile radio business, while they are joined by Collins Radio and RCA in supplying 75 percent of the $50 million microwave market. Factory sales of CCTV grew from $2.1 million in 1955 to $7.2 million in 1958 and $11.5 million in 1961; about 40 percent of the sales are electronic equipment.

Sales of aviation/marine communication and navigation equipment exceeds $200 million annually with 70 percent in navigational aids. Complex equipment is manufactured by such firms as Collins Radio and Bendix, while suppliers of small craft equipment include National Aeronautical Corporation, Lear, and Aircraft Radio Corporation in the aviation field; and Raytheon's Applied Electronics Division, Kaar Engineering Corporation, and Bendix in the marine end. With the number of radio-equipped aircraft growing from 70 to 100 thousand between 1961–1970 and the Mach 2.0 and 3.0 transports, the Federal Aviation Agency (FAA) expects to spend $250 million for ground installations by 1970 (see Exhibit 11).

The last two segments—broadcasting and commercial sound equipment—are more stable. Color TV and stereo provide the impetus for in-

[4] *Computers and Automation,* February, 1963, p. 26.

creased broadcasting equipment business which runs about $30 million yearly. General Electric, RCA, Dage Radio, Collins, and Ampex account for 80 percent of this market. Commercial sound equipment totals some $200 million with no firm or even type of company dominating.

Nuclear, Medical, and Miscellaneous

Nuclear electronic apparatus has shown continued growth from $33.4 million in 1957 to $50.8 million in 1959 and $65.0 million in 1961. Reactor control instruments account for $19.5 million, radiation detection and monitoring devices total $35.5 million, and radioactive isotope measuring devices sell for $10.0 million. Reactor control instrumentation is supplied by such companies as Westinghouse, General Electric, and Bendix, while other types of equipment come from numerous small firms like Nuclear Chicago, Baird-Atomic, Tracerlab, Radiation Counter Laboratories, and Industrial Nucleonics. One indication of growth is the over 100 percent expansion since 1956 of Atomic Energy Commission licenses to use radioisotopes; use by medical institutions and physicians increased 88 percent.

Although X-ray systems still account for the majority of medical electronic sales, the 110 percent growth between 1956–1961 when sales were $150 million was largely attributable to new products. These included ultraviolet microscopes for cancer detection, infrared devices to study viruses, and ultrasonics for instrument cleaning, surgery, and dental drilling. General Electric and Picker X-ray Corporation are the main suppliers of medical X-ray units, but other medical electronic products are made by Hewlett-Packard's Sanborn Instruments Division, Burdick, Radiation, Inc., Edin Division of Epsco, Inc., Cambridge Instruments, and a host of newcomers.

THE GOVERNMENT MARKET

The largest single customer of the electronics industry in 1962 was the U.S. government, represented primarily by the Department of Defense (DOD) and the National Aeronautics and Space Agency (NASA). NASA is charged with developing a comprehensive program for the study and peaceful utilization of space and the DOD is responsible for defending the nation against, as well as competing in, missile and aerospace warfare. In addition to these two agencies, the FAA, the Atomic Energy Commission (AEC), and the Weather Bureau are substantial electronic customers (see Exhibits 11 and 12).

The rapid growth of liberal spending for military electronics (see Exhibit 1) may be attributed primarily to: (1) expanding missile and space programs; (2) the rising electronic content of weapons systems; and (3) increasing command and control communication requirements. Prior to World War II, military electronic hardware essentially was "beefed up" commercial communication equipment. The war brought special purpose items, such as the "Walkie-Talkie," that were designed not to fail in combat and accelerated research in such areas as radar and missiles. Electronic and communications expenditures totaled $4.5 billion in 1945. The next breakthrough was airborne automatic weapons control that came in 1948 when Hughes Aircraft Company combined a gunsight with radar and a computer. In this system the pilot was told the best intercept course, when to start firing, and when to break off the attack. Succeeding steps were integrated electronic defense systems such as the DEW Line (Distant Early Warning) radar screen and the inclusion of a miniaturized electronic guidance system in a missile. These developments were hastened by the Korean War which increased DOD electronic expenditures five-fold to $3 billion in 1953.

The first category within the military field is aircraft electronic equipment which in turn may be subdivided into five segments.[5] The first is navigation, guidance and control equipment that accounts for 40–45 percent of the total, while the second is ordnance equipment amounting to 20 percent. The third category is communication installations, making up 15–20 percent of the aircraft electronic market, but which is expected to decline to 10 percent by 1965 with the greater utilization of cargo and utility planes. Reconnaissance and surveillance systems, the fourth segment, is being transferred to astronautics and its share will drop from 10 to 5 percent by 1965. The final category is countermeasure equipment that degrades an electronic system for guidance, communications, or other similiar

[5] Small Business Administration, *A Study of Small Business in the Electronics Industry,* 1961, pp. 45–61.

functions; its share is 10 percent. For the aircraft electronic category as a whole, Air Force procurement accounts for two thirds, the Navy 30 percent, and the Army 4 percent.

Missiles and astronautics is the most rapidly growing category and is expected to equal some 45 percent of the 1965 procurement and productions expenditures by the Department of Defense and 55 percent of the electronic content. The electronics portion of missiles expenditures is estimated at 35–55 percent for defense interceptor; 45–55 percent for air-to-air interceptor, radar; 50–80 percent for air-to-air interceptor, infrared; 25–30 percent for ballistic with inertial guidance; and 50–60 percent short range battlefield missiles. Airborne equipment—almost all guidance and control systems as shown in Exhibit 12-A—accounts for two thirds of the total, while the remaining third is divided into guidance equipment (40 percent), launching and tracking equipment (35 percent), and automatic checkout systems (25 percent). The Air Force buys 65 percent of the missile electronics, the Army 20 percent, and the Navy 15 percent.

Three other categories make up most of the remaining DOD electronic expenditures. (1) Electronics and communications equipment is almost entirely electronic and embraces hand radio receivers and the Ballistic Missile Early Warning System (BMEWS), (2) Electronic equipment for ships varies from 5 percent of a $300 million carrier to 20 percent of a $57 million submarine, (3) The portion of Research, Development, Test, and Evaluation (RDT&E) going for electronic equipment doubled to 25 percent between 1951–1961; missiles and communications/electronics each accounted for one third in 1961.

Government Purchasing Practices

The government is a unique customer who sets the rules to be followed and requires rigorous adherence to paperwork, design, manufacturing, and inspection procedures. First there is the bidding procedure of open or negotiated bids. For open bids, the contracting agency publishes a notification of contract availability and invites potential qualified contractors to submit a proposal. A contract award is based not only on price but also on technical competence, past performance, related experience, available facilities, time of start and completion, and the amount of Government Furnished Equipment (GFE) required, be it test equipment or an airplane. Negotiated bids involve the same procedures except only a single potential supplier is invited to bid. Use of this later form of bid has increased with the advent of the total weapons system procurement concept, although it is also used when a concern has unique competence, resources, or proprietary rights.

The successful bidder must submit a variety of progress reports and adhere to military standards. These include specifications as to equipment, manufacturing processes, approved components suppliers, security clearances, and performance tests. If the final result passes military inspection, the contractor usually is still subject to renegotiation on a contract by contract basis. Renegotiation generally limits returns to 7 percent, to 9 percent on Major Procurement-Production (MP-P) contracts and 5–6 percent on R&D ones.

THE COMPONENTS MARKET

Electronic components are products which amplify, switch, resist, store, or otherwise affect an electrical circuit when combined with other components in an electric circuit, equipment, or system. They may be classified as active or passive. Active components primarily include semiconductors (transistors, diodes, rectifiers), and vacuum (or electron) tubes that do the switching or amplifying. Passive components include capacitors, resistors, transformers, tuners, filters, speakers, and hardware (sockets, wire, printed circuit boards, etc.). These passive devices feed the tube or transistor the right amount of signal or power in addition to adjusting its output for presentation to the next circuit (see Exhibit 13). The problem of simplifying and reducing the number and complexity of passive components occupied much of the research since 1956.

The importance of these components to an appliance such as a TV set may be gleaned from the following estimated materials cost for a 21-inch TV set with a $100 factory price:

Picture tube	$19.00	Capacitors	$ 3.00
Cabinet	8.50	Minor parts	13.00
Tuner	7.50	Labels and knobs	5.90
Receiving-type tubes	7.50		
Transformer	7.00	Total	$71.40

Active Components

Vacuum Tubes—Having gone through "shakeouts," both the receiving and picture tube businesses are in the hands of established companies (see Exhibits 13 and 14). Thanks to the highly competitive 1930's, RCA, General Electric, and Sylvania accounted for 70 percent of the 1961 receiving tube business, while 12 survivors of the 1957 cutback had the picture tube end. The latter is plagued by frequent changes in tube size and shape and by competition from rebuilders (see Exhibit 14). These rebuilders reclaim the glass from old tubes and can produce low-cost renewal tubes since new glass bulbs represent 50–65 percent of the tube cost. With rebuilders holding an estimated 50 percent of the renewal market, the industry operates below its 15 million tube capacity.

Power and Special Purpose Tubes—"Power tubes" such as "klystrons," "magnetrons," and "thyratrons" have such uses as the transmission of radio and TV signals and of radar pulses. "Special purpose" tubes find use as radiation detector tubes used in nuclear instruments, photo tubes used in light meters, television pick-up tubes, X-ray tubes, and so on.

Semiconductors—Despite mounting competition and predictions of a shakeout, semiconductors are still the glamorous components (see Exhibit 16). All the major tube manufacturers entered the field, but the rapidly shifting technology enabled unknowns to join the top 15 firms that have 85 percent of the business. A notable example is Texas Instruments (T.I.), formerly a small company offering seismograph services and producing geophysical instruments, climbed to the top by developing the first silicon transistor in 1954. Not all the entrants are unknowns: in 1962 IBM announced that it planned to integrate into manufacturing silicon transistors of which T.I. was the chief supplier.

Technological advances followed swiftly upon the Bell Telephone Laboratories' 1948 announcement of the transistor. Three years later the alloy-junction was developed, followed by: the silicon junction diode in 1952, the drift version in 1953, zone refining and silicon transistors in 1954, diffusion and mesa transistors in 1956, integrated semiconductor circuits in 1958, the epitaxial and planar transistors in 1960, thin film devices in 1961, and the gallium arsenide transistor in 1963. These developments reflect the need (especially by the military) for substances to withstand higher temperatures without loss in reliability. Germanium has a maximum operating temperature of 100°C., silicon 200°C., gallium arsenide 400°C., and silicon carbide 600°C. On the other hand, silicon tends to produce more noise than germanium, making it unsuitable for the detecting and tuning functions of TV sets. Prices and trends of silicon and germanium transistors are shown in Exhibit 19.

Although solid state[6] devices can perform 75 percent of vacuum tube functions, most transistors are used in new rather than replacement applications. Increasingly, designers have specified transistors where superior operating characteristics outweigh higher unit costs. For example, in 1957 the major transistor market was in portable and auto radios that accounted for 40 percent of unit production; however, by 1962 industrial and military applications far surpassed the consumer products volume. For example, an IBM 1401 computer system uses 4,300 to 9,800 transistors, a Univac 1107 has 25,500, while a Philco 2000 uses 56,000 and an IBM Stretch 200,000! On the military side, a B52 has 19,951 transistors; the fire control system on a Polaris submarine, 15,000; the Atlas missile 5,393 and its ground-based guidance control and launch system 61,443! On the other hand, if TV sets were converted to transistors they could use 150 to 200 million units annually.

As explained in the process note, diodes are one-way electrical gates and are used as switching devices or for converting alternating into pulsating direct current. Rectifiers perform the same functions for higher power loads (see Exhibit 17).

Passive Components

Resistors—Over the past 10 years, the resistor industry has seen considerable change in manufacturers and product. From 22 competitors in 1952, the group has grown to 110 of which 23 do the majority of the volume. Productwise, resistors have become more specialized; for example, special purpose resistors have been developed for micro-miniature circuitry and high performance precision ones for the military.

[6] Solid state devices: elements that can control current without moving parts, heater filaments or vacuum gaps. Transistors, diodes, and rectifers are primary examples.

Capacitors—These components are designed to "block" the flow of direct current, store electric energy, or "release" the flow of alternating current at a rate which is a function of their capacity. Primary growth has come from tantalum electrolytic capacitors going from $2 million in 1955 to $8 million in 1958 and $62 million in 1961.

Complex Components—Despite their small percentage market share, complex components promise to affect significantly the entire electronics industry. They are made by three methods:

(1) Modular circuits of "conventional" or specially designed components on wafers are soldered or welded together and encapsulated in a parallelogramic shell.

(2) Successive *thin films* of conductive metals and insulating materials are placed (by vacuum depositing or evaporating) in geometric patterns on a passive substrate (glass or ceramic) to make resistors and capacitors for later combination with semiconductors into circuits. The material may be deposited through a masking stencil or in a uniform layer and then unwanted sections etched away. The resulting crystal structure is a disorderly jumble and hence it is difficult to deposit diodes or transistors which require perfect single crystals. (One solution may be the thin-film triode, built of layers of electronic and insulating materials, that is a solid-state analog of the vacuum tube.)

While most thin films have been used for complex close tolerance, small volume applications, the process lends itself to automation: one machine, with a turntable to bring the raw materials to the heater in proper sequence and a changer to switch masks, can deposit 10,000 four-layer circuits per eight-hour shift. They are a bit over 100 angstrom units thick and may be switched in one nanosecond.[7] Magnetic films make possible a theoretical increase in speeds of 100 times —provided the retrieval circuits could keep pace; the actual increase is 5 to 10 times.

(3) An *integrated circuit* is made on or within a silicon slab by epitaxial growing, diffusing, alloying, etc. (as was done with a mesa). An oxide layer is grown on the silicon slice to protect and mask the surface. Active and passive components are produced by etching away areas of the coating, and successively diffusing impurities. A final etching step uncovers spots for external connections and the circuit is ready for deposition of aluminum film to interconnect the spots. A circuit on a 65 to 90 mil silicon chip can handle all functions in a conventional circuit of 11 resistors, 5 transistors, and 1 diode. Or, a digital computer with integrated circuits weighs only 10 ounces, occupies 6.3 cubic inches, and does the work of a conventional unit 150 times larger.

Costs and limited control of electrical characteristics have kept integrated circuits to high-reliability military switching needs (such as airborne computers and the ICBM), although consumer switching and amplifier applications may begin in 1965. For example, one high-reliability circuit cost in 1962 $30 to $50 in discrete components or $16 to $66 in integrated form, while the commercial grade components ran $6 to $8 and the integrated circuit, $25; however, one company estimated that its 1962 $125 "flip-flop" circuit for computers would go for $4 to $6 in 1965.[8]

Integrated circuits are marketed two ways: (1) as a complete circuit (either standard or designed for a specific customer), or (2) as a "universal chip" with functions built in but not connected into specific circuits. A single chip might contain several thousand transistors, diodes, capacitors, and resistors. The customer specifies the circuitry desired (utilizing any or all of the components), while the manufacturer vacuum deposits the aluminum wiring and slices the chip into individual circuits. The result is two alignment and masking operations substituted for the seven of a custom-made circuit.

Sales of the integrated circuit are predicted at $20–30 million in 1963, $50 million in 1964, and $200 million in 1967.

DISTRIBUTION CHANNELS

While company salesmen sell about 80 percent of the original equipment direct, some 1,500 manufacturer's representatives and radio parts distributors handle most components. Representatives sell to original equipment manufacturers, while distributors cover the replacement trade. Some 70 percent of the latter's sales are to radio and TV servicemen and retail

[7] An angstrom unit is 1/254 millionth of an inch; a nanosecond is one billionth of a second.

[8] *Electronics*, May 10, 1963, p. 24.

dealers, 20 percent to industrial users, and 10 percent to amateur operators. A manufacturer can get nationwide coverage with about 15 representatives; about 25 percent are equipped to install and service electronic gear and 53 percent have warehouses. A typical distributor may buy from 100 suppliers and stock 10,000 to 50,000 items.

FOREIGN COMPETITION

Despite the much-publicized threat of Japanese competition, the United States exports about three times the dollar value of imports (see Exhibit 18). Typically, exports consist of military and industrial products and over two thirds went to industrially advanced countries in 1961; on the other hand, imports are mostly mass-produced items such as radios and components. In terms of specific countries, Canada bought the most in 1961 (19.2 percent), followed by Germany (9.0 percent), France (7.4 percent), and Japan (7.0 percent); while Japan sold the most to the U.S. (54.8 percent), followed by Canada (12.8 percent), West Germany (12.2 percent), United Kingdom (11.9 percent), and the Netherlands (3.1 percent).

The Japanese electronics industry is second in the world. Production has expanded from \$247 million in 1956 to \$498 million in 1958, \$1.2 billion in 1960 and \$1.6 billion in 1962, with consumer products averaging about 55 percent. Exports to the United States increased from \$3.3 million in 1956 to \$119 million in 1961 (see Exhibit 18-C). Besides the deluge of transistor radios, the imports included in 1963 a 5½ inch, 8-pound transistor TV set for \$190, and a 14-inch 70-pound color set for \$369.

FUTURE TRENDS

In looking into the future, industry leaders saw several trends and questions. They included: (1) rapid substitution of microminiature complex for discrete components to reduce the "tyranny of numbers"; (2) a slowing down of the miniaturization trend and an increasing concern for reliability; and (3) a leveling off of the rate of technological change and the substitution of increased cost cutting techniques (such as encasing a silicon transistor in epoxy plastic, not a metal can, and bringing the price down to germanium entertainment-type level). Many predicted that microminiaturization would bring high reliability and low cost with it. Success in the electronics industry would increasingly depend on "command over materials" rather than on the "circuit concept" of putting components together for each particular job.

1. ELECTRONICS INDUSTRY

Factory Sales of Electronic Products by Selected Years, 1914-1962*
(In Millions of Dollars)

Year	Consumer Products	Replacement parts, tubes Semiconductors	Industrial Products	Military and Space Products	Total
1914					$ 1
1919					8
1921					11
1923	$ 13				54
1925	93**				180
1926	94**				187
1927	95**				200
1929	275**				465
1931	125**				220
1933	73				135
1935	135			$ 20	240
1937	182			28	350
1939	186			37	340
1947	810			680	1,750
1950	1,500	$ 215	$ 350	655	2,720
1951	1,400	225	450	1,193	3,268
1952	1,300	240	500	3,100	5,140
1953	1,400	290	600	3,230	5,520
1954	1,400	305	650	3,100	5,455
1955	1,500	335	750	3,332	5,917
1956	1,600	395	950	3,595	6,540
1957	1,797	440	1,300	4,130	7,667
1958	1,647	475	1,380	4,725	8,227
1959	2,098	530	1,600	5,373	9,601
1960	2,101	555	1,850	6,124	10,630
1961	2,087	580	2,200	7,190	12,057
1962	2,287	620	2,450	8,348	13,705
1965E	2,700	1,100	3,200	8,000	15,000

*All available information is shown. Data covers manufacturers' shipments from 1947 and production prior to that date. Between 1941-1945 military purchases of electronics and communication equipment totaled $7.5 billion.

**Includes all radio receivers, commercial as well as home-type.

Sources: Electronics Division, Business and Defense Services Administration, Bureau of the Census, and Electronics Industry Association (EIA); and Stanford Research Institute (Small Business Administration, A Study of Small Business In the Electronics Industry, p. 4) for the 1965 estimate.

2. ELECTRONICS INDUSTRY

Distribution of Manufacturers by Sales Volume, Geographical Region, Engineers, Nonengineers, 1962

Region	Total Firms	Number Replying	Annual Sales Volume* A	B	C	D	E	F	G	Engineers** (Thousands)	Nonengineers*** (Thousands)
New England	709	456	52	81	79	80	160	46	48	16.6	178.6
Middle Atlantic	1,802	1,163	101	162	158	216	338	57	131	42.0	421.2
E. North Central	938	586	46	55	64	85	185	45	106	32.8	275.0
W. North Central	177	110	11	7	15	20	37	8	12	9.4	65.0
S. Atlantic	174	128	11	14	16	24	33	12	18	9.4	47.2
E. South Central	24	16	2	---	3	1	5	---	5	.3	6.1
W. South Central	59	46	10	8	7	4	10	2	5	1.4	9.1
Mountain	54	41	8	8	6	4	9	4	2	1.7	10.4
Pacific	820	574	81	79	78	100	149	38	49	21.6	153.2
Total	4,757	3,120	322	414	426	534	926	212	376	135.2	1,165.8

*Sales Volume Categories: A - up to $100,000; B - $100,000-$250,000; C - $250,000-$500,000; D - $500,000-$1 million; E - $1 million-$5 million; F - $5 million-$10 million; G - over $10 million.

**Some 1,612 plants had 1-5 engineers; 441 had 6-9; 447 had 10-20; 317 had 21-50; 124 had 51-100; 62 had 101-250; 81 had over 250.

***Some 324 plants had 1-10 employees; 718 had 11-30; 404 had 31-50; 865 had 51-151; 649 had 151-50; 189 had 501 to 1,000; 217 had over 1,000.

Source: Electronics, "Small Companies Continue to Dominate Electronics Industry," December 7, 1962, pp. 28-29.

3. ELECTRONICS INDUSTRY

Factory Sales of Consumer Electronic Products, 1957-1961*
(In Millions of Dollars)

Category	1957	1958	1959	1960	1961	1962
Television Receivers**	$ 831	$ 686	$ 886	$ 825	$ 832	$ 833
Home Radios	240	241	211	209	209	205
Auto Radios	143	96	130	154	134	181
Phonographs	187	198	373	395	335	385
Records and Magnetic Tapes	190	213	248	246	265	325
Hi-fi Components	34	36	38	32	42	48
Other Consumer Products	172	177	212	240	270	310
Total	$1,797	$1,647	$2,098	$2,101	$2,087	$2,287

*Information for previous years not available.
**Monochrome only.
Source: EIA, Electronic Industries, 1962 Yearbook.

4. ELECTRONICS INDUSTRY

Production and Sales to Retailers of Radio and Monochrome Television Sets, for Selected Years 1925-1962
(Production Units in Thousands, Dollars in Millions)

A. RADIO PRODUCTION:

Year	Home	Clock	Portable***	Auto	Total	Mfrs. Value
1925	2,000				2,000	$ 82.5
1929	4,428				4,428	222.0
1931	3,484			110	3,594	104.7
1935	4,840			1,190	6,030	128.4
1937	6,193			1,890	8,803	165.4
1939	8,547		616	1,600	10,763	153.4
1942	3,374*		573*	360*	4,307*	103.0*
1946	13,276		1,069	1,610	15,955	434.2
1947	14,083		2,458	3,459	20,000	650.0
1948	9,630		2,630	4,240	16,500	525.0
1949	5,961		1,843	3,596	11,400	310.0
1950**	8,175		1,675	4,740	14,590	375.0
1951	5,974	777	1,333	4,543	12,627	315.9
1952	4,043	1,929	1,720	3,243	10,935	249.8
1953	4,403	2,041	1,742	5,183	13,369	298.0
1954	3,068	1,875	1,333	4,124	10,400	228.8
1955	3,394	2,244	2,027	6,864	14,529	291.2
1956	3,037	2,311	3,113	5,057	13,982	294.0
1957	3,228	2,516	3,265	5,496	14,505	351.6
1958	2,621	2,038	3,373	3,715	11,747	314.6
1959	3,145	2,794	4,128	5,555	15,622	330.9
1960	3,440	2,720	4,535	6,432	17,127	340.5
1961	3,042	3,017	5,747	5,568	17,374	313.5
1962	3,015	3,257	5,640	7,250	19,162	386.0

Exhibit 4 (continued)

B. TELEVISION PRODUCTION:+

Year	Portable Table	Console	Phono. Comb.	Total	Mfrs. Value
1947	116	37	25	179	$ 50
1948	647	179	149	975	230
1949	1,793	989	218	3,000	580
1950	2,942	3,820	702	7,464	1,350
1951	2,276	2,775	334	5,385	957
1952	2,838	3,039	220	6,096	1,049
1953	3,225	3,755	236	7,216	1,230
1954	4,249	3,012	86	7,347	1,029
1955	4,440	3,200	117	7,757	1,071
1956	4,755	2,557	75	7,387	939
1957	3,846	2,433	120	6,399	833
1958	2,717	2,069	135	4,920	668
1959	3,613	2,567	170	6,349	896
1960	3,274	2,211	223	5,708	826
1961	3,812	2,135	230	6,178	835

C. RADIO SALES TO RETAILERS:

Year	Home	Clock	Portable	Total
1952	4,287,410	1,816,075	1,571,038	7,674,523
1953	3,824,284	1,792,151	1,593,446	7,209,881
1954	2,932,576	1,901,721	1,353,206	6,187,503
1955	3,056,368	2,060,081	1,960,273	7,076,722
1956	3,392,324	2,281,457	2,749,042	8,422,823
1957	3,987,509	2,381,257	3,207,046	9,575,812
1958	3,329,725	2,110,740	3,297,732	8,738,197
1959	3,025,299	2,625,397	3,884,470	9,535,166
1960	3,271,667	2,669,396	4,512,636	10,453,699
1961	2,917,150	2,945,341	5,362,519	11,225,010
1962	2,983,360	3,216,963	5,556,770	11,757,093

D. TELEVISION SALES TO RETAILERS:

Year	Table and Portable	Console	Combination	Total
1952	2,823,443	3,114,218	236,845	6,174,506
1953	3,047,453	3,439,790	212,242	6,699,485
1954	3,983,809	3,069,237	108,316	7,161,362
1955	4,243,661	3,071,206	107,111	7,421,978
1956	4,408,314	2,542,146	77,996	7,028,456
1957	3,808,278	2,379,825	97,716	6,285,819
1958	2,875,843	2,058,782	127,226	5,061,851
1959	3,340,226	2,486,230	186,523	6,012,979
1960	3,214,709	2,221,945	214,313	5,650,967
1961	3,401,716	2,146,035	226,810	5,774,561
1962	4,040,892	1,982,262	278,186	6,301,340

*Civilian production terminated April, 1942.

**Radio-Phonograph Combinations are included in figures prior to 1950.

***Numbers of receivers with one or more transistors for 1956 totaled 986 thousand, for 1957 totaled 1.6 million, for 1958 totaled 2.7 million, for 1959 totaled 3.9 million, and more than 95% for 1960 and 1961.

+Includes monochrome only.

Source: EIA, Electronic Industries, 1962 Yearbook.

5. ELECTRONICS INDUSTRY

Selected Statistics on TV Set Production, Sales, Scrappage and Inventory, 1956 and 1962

(A) Quarterly Set Data, 1956
(In Thousands of Units)

	Portables	Under 18 In.	19 - 21	Over 22 In.	Color	Portables	Under 18 In.	19 - 21	Over 22 In.	Color
		Factory Production					Retail Sales			
1st Quarter	109	181	1,372	183	30	90	190	1,191	217	20
2nd Quarter	388	129	956	98	35	161	140	801	77	25
3rd Quarter	593	15	1,037	198	40	373	57	1,116	189	30
4th Quarter	865	115	1,060	170	45	735	125	1,135	205	45
		Distributors' Sales					Sets Scrapped			
1st Quarter	97	177	1,234	194	30	0	377	168	6	0
2nd Quarter	182	129	671	90	25	0	436	193	7	0
3rd Quarter	415	50	1,158	192	35	1	502	223	8	0
4th Quarter	745	130	1,215	210	40	2	523	231	9	1
		Sets in Use					Percent of Sets in Use			
1st Quarter	328	16,656	20,009	1,335	60	0.8	43.4	52.1	3.5	0.2
2nd Quarter	489	16,360	20,617	1,405	85	1.3	42.0	52.9	3.6	0.2
3rd Quarter	861	15,916	21,510	1,585	115	2.2	39.8	53.8	3.9	0.3
4th Quarter	1,592	15,516	22,412	1,785	159	3.9	37.4	54.0	4.3	0.4

Source: The Television Factbook, Spring-Summer, 1957, p. 24. Prepared by Frank W. Mansfield, director of Sales Research, Sylvania Electric Products, Inc.

(B) Trends in Television Receiver Production, Retail Sales, and Scrappage, 1956-1962
(Monochrome only. Units and Dollars in Thousands)

Year	Production: Tables Portables	Console	Combination	Total (Units)	Value (Dollars)	Retail Sales (Units)	Scrappage
1956	4,755	2,557	75	7,387	$938,596	6,840	1,400
1957	3,846	2,433	120	6,399	832,747	6,560	2,745
1958	2,717	2,069	135	4,921	667,899	5,160	1,990
1959	3,613	2,567	170	6,350	896,405	5,749	2,759
1960	3,274	2,211	223	5,708	825,501	5,945	3,585
1961	3,812	2,135	230	6,177	835,423	6,200	3,700
1962	n.a.	n.a.	n.a.	6,400*	896,000*	6,500	4,300

*Estimated.

Sources: (Production figures) Electronics Industries Association, Electronic Industries Yearbook, 1962, except for 1962 estimates from Television Digest, Inc., Television Factbook 1962-63 edition (#33); (Sales and Scrappage) Television Digest, Inc., Television Factbook, 1962-63 edition (#33).

Exhibit 5 (continued)

(C) Inventories, 1955-1956, 1961-1962:
(in thousands)

	Production	Dist. Sales	Retail Sales	Inventories, End of Period Factory	Distrib.	Retail	Total
1954 4th quarter				407	575	861	1,843
1955 1st quarter	2,188	1,992	1,944	455	723	885	2,063
2nd "	1,641	1,154	1,259	919	746	742	2,407
3rd "	1,932	2,212	1,947	502	974	886	2,362
4th "	1,996	2,266	2,271	426	780	862	2,068
1956 1st quarter	1,845	1,745	1,689	538	768	875	2,181
2nd "	1,571	1,112	1,179	879	886	768	2,533
3rd "	1,844	1,859	1,735	438	1,312	848	2,598
4th "	2,127	2,468	2,201	462	929	1,085	2,476
1961 1st quarter	1,309	1,334	n.a.	373	603	n.a.	n.a.
2nd "	1,491	1,159	n.a.	524	734	n.a.	n.a.
3rd "	1,593	1,559	"	417	811	"	"
4th "	1,785	1,723	"	437	770	"	"
1962 1st quarter	1,690	1,568	"	447	808	"	"
2nd "	1,606	1,157	"	598	1,034	"	"
3rd "	1,569	1,699	"	430	1,018	"	"
4th "	1,606	1,877	"	373	750	"	"

Source: EIA, Electronic Industries, 1962 Yearbook.

6. ELECTRONICS INDUSTRY

Seasonality of Television Sets, 1955 - 1963

A. Monthly Television Set Trends, 1955-1956:

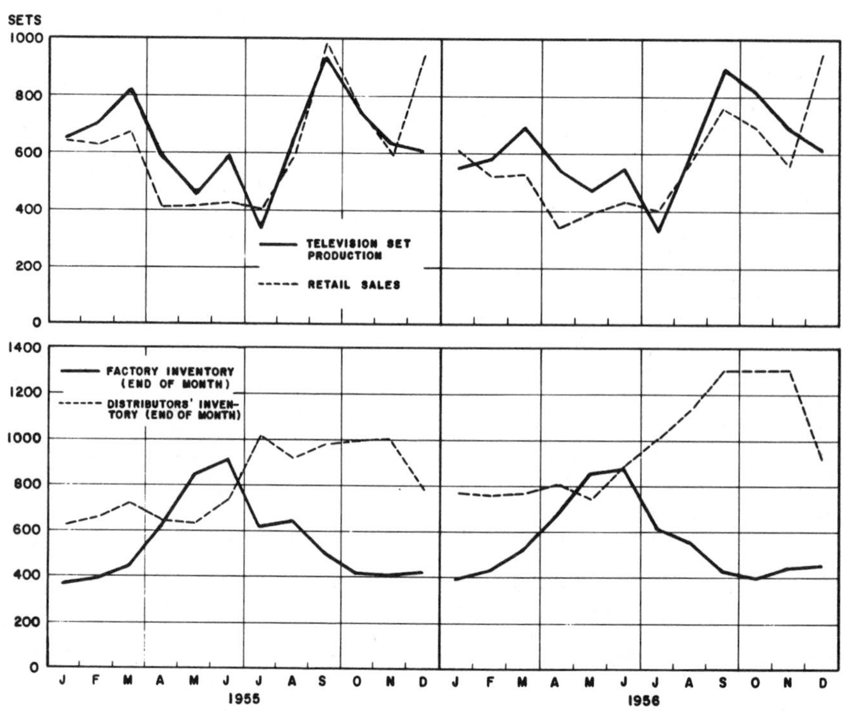

Source: E.I.A.

B. Seasonality Indexes, 1963:

	Factory Sales to Distributor			Distributor Sales to Dealer			Dealer Sales to Public		
	Monthly	Cumulative	3 Months' Moving Total	Monthly	Cumulative	3 Months' Moving Total	Monthly	Cumulative	3 Months' Moving Total
January	7.6%	7.6%	25.1%	8.0%	8.0%	29.4%	9.2%	9.2%	31.8%
February	7.7	15.3	23.8	7.6	15.6	27.6	7.9	17.1	30.6
March	7.8	23.1	23.1*	7.9	23.5	23.5*	7.9	25.0	25.0*
April	5.0	28.1	20.5	4.8	28.3	20.3	5.0	30.0	20.8
May	4.2	32.3	17.0	4.7	33.0	17.4	5.4	35.4	18.3
June	7.5	39.8	16.7*	5.9	38.9	15.4*	5.8	41.2	16.2*
July	7.1	46.9	18.8	6.7	45.6	17.3	5.9	47.1	17.1
August	10.3	57.2	24.9	8.8	54.4	21.4	8.3	55.4	20.0
September	14.1	71.3	31.5*	13.0	67.4	28.5*	12.0	67.4	26.2*
October	11.2	82.5	35.6	11.2	78.6	33.0	10.0	77.4	30.3
November	9.0	91.5	34.3	9.4	88.0	33.6	9.1	86.5	31.1
December	8.5	100.0	28.7*	12.0	100.0	32.6*	13.5	100.0	32.6*

*Quarterly Seasonal.

NOTE: This data was based on adjusted monthly sales over a five-year period; it has not been necessary to revise the seasonals since 1959.

Source: Calculated by an electronics manufacturer from E.I.A. statistics.

7. ELECTRONICS INDUSTRY

Seasonality of Radio Sets, Phonographs, Picture Tubes, and Receiving Tubes, 1963

	A. HOME SETS EXCLUDING PORTABLES — Factory Sales to Distributor			B. HOME SETS EXCLUDING PORTABLES — Dealer Sales to Public			C. PORTABLE RADIOS — Factory Sales to Distributor		
	Monthly	Cumulative	3 Months' Moving Total	Monthly	Cumulative	3 Months' Moving Total	Monthly	Cumulative	3 Months' Moving Total
January	5.5%	5.5%	28.7%	7.3%	7.3%	38.9%	6.1%	6.1%	24.6%
February	6.3	11.8	23.3	5.2	12.5	33.2	8.5	14.6	23.6
March	6.8	18.6	18.6*	6.8	19.3	19.3*	9.5	24.1	24.1*
April	4.8	23.4	17.9	4.5	23.8	16.5	7.2	31.3	25.2
May	3.9	27.3	15.5	5.2	29.0	16.5	6.5	37.8	23.2
June	6.8	34.1	15.5*	6.8	35.8	16.5*	9.0	46.8	22.7*
July	6.6	40.7	17.3	5.3	41.1	17.3	6.1	52.9	21.6
August	9.5	50.2	22.9	7.5	48.6	19.6	7.7	60.6	22.8
September	14.2	64.4	30.3*	10.2	58.8	23.0*	11.2	71.8	25.0*
October	12.4	76.8	36.1	9.6	68.4	27.3	9.7	81.5	28.6
November	11.7	88.5	38.3	10.9	79.3	30.7	9.5	91.0	30.4
December	11.5	100.0	35.6*	20.7	100.0	41.2*	9.0	100.0	28.2*

	D. PORTABLE RADIOS — Dealer Sales to Public			E. PHONOGRAPHS (Including RADIO-PHONOS) — Factory Sales			F. RECEIVING TUBES--EQUIPMENT		
	Monthly	Cumulative	3 Months' Moving Total	Monthly	Cumulative	3 Months' Moving Total	Monthly	Cumulative	3 Months' Moving Total
January	7.0%	7.0%	33.9%	7.3%	7.3%	32.5%	7.5%	7.5%	23.9%
February	6.1	13.1	30.8	7.0	14.3	26.3	7.6	15.1	22.5
March	6.4	19.5	19.5*	6.4	20.7	20.7*	7.4	22.5	22.5*
April	6.0	25.5	18.5	3.8	24.5	17.2	7.0	29.5	22.0
May	6.2	31.7	18.6	3.0	27.5	13.2	7.5	37.0	21.9
June	9.9	41.6	22.1*	5.1	32.6	11.9*	7.7	44.7	22.2*
July	7.0	48.6	23.1	4.9	37.5	13.0	6.9	51.6	22.1
August	7.8	56.4	24.7	10.1	47.6	20.1	10.0	61.6	24.6
September	8.5	64.9	23.3*	13.0	60.6	28.0*	11.1	72.7	28.0*
October	8.2	73.1	24.5	14.2	74.8	37.3	10.9	83.6	32.0
November	9.2	82.3	25.9	13.2	88.0	40.4	9.0	92.6	31.0
December	17.7	100.0	35.1*	12.0	100.0	39.4*	7.4	100.0	27.3*

Exhibit 7 (continued)

	G. TV PICTURE TUBES--EQUIPMENT			H. RECEIVING TUBES--RENEWAL			I. TV PICTURE TUBES--RENEWAL		
	Monthly	Cumulative	3 Months' Moving Total	Monthly	Cumulative	3 Months' Moving Total	Monthly	Cumulative	3 Months' Moving Total
January	7.5%	7.5%	24.5%	8.1%	8.1%	23.6%	8.8%	8.8%	25.8%
February	7.1	14.6	21.9	8.9	17.0	23.6	9.1	17.9	26.2
March	7.7	22.3	22.3*	10.7	27.7	27.7*	9.1	27.0	27.0*
April	6.5	28.8	21.3	7.2	34.9	26.8	8.6	35.6	26.8
May	7.2	36.0	21.4	7.2	42.1	25.1	7.6	43.2	25.3
June	8.7	44.7	22.4*	9.7	51.8	24.1*	7.3	50.5	23.5*
July	5.6	50.3	21.5	8.0	59.8	24.9	6.2	56.7	21.1
August	9.6	59.9	23.9	7.5	67.3	25.2	8.3	65.0	21.8
September	11.6	71.5	26.8*	8.2	75.5	23.7*	9.1	74.1	23.6*
October	11.5	83.0	32.7	9.0	84.5	24.7	8.9	83.0	26.3
November	9.7	92.7	32.8	8.9	93.4	26.1	8.7	91.7	26.7
December	7.3	100.0	28.5*	6.6	100.0	24.5*	8.3	100.0	25.9*

*Quarterly Seasonal.

NOTE: The seasonality of radio sets changed since World War II. In the 1930's it was: January, 9%; February, 6%; March, 5%; April, 4%; May, 2%; June, 5%; July, 4%; August, 8%; September, 12%; October, 14%; November, 15%; December, 16%.

Source: See Exhibit 6.

8. ELECTRONICS INDUSTRY

A. Factory Sales of Phonographs and Hi-Fi Components, 1947-1962

Year	Phonographs (000 Units) Single Phono-graphs	Radio-Phono-graph Combina-tion	Attach-ments	Total	Hi-Fi Components (Millions of Dollars) Amplifiers	Speakers	Tuners	Total
1947	468	3,045	718	4,231				-
1948	351	2,229	-	-				-
1949	384	1,286	-	-				-
1950	-	-	-	-				1.9
1951	-	-	-	-				-
1952	322	538	490	1,350				7.5
1953	724	491	390	1,605				-
1954	1,886	358	439	2,683				15.4
1955	2,234	393	379	3,006				19.0
1956	3,338	526	312	4,176	7.5	12.8	6.5	26.8
1957	3,718	1,048	213	4,979	11.2	14.4	7.9	33.5
1958	3,212	801	124	4,137	14.0	14.0	8.0	36.0
1959	3,475	829	86	4,390	14.2	14.3	9.4	37.9
1960	3,681	842	104	4,627	10.9	11.3	9.9	32.1
1961	2,979	1,010	N.A.	3,932	14.0	15.1	13.1	42.2
1962	3,859	1,227	N.A.	5,085	14.0	16.5	17.3	47.8

B. Factory Sales of Phonographs by Monaural and Stereophonic Types, 1958-1961

	1958		1959		1960		1961		1962	
Monaural	3,008	73.1%	1,268	29.5%	1,183	26.2%	1,089	27.3%	1,353	27.3%
Stereophonic	1,105	26.9%	3,036	70.5%	3,340	73.8%	2,900	72.7%	3,601	72.7%
	4,113	100.0%	4,304	100.0%	4,523	100.0%	2,989	100.0%	4,954	100.0%

Source: EIA, Electronic Industries, 1962 Yearbook.

9. ELECTRONICS INDUSTRY

Factory Sales of Industrial Products, 1957-1962
(In Millions of Dollars)

Equipment	1957	1958	1959	1960	1961	1962
Computing, Data Processing and Industrial Control and Processing	$ 495	$ 525	$ 625	$ 800	$1,030	$1,190
Testing and Measuring	210	220	245	265	290	315
Communications, Navigational Aids and Broadcast and Commercial Sound	470	485	530	560	615	650
Nuclear, Medical and Miscellaneous .	125	150	200	225	265	295
Total	$1,300	$1,380	$1,600	$1,850	$2,200	$2,450

Source: EIA, Electronic Industries, 1962 Yearbook.

10. ELECTRONICS INDUSTRY

Sales of Testing and Measuring Equipment, for Selected Years, 1947-1962
(In Millions of Dollars)

Description	1947	1954	1958	1959	1960	1961	1962
EQUIPMENT SALES FOR INDUSTRIAL AND MILITARY MARKET:							
Voltage current & power measuring	*	*	$ 22.4)				
			)	$ 42.0	$ 45.0	$ 49.0	
Tube characteristics measuring	$ 2.1	$ 5.8	11.6)				
Microwave testing	2.5	8.5	30.3)				
			)	56.0	58.0	61.0	
Frequency measuring	1.8	13.8	18.4)				
Oscilloscopes	4.8	25.0	42.4)				
			)	65.0	68.0	72.0	
Internal-combustion engine analyzing & measuring	15.2	23.2	) 14.0)				
Signal generating	3.8	15.2	31.6	35.0	37.0	40.0	
Communications circuit testing	*	5.7	22.4)				
			)	205.1	210.4	217.0	
Other testing & measuring equipment	24.2	81.4	139.3)				
Parts for testing & measuring equip. (sold separately)	.5	11.4	)) 9.5)				
Total	$ 54.9	$190.0	$341.9	$403.1	$418.4	$439.0	
EQUIPMENT SALES, INDUSTRIAL VS. MILITARY MARKET:							
Industrial	n.a.	$110.0	$220.0	$245.0	$265.0	$290.0	
Military & other nonindustrial	n.a.	80.0	121.9	158.1	153.4	149.0	
Total	$ 54.9	$190.0	$341.9	$403.1	$418.4	$439.0	

*Not available separately; included in the Other Testing and Measuring Equipment category.

Sources: For 1947, 1954, and 1958, all information is from the U.S. Census of Manufacturers. Total data for 1959 and 1960 is from the Annual Survey of Manufacturers, U.S. Dept. of Commerce. The 1961 total, detailed information for the years 1959, 1960, and 1961, and the "Industrial vs. Military" figures are estimates by the EIA Marketing Services Department.

11. ELECTRONICS INDUSTRY

Department of Defense Expenditures, N.A.S.A., F.A.A., Electronic Content and Total Federal Budget*
Fiscal Years, 1955-1963
(Millions of Dollars)

Category	1955	1956	1957	1958	1959	1960	1961	1962	1963
Department of Defense (DOD)									
Procurement									
Aircraft	$ 8,804	$ 7,835	$ 8,647	$ 8,793	$ 7,730	$ 6,272	$ 5,898	$ 6,449	$ 5,568
Missiles	604	1,005	1,855	2,434	3,337	3,027	2,972	3,522	3,899
Ships	944	858	842	1,105	1,491	1,744	1,801	2,049	2,308
Ordnance, Vehicles, etc.	1,191	1,260	674	365	399	443	675	1,135	1,717
Electronics and Communications	441	660	704	663	721	1,093	1,042	1,196	1,208
Other	854	608	767	723	731	755	707	485	656
Total	$12,838	$12,227	$13,489	$14,083	$14,409	$13,334	$13,095	$14,836	$15,356
Operation and Maintenance	7,931	8,400	9,487	9,761	10,378	10,233	10,611	11,595	11,511
Research, Development, Test and Evaluation	3,261	2,101	2,406	2,504	2,866	4,710	6,131	6,039	6,650
Military Construction	1,715	2,079	1,968	1,753	1,948	1,626	1,605	1,250	1,189
Other	9,788	10,984	7,088	10,961	11,632	11,312	11,785	14,530	14,994
Total DOD	$35,533	$35,791	$34,438	$39,062	$41,233	$41,215	$43,227	$48,250	$49,700
Electronic Content									
DOD	$ 3,225	$ 3,440	$ 3,878	$ 4,382	$ 4,940	$ 5,670	$ 6,238	$ 7,235	$ 7,921
As % of total DOD	9.1%	9.6%	11.3%	11.2%	12.0%	13.8%	14.4%	15.0%	15.9%
NASA							241	377	742
FAA							130	160	160
Federal Budget, Total									
In Dollars	$64,600	$66,500	$69,400	$71,900	$80,300	$76,500	$81,500	$89,100	$92,500
Total DOD as %	55.0%	53.9%	49.6%	54.3%	51.3%	53.9%	53.0%	54.2%	53.6%

*Differs from Exhibit 1; this table is in terms of fiscal years while Table One is for calendar years. Fiscal years end June 30.

Source: EIA, Electronics Industries, 1962.

12. ELECTRONICS INDUSTRY

Electronic Content of Fiscal Year 1963 Department of Defense Programmed Expenditures (In Millions of Dollars)

Category	Dollar Expenditures	Electronics Content	Percent Electronics
Procurement:			
Aircraft	$ 5,568	$1,169.0	21.0%
Missiles	3,899	1,599.0	41.0
Ships	2,308	496.0	21.5
Vehicles, Ordnance and Related Equipment	1,717	85.0	5.0
Electronics and Communications	1,208	1,026.0	84.9
Other	656	13.0	2.0
Total	$15,356	$4,388.0	28.6
Operations and Maintenance	11,511	1,735.0	15.1
Research, Development, Test and Evaluation	6,650	1,733.0	26.1
Military Construction	1,189		
		65.0	.4
Other	14,994		
Total	$49,700	$7,921.0	15.9

Source: EIA, Electronic Industries, 1962 Yearbook.

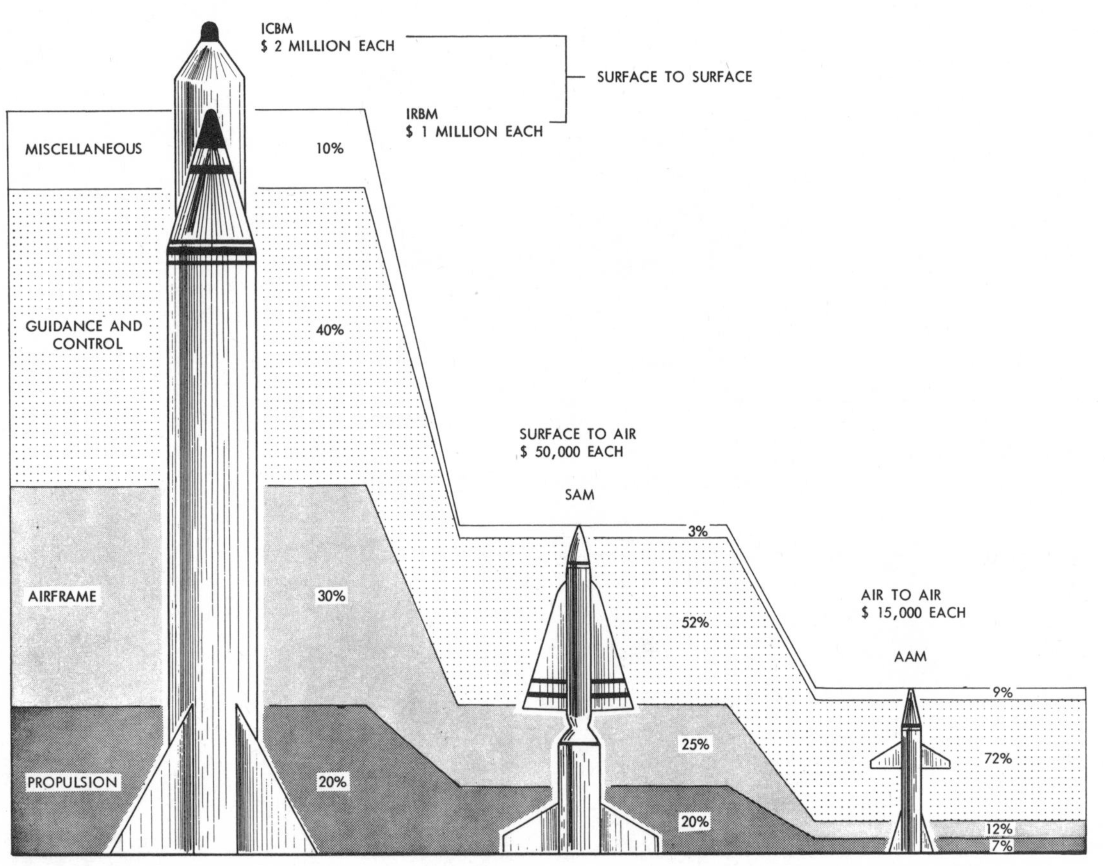

Source: Stanford Research Institute.

12A. ELECTRONICS INDUSTRY

Typical Missile Production Costs

13. ELECTRONICS INDUSTRY

Manufacturers' Component Sales, 1954-1962
(In Millions of Dollars)

	1954	1955	1956	1957	1958	1959	1960	1961	1962
DISCRETE COMPONENTS									
Active									
Electron Tubes									
Receiving	$ 276.0	$ 358.1	$ 374.2	$ 384.4	$ 341.9	$ 368.9	$ 331.7	$ 311.1	301.5
TV Picture	206.1	209.0	196.2	183.2	163.5	183.8	180.8	185.6	173.7
Power and Special Purpose	152.0	148.0	161.0	185.0	215.0	252.0	252.0	285.0	325.0
Total	$ 634.1	$ 715.1	$ 731.4	$ 752.6	$ 720.4	$ 804.7	$ 764.5	$ 781.7	$ 800.2
Semiconductors									
Transistors	$ 5.1	$ 12.3	$ 37.4	$ 69.7	$ 112.7	$ 222.0	$ 301.4	$ 299.5	$ 291.4
Diodes and Rectifiers	N.A.	N.A.	76.0	102.3	112.8	166.3	224.0	200.0	203.7
Other	N.A.	N.A.	N.A.	5.0	10.0	20.0	35.0	65.0	68.0
Total	N.A.	N.A	N.A.	$ 177.0	$ 235.5	$ 408.3	$ 560.4	$ 564.5	$ 563.1
Passive									
Capacitors	$ 200.0	$ 215.0	$ 224.0	$ 225.0	$ 218.0	$ 267.0	$ 295.0	$ 338.0	$ 340.0
Quartz Crystals	-	8.0	10.0	11.0	9.0	12.0	22.0	28.0	N.A.
Resistors	130.0	150.0	175.0	171.0	158.0	194.0	227.0	295.0	315.0
Inductors	175.0	165.0	160.0	183.0	201.0	224.0	204.0	231.0	230.0
Other	795.0	862.0	858.0	920.0	825.0	984.0	1,017.0	1,071.0	1,115.0
Total	$1,300.0	$1,400.0	$1,427.0	$1,510.0	$1,411.0	$1,681.0	$1,765.0	$1,963.0	$2,000.0
COMPLEX COMPONENTS									
"Nonminiaturized"*	N.A.	N.A.	N.A.	35.0)	45.0)	60.0)	90.0	85.0	95.0
"Miniaturized"	-0-	-0-	-0-	)	)	)		60.0	90.0
Total	N.A.	N.A.	N.A.	$ 35.0	$ 45.0	$ 60.0	$ 90.0	$ 145.0	$ 185.0
GRAND TOTAL	N.A.	N.A.	N.A.	$2,274.6	$2,411.9	$2,954.0	$3,179.9	$3,454.2	$3,548.0

*Includes modules with discrete active combined with passive components to perform a circuit function; planar, integrated and molecular circuits, thin circuits with and without active components.

Source: EIA, Electronic Industries, 1962 Yearbook.

14. ELECTRONICS INDUSTRY

Manufacturers' Sales of Picture Tubes, 1947-1962

	1947	1948	1949	1950	1951	1952	1953	1954	1955	1956	1957	1958	1959	1960	1961	1962
Dollar sales (millions)	$7.8	$33.5	$98.1	$210.7	$122.2	$170.7	$234.9	$206.1	$209.0	$196.2	$183.2	$163.5	$183.8	$180.8	$185.6	$173.7
Unit sales (thousands)	274	1,309	3,513	7,957	5,136	7,635	9,839	9,914	10,874	10,998	9,723	8,254	9,523	9,014	9,309	9,070
Unit Sales by End Use																
Initial			3,306	7,474	4,434	6,120	7,583	7,515	7,752	7,540	6,175	4,955	6,135	5,715	6,022	6,457
Renewal			203	472	674	1,432	1,800	1,807	2,361	2,726	2,779	2,503	2,630	2,406	2,112	1,698
Export			4	11	22	83	452	590	760	721	767	794	757	893	1,173	914
Government					6		4		1	1	2	2	1	*	2	*
Unit Sales by Screen Size																
15" and under		1,146	3,316	2,365	437	297	267	236	412	1,596	518	289	156	74	66	43
16" to 18"		9	180	5,356	3,587	3,005	3,065	2,086	1,805	1,909	2,231	2,064	2,932	1,540	581	656
19" to 21"				212	973	4,296	6,105	7,223	7,674	6,713	6,415	5.511	5,644	4,413	4,300	4,599
22" to 25"					121	30	276	319	948	742	535	371	779	2,724	4,123	3,534
26" and over							120	47	35	27	22	17	12	264	238	238
Projection		154	17	24	18	7	6	3	*	*	*	*	-0-	-0-	-0-	-0-

*Included with 15" and under.

Source: EIA, Electronic Industries, 1947-1962 Yearbooks.

15. ELECTRONICS INDUSTRY

Manufacturer's Sales of Receiving Tubes by End Use, 1935-1962
(Thousands of Units)

Year	Initial	Renewal	Export	Government*	Total	Value
1935	41,006	28,060	6,896		75,962	26,565
1936	58,579	30,882	8,843		98,304	31,942
1937	54,599	27,210	10,247		92,056	29,871
1938	42,373	24,917	7,401		74,691	23,093
1939	65,284	25,375	7,841		98,500	27,985
1940	72,249	28,994	7,233		108,476	27,610
1941	92,031	33,782	10,025		135,838	47,500
1942	64,640	36,495	6,612		107,747	43,000
1943	54,507	19,637	3,106	32,828	110,078	51,000
1944	60,207	20,899	4,552	43,405	129,063	62,140
1945	57,235	40,462	4,995	36,786	139,478	68,500
1946	129,637	65,228	9,991	361	205,217	101,000
1947	131,987	43,530	23,184	833	199,534	107,000
1948	146,162	47,056	10,687	815	204,720	112,000
1949	147,298	39,696	10,073	1,686	198,753	119,000
1950	301,483	69,325	10,768	1,385	382,961	250,000
1951	247,855	94,597	24,438	8,754	375,644	261,000
1952	241,406	83,843	13,935	29,335	368,519	259,116
1953	293,601	112,785	20,614	10,091	437,091	303,675
1954	246,729	115,358	15,922	7,080	385,089	275,999
1955	288,810	150,718	24,442	15,832	479,802	358,110
1956	262,898	166,558	25,397	9,333	464,186	374,186
1957	240,708	184,493	23,378	7,845	456,424	384,402
1958	191,832	167,805	24,597	13,132	397,366	341,929
1959	227,729	170,729	19,969	14,569	432,936	368,872
1960	200,362	161,092	21,375	10,226	393,055	331,742
1961	188,176	150,249	22,245	14,336	375,006	311,098
1962	190,140	134,390	19,804	16,905	361,239	301,525

*Includes only Direct Sales after 1954.

Source: EIA, Electronic Industries, 1962 Yearbook.

16. ELECTRONICS INDUSTRY

Factory Sales of Transistors, 1954-1962
(Thousands of Units)

	1954	1955	1956	1957	1958	1959	1960	1961	1962
Nonconsumer--by Market									
Original Equipment									
Units	1,095	2,303	4,913	7,991	13,595	33,051	65,441	114,882	142,696
Dollars	$4,493	$ 9,448	$21,040	$39,998	$ 68,405	$152,952	$216,204	$218,202	198,245
Distributor									
Units	12	100		458		3,314	6,728	9,839	15,010
Dollars	130	235		1,138		22,977	36,388	33,882	43,349
			536		2,423				
Other			$ 3,972		$ 12,102				
Units	13	29		881		1,569	2,883	6,111	7,258
Dollars	137	178		1,998		4,811	7,894	11,876	13,280
Total Nonconsumer									
Units	1,120	2,432	5,449	9,357	16,018	37,934	75,052	130,832	164,960
Dollars	$4,760	$ 9,861	$25,012	$43,134	$ 80,507	$180,740	$260,486	$263,960	254,874
Consumer--all Markets									
Units	198	1,215	7,391	19,408	31,033	44,360	52,877	60,084	75,339
Dollars	$ 362	$ 2,392	$12,340	$26,605	$ 32,223	$ 41,270	$ 40,946	$ 35,579	36,530
Grand Total--all Markets									
Units	1,318	3,647	12,840	28,765	47,051	82,294	127,929	190,916	240,229
Dollars	$5,122	$12,253	$37,352	$69,739	$112,730	$222,010	$301,432	$299,539	291,404

Source: EIA, Electronic Industries, 1962.

17. ELECTRONICS INDUSTRY

Manufacturers' Sales of Diodes and Rectifiers, 1954-1962
(Millions of Units and Dollars)

Material	1954	1955	1956	1957	1958	1959	1960	1961	1962
Germanium									
Units	13.2	16.5	30.0	41.2	45.8	66.5		171.4	190.0
Dollars.	$ 8.5	$11.2	$19.6	$ 29.5	$ 27.6	$ 31.8		$ 47.3	34.3
							185.4		
Silicon							$176.8		
Units	5.9	7.0	11.4	14.5	26.2	53.6		107.5	102.3
Dollars.	$11.5	$18.8	$30.4	$ 43.7	$ 67.8	$101.2		$ 98.2	109.6
Other									
Units	na	na	na	15.8	13.1	na	na	na	na
Dollars.			$26.0	$ 29.6	$ 17.4	$ 33.3	$ 47.2	$ 54.5	59.8
Total									
Units	na	na	na	71.5	85.1	na	na	na	na
Dollars.			$76.0	$102.8	$112.8	$166.3	$224.0	$200.0	203.7

Source: EIA, Electronic Industries, 1962 Yearbook.

18. ELECTRONICS INDUSTRY

Trends and Prices of Germanium and Silicon Transistors

A. Trends

	Germanium		Silicon		All Transistors	
	Production (1,000 Units)	Average Value	Production (1,000 Units)	Average Value	Production (1,000 Units)	Average Value
1954					2,000	$4.96
1955					4,000	3.37
1956					14,000	2.73
1957					28,000	2.45
1958					46,000	2.43
1959					83,477	2.73
	0-999 mw		All Silicon Transistors			
1960 1st quarter	25,413	$1.85	2,057	$12.15	32,880	2.53
2nd "	24,285	1.72	2,030	12.83	29,621	2.61
3rd "	22,960	1.50	3,545	7.78	29,787	2.36
4th "	32,587	1.40	2,916	9.61	39,534	2.10
Total	105,245	1.60	10,548	10.11	131,822	2.38
			0-999 mw			
1961 1st quarter	34,985	1.30	1,973	6.40	41,376	2.04
2nd "	42,441	1.14	1,644	5.88	49,144	1.70
3rd "	38,714	1.01	1,862	4.69	45,750	1.51
4th "	47,665	0.91	3,150	4.69	56,779	1.40
Total	163,805	1.08	8,629	5.31	193,049	1.64
1962 1st quarter	52,692	0.93	3,914	4.35	62,787	1.28

Source: U.S. Department of Commerce, Business and Defense Services Administration, Electronics Division, Electronic Components: Production and Related Data 1952-1959 and subsequent quarterly surveys.

B. Prices

	NPN Germanium Alloy	PNP Germanium Alloy	NPN Silicon Mesa	PNP Silicon Mesa
1960				
January	$2.95	$1.45	-	-
April	2.84	1.30	-	-
July	2.67	1.00	-	$1.95
October	2.00	.67	-	1.95
1961				
January	1.80	.60	-	1.95
April	1.70	.55	$4.55	1.75
July	1.45	.45	1.05	3.20
October	.82	.42	3.20	1.01
1962				
January	.74	.42	2.80	.97
April	.74	.38	2.23	.89
July	.85	.45	1.73	.89
October	.36	.45	.94	.69
1963				
January	.36	.30	.94	.68
April	-	.30	.94	.68

NOTE: All prices are list, although sales were made 25% or more off list. For example, the second transistor which is similar to the 2N404, was being offered for $.19 in April, 1963.
Source: A major electronics company.

19. ELECTRONICS INDUSTRY

U.S. Exports and Imports of Electronic Products
(Thousands of Dollars)

	1959	1960	1961
A. Domestic Exports:			
Television receivers	$ 17,631	$ 14,713	$ 16,809
Television chassis	2,901	3,968	11,468
Radios:			
Automobile	1,782	1,395	2,015
Home	4,086	2,861	3,616
Chassis	935	876	735
Radio-phonograph	916	515	726
Phonographs, records	33,840	31,285	27,786
Recorders	10,986	12,971	14,603
Other	3,317	2,798	3,626
Total Consumer	$ 76,394	$ 71,382	$ 81,384
Industrial and Military:			
Radio and TV broadcast	$ 18,456	$ 20,838	$ 23,455
Communication	90,691	94,299	107,445
Detection and navigation	45,809	50,538	72,268
Other	55,904	86,703	159,519
Total	$210,860	$252,328	$362,687
Components:			
Receiving tubes	$ 14,671	$ 14,382	$ 16,400
TV picture	13,757	21,304	21,320
Other tubes	20,898	28,405	28,299
Semiconductor devices	9,148	15,973	20,788
Other	54,997	62,688	82,153
Total	$113,471	$142,752	$168,960
Grand Total	$400,725	$466,462	$613,031
B. Domestic Imports:			
Radios	$ 72,724	$ 92,653	$111,188
Portable (tube)	N.A.	2,512	1,784
Transistor	N.A.	55,849	66,688
Other	N.A.	9,303	13,424
Tubes	N.A.	10,099	12,524
Parts	N.A.	14,890	16,768
Radio-phonographs	N.A.	8,643	12,940
Phonographs, records	6,327	14,259	19,361
Testing equipment	N.A.	8,767	6,878
Radar	N.A.	4,434	10,561
Loud speakers	N.A.	1,747	2,320
TV cameras, parts	1,302	3,502	5,817
Photocells, tubes	1,358	2,394	3,816
Other	N.A.	4,842	6,387
Total	N.A.	$142,385	$179,268

Exhibit 19 (continued)

C. U.S. Imports from Japan:	1956	1957	1958	1959	1960	1961
Radio receivers	$2,646	$5,294	$17,904	$62,373	$69,315	$ 74,638
Tube-type	N.A.	N.A.	N.A.	2,552	6,277	14,171
Transistor.	N.A.	N.A.	N.A.	57,272	55,130	48,153
Other	N.A.	N.A.	N.A.	2,549	7,908	12,314
TV receivers	-	-	-	-	507	1,721
Radio-phonographs . . . .)	5	139	511	547	1,252	2,698
Sound recorders, reprod. . . . .)				1,617	6,068	15,554
Electron tubes	7	8	314	2,088	4,599	5,780
Semiconductor devices.	4	1	7	1,673	1,846	2,400
Other components	26	865	1,550	3,348	4,517	7,683
Other products*	611	1,275	1,489	3,996	5,909	9,404
Total	$3,299	$7,582	$21,775	$75,642	$94,013	$119,878

*Includes amplifiers, microphones, speakers, receivers, and phonograph parts.

NOTE: Imports are understated due to being reported under non-electronic categories, and due to products of U.S. overseas plants not being included. Exports do not reflect electronic equipment incorporated in weapons systems under military assistance programs for exported "know-how."

Source: U.S. Department of Commerce, Bureau of the Census, Report No. FT-410, FT-110, and EIA.

Sentinel Radio Corporation

The Sentinel Radio Corporation of Evanston, Illinois, was an independent manufacturer of radio and television sets, with a net worth of $3 million and a sales volume of $15 million in 1953. In the promotion of television sets under its own brand name "Sentinel," the company was in direct competition with other independent manufacturers more than ten times its size and with divisions of large diversified corporations. The Sentinel organization placed particular emphasis on the performance characteristics and reliability of its television sets, which were sold in the medium price range.

The executives of the Sentinel Radio Corporation believed that the company was in sound financial condition, had excellent manufacturing facilities, enjoyed fine labor relations and loyal staff support, and produced a television set that was recognized in the trade to be particularly free from service difficulties. In March, 1954, the impending development of color television and the moderate decline in general business conditions combined to create severe price competition in black-and-white TV sets. The executives wanted to choose the short- and long-range program most likely to establish Sentinel in its proper niche in the industry. Balance sheets and income statements for 1947–1954 are shown in Exhibits 1 and 2.

COMPANY HISTORY

The Sentinel company was organized in 1931 by Mr. Ernest Alschuler, with an original capital of $11,000. The name Electrical Research Laboratories, Inc. was used until 1945, when the company became the Sentinel Radio Corporation.

Between 1933 and 1941, the annual sales of Electrical Research Laboratories, Inc., increased from $319,000 to $3,004,000 while the company shifted from supplying private band radios to retail chains and mail-order houses to selling small radios under the Sentinel name to consumers. Mr. Alschuler established a reputation for dependable sets and obtained contracts as a supplemental supplier of radio chassis to a large manufacturer serving the high-quality market.

In the competitive market of the 1930's, one of the few areas then untouched by active sales promotion was the region of isolated farmhouses in the South and Middle West. Since widespread rural electrification had not developed, special radios had to be designed for farms which were not wired for electricity. The Sentinel company pioneered the development of a 1½ volt farm radio using a 1,000 hour battery pack. Promoted under the Sentinel name, farm sets accounted for almost 30 percent of the company's sales by 1935.

In the late 1930's, Mr. Alschuler became interested in the market for portable radios to offset the seasonal lull in sales during the summer months. In cooperation with a large electrical manufacturing corporation, the company designed and patented a portable radio designed to look like a camera. Although a substantial part of the camera type radios were sold under a private brand name, they accounted for 20 percent of the company's sales in 1941.

When commercial radio production was halted by government order in March, 1942, more than half of the company's sales were under its own brand name Sentinel. At that time the company was producing 281,000 radio sets a year, or 2½ percent of the industry total. Its sales volume of $3,828,000 was only 1½ percent of the industry, however, because of its concentration on small sets. Sales were made through 75 distributors to 10,000 retail outlets. The following table shows the product distribution in 1941:

Product	
Table and console radios and table radio-phonographs	34%
Portable radios, battery and electric	26
Battery operated farm sets	26
Export sets designed for radio reception in foreign countries	9
Battery replacements and other	5

War Business

As a result of the military demand for radio equipment during World War II, annual sales of the Sentinel company increased from $3,828,000 to almost $17,000,000 in two years. During the war, the company produced $38,000,000 of military products, which yielded a net profit after taxes of approximately $550,000. The company received the Army-Navy "E" for excellence as well as the Navy Certificate of Achievement.

In order to accomplish its wartime expansion, the company enlarged its personnel from 450 to 700 persons, 70 percent of whom were women.

The engineering staff was increased to 32 men. The principal difficulty, however, was to find adequate production facilities for the expanded scale of operations. The main plant consisted of a leased four-story building with a basement, located in Evanston. It contained 64,000 square feet of floor space. By 1945, the company was obliged to operate in six widely separated emergency locations as well as in the main plant. Meanwhile, annual plant rental costs had been increased from $12,800 to $80,000.

In order to provide adequate facilities and eliminate rental fees, the Sentinel executives decided to build a new plant in 1945. The building was designed to provide the most modern assembly and storage facilities, engineering space, and executive offices. With a subsequent addition, the plant contained 124,000 square feet of space in a one-story fireproof brick building located on 9½ acres of land. Construction of the new plant, which cost over $800,000, increased the company's net fixed assets from $72,000 in 1942 to $946,000 in 1946 and reduced its working capital. An issue of common stock was floated in order to gain $450,000 in new funds to carry the company through the period when military contracts were being canceled.

ORGANIZATION

The Sentinel Radio Corporation was administered by three senior officers, who were members of the board of directors, and a six-man management group.

Engineering and Design

Mr. Schnell, director of engineering, had been chief engineer for the Sentinel company for 25 years. He was a senior member in the Institute of Radio Engineers and had obtained more than two dozen patents for electrical inventions, many of which were in commercial use. In 1953, he took an active part in the development of technical standards for color television by the National Television System Committee.

The engineering department was responsible for the design details of television and radio sets as well as for research and development work on electrical circuits. New designs for Sentinel brands were developed under the close supervision of the sales executives; new designs for private brands were developed according to customers' specifications. Component specifications were strictly controlled; Sentinel made some parts (such as coils) to ensure quality. The housings for the company's line of portable radios were designed for injection molding in plastic, but all television cabinets were of more conservative style, making use of solid and veneered wood construction. The use of wood not only maintained a high-quality product but avoided the initial investment of $30,000 to $50,000 in dies necessary for the compression molding of a plastic television cabinet.

In 1954, research and development of color television was becoming a major program in the department. The Sentinel company had authorized $80,000 for engineering and $60,000 for production color test equipment. The facilities for complete color testing were nearly finished in March, 1954, and included equipment for transmitting color test signals, synchronizing and monitoring signals in accordance with industry standards, set alignment, and racks for the spot check and life testing of color sets.

The Sentinel Radio Corporation had built several color television sets for its distributors to use for demonstration purposes. Although the circuit of the color television set was extremely complex and required careful shielding and alignment, most of the basic circuit designs were established by March, 1954. The principal delay in production was due to the selection of a picture tube. Mr. Schnell believed that the current 15-inch size was too small to be accepted by consumers and wished to wait until a 19-inch tube was available. The production of color picture tubes was in a confused state due to the fact that there were three competing tube designs, one of which required a different circuit than the others, and none of which was as yet in full production in a 19-inch size.

Manufacturing

Mr. Irving J. Jacobsen, director of manufacturing, had owned a company manufacturing electrical and radio products before joining the Sentinel organization. By 1954, he had been in charge of production at Sentinel for almost 20 years. The principal problems facing Mr. Jacobsen were planning of assembly schedules and supervision of factory personnel.

The Sentinel production facilities were such that they could be adjusted to changing requirements fairly easily, although storage space for finished inventory was relatively small. The plant had originally been designed to manufacture 5,000 small radios per day, but had been converted to two assembly lines for a maximum potential of 3,000 small radios and 1,000 television sets. The storage space for incoming shipments was located adjacent to the start of the two assembly lines. Purchased components were checked at this point and any indications of poor quality resulted in a 100 percent check and return of the defective parts. The workers were instructed to work carefully without undue speed so as to ensure reliable workmanship.

The design of television and radio sets was revised twice a year before the January and June distributors' meetings. Although Sentinel sometimes had as many as 20 different cabinet styles or finishes for television sets, it manufactured only three basic chassis models: table, console, and superchassis. The superchassis which had special circuiting to permit reception in isolated areas was eliminated in 1954, leaving two basic chassis types to be used for all models. These two types were modified as required to permit the installation of UHF tuning components and large-sized picture tubes.

Whenever a completely new chassis was introduced, the engineering department provided a working model which was checked carefully for processing and component requirements. A pilot run of 50 to 100 sets was made. Next, a full month was devoted to trouble shooting production problems, forestalling service difficulties, obtaining new parts from outside suppliers, and developing time standards and work methods.

It was occasionally necessary to switch the television line from one established chassis type to another, such as from table to console models. In these cases only a few hours were ordinarily required to start the line on the new model since the necessary jigs and fixtures were located near the line on trucks. Mr. Jacobsen liked to run a full week on each chassis before changing to the other. Less than a week on each model ordinarily led to losses in setup time and production efficiencies, since the workers usually reached their peak of dexterity on the fourth day. Due to the lack of space for finished inventory, more than a week on each model was not feasible except during periods when immediate shipment could be made.

Changes in production requirements ordinarily affected the size of the work force in the plant. When the television line was on a one-minute cycle, 500 sets could be produced in one day with 120 women on the assembly line alone (exclusive of test and alignment personnel). Each worker made four or five wiring connections. When production dropped to 150 sets per day, the cycle was increased to 3 minutes and 38 women could operate the line, making 7 to 10 connections each. On the radio assembly line the wiring job was less complicated, and 16 women could assemble 400 sets per day.

The Sentinel executives wished to maintain the labor force as steady as possible throughout the year; however, financial pressures forced layoffs during the slack seasons. The growing industrialization of the area made it increasingly difficult to obtain help after long periods of layoffs.

Many of the 700 employees had worked for the company for more than 10 years. Attempts were made to protect the workers from seasonal unemployment through the development of fringe benefits and a high-base pay. The workers were represented by the Independent Radio Workers Union, which had no affiliations with the AFL or CIO and maintained cordial relationships with the company. Women assembly workers were paid \$1.29 per hour to start as trainees, and would ordinarily earn as much as \$1.65 per hour in eight months, with continual increases thereafter. Test and alignment men earned about \$2 per hour. Due to the nature of the assembly line, there were no piece rates or incentive pay scales, though the operations of individual workers were time studied under the supervision of an industrial engineer.

Sales and Advertising

The responsibility for sales of the Sentinel products was shared by the director of sales and the general sales manager. Mr. E. G. May, the director of sales, had been with the company since the 1930's. Mr. R. B. Parks, the general sales manager, had come to the company in 1952 from the sales division of the Firestone Tire and Rubber Corporation. The arrival of Mr. Parks coincided with a new program undertaken by Sentinel in 1952 to develop and expand its field operations and distributor relations.

The following table indicates the proportion

of branded and unbranded products as a percentage of total sales:

	Sales (1,000)	Sentinel	Private	Gov't.
1948	$ 6,543	85%	15%	—
1949	6,079	80	20	—
1950	9,073	80	20	—
1951	20,091	85	15	—
1952	10,126	70	15	15%
1953	15,143	50	20	30
Objective		60	25	15

The Sentinel Radio Corporation sold its products in 11 sales territories through 110 distributors who in turn worked with 20,000 retail dealers. All distributors were independent firms and were responsible for their own relationships with retailers, except in the Chicago–St. Louis–Memphis territory where the company had its own distributing organization. Sixty of the distributors handled both radio and teleivsion sets, but 50 were in areas which did not yet have television broadcasting and hence handled only radio sets.

Mr. Parks considered the sales coverage to be good with the exception of a few weak areas. The company maintained a force of 13 salesmen or commission representatives to service the distributors. The salesmen were instructed to give considerable selling help and even financial advice to the distributors. Relationships between the headquarters office and the selling offices were regarded as unusually favorable.

Because the company's products were considered dependable and its selling policies conservative, many distributors viewed the Sentinel line as a "safe" line with sound growth prospects. The conservative company policies had prevented rapid expansion in 1950 and had resulted in a relatively narrow line of television models. As a result, although the distributors often expected to do a smaller volume with the Sentinel line than would be the case with competing lines, they had smaller inventory commitments and fewer financial problems and risks.

The Sentinel Radio Corporation undertook both national and local advertising. After 1952 the total advertising expenditures varied between 4½ and 7 percent of sales, and averaged approximately $500,000 per year. The national advertising campaign was conducted through magazines such as *Time,* the *Saturday Evening Post, Newsweek,* and *Better Homes & Gardens.* It was recognized that the resources of the company were inadequate to provide intensive advertising throughout the nation. Expenditures for national campaigns were therefore limited to selected magazine insertions.

Almost 45 percent of the total advertising budget was directed to local campaigns in support of key distributors through a cooperative plan. Although Sentinel sales were small in certain cities, they ran second in the entire television industry in Rochester, New York, and Springfield, Illinois, and were just below the five major producers in Chicago and San Francisco.

In 1947 and 1950, Duff, Anderson, and Clark, a firm of security analysts, made a survey of private brand customers, Sentinel distributors, and Sentinel dealers, to determine the trade acceptance of the company's products. The subsequent report contained the following statement:

> Almost all of these companies have handled the Sentinel line for many years. Their replies to the questions asked are almost identical in nearly every case. They agree that the performance of Sentinel radios is excellent; that appearance is fair and leaves something to be desired (with the exception of certain models, notably the "Treasure Chest," which is extremely popular); that Sentinel radios are exceptionally free of service troubles, giving far better satisfaction in this respect than most radios; that dealer and consumer acceptance is improving rapidly. They agree that the company is competitive from the standpoint of price, although one reply states that certain models are slightly overpriced. They agree that the company's sales program is rapidly becoming more satisfactory. They want more sales helps of the type which the company has recently begun to supply. They agree that the line has suffered in past years from lack of consumer advertising, but that the consumer advertising program the company has now begun is showing spectacular results. They are all most positive in their statement that their general business relations with the company have always been extremely satisfactory.

Partly in response to the report, Sentinel launched a more intensive campaign to build consumer sales demand for its branded sets, and devoted special attention to styling, merchandising, and distributor support. An example of the new advertising and style effort is contained in Exhibit 6.

Purchasing

Mr. Lawrence Priscal, director of purchases, had joined the predecessor of the Sentinel Radio Corporation before its reorganization in 1931. Mr. Priscal supervised the work of five buyers who collectively spent about $10,000,000 a year for materials and component parts. Exhibit 3 includes information of the cost of products sold and Exhibit 4 shows selling, administrative, and general expenses. In 1953, the major categories of expenditures for each Sentinel sales dollar were as follows: direct labor, 7.4 percent; royalties, 1.4 percent; wages and salaries, 7.0 percent; and purchased materials, 68.6 percent.

The purchasing power of the Sentinel Radio Corporation was considered small relative to that of its major competitors. Prior to 1953, the heavy demand for television set components made it difficult for the company to ensure adequate supplies of materials. Moreover, Mr. Priscal estimated that he could obtain cabinets for 10 percent below his current price if he were able to purchase in larger lots than 2,000 units. Certain of the cabinet styles often required 10,000 or 15,000 units per year. In order to obtain larger quantity discounts, it was necessary for the company to contract for a full year's supply of cabinets at one time and to forego the option of revising its requirements on a quarterly basis.

In 1953, the company had made its purchase commitments on an annual basis, but the autumn sales increase generally anticipated throughout the industry did not materialize. Since the procurement lead time was about 12 weeks, it was impossible to cut back orders for November and December when the sales volume in October did not meet the company's expectations. Exhibit 5 indicates the production and sales of units in the major product lines during 1953 and 1954. As can be seen from this exhibit, production of console television sets exceeded sales during the April and July quarters of 1953 by 7,500 sets. Sales in the October quarter were not sufficient to accomplish any major reduction in inventories, but total production was cut back only slightly during the fall quarter because of the difficulties of cancelling purchase commitments. The company did, however, shift its production so as to reduce the output of console models and increase the output of table models.

Production was not substantially reduced until the January quarter of 1954. Meanwhile, the company was obliged to rent space in an empty building in Evanston to store the additional inventory of television sets which the main plant could not provide. The additional cost of shipping sets to the rented warehouse and maintaining separate inventory files suggested the desirability of building an addition to the main plant to provide more storage space.

Finance

As acting treasurer of the Sentinel Radio Corporation, Mr. Lawton was concerned with financial problems arising from the seasonal nature of the television business. One manufacturing season ordinarily ended on March 31, when the fiscal year closed and inventory was taken. April, May, and June were slack months, since distributors were watching for advance indications of fall buying trends, and manufacturers were waiting for the distributors' orders to be taken during the furniture show in the week of July 1. The television plants ordinarily closed for two weeks' vacation, July 1–15. Production volume usually built up in August and September to a peak in October and November and then gradually declined. Since Sentinel enjoyed good bank credit, it ordinarily financed with short-term bank loans its seasonal extension in receivables and inventory, which usually were at a maximum of about $1,000,000 in October.

Mr. Lawton believed that it was impossible to predict the fall trends as early as the April quarter. Furthermore, since the procurement cycle was twelve weeks, it was even difficult to stockpile in July, unless market predictions were made prior to the summer model showing. Rather than run the market and financial risks associated with the accumulation of inventories, he believed that the company should seek to level out its production operations (*a*) by obtaining private brand business during the April quarter, and (*b*) by developing new products which would offset the summer slump in the television business.

The company's anticipated production program for the last three quarters of 1954 is shown in Exhibit 5.

PRODUCT POLICIES

In the fall of 1953, the anticipated seasonal increase in television sales did not materialize, in part because of consumer interest in color television which resulted in a curtailment of monochrome set purchases. By March, 1954, severe price competition began to appear in the industry as a result of excess inventories.

The executives of the Sentinel Radio Corporation predicted that consumers would have a strong preference for low-priced sets until color television became a factor in the market. In planning the 1954 fall line, therefore, they decided to concentrate on the models at the lower end of the Sentinel price range as a means of staying in competition without reducing quality. Table models, for example, were increased from 38 to 57 percent of the company's scheduled output. The 27-inch set was eliminated so as to reduce the number of special circuit components and costly folded-door cabinets. The "superchassis" for fringe area reception was also eliminated since higher power telecasting stations currently under construction would improve reception. Certain special cabinet sizes were discontinued so that the percentage of staple models could be increased from 75 to 92 percent. The executives believed that conservative merchandising and sound financing would enable their company to remain strong during the current buyer's market and permit it to prepare for the development of the color television market.

In making plans for the introduction of color television, the Sentinel executives were faced with conflicting information and opinions from industry sources. Certain industry spokesmen claimed that color television was at least two years away due to technical difficulties in the manufacture of the picture tube and to the high cost of producing color sets until full mass-production was attained. The Westinghouse Electric Corporation placed color sets on the market in February, 1954, conducted a major sales campaign, and sold only 30 sets in two months. The General Electric Company adopted a "wait-and-see" policy, confining its activity to laboratory development until the market picture clarified. Philco, Dumont, and Magnavox were among the companies which had no current plans for selling color television sets. The Emerson Company announced that it would rent color sets in the belief that the initial cost would be too high for outright consumer purchase. Mr. Lawton heard talk in the trade during April, 1954, that the small-tube sizes were very difficult to promote. Several manufacturers such as Admiral corporation stopped marketing 15-inch color sets because customers seemed to be waiting for 19-inch and 21-inch tubes.

On the other hand, many industry leaders were predicting that up to 100,000 color television sets would be produced during 1954 at retail prices of $1,000 to $1,500 each, with production increasing to 350,000 in 1955, 1,780,000 in 1956, 3,000,000 in 1957 and 5,000,000 in 1958. Zenith, Motorola, and other companies announced plans for the introduction of color sets during the fall of 1954. Meanwhile, the Radio Corporation of America was producing color sets at the rate of 2,000 per month.

The production costs of color television sets were considerably greater than those for monochrome sets. Not only did color sets require three times as many tubes, but the picture tube itself was five to ten times as expensive. The entire set required very careful test and alignment as well as quality control during assembly. Additional test equipment for color had already cost the company $140,000 for engineering and production control. Moreover, a color assembly line required four times as many workers as an equivalent monochrome television line.

Color posed a production problem. If the monochrome assembly line were used for color sets one week per month, the changeover cost would be very high. On the other hand, if a separate line for color were installed, space limitations might require additional plant expansion.

LONG-RANGE PLANS

Until the reappearance of the seller's market, Sentinel executives believed that the company would be under a certain amount of pressure from its distributors for help in maintaining their market positions. The distributors had always been exceptionally loyal to the company and their conservative inventory policies had placed them in a position to withstand a market downturn. Moreover, the new products which the company planned to offer during the coming year would give the distributors a lower priced line without reducing Sentinel quality.

Nevertheless, hard times were believed to be in prospect. One large corporation, for example, was rumored to be ready to lose $21½ million in 1954 if necessary to hold its market position for the future. It was anticipated that such losses would be incurred by companies entering the color television market early because the cost of telecasting programs and manuafcturing color sets would exceed selling prices until a mass market developed. A second indication of an immediate buyer's market occurred in March, 1954, when a competing manufacturer announced a 17-inch table model black-and-white set for only $139 retail list price. It was believed that the manufacturer was able to offer such a low selling price only as a result of cost savings from large volume purchases and from long production runs obtained by stopping work on all other models in the line. The increasing intensity of competition in the industry was also indicated by the strong efforts of all television companies to take distributors away from one another.

Mr. Lawton was considering two alternative courses of action to meet the difficult transitional period. The first proposal involved the granting of additional margins to distributors. There was a strong likelihood that distributors might exert pressure for such margin increases instead of placing strong emphasis on the lower priced lines offered by Sentinel. The current reduced factory prices of 50 to 60 percent off original list price were on a par with those of most companies in the industry. The Sentinel executives believed that the only feasible means by which the company could increase dealer margins would be by raising the list prices of its products.

A second possible method of improving the company's market position in the transition period was to add new product lines such as electric appliances. One objective of such a program would be to increase consumer recognition of the Sentinel name. It was estimated that in 1953 certain of the independent television manufacturers were spending over $8 million a year in advertising, while others such as RCA, General Electric, and Westinghouse had well-known corporation names to rely upon. Another objective of a more extensive line would be to offset the summer lull and thus maintain a steady work force throughout the year.

The Sentinel executives considered it important that any new products added to the company's line should fit satisfactorily into the company's present price ranges. Sentinel produced table model and portable radios in a price range from $22 to $39.95 and television sets in a range from $179 to $595. Distributors carried Sentinel radio and television products exclusively in addition to a large number of other types of electric appliances. Retail dealers, however, often carried competing television lines.

Mr. Parks believed that, in general, the reputation acquired by the Sentinel name in radios was helpful in promoting television. For example, the first television advertisement in the *Saturday Evening Post* resulted in a large number of unsolicited letters from rural consumers who had had satisfactory performance from the company's battery-operated farm sets before World War II. At the same time, however, Mr. Parks believed that the difference between selling a $30 radio and a $300 television set was so great that the same distributors were not always successful with both. Salesmen accustomed to the large commission available from selling a few television sets were not always interested in promoting table radios; salesmen accustomed to "catalogue selling" of small items such as table radios, clocks, and toasters, did not always have the patience required to sell a major appliance like a television set. For this reason, the Sentinel executives believed that any new products added to the company's line should be in about the same price range as its television sets.

Certain electric appliances in the television price range had been investigated. At one time, negotiations had been started with a major manufacturer of electric ranges in order to add a "white line" of kitchen products under the Sentinel name. It was decided, however, that it would be difficult to ensure supply from a large manufacturer that had its own branded line to produce. The possibility of making room air-conditioners was also studied. Although the market potential appeared to be excellent and the sales peak was in the summer, the Sentinel plant was not particularly well organized to manufacture such a product. Since none of the parts were electronic and the company had no large stamping or production machine facilities, all air-conditioner components would have to be purchased and the process would not supplement Sentinel's own operations. The Sentinel executives noted, however, that the Emerson Radio and Phonograph Corporation had recently announced plans for the production and sale of room air-conditioning units.

Other possibilities for new products were the manufacture of high-fidelity phonograph sets and tape recorders. Executives believed that these products would supplement their distribution program and make use of the company's engineering and production skills. They would not, however, be particularly helpful in offsetting the seasonal slump during the slack summer period.

1. SENTINEL RADIO CORPORATION
Balance Sheets, 1947-1954 (Year Ended March 31))
(In Thousands)

ASSETS	1947	1948	1949	1950	1951	1952	1953	1954
Cash	$ 142	$ 183	$ 290	$ 247	$1,766	$1,175	$1,101	$1,233
U. S. Treasury Bills	41	195						
Accounts Receivable	669	228	682	748	1,573	1,286	2,020	1,160
Refund Federal Taxes	13	43						29
Inventories	1,738	1,034	1,160	1,284	1,400	878	1,600	1,312
Total Current Assets	$2,603	$1,683	$2,132	$2,279	$4,739	$3,339	$4,721	$3,734
Other Assets	24	15	9	7	9			
Property, Plant, and Equipment	1,051	1,842	1,174	1,186	1,263	1,313	1,338	1,386
Depreciation	(105)	(880)	(187)	(220)	(259)	(333)	(388)	(419)
Deferred Charges	20	31	33	28	34	37	24	18
TOTAL ASSETS	$3,593	$2,691	$3,161	$3,280	$5,786	$4,356	$5,695	$4,719
LIABILITIES								
Notes Payable	$ 750		$ 275				$ 300	
Accounts Payable	521	$ 197	486	$ 472	$ 423	$ 359	494	$ 545
Federal Taxes	42	-	26	56	1,238	245	723	195
Other Liabilities	488	248	240	279	843	384	562	357
Total Current Liabilities	$1,801	$ 445	$1,027	$ 807	$2,504	$ 988	$2,079	$1,097
Long-Term Debt	279	889	761	894	710	503	413	353
Product Warranties					225	175	175	175
Common Stock	$ 320	$ 320	$ 320	$ 360	$ 360	$ 380	$ 380	$ 380
Paid-In Surplus	366	366	366	484	484	544	544	544
Earned Surplus	827	671	687	735	1,503	1,766	2,104	2,170
Capital Stock and Surplus	$1,513	$1,357	$1,373	$1,579	$2,347	$2,690	$3,028	$3,094
TOTAL LIABILITIES	$3,593	$2,691	$3,161	$3,280	$5,786	$4,356	$5,695	$4,719

2. SENTINEL RADIO CORPORATION
Income Statements, 1947-1954 (Year Ended March 31)
(In Thousands)

	1947	1948	1949	1950	1951	1952	1953	1954
Net Sales	$6,240	$6,543	$6,079	$9,073	$20,091	$10,126	$15,143	$13,532
Cost of Products Sold	5,342	6,143	5,492	8,152	16,686	8,284	12,718	11,775
Gross Profit	$ 898	$ 400	$ 587	$ 921	$ 3,405	$ 1,842	$ 2,425	$ 1,757
General Expenses	708	552	511	770	1,368	1,179	1,157	1,258
Profit	$ 190	$ (152)	$ 76	$ 151	$ 2,037	$ 663	$ 1,268	$ 499
Other Income	13	17	16	3	18	24	9	10
	$ 203	$ (135)	$ 92	$ 154	$ 2,055	$ 687	$ 1,277	$ 509
Other Charges								
Interest	$ 24	$ 40	$ 55	$ 43	$ 46	$ 50	$ 55	-
Retirement Fund	51	8	17	30	107	108	103	$ 122
Amortization of Mortgage	-	2	3	3	3	8	-	-
Sundry	24	18	-	-	-	-	-	74
Total Other Charges	$ 99	$ 68	$ 75	$ 76	$ 156	$ 166	$ 158	$ 196
Profit before Income Taxes	$ 104	$ (203)	$ 17	$ 78	$ 1,899	$ 521	$ 1,119	$ 313
Federal Taxes	40	(63)	1	30	1,193	257	715	162
Net Profit after Taxes	$ 64	$ (140)	$ 16	$ 48	$ 706	$ 264	$ 404	$ 151

3. SENTINEL RADIO CORPORATION
Cost of Products Sold
Year Ending March 31, 1954

Inventory at April 1, 1953			$ 1,599,734
Purchases, less cash discounts of $106,660 in 1954			8,737,643
Direct labor			1,049,811
Manufacturing expenses:			
Wages and salaries:			
Indirect labor	$953,212		
Employees' bonus	30,429		
Vacations	66,813	$1,050,454	
Provision for depreciation		142,845	
Real estate and personal property taxes		29,964	
Payroll taxes		39,231	
Heat, light, and power		26,121	
Rent		34,502	
Supplies		58,847	
Samples		17,803	
Small tools		4,101	
Maintenance and repairs		20,910	
Insurance		20,691	
Professional services		2,529	
Travel		18,796	
Automobile expense		1,319	
Dues and subscriptions		1,139	
Employees' welfare		6,140	
Tooling and equipment costs relating to United States government defense contracts		45	
Miscellaneous		8,625	
		$1,484,062	
Loss on cafeteria operations		10,749	
Royalty expense		178,518	
Warranty expense		26,151	1,699,480
			$13,086,668
Less inventory at March 31, 1954			1,311,889
COST OF PRODUCTS SOLD			$11,774,779

4. SENTINEL RADIO CORPORATION
Selling, Administrative, and General Expense
Year Ending March 31, 1954

Selling expenses:		
Wages and salaries		$ 167,190
Commissions		223,666
Advertising:		
Cooperative	$141,037	
Magazine space	114,724	
Newspaper	65,792	
Catalogues	48,702	
Other	66,656	436,911
Sales promotion		24,019
Dues and subscriptions		2,288
Travel		28,101
Telephone and telegraph		8,542
Provision for depreciation		3,410
Rent—branch office		11,835
Warehousing and handling costs		12,331
Printing, stationery, and supplies		8,434
Franchise and payroll taxes		4,881
Provision for doubtful accounts		18,628
Miscellaneous		6,994
TOTAL SELLING EXPENSES		$ 957,230

4. (Continued)

Administrative and general expenses:	
Wages and salaries	$ 175,653
Dues and subscriptions	11,038
Travel	10,987
Donations	2,638
Professional services	25,978
Telephone and telegraph	27,368
Insurance	10,907
Provision for depreciation	6,173
Printing, stationery, and supplies	16,598
Provision for doubtful accounts	-0-
Franchise and payroll taxes	2,763
Registrar and stock transfer fees	2,537
Repair and Maintenance	2,051
Miscellaneous	6,020
TOTAL ADMINISTRATIVE AND GENERAL EXPENSES	$ 300,711
TOTAL	$1,257,941

5. SENTINEL RADIO CORPORATION

Quarterly Production and Sales by Units, 1953-1954

Quarterly Production
(Quantities Only)

	Radio	Table Model TV	Console TV Leader Models	Console TV DeLuxe Models
Quarter Ended 3/31/53	21,700	4,200	8,100	3,300
Quarter Ended 6/30/53	23,000	5,100	8,800	1,900
Quarter Ended 9/30/53	21,700	5,100	5,200	6,300
Quarter Ended 12/31/53	24,200	8,300	5,100	1,100
Quarter Ended 3/31/54	16,900	5,400	2,600	150
Quarter Ended 6/30/54 (Est.)	24,000	3,000	8,000	-0-
	(5,000*		(12,000*	**
Quarter Ended 9/30/54 (Est.)	(10,000	6,000	(6,000	
			(12,000*	**
Quarter Ended 12/31/54 (Est.)	7,500	6,000	(6,000	

Quarterly Sales
(Quantities Only)

	Radio	Table Model TV	Console TV Leader Models	Console TV DeLuxe Models
Quarter Ended 3/31/53	21,800	4,000	8,100	3,200
Quarter Ended 6/30/53	21,400	3,500	4,600	1,000
Quarter Ended 9/30/53	24,200	8,000	4,200	4,900
Quarter Ended 12/31/53	19,200	7,600	6,900	1,400
Quarter Ended 3/31/54	18,400	4,900	5,600	400
Quarter Ended 6/30/54 (Est.)	20,000	1,400	2,000	250
	(4,000*		(11,000*	
Quarter Ended 9/30/54 (Est.)	(14,000	8,000	(10,550	1,000
	(1,000*		(13,000*	
Quarter Ended 12/31/54 (Est.)	(7,000	6,000	(6,500	700
Inventory 1/1/53 (no. of sets)	2,000	700	150	100
Average Selling Price (to Distributor)	$17	$155	$190	$250

*Private brand.
**Experimental color set production.

6. SENTINEL RADIO CORPORATION

Sample of Consumer Advertising of Television Sets

The "sandman" was forgotten...

Model illustrated with 21-inch picture at \$339.95* Choose from 18 models, starting at \$199.95*

Sentinel Picture Sealed TV

Power Factor Glass & Living Picture Television Perfection for 31 Years

...the picture stayed clear and steady!

Night after night...month after month...through the years...that Sentinel you bought for Christmas brings in clear, big pictures without "flip, flap, or flutter"!—because Sentinel —and Sentinel alone—offers *Picture-Sealed* TV. So, whether you live right next door to a telecasting station or out on the "fringe," you enjoy perfect, sharp reception on all channels, including VHF and the new UHF stations now being licensed.

Sentinel's much envied *Studio Tone* brings you the richness of hi-fidelity. Its authentic *Decorator-Approved* cabinet styling graces your home with the restrained simplicity and friendly charm found only in fine furniture, traditional or modern.

Treat yourself to the new 1953 Picture-Sealed Sentinel TV this Christmas! Your dealer will gladly arrange a home demonstration. He's waiting for your call...today.

Sentinel Radio Corporation, Evanston, Illinois

Famous Sentinel Power-Factor Chassis

Cascode UHF-VHF Tuner

Reflection Eliminator Safety Glass

Automatic Gain Control

Inter-Carrier System

Locality Adjuster

Truly Automatic Tuning

Full Range Tone Control

THE PICTURES STAY CLEAR...YEAR AFTER YEAR!

Owners proudly recommend

Sentinel TV

For more than a quarter of a century, producers of America's premier quality radio and television receivers.

**Prices slightly higher South and West. All Sentinel prices include Federal Tax and one year warranty on picture tube and all parts.*

SENTINEL RADIO SETS... TABLE, PORTABLE AND CLOCK MODELS... FOR STUDIO TONE IN YOUR HOME

Emerson Radio and Phonograph Corporation (A)

In 1949 the Emerson Radio and Phonograph Corporation was one of the leading manufacturers of small radio receiving sets and television sets. Its products were advertised and distributed nationally under the Emerson brand name through 70 distributors and 25,000 retail dealers located in all parts of the United States. The company had four wholly owned subsidiaries: the Plastimold Corporation, a manufacturer of plastic radio cabinets and other plastic products; Jefferson-Travis, Inc., a firm which sold a small volume of radio telephone equipment manufactured by the parent company; the Emerson Television Service Corporation, a company organized in 1947 for the purpose of installing and servicing Emerson television sets sold by dealers in the New York City area; and the Emerson Radio Export Corporation, a concern which promoted the sale of Emerson products in foreign countries. Consolidated income statements and balance sheets for the parent company are shown in Exhibits 1 and 2.

The Emerson Radio and Phonograph Corporation was organized in 1924 but did not become a significant producer of radios until 1932, at which time it successfully promoted a compact radio selling at a retail price of $25. In 1932 the company manufactured 39,000 radio sets. Production increased each year thereafter (in spite of the general depression in the United States during the 1930's) and reached a prewar peak in 1941 when 1,165,000 sets were produced. In January, 1949, the company's ten millionth radio set came off the production lines.

In May, 1948, the company began the large-scale production of television receivers, with an initial output of 150 units a day. The demand for television receivers in the United States was growing, and the company increased its production rate to over 1,100 television sets a day in the fall of 1949; however, demand increased far faster than the rate of production, and in September, 1949, the company was forced to ship to distributors on an allotment basis. Production was expected to reach 1,500 units a day in December. On September 24 the company president, Mr. Benjamin Abrams, said: "The demand is so great that we could sell four or five times as many television sets as we are now making." The company sales manager estimated that the company was "oversold" by $10,000,000.

The executives estimated that the company's total sales volume for 1949 would be approximately $40 million and would exceed by four times the company's largest annual prewar sales volume of a little over $10 million in 1941. It was anticipated that 70 percent of the total dollar volume in 1949 would come from the sale of television sets and the remaining 30 percent from the sale of radio sets. In September, 1949, the unit rate of production of radio and television sets was approximately equal. Mr. Abrams anticipated sales of 500,000 television sets in 1950, but believed that radio sets would always constitute an important factor in the company's operations.

The executives were very optimistic about the future of the television industry and about the company's possibilities for expansion in it. For example, Mr. Abrams said, "We expect to increase our business ten times in the future." In September, 1949, Mr. Max Abrams, company secretary-treasurer, declared, "Authorities in the industry are estimating production of 2½ million television sets this year (1949), and they predict that it might increase to 5 million sets next year."

In the summer of 1949, according to Mr. Benjamin Abrams there were for the first time indications that the seasonal pattern of the radio industry would be duplicated in the television industry. A slowing down of consumer sales appeared in the middle of May and lasted until the middle of July. A considerable amount of price-cutting occurred, with the retail price of a 10-inch table model set dropping from $269 to $199.50 between the spring and fall of 1949.

In regard to the 1949 seasonal pattern in the television industry, Mr. Benjamin Abrams said, "We were able to revive consumer interest in television to some extent during the summer by reducing prices. Price reductions were possible at that time because television profit margins were good. The reductions have been made, and we can't hold out hope for that next year. We now have to get down to brass tacks."

COMPANY HISTORY

The Emerson Radio and Phonograph Corporation was organized in 1924 as a result of a merger of the Emerson Phonograph Company,

Inc. and the Emerson Radio Corporation. At the outset the company specialized in the production and sale of phonograph records, while its radio and phonograph business was small. The company at that time was one of the three largest producers of phonograph records and made and sold as many as 100,000 records a day. After the merger the company sold a line of large, expensive radios and phonographs in common with the rest of the industry.

Development of Small Radios: Emerson's $25 compact radio evolved after the technical problems of making bulky $45 and up sets had stabilized. Mr. Benjamin Abrams thought that the styling factor had been overlooked:

> While visiting a friend who was in the clock business in New England, one clock in his showroom caught my eye. The case of the clock was 10″ high, 6″ wide, and 4″ deep. The thought occurred to me that if the dimensions could be reversed to 6″ high, 10″ wide and 4″ deep, it would make a very compact cabinet for a radio set which would be attractive because of the quality of the veneers and the finish of the cabinet. I had a sample of the cabinet made to my specifications and took it back to my engineers. I told them to make a radio chassis that was suitable for this cabinet. They did not think it was possible, but I told them to come up with it in four or five weeks. Before then, the customary practice in the industry was to build a chassis and then make a cabinet to house it.
>
> We ordered our first production release for 1,000 sets and soon built up our production to 1,000 sets a day. The set was in such high demand that dealers would come to the factory with money in their hands to carry away sets as they came off the assembly line. This was in 1932, at the height of the depression, and it began a radio boom.

After 1932 the Emerson Radio and Phonograph Corporation specialized in the production of small radios, introducing each year new and more compact models. In 1937 the company sold a five-tube radio set retailing for $9.95.

Small radios received such substantial public acceptance that, according to Mr. Abrams, they accounted for 80 percent of all radio production by 1936. Besides introducing radios which were more compact and which sold at lower prices than the conventional models on the market, the Emerson Radio and Phonograph Corporation incorporated many novel style features in its radio designs. For example, the company introduced a combination radio and clock as a compact unit; a small radio featuring the "stabent" or curved cabinet of molded plywood construction; a small table model with cabinet designs featuring Walt Disney characters such as Mickey Mouse; and a "Snow White and the Seven Dwarfs' model.

Another novel radio model was "The Patriot," designed in 1940 by the industrial designer Norman Bel Geddes. The Patriot was intended to appeal to the strong patriotic sentiments prevailing at the time and featured a red, white, and blue plastic cabinet. The unit retailed for $15. Referring to The Patriot model in a company publication called *Small Radio,* Mr. Abrams wrote, "The sale of this (The Patriot) receiver, which might have been considered a novelty, reached unexpectedly large proportions and again indicated that style, timing, and the current affairs of people should always be considered by radio engineers."

War Production: War-time electronic devices made by the Emerson Radio and Phonograph Corporation included: many varieties of navigational equipment, submarine detecting equipment, radar and radar training equipment, two-way portable radios, hand-operated portable power generating equipment and pocket radio receivers for the armed forces. The company also produced the V–T proximity fuse in large quantities.

The research and engineering personnel and facilities of the company were also engaged in work on government contracts during the war. The number of scientists, technicians, and laboratory personnel was increased ten times over the prewar level. In 1944, the company spent more than $1,000,000 on research and engineering work.

Entry into the Television Business: By the latter part of 1947, the pent-up consumer radio demand was almost satisfied, and Emerson began switching facilities from radio to television production. Unit for unit, the manufacture of television sets required over ten times as much space, assembly work, and materials as radio sets.

Mr. Benjamin Abrams summarized the company's objectives in the television industry as follows: "Emerson is now trying to do the same thing in television as it did in radio—namely, to develop compact television sets with good picture quality and with emphasis on good styling."

PRODUCT LINE AND PRICING

The company presented a line of radio and television sets to the trade in the fall of 1949 known as the "Emerson '50 Line" which was "priced for the mass market." In the radio line, there were ten table model AM radios priced from $14.95 to $79.95 (retail). There was an FM table model radio retailing at $29.95, a combination AM-FM table model for $49.95 and a table model phonograph-radio combination for $49.95. The company offered four portable radios priced from $16.95 to $39.95.

To complete the company's line, there was an automatic 45 rpm record player for $39.95 and a standard automatic record player for $29.95.

The television line was divided into five groups. (1) six table models, including a 7-inch picture for $129.95, a 10-inch for $179.95 and a 16-inch for $329.50; (2) a combination 10-inch television and AM-FM radio table model for $269.50; (3) three console models, including a 10-inch set for $249.50 and a 16-inch set for $449.50; (4) three television, radio, phonograph combinations priced between $369.50 and $599.50; and (5) a projection television console for $599.50.

An important aspect of the company's price policies was its price guarantee arrangement with dealers, considered by the sales vice-president to be unique in the industry. At the height of the June, 1959 price-cutting, the company announced that in case it reduced prices on any of its products, distributors would refund to all dealers the difference between the old price and the new on all merchandise purchased within 30 days preceding the day of the new price announcements. The outstanding feature of the price guarantee was the fact that the refunds applied to all merchandise, irrespective of whether or not it was still in dealers' inventories. In turn, the dealers extended the guarantee to retail purchasers. The purpose was to maintain dealer confidence in Emerson sets and their price stability.

SALES PROGRAM

Emerson radio and television sets were advertised and sold nationally. The distribution channels used by the company were, in general similar to those used by other radio and electric appliance manufacturers. The company sold its products to wholesale distributors who in turn sold to various types of retail outlets.

Distribution and Dealer Organization: The company gave exclusive franchises to 70 distributors located in all major market centers in the United States. These distributors used 600 salesmen to warehouse and sell Emerson television and radio sets and noncompetitive appliances to approximately 25,000 dealers. Three Emerson regional sales managers and 12 salesmen assisted the distributors in missionary work.

The dealers included radio stores, phonograph record stores, department stores, electrical appliance stores, both chain and nonchain as well as furniture and jewelry stores. The dealers had a nonexclusive selling agreement with the Emerson Radio and Phonograph Corporation under which they were permitted to carry competitive radio and television receivers. All distributors and dealers sold the complete Emerson line with the exception that those located in areas where television programs were not yet available did not carry television receivers.

Sales objectives were established for each territory based on the estimated potential demand in the area. The company then allocated a certain part of its output to each distributor. In 1948, 35 percent of the company's consolidated net sales were derived from five major distributors in: Metropolitan New York, Northern New Jersey, Eastern Pennsylvania, Southern New Jersey and Northern Deleware, and the District of Columbia.

Emerson product lines were introduced to the trade at semiannual distributor shows held in Chicago and New York in January and July. "Convention terms" permitted dealers to pay for any merchandise ordered 90 days later instead of the usual 10.

Advertising effort involved some $6 million in cooperative in 1949 and a national campaign that included color spreads in *Life* and Sunday rotogravue sections of newspapers. An example of the latter testimonial-type ad is shown in Exhibit 4.

MANUFACTURING

Company executives decided in 1932 to assemble radio sets instead of buying them on contract. In speaking of this decision Mr. Norman D. Israel, the executive vice-president, stated that the company had found it difficult to get delivery of sets during the height of the season because the manufacturers who contracted for the Emerson work also produced their own radio sets and were more apt to concentrate on their own production when demand was at its peak.

In 1945, the company purchased all of the stock of Radio Speakers, Inc., a firm which manufactured speakers for radio and television sets. This subsidiary was sold in 1949; thereafter, Emerson bought its speakers from outside suppliers.

Factory Space: The company rented factory space in two buildings in New York City. In the main headquarters building at 111 Eighth Avenue, the company rented space on four floors. On the second floor, there were 160,000 square feet of which 75,000 were used for production and 25,000 for the storage of finished units. The remaining space was used for offices, laboratories and for material stores. On the fourth floor there were 20,000 square feet of floor area of which 16,000 were allotted to storage of materials. On the sixth floor 15,000 square feet out of a total of 40,000 square feet were used for manufacturing and the balance for production services, U.S. Government laboratories and for material stores. The space available on the thirteenth floor after providing for service and parts sales functions, was set aside for the storage of finished goods. Of the 70,000 square feet of floor space rented in a second New York building, 12,000 were used for manufacturing, 3,000 for storage of finished goods, and 26,000 for the storage of television and radio cabinets.

Operation of Production Units: The production of radio and television sets consisted mainly of assembling components purchased from suppliers. The assembly work was done in assembly lines which were referred to as production units. The units consisted of long, "snaking" tables along which operators, mostly girls, were stationed. Each girl had certain specific assembly steps to perform. After her work was completed, the chassis was moved along the line to the next girl. The tools used in the assembly work consisted of hand pliers, soldering irons, air gun screwdrivers, and nut runners. The most expensive pieces of equipment used were riveting machines for riveting tube sockets to the metal television chassis, oscilloscopes and other electronic equipment for testing the television sets.

There were seven separate production units used for the assembly of the company's five basic television chassis and its several radio chassis. There was also one production unit for building television subassemblies. In this unit wire, resisters, and other components were wired to tube sockets and the tube sockets were riveted to the television chassis. The subassembly then went to the appropriate main line.

There were two systems for moving the chassis along the lines. In the first method the chassis were slid along guide rails which also supported them at the proper angle for assembly. In the second method the chassis were mounted on a dolly which was moved from operator to operator on the line, guided by a center track which was built in the assembly tables. The latter method was an innovation in the work setup. Radio chassis, because of their small size, were slid along a metal worktable from one operator to the next. The company did not use mechanized belt conveyors on its assembly work although there were conveyors in the radio section for moving completed chassis to the cabinet assembly.

After assembly, the sets were tested. For radios the test was simple and did not involve expensive equipment. Television testing required special equipment including a set of closed circuit pictures. Before testing began, the cathode ray picture tube was installed. Operators did not need technical training to adjust the sets. If any major difficulty was detected, the sets went to off-line repairers.

The final step was cabinet assembly in which the chassis was installed along with speaker and record player if required. Several production units fed one cabinet line. Television sets were also given a final inspection and adjustment.

The production cycle for the radio sets ranged from one to two hours, while for the television sets it went from four to twelve hours, depending on the model. Exhibit 3A contains data on the daily production capacity of and employment on the production units.

Because the floors were long and narrow, the assembly line tables "snaked" or wound across the floor as a continuous unit. Exhibit 3B is a floor plan of the company's main production floor (the second) at 111 Eighth Avenue. Exhibit 3C shows in detail television production unit #2.

Procurement of Components: Material costs constituted 70 to 80 percent of the total factory cost of the radio and television sets. The remainder of the cost consisted of labor and overhead in about equal amounts. Each television set had between 1,500 and 2,500 parts which were purchased from outside suppliers.

Labor Force: Emerson employed about 1,500 factory workers in September, 1949, of whom about 1,200 were on direct labor. The total was increased to about 2,000 by the end of 1949. Of the direct labor workers about 50 percent were unskilled, and most of them were women. The unskilled workers were usually placed on assembly jobs. Twenty-five percent of the employees were semiskilled workers; this group included inspectors, testers, and repairmen. The remaining 25 percent of the factory employees held skilled jobs, such as that of group leaders, trouble-shooters, and test technicians.

The company employed about 30 foremen, and there was one working group leader for each 15 to 20 workers.

Production Scheduling: Production schedules were prepared in the form of "releases" or commitments to manufacture for each model in the line. The quantity involved in a release as well as the daily rate of production to reach the desired quantity were decisions made by the top management of the company.

Two types of releases were used: "block quantity" releases and "flexible" releases. A block quantity release was an order to build a definite and fixed quantity of sets at a fixed rate each day; for example, 10,000 television sets of a certain model at the rate of 500 units a day. A flexible release was an order to produce a definite number of units a day of a given model until further notice; for example, 500 units a day for an indefinite period of time. When a flexible release of 500 units a day was issued, the purchasing department arranged with suppliers for the delivery of components in lots of 2,500 each week.

In scheduling the production of radios, it had been the policy of the company to produce in the off season for inventory, thereby maintaining stable production and employment and increasing the opportunities for savings on the procurement of materials. The company executives expected to carry this policy into television as soon as a predictable seasonal pattern was established.

An important factor in scheduling production was the length of time required to get the assembly lines up to normal output on a new model. The period varied depending on the extent to which a new model differed from models in production. Starting the production of a new model required a process analysis, a breakdown of the production steps for each operation on the line, planning and setting the layout of the assembly line, and the placement of parts, work tools, jigs and fixtures along the line. In addition, a certain period of learning time was necessary for the operators to become acquainted with the operations and to build up to a standard production speed.

On new television models that differed radically from existing models, it sometimes took as long as four weeks to get into quantity production. Introducing new models with less extensive changes required up to two weeks before normal output could be achieved. Because of the long period required to get new television models into production, Mr. Israel believed that it was not economical to introduce a new model for a quantity less than 25,000 units.

Changing over to new radio models was less complicated than changing over to new television models. For a new radio model that did not differ to a marked extent from existing models, normal production could usually be attained in a few days.

Commenting on the problem of changing production, one of the company's industrial engineers stated, perhaps with exaggeration, that before the war changes were sometimes made so abruptly that a foreman of a radio production unit would find his line changed over upon returning from lunch.

1. EMERSON RADIO AND PHONOGRAPH CORPORATION (A)

Balance Sheets, 1943-1949 (Year End Oct. 31)

ASSETS	1943	1944	1945	1946	1947	1948	1949
Cash	$1,472,969	$ 1,991,858	$ 2,560,019	$1,744,093	$ 3,066,030	$ 3,332,659	$ 5,980,706
U.S. Government Notes	1,520,000	2,500,000	2,561,701	700,000		500,099	1,650,059
Receivables	1,511,452	4,028,607	4,730,348	3,009,446	3,668,148	4,010,031	3,321,854
Inventories	2,503,941	4,587,686	2,410,682	3,484,094	3,988,470	3,824,729	3,585,984
Due from U.S. Govt.	51,389	58,116					
Other	1,643	5,845	9,160	2,543			
Current Assets	$7,061,394	$13,172,112	$12,271,910	$8,940,176	$10,722,648	$11,667,518	$14,538,603
Fixed Assets	$ 165,164	$ 190,167	$ 319,457	$ 595,474	$ 637,242	$ 680,443	$ 657,243
Less Depreciation	109,646	123,672	138,934	173,736	263,417	352,748	393,997
Net Fixed Assets	$ 55,518	$ 66,495	$ 180,523	$ 421,738	$ 373,825	$ 327,695	$ 263,246
Patents	$ 1	$ 1	$ 1	$ 1	$ 1	$ 1	$ 1
Tax Refund Credit	129,600	120,928					
Value of Insurance	15,734	17,830	22,355	20,304	23,535	25,475	
Due from Employees				209,306	207,401	188,902	75,545
Other Assets	854	1,746	36,030	11,604	7,589	17,549	30,181
Deferred Charges	238,457*	533,891*	147,789*	154,641*	90,548*	64,180*	104,424
Total Assets	$7,501,558	$13,913,003	$12,658,608	$9,757,770	$11,425,547	$12,291,320	$15,012,000
LIABILITIES							
Accounts Payable	$ 598,216	$ 1,954,138	$ 3,414,602	$2,719,937	$ 2,551,659	$ 1,894,896	$ 2,193,225
Notes Payable	1,000,000	3,750,000	1,794,806	91,565			
Accruals	316,474	491,577	771,221	528,110	870,385	808,514	900,636
Renegotiation Refund	100,000	500,000					
Renegotiation Provision	500,000(	3,690,413(	2,704,407(	1,384,230			
Provision for Tax	1,675,000(	(	(		1,586,550	1,520,557	1,803,125
Current Liabilities	$4,189,690	$10,386,128	$ 8,685,036	$4,723,842	$ 5,008,594	$ 4,223,967	$ 4,896,986
Notes Payable**				120,000			
Deferred Income						28,630	80,640
Capital Stock ($5)	2,000,000	2,000,000	2,000,000	2,000,000	2,000,000	4,000,000	4,000,000
Capital Surplus	228,123	228,123	228,123	228,123	228,123	456,248	456,247
Earned Surplus	1,083,745	1,298,752	1,745,449	2,685,805	4,188,830	3,582,475	5,578,127
Total Liabilities	$7,501,558	$13,913,003	$12,658,608	$9,757,770	$11,425,547	$12,291,320	$15,012,000

*Most of the amount shown represents unamortized tools, dies, molds, and laboratory charges.
**Non-interest-bearing—$30,000 due annually on August 15, 1948 to 1951, inclusive.

2. EMERSON RADIO AND PHONOGRAPH CORPORATION (A)

Income Statements, 1943-1949

	1942	1943	1944	1945	1946	1947	1948	1949
Net sales	$8,991,782	$11,857,771	$23,043,363	$32,490,805	$23,088,881	$32,658,122	$30,926,842	$40,543,925
Cost of sales	7,181,452	8,224,155	17,770,522	27,205,004	19,010,709	26,737,470	24,513,408	32,995,664
Selling and admin.	640,835	744,707	1,131,761	1,870,797	1,461,702	2,424,330	2,616,300	2,921,364
Operating profit	$1,169,495	$ 2,888,909	$ 4,141,080	$ 3,415,004	$ 2,616,470	$ 3,496,322	$ 3,797,134	$ 4,626,897
Other income		13,921	35,239	36,247	60,755	276,316	28,236	121,896
Total income	$1,169,495	$ 2,902,830	$ 4,176,319	$ 3,451,251	$ 2,677,225	$ 3,772,638	$ 3,825,370	$ 4,748,793
Interest	32,671	18,593	70,073	114,470	20,836			
Excess cost of subsidiary					27,357			
Renegotiation refund		500,000(	(	(				
Federal tax	350,564	404,100(	(	(		1,509,614	1,422,601	1,713,141
Excess profits tax	137,296	1,271,000(	3,377,702(	2,530,083(	1,288,904			
Postwar tax credit	2,500	127,000(	(					
Net income	$ 651,464	$ 836,137	$ 728,544	$ 806,698	$ 1,340,128	$ 2,263,024	$ 2,402,769	$ 3,035,652
Dividends	*	60,000	280,000	360,000	400,000	760,000	780,000***	1,040,000
Surplus for year	$ 651,464	$ 776,137	$ 215,009**	$ 446,698	$ 940,128	$ 1,503,024	$ 1,622,769	$ 1,995,652
Previous earned surplus	946,169	307,509	1,083,745	1,298,752	1,745,449	2,685,806	4,188,830	3,582,475
Earned Surplus October 31	307,509	1,083,745	1,298,752	1,745,449	2,685,805	4,188,830	3,582,475	5,578,127

*Stock dividend of $1,290,125.

**Contract renegotiation adjustment of $233,535 for year ended October 31, 1943, charged to earned surplus.

***Transferred $2,228,124 to capital stock and capital surplus.

3A. EMERSON RADIO AND PHONOGRAPH CORPORATION (A)

Production Capacity and Personnel of the Production Units

Television Production Unit #	Daily Capacity	Personnel
1	225 units	175
2	345 "	309
3	140 "	119
4	235 "	137
5 (subassembly)	------	100
6	145 units	180
Radio		
7	671 "	93
8	231 "	60

Unit Sales of Radio and Television Sets

	Radio	Television
1946	1,130,805	14
1947	1,839,739	1,137
1948	1,074,743	43,714
1949 est.	660,000	190,000
1950 est.	800,000	500,000

3B. EMERSON RADIO AND PHONOGRAPH CORPORATION (A)

Floor Plan—Second Floor

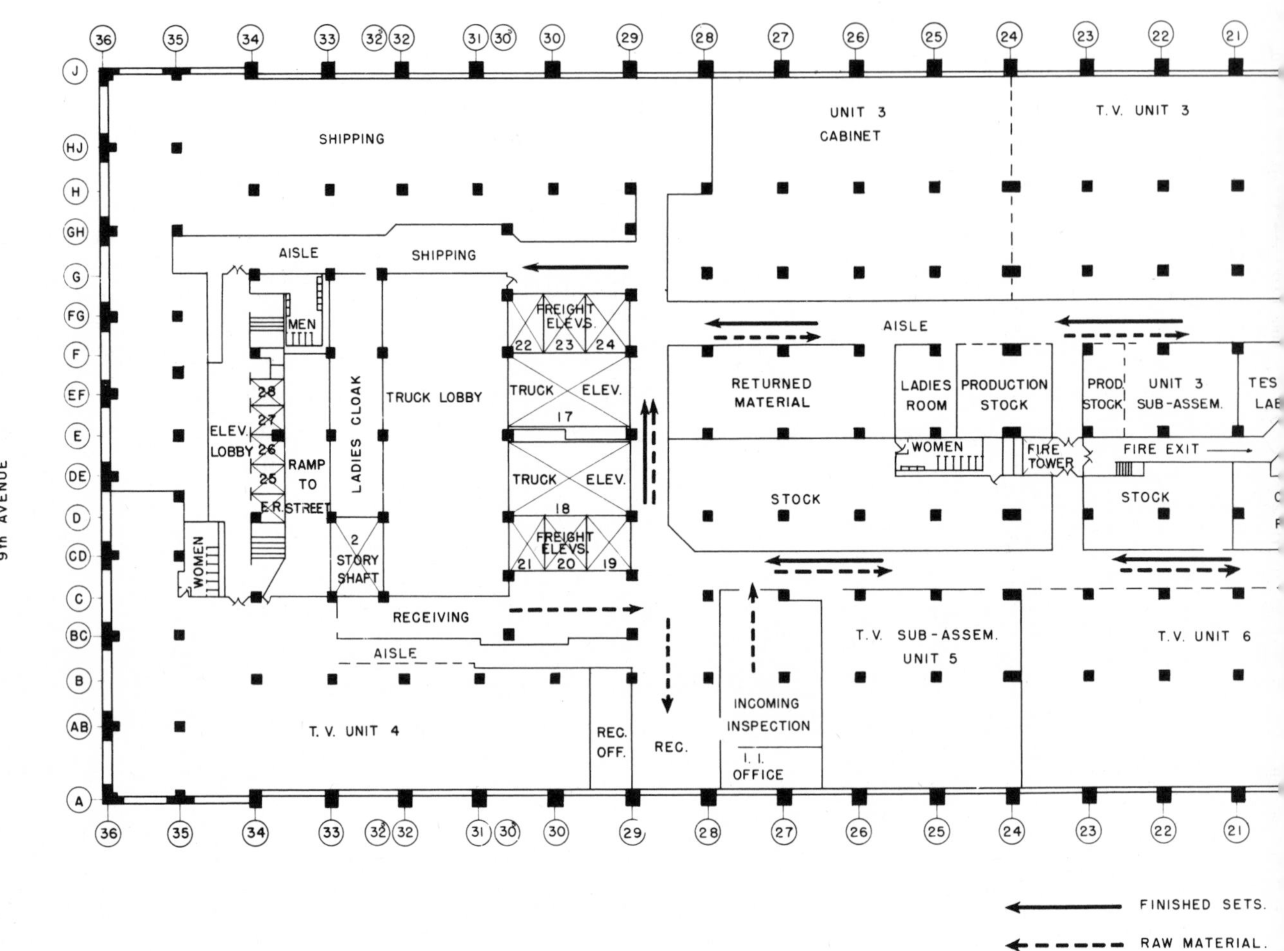

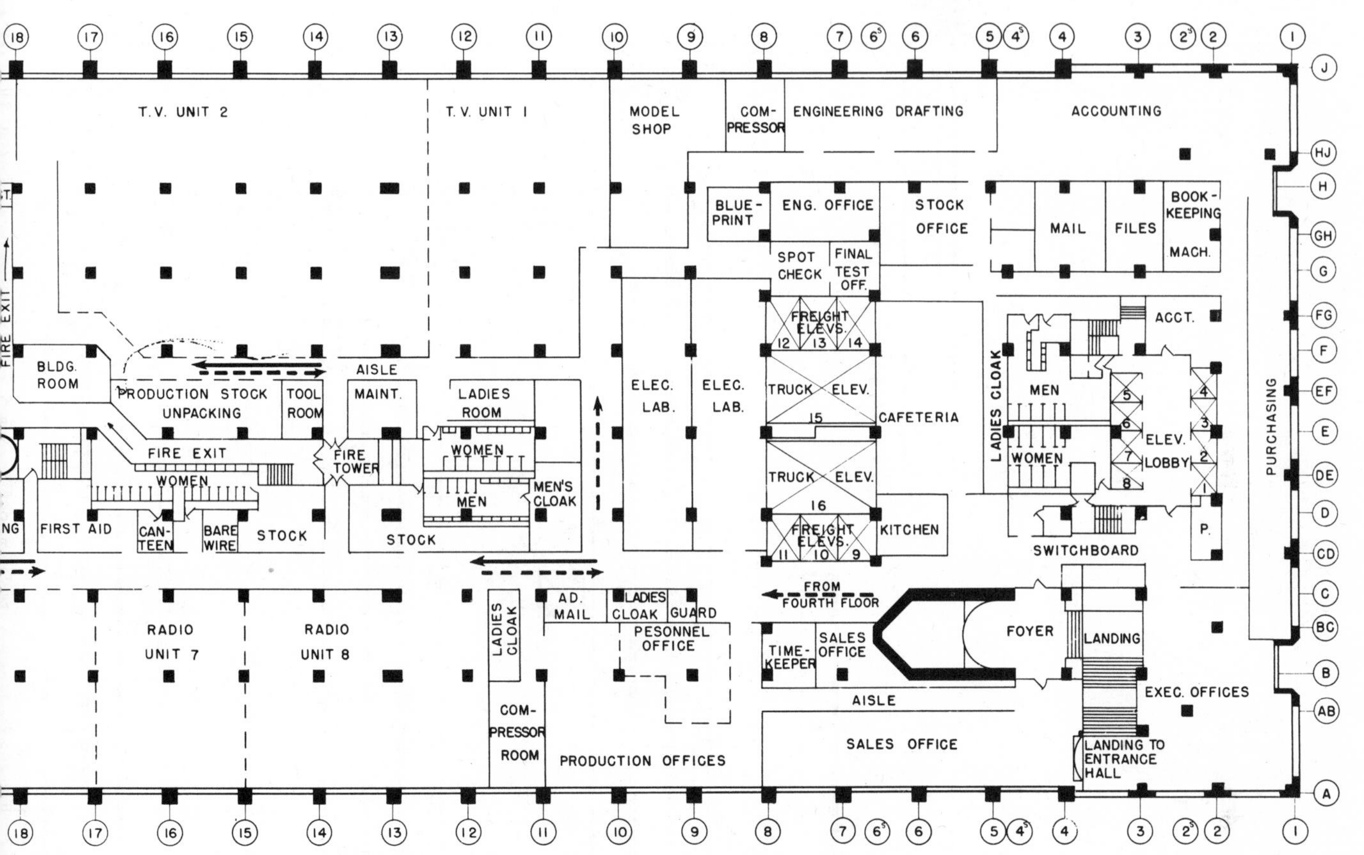

WEST 16th STREET
T.V. UNIT 2
T.V. UNIT 1
MODEL SHOP
COM-PRESSOR
ENGINEERING DRAFTING
ACCOUNTING
BLUE-PRINT
ENG. OFFICE
STOCK OFFICE
MAIL
FILES
BOOK-KEEPING MACH.
SPOT CHECK
FINAL TEST OFF.
FREIGHT ELEVS.
ACCT.
BLDG. ROOM
AISLE
PRODUCTION STOCK UNPACKING
TOOL ROOM
MAINT.
LADIES ROOM
ELEC. LAB.
ELEC. LAB.
TRUCK ELEV.
CAFETERIA
LADIES CLOAK
MEN
ELEV. LOBBY
PURCHASING
FIRE EXIT
FIRE TOWER
WOMEN
WOMEN
MEN
MEN'S CLOAK
WOMEN
FIRST AID
CAN-TEEN
BARE WIRE
STOCK
STOCK
KITCHEN
SWITCHBOARD
P.
8th AVENUE
RADIO UNIT 7
RADIO UNIT 8
LADIES CLOAK
AD. MAIL
LADIES CLOAK
GUARD
PESONNEL OFFICE
FROM FOURTH FLOOR
TIME-KEEPER
SALES OFFICE
FOYER
LANDING
EXEC. OFFICES
AISLE
COM-PRESSOR ROOM
PRODUCTION OFFICES
SALES OFFICE
LANDING TO ENTRANCE HALL
15th STREET
SCALE 5 10 20 30 40 50 FEET

3C. EMERSON RADIO AND PHONOGRAPH CORPORATION (A)

Layout of Production Units No. 1 and No. 2

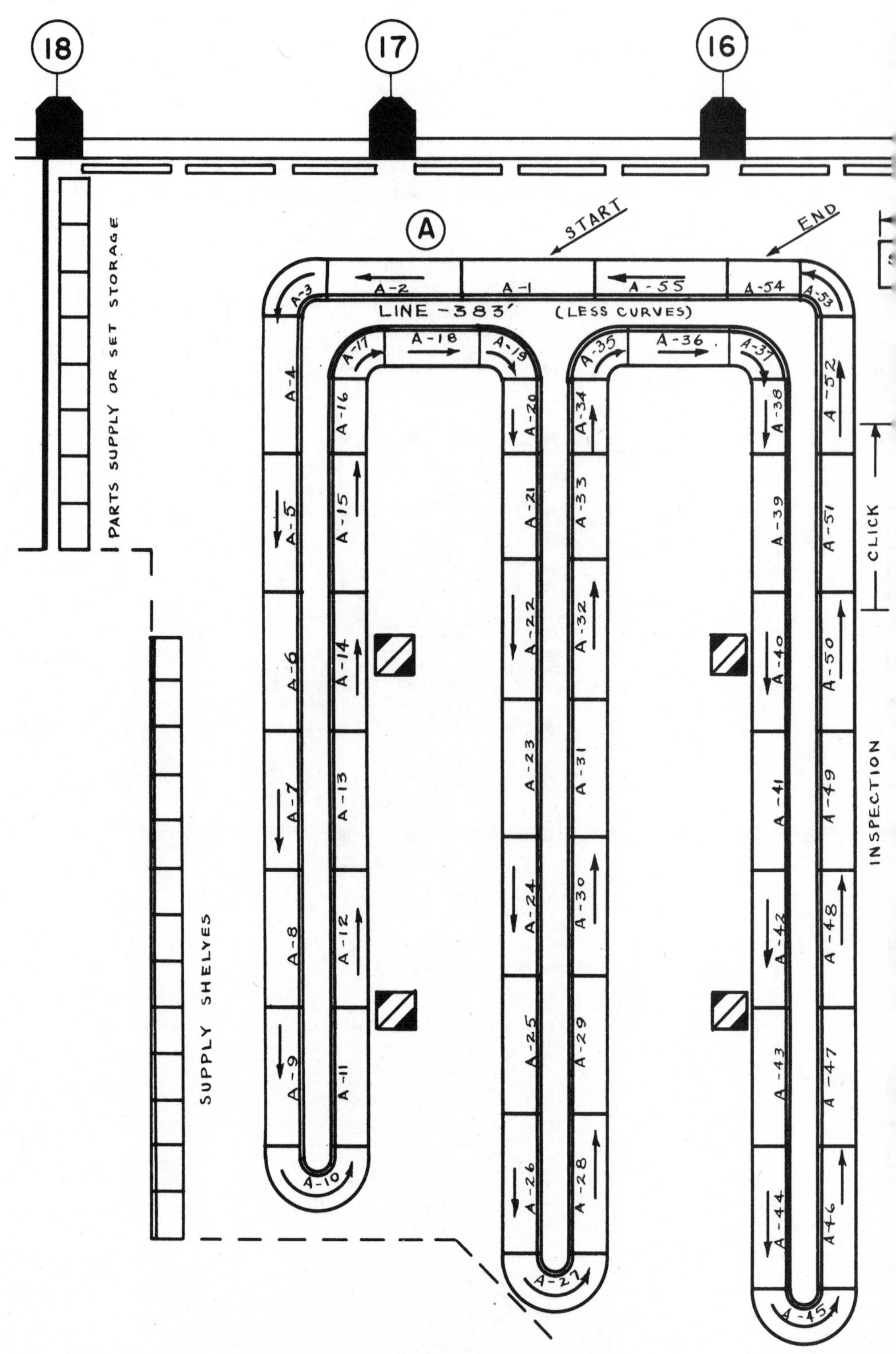

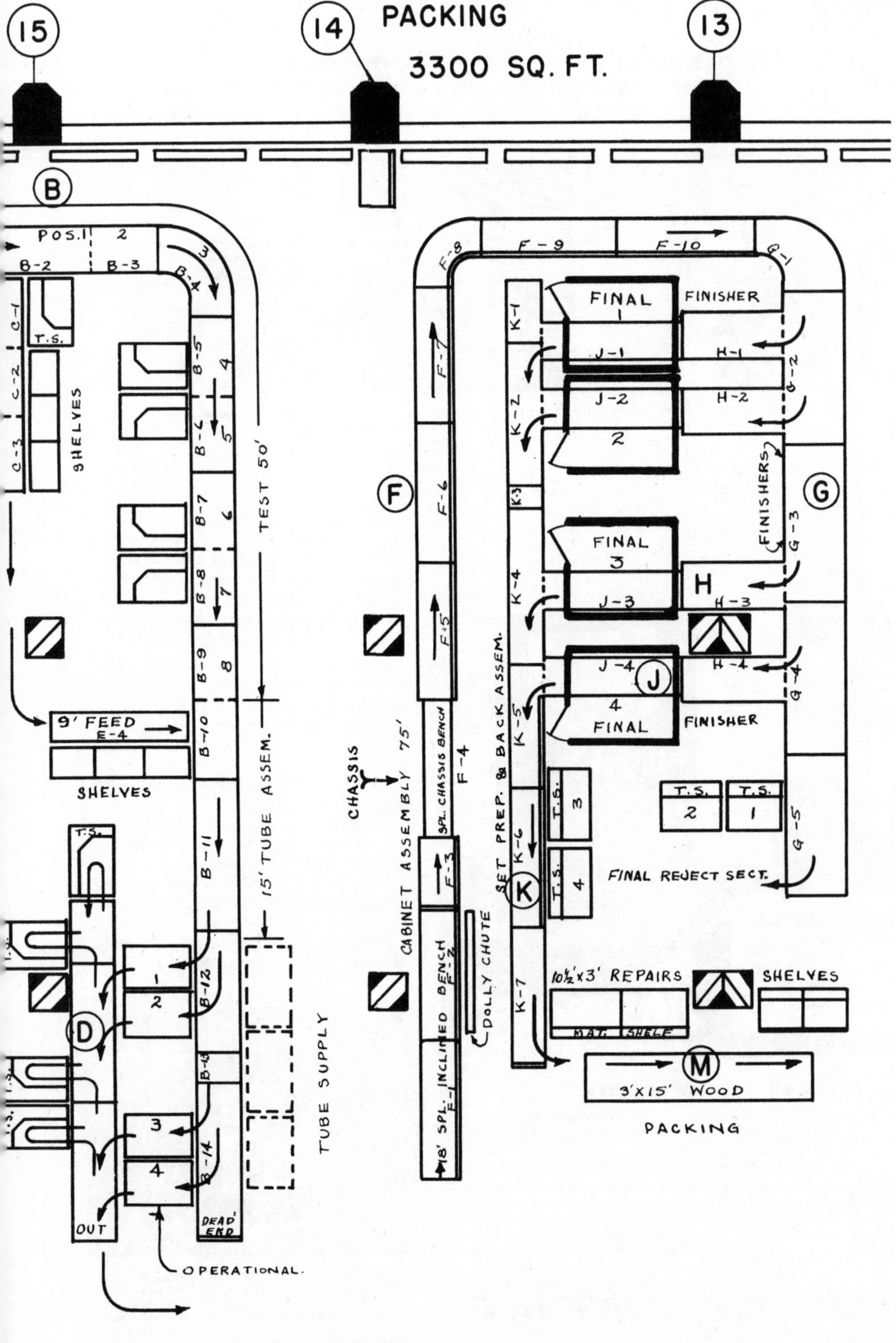
CABINET ASSEM.
FINAL TEST
PACKING
3300 SQ. FT.
15
14
13
B
F
G
H
J
K
D
M
FINAL 1
FINAL 3
4 FINAL
FINISHER
FINISHERS
9' FEED E-4
SHELVES
TEST 50'
15' TUBE ASSEM.
TUBE SUPPLY
CHASSIS
CABINET ASSEMBLY 75'
SPL. CHASSIS BENCH
SET PREP. & BACK ASSEM.
DOLLY CHUTE
18' SPL. INCLINED BENCH
FINAL REJECT SECT.
10½'x3' REPAIRS
MAT. SHELF
3'X15' WOOD
PACKING
OPERATIONAL
OUT
DEAD END

4. EMERSON RADIO AND PHONOGRAPH CORPORATION (A)

Example of Advertisement

Read why these Independent Television Service Men say—

"Emerson is your BEST BUY!"

Before you buy *any* television receiver, read what these experts—*who make their living installing and servicing all* television receivers—say about Emerson:

CARRY IT WITH YOU... Brilliant, console-quality television in this handsome, simulated pigskin carrying case. Only 25 pounds. Comes complete with antenna. No installation. Just take it with you . . . plug it in anywhere, AC-DC current. Only..... $169^{95}

Inspected and Tested 225 Times MODEL 600

"I appreciate good television engineering—that's why I have such high respect for the Emerson receivers," says M. A. Gribin of Los Angeles. "I work with all makes and I know what makes them different. For real quality, Emerson's your best buy."

"Television is my business. I have no stake in any set . . . I install and service them all," says Henry Pierro of Yonkers, New York. "And I can tell you that they don't come any better than the Emerson. It's the best buy for your money in television today."

"Sometimes I'm surprised myself at the ability of the Emerson receivers to bring in excellent reception in areas where other sets fail," says John W. Sandquist of Chicago. "I service all makes and, you can take it from me, Emerson's your best buy."

MAHOGANY CONSOLE SENSATION

The greatest dollar's worth in television, bar none. Giant size ten-inch tube in magnificent mahogany veneer CONSOLE cabinet. Super Powered Long Distance Reception on all television channels.............. $249^{50}

Inspected and Tested 225 Times MODEL 638

Model for model, screen size for screen size, Emerson's new television receivers are today's greatest values, *according to these men who make their living installing and servicing* all makes.

If you were buying a car, you'd *know* that an independent garage mechanic could give you the most impartial advice.

And—if you're buying a television receiver, you can't do better than to be guided by independent television servicemen—experts who do not sell television, but *install and service all makes*.

See Emerson's brilliant new television receivers for yourself. You'll be honestly impressed by Emerson's easy tuning, amazing Long Distance reception, beautiful styling —and Emerson's revolutionary low prices, in themselves an engineering achievement.

No wonder independent television service men say, "*Emerson* is your *best buy!*"

4-WAY, GIANT 10" TELEVISION—This amazing receiver gives you (1) Long Distance Television (2) A full FM radio (3) A full AM radio (4) A plug-in switch and dial control for attachment of any speed record player . . . all in a revolutionary *single* chassis, and smart mahogany veneer cabinet. $269^{50}

Inspected and Tested 225 Times MODEL 621

Emerson gives you all these advantages:

1. **NO OUTDOOR ANTENNA NECESSARY**—in most localities. Your new Emerson is delivered *fully* assembled, quicker and easier to plug in.
2. **EASIER TO TUNE**—Complicated controls are eliminated. Even a child can operate it. All Emerson receivers are solidly, precision built—made to last for years.
3. **EASIER TO LOOK AT**—Emerson has *6 times the brightness of home movies without glare.* And the decorator styling of Emerson cabinets makes *them* easier to look at, too.
4. **EASIER TO PICK UP RECEPTION**—Emerson's exclusive Long-Distance Circuit pulls in signals of faraway stations, adjusts overly-strong signals in nearby areas. You'll find that—*no matter where you are, wherever there's a signal, you get it on an Emerson.*
5. **EASIER TO OWN**—Emerson gives you *more* for your money, model for model, screen size for screen size, quality for quality. The Emerson brand name is your best assurance of dependability. The Emerson you buy is inspected and tested 225 times before it reaches your home.

Emerson  **Television**

Emerson Radio and Phonograph Corporation, New York 11, N. Y.

For Better Vision, Style, Tone, Performance, Value . . . *EMERSONIZE YOUR HOME*

Emerson Radio and Phonograph Corporation (B)

By 1956, the Emerson Radio and Phonograph Corporation had become well established as one of the ten companies that together manufactured over 80 percent of the television sets in the United States. Mr. Benjamin Abrams, president, while confident that Emerson was equipped to face the increasing competition, still was interested in production cost reduction, aggressive promotional campaigns, and in new products. Balance sheets and income statements for 1949–1955 are shown in Exhibits 1 and 2.

GROWTH BETWEEN 1948 AND 1955

A sharp increase in the rate of television production in 1949 had been made possible by the conversion of radio set assembly lines. The conversion, however, required large amounts of factory space, since unit for unit, the manufacture of television sets required more than ten times as much space, assembly work, and materials as the manufacture of radio sets. Television sets were assembled on five production lines, each with an average daily output of 220 sets. The company rented 290,000 square feet of space in Manhattan, of which 112,000 was used for production, 51,000 for finished inventory, and 127,000 for laboratories, offices, raw materials, and service needs.

In order to provide adequate facilities for more rapid assembly, the Emerson company purchased an empty plant in Jersey City in April, 1950. The five-story New Jersey plant had 450,000 square feet of space, but was expanded to 600,000 square feet in 1953 at a total cost of more than $2 million for land and buildings. A manufacturing plant with 90,000 square feet of space in Brooklyn was also established to supply wood television cabinets.

In 1953, Emerson acquired the Quiet Heet Manufacturing Corporation, which manufactured oil burners and air conditioners in 108,000 square feet of space in Newark, New Jersey. The subsidiary produced oil and gas burners under the Quiet Heet name as well as under private labels for furnace and burner manufacturers, and room, residential, and commercial air conditioners under the Emerson-Quiet Kool label.

Other facilities were scattered around the country. In 1954, Emerson leased facilities in Washington, D.C. to house the Emerson Research Laboratories, which were utilized for defense electronics projects for national defense. The company also had wholly owned distributing subsidiaries in New York City, Buffalo, Chicago, Detroit, Cleveland, San Francisco, Fresno, and Portland (Oregon). The distributors in Los Angeles and Boston were 50 percent owned by the company. A separate subsidiary was established in 1955 to promote the rental and sale of air conditioners and television sets to hotels, motels, and other commercial establishments.

With the start of the Korean War in 1950, the company's wartime military experience was again utilized. In 1951, approximately 80 percent of the Emerson company's electronic and mechanical engineers were engaged in government work. By 1952, the backlog of undelivered defense contracts amounted to $50 million. A trend in military electronics work became established away from simple devices in long production runs and toward complex systems requiring great engineering skills, much special plant equipment, and a long lead time. In 1955, government sales were approximately 50 percent higher than in 1952, and accounted for about one fifth of the company's total sales volume. At that time, television sets accounted for about one half the sales, and radio sets about one tenth.

The company's gross plant, which was $657,000 in 1949, had grown to $4,604,000 in 1955. Of the latter figure, $2,839,000 was for buildings, $1,608,000 for machinery and equipment, and $383,000 for land. The annual account for maintenance and repairs had increased from $27,000 in 1948 to $282,000 in 1955 and charges for depreciation from $99,000 in 1948 to $530,000 in 1955. The number of employees grew from 2,200 in 1949 to about 8,000 in 1955, including all branches of the company.

Until 1943, the Abrams family owned the entire common stock of the Emerson corporation. In 1949, members of the family offered to the public 235,000 of the 800,000 shares then outstanding. As a result of the offering, the number of stockholders increased from 2,100 in 1949 to 7,500 in 1955 and the share of ownership of the Abrams family declined from 52.2 to 24.6 percent. Between 1949 and 1955, net worth increased from $10.0 million to $21.8 million and a long term 4¼ percent note for $7.5 million was obtained to provide additional funds. In April, 1956, 1,936,000 shares of common stock were outstanding and were quoted on the New York Stock Exchange for approximately $12 per share.

MARKET POLICIES

Emerson increased the portion of its own net sales due to television from 18 percent in 1948, when the industry sold a million sets, to 77 percent in 1950, when the industry sold seven million sets. During the period subsequent to 1950 when market saturation became more complete and the demand for sets levelled off, the television industry became very competitive and prices declined markedly. The number of television models in the Emerson line increased from 14 in 1949 to 23 in 1955. Prior to 1948, a 10-inch television set might have been priced to sell at retail between $300 and $500; in 1949, a 10-inch set was priced between $200 and $350. Continual technological progress and design simplification made it difficult to compare sets, but a 16-inch table model Emerson set priced retail at $329 in 1949 could be replaced in 1956 by a 17-inch table model set priced at $138. Mr. Abrams believed that despite increased competition, the Emerson company could increase its strength through production efficiencies and through intensive merchandising, advertising, and selling effort. In order to support the growth of educational television broadcasts, for example, Mr. Abrams awarded a prize of $10,000 to each of the first ten educational stations that started up in 1953.

Merchandising

In the design of its products, the Emerson company emphasized compactness, color, and special features, for the lower price market. Emerson often took the lead in offering new promotional features. For example, in 1954, a 17-inch table model television set was introduced for a suggested list price of only $129. In 1955, pastel colored television sets were placed on the market, to harmonize with interior decorations. The same year, a portable air conditioner was placed on the market which enabled the consumer to move the unit from room to room. In 1956, the Emerson air conditioner was provided with an electronic purification device which was advertised as an "electronic germkiller." The company continued its pioneer design work in the field of small radios by introducing a pocket radio which had a volume of only 26 cubic inches and weighed less than one pound. The radio was later transistorized to increase its battery life an estimated ten times.

Most of the 23 television models in the Emerson line used two or three basic chassis designs. Variations were obtained by mounting a different type of picture tube or cabinet on the same chassis, or by adding special subassemblies, such as ultrahigh frequency tuning and remote control dialing. Photographs of the three most popular models in the line in 1956 are included in Exhibit 3B.

The Emerson company originated many novel programs to help "move" merchandise in sluggish periods. For example, since air conditioners were a highly seasonal item, it had always proved difficult to sell these products in the autumn months. The Emerson company therefore offered to sell air conditioners for $100 below retail list price during the month of September, with lesser amounts of discount during succeeding months until the product returned to list price in January. When necessary to promote the sale of regular television sets, the company offered its distributors "convention terms" under which they could take immediate delivery of new sets from inventory and postpone payment for periods up to 90 days. Other programs were devised to help the sale of color television sets or to facilitate the development of color television without reducing the market for black-and-white sets. For example, when the initial retail price of $1,000 for a color set appeared to be too high and the prospect of obsolescence too immediate to stimulate sales, the Emerson company offered to lease color sets rather than sell them outright. Another example occurred in April, 1953, when industry executives feared the reluctance of prospective purchasers to invest in black-and-white receivers in view of the anticipated introduction of color television. At that time, Emerson issued an unqualified guarantee that a purchaser of any 1953 Emerson television model, upon surrender of the set before June 30, 1954, would receive the total purchase price paid as partial payment for any color receiver, regardless of make, which he might buy before the expiration date of the offer.

Selling

By 1956, the Emerson company had approximately 100 distributors who sold Emerson television receivers, radios, phonographs, and air conditioners to approximately 30,000 dealers throughout the country. The largest volume accounts were located in New York City, Los Angeles, San Francisco, Philadelphia, and sections of New Jersey.

Television sets initiated a change to higher quality, more strongly capitalized dealers. Instead of the $10 and up cost for a radio or phonograph, TV sets cost $100 or more and created storage problems. Margins were reportedly 22 to 35 percent off retail for dealers and 10 percent off dealer price for distributors. The lower margins were for portables and price leaders. About 25 percent of 1956 sales were for replacement or second set sales.

Advertising

Cooperative and national advertising ran $4 million annually in 1955 and 1956. National advertising emphasized the versatility of small radios, room air conditioners, and TV sets with the theme "Wherever you look—There's Emerson" (see Exhibit 4). The cartoons were done by Steinberg, Soglow, or Steig and reproduced on a variety of ash trays, napkins, playing cards, and other small items. In addition, a large mockup was made of the "lady in a bathtub" cartoon so that each distributor could be photographed looking out of the TV screen in the illustration. The distributors continued to campaign by using the cartoon and slogan wherever possible.

MANUFACTURING

Between 1949 and 1956, television set design was greatly simplified and the number of component parts reduced. Whereas in 1949 a television set was considered to be ten times as complex and costly as a radio set, in 1956 a factor of seven was considered more reliable. Color sets, however, were about six times as costly as black-and-white television in materials, labor, and difficulty of assembly.

Automation

In view of the high volume of output, the expenditures for wages, and the pressure of price competition, Emerson became increasingly interested in machine processes that would increase production efficiency. By 1955 the company had invested several hundred thousand dollars in an automated subassembly line of advanced design for the preparation of wired boards for a new chassis.

The new line was a fully automatic, 30-position machine designed to assemble components on a printed circuit board (see Exhibit 6). The printed boards, which were purchased from an outside concern, were loaded at one end of the moving conveyor. Each position dropped a particular component through prepunched holes in the board, and bent the wires across the underside. Once the heads were in proper alignment and the components loaded at each position, the machine could turn out approximately 24 boards in one minute. Approximately one hour was required to re-align the machine for a second run to place additional components on the same board. Although all the required components could not be assembled by machine, it eliminated twenty-two assembly operations in each of two boards used in the 1956 chassis. The boards were then delivered to the main assembly line. Assembly workers added the final components and placed each board into the dip-solder bath where all connections were simultaneously fluxed and then soldered in one pass through the hot solder bath.

Modules

An alternative to automation with printed circuits was introduced at the Emerson plant in 1956 in the use of modular assemblies of components. Modular construction, developed for the Navy Department Bureau of Aeronautics under the title "Project Tinkertoy," was designed to enable groups of special components to be assembled as a stack of ceramic wafers ⅞ inch square and spaced $^3/_{16}$ inch apart. The wafers were held together by twelve riser wires which also served as connectors. Each wafer could carry from one to four capacitors or resistors and one or two conductors. The advantages of modular construction were as follows: (1) it was highly adaptable to mass production, since all wafers were of a standard size and could be mounted on top of one another on a standard connecting unit; (2) it simplified repairs in that an entire modular unit could be removed and replaced without requiring repair work on the chassis; (3) it eliminated the problem of cross-over wires which occurred in printed circuits due to their two-dimensional design. The major problem with modular construction seemed to be that all components had to be redesigned to meet the wafer design. An additional difficulty lay in the fact that modules were coated with an insulating compound which had to be removed and replaced when repair work was undertaken.

1. EMERSON RADIO AND PHONOGRAPH CORPORATION (B)

Balance Sheets, 1950-1955 (Year End Oct. 31)
(In Thousands)

ASSETS	1950	1951	1952	1953	1954	1955
Cash and Securities	$ 9,313	$ 4,099	$ 4,983	$ 4,235	$ 6,658	$ 7,377
Receivables	8,272	10,738	6,843	13,786	14,979	17,880
Inventories						
Raw and in Process	6,695	5,483	9,366	7,386	7,041	5,771
Finished	857	12,440	1,872	7,061	7,360	7,866
Other		743*		1,512**	369**	331**
Current Assets	$25,137	$33,503	$23,064	$33,980	$36,407	$39,225
Fixed Assets	$ 2,343	$ 2,608	$ 3,003	$ 4,593	$ 5,107	$ 5,604
Less Depreciation	336	799	1,129	1,515	2,010	2,437
Net Fixed Assets	$ 2,007	$ 1,809	$ 1,874	$ 3,078	$ 3,097	$ 3,167
Patents	$ 1	$ 1	$ 1	$ 1	$ 1	$ 1
Value of Insurance	29	31	28			
Due from Employees			142			
Other Assets	3	32		1,286***	1,466***	1,167***
Deferred Charges	144	1,152	1,040			
Total Assets	$27,321	$36,528	$26,149	$38,345	$40,971	$43,560
LIABILITIES						
Accounts Payable	$ 4,675	$ 4,248	$ 3,773	$ 6,954	$ 8,547	$ 8,624
Notes Payable		8,500		4,920	7,500	7,500
Accruals	1,908	2,172	2,087	2,995	2,697	3,237
Provision for Tax	5,495	4,717	2,500	3,673	1,710	2,394
Current Liabilities	$12,078	$19,637	$ 8,360	$18,542	$20,454	$21,755
Parts Warranty	105	102				
Other Liabilities			91	85	70	49
Capital Stock	8,798	9,676	9,676	9,676	9,678	9,679
Capital Surplus		1,580	1,580	1,580	1,583	1,584
Earned Surplus	6,340	5,533	6,442	8,462	9,186	10,493
Total Liabilities	$27,321	$36,528	$26,149	$38,345	$40,971	$43,560

*Unbilled costs under U.S. Government contracts.

**Includes $473,000 for goodwill in connection with acquisition of subsidiary company.

***Prepaid taxes, insurance, etc., and investment in securities of subsidiaries not consolidated (at cost).

2. EMERSON RADIO AND PHONOGRAPH CORPORATION (B)

Income Statements, 1950-1955 (Year End Oct. 31)
(In Thousands)

	1950	1951	1952	1953	1954	1955
Net Sales	$74,188	$55,798	$57,664	$75,926	$80,560	$87,383
Cost of Sales	56,933	44,039	48,202	62,694	69,959	74,544
Gross Profit	$17,255	$11,759	$ 9,462	$13,232	$10,601	$12,839
Selling, General and Administrative Expenses	5,362	4,979	4,873	6,837	7,776	8,231
Profit	$11,893	$ 6,780	$ 4,589	$ 6,395	$ 2,825	$ 4,608
Other Income	77	95	62	104	624	162
Income before Taxes	$11,970	$ 6,875	$ 4,651	$ 6,499	$ 3,449	$ 4,770
Provision for Taxes	5,455	3,283	2,389	3,511	1,564	2,302
Net Income	$ 6,515	$ 3,592	$ 2,262	$ 2,988	$ 1,885	$ 2,468

*Includes $109,000 for royalties.

Company and Industry Output of Television and Radio Sets, 1948 to 1955

	Television Emerson Sales*	Radio Emerson Sales*
1948	$ 5,554,000	$21,202,000
1949	26,353,000	11,001,000
1950	56,805,000	12,944,000
1951	39,579,000	9,049,000
1952	30,779,000	6,611,000
1953	44,667,000	7,830,000
1954	38,721,000	7,471,000
1955	40,268,000	8,729,000

*Company sales excluding excise and warranty; for fiscal year ending October 31.

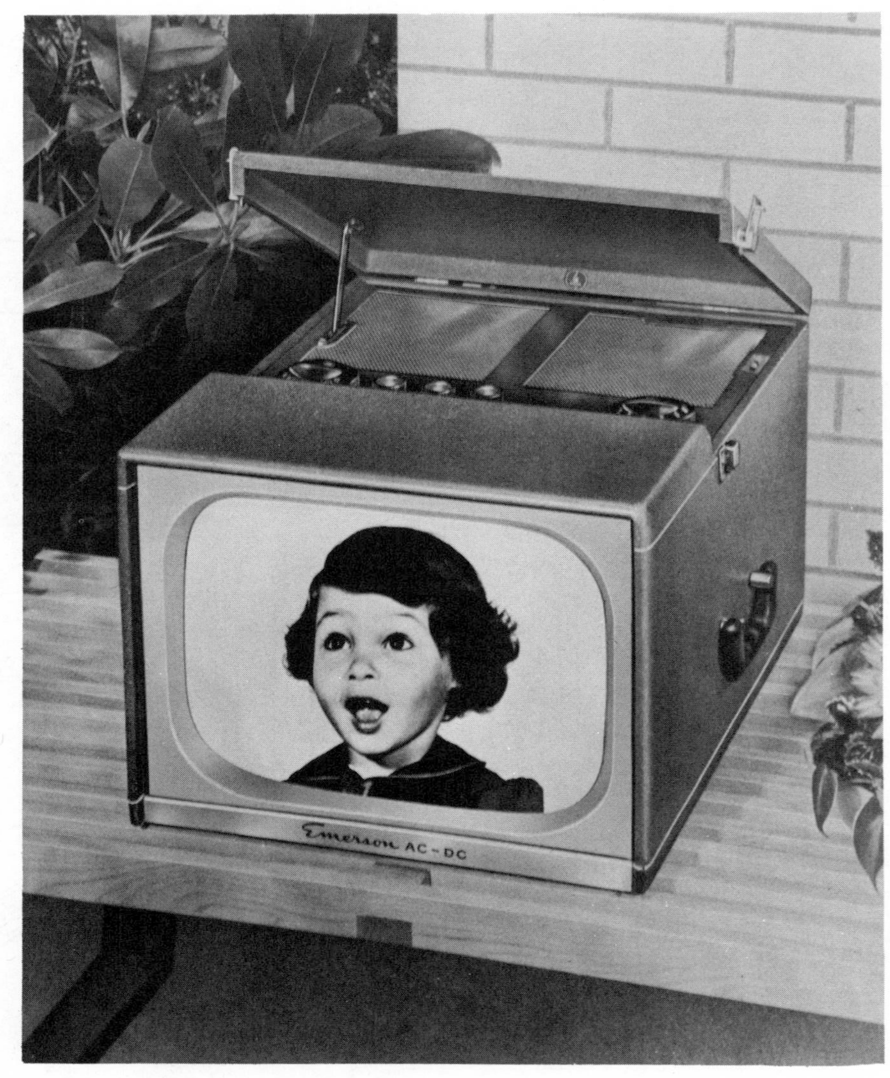

3. EMERSON RADIO AND PHONOGRAPH CORPORATION (B)

Upper left: 17-inch table model; pastel colors; retail price $138
Lower left: 21-inch consolette; mahogany, walnut, or blond wood; retail price $214
Right: 14-inch portable; wood, red, white, or blue; retail price $168

4. EMERSON RADIO AND PHONOGRAPH CORPORATION (B)

"Lady in a Bathtub" Advertisement

Wherever you look . . . there's Emerson

The lady could, of course, be watching a soap opera... but the chances are she's merely bathing in the luxury of viewing her 1956 Emerson TV Model 1102...available in *8 decorator colors* to harmonize with *any* room in your house. It's a gem of a set, with lines as clean as newly washed marble. Because of Emerson's exclusive Dyna-Power chassis, the picture is the sharpest, brightest this side of a movie palace. Or *in* a movie palace, for that matter. Trouble-free, it costs as little as *half* as much to operate—and parts last up to *ten times* longer. Your choice of colors...$138. *Wherever you look...look for Emerson TV, radios, phonographs, air conditioners.*

*Reg. U. S. Pat. Off. Emerson Radio & Phonograph Corp., Jersey City, N. J.

Over 16,000,000 satisfied owners

As Advertised in Farm Journal October, 1955

5. EMERSON RADIO AND PHONOGRAPH CORPORATION (B)

Monthly Dollar Sales to Distributors, 1954 and 1955

	1954		1955	
	TV	Radio	TV	Radio
January	$4,875,808	$ 672,686	$4,544,496	$ 532,690
February	3,574,894	457,416	3,942,831	545,067
March	2,707,647	383,036	3,367,074	530,784
April	3,154,602	418,327	1,661,549	282,234
May	1,414,429	235,853	999,566	489,066
June	954,155	248,485	1,057,600	458,500
July	2,764,186	875,552	5,713,182	1,002,762
August	3,796,594	331,402	3,284,680	579,943
September	3,910,530	526,362	3,631,438	859,972
October	5,339,654	1,165,005	5,004,867	1,429,562
November	3,532,419	507,360	3,277,811	785,555
December	3,367,171	849,270	2,239,854	1,045,944

Television Average Price to Distributors (UHF only)

	1954	1955
17-inch Table	$113.50	$101.00
21-inch Table	150.00	116.50
Consoles (consolettes)	203.00	167.75

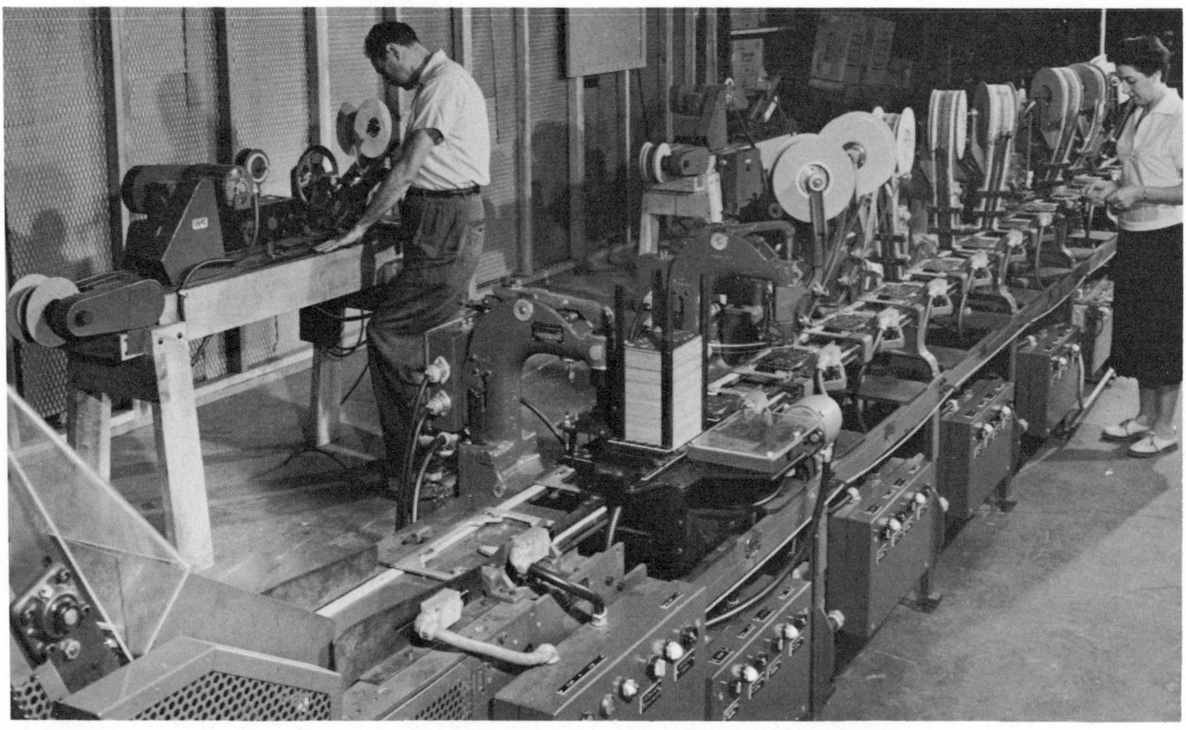

6. EMERSON RADIO AND PHONOGRAPH CORPORATION (B)

Top: Assembly line.

Bottom: Start of automated line. Boards are loaded at left and move right to subsequent positions. Machine at rear prepares components for loading on line in reels.

National Video Corporation

Throughout its history, the National Video Corporation of Chicago has remained the largest independent manufacturer of television picture tubes and an important supplier to midwestern set assemblers. Founded in 1948 with $100,000 and a 24,000 square foot rented plant, the company grew in eight years to over $1 million in net worth, with $9.7 million in sales and a 172,000 square foot building equipped with modern automatic machinery and six conveyor systems. By mid-1956 management claimed that 10 percent of the television receivers in use in the United States contained National Video picture tubes.

Except for a diversification loss in 1952, operations were profitable until competition intensified in 1954. A break-even point was reached in 1956 and in October, 1956, the company had a gross margin of $150,000 and profits of $60,000 on $1,140,000 sales for the month. The excess of industry production over demand affected National Video sales the next month and at the beginning of December, production was cut back.

In December, 1956, Mr. Asher Cole, president, was considering installing a second screening belt conveyor and two automatic settling solution dispensers in the screening room. By investing approximately $90,000, the screening room labor force would be reduced and the reject rate cut. On the other hand, the equipment might lead to higher maintenance costs and a loss of production flexibility.

COMPANY HISTORY

The National Video Corporation was founded in December, 1948, by Mr. Cole and five partners. Mr. Cole had spent the period since 1931 as television research engineer for a research corporation, and in that position "barnstormed" around the country during the 1930's demonstrating television at fairs, expositions, conventions, and retail stores. In 1948 he resigned his position as vice-president of the research company to start a business in partnership with three other engineers and two outside investors.

Mr. Cole and his engineer-partners not only designed and built the production machinery but operated the machines to produce their first tubes in March, 1949. The first three months' output totaled 7,000 tubes and brought in profits of $70,000 before taxes. Two years later one of the partners retired and received $535,000 in return for his original investment of $20,000.

Sales of National Video tubes rose to a peak during the 1950 television boom, but began to decline sharply during early 1951 with output dropping from 55,000 to 25,000 tubes per month. A factor in this decline was the demand for receiving tubes, the supply of which had been insufficient to meet industry needs since the outbreak of hostilities in Korea. Mr. Cole felt that companies which produced both receiving and picture tubes were giving preference on receiving tube shipments to set assembly companies which also bought their picture tubes.

To offset his company's competitive disadvantage in this respect, Mr. Cole decided to enter the receiving tube field. Accordingly, in June, 1951, the National Video Corporation purchased a 53,000 square foot plant in Grayslake, Illinois, a small town about 30 miles north of Chicago. It was estimated that with an investment of $1,000,000 in equipment, in addition to the $500,000 which had been spent on the plant, the company would be able to produce 100,000 receiving tubes per day. Before the receiving tube plant began operations, however, the general shortage of tubes had been relieved by expansion of other companies' capacities. National Video's decision to undertake production of receiving tubes had been motivated by a desire to sustain the company's sales of picture tubes; when the receiving tube shortage disappeared, it was decided to liquidate the receiving tube plant, with National Video taking a loss of $1,400,000 on the venture.

The rapid growth of the company required constant expansion of personnel and physical facilities. By 1952 the company was using 65,000 square feet on two stories of the original plant. This plant, however, had no in-line exhaust facilities and only one conveyor. Therefore in 1952, a new 117,000 square foot company-owned building was constructed in the same neighborhood. Before this new plant had been fully completed, ground was broken for a 55,000 square foot addition. All of the original production equipment in both plants had been designed and installed by the company's engineers.

Two changes in the corporate structure were

made subsequent to the company's founding. In April, 1951, a new company, Navidico, Inc., was established to handle sales of National Video picture tubes to the replacement market. The management and ownership of Navidico were identical to that of National Video. In January, 1953, another company, Rico Electronics, Inc., was established in Puerto Rico to manufacture electron guns for assembly in National Video tubes. The Rico corporation, which proved to be very profitable, provided a means of offering an ownership share to deserving executives of the National Video Corporation without diluting the equity of the parent company. Worker productivity in Puerto Rico was found to be much higher than at the Chicago plant, and by 1956, two thirds of the guns used by National Video were being produced by the Rico company and shipped by Air Freight to Chicago. Combined Balance Sheets and Income Statements for the three associated corporations for 1949–1956 are given in Exhibits 1 and 2.

In 1956, the National Video Corporation employed 700 persons, 600 of whom were unionized production workers. The average hourly wage paid was approximately $1.60, and Mr. Cole estimated that fringe benefits cost the company an added thirty cents per hour. Wages had been increased by 8 cents per hour in February, 1956, after having remained level for approximately two years. Most of the operations on the tube production line were unskilled or semiskilled.

MARKETING

From 1949 to mid-1956 the National Video Corporation produced and sold more than four million television picture tubes. In 1956, sales of picture tubes, the company's only product, were running at an average monthly rate of 70,000 units, although a peak of 90,000 had been reached in one month. About 11 percent of the company's 1956 sales were to the replacement market.

Product Characteristics

Specifications for picture tubes were prepared by an industry committee with the result that, with only a few exceptions, tubes were a standard product. The important physical characteristics of a tube were the diameter and shape of the screen, angle of sweep of the electron gun, neck diameter, and inner chemical coating. Set assemblers, having specified a particular tube type, were concerned with performance specifications such as: maximum possible voltage, light output and precise color of the screen, and tube life. Products of different tube manufacturers, while produced to standard specifications, could be differentiated with respect to those performance features. All manufacturers offered a one-year warranty on picture tubes, and although most tubes would last three to five years, about 5 percent would be returned during the warranty period.

Nature of Market

Picture tubes were sold directly to television set assemblers for use as original equipment and, through distributors, to television servicemen for replacement purposes. The nature of the product had undergone a rapid and continuing evolution since 1948. The first tubes sold by National Video had 10-inch screens and a deflection of 52 degrees; in 1956, tubes were made with 90 degree deflections and sizes ran from 10 inches up to 27 inches. Bulb construction changed from glass and metal combinations to all glass, and glass bulb shapes evolved from circular to rectangular.

None of these changes came about easily, however, and not all were successful. When the first all-glass rectangular-screen bulbs were developed in 1950 Mr. Cole helped to promote the new screen among industry users. As a result, the National Video company was committed to large advance orders for the new bulbs and thus enjoyed an advantage when the sudden popularity of the new shape caused a shortage of bulbs. Since that date the all-glass rectangular bulb has been standard for all tubes. On the other hand, companies who believed tube sizes would continue to increase incurred losses on 24- and 27-inch bulb facilities when consumers decided 21 inches was sufficient.

In the sale of tubes to set assemblers price competition was usually quite severe. Twelve-inch tubes had been sold for $35 in 1949, while in 1956 the price of 24-inch tubes was $26 and 10-inch tubes were sold for only $10. The continued downward trend in prices held true for all tube sizes and types. The first 17-inch tubes in 1950 were priced at $35, and one year later 21-inch tubes were introduced at a $40 price.

In 1953, 24-inch and 27-inch tubes were introduced at prices of $42 and $50, and the price of 21-inch tubes had dropped to $23.

In late 1956 the latest product development was a new tube with a 110-degree sweep and 1⅛-inch diameter neck. Although this offered the advantages of a smaller and lighter weight product, it was expected that the cost would be greater than for the then current 90-degree tube with 1⅝-inch neck diameter. National Video was preparing for total conversion to production of this new tube, but could not forecast when it would happen. In early 1957 a large manufacturer of picture tubes and television receivers made public the following comparison of dimensions and costs of 90-degree versus 110-degree tubes:

Tube Type	*Length (inches)*	*Weight (pounds)*	*Approx. Cost*[1]
17-inch 110-degree	12 13/16	10½	$15.00
17-inch 90-degree	16	13½	13.25
21-inch 110-degree	14¾	22	19.50
21-inch 90-degree	20⅜	24	17.50
24-inch 110-degree	14¼	30	25.25
24-inch 90-degree	21½	35	22.75

[1] Approximate list price to original equipment manufacturers.

Although volume demand for color tubes seemed far distant, National Video had spent $200,000 in 1955 on pilot runs of color tubes. Mr. Cole felt that the complexity of present tube designs would prohibit volume sales of color sets. He believed that the market for color would appear only after a major new invention had eliminated the complexities which resulted in high costs and especially high shrinkage in production.

Sales to Set Assemblers

Many of the largest manufacturers of television receivers were vertically integrated to produce all or part of their picture tube requirements. In 1956 National Video was one of two remaining companies which manufactured only picture tubes, the other company being located in New Jersey. National Video's customers were located in the Chicago area, and included two large nonintegrated set manufacturers, the Admiral Corporation and Motorola, Inc., plus six smaller manufacturers. In selling to these companies National Video competed against several large integrated companies which sold their excess picture tubes to outsiders. National Video had always concentrated its selling efforts in the Midwest, where it could provide maximum service in both engineering and delivery. In the industry, tube manufacturers shipped tubes freight prepaid, a practice which reduced the profitability of selling to distant markets. The rental and operating cost for a leased truck would amount to about $400 for a load of 400 21-inch tubes shipped to the East Coast from Chicago.

The year 1956 was a difficult one for most of the television receiver manufacturers; eight important set assembly companies ceased operations during the year. One of these, The Raytheon Manufacturing Co., sold its set assembly facilities in Chicago but continued to produce and sell picture tubes at a plant in Massachusetts. The CBS-Columbia Division of Columbia Broadcasting System stopped its set assembly operations in July, 1956, and at the same time the CBS-Hytron Division closed a 275,000 square foot picture tube plant in Kalamazoo, Michigan. CBS-Hytron continued to produce color and black-and-white tubes in the East, however. Service and contacts with the top managements of one's customers were important in selling; most companies, including National Video, met any competitive prices. Most set assemblers maintained tube inventories of less than three days' requirements.

Replacement Sales

The market for replacement tubes was one that was increasing in size each year. Known consumer brands, such as RCA, General Electric, and Sylvania, seemed to dominate the market in 1956, but smaller manufacturers were also a factor. In large cities many "rebuilders" had appeared; they operated in garages and small shops and rebuilt burnt-out tubes by salvaging the glass and other usable components. Mr. Harold Cole, sales manager, thought that as much as 40 percent of replacement sales went to such companies, despite the apparent inferiority of their product.

National Video, through Navidico, Inc., sold to independent distributors and to franchised distributors of the Admiral and Motorola companies, which, in turn, sold tubes to TV servicemen. These tubes carried the set assembler's brand and were shipped direct to distributors by Navidico. Navidico's price included a small markup over the National Video list price to cover costs of individual handling, packing, and freight. Tubes for set assemblers were shipped in truckload lots on pallets; replacement tubes, however, were individually packed in cartons, and shipped in smaller lots with a resulting higher unit freight cost. Although price competition had become severe in the replacement tube market and margins barely covered the added selling costs, Navidico sales served to build volume for tube production, and gave the company an entry into a market that Mr. Cole expected to reach a volume double that of the market for original equipment.

A Navidico catalogue issued to distributors in 1956 listed 250 tube types, any of which might be ordered for replacement purposes. The efficient production in small volume of these many and diverse items was a continuing problem.

MANUFACTURING

The manufacture of picture tubes utilized a highly automated, conveyorized, continuous process, which was operated 24 hours, 5 days weekly. Purchased glass bulbs were cleaned, coated with screen phosphors and other chemicals, fitted with an electron gun, evacuated, sealed, and tested. The process described below was used by the National Video Corporation to produce the tubes which sold in large volume. These 21 tube types accounted for 99 percent of the company's sales in late 1956. Production for each of these types ranged from 400 to 5,500 tubes per month. A diagram of one portion of the National Video plant is shown as Exhibit 3, a Flow Chart as Exhibit 4, and pictures of some manufacturing operations as Exhibits 5–8. The bulbs were carried through the plant on overhead monorail conveyors with hangers located every 3½ feet. The length of time required for each conveyor to travel 3½ feet was as follows:

Conveyor	*Time*
(*A*) "Wash"	6 seconds
(*B*) "Spray lacquer"	10 "
(*C*) "Preheat"	9 "
(*D*) "Sealing"	12 "
(*E*) "Pump"	18 "
(*F*) "Forming and Aging"	15 "

(*A*) *"Wash" Conveyor*

Incoming bulbs were stored in cartons near the conveyor loading station. Two men removed bulbs from cartons, visually inspected the glass, and placed the bulbs on the first, or "wash," conveyor (see Exhibit 5). Bulbs were grouped to coincide with the screening schedule, and labelled with colored and numbered pieces of tape. For washing, the bulbs were removed from the monorail and placed in one of three fully automatic machines, each attended by one worker. A fourth machine was under construction in late 1956. Bulbs placed in the washers were automatically indexed every 15 seconds through 10 wash stations and then reached the "unload" position from which they were returned to the "wash" conveyor and carried into the screening room.

The screening room contained one settling belt conveyor and twenty tilting tables, called "tippers." The belt and tippers served to hold bulbs steady while the phosphors settled onto the bulb face, and to decant the excess solution from the bulbs after the settling period. The belt conveyor could accommodate only 21-inch bulbs, while the tables could be set up for any size. The tippers were laid out in groups of four tables, called "merry-go-rounds," with three men handling each merry-go-round. Each table could handle from 10 to 20 bulbs, depending on the bulb size. Pictures of the tipper tables are shown in Exhibit 6.

The monorail conveyor passed by each table and the settling belt conveyor. Bulbs were unloaded directly onto the tables and clamped in place, neck up. When the table was full, the workers poured phosphor and electrolyte solutions into the bulbs and switched on an automatic mechanism to operate the table. At the end of a twenty minute settling period, the table would automatically begin to tip, thus draining the solution from the bulbs. The crew would work in turn on each table in their merry-go-round, completing a full cycle in about one hour. After the bulbs were emptied they were removed from the table, air-dried briefly, and replaced on the overhead conveyor.

The tables could be set up to handle any bulb size by changing the number of the clamps. Each table would hold ten 24-inch or 27-inch bulbs, fourteen 20-inch or 21-inch bulbs, or twenty 10-inch through 17-inch bulbs. Changing the clamps took at least one hour, but changes within each of the three size groups would not require down time. Thus no production would be lost in a change from 10-inch to 17-inch size, while a setup would be required to go from 17-inch to 20-inch. No time was lost in changing from one phosphor solution formula to another.

The settling belt conveyor did not have equipment to automatically dispense the screening solution, and was operated by five men who loaded and unloaded bulbs and poured the proper settling solutions into the bulbs. The belt would handle only 21-inch bulbs and carried them in twenty-six rows of three bulbs. The output was approximately 75 bulbs per hour.

As the bulbs emerged from the screening room each one was carefully inspected while on the monorail conveyor and rejects were marked to be rewashed and screened once again. The reject rate on bulbs from the tippers was about 25 percent, but was one-third less for bulbs from the settling conveyors. The monthly average reject rate for screening was subject to continuing fluctuation, some months going below 10 percent, at other times reaching as high as 30 percent. A reject caught at this stage cost only about 35 cents to rework, while after the next operation the cost of rework would be 91 cents for an aluminized bulb and 50 cents for one not aluminized.

(B) "Spray Lacquer" Conveyor

Bulbs which passed inspection were removed from the "wash" conveyor. Bulbs to be aluminized were grouped by size and placed on a transfer conveyor, called the "spray lacquer" conveyor, which carried them into the spray-lacquer room. These bulbs were identified by the color of the label attached in loading. Non-aluminized bulbs were processed to apply the inner carbon coating, while all rejects remained on the "wash" conveyor and returned on it for rework.

In the spray-lacquer room the inside of the bulb to be aluminized was sprayed with water and then the bulb placed neck down in a machine which rotated it for 10 to 25 seconds while coating the inside with a lacquer film. The film provided a smooth surface for aluminum to adhere to. The bulbs were transferred after lacquer spray to a similar machine which sprayed water inside away from the face level so that lacquer remained only on the bulb face. The neck of each bulb was dried manually with a sponge and then the bulb was dried in a rack by warm air before being returned to the spray lacquer conveyor. Minor adjustments in the spray nozzle had to be made when the bulb size was changed.

The monorail conveyor returned lacquered bulbs to the main production area where a graphite coating, known as a "dag" coat, was applied to the inside of each bulb. The graphite was the simplest type of electrical conductor to apply, and served to complete the circuit inside the tube. Only the neck and a strip for a high voltage anode were "dagged" on bulbs to be aluminized. Other bulbs received a "full dag," which meant that all of the inside of the cone was coated. Full dag bulbs were placed in vacuum driers, those to be aluminized were moved to the aluminizing machines. All but two of the aluminizing machines were fully automatic once the bulb was inserted, and operated on about an eight-minute cycle. Pictures of graphite coating and aluminizing machines are given in Exhibit 7.

An intermediate inventory of graphite coated and aluminized bulbs was maintained adjacent to the aluminizing machines. This buffer absorbed fluctuations in the output of screening operations so that maximum efficiency could be realized on the sealing and exhaust machines. The inventory amounted to 1½ to 2 shifts output and was drawn down during the last shift each week when the screen room was shut down for cleaning.

(C) "Preheat" Conveyor

Two men handled the buffer inventory and rescheduled and loaded bulbs onto the "preheat" conveyor in the area next to aluminizing and dagging operators. The bulbs were loaded in sequence to match the schedule of the sealing and exhaust machines.

All bulbs passed a second inspection point just prior to the preheat oven. Two men counted the bulbs by type, made a visual check of glass and screen condition, and used an electrical probe to gauge the thickness of the aluminum coating. Bulbs which passed this inspection were loaded by one man onto the belt conveyor leading into the oven.

Baking out the bulbs annealed the glass, dried the chemical coatings, and evaporated the lacquer used for aluminizing. Some bulbs broke during the heating, usually because of a glass defect. Bulbs traveled through the 130-foot oven on a 10-foot wide belt conveyor moving at 11 inches per minute. Baking-out required temperatures above 840 degrees Fahrenheit, and because glass will not withstand temperature changes above 30 degrees per minute, both the belt speed and "temperature curve" within the oven were important factors in controlling breakage. Management felt that National Video's oven breakage was far below the usual rate for the industry. Pictures of the preheat oven and sealing machines are given in Exhibit 8.

Upon leaving the oven, bulbs were loaded again onto the "preheat" conveyor which traveled past an inspection point and then brought them to the sealing machines. Each bulb was inspected on the conveyor under ultraviolet light to detect defects in the screen. One man also marked the neck to indicate the position for the gun mount seal.

The company used three semiautomatic ten-station rotary indexing sealing machines. One man at each machine loaded bulbs taken from the "preheat" conveyor and unloaded bulbs from the sealing machine onto the "sealing" conveyor. Each bulb was indexed through four stations to heat the neck, and at the fifth station the mount was manuallly inserted and sealed-in by an operator. The bulb then passed through three stations where the glass was annealed for greater strength. At the tenth position the bulb was removed from the sealing machine. Because the mounts varied from one tube type to another two workers were needed to sort the mounts and distribute them in the proper order to the three sealing operators. The output of each machine had to balance that of an exhaust machine, therefore the sealing machines operated on a 42-second index.

(D) "Sealing" Conveyor

As the conveyor carried sealed tubes to the in-line exhaust machines a random sample was checked with polarized light to detect strains in the mount seal. A buffer inventory of sealed tubes was maintained to insure maximum utilization of exhaust capacity.

Each of the three in-line exhausts used 108 exhaust carts. The bulbs were loaded into and unloaded from the carts by men on platforms running between the in-line ovens; three men tended in-lines #2 and #3 together, while two men tended #1. The in-lines indexed on a cycle of 50 to 90 seconds, depending upon the tube size. At each index one cart emerged from the oven, all those in the oven advanced one position, and one cart moved into the oven. The oven held 78 carts. One man at the end of each oven tipped off the tubes, sealing the glass stem so that the tube could be removed from the cart without loss of vacuum. The tip-off was done while the tube was hot because this was thought to result in higher quality.

Careful heating and cooling was necessary in the exhaust oven to avoid breakage of glass. The tubes cooled while the cart moved down an uncovered track; individual sheet metal covers on the carts protected workers from explosions which sometimes occurred during cooling. The principal advantage of the covers, however, was to diffuse the heat when the tube was in the oven, thus permitting the tube to enter and leave at a higher temperature. (Some companies subjected the glass to extreme heat in the baking-out, and thus could run the surviving bulbs through the in-lines more rapidly.) At the end of the cooling tracks, which ran parallel to the in-line ovens, were the load platforms where the tubes were removed and placed onto the "pump" conveyor which carried them to the basing operation.

The in-lines could be used for any size or type tube. A size change, however, required a change in cycle time and oven temperature, and usually a setup change on the carts. Setups were done by maintenance men and required at least one hour. Changing from a 21-inch to 24-inch size, however, required only an increase in cycle time from 62 seconds to 75 seconds, and if desired those two sizes could be run intermixed by using the longer cycle time; in addition, the carts and oven could be set to run mixed bulbs up to a maximum size of 17 inches.

Installation of in-line #3 in 1956 increased production capacity some 700 units per day by replacing stationary exhaust banks which required four operators but were limited to only 600 units daily. The company continued to use three stationary exhaust banks. The banks held a total of 18 tubes and operated on a four-hour cycle. They were used primarily for 27-inch tubes and other small-volume odd sizes.

(E) "Pump" Conveyor

Bases were attached to the tubes on the monorail "pump" conveyor as they passed the basing platform. From that point the coneyor entered the basing oven which baked the cement. The speed of the "pump" conveyor was set to provide the proper exposure to heat in the basing oven. After passing through the oven, tubes were removed from the conveyor for getter flashing and then returned to the same conveyor. While moving on the conveyor the leads were soldered to the base pins and 45 thousand volts applied to the anode as a high-voltage "cleanup." When all three in-lines were operating three men attached bases, two men handled getter flashing and one man did base soldering. High-voltage cleanup was done fully automatically without a worker.

(F) "Forming and Aging" Conveyor

Before forming and aging, the tubes were removed from the "pump" conveyor for application of the outer graphite coating. This "outer dag" was applied in a spray booth, and three men were used to spray the output of three in-lines. After the spraying operation the tubes were dried in a rack where base connections were checked and faulty bases replaced. The tubes were then placed on the "forming and aging" monorail conveyor. One man loaded the conveyor and attached the proper connections to the tube. All operations were performed automatically as the tubes moved overhead on the conveyor, although one worker was needed to remove base connections before the final high-voltage application.

Inspection and Test

After aging, all tubes passed through one of two test operations. A new fully automatic test mechanism developed by National Video made it possible to rapidly test tubes without removing them from the conveyor. One half of the output was checked by unskilled workers using test equipment that checked vacuum, gas, and electrical characteristics and flashed red or green lights to indicate acceptability. Other tubes were removed from the conveyor to be screen checked in the conventional manner by skilled technicians. The company hoped to convert all test operations to the fully automatic method.

Tubes were held for 24 hours and retested by the "product acceptance" inspectors before being shipped. Tubes which failed either of the final tests, as well as bulbs damaged in production and defective tubes returned under warrantee or traded in on purchase of replacement tubes, were processed whenever possible to salvage the glass envelope. This was done by cutting off the neck, washing the glass to remove all chemicals, splicing on a new neck, and restarting the bulbs just like new ones. The quality of these reclaimed bulbs was in no way inferior to new glass. The company also maintained a buffing department to remove scratches and rough spots from rejected and reclaimed bulbs.

PLANNING AND CONTROL

The objectives of the purchasing and scheduling departments were to permit rapid response to customers' orders while maintaining minimum inventory levels and reasonably level production flow. The job of cost control was closely integrated with these functions and required constant awareness of trends in reject rates and causes and in worker productivity.

Purchasing

The cost of purchased material represented 52 to 61 percent of the selling price of picture tubes. Three items, the glass bulb, screen chemicals, and electron gun accounted for the major portion of the materials used. Guns were largely bought from Rico Electronics. Bulbs were bought from the Corning Glass Company and the Kimble Glass Works division of Owens-Illinois Glass Company. These companies produced standard items sold at the same price to all purchasers, without volume discounts. During 1956, National Video had also bought glass from a third, and much smaller, company which manufactured a special size tube for Admiral from molds owned by Admiral. Screen phosphor was bought from U. S. Radium Corporation and E. I. duPont de Nemours & Company. The markets for both these important raw materials were not affected by the severe competitive conditions which marked the picture tube market, with the result that the National Video company's purchase costs were far more stable than its selling prices. Bulbs were received daily in truckloads scheduled as close as possible to production requirements. The purchasing director estimated that delivery could be obtained within 8 to 24 hours in an emergency. Inward freight paid by National Video amounted to about 20 cents per bulb, based on shipment from Albion, Michigan.

Scheduling

Each week a tentative weekly production schedule was prepared in accordance with customers' advance orders. Firm schedules were prepared daily, but were often revised during the couse of the day. Production of replacement tubes was planned to maintain an inventory for Navidico equal to one to three weeks' requirements, resulting in a total stock of 5,000 units including approximately 40 different tube types. Original equipment bulbs were scheduled to order whenever possible, with some production for inventory on standard, high-volume bulbs during slack times. For these latter items, a finished inventory of five days' requirements would be considered high.

Control

The production control department prepared daily reports of unit production and man-hours of labor by department and shift plus daily detailed counts of good tubes packed, intermediate bulb and tube inventories, and finished inventories. Reject analysis forms presented a daily count of rejects by shift, department, and cause, and a daily report of the number of bulbs started and tubes packed as well as summaries of rejects, renecks, and bulbs lost by shift and department. A summary of the daily reports of production versus man-hours for November 30, 1955, and November 28 and December 3, 1956, is given in Exhibit 9. Reject analysis reports were summarized monthly; the monthly summaries for October, 1955 and 1956 are given in Exhibit 10.

Product Cost Analysis

At the end of each month a cost sheet prepared by the controller summarized the cost of each of the 20 most important tube types in production. This report showed average selling price for each type, costs of producing and selling, and volume of production and sales. The product cost contained the following components: *Direct Materials,* including glass, various chemicals, incoming freight cost, and shipping carton; *Gun,* this subassembly cost about $1.40; *Direct Labor,* allocated to each bulb at a rate per inch of screen diameter derived by dividing the month's total direct labor cost by total inches produced; *Shrinkage,* an allowance for material shrinkage in production based on actual reject cost experience for the month; *Factory Overhead,* allocated on the basis of screen diameter, usually amounting to about 140 percent of direct labor cost; *Returns Allowance,* a 5 percent allowance on total factory cost to reflect probable returns within warrantee; *General Overhead,* a fixed rate per tube, which averaged about $1.25 per unit, although the charge varied from month to month between 95 cents and $1.66. In addition to the product cost calculation, the controller prepared a calculation of labor and material reject costs by department.

The monthly product cost sheet for October, 1956, listed 21 tube types in seven screen sizes. Although other types had been produced in small quantities, total factory labor and expense were charged to the 21 high-volume items. Trends in production, costs, and sales by tube size are illustrated in Exhibit 11.

EQUIPMENT REPLACEMENT

The expected industry conversion to 110° narrow-neck tubes would have implications for most production operations, especially the sealing operation. The new tubes would be several inches shorter than 90° tubes, and neck diameter would be cut from 1⅝ to 1⅛ inches. Jigs and fixtures, hangers, and clamps would have to be altered, and nozzles, tubes, and brushes to be inserted in the bulbs would have to be reduced in size.

Because the tube connectors would be incorporated in the mount, instead of being in the base, hand sealing would not be satisfactory on the 110° tubes. Automatic sealing mechanisms could, when necessary, be added to the existing three semiautomatic sealing machines. In late 1956, however, the management decided to construct a fourth sealing machine. This would be fully automatic and was scheduled to be in operation in early 1957.

Belt Screening

Although the screen room was built with a ceiling high enough to permit future installation of settling belt conveyors, tipper tables had been installed in 1952 as an expedient. The first belt conveyor was purchased in 1956 in order to get production started. Mr. Hayes hoped to install an automatic dispenser on this conveyor and thus reduce the required personnel from five men to two men, with one of the two men loading bulbs and the other attending the dispenser. A dispenser for this purpose would cost aproximately $12,000.

Mr. M. S. Hayes, chief mechanical engineer, was also designing a second settling belt, complete with automatic dispenser. The belt and its dispenser would cost $60,000 to construct, and the 150 bulb holders would cost about $100 each. Because as many as four automatic dispensers could be attended by one man, the two belts would require only three workers, two of them loading bulbs and the third attending the two dispensers. Installation of the belt would require removal of eight of the twenty tipper tables presently operating in the screening room.

The proposed belt would be more than forty feet long and six feet wide. The flat sections, top and bottom, would measure forty feet in length, and the ends would curve 180 degrees around a five-foot diameter. Bulb holders would be attached in three longitudinal rows of fifty holders each. Thus the new belt would be larger than the present one, which held only 78, rather than 150 bulbs, and had a three-foot diameter at the ends. The three rows of holders on the proposed belt would be spaced far enough apart to carry bulbs up to 24 inches in size, and the holders would be adjustable to hold any size from 24 inches down to the smallest bulbs. The bulbs within each row would be twenty inches between centers, and the belt speed could be adjusted between eight and twenty inches per minute. Thus at the maximum belt speed it would be possible to apply screens to three bulbs per minute.

Pouring the settling solution from the bulbs would hold output well below the maximum rate, although Mr. Hayes hoped that average production of 120 bulbs per hour could be achieved. Bulbs would be fastened to the belt at one end of the loop, called the "loading" end. They would pass under the automatic dispenser and then traverse the top "flat" section while the phosphors settled. When the "pouring end" was reached the bulbs would be turned upside-down gradually and the solution decanted. When the bulb had turned the full 180° it would start on the bottom "flat." Among this portion of the machine, sponges were automatically inserted to clean the bulb neck, and air blown into the bulb to dry the screen. All of the solution had to be poured out before the bulb could start on this part of the operation. Finally, the bulb was returned to the "loading" end, and removed from the belt.

The impending change to narrow neck tubes complicated the pouring problem. The narrow necks would permit a pouring rate less than half that of the present bulbs. For narrow neck tubes with large screen diameters, seven to eight minutes would probably be required to empty all the electrolyte. The length of the portion of the belt that curved around the "pouring" end, however, was only 8½ feet, and, of course, only during the bottom half of that curve would the bulb neck be pointing downward. One possible improvement could result from the use of "breather" tubes, inserted in the neck of the bulb to speed decanting. These were thought to be unsatisfactory, however, since insertion would require an additional man, and, in addition, the tubes tended to become polluted and spoiled the screen chemicals. Mr. Hayes was hoping, instead, to be able to remove some solution from the bulbs with automatic siphons inserted as soon as they reached the "pouring" end. This would remove some of the liquid before the bulb turned far enough to pour by itself.

The automatic dispenser would limit the number of different sizes that could be run simultaneously on the belt, as well as requiring substantial set-up work whenever a change had to be made. Because the dispenser had to be set for a specific neck length and quantity of solution, each of the rows on the belt could be used for only one bulb size at a time. Thus only three sizes could be screened on the belt at any given time. Changes from one size to another required adjustment of the clamp which held the bulb to the belt, and of the length of the dispenser nozzle and quantity of solution dispensed. However, the belt could be operated during this changeover if it was desired to keep the other two rows in production. A change in one row would require about 2½ hours of work on that row's dispenser nozzle and belt clamps, during which time the row would be completely out of production.

Mr. Hayes was hopeful that installation of the second settling belt would result in substantial savings in labor costs and reject rates. He thought that experience with this new belt would lead to construction of a third belt, which would probably handle the remainder of the company's production requirements. The room had space for a fourth settling belt, should the need arise.

1. NATIONAL VIDEO CORPORATION
Combined Comparative Balance Sheets
May 31, 1949 to 1956, Oct. 31, 1956

	1949	1950	1951	1952	1953	1954	1955	1956	Oct. 31, 1956
ASSETS									
Current Assets:									
Cash	$ 6,418	$ 379,202	$ 250,380	$ 88,672	$ 302,087	$ 147,180	$ 175,516	$ 252,420	$ 321,178
Accounts Receivable	26,997	526,697	269,184	489,918	280,307	77,264	239,460	509,177	668,463
Inventories	213,203	216,479	611,943	407,407	1,172,855	722,839	596,327	551,794	693,221
Government Bonds			1,149,426	37,997	121,876	36,981	24,007		
Total Current Assets	$246,618	$1,122,378	$2,280,933	$1,023,994	$1,877,125	$ 984,264	$1,035,310	$1,313,391	$1,682,862
Fixed Assets:									
Building Machinery	86,008	366,039	586,437	681,428	1,824,938	2,636,094	2,934,128	3,021,756	3,167,134
Land			42,460		112,483	117,948	117,948	117,948	187,948
Less: Depreciation	(7,032)	(79,836)	(217,108)	(371,361)	(576,544)	(898,806)	(1,323,424)	(1,690,610)	(1,780,131)
Other Assets	5,402	64,656	152,499	77,566	207,628	138,771	141,843	60,586	61,476
TOTAL ASSETS	$330,996	$1,473,237	$2,845,221	$1,411,627	$3,445,630	$2,978,271	$2,905,805	$2,823,071	$3,319,289
LIABILITIES									
Current Liabilities:									
Accounts Payable	$139,373	$ 254,089	$ 151,538	$ 355,125	$ 657,234	$ 318,285	$ 257,386	$ 304,133	$ 461,514
Notes Payable	34,808			203,316	28,553	186,336	113,578	40,957	156,709
Accruals	38,898	65,250	73,661	95,376	322,297	516,588	689,774	786,537	786,736
Liabilities			2,776	15,936	44,777	203,985	143,784	187,599	244,150
Federal Taxes		394,723	1,292,681		544,101				
Total Current Liabilities	$213,079	$ 714,062	$1,520,656	$ 669,753	$1,596,962	$1,225,194	$1,204,522	$1,319,226	$1,649,109
Long-Term Debt			210,000	4,250	576,673	708,030	669,453	628,495	610,693
Capital Stock	100,000	100,000	100,000	110,000	152,800	110,000	110,000	110,000	110,000
Surplus	17,917	659,175	1,014,565	627,624	1,119,195	935,047	921,830	765,350	949,487
TOTAL LIABILITIES	$330,996	$1,473,237	$2,845,221	$1,411,627	$3,445,630	$2,978,271	$2,905,805	$2,823,071	$3,319,289

Note: These figures and those on Exhibit 2 are the result of a combination of the statements of the three associated companies. It should be realized that the original statements reflected both a very conservative policy with regard to capitalization of assets and a policy of depreciation of assets within three years. The combination of statements was intended to eliminate intercompany balances with the result that some approximations are included.

2. NATIONAL VIDEO CORPORATION
Combined Comparative Income Statement (1949-1956)
(Year End May 31)

	1949*	1950	1951	1952	1953	1954	1955	1956
Net sales	$293,223	$5,730,652	$11,552,925	$6,868,061	$11,435,714	$11,324,679	$11,160,932	$9,738,548
Cost of goods sold	235,056	4,358,425	8,201,488	6,250,855	9,259,633	10,512,480	10,109,415	8,608,393
Gross profit	$ 58,167	$1,372,227	$ 3,351,437	$ 617,206	$ 2,176,081	$ 812,199	$ 1,051,517	$1,130,155
General overhead	36,802	384,345	997,341	1,307,696	1,470,461	1,745,695**	1,470,173	1,391,468
Operating income	$ 21,365	$ 987,882	$ 2,354,096	($ 690,490)	$ 705,620	($ 933,496)	($ 418,656)	($ 261,313)
Other income (loss)	1,857	37,778	(215,426)	(227,091)	101,999	193,719	158,282	147,037
Income taxes (refund)	5,305	389,751	1,285,950	(540,935)	354,216	(526,711)	(192,028)	1,940
Net profit	$ 17,917	$ 635,909	$ 852,720	($ 376,646)	$ 453,403	($ 213,066)	($ 68,346)	($ 116,216)
Beginning inventory		$ 213,203	$ 216,478	$ 611,942	$ 407,407	$ 1,163,766	$ 722,839	$ 596,327
Purchases	$336,669	3,309,845	6,571,530	4,110,358	6,467,456	6,144,533	5,808,896	5,099,265
Salaries and wages	73,856	769,479	1,494,178	1,426,800	2,577,302	2,911,707	3,027,434	2,553,006
Factory expense	30,702	209,572	393,972	354,909	766,565	699,348	731,144	553,897
Depreciation	7,032	72,804	137,272	154,253	204,669	315,965	415,429	357,691
Total	$448,259	$4,574,903	$ 8,813,430	$6,658,262	$10,423,399	$11,235,319	$10,705,742	$9,160,186
Less: Ending inventory	213,203	216,478	611,942	407,407	1,163,766	722,839	596,327	551,793
Cost of goods sold	$235,056	$4,358,425	$ 8,201,488	$6,250,855	$ 9,259,633	$10,512,480	$10,109,415	$8,608,393

*Six months only.
**Bad debt loss of $230,000.

3. NATIONAL VIDEO CORPORATION

Layout of Part of National Video Plant

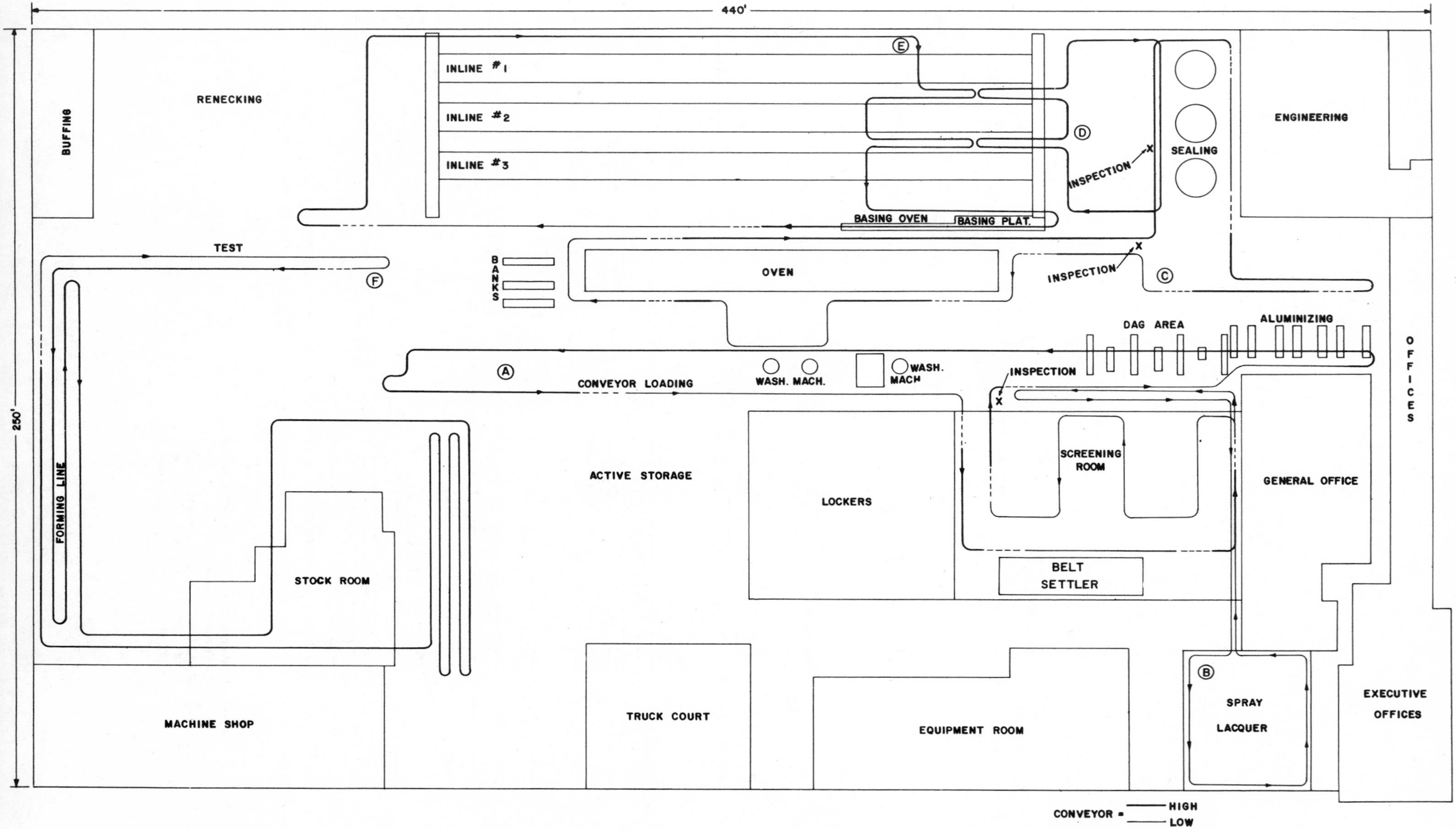

440'
250'
BUFFING
RENECKING
INLINE #1
INLINE #2
INLINE #3
(E)
(D)
SEALING
INSPECTION
X
ENGINEERING
BASING OVEN
BASING PLAT.
TEST
(F)
BANKS
OVEN
INSPECTION
X
(C)
DAG AREA
ALUMINIZING
OFFICES
(A)
CONVEYOR LOADING
WASH. MACH.
WASH. MACH
INSPECTION
X
SCREENING ROOM
FORMING LINE
ACTIVE STORAGE
LOCKERS
GENERAL OFFICE
STOCK ROOM
BELT SETTLER
(B)
SPRAY LACQUER
EXECUTIVE OFFICES
MACHINE SHOP
TRUCK COURT
EQUIPMENT ROOM
CONVEYOR = HIGH / LOW

Remainder of plant is a 180 × 275 foot area located at left of this portion. It is used primarily for shipping and storage, except for 225 square feet used for mount assembly. The six conveyors shown here are indicated by letters (A)-(F) corresponding to Exhibit 4.

4. NATIONAL VIDEO CORPORATION

Process Flow Diagram

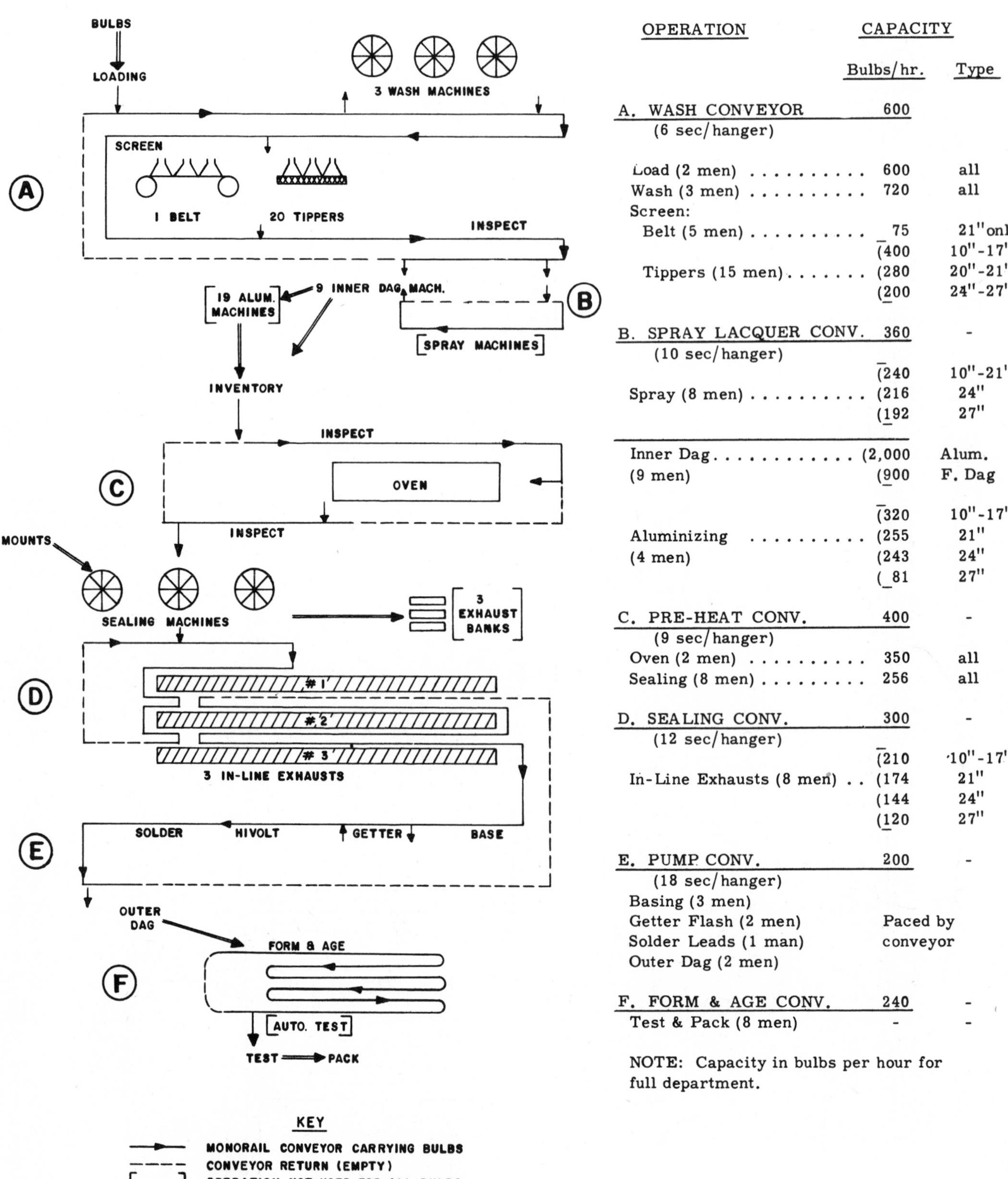

OPERATION	CAPACITY Bulbs/hr.	Type
A. WASH CONVEYOR (6 sec/hanger)	600	
Load (2 men)	600	all
Wash (3 men)	720	all
Screen:		
Belt (5 men)	75	21" only
	(400	10"-17"
Tippers (15 men)	(280	20"-21"
	(200	24"-27"
B. SPRAY LACQUER CONV. (10 sec/hanger)	360	-
	(240	10"-21"
Spray (8 men)	(216	24"
	(192	27"
Inner Dag	(2,000	Alum.
(9 men)	(900	F. Dag
	(320	10"-17"
Aluminizing	(255	21"
(4 men)	(243	24"
	(81	27"
C. PRE-HEAT CONV. (9 sec/hanger)	400	-
Oven (2 men)	350	all
Sealing (8 men)	256	all
D. SEALING CONV. (12 sec/hanger)	300	-
	(210	10"-17"
In-Line Exhausts (8 men)	(174	21"
	(144	24"
	(120	27"
E. PUMP CONV. (18 sec/hanger)	200	-
Basing (3 men)	Paced by conveyor	
Getter Flash (2 men)		
Solder Leads (1 man)		
Outer Dag (2 men)		
F. FORM & AGE CONV.	240	-
Test & Pack (8 men)	-	-

NOTE: Capacity in bulbs per hour for full department.

Designed and built by National Video this utilizes acid to obtain a chemically pure inner surface for further processes.

5. NATIONAL VIDEO CORPORATION

Bulb Washing Machine

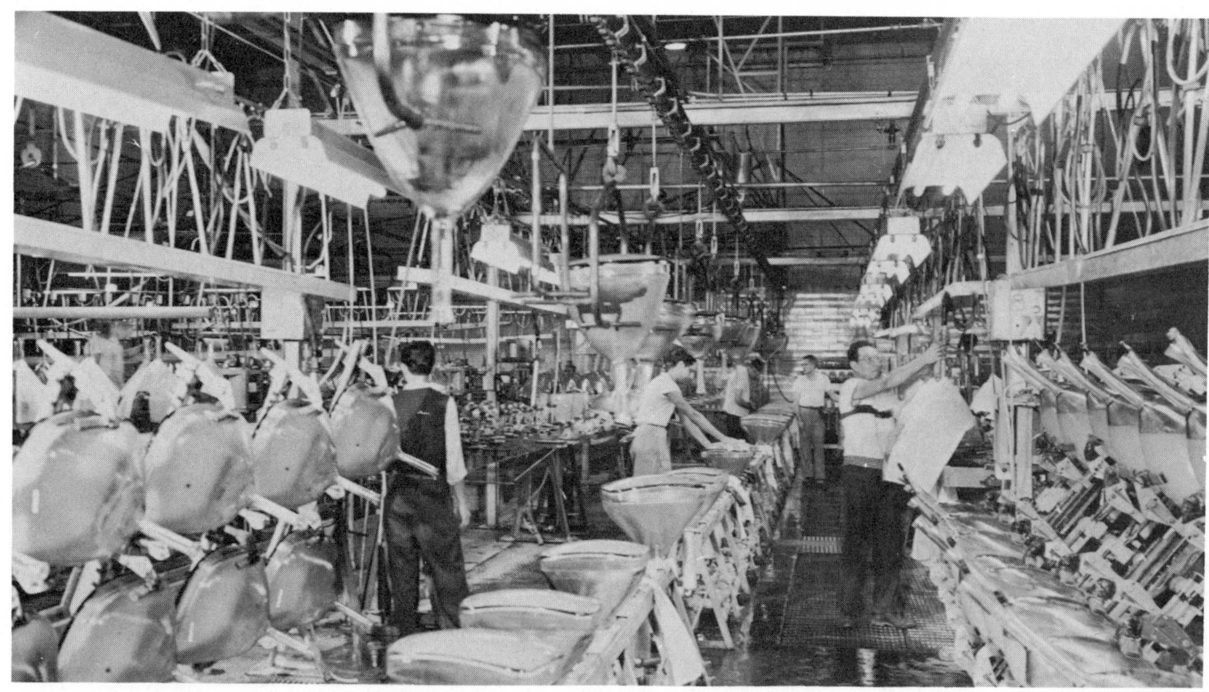

A. Screening Room. Bulbs at left and right in foreground contain settling solution and are slowly being tipped. Floor rack in center is for drying; the monorail conveyor can be seen running overhead at center of photo. The man at right is pouring electrolyte into bulbs on a tipper.

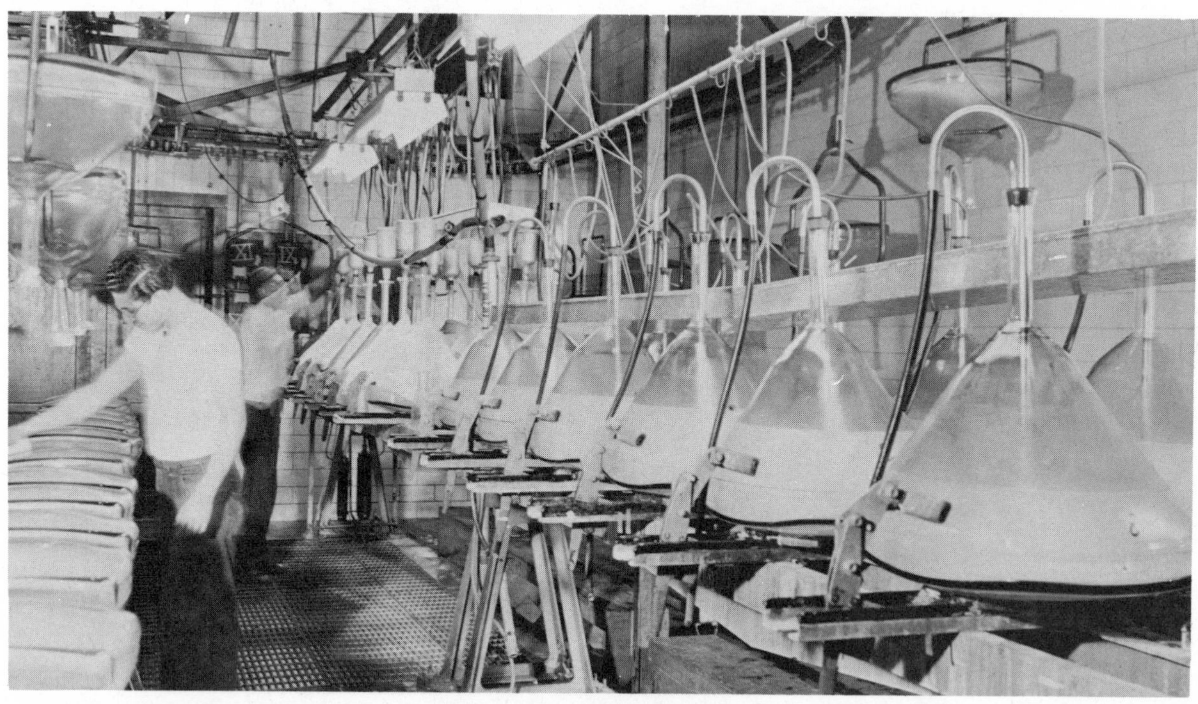

B. Close-up of Tipper. Bulbs at right are settling; man in background is pouring phosphor solution into bulbs on another tipper. The monorail conveyor is overhead at left.

6. NATIONAL VIDEO CORPORATION

Screening Room

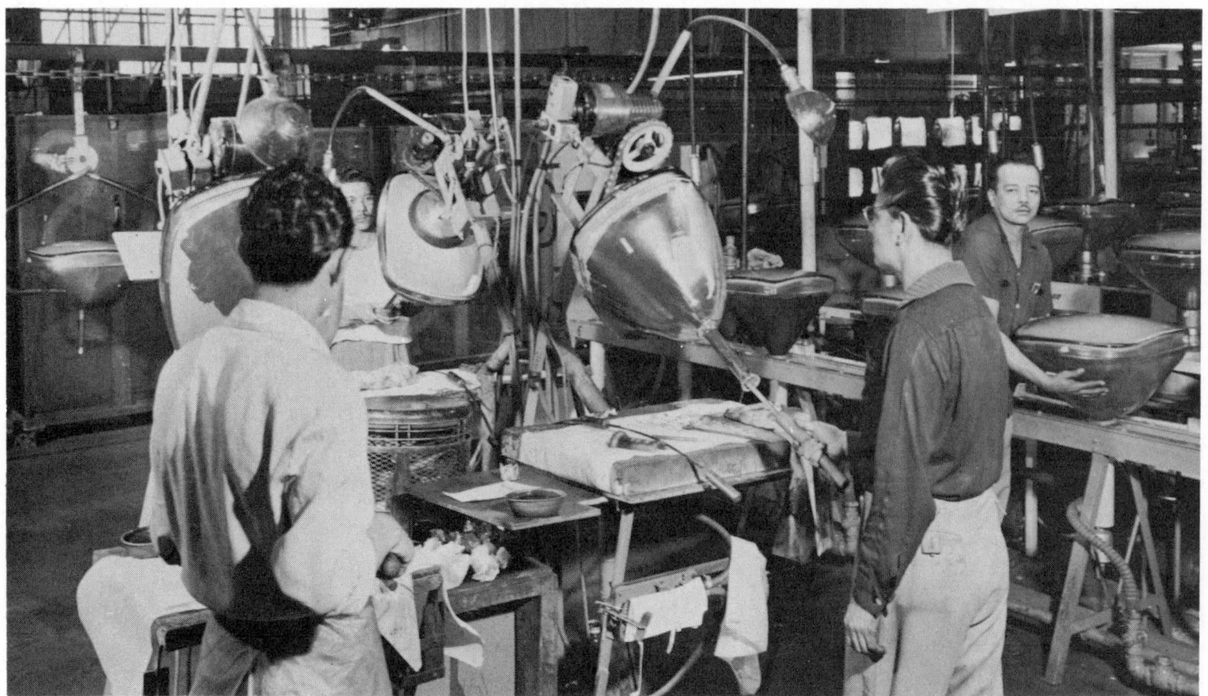

A. Application of Inner Dag Coat. Men in center are applying graphite to bulbs rotating on special fixtures. Man at right is placing coated bulb in air-drying rack.

B. Aluminizing Machines. Bulbs are placed in machine which automatically evacuates the bulb and evaporates piece of aluminum.

7. NATIONAL VIDEO CORPORATION

Graphite Coating and Aluminizing

A. Preheat Oven. Bulbs are unloaded at this end of the oven and placed on hangers of the "preheat" conveyor in the foreground.

B. Sealing Machine. Bulbs are loaded on the far side. The fixtures index automatically, bringing bulb to operator's position where mount is sealed in. The clamps rapidly rotate to ensure even heating of the bulb necks. A bulb on the "preheat" conveyor can be seen at right of operator's head.

8. NATIONAL VIDEO CORPORATION

Baking-Out and Sealing

9. NATIONAL VIDEO CORPORATION
Daily Report of Production versus Man-Hours
(Totals for Three Shifts)

	Nov. 30, 1955			Thursday Nov. 28, 1956			Monday Dec. 3, 1956		
Direct Labor	Net Prod'n.	Hours Used	Tubes per Hr.	Net Prod'n.	Hours Used	Tubes per Hr.	Net Prod'n.	Hours Used	Tubes per Hr.
Bulb Preparation	2,927	1,379	2.1	3,473	1,434.0	2.42	2,598	1,064	2.44
Tube Preparation	2,987	649	4.8	3,966	686.0	5.78	2,558	560	4.57
Tube Finish Production	n.a.	n.a.	n.a.	3,733	373.0	10.01	2,679	325	8.24
Reneck	822	429	1.9	658	218.0	3.02	579	165	3.51
Buff	1,116	421	2.6	1,935	112.0	17.28	1,582	96	16.48
Test	2,782	489	5.69	3,733	492.0	7.59	2,679	416	6.44
Production Acceptance	1,651	152	10.8	2,577	234.0	11.01	1,755	169	10.38
Production Engineering		113			128.0			128	
Scheduling		n.a.			87.5			80	
Production Control		210			72.0			72	
SUBTOTAL	2,782	3,840	.724	3,733	3,836.5	.973	2,679	3,075	.871
Indirect Labor									
Shipping		85			72.5			70.5	
Nav. Return Line	588	87	6.7	437	88.0	4.97	392	72.0	5.44
Nav. Test and Pack	334	69	4.8	553	94.0	6.88	465	88.0	5.28
Plant Cleanup		88			72.0			72.0	
Maintenance and Machine Shop		456			504.0			504.0	
Plant Staff		128			128.0			128.0	
SUBTOTAL		881			958.5			934.5	

Note: BULB PREP - Conveyor loading, Screening, Lacquer, Inner Dag, Aluminizing. (Conveyors A & B)
TUBE PREP - Preheat, Sealing, Exhaust. (Conveyors C & D)
TUBE FINISH PROD - Basing and flashing, Solder, Outer Dag. (Conveyor E)
TEST - Forming, Inspection, Test, Pack. (Conveyor F)

10. NATIONAL VIDEO CORPORATION
Monthly Reject Summary
October, 1955-1956

	BULBS STARTED		TUBES PACKED	
	Oct. 1955	Oct. 1956	Oct. 1955	Oct. 1956
Alum.	77,623	113,792	34,075	53,792
Full Dag	22,071	40,947	13,613	24,921
Total	99,694	154,739	47,688	78,713

DEPARTMENT REJECTS

	Oct. 1955		Oct. 1956	
	Rejects	Per Cent	Rejects	Per Cent
Screen Alum.	24,598	31.7	25,427	22.3
Screen Full Dag	6,653	30.1	6,814	16.6
Lacquer Spray	10,283	17.4	19,177	21.7
Inner Dag	1,555	2.0	5,153	5.0
Alum. Dept.	4,398	8.1	8,334	8.1
Sealing	580	1.1	1,046	1.2
Exhaust	1,832	3.4	2,789	3.1

Units 1955	Units 1956	Tubes Renecked From:	Per Cent 1955	Per Cent 1956
701	545	Screen	1.2	.61
1,152	346	Film-Dag-Alum	2.1	.39
575	1,015	Seal	1.0	1.14
1,643	2,060	Exhaust	2.9	2.33
1,279	1,758	Form Test	2.2	1.98
1,552	1,026	Final Test #1	2.8	1.16
	660	Final Test #2		.74
681	709	Other		
7,583	8,119	Cur Prod Ren Pct	13.6	9.16
666	1,638	Cur Prod Tot Loss	1.2	1.85
8,249	9,757	Tot Loss & Ren	14.8	11.01

Total Loss by Dept.	Units 1955	Units 1956
Screen	43	86
Film-Dag-Alum	11	155
Preheat	206	113
Seal	5	31
Exhaust	189	729
Reclaim-Nav.	192	477
Other	20	47
Total	666	1,638
Per cent	1.2	1.85

DEPARTMENTAL REJECT COST
Month of October, 1956

Department	Labor	Material	Total	Per Cent	Labor & Mat. per Unit Sept.	Labor & Mat. per Unit Oct.
Screen	$ 8,919	$ 7,628	$16,547	25.19%	.483	.563
Film	5,896	4,686	10,582	21.86	.668	.683
Aluminize	2,546	3,222	5,768	11.92	.806	.916
Inner Dag	1,343	972	2,315	04.78	.595	.574
Pre-Heat	180	1,026	1,206	02.49	4.41	5.24
Seal	1,197	678	1,875	03.87	1.90	1.79
Pump Banks	85	227	312	00.65	8.95	3.51
In-Lines	2,577	7,210	9,787	20.24	3.19	3.76
	$22,743	$25,649	$48,392	100.00%	.735	.818

RENECK COST
(Included in above Costs)

Buff - 23,045 Units	@ .23		$ 5,000
Reneck - 8,066 Units*	@ .79 - labor	- $6,372	
	@ .10 - material -	807	7,179
	Total		$12,179

*928 without guns.
7,138 with guns.

11. NATIONAL VIDEO CORPORATION

Trends in Sales, Production, and Costs

SALES

Bulb Size	Selling Prices*		Unit Sales
	Jan. 1955	Oct. 1956	Oct. 1956
10"	n.a.	$10.00	3,486
14"	n.a.	12.50	12,831
17"	$15.00	13.50	15,021
21"	20.50	18.25	26,108
24"	29.00	26.00	8,317
27"	49.00	49.00	711

*Manufacturer's list to set assemblers, nonaluminized bulbs. Add 50 cents for aluminized.

UNIT PRODUCTION

	Oct. 1954	Oct. 1955	Oct. 1956
10"	n.a.	n.a.	2,914
14"	n.a.	n.a.	13,722
17"	2,600	2,200	15,316
21"	47,000	35,000	34,132
24"	2,300	5,000	10,070
27"	2,600	1,000	615
Misc.	2,000	4,000	1,000

BULB COSTS**

	Oct. 1954	Oct. 1955	Oct. 1956
10"	n.a.	n.a.	$ 3.00
14"	n.a.	n.a.	4.15
17"	$ 6.15	$ 6.15	6.15
21"	8.35	8.35	8.35
24"	12.00	11.00	11.00
27"	18.00	18.00	18.00

**Purchase cost of glass bulb, including inward freight. Does not include any other material costs.

Company's average actual costs for carton, freight-out, and chemicals for an average tube was $2.00 in 1954, $1.60 in 1955, and $1.56 in 1956. Prices did not significantly decline in this period.

Radio Corporation of America

The Radio Corporation of America (RCA) was the world's largest all-electronic company in 1963. It was a diversified manufacturer of consumer, industrial, and military electronic products and also engaged in radio and television broadcasting, servicing of electronic devices, transoceanic communications and technical training; 1962 sales and earnings reached an all-time high of $1.75 billion and $51.5 million respectively (see Exhibit 1).

Mr. David Sarnoff, chairman of the board, believed research was basic to the corporation's growth and survival. When chided about the stock selling in 1963 at the 1953 price, Mr. Sarnoff reported, "If it were not for pioneering and research, there would be no profits."[1] Until a 1958 antitrust consent decree, RCA nurtured a "package of patents" numbering 10,000 that earned up to $15 million annually in royalties. This policy of licensing all comers helped establish many of the smaller electronic companies in the consumer entertainment end of the field. Since the middle 1950's, RCA increased its efforts in the industrial, component, and military fields to broaden the sales base.

The company was organized under three group vice-presidents into 19 divisions and subsidiaries which could be classified as research laboratories, consumer products, industrial products, military products, international operations, components, and broadcasting (see Exhibit 2). Corporate policy stated that inter-divisional transactions were to be at "arms length"; in other words, the tube division would offer a new product to all comers, not just an RCA division. Each segment is described briefly below:

A. Research Laboratories

Basic and some applied research in all phases of electronics and the supporting sciences was done at the David Sarnoff Research Center at Princeton, New Jersey.

B. Consumer Products

The RCA Victor Home Instruments Division manufactured black-and-white and color television receivers, radios, tape recorders, and phonographs, all of which were sold through two sales companies and serviced by a third; the RCA Institutes, Inc., provided technical education. The RCA Victor Record Division made and merchandised records. The consumer products area sales approximated $280 million in 1962 plus $55 million in sales and service activities, the same as in 1957.

C. Industrial Products

Three divisions comprised this area. They were: (1) Electronic Data Processing, with products ranging from computers to motion picture recording devices to medical instruments; (2) Broadcast and Communications Products Division that made television cameras, broadcasting apparatus, electron microscopes, and mobile, microwave, and marine communications equipment; and (3) RCA Communications, Inc., operators of an international radio-telegraph service. The 1962 sales of the first two divisions were estimated at $200 million, up from $70 million in 1957.

D. Military Products

The five Defense Electronics Divisions designed a variety of equipment from walkie-talkies to infrared detection devices to the Ballistics Missile Early Warning System and satellites.

E. International Operations

The International Division exported RCA and related products, supervised foreign subsidiaries, licensed companies, and furnished technical assistance.

F. Components

Color and black-and-white television picture tubes were included in the output of the Electron Tube Division, while both silicon and germanium transistors were made by the Semi-Conductor and Materials Division. Component sales were about $170 million in 1962 as they were in 1957.

G. Broadcasting

The National Broadcasting Company owned and operated television and radio broadcasting stations and networks. Of the 206 television stations in the network, 158 could transmit and 53 could originate color programs. There were 203 affiliated radio stations.

[1] *Forbes*, February 1, 1963, p. 19.

The remaining paragraphs detail some of the highlights of the corporation's history.

EARLY HISTORY, 1919–1929

Organized in 1919 by General Electric with the encouragement of the Navy Department, RCA was largely concerned prior to 1929 with international and marine communication in this country's efforts to establish its own world-wide system. General Electric owned the patents on the high-frequency alternator used for long-distance transmission and before and after World War I negotiated to sell the rights and alternators to the British-owned Marconi Wireless Telegraph Company of America. Unwilling to rely on a foreign company, the Navy Department interjected the suggestion that an American company be formed to take over the Marconi Company assets; consequently, on October 17, 1919, RCA was incorporated with General Electric a substantial shareholder.

Cross-licensing agreements with General Electric, American Telephone and Telegraph Company, and the Westinghouse Electric Manufacturing Company augmented the initial "package of patents." The latter two cemented the deal by purchasing stock. Commercial radio telegraph communication between the United States and foreign countries was inaugurated by RCA the next year.

The next step was radio telephony. Seven months after the Westinghouse's pioneering KDKA started, RCA entered the field with a one-day broadcast; at the end of 1921 RCA and Westinghouse formed a partnership to manage Newark's station WJZ. The next year RCA initiated the sale of radio sets manufactured by Westinghouse and General Electric. Then in 1926 RCA and its associates established the National Broadcasting Company; it started with three RCA stations and one AT&T one. The pre-eminence of RCA in the broadcast field finally led the company in 1926 to license all other manufacturers that applied on a royalty basis.

During the 1920's the corporation made progress in related fields. Photographs were transmitted by transatlantic radio. In 1925 new receivers were developed, one for short wave and one to run on household current instead of batteries. Apparatus was made to record and reproduce records electrically. Ship-to-shore telegraph business expanded and was segregated into a subsidiary, the Radiomarine Corporation of America. The RCA Photophone, Inc., was organized in 1928 to exploit the General Electric process of recording sound on film and projecting it. Subsequently, RCA acquired a substantial stock interest in its customer, Radio-Keith-Orpheum Corporation, a producer, distributor, and exhibitor of sound-motion pictures.

CORPORATE INDEPENDENCE, 1929–1932

Under the leadership of general manager Sarnoff, who first got national publicity as the radio officer who picked up signals from the *Titanic,* RCA won its independence from General Electric and Westinghouse. Mr. Sarnoff thought being just a sales agent was a slow, cumbersome way to compete with integrated competitors; even to standardize tubes required a tri-company committee with numerous subgroups and the results were regarded as unsatisfactory. His first move was to purchase for stock the Victor Talking Machine Company; the deal brought a declining phonograph business, a trademark ("His Master's Voice"), and most important—manufacturing facilities. Then General Electric and Westinghouse were persuaded to exchange tube plants and manufacturing patents for stock on January 1, 1930. That year the government sued RCA and its parent for exclusive agreements violating the Clayton Act. The November, 1932 consent decree stipulated that General Electric and Westinghouse spin off their RCA stockholdings. The cross-licenses were made nonexclusive and RCA given the right to sublicense any General Electric or Westinghouse patent until December 31, 1954.

TRANSITION TO DIVERSIFICATION, 1932–1945

During the 1930's the company weathered the Depression with losses in 1932–1933, improved its communications products and services to embrace 45 countries and 12 U.S. cities with direct circuits, and embarked into related fields. Most of the innovations—home sound movies, lapel microphones, flexible records, electrical musical instruments, facsimile radio communications, all-metal receiving tubes, the first full-size orchestra exclusively for radio—were extensions of its original product lines; the one that received the most interest was television.

RCA began experimenting with a mechanical 48-line picture TV transmitter in 1928 and eleven years later sold its first sets. In between, each annual report detailed progress: the all-electronic receiver (1929), all-electronic transmitter-receiver system with 240 lines and 24 frames per second (1933), 441 lines (1937), transmitters sold (1938), and receiving sets (1939). On April 30, 1939, Mr. Sarnoff "added sight to sound" by televising the opening of the New York World's Fair. Experimental programs eminated from the Empire State Building and were watched on 9- and 12-inch screens.

World War II effectively interrupted the exploitation of television, but paved the way for broadening the electronics sales base. With prewar experience in radar, underwater sound, and airborne electronics, RCA was almost completely converted to military radios, radar, tubes, altimeters, accoustical devices, proximity fuses, and navigation systems by Pearl Harbor. Increasing military demands led to the 1942 consolidation of the research program in the David Sarnoff Research Center.

THE DECADE OF TELEVISION, 1945–1955

The growth of television dominated the first postwar decade. The war-developed electron tubes were incorporated in the 10-inch 630TS set that RCA marked for $375 in September, 1946; it was the country's first quantity-produced receiver. The next year saw eight models, ranging in price from $250 to $1,195. Sales were helped by NBC's pioneering television broadcasting with its TV stations growing from 4 in 1946 to 16 in 1947 and 55 in 1948. Set demand exceeded supply in both 1948 and 1949 and by February, 1950, RCA had produced its millionth TV receiver. Meanwhile, the size of the tube increased to 16 inches in 1949, 19 inches in 1950, and 21 inches in 1952. As the decade closed, RCA produced an estimated 1.4 million TV sets in 1955 alone.

Overshadowing RCA's constant patent litigation squabbles was the color TV fight. The company's first color set was demonstrated in 1945 and engineers predicted commercial production five years away. Although mechanical techniques promised quicker commercial return, RCA strived for an all-electronic system fully compatible with black-and-white; Columbia Broadcasting System went the other route. FCC hearings in 1946–1947 concluded with color being relegated to further experimental work. In 1949 hearings resumed and the FCC authorized the CBS system in October, 1950. Court restraining orders delayed production and in October, 1951, the National Production Authority prohibited manufacturing in order to conserve materials and release engineers.

By the time the N.P.A. ban was revoked, a new compatible color system was ready and CBS never resumed production of its version. The new system was developed by an industry group culled from some 90 companies and the result was patterned after the RCA system. It won FCC approval in December, 1953.

Winning the battle proved to be a mixed blessing. Developing radio cost a reported $50 million, black-and-white television another $30 million, while color TV was to cost $130 million (including $30 million in NBC facilities), before it was profitable. In April, 1954, the first color sets with 15-inch tubes were sold at $1,000 followed by 21-inch at $895 that fall. Tubes wholesaled for $175, then $100. Only 5,000 sets were sold and almost all stayed on dealers' shelves. The next year others in the industry began to berate color because it was holding back monochrome second and replacement set sales. By 1957, RCA had sold 100,000 of the 130,000 sets but was not to break even until 1959 or make a substantial profit until 1962 on 70 percent of the market.

Other major developments included 45 rpm long-playing records in 1949, experimental UHF in 1949–1950 and hi-fi sets and transistorized radios in 1955. The company entered the air-conditioning business in 1951 and the range business in 1952, but sold out to Whirlpool-Seeger Corporation in 1955 for 20 percent of the common (sold in 1962 for a $6.96 million capital gain).

BROADENING THE PRODUCT BASE, 1955–1963

The last decade saw RCA add computation and control systems to its wares and pay the price of late entry. Most of its increasing defense business (see Exhibit 1) was in communications; one way of increasing volume was data processing. In addition, the company had the basic research skills and made many of the components for competitors. Also the company had experience with an analog computer in 1949 and developed the first big digital one in 1954. The decision to expand was made in 1957.

The initial product was the first fully transistorized computer, the middle range 501. An insurance company rented one in June, 1959, and 91 other units were placed over the next three years (more than any other comparable computer except IBM's 7070). A smaller computer, the 301, followed, but perfecting and marketing a complex ultrahigh speed, fast-memory 601 proved difficult. Delays—partly caused by work on the $50 million Communications Logistical Network—caused cancellations before the first unit was delivered in October, 1962. The same year the company withdrew from the industrial-control computer field. Although RCA with 1962 sales of about $225 million would be number two or four in data processing, entering the field had cost $100 million and losses were continuing.

Looking into the future, Mr. Sarnoff was undaunted. He predicted 1970 data processing sales would equal the company's 1960 volume. He could have pointed out that RCA was prominent in all major segments of electronics and, for example, first in color TV, second in black-and-white, second in transistors, and a major defense contractor. As for 1963, "We are just approaching escape velocity. This is going to be our record year."[2]

[2] *Fortune,* "RCA: The General Never Got Butterflies," October, 1962, p. 143.

1. RADIO CORPORATION OF AMERICA

Selected Financial Data for Selected Years
(Dollars in Millions)

	1921	1925	1935	1939	1946	1950	1955	1958	1959	1960	1961	1962
Sales												
Commercial	)	)	)	)$ 60	)$156	)$471	$ 558	$ 533	$ 568	$ 576	$ 584	$ 717
U.S. Government	)	)$46	)$77	)	)	)	229	305	471	552	582	615
Broadcasting (NBC)	-	)	)	41	61	92	246	309	323	330	341	379
R.C.A. Communications, Inc.	$ 3	4	)	9	20	22	21	26	30	33	35	37
Training Institutes	-	-	-	-	-	1	1	3	3	4	4	4
	$ 4	$50	$77	$110	$237	$586	$1,055	$1,176	$1,395	$1,495	$1,546	$1,752
Profits before Taxes	$ .4		$ 6	$ 13	$ 14	$ 97	$ 100	$ 60	$ 78	$ 67	$ 65	$ 108
Profits after Taxes	.4		5	9	11	46	48	31	40	35	35	52
Current Assets	5	26	57	44	129	210	480	483	542	513	619	744
Current Liabilities.	1	8	11	19	54	79	153	175	226	218	246	296
Working Capital.	4	18	46	25	75	131	327	308	316	295	374	449
Net Plant	12	9	38	40	49	87	158	198	210	240	257	264
Long-Term Debt	.6	.5	2	4	30	60	250	250	245	152	235	255
Net Worth.	34	52	89	71	102	173	258	295	323	433	449	489

Source: Annual Reports.

2. RADIO CORPORATION OF AMERICA

Condensed Organization Chart, 1963

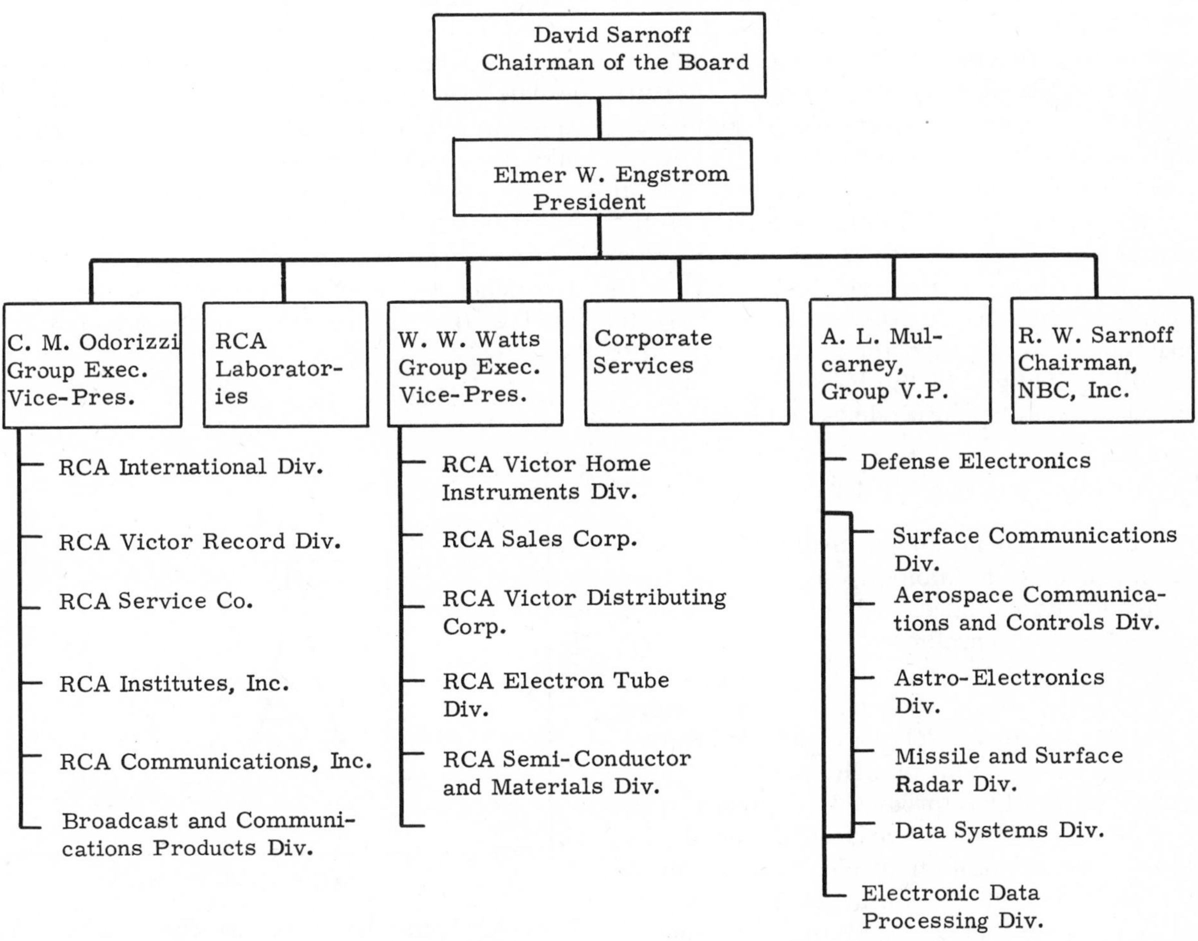

Source: Various periodical articles.

Lansing Corporation

In April, 1962, Mr. Harold B. Hart, director of manufacturing for the Special Products Division of the Lansing Corporation, was analyzing the filter sales forecast for the remainder of fiscal 1962 recently received from Mr. Foster K. Ryan, president of Special Products. It was Mr. Hart's responsibility to take the necessary steps to see that the sales goal of $2 million was achieved by September 30, 1962, the end of Special Products' fiscal year. Divisional Balance Sheets and Income Statements for selected periods are shown in Exhibits 1 and 2.

The use of crystal filters dated to World War II, but increased greatly after 1957. Industry sales of these devices, estimated at about $11 million in 1962, were primarily to the government or prime government contractors. Special Products executives felt that the cost of the crystal filters precluded their use in fields other than for military applications for some time to come. Consequently, they were anxious to maintain and enhance their position in this rapidly growing field by developing a reputation for reliability in products and service.

PRODUCT LINES

Lansing Corporation was involved in the field of information technology. The several divisions, including Special Products, were concerned with the problem of handling, storing, retrieving, and using information in various forms, such as the spoken or written word, computer languages, photographs, or information carried by radio or light waves.

Special Products produced frequency selective devices utilizing piezo-electric[1] crystal resonators; the application of electrical energy to the quartz crystal causes it to resonate mechanically at a very precise and stable frequency. Components and instruments included crystal discriminators, spectrum analyzers, frequency synthesizers, and compressed gain amplifiers—all related to the major line, crystal filters.

Filters may be classified as acoustical (such as automobile mufflers), optical (such as photographical color filters), and electrical; the latter is a transmission network used in electrical systems for the selective enhancement of a given class of input signals. Like a color filter, the electrical version transmits some frequencies (the pass bands) and attenuates others (stop bands). For example, filters in a radio receiver select the desired frequency components for amplification, thus attenuating the undesired signals and noise in surrounding frequency ranges. Likewise, a system of filters separate audio and visual signals for further processing in the TV receiver. Filters are also employed to isolate various sections of a complete system and thus prevent undesired interactions; for example, power supply filters are used to remove the AC components of a rectifier output and leave the DC signal.

Crystal filters can select relatively narrow frequency bands over the range of 50 cps to 60 cps (see Figure 1). The width and frequency of the band passed through can be varied by adding more filters and other components or by modifying the physical properties of the crystal (through varying the length, thickness, diameter, shape, or axis of cut). The advantages of these filters include low weight, stability over a wide range of temperatures, adaptability for miniaturized packaging, and the flexibility of specifications. The major limitation is developing new applications.

FIGURE 1

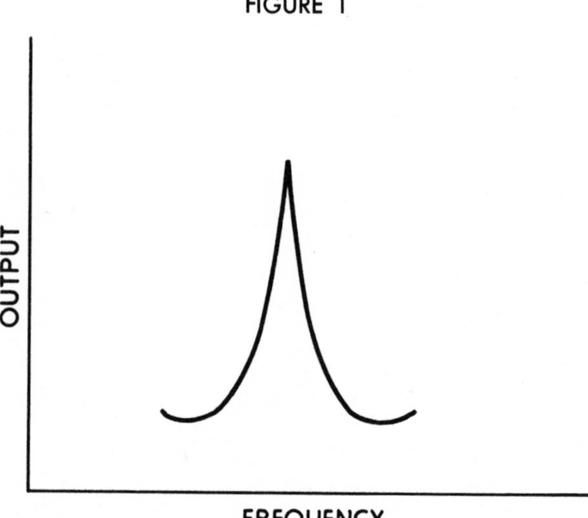

Special Products' crystal filters were used in two-way radio communications systems, radar

[1] Electricity produced by subjecting a quartz crystal to pressure. Under pressure, charges appear on the crystal surfaces, positive on some faces and negative on others. The flow of electrons from the negative to positive faces results in an electric current.

systems, carrier communication devices, telemetering systems, single side band equipment, noise analyzers, telephone channeling devices, and high selectivity amplifiers of all types. The simpler types of crystal filters made by Special Products sold for about $25 to $50 but the more complex ones ranged to $600. Conventional coil and capacitor filters, such as are used in radio and TV receivers, sold for about $1.

CRYSTAL FILTER SALES

One of the leaders in the field of crystal filter technology, Special Products had only recently decided to undertake the volume production of these items. Prior to August, 1961, all crystal filters produced by Special Products were designed and built to individual customers' specifications; some 93 percent of the orders received were for five units or less.

After the decision to develop its own line of filters was made, Special Products' first move was to expand the sales force from three to twelve manufacturers representatives and add five additional company salesmen. In commenting on this decision, Mr. Hart said:

> That concentrated sales effort really paid off as far as volume was concerned. Orders came in continuously, and before we knew it, we had quite a substantial backlog of work. But our troubles were just beginning. We were not at all selective in our willingness to accept orders; we took anything that came along. As a result a number of difficulties arose. First, many of the specifications on these orders were too tight. It would have taken months just to do a proper design job. So we had to schedule many jobs into production before we had a chance to do any prototype or process engineering work.
>
> Second, our pricing was way off. With little prior experience to go on, we had an awful job estimating our costs on these large orders. In too many instances, we had to guess what the traffic would bear and work backwards from that figure. The results of this are clear from an inspection of our P&L sheets.
>
> And we are still not out of the woods. From now until the end of the year we have to run these A filters, which were one of the types that was never properly engineered for production. We put them off as long as we could, but now the customer is beginning to holler and we can't afford to lose the account. You can see the difference that proper design has on production by comparing this A type filter[2] with our B type, which we ran from October 1 to October 20, 1961, and again from November 24 to December 29, 1961. The A type accounts for most of the other units shipped since the beginning of our fiscal year.

CRYSTAL FILTER PRODUCTION

Both types of filters are composed of one or more quartz crystals, coils (a hybrid transformer which gives a 180° phase shift), capacitors, and other hardware. The key element, however, is the quartz crystal, which can be made from either natural or synthetic quartz.

Production of high-frequency crystal filters involves the preparation of the crystal blanks or wafers, assembly of the crystal wafers and other components, and alignment or test of the finished filter.

Preparation of the crystal blanks embraces the cutting, lapping,[3] and finishing of the crystal wafers. The starting material is a five-sided natural or synthetic quartz stone or blank about six inches long and three inches in diameter. This quartz stone is mounted with wax on a tile square after which it is cut lengthwise down the center. Still mounted on the tile, the stone is placed in a converted milling machine for cutting at a definite angle and thickness. Each side of the quartz blank produces about 75 wafers, which are lapped down to a thickness of about 11 to 16 thousandths of an inch in groups of 20. After cleaning in alcohol, each wafer is X-rayed for an exact determination of its axis alignment and sorted into categories. Although the machine is set to cut at a certain angle, say 35° 21 minutes, cut wafers could vary plus or minus 10 minutes.

The next process is lapping. Upon receipt

[2] "A" type filter averaged two quartz wafers per filter while the "B" type averaged one quartz wafer per filter.

[3] An abrasive grinding process in which about 20 single wafers are placed in holes in a carrier frame of the desired thickness. The carrier frames, along with a fine abrasive powder, are placed on a rotating wheel and weighted down by the carrier cover. The rotating motion reduces the thickness of the wafer to that of the carrier frame.

of an order for a particular angle, about 80 to 90 wafers are placed in a small metal clamp, dipped in beeswax to hold them together, and then put in a small lathe where the wafers are ground by a diamond wheel to a cylindrical shape. The wax is then dissolved in chlorothene and the individual wafers are further lapped in groups of 20 to a thickness of about six to nine thousandths of an inch. A third lapping reduces thickness to between two and four thousandths of an inch, depending on the frequency selectivity desired. Abrasive contouring follows in which the individual wafers are mounted on a rotating spindle and turned against a diamond wheel; the result is a convex-shaped wafer. This process allows for freer oscillation and/or elimination of unwanted peaks within the band width. Before being sent to the finishing department the wafers are again cleaned and dried.

Operations in the finishing room are divided into three sections: base-plating, finishing, and sealing. In the base plate section, the 80–90 wafers first are cleaned and etched in a fluoride solution using an ultrasonic vibrator. The etching process produces a rough finish on the crystal surface by rubbing off one or two atomic layers. This allows for a better bond between the crystal surface and the base.

Next, 60 wafers are inserted in a metal masking holder that exposes only the wafer center and two thin strips or radii going from the center to the outside edge. The holders are placed in a vacuum chamber where silver is evaporated and deposited on the exposed wafer surfaces. The area and configuration of the silver on the wafer determines the electrical characteristics while the two silver radii act as electrical leads. After the silver deposition, the wafer is handmounted into a thin wire holder and baked in an oven for 90 minutes.

Finishing is the next step. Those wafers within the desired frequency are repeatedly hand-dipped in a nickel solution until the exact frequency sensitivity is obtained; one or two dips by an experienced operator are usually sufficient. If the wafer is not within the desired frequency, the base plating process must be repeated. Finally, the nickel-plated wafer is sent to the sealing section for cleaning, lining, baking, encapsulating in a metal can, and final inspection.

The finished wafers along with the necessary coils, printed wiring boards, and metal parts (all of which were produced by Lansing) such as panels, chassis, covers, and so forth, come together in the 18-girl assembly department. Filter assembly is done by hand and involves preparing the board by drilling necessary holes and installing eyelets and terminals; mounting coils and other components and then soldering them into place; installing and soldering of the crystal wafers. Each girl concentrates on one or more operations. The electrical and mechanical connections are checked visually. At Lansing, assembly time ran between 10 and 60 minutes, depending upon the number of crystal wafers (1 to 10), coils (2 to 8), and other passive components (2 to 8) involved (see Exhibits 4 and 5). The "A" filter averaged 40 minutes; the "B" 25 minutes.

After assembly the completed filter is sent to the alignment or test department. At Lansing, this department consisted of 13 stations, each station equipped with approximately $12,000 worth of electrical test equipment. A number of operations are performed which include adjustments, replacement of damaged components, cementing the components into place, sealing the filter, painting, testing, and final checking of the electrical properties against the customer specifications. Typically, there is no established procedure for pinpointing the reason for failure which might be due to improper grounding, wrong capacitor values, imbalance between wafers, or even fingerprints on the wafer surface. At Lansing, it was almost always possible to locate and remedy the source of trouble hence, no allowance was made for fallout. Depending upon the cause of the difficulty and the skill of the aligner (who took four weeks to train), alignment time could run as high as 4 hours per filter (see Exhibit 5). An average of 2.5 hours was used for scheduling purposes.

The learning curves for each job vary. On the basis of his experience in the industry, Mr. Hart had classified jobs into categories 1 through 4 indicating the number of weeks of the learning curve and A type and B type to represent the transferability of manual dexterity. The learning curve was as follows:

Weeks	*Job Classification* 1	2	3	4
1	100%	65%	60%	58%
2		100	78	74
3			100	88
4				100

Going from an A to another A job reduced the learning time 50 percent; from an A to a B job, 30 percent; from a B to an A job, 25 percent; and from a B to a B job, 10 percent.

Jobs were classified as follows: All crystal cutting and preliminary lapping (see Exhibit 5) were 1–B jobs except cutting wafers (2–B), lapping (2–B), and round on lathe (3–B). Lapping were all 2–B jobs except contour each wafer, which was 3–B. Finishing were all 1–B jobs except mounting, inspection and nickel plate which were 3–A and insert liner and assemble wafer can which were 2–A. Assembly were all 2–B jobs, except soldering which was 3–B. Alignment was a 4–A job.

PRODUCTION SCHEDULE

The sales shipments and production schedules for fiscal 1962 were as follows:

	Shipment	*Produced*
October, 1961	$ 48,000	$149,195
November	54,000	63,092
December	193,000	163,582
January, 1962	180,000	82,133
February	64,000	62,191
March	160,000	157,114
April	215,000	
May	255,000	
June	285,000	
July	235,000	
August	100,000	
September	286,000	
Total	$2,075,000	$677,307

Mr. Hart was uncertain how to schedule the 12,700 A units (at an estimated $110 a unit) needed to produce $1.4 million in sales from April 1 through September. He knew that he had no inventory backlog of type A and only $21,000 of type B, but he didn't want to build up too much inventory because the orders from July-December inclusive were not absolutely certain. In addition, he wanted to consider all the short- and long-term effects of any proposed schedule upon the division's operations.

1. LANSING CORPORATION

Comparative Balance Sheets of the Special Products
Division for Selected Periods, November, 1961 to March, 1962
(Dollars in Thousands)

	March 31, 1962	Feb. 24, 1962	Jan. 27, 1962	Dec. 30, 1961	Nov. 25, 1961
Current Assets					
Cash	$ 8	$ 42	$ 12	$ 38	$ 27
Receivables (net).	570	476	547	420	405
Inventory* (net).	378	469	439	480	421
Unbilled contracts (net).	37	79	83	85	84
Other.	23	39	15	13	32
Total.	$1,016	$1,105	$1,096	$1,036	$ 969
Fixed Assets (net)	372	365	365	364	370
Total Assets.	$1,388	$1,470	$1,461	$1,400	$1,339
Current Liabilities					
Accounts payable.	$ 47	$ 38	$ 56	$ 29	$ 85
Notes payable	52	52	-	-	-
Accruals	199	172	166	205	143
Other.	165	128	53	49	41
Total.	$ 463	$ 390	$ 275	$ 283	$ 269
Corporate Investment					
Common stock-subsidiary.	$ 50	$ 50	$ -	$ -	$ -
Permanent corporation advance . .	794	794	794	794	794
Account current-corporation	456	462	445	381	324
Retained earnings-subsidiary (prior to 10/1/61)	(105)	(105)	-	-	-
Retained earnings-current					
Special products	(289)	(127)	(54)	(58)	(48)
Subsidiary	20	6	-	-	-
Total Investment	$ 925	$1,080	$1,186	$1,117	$1,070
Total Liabilities	$1,388	$1,470	$1,461	$1,400	$1,339
*Reserve for inventory evaluation. . . .	$ 265	$ 300	$ 300	$ 299	$ 303
Backlog	1,170	1,230	1,300	1,500	1,551

Source: Company records.

2. LANSING CORPORATION

Comparative Income Statements of the Special Products Division
for Selected Periods, November, 1961 to March, 1962
(Dollars in Thousands)

	March 31, 1962	Feb. 24, 1962	Jan. 27, 1962	Dec. 30, 1961	Nov. 25, 1961
Filter Sales	$ 160	$ 64	$180	$193	$ 54
Other Sales	112	72	70	46	53
Total	$ 272	$136	$259	$239	$107
Cost of Goods Sold	257	133	168	153	73
Gross Profit	$ 15	$ 3	$ 91	$ 86	$ 34
Selling Expense	54	22	37	36	25
General and Administrative	46	24	31	46	29
Corp. Allocation	7	5	5	5	4
Product Development	40	25	14	7	14
Other	30	-	-	2	2
Net Profit	$(162)	$ (73)	$ 4	$ (10)	$ (40)
Filter Cost of Goods Sold					
Materials	$ 13	$ 5	$ 8	$ 7	$ 5
Labor	51	21	47	33	16
Overhead	102	41	94	66	32
Total	$ 166	$ 67	$149	$106	$ 53

Source: Company Records.

3. LANSING CORPORATION

Production Analysis

Month	Week Ending	Days/Week	Production Dollar Value	Units Produced	Alignment Time Man-Hours/Week
October, 1961	6	5	$13,064	130	500
	13	5	31,600	260	540
	20	5	79,918	530	560
	27	5	24,613	90	580
November, 1961.	3	5	29,567	190	520
	10	5	10,223	120	500
	17	5	10,302	90	600
	24	3	13,000	100	300
December, 1961.	1	5	11,653	190	500
	8	5	13,085	300	400
	15	5	23,620	200	600
	22	5	78,778	550	500
	29	4	36,446	250	400
January, 1962	5	4	12,468	100	400
	12	5	13,107	50	500
	19	5	29,191	250	700
	26	5	27,367	250	700
February, 1962	2	5	8,114	50	500
	9	5	22,543	300	700
	16	5	17,217	100	500
	23	4	14,317	150	500
March, 1962	2	5	36,770	250	800
	9	5	22,866	250	700
	16	5	22,447	250	1,000
	23	5	43,231	400	500
	30	5	31,800	400	1,000
April, 1962	6	5			
	13	5			
	20	4			
	27	5			
May, 1962.	4	5			
	11	5			
	18	5			
	25	5			
June, 1962	1	4			
	8	5			
	15	5			
	22	5			
	29	5			
July, 1962	6	4			
	13	5			
	20	5			
August, 1962*	17	5			
	24	5			
	31	5			
September, 1962	7	4			
	14	5			
	21	5			
	28	5			

Date	Filter Type
Oct. 1 - Oct. 20, 1961	B
Oct. 20 - Nov. 24, 1961	A
Nov. 24 - Dec. 29, 1961	B
Dec. 29--	A

*Plant closed two weeks annual vacation.

Source: Company records.

4. LANSING CORPORATION

Production Department Organization Chart

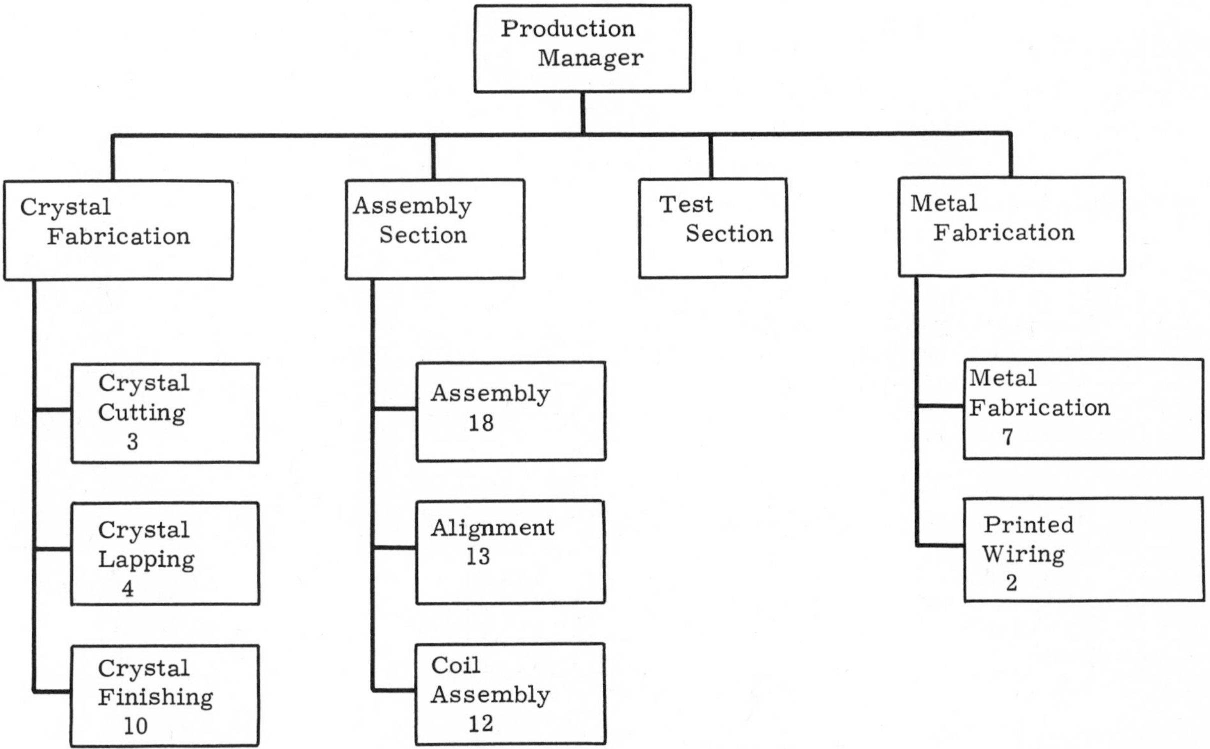

NOTE: Numbers refer to number of people in each department.

Source: Company records.

5. LANSING CORPORATION

Simplified Process Charts--Crystal Filters

Operation	Setup Time (Minutes)	Operating Time (Minutes)
I. CRYSTAL CUTTING AND PRELIMINARY LAPPING*		
1. Mount and slice quartz blank	-	6
2. Set up milling machine	9	-
3. Cut wafers	-	7
4. Lap wafers	1	1
5. Clean and dry	-	1
6. X-ray and sort (each wafer)	-	0.15
7. Round on lathe	2	2
8. Clean and dry	-	1
9. Lap	1	1
10. Clean and dry	-	1
II. LAPPING**		
1. Lap to final thickness	2	1
2. Contour each wafer	7	8
3. Clean and dry	-	1
III. FINISHING***		
1. Base plate		
a. Clean and etch	-	5
b. Baseplate--one side (60 wafers)	5	7
c. Baseplate--one side (60 wafers)	5	7
d. Mount (each wafer)	-	6
e. Bake	-	90
f. Inspection	-	4
2. Finish		
a. Nickle-plate (each wafer)	-	2-6
b. Bake	-	30
3. Seal		
a. Clean, dry, and insert liner	-	3
b. Bake	-	30
c. Assemble wafer can	-	5
d. Bake	-	30
e. Seal	-	0.1
IV. ASSEMBLY		
1. Printed circuit boards		
a. Drill	-	4.5
b. Install eyelets	-	4.5
c. Install terminals	-	4.5
2. Assembly		
a. Install coils and other components	-	2-32
b. Solder	-	1-12
3. Crystal assembly		
a. Install cyrstals	-	0.5-8
b. Solder	-	2-4
V. ALIGNMENT	-	60-240

*Equipment includes: 1 milling machine, 1 bench lathe, 1 X-ray machine, and 1 lapper.
**Equipment includes: 2 lappers and 6 contouring machines.
***Equipment includes: 1 cleaner, 2 vacuum systems for baseplating, and 2 ovens for baking.
NOTE: The times refer to the amount required for the entire operation (e.g., slicing an entire quartz blank takes six minutes and all the wafers produced another seven minutes while drilling takes 4.5 minutes per filter).
Source: Foremen's estimates.

Steel Industry Process Notes

FLOW CHART OF THE

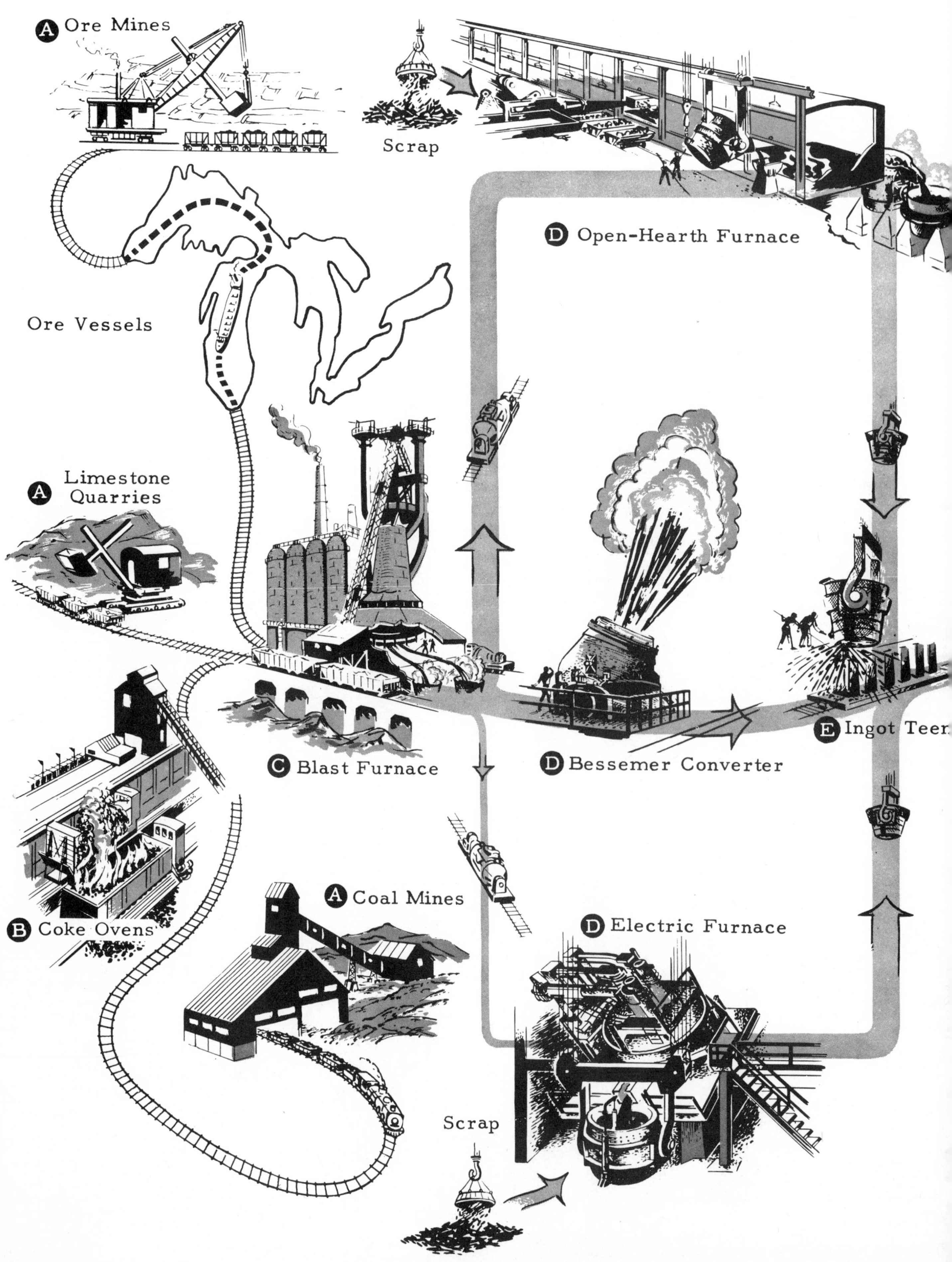

A Ore Mines
Scrap
Ore Vessels
D Open-Hearth Furnace
A Limestone Quarries
E Ingot Teem
C Blast Furnace
D Bessemer Converter
A Coal Mines
B Coke Ovens
D Electric Furnace
Scrap

EEL MAKING PROCESS

A The three principal raw materials, iron ore, coal, and limestone, are mined and shipped over water and rail routes to the steel mills.

B Coal is converted into coke in by-product coke ovens.

C Pig iron is extracted from iron ore in the blast furnace. The coke and limestone are the reducing and purifying agents.

D Steel is made by refining pig iron and scrap in the open-hearth furnace, Bessemer converter and electric furnace. Pig iron and scrap are used in about equal proportions in the open-hearth furnace; pig iron accounts for almost the entire charge in the Bessemer converter; scrap iron and steel account for almost the entire charge in the electric furnace.

E The steel-making furnaces are tapped and the molten steel is poured or "teemed" into an ingot mold.

F After cooling the mold is stripped away from the ingot.

G Ingots are heated in soaking pits to a uniform rolling temperature.

H Ingots are rolled into three semi-finished forms: (1) blooms in the blooming mill, (2) slabs in the slabbing mill, and (3) billets in the billet mill. To roll billets the ingot is first reduced to a bloom, which is then further reduced to a billet in the billet mill.

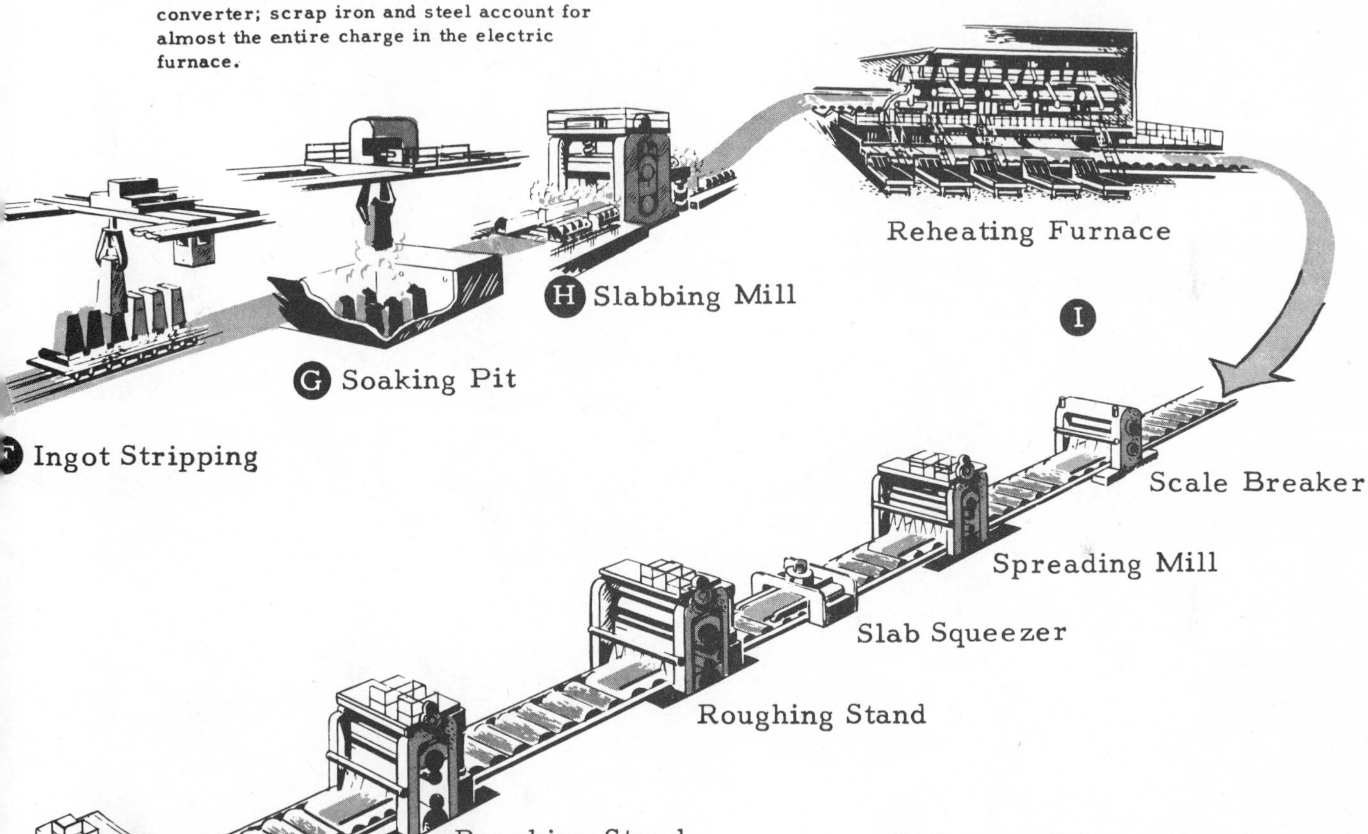

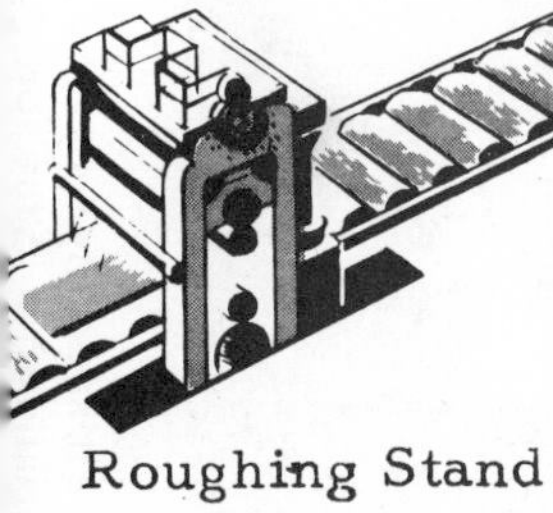

Semi-finished forms are rolled into a variety of products in hot finishing mills: (1) blooms are rolled into structural shapes and rails in structural and rail mills, (2) slabs are rolled into flat-rolled products such as coil, sheet and strip in continuous hot strip mills, and (3) billets are rolled into rod in continuous rod mills. The hot finishing process illustrated below is the continuous rolling of slabs into coil, sheet and strip. Further finishing of flat-rolled products is frequently performed in cold finishing mills. The coil is given a further reduction in thickness and a variety of coated finishes depending on the end use of the product.

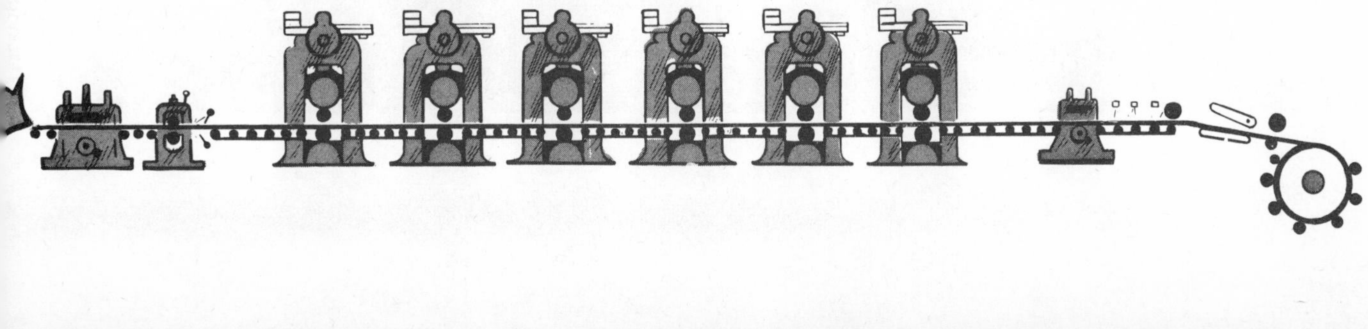

United States Steel Corporation's Fairless Works, Fairless Hills, Pennsylvania

The largest integrated steel mill ever built at one time, Fairless started operations in December, 1952 and had a 1960 capacity of 2,687,000 ingot tons. Docking facilities are in the foreground, open hearths in the center, and rolling mills in the upper right.

RAW MATERIALS

1. Mining Iron Ore. Iron is found in nature as an oxide mixed with other compounds. The ore must contain between 35–65 percent iron to be usable directly after mining and possibly mechanical screening. Ore from the Lake Superior Mesabi Range, major source in the United States, averages 51 percent iron content.

Approximately 88 percent of all ore mined in the United States is by the open pit method, while the remainder is mined underground. In open pit mining, a surface layer of boulders, sand and gravel is removed, after which shovels scoop up the ore and load it into railroad cars. Underground mining resembles coal mining with shafts sunk to varying depths and passageways dug into the ore bodies. Blasting loosens the ore and it is then hauled to the main shaft for transportation to the surface in skip cars. Underground mining is more expensive than open pit, but it is not subject to curtailment during the winter.

Large capital expenditures are required to develop ore sites. For example, some $250 million has been invested in the Quebec-Labrador ore fields for town sites, 400–500 miles of railroad, and for mine operating equipment. United States Steel Corporation alone has poured $170 million into its Venezuelan ore mines.

2. Beneficiation. Only about 40 percent of the ore found in the United States is suitable for shipping directly after mining or after simple screening; the rest must be treated or beneficiated. Beneficiation may involve crushing and then washing, jigging, or other gravity processes separating according to density, or it may mean the fine grinding and magnetic separation given Taconite. This ore, containing about 32 percent iron, is crushed and then reduced to muddy sand first in a rod mill and then in a ball mill. Between grinding operations, the iron-bearing materials are removed in magnetic separators. Water is drained by vacuum, forming magnetite (containing 62 percent iron) into thick mud, which is in turn rolled into small round pellets in a balling drum and baked.

Beneficiation requires a major capital investment. A 4.2-million net annual ton capacity Taconite plant costs about $112 million. Investment for pelletizing machinery alone runs about $6.50–$7.50 per annual ton of capacity in 2,500 tons per day plants and operating costs are $1.50–$2.00 per ton (exclusive of depreciation).

Another way of improving ore is called sintering, a process that makes fine ore particles and flue dust, which otherwise might be wasted, into compact lumps. Very soft ores, fines from beneficiating, and blast flue dust is mixed with fine coke, deposited on a moving conveyor, and ignited. The burning coke and air fuse together the surfaces of the ore and dust particles which are then chewed into fairly uniform lumps by rotating steel sinter breakers. A sinter plant with an annual capacity of 2.5 million net tons might be as high as an eight-story building, cover five acres, cost $17 million, with operating costs of $1.80 per ton.

Photo, Courtesy of McLouth Steel Corp.

3. Ore Boat Unloading at Lake Port

3. Transportation. Iron ore is transported from the mines to the blast furnaces by railroad and boat. Railroads carry ores the 65–80 miles from mines to the sorting yards near the lake where the ore is classified by chemical content before going to the loading dock. The ore stored in loading docks, which may hold over 150,000 tons, is gravity-fed into ore boats of about 12,000-ton average capacity. The loading operation requires from three to six hours. The vessels proceed to the lower lake ports where electric unloaders with 17-ton scoops unload a boat in five hours. The ore is then trans-shipped by rail to the blast furnaces or is stockpiled for use when winter closes lake shipping.

Equipment required for ore movement is specialized and costly. A unit of five 17-ton unloaders, five bridges for further handling, and docking facilities costs over $17.5 million; a modern 18,500-ton ore boat costs about $5 million.

4. Coke and Limestone. Coke is used as a reducing agent and a source of heat and carbon in producing pig iron. Consisting of 90 percent carbon, it is produced by heating special metallurgical coal in a closed vessel. Coke is superior to ordinary coal, charcoal, or wood for use in the blast furnace because of its higher carbon content and greater strength and porosity. Some 98 percent of coke is manufactured by the by-product method in which outgoing gases are captured for conversion into raw materials for such chemical products as aviation gasoline, dyes, and explosives. The remaining amount of coke is produced in beehive-shaped ovens in which controlled amounts of air burn the volatile products of coal and generate heat for further distillation. Appropriately called the beehive process, it is more flexible in operation and more economical at peak levels than the by-product method.

The by-product coking process is carried out in a battery of as many as 90 rectangular ovens in a row, each from 30 to 40 feet long, 6 to 14 feet high, and 11 to 22 inches wide. Some 16 to 20 tons of crushed coal are charged into each oven and heated by gas-heating chambers on each side. After about 19 hours of heating at 1,600° to 2,100°F., the doors on both ends of an oven are opened. A power ram proceeding down the track from one oven to the next pushes the coke out the opposite end into a "hot car." The coke is then water-quenched, screened, and delivered to storage bins. A battery of 30 by-product coke ovens costs $2 million and has an average life of 17 years.

The third major raw material is limestone, an abundant rock whose main constituent is calcium carbonate. It is usually quarried near blast furnaces and delivered crushed and screened. In both iron- and steelmaking the limestone combines with impurities to form a slag that floats on top of the molten metal and may be drawn off separately.

Photo, Courtesy United States Steel Corp.

4A. Power Ram Pushing Coke through Ovens

Photo, Courtesy United States Steel Corp.

4B. Fairless Works: Coke Falling into Quencher Car

5. *Blast Furnace.* Pig iron is produced in the blast furnace from iron ore, coke, and limestone. Pig iron may be used in foundries for making gray iron castings or may be processed into steel in steelmaking furnaces. Pig iron differs from steel primarily in that it has a higher carbon content and contains impurities such as phosphorous, silicon, sulfur, and manganese. It is hard and brittle and must be shaped by casting rather than by rolling.

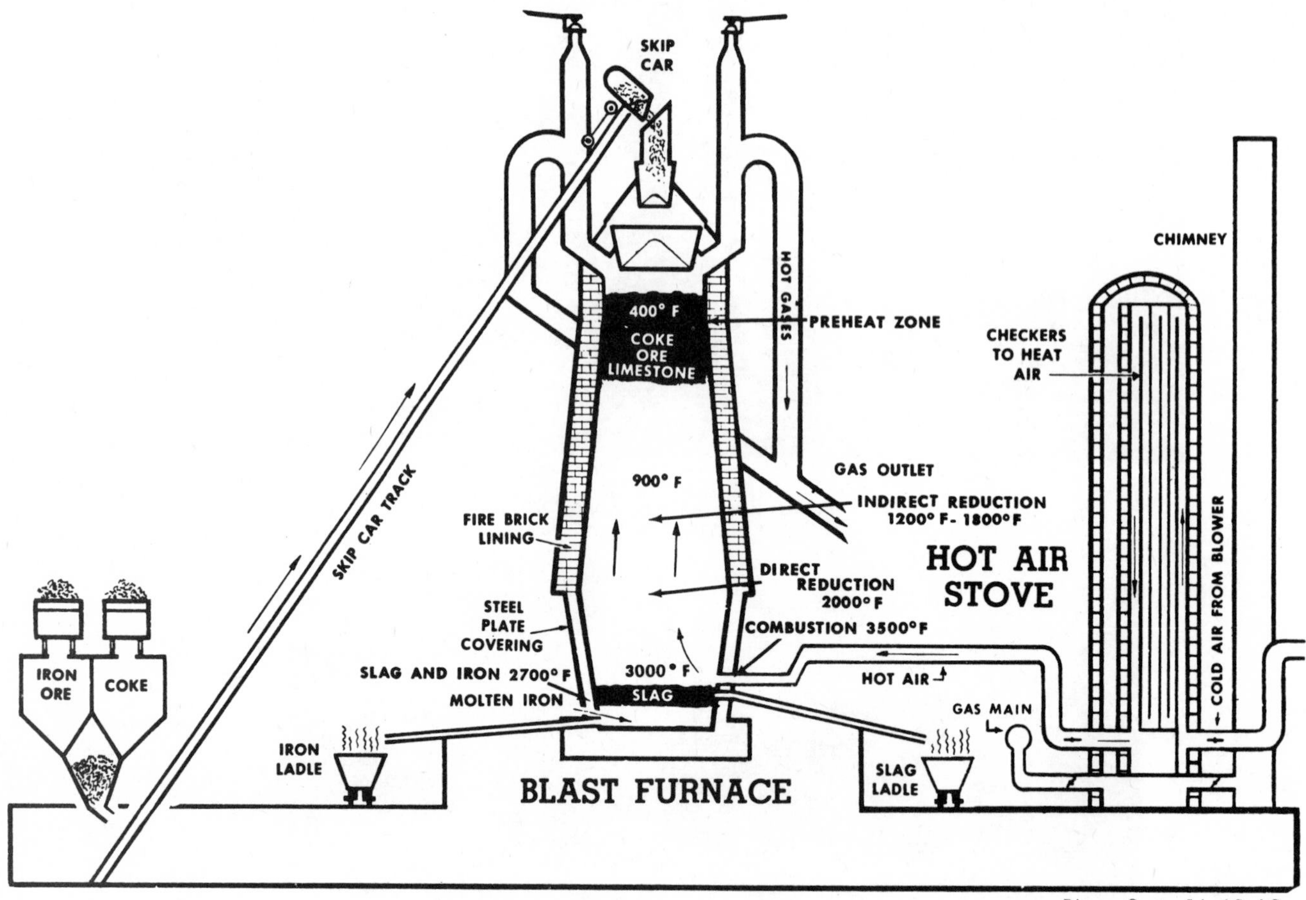

Diagram Courtesy Inland Steel Co.

5A. Diagram of Blast Furnace

The operation of a blast furnace is simple to sketch, although the exact metallurgy of the process is still shrouded in mystery. Skip cars running up an inclined track charge iron ore, coke, and limestone into the top hopper of a blast furnace in alternate layers. Blasts of hot air are injected through 10 to 20 pipes or "tuyeres," arranged around the bottom circumference of the furnace and extending several inches inside. In the "combustion zone," the hot air supports the burning of coke or fuel and the production of carbon monoxide. The latter combines with some of the oxygen in the ore to produce carbon dioxide in the "indirect reduction zone." The charge, or "burden," moves downward gradually into progressively higher temperatures until it hits an up-to-now undetermined "melt zone" where it becomes molten and falls to the furnace bottom. The limestone forms a slag with the coke ash and some of the silicon, manganese, and sulfur from the iron ore. The slag floats on top of the metal bath and is tapped periodically during the heat into a slag car.

The "hot blast" is produced in three of four hot air stoves. Filtered hot gases generated during the heat are fed through the stoves' checkerboard system of brick. When the bricks are heated, cold air is substituted for hot gases and, after circulating, is forced into the furnace through the tuyeres. After the bricks have cooled, hot gas enters the stoves and the cycle is repeated. Surplus hot gases may be used as fuel for the open-hearth furnaces.

Because of the desire to reduce coke consumption, the hot blast temperature is a critical factor in furnace operation. Heat is supplied from two sources: (1) the combustion of coke and fuel and (2) the

Photo, Courtesy United States Steel Corp.

5B. Fairless Works: One of Three Blast Furnaces and Heating Stoves. Total Annual Capacity Is 1,878,000 Tons.

hot blast. The higher the hot blast temperature, the less wind needed to be blown per ton of hot metal produced. The limit is reached when there is insufficient carbon monoxide produced for full indirect reduction. As the unreduced iron oxide descends, it meets hot coke and is reduced to metallic iron below its melting point. The iron will freeze on the coke to make a ridge of iron and coke and the burden will not descend or "hang."

One way of increasing the reduction rate, and the temperature, is through adding steam or auxiliary fuel. Based on a blast furnace operating at 1,200°F. producing 1,800 net tons per day, and using 1,300 pounds of coke per net ton of hot metal, the following quantities of injected fuels were required to replace 100 pounds of coke:

	Quantity Required per NTHM	*Hot Blast Required, °F.*
Fuel Oil (40%) and High Volatile Coal (60%) Slurry	3.61 gal. / 45.22 lbs.	1,273
Water (35%) and High Volatile Coal (65%) Slurry	6.246 gal. / 96.81 lbs.	1,480

	Quantity Required per NTHM	*Hot Blast Required, °F.*
High Volatile Coal	83.10 lbs.	1,236
Blast Furnace Gas	8,950 s.c.f.	2,020
Propane	14.33 gal.	1,355
Ammonia	154.31 lbs.	1,810
Natural Gas	1,292 s.c.f.	1,422
Fuel Oil	7.909 gal.	1,302

Photo, Courtesy United States Steel Corp.

5C. Fairless Works: One of the Five Daily Blast Furnace Tappings

As shown above, coal has the least chilling effect on furnace temperature; for example, operating at 1,800°F., 198 pounds of coal per net ton of hot metal (NTHM) can save 231 pounds of coke per NTHM, or 14.24 gallons of fuel oil per NTHM replaces 180 pounds of coke per NTHM, or 1,600 s.c.f. of natural gas can substitute for 108 pounds of coke. Bulk fuel cost about $.06 per gallon in 1963, coal $8.30 per ton delivered, the natural gas or coal-fuel injection systems required a $120,000–$150,000 investment, and the dry coal injection ran $1–$1.5 million per installation.

Another method of decreasing reduction time is the use of beneficiated pellets containing 62 percent iron. Done with and without natural gas, the results were as follows:

Without Gas

Pellet Charge	5%	40%	60%
Output (tons/day)	1,933	2,260	2,345
Coke (lbs./ton)	1,424	1,362	1,369
Iron content (%)	56.84	58.39	59.01

With Gas

Iron Content	56%	58%	59%
Gas Rate (c.f.m.)	0	2,602	3,653
Gas Charge (%)	0	2.63	3.65
Coke (lbs./ton)	1,302	1,119	1,125
Output (tons/day)	2,256	2,356	2,344

The company doing this experiment concluded that increasing natural gas saved coke, but the production gain was due to both the higher iron content and gas.

The blast furnace is a continuous operation. Every four to six hours it is tapped and the molten iron flows out into a big ladle or into a "thermos-bottle" car for transporting directly to the open-hearth furnaces. About once every five to ten years the blast furnace must be shut down for relining. This usually requires three months and $200,000 to $1,000,000.

Increasing size, capacities, temperatures, and pressure levels are reflected in the cost of a blast furnace. Normal hearth diameter is about 28 feet. With coke consumption at 1.1 to 1.2 pounds per hour per square inch of cross section and melting rates going from 1.8 to 3.6 pounds of iron per square inch per hour, capacities range around 550,000 tons a year and go as high as 908,000 tons. Temperatures are normally 1,200°–1,500°F., although a few operate at 2,000°F. Top pressures used to be about 11–13 p.s.i., but now they are 30 p.s.i. with as much as 35 percent increase in capacity. The cost of all this is $21–27 million for a 750,000-ton furnace plus a foreman and 50–100 men on each shift. Materials side the furnace is generally too violent for good control; above 70 percent cold scrap, too much carbon is removed and melt time becomes excessively long. Typically, about half the scrap is "home scrap" and consists of end croppings from billets, ingots, and other rolled products; the rest is purchased from dealers.

In charging the open hearth, the solid materials—limestone, iron ore, and scrap—are loaded first. Flat cars deliver open steel boxes containing predetermined quantities of these materials. A charging machine running the length of the open-hearth floor picks up each box with a long steel arm. The box is inserted into the furnace, its contents emptied, and the empty box replaced on the flat car. Molten pig iron may be poured from a ladle into the furnace either right away or about 2 hours later, when the cold charge has melted.

The heat lasts 4 to 10 hours, depending mostly upon the age of the furnace, proportion of hot metal in the charge, and the finished product characteristics desired. For example, one mill reported in 1962 that charge-to-tap time for its 275-ton furnaces was 3 hours and 42 minutes at 60 percent hot metal, 5 hours and 54 minutes at 50 percent, and 6 hours and 30 minutes at 35 percent. Furnace yield rose from 87.5 percent at 60 percent to 91 percent at 35 percent hot metal. Special characteristics in the finished steel might have required more samples and pyrometer temperature tests and lengthened these times.

Upon completion of the heat, the furnace is tapped. The clay sealing the tapping hole is bored and burned away and the molten metal flows into a ladle. The slag floats on top of the molten steel and overflows onto the floor or into slag pots. Tapping time is 5 to 10 minutes.

Of the three main steelmaking processes, the open hearth involves the largest fixed investment, but, depending upon the price of scrap, it can have the lowest operating costs. Furnaces are usually 200 to 300 tons per heat in size, although they can run to 550 tons, and are operable for some 25 years. Relining is necessary every 60–180 heats for the roof, 85 to 125 heats for the front walls, and 450–550 heats for the end walls. A bank of six furnaces requires a melter and 18 helpers. Investment figures for the open hearth are shown in Exhibit 1 and operating costs in Exhibit 2. (see pp. 570–1)

7. *The Bessemer Converter.* The Bessemer converter is a pear-shaped vessel in which 5 to 25 tons of steel are made by blasting cold air under 20–30 pounds per square inch of pressure through the metal (see Figure 8). The converter has a perforated bottom to admit cold air and a refractory brick lining.

The converter produces steel fast. Molten pig is charged while the furnace is in a horizontal position in order not to clog the air holes or "tuyeres." The air is turned on as the furnace is rotated to an upright position. Oxygen in the air combines with silicon and manganese to form a slag and with carbon to form carbon monoxide. The chemical reaction generates sufficient heat to keep the metal molten. With a blow time of 12–18 minutes, bottom relining every 20 blows, and complete relining every 650 blows, a furnace can produce 830 tons of steel per day.

Despite this speed, the Bessemer converter is being displaced. The main reasons are the process' inability to: (1) remove phosphorus and sulfur, (2) take more than a 7 percent scrap charge, and (3) allow adjustments during a blow.

8. *The Oxygen Converter.* This refractory-lined furnace resembles its predecessor, the Bessemer converter; however, instead of using bottom blown air, oxygen is blown in from the *top* by means of water-cooled lances.[1] The furnace is a melon-shaped crucible resting on trunions which permit it to be tilted from side to side. It is 26 feet 9 inches long and 17 feet 8 inches in diameter and weighs 116 tons unlined. The permanent lining is of burned magnesite brick. The working lining consists of tarbonded dolomite brick with a magnesia content of 55 percent. The two linings add another 210 tons to the weight of the furnace. Lining life averages slightly in excess of 300 heats. Relining involves 96–112 hours as follows: cooling, 8 hours; removal of outer lining, 32–48 hours; addition of new lining (eight men) 56 hours.

In operation, the furnace is first tilted and charged with the necessary amount of scrap, generally amounting to 26–32 percent of the metallic charge. Following the scrap, the iron is poured into the furnace, which is then raised to a vertical position. The oxygen lance is lowered and the oxygen is turned on to a flow of 5,000 to 6,000 c.f.m. and a pressure between 140 and 160 p.s.i. Under usual or normal conditions, the lance distance is about 70 inches above the metal surface.

An immediate oxidation begins, silicon and manganese in the iron burning to their oxides and raising the temperature of the bath. Carbon also burns to carbon monoxide and some iron is oxidized to iron oxide, which diffuses through the bath. The carbon monoxide, unable to escape in the area of oxygen bath contact, is forced to the bath circumference and causes the stirring action which mixes the carbon

[1] Data for the description of the process is drawn mainly from: D. R. Loughrey, "The Basic Oxygen Process, Jones & Laughlin Steel Corporation," *Iron and Steel Engineer,* December, 1959 and November, 1960.

EXHIBIT 1

Comparative Investment Costs for Oxygen, Open-Hearth, Electric, and Bessemer Furnaces
(In Millions of Dollars)

A. 500,000 Tons Annual Capacity

	Oxygen	Open Hearth	Electric	Basic Bessemer
Buildings	$ 0.9	$ 5.7	$ 2.5	$ 1.8
Equipment	1.9	10.0	7.25	6.5
Utilities	2.6	1.6	0.5	.7
Air Pollution Control	1.5	1.5	--	--
Storage and Miscellaneous	2.2	2.0	1.2*	3.5
Total	9.1	20.8	11.45	12.5
Cost per Ton	$20.22	$39.61	$22.90	$24.93

For the 500,000 tons annual capacity, the following facilities were assumed:

(1) An oxygen plant with two 35-ton vessels (one operating and one standby);
(2) An open-hearth shop with three 275-ton furnaces;
(3) An electric shop with four 20-foot furnaces;
(4) A Basic Bessemer with three 23-ton converters and two 14-foot electric furnaces for scrap melting.

The difference in the cost for the open hearth was due primarily to the greater size of building foundations, charging, and auxiliary equipment, etc.

B. 1,000,000 Tons Annual Capacity

	Oxygen	Open Hearth	Electric	Basic Bessemer
Buildings	$ 1.2	$ 9.3	$ 3.5	$ 2.8
Equipment	2.4	19.3	11.25	11.0
Utilities	3.4	1.9	.75	1.0
Air Pollution Control	2.0	3.0	--	--
Storage and Miscellaneous	2.4	2.0	1.2	5.0
Total	11.4	35.4	16.70	20.8
Cost per Ton	$12.67	$33.71	$16.70	$19.81

For a mill with a million ingot-tons of annual capacity, there were some significant differences:

(1) An oxygen shop with three 35-ton vessels (two operating in sequence and one standby);
(2) An open-hearth shop with six 275-ton furnaces;
(3) An electric shop predicated on eight 20-foot electric furnaces;
(4) A Basic Bessemer with three 44-ton converters and two 18-foot electric furnaces.

The reason for the smaller rate of increase for the oxygen shop was due to the fact that at the lower capacity, virtually 100 percent standby equipment was required. (Production cycle of a 35-ton converter was 20 minutes for blowing and 20 minutes idle for skimming, testing, pouring, and charging. The second converter was used when the first one was idle and vice versa.)

Source: W. C. Rueckel and J. W. Irvin, "Economic Aspects of the Oxygen Converter," Iron and Steel Engineer, March, 1955; David D. Moore, "Cost Comparisons of the Open Hearth and Electric Furnace," Iron and Steel Engineer, March, 1950.

EXHIBIT 2

Comparative Operating Costs for Oxygen, Open-Hearth, and Electric Furnaces

(Costs per Ton of Steel)

A. Metallics

	Oxygen		Open Hearth						Electric			
			77% Not Metal		50% Hot Metal		0% Hot Metal		50% Hot Metal		0% Hot Metal	
	Lbs./Net Ton	$/Net Ton	Lbs./Net Ton	$/Net Ton	Lbs./Net Ton	$/Net Ton	Lbs./Net Ton	$/Net Ton	Lbs./Net Ton	$/Net Ton	Lbs./Net Ton	$/Net Ton
Steel Scrap at $43/gross ton	475	$ 9.12	438	$ 8.41	1,096	$21.04	1,623	$31.15	1,073	$20.60	1,930	$37.05
Hot Metal at $33/net ton	1,650	27.23	1,465	24.17	1,096	18.08	---	---	1,073	17.70	---	---
Cold Pig at $33/net ton	---	---	---	---	---	---	541	8.93	---	---	168	2.77
Iron Ore at $14/gross ton	---	---	380	2.42	150	.95	24	.15	120	.76	50	.31
Ferromanganese at $225/gross ton	7.5	.77	12	1.23	12	1.23	12	1.23	12	1.23	12	1.23
Scale	---	.40	---	.60	---	.60	---	.60	---	.40	---	.40
Cost per Ton of Steel		$37.52		$36.83		$41.90		$42.06		$40.69		$41.76

B. "Cost Above" Materials

	500,000 Tons						1,000,000 Tons					
	Oxygen	Open Hearth			Electric		Oxygen	Open Hearth			Electric	
		77% Hot Metal	50% Hot Metal	0% Hot Metal	50% Hot Metal	0% Hot Metal		77% Hot Metal	50% Hot Metal	0% Hot Metal	50% Hot Metal	0% Hot Metal
1. Fuel or Power	--	$ 1.98	$ 1.98	$ 2.76	$ 4.25	$ 4.70	--	$ 1.98	$ 1.98	$ 2.76	$ 4.25	$ 4.70
2. Electrodes	--	--	--	--	1.80	2.15	--	--	--	--	1.80	2.15
3. Fluxes	$1.17	.50	.50	.69	.67	.62	$1.17	.50	.50	.69	.67	.62
4. Refractories	.45	.85	.85	.85	.60	.65	.45	.85	.85	.85	.60	.65
5. Repairs	1.25	2.15	2.15	2.25	2.05	2.15	1.25	2.15	2.15	2.25	2.05	2.15
6. Oxygen or Air	1.00	.20	.20	--	.28	.28	1.00	.20	.20	--	.28	.28
7. Prod. Labor ($2/hr.)	.80	1.60	1.60	2.00	1.25	1.35	.80	1.60	1.60	2.00	1.25	1.35
8. Maint. Labor, Mtls.	.42	.70	.70	.85	.70	.80	.33	.55	.55	.70	.55	.65
9. Ind. Labor (inc. sup.)	.20	.20	.20	.25	.25	.25	.20	.20	.20	.20	.20	.20
10. Supplies, utilities	.96	1.00	1.00	1.10	.95	.95	.96	1.00	1.00	1.10	.95	.95
11. Employee Benefits	.30	.30	.30	.35	.23	.25	.30	.30	.30	.35	.23	.25
12. Overhead	.40	.40	.40	.50	.40	.40	.40	.40	.40	.45	.40	.40
13. Fixed Charges (12% of capital)	2.43	4.75	4.75	4.75	2.75	2.75	1.52	4.04	4.04	4.04	2.00	2.00
Total	$9.38	$14.63	$14.63	$16.35	$16.18	$17.30	$8.38	$13.77	$13.77	$15.39	$15.23	$16.35

*For comparison with the oxygen process, the hot metal ratio was increased in the Rueckel and Irvin study (see sources below) to 77 percent rather than the normal 50-60 percent. The Moore study compared the 50 per cent hot metal ratio and a cold charge to an electric furnace, usually run with a cold scrap charge.

Source: Adapted from W. A. Rueckel and J. W. Irvin, "Economic Aspects of the Oxygen Converter," *op. cit.*; David D. Moore, "Cost Comparisons of the Open Hearth and Electric Furnace," *op. cit.*

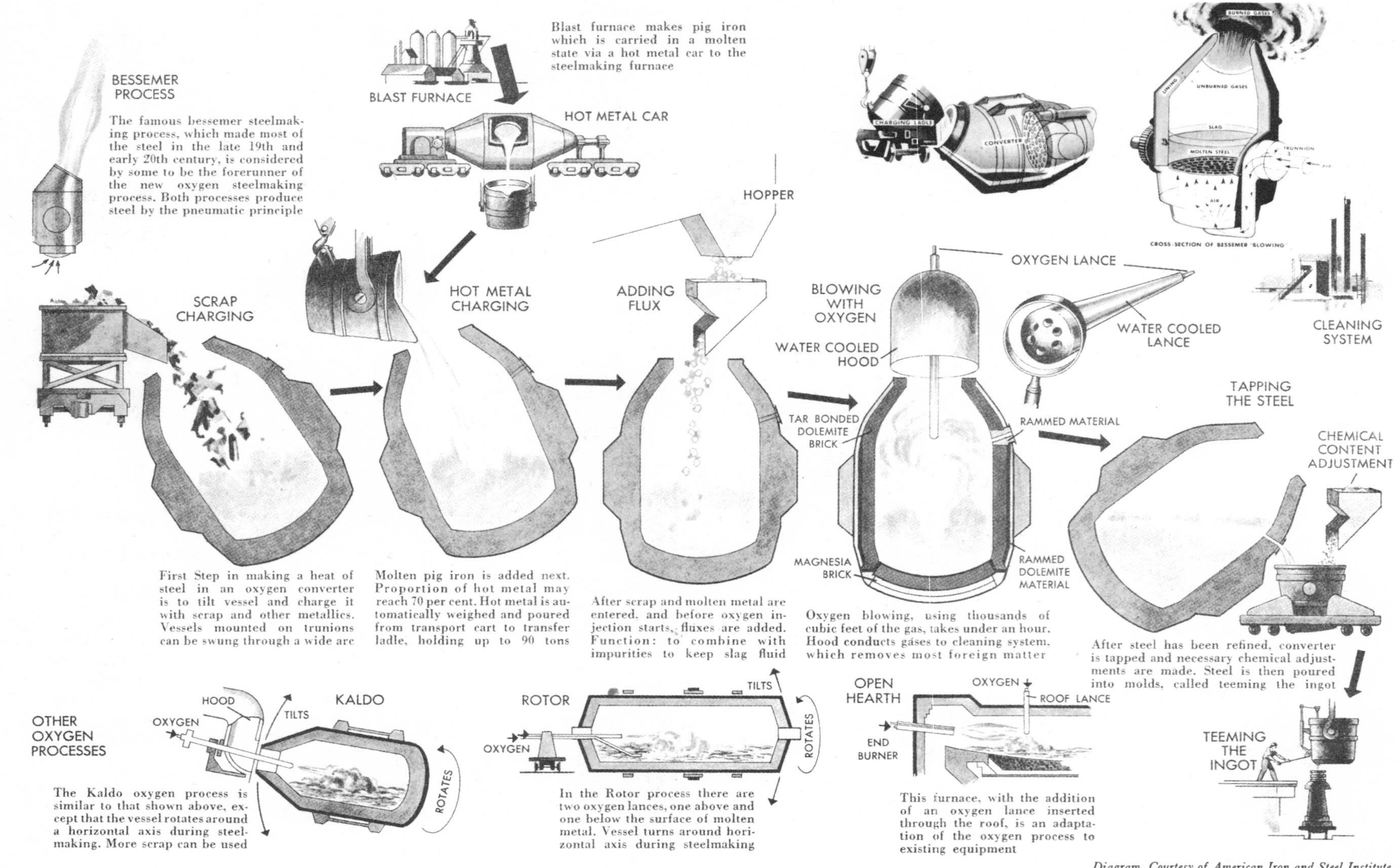
BESSEMER PROCESS
The famous bessemer steelmaking process, which made most of the steel in the late 19th and early 20th century, is considered by some to be the forerunner of the new oxygen steelmaking process. Both processes produce steel by the pneumatic principle
BLAST FURNACE
Blast furnace makes pig iron which is carried in a molten state via a hot metal car to the steelmaking furnace
HOT METAL CAR
HOPPER
SCRAP CHARGING
HOT METAL CHARGING
ADDING FLUX
BLOWING WITH OXYGEN
WATER COOLED HOOD
OXYGEN LANCE
WATER COOLED LANCE
CLEANING SYSTEM
CHARGING LADLE
CONVERTER
BURNED GASES
UNBURNED GASES
SLAG
MOLTEN STEEL
TRUNNION
CROSS-SECTION OF BESSEMER "BLOWING"
TAPPING THE STEEL
TAR BONDED DOLEMITE BRICK
RAMMED MATERIAL
MAGNESIA BRICK
RAMMED DOLEMITE MATERIAL
CHEMICAL CONTENT ADJUSTMENT
First Step in making a heat of steel in an oxygen converter is to tilt vessel and charge it with scrap and other metallics. Vessels mounted on trunions can be swung through a wide arc
Molten pig iron is added next. Proportion of hot metal may reach 70 per cent. Hot metal is automatically weighed and poured from transport cart to transfer ladle, holding up to 90 tons
After scrap and molten metal are entered, and before oxygen injection starts, fluxes are added. Function: to combine with impurities to keep slag fluid
Oxygen blowing, using thousands of cubic feet of the gas, takes under an hour. Hood conducts gases to cleaning system, which removes most foreign matter
After steel has been refined, converter is tapped and necessary chemical adjustments are made. Steel is then poured into molds, called teeming the ingot
TEEMING THE INGOT
OTHER OXYGEN PROCESSES
HOOD
OXYGEN
TILTS
KALDO
ROTATES
The Kaldo oxygen process is similar to that shown above, except that the vessel rotates around a horizontal axis during steelmaking. More scrap can be used
ROTOR
OXYGEN
TILTS
ROTATES
In the Rotor process there are two oxygen lances, one above and one below the surface of molten metal. Vessel turns around horizontal axis during steelmaking
OPEN HEARTH
OXYGEN
ROOF LANCE
END BURNER
This furnace, with the addition of an oxygen lance inserted through the roof, is an adaptation of the oxygen process to existing equipment

Diagram, Courtesy of American Iron and Steel Institute

8A. The Bessemer and Oxygen Converter

Photo, Courtesy McLouth Steel Corp.

8B. An Oxygen Converter

reaction throughout the vessel. The combination of high temperature and turbulence set up by the carbon monoxide results in a rapid oxidation.

Progress of the blow is judged by observation and experience. The end of the process is marked by a clearly visible drop in the flame at the vessel nose. The oxygen then is shut off, the lance is retracted through the hood, and the furnace is rotated to a position facing the teaming aisle. The furnace is lowered until the slag approaches the lip and the metal flows into the ladle without slag contamination.

The blows usually last 20 to 21 minutes, and heats run from 81 to 83 tons. With a 67.9 percent hot metal charge, one furnace averaged 34.45 minutes charge-to-tap time, 46.21 minutes tap-to-tap time for production of 107.96 tons per furnace hour with oxygen consumption of 1,615 cubic feet per ton. Some 12.4 pounds of alloy and 139.4 pounds of flux were charged per ton of steel and the yield was 86.9 percent of the gross charge in ingots and 4 percent in dust and butts. A crew consists of: 13 top side, 11 in the pit, 6 in the stock house and 7 maintenance. Included are 3 foremen.

Oxygen steel has low carbon, sulphur, and phosphorus content (below .09 percent, .017 percent, and .01 percent respectively), and extreme purity overall (although the carbon end-point is difficult to control) and thus has found many applications. It is superior to open-hearth steel and in cold working and deep drawing because cold reduction hardens steel and the degree of work-hardening varies with the impurities in the metal. In hot formability, yield-point strength relations, and impact values, oxygen steel at least matches open-hearth products, although tensile strength appears to be somewhat lower.

As shown in the Figure 8 diagram, oxygen is used in the Kaldo Furnace (similar to the converter although it takes up to 45 percent scrap) and in the open-hearth and electric furnaces. In the latter two processes, conversion to oxygen involves modification of the roof to receive the oxygen lances. Experiments with lancing started in 1946 and the results vary greatly. Generally the introduction of 150–250 cubic feet of oxygen per ton reduces heat time 20–25 percent. One 300-ton furnace combined oxygen with dumping in 58 percent hot metal immediately after scrap charge and got the following results: oxygen usage increased from 404 c.f. per ton hour to 695 c.f. per ton hour; fuel consumption reduced from 2.40 million b.t.u. per ton to 1.29 million; tap-to-tap time reduced from 8 hours and 26 minutes to 4 hours and 37 minutes; and steel tons per hour increased from 38.03 to 70.48. Meanwhile, the temperature of the reaction increased from 3,400° up to 5,000°F.

Oxygen may be purchased for about $12 per ton, but some steel mills build their own plants. To produce 250 tons daily of 99.5 percent gaseous oxygen delivered at 150 pounds pressure entails a $3.2 million investment and $5 a ton operating costs, excluding depreciation. (One ton equals 24,000 cubic feet.)

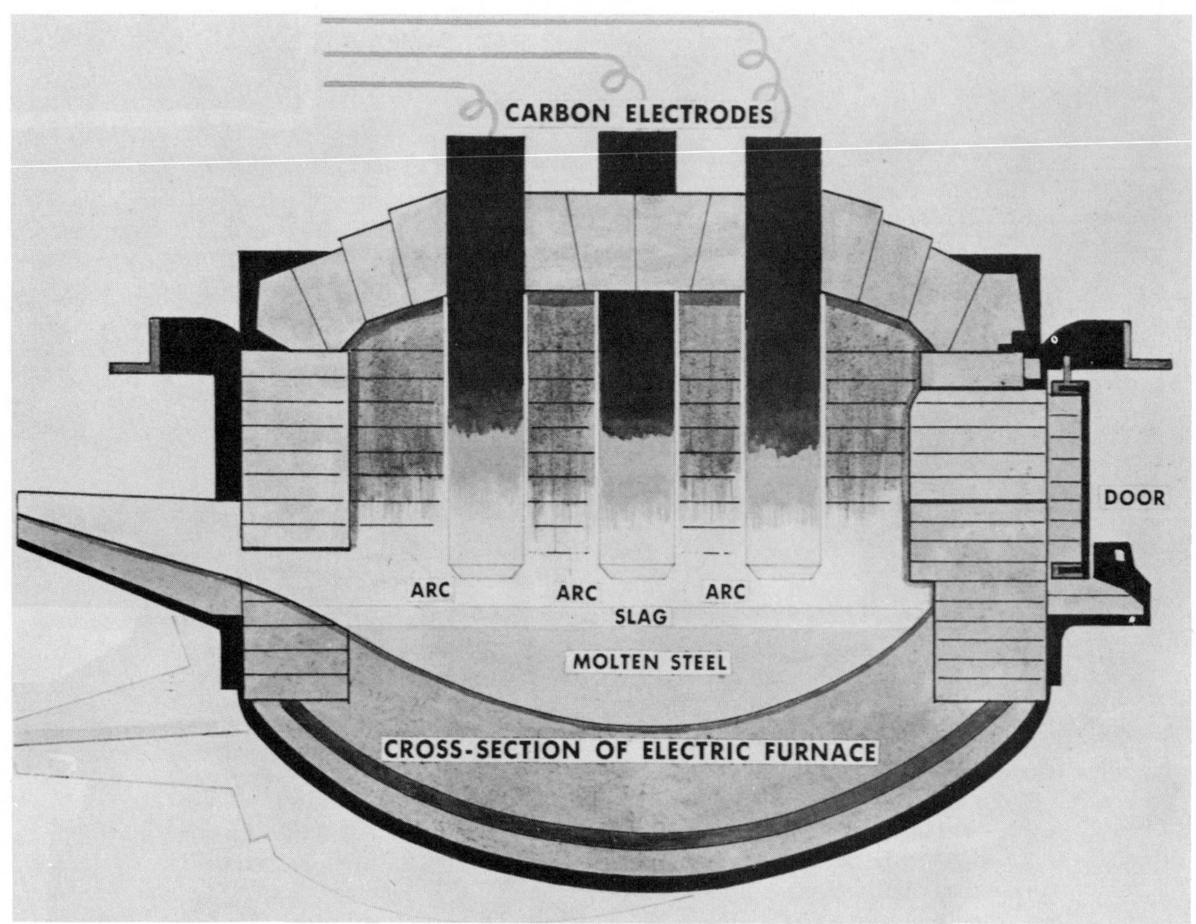

Diagram, Courtesy American Iron and Steel Institute

9A. Cross Section of an Electric Furnace

9. The Electric Furnace. Resembling a tea kettle, the electric furnace is used primarily for the production of high alloy steels. It consists of: (1) a cylindrical steel shell with a domed top and refractory brick lining; (2) three electrodes, which carry the charge, protruding through holes in the top cover, and (3) rockers so that the furnace can be tilted and steel and slag poured out.

The first step in electric furnace refining is to melt the charge. Scrap is loaded into the furnaces through the top with a bottom opening charging bucket. The cover is replaced, the electrodes are lowered to within an inch of the charge, and current passes from one electrode to another through the metal and produces a temperature at the arcs in excess of 3,000°F. The current applied might be 12,000

Photo, Courtesy United States Steel Corp.

9B. South Works: Tapping an Electric Furnace (There Are No Electrics at Fairless)

amperes at 140 volts. The charge becomes molten and is constantly circulated since the metal immediately under the electrodes is hotter than the metal near the walls of the furnace.

The actual refining is done in two stages. First, iron ore is added to remove manganese and phosphorus and reduce the carbon content. The resulting floating slag is skimmed off with wooden rakes. In the second stage, other compounds are added and periodic samples of the melt analyzed to meet the desired specifications. The heat is tapped by tilting the furnace; the slag is prevented from flowing by a skimmer on the furnace spout. A melter and two helpers can average a tap-to-tap time of 4.8 hours with charges of 64 tons, 88 tons and 152 tons in 18-, 20-, and 24-foot furnaces respectively. Relining roofs takes 2 to 5 hours every 75 heats and the sides 10 to 20 hours every 300 heats; bottoms need relining every several years. Investment and operating costs are shown in Exhibits 1 and 2.

The electric furnace enjoys several advantages over other processes. They are: (1) ability to take 100 percent scrap charge; (2) higher and accurately controllable temperatures; (3) more exact product specifications attainable through controlled use of oxygen; (4) and minimal loss of costly alloying elements through oxidation. These advantages often outweigh such drawbacks as the low productive capacity and power costs.

EXHIBIT 3

Investment and Operating Costs for the Hot Blast Cupola

A. Investment Costs

Annual Capacity (Tons)	100,000	250,000	500,000
Buildings	$149,000	$ 262,500	$ 398,000
Cupola, preheater	241,800	483,500	729,000
Cranes	99,000	159,500	198,000
Utilities	67,000	127,800	141,400
Scrap Handling Equipment	35,000	69,000	72,000
Coke Handling	217,000	378,000	556,000
Electrical System	72,000	95,000	137,000
	880,800	1,575,300	2,231,400
Engineering	88,000	158,000	223,000
Total*	$968,800	$1,733,300	$2,454,400
Cost per Ton	$9.68	$6.93	$4.91

B. Operating Costs

Metallics	Lbs./Net Ton	$/Net Ton
Scrap @ $43/gross ton	1,746	$33.52
Pig Iron @ $33/net ton	202	3.33
Molds, stools @ $45/net ton	52	1.17
		$38.02

"Cost Above" Materials (Per Ton)	(Annual Capacity (Tons) 100,000	250,000	500,000
Coke 7/1 ratio at $15.13	$ 2.16	$ 2.16	$ 2.16
Stove 100 lbs. at $5	.25	.25	.25
Utilities	.64	.49	.35
Refactories	.20	.18	.17
Labor and Superv.	3.50	2.20	1.20
Water, Supplies	.65	.60	.55
	$ 7.40	$ 5.88	$ 4.68
General Plant Overhead	1.65	1.43	1.20
Fixed Charges (12% of Capital)	1.16	.84	.59
	$10.21	$ 8.15	$ 6.47
Metallics Cost	38.02	38.02	38.02
Total Cost	$48.23	$46.17	$44.49

The following facilities were assumed: one 66-inch cupola for the 100,000-ton level, two 66-inch cupolas for the 250,000 level, and two 102-inch cupolas for the 500,000 ton level.

*NOTE: Not included are hot metal mixers to act as reservoirs for cupola iron moving to the L-D shop. Costs are $137,500, $310,000, and $143,000 for capacities of 100,000 tons, 250,000 tons, and 500,000 tons, respectively.

Source: Adapted from D. A. Sutch and H. C. Manley, "Electric Furnace or Cupola, Basic Oxygen Converter for the Non-Integrated Steel Plant," Iron and Steel Engineer, July, 1961, and Ramseyer and Miller, Inc.

The minor impurities and defects in electric furnace specialty steels are usually not apparent and unimportant; however, where greater uniformity and toughness is required— such as in jet engine and missile parts—vacuum melted alloys are used. These are produced in vacuum induction or consumable electrode furnaces, where there is no danger of the alloy oxidizing. The result is steel with (*a*) low gas (hydrogen, oxygen, nitrogen) content and the advantages of greater cleanliness, toughness, hot strength, and wider choice of alloys, and (*b*) more homogeneous and sound ingot structure and the advantages of increased fatigue strength, traverse ductility, and impact strength. Uses for such steels include gas turbines, airborne structures, ball bearings, power transmission gears, tools, and nuclear reactor shielding. Total U.S. vacuum melting capacity was about 280 million pounds in 1963.

The two vacuum methods are used separately or in tandemn. In the vacuum induction process, the steel is melted and refined in a nose-tilting crucible surrounded by an electrical coil and suspended in a vacuum chamber. The metal is heated by its resistance to the induced current and melts at the rate of half a ton per hour. After refining, the steel is teemed into ingots in the same or an adjoining chamber. A two-ton furnace costs about $455,000 installed with per pound melting costs running $.0225 for labor, $.015 for power, and $.1125 for overhead. In the vacuum arc or consumable electrode process, a stalactite electrode of steel suspended in a vacuum is remelted by an electric arc and builds up a stalagmite ingot in a center-cooled copper mold. The technique is similar to electric arc welding in which the welding stock is melted in the arc and deposited on the part being welded. With a melting rate of .6 tons per hour, a 1.8-ton furnace costs about $220,000 installed, and operating costs are similar to induction furnaces although power is less.

10. Hot Blast Cupola. One means of supplying hot metal for any of the steelmaking processes is the hot blast water-cooled cupola. Resembling a blast furnace, the cupola has a coke burning shaft from 42–132 inches in diameter and 6 to 8 diameters in height within which the descending pig iron, or scrap charge, is melted with a hot blast of 1,000° to 1,800°F. With 100 percent scrap, it is difficult to reduce carbon content below 2.2 percent. Coke consumption runs 1.1 to 1.2 pounds per hour per square inch of cross-section area and melting rates range from 8 to 16 pounds per hour per square inch. Capital and operating costs are given in Exhibit 3.

Photo, Courtesy United States Steel Corp

11. Fairless Works: Teeming Steel into Ingot Molds

11. Teeming Ingots. Molten steel tapped from the steelmaking furnaces must be solidified into ingot form for semifinishing. The steel flows from the furnaces into a refractory-lined ladle with a capacity up to 225 tons and a controllable spout at the bottom. The ladle is carried by crane to a line of molds in flat cars and fills each one from the top or from the bottom with a runner guiding the flow of metal. "Bottom pouring" prevents the steel from splashing against the side of the mold as it does during conventional casting. Prior to teeming, the molds are preheated and coated with tar, creosote, or soot to facilitate the subsequent stripping operation. Molds last for about 65 casts. The ingot casts range from 5 to 25 tons for open-hearth steel and from 1 to 5 tons for electric furnace steel.

To improve the cleanliness and uniformity of the steel and reduce the hydrogen content, steel may be teemed in a vacuum chamber. In vacuum degasing, the mold is placed in a vacuum chamber and the molten steel poured into an intermediate ladle and through a vacuum lock at the bottom into the mold. Alternatively, the ladle itself may be placed in the chamber and degased. A 200-ton degasing unit costs $200,000 and operating costs are about $3.50 per ton.

Photo, Courtesy United States Steel Corp.

12. Fairless Works: A 150-Ton Crane Stripping Molds from a Line of Ingots

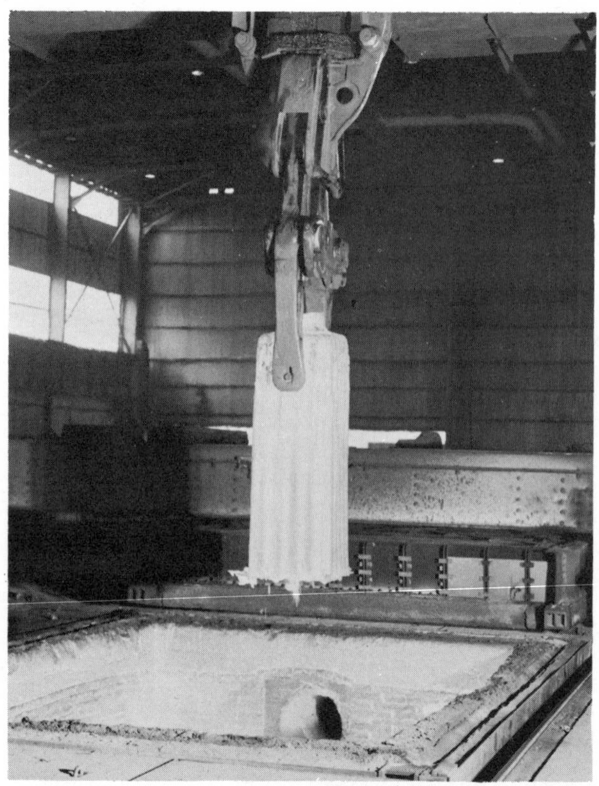

Photo, Courtesy United States Steel Corp.

13. Fairless Works: A 6-Ton Ingot Being Hoisted from One of 20 Soaking Pits of 150-Ton Capacity

12. Stripping. The steel is allowed to cool in the ingot molds for approximately one hour during which time it solidifies and shrinks sufficiently to permit stripping. An "ingot stripper" engages lugs on the sides of the mold while a plunger between the jaws of the stripper holds the ingot down until the mold is pulled free. The molds are stripped as soon after teeming as possible in order to minimize the time required to heat the ingots back up to rolling temperatures.

13. Soaking Pits. The ingots must be reheated to rolling temperature because a certain loss of heat after teeming cannot be avoided. The heating takes place in the soaking pit which is a gas- or oil-fired floor furnace. Overhead cranes carry the stripped ingots and lower them into the pit, where they remain for four to six hours at 2,200° F. Soaking pits can usually hold four to eight ingots, and cost new about $200,000.

SEMIFINISHING

In the semifinishing operations ingots are reduced to more convenient shapes for final working, and the physical properties changed. Ductility especially is improved by the elimination of cavities and the breakdown of coarse crystal formations.

Semifinishing mills are classified both as to construction and product. The terms "two-high," "three-high," and "four-high" designate the number of rolls in each stand. A two-high mill consists of two working rolls between which the steel is passed. A three-high mill has three working rolls; the steel is worked back and forth in such a mill, passing in one direction through the lower and middle rolls and in the other direction through the middle and upper rolls. A four-high mill consists of two working rolls supported by two backing-up rolls which serve to keep the working rolls from bending. The two-high and four-high mills may run continuously in one direction or be reversed to permit the steel to be worked back and forth for several passes.

The terms "blooming," "billet," and "slabbing mill" refer to the semifinished products rolled. A bloom is square or rectangular in cross-section with an area 36 inches square or more. A similarly shaped product with a cross-sectional area of 2¼ to 36 inches is a billet. A slab is not limited as to cross-sectional area. Shapes in either the bloom or billet cross-sectional area range are termed slabs if their width equals or exceeds twice their thickness. While a blooming mill may also be used to produce both billets and slabs, these products usually are turned out on specialized billet or slabbing mills.

14. Blooming Mill. A blooming mill, such as a single two-high reversing stand, is used to reduce ingots to blooms. The first pass breaks the oxide scale, which is flushed off by high-pressure water to prevent its being pressed into the steel. As many as 20 subsequent passes may be needed to attain the desired size and shape. A "roller" and his assistants in a "pulpit" overlooking the mill control the speed and direction of the rolls, the space between the rolls, and the manipulators that turn the ingots between passes. The roller must balance ingot temperature against speed and amount of reduction per pass: excessive temperature eliminates many expected improvements in the physical properties, while too low temperature risks roll breakage as resistance to deformation is raised. A two-high blooming mill with rolls 46 inches in diameter and a 7,000-H.P. motor capable of rolling slabs up to 52 inches in width costs about $12 million.

A three-high stand blooming mill operates on the same principle. The top and bottom rolls turn in the same direction and the middle roll in the opposite direction; the ingot may be passed back and forth without changing the direction of roll rotation. Tables at each side of the stand are raised and lowered in order that the bloom alternately passes between the top and bottom pair of rolls.

15. Billet Mill. The billet mill follows the blooming mill in the sequence of operations and reduces blooms to billets. The mill may consist of a single three-high stand (similar to the blooming version) or of a series of two-high stands set in tandem, called a continuous mill. In the continuous mill, the steel moves from stand to stand and the necessity for reversal of motion or adjustment of roll clearance between passes is eliminated. A typical mill has 10 stands, with the bloom entering the first at a speed of about one-half mile per hour and leaving the last at nearly five miles per hour.

Photo, Courtesy United States Steel Corp.

16A. Fairless Works: A 45-Inch Slabbing Mill

Photo, Courtesy United States Steel Corp.

16B. Fairless Works: Slab-Heating Furnaces

16. Slabbing Mill. The slabbing mill, consisting of a single two-high or four-high stand, is used to reduce ingots to slabs. In the four-high stand only two of the rolls make contact with the ingot. These are known as the "working" rolls and may be of smaller diameter than the rolls of a comparable two-high mill. The decrease in size lessens the power required to make a given reduction in steel thickness per pass and makes possible a better working of the steel. The "backup" rolls are of larger diameter than the working rolls and are not power driven.

FINISHING

The steel finishing processes may be divided into two broad categories depending on whether the steel is worked hot or cold. In most instances, cold finishing operations are proceeded by hot finishing.

The following discussion will be confined to the processing of hot and cold rolled strip,[2] although this is but one of many products formed by one of many finishing processes. For instance, rails and structural sections are rolled directly from blooms. Bars of various shapes, seamless tubing, and wire are made from billets. Plate, sheet, and strip are rolled from slabs. Pipe and tubes are formed from strip.

[2] The terms "sheet" and "strip" are often used interchangeably in the steel trade. Technically, however, strip is defined as steel not over 1/4 inch thick and not over 12 inches wide. Sheet is defined as steel not over 1/4 inch thick but over 12 inches wide. Plate is the term generally used for steel between 1/4 and 1 inch in thickness.

Photo, Courtesy United States Steel Corp.

17A. Fairless Works: An 80-Inch Continuous Hot Strip Mill

Photo, Courtesy United States Steel Corp.

17B. Fairless Works: Six Finishing Stands

The steel leaves the stand in the foreground at 2,330 feet per minute and travels 402 feet to the coilers.

Photo, Courtesy United States Steel Corp.

17C. Fairless Works: Operator in Control Pulpit of Continuous Butt Weld Pipe Mill

17. Hot Finishing. Hot rolled strip is suitable without further processing for purposes where a smooth, scale-free surface is not required. In hot rolling, the semifinished shape, which may be a slab or billet, is first raised to the proper temperature, 2,200° to 2,400° F., in a gas-fired furnace. Then it is pushed onto a conveyor leading to the continuous strip mill. In the first stand of rolls, called a scale-breaker, the scale is loosened by the action of the rolls and removed by jets of water at 1,000 pounds per square inch.

The continuous hot strip mill consists of a succession of four-high stands in tandem connected with roller tables. The first group, known as roughing stands, are spaced so that only one stand will engage the metal at a time. The second and last group, known as the finishing train, are spaced close together and all stands are frequently in contact with the same piece of steel simultaneously. As the steel is reduced in thickness, its length increases; therefore, the rollers in the successive stands operate at progressively higher speeds to prevent buckling between stands.

Hot rolling mills are becoming bigger, faster, and more expensive. In 1962, most new mills were 80-inch, used 30-ton ingots, delivered 60,000-pound coils at 3,000 feet per minute, and cost $1 million per inch of width; back in the 1930's narrower mills delivered coils weighing 350 pounds per inch of width at 1,250 feet per minute. An example of the new type is the Great Lakes Steel Corporation's computer controlled Detroit mill that delivers 80-inch coils at 3,000 feet per minute, cost $100 million, and has a 3.6 million-ton annual capacity. About 38 skilled workers are required for a continuous hot mill. Some operators control the equipment by levers and buttons in pulpits above or to the side of the mill. Others are shear operators, coiling machine operators, samplers, weighers, inspectors, cranemen, or maintence men.

18. Cropping and Inspection. Since the bottoms and tops of ingots do not produce good steel, the hot strip ends are cropped by shears. The pieces are then inspected for imperfections and any seams, slivers, and scabs removed by chipping, grinding, or burning.

Photo, Courtesy United States Steel Corp.

19A. Fairless Works: A 48-Inch, Five-Stand Cold Reduction Mill Reduces Steel at 7,000 Feet per Minute

Photo, Courtesy United States Steel Corp.

19B. Fairless Works: Continuous Annealing Line

Photo, Courtesy United States Steel Corp.

19C. Fairless Works: Electrolytic Tinning Line with a 102,000 Annual Ton Capacity

19. Cold Reduction. Cold rolling serves (1) to reduce sheet and strip to gages below 0.05 inch, (2) to increase strength, hardness, and stiffness, and (3) to improve surface finish. For a $35 million investment, the process takes hot strip through the following steps:

(*a*) Scale Breaker: The steel is first passed through a set of rollers and under water jets to remove the mill scale.

(*b*) Continuous Pickler: The strip metal is next drawn through a 190° F. bath of 8 to 12 percent sulfuric acid in order to remove oxide from the surface. The strip is cold water rinsed, hot water rinsed, steamed, dried, and finally oiled to prevent rust.

(*c*) Cold Reduction Mill: The strip, at atmospheric temperature, is passed through a varying number of four-high stands, depending on the thickness desired. Sensitive controls regulate the speed and metal thickness to achieve a thickness reduction of 40–85 percent. For example, a five-stand mill can reduce a coil of strip metal originally 1/16 of an inch thick and 1,400 feet long to a thickness of 1/90 inch and a length of 7,600 feet in about 4¾ minutes. Such a mill will produce finished steel at a linear speed of up to 66 miles per hour.

(*d*) Annealing Furnace: The steel usually has to be annealed because it tends to work-harden during the rolling process. By heating in a furnace to 1,300° F. and cooling slowly for a total of 36 to 72 hours, the steel is softened and internal stresses relieved. Deep drawing and other further processing are then possible.

(*e*) Tempering Mill: The step is given a 1 to 3 percent reduction in a single-stand, four-high tempering mill. This rolling operation brings the steel up to the desired hardness, stiffness, and surface finish.

After these cold rolling processes, the steel may go through further finishing processes such as galvanizing, tinning, or protective coating.

SUMMARY

The preceding pages have outlined the major operations in the iron and steel-making process. The following diagram indicates the balance of equipment in an integrated steel mill.

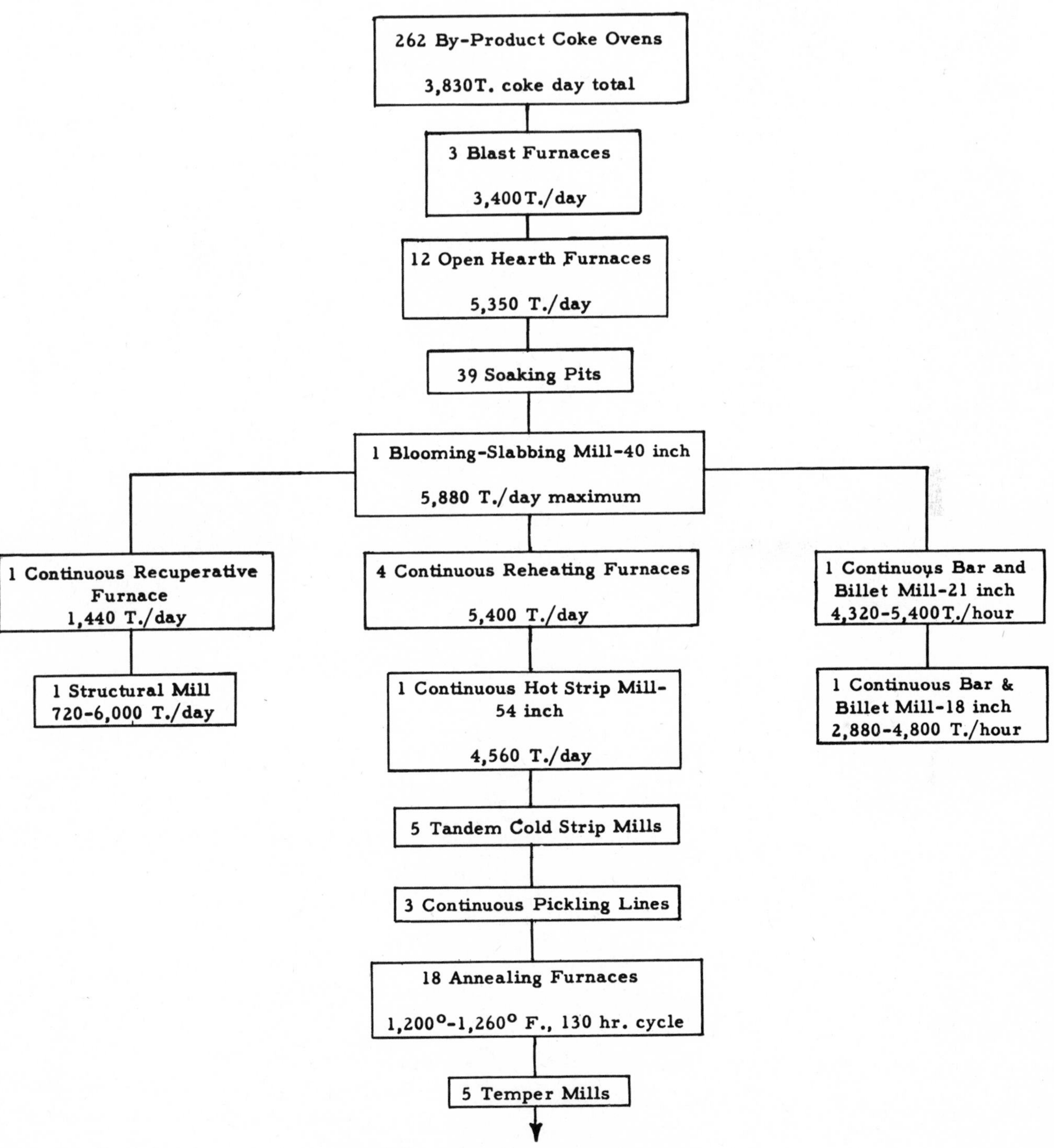

Steel Industry Reference Notes

From a small beginning, the United States iron and steel industry has grown to be the largest in the world; however, despite installations of new capacity and the development of new techniques and processes, its share of world production has dropped steadily since 1945 (see Exhibits 1 and 2). For example, United States production rose 122 percent from 52.8 million tons in 1939 to a peak of 117 million tons in 1955, but market share rose only from 33.4 to 39.4 percent. By 1962, the share was only 24.5 percent. Statistics on United States production and capacity since 1929 are shown in Exhibit 3.

Domestically, in 1962, the iron and steel industry was the largest manufacturing industry in the United States in terms of value added by manufacture, number of persons employed, and wages paid. There were 673,796 employees earning a total of $5.5 billion including pensions, insurance, social security, and vacation pay. Total investment in the industry was $14.3 billion. The industry earned about $566 million on sales of $13.8 billion. In the period 1946–1962, the industry spent more than $15 billion to modernize and expand capacity and increased its long-term debt from $0.5 billion in 1946 to $3.0 billion in 1962. Balance sheets and income statements for the industry as a whole are included in Exhibits 4 and 5.

ORGANIZATION OF THE INDUSTRY

The iron and steel industry, as defined in these notes, consists of enterprises engaged in operations which range from the mining of iron ore to the production of semifinished and finished hot rolled products and certain products beyond the hot rolled stage. It includes iron ore and coal mines, blast furnaces, steel works, rolling mills, finishing facilities (such as wire drawing and pipe and tool plants) as well as iron and steel foundries and forging plants.

The industry includes five major processing divisions: (1) iron ore mining, (2) pig iron producing, (3) steelmaking, (4) steel rolling, and (5) steel forgings and iron and steel casting.

Individual concerns which make up the industry are classed as (1) integrated: firms that combine the production of raw materials, pig iron, rolled steel products, and in some cases the production of more advanced products such as ships, bridges, and prefabricated houses; (2) semi-integrated: firms that purchase pig iron to make steel and rolled products; and (3) nonintegrated: firms that make only pig iron for sale, or that buy ingots of semifinished steel for rolling and further processing. In 1961, there were approximately 22 integrated concerns, 60 semi-integrated companies, and over 150 nonintegrated producers.

The United States iron and steel industry is characterized by vertical integration and concentration of ownership. The comparatively few large integrated concerns control most of the iron ore reserves, blast furnaces, steel works, and rolling mills (see Exhibit 6). Concentration of control is usually greatest in the production of bulky products of low-unit value such as iron ore, pig iron, and steel ingots. In fact, in 1960, the three largest companies, U.S. Steel, Bethlehem, and Republic, together owned 55 percent of the nation's coke, 50 percent of the nation's pig, and 52 percent of the nation's ingot-making capacity. Most of the pig iron and steel ingots and some of the finished steel produced by these large companies were used in their own vertically integrated operations.

LOCATION OF THE INDUSTRY

In 1961, 83 percent of the nation's steelmaking capacity was located in the seven east-north-central states of Pennsylvania, Ohio, Indiana, Illinois, New York, Michigan, and Maryland. The remaining capacity was divided between the Atlantic Coast, the Birmingham, Alabama district, and the Western states. Most of the industry's production facilities were located close to the ore and coal sources and reasonably close to the large domestic consuming centers. Eighty percent of the iron ore mined in the United States came from the Lake Superior district; 57 percent of the coking coal came from Pennsylvania, Ohio, and Indiana while the major domestic markets were located in the east-north-central area. Exhibits 7 and 8 show steel capacities and consumption by states.

Historically, proximity to source of raw material has been the prime determinant of the location of the steel industry because of the large tonnages of raw materials required for each ton of finished steel produced (see Exhibit 9). Furthermore, unlike the iron and steel industries of most other producing countries, the major portion of the United States' industry is situated nearer the sources of coking coal than those of iron ore, even though somewhat more ore than coal is used in making pig iron. Coking coal is found closer to the consuming centers and is more expensive to transport than iron ore.

RAW MATERIALS

The growth of the iron and steel industry in the United States to its present size has been due largely to the abundant native supply of the required raw materials. The principal materials used in the production of pig iron are iron ore, coking coal, and limestone and in the production of steel, pig iron and iron and steel scrap. Data on iron ore sources are shown in Exhibit 10 and on ore shipments in Exhibit 11, while the consumption and sources of scrap for 1946–1961 are shown in Exhibit 12.

1. *Iron Ore:* Iron ore occurs in vast deposits in certain parts of the United States. According to 1959 estimates, the United States has 4.5 billion tons of direct shipping ores and 60.4 billion tons of ore requiring beneficiation. The iron content of these domestic sources was estimated at 20.1 billion tons.[1] The largest and richest ore deposits were in the Lake Superior district, which contained 742 million gross tons of the country's total high-grade ore reserves and most of the taconite reserves. Lake Superior ore averages between 50–55 percent iron, compared with 35–40 percent in other districts. About 80 percent of the Lake Superior ore shipments come from the Minnesota Mesabi Range, where the ore is 10 to 150 feet below the surface, and mined by the open-pit method.

The proportion of ore mined in open pits has increased, despite the problems of weather, due mostly to the labor costs being one fifth those of underground mining. For example, the 1954 production was 108.9 million long tons, of which 84.7 million were from open pits, while the 1961 yield was 135.9 million, with 120.1 million from open pits. The value of ore shipped was $547.2 million in 1954 and $650.5 million in 1961.

[1] *Engineering and Mining Journal,* October, 1959, p. 128.

Since the largest portion of the iron reserves are owned by integrated companies, the open market for ore is relatively unimportant. Typically, about 85 percent of the ore shipments go to large integrated steel producers.

Although in the past the Lake Superior district has consistently supplied over 80 percent of the total United States ore production, the district's rich deposits are rapidly approaching exhaustion. In 1962, two trends were discernible. The first was the increasing use of imported ores especially from Canada and South America (see Exhibit 10). These ores had a richer iron content and were being delivered at Pittsburgh at only a slight premium above high-grade domestic ore. The second was the increasing use of agglomerated pellets and sinters. Prior to 1956, negligible quantities of pellets were being produced in the Lake Superior region, but by 1962 there were 12 plants with 19.4 million net tons of annual capacity; about 80 percent of the output was in taconite pellets. Sintering capacity rose from 10 million annual net tons in 1949 to 35.8 million in 1955 to 71.5 million in 1962. Production of agglomerates was as follows[2] (in thousands of net tons):

	1955	*1957*	*1958*	*1959*	*1960*	*1961*	*1962*
Pellets	1,144	5,641	9,575	9,401	15,192	16,098	20,220
Sinter	25,881	31,147	28,557	33,336	44,939	45,109	46,303
Briquettes, etc	1,048	895	736	590	720	1,045	727
Total	28,073	37,683	38,868	43,327	60,851	62,252	67,250

Pellets produce operating and transportation savings, although they usually commanded a 13 percent price premium over ore. For example, in 1962 one Armco blast furnace was claimed to have increased daily output from 1,500 tons to 2,900 tons on long runs by switching from ore to pellets.[3]

2. *Pig Iron:* Pig iron is the product of the blast furnace and the principal raw material for steel ingots and other ferrous products. Amounts and proportions used by the different steelmaking processes are shown in Exhibit 9.

The market for pig iron is relatively small because most is produced by integrated producers for use in their adjacent mills. In recent years, 90–93 percent of total pig iron production was for the maker's use, while 7–10 percent was sold as merchant pig. Such sales were usu-

[2] AISI, *Annual Statistical Reports,* 1955–62.
[3] *Iron Age,* March 31, 1962, p. 97.

ally made through an agent or broker with the pig iron being shipped directly from the blast furnace to the customer.

3. *Iron and Steel Scrap:* Along with pig iron, iron and steel scrap is a major raw material in steelmaking (see Exhibit 12.) The growth of the scrap industry has been due primarily to the predominant use of open-hearth furnaces, averaging a 40 percent scrap charge, and the decline of the Bessemer, with a 7 percent maximum scrap charge (see Exhibit 9). About 75 percent of all scrap is used by steel mills, and 20 percent by foundries.

Classified as to source, there are two categories of scrap: home scrap and purchased scrap. Home scrap is produced by the iron and steel industry; roughly 30 percent of the weight of all ingots cast becomes scrap during the various processing steps. In 1961, 60 percent of all scrap consumed was home scrap.

Purchased scrap is harvested from a variety of places. In 1961, the amount of scrap collected was 30.9 million gross tons, from eight major sources.[4] (1) About 9.6 million tons was "prompt industrial scrap," from steel fabricating plants. Assuming that fabrication involves a 15 percent scrap loss, the loss for 60.4 million gross tons of steel products shipped was 9 million; likewise, assuming a 5 percent machine loss, castings yielded .6 million tons of scrap. The largest contributor to prompt scrap was the automotive industry with 4 million gross tons, industrial machinery with .9 million, containers with .8, electrical machinery with .5, contractors products with .3, and appliances with .3. (2) Automobile scrappage was estimated at 4.3 million gross tons. (3) Railroads provided 2.7 million gross tons. (4) Shipbreaking yielded only .3 million gross tons. (5) Increased construction boosted building demolition to 2 million gross tons of scrap. (6) Farmers parted with 1 million tons. (7) Public utilities and government agencies were credited with .8 million. (8) Detinning and shredding of tin cans accounted for .85 million gross tons.

Classified as to type, there are about 75 recognized grades. No. 1 heavy melting steel, the bellweather of the industry, accounted for almost 40 percent of the 1961 home scrap and 20.2 percent of purchased scrap. Most of the steel scrap is used by steelmakers, and most of the cast iron scrap by iron foundries. Borings and turnings are used largely in blast furnaces.

[4] Institute of Scrap Iron and Steel, *Yearbook* (1962).

Scrap supply follows the business cycle closely. When industrial activity is low, scrap accumulates in the yards of mills and dealers and when activity increases, these accumulations act as reservoirs from which the nation's furnaces are fed. During prolonged periods of capacity production and expansion, such as during World War II and the postwar period, these reservoirs were empty and the scrap drives were necessary to meet requirements. Prices fluctuate accordingly. For example, record steel production in 1955 resulted in steadily rising prices for scrap until, in the spring of 1956, prices exceeded $50 a ton. In the 1958 recession, scrap prices remained in a $32–44 range.

Scrap is accumulated by dealers and their sales constitute a $1.7 billion business. In 1958, there were 4,948 scrap dealers and brokers (of which 2,781 owned their own processing equipment), and they employed 37,929 people.

STEELMAKING

The increasing use of oxygen in steelmaking is often called the most significant change in steelmaking over the past decade. In 1935, the industry used about 38 cubic feet of oxygen per ton of steel produced; by 1962, this figure was 850 cubic feet. Since 1956 alone, total steel industry use went from 24 billion cubic feet to 83.8 billion.

Oxygen in a modern steel mill does a variety of jobs. The major categories in millions of gaseous cubic feet are shown below:[5]

	1962	*1961*	*1960*	*1959*
Purchased	72,126	55,844	36,143	25,260
Produced	11,660	13,559	12,120	9,211
Consumption:				
Conditioning	12,047	10,360	9,775	8,139
Scrap	1,445	1,507	1,540	1,267
Burning, welding	1,684	1,842	1,309	1,270
Blast furnaces	11,411	8,894	4,362	4,484
Steelmaking	54,675	44,170	29,213	18,307
Maintenance	1,004	1,002	1,272	308
All other	1,520	1,628	812	696
Total	83,786	69,403	48,263	34,471

Part of the growth in the use of oxygen was the use of the oxygen converter in the Linz-Donawitz (LD) process. Experiments on this process

[5] AISI, *Annual Statistical Reports,* 1959–62.

started in 1933, the first successful test was done in 1948, and commercial production began at the United Austrian Iron and Steel Works in Linz in 1952. The first plant outside Austria was Canada's Dominion Foundries & Steel, Ltd., in August, 1954, followed by McLouth Steel Corporation the next March.

United States oxygen capacity in 1960 was estimated to be in excess of 4 million tons (2.7 percent of the total), compared to a half million tons in 1957. This capacity was divided between the following four companies: (1) Acme Steel in Chicago had two vessels which were rated at 452,000 tons of ingot capacity; (2) Jones and Laughlin in Pittsburgh had two vessels which were rated at 880,000 ingot tons; (3) Kaiser Steel on the West Coast had three vessels rated at 1,440,000 ingot tons; and (4) McLouth Steel had five vessels which were rated at 1,400,000 ingot tons. Oxygen steel capacity represented about 31 percent of the total steel capacity of 13.6 million tons of these four companies.

Another 3.5 million tons capacity was added during 1962 while the industry debated what was the most economic furnace size. The first American units installed were rated for 30-ton heats, and the second round of construction saw the rating jump to 80–100 tons. Then in January, 1962, Jones and Laughlin installed at its Cleveland plant two 200-ton vessels capable of producing 1.5 million ingot tons annually, and in the fall National Steel followed suit with two 300-ton units at its Great Lakes unit with a rating of two million tons. Finally, in September, United States Steel announced plans for two 150-ton vessels with a 1.5 million annual ton rating; these would be the first oxygen steelmaking units to be installed by any of the "big three."

With the help of improved refractories, oxygen is being introduced in increasing amounts into open-hearth, electric, and blast furnaces. Until about 1959, the silica roof temperature ceiling of 3,100° F. restricted oxygen lancing in open hearths. Then a practical design was found to make furnace roofs of basic brick, composed of magnesite and chrome ore, that withstood 3,400° F. Basic brick costs five times as much as silica, may reduce heat time 10 percent, and lasts 400–500 heats instead of 200. Seemingly, synthetics will be needed for the 3,600° F. and above range; one glass company developed in 1962 a refractory to withstand 4,500° F.

STRUCTURE AND LOCATION OF MARKETS

1. *Foreign Market:* The long-established position of the United States as a net exporter of steel products ended in 1959 (see Exhibit 1C). Initially this was a result of the 116-day steel strike, but the continuation of the trade balance reflects the buildup of steelmaking capacity abroad. The losses are felt across the board with the exception of sheet and strip in 1960 when European automobile makers increased purchases. China and Japan are responsible for the bulk of the export drop, and Japan, the Common Market, and the United Kingdom are making inroads into other U.S. foreign markets.

2. *Domestic Market:* The main domestic markets for the products of the iron and steel industry are located in roughly the east-north-central area and Michigan and Minnesota (see Exhibit 8). During and since World War II, there has been a significant growth of steel markets in the West and Far West. The increased consumption has been attributed to the expansion and construction, oil-producing facilities, and pipelines, and to the general increase in consumer durable goods industries. The major consuming industries of steel products in the United States are the automotive, construction, container, machinery, and oil and gas industries in that order (see Exhibits 13 and 14).

3. *Direct Selling:* A significant characteristic of the sale of iron and steel products is the predominance of direct selling from the mill to the consumer, rather than through wholesalers or jobbers. Exhibits 15 through 17 document this trend and indicate major markets.

PRICING AND PRICING POLICIES

1. *Pricing Behavior:* Prices in the iron and steel industry fluctuates less than those in most industries making basic materials despite the unusually wide fluctuations in the demand for iron and steel (see Exhibit 13 and 18). This relative stability in prices is especially true of iron ore and of semifinished and finished steel products. One increase and no reductions occurred in the annual average published price of iron ore during the entire period 1929 to 1939.

During the same period, there were relatively few price reductions on semifinished and finished steel, and they were much less marked than might have been expected from the increase in demand. Published prices of pig iron tended to fluctuate more in response to variations in demand than prices of ore and semifinished and finished steel. Pig iron competes to a large extent with steel scrap and steelmaking, and prices of scrap have always been extremely sensitive to fluctuations in the production of steel.

The characteristic stability of steel prices have been severely criticized by the government and other groups. It has been claimed that stable prices are evidence of a lack of competition and the existence of a monopoly power. In addition, the charge has been made that stable prices for a basic commodity such as steel tend to increase the severity of depression.

Industry groups, on the other hand, have pointed out that price behavior per se is not evidence of competition or a lack of it, since other factors such as quality, product development, and service enter into the picture. With regard to the effects of steel prices on economic activity, industry sources have claimed that prices of iron and steel products have little effect on the demand for steel. They point out that the demand for steel depends on the demand for end products which use steel and that the cost of steel is a relatively small fraction of end-product prices. For example, the estimated cost of steel in an electric toaster selling for $22 was $0.35 and $77 in a farm tractor selling for $1,700.

2. *The Basing Point Method of Pricing:* Under the basing point system, steel was sold on a delivered price basis. The price to the buyer included the following: (1) a base price which was quoted for a specified type or grade of steel at a particular central point designated by the industry as the basing point for the area;[6] (2) the cost of transporting the article from the basing point to the point of delivery specified in the order, irrespective of the location of the producer making the shipment; and (3) price adjustments if the product varied from standard specifications. Transportation costs were generally based on published railroad rates irrespective of the actual means of transportation used. Extras and deductions were generally standardized throughout the industry.

As practiced by the steel industry, publicly quoted delivered prices at any given point were, as a rule, identical for all producers. Producers, whose plants were closer to a particular market than a basing point and/or who had transportation available at a lower cost than rail, received so-called "phantom freight" or the difference between the railroad freight cost from freight point to consumer and the lower actual freight.

In 1948, the Supreme Court upheld the finding of the Federal Trade Commission that the basing point system as used by the cement industry was an unfair trade practice. Later that year, nearly all of the major steel producers, making it clear that they were not involved in any sort of collusive action, announced that they were abandoning the multiple basing point system of pricing and would in the future quote f.o.b. mill prices to all customers. This voluntary action did not settle the legal status of the system.

The demise of the basing point system was the start of the gradual elimination of regional pricing. The succeeding moves involved freight absorption and premiums: (1) On October 8, 1953, U.S. Steel Corporation announced a policy of freight absorption and other companies followed suit. This meant that a mill located in a steel export area such as Pittsburgh (which produces more steel than it uses) would absorb enough of the freight to, say, Chicago to make its delivered price equal to that of a local mill. Both before and after this move, its legality was strongly opposed by the Federal Trade Commission, and attempts to introduce clarifying legislation failed. By 1954, absorption was costing $70 million a year, with Pittsburgh mills hardest hit. (2) In June, 1958, regional premiums started to vanish when the $2 premium on sheet was eliminated. In March, 1961, the tinplate premiums for the South and East Coast were eliminated. Then in October, 1962, the West Coast's historical premium essentially was erased with the announcement that Kaiser Steel Corporation was reducing prices an average of $12 a ton.

Some regional premiums remain. They in-

[6] The base price was designated f.o.b. a particular location. For each product there was at least one basing point, and for most products there was more than one; each basing point was usually an important producing center.

clude, for example: structurals at Bethlehem, Buffalo, Johnstown, Atlanta, Houston; sheets at Fairless and Granite City; galvanized at Granite City and the West Coast; bars at Fairless, Atlanta and Houston; plates at Granite City and Houston.

3. *The Attempted 1962 Price Increase:* The endless debate over steel pricing policies and practices came to a much-publicized head in April, 1962. On Tuesday, April 10, the day after signing a 10-cent per hour labor agreement, United States Steel Corporation announced a $6 per ton price increase. Led by Bethlehem Steel, the majors—with the exception of Inland Steel and Armco—followed suit the following day.[7]

Mr. L. B. Worthington, President of U.S. Steel, said that since 1958 prices had, if anything, "declined somewhat . . . due to competitive pressures from the domestic producers and from imports of foreign-made steel as well as from other materials which are used as substitutes for steel." Conceding severe competition still existed, he continued: "We have reluctantly concluded that a modest price adjustment can no longer be avoided in the light of production cost increases." Profits, he said, were inadequate to maintain competitive low-cost facilities.

The reaction of President Kennedy was quick and dramatic. For the past year the administration had applied pressure on both steel labor and management to exercise restraint on prices and wages, and Mr. Kennedy had hailed the new contract as a "non-inflationary" one that would make any price increase unnecessary. The day after the U.S. Steel announcement, President Kennedy called the increase "a wholly unjustifiable and irresponsible defiance of the public interest" and predicted labor costs per ton would decline in the coming year.

On Thursday, April 12, a grand jury investigation was initiated and Roger M. Blough, Chairman of U.S. Steel, discussed his position at a news conference. He denied any political motivation to the decision and indicated that if Inland and Armco did not follow suit it would be very difficult to maintain the price increase.

The next day, April 13, the price increase collapsed. First, Inland Steel announced it would not raise prices, then the Defense Department made official the rumor that defense business would be shifted to companies not raising prices, and then Kaiser Steel and Bethlehem joined the Inland position. Finally, U.S. Steel rescinded its increase and the others followed.

[7] *The New York Times,* April 11–14, 1962.

LABOR

1. *Employment, Hours, and Wages:* Historically, employment has fluctuated to a lesser degree than average weekly hours of work in response to fluctuations in demand and output. From 1937–1938 output fell 44 percent, average weekly hours 22 percent, but employment only 13.7 percent. From 1941 to 1944 the production rose 8.2 percent, average weekly hours 25.3 percent, but employment only 0.7 percent.

Average hourly earnings have risen steadily from $0.921 an hour in 1934 to $3.33 an hour in 1962. Earnings vary within the industry, depending upon the differences in skill, method of wage payment, and branch of the industry involved. In 1961, total employment costs per hour increased 441 percent above the 1940 level. After the affects of inflation are eliminated, steel workers received 180 percent greater hourly earnings in 1961 than in 1940 (see Exhibit 19).

Regional variations in wage rates have been minimized as a result of the almost complete unionization of the steel industry. Differences in overall regional rates that do exist are mainly attributed to the composition of the labor force; for example, a region in which the balance of facilities is weighted toward rolling processes probably has a higher average wage rate than a region in which the blast furnace predominates.

2. *Productivity:* Output per man-hour has not been affected greatly by the industry's level of output but instead has tended to increase because of technological innovations (see Exhibit 19). From 1929–1932, total output declined by 76.2 percent, and open-hearth output per man-hour decreased only 26.4 percent. Since 1932, output per man-hour has increased steadily except during the 1938 recession and the World War II period when obsolete equipment was pressed into use. In 1960, output per man-hour was 166 percent above the 1940 level. The gain

in productivity resulted primarily from such technological innovations as the more extensive utilization of continuous mills for the production of strip and sheet.

3. *Unions:* The United Steel Workers of America, CIO, is the chief bargaining agent for employees in the iron and steel industry. For the single union representing most of the employees, bargaining is on an industry-wide basis. As was the case in the union organization of the industry, the results of contract negotiations with the United States Steel Corporation set the pattern for union bargaining with the rest of the industry. Occasionally the terms are tempered to an individual company situation. The results of the 1945–1962 negotiations are shown in Exhibit 20.

Industry-wide bargaining has also resulted in industry-wide strikes, such as those which occurred in 1946, 1949, 1952, 1956, and 1959. When United States Steel Corporation did not concede to union demands, the smaller producers also resisted; therefore, strikes took place which involved most of the producers in the industry.

Besides setting a wage pattern for the rest of the steel industry, the results of contract negotiations with "Big Steel" also influence the wage package pattern for a large part of the economy. For example, managements in both steel and other industries were wondering about the impact on workforce scheduling and utilization of two provisions in the July, 1962 contract: (1) payment to employees with two or more years of service of a "short work week benefit" for any week in which some, but less than 22, hours are worked; (2) creation of seniority pools to cushion the shock of technological change. Seniority rights were broadened to permit long-service men to bump juniors within an entire operating unit, such as a blast furnace or open hearth; however, at the beginning of 1963 few companies had reached final agreement with union representatives as to the make-up of the pool.

Even those outside the "Big Three" can influence collective bargaining within and outside the steel industry. Kaiser Steel Corporation's 1962 agreement is a case in point. The four-year plan incorporated: (1) a plant-wide labor pool for automation-eliminated workers who would be paid at their old rate times at least the average hours worked in the plant for up to a year; (2) payment to workers of 32.5 percent of cost savings[8] above a 1961 labor-plus-materials base regardless of the reason for improvement or company profits; (3) elimination of incentive plans and a freer hand for management in work assignments. Multiplant major companies were leery of the idea.

FUTURE TRENDS

Steelmen looking into the future in 1962 saw five major trends. They were: (1) increasing foreign competition; (2) displacement of steel by other materials; (3) rapid technological developments; (4) growing, but varied, expansion costs; and (5) mounting concern over air and water pollution.

1. *Foreign Competition:* Efficient new plants, lower wage rates, and different pricing policies would continue to accelerate the pressure of imports. Foreign firms were continuing to modernize and to expand in 1962 with $5 billion earmarked for the year's capital expenditures; however, steelmen singled out lower wage rates as the prime cause of prices below the United States. For example, in 1962, hourly employment costs were $3.99 in the United States versus $0.63 in Japan, $1.04 in Italy, $1.11 in France, $1.17 in the United Kingdom, and $1.37 in West Germany. (The 1952 rates were $2.32, $0.32, $0.63, $0.72, $0.64, and $0.69 in the same countries.) Raw material costs are about 5 percent higher in Europe, 10 percent higher in Japan, than in the United States. The net result was that in 1962, structural steel, for example, sold for $100 per metric ton[9] f.o.b. Antwerp compared with the U.S. price of $110 per ton.

2. *Displacement of Steel:* More lighter and cheaper substitute materials presaged more competition for steel's traditional markets. For example, prestressed concrete and glass are sub-

[8] Savings would be adjusted to reflect cost reducing capital expenditures on *existing* facilities, but not on new or increased capacity.

[9] A net or short ton is 2,000 pounds; a gross or long ton is 2,240 pounds; and a metric ton is 2,204.6 pounds.

stituting for structural steels; copper and plastic are making inroads into the piping business; and aluminum is seeking to replace steel in the container market. In response, steel products have been upgraded, with structurals between 1959–1962 being reduced 16–25 percent in weight for the same strength, oil and gas pipes weighing 80 percent of the 1958 version, and tin cans weighing only 60 percent of what the product did in mid-1960.

3. *Technological Developments:* Of the burgeoning number of innovations, two—direct reduction of ore and continuous casting—seem to hold the most promise.

In direct reduction, hot reducing gas of hydrogen and carbon monoxide is sent through an ore-filled reactor where it combines with the oxygen in the ore to form water and carbon dioxide and leave a nonliquid "sponge iron" with 90 percent of the oxygen removed and 85 percent metallization. The process is the fluidizing of solids techniques (used in the petroleum industry) with the hydrogen being forced up through a column of crushed ore particles and keeping them in turbulent or boiling motion. The reactor has a 12-hour cycle with four three-hour steps: loading, preheating, reducing, and cooling.

In 1962, the major commercial installation was in Monterrey, Mexico. The largest unit in the world was there, with a capacity of 500 metric tons a day. Built in 1960, the investment in five reformer furnaces (to convert natural gas to hydrogen and carbon monoxide), four reducing reactors, and related equipment including utility distribution systems and offices cost $6.1 million. Eight men per shift were required with the following operating costs:[10]

Cost Factor	*Unit Cost*	*Quantity*	*$/Year*
Natural gas	0.30/MCF	3,465,000 MCF	$1,040,000
Water make-up	0.027/M Gal.	194,500 M Gal.	5,300
Catalyst and chemicals			40,000
Operating labor	0.80/Man-hour	54,000 Man-hour	43,200
Supervision	1.25/Man-hour	9,000 Man-hour	11,200
Maintenance	4% cap. invest.		245,000
Gen'l overhead	100% labor and supervision		54,400
Misc. supplies			30,000
Royalty	1.00/Ton Fe		165,000
Net operating cost/year	$9.91/Ton	165,000 Tons	$1,634,100

Several American companies were investigating direct reduction processes and alternatives of adding powdered coal, oil slurry, or oxygen to the blast furnace charge.

In continuous casting, molten steel is poured into the top of a water-cooled mold of billet size, and a solid hot billet ready for rolling is drawn from the bottom and cut to desired lengths; the process eliminates ingot casting, soaking pits, and blooming mills. The ladle usually holds 1–75 tons, but some can handle 200 tons; the main limitation is that the heat be poured within an hour. The hot metal is poured on top of a starting bar inserted in a water-cooled mold. The bar is then withdrawn slowly, followed by the metal which is surface-chilled and solidified. The billet emerges at a speed of 4–5 feet per minute, or even seven feet, and the yield is 95–98 percent versus the conventional 86 percent due to lower cropping scrappage. A four-strand machine with a 240,000 annual metric ton capacity might cost with all auxiliary equipment between $2.0–2.5 million; require six operators per shift and one maintenance man; and incur $.94 in direct operating costs excluding labor (a total saving of about 7 percent of the hot-rolled bar cost).

There were 37 continuous casting machines producing two million tons of steel in 1962, but none were in the United States, although Atlas Steels Ltd. installed a unit for specialty steels in Welland, Ontario, in November, 1954. In October, 1962, National Steel announced plans for a 300-ton batch unit to cast a million tons a year and McLouth Steel scheduled a 75–100 ton batch unit with an annual output of 250–300,000 tons.

4. *Growing Expansion Costs:* Many steelmen wondered whether the industry would be able to take advantage of technological developments in view of increasing cost per ton for new and for incremental capacity (these costs may be estimated from Exhibits 3–5) and the small cash flow per ton of the industry.

5. *Pollution:* The abatement of air and water pollution would become increasingly necessary. Air pollution came to the fore with the increasing use of oxygen: at 1,700° to 1,800° C. the oxygen reaction gives off a brown fume of very fine particles. Almost all of the oxygen converters but only 40 of the 900 open hearths were equipped with electrostatic precipitators

[10] The M. W. Kellog Company, "Steelmaking with Gas."

costing between $500,000 and $1 million each (depending on whether or not waste boilers are included) in 1962. Since steel production needs 265 tons of water per ton of steel, water pollution has always been a potential problem. As of 1962, water pollution facilities in the United States had a replacement value of $100,000,000; the cost of making all water the oft-suggested standard "of trout stream purity" was beyond estimate.

1. STEEL INDUSTRY

Position of Steel in the World and American Economy

A. World Steel Ingot Production (Millions of Net Tons)

	1939	1945	1947	1950	1955	1958	1959	1960	1961	1962*
United States	52.8	79.7	84.9	96.8	117.0	85.3	93.4	99.3	98.0	98.2
ECSC***.	42.8**	8.8**	18.0	32.3	54.4	60.1	65.7	80.2	80.7	80.4
United Kingdom	14.8	13.2	12.2	18.2	22.2	21.9	22.6	27.2	24.8	23.0
U.S.S.R.	20.7	12.3*	14.7*	29.8	49.9	60.5	66.1	72.0	77.9	80.0
Japan.	8.1	1.2	1.0	5.3	10.4	13.4	18.3	24.4	31.2	30.0
All Other	11.6	10.7*	16.4*	21.9	43.1	57.8	70.6	78.6	83.9	88.6
Total	150.8	125.9*	147.2*	204.3	297.0	299.0	336.7	381.7	396.5	400.2

*Estimated.

**Includes total Germany.

***European Coal Steel Community (Belgium, Netherlands, Luxemburg, France, West Germany, Italy).

Source: Iron Age, January 3, 1963, p. 159.

B. Relationships between Steel and Industrial Production, 1929-1961

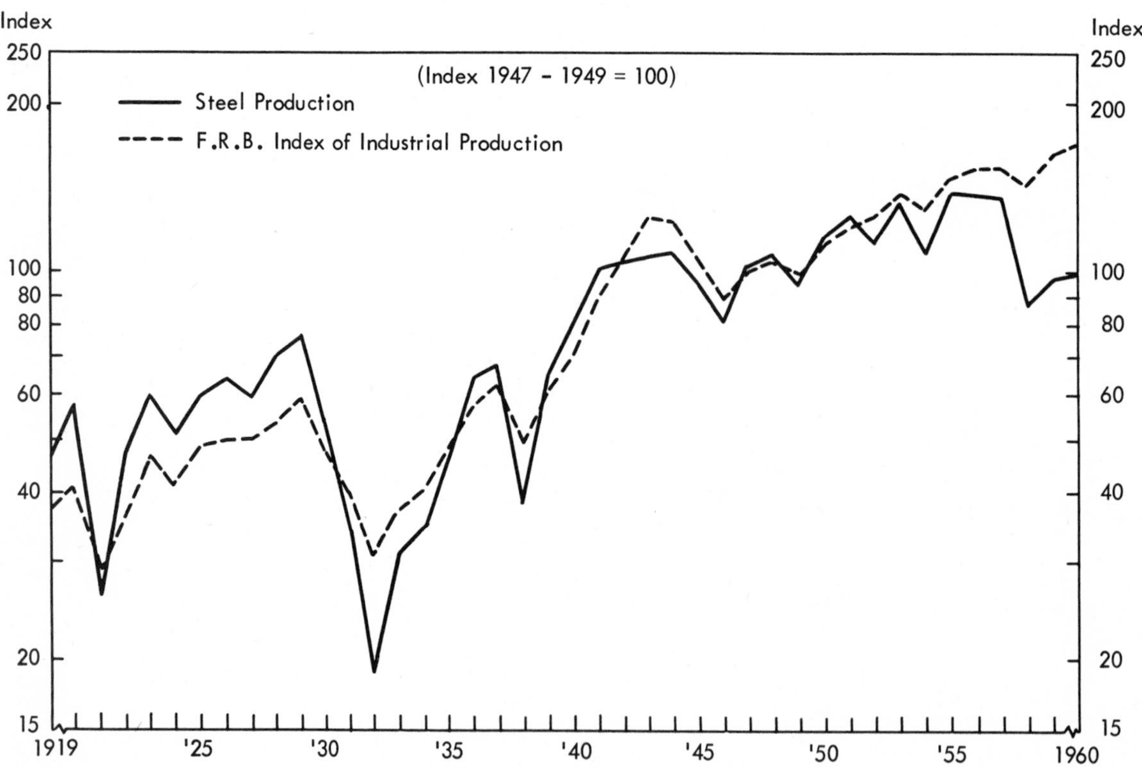

Exhibit 1 (continued)

C. Imports and Exports to the United States

Imports of Iron and Steel Products, 1955-1961 (Thousands of Tons)

Products	1955	1956	1957	1958	1959	1960	1961*
Steel Mill Products:							
Semifinished	194	92	63	200	540	477	631
Shapes, Plates, and Piling	112	400	291	171	798	529	331
Rails and Accessories	7	8	5	5	10	10	23
Bars and Tool Steel	283	396	263	649	1,339	841	907
Pipe and Tubing	77	140	191	200	553	480	521
Wire and Wire Products	245	248	301	432	703	547	562
Tin Mill Products	0.1	1	0.1	0.2	67	39	19
Sheets and Strip	55	55	41	50	386	436	171
Total Steel Mill Products	973	1,341	1,155	1,707	4,396	3,359	3,164
Other Steel Products	102	140	149	124	232	219	158
Total Steel Products	1,075	1,481	1,304	1,831	4,628	3,578	3,322
Iron Products and Ferroalloys	394	519	549	305	895	510	604
Grand Total	1,470	2,000	1,853	2,136	5,524	4,088	3,927

Exports of Iron and Steel Products, 1955-61 (Thousands of Tons)

Products	1955	1956	1957	1958	1959	1960	1961*
Steel Mill Products:							
Semifinished	721	529	721	124	35	129	185
Shapes, Plates, and Piling	505	672	1,075	554	306	386	320
Rails and Accessories	68	87	235	165	82	134	109
Bars and Tool Steel	206	298	215	123	68	85	91
Pipe and Tubing	350	783	1,185	623	266	195	211
Wire and Wire Products	49	56	39	35	26	29	26
Tin Mill Products	968	848	802	495	460	686	481
Sheets and Strip	1,194	1,075	1,074	703	435	1,333	566
Total Steel Mill Products	4,061	4,348	5,358	2,823	1,677	2,977	1,989
Other Steel Products	349	421	607	414	306	247	239
Total Steel Products	4,410	4,769	5,955	3,237	1,983	3,224	2,228
Iron Products and Ferroalloys	184	448	1,054	226	145	246	558
Grand Total	4,595	5,216	7,009	3,463	2,128	3,470	2,786

*Preliminary.

Source: American Iron and Steel Institute, Annual Statistical Reports, 1955-1961.

2. STEEL INDUSTRY

Comparative Indicators for the American Economy and the Steel Industry, 1929-1962
(In Billions of Dollars)

Year	Pop. (Mil.)	GNP*	Personal Exp. on Durables*	Invest. for Prod. Dur. Equip.*	Price Indexes for Durables 1957-59=100: Consum.	Price Indexes for Durables 1957-59=100: Wholesale	Construction Cost Index 1957-59=100	Prod. Indexes 1957=100: All Ind.	Prod. Indexes 1957=100: Steel	Price Indexes 1957-59=100: All Ind.	Price Indexes 1957-59=100: Steel
1929	121.9	181.8	14.9	11.1	N.A.	N.A.	36.2	38	54.8	51.7	37.6
1935	127.4	152.9	10.7	6.7	48.1	N.A.	31.5	31	33.9	44.0	34.4
1939	131.0	189.3	13.3	8.5	51.7	N.A.	37.5	38	46.8	45.9	38.0
1940	132.1	205.8	15.3	10.9	51.3	N.A.	38.5	44	59.4	46.9	37.7
1941	133.4	238.1	17.6	12.9	54.8	N.A.	40.1	56	73.5	50.3	38.3
1942	134.9	266.9	10.9	7.4	62.2	N.A.	42.2	69	76.3	54.0	38.6
1943	136.7	296.7	9.4	6.9	64.3	N.A.	43.4	82	78.8	54.7	39.6
1944	138.4	317.9	8.6	9.2	70.2	N.A.	44.5	81	79.5	55.6	38.5
1945	139.9	314.0	9.8	12.7	75.5	N.A.	45.4	70	70.7	56.3	39.3
1946	141.4	282.5	19.4	16.1	79.0	N.A.	49.8	59	59.1	61.9	43.6
1947	144.1	283.2	23.3	21.7	85.6	64.8	59.4	65	75.3	75.3	53.1
1948	146.6	293.1	24.6	22.8	91.9	71.5	65.4	68	78.6	81.7	61.7
1949	149.2	292.7	26.3	19.8	93.2	73.0	66.7	64	69.2	80.0	62.7
1950	151.7	318.1	32.1	21.3	94.2	75.9	71.2	74	85.9	83.0	66.9
1951	154.4	341.8	29.2	22.0	101.4	83.2	76.0	81	93.3	91.6	72.9
1952	157.0	353.5	28.5	21.8	102.7	83.6	78.8	84	82.7	89.4	73.8
1953	159.6	369.0	33.1	22.5	101.6	85.2	81.7	91	99.0	90.1	77.7
1954	162.4	363.1	32.4	20.8	97.7	86.0	84.6	85	78.3	90.5	78.7
1955	165.2	392.7	39.6	22.5	94.9	89.5	88.9	96	103.8	92.4	83.2
1956	168.2	400.9	38.0	25.0	94.9	95.4	93.1	99	102.2	96.5	91.6
1957	171.2	403.6	38.5	24.6	98.2	98.6	96.5	100	100.0	99.2	98.4
1958	174.1	401.3	35.5	19.4	99.7	99.6	99.5	93	75.6	99.5	99.9
1959	177.3	428.6	41.0	21.4	102.0	101.8	103.9	105	82.9	99.8	101.8
1960	180.7	440.2	42.2	22.7	100.7	101.7	106.1	108	88.1	101.3	100.6
1961	183.6	447.9	41.6	21.1	100.5	101.3	107.8	109	87.0	100.8	100.7
1962	186.6	471.9	45.2	23.8	101.5	101.0	110.1	118	87.2	100.8	99.3

In constant dollars (e.g., deflated by appropriate price indexes; for derivation see Business Statistics, 1961, p. 200).

Sources: U.S. Department of Commerce, Office of Business Economics, Business Statistics, 1961 and Survey of Current Business, October, May, 1963, for all items except steel production. Steel production index compiled from basic data in AISI, Annual Statistical Report, 1961. Construction index compiled by Engineering News-Record by weighing prices of structural steel, cement, lumber, and the common labor rate.

3. STEEL INDUSTRY

American Steel Ingot Production and Capacity by Type of Furnace, 1929-1962
(Thousands of Net Tons)

	Total			Open Hearth		Electric		Basic Oxygen		Bessemer	
Year	Capacity	Production	%	Production	% Cap.	Production	% Cap.	Production	% Cap.	Production	% Cap.
1929	69,584	61,742	88.7	53,152	96.2	643	48.3	-	-	7,945	92.6
1935	78,452	38,184	48.7	34,401	50.2	608	57.0	-	-	3,175	35.9
1939	81,829	52,799	64.5	48,410	66.4	1,030	59.5	-	-	3,359	47.1
1940	81,620	66,983	82.1	61,573	83.5	1,701	90.1	-	-	3,708	61.7
1941	84,152	82,839	98.4	74,390	99.8	2,872	110.9	-	-	5,578	79.7
1942	88,570	86,032	97.1	76,502	97.9	3,976	106.3	-	-	5,553	82.6
1943	90,293	88,837	98.4	78,622	99.3	4,859	100.7	-	-	5,625	85.8
1944	93,652	89,642	95.7	80,364	97.7	4,238	79.1	-	-	5,040	83.0
1945	95,505	79,702	83.5	71,940	85.5	3,457	63.3	-	-	4,305	73.3
1946	91,890	66,603	72.5	60,712	74.7	2,563	46.6	-	-	3,328	64.6
1947	91,241	84,894	93.0	76,874	94.9	3,788	74.6	-	-	4,232	82.1
1948	94,234	88,640	94.1	79,340	94.9	5,057	93.7	-	-	4,243	81.2
1949	96,121	77,978	81.1	70,249	82.8	3,783	61.9	-	-	3,947	76.0
1950	99,393	96,836	97.4	86,282	99.2	6,039	87.9	-	-	4,534	81.9
1951	104,230	105,200	100.9	93,166	102.3	7,142	94.5	-	-	4,891	87.0
1952	108,588	93,168	85.8	82,846	87.2	6,798	82.6	-	-	3,524	65.5
1953	117,547	111,610	94.9	100,474	97.9	7,280	71.1	-	-	3,856	83.2
1954	124,331	88,312	71.0	80,327	73.6	5,436	52.0	-	-	2,548	53.2
1955	125,828	117,036	93.0	105,359	95.6	8,050	74.5	307		3,320	69.4
1956	128,363	115,216	89.8	102,840	91.6	8,641	80.6	506	93.7	3,228	67.4
1957	133,459	112,715	84.4	101,658	87.0	7,970	69.3	612	113.3	2,475	54.9
1958	140,742	85,255	60.6	75,879	62.0	6,656	50.0	1,323	122.4	1,396	34.7
1959	147,639	93,446	63.3	81,669	64.5	8,532	63.2	1,864	46.2	1,380	38.6
1960	148,571	99,282	66.8	86,368	68.2	8,379	58.2	3,346	80.5	1,189	35.0
1961	N.A.	98,014	N.A.	84,502	N.A.	8,664	N.A.	3,967	N.A.	881	N.A.
1962*	N.A.	98,327	N.A.	82,957	N.A.	9,013	N.A.	5,553	N.A.	804	N.A.

*Estimate
Note: In 1961, the major steel companies ceased furnishing capacity figures.
Source: AISI, Annual Statistical Report, 1962. Percentages prepared by Harvard Business School, Bureau of Business Research.

4. STEEL INDUSTRY

Comparative Industry Balance Sheets as of December 31, 1948-1962
(In Millions)

	1948	1949	1950	1951	1952	1953	1954	1955	1956	1957	1958	1959	1960	1961	1962
ASSETS															
Current Assets:															
Cash	$ 693	$ 721	$ 857	$ 924	$ 837	$ 829	$ 829	$ 973	$ 930	$ 973	$ 958	$ 973	$ 917	$ 892	$ 903
Securities	587	693	940	1,407	741	1,031	1,003	1,459	1,186	945	782	1,307	1,031	1,035	1,214
Accounts Receivable	625	514	764	818	911	812	792	1,122	1,253	1,017	1,131	1,390	994	1,217	1,110
Inventories	1,260	1,229	1,384	1,578	1,796	2,027	1,933	2,076	2,426	2,720	2,835	2,696	2,991	3,210	2,946
Total Current	$3,165	$3,157	$3,945	$4,727	$ 4,285	$ 4,699	$ 4,557	$ 5,630	$ 5,795	$ 5,655	$ 5,706	$ 6,366	$ 5,933	$ 6,354	$ 6,173
Miscellaneous Investments	$ 386	$ 394	$ 522	$ 608	$ 399	$ 391	$ 409	$ 741	$ 1,099	$ 1,101	$ 1,219	$ 1,214	$ 1,021	$ 1,072	$ 1,090
Fixed Assets:															
Plant and Equipment	$7,074	$7,467	$8,061	$9,080	$10,375	$11,196	$11,656	$12,212	$13,440	$15,143	$16,190	$16,971	$18,316	$18,976	$19,463
Less: Depreciation	3,856	4,060	4,325	4,621	5,022	5,502	6,043	6,647	7,300	7,894	8,468	8,955	9,485	9,980	10,590
Net Plant	$3,218	$3,407	$3,736	$4,459	$ 5,353	$ 5,684	$ 5,613	$ 5,565	$ 6,139	$ 7,249	$ 7,722	$ 8,016	$ 8,831	$ 8,996	$ 8,873
Deferred Charges	$ 47	$ 53	$ 70	$ 70	$ 70	$ 72	$ 74	$ 76	$ 83	$ 99	$ 122	$ 130	$ 152	$ 163	$ 158
Total Assets	$6,816	$7,011	$8,273	$9,864	$10,107	$10,836	$10,653	$12,012	$13,116	$14,104	$14,769	$15,726	$15,937	$16,585	$16,294
LIABILITIES															
Current Liabilities:															
Accrued Taxes	$ 557	$ 509	$ 933	$1,454	$ 754	$ 1,201	$ 663	$ 923	$ 869	$ 880	$ 783	$ 885	$ 896	$ 853	$ 725
All Other	770	658	864	1,083	1,278	1,253	1,042	1,282	1,568	1,474	1,406	1,723	1,430	1,528	1,424
Total Current	$1,327	$1,167	$1,797	$2,537	$ 2,032	$ 2,454	$ 1,705	$ 2,205	$ 2,437	$ 2,354	$ 2,189	$ 2,608	$ 2,326	$ 2,381	$ 2,149
Long-Term Debt	$ 649	$ 681	$ 763	$1,030	$ 1,447	$ 1,327	$ 1,486	$ 1,538	$ 1,568	$ 1,801	$ 2,145	$ 2,303	$ 2,488	$ 2,968	$ 2,853
Deferred Credits	4	5	3	5	5	41	55	64	84	71	89	130	-	-	-
	$ 653	$ 686	$ 766	$1,035	$ 1,452	$ 1,368	$ 1,541	$ 1,602	$ 1,652	$ 1,872	$ 2,234	$ 2,433	$ 2,488	$ 2,968	$ 2,853
Reserves:															
Contingencies	$ 126	$ 124	$ 83	$ 82	$ 71	$ 70	$ 102	$ 133	$ 173	$ 200	$ 244	-*	-*	-*	-*
Insurance	80	80	90	91	91	100	101	104	110	114	129	-	-	-	-
Other	60	66	76	78	85	60	61	67	71	75	67	-	-	-	-
Total	$ 266	$ 270	$ 249	$ 251	$ 247	$ 230	$ 264	$ 304	$ 354	$ 389	$ 440	$ 434	$ 576	$ 584	$ 613
Minority Interest	$ 3	$ 3	$ 3	$ 3	$ 3	$ 3	$ 3	$ 4	$ 7	$ 6	$ 2	$ 3	$ 2	$ 2	$ 2
Stockholder Equity:															
Preferred Stock	$ 653	$ 654	$ 643	$ 685	$ 692	$ 702	$ 670	$ 635	$ 629	$ 654	$ 673	$ 665	$ 650	$ 644	$ 642
Common Stock	1,854	1,893	1,929	1,924	1,968	1,970	2,034	2,139	2,258	2,415	2,465	2,504	2,524	2,538	2,554
Capital Surplus	264	265	293	507	512	530	572	631	707	826	842	886	913	906	918
Earned Surplus	1,796	2,075	2,593	2,904	3,201	3,579	3,864	4,492	5,071	5,571	5,918	6,193	6,458	6,561	6,572
Total	$4,567	$4,885	$5,458	$6,038	$ 6,373	$ 6,781	$ 7,140	$ 7,897	$ 8,665	$ 9,466	$ 9,898	$10,248	$10,545	$10,649	$10,676
Total Liabilities	$6,816	$7,011	$8,273	$9,864	$10,107	$10,836	$10,653	$12,012	$13,116	$14,104	$14,769	$15,726	$15,937	$16,685	$16,294
Capital Expenditures	646	483	501	1,038	1,287	990	609	708	1,299	1,728	1,131	937	1,521	978	904
Cost to Complete	627	478	1,539	1,588	1,176	720	651	1,477	1,975	1,398	1,285	1,759	1,162	1,073	1,474

*1959, 1960, 1961, and 1962 reserves give totals only.
Source: AISI, Annual Statistical Reports, 1948-1962.

5. STEEL INDUSTRY

Comparative Industry Income Statements as of December 31, 1946-1961
(In Millions)

	1946	1947	1948	1949	1950	1951	1952	1953	1954	1955	1956	1957	1958	1959	1960	1961	1962
Revenue																	
Net billings	$4,778	$6,691	$8,081	$7,392	$9,486	$11,782	$10,804	$13,091	$10,533	$13,885	$15,151	$15,469	$12,442	$14,089	$14,056	$13,142	$13,835
Other income	34	30	38	44	49	63	54	65	60	88	111	123	109	144	165	153	142
Total Revenue	$4,812	$6,720	$8,119	$7,436	$9,535	$11,845	$10,858	$13,156	$10,593	$13,973	$15,272	$15,592	$12,551	$14,232	$14,221	$13,295	$13,977
Employment costs																	
Wages and salaries*	**	**	$2,730	$2,489	$2,852	$ 3,495	$ 3,474	$ 4,093	$ 3,532	$ 4,236	$ 4,566	$ 4,939	$ 4,353	$ 4,576	$ 4,838	$ 4,673	$ 4,762
Social security, etc.	42	50	73	71	124	149	142	164	157	214	242	273	251	296	470	466	546
Pensions	20	26	28	41	175	185	173	219	199	234	272	316	188	266	228	213	171
Total	$ 62	$ 76	$2,831	$2,601	$3,151	$ 3,829	$ 3,789	$ 4,476	$ 3,888	$ 4,684	$ 5,082	$ 5,528	$ 4,792	$ 5,138	$ 5,536	$ 5,352	$ 5,479
Materials, freight	4,087	5,589	3,931	3,517	4,356	5,488	5,352	6,088	4,578	6,086	7,001	6,745	5,245	6,442	6,011	5,528	6,127
Depreciation	169	233	302	277	327	374	500	614	671	735	748	766	673	665	698	739	928
Interest	27	21	20	22	25	29	43	55	53	53	55	65	79	94	101	123	133
State, local taxes	70	92	105	113	132	164	150	191	173	213	227	276	240	259	293	268	270
Federal taxes	133	286	389	377	777	1,279	483	997	593	1,104	1,046	1,081	735	806	772	596	473
Total Costs	$4,548	$6,297	$7,578	$6,907	$8,768	$11,163	$10,317	$12,421	$ 9,956	$12,875	$14,159	$14,460	$11,764	$13,403	$13,410	$12,606	$13,410
Net Income	$ 264	$ 423	$ 541	$ 529	$ 767	$ 682	$ 541	$ 735	$ 637	$ 1,098	$ 1,113	$ 1,132	$ 788	$ 830	$ 811	$ 689	$ 567
Cash Dividend	$ 147	$ 184	$ 205	$ 222	$ 311	$ 312	$ 316	$ 324	$ 343	$ 438	$ 508	$ 566	$ 540	$ 554	$ 564	$ 557	$ 508

*Omits payroll charged to construction or other nonoperating accounts.
**Included in materials and freight.

Source: AISI, Annual Statistical Reports, 1946-1962.

6. STEEL INDUSTRY

Steel Capacity by Principal Companies, 1938, 1954, and 1960*
(In Millions of Net Tons)

Company	Coke 1938	Coke 1948	Coke 1954	Coke 1960	Pig Iron 1938	Pig Iron 1948	Pig Iron 1954	Pig Iron 1960
U.S. Steel	18.6	23.6	24.6	22.4	22.9	24.9	28.0	31.7
Bethlehem Steel	7.1	8.7	11.3	11.4	7.4	9.9	12.4	15.0
Republic Steel	3.8	4.6	6.9	6.3	4.3	6.3	7.2	8.1
Subtotal	29.5	36.9	42.8	40.1	34.6	41.1	47.6	54.8
Jones & Laughlin	3.5	3.5	4.1	3.1	3.5	4.1	4.5	5.1
National Steel	1.6	2.5	4.0	4.5	2.4	3.1	4.5	5.9
Youngstown Sheet & Tube	2.9	2.8	3.2	4.4	3.2	3.5	4.1	4.1
Inland Steel	1.3	2.1	2.1	2.8	1.5	3.0	2.6	3.6
Armco Steel		.7	1.3	1.4	.8	1.6	2.2	3.1
Colorado Fuel & Iron	1.0	1.0	1.1	1.0	.6	1.2	1.4	1.5
Wheeling Steel	1.2	.7	1.7	1.7	1.2	.8	1.8	2.0
Sharon Steel		.7	.6	.4	.2	.7	.7	.9
Kaiser Steel		.4	1.1	1.5		.4	1.3	2.0
Crucible Steel	.4	.5	.8	.8	.5	.5	.9	.9
Pittsburgh Steel	.9	.5	.9	.8	.5	.6	1.0	1.0
Detroit Steel			.6	.6			.8	.8
McLouth Steel								1.4
Granite City Steel	.5		.5	.5	.4		.5	.8
Subtotal	42.8	52.3	64.8	63.6	49.4	60.6	73.9	87.9
All other**	8.7	10.2	8.2	9.7	8.2	6.8	8.1	9.0
Total	51.5	62.5	73.0	73.3	57.6	67.4	82.0	96.9
(Number of companies)	(26)	(28)	(26)	(26)	(52)	(32)	(34)	(34)

Company	Steel Ingots 1938	Steel Ingots 1948	Steel Ingots 1954	Steel Ingots 1960	Hot Rolled 1938	Hot Rolled 1948	Hot Rolled 1954	Hot Rolled 1960
U.S. Steel	28.9	31.2	38.7	42.0	20.1	25.0	28.5	29.8
Bethlehem Steel	11.2	13.9	18.5	23.0	8.2	10.5	14.6	17.6
Republic Steel	7.3	8.7	10.3	12.7	5.7	7.1	7.8	10.1
Subtotal	47.4	53.8	67.5	77.7	34.0	42.6	50.9	57.5
Jones & Laughlin	4.1	4.7	6.2	8.1	3.2	3.7	4.9	6.3
National Steel	3.8	4.1	6.0	7.0	3.7	3.2	5.0	5.9
Youngstown Sheet & Tube	3.5	4.0	5.5	6.8	2.4	3.2	4.4	5.4
Inland Steel	3.1	3.4	4.7	6.5	2.4	2.5	3.8	5.1
Armco Steel	3.0	3.4	3.2	6.8	2.2	2.3	3.6	5.5
Colorado Fuel & Iron	1.0	1.5	2.4	2.6	.7	1.1	1.7	2.1
Wheeling Steel	2.0	1.4	2.1	2.4	1.1	1.3	1.7	2.0
Sharon Steel	.6	1.6	1.6	2.0	.4	.8	1.0	1.1
Kaiser Steel		.9	1.5	3.0		.6	1.2	2.2
Crucible Steel	1.0	1.3	1.4	1.4	.8	.7	.7	1.0
Pittsburgh Steel	1.0	1.1	1.4	1.6	.6	.7	1.2	1.3
Detroit Steel			1.3	1.0			1.1	.8
McLouth Steel			1.0	2.0			.7	1.7
Granite City Steel	.5	.6	1.3	1.4	.3	.4	.9	1.2
Subtotal	71.0	81.8	107.1	130.3	51.8	63.1	82.8	99.1
All other**	11.2	12.4	17.4	18.3	12.2	11.2	14.0	14.7
Total	82.2	94.2	124.5	148.6	64.0	74.3	96.8	113.8
(Number of companies)	(74)	(78)	(85)	(84)	(124)	(100)	(94)	(88)

*As of July 1, 1938, and January 1, 1948, 1954, 1960.

**Capacities of integrated companies in other industries are included. For example, the Ford Motor Company's capacities in 1954 included over one million tons of coke and over 1.75 million tons for ingots and steel for castings. Its capacities in 1960 included 1.46 million tons of coke and 1.3 million tons of pig iron, and 1.94 million tons of basic steel.

Source: AISI, Iron and Steel Works Directory of the United States and Canada, 1938, 1948, 1954, 1960.

7. STEEL INDUSTRY

Steel Capacities by States, 1938-1960
(In Millions of Net Tons)

	Coke				Pig Iron				Steel Ingots				Hot-Rolled Products			
	1938	1948	1954	1960	1938	1948	1954	1960	1938	1948	1954	1960	1938	1948	1954	1960
Alabama	3.9	5.4	5.5	6.2	3.2	4.1	5.3	5.8	2.3	3.6	4.7	5.5	1.9	3.2	3.7	4.0
California		0.4	1.0	1.5		0.4	1.3	2.0	0.8	2.1	3.2	4.8	0.6	2.0	2.4	3.5
Colorado	1.0	1.0	1.2	1.0	0.6	0.9	0.9	1.0	0.9	1.3	1.5	1.8	0.7	1.0	1.0	1.3
Delaware									0.4	0.5	0.5	0.5	0.3	0.3	0.3	0.3
Georgia									0.1	0.2	0.3	0.3	0.1	0.1	0.2	0.3
Illinois	3.7	3.5	3.5	2.6	5.7	6.2	7.1	8.0	6.3	8.3	10.9	12.8	4.5	6.1	7.7	9.4
Indiana	6.6	8.5	9.2	9.8	5.4	8.0	8.7	10.3	9.2	11.1	15.0	18.4	7.0	9.4	12.6	14.8
Kentucky					0.3	0.7	0.8	1.1	1.0	1.2	1.8	1.8	0.7	0.6	1.3	1.5
Maryland	1.6	2.6	3.8	4.1	1.9	3.3	4.1	5.5	3.0	4.7	5.9	8.4	2.1	3.8	5.6	7.2
Massachusetts		1.1	0.7	0.7	0.2	0.2	0.2	0.2	0.2	0.3	0.3		0.2	0.2	0.3	0.2
Michigan	2.3	2.6	3.0	3.5	1.3	1.6	2.8	5.3	3.0	3.5	6.6	8.0	3.0	2.7	5.0	6.4
Minnesota	0.6	0.7	0.9	0.9	0.3	0.6	0.6	0.7	0.3	0.7	1.0	1.0	0.2	0.2	0.3	0.2
Missouri					0.1				0.6	0.4	0.6	0.8	0.6	0.4	0.5	0.7
New Jersey									0.2	0.3	0.2	0.2	0.2	0.2	0.2	0.2
New York	2.0	3.2	4.0	3.6	3.7	4.3	5.3	6.0	3.6	4.3	6.3	7.4	2.7	3.5	5.1	6.0
Ohio	8.1	9.5	11.1	11.3	11.1	13.6	16.8	18.8	15.6	18.8	24.4	28.3	11.1	15.6	19.0	21.6
Pennsylvania	16.1	19.8	23.5	20.7	16.6	20.0	23.2	26.3	23.4	28.1	34.0	39.1	19.0	20.8	25.0	28.0
Tennessee		0.2	0.3	0.3	0.1	0.1	0.2	0.2					0.1	0.1	0.1	0.1
Texas		0.6	0.8	0.8		0.7	0.7	1.0		0.6	1.8	2.5		0.5	1.4	1.9
Utah	0.2	1.2	1.3	1.4	0.2	1.3	1.7	1.8		1.3	1.9	2.3		1.0	1.4	2.0
Washington									0.2	0.3	0.4	0.4	0.1	0.2	0.3	0.2
West Virginia	0.6	2.6	3.6	3.9	0.8	1.5	2.2	2.6	1.9	2.3	2.7	3.4	2.0	2.1	2.8	3.4
Others								0.1	0.3	0.5	0.5	0.4	0.1	0.5	0.5	0.3
Total	46.7	62.9	73.4	72.3	51.5	67.5	81.9	96.7	73.3	94.4	124.5	148.1	57.2	74.4	96.7	113.5

Source: AISI, *Iron and Steel Works Directory of the United States and Canada*, 1938, 1948, 1954, 1960.

8. STEEL INDUSTRY

Capacity and Consumption of Selected Steel Products, 1957-1962
(Thousands of Net Tons)

	Carbon Plates				Carbon-Rolled Bars: All Carbon-Rolled Bars		Carbon-Rolled Bars: Carbon Hot-Rolled Bars			Galvanized Sheet		
	1957 Capacity	1958 Consumption	1960 Capacity	Estimated 1962 Consumption	1957 Capacity	1958 Consumption	1957 Capacity	1960 Capacity	Estimated 1962 Consumption	1957 Capacity	1960 Capacity	Estimated 1962 Consumption
Alabama	469	140	495	*	461	84	401	410	*	364	402	*
California	178	359	527	386	557	231	483	414	227	133	151	238
Colorado	7	25	7	*	80	20	80	80	*	---	---	*
Connecticut	---	25	---	112	321	52	66	35	103	---	---	46
Delaware	300	55	300	*	---	5	---	---	*	---	---	*
Georgia	---	40	---	*	90	20	90	90	*	---	---	*
Illinois	1,036	434	1,238	555	2,298	816	1,843	2,194	659	214	225	341
Indiana	1,189	234	1,238	240	2,677	288	2,154	2,147	250	595	655	204
Kentucky	261	45	321	*	25	36	25	24	*	343	343	*
Maryland	930	101	1,074	70	99	30	28	31	25	360	336	39
Massachusetts	---	106	---	147	60	81	---	---	104	---	---	68
Michigan	---	204	---	337	642	870	290	461	814	---	---	324
Minnesota	---	40	---	60	134	60	134	39	49	---	---	46
Missouri	---	83	---	115	198	73	198	297	61	---	---	76
New Jersey	---	155	---	214	172	101	30	30	110	---	---	102
New York	73	255	72	350	1,849	252	1,570	1,561	267	---	---	235
Ohio	544	438	316	598	3,995	564	3,332	3,374	462	956	1,112	366
Pennsylvania	3,250	889	3,830	793	4,960	466	3,808	3,706	373	360	395	295
Tennessee	---	71	---	*	65	39	65	65	*	---	---	*
Texas	598	254	772	171	135	126	135	149	74	---	---	68
Utah	584	75	657	*	---	8	---	2	*	---	---	*
Washington	18	49	18	*	97	25	93	86	*	---	---	*
West Virginia	---	101	---	*	82	17	82	82	*	432	535	*
Wisconsin	---	216	---	235	44	243	24	24	209	---	---	136
Others	---	444	---	*	83	387	83	118	*	---	---	*
Total	9,437	4,838	10,985	*	19,124	4,894	15,114	15,419	*	3,756	4,154	*

*Not available.

Exhibit 8 (continued)

	Carbon-Rolled Sheet and Strip: All Rolled Sheet and Strip		Hot-Rolled Sheet and Strip			Cold-Rolled Sheet and Strip			Stainless Steel: Stainless Steel Mill Shapes and Forms	Stainless Steel Sheet and Strip
	1957 Capacity	1958 Consumption	1957 Capacity	1960 Capacity	Estimated 1962 Consumption	1957 Capacity	1960 Capacity	Estimated 1962 Consumption	1958 Consumption	1962 Estimated Consumption
Alabama	1,157	79	767	1,246	*	390	730	*	1	*
California	524	582	176	439	336	348	446	630	30	20
Colorado	---	27	---	2	*	---	---	*	1	*
Connecticut	---	173	---	---	113	---	248	170	17	9
Delaware	---	14	---	---	*	---	---	*	1	*
Georgia	---	62	---	66	*	---	---	*	5	*
Illinois	1,459	2,140	762	1,623	993	697	677	1,684	31	25
Indiana	7,883	1,171	5,796	6,578	502	2,087	3,455	981	18	16
Kentucky	1,228	250	948	1,069	*	280	438	*	6	*
Maryland	3,586	126	2,610	2,961	64	976	1,118	106	3	3
Massachusetts	54	203	---	---	125	54	54	195	15	14
Michigan	8,903	3,920	5,071	5,943	1,868	3,832	4,071	3,565	45	51
Minnesota	---	313	---	2	75	---	---	143	5	4
Missouri	---	328	---	---	126	---	---	202	6	5
New Jersey	67	349	---	12	210	67	69	345	22	14
New York	4,401	1,153	2,535	2,641	582	1,866	1,960	1,122	35	29
Ohio	14,665	3,354	8,664	10,708	1,360	6,001	7,445	2,527	51	44
Pennsylvania	19,301	1,501	5,610	8,096	780	3,691	3,837	1,244	31	24
Tennessee	---	180	---	2	*	---	---	*	2	*
Texas	---	254	---	---	120	---	---	174	8	4
Utah	524	12	524	650	*	---	---	*	--	*
Washington	---	42	---	---	*	---	---	*	2	*
West Virginia	1,126	192	66	---	*	1,060	1,060	*	--	*
Wisconsin	---	850	---	---	400	---	---	690	30	20
Others	32	775	---	32	*	32	29	*	22	*
Total	63,867	18,050	33,529	42,070	*	21,381	25,637	*	387	*

Sources: 1957 Capacity Directory of Iron and Steel Works of the United States and Canada (AISI) 1957.
1958 Consumption 1958 Census of Manufactures, Vol. I, pp. 7-62.
1961 Capacity Directory of Iron and Steel Works of the United States and Canada (AISI) 1960.
1962 Consumption estimated by Iron Age, December 27, 1962.

9. STEEL INDUSTRY

Consumption of Materials Used in Making Pig Iron and Steel, 1946-1962

A. Blast Furnace--Materials Used to Produce One Ton of Pig, 1946-1962 (Net Tons)

Year	Iron Ore	Scrap	Scale	Total	Lime-stone	Coke	Year	Iron Ore	Scrap	Scale	Total	Lime-stone	Coke
1946	1.725	.033	.136	1.894	.406	.934	1954	1.656	.050	.153	1.859	.395	.873
1947	1.748	.030	.127	1.905	.412	.950	1955	1.662	.049	.149	1.860	.387	.873
1948	1.767	.035	.126	1.928	.440	.954	1956	1.630	.045	.127	1.802	.362	.850
1949	1.753	.042	.123	1.918	.428	.935	1957	1.642	.040	.125	1.807	.355	.708
1950	1.737	.056	.110	1.903	.429	.922	1958	1.603	.036	.120	1.759	.329	.799
1951	1.725	.054	.102	1.881	.432	.924	1959	1.588	.039	.106	1.733	.314	.785
1952	1.710	.055	.110	1.875	.426	.922	1960	1.573	.042	.094	1.709	.303	.749
1953	1.691	.053	.125	1.869	.418	.906	1961	1.577	.043	.091	1.711	.301	.708
							1962	1.557	.044	.094	1.695	.282	.690

B. Cupolas--Materials Used, 1949-1962 (Thousands of Net Tons)

	1949	1950	1951	1952	1953	1954	1955	1956	1957	1958	1959	1960	1961	1962
Scrap	110	106	122	88	94	732	1,006	752	832	641	1,046	1,123	1,220	1,330
Pig Iron	299	369	459	366	417	680	830	666	636	481	581	599	407	321
Total	409	475	582	454	511	1,412	1,836	1,418	1,467	1,122	1,627	1,722	1,627	1,651

B. Steelmaking Furnaces--Materials Used, 1946-1962 (Thousands of Net Tons)

	Open Hearth			Electric			Basic Oxygen			Bessemer		
	Scrap	Pig Iron	Total	Scrap	Pig Iron	Total	Scrap	Pig Iron*	Total	Scrap	Pig Iron	Total
1949	34,795	41,817	76,613	3,712	66	3,778	--	--	--	159	4,572	4,731
1950	42,762	50,702	93,464	6,069	109	6,178	--	--	--	247	5,569	5,816
1951	45,668	55,435	101,103	7,082	84	7,166	--	--	--	293	6,135	6,428
1952	41,736	49,294	91,030	6,836	68	6,905	--	--	--	175	3,864	4,039
1953	46,698	61,106	107,804	7,328	134	7,462	--	--	--	219	4,249	4,468
1954	38,065	48,511	86,576	5,143	122	5,265	--	--	--	146	2,787	2,933
1955	50,074	63,473	113,547	7,961	487	8,448	--	--	--	196	3,610	3,806
1956	49,089	61,824	110,913	8,469	586	9,055	**	**	**	187	3,537	3,724
1957	44,928	64,800	109,728	7,742	738	8,480	**	**	**	125	2,762	2,887
1958	33,533	48,301	81,834	6,696	1,310	8,006	**	**	**	103	1,503	1,606
1959	37,244	50,926	88,170	7,910	354	8,264	569	1,553	2,122	123	1,459	1,582
1960	38,543	55,037	93,580	7,662	312	7,974	960	2,883	3,843	88	1,272	1,360
1961	37,036	54,439	91,475	7,836	231	8,067	1,063	3,487	4,550	52	956	1,007
1962	35,958	54,278	90,236	8,381	166	8,547	1,527	4,878	6,405	52	877	929

*Includes molden metal.
**Included in Electric Furnace Consumption.
Source: AISI, Annual Statistical Reports, 1946-1962.

Iron Ore: U.S. Production, Percent Beneficiated, and Imports, 1939-1961
(In Thousands of Gross Tons)

	Production					%	Imports							
Year	Total U.S.	L. Sup.	South	East	Other	Benefi-ciated	Total	Canada	Venezuela	Peru	Sweden	Chile	Brazil	Liberia
1945	88,376	74,821	6,050	3,615	3,890	22.4	1,189	700	-0-	-0-	-0-	215	-0-	-0-
1946	70,843	59,042	5,903	2,593	3,305	22.4	2,813	1,111	-0-	-0-	233	1,096	-0-	-0-
1947	93,092	76,384	7,197	3,987	5,524	23.1	4,889	1,540	-0-	-0-	1,287	1,670	86	-0-
1948	101,003	82,277	7,751	4,415	6,560	23.6	6,086	963	-0-	-0-	1,331	2,632	296	-0-
1949	84,937	68,494	7,602	3,864	4,977	24.5	7,395	1,596	-0-	-0-	2,047	2,627	355	-0-
1950	98,045	79,627	7,507	4,475	6,436	27.5	8,216	1,843	-0-	-0-	2,037	2,570	692	-0-
1951	116,505	93,947	8,588	5,181	8,789	26.5	10,145	1,968	635	-0-	2,521	2,767	1,038	110
1952	97,918	77,095	7,624	4,426	8,773	27.8	9,761	1,822	1,846	-0-	2,111	1,862	1,011	572
1953	117,995	95,655	7,692	5,162	9,486	30.6	11,085	1,842	1,950	845	2,098	2,363	458	720
1954	78,094	60,994	6,150	4,084	6,866	36.5	15,783	3,537	5,210	1,922	1,544	1,664	596	765
1955	103,002	83,255	7,616	5,440	8,752	34.4	23,443	10,072	7,120	1,544	1,221	1,059	1,010	928
1956	97,877	77,817	6,035	4,867	9,158	39.4	30,358	13,720	9,246	1,814	1,002	1,538	1,214	1,218
1957	106,148	83,531	6,749	4,961	10,851	40.3	33,653	12,537	12,293	2,359	677	2,741	1,431	1,013
1958	67,709	51,777	3,827	3,412	8,693	48.2	27,833	8,295	12,170	1,966	113	3,257	832	838
1959	60,276	43,950	4,350	3,669	8,307	51.3	35,623	13,453	13,543	2,271	136	3,577	1,200	1,090
1960	88,784	71,792	4,365	4,125	8,502	55.5	34,590	10,603	14,556	2,762	94	3,942	1,461	907
1961	71,543	53,680	3,764	4,734	9,365	63.7	25,843	9,685	10,515	1,211	78	2,599	888	719

Note: Because of the differences in ore, the values differ considerably: In 1961 the f.o.b. values in millions were:

Canada $99.1 ($10.24/ton)
Peru 11.8 ($9.72/ton)
Chile 21.9 ($8.42/ton)
Liberia 6.7 ($9.41/ton)
Venezuela $99.2 ($9.46/ton)
Sweden 1.2 ($14.75/ton)
Brazil. 9.6 ($10.82/ton)

Sources: U.S. Department of the Interior, Bureau of Mines, 1961 Minerals Yearbook and Mineral Industry Surveys, December, 1961, and 1961 Annual Issue for percent U.S. mine shipments beneficiated and values of imports. AISI, Annual Statistical Reports, 1945-1961 for all other figures.

11. STEEL INDUSTRY

Lake Superior Ore: Monthly Shipments, Inventory at Furnaces and Consumption, 1958-1961

(In Thousands of Iron Tons)

Month	Shipments				E.O.M. Inventory at Furnace				Consumption			
	1958	1959	1960	1961	1958	1959	1960	1961	1958	1959	1960	1961
January	0	0	0	0	57,349	53,140	49,411	63,592	7,605	9,832	11,856	6,214
February	0	0	0	0	50,379	46,473	42,505	59,980	6,484	9,707	11,337	6,060
March	0	0	28	0	46,272	38,504	35,016	55,923	6,947	11,512	11,788	6,953
April	62	2,980	5,648	213	43,437	32,816	32,667	51,570	5,888	11,540	10,433	7,109
May	4,061	12,765	12,474	5,237	43,382	37,017	38,852	50,398	6,203	11,848	9,740	8,301
June	8,041	12,987	12,026	8,785	47,904	43,649	47,086	53,155	6,674	11,131	8,060	8,545
July	9,589	6,845	12,066	9,936	53,725	47,924	55,776	57,318	6,624	5,632	7,014	8,518
August,	9,324	798	10,064	9,928	58,075	49,498	62,942	62,086	7,417	1,508	6,728	8,767
September	8,706	758	8,375	9,025	62,325	51,592	67,634	65,238	7,898	1,464	6,356	8,964
October	8,481	1,096	7,002	8,324	65,842	53,024	70,846	67,556	9,123	1,593	6,694	9,681
November	4,528	5,311	1,943	5,845	65,904	57,537	70,351	68,057	9,250	7,091	6,362	9,058
December	75	3,165	0	128	60,265	56,941	67,116	62,605	9,573	11,539	5,895	9,532
Total	52,868	46,705	69,626	57,422	---	----	----	----	89,686	94,398	102,263	97,712

Source: American Iron Ore Association, Iron Ore, 1958, 1959, 1960, 1961.

12. STEEL INDUSTRY

Consumption and Sources of Scrap, 1946-1961

A. Annual Consumption of Ferrous Scrap (Thousands of Gross Tons)

Year	Consumption of Ferrous Scrap			Foreign Trade in Scrap	
	Total	Purchased	Home	Exports	Imports
1946	44,182	20,848	23,334	122	27
1947	54,343	26,148	28,195	197	32
1948	58,003	29,057	28,946	186	388
1949	48,516	22,475	26,041	203	977
1950	61,497	29,402	32,095	186	652
1951	68,518	33,822	34,696	196	334
1952	61,626	30,521	31,105	300	88
1953	69,026	35,592	36,434	271	116
1954	54,790	25,200	29,590	1,346	184
1955	72,655	34,511	38,144	4,537	204
1956	71,709	35,109	36,600	5,363	232
1957	65,669	29,618	36,051	5,921	213
1958	50,243	22,127	28,116	2,686	296
1959	58,980	25,701	33,279	4,336	276
1960	59,347	23,567	35,780	6,412	162
1961	57,434	22,464	34,770	8,683	240
1962*	53,600	22,230	31,370	4,500	N.A.

B. Scrap Purchased, Received, Consumed by Sheets, 1961 (Gross Tons)

State	Home Scrap Produced	Purchased Scrap Received	Total Scrap for Consumption	Total Scrap Consumed
New England	213,843	221,349	435,192	415,327
New York	1,472,693	1,031,497	2,504,190	2,401,759
Pennsylvania (East)	2,113,016	1,498,838	3,611,854	3,625,965
Pennsylvania (West)	5,756,189	2,442,893	8,199,082	7,519,327
Illinois	3,039,074	3,026,564	6,065,638	6,065,038
Indiana	4,321,447	2,293,035	6,614,482	6,567,657
Michigan	2,752,833	2,112,791	4,865,624	4,892,246
Ohio (East)	4,837,936	2,921,589	7,759,525	7,553,420
Ohio (West)	1,186,075	677,778	1,863,853	1,968,883
Delaware, D.C. and Maryland	2,062,087	683,338	2,745,425	2,711,915
Virginia and West Virginia	692,936	874,850	1,567,786	1,547,662
Alabama	1,273,449	1,096,222	2,369,671	2,178,882
Kentucky, Mississippi and Tennessee	532,783	921,559	1,454,342	1,353,762
Texas	625,867	861,951	1,487,818	1,391,294
Colorado, Utah, Idaho, and Montana	939,284	381,055	1,320,339	1,348,413
California	1,165,814	976,764	2,142,578	2,008,878
Other	1,367,408	2,579,169	3,946,577	3,884,124
Total	34,352,734	24,601,242	58,953,976	56,434,552

*Estimate.

Source: Institute of Scrap Iron and Steel, Yearbook (1962), Blast Furnace and Steel Plant, February, 1963, p. 151.

13. STEEL INDUSTRY

Shipments of Products by Type of Steel, 1946-1962
(In Millions of Net Tons)

Steel Products	1929	1935	1939	1946	1947	1948	1949	1950	1951	1952	1953	1954	1955	1956	1957	1958	1959	1960	1961	1962
Semifinished	*	.8	1.3	2.9	3.8	3.8	2.9	4.1	4.6	4.3	4.5	2.7	4.8	4.3	3.4	2.4	2.9	2.8	3.9	3.9
Structural, piling	4.6	1.4	2.7	3.7	4.8	4.6	4.0	4.5	5.2	4.4	5.4	4.9	5.1	5.8	7.4	4.4	4.4	5.3	4.7	4.8
Plates	4.4	1.6	3.3	4.1	6.3	7.0	5.8	5.7	7.9	7.0	7.7	5.3	6.8	7.7	9.3	5.3	5.8	6.1	6.3	6.7
Rails	2.7	.9	1.8	3.1	3.8	3.5	2.9	2.9	3.2	2.5	3.1	1.8	2.1	2.3	2.3	1.0	1.2	1.2	0.8	1.0
Bars, tool steel	7.7	4.0	5.9	9.2	11.2	11.4	9.3	11.4	12.9	12.0	13.5	9.3	13.0	13.2	11.3	8.8	10.6	10.6	10.7	11.7
Standard pipe						2.3	2.2	2.6	2.9	2.4	2.8	2.3	3.0	2.9	2.7	2.2	2.2	2.1	2.1	2.2
Oil country goods						1.5	1.4	1.7	1.9	1.6	2.0	2.3	2.5	2.6	2.8	1.2	2.1	1.2	1.6	1.6
Line pipe	4.4	1.8	3.5	4.7	6.1	2.0	2.5	3.7	3.2	2.9	3.5	2.6	3.1	3.4	4.2	2.6	2.8	2.7	2.6	2.5
Tubing						1.0	0.8	1.0	1.3	1.4	1.5	0.9	1.2	1.3	1.1	0.8	1.2	1.0	1.0	1.0
Wire products	2.9	1.8	3.2	3.3	4.2	4.3	3.5	4.5	4.8	3.9	3.8	3.5	4.3	3.9	3.4	3.0	3.4	3.0	3.1	3.1
Tin mill products	2.0	1.9	2.6	3.7	4.5	4.8	4.1	5.3	5.6	5.1	5.4	5.1	6.4	6.3	5.9	6.1	5.8	6.0	6.1	6.1
Sheets, hot rolled		2.5	4.6	5.5	7.3	7.1	6.2	7.8	8.2	6.1	7.7	6.1	9.4	8.8	7.8	6.3	7.8	7.9	7.4	8.3
Sheets, cold rolled		1.6	2.0	4.1	5.7	7.0	7.1	9.6	9.8	8.2	11.5	9.8	15.2	13.3	11.9	10.3	12.7	14.5	12.2	13.6
Sheets, galvanized	6.1	.9	1.4	1.5	1.6	1.6	1.8	2.3	2.0	2.0	2.3	2.4	2.9	3.0	2.4	2.8	2.8	3.1	3.3	3.5
Sheets, other coated		.4	.5	*	*	0.1	0.1	0.2	0.3	0.2	0.3	0.2	0.3	0.2	0.2	0.2	0.3	0.3	0.3	0.3
Electrical sheets, strip		*	*	0.3	0.5	0.5	0.4	0.7	0.8	0.6	0.8	0.6	0.8	0.8	0.6	0.5	0.6	0.6	0.5	0.6
Strip, hot rolled	2.5	1.7	1.2	1.4	1.7	1.7	1.6	2.3	2.2	1.8	2.2	1.5	2.1	1.8	1.4	1.0	1.3	1.3	1.5	1.6
Strip, cold rolled		.5	.7	1.3	1.5	1.7	1.9	1.9	2.1	1.7	2.2	1.3	1.7	1.5	1.3	1.0	1.4	1.3	1.3	1.5
	37.3	21.8	34.7	48.8	63.1	66.0	58.1	72.2	78.9	68.0	80.2	62.6	84.7	83.3	79.9	59.9	69.4	71.1	69.5	74.0
Carbon	40.6	21.8	34.7	45.1	58.6	61.0	54.4	67.1	72.7	62.3	73.7	58.9	78.4	77.0	74.5	55.1	64.2	66.2	64.5	68.2
Stainless, heat resistance	*	*	*	0.3	0.3	0.3	0.3	0.5	0.5	0.6	0.6	0.4	0.7	0.7	0.6	0.5	0.6	0.6	0.7	0.7
Alloy (exclusive of stainless)	*	*	*	3.3	4.1	4.7	3.5	4.7	5.7	5.1	5.8	3.8	5.6	5.6	4.7	3.3	4.6	4.4	4.3	5.1

*Included in another category.

Source: Iron Age, January 2, 1930, pp. 10-11 for 1929 figures; January 2, 1936, p. 53, for 1935 alloy shipments; AISI, Annual Statistical Reports, 1935, 1939, 1946-61 for all others.

14. STEEL INDUSTRY

Distribution of Steel by Market, 1929-1962
(In Millions of Net Tons)

Market	1929	1935	1939	1946	1947	1948	1949	1950	1951	1952	1953	1954	1955	1956	1957	1958	1959	1960	1961	1962
Converting, Processing . . .			.8	1.9	2.8	3.4	2.5	3.9	4.2	3.0	3.5	2.4	3.7	3.8	3.4	2.8	3.1	2.9	2.4	2.3
Forgings (exclusive of Auto)	.3	N.A.	.1	.7	.7	0.9	0.8	1.1	1.5	1.4	1.4	0.8	1.3	1.5	1.1	0.8	1.0	0.8	0.8	0.9
Bolts, Nuts	.7	.3	.3	1.1	1.3	1.3	0.9	1.4	1.6	1.3	1.3	1.0	1.5	1.5	1.1	0.9	1.1	1.1	1.0	1.1
Warehouses	3.6	2.5	4.8	8.4	9.6	10.0	8.9	11.7	12.7	11.9	13.1	9.9	13.6	14.5	12.2	9.9	11.2	11.3	10.8	10.8
Construction	3.5	1.7	3.5	4.1	5.3	5.1	4.9	5.6	6.9	5.5	7.0	6.6	7.2	7.9	9.1	6.6	6.3	7.5	7.2	7.3
Contractor's Products	1.0	.3	1.2	1.6	2.2	2.5	2.1	3.1	3.1	2.6	3.3	3.0	4.0	4.1	3.4	3.5	3.6	3.6	3.8	4.2
Automotive	5.4	4.6	5.4	6.6	9.3	10.2	11.0	14.5	13.0	10.9	14.7	11.8	18.7	14.1	14.2	10.1	14.2	14.6	12.6	15.2
Rail Transportation.	6.2	1.4	3.1	3.8	4.9	5.2	3.7	4.3	5.8	4.0	4.8	2.5	3.5	4.2	4.1	1.5	2.4	2.5	1.6	2.0
Ships	.3	.1	.5	.3	.3	0.7	0.7	0.3	0.9	1.0	0.9	0.5	0.6	0.8	1.3	0.8	0.6	0.6	0.7	0.7
Aircraft	-	-	-	-	-	0.0	0.0	0.0	0.2	0.1	0.2	0.1	0.1	0.1	0.1	0.0	0.1	0.1	0.1	0.1
Oil and Gas	2.5	.7	1.6	2.0	3.2	4.3	4.5	5.3	5.2	4.5	5.5	4.7	5.4	5.6	6.5	3.4	4.7	3.7	3.9	3.8
Mining, Lumbering	.2	.1	.1	.2	.3	0.3	0.3	0.3	0.4	0.3	0.3	0.2	0.3	0.4	0.3	0.2	0.2	0.3	0.3	0.3
Agricultural.	1.6	1.0	.8	1.0	1.2	1.4	1.5	1.5	1.6	1.3	1.2	1.2	1.3	1.1	1.1	1.2	1.3	1.0	1.0	1.1
Machinery, Tools	.7	.4	.6	2.4	3.0	3.2	2.7	3.5	4.2	3.8	4.3	3.5	4.7	5.0	4.5	3.2	4.2	4.0	3.8	4.2
Electrical Equipment	.7	.5	.6	1.2	1.6	1.6	1.2	1.8	2.0	1.6	2.1	1.7	2.3	2.4	2.1	1.8	2.0	2.1	2.0	2.2
Appliances, etc.	.5	.3	1.1	1.2	1.6	2.0	1.3	2.1	1.8	1.4	2.1	1.4	2.2	2.1	1.6	1.6	1.8	1.8	1.7	1.9
Other Domestic Equipment.	1.1	.3	.6	1.4	1.7	1.7	1.3	1.8	2.0	1.6	2.1	1.7	2.2	2.3	1.8	1.7	1.8	2.0	1.8	1.9
Containers	1.8	2.1	2.7	4.3	5.1	5.3	4.7	5.9	6.5	5.6	6.1	5.9	6.7	6.8	6.2	6.6	6.3	6.4	6.6	6.7
Military	-	-	-	-	-	0.0	0.0	0.2	1.2	2.1	2.7	1.0	0.9	0.5	0.4	0.2	0.1	0.2	0.2	0.2
Nonclassified Shipments. . .	5.5	3.9	2.5	3.6	4.7	3.6	1.6	1.3	1.3	0.8	0.9	0.7	0.9	0.9	0.8	0.7	2.0	2.1	2.1	2.1
Total Domestic.	35.6	20.2	30.3	45.8	58.8	62.7	54.6	69.6	76.1	64.7	77.5	60.6	81.8	79.6	75.3	57.5	68.0	68.6	64.4	69.0
Export	1.9	.8	2.1	3.0	4.2	3.3	3.5	2.6	2.8	3.3	2.7	2.5	3.6	3.6	4.6	2.4	1.4	2.5	1.7	1.6
Total Shipments	37.5	21.0	32.4	48.8	63.0	66.0	58.1	72.2	78.9	68.0	80.2	63.1	84.7	83.2	79.9	59.9	69.4	71.1	66.1	70.6

Source: Iron Age, January 2, 1930, pp. 8-11 for 1929; January 2, 1936, pp. 53-54 for 1935, and March 21, 1940 p. 79c for 1939; AISI, Annual Statistical Reports, 1946-62 for all other years.

15. STEEL INDUSTRY

Distribution of Carbon, Alloy, and Stainless Steel by Type of Channel--1947, 1957, 1967
(Net Tons)

	Net Direct Mill Shipments*			Service Center Shipments			Total Shipments		
	1947	1957	1967	1947	1957	1967	1947	1957	1967
Carbon Steel	48,397,095	60,744,490	80,713,293	10,208,591	13,787,119	20,271,707	58,605,596	74,531,609	100,985,000
Alloy Steel	3,933,729	4,229,308	6,529,681	222,279	513,905	968,319	4,156,008	4,743,213	7,498,000
Total Stainless Steel Shipments	242,182	413,471	720,193	53,364	206,284	419,557	295,546	619,755	1,139,750
Plates	8,560	18,147	36,208	2,713	20,549	37,115	11,273	38,696	73,323
H. R. Bars	21,946	40,194	78,018	3,230	13,170	25,927	25,176	53,364	103,945
C. F. Bars	18,013	24,584	50,590	4,749	31,018	67,147	22,762	55,602	117,737
Mech. Tub.	1,857	3,363	7,288	786	850	1,539	2,643	4,213	8,827
Press. Tub.	**	20,160	43,305	**	3,477	7,058	**	23,637	50,363
Wire Drawn	7,332	17,476	35,161	1,559	9,634	22,735	8,891	27,110	57,896
H. R. Sheets	22,086	20,215	28,437	10,272	5,832	12,051	32,358	26,047	40,488
C. R. Sheets	44,040	47,863	80,536	23,440	89,054	184,773	67,480	136,917	265,309
H. R. Strip	997	8,725	9,003	37	98	104	1,034	8,823	9,107
C. R. Strip	96,875	175,618	306,462	4,413	20,236	40,599	101,288	195,854	347,061
All other	20,476	37,126	45,185	2,165	12,366	20,509	22,641	49,492	65,694
Grand Total	52,573,006	65,387,269	88,235,167	10,484,144	14,507,308	21,659,583	63,057,150	79,894,577	109,894,750

*Excluding shipments to warehouses (service centers).
**Included in Mech. Tub.
Source: The International Nickel Co., Inc., Stainless Steel Market Study, 1961 (Outlook & Summary).

16. STEEL INDUSTRY

Top 13 Market Areas for Stainless Steel, 1957, 1967
(Net Tons)

Area	1957	1967
Detroit	58,213	80,924
New York	43,717	76,356
Chicago	42,584	75,356
Cleveland	26,006	43,200
Los Angeles	24,800	56,818
Philadelphia	21,254	34,432
Boston	13,922	26,574
Hartford	12,806	21,583
Cincinnati	10,535	20,685
Buffalo	10,213	14,246
Pittsburgh	9,813	16,925
Milwaukee	9,428	17,654
Columbus	8,402	19,057

Source: The International Nickel Co., Inc., Stainless Steel Market Study, 1961 (Outlook & Summary).

Distribution of Cold Rolled Stainless Sheet, 1947, 1957, 1967
(Net Tons)

Major Market Class	Direct Mill Shipments			Service Center Shipments			Total Shipments		
	1947	1957	1967	1947	1957	1967	1947	1957	1967
Net Conversion and Forgings (Exclusive of Auto)	493	853	862	36	153	155	529	1,006	1,017
Bolts, Nuts, Rivets, and Screws	7	8	21	289	1,444	3,765	296	1,452	3,786
Construction, Contractors' Products	1,744	4,019	8,399	3,181	18,047	37,716	4,925	22,066	46,116
Automotive	417	3,483	5,709	57	1,178	1,931	474	4,661	7,640
Rail Transportation	1,567	382	397	600	360	373	2,167	742	770
Shipbuilding and Marine Equipment	305	210	403	1,282	2,173	4,167	1,587	2,383	4,570
Aircraft	1,503	3,617	5,677	1,037	6,145	9,645	2,540	9,762	15,322
Oil and Gas Drilling	6	15	23	*	*	*	6	15	23
Mining, Quarrying, and Lumbering	25	88	120	29	252	342	54	340	462
Agricultural	86	211	405	41	249	509	127	460	914
General Purpose Industrial Equipment	535	1,976	5,796	623	5,666	16,622	1,158	7,642	22,418
Chemical Industry Equipment	516	707	1,080	1,201	4,054	6,196	1,717	4,761	7,276
Construction and Related Equipment	*	37	121	1	98	319	1	135	440
Food Processing Equipment	2,407	4,020	8,619	2,332	9,589	20,561	4,739	13,609	29,180
Metal Working Equipment	60	1,725	3,977	78	5,542	12,779	138	7,267	16,756
Pulp and Paper Equipment	29	78	150	153	1,015	1,956	182	1,093	2,106
Textile Equipment	309	108	125	3,776	3,248	3,762	4,085	3,356	3,887
Other Special Industrial Equipment	781	2,212	6,415	893	6,227	18,057	1,674	8,439	24,472
Tractors	*	3	4	1	9	11	1	12	15
Hand Tools	*	19	23	1	54	68	1	73	91
Electrical Machinery and Equipment	553	460	946	524	1,073	2,208	1,077	1,533	3,154
Appliances, Utensils, and Cutlery	8,014	3,614	7,186	2,133	2,368	4,709	10,147	5,982	11,895
Other Domestic and Commercial Equipment	2,177	3,851	7,893	4,039	17,592	36,056	6,216	21,443	43,949
Containers	2,076	647	1,033	828	636	1,015	2,904	1,283	2,048
Ordnance	23	564	565	15	909	910	38	1,473	1,475
Nonreporting	9,445	*	*	*	*	*	9,445	*	*
Warehouse	23,440	89,054	184,773	*	*	*	*	*	*
Total Domestic	56,518	121,961	250,722	23,150	88,081	183,832	56,228	120,988	249,781
Export	10,962	14,956	14,587	290	973	941	11,252	15,929	15,528
Grand Total	67,480	136,917	265,309	23,440	89,054	184,773	67,480	136,917	265,309

*Included in Mech. Tub.

Source: The International Nickel Co., Inc., Stainless Steel Market Study, 1961 (Outlook & Summary).

18. STEEL INDUSTRY

Iron Ore, Coke, Pig Iron, Scrap, and Finished Steel Prices, 1929-1962
(Annual Averages per Net Ton)

	Iron Ore**	Coke***	Pig Iron#	Scrap##	Steel (Composite)###	Hot Rolled HR Strip+	Hot Rolled A Sheet+	Cold Rolled A Strip+	Cold Rolled A Sheet+	Galvanized Sheet+	Plates+	Stainless Sheet+
1929	$ 4.02	$ 2.75	$16.46	$16.03	$ 50.80	$ 37.60	$ 42.40	$ 55.40	$ 81.20	$ 71.00	$ 38.60	N.A.
1935	4.02	3.61	16.10	11.56	48.80	37.00	37.00	52.00	59.00	62.00	36.00	$ 720.00
1939	4.42	4.09	18.92	15.37	52.80	41.20	41.20	57.20	62.00	70.00	42.00	720.00
1943	3.97	6.45	21.09	18.86	53.00	42.00	42.00	56.00	61.00	70.00	42.00	720.00
1946	4.29	8.10	24.35	18.59	60.00	46.60	48.00	60.60	64.84	79.80	49.40	763.00
1947	4.96	10.83	30.66	32.41	68.40	52.60	52.60	67.00	67.00	74.40	56.00	779.80
1948	5.31	13.63	38.20	36.90	78.20	60.60	60.00	75.20	74.60	82.60	63.80	795.80
1949	6.43	14.58	41.23	28.63	84.20	65.20	65.20	80.20	80.00	88.00	68.60	801.00
1950	6.88	14.20	42.72	35.05	88.00	65.40	67.40	85.00	82.40	88.60	70.40	807.60
1951	7.41	14.65	47.05	40.34	94.20	70.00	72.00	95.00	87.00	96.00	74.00	862.50
1952	7.75	14.75	48.06	39.29	96.40	72.12	73.52	97.00	88.98	98.38	75.60	882.60
1953	8.75	14.64	49.96	36.61	102.60	76.64	77.10	105.80	93.64	103.64	80.20	948.60
1954	8.84	14.38	50.53	26.63	106.60	79.74	79.74	112.00	97.24	107.24	83.24	912.40
1955	9.02	13.69	51.59	36.20	112.20	83.62	83.78	119.60	102.54	112.80	87.12	916.20
1956	9.70	14.62	54.59	48.35	120.00	89.18	89.18	129.60	109.76	120.46	92.60	963.00
1957	10.22	15.38	58.17	42.44	131.00	96.00	96.00	140.20	118.00	129.00	99.60	1,087.60
1958	10.22	15.01	59.34	35.20	137.20	99.96	99.90	145.52	122.86	134.30	103.90	1,100.00
1959	10.22	14.96	59.30	38.76	130.60	102.00	102.00	148.50	125.50	137.50	106.00	1,100.00
1960	10.22	15.13	59.28	29.44	139.60	102.00	102.00	148.50	125.50	137.50	106.00	1,080.00
1961	10.22	15.13	59.32	31.15*	139.60	102.00	102.00	148.50	125.50	137.50	106.00	1,040.00
1962	9.51	15.13	58.85	25.47*	139.60	102.00	102.00	148.50	125.50	137.50	106.00	1,005.40

*Estimate.
**Mesabi non-Bessemer at lower lake ports, converted to net ton.
***Connellsville furnace coke.
#Composite of basic pig at six locations, converted to net ton.
##Heavy melting scrap, Pittsburgh, converted to net ton.
###Composite compiled by American Metals Market. Weighted average of bars, plates, pipe, sheets, structural shapes, wire nails, hot rolled strips, and tin plate.
+At Pittsburgh.

NOTE: All prices held firm during the year 1962 except iron ore, which was cut $.80 a gross ton in January and scrap which fluctuated as follows: January, $34.15; February, $32.36; March, $29.02; April, $27.41; May, $24.11; June, $22.77; July, $23.66; August, $24.37; September, $23.06; October, $20.98; November, $20.53; December, $23.21.

Source: The Iron Age, Annual Review issue (first issue in January) for iron ore, pig iron, and all steel prices except steel composite. Department of Commerce, Business Statistics, 1961, and Survey of Current Business, February, 1963.

19. STEEL INDUSTRY

Employees, Average Earnings, Real Earnings, Total Employment Costs, Man-Hours, and Output per Man-Hour, 1939-1962

Year	No. of Hourly Workers (Thousands)	Average Hourly Earnings*	Real Earnings in 1957-59 Purchasing Power**	Total Employment Costs per Hour for Workers***	Total Hourly Worker Man-Hours (Millions)	Output for Hourly Worker Man-Hours (1947=100)
1940	454.0	$ .843	$1.727	$ .905	857.8	82.0
1943	487.2	1.121	1.859	1.190	1,089.8	#
1946	458.2	1.279	1.881	1.404	836.9	#
1947	489.1	1.456	1.871	1.563	984.4	100.0
1948	503.4	1.573	1.877	1.679	1,028.5	100.4
1949	491.6	1.633	1.967	1.753	884.7	102.8
1950	503.3	1.681	2.006	1.908	1,023.1	111.9
1951	540.4	1.872	2.068	2.114	1,132.2	113.0
1952	519.2	2.044	2.210	2.315	970.7	117.6
1953	544.3	2.145	2.302	2.440	1,119.3	118.8
1954	478.0	2.190	2.340	2.512	900.6	115.9
1955	519.1	2.376	3.547	2.722	1,062.4	129.4
1956	509.2	2.542	2.684	2.954	1,027.2	130.3
1957	508.4	2.729	2.785	3.216	986.5	128.8
1958	411.6	2.931	2.911	3.513	756.4	126.5
1959	399.7	3.144	3.098	3.798	769.2	141.8
1960	449.9	3.094	3.001	3.820	840.3	136.4
1961	405.9	3.241	3.110	3.989	775.0	141.6
1962	402.7	3.332	3.160	4.155	768.5	N.A.

*Includes shift, overtime, and holiday pay and premiums of steel workers, but before deductions such as insurance, social security, and income tax.

**Average hourly earnings of steel workers as related to the consumer price index.

***Includes expense incurred for vacations, adjustments, pensions, insurance, and social security.

#Not shown because of unusual wartime production mix.

Sources: AISI, Annual Statistical Report, 1940-1961, for average hourly earnings, workers, man-hours, and total employment costs per hour; U.S. Department of Labor, Bureau of Labor Statistics, Man-Hours per Unit of Output in the Basic Steel Industry, 1939-1961, and Indexes of Output per Man-Hour for Selected Industries, 1939 and 1947-1961.

20. STEEL INDUSTRY

Results of Steel Labor Negotiations, 1945-1962

Negotiations Started	Result	Wage Increase	Insurance and Pension	New Average Wage	Amount	Date
10/11/45	Strike, 1/21-2/16/46	$.185	-	$1.35	$5.00	2/15/46
					$2.50	12/46
1/47	No strike	$.16	-	$1.53	$5.00	7/20/47
4/5/58	No strike	$.13	-	$1.68	$10.00	7/20/48
6/15/49	Strike, 10/1-11/15/49	-	$.10	$1.68	$4.00	12/16/49
10/16/50	No strike	$.16	-	$1.96	$5.58	11/30/50
11/26/51	Strike, 4/29-6/27/52	$.16	-	$2.17	$5.10	7/24/52
5/14/53	No strike	$.085	-	$2.31	$4.00	6/19/53
5/18/54	No strike	$.09	-	$2.36	$1 to $321	7/1/54
6/7/55	1/2-day strike	$.152	-	$2.60	$7.50	7/2/55
5/28/56	Strike, 6/1-7/7/56	$.259 (over 3 yrs.)	$.191	$2.78	$8.50	8/6/56
					$4.50	7/31/58
5/5/59	Strike, 6/15-10/8/59	$.083 (12/1/60) $.071 (10/1/61)	$.251	$3.59	-	-
2/14/62	No strike	-	$.10	$3.59	-	-

Source: Steel, "Here's What Happened in Last 12 Settlements," April 16, 1962, p. 91.

Sharon Steel Corporation

In 1947 the Sharon Steel Corporation ranked as the ninth largest producer of steel in the United States. The company was located in Sharon, Pennsylvania, a small town on the Shenango River[1] about 16 miles from Youngstown, Ohio. The company and its subsidiaries manufactured and sold hot- and cold-rolled carbon steel strip, stainless and alloy steel strip, steel sheets, carbon and alloy seamless tubing, galvanized and other coated products, and certain miscellaneous items.

In the years 1945 to 1947 the company initiated an extensive program of expansion and integration. The program was designed: (1) to enlarge the company's steel ingot producing capacity, and (2) to secure manufacturing subsidiaries which could further process the steel the company had been selling as hot-rolled strip and thereby enable the company to "take its products to market at higher levels of price."

In 1946 the company's sales totaled $54,000,000; in 1947 it was estimated that sales would be slightly over $90,000,000. Comparative balance sheets and income statements for the period 1940 to 1946 are presented in Exhibits 1 and 2. Exhibit 3 contains a summary record of earnings from 1920 to 1946 and Exhibit 4 a record of production, purchases, and shipments from 1936 to 1946. As indicated in the financial records, the company retired its preferred stock in 1946. It was thus left with nothing other than common stock outstanding, a position unique and unusual in the steel industry. Capital charges on a bank loan of approximately $4,000,000 were very low as related to the size of the company and its total ingot producing capacity.

COMPANY HISTORY

The Sharon Steel Corporation was founded as the Sharon Steel Hoop Company[2] by a small group of businessmen in October, 1900. The authorized capital consisted of 4,000 shares of stock with a par value of $50.

The new company purchased a site of land along the Shenango River adjacent to a steel company which later became the Farrell Works of the Carnegie-Illinois Steel Corporation. Construction of an 8-inch and a 9-inch hand-fed hot strip mill was begun almost immediately, and by May of the following year both mills were in production. The two mills were equipped to roll hot strip in a range of sizes from 1/4 to 4 inches wide. The majority of the output was sold for use as cooperage hoop to about a dozen manufacturers, most of whom were business and personal friends of the company's founders.

Early Growth: The company had originally contracted to secure its requirements of steel billets from the adjacent steel company. Within a short time, however, that company was absorbed by the United States Steel Corporation, and it soon became difficult to secure an adequate supply of billets. As a result, in 1902 the Sharon Steel Hoop Company undertook construction of four open-hearth furnaces, a blooming mill, and a billet mill. These facilities, which were brought into production in 1903, gave the company an ample supply of steel billets for its cooperage trade.

In 1917 the company acquired the properties of the Youngstown Iron and Steel Company which had two plants, one at Lowellville and the other at Youngstown, Ohio. The equipment at the Lowellville plant consisted of four open hearths, three soaking pits, a blooming mill for making sheet bar and a universal plate mill for making slabs.

The Youngstown Pressed Steel Company was organized as a wholly owned subsidiary in November, 1917, to take over the operation of the pressed steel and the roofing and expanded metal departments at the Youngstown plant along with certain of the fabricating departments at the Sharon Works. In 1919 this subsidiary moved all of its equipment into a new plant in Warren, Ohio, where it subsequently conducted a general stamping business and manufactured steel lathe and other steel building products.

A source of supply for the open hearths at Lowellville was secured in 1918 by the purchase of the nearby "Mary" furnace from the Ohio Iron and Steel Company. This furnace was

[1] The Shenango Valley together with the adjacent Mahoning Valley constituted one of the most important steel producing districts in the United States.

[2] The name was changed to the Sharon Steel Corporation in 1936, by which time hoop steel had become a small part of the company's overall production.

constructed in 1846 and was the first blast furnace in the United States to manufacture pig iron successfully with raw bituminous coal.

The executives of the company early foresaw the demand which was to develop for cold-rolled strip steel. To supply this market and to meet an increased demand for hot-rolled coils with a better surface finish, the construction of a continuous high-speed hot strip mill, a new pickling department, and a cold-rolling department was under taken. The first steel was cold rolled in August, 1928, and in the following year the new continuous hot strip mill was started in operation. With this mill and the hand-fed mills, the company was able to roll strip steel in widths from 1/4 inch to 17 inches.[3]

The year 1930 marked the company's entry into a new field, the manufacture of stainless strip steels and alloy steels. For these products the company subsequently became one of the largest and most successful independent producers.

In 1931, when Mr. Henry A. Roemer became president, the company's manufacturing properties consisted of four plants located at Sharon, Pennsylvania, Lowellville, Ohio, Youngstown, Ohio, and Warren, Ohio. The latter three plants were about 21, 16, and 17 miles distant from Sharon, respectively.

At the Lowellville Works the company operated a blast furnace, four open-hearth furnaces, a blooming mill, and a billet and bar mill. The Lowellville Works produced the semifinished steel (billets, slabs, and sheet bar) which was used in the plants at Sharon and Youngstown. The majority of the output consisted of carbon steel but, as noted above, beginning in 1930 a small volume of stainless steel was also produced.

The equipment at the Sharon Works included the four hand-fed hot strip mills and the new continuous hot strip mill. With this equipment the company produced strip steel in all widths from 1/4 of an inch to 17 inches wide and in a great variety of gauges and lengths. The Sharon plant also contained pickling equipment and the cold strip mill which was capable of handling strip steel up to 22 inches in width.

[3] Although hot-rolled steel over 12 inches in width is usually designated commercially as sheet steel, it was the practice of the company to refer to the products of its continuous hot mill as "strip."

At the Youngstown Works the company operated nine sheet mills (acquired in 1917 from the Youngstown Iron and Steel Company) which were used to produce black, blue annealed, pickled, cold-rolled, heat treated, deep drawing, and extra deep drawing sheets. The products of this division were sold primarily as automobile frame stock and sheet steel for the steel barrel trade.

The Warren Works was operated by the wholly owned subsidiary, the Youngstown Pressed Steel Company. In 1930 this company was manufacturing pressed steel stampings and a wide variety of drawn products for use by the automotive, household equipment, gasoline, oil, machine shop, and stove industries. The company also produced handling equipment for industrial plants and operated a vitreous enameling department.

PROGRAM OF EXPANSION AND ACQUISITION

In 1930 and the years which followed, the company suffered severe operating losses (see Exhibit 3), and its financial position deteriorated rapidly. At one point, Mr. Roemer had to "hock everything in the box" to get the money required to meet the payrolls and the current bills. Many observers in the industry believed the company was doomed. During this period, however, Mr. Roemer built around himself a strong and competent organization and proceeded with the rehabilitation of the company.

As a first step, Mr. Roemer made a number of changes in the company's plant equipment and manufacturing activities which were designed to accomplish economies in operating and administrative costs, to conserve the company's assets, and to place it in a better competitive position. He then initiated a long-run program designed to expand the company's operations and to place its finishing capacity in approximate balance with its steel producing capacity. Mr. Roemer believed that the acquisition of additional finishing capacity would permit the company to sell its products at higher price levels and to secure better profit margins.

Over a period of about 15 years, Mr. Roemer had noted that the profit margins on hot-rolled strip had become very small. However, the margins secured by the converters who reduced the strip to finished steel and various specialty products appeared to be entirely satisfactory. Mr. Roemer had also noted that most of the large companies were gradually integrating forward and were thus taking advantage of the margins available on finished items. Mr. Roemer was convinced that Sharon could improve its situation by further processing its hot-rolled strip and by "fanning the steel out" into a large number of specialty, finished steel markets.

The program which was initiated and carried out by Mr. Roemer and his staff was as follows:

Developments, 1930 to 1935: During the period 1930 to 1935, attention was directed primarily to the improvement of plant facilities and the reduction of operating costs. In 1931 the "Mary" blast furnace at Lowellville was shut down, and for six years thereafter the company purchased its pig iron from outside sources. The furnace was one of the oldest in the United States and could not be operated economically under the conditions which prevailed during the depression years. It was put back into production in 1937, after it had been reconditioned at a cost of $150,000:

In 1932 operations at the sheet mills in Youngstown were discontinued because the equipment was found to be obsolete and inefficient. In subsequent years the plant was dismantled and the property sold.

Throughout the period 1930 to 1935 a certain amount of new, modern equipment was installed which enlarged the company's hot- and cold-rolling facilities and increased its capacity for the production of stainless steel.

Formation of the Niles Rolling Mill Company: The first major step in the expansion program was the formation of the Niles Rolling Mill Company in 1935. The Sharon Steel Corporation acquired 70 percent of the common and 75 percent of the preferred stock in the new company.[4] The new concern purchased a sheet mill located at Niles, Ohio, about 16 miles from the Sharon Works. Some new equipment was installed, and the existing facilities were modernized. When this work was completed, the plant contained three hot sheet mills with an annual capacity of about 55,000 net tons of finished sheets, a modern pickling and galvanizing department, and a number of annealing furnaces. It thus provided facilities for processing a substantial portion of the semifinished steel produced at the Lowellville Works.

[4] In 1947 the Sharon Steel Corporation acquired the minority interest in the Niles Rolling Mill Company in exchange for 8,905 shares of its own common stock. The minority interest had been held by the Sears Roebuck & Company which aided in the organization of the concern in 1935.

Merger of Youngstown Pressed Steel Company: The company's subsidiary, the Youngstown Pressed Steel Company, suffered severely during the depression years, and was in a precarious financial position by 1936. The Mullins Manufacturing Corporation of Salem, Ohio, another stamping concern, had also encountered serious financial difficulties during the depression years. After being approached by certain large stockholders of the Mullins Manufacturing Corporation, Mr. Roemer brought about a merger of the two firms on May 1, 1937. The Sharon Steel Corporation transferred the plant, property, and assets of the Youngstown Pressed Steel Company to the Mullins Manufacturing Corporation. In return the Sharon Steel Corporation received 200,000 shares of the Class B common stock of the Mullins Manufacturing Corporation.

Prior to the merger, the Mullins Manufacturing Corporation had been a competitor of the Youngstown Pressed Steel Company. The corporation had operated two plants in Salem, Ohio, which produced various pressed steel and enameled products, including automotive parts, washing machine tubs and wringers, refrigerator parts, cabinet sinks, and kitchen cabinets. The plant included over 125 stamping presses, a die sinking department, a vitreous enameling department, and an assembly department for the manufacture of kitchen cabinets and sinks.

Shortly after the merger, the manufacture of kitchen equipment was concentrated at the Warren plant of the Youngstown Pressed Steel Company. This equipment was marketed under the brand name "Youngstown Kitchens." The two plants in Salem were then used primarily for the production of porcelain enameled washing machine tubs.

Before the merger, the annual sales of the Youngstown Pressed Steel Company amounted to about $3,500,000, while those of the Mullins Manufacturing Corporation amounted to about

$6,600,000. In the years following the merger, the company developed into one of the largest stamping and enameling concerns in the world and secured an outstanding position as a producer of steel kitchen equipment.

Acquisition of the Detroit Seamless Steel Tubes Company: At the close of the war, the company resumed its long-run program of development. On April 1, 1945, Mr. Roemer completed negotiations for the purchase of the Detroit Seamless Steel Tubes Company. The Sharon Steel Corporation acquired all of the outstanding capital stock of the Detroit Seamless Steel Tubes Company for $1,000,000 in cash. The book value of the underlying net assets thus acquired was $1,832,314. It was reported that the transaction cost the Sharon Steel Corporation $132,000 net, after deducting cash on hand, inventory value, and accounts receivable.

The plant, which was located in Detroit, Michigan, had excellent facilities and was equipped for about 36,000 tons of seamless steel tubes per year. The company had a reputation in the trade for producing high quality products; over a period of years returned and defective materials had averaged less than two tenths of 1 percent of total shipments. The majority of the company's output was sold to the automotive industry; a substantial volume was also sold to the oil industry.

The acquisition gave the Sharon Steel Corporation a new line of products, an outlet for semifinished steel, and a position in the important Michigan market.

Acquisition of the Farrell Works: On November 9, 1945, Mr. Roemer completed negotiations for the purchase of the Farrell Works of the Carnegie-Illinois Steel Corporation which were located in Farrell, Pennsylvania, immediately adjacent to the company's finishing mills at the Sharon site. The property included two 800-ton blast furnaces with ore handling equipment and all other facilities necessary for the production of approximately 500,000 tons of pig iron per year, 15 open-hearth furnaces with an annual ingot capacity of approximately 900,000 tons of steel, a 36-inch blooming mill, a 24-inch bar mill, and an 18-inch bar mill. The purchase thus enabled the company to increase its ingot capacity from about 600,000 to 1,500,000 net tons per year.

The Farrell Works was clearly visible from Mr. Roemer's office window, and for many years he had had in mind the hope that it might some day be added to the properties of the Sharon Steel Corporation. To that end he had purchased bit by bit the few pieces of land which lay between the two mills. In 1938 he began negotiations on the transaction with Mr. Benjamin Fairless, president of the United States Steel Corporation, who had been his good friend for a great many years. Mr. Fairless had previously remarked that the Farrell Works did not fit particularly well into the long-run plans which the United States Steel Corporation was developing for the consolidation of its properties. The Farrell Works had originally been a completely integrated unit with a sheet mill, tin mill, and a wire mill. The sheet, tin, and wire mills, however, had been dismantled during the 1930's, and by 1938 the Farrell Works had only facilities for the production of semifinished steel as noted above.

Circumstances were not quite favorable to the transfer in 1938 or 1939. During the war years the Carnegie-Illinois Steel Corporation continued to operate the properties at the request of the Government, and it was not until June, 1945, that Mr. Roemer was able to resume negotiations for the purchase.

The executives of the Sharon Steel Corporation were particularly anxious to acquire the Farrell Works at that time because they realized that the Mary blast furnace at Lowellville would inevitably pass out of operation in the near future and leave the company in a very precarious position with regard to its supply of pig iron. The construction of a new blast furnace was regarded as quite unfeasible because the prevailing costs for new construction work were highly inflated. The alternative of purchasing pig iron in the open market was likewise regarded as undesirable because it would greatly increase the company's pig iron costs and expose the company to uncertainties in supply. Moreover, it appeared that the use of a cold metal pig iron charge in the open hearths would increase ingot costs to the point where it would be more economical to purchase semifinished steel than to make it.

It was anticipated that the acquisition of the Farrell Works would enable the company to produce its entire requirements of pig iron and eliminate the purchasing of pig iron, steel ingots, and semifinished steel in the open market which had been necessary in recent years. It also appeared that the operation of the Farrell Works would enable the corporation to improve the quality of its steel and permit a reduction in operating costs through using a higher percentage of hot metal in the open-hearth charge than had been possible at Lowellville where it was necessary to use a fairly high ratio of cold metal and scrap. Finally, it was clear that the acquisition would eliminate the substantial freight charges currently being paid to ship semifinished steel from the Lowellville plant to the company's finishing mills at Sharon, a distance of 21 rail miles. Overall savings from the operation of the Farrell Works were estimated at about $5 per ton of ingots.

The purchase arrangements provided for a payment by the Sharon Steel Corporation of $4,250,000 in cash for the Farrell plant and $3,835,004 in cash for the inventories of raw materials and supplies. The funds for the inventories and supplies were secured by bank borrowing while the funds for the plant were drawn from the company's cash balances.

A very important provision of the purchase agreement provided that the subsidiaries of the United States Steel Corporation would supply the Farrell Works with iron ore for a period of ten years and with coke until the company was able to provide its own supply. Limestone for the open-hearth and blast furnaces at Farrell was to be purchased from the Pittsburgh Limestone Corporation pursuant to a ten-year contract negotiated in 1945.

Lease of Morgantown Coke Plant: Shortly after the acquisition of the Farrell Works, arrangements were made to lease a by-product coke plant, located at Morgantown, West Virginia, from the United States Government for a period of five years beginning on July 1, 1946. The lease agreement provided that the company would pay an annual rental of $233,496. It was estimated that about $100,000 would have to be spent to place the property in operating condition, and this amount was to be deductible from the rental for the first year.

In full operation the coke ovens produced about 11 tons of coke every 16 minutes or about 400,000 tons per year. After certain current commitments to the Government were fulfilled, it was anticipated that the coke ovens would be able to supply all of the coke required by the blast furnaces at the Farrell Works.

Acquisition of Bopp Steel Corporation: On October 31, 1946, the Sharon Steel Corporation acquired all of the common stock of the Bopp Steel Corporation. This company, a privately owned concern, had established an excellent reputation and a record for profitable operations, even during the lean years of the depression. The three principal stockholders were anxious to get their investment transferred into a listed security which would be more readily negotiable and were willing, therefore, to accept a trade with the Sharon Steel Corporation for their interests. In this transaction, 1.3 shares of Sharon common stock were exchanged for each share of Bopp stock. The net assets thus acquired totaled $1,633,299 as of December 31, 1946.

The plant, which was located in Dearborn, Michigan, contained three cold-rolling mills with an annual capacity of 55,000 tons of cold-rolled steel in various grades and finishes. Approximately 80 to 90 percent of the company's output was sold to customers in the automobile industry.

With the Bopp Steel Corporation, the Sharon Steel Corporation acquired its wholly owned subsidiary, Steel Trucking, Inc. This concern operated a fleet of 20 diesel trucks and trailers. In the future it was anticipated that this equipment would be used to haul hot-rolled billets and strip from Sharon to the Detroit Seamless Steel Tubes Company and to the Bopp Steel Corporation. On the return trip the trucks would haul scrap from the automobile plants in Detroit to the Farrell Works.

Acquisition of Brainard Steel Corporation: On December 31, 1946, arrangements were completed for the acquisition of the common stock of the Brainard Steel Corporation. One share of Sharon stock was exchanged for each 2.5 shares of Brainard stock. A total of 30,632 shares of Sharon stock were issued for this purpose. Sharon stock was selling on the market at about $31⅜, and the purchase price was thus about $1,000,000. The net assets of the new subsidiary totaled $802,431 as of December 31, 1946; the annual sales volume was between $3,000,000 and $4,000,000.

It was anticipated that the Brainard Steel Corporation would be developed as a producer of steel specialties. The plant, which was located in Warren, Ohio, contained three cold reducing and three cold finishing mills; it had an annual capacity of 35,000 tons of cold-rolled strip steel, electro galvanized strip steel, welded tubing, box strapping, and cooperage hoop.

At the time of acquisition, the company's principal product was steel strapping to reinforce shipping containers. In this field it ranked as the third largest producer in the country.

Formation of Sharonsteel Products Company: In the early part of 1947 the company established the Sharonsteel Products Company as a wholly owned subsidiary. The function of the subsidiary was to set up and operate a steel warehouse in Detroit. It was intended that the warehouse would draw finished steel from the parent company's several finishing mills and maintain an inventory from which sales could be made to small customers or to customers who required quick deliveries. It was anticipated that the average sale made by the warehouse would be for a quantity somewhere between 100 and 500 pounds. It was hoped that the warehouse would develop a sales volume of about 1,000 tons per month.

Formation of Detroit Tube and Steel Company: In April, 1947, a new subsidiary was formed to take over the operations of the Detroit Seamless Steel Tubes Company and the Bopp Steel Corporation. The company, which was wholly owned by the Sharon Steel Corporation, was known as the Detroit Tube and Steel Company.

OPERATIONS IN 1947

In the months following the end of the war, the Sharon Steel Corporation took a number of steps to improve further the operating efficiency of its several plants. A considerable amount of new equipment was added and much old equipment was modernized or dismantled. The facilities which the company had in operation in the summer of 1947 are outlined in Exhibit 5. This exhibit also shows the approximate volume of production and interplant shipments for the month of May, 1947.

Lowellville Works: The Lowellville Works was being used for the production of both carbon and alloy steel ingots. These ingots were rolled into slabs, billets, and sheet bar and then shipped to the finishing mills in Sharon, Niles, or Detroit or sold to outside customers (see Exhibit 5). The pig iron for the open hearths at the Lowellville Works was produced by the Mary blast furnace. The Mary furnace was producing about 12,000 tons of pig iron per month while the open hearths were producing about 41,000 tons of steel ingots per month. The percentage of pig iron in the charge to the open hearths was thus about 30 percent. The executives would have preferred a higher ratio of pig iron in the charge, but during the summer months of 1947 it was not possible to purchase pig iron on the open market at any reasonable price.

Shortly after the Farrell Works was acquired, Mr. Roemer undertook negotiations for the sale of the Lowellville Works to four nonintegrated steel finishing companies. These arrangements were not consummated, however, and the company continued to operate the properties. It was anticipated that the Lowellville facilities would be continued in use for an indefinite period and that the production of stainless steel would eventually be concentrated there.

Farrell Works: The two blast furnaces at the Farrell Works were being operated as close to capacity as was possible and were producing about 44,000 tons of pig iron per month. This metal was charged hot to the open-hearth furnaces. The company was operating ten open hearths, each of which had an output of about 7,000 tons of steel ingots per month. The charge to the open-hearth furnaces was made up of about 58 percent pig iron and 42 percent scrap iron. Each furnace was tapped every 10 to 11 hours and produced slightly over 100 tons per heat.

The company officials had found that the optimum ratio of pig iron in the metal charge for the open-hearth furnaces was somewhere between 62 and 65 percent. A higher proportion of pig iron resulted in certain process difficulties; a lower proportion increased the time per heat because of the larger amount of cold scrap which had to be melted. Under normal circumstances the furnaces were never operated with less than 50 percent or more than 70 percent pig iron in the charge. Above 70 percent pig iron the furnace reaction became so violent that it was somewhat uncontrollable. Below 50 percent pig iron, the furnace reaction removed too much of the carbon from the metal, and it became necessary to go to the cost and trouble of adding carbon to the melt. Moreover, with more than 50 percent cold scrap in the charge the melting times became excessively long.

The steel ingots were reduced in the blooming and semifinishing mills at the Farrell Works to slabs, billets, and sheet bar. This steel was then transferred to the finishing mills at Sharon, Niles, or Detroit. As may be seen from Exhibit 5, a small volume was also sold to outside customers.

Sharon Works: In 1947 the Sharon Works was operating four hot strip mills. One of these was a modern continuous strip mill, while the other three mills were older-type, hand-fed mills. The continuous mill was used for strip ranging between 5 and 22 inches in width. The 8-inch hand-fed mill was used for strip between 3/8 and 1 1/4 inches in width, the 9-inch mill for strip between 1 and 2 1/4 inches in width, and the 10-inch mill for strip between 2 and 5 1/4 inches in width.

A substantial proportion of the hot strip was further processed on the company's cold finishing equipment. This equipment is listed in Exhibit 5. Other processing facilities at the Sharon Works included 4 continuous heating furnaces, 4 double box annealing furnaces, 21 heated box type annealing furnaces, 4 normalizing furnaces, 7 pickling machines, and 6 galvanizing, tin, and terne pots.

The approximate distribution given to the output of the Sharon Works is shown in Exhibit 5. The hot-rolled strip which was not transferred to the subsidiaries was sold to customers in many different industries for fabrication into a very wide range of end products. In a typical month the tonnage of hot-rolled strip might be sold as follows:

10,000 tons to other converters for processing into hot- and cold-rolled sheets
3,800 tons to manufacturers of automobile parts, accessories, and supplies
3,300 tons to manufacturers of heavy industrial machinery and equipment
2,500 tons for use in contractor's products
2,300 tons for use in cooperage, box strapping, and containers
2,100 tons to manufacturers of agricultural machinery
1,400 tons to steel jobbers
1,300 tons to manufacturers of appliances, utensils, and cutlery
12,300 tons to a variety of miscellaneous users.

The customers for the output of the Sharon Works included the Mullins Manufacturing Company. This concern, however, received only 1 or 2 percent of the total volume.

Subsidiaries: The activities carried on by the several subsidiary companies in the summer of 1947 may be summarized as follows:

The Niles Rolling Mill Company secured sheet bar from the Lowellville and Farrell Works and reduced it to hot-rolled sheet of several different grades and finishes (see Exhibit 5). For the first four or five years after the company was formed its output was sold to about 25 accounts, the majority of which were in the automobile industry. It had been found very difficult, however, to compete with the large integrated steel concerns for the automobile business. Accordingly, the direction of the company's sales effort was gradually changed. In 1947 the majority of the sheet steel was sold to manufacturers of such products as refrigerators, stoves, washing machines, furnaces, and fractional horse power motors; none of the output went to the automobile industry. The total number of accounts was about 100. The Mullins Manufacturing Company was an important customer and accounted for about 20 percent of the company's sales volume.

The Detroit Tube and Steel Company operated the tube plant in Detroit and the cold-rolling mill in Dearborn (formerly Bopp Steel Corporation). The tube plant secured about 20 percent of its requirements of steel rounds from the Lowellville Works and purchased the remainder on the open market. The Lowellville Works did not have sufficient equipment to produce all of the different sizes and types of rounds required in the tube plant. Additional equipment was to be installed for rolling rounds, but it was anticipated that the tube plant would always buy some of its steel from other companies. As noted above, the output of the tube plant was sold primarily to the automobile and oil industries.

The cold-rolling plant in Dearborn secured all of its requirements of hot-rolled strip from the Sharon Works. About 80 to 90 percent of the output of this plant was sold to customers in the automobile industry and the remainder to miscellaneous steel stamping companies.

The Brainard Steel Corporation operated cold reducing and cold finishing mills as indicated in Exhibit 5. The requirements of hot-rolled strip were secured from the Sharon Works. The finished products of the company were sold to a large number of relatively small customers in all sections of the country. The most important item in the company's line was box strapping.

The distribution of the Sharon Steel Corporation's sales volume, including the sales of subsidiaries, broken down by principle product groups for the period 1936 to 1945 is shown in Exhibit 4.

Manufacturing Costs: Illustrative manufacturing costs for the summer of 1947 are presented in Exhibit 6. These figures have been simplified in several respects and do not, therefore, represent the actual company costs for any particular period.

MARKETING PROGRAM

The general sales organization of the Sharon Steel Corporation in 1947 consisted of approximately 24 salesmen. District offices were maintained in New York, Philadelphia, Rochester, Cleveland, Detroit, Chicago, Indianapolis, Cincinnati, and Sharon. The largest office was in Detroit where four salesmen were located. The Indianapolis and Cincinnati offices each had one salesman; the remaining offices had three salesmen each. In addition to its own sales force, the company maintained commission offices in Toronto, Montreal, St. Louis, San Francisco, and Los Angeles.

Each of the subsidiaries maintained a separate sales staff. The field organizations of the subsidiaries, however, were gradually being merged into that of the parent company. It was anticipated that each subsidiary would retain a few sales executives in its organization who would have a general responsibility for the sale of the products which the subsidiary produced.

By 1947 the sales organization of the Niles Rolling Mill Company had been merged almost entirely with that of the Sharon Steel Corporation. The company had three sales executives of its own, one of whom was the vice-president in charge of sales. The bulk of the company's output was sold within a radius of 100 miles of the mill.

The Detroit Tube and Steel Company had about five salesmen at its main office in Detroit, one man at a district office in Detroit, and one man at a district office in Chicago. In addition, the Cleveland office of the parent company served a certain number of accounts for the Detroit Tube and Steel Company. Most of the subsidiary's products were sold in a restricted territory in and about Detroit, Chicago, Indiana, and Cleveland.

The sales organization of the Brainard Steel Corporation consisted of approximately 20 men. This subsidiary sold its products on a national basis to a substantially larger number of customers than did the parent company. The unit of sale was usually small in terms of tonnage.

All of the salesmen for the corporation and its subsidiaries were paid on a straight salary basis. The majority of them had been trained in the company's training program which involved about 1 to 1½ years of work in the mills.

Advertising and Promotion: The Sharon Steel Corporation spent a relatively small amount for advertising and sales promotion purposes. The program was designed to develop the reputation of the company as a producer of specialty steels. The advertising appeared primarily in the steel trade papers, but a small amount of institutional advertising was done in such magazines as *Fortune* and *The Saturday Evening Post* and in some of the financial papers. In advertisements featuring the products of a subsidiary, the subsidiary was identified as a "Division of the Sharon Steel Corporation."

Basis of Competition: The company completed for small volume orders on certain specialty items. For example, a customer might wish to buy hot-rolled strip 18½ inches in width and .090 inches in thickness. Sharon could roll such steel in its continuous hot mill at a rate of perhaps 500 tons per eight-hour shift. A big producer with large equipment, however, would probably be able to roll the same steel in 37-inch or 54-inch widths at a rate of perhaps 1,000 to 2,000 tons per eight-hour shift. The large widths could then be quickly slit to the desired dimension of 18½ inches. In a situation of this type the conversion costs of the big producer would unquestionably be lower. Sharon could compete, however, if the customer wished to buy in small lots, insisted on having "mill" rather than "sheared" edges on the steel,[5] or wished a very high carbon steel or unusually close tolerances on the gauge. The company made no attempt to solicit business in such markets as automobile sheet steel where the contracts were let for very large tonnages of standard grades and finishes.

During the summer of 1947, steel prices were such that the Sharon Steel Corporation could have met competitive prices and secured a fair rate of return in almost any market. In the long run, however, the executives believed that the company's interests would best be served by developing those markets which the large producers were not too well equipped to serve.

As a result of its sales policies, the company had established a position as one of the most important producers in the field of special and coated steels. It ranked as perhaps the largest producer of cutlery and cooperage steels in the United States. It was also one of the most important producers of high carbon steels.

PLANS AND OBJECTIVES

Mr. Roemer planned to continue the Sharon Steel Corporation's program of expansion until finishing capacity was approximately in balance with semifinished steel production. He believed that under existing circumstances the expansion could probably be accomplished more advantageously through the acquisition of additional subsidiaries than through the installation of more equipment at existing plants. The cost of new equipment and new construction in 1947 was extremely high. Moreover, when a subsidiary was acquired it usually brought with it an established business and clientele. During the first half of 1947, the subsidiaries accounted for 38 percent of the corporation's net profit, which was reported at $3,385,000.

Mr. Roemer anticipated that the company would also continue its program of establishing warehouse facilities for the wholesaling of steel to small customers and customers who required emergency deliveries. In August, 1947, a second warehouse company, the Sharonsteel Products Company of Pennsylvania, was being incorporated and was expected to commence operations in the near future. Mr. Roemer believed that perhaps five additional warehouse companies might be incorporated in nearby states. Freight costs made it unfeasible to extend the warehouse organization into states far removed from the company's plants.

A third program of development involved the expansion of facilities for the production of stainless, alloy, and special steels. Two new electric furnaces were under construction at the Lowellville Works which were designed to increase the company's electric furnace steel capacity to approximately 100,000 tons per year. A new battery of soaking pits for heating specialized products had just been completed, and grinding equipment was being installed for the preparation of semifinished stainless steel.

Finally, the executives of the company intended to continue the modernization and improvement of existing plant equipment wherever circumstances seemed to warrant it. They hoped, for example, that the 8-, 9-, and 10-inch hand-fed, hot strip mills might be replaced in the near future with two modern, continuous hot strip mills. One of these mills would roll strip ¾ to 3 inches in width and the other strip from 3½ inches to 9 inches in width. The company's existing continuous hot mill was capable of rolling strip from 9 inches to 22 inches in width.

[5] A "mill" edge was the edge resulting from normal hot-rolling operations; a "sheared" edge was the edge left after shearing operations.

1. SHARON STEEL CORPORATION

Balance Sheets, 1940-46
(In Thousands)

ASSETS	1940	1941	1942	1943	1944	(1) 1945	(2) 1946
Cash	$ 3,149	$ 4,042	$ 3,225	$ 3,672	$ 8,396	$ 4,234	$ 6,942
U.S. Treasury certificates	-0-	-0-	-0-	-0-	-0-	650	61
War contract claims	-0-	-0-	-0-	-0-	-0-	640	-0-
Tax refunds including refund bonds	-0-	-0-	-0-	-0-	-0-	469	37
Notes and accounts receivable (net)	2,648	2,484	2,413	2,227	2,060	2,443	4,990
Inventories	4,963	5,094	6,012	7,256	5,312	11,226	13,692
Total Current Assets	$10,760	$11,620	$11,650	$13,155	$15,768	$19,662	$25,722
(3) Securities of subsidiaries	$ 570	$ 570	$ 570	$ 570	$ 570	-0-	-0-
(4) Securities of assoc. companies	2,769	2,769	2,769	2,769	2,769	$ 2,769	$ 1,378
Adv. to assoc. companies	112	99	53	70	86	-0-	-0-
Miscellaneous investments	99	69	65	65	28	37	37
Postwar credit-excess profits tax	-0-	-0-	75	95	228	-0-	-0-
Lease improvement, net	-0-	-0-	-0-	-0-	-0-	-0-	311
Land						597	667
Buildings, machinery, and equipment	$18,018	$18,048	$17,868	$17,919	$17,925	$24,952	$28,835
Less: Reserve for depreciation	11,341	12,027	12,697	13,357	13,932	15,804	17,547
Net Buildings and Machinery	$ 6,677	$ 6,021	$ 5,171	$ 4,562	$ 3,993	$ 9,148	$11,288
Special facilities	-0-	$ 1,754	$ 2,408	$ 2,495	$ 2,495	$ 2,495	$ 2,598
Less: Amortization reserve	-0-	102	501	1,001	1,500	2,495	2,598
Net Special Facilities	-0-	$ 1,652	$ 1,907	$ 1,494	$ 995	-0-	-0-
Deferred charges	$ 26	$ 103	$ 212	$ 188	$ 292	$ 201	$ 227
Insurance, cost value	-0-	-0-	-0-	-0-	-0-	-0-	60
Total Assets	$21,013	$22,903	$22,472	$22,968	$24,729	$32,414	$39,690
LIABILITIES							
Notes payable to banks	-0-	-0-	-0-	-0-	$ 400	-0-	$ 680
Accounts payable	$ 898	$ 1,285	$ 1,277	$ 765	$ 881	$ 2,273	$ 4,552
Ore contracts payable	198	365	61	22	-0-	-0-	-0-
Accrued interest	274	394	344	380	769	1,192	2,161
Taxes other than income	150	219	242	261	205	167	296
Provision for income taxes	530	1,195	1,042	1,923	1,039	1,819	2,320
Accrued interest	1	7	4	-0-	8	4	27
Other current liabilities	169	154	226	405	353	423	282
Total Current Liabilities	$ 2,220	$ 3,619	$ 3,196	$ 3,756	$ 3,655	$ 5,878	$10,318
Notes payable to banks	2,000	1,600	900	-0-	1,600	5,000	4,500
Reserve for repairs	277	225	225	225	225	244	258
Reserve for insurance, etc.	100	100	100	100	100	107	107
Reserve for postwar contingencies	-0-	-0-	-0-	600	600	600	-0-
Minority interest	-0-	-0-	-0-	-0-	-0-	301	-0-
$5 cum. conv. preferred stock (59,720 no-par shares)	5,972	5,972	5,972	5,972	5,972	5,972	-0-
Common stock (392,331 shares)	3,975	3,975	3,975	3,975	3,975	3,975	6,233
(5) Capital surplus	4,923	4,923	4,923	4,923	4,923	5,756	11,362
Earned Surplus	1,546	2,489	3,181	3,417	3,679	4,581	6,912
Total Liabilities	$21,013	$22,903	$22,472	$22,968	$24,729	$32,414	$39,690

(1) Consolidated, includes Niles Rolling and Detroit Seamless.

(2) Consolidated, reflects accounts of Niles Rolling, Detroit Seamless, Bopp Steel, and Steel Trucking, and net assets acquired from Brainard.

(3) Consists of capital stock of Niles Rolling Mill Co.

(4) Comprising $1,110,651 Mullins stock and $267,277 Pittsburgh Steel Co. stock.

(5) Balance Jan. 1, 1946, $5,755,836. Add: Net excess of book values of net assets of subsidiaries at dates of acquisition, $429,505; excess of investments in subsidiaries acquired in exchange for capital stock, $1,379,403; excess on sale of common stock, less $27,579 financing expenses, $3,797,421; balance, Dec. 31, 1946, $11,362,165.

Source: Company records.

2. SHARON STEEL CORPORATION
Income Statements, 1940-1946
(In Thousands)

	1940	1941	1942	1943	1944	(1) 1945	(2) 1946
Net sales	$21,573	$31,949	$35,780	$39,916	$35,335	$40,603	$54,164
(3) Cost of sales	16,650	23,378	25,926	28,893	27,112	31,726	42,837
Maintenance and repairs	1,339	1,923	2,191	2,411	2,385	2,447	3,504
Depreciation	591	798	739	672	588	712	1,158
Amortization		102	399	500	499	512	
Selling, general, and admin. expenses	895	1,003	979	928	1,129	1,351	1,891
Taxes other than income	329	488	505	607	426	349	725
Pension plan					59	66	80
Doubtful accounts	6	26					
Operating profit	$ 1,763	$ 4,231	$ 5,041	$ 5,905	$ 3,137	$ 3,440	$ 3,969
Other income, dividends, etc.	102	101	72	93	228	201	857
Total income	$ 1,865	$ 4,332	$ 5,113	$ 5,998	$ 3,365	$ 3,641	$ 4,826
Interest paid, etc.	28	48	30	15	45	46	142
Balance	$ 1,837	$ 4,284	$ 5,083	$ 5,983	$ 3,320	$ 3,595	$ 4,684
Provision for federal taxes	400	725	450	470	453	530	1,675
Provision for state taxes	40	50	50	145	60	65	100
Excess profits tax	60	1,875	3,200	3,760	1,737	1,951	
Postwar contingencies				600			
Minority interest						20	51
Net income to surplus	$ 1,337	$ 1,634	$ 1,383	$ 1,008	$ 1,070	$ 1,029	$ 2,858
Surplus beginning of year	671	1,546	2,488	3,181	3,417	3,679	4,581
Other surplus credits						1,046	600
Preferred dividends	299	299	299	299	299	299	149
Common dividends	98	392	392	392	392	392	680
Other surplus debits	65			81	117	482	298
Surplus end of year	$ 1,546	$ 2,489	$ 3,181	$ 3,417	$ 3,679	$ 4,581	$ 6,912
Equity in earnings of uncons. subs.	$ 139	$ 158,	$ 103	$ 88	$ 88		
Dividends from uncons. subsidiaries					34		

(1) Consolidated, including Niles Rolling Mill Co. and Detroit Seamless Steel Tubes Co. from April 1, 1945, date acquisition.

(2) Includes profit of Bopp Steel Corp. and Steel Trucking Inc. for two months from date of acquisition only.

(3) Includes $3,503,950 (1945, $2,446,501) repairs and maintenance and in 1946 approximately $1,300,000 idle pla expense attributable to strikes.

Source: Company records.

3. SHARON STEEL CORPORATION

Summary of Earnings, 1929-1946

	(In Millions)					Common Stock		
	Net Sales	% Oper. Inc. of Sales	Depreciation	Income Taxes	Net Income	Earnings	Dividends Paid	Price Range
1929	$22.94	$12.1	$0.95	$0.14	$1.34	$3.52	$1.43	
1930	14.83	3.1	0.90		d0.75			
1931	10.70	d 1.3	0.93		d1.40			
1932	6.27	d11.3	0.94		d2.02	d5.38	Nil	$ 7-$ 1
1933	10.14	10.2	0.95		d0.27	d0.73	Nil	12- 1
1934	11.25	11.6	0.96	0.22	d0.01	d0.03	Nil	13- 5
1935	15.63	15.1	0.97	0.07	1.01	2.69	Nil	25- 9
1936	21.19	11.4	0.84	0.27	1.31	3.04	1.05	32- 20
1937	20.21	11.6	0.69	0.38	1.35	2.83	1.20	42- 15
1938	10.51	4.3	0.58		d0.10	d1.01	Nil	23- 10
1939	16.18	5.4	0.59	0.05	0.26	d0.11	Nil	21- 10
1940	21.57	10.9	0.59	0.50	1.34	2.65	0.25	16- 8
1941	31.95	16.1	0.90	2.65	1.63	3.40	1.00	14- 7
1942	35.36	16.3	1.14	3.36	1.30	2.56	1.00	10- 8
1943	39.29	16.4	1.17	3.86	0.89	1.51	1.00	17- 9
1944	35.34	12.0	1.09	2.25	1.07	1.97	1.00	18- 13
1945	40.60	11.5	1.22	2.55	1.03	1.86	1.00	28- 16
1946	54.16	9.5	1.16	1.78	2.86	4.39	1.30	40- 23

d = Deficit.

4. SHARON STEEL CORPORATION

Operating Data, 1936-1946

	Consolidated Operations (Net Tons)				Breakdown of Consolidated Sales (Per Cent of Dollar Volume)					
	Pig Iron Produced	Pig Iron Purchased	Ingots Produced	Steel Shipments	Hot Rolled Strip	Cold Rolled Strip	Stainless Strip	Sheet	Seamless Tubing	Misc.
1936	-0-	176,651	486,837	372,444	49.0%	13.0%	7.6%	14.5%	10.0%	5.9%
1937	76,073	98,791	461,881	372,257	49.1	11.3	7.6	16.5	8.8	6.7
1938	113,807	-0-	272,973	205,272	50.3	11.3	5.9	17.0	7.5	8.0
1939	93,868	16,239	443,636	335,714	44.7	12.7	7.6	19.4	8.5	7.1
1940	172,601	60,152	530,010	398,170	45.6	11.6	11.9	17.1	8.1	5.7
1941	151,995	62,364	641,654	503,575	42.1	8.1	19.8	13.3	9.6	7.1
1942	166,629	80,841	640,442	524,270	34.8	11.7	24.9	11.4	11.8	5.4
1943	175,703	93,755	646,428	523,464	29.8	10.2	34.8	11.3	9.6	4.3
1944	149,822	36,504	596,760	485,219	34.2	12.1	26.4	13.1	9.8	4.4
1945	166,113	26,118	582,126	467,828	34.0	11.8	27.2	12.5	8.6	5.9
1946	416,363	27,455	874,190	677,566						

Source: Company records.

5. SHARON STEEL CORPORATION

Manufacturing Properties and Production for May, 1947

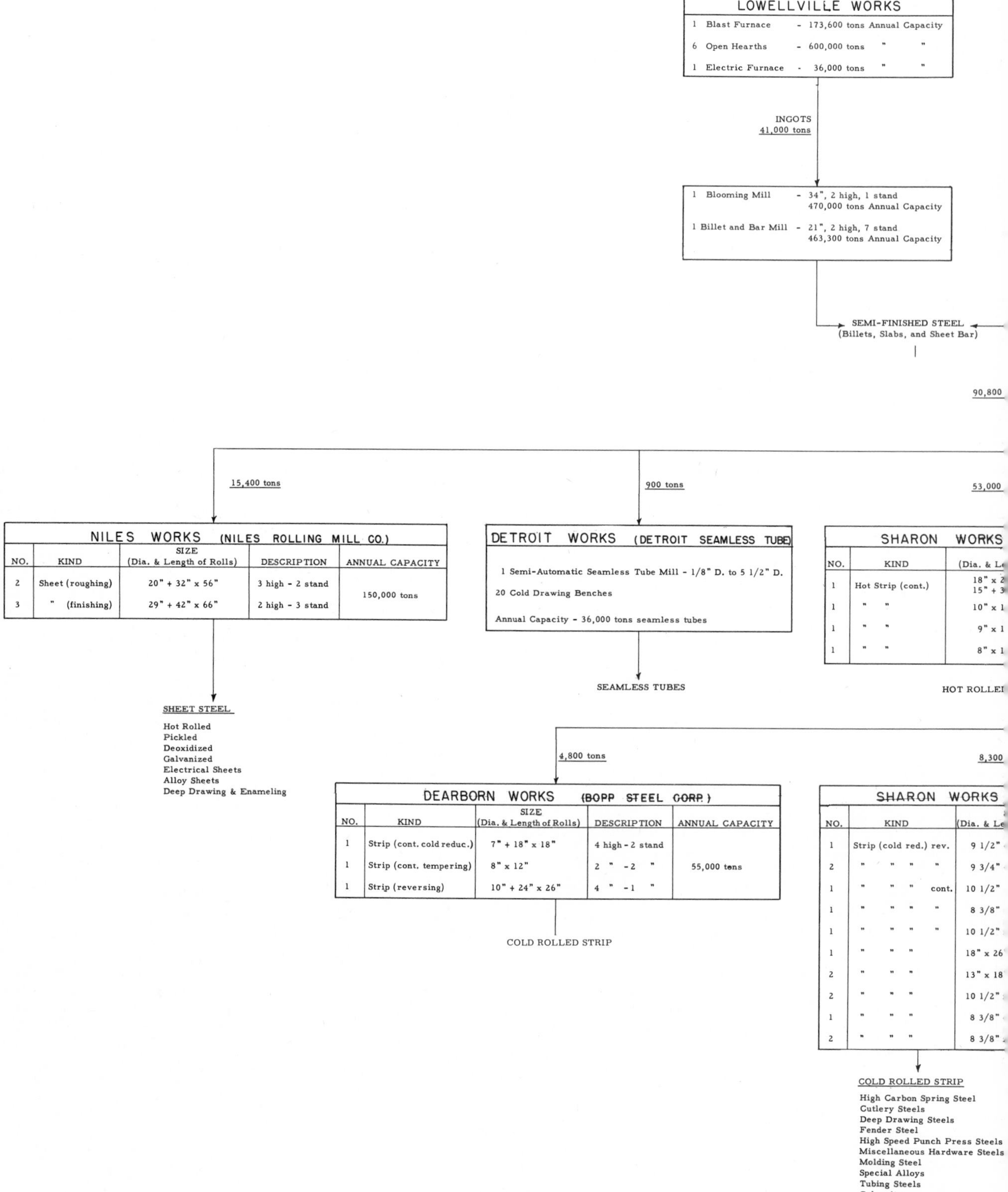

LOWELLVILLE WORKS
1 Blast Furnace - 173,600 tons Annual Capacity
6 Open Hearths - 600,000 tons " "
1 Electric Furnace - 36,000 tons " "
INGOTS
41,000 tons
1 Blooming Mill - 34", 2 high, 1 stand
470,000 tons Annual Capacity
1 Billet and Bar Mill - 21", 2 high, 7 stand
463,300 tons Annual Capacity
SEMI-FINISHED STEEL
(Billets, Slabs, and Sheet Bar)
90,800
15,400 tons
900 tons
53,000
NILES WORKS (NILES ROLLING MILL CO.)
NO.
KIND
SIZE (Dia. & Length of Rolls)
DESCRIPTION
ANNUAL CAPACITY
2 Sheet (roughing) 20" + 32" x 56" 3 high - 2 stand
3 " (finishing) 29" + 42" x 66" 2 high - 3 stand
150,000 tons
DETROIT WORKS (DETROIT SEAMLESS TUBE)
1 Semi-Automatic Seamless Tube Mill - 1/8" D. to 5 1/2" D.
20 Cold Drawing Benches
Annual Capacity - 36,000 tons seamless tubes
SHARON WORKS
NO.
KIND
(Dia. & L
1 Hot Strip (cont.) 18" x 2
15" + 3
1 " " 10" x 1
1 " " 9" x 1
1 " " 8" x 1
SHEET STEEL
Hot Rolled
Pickled
Deoxidized
Galvanized
Electrical Sheets
Alloy Sheets
Deep Drawing & Enameling
SEAMLESS TUBES
HOT ROLLE
4,800 tons
8,300
DEARBORN WORKS (BOPP STEEL CORP.)
NO.
KIND
SIZE (Dia. & Length of Rolls)
DESCRIPTION
ANNUAL CAPACITY
1 Strip (cont. cold reduc.) 7" + 18" x 18" 4 high - 2 stand
1 Strip (cont. tempering) 8" x 12" 2 " - 2 "
1 Strip (reversing) 10" + 24" x 26" 4 " - 1 "
55,000 tons
COLD ROLLED STRIP
SHARON WORKS
NO.
KIND
(Dia. & Le
1 Strip (cold red.) rev. 9 1/2"
2 " " " " 9 3/4"
1 " " " cont. 10 1/2"
1 " " " " 8 3/8"
1 " " " " 10 1/2"
1 " " " 18" x 26
2 " " " 13" x 18
2 " " " 10 1/2"
1 " " " 8 3/8"
2 " " " 8 3/8"
COLD ROLLED STRIP
High Carbon Spring Steel
Cutlery Steels
Deep Drawing Steels
Fender Steel
High Speed Punch Press Steels
Miscellaneous Hardware Steels
Molding Steel
Special Alloys
Tubing Steels
Galvanite
Special Alloy Coated
Tin Coated

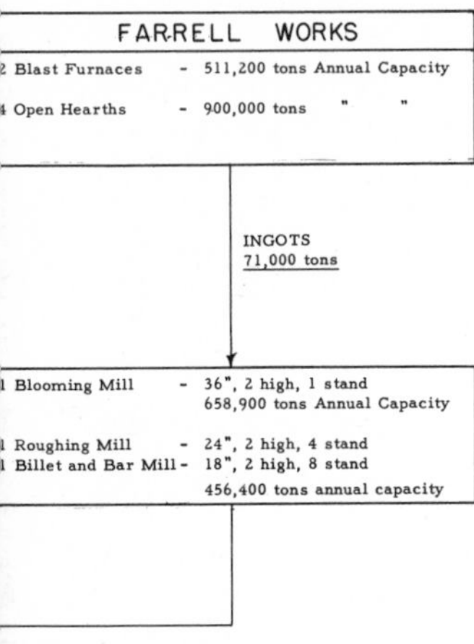

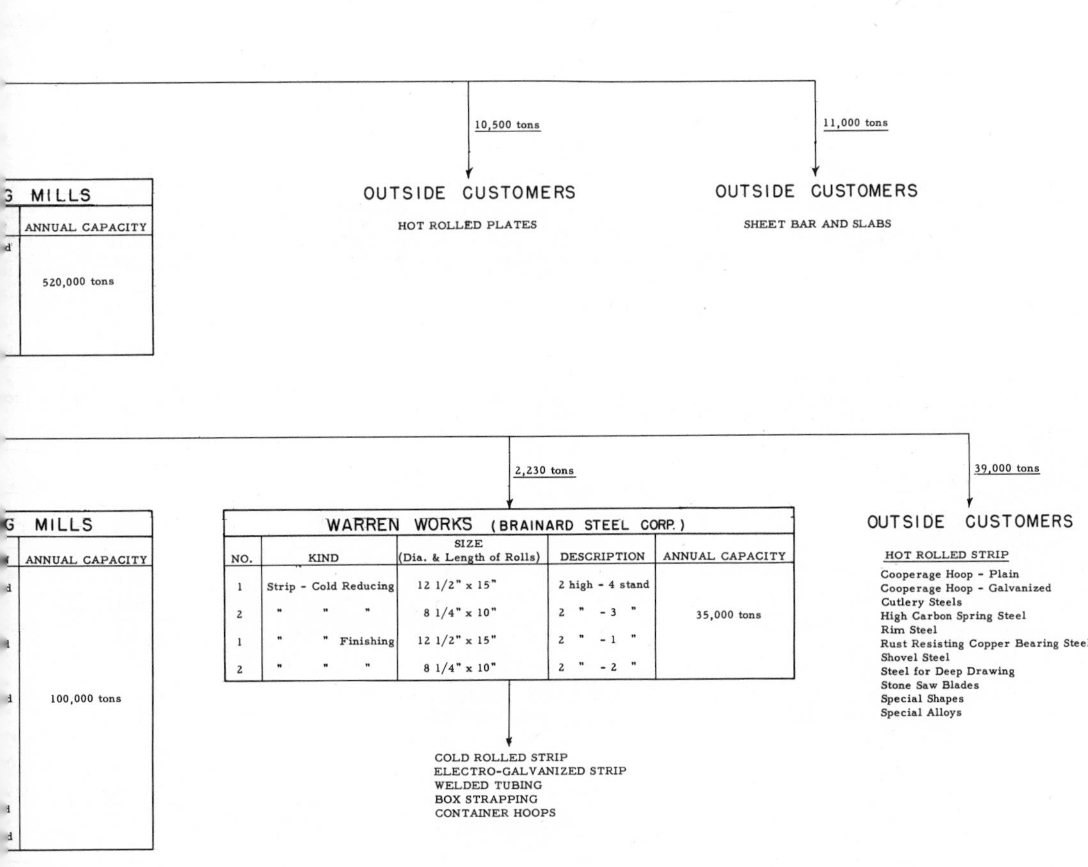

NO.	KIND	SIZE (Dia. & Length of Rolls)	DESCRIPTION	ANNUAL CAPACITY
1	Strip - Cold Reducing	12 1/2" x 15"	2 high - 4 stand	35,000 tons
2	" " "	8 1/4" x 10"	2 " - 3 "	
1	" " Finishing	12 1/2" x 15"	2 " - 1 "	
2	" " "	8 1/4" x 10"	2 " - 2 "	

6. SHARON STEEL CORPORATION

Illustrative Manufacturing Costs, Summer of 1947

BLAST FURNACE #2

METALS CHARGED: (In period of one month)		
Iron Ore	39,683 tons at $ 4.93 per ton =	$195,637
Scrap	20 " at 14.04 " =	281
Sintered Flue Dust	1,837 " at 7.09 " =	13,024
Cinder and Slag	3,697 " at .81 " =	2,989
	45,237	$211,931
LIMESTONE CHARGED:	9,445 tons at $ 1.80 per ton =	17,001
COKE CHARGED:	23,096 tons at 10.53 per ton =	243,201
LABOR AND OTHER OPERATING EXPENSES (except depreciation):		71,000
TONS OF PIG IRON PRODUCED; 22,971 tons; Total Cost:		$543,133

Cost of Metal	=	$ 9.22 per ton of pig
Cost above Metal	=	14.42 per ton of pig
NET COST OF PIG IRON:	=	$23.64 per ton

OPEN HEARTHS - TEN FURNACES OPERATING

(70,000 Tons per Month)

METALS CHARGED PER TON OF INGOTS PRODUCED:		
Pig Iron	1,302 lbs. at $23.64 per ton =	$15.37
Scrap	940 lbs. at 38.00 per G.T. =	15.96
Ore (Metallic Content)	111 lbs. at 11.30 per ton =	63
Misc. Metals	13 lbs. at 155.00 per ton =	1.01
		$32.97
Scrap Credit		1.00
METAL COST PER TON OF INGOTS:		$31.97
COST ABOVE METAL (labor and other expenses, excluding depreciation):		7.57
FLUXES:		.63
MOLDS AND STOOLS:		.44
NET COST OF INGOTS:		$40.61

BLOOMING, BILLET, AND BAR MILLS

(Cost per Ton for Slab Production)

GROSS METAL COST (Yield, 84.3%):	$48.17
Scrap Credit (13.7% salvaged)	5.51
NET METAL COST:	$42.66
COST ABOVE METAL:	3.09
CONDITIONING AND SHIPPING:	1.06
NET COST OF SLABS	$46.81

CONTINUOUS HOT ROLLING MILL

(Cost per Ton for Rolling Slabs into HR Strip)

GROSS METAL COST (Yield, 93.6%):	$50.01
Scrap Credit (6% salvaged)	2.17
NET METAL COST:	$47.84
COST ABOVE METAL:	6.85
LOADING AND SHIPPING:	.73
NET COST OF HR STRIP:	$55.42
AVERAGE SELLING PRICE OF HR STRIP:	$65.00

Source: Company records.

Armco Steel Corporation (A)

The Armco Steel Corporation was a fully integrated steel producer with facilities for performing all steps in the steel process from the mining of coal and iron ore to the manufacture of finished steel products. The company specialized in the production of flat-rolled sheet and strip in standard and special purpose grades sold in hot- or cold-rolled form or with a variety of metal alloy coatings. The company, through its subsidiaries, also manufactured many other items such as structural shapes, pipe, wire fencing, and nails. The products were sold throughout the United States and in most foreign countries. The largest markets were in the automobile, household appliance, and construction industries.

In 1950 the Armco Steel Corporation was approximately the seventh largest producer in the industry. On December 31, 1949, the company's invested capital, including funded debt, totaled over $260,000,000. The sales volume of the company and its subsidiaries for 1949 was approximately $350,000,000; ingot production was about 3¼ million tons. Exhibits 1 and 2 contain consolidated balance sheet and income statements for the corporation for the years 1940–1949.

The parent company's general offices were located in Middletown, Ohio. Steel producing plants were located at Middletown, Ohio; Ashland, Kentucky; Butler, Pennsylvania; and Baltimore, Maryland. The combined annual ingot capacity of these plants in January, 1950, was about 2½ million tons. The Middletown plant was by far the largest of the group and had an annual ingot capacity of 1,128,000 net tons. The Ashland, Butler, and Baltimore plants had capacities of 853,000, 468,000, and 102,000 net tons, respectively. The Baltimore plant operated six electric furnaces and specialized exclusively in the production of stainless steel ingots and rolled products. In addition to the plants listed above, the company operated a small rolling mill in Zanesville, Ohio, and a welded tube plant in Piqua, Ohio.

The Armco Steel Corporation had three wholly owned subsidiaries: the Sheffield Steel Corporation, Armco Drainage and Metal Products, Inc., and the Armco International Corporation. The Sheffield Steel Corporation operated steel producing and fabricating plants in Kansas City, Missouri; Sand Springs, Oklahoma; and Houston, Texas. The company produced a wide variety of steel products such as wire fencing, nails, bolts and nuts, structural steel shapes, and pipe to serve the agricultural, railroad, and oil industries in its localities.

Armco Drainage and Metal Products, Inc., operated more than 40 small fabricating plants located in all parts of the United States and Canada. This subsidiary purchased flat-rolled sheet and strip from the parent company and manufactured metal drainage products such as culverts and pipe and other steel items such as prefabricated steel buildings. These products were sold through the subsidiary's own sales organization to road building and construction concerns.

Armco International Corporation, the third wholly owned subsidiary, conducted all of the export business for the parent corporation. In addition to selling Armco products abroad, Armco International operated steel producing and fabricating plants in foreign countries and licensed the company's processing techniques to foreign concerns.

COMPANY HISTORY

The Armco Steel Corporation was organized in 1900 as the American Rolling Mill Company by Mr. George M. Verity. The first plant consisted of an open-hearth furnace for the production of ingots and rolling facilities for converting the ingots to steel sheet. The company expanded over the years and acquired or merged with other steel producers. Exhibit 3 presents consolidated ingot production, shipments, and net sales for the company for the years 1901 to 1949.

1. *Early History:* At the end of the 19th century, Mr. Verity was the operating head of a metal roofing manufacturing company located in Cincinnati, Ohio. His firm purchased sheet metal from rolling mills and manufactured it into roofing and metal siding. Mr. Verity became interested in plans for a steel rolling mill to supply the roofing concern, and undertook the responsibility for acquiring the initial capital of $500,000, choosing the plant location, gathering the personnel, and supervising construction of

the mill. To avoid being dependent on other mills for steel ingots, Mr. Verity included in his plans an open-hearth furnace, which was a new ingot producing method at that time. Middletown, Ohio, in the Miami Valley, was selected for the mill site, although it was not considered a favorable location for a steel producing plant because of its distance from raw material sources and in seemingly unfavorable position with respect to the markets for steel. The site was chosen, however, because it was close to Cincinnati where Mr. Verity's roofing concern was located. The first heat was tapped in February, 1901, and the first sheet came off the rolling mills shortly thereafter. The production of this first sheet came almost simultaneously with the announcement of the formation of the U.S. Steel Corporation which was organized after a series of steel company mergers and the spectacular purchase by J. P. Morgan of Andrew Carnegie's steel works for $493,000,000.

In the face of the severe competition from the larger companies in the steel industry, the American Rolling Mill Company went through a difficult and trying period in its early days. Mr. Verity believed that his company could not compete on a cost basis on the standard steel items which his competitors were producing. The best chance for success, he believed, was in the production of specialty sheet to meet rigid specifications of buyers. Mr. Verity was of the opinion that the large steel producers would not be interested in the specialty business in view of their size and need for large volume production. In its search for specialty markets, the company offered to cooperate with the Westinghouse Electric and Manufacturing Company in the development of steel sheet with the proper magnetic characteristics for use in electric generators and transformers. With the aid of a Westinghouse research man the company successfully produced an electrical sheet in 1904 which subsequently provided an entree into the large and expanding electrical generating and transmission equipment market.

The demand for sheet increased rapidly, and the company soon found it necessary to increase its rolling capacity. Since the company had ample ingot producing capacity, it arranged a merger with a rolling mill in Zanesville which had no ingot producing facilities.

A second major turning point in the company's effort to attain a position as a producer of specialty steel sheets came in 1909 when it successfully produced a corrosion-resistant steel which became known as Armco ingot iron. The company began its work on a corrosion-resistant steel sheet in an effort to supply the large potential market for steel culverts. Steel for culverts before 1909 was unsatisfactory because it corroded through water contact. A chemist in the Department of Agriculture found that the alloys in steel caused much of the corrosion. The company's problem then became one of producing ingots with a minimum of impurities such as phosphorous, sulphur, and carbon. After much experimentation over a period of five years, the company turned out ingots from its open-hearth furnaces that were guaranteed to be "99.84 per cent pure." The expansion of road building in the United States provided a large demand for steel culverts made out of ingot iron and the demand for the company's flat-rolled sheet increased accordingly. Other uses for corrosion-resistant steels were soon discovered which further increased the company's market. It was found, for example, that ingot iron sheet was especially suitable as a base for the porcelain-enamel coating used in refrigerators and kitchen ware. The increased production of other home electrical appliances also enlarged the market for ingot iron sheet.

In 1909, the company built an entirely new open-hearth shop and rolling mill at a cost of $3,000,000 in Middletown. The original plant later became a fabricating plant and all ingot production and rolling facilities were centralized at the new plant, which became known as the East Works. The decision to build the new open-hearth shop and rolling mill resulted from a recognition by company officials of a need for a more economical production process. In the original plant, the molten steel was cast into small ingots which were then broken down into sheet bar for further processing in the rolling mill. In the new plant a blooming mill was installed which made it possible to process ingots of much larger size.

World War I taxed the steel producing facilities of the company as well as those of the entire steel industry. The high rate of activity throughout the war years enabled the company to strengthen its financial position.

Prior to 1918, the company purchased pig

iron for use in its open-hearth furnaces. In order to gain control of a source of pig iron, the company purchased the assets of the Columbus Iron and Steel Company located in Columbus, Ohio, in 1918. The Columbus Iron and Steel Company operated coke ovens and a blast furnace and owned coal, ore, and limestone reserves and ships for transporting ore to its blast furnace. The acquisition of the assets of the Columbus Iron and Steel Company gave Armco a fully integrated operation from raw materials to rolled steel.

To further strengthen its position with regard to pig iron supply, the company in 1928 purchased a blast furnace located in Hamilton, Ohio, which was 12 miles from the East Works in Middletown. The company then moved its entire coke and pig iron production from Columbus to Hamilton. A special railroad was constructed between Hamilton and the East Works to attain the economy of charging hot pig iron into the open hearths.

2. *Development of the Continuous Hot Strip Mill:* Before 1927, the hot-rolling of steel sheet had involved a large amount of manual work. Workers in the hot-rolling mills would "catch" the sheet as it completed a pass through a rolling stand and would feed the sheet back and forth through the rolls until it was reduced to the desired thickness. Mr. John Tytus, who had come to the company in 1904 as a "spare hand" and who later became a vice-president, thought it would be possible to develop a continuous hot-rolling process that would eliminate the need for manual feeding. Over the years he discussed this project with Mr. C. R. Hook, who was then superintendent of the mill and who later became chairman of the board and chief executive officer. Mr. Tytus experimented on the project from time to time, but because of high demand for sheet, funds were allocated to expanding the manually operated mills. A definite amount of production could be attained on those mills, while it was still very uncertain as to the practicability of the continuous process.

In 1922, the company purchased the properties of the Ashland Iron and Mining Company which consisted of coal mines, blast furnaces, open-hearth furnaces, and a blooming mill. Included in the purchase was a 20-mile railroad and certain gas producing facilities. These properties were sold at a price about equal to the cost of the entire purchase. The Ashland plant lacked finishing mills so the company's board of directors authorized Mr. Tytus to build a continuous hot-rolling mill there. Ten million dollars was appropriated for the project. Later Mr. Hook, chairman of the board, said with regard to this appropriation, "The board of directors voted to take the risk in appropriating $10 million of borrowed money to the continuous rolling project. There was no assurance that it would prove successful, and if it hadn't the company might not have survived."

The continuous hot-rolling mill was built at Ashland and the first sheet was rolled successfully in early 1924. Patents were acquired on the new process. It was found in 1927 that similar work was being done at a steel plant in Butler, Pennsylvania, which in the opinion of the company officials infringed the American Rolling Mill patents. The process at Butler provided for the continuous hot-rolling of strip several hundred feet long; the process at Ashland was limited to the rolling of individual sheets. The company purchased the Butler plant and thereby acquired the continuous hot strip mill as well as a shop for producing forged-steel railway car wheels. The car wheel shop represented the company's first steel product outside of the flat-rolled category.

After the successful development of the continuous hot-rolling process, the American Rolling Mill Company licensed its use to other steel manufacturers including the U.S. Steel Corporation, Republic Steel Corporation, and the Youngstown Sheet and Tube Company. In 1937, twelve domestic and two foreign steel companies had licenses under the company's patents. Royalty income in that year totaled $806,000. Under the license agreements royalty payments ceased after 1945.

The sheet and strip capacity of the industry increased substantially with the continuous process and the resultant lower price of steel sheet encouraged the production of all-steel automobile bodies, which provided a huge market for flat-rolled sheet. Mr. C. R. Hook, in speaking of the continuous hot-rolling process and the use of steel in automobile bodies said, "In 1923, before the development of continuous rolling, deep drawing sheet for automobile fenders sold for $135 a ton. By 1939 a better quality steel sheet for fenders sold for $62 a ton. Without the continuous rolling of sheet, this reduction in cost would not have been possible."

3. *Armco Drainage and Metal Products, Inc., and Armco International Corporation:* Armco Drainage and Metal Products, Inc., was organized as a wholly owned subsidiary in 1941 to centralize control of the company's operations in the drainage and fabricated products business which had been carried on previously by 22 separate, wholly owned subsidiaries. The Armco Drainage subsidiary became responsible for the fabrication and sale of a wide variety of fabricated metal products including culverts, drainage pipe of many kinds, and sewage equipment. In addition it produced light and heavy prefabricated steel buildings known as Steelox buildings. The subsidiary's products were sold to the construction industry, railroads, airports, and soil conservation services. In 1950, Armco Drainage and Metal Products, Inc., operated over 40 fabricating plants. A typical fabricating plant employed about 250 workers. These plants purchased steel sheet and strip from the parent company and further processed it into finished steel products of the types listed above.

The parent company's activities in the drainage products business dated back to 1904 when work was begun with the Corrugated Iron Culvert Manufacturers Association to promote the use of steel for culverts instead of concrete. With the successful production of Armco ingot iron described above a suitable corrosion-resistant steel was made available to culvert manufacturers and this market provided a substantial proportion of the company's sales throughout the following years.

In the 1930's, with the advent of the severe nationwide depression, road building activity declined sharply and the independent culvert manufacturers were placed in a precarious position. These firms were typically small companies unable to withstand any prolonged reduction in their volume of sales. The Armco Steel Corporation encouraged the culvert manufacturers to bid on road-building contracts at lower prices. The company in turn hoped to supply the culvert manufacturers with steel to maintain its volume. Many of the culvert manufacturers indicated that they planned to liquidate their businesses. Rather than lose whatever volume of steel these firms could provide, the Armco Steel Corporation decided to buy them out. By 1941, when Armco Drainage and Metal Products, Inc., was organized, the company had acquired 22 subsidiaries in the fabricating field.

The Armco International Corporation was organized as a wholly owned subsidiary in 1924. AIC was responsible for the foreign sale of the company's products as well as the operation of steel plants in Europe and South America.

The company's foreign business stemmed from an order for culverts from Brazil in 1912. To provide the proper type of steel for this order, the company had to study the requirements of its Brazilian customer. The study led to visits to South America by several company executives and the eventual establishment of a foreign office in Rio de Janeiro. The company subsequently expanded its foreign operations by establishing fabricating plants in South America and Europe. Another major activity of Armco International was the licensing of steel mills in foreign countries. The company received royalty payments for assisting in the construction of the mills and advising as to their operation.

4. *Product Diversification:* The company had originally intended to establish a position for itself in the steel industry by concentrating on special grade, flat-rolled sheet. With the development of the continuous hot-rolling process, the company sought large volume orders for flat-rolled sheet and strip in standard and general purpose grades. The company continued, however, to restrict its operations to flat-rolled items with the exception of the forged railway car wheel business which was acquired with the purchase of the Butler plant.

In the latter part of the 1920's, the company's officials became concerned about the possible adverse effects of a reduction in demand for sheet and strip. They decided, therefore, that the company should embark on a program of product diversification.

In 1930, the company purchased the Sheffield Steel Corporation which had its main plant in Kansas City, Missouri. The purchase involved an exchange of stock between the two concerns so that Sheffield became a wholly owned subsidiary of the Armco Steel Corporation. The products and markets of the Sheffield Steel Corporation supplemented those of the parent company. Whereas Armco specialized in flat-rolled sheet and strip for the automobile, electrical appliance, and drainage product markets, Sheffield produced wire and wire products such as bolts, nails, barbed wire fencing, and pipe for the agricultural, railroad, and oil industries. Throughout the depression of the 1930's, the Sheffield Steel Corporation was able to maintain its sales volume and profitable operations.

In 1950, the Sheffield Steel Corporation, which operated as an autonomous unit, owned open-hearth furnaces and rolling mills in Kansas City, Missouri, and Sand Springs, Oklahoma. In addition, Sheffield operated in Houston, Texas, Armco owned coke ovens, a blast furnace, open-hearth furnaces, and a rolling mill. In 1950, the Armco Steel Corporation was constructing a $5,000,000 welded steel pipe plant in Houston, Texas, in cooperation with the A. O. Smith Corporation. This joint venture was undertaken to serve the expanding market in Texas for pipe used in the transmission of oil and natural gas. When completed, it was intended that the new pipe plant would be operated jointly by the Sheffield Steel Corporation and the A. O. Smith Corporation.

In 1934, Armco decided to enter the flat-rolled stainless steel sheet business as an additional step in its product diversification program. The Butler plant, which was a comparatively high cost producer because it lacked hot metal for charging the open-hearth furnaces, was selected as the rolling mill. At that time price was a less important factor than quality in the sale of stainless steel sheet. The company lacked stainless steel ingot capacity to supply the Butler mill and acquired, therefore, in 1937, a 40 percent stock interest in the Rustless Iron and Steel Corporation in Baltimore, Maryland. The Rustless Corporation had developed a process for the direct reduction of chromium ore, an important alloy element in the manufacture of stainless steel ingots. The Rustless Corporation rolled and forged stainless steel products in angles and shapes which did not compete with Armco's flat-rolled products.

The proportion of stock ownership in the Rustless Corporation was gradually increased to more than 50 percent; in 1945 all of the remaining stock was secured. The two companies were merged in 1945 and thereafter the Rustless properties were operated as the Rustless division of the Armco Steel Corporation.

A final step in the company's product and market diversification program was taken in 1948. In that year, the company purchased the assets of the Jackson Tube Company located in Piqua, Ohio. The Jackson plant was subsequently operated as the tubing division of the company and manufactured mechanical tubing by a continuous welding process for the bicycle, automobile, furniture, and household appliance industries.

Exhibits 4 to 6 present data on the company's physical output, operating rate, earnings, dividends, and investment ratios for the years 1925 to 1949.

1. *Plant Locations and Facilities:* The eight divisions of the operations department were: Middletown, Ashland, Butler, Rustless, Zanesville, fabricating, tubing, and mining. Exhibit 7 is a map of the United States showing the location and facilities of each division as well as those of the Sheffield Steel Corporation. The map also shows the location of ore reserves, coal mines, water transportation facilities, and the fabricating plants of Armco Drainage and Metal Products, Inc. Exhibit 8A lists the plant capacities of the various divisions.

(*a*) *Middletown Division:* The Middletown division which was located in Middletown and Hamilton, Ohio, was the largest unit in the operations department. The division operated 110 coke ovens and 2 blast furnaces at the Hamilton works and 8 open-hearth furnaces, 2 electric furnaces, and hot- and cold-rolling mills at the Middletown plants. The Middletown division specialized primarily in the production of standard grades of sheet such as those used for automobile body stampings. In addition, the division produced light gauge zinc and terne-coated sheet[1] as well as the heavier gauges of stainless steel sheet.

Molten pig iron was tapped from the Hamilton blast furnaces into special "thermos bottle" railway cars which were moved over the company's railroad to the open-hearth shop at the East Works in Middletown, 12 miles away. The pig iron, still in a molten state, was then poured into the open-hearth furnaces. Steel ingots were

[1] Terne-coated sheet had a lead and tin coating.

rolled into slabs and the slabs into coils in a continuous blooming and hot strip mill at the East Works and then finished in cold reduction and coating operations to product specifications. Exhibit 9 is a flow chart tracing the input and output at the different production stages at the Middletown division for the year 1948. During 1948 operations at the Middletown division were at almost full capacity. Between 1948 and January 1, 1950, there were no significant changes in the ingot production capacity of the Middletown division except for an increase in electric furnace capacity.

As of January, 1950, the Middletown division had an excess of rolling and finishing capacity over its ingot production capacity. To utilize the excess rolling capacity the Middletown division had been processing cold ingots shipped from the Ashland division. In addition, the Middletown division had been doing some rolling work for customers who had ingots which they wished processed into sheet and strip. By January, 1950, the volume of outside rolling work available was reduced. It was expected, however, that by the fall of 1950 three new open-hearth furnaces would be completed at the East Works which would bring the operations of the Middletown division into full balance, even to the extent of eliminating the processing of ingots produced at the Ashland division. The open-hearth expansion project at Middletown will be discussed more fully when the company's postwar expansion program is considered.

(*b*) *Ashland Division:* The Ashland division, located on the Ohio River in Ashland, Kentucky, operated three blast furnaces, eight open-hearth furnaces, and a continuous hot-rolling mill. The division specialized in the production of heavy plain and galvanized sheeting from 16-gauge upwards. The finishing facilities at Ashland were limited to the continuous hot-rolling mill.

The Ashland division had excess ingot producing capacity in relation to its finishing capacity. As mentioned previously, cold ingots were shipped from Ashland to Middletown where the finishing operations were performed.

(*c*) *Butler Division:* The plants of the Butler division were located in Butler, Pennsylvania, a few miles north of Pittsburgh. The Butler division had six open-hearth furnaces, one electric furnace, and hot and cold reduction mills for the narrower widths of strip. Most of the division's output consisted of specialty grades, such as the electrical steels (silicon steels) and the lighter gauges of stainless steel sheet. In addition, the Butler division forged railway car wheels.

The Butler division had no blast furnaces, and therefore pig iron for charging the open-hearth furnaces was purchased in its area. The pig iron was purchased in cast pig form and charged cold into the open-hearth furnaces.

(*d*) *Rustless Division:* The Rustless division specialized in the production of stainless steel. The division had six electric furnaces, hot-rolling mills, and cold drawing mills located in Baltimore, Maryland. Stainless steel ingots were produced by a patented process in which chrome ore and scrap were reduced in one operation in the electric furnaces. The Rustless division supplied Middletown and Butler with ingots which were then rolled into sheet. The Rustless plant did not produce sheet, but rather specialized in semifinished forms and finished stainless steel products such as wire, rod, angles, and a variety of other shapes.

(*e*) *Zanesville Division:* The Zanesville division plant was located in Zanesville, Ohio, and its facilities were limited to a hot-rolling mill. The Zanesville division rolled high-grade specialty sheet such as the silicon steel sheet used in electric generators and transformers. Bars were shipped to Zanesville from the other Armco plants for the hot-rolling and finishing operations.

(*f*) *Fabricating Division:* The fabricating division had its plant in Middletown at the site of the company's original works. This division fabricated steel products out of sheet produced in the East Works. Its products which were sold by Armco Drainage and Metal Products, Inc., included Steelox prefabricated buildings, spiral welded pipe, and drainage products.

(*g*) *Tubing Division:* The tubing division, located in Piqua, Ohio, manufactured cold drawn, small diameter, welded tubing for use in metal framed furniture and bicycles. Steel strip was supplied to the tubing division by the Middletown division.

(*h*) *Mining Division:* The mining division operated the company's coal mines which will be described below.

2. *Raw Materials Supply:* The Armco Steel Corporation owned wholly, or had an interest in, properties containing its two basic raw materials, coal and iron ore. In addition, the company owned river boats for transporting coal from the mines to its plants and owned stock in a Great Lakes transportation concern that operated lake boats from the Lake Superior region to southern Great Lakes ports.

The company owned and operated six coal mines in West Virginia which produced high volatile coal for making coke. Low volatile coal was purchased on the open market. Coal for the coke ovens at the Hamilton works was shipped from Harewood and Huntington, West Virginia, on company-owned boats and barges to Cincinnati, Ohio, and from there to the works by rail. The Ashland plant had no coke ovens and hence purchased coke for its blast furnaces.

All of the Armco Steel Corporation's iron ore requirements came from the Lake Superior district; the ore was shipped by lake boats to Cleveland and trans-shipped by rail to the plants. Company executives estimated that the Lake Superior ore reserves were sufficient to meet production needs for at least 10 years. The company had augmented its Mesabi ore reserves by its purchase of approximately a third interest in the Consumers Ore Company. The Consumers Ore Company was organized by the Armco Steel Corporation, the Inland Steel Company, and the Wheeling Steel Corporation in 1948. The Consumers Ore Company in turn purchased a 75 percent interest in Butler Brothers, a large iron ore producer in the Mesabi Range.

To prepare for the eventual depletion of the high-grade iron ore in the Lake Superior region, the company was engaged in two cooperative projects: (1) the benefication of taconite (ore-bearing rock with a 25 to 30 percent iron content) and (2) the development of the high-grade ore mines in Labrador.

In 1947, the Armco Steel Corporation, the Wheeling Steel Corporation, Cleveland-Cliffs Iron Company, and Oglebay-Norten and Company formed the Reserve Mining Company with Armco owning a 1/3 interest. The Reserve Mining Company was organized to acquire substantial reserves of magnetic taconite rock and to develop a process for the economical concentration of the iron ore content in the taconite. In 1949, the construction of a pilot plant for the benefication of taconite was undertaken at Armco's Ashland division. The benefication process when fully developed was expected to produce 5 million tons a year of concentrated ore suitable for use in blast furnaces.

The second project by which the Armco Steel Corporation planned to meet its long-term iron ore requirements was the development of the iron reserves located in Labrador and Quebec. Geological explorations in that area had confirmed the existence of 300 million tons of iron ore reserves with an average iron content of about 60 percent and in some deposits as high as 65 percent. Iron ore being shipped from the Mesabi Range averaged 51 percent in iron content.

To exploit the iron ore reserves in the Labrador-Quebec region, two companies were organized, Iron Ore Company of Canada and Hollinger-Hanna, Ltd. The Iron Ore Company of Canada was formed by the Armco Steel Corporation, National Steel Corporation, Wheeling Steel Corporation, and Youngstown Sheet and Tube Company. These firms all consumed iron ore in large quantities and would presumably purchase iron ore coming from the Labrador-Quebec region. Hollinger-Hanna, Ltd. was organized by four mining concerns to supervise the ore development and mining operations for the Iron Ore Company of Canada. For this service it was to receive a fee of 10 cents a ton of ore mined.

The total capital requirement for the project was estimated at between $150,000,000 and $200,000,000, of which Iron Ore Company of Canada was to supply about $75,000,000. Since the project was to extract hitherto untapped ore reserves, it required the construction of mining equipment, hydroelectric power facilities to supply the mining equipment and the community, and a railroad to carry ore from the mines to a terminal point at Seven Islands on the St. Lawrence River. The railroad when completed would be 360 miles long.

DISTRIBUTION

The parent company's products fell into three major categories: (1) flat-rolled steel and stainless steel sheet, plate, and strip, (2) stainless steel bar and wire, and (3) forged steel wheels.

The product grades ranged from general purpose standard steels to a variety of premium and special alloy steels. The company's growth was in large measure a result of its specialization in premium grades and it continued to emphasize this business although it produced a large tonnage of standard sheets and strip.

The products and their order of importance in terms of tonnage produced were as follows: cold rolled, hot-rolled, zinc coated, enameling iron, electrical steel, alloy coated steels, and stainless steel. The company's markets in order of importance were the automobile, household appliance, construction, and agricultural equipment industries.

The company's marketing organization was headed by a vice-president in charge of distribution. The organization was divided into two major groups, sales and market development.

1. *Sales:* The company's products were sold directly to large customers and through jobbers to small customers. The jobbers purchased steel products in large quantities and stored them in warehouses from which they made shipments to small consumers. The company did not own or operate warehouses and hence relied heavily on the jobbers as a channel of distribution.

The United States was divided into three major sales areas, eastern, central, and western, each of which was under the supervision of an area sales manager. Reporting to the area sales managers were 17 district sales managers.

2. *Market Development:* From its inception the company made it a basic sales policy to search out markets and to educate steel fabricating customers on the uses of Armco products. The development of electrical steel and ingot iron in the early days of the company's history are examples of this policy. The company was also the first in the steel industry to advertise the steel producer's name directly to the ultimate consumers of steel and to stamp a company trademark on its products.

The market development program was the responsibility of the market development division in the distribution organization. The market development manager reported directly to the vice-president in charge of distribution. The market development division was divided into four departments: development engineering, commercial research, advertising, and market services.

3. *Pricing Policies:* Prior to the summer of 1948, the Armco Steel Corporation priced its products on the basing point system which was commonly used throughout the steel industry. The price charged a particular customer was the base price at the nearest basing point plus rail freight from that point to the customer's plant, irrespective of the point of actual shipment. In some cases, the rail freight from the basing point was less than the actual transportation cost; in other cases the rail freight from the basing point was more than the actual cost and the company "absorbed" the difference.

In the summer of 1948, following the Supreme Court's reversal of the Circuit Court of Appeals decision on the Cement Case, the company changed its pricing practices along with most other producers in the industry and sold its products on an f.o.b. mill basis.

The immediate effect of f.o.b. pricing on the company's sales volume was insignificant because of the high demand for steel. For the longer term, company executives believed the Middletown plants would be in a favorable position under f.o.b. mill pricing because their market studies indicated that the potential steel demand in the adjacent area exceeded supply. In the case of the Rustless division, the situation was just the reverse. Company executives pointed out that the plants of this division were located in Baltimore, Maryland, while its primary markets were in the Midwest and that it was, therefore, at a serious competitive disadvantage under the f.o.b. pricing system. In 1949, sales of the Rustless division declined. To meet this situation, the company resumed the practice of absorbing freight on shipments from the Rustless plants.

FUTURE PROBLEMS AND PROSPECTS

In reviewing the future prospects of the company, the executives cited several problems to which they expected to give continuing attention. The problems discussed most frequently were related to the demand for steel products, the status of raw materials reserves, and the direction of the company's research program.

1. *Demand for Steel Products:* The company's future prospects hinged to a considerable degree on the general level of demand for steel products. For the very near future, the outlook on demand appeared favorable. In January, 1950, the company's plants were operating at full capacity and forecasts indicated that a high level of operations would be continued for at least six months. In the summer of 1949 demand had tapered off for the company and the steel industry as a whole. The effect of the "pension" steel strike in the fall of 1949, however, was to create a pent-up demand for steel products which required the maximum output of the steel industry in the early part of 1950. On the other hand, there was considerable debate as to the demand for steel in the longer run.

2. *Raw Materials Reserves:* A second problem was the status of the raw materials reserves. The company's efforts to strengthen its position with regard to the supply of iron ore through the beneficiation of taconite and the development of the iron ore mines in Labrador have been discussed. It was expected that if these two projects were carried through successfully, the company would be assured of an abundance of iron ore for its blast furnaces for many years to come. The company was also searching in 1950 for additional coal reserves to keep its coke ovens supplied.

Competitors of the Armco Steel Corporation were also active in extending their reserves of high-grade iron ore. One such venture which was receiving considerable publicity was the Venezuelan mining venture of the United States Steel Corporation. Early in 1950 the United States Steel Corporation announced the discovery of very large and rich iron ore deposits in Venezuela. The corporation was proceeding with the construction of transportation facilities to carry the ore to seaports for shipment to blast furnaces in the United States. Almost in conjunction with the announcement of the Venezuelan ore find, the United States Steel Corporation announced the acquisition of a huge tract of land in the New Jersey-Pennsylvania area bounding the Delaware River near Trenton. It was rumored that the corporation planned the construction of a 2,000,000-ton integrated steel mill on the site. The Venezuelan mines would be the chief source of ore supply for this mill. The ore would be carried to the mill by sea-going vessels up the Delaware River. It was uncertain how the costs of ore imported from the Venezuelan mines would compare with the costs of ore brought from Labrador.

3. *Direction of Research:* The executives were giving considerable thought to the nature and extent of the company's technical research program. Mr. W. W. Sebald, president of the Armco Steel Corporation, pointed to the role of new product development in the company's growth in the past and emphasized that research efforts toward developing new steel products would be continued. In 1948, the Armco Steel Corporation spent $1,150,000 on research, and it was stated that such a high level of research expenditures was a continuing necessity.

1. ARMCO STEEL CORPORATION (A)

Balance Sheets, 1941 to 1949
(In Thousands)

	1941	1942	1943	1944	1945	1946	1947	1948	1949
ASSETS									
Cash and Gov't Notes	$ 35,306	$ 25,139	$ 24,300	$ 31,641	$ 36,689	$ 41,515	$ 25,228	$ 53,880	$ 59,107
Receivables	16,215	15,742	13,803	14,209	25,394	20,009	24,464	30,692	24,782
Inventories	32,182	45,507	45,854	44,073	50,434	61,208	72,395	83,877	71,355
TOTAL CURRENT ASSETS	$ 83,703	$ 86,388	$ 83,957	$ 89,923	$112,517	$122,732	$122,087	$168,449	$155,244
Investments--Net	10,198	11,377	11,072	12,736	5,656	5,073	4,186	9,633	13,380
Plant, Equipment, Less Depr.	94,149	101,439	93,844	85,995	87,565	97,804	119,671	133,720	142,857
Prepaid Expenses	1,061	951	1,137	1,127	1,231	1,540	2,848	4,402	3,264
TOTAL ASSETS	$189,111	$200,155	$190,010	$189,781	$206,969	$227,149	$248,792	$316,204	$314,745
LIABILITIES									
Total Current Liabilities	$ 27,798	$ 32,360	$ 26,254	$ 26,236	$ 32,010	$ 40,155	$ 45,265	$ 55,916	$ 48,032
Long-Term Debt	23,300	24,828	17,750	14,750	14,000	38,500	37,000	69,160	64,290
Current Operating Reserves	2,063	2,514	3,269	3,070	2,924	3,545	3,956	4,610	4,815
TOTAL LIABILITIES	$ 53,161	$ 59,702	$ 47,273	$ 44,056	$ 48,934	$ 82,200	$ 86,221	$129,686	$117,137
Stockholders' Equity	135,950	140,453	142,737	145,725	158,035	144,949	162,571	186,518	197,608
TOTAL LIAB. & EQUITY	$189,111	$200,155	$190,010	$189,781	$206,969	$227,149	$248,792	$316,204	$314,745
CAPITAL STOCK:									
Preferred	$ 44,993	$ 44,993	$ 44,993	$ 44,993	$ 44,993	$ 19,993	$ 19,993	$ 19,993	$ 20,000
Common	71,739	71,739	71,739	71,739	32,413	32,413	32,413	39,093	39,094
Reserve for Contingencies	1,000	2,500	3,580	5,820	3,070	3,070	3,070	-0-	-0-
Capital Surplus	4,795	4,795	4,795	4,795	47,839	47,838	47,838	57,960	57,959
Earned Surplus	13,423	16,426	17,630	18,378	29,720	41,635	59,257	69,472	80,554
TOTAL EQUITY	$135,950	$140,453	$142,737	$145,725	$158,035	$144,949	$162,571	$186,518	$197,608

Source: Company records.

2. ARMCO STEEL CORPORATION (A)

Income Statements, 1941 to 1949
(In Thousands)

	1941	1942	1943	1944	1945	1946	1947	1948	1949
Sales	$169,178	$180,979	$199,266	$200,819	$220,145	$231,931	$311,685	$382,564	$341,350
Other revenues	2,229	1,908	2,081	2,497	2,444	2,320	2,415	3,262	7,699
	$171,407	$182,887	$201,347	$203,316	$222,589	$234,251	$314,100	$385,826	$349,049
Employment costs:									
Wages and salaries	$ 42,123	$ 48,055	$ 55,790	$ 64,145	$ 70,231	$ 73,765	$ 91,284	$104,025	$ 95,219
Social security taxes	1,536	1,187	1,355	1,296	1,438	1,438	1,501	1,473	1,414
Pensions and insurance	965	104	223	169	1,002	1,226	1,514	1,917	2,223
	$ 44,624	$ 49,346	$ 57,368	$ 65,610	$ 72,671	$ 76,429	$ 94,299	$107,415	$ 98,856
Materials and services	$ 92,558	$ 97,571	$113,290	$110,279	$118,905	$118,916	$166,802	$211,804	$184,983
Depreciation	5,134	7,332	10,701	11,051	8,954	5,001	6,952	8,161	9,591
Loss on assets	1,351	338	546	397	665	376	911	662	444
Interest	536	1,007	901	564	1,086	828	1,075	1,825	2,022
Other charges	459	2,912	470	630	3,378	781	371	939	343
State, local, and misc. taxes	1,803	1,732	2,081	2,104	2,095	1,917	2,223	2,917	2,761
Federal income taxes	12,714	13,368	8,812	5,373	5,420	11,450	16,465	20,072	19,131
	$114,555	$124,260	$136,801	$130,398	$140,503	$139,269	$194,799	$246,380	$219,275
TOTAL	$159,179	$173,606	$194,169	$196,008	$213,174	$215,698	$289,098	$353,795	$318,131
Income before Contingencies	$ 12,228	$ 9,281	$ 7,178	$ 7,308	$ 9,415	$ 18,553	$ 25,002	$ 32,031	$ 30,918
Contingencies	1,000	1,500	1,080	2,240	3,977*	-0-	-0-	-0-	-0-
Income for the Year	$ 11,228	$ 7,781	$ 6,098	$ 5,068	$ 13,392	$ 18,553	$ 25,002	$ 32,031	$ 30,918

*Addition to income.
Source: Company records.

3. ARMCO STEEL CORPORATION (A)

Consolidated Ingot Production, Shipments and Net Sales, 1901–49

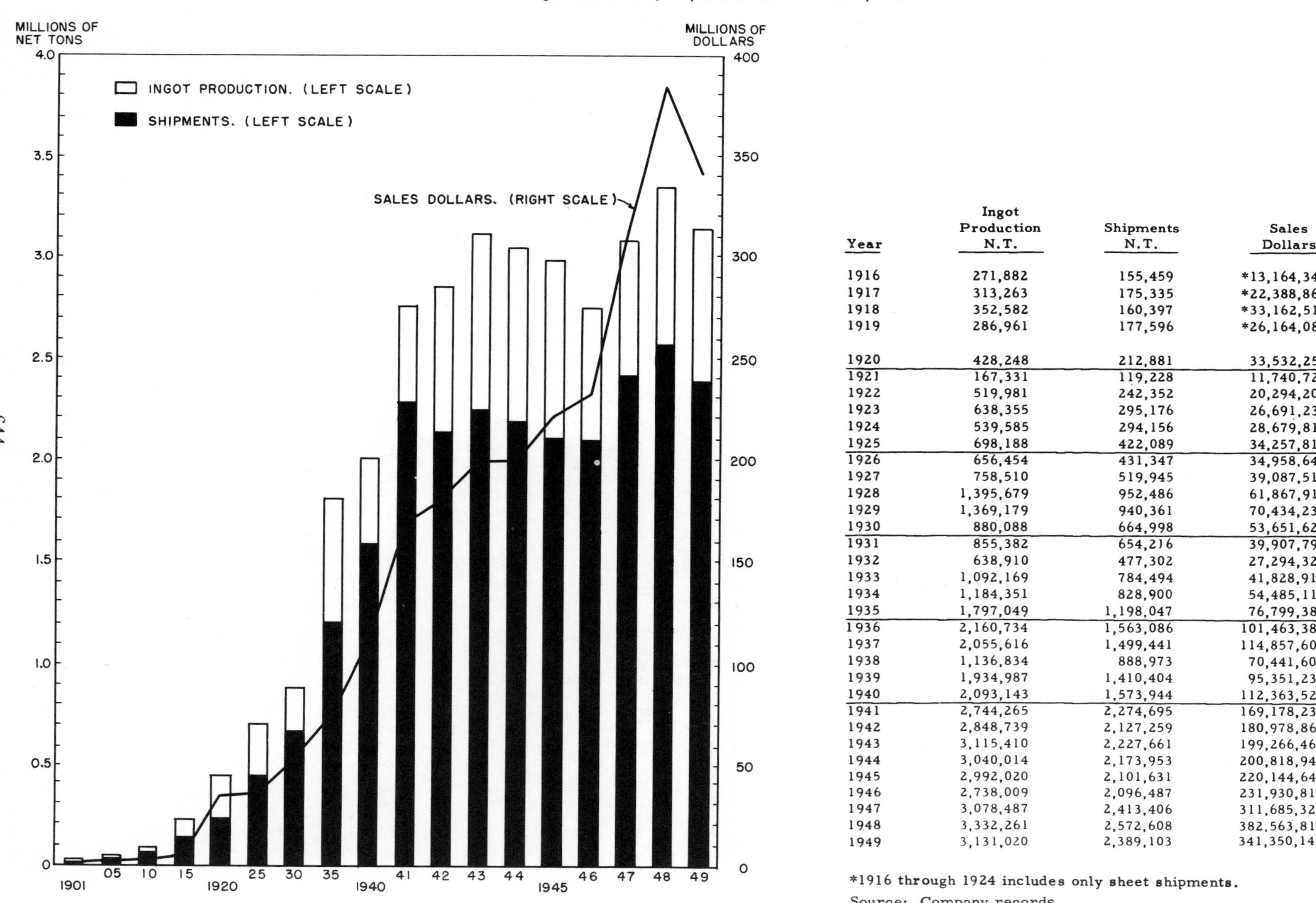

Year	Ingot Production N.T.	Shipments N.T.	Sales Dollars
1916	271,882	155,459	*13,164,344
1917	313,263	175,335	*22,388,862
1918	352,582	160,397	*33,162,516
1919	286,961	177,596	*26,164,084
1920	428,248	212,881	33,532,254
1921	167,331	119,228	11,740,728
1922	519,981	242,352	20,294,205
1923	638,355	295,176	26,691,235
1924	539,585	294,156	28,679,818
1925	698,188	422,089	34,257,812
1926	656,454	431,347	34,958,643
1927	758,510	519,945	39,087,519
1928	1,395,679	952,486	61,867,914
1929	1,369,179	940,361	70,434,233
1930	880,088	664,998	53,651,626
1931	855,382	654,216	39,907,797
1932	638,910	477,302	27,294,322
1933	1,092,169	784,494	41,828,918
1934	1,184,351	828,900	54,485,115
1935	1,797,049	1,198,047	76,799,385
1936	2,160,734	1,563,086	101,463,383
1937	2,055,616	1,499,441	114,857,600
1938	1,136,834	888,973	70,441,606
1939	1,934,987	1,410,404	95,351,230
1940	2,093,143	1,573,944	112,363,529
1941	2,744,265	2,274,695	169,178,239
1942	2,848,739	2,127,259	180,978,867
1943	3,115,410	2,227,661	199,266,466
1944	3,040,014	2,173,953	200,818,944
1945	2,992,020	2,101,631	220,144,648
1946	2,738,009	2,096,487	231,930,811
1947	3,078,487	2,413,406	311,685,322
1948	3,332,261	2,572,608	382,563,811
1949	3,131,020	2,389,103	341,350,147

*1916 through 1924 includes only sheet shipments.

Source: Company records.

4. ARMCO STEEL CORPORATION (A)
Physical Output and Operating Rate, 1925–59

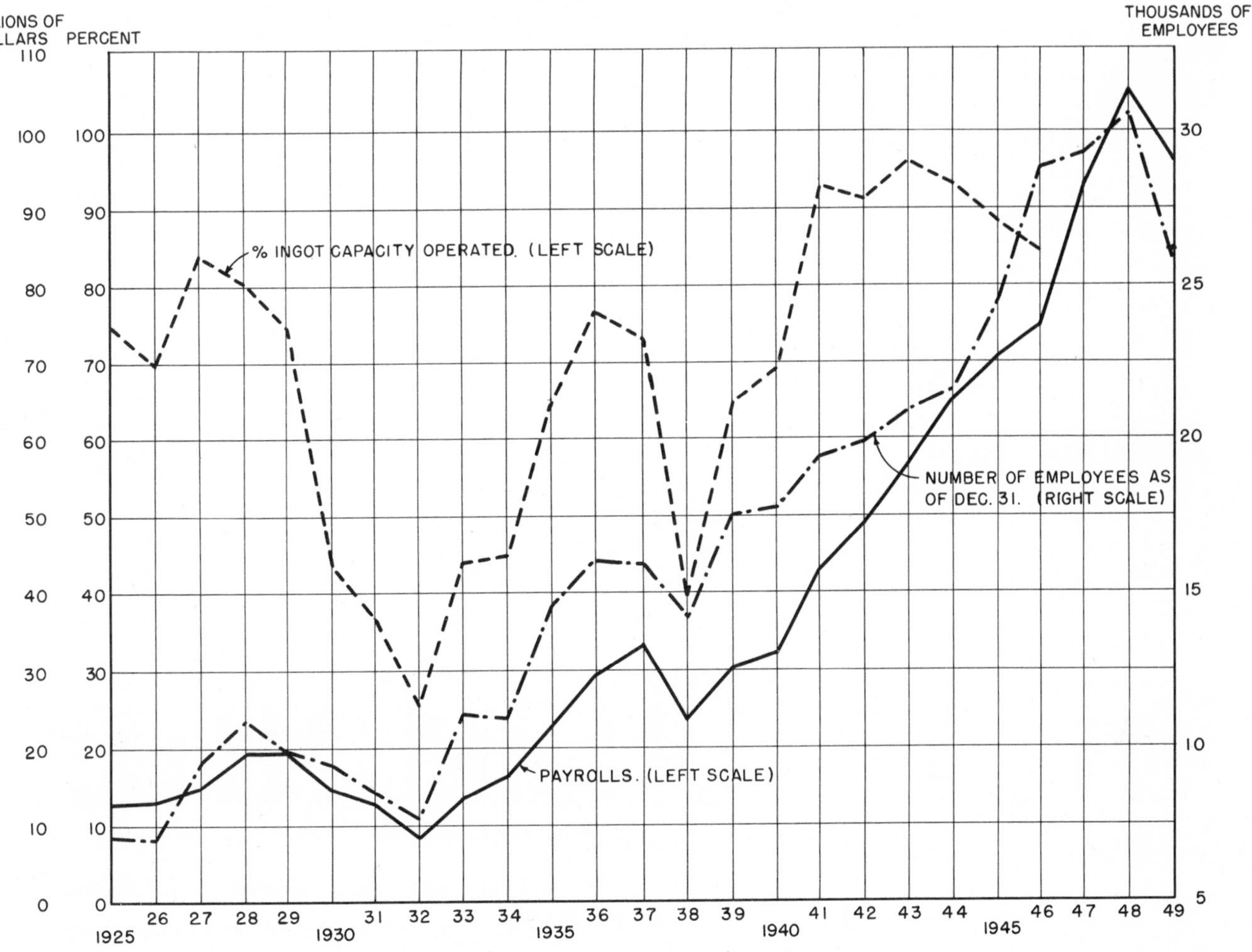

Year	Ingots Produced (Net Tons)	% Ingot Capacity Operated	Product Shipments (Net Tons)	Number of Employees	Payrolls
1932	638,910	25.8	477,302	7,660	8,713,310
1933	1,092,169	44.1	784,494	11,293	13,234,170
1934	1,184,351	45.4	828,900	11,177	16,872,260
1935	1,797,049	66.0	1,198,047	14,503	22,440,420
1936	2,160,734	77.7	1,563,086	16,536	29,327,120
1937	2,055,616	72.5	1,499,441	16,204	33,769,160
1938	1,136,834	39.4	888,973	14,295	23,747,729
1939	1,934,987	64.7	1,410,404	17,583	30,395,267
1940	2,093,143	69.1	1,573,944	17,777	31,945,335
1941	2,744,265	92.8	2,274,695	19,345	43,045,749
1942	2,848,739	90.9	2,127,259	19,995	48,902,953
1943	3,115,410	96.8	2,227,661	21,052	56,377,766
1944	3,040,014	93.1	2,173,953	21,957	64,786,517
1945	2,992,020	88.5	2,101,631	24,569	70,868,905
1946	2,738,009	84.6	2,096,487	28,432	74,896,811
1947	3,078,487		2,413,406*	28,982	92,787,405
1948	3,332,261		2,572,608*	30,617	105,412,258
1949	3,131,020	84.5	2,389,103	26,048	96,404,964

*Includes products manufactured from ingots of other producers.
Source: Company records.

5. ARMCO STEEL CORPORATION (A)

Summary of Company Earnings and Dividend Record, 1925–49

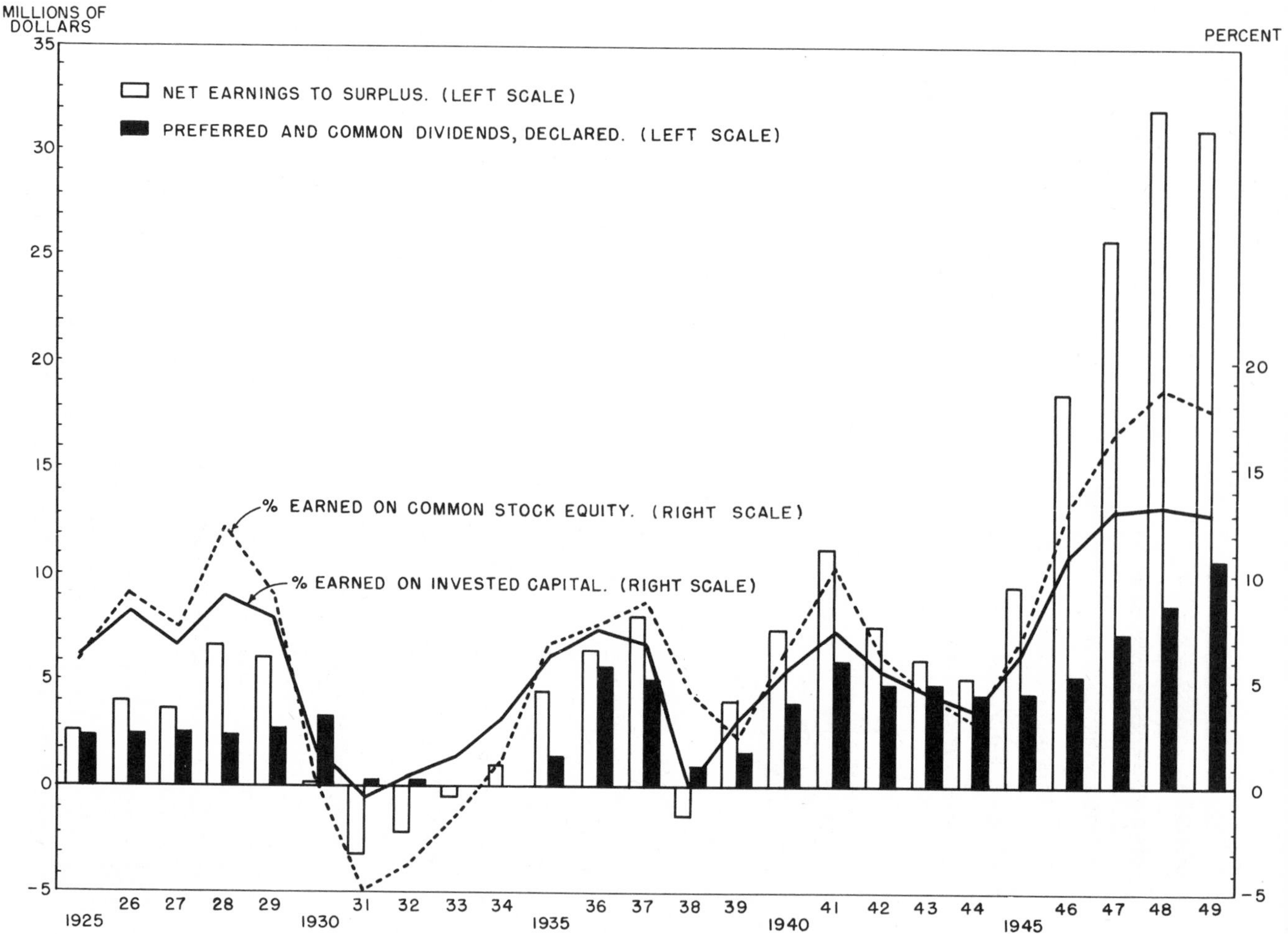

Year	Earnings on Invested Capital	Interest on Debt	Net Earnings to Surplus	Preferred & Common Dividends	Earnings Retained	% Earned on Invested Capital‡	Earnings Per Share Common	% Earned on Common Stock
1932	$ 210,800	$2,240,402	$ 2,029,602*	$ 118,620	$ 2,148,222*	.24	$1.26*	3.61*
1933	1,471,604	2,144,693	673,089*	---	673,089*	1.53	.46*	1.38*
1934	3,149,738	2,183,172	966,566	---	966,566	3.18	.50	1.49
1935	6,698,303	2,388,173	4,310,130	1,416,653	2,893,477	6.12	2.41	6.74
1936	8,235,031	1,793,354	6,441,677	5,749,027	692,650	7.51	2.73	7.64
1937	9,140,629	909,294	8,231,335	4,988,294	3,243,041	6.89	2.55	8.67
1938	1,200,996*	106,884	1,307,880*	1,012,523	2,320,403*	.93	1.16*	4.09
1939	4,095,837	83,928	4,011,909	1,800,000	2,211,909	3.17	.69	2.44
1940	7,816,244	173,530	7,642,714	3,979,705	3,663,009	5.59	1.96	6.58
1941	11,764,467	535,992	11,228,475	6,040,778	5,187,697	7.43	3.21	10.23
1942	8,787,739	1,006,751	7,780,988	4,893,420	2,887,568	5.40	2.01	6.19
1943	6,999,097	901,023	6,098,074	4,893,446	1,204,628	4.46	1.42	4.33
1944	5,631,916	563,925	5,067,991	4,319,722	748,269	3.64	1.06	3.21
1945	10,501,039	1,086,392	9,414,647	4,319,739	5,094,908	6.21	2.58	6.72
1946	19,380,678	828,187	18,552,491	5,231,725	13,320,766	10.74	5.35	14.21
1947	26,077,023	1,074,812	25,002,211	7,380,755	17,621,456	13.07	7.44	16.90
1948	33,855,670	1,824,958	32,030,712	8,682,739	23,347,953	13.24	8.00	18.69
1949	32,940,495	2,022,293	30,918,202	10,667,783	20,250,419	12.96	7.68	17.92

* Loss.
Source: Company records.

6. ARMCO STEEL CORPORATION (A)

Table of Investment Ratios, 1925–49

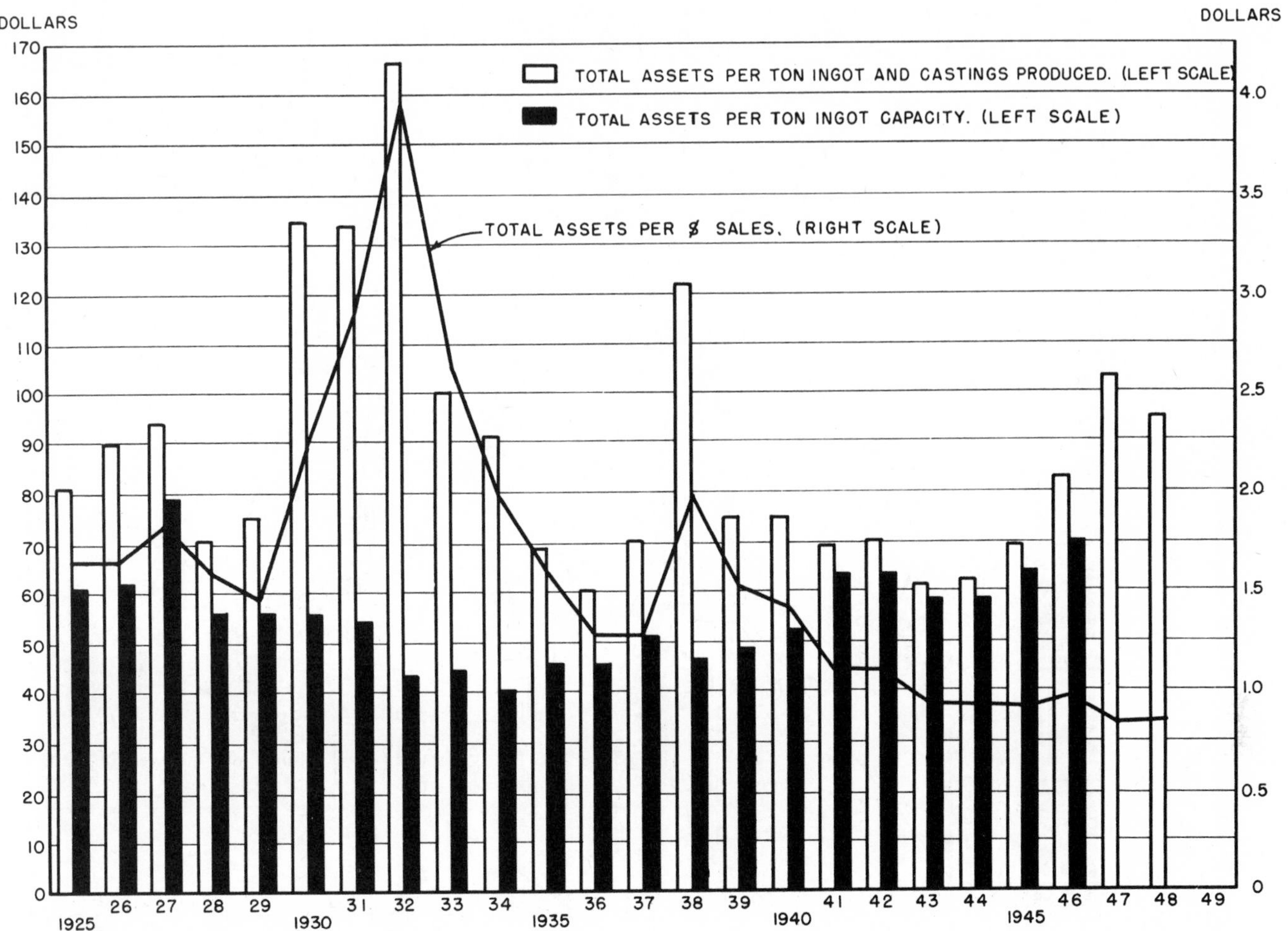

Year	Total Assets per Ton Produced	Total Assets per Ton Ingot Capacity	Total Assets per $ Sales	Total Assets per Employee
1932	$167	$43	$3.92	$13,925
1933	99	44	2.59	9,554
1934	91	40	1.98	9,645
1935	68	45	1.60	8,458
1936	60	45	1.27	7,777
1937	70	51	1.26	8,927
1938	122	46	1.98	9,711
1939	75	48	1.52	8,208
1940	75	52	1.40	8,833
1941	69	63	1.12	9,776
1942	70	63	1.11	10,010
1943	61	58	.95	9,026
1944	62	58	.95	8,643
1945	69	64	.94	8,424
1946	83	70	.98	7,989
1947	103		.80	8,584
1948	95		.82	10,328
1949				

Source: Company records.

7. ARMCO STEEL CORPORATION (A)

Map of the U.S. with Plant Facilities

HOUSTON TEXAS 47 8
SAND SPRINGS OKLAHOMA 1
KANSAS CITY MISSOURI 5
HAMILTON OHIO 110 2
MIDDLETOWN OHIO 8 2
PIQUA OHIO MECHANICAL TUBING
ASHLAND KENTUCKY 3 8
ZANESVILLE OHIO
BUTLER PENNSYLVANIA 6 1
BALTIMORE MARYLAND 6

LEGEND

- COKE OVENS
- BLAST FURNACES
- OPEN HEARTHS
- ELECTRIC FURNACES
- ROLLING MILLS
- △ ARMCO FABRICATING PLANT
- ▽ AD&MP PLANTS
- C COAL RESOURCES
- ^^ ORE RESOURCES
- RIVER TRANSPORTATION
- LAKE TRANSPORTATION OF ASSOCIATED COMPANIES

SALES OFFICES

- A ARMCO
- S SHEFFIELD
- B AD&MP
- C ARMCO & AD&MP
- D ARMCO, AD&MP & AIC
- E ARMCO & SHEFFIELD
- F SHEFFIELD & AD&MP
- G ARMCO, SHEFFIELD & AD&MP
- H AD&MP & AIC

Source: Company records.

8A. ARMCO STEEL CORPORATION (A)
Plant Capacities of Various Divisions
Coke, Blast Furnaces and Steel Capacities (Net Tons)
January 1, 1950

	Monthly		Annual
Hamilton 110 ovens	40,000		480,000
Houston 47 ovens	21,000		252,000
Total Coke Capacity	61,000		732,000
Ashland #1 } 3 Blast Furnaces	11,917	Ashland Blast Furnaces	143,000
Norten } 3 Blast Furnaces	14,833	Ashland Blast Furnaces	178,000
Bellefonte } 3 Blast Furnaces	36,000	Ashland Blast Furnaces	432,000
Hamilton #1	22,000		264,000
Hamilton #2	25,000		300,000
Total Parent Co.	109,750		1,317,000
Houston	22,833		274,000
Total Blast Furnace Capacity	132,583		1,591,000
Ashland O.H. 8 furnaces	71,083		853,000
Butler O.H. 6 "	34,000		408,000
" Elect. 1 "	5,000		60,000
Middletown O.H. 8 "	76,000		912,000
" Elect. 2 "	18,000		216,000
Rustless - Elect 6 "	8,500		102,000
Total Parent Co.	212,583		2,551,000
Kansas O.H. 5 "	35,000		420,000
Sand Springs O.H. 1 "	4,500		54,000
Houston O.H. 8 "	64,000		768,000
Total Sheffield	103,500		1,242,000
Total Steel Capacity	316,083		3,793,000

8B. ARMCO STEEL CORPORATION (A)
Investments in Iron Ore Concerns and Shipping Company

Associated Companies:	Percentage of Ownership	Investment 12/31/48 At Cost	Equity per Reports of Associates
Hanna Ore Mining Company	15	$ 660,383	$ 918,715
The Castile Mining Company	25	579,416	603,678
Richmond Iron Company	33.33	27,629	118,263
The St. James Mining Company	25	293,513	293,513
Reserve Mining Company	33.33	1,012,667	1,012,667
Consumers Ore Company			
Class A	28)	5,600,000	5,793,607
Class B	40)		
Columbia Transportation (shipping)	11.49	258,043	427,660
United Dominion Mining Company	6.67	14,501	22,512
Total		$8,446,152	$9,190,615

Source: Company records.

9. ARMCO STEEL CORPORATION (A)

Flow Chart of Input and Output, Middletown, 1948

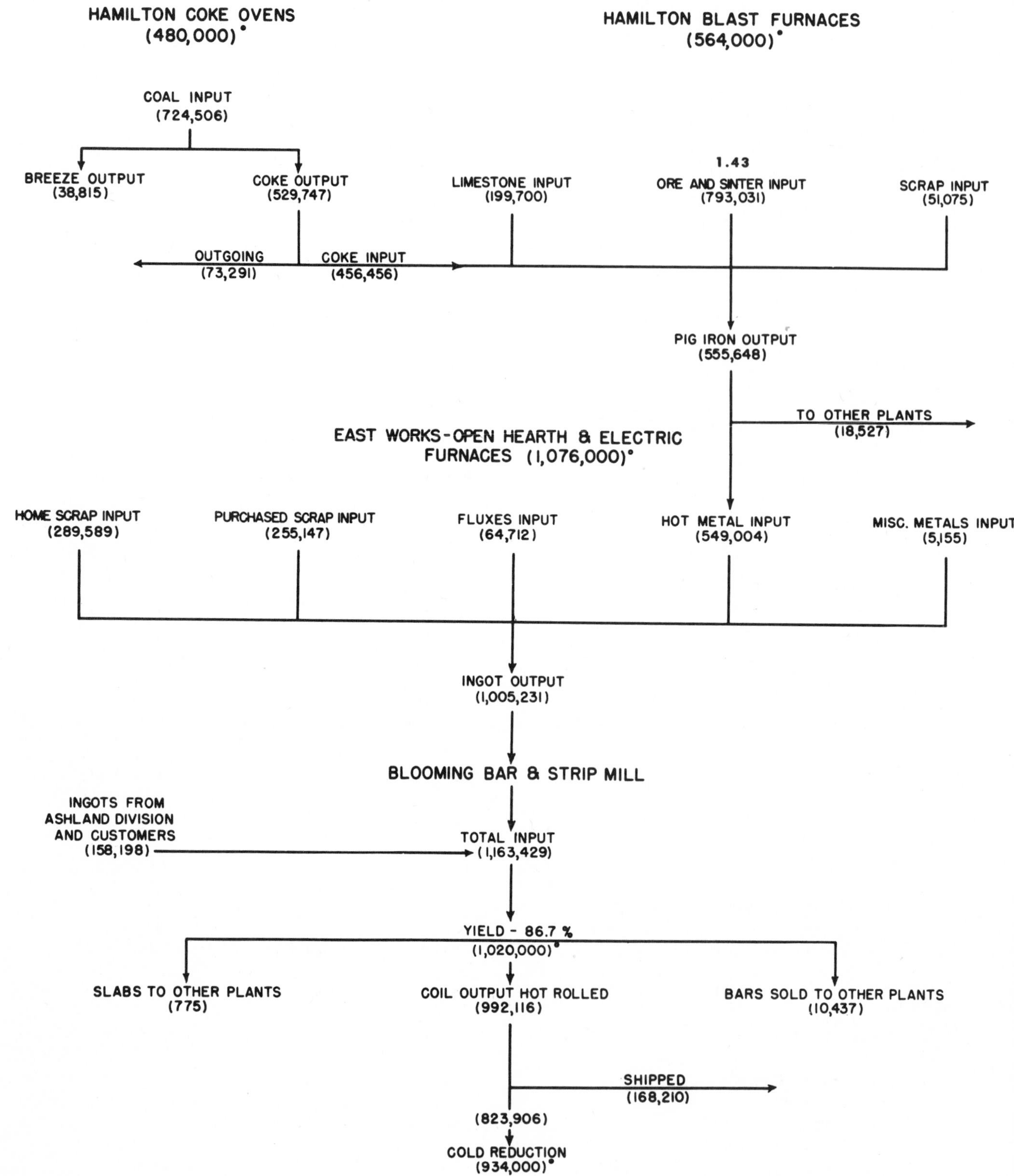

Note: ° indicates capacities. All other figures are inputs and outputs.
All figures in net tons.
Source: Company records.

Armco Steel Corporation (B)

In 1944, the Armco Steel Corporation organized a postwar planning committee of its top executives in order to analyze the status of the company's plant facilities and to make recommendations for a postwar capital improvements and expansion program. The committee recommended a construction program to cost $40 million; this total was later increased to about $55 million.

After the cessation of hostilities in 1945, the company began the execution of its postwar expansion plans. The amounts spent on capital projects are listed below. These amounts included the expenditures for the new construction program as well as expenditures for the replacement of old equipment.

1945	$ 8,434,868
1946	16,170,428
1947	28,568,018
1948	21,348,909
1949	24,000,000
	$98,522,223

In the period 1945 to 1949 the expansion program increased the company's ingot capacity by 422,000 tons or 13 percent. The finishing capacity was increased to keep pace with the added ingot producing capacity. Exhibit 1 is a schedule of capital expenditures for the Armco Steel Corporation from 1925 to 1949.

The capital development program was financed largely through the reinvestment of earnings and funds available from annual depreciation charges. In 1946 the company negotiated a long-term loan of $40,000,000 from the Equitable Life Assurance Company. The loan consisted of 2¾ percent debentures maturing in 20 years and repayable in annual installments of $1,500,000 beginning in 1947. With these funds the company retired an outstanding bank loan of $15,000,000 and $25,000,000 of outstanding 4½ percent cumulative convertible preferred stock.

In February, 1948, the company sold an additional $30,000,000 of 20-year 3 percent debentures to the Equitable Life Assurance Company. With these funds, the company planned to continue its program of improvements and expansion and to proceed with its project for the beneficiation of taconite rock. An additional $5,000,000 of debentures was sold to the assurance company late in 1948 to help cover the purchase of the Defense Plant Corporation's blast furnace in Houston, Texas, which was being operated by the Sheffield Steel Corporation.

It was proposed to continue the company's plant expansion program into 1950 by additional investment of $30,000,000 for new facilities. A major project under consideration in 1949 was the construction of three new open-hearth furnaces at the East Works of the Middletown division. This project will be discussed in detail below.

EXPANSION OF THE OPEN-HEARTH SHOP AT THE EAST WORKS

If approved, construction of the three new open-hearth furnaces at the East Works would be started in the fall of 1949. It was estimated that the furnaces would cost $12,000,000 and would have an ingot output of 32,600 net tons a month. The project was under consideration by the company's board of directors in the summer of 1949, based upon the report and recommendations of a management committee which had been studying the problem for two years.

In its report to the board of directors, the management committee considered four major factors: (1) the need for bringing the Middletown ingot capacity into balance with the rolling and finishing capacity, (2) the comparative production cost of ingots from the existing and new open-hearth furnaces, (3) the cost of rebuilding the existing eight open-hearth furnaces, which were in need of a major overhauling, with and without the new construction program, and (4) the market for sheet and strip in the company's favored market area.

1. *Balance of Ingot Capacity with Rolling and Finishing Capacity:* In January, 1950, the Middletown division's facilities would be set up to process 120,000 ingot tons a month. The existing eight open-hearth furnaces could produce 72,000 tons a month and the two electric furnaces 20,000 tons a month at a 90 percent operating rate.[1] The ingot capacity thus totaled 92,000 tons a month and was 28,000 tons short of the rolling and finishing capacity.

[1] The management committee based all of its production output cost calculations on a 90 percent operating rate.

Prior to 1950, the ingot deficiency had been made up by ingots shipped from the Ashland division to Middletown and by ingots supplied by customers for processing in the Middletown rolling mill. The management committee pointed out that the business of converting customers' ingots had declined in 1949 and that such business would probably be unavailable in the future. The committee also reported that the maximum tonnage which could be shipped from Ashland in the future would be only 11,000 net tons a month. The ingots from Ashland cost about $4.25 a ton more than the ingots produced at Middletown because of the transportation costs and the costs of reheating the cold ingots. Since a ton of ingots yielded an average of .7 of a ton of finished sheet, a cost difference of $4.25 a ton on the ingots amount to $6.07 a ton on finished sheet. At an operating level of 120,000 tons per month, the company obtained an estimated $30 per ton of finished sheet steel as contribution to depreciation charges and out-of-pocket fixed costs. Due to steel losses during the rolling operation, which reduced the yield of finished steel to 70 percent of the ingot input, contribution earned per ton of Middletown open-hearth ingot was $21. Any Ashland ingots not needed at Middletown could be sold at Ashland at a contribution of about $5 per ton. It was believed that by 1950 the company would no longer be able to buy ingots from outside sources for rolling at Middletown at a price which would permit profitable operations.

It was anticipated that the three new open-hearth furnaces would make an additional 28,000 tons of ingots a month available to the Middletown rolling and finishing mills. The new furnaces had an output of 32,600 tons operating at 90 percent of capacity. It was anticipated, however, that the operation of the new furnaces would involve a reduction in the output of the existing furnaces by 4,100 tons a month, because the molten pig used in the existing furnaces would have to be reduced.

The existing eight open-hearth furnaces received molten pig iron from the Hamilton blast furnaces. The monthly capacity of the blast furnaces was approximately 48,000 tons a month. The eight open-hearth furnaces consumed 45,000 tons of molten pig a month and operated on a charging ratio of approximately 55 percent pig to 45 percent scrap. It was anticipated that when the new furnaces were completed the available molten pig iron would be distributed between the old and new furnaces as shown in the "tons per month" figure in Exhibit 2B. The reduction in the molten pig available to the eight existing furnaces would reduce their output by 4,100 tons a month because of the additional time required to charge and melt the additional scrap. The net increase in ingot output at Middletown from the new furnaces was thus estimated at 32,600 tons minus 4,100 tons or 28,500 tons.

2. *Comparative Production Costs:* Exhibit 2A shows the estimated cost of ingots from the existing and new furnaces for different pig to scrap charging ratios and for scrap prices of $25 and $30 a ton. It also shows the ingot costs which would develop in the new and existing furnaces with the available supply of molten pig limited to 48,000 tons a month as discussed above.

As indicated in Exhibit 2B, the equivalent of 6.3 of the existing furnaces would operate with a charge of 50 percent hot pig and the equivalent of .9 of a furnace with a charge of 32 percent hot pig. The equivalent of 2.4 of the new furnaces would operate with a charge of 32 percent hot pig and the equivalent of .3 of a furnace with a charge of 32 percent cold pig.[2] The cold pig was to be shipped from the Ashland blast furnaces at the rate of 1,150 tons a month. The ratios of hot metal to scrap were below the optimum for economical operation but would be necessary because of the limitations on the available supply of hot pig. Since the new furnaces would have more efficient scrap charging facilities than the existing furnaces, it was planned to run them on a higher proportion of scrap than the existing furnaces. From the data in Exhibit 2 the committee could calculate how much less the cost of ingots would be from the new furnaces at scrap prices of both $25 and $30 per ton.

The committee stated that the maximum economy from the operation of the new open-hearth shop would not be realized until another blast furnace could be constructed to provide a greater quantity of molten pig iron. When ample hot pig became available, the committee

[2] On the 90 percent basis of calculation, 8 existing furnaces equaled 7.2 operating furnaces and 3 new furnaces equaled 2.7 operating furnaces.

estimated that the cost of ingots from the new furnaces would be about $1.50 a ton less than the cost of ingots from the existing furnaces (see Exhibit 2A).

3. *Cost of Rebuilding Old Furnaces:* The third major factor considered by the committee was the cost of rebuilding the eight existing open-hearth furnaces if the new furnaces were built and if they were not built. The committee stated in its report that the eight existing open-hearth furnaces were in need of a major rebuilding work, including the construction of new foundations and the installation of auxiliary equipment to improve charging and other operations. The committee reported that if the three new open-hearth furnaces were not authorized, the rebuilding would be spaced over a two-year period at a cost of $3,348,000. In addition, there would be a loss in production of 180,000 ingot tons over the two-year period because of "downtime" which would result in an estimated reduction in profits of $1,260,000 on the sale of finished sheet. If the three new open-hearth furnaces were authorized, the existing furnaces could be rebuilt over a four-year period and at a schedule to coincide with the normal dates for rebuilding the furnaces. The cost of the major rebuilding job under these conditions was estimated at $1,976,000 with a loss of 90,000 ingot tons over the four-year period or the equivalent of an estimated $630,000 in the profits on sheet steel. The total savings on the rebuilding job resulting from the authorization of the new open-hearth furnaces were thus calculated at $2,002,000 (see Exhibit 3A).

4. *Study of Market for Sheet and Strip:* The fourth major consideration in the open-hearth expansion project was the market potential for the increased production and for the company's products as a whole. In July of 1948, after the Cement Case decision when the steel industry shifted to f.o.b. mill pricing, the company's market development department made a study of the market potential for the company's products in the areas surrounding each of the plants. The company executives stated that this study indicated that there was a favorable balance of potential market demand to producing capacity in the area in which the Middletown division had a freight advantage over competing mills. Mr. Sebald stated that the market report was a basic factor leading to the decision to build the three additional open-hearth furnaces. He also stated that Middletown's favorable location with respect to the market was a relatively recent development; prior to 1938, he said, there was excess capacity in relation to demand in the Middletown market area. The company had been engaged in a program to attract new steel sheet consuming industries to the Middletown region.

As an incidental part of its study, the committee compared production costs in the electric furnaces and the open-hearth furnaces. The electric furnaces required a 100 percent scrap charge and therefore the ingot costs varied considerably with the price of scrap. The committee calculated that the cost of ingots from the electric furnaces would equal the cost of ingots from the existing open-hearth furnaces when scrap was selling at $18 a ton. Any scrap price in excess of $18 a ton would make electric furnace ingots more expensive than ingots from the existing open-hearth furnaces. Assuming an 87½ percent yield from the open hearths and a 99 percent yield from the electrics, it was calculated that electric furnace steel would cost $42.71 per ton at a scrap price of $25 and $47.74 per ton at a scrap price of $30. The committee, therefore, viewed the electric furnaces in operation at Middletown as long-term stand-by equipment, to be used when the demand was high enough to warrant their operation or when the price of scrap was low enough to make their use more economical than use of the open-hearth furnaces. To balance ingot production with hot strip mill capacity, however, would require the full-time operation of the electric furnaces even after the new open-hearth furnaces were in full production.

Completion of the three new open-hearth furnaces was expected to place the Middletown division in a better competitive position from a cost standpoint. Mr. Sebald, president of the company, pointed out, however, that the open-hearth project could not be considered apart from a longer-range program involving the construction of a new blast furnace and then possibly additional open-hearth furnaces in the Middletown division to keep the pig iron capacity in balance with ingot capacity. These steps, Mr. Sebald stated, involved consideration of the adequacy of the company's iron ore and coal reserves to meet the blast furnace requirements. Mr. Sebald pointed out that the decision to build additional open-hearth capacity in Middletown involved highly complex considerations requiring long-range thinking on the part of the company's executives.

1. ARMCO STEEL CORPORATION (B)

Schedule of Capital Expenditures, 1925–49

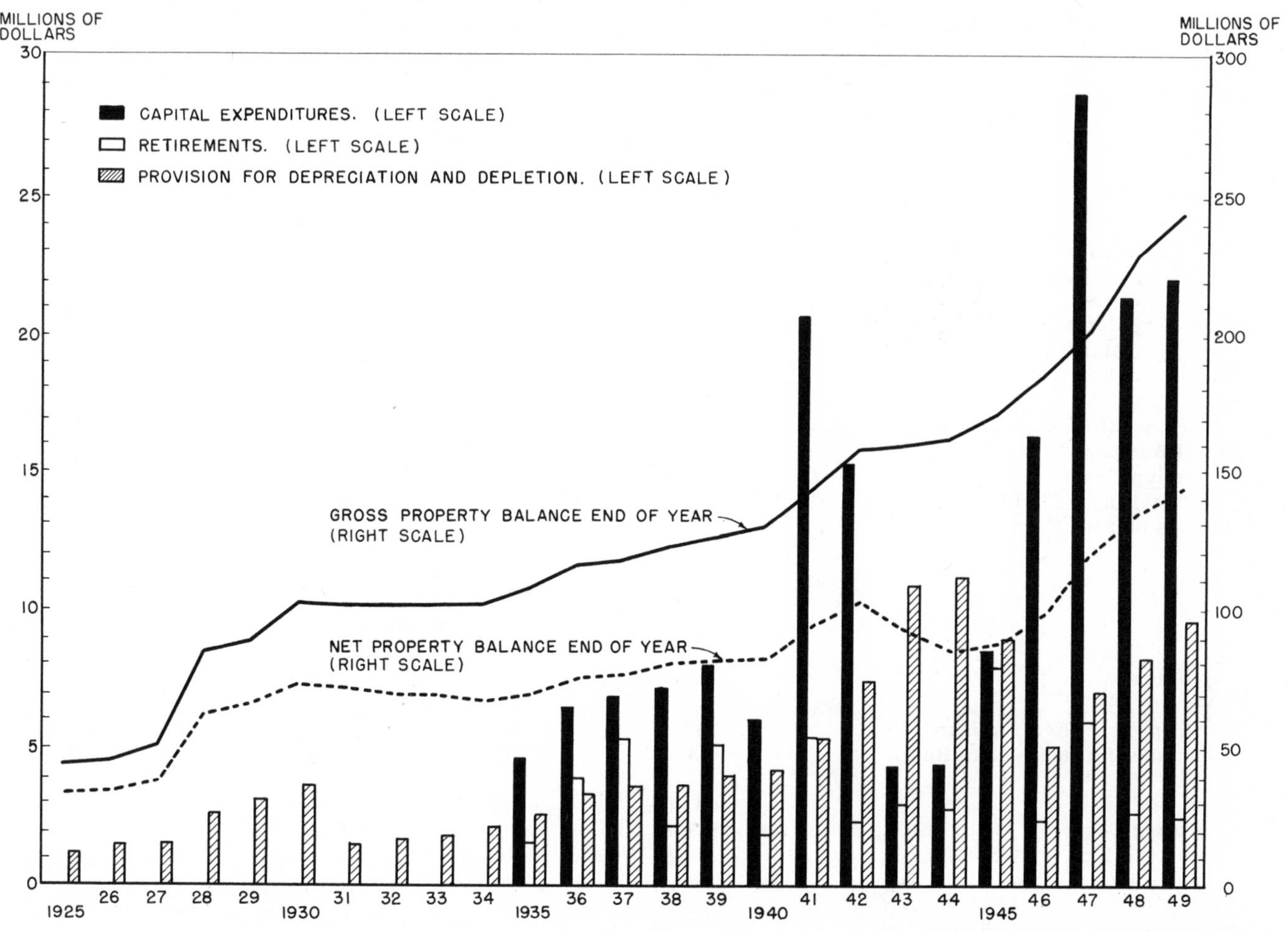

	PROPERTY, PLANT, AND EQUIPMENT				DEPRECIATION AND DEPLETION	
Year	Capital Expenditures	Retirements	Gross Property	Net Property	Depreciation*	Depreciation Reserve
1935	$ 4,453,986	$1,547,827	$106,383,041	$ 70,324,945	$ 2,344,751	$36,058,096
1936	6,448,555	3,821,871	116,256,173	75,925,056	3,180,022	40,331,117
1937	6,782,037	5,198,455	117,810,818	76,625,268	3,369,386	41,185,550
1938	7,134,792	2,129,178	122,574,002	79,343,228	3,516,405	43,230,774
1939	7,816,879	5,081,585	125,523,912	80,360,750	3,970,173	45,163,162
1940	5,899,027	1,759,172	129,379,257	80,800,311	4,208,803	48,578,946
1941	20,688,993	5,202,009	144,730,116	94,148,957	5,133,899	50,581,159
1942	15,152,000	2,219,411	157,514,559	101,438,786	7,331,872	56,075,773
1943	4,093,540	2,804,465	159,335,854	93,844,032	10,701,387	65,491,822
1944	4,288,069	2,697,915	160,780,438	85,995,118	11,050,456	74,785,320
1945	8,434,868	7,797,267	171,298,364	87,564,743	8,953,949	83,733,621
1946	16,170,428	2,333,768	185,135,024	97,803,804	5,000,811	87,331,220
1947	28,568,018	5,807,846	209,340,804	119,670,866	6,951,619	89,669,938
1948	21,348,909	2,519,716	229,069,997	133,720,154	8,161,074	95,349,843
1949	22,032,888	2,301,782	244,722,003	142,856,480	9,591,016	101,865,523

*Includes depletion
Source: Company records.

2A. ARMCO STEEL CORPORATION (B)
Data on Comparative Economy of Operations

	Existing Furnaces			New Furnaces		
Percentage Molten Pig Iron Charged						
at Scrap Cost of $25/Ton	55%	40%	30%	55%	40%	30%
Metal Additions	31.89	31.44	31.36	31.89	31.44	31.36
Operating Costs	$7.40	$7.75	$8.11	$5.82	$6.21	$6.38
Total Ingot Costs	39.29	39.19	39.47	37.71	37.65	37.74
Savings on New Furnaces				1.58	1.54	1.73
At Scrap Cost of $30/Ton						
Metal Additions	34.17	34.81	35.29	34.17	34.81	35.29
Operating Costs	7.40	7.75	8.11	5.82	6.21	6.38
Total Ingot Costs	41.57	42.56	43.40	39.99	41.02	41.67
Savings on New Furnaces				1.58	1.54	1.73

2B. ARMCO STEEL CORPORATION (B)
Ingot Costs on Basis of Limited Molten Pig Iron Availability

New Situation		Existing Furnaces		New Furnaces	
Per Cent of Molten Pig Iron		50%	32%	32%	32% (cold pig)
Number of Furnaces (90% Rate)		6.3	0.9	2.4	0.3
Tons per Month		60,000	7,900	29,400	3,200
Operating Cost		$ 7.49	$ 7.92	$ 6.38	$ 6.97
Molten Pig Iron	@ $25.80/Ton	14.89	9.28	9.28	
Cold Pig Iron	@ 31.90/Ton				11.47
Charge Ore	@ 11.00/Ton	1.10			
Scrap	@ 25.00/Ton	12.68	19.14	19.14	19.14
Alloys and Flux		3.00	3.00	3.00	3.00
Total Cost		$39.16	$39.34	$37.80	$40.58
Additional Cost—Scrap @ $30.00/Ton		2.54	3.83	3.83	3.83
Total Cost		$41.70	$43.17	$41.63	$44.41

Note: Figures for tons per month are: 60,000 - 7,900 - 29,400 - 3,200.

Source: Company records.

3A. ARMCO STEEL CORPORATION (B)
Costs of Rebuilding Eight Existing Open Hearth Furnaces

	Normal*	Accelerated**
Costs of Rebuilding Eight Existing Open Hearth Furnaces:		
Cost of Rebuilding Eight Open Hearth Furnaces	$1,300,000	$2,672,000
Cost of Auxiliary Equipment and Repairs	676,000	676,000
Total Cost	$1,976,000	$3,348,000
Loss in Production Due to "Down Time":		
Down Time for Each Furnace	2 months	2 months
Down time for Normal (Recurring) Overhaul	1 month	
Net Time Lost Chargeable Directly to Rebuilding	1 month	2 months
Loss of Ingot Tonnage per Furnace per Month	10,000 tons	10,000 tons
Loss of Ingot Tonnage (8 Furnaces Times No. of Months)	80,000 tons	160,000 tons
Added Loss of Ingot Tonnage Because of Interference with Adjacent Furnaces	10,000 tons	20,000 tons
Total Loss of Ingot Tonnage	90,000 tons	180,000 tons
Number of Years for Rebuilding Furnaces	4 years	2 years
Yearly Loss of Ingot Tonnage	22,500 tons	90,000 tons
Yearly Loss of Equivalent Finished Sheet (70%)	15,750 tons	63,000 tons
Estimated Yearly Loss in Profits (@ Profit Rate of $10/Ton)	$ 157,500	$ 630,000
Estimated Loss in Profit over Entire Rebuilding Period	630,000	1,260,000
Calculation of Savings:		
Difference in Cost of Rebuilding	$1,372,000	
Difference in Loss in Profits	630,000	
Total Rebuilding Savings under "Normal" Program	$2,002,000	

*Normal refers to costs of rebuilding existing open hearth furnaces assuming the proposed three new open hearth furnaces were constructed (4-year project).

**Accelerated refers to costs of rebuilding existing open hearth furnaces assuming the proposed three new open hearth furnaces were not constructed (2-year project).

3B. ARMCO STEEL CORPORATION (B)
Facilities Utilized at Varying Levels of Market Demand

I. Market demand of 120,500 tons per month:

Present Operations		Proposed Operations	
Existing open hearths (8) =	72,000 tons	Existing open hearths (8) =	67,900 tons
Electric furnaces (2) =	20,000 tons	Electric furnaces (2) =	20,000 tons
Ashland ingots =	11,000 tons	New open hearths (3) =	32,600 tons
	103,000 tons		120,500 tons
Ashland ingots for sale	0 tons	Ashland ingots for sale	11,000 tons

II. Market demand of 100,500 tons per month:

Present Operations		Proposed Operations	
Existing open hearths (8) =	72,000 tons	Existing open hearths (8) =	67,900 tons
Electric furnaces (2) =	20,000 tons	New open hearths (3) =	32,600 tons
Ashland ingots =	8,500 tons		
	100,500 tons		100,500 tons
Ashland ingots for sale	2,500 tons	Ashland ingots for sale	11,000 tons

Note: Numbers in parentheses (8) indicate number of furnaces.
Source: Company records.

McLouth Steel Corporation

The McLouth Steel Corporation of Detroit, Michigan entered the steel industry with limited financial resources but soon became an integrated corporation with facilities for all stages of the steelmaking process from blast furnace to cold rolling. Although it was incorporated in 1934 with the limited objective of processing steel slabs purchased from the large mills, McLouth Steel constructed its own iron and steelmaking facilities subsequent to World War II. During the postwar period, the company doubled its size every two years and became an increasingly important supplier of steel to Detroit's automobile manufacturers. Between 1947 and 1954, total assets of the company increased from $7½ million to $149 million, and net plant from $3 million to $101 million. Net sales which were $18 million in 1947 were estimated to be $140 million in 1955 at the completion of the expansion program. Comparative income statements and balance sheets are shown in Exhibit 1 and 2.

In 1955 McLouth executives were pioneering the first oxygen converter installation in the United States. The company's market was concentrated on the automobile industry and on stainless steels. In the midst of the major expansion program, in July, 1954, the founder of the company died; therefore, the security of the organization depended on the ability of the new management to establish the company in a permanent niche in the industry.

HISTORY OF THE COMPANY

The McLouth Steel Corporation was organized in 1934 to process steel slabs into hot-rolled strip for the Detroit market. The founder of the company, Mr. Donald B. McLouth, had been engaged since the early 1920's in the purchase and resale of secondary steels.

In 1934 the major item of equipment of the McLouth Steel Corporation was a single stand reversing hot mill which the company purchased for only $350,000 plus royalty payments based on output. The mill was unique in that all the rolling operations were made by reversing the steel back and forth through the one stand, rather than passing steel continuously through multiple stands as in the case of modern rolling equipment. It later became known familiarly in the company as the "coffee grinder." Since the company had no melting facilities, the purchased slabs were heated and passed into the "coffee grinder," which contained coilers housed in small furnaces on either side of the rolls. As the steel was passed through the rolls it was successively coiled and uncoiled and heated to enable the one stand to perform the entire operation. A picture of the "coffee grinder" is shown in Exhibit 3.

The remarkable aspect of the reversing hot mill was that its construction was so simple that it could operate at very low cost if it could be made to operate at all. Since there was only one stand, its initial purchase price was far below that of a multiple stand mill. Because of the coiling action, the space required for the run-out table was shorter than that necessitated by a continuous mill.

Its peculiarities, however, did not make the "coffee grinder" simple to operate. Since Mr. McLouth was a salesman and organizer rather than a production specialist, he needed an experienced steelmaker with a reliable production crew. Ivor Bryn, with 14 years experience in steel production, was placed in charge of operations. Although Mr. Bryn was able to put the reversing mill in operation, it required two years and much rebuilding to make it effective.

The expense of bringing the reversing mill into operation had been so great, however, that by 1936, McLouth Steel was in precarious financial condition. At this time, Mr. Merlin A. Cudlip left his position as vice-president and secretary of the Packard Motor Company to join McLouth. Mr. Cudlip was named treasurer and director of McLouth Steel and immediately embarked upon a vigorous financial program. By 1939, the net working capital had improved from a deficit of $290,000 to a surplus of $495,000. Furthermore, a four-high cold-rolling mill had been constructed, together with annealing furnaces and related equipment and buildings at a cost of $730,000.

During World War II McLouth Steel manufactured certain products such as armor plate sections for tank louvers, steel shell case stock, and bullet jacket cups. By this time, the reversing hot mill was operating on a very profitable basis. The provisions of the excess profits tax threatened to penalize profits severely, however, since the base period upon which tax assessments were calculated had been a difficult period for the company. The company's case was appealed, and eventually a $380,000 rebate obtained. Partly as a result of the vigorous representation in Washington, an amendment was made to the tax law which relieved recently established corporations of undue burden from the excess profits tax.

In October, 1945, McLouth Steel obtained a ten-year loan of $1,750,000 to construct facilities for the manufacture of stainless steel. The new facilities included two cold-rolling mills, continuous annealing and pickling equipment, tempering mills, slitters, power facilities, and enlarged buildings. The company was able to repay the entire loan by June, 1948. At that time, shipments of strip steels were at the following volume in net tons per year:

carbon hot-rolled	81,200
carbon cold-rolled	64,500
stainless	8,000

Organization in 1947

Mr. McLouth was a dynamic person, known in the industry as a supersalesman. Much of his activity was expended outside the office, in negotiations with leading industrial and political figures of Michigan. He was an enthusiastic hunter and fisherman and became chairman of the State Conservation Commission. He formed many close personal associations with leading executives in the automobile industry.

Mr. Cudlip paid particular attention to the financial and legal problems of the company and to the analysis of costs and development of markets. After establishing the company on a firm financial base by 1939, he had become increasingly interested in products and facilities. It was largely as a result of his interest in the opportunities afforded by specialty alloys that the company engaged in the production of stainless steels.

Mr. Bryn was a big Welshman with many years of production experience in the steel industry. He was recognized as an outstanding production executive.

Backward Integration into Melting Facilities

In 1947, McLouth's supplier of carbon steel slabs notified the company that it would discontinue semifinished steel shipments after 1948. The reason was the heavy demand for steel on the part of the supplying corporation's other customers. Since the corporation had capacity to finish its own steel slabs, it was unwilling to lose potential business while McLouth Steel made a profit by finishing the slabs.

The threatened loss of steel deliveries placed McLouth Steel in a dangerous position. The only alternatives available to the company were to integrate backward in order to obtain its own steel melting facilities or else to go out of business entirely. At this time, the net worth of McLouth Steel was only $4.3 million. A possible solution, however, seemed to exist in the purchase of special inexpensive melting equipment obtained through extraordinary financial measures.

In their search for steelmaking facilities, McLouth executives discovered that the War Assets Administration was offering for sale a steel ingot plant in Indiana, using 60-ton electric furnaces. The cost of purchasing and installing such a plant, together with associated equipment, would be substantial. The government was willing to sell the plant at competitive bids to a company that would keep it operating as an emergency standby facility.

The automobile leaders had confidence in McLouth and wished to see an additional assured supply of flat-rolled steel in the Detroit area. They therefore agreed to take $8 million in second mortgage notes if the Reconstruction Finance Corporation invested $10½ million. Actual construction, installation, and start-up costs exceeded the original estimates by $4 million, which the Reconstruction Finance Corporation finally approved.

BACKWARD INTEGRATION INTO BLAST FURNACE PRODUCTION

By 1949, McLouth Steel owned four 60-ton electric furnaces which were then among the largest in the world at its 210-acre Trenton, Michigan plant; however, three factors tended to make operating costs difficult to control: (1) loading operations consumed half the operating time, because the side charging boxes were small; (2) electricity requirements were very large in the electric furnace process and the local power company considered it impossible to reduce power rates to the level requested by the company; (3) the dependence of the electric furnaces solely upon scrap steel meant that the operating cost fluctuated with scrap prices.

In order to improve the efficiency of the furnace operation, McLouth Steel spent an additional $1.8 million in 1950 to change from side to top charging. Under the top charging system, the entire top of the electric furnace was swung aside, and a clam-shell bucket emptied 20 tons of scrap into the furnace at one drop. Only three bucket loads were required to charge a furnace to capacity. The new program increased the company's ingot capacity by 33 percent and paid for itself in little over one year.

The problem of electricity and scrap prices remained. For example, scrap prices in Detroit increased from $19 per ton in 1949 to $31 per ton in 1950. McLouth Steel management was anxious to make further changes in its plant facilities in order to fit the electric furnaces into a more economical operating plan.

In 1952, McLouth conceived the idea of constructing an integrated steel mill. Since the automobile industry took 75 percent of the company's output, McLouth management decided to discuss the plan with executives of the leading automobile companies in Detroit. The reaction was favorable for two main reasons. First, production bottlenecks and assembly schedule revisions might be most easily handled by a local steel supplier who could deliver immediately upon receipt of telephone requests. Two, the existence of a strong independent mill in Detroit might induce other steel companies to reduce delivered prices by the margin of the freight cost from Pittsburgh to Detroit.

McLouth executives believed that by using bessemer converters they could reduce the cost of operating the electric furnaces. Although the quality of bessemer steel was not adequate for the company's products, the steel could be "duplexed" or added to the scrap in the electric furnaces and so shorten the heat time. In order to produce bessemer steel, however, molten iron would be needed, which McLouth wished to provide from its own blast furnace. The objective was to build a large blast furnace, but to purchase the iron ore and coke from outside suppliers to avoid expenditures for ore reserves, ore vessels, and coke ovens. Furthermore, McLouth Steel planned to install two 200-ton electric furnaces, the largest ever built, in an attempt to reduce unit operating costs. By making these economies, McLouth executives believed they could construct an almost fully integrated mill capable of producing 1,460,000 tons of carbon steel annually.

PROGRESS OF THE EXPANSION PROGRAM

The objective of the expansion program was to achieve a large-scale, efficient, and integrated plant despite the fact that McLouth Steel could not itself provide the huge capital resources that integrated steel operations typically require. At the end of 1952, the net worth of the company was $24.8 million and long-term debt was $11.3 million. In order to build an integrated plant upon such a capital base, two approaches were explored. The first was a campaign to obtain capital from certain automobile and insurance companies. The second was an open-minded, experimental attitude toward unorthodox types of steelmaking equipment which might provide capacity at an unusually low initial investment.

The financial campaign was assured of success when the General Motors Corporation agreed to take $25 million of the net debt as 5¼ percent participating cumulative preferred stock, and the American Metal Products company invested an additional $2 million. With the participation of General Motors, it was less difficult to interest four banks in $14 million of 3¾ percent notes and to obtain $64 million from the Metropolitan Life Insurance Company and the Prudential Insurance Company of America in 4¼ percent mortgage bonds and 5¼ percent income notes. Provision was made for a sinking fund and a formula was calculated to apply a portion of profits to the repayment of the debt ahead of schedule.

The methods used to bring about its expansion necessarily committed McLouth Steel to certain policies. The close financial association with the General Motors Corporation meant that McLouth Steel intended to concentrate its major market effort in the automobile industry. The trial of unorthodox equipment meant that the production executives were obliged to experiment with unpredictable machinery just at a time when every ton of production was required in order to meet the new financial obligations.

Its concentration in automobile steel was a natural development of McLouth Steel's location in Detroit. The State of Michigan had the greatest disparity in the nation between steel consumption and production. In 1954 the automobile industry consumed 11.8 million tons of steel. The State of Michigan produced only 5.5 percent of the nation's steel, while consuming about 15 percent. Reshipment costs between Detroit and Pittsburgh meant that Detroit steel mills paid about $3.52 per net ton of molten iron less than Pittsburgh mills for delivered iron ore, though paying $2.93 per net ton of molten iron more for delivered coke.

Concentration in automobile steels imposed certain production and marketing requirements. Cold-rolled sheet was the product in greatest demand in the automobile industry. Since McLouth Steel had previously specialized in hot-rolled strip and in stainless steels, the shift to cold rolling and to sheet steel meant that the company was emerging from the specialty business into the arena of direct competition with the major producers. In order to manufacture such a product in quantity successfully, the company had to develop low-cost production facilities.

Construction of Blast Furnace and Purchase of Coke and Ore

A new 1,350-ton blast furnace was completed in 1954. The engineer-contractors who designed the blast furnace originally estimated that the company could reduce the cost of producing molten iron by installing its own coke ovens. The most efficient size of the coke ovens, however, was large enough to supply two blast furnaces. McLouth, therefore, wished to postpone an investment in coke ovens until they could also add a second blast furnace.

The McLouth Steel company held contracts for the supply of ore at market price through 1969 from Oliver Mining Division of the U.S. Steel Company and from Cleveland-Cliffs Iron Company. In addition, McLouth Steel had a sizeable optionable interest in the Ashland Mining Corporation which held options to lease certain Wisconsin properties estimated to contain 160 million gross tons of taconite (average 29 percent iron). Development of these ores awaited further metallurgical studies; it was not planned at this time to construct a beneficiation plant.

The 200-Ton Electric Furnaces

The two new 200-ton electric furnaces were by far the largest in the world. Although the large size was believed to be more economical than the four 60-ton furnaces, it was difficult for the production executives to prove this assumption. The cost of operating electric furnaces depended largely upon the cost of electricity and of steel scrap. The amount of steel that could be poured in a single heat, however, depended also upon the skill of workers and the characteristics of the furnace. In order to produce a ton of steel, electric furnaces generally used about 500 kilowatts of electricity at $.0094 per kilowatt-hour, 12 pounds of electrodes at 22 cents per pound, and 1.1 tons of scrap at $31 per net ton at 1954 prices.

Before the 200-ton furnaces were installed, each of the four 60-ton electrics produced steadily at about 17 tons per operating hour and consistently poured 25 percent more steel than its rated capacity. The 200-ton electrics were designed to produce about 23 tons each per hour, despite the fact that their large size caused special operating problems. It was expected that if hot blown metal from the Bessemers were used in the electrics, it would help melt the scrap and reduce the electricity requirements from 500 kilowatts to 350 kilowatts per ton of steel.

Another factor affecting the operation of the electrics was the price of scrap. When the electric furnace program was planned, scrap prices in Detroit were about $7 per net ton lower than Pittsburgh. The price differential was due to the fact that the large number of metalworking plants in Detroit generated a substantial supply of scrap, while the relatively small steelmaking facilities created little demand. However, as steelmaking actively rose in 1955, scrap prices increased all over the nation, making freight charges a relatively less important factor and allowing other steelmaking centers to draw upon Detroit scrap as a source of supply. At the same time, exports of scrap to Canada placed a substantial drain on the supply and caused Detroit scrap prices to approximate more closely those in other areas. Steel executives were concerned that the proposed St. Lawrence Seaway would extend the export of scrap from Detroit and increase prices still further.

Oxygen Inverters

As noted above, the company intended to use bessemer steel, but a serious problem developed as plans for construction went ahead. Ordinances of the town of Trenton prevented the use of Bessemers due to the large amount of smoke released into the atmosphere during the "blowing" operation. Conferences with town officials failed to effect any compromise whatever. The only alternative available to the McLouth engineers was to install a $1 million smoke disposal unit and to redesign the Bessemer converters to act as oxygen inverters.

Oxygen inverters had never been used in the Western Hemisphere. The process had been developed in Europe where oxygen was available for industrial purposes on a tonnage basis. Kaiser Engineering Inc. held the American licensed rights to the process and agreed to license McLouth Steel. McLouth executives were at first unwilling to attempt an untried process. Some of the executives were convinced, however, that the oxygen process offered a remarkable opportunity to reduce operating costs if the equipment were successful. The company therefore proceeded to invest in 500,000 annual tons of oxygen inverter steel capacity.

The development of the oxygen inverter was of such importance that some observers believed it might eventually supplant the open-hearth process. In *Iron Age* magazine for March 31, 1955, a report of the process at the McLouth company included the following statements:

> The first U.S. installation[1] of the oxygen process for steelmaking using high-pressure, high-purity oxygen to refine a charge of 80 percent molten pig iron and 20 percent scrap is producing 40-ton heats of controlled quality steel at McLouth Steel Corporation, Detroit, in 18–23 minutes blowing time. . . .
>
> In addition to high production per hour, the oxygen process offers (1) lower investment per ton than conventional steelmaking, (2) ability to cast high quality steel in ingot form direct from the oxygen process without duplexing in an electric furnace or open-hearth.
>
> McLouth has produced heats with nitrogen as low as 0.0013 percent. This is well below the usual open-hearth lower limit for nitrogen. Sulphur and phosphorous are being held far below standard specifications of 0.040 percent maximum. . . .
>
> Three oxygen vessels are installed, of which two can be operated simultaneously, thereby at least doubling present daily ingot output of oxygen process steel.

The entire oxygen inverter program at McLouth proceeded upon a tentative schedule, subject to many changes as advantages were discovered or obstacles presented themselves. Although the process had been used in Austria, it had never been attempted on the scale required by McLouth to balance its 1,350-ton blast furnace. The company needed a plant capable of turning out oxygen 99.5 percent pure at the rate of 3.5 million cubic feet per day as well as three inverters each producing 40 tons of steel in a 20-minute blow.

The original plan was to duplex the blown steel into the electric furnaces. When the first blows were made in December, 1954, however, it was discovered that the oxygen process produced such a superior quality of steel that it not only did not require duplexing, but even was superior to the product of an electric furnace. The reason was that the oxygen used to make the blow removed carbon and other impurities and, unlike most open hearths or electrics, eliminated nitrogen as well. The low nitrogen content of the steel gave it superior characteristics which made it excellent for deep drawing in products such as automobile fenders. In addition, it was believed that when the process was placed on an efficient production basis it could produce steel for $3 less per ton than the electric furnaces at scrap prices prevailing in 1954.

In early 1955 the oxygen inverters were not at their peak production potential. Under an oxygen lance, the temperature of the large inverters rose to about 3,100 degrees at the surface and well beyond the limit of the measuring apparatus (3,500 degrees) at certain areas. The high temperature wore out 20 pounds of refractory material per ton of steel. At the same time,

[1] The Dominion Foundries and Steel Ltd. at Hamilton, Ontario had one 40-ton oxygen inverter in operation during 1955. It was subsequently reported that the Russians were working on the oxygen steel process.

the oxygen plant, which provided 2,000 cubic feet per ton of metal, cost McLouth Steel only 50 cents per ton of tapped steel. There were still many unknown factors, such as the proper percentage of scrap (which varied from 10 to 30 percent), the shape of the hood, the best method of loading scrap and molten pig iron, the distance of the oxygen lance from the melt surface, and the optimum pressure of the oxygen. Day by day, the crews were gaining considerable operating know how that was unavailable elsewhere.

Rolling Mills

The two new 200-ton electric furnaces were completed in August, 1954; the blast furnace in September, 1954; and the hot-rolling mill in December, 1954. The cold-rolling mill and the oxygen inverters were still in the process of starting up at the end of 1954.

By 1955, it was believed that McLouth Steel's new hot-and cold-rolling mills would provide facilities for steel processing that were the peer of any in the nation. Using standard equipment of tested design, they incorporated the most modern features available, such as highly automatic controls, automatic cropping and testing devices, complete materials handling facilities, roll grinding machinery immediately adjacent to the rolling mills, safety devices, high-speed mills, and so on. The new six-stand hot-rolling mill at Trenton was quite a contrast to the old "coffee grinder." The distance of the new rolling table, from blooming mill to take-up coil, was 1,325 feet, almost seven times as long as the original mill.

Meanwhile, an 860-acre site near Trenton had been purchased and a modern four stand 4-high continuous cold reducing mill constructed there. The company possessed over 1,000 acres of land and 1.8 million square feet of buildings. The cost of the new plant was only $104 per ton of annual ingot capacity, which compared with $275 per ton of capacity for a larger, diversified, fully integrated plant constructed in 1953 on the Atlantic Coast. The relatively low plant investment was due almost entirely to using oxygen inverters; for example, the rolling mills were somewhat advanced design of standard equipment. The flow chart at capacity operations in 1955 is shown in Exhibit 4.

FINANCIAL COMMITMENTS

The financial commitments included interest, sinking fund requirements, participation in common dividends by the preferred stock, a pension fund and delayed tax obligations resulting from rapid amortization. The following table indicates peak interest and dividend commitments:

$ 14,000,000	bank notes at	3¾%	$ 525,000
56,000,000	mortgage bonds at	4¼%	2,380,000
8,000,000	income notes at	5¼%	420,000
27,000,000	preferred stock at	5¼%	1,417,000
$105,000,000			$4,742,000

The bank notes were scheduled to be repaid at $3,500,000 per year. Upon repayment of the bank notes by the end of 1958, a sinking fund for the mortgage bonds was to commence, at $3,500,000 per year until 1972. In addition, starting in 1956, whenever the net income plus depreciation and amortization less preferred dividends totaled more than $3,500,000, 60 percent of the excess (50 percent after 1960) was to be paid to a contingent sinking fund to reduce the outstanding debt.

No dividends could be declared on the common stock until 1959. In 1959, dividends could be paid only if net current assets were greater than $25,000,000. Such dividends were to be no greater than 25 percent of net earnings less preferred dividends. Each dollar of common dividends was to be equaled by a dollar to the preferred stockholders in addition to their 5¼ percent cumulative dividend.

Pensions and delayed taxes were additional obligations. In 1954, McLouth Steel paid $545,200 for the minimum retirement benefits for workers under the "New Steel Formula." For book purposes, the company depreciated its new equipment on the basis of remaining useful life. However, for tax purposes, the company amortized 70 percent of the new expenditures over a 60-month period. Exhibit 5 is a comparison of McLouth Steel's debt structure with that of other companies in the industry.

The Status of Operating Costs

During the planning for the oxygen inverter operation, estimates made by engineers indicated that inverter steel would cost $3.13 less per ton than electric furnace steel based upon prices in 1954. It was believed that the company could make its own coke for $3.54 less per ton by investing $17 million in a battery of coke ovens and $8 million for an additional blast furnace. Exhibit 6[1] shows the estimated cost structure under favorable operating conditions at capacity operations.

The company's peak ore commitments coincided with the loss in automobile sales due to the annual model changeover. Since the ore season ended about November 15 when the Great Lakes began to freeze, it was necessary to build up inventories at that time to meet winter needs; however, the automobile model changeover began around September 15. During the succeeding four weeks, if the automobile industry anticipated a poor year, the company ordinarily lost sales of 40,000 tons of hot rolled steel. This loss totaled $4.5 million and occurred during the period of accumulating an additional ore inventory of $1.6 million. However, if the automobile companies anticipated a good year, they wished to increase their steel inventories at this time and maintained their steel receipts at the regular level.

Potential Market Demand

Under an agreement established during financial negotiations, the General Motors Corporation committed itself to purchase at least 5 percent of its annual United States requirements of steel from McLouth Steel, but not exceeding 252,000 tons of hot-rolled and 124,200 tons of cold-rolled carbon steel and 20,400 tons of rolled stainless. The General Motors company had the option to purchase up to 92.6 percent of the McLouth company's cold-rolled carbon sheet, 50 percent of its cold-rolled carbon strip and hot-rolled carbon sheet and strip, and 40 percent of its stainless.

The character of the McLouth Steel Corporation's sales in 1952, 1953, and 1954 is shown in Exhibit 7. The decrease in steel sales during 1954 was attributed to the heavy steel inventories carried by automobile companies at the start of the year. Exhibit 8 shows the steel specifications for a typical automobile. Exhibit 9 is a prediction of future automobile demand. Exhibit 10 shows the actual production in the automobile industry during 1952, 1953, and 1954. Exhibit 11 shows selected operating figures in the steel industry as of December, 1955.

[1] Operating figures, as indicated in Exhibit 6, represent engineering estimates made during 1954, prior to actual operating experience in large tonnages.

Stainless steel presented the most immediate opportunity for McLouth Steel to diversify its production in markets not directly dependent upon the economics of the automobile industry. By this means, the executives hoped to stabilize the company's production during the 6-week period of model changeover as well as partially protecting itself against a major slump in the Detroit market.

Although freight costs put a high charge on the company's carbon steel when shipped outside the Michigan area, the fact that the price of stainless was eight times as high as carbon steel made freight charges a relatively minor consideration. When the new facilities were put into operation, it became desirable to distribute nationally because no regional distribution the company could obtain was able to absorb a significant proportion of its production. National distribution enabled the company to make use of national advertising media.

The market for stainless steel as a whole was a small percentage of the total steel consumption, and consisted of diverse products in many scattered industries. "We produce stainless in tons and sell it in pounds," remarked a McLouth executive. The most promising markets were for food handling equipment in restaurants and home kitchens, for architectural trim, meat packing equipment, chemical and petroleum apparatus, plumbing fixtures, containers, and so on. Since stainless steel was rustproof throughout the lifetime of the product, it was specified by state law in some regions for use in the dairy industry and public restaurants. Partly as a result of such laws, and partly due to the rapid increase in population, the West Coast and Texas areas offered particularly good opportunities for sales growth.

The great majority of stainless steel was sold in small quantities, through jobbers and warehousemen. Since McLouth Steel had entered the stainless market only in 1947, it was still in the process of establishing a nationwide distribution system by locating reliable independent steel warehouse companies. It was considered advisable to give each distributor exclusive rights in his area so as to concentrate the promotional effort. The nine company salesmen outside the Detroit area concentrated on locating new distributors, building sales relationships, and trying to locate the proper industry associations, technical groups, purchasing agents, or designers who could make adequate value analyses of stainless steel for their products.

The McLouth Steel company advertised its stainless steel extensively in management and industry magazines. During the 1954–55 season, the company had 8 full-page color advertisements each in *Business Week* and *U.S. News and World Report,* 10 in *Steel, Iron Age, Automotive Industries, SAE Journal,* 5 or 6 each in *Product Engineering, Purchasing,* and *Materials and Methods,* as well as 6 black-and-white pages each in *Architectural Forum, Architectural Record, American Milk Review,* and *Chemical Engineering,* and 10 black-and-white pages in each of 14 regional purchasing magazines. A sample advertisement is included in Exhibit 12.

McLouth stainless had appeared on the scene after its major competitors had already established strong national warehouse organizations. Nevertheless, McLouth executives believed there were plenty of "pound distributors" available to work with. McLouth was third in the production of flat-rolled stainless steel, with about 5 percent of the U.S. stainless market of one million tons. It ranked behind the United States Steel, the Alleghany Ludlum, Armco, and Republic companies, and with the Sharon, the Crucible, and other companies. Since prices and commissions were generally the same throughout the industry, sales were made on the basis of service and quality.

Since the supply and price of nickel was the most important aspect in the production of nickel-bearing steel, stainless prices often reflected changes in the price of electrolytic nickel. In 18–8 stainless, for example, 360 pounds of chromium (at 22½ cents per pound) and 160 pounds of nickel were required per ton of steel. The established quoted price of nickel partly reflected mining costs and partly currency exchange rates between Canada and the United States. The importance of currency rates was due to the fact that the principal producer, International Nickel Company of Canada, paid wages in Canadian dollars and sold nickel principally in American markets for United States dollars. Thus, in January, 1953, International Nickel raised its prices 3½ cents and in November, 1954, 4½ cents per pound to 64½ cents, in response to the rising value of the Canadian dollar.

However, the quoted price of 64½ cents was not as important as the extreme shortage of nickel, which would make it necessary for producers of stainless steel to pay $2.00 per pound for amounts in excess of those allocated to them by International Nickel company. McLouth Steel was at a disadvantage in its nickel allocations because it had made no stainless ingots during the base period 1946 to 1949. McLouth Steel received enough nickel from International Nickel to make about 30 percent of its requirements by using the stainless scrap generated within its own plant. The company was obliged to buy the remainder of its requirements at premium prices.

The most severe competition to stainless steel at 50 cents per pound was from aluminum at 43 cents and carbon steel at 8 cents. Carbon steel could be plated first in copper which would serve as a bonding agent for a subsequent coating of nickel, and finally finished in a light coat of chromium to prevent the nickel from corroding. Aluminum weighed so little that a pound of the metal took up three times the volume of steel. Plated steel had the advantage of lower cost in many applications as well as ability to be formed in larger shapes and thicknesses than stainless. In competition with these metals, stainless steel had to justify its higher price on qualities such as purity, strength, and durability. For example, stainless steel was strong enough to carry weight and strains without the support of another metal, as the weaker structure of aluminum required in its "Alclad" types. The clear surface of stainless never wore away as plated products did. On the other hand, although stainless could be deep-drawn, it did not machine easily. It lacked the light weight of aluminum and the brilliant shine of nickel-chrome plate.

1. McLOUTH STEEL CORPORATION
Comparative Income Statements and Selected Operating Data, 1945-1954
(In Thousands except where Marked)

	1945	1946	1947	1948	1949	1950	1951	1952	1953	1954
Net sales	$9,108	$11,927	$17,964	$24,449	$33,738	$57,801	$78,948	$79,171	$96,384	$59,134
Cost of products sold	8,205	10,089	14,238	18,210	28,625	42,935	57,069	59,549	72,005	52,455
Gross profit	$ 903	$ 1,838	$ 3,726	$ 6,239	$ 5,113	$14,866	$21,879	$19,622	$24,379	$ 6,679
Selling and admin. expenses	398	433	543	814	812	935	1,249	1,500	2,476	3,022
Operating profit	$ 505	$ 1,405	$ 3,183	$ 5,425	$ 4,301	$13,931	$20,630	$18,122	$21,903	$ 3,657
Interest income	$ 3	$ 2	$ -0-	$ -0-	$ 21	$ 3	$ -0-	$ 4	$ 396	$ 970
Other income	2	5	-0-	-0-	-0-	3	12	11	72	299
	$ 5	$ 7	$ -0-	$ -0-	$ 21	$ 6	$ 12	$ 15	$ 468	$ 1,269
	$ 510	$ 1,412	$ 3,183	$ 5,425	$ 4,322	$13,937	$20,642	$18,137	$22,371	$ 4,926
Interest on debt	$ 15	$ 58	$ 44	$ 48	$ 580	$ 865	$ 714	$ 503	$ 1,665	$ 3,250
Other interest expense	17	29	37	52	23	-0-	8	-0-	-0-	8
Other deductions	-0-	-0-	3	45	25	-0-	-0-	-0-	-0-	114
	$ 32	$ 87	$ 84	$ 145	$ 628	$ 865	$ 722	$ 503	$ 1,665	$ 3,372
Earnings before depr. and taxes on income	$ 478	$ 1,325	$ 3,099	$ 5,280	$ 3,694	$13,072	$19,920	$17,634	$20,706	$ 1,554
Depreciation	134	126	176	206	298	1,875	3,429	3,806	3,905	1,949*
Net profit (B.T.)	$ 344	$ 1,199	$ 2,923	$ 5,074	$ 3,396	$11,197	$16,491	$13,828	$16,801	$ (395)
Federal taxes on income:										
Normal income tax	$ 124	$ 465	$ 1,165	$ 1,960	$ 1,260	$ 4,585	$ 8,410	$ 7,145	$ 8,640	$(3,090)
Excess profits tax	-0-	-0-	-0-	-0-	-0-	855	2,930	2,455	2,820	(1,760)
Future income taxes	-0-	-0-	-0-	-0-	-0-	-0-	-0-	-0-	100	2,760
	$ 124	$ 465	$ 1,165	$ 1,960	$ 1,260	$ 5,440	$11,340	$ 9,600	$11,560	$(2,090)
Net profit	$ 220	$ 734	$ 1,758	$ 3,114	$ 2,136	$ 5,757	$ 5,151	$ 4,228	$ 5,241	$ 1,695
Dividends										
Preferred	-0-	-0-	-0-	-0-	-0-	-0-	-0-	-0-	-0-	709
Earnings for common	$ 220	$ 734	$ 1,758	$ 3,114	$ 2,136	$ 5,757	$ 5,151	$ 4,228	$ 5,241	$ 986
Earned surplus	1,279	1,344	2,078	3,479	6,236	8,372	8,181	13,332	17,560	17,091
	$1,499	$ 2,078	$ 3,836	$ 6,593	$ 8,372	$14,129	$13,332	$17,560	$22,801	$18,077
Steel products shipped (N.T.)	124	118	150	165	269	450	536	577	632	360
Av. number of employees**	353	475	566	591	802	1,393	1,514	1,618	1,671	1,782
Av. hourly earnings**	$1.208	$1.368	$1.491	$1.690	$1.756	$1.799	$1.986	$2.179	$2.301	$2.340
Av. hours worked/week**	47.6	43.5	46.1	46.8	45.6	44.5	42.1	37.7	40.9	36.6

*Provisions for depreciation and amortization of certain defense facilities were reduced, effective January 1, 1954, in recognition of the estimated longer useful life of the facilities, although amortization thereof for income tax purposes was continued on a 60-month basis. Depreciation and amortization for 1954 for book purposes would have been $2,833,000 greater if the same method of computation had been followed as in the previous year and net earnings would have been $1,360,000 less.

**Not in thousands.

Source: Company records.

2. McLOUTH STEEL CORPORATION
Comparative Balance Sheets, 1945-1954
(In Thousands)

Assets	1945	1946	1947	1948	1949	1950	1951	1952	1953	1954
Cash	$1,042	$1,178	$1,926	$ 4,613	$ 2,980	$ 9,940	$16,585	$16,676	$ 12,770	$ 1,304
Accounts Receivable	551	1,433	1,325	1,916	2,337	4,018	5,208	4,933	4,676	4,530
Refund Federal Taxes	169						280	280	570	4,549
Inventories	1,654	1,384	1,206	1,658	4,395	5,283	7,156	7,600	10,308	18,742
Total Current Assets	$3,416	$3,995	$4,457	$ 8,187	$ 9,712	$19,241	$29,229	$29,489	$ 28,324	$ 29,125
Other Assets	30	39	54	13,933	352	537	292	292	49,282	17,279
Property, Plant, and Equipment	2,188	3,309	3,610	5,252	27,297	28,112	30,081	31,575	35,131	102,178
Depreciation	(516)	(624)	(789)	(970)	(1,175)	(2,974)	(6,308)	(10,079)	(13,895)	(13,965)
Construction in Progress	900			4,604					11,305	12,959
Deferred Charges	59	96	126	160	297	574	573	764	1,193	1,505
Total Assets	$6,077	$6,815	$7,458	$31,166	$36,483	$45,490	$53,867	$52,041	$111,340	$149,081
Liabilities										
Accounts Payable	$ 398	$ 702	$ 492	$ 2,699	$ 2,383	$ 2,453	$ 3,490	$ 4,191	$ 4,756	$ 8,968
Payroll Withholding Taxes	81	126	144	138	334	423	497	348	354	614
Federal Taxes	581	999	1,469	1,972	1,064	5,444	11,547	9,611	11,807	30
Accrued Interest					552	713	625			
Other Liabilities	1,024	471	660	553	1,450	3,816	5,556	1,855	296	4,095
Total Current Liabilities	$2,084	$2,298	$2,765	$ 5,362	$ 5,783	$12,849	$21,715	$16,005	$ 17,213	$ 13,707
Long-Term Debt	$1,750	$1,575	$ 350	$18,500	$21,050	$17,234	$11,594	$11,250	$ 64,000	$ 74,500
Other Liabilities									100	2,860
Capital Stock and Surplus:										
Preferred										$ 27,000
Common	$1,190	$1,190	$1,190	$ 1,190	$ 1,190	$ 2,379	$ 2,379	$ 2,379	$ 2,974	2,974
Capital Surplus	88	88	88	88	88	4,847	4,847	4,847	9,962	9,962
Earned Surplus	965	1,664	3,065	6,026	8,372	8,181	13,332	17,560	17,091	18,078
	$2,243	$2,942	$4,343	$ 7,304	$ 9,650	$15,407	$20,558	$24,786	$ 30,027	$ 58,014
Total Liabilities	$6,077	$6,815	$7,458	$31,166	$36,483	$45,490	$53,867	$52,041	$111,340	$149,081

Source: Company records.

3. McLOUTH STEEL CORPORATION

Original Hot Strip Mill in 1934, the "Coffee Grinder"

Slabs pushed from a preheating furnace to the right are rolled back and forth in the mill in front of the operator. Coils in the upper part of the mill keep the strip hot while it is worked. Run-out table at the left extends up toward the roof so as to take up less plant space.

4. McLOUTH STEEL CORPORATION

Flow Chart at Capacity in January, 1955*

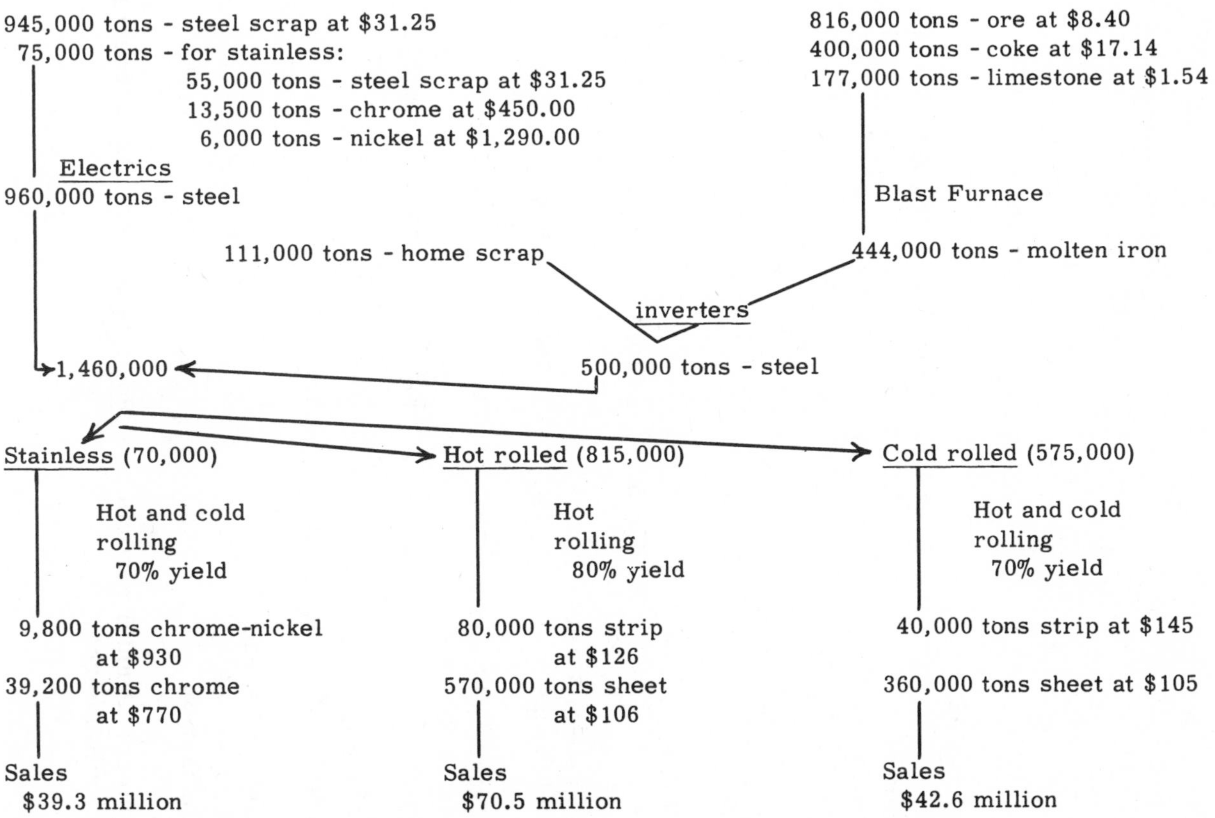

*Published selling prices as of August, 1954, have been used.
Source: Company records.

5. McLOUTH STEEL CORPORATION

Debt Structure of Nine Steel Companies as of Dec. 31, 1954
(In Thousands)

	McLouth Steel	Allegheny Ludlum	Armco Steel	Bethlehem Steel	Jones & Laughlin	National Steel	Republic Steel	Rotary Electric	U.S. Steel
Capitalization									
Debt	$ 74,500	$ 32,507	$ 64,094	$ 343,833	$113,972	$ 55,000	$ 77,447	$ 3,198	$ 324,120
Preferred	27,000	8,134		93,389	29,357				360,281
Common and Surplus	31,014	71,938	339,656	986,532	354,110	372,082	537,849	15,582	1,988,432
Total	$132,514	$ 112,579	$403,750	$1,423,754	$497,439	$427,082	$615,296	$18,780	$2,672,833
Number of Common Shares	1,189,600	1,689,360	5,228,307	9,582,942	6,196,554	7,341,680	7,325,956	696,700	26,391,022
Book Value per Share	$26.50	$42.69	$65.04	$102.95	$58.60	$50.92	$74.17	$22.37	$75.50
Market as Per Cent of Book Value	143%	112%	122%	134%	65%	137%	115%	132%	115%
Long-Term Debt and Equity as Share of Common	$111	$67	$77	$149	$80	$58	$84	$27	$101
Ratio of Capitalization to Book Value	4.2	1.6	1.2	1.4	1.4	1.1	1.1	1.2	1.3
Debt and Preferred as Per Cent of Capitalization	76%	36%	16%	31%	29%	13%	13%	17%	26%

Source: Annual reports and Moody's Industrials; percentages prepared by Harvard Business School, Bureau of Business Research.

6. McLOUTH STEEL CORPORATION

Estimated Costs at Capacity in January, 1955*

I. PIG IRON - 41,500 tons per month:**

Materials:			
Iron Ore	- 1.84 tons at $ 8.40		$15.46
Scale	- .06 tons at 6.00		.36
Coke	- .90 tons at 17.14		15.43
Limestone	- .40 tons at 1.54		.62
Gross Material Cost			$31.87
Material Credits:			
Slag	- .4 tons at $ .35	$.14	
Flue Dust	- .1 tons at 1.00	.10	
Coke Breeze	- .036 tons at 4.00	.14	
BF Gas	- .80 MCF at .01	. .80	(1.18)
Net Material Cost			$30.69
Cost above Materials			5.78
Total Cost of Molten Iron			$36.47
(Cost to Pig)			(1.23)
(Total Cost of Pig Iron)			($37.70)

II. OXYGEN INVERTER STEEL INGOTS:*

Materials:		
Molten Iron	- .90 tons at $36.47	$32.82
Steel Scrap	- .22 tons at 31.25***	6.88
Limestone and Burnt Lime		.42
Scrap Credit	- .0225 tons at 31.25	(.70)
New Material Cost		$39.42
Inverter Labor		1.00
Other Cost above Materials		2.10
Total Cost of Blown Metal for Duplex		$42.52
Cost of Ferro-Alloys		.49
Cost to Prepare Ingots		1.44
Total Cost of Ingots from Blown Metal		$44.45

III. ELECTRIC FURNACE STEEL INGOTS:****

Materials:		
Steel Scrap	- 1.0375 tons at $31.25	$32.42
Ingot Mold Scrap	- .0250 tons at 31.25	.78
Iron Ore (FE 60%)	- .0170 tons at 12.50	.21
Ferro-Alloys	- .0100 tons at 170.00	1.70
Fluxes		.64
Less: Scrap Credit	- .023 tons at 31.25	(.72)
Net Material Cost		$35.03
Cost above Materials:		
Melt Labor		$ 3.75
Power		4.75
Electrodes		2.75
Other Cost		1.30
		$12.55
Total Cost Electric Furnace Ingots Produced Wholly from Scrap		$47.58

*Costs estimated by engineers prior to actual operation. Does not include depreciation.

**41,500 tons of molten iron blows out to 44,820 tons of blown metal with 20% scrap added, 90% yield.

***Equivalent to $35 per gross ton (2,240 lbs.).

****Using 100% steel scrap on the new 200-ton furnaces.

Source: Company records.

7. McLOUTH STEEL CORPORATION
Market Analysis of Steel Shipments

McLouth Steel Shipments

Market Classification	1952 Carbon	1952 Stainless	1953 Carbon	1953 Stainless	1954 Carbon	1954 Stainless
			(net tons)			
Automotive	302,201	15,741	432,258	28,383	276,780	20,934
Steel for Converting and Processing	74,245	422	59,945	42	18,282	178
Export	46,020	215	7,069	387	3,753	242
Jobbers	36,678	908	39,579	1,282	14,268	1,171
Ordnance and Other Military	21,997	11	2,086	23	338	
Agricultural	17,686		10,017		1,219	3
Machinery, Industrial Equipment, and Tool	14,565	48	.6,461	70	5,701	67
All Other	43,926	3,082	40,591	4,190	13,832	3,328
Total	557,318	20,427	598,006	34,377	334,173	25,923
Per Cent of Capacity at McLouth	89%		91%		62%	
Per Cent of Capacity in Industry	85%		95%		71%	

Market for Carbon and Stainless Steels
All Companies

Carbon		Stainless	
Automotive and aircraft	16.78%	Automotive and aircraft	23:04%
Warehouses and distributors	19.55	Warehouses and distributors	27.31
Construction	15.16	Appliances, utensils, and cutlery	6.84
Containers	11.00	Machinery	6.46
Contractors' products	4.97	For converting and processing	6.25
Machinery	4.62	Export	3.34
Rail	4.44		
Export	4.06		

Source: Automotive Industries, 37th Annual Statistical Issue, March 31, 1955, McLouth Steel Corporation records.

8. McLOUTH STEEL CORPORATION

Steel Required for 1952 Four-Door Sedan (In Pounds)

	Steel Bars			Strip Steel		Sheet Steel						
	Hot Rolled	Cold Rolled	Forgings	Hot Rolled	Cold Rolled	Hot Rolled	Cold Rolled	Wire Products	Steel Plates	Terne Plate	Structural and Tubes	Totals
Steering Mechanism	20.5	10.3	1.2	1.4	0.9	6.2	7.2	3.6	0.3			51.6
Engine and Clutch	28.4	34.8	137.5	31.6	23.7	42.7	22.1	17.4	7.9	10.8		356.9
Front End Suspension	47.2	7.7	57.4	9.5	2.2	18.2	0.2	2.6				145.0
Brakes, Wheels, and Tires	3.5	10.1	0.4	146.4	1.5	69.3	11.0	13.6				255.8
Bumpers, Guards, Etc.	5.4	1.4	25.1	26.7	78.2	7.4	51.7	3.4			5.8	205.1
Fuel Tank and Exhaust System	1.1	0.7		1.6	23.8	3.4	20.6	0.5		17.3	0.7	69.7
Frame						248.5	45.4	5.7				299.6
Electrical System	0.5	2.9		5.1	5.3	3.1	17.4	2.8		0.1		37.2
Transmission	4.6	22.4	42.9	1.0	2.1	0.4	4.1	2.1				79.6
Radiator and Grill	0.5			4.2	1.8	14.7	51.1	0.9		5.3	0.4	78.9
Body, Hood, and Fenders	7.5	8.3	0.9	53.9	115.7	160.2	1,185.7	96.1		22.9	0.1	1,651.3
Rear Axle and Rear-End Suspension	84.9	15.8	54.9	10.8	2.4	94.6	13.1	6.7	18.2	—	9.8	311.2
Totals	204.1	114.4	320.3	292.2	257.6	668.7	1,429.6	155.4	26.4	56.4	16.8	3,541.9

Source: American Iron and Steel Institute, October, 1953.

9. McLOUTH STEEL CORPORATION

Consultant's Forecast of Automobile Demand, 1954

Passenger Cars

I. Personal Expenditures for Automobiles and Parts ($Billions)

	1939	1940	1947	1948	1949	1950	1951	1952	1953
Expenditures	2.2	2.7	6.3	7.3	9.5	12.4	10.9	10.6	13.1
% Disposable Income	3.1%	3.5%	3.7%	3.9%	5.0%	6.0%	4.8%	4.5%	5.2%

II. Registrations - Units, Year End (Millions) (U.S. Bureau of Public Roads)

1929	1933	1939	1941	1946	1947	1948	1949	1950	1951	1952	1953	1954E	1958E
23.0	20.6	26.1	29.5	28.2	30.8	33.4	36.4	40.3	42.7	43.8	46.5	48.1	54.7

III. Demand - Breakdown - Units (Thousands)

	1929	1932	1937	1938	1947	1948	1949	1950	1951	1952	1953
New Sales	1,756	Neg.	1,427	Neg.	2,700	2,295	3,177	3,888	2,477	1,007	2,767
Placement Sales	2,297	1,715	2,219	2,178	590	1,374	1,780	2,616	2,591	3,141	3,160
Exports	402	65	283	198	261	233	156	153	247	167	186
Total	4,455	1,103	3,929	2,020	3,551	3,902	5,113	6,657	5,315	4,315	6,113

IV. Forecast of Demand - Units (Thousands)

Passenger Cars	1954	1955	1956	1957	1958	5-Year Average
New Sales	1,750	1,800	1,800	1,800	1,900	1,810
Replacement Sales	3,350	3,850	3,850	4,050	4,150	3,810
Exports	200	200	200	200	200	200
Car Total	5,300	5,850	5,850	6,050	6,250	5,820

V. Saturation

	1929	1939	1941	1946	1950	1951	1952	1953	1958E
Passenger Cars per Family	.78	.76	.83	.74	.93	.96	.97	.99	1.06
Age of Cars in Service - July 1 (Millions) (R. L. Polk)									
Less than 5 years old	17.0	7.4	14.0	1.4	16.0	19.9	21.3	23.3	24.4
5-9 years old	6.0	12.6	8.8	14.8	4.9	2.9	4.8	7.7	23.0
10 years and older		4.2	4.7	8.7	14.8	15.5	13.7	11.2	1.6
Total	23.0	24.2	27.5	24.9	35.7	38.3	39.8	42.2	49.0
Age Groups as Percentages									
Less than 5 years	78%	31%	51%	6%	45%	51%	53%	55%	51%
5-9 years old	22	52	32	59	14	5	12	18	47
10 years and older		17	17	35	41	44	35	27	2
Total	100%	100%	100%	100%	100%	100%	100%	100%	100%

VI. Average Life Expectancy - 12 years

	1941	1946	1951	1952	1953	1958E
Average Age per Car (Years)	5.5	9.0	7.1	6.7	6.5	5.0

Source: Consultant's report.

10. McLOUTH STEEL CORPORATION

Actual Passenger Car Production, 1952, 1953, and 1954

	1952	1953	1954
Chrysler Group			
Chrysler	120,678	160,410	101,743
DeSoto	97,558	129,983	69,844
Dodge	259,519	293,714	151,766
Plymouth	474,837	662,515	399,900
	952,592	1,246,622	723,253
Ford Group			
Lincoln	31,992	41,962	35,733
Mercury	195,261	320,369	256,731
Ford	777,731	1,184,187	1,394,762
	1,004,984	1,546,518	1,687,226
General Motors			
Cadillac	96,844	103,538	123,746
Buick	321,048	485,383	531,463
Oldsmobile	228,452	319,414	433,810
Pontiac	277,156	414,011	370,887
Chevrolet	877,950	1,477,299	1,414,365
	1,801,450	2,799,645	2,874,271
American Motors			
Hudson	76,348	76,331	31,566
Nash	152,141	134,486	64,870
	228,489	210,817	96,436
Kaiser Group			
Henry J and Kaiser	74,862	21,092	5,818
Willys	50,836	40,186	10,941
	125,698	61,278	16,759
Studebaker-Packard			
Packard	62,878	81,298	27,592
Studebaker	161,520	186,484	85,369
	224,398	267,782	112,961
Total Passenger Car Production	4,337,611	6,132,662	5,510,906

Source: Automotive Industries Magazine, January 15, 1954, p. 20 and January 15, 1955, p. 39.

Percentages of McLouth Dollar Sales to Customers in the Automobile Industry

	1953	1954
Chrysler and Briggs	9.8	3.2
Ford	10.1	7.2
General Motors	27.8	38.2
American Metal	7.2	6.3

Source: Company records.

11. McLOUTH STEEL CORPORATION

Steel Industry Operating Figures, December, 1955

I. Prices in Detroit Area:

Steel Scrap, per net ton	$ 47.00
Nickel, allocated price	1,290.00
Nickel, composite price	3,200.00
Nickel, premium price	1,910.00
Iron ore	9.25

II. Price Increases from August, 1954, to December, 1955:

Steel Selling Price	12%
Wages	3

III. Selected Steel Prices, per net ton:

	December 1953	December 1954	December 1955
Rerolling billets, carbon steel	$ 62.00	$ 64.00	$ 68.50
Hot Rolled Sheet, Pittsburgh, Mill	78.50	81.00	86.50
Hot Rolled Sheet, Pittsburgh, Warehouse	120.00	127.60	136.00
Cold Rolled Sheet, Pittsburgh, Mill	95.50	99.00	106.50
Cold Rolled Sheet, Pittsburgh, Warehouse	136.40	147.60	161.80
Cold Rolled Sheet, Detroit, Mill	99.50	101.00	108.50
Cold Rolled Sheet, Detroit, Warehouse	145.50	151.40	165.60
Scrap, #1 heavy melting, Pittsburgh (net ton)	30.00	30.00	51.00
Scrap, #1 heavy melting, Detroit (net ton)	23.50	23.50	47.00
Stainless, #304, cold rolled strip, mill	875.00	890.00	940.50

IV.

a. Passenger Car Factory Sales

1952	4,321,000
1953	6,117,000
1954	5,530,000
1955	7,960,000 (estimated)
1956	6,500,000 (predicted)

b. Approximate production, 1955

Chrysler Group	1,361,000
Ford Group	2,249,000
General Motors	4,007,000
American Motors	158,000
Kaiser Group	7,000
Studebaker-Packard	178,000

c. New Car Stocks

Dealers unsold cars in field or in transit, December 1:

1953	459,876
1954	265,153
1955	709,689

12. McLOUTH STEEL CORPORATION

Advertisement for McLouth Stainless Steel

Monongahela Steel Company (A)

In January, 1963, the executive committee of the Monongahela Steel Company of Pittsburgh, Pennsylvania, was trying to decide whether to invest up to $117.5 million for rolling facilities that would enable the company to convert a greater proportion of its ingots into finished steel products with expected high margins and steady demands.

Monongahela was a growing, integrated specialty steel producer with a main plant in Pittsburgh and cold-rolling facilities at Columbus, Ohio, and Detroit, Michigan. Started in 1910, the company grew primarily by a series of mergers and acquisitions until 1952 when a program of facilities consolidation and modernization began. Between 1952 and 1962, over $78 million was invested in fixed assets; during 1962 alone, steelmaking capacity expanded 23 percent with the modernization of four open hearths. Substantial additional funds were spent on maintenance and repair of existing facilities. Financial and operating data are shown in Exhibits 1–3, while a breakdown of annual capacity by product line and by plant is given in Exhibit 4.

PRODUCTION FACILITIES, 1963

Monongahela was a fully integrated, although not balanced, producer of specialty steels. Production equipment consisted of a coke plant, blast furnaces, open-hearth and electric furnaces, and hot-rolling mills and finishing facilities (see Exhibit 4).

1. *Coke Plant:* Acquired in 1949, the coke plant was located 65 miles from Pittsburgh in Fairmont, West Virginia, and had a capacity of over 500,000 net tons annually (see Exhibit 4). About 50 percent of the coal requirements were supplied from company-owned mines at a cost averaging 15 percent under the open market price.

2. *Blast Furnaces:* The four blast furnaces varied as to age, raw materials requirements and productivity. In age, they ranged from #1, built in 1910, to #4, constructed in 1952. With respect to consumption, furnace #1 used 100 percent Masabi iron ore and 1,800 pounds of coke per ton of hot metal produced, while the others took a charge of 60 percent Masabi ore, 16 percent Venezuelan ore, and 24 percent roll scrap and trimmings and needed 1,700 pounds of coke per ton of hot pig. As to productivity, during the 1959 relining facilities for high top pressure were installed in furnaces #3 and #4, with a resultant 35 percent increase in capacity.

3. *Open Hearths:* The 26 open hearths were divided into two main categories: (1) eighteen 200-ton units designed for a 35 to 70 percent hot metal charge and (2) eight 170-ton units designed for a 30 percent hot charge. The blast furnace capacity limited the charge to 58 percent hot pig in the 200-ton units and 25 percent hot metal plus 12 percent cold iron in the 170-ton ones. (The latter units could not handle over 30 percent hot metal without being rebuilt.)

Furnace yields and times varied with the hot metal charge. The ingot yield was 87.5 at 60 percent hot metal and rose steadily to 91 percent as the hot metal charge was reduced to 35 percent. Charge-to-tap time was three hours and 42 minutes at 60 percent hot metal, five hours and 54 minutes at 50 percent, and six hours and 30 minutes at 35 percent.

The two categories of furnaces produced ingots of different carbon content. Some 50 percent of the steel produced in the 200-ton units was below .10 percent carbon, and 10 percent above .30 percent carbon. For the 170-ton units, the figure was 42 percent under .10 percent carbon and 30 percent over .30 percent carbon.

4. *Electric Furnaces:* The electric furnace capacity was to be increased 131 percent during 1963 with the installation of two furnaces (see Exhibit 4). In 1962, $8.2 million was appropriated and construction was to begin in April, 1963. The furnaces were expected to produce 10,717 net tons per month of stainless and add $5.9 million in annual gross profit. All the furnaces operated on an all-scrap charge with a 99 percent yield.

5. *Semifinishing Facilities:* The company's blooming, slabbing, and roughing mills were more than sufficient to convert all steel produced. Blooming capacity was increased almost

50 percent in December, 1962, with the installation of a $14 million, 44-inch blooming and slabbing mill that replaced a 36-inch mill. The ability to use 35-ton rather than 15-ton ingots accounted for the capacity increase.

6. *Hot-Rolling Facilities:* The company's four hot-rolling mills had an annual capacity of almost 1.5 million tons of strip and plate up to 22 inches in width (see Exhibit 4).

7. *Cold-Rolling Mills:* Some 28 continuous and reversing cold mills could reduce, temper, and finish over 400,000 annual tons; about half of this capacity was located outside of the main Pittsburgh plant (see Exhibit 4). Width limitations were 22 inches, except stainless which had a maximum of 18 inches.

FINANCIAL POLICIES

According to the treasurer, Monongahela Steel's financial policies were "prudently conservative." The company increased its long-term debt to $13.4 million in 1954 with an $8 million loan at 3⅜ percent interest; subsequent repayments reduced the 1962 balance to $6.3 million, payable in $520,000 annual installments. In addition, a $13 million line of credit at 4.5 percent interest was held with three banks. The credit could be drawn upon before December 31, 1963, and the funds held until 1971. Corporate debt limit was $65 million.

SALES POLICIES

In 1963, Monongahela was a specialty steel producer selling rolled flat products up to 22 inches in width. Sales were made through six district offices in Michigan, Illinois, Indiana, Ohio, and Pennsylvania, although about half of the company's tonnage was sold in the Pittsburgh triangle where Ohio, West Virginia, and Pennsylvania meet. Customers were divided into two groups: (1) the automobile manufacturers and the fabricators of automotive products, who together took 45 percent of the company's tonnage, primarily as hot-rolled strip, and (2) 150 diversified purchasers of cold-rolled steel. The latter included the home building field (buyers of galvanite, tinplate, and other coated products) and cutlery and houseware companies (users of stainless steel).

The company's objective was to decrease its dependence upon hot-rolled carbon strip by "selling dollars instead of tons." The vice-president of sales pointed out that stainless sales showed the greatest stability with operations during the past few years at 90 percent of capacity or above. In contrast, hot-rolled carbon sales usually fell more than most in periods of dropping steel demand. A sales analysis by product line and by market for selected years is shown in Exhibit 5A.

Based on a consultant's survey of 1960 steel consumption, management estimated that the total market for flat-rolled steel in its Pittsburgh sales area was 22.4 million tons. Less than 25 percent of this consumption consisted of products Monongahela could make; however, Monongahela's market share of product made ranged up to 20.9 percent as shown in Exhibit 5B.

The consultant stated that steel users doing their own slitting was causing the drop in strip consumption (expressed as percentage of strip plus sheet consumption). Improved technology permitted rolling wide steel to close tolerances, thus removing a quality objection to slitting. One user reported purchasing 36-inch coils for $108 per ton and slitting them for a total cost of $6 per ton; the resulting cost of $114 per ton was below Monongahela's price of $149. In a study of 106 steel buyers in the Pittsburgh sales area, 59 companies consuming 2.5 million tons of strip and sheet in 1960 reported a major shift toward slit sheet in recent years. There were only 47 companies reporting no such shift and they used 570,000 tons in 1960.

ROLLING MILL PLAN

The first of the two long-range plans involved building a plate mill, a cold-rolling stainless mill, and a 60-inch hot sheet mill. Monongahela hired a consultant to prepare the basic analyses of the three proposals.

1. *Plate Mill:* The consultants recommended construction of a four-high single stand 120-inch plate mill that would roll steel up to 100 inches in width and serve as the roughing stand should a 60-inch hot sheet mill be built. They estimated the mill would produce 47,800 tons per month, 60 percent with an average width of 36 inches and 40 percent with a width

of 76 inches. Average thickness would be 3/8 of an inch. About 85 percent would be low carbon steel, the remainder alloys. Although the blooming and slabbing mill would not be able to roll widths greater than 60 inches, 110-inch slabs could be obtained by rolling to that length and turning the slab 90 degrees before entry into the plate mill. The cost of this mill would approximate $41 million.

The 1960 market for plate in the Pittsburgh area was believed to be over 3 million tons (see Exhibit 5B). More than 300 firms used plate in this area; for example, one railroad tank car manufacturer used 60,000 tons of wide plate annually and was located adjacent to the Monongahela plant.

The consultants predicted steady sales, inasmuch as only twice during the past decade (fall of 1950 and spring of 1954) had supply been sufficient to meet demand. Large consumers estimated that in times of high consumption, supply was 25 percent short.

Customers in the Pittsburgh area used more than the average percentage of narrow sheet. The consultants estimated that 75 percent of the tonnage would be over 48 inches in width and between 20 and 40 percent, 110 inches and over. By comparison, of the 9-million ton U.S. plate capacity, 30 percent was in widths of 97–120 inches and 40 percent over 120 inches.

2. *Cold-Rolling Mill:* The installation of a $20 million, 50-inch cold strip mill was expected to increase stainless sales by almost 2,700 tons a month, or over 100 percent. Half the production would end up as slit sheets under 18 inches in width and half from 18–48 inches in width. All the ingots would come from the new electric furnaces and be rolled on the new 44-inch blooming mill. Since Monongahela had no wide hot-rolling facilities, the ingots would be shipped to another company for hot rolling and returned for cold rolling.

Addition of wide stainless products would necessitate changes in the sales organization since stainless was sold in small and large quantities and through both warehouses and direct. Monongahela's costs would include a 10 percent commission to the warehouse, a new home office product manager, and at least one new field salesman.

3. *60-Inch Hot-Rolling Mill:* Construction of a 60-inch hot rolling mill, if the proposed 120-inch plate mill were available as a roughing stand, would permit operation of a semicontinuous hot sheet mill. The results would be: (1) stainless slabs for the proposed cold-roll mill could be converted at Monongahela rather than outside; (2) some 27,000 tons monthly output of the plate mill could be converted into more profitable hot-rolled strip and sheet; and (3) hot-rolled sheet could be slit to strip, which otherwise would be produced on the existing 24-inch hot mill. Total cost of the semicontinuous mill, *in addition* to the plate mill, would be $56 million.

THE CONSULTANT'S CALCULATIONS

In preparing his recommendations, the consultant first forecast the monthly sales in tons and dollars following installation of the proposed plate and cold-rolling mill, but not the hot-rolling mill (see Exhibit 6).

Next, the consultant estimated the probable operating costs and gross profit contributions for the current and new facilities (see Exhibit 7). He concluded that gross profit would run $64.9 million annually (see Exhibit 7A) and that the proposed facilities would contribute almost $21.6 million to that amount (see Exhibit 7B). In arriving at these figures, he made three major assumptions: (1) that the blooming mill yield was 80 percent, the hot-roll mill 95 percent, and the cold-roll mill 90 percent; (2) that purchased scrap at $53 per gross ton equalled 35 percent of the ingot tonnage produced and "home" scrap another 20 percent; (3) and that conversion costs for the hot-roll stainless sheets done outside would be $85 per ton *plus* freight.

The third step was calculating the incremental profit contribution of the plate mill and of the cold-roll mill (see Exhibit 7C). After deducting variable overhead expenses, he concluded the plate mill would yield an annual incremental profit of $2,794,000 and the cold-roll mill $13,186,000 for returns on investment of 6.8 and 64 percent respectively. He believed the return on the plate mill was inadequate, but hoped it might be better in the future through substituting alloy and stainless for carbon plate, through increased sales during shortages, through price premiums on scarce plate, and through future improvements in process and profits for the industry as a whole.

Incremental profits for the semicontinuous strip mill would come from three main sources. The first was the $5.8 million profit earned from producing the new mix shown in Exhibit 7D-I. The second was the use of the new mill to convert the 15,707 tons of hot-rolled strip and the 17,442 tons of cold-rolled strip and sheet scheduled to be processed monthly on the 24-inch mill (see Exhibit 6) and retire the latter unit. Savings would amount to $4.50 per ton or $149,000 per month. The third source of savings would be from rolling the wide stainless slabs instead of shipping them outside; the saving would be $235,000 monthly, or $86 a ton. The three sources totaled annual savings of $10.4 million or a 10.7 percent return on investment.

THE MANUFACTURING VICE-PRESIDENT'S VIEWPOINT

Mr. James L. Hewett, vice-president of manufacturing, was uncertain what to recommend to the executive committee with regard to production facilities. Installing rolling facilities for specialty steels seemed attractive because of the increased gross margin[1] potential: 17.5 percent on sales for specialties (narrow 8–10-inch hot-rolled strip, stainless, cold-rolled and coated products) versus 6.5 percent on semifinished and hot-rolled, and 8.6 percent on ingots. On the other hand he wanted to be sure he recognized all the long-range implications for the corporate strategy of such a decision.

[1] Profit before general overhead, depreciation and taxes.

1. MONONGAHELA STEEL COMPANY (A)

Comparative Balance Sheets for the Years Ending December 31, 1957-1962
(In Thousands of Dollars)

	1957	1958	1959	1960	1961	1962
ASSETS						
Cash	$ 24,542	$ 13,224	$ 15,280	$ 14,344	$ 12,515	$ 13,038
Securities	29,301	11,824	17,299	7,077	11,513	8,696
Accounts receivable	15,465	12,213	9,728	13,038	17,278	19,980
Inventories	38,418	41,051	40,001	35,653	40,892	43,553
Total Current	$107,726	$ 78,312	$ 82,308	$ 70,112	$ 82,198	$ 85,267
Investments	$ 7,247	$ 7,341	$ 8,000	$ 9,323	$ 11,782	$ 17,068
Fixed assets (net)	33,066	36,452	37,184	37,926	42,179	47,610
Miscellaneous	1,433	783	463	427	303	391
Total Assets	$149,472	$122,888	$127,955	$117,788	$136,462	$150,336
LIABILITIES						
Notes payable	$ 1,367	$ 1,367	$ 1,367	$ 1,367	$ 273	$ 547
Accounts payable	17,837	11,397	9,489	10,020	13,355	15,423
Accrued taxes	27,005	6,298	11,237	3,525	10,797	10,515
Accrued liabilities	9,205	10,151	10,533	8,387	12,112	10,780
Total Current	$ 55,414	$ 29,213	$ 32,626	$ 23,299	$ 36,537	$ 37,265
Notes payable	$ 12,098	$ 10,731	$ 9,364	$ 7,997	$ 6,835	$ 6,288
Other liabilities	697	697	560	561	-	-
Common stock	$ 15,119	$ 15,119	$ 15,119	$ 15,119	$ 15,119	$ 15,119
Capital surplus	30,324	30,324	30,324	30,324	30,324	30,324
Retained earnings	35,820	36,804	39,962	40,488	47,647	61,340
Total Net Worth	$ 81,263	$ 82,247	$ 85,405	$ 85,931	$ 93,090	$106,783
Total Liabilities	$149,472	$122,888	$127,955	$117,788	$136,462	$150,336

Source: Company records.

2. MONONGAHELA STEEL COMPANY (A)

Comparative Statements of Profit or Loss for the Years Ending December 31, 1957-1962
(In Thousands of Dollars)

	1957	1958	1959	1960	1961	1962
Gross Sales	$232,338	$180,958	$230,024	$135,809	$236,622	$246,120
Cost of Goods Sold						
Labor and Materials	$179,104	$155,187	$192,569	$113,617	$195,301	$210,813
Pensions	3,458	3,137	4,477	2,201	4,258	3,613
Depreciation, Other	3,560	4,134	4,946	5,433	6,446	5,564
Total	$186,122	$162,458	$201,992	$121,251	$206,005	$219,990
Gross Profit	46,216	18,500	28,032	14,558	30,617	26,130
Selling and Administration	$ 7,505	$ 7,121	$ 8,097	$ 7,293	$ 8,210	$ 7,565
Interest	379	381	373	314	280	277
Net Profit before Tax	$ 38,332	$ 10,998	$ 19,562	$ 6,951	$ 22,127	$ 18,288
Taxes	$ 26,219	$ 3,998	$ 10,389	$ 2,666	$ 11,209	$ 8,849
Net Profit	$ 12,113	$ 6,999	$ 9,173	$ 4,285	$ 10,918	$ 9,439*

*In addition, $3,718,000 was realized from sale of facilities and $5,047,000 from sale of stock.
Source: Company records.

3. MONONGAHELA STEEL COMPANY (A)

Summary of Operating Data, 1957-1962

Year	Net Earnings Per Share	Net Earnings % Sales	Dividends per Share	Steel* (Thousand Net Tons) Ingots Produced	Steel* (Thousand Net Tons) Products Shipped	Expenditures (Millions) Plant Additions	Expenditures (Millions) Repairs and Maint.**	Number of Employees
1957	$11.02	5.2	$4.80	2,187	1,542	$ 6.42		13,905
1958	6.36	3.9	5.50	1,755	1,292	7.66		13,814
1959	8.34	4.0	5.50	2,087	1,564	6.01	$3.14	13,777
1960	3.90	3.2	3.40	1,158	837	6.56		11,136
1961	9.92	4.6	3.40	2,090	1,494	12.85	2.87	12,386
1962	8.58	3.8	4.10	2,063	1,541	12.85	2.60	11,700

*Rated capacity was 2,119 thousand tons through 1961, and 2,410 thousand tons in 1962.
**Selected years only.
Source: Company records.

4. MONONGAHELA STEEL COMPANY (A)

Annual Capacities, January, 1963
(Net Tons)

	Total	Plant #1 Pa.	Plant #2 Ohio	Plant #3 Mich.
COKE				
By-product	307,575	307,575		
Beehive	218,720	218,720		
PIG IRON	1,113,285	1,113,285		
STEEL				
Basic open hearth	2,496,142	2,496,142		
Electric	98,424	98,424		
Total	2,594,566	2,594,566		
HOT-ROLLED STEEL PRODUCTS (a)				
Plates--Universal	213,252	213,252		
Sheets	563,204	563,204		
Strip	702,638	702,638		
Blooms and billets for forging	27,340	27,340		
Total	1,506,434	1,506,434		
OTHER FINISHED PRODUCTS (b)				
Strip--Cold-Rolled	304,841	164,040	34,175	106,626
Strip--Galvanized and terne coated	86,121	65,616	20,505	
Strip--Galvanized (electro)	13,670		13,670	
Electric weld tubing	84,344		84,344	

(a) Capacities of hot-rolled products are limited to steel available from own ingot capacity plus estimated steel supply normally obtained from others.

(b) Capacities of other finished products are annual capacities without regard to the available supply of ingots or semifinished steel or hot-rolled products.

Source: Company records.

5. MONONGAHELA STEEL COMPANY (A)

Market Analyses, 1951-1962

A. Sales Analysis

Percent of Dollar Sales

Product	1951	1954	1957	1960	1962
Hot-Rolled Carbon	35	23	26	33	39
Cold-Rolled Carbon	12	16	17	16	11
Sheets	13	13	14	13	5
Stainless and Alloy Strip	28	10	13	13	16
Electric Weld Tubing	-	2	5	5	3
Semifinished	-	12	2	2	5
Coated Products	5	5	5	5	4
Plates	-	5	4	4	7
Ingots	-	-	-	-	3
Strapping	-	2	4	4	3
Miscellaneous	7	12	5	5	4

Percent of Tonnage

Market	1951	1954	1957	1960	1962
Automotive	14	20	27	31	28
Steel for further fabrication*	25	26	25	26	32
Construction	6	7	7	5	4
Electrical Mach.	3	6	6	8	7
Containers	8	3	6	4	3
Jobbers	9	4	2	2	2
Machinery and Tools	6	7	4	5	5
Contractor's Products	-	9	5	8	6
Miscellaneous	29	18	18	11	13

*Included semifinished steel for conversion by others.

Exhibit 5 (continued)

B. Consultant's Estimate of Market in Pittsburgh Sales Area

	Estimated Market Consumption-1960* (Thousand Tons)	Monongahela Sales-1960 (Thousand Tons)	Monongahela Percent Total
Carbon Steel			
Strip (up to 22")	2,808	588	20.9%
Sheet	10,335	-	-
Galvanized Strip	679	59	8.6
Galvanized Sheet	593	-	-
Plates	3,375	48	1.4
Tin Plate	2,078	-	-
Other Coated	130	-	-
Semifinished	793	138	17.4
Total	20,791	833	4.0%
Stainless Steel			
Strip	195	15	7.7%
Sheet	129	-	-
Plates	19	-	-
Semifinished	36	-	-
Total	379	15	4.0%
Alloy Steel			
Strip	36	10	27.0%
Sheet	314	-	-
Semifinished	869	0.3	-
Total	1,219	10	0.8%

*Selected flat-rolled products only. Study of use of steel bars in 1960 indicated following use of bar (thousand tons):

Carbon Steel	3,355
Stainless	86
Alloy	1,941

Source: Consultants' Report.

6. MONONGAHELA STEEL COMPANY (A)

Consultant's Forecast of 1963 Monthly Sales and 1962 Actual Tonnage
(Net Tons)

Product	1962 Monthly Tonnages*	1963 Forecast Monthly Tonnages	1963 Forecast Sales (Thousands)	1963 Forecast Price per Ton
INGOTS				
Carbon	10,280	1,367**	$ 116	$ 85
Alloy	396	1,367	166	121
Stainless	96	342	156	456
SEMIFINISHED				
Carbon Steel	1,381	7,518	767	102
Sheet Bar	17,320	18,865	1,830	97
Alloy Slabs	1,641	5,468	902	165
Stainless	14	684	504	737
PLATES***				
Narrow	12,440	13,670	1,586	116
Wide	-	47,845	4,832	101
HOT-ROLLED STRIP				
Carbon 8" Mill	2,256	2,734	418	153
Carbon 10" Mill	8,858	8,202	1,083	132
Carbon 14" Mill	31,263	23,827	2,812	118
Carbon 24" Mill	34,954	9.419	1,083	115
Specialties	232	3,691	576	156
Alloy Steel	2,092	2,324	578	249
Stainless Steel	191	273	195	715
COLD-ROLLED STRIP AND SHEETS				
Carbon Steel	8,981	8,557	1,673	195
Alloy Steel	232	410	204	496
Stainless Strip	2,556	2,734	2,618	958
Stainless Sheet and Slit Sheet	-	2,734	3,080	1,126
COATED STRIP				
Galvanite and Terne	5,700	5,741	1,073	187
TOTALS	140,883	167,772	$26,252	$ 156

*Based on average of January through March, 1962.
**Forging quality ingots.
***85% carbon steel; 15% alloy.

Source: Consultants' Report.

7. MONONGAHELA STEEL COMPANY (A)

Summary of Costs and Savings of Proposed Facilities, 1963
(All Dollars in Thousands)

A. Gross Profit Forecast:

Forecast monthly revenues (Ex. 6)	$26,252
Forecast costs of production	20,223
	$ 6,029
Current works admin. expense, prop. tax, and insurance	615
Forecast gross profit--monthly	$ 5,414
annual	64,960

B. Analysis of Annual Gross Profit:

Current operations	$37,456
New electric furnaces	5,878
Proposed plate mill	6,835
Proposed cold-rolled mill	14,764
	$64,933

C. Forecast Annual Returns on Investments:

	Plate Mill	CR Mill
Incremental sales (Ex. 6)	$57,961	$36,958
Incremental gross profit	6,835	14,764
Freight, discounts, returns (2% sales)	1,159	740
General and administrative expense (2% sales)	1,159	740
Works administration, taxes, insurance ($3/ton)	1,723	98
Incremental profit before tax	$ 2,794	$13,186
Investment	$41,010	$20,505
Return on investment	6.8%	64%

D. Semicontinuous Strip Mill Savings and Return:

1. Semicontinuous mill monthly output--24,606 tons - Plate
   8,886 tons - Hot-rolled sheet--sold
   15,037 tons - Hot-rolled sheet--converted
   1,367 tons - Hot-rolled sheet--converted and coated

2. Profit from the new sales mix

Profit from the new sales mix		$9,830
Less: Freight, discount, allowance (2%)	$1,159	
General and administrative expense (2%)	1,159	
Works administration, taxes, insurance ($3/ton)	1,723	
Incremental Net Profit		$5,789

3. Operating savings on conversion

a. 33,149 tons for 24" mill	$ 149/month
b. 2,734 tons of stainless slabs	235/month
Total monthly	$ 384/month
Annual savings	$4,608

4. Profit from sales mix change

Profit from sales mix change	$ 5,789
Savings on conversion	4,608
Incremental profit from continuous mill	$10,397
Investment	97,057
Return on investment	10.7%

Source: Consultants' Report.

Monongahela Steel Company (B)

The Monongahela executive committee had an alternative plan to investing in finishing facilities [see Monongahela Steel Company (A)]. The other plan—and the one initially favored by the vice-president of manufacturing—meant investing up to $171 million to modernize and integrate basic steel facilities in order to increase the profitability of the existing product line.

FACILITIES MODERNIZATION PLAN

The second plan was also based on the consultant's forecast of 1963 tonnage and sales and posed four not mutually exclusive alternatives. Using his forecast shown in Monongahela (A), Exhibit 6, the consultant estimated the costs of producing 209,151 ingot tons of steel per month on the existing open-hearth facilities (see Exhibit 1). In all his calculations he assumed that home scrap generated would equal 20 percent of ingot production. The alternatives presented for reducing these costs were: constructing four or eight open-hearth furnaces; installing oxygen converters; erecting a blast furnace for additional or replacement capacity; or building a coke oven plant.

1. *Open-Hearth Furnaces:* The first project was the proposed construction of a new shop with eight new 250-ton open-hearth furnaces designed to produce a total of 146,300 tons per month and exactly replace the eighteen 200-ton units. With no change from the present materials charge, the cost above metals for these new furnaces was estimated at $12 a ton. Construction of the furnaces, a building, and the necessary auxiliary facilities would require about $75 million.

Should the executive committee decide to conserve funds, a partial installation was possible. Four furnaces with the building and auxiliary equipment for eight would cost $47.8 million. The nine most inefficient furnaces would be replaced resulting in a one dollar reduction (to $14.75) in the cost above metals for the old furnaces remaining (see Exhibit 1).

2. *Oxygen Converters:* The second project was the installation of 50,600 tons per month of oxygen converter capacity. The process was most satisfactory for low carbon steel; the expected future operating schedule called for 54,700 tons per month of steel less than .10 percent carbon. Cost above materials would be $8 per ton, and the facilities cost $16.4 million. Since the converters took an 80 percent hot metal charge, the materials requirements for the monthly production of 209,000 ingot tons changed as shown in Exhibit 1, column I.

3. *Blast Furnace:* A fifth blast furnace would be needed if the company were to operate at the 209,151 ingot ton per month level with optimal hot metal charges. Some 131,200 tons of hot metal would be required to achieve a 60 percent optimum charge for the open hearths. If oxygen converters were installed, the total would rise to 144,100 because the converters needed 80 percent hot metal (see Exhibit 1, column III). Construction of a blast furnace, with a monthly capacity of 45,500 tons per month, and an ore screening and sintering plant would cost about $36 million. The furnace would consume 1,600 pounds of by-product coke per ton of hot metal and produce iron at $41.40 per ton.

The vice-president of research and development wanted the new furnace to replace unit #1, the company's oldest, that produced 203,136 tons of pig iron per year at capacity. He pointed out that the unit was technologically outmoded, of small capacity, and had a production cost $8 per ton above the other blast furnaces.

4. *Coke Oven Plant:* The fourth proposal was to integrate backwards and manufacture all coke needed. During the first quarter of 1962, Monongahela consumed 60,000 tons monthly. A new coke plant could produce coke at $12 per ton, based upon a cost of $9 per ton for coal delivered. The cost of the plant would depend upon the capacity: a 54,700-ton per month plant would cost $27.3 million, while an 89,000-ton per month unit would run $43.7 million.

In 1962, Monongahela produced 2,061,000 ingot tons, or 74.9 percent of 1963 ingot capacity. The treasurer estimated the company should earn $9 million after taxes in 1963 at 100 percent capacity or $2.7 million at 50 percent capacity.

1. MONONGAHELA STEEL COMPANY (B)

Costs of Present and Proposed Steelmaking Facilities, 1963

A. Present Cost to Produce 209,151 Net Tons of Open-Hearth Ingots per Month:

	Tons	Cost/Ton	Total Cost
Hot Metal	98,971	$42.15	$4,172,000
Purchased Scrap	74,638	31.10	2,321,000
Limestone	7,518	2.80	21,000
Burned Lime	8,339	18.40	153,000
Ore	17,771	10.22	182,000
	207,237		$6,849,000

Cost above Materials: $15.75 per ton

B. Charge Materials to Produce 209,151 Tons/Month of Ingots under Proposed Conditions (In Thousand Tons):

	I	II	III
Hot Metal	99.0	131.2	144.1
Purchased Scrap	80.1	38.4	33.1
Limestone	4.0	16.7	12.2
Burned Lime	9.7	1.1	4.1
Ore	4.8	24.3	11.8

I. After construction of proposed oxygen steelmaking plant.
II. After construction of proposed blast furnace.
III. After construction of blast furnace and oxygen converters.

Note: Home scrap was equal to 20% of ingot production.

Source: Consultants' Report.

Armco Steel Corporation (C)

During the six-year period 1949 to 1954, the Armco Steel Corporation expanded from a sales volume of $341 million and an ingot production of 3.14 million tons, to a sales volume of $532 million and an ingot production of 4.46 million tons. Between 1949 and 1954 the company spent $232 million for expansion and modernization, increasing its capacity from 3.86 to 4.95 million ingot tons (Balance sheets and income statements are shown in Exhibits 1 and 2).

As a result of this successful record, executives of the Armco company decided early in 1955 to proceed with a second large-scale expansion and modernization program, involving some $328 million of capital expenditures during the six-year period from 1955 to 1960. The new program, financed largely through internally generated funds, proceeded favorably for the first three years, and in 1957 the company attained a sales volume of $777 million and ingot production of 5.42 million tons. However, in 1958 a recession hit the steel industry, which operated as a whole at only 60 percent of rated capacity during the year. Since the outlook was that internally generated funds would be insufficient to maintain its capital investment program, the Armco corporation stopped all projects that were not already under construction in February, 1958.

As a result of this situation, the management was obliged to review the status of the two principal projects that had been planned but not yet begun. One project included $51 million for a new blast furnace and steelmaking facilities at the Ashland, Kentucky Works to provide the additional steel ingot tonnage which this plant was capable of rolling and finishing. The other included $17 million for cold-rolling, processing and finishing facilities to enable the Butler, Pennsylvania Works to make full use of its hot-rolling facilities and increase capacity for stainless steel from 29,000 to 54,000 tons. Due to the shortage of funds, the management had to decide whether to defer both projects or seek new sources of capital and go ahead with one or both projects.

DEVELOPMENTS BETWEEN 1949 AND 1958

The capital investment program of 1949–54 increased ingot capacity by 1,100,000 tons. This increase came about through a new blast furnace and open-hearth furnaces in Middletown, a new open-hearth furnace in Houston, and new electric furnaces in Kansas City and Houston. At the same time the rolling capacity was increased through the completion of a new plate mill in Houston to roll the metal for the new pipe mill jointly owned by the A. O. Smith Company and Armco Steel Corporation. The old hot strip mill in Ashland was replaced by a new 72-inch wide mill and additional cold-rolling facilities were added to bring the annual cold-rolling capacity at this location to 370,000 tons. A new blooming mill was constructed in Kansas City and a new stainless steel bar mill was started in Baltimore.

Meanwhile, the Armco corporation continued its development of new steel products, while concentrating on cold-rolled sheet and strip at its Middletown and Ashland plants. In 1950, the company developed ORTHONIK alloys for use in electronic controls in industry and defense. This was followed in 1951 by the introduction of 17–10 P, a nonmagnetic stainless steel for naval minesweepers, and 21–4 N, a stainless steel used for valves in high compression auto engines. In 1952, the company added ALUMINIZED STEEL Type II to its line of aluminum coated steels. This new product offered great resistance to atmospheric corrosion. In 1953, ultra-thin electrical steel for use in memory cores of electronic computers was produced. Continued research into precipitation hardening stainless steels, originally developed by Armco, produced PH 15–7 Mo in 1957 which provided the high strength at elevated temperatures required by American supersonic defense planes and missiles. A new process for porcelain coating steel in a one-coat, one-fire process rather than the old two-coat, two-fire process was invented in 1957 and the company began limited sales in 1958 of UNIVIT, the steel to take this porcelain enameling process.

The company also continued to improve its silicon steels for electrical uses. Armco pioneered in the development of silicon steels which are used to make laminations in the cores of electrical transformers, improving their ability to contain magnetic lines of force. Armco scientists established that magnetic properties depended upon the alignment of silicon crystals in the steel. The Armco technologists developed means of orienting the crystals through rigid controls over the chemistry of the ingot, as well as maintaining control over temperature changes and rolling deformations. The steel was made in open-hearth furnaces at the Butler Works, was annealed and pickled between successive cold reductions, and was given a special CARLITE coating to provide surface insulating properties.

During the early 1950's, the corporation consisted of the parent company with plants at Middletown, Hamilton, Piqua, and Zanesville, Ohio; Ashland, Kentucky; Butler, Pennsylvania; and Baltimore, Maryland, and three wholly owned subsidiaries, Sheffield Steel Corporation, Armco Drainage & Metal Products, Inc., and the Armco International Corporation. The principal products of the parent company plants were hot- and cold-rolled steels and special purpose flat-rolled steels, manufactured steel products, railroad wheels and tubing. Sheffield plants, located at Houston, Kansas City and Sand Springs, Oklahoma, produced bar and wire products, structural shapes and plates. Armco Drainage manufactured a diversified line of manufactured steel products, including drainage structures and related construction items and prefabricated steel buildings, in 46 plants in the United States and Canada. Armco International distributed and manufactured Armco products outside the United States and Canada.

In 1954, Sheffield Steel Corporation became a division of Armco Steel Corporation. During the same year, Southwest Steel Products, a small manufacturer of bar joists, roof decks and other steel construction products in Houston, was acquired and became a part of the Sheffield Division.

During the five years from 1950 through 1954, Armco Drainage and Metal Products built three new plants and expanded several others. In view of the expected federal program to increase highway construction, Armco executives were very optimistic about this part of the company's activities.

Armco International Corporation set new sales records in 1950, 1952, and 1954. New plants were constructed for tubing, welding electrodes, and drainage products in England, France, Italy, South Africa, and Colombia.

In November, 1957, Armco Steel Corporation exchanged 264,000 Armco shares for the entire 660,000 outstanding shares of the Union Wire Rope Corporation of Kansas City, Missouri. The latter firm manufactured high carbon steel wire and stranded some of this wire into wire rope. The plant had a capacity of 72,000 net tons of wire including 37,000 tons of wire rope. The principal customers of this firm were in the mining, oil and gas, construction, logging, transportation, ship building, national defense, and other heavy industries.

The National Supply Company was merged into Armco Steel Corporation on April 30, 1958, by an exchange of 2,500,000 shares of Armco common stock for the 2,940,000 shares outstanding of The National Supply Company. The National Supply Company was one of the largest manufacturers and distributors of oil and gas well equipment. About 45 percent of its sales were tubular products manufactured in two large plants in western Pennsylvania. Another 15 percent of its sales were drilling and pumping equipment manufactured in five plants in California, Texas, Ohio, and Illinois.

Products and supplies for the oil and gas industry manufactured by other firms and sold through the 124 national outlets in major oil fields throughout the Western hemisphere made up another 33 percent. The other 7 percent was miscellaneous parts and tools manufactured by the National Supply Company for many industries.

The National Supply Company had been purchasing about 750,000 tons of steel annually, primarily for its pipe and tube plants in Pennsylvania. Seventy-five percent of these requirements were purchased from United States Steel Corporation on a firm contract lasting until August 31, 1966. The remaining 25 percent was purchased from Crucible Steel Company on a contract terminating on December 31, 1961.

In 1958 Armco Steel Corporation's sales were broken down approximately as follows:

Armco Division	35%
National Supply	23
Sheffield Division	20
Armco Drainage	10
Armco International	10
Union Wire Rope	2

NEW CAPITAL EQUIPMENT PROGRAMS

Armco Steel Corporation planned to devote very considerable resources during the 1950's to capital equipment programs designed to provide new reserves of iron ore, modernize its processing facilities, and balance its mills on a vertically integrated basis.

The Armco company was one of the first major steel companies to use iron ore pellets beneficiated from taconite. In 1949 it had shared equally with Republic Steel Corporation in the establishment of the Reserve Mining Company. The Reserve company had borrowed some $150 million in mortgage bonds to finance its mining and processing operations in Minnesota. Armco also owned 6.67 percent of the common stock of Iron Ore Company of Canada, which opened up the new ore reserves in Labrador. It also purchased coal and ore reserves in Texas to supply its Sheffield Division. By 1958 Armco Steel Corporation received almost all of its iron ore from three sources. The Iron Ore Company of Canada could supply 1,000,000 gross tons, Reserve Mining Company could supply 2,500,000 gross tons, and leased or owned Texas sources could supply up to 900,000 tons. Armco's share of the reserves in these three locations was approximately 40,000,000 gross tons, 250,000,000 gross tons, and 48,000,000 gross tons.

In 1955 the company developed a new capital equipment program intended to expend some $328 million by 1960 (see Exhibit 3). Of this sum, $154 million was allocated to a program to expand and modernize sheet and strip facilities, including $80 million for specialty steels at Butler, $50 million at Middletown, and $24 million at Ashland. Of the remaining $174 million, $66 million went to Sheffield and $34 million to other subsidiaries. The other $74 million was for the Armco Division, including $10 million a year for normal replacement and $14 million for facilities such as sintering plants.

The main purpose at Middletown was to take advantage of the new blast furnace and openhearth facilities installed there in the 1949–54 period. This involved revamping the hot strip mill to increase its rolling capacity, modernization of cold-rolling mills to allow bigger coils and faster speeds and expansion of annealing and pickling facilities. At Ashland, additional cold rolling, processing and finishing facilities were required to match the steelmaking capacity of this plant. However, the hot strip mill in this plant which had been installed new in 1953 had a capacity to roll steel well in excess of the plant's steelmaking capacity. The 1955 plan was therefore later enlarged to include additional steelmaking capacity. The Butler and Ashland programs will be described in greater detail below.

The company hoped to meet these capital costs partly through the sale of one million shares of common stock and the balance through the internal generation of cash funds.

The program proceeded well until the late summer of 1957, when a severe decline started to take place in the steel industry. At Armco, although its total ingot capacity had increased about 24 percent since 1955, its actual output of ingots was declining about 10 percent from the 1955 level. The rest of the industry was under more serious pressure, however, since Armco was actually increasing its share of the industry's total ingot production from 4.4 percent in 1955 to 5.0 percent at the end of 1957. Monthly shipments of stainless and heat-resistant steels, which were running at 60,000 tons for the industry in late 1955, declined to 40,000 tons monthly in late 1957.

During 1957 Armco borrowed $50 million at 3½ percent interest from several New York and other large city banks and sold an additional 1,088,000 common shares at $56 per share. In February, 1958, the stock was selling at a price of $45 per share.

Armco's long-term debt required annual sinking fund payments of $5,870,000 through 1962 and reduced annual payments thereafter to maturity in 1966. In addition the $50 million loan was to be paid off in approximately equal installments in 1962, 1963, and 1964. In 1956 the company had increased its dividend rate to 75 cents per quarter. The company placed a very high priority on its $3 dividend in order to maintain the confidence of its investors. Despite the large scale of the announced merger with National Supply, no major cash impact was anticipated from this source, since common shares were to be exchanged and the increased income and depreciation would be about balanced by increased dividends and capital expenditures.

The inadequacy of depreciation funds in covering replacement of facilities was a source of major concern to management. Because several facilities carrying rapid amortization certificates were reaching full depreciation, cash flows were not expected to rise greatly due to the new expansion program. Depreciation funds were expected to be $36 million in 1958 and $40 million in 1959.

The Armco management reconsidered the program they had undertaken, taking into account the financial resources they could depend on, the effect of the changed business situation on the urgency of going ahead with certain projects, and the future trends they should prepare for. As a result of the reduced level of operations, Armco decided in February, 1958, to halt all parts of the special sheet and strip program that were not already under construction. (Projects under construction at that time together with normal replacement were estimated to require total capital expenditures of $60 million for 1958, $40 million for 1959, and $30 million for 1960.) The two projects which were most seriously affected were the newly planned $51 million blast furnace and oxygen converter program for Ashland and the $17 million cold-rolling, processing and finishing facilities for making stainless steel at Butler.

ASHLAND AND BUTLER PROGRAMS

The Ashland and Middletown Works were the mainstay of the company's sheet and strip production, which supplied principally appliance and automotive customers within 150 miles of their Ohio and Kentucky locations. The company wished to make use of new steelmaking techniques and to keep both plants as balanced as possible in their vertical integration in order to obtain the maximum production efficiencies. The Armco management had already spent very large sums to assure ore supplies, balance the Middletown Works, and obtain a better balance in the Ashland rolling facilities.

As the Ashland program developed it became clear that iron and steelmaking facilities were insufficient to meet the 1,800,000 annual tons of capacity in the Ashland hot strip mill. The three blast furnaces and eight open-hearth furnaces could provide 1,038,000 tons of ingot steel. In order to obtain comparable steel capacity, the company would have to provide a new blast furnace and oxygen converters. The new program would cost $51 million and take five years to complete.

The Butler Works, located 35 miles north of Pittsburgh, had been acquired in 1927. It contained a continuous hot strip mill which had been built about the same time as the original Ashland continuous strip mill which had been replaced in 1953. The purchase had allowed Armco to consolidate its patent position on continuous mills. After the acquisition, the Butler Works was used for hot-rolled, cold-rolled and other so-called commodity grades, in addition to forged railroad wheels. As new stronger and wider strip mills were developed in the other steelmaking plants around the country, the inherent disadvantages of this mill showed up in the form of continuing losses on the standard market products. Among these disadvantages were: the small scale of operations, the narrow width of the hot strip mill, the high cost of producing ingots due to the lack of a blast furnace and the resultant use of cold pig iron, and the increasing obsolescence of the mill.

Although there was frequent talk of expanding the mill and putting in a blast furnace, particularly during World War II and the Korean War when the government directly or indirectly might have assisted in the financing, the problem of adequate space prevented this kind of a major expansion. The Butler Works lies in a narrow valley and there is insufficient flat land for the improvements. In view of these limitations, the Armco management decided to use the Butler plant on specialty products. As the specialties developed, four principal products, namely railroad wheels, and stainless, electrical and coated steel sheet and strip products, made up the majority of the Butler shipments.

In February, 1958, the Butler Works employed 3,300 people, including 2,800 hourly employees. The main plant contained the open-hearth and electric furnaces, a new hot strip mill and numerous processing and finishing facilities including a tandem cold mill and a 36-inch Sendzimir mill, both of which were used for cold rolling stainless steel. The furnaces used purchased pig iron supplemented by stainless ingot supplied by the Baltimore

Works. The new hot strip mill rolled all products. The Sendzimir mill rolled narrow width stainless steel in small coils at a rate of three tons an hour, or 1,500 tons per month.

In addition to the main plant, there was also a nearby wheelworks and an adjacent empty plant that had been acquired for stainless steel processing and finishing operations. The plant management wanted a new 48-inch Sendzimir mill. The rest of the stainless steel could be rolled with this new mill after initial cold rolling on the tandem mill. The main plant operations also needed the space which would be available if stainless steel operations were removed.

The Butler Works had a capacity to produce 285,000 tons of steel products per year including 192,000 tons of electrical and coated steels, 65,000 tons of railroad wheels and 29,000 tons of stainless steels. The main elements of the total Butler program included $26 million for the new powerful 54-inch wide continuous hot strip mill which replaced the old 38-inch mill, another $10 million for general facilities such as space relocation and water and power facilities, $26 million for rolling and processing silicon-oriented electrical steels and $17 million for rolling and processing facilities for stainless steels. By February, 1958, most of these programs had been substantially completed except for the stainless steel facilities.

BUTLER STAINLESS STEEL FACILITIES

The main features of the halted $17 million stainless program, which was expected to take about 20 months to complete, were the following:

1. *Revamping Purchased Plant Space, $4,-050,000:* In 1956, an empty plant adjacent to the main Butler plant had been purchased and earmarked for all stainless steel processing once the steel had received its first cold-rolling reduction. This would include annealing, pickling, cold reduction, tempering, slitting, banding, shearing, inspection, and shipping. It would remove the stainless steels from the heavy concentration of oxides, dust and smoke created in hot-rolling silicon steels. It was anticipated that the steel would be transported in coils on trucks or rail cars after the initial reduction on the tandem mill. The new plant was to be built to handle 3,500 tons per month of chrome-nickel grades, while the main plant handled 1,000 tons of chrome grades.

2. *New Sendzimir Mill, $3,480,000:* The Sendzimir mill was a cold-rolling mill designed to take large and accurate reductions and hence eliminate some annealing and pickling operations that would be necessary to soften the hard surface of stainless steels between reductions on a regular mill. The Sendzimir mill had very small work rolls held in place by three sets of larger back-up rolls which prevented distortion laterally as well as vertically. The work rolls were designed to be easily removed for regrinding, which was required every 90 minutes. The mill processed about four tons per hour. The general rule of thumb was that each trip through the anneal and pickle line cost about $30 per ton and the Sendzimir mill was expected to eliminate from one to four trips, according to the final thickness of the steel. It was also expected to reduce scrap by about 3 or 4 percent. Present yields ran 60 to 70 percent.

3. *Pickling and Annealing Lines, $4,030,000:* About $2,680,000 was for a new annealing and pickling line for chrome-nickel stainless in the new plant, with a capacity of 10 tons per hour. The rest was to rebuild the two old lines in the main plant, one to process chrome-nickel and the other chrome stainless as they came off the hot strip mill.

4. *Other Facilities:* Other facilities included increased power on the main tandem cold-rolling mill, larger coil winding and slitting equipment, new grinders, and so on.

The major objectives of this program were:

a) Capacity. Present stainless steel capacity at the Butler Works was 2,400 to 2,500 tons per month. The new hot strip mill had removed one of the limiting factors on this capacity, but the Butler Works was still limited by annealing and pickling capacity and rewinding and slitting equipment. Slab grinding, cold-rolling, and coil grinding were also very close to the same capacity level and under certain conditions of product mix and quality control became limiting factors. Except for very short periods in 1949 and 1954, stainless steel production at the Butler Works held at capacity levels until the late summer of 1957. By March of 1958, production had fallen to approximately two thirds of capacity.

b) Width of Coil. There was one anneal and pickle line capable of handling 50-inch strips and one single stand reversing mill wide enough for these strips. However, processing through this single stand mill required so many passes and so many anneals that capacity limitations in the annealing and pickling prevented these facilities from being used for this purpose. The width permissible on all the other equipment was 36 inches except for the new hot strip mill. On all equipment except the tandem mill the problem was the actual width of the rolls and the dimensions inside the equipment. On the tandem mill the problem was that the mill was not powered sufficiently to take the desired reduction in a single pass. Intermediate anneals would be required.

The larger width was very important for use in the aircraft industry where additional seams or joints add weight and expense to the aircraft and was also important to other stainless steel users either because of the size of the finished piece or the economy of handling large widths prior to cutting or stamping.

Armco was able to supply hand-rolled stainless steel sheets from Middletown in widths up to 80 inches. However, the quality of these hand-rolled sheets was not acceptable to some users. They could only be produced in sheet rather than coil form. The costs of production, particularly on the lighter gauges were extremely high.

Armco had considered the possibility of installing facilities at Butler to handle wider widths. The product manager estimated that Armco's sales of stainless strip might be increased by 3 or 4 percent if the mill could produce 60-inch wide strip but this would add $30 million to the cost of the Butler expansion program. The 48-inch width provided some production economies for Armco compared to the previous widths. For instance, an order for 24-inch wide strip could be manufactured most economically by producing 48-inch wide strip and then at the last stage in the production process slitting in half to 24-inch widths.

c) Size of Coil. Many fabricators of stainless steel preferred heavier and longer coils in order to reduce the setup costs of loading coils into their stamping or forming equipment. The capacity of the coilers on the old hot strip mill had forced Armco to divide 11,000-pound ingots to three or four coils. The new hot strip mill allowed the production of full ingot coils and the balance of the stainless steel program included the capacity for welding coils at the first anneal and pickle line to build up two ingot coils. Subsequent processing equipment was designed to handle 33,000-pound coils for processing economies (less yield loss at the ends and decreased handling) and customer satisfaction. Armco would be able to supply 11,000-pound coils for those customers who could not accept welds and larger coils for other customers.

d) Quality. The substitution of stainless steel from Butler for the hand-rolled sheets from Middletown would result in a real improvement in the quality of the product reaching the customer from the standpoint of dimensional tolerances and surface quality.

Most of the other quality improvements were translated into higher yields for the Butler Works. A significant reduction in scratches and marks occurs due to the decreased handling when rolled on a Sendzimir mill as opposed to many more passes through other types of mills and the additional annealing and pickling required. Other gains would be attained through the better condition of the hot strip mill. The removal of most of the stainless steel processing from the main plant with its heavy concentration of oxides in smoke and dust was also expected to improve the quality.

e) Tolerances. A conventional four-high single stand rolling mill was not rigid enough to attain the same tolerances that a Sendzimir mill could. Since almost all of their competitors were producing all stainless steel sheet and strip in widths up to 48 inches on Sendzimir mills and since the customers were pressing for closer tolerances, the Armco management knew there would be continual pressure to reduce the standard mill tolerance from the existing ±10 percent. If it were reduced to ±5 percent as expected, material off the single stand mills would not be commercially acceptable.

Military aircraft steel requirements were

known to be extremely rigid. In order to meet the proposed tolerance of +0 −.002 of an inch, Armco would have to have the best and most accurate Sendzimir.

f) Space. When the hot strip mill was completed and if the silicon oriented steel program attained capacity operations, the Butler Works anticipated severe space and handling problems. In order to allow for proper storage of coils off the hot strip mill, the plant management was extremely anxious to move the stainless steel operations out of the main plant.

g) Costs. Major cost savings anticipated were:

(*a*) Elimination of anneal and pickle line operations at $30 per ton.
(*b*) Increased yield of 3 or 4 percent.
(*c*) Reduction of materials handling due to larger coils, space and better layout.

MARKET PROSPECTS

In evaluating the relative merits of the Ashland versus the Butler program, the following March, 1958, prices per ton might be considered:[1]

	Carbon Steel	*#430 Stainless*	*#302 Stainless*
Ingot	$ 77.60	$340	$ 505
Hot-rolled	99.60	640	810
Cold-rolled	152.00	815	1,040

The carbon steel from Ashland went largely to appliance and automotive customers in the Ohio and Kentucky areas. Stainless type #430 was a ferritic chrome steel. The 17 percent chrome content gave it high corrosion resistance suitable to automotive and architectural trim.

[1] The price differential between stainless steel and carbon steel had to cover additional costs including the following: more expensive alloying metals; decreased yields; increased resistance to rolling deformation which required more powerful and more expensive mills, an increase in the number of passes and/or a decrease in rolling speeds; increased electric power consumption; increased inspection; additional slab grinding; and the extra work of placing interleaving paper in the stainless coils to protect the finish.

Stainless type #302 was an austenitic chrome-nickel steel known as 18–8 (18 percent chrome, 8 percent nickel). The austenitic structure gave it good ductility suitable for deep drawing. It was widely used in kitchen equipment and utensils, dairy installations, transportation equipment, and oil, paper, chemical, and food-processing machinery. The Butler Works served a national market. A major portion of its production was sold through distributors who had begun handling products of some other companies in the past when Armco had been unable to fully satisfy their demands. Armco was the principal producer of continuously rolled stainless steel sheets during the early and middle thirties. It had been joined by United States Steel and Republic before the war. Right after the end of the war Armco was the third largest producer of stainless steel sheet and strip. In the postwar era the other firms significantly increased their capacity and several additional producers entered the field. By 1958, Armco's share of the total flat-rolled stainless steel production had declined significantly.

In addition to the $17 million capital investment, the Butler program would require approximately $8 million for additional working capital.

The Armco company hoped that about half of the increase in its stainless steel capacity would eventually be filled by its new precipitation hardening stainless steels, one example of which was PH 15–7 Mo which was to be used in the B-70 supersonic bomber program. This patented steel, made in an electric furnace, was processed under controlled conditions in such a way that it remained soft until a final heat treatment in the customer's plants hardened it. The softness enabled the steel to be rolled into very thin sections, thus keeping the weight low on supersonic aircraft. If the new Butler program did not proceed and if the B-70 program did proceed, the company would have to license the process to another manufacturer.

1. ARMCO STEEL CORPORATION (C)

Comparative Balance Sheets for the Years Ending December 31, 1949-1957
(In Millions)

	1949	1950	1951	1952	1953	1954	1955	1956	1957
Assets									
Cash and government notes . .	$ 59.1	$ 56.2	$ 54.6	$ 56.7	$ 48.2	$ 59.2	$ 85.1	$ 53.8	$ 88.0
Receivables	24.8	36.6	36.4	43.0	39.5	39.8	56.7	66.4	54.2
Inventories	71.3	94.1	98.8	105.0	114.1	122.7	147.4	187.9	177.5
Total current assets.	155.2	186.9	189.8	204.8	201.8	221.6	289.2	308.0	319.8
Cash set aside for modernization and expansion									50.0
Investments--net.	13.4	16.4	23.8	23.0	26.2	32.1	39.3	36.4	37.8
Plant and equipment less depreciation.	142.9	164.0	197.2	230.0	231.3	231.7	231.7	263.6	311.0
Prepaid expenses.	3.3	4.7	5.2	6.3	5.4	4.7	2.9	4.8	4.8
Total assets	314.7	372.1	416.0	464.1	464.7	490.2	563.1	612.8	723.4
Liabilities									
Total current liabilities	48.0	77.7	70.8	80.8	67.7	78.4	106.4	116.7	99.7
Long-term debt.	64.3	60.9	59.1	80.5	75.3	64.1	57.3	51.3	95.5
Current operating reserves and deferred credits. . . .	4.8	5.5	6.5	7.3	8.1	8.1	12.6	15.8	20.6
Total liabilities, reserves	117.1	144.1	136.3	168.7	151.0	150.5	176.4	183.8	215.7
Stockholders' equity	197.6	228.0	279.7	295.4	313.6	339.7	386.7	429.0	507.7
Total liabilities and equity.	314.7	372.1	416.1	464.1	464.7	490.2	563.1	612.8	723.4
Capital stock									
Preferred.	20.0	18.2	-	-	-	-	-	-	-
Common.	39.1	39.5	52.1	52.1	52.1	52.3	106.3	108.8	119.9
Reserve for contingencies	-	-	-	-	-	-	-	-	-
Capital surplus	58.0	59.3	96.5	96.5	96.5	96.9	46.2	48.1	96.6
Earned surplus	80.6	111.0	131.0	146.7	165.0	190.5	234.2	272.1	291.2
Ingot capacity (millions of tons) . .	3.60	3.86	4.33	4.525	4.718	4.902	4.950	5.15	6.00
Percent of industry total.	3.7%	3.9%	4.2%	4.2%	4.0%	3.9%	3.9%	4.0%	4.5%

Source: Company records.

2. ARMCO STEEL CORPORATION (C)

Comparative Income Statements for the Years Ending December 31, 1949-1957, and 1st Quarters 1957 and 1958
(In Millions)

	1949	1950	1951	1952	1953	1954	1955	1956	1957
Sales	$341.4	$439.3	$534.8	$518.6	$588.9	$532.0	$692.7	$761.8	$776.7
Other revenues	7.7	5.0	6.4	5.9	6.9	9.1	8.3	12.3	14.6
	$349.0	$444.3	$541.3	$524.5	$595.8	$541.2	$701.0	$774.1	$791.3
Wages and salaries	$ 95.2	$110.1	$125.7	$131.5	$150.3	$154.8	$176.8	$195.4	$206.7
Social security taxes	1.4	2.0	2.3	2.2	2.2	2.4	3.3	3.6	3.8
Pensions and insurance	2.2	7.6	10.1	10.8	11.3	9.3	9.8	13.8	16.6
	$ 98.9	$119.8	$138.1	$144.6	$163.8	$166.6	$189.9	$212.8	$227.2
Materials and services	$185.0	$212.8	$278.5	$281.2	$311.0	$250.3	$336.3	$394.0	$408.4
Depreciation	9.6	10.8	14.2	16.7	26.9	32.2	33.9	33.3	34.6
Loss on assets	.4	.3	.2	.6	.9	.4	.9	.3	1.6
Interest	2.0	1.9	1.9	2.6	2.5	2.4	2.0	2.0	2.1
Other charges	.2	.2	.3	.4	1.2	.5	.8	.2	.3
State, local and misc. taxes	2.8	3.4	3.9	3.9	4.8	5.2	6.1	6.5	8.2
Fed. income taxes	19.3	48.2	69.1	43.1	50.8	42.5	66.6	62.3	54.4
	$318.1	$397.3	$506.2	$493.1	$561.9	$500.1	$636.6	$711.5	$736.8
Income before contingencies	30.9	47.0	35.0	31.3	33.9	41.1	64.4	62.6	54.5
Contingencies (extraordinary credits)								(3.0)	(.5)
Income for year	30.9	47.0	35.0	31.3	33.9	41.1	64.4	65.6	55.0
Cash dividends	10.7	16.6	14.9	15.6	15.6	15.6	20.6	27.7	36.0
Ingot production (million tons)	3.131	3.958	4.358	4.042	4.705	4.449	5.100	5.220	5.407
Shipments (million tons)	2.389	2.976	3.387	3.079	3.376	3.171	4.004	3.936	3.808
Employees	26,048	27,888	28,032	28,339	28,644	29,145	31,504	32,358	30,596
% of ingot capacity operated	84.5	102.6	99.4	87.5	97.8	90.8	103.0	94.1	90.9

	1st Quarter 1957	1st Quarter 1958
Net sales	$198.2	$143.0
Cost of sales	158.1	117.2
includes deprec., depletion	8.5	7.8
Selling, etc. expenses	10.5	10.4
Operating profit	29.6	15.4
Royalty, etc. income	1.1	.9
Dividends rec'd.	.8	1.6
Other income	.9	.6
Total income	32.3	18.5
Interest	.5	.9
Fed. income tax	15.5	8.2
Foreign income tax	.3	.1
State, etc., income tax	.4	.2
Net profit	15.5	9.2
Common dividends	9.0	9.2

Source: Company records.

3. ARMCO STEEL CORPORATION (C)

3A. Capital Expenditure Program
(All Figures in Millions)

	1955	1956	1957	1958	1959	1960	1955-1960
Special sheet and strip program							
Butler							
General.	$ 7	$11	$13	$ 2	$ 2	$ 0	$ 35
Silicon steel	0	2	10	8	3	3	26
Stainless.	0	0	1	7	7	4	19
Total Butler.	7	13	24	17	12	7	80
Total Ashland	3	6	8	7*	0	0	24*
Total Middletown	3	14	18	15	0	0	50
Total special sheet and strip program	13	33	50	39	12	7	154
Other Armco Division**.	14	13	14	11	11	11	74
Total Armco Division	27	46	64	50	23	18	228
Total Sheffield Division	5	15	15	10	11	10	66
Total Armco Subsidiaries.	5	6	6	7	5	5	34
Total capital expenditures	$37	$67	$85	$67	$39	$33	$328

*The new $51 million program for Ashland was decided upon after 1955 but postponed in 1958.

**Includes expenditures for normal replacements in Butler, Ashland, Middletown, Baltimore, Zanesville, and other plants, offices, and mines of Armco Division of about $10 million per year.

3B. Ashland Expenditure Program

New blast furnace.	$25,500,000
Pressure top.	500,000
Oxygen converters	12,000,000
Additional soaking pits	6,500,000
Slab shear layout	1,500,000
Slab handling layout	1,500,000
Third slab furnace	800,000
Third coiler	800,000
Additional crane.	150,000
Rebuild box anneal	500,000
Other.	1,330,000
	$51,080,000

Source: Company records.

4. ARMCO STEEL CORPORATION (C)

Steel Industry Shipments of Selected Products
(Thousands of Net Tons)

	Shipments of Stainless Steel				Shipments of Carbon Steel			
	Sheet		Strip		Sheet		Strip	
	Hot-Rolled	Cold-Rolled	Hot-Rolled	Cold-Rolled	Hot-Rolled	Cold-Rolled	Hot-Rolled	Cold-Rolled
1949	15.5	54.8	5.7	105.1	5,995	6,737	1,570	1,255
1950	27.4	109.3	7.8	172.0	7,508	9,118	2,277	1,704
1951	38.6	108.1	8.1	191.3	7,836	9,421	2,160	1,856
1952	26.4	108.3	3.5	146.1	5,823	7,812	1,793	1,548
1953	16.3	121.1	3.9	227.7	7,379	11,030	2,172	1,916
1954	15.0	96.9	3.6	167.3	5,876	9,466	1,458	1,104
1955	35.4	143.4	5.4	268.2	9,022	14,964	2,051	1,451
1956	27.8	159.1	5.6	208.3	8,368	13,099	1,757	1,318
1957	26.0	136.9	8.8	195.9	7,492	11,701	1,354	1,057
1958	29.7	112.5	8.6	156.1	6,046	10,176	1,022	813

	Carbon Steel for Automotive Use				Carbon Steel for Appliance Use			
	Sheet		Strip		Sheet		Strip	
	Hot-Rolled	Cold-Rolled	Hot-Rolled	Cold-Rolled	Hot-Rolled	Cold-Rolled	Hot-Rolled	Cold-Rolled
1954	2,318	4,994	625	384	135	758	14	104
1955	3,848	7,905	849	611	199	1,429	21	145
1956	3,056	5,950	551	408	173	1,399	124	129
1957	3,220	6,212	476	399	116	1,011	22	95
1958	2,279	4,427	299	263	103	1,057	19	93

Monthly Shipments of Stainless and Heat Resisting Steels

	Jan.	Feb.	March	April	May	June	July	Aug.	Sept.	Oct.	Nov.	Dec.
1955	48.1	48.8	58.4	57.8	58.4	65.3	48.4	56.2	59.3	62.7	62.1	60.9
1956	61.1	59.3	58.3	58.1	60.9	67.7	22.8	47.0	59.3	66.9	63.9	62.4
1957	65.3	59.2	61.7	58.3	53.2	59.3	43.8	44.6	43.7	49.5	43.7	35.5
1958	41.6	35.2	35.4	33.9								

Source: AISI, Annual Statistical Reports, 1949-1958.

Oil Industry Process Notes

Crude oil, as it comes to the refinery from its underground pools, is a mixture of hundreds of hydrocarbons together with some impurities. This mixture varies from pool to pool, some crude oils being high in the lighter hydrocarbons which are usually more valuable, others high in the heavy materials which are difficult to convert to gasoline. The purpose of the refinery is to separate the mixtures into useable cuts, purify them, and upgrade them to meet product specifications. In this process, the most important manufacturing equipment include the fractionating or "bubble" tower and the catalytic reactor, with their associated service equipment such as furnaces, heat exchangers, pumps and compressors.

The fractionating tower is a continuous flow distillation process that separates the mixed feedstock according to the different boiling points of the cuts. Fractionation is used first to distill the crude oil into light ends (boiling below 100° F.), naphthas (from about 100° F. to about 400° F., in the gasoline range), feedstock for kerosene, diesel fuel and heating oil (about 350° to 640° F.), gas oils (600° to 950° F.), and residual material (over 950° F.). Atmospheric pressure distillation is adequate for material as heavy as gas oil, but vacuum fractionation is necessary to separate the heavy gas oils from residual fuel. Smaller fractionating towers are also used extensively throughout the refinery to prepare feedstock for certain process units or to separate the product effluent. A fractionating tower used to remove butanes and lighter gases is called a stabilizer, because it frees the material of vapors that will escape during storage. Other towers are used as depentanizers (to remove the C_5 hydrocarbons) or splitters (to separate light overhead stock from heavier bottoms). Since clean separation is usually difficult, many process units recycle some portion of the effluent back into the feedstock.

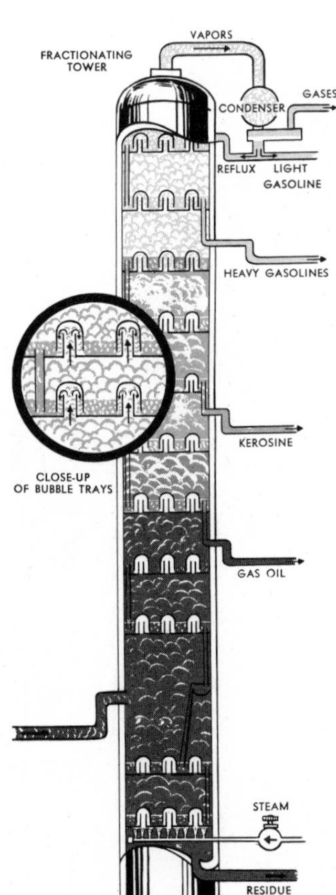

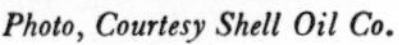

Photo, Courtesy Shell Oil Co. *Illustration, Courtesy Harbridge House, Inc.*

Fractionating Towers at an Oil Refinery

During the 1920's and 1930's, high temperatures were used to "crack" heavy material to lighter products or to "reform" naphthas to higher octane gasoline. Thermal cracking and reforming, however, have largely been replaced by the more effective catalytic processes developed in the 1940's and 1950's. For cracking heavy naphthas and light gas oils into high-octane gasoline, small beads or microspheres of alumina-silica are fed in large quantities into reactors, where they change the chemical structure of the hydrocarbons and accumulate a coating of coke. The coated catalyst is then moved to a regenerator where hot air removes the coke and allows the catalyst to be recycled. For reforming light naphthas, an alumina catalyst with a small amount of platinum is used under high pressure. The catalyst is usually placed in fixed beds within a series of reactors, and the naphtha is fed through each heated and pressurized reactor in turn. Cokers have also been developed to take the heavy gas oils and residuum from crude distillation and remove the coke so as to provide lighter gas oils capable of being fed to the catalytic cracker.

A refinery can use a wide variety of materials to heat its process units, such as natural gas, by-product gases, heavy residual fuel oil, coke, or other material, depending upon its particular sources of cheap materials and their British thermal units (B.T.U.) of heat energy. About 8½ percent of the crude input may be used up as process fuel within the refinery. To preserve the furnace heat, most process units have numbers of heat exchangers that pass hot by-product gases or liquids through pipes intermingled with a counterflow of pipes containing cool material to be heated. A considerable number of pumping units and compressors are required to move the material through the process units, and these may be driven by steam or by electricity. Large quantities of cooling water are also needed to dissipate heat and keep the units at constant temperature. The variable costs of each process unit can therefore be roughly defined according to the fuel required per barrel of feed (in B.T.U.), the steam (in pounds), the electricity (in watts), the cooling water (in gallons), and the catalyst or solvent (in pounds). The barrel is used as the unit of measure for crude oil, equivalent to 42 gallons.

In order to visualize the process units in an oil refinery, we will describe one large modern refinery,[1] the Tidewater plant in Delaware.

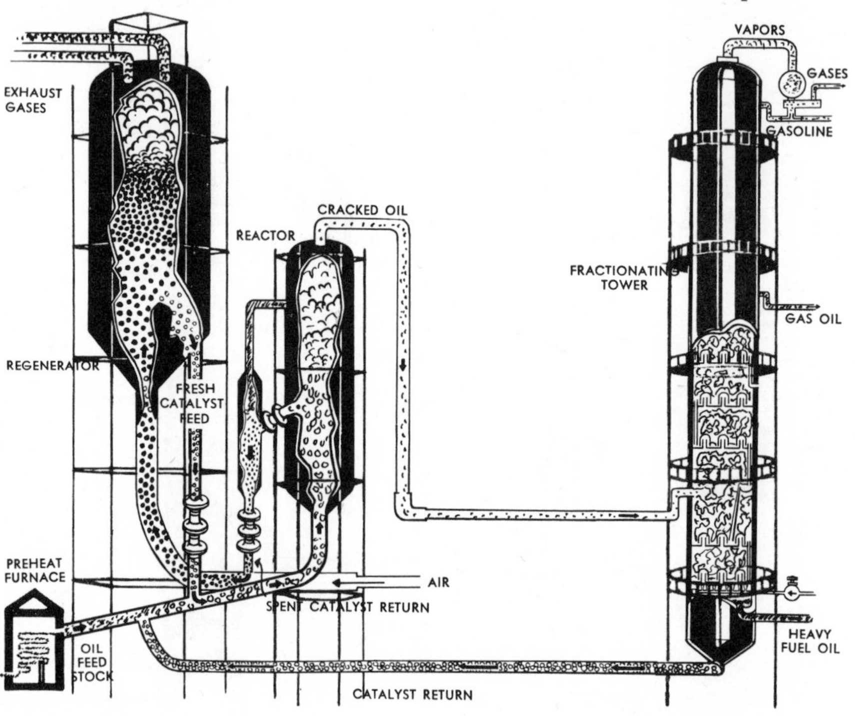

Illustration, Courtesy Harbridge House, Inc.

Fluid Catalytic Cracker

THE TIDEWATER REFINERY IN DELAWARE[1]

In the spring of 1957, the Tidewater Oil Company put on stream a new refinery on 5,000 acres of land by the Delaware River 15 miles south of Wilmington, Delaware. The refinery capacity was 130,000 barrels of crude oil per stream day, making it about tenth in size among American refineries, the largest of which could handle more than 350,000 barrels. However, the Tidewater refinery was a "grass roots" plant, new from the ground up, and therefore considered to be the most modern single integrated plant of its kind. While other refiners achieved capacity through additional units, Tidewater spent about $200 million to achieve maximum efficiency from the latest designs. It did so by installing six of the largest single-process units ever built—a 130,000-barrel crude unit, a 102,000-barrel cat cracker, a 42,000-barrel fluid coker, a 45,500-barrel reformer, a 45,000-barrel extraction unit, and a 88,000-barrel desulfurizer. It was designed to charge low-gravity, high sulfur crude and to obtain better than 100-octane gasoline and high-quality fuels.

Tidewater's previous East Coast refinery had been located at Bayonne, New Jersey, where it employed 2,200 people and processed 85,000 barrels per day of crude oil. The company became concerned about its high local taxes, limited 230-acre land, and old equipment, including a wartime fixed-bed cat cracker. It lacked both a catalytic reformer and an alkylation unit, and some of its units were designed for lubricating oils and waxes, rather than fuels.

The Delaware site was chosen, in part, for its market location, land availability, and deep-water access. Some units, like the catalytic cracker, which was constructed on site, were very large in size. Other units, such as the catalytic reformer reactors and the extraction towers, were duplicated in twin trains to provide operating flexibility or to allow the 70 fractionating towers to be prefabricated. Even so, some of the larger towers weighed 75 tons and required special handling during construction.

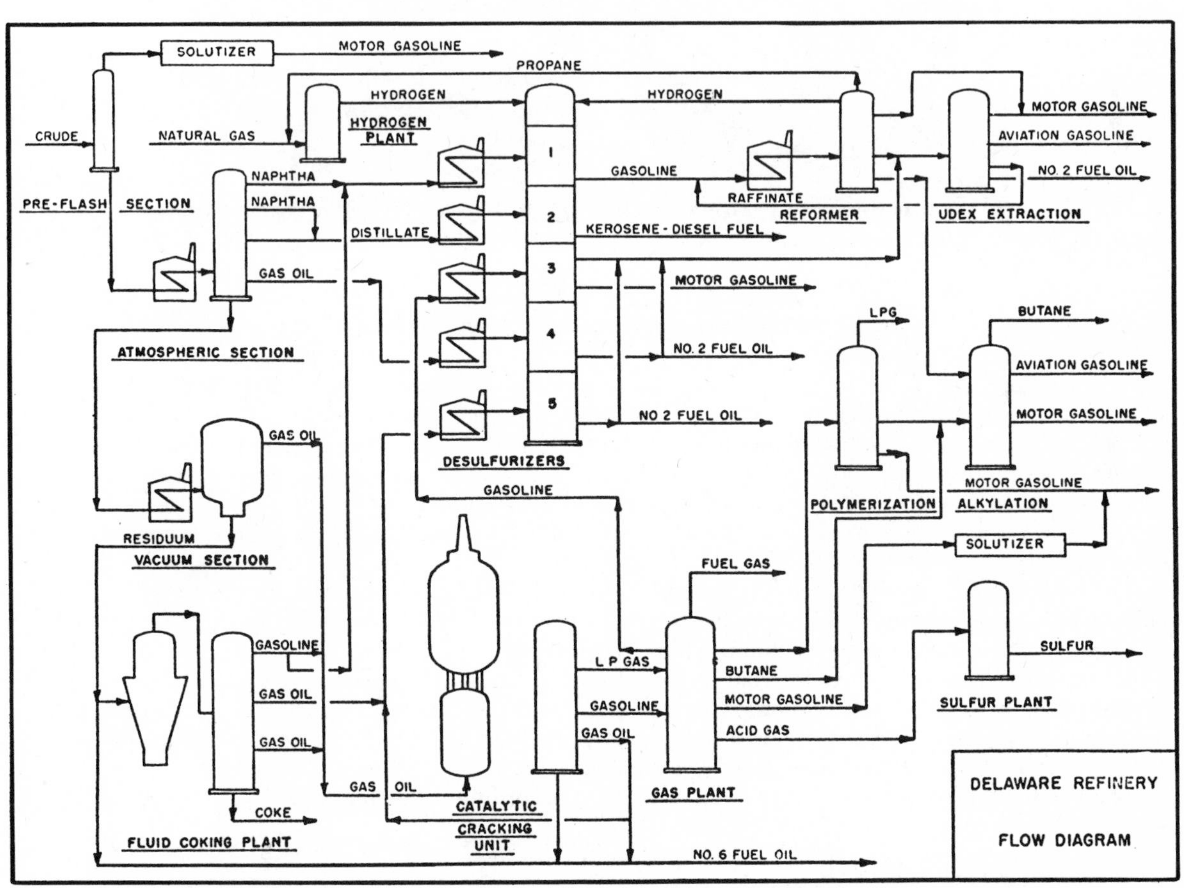

Illustration, Tidewater Oil Co.

Tidewater Delaware Refinery: Flow Diagram

[1] Much of the material in this section is drawn from a special issue of "Petroleum Processing" for July, 1957, featuring the new refinery.

Photo, Tidewater Oil Co.

1. Crude Unit

Atmospheric column is left, vacuum column is in the center.

1. Crude Distillation. The crude unit was capable of distilling 130,000 barrels of crude oil per day into eight product yields for further processing. Distillation was done in three stages. The gasoline column yielded light ends and straight-run gasoline. The atmospheric column yielded intermediate and heavy naphthas, virgin distillate, and light gas oil. The vacuum column yielded heavy gas oil and residuum.

The crude oil was desalted by electrical precipitation in a series of drums, then heated to 400° F. for entry to the gasoline column. The light ends went to the gas plant and the gasoline was condensed for blending into the final product.

The bottoms of the gasoline column were put through a fired heater to raise the temperature for the large atmospheric column, which was 23 feet in diameter. The bottoms were again fire-heated and passed at 750° F. to the vacuum column which provided heavy gas oil to the catalytic cracker and residuum to the fluid coker. The internal linings of much of the atmospheric and vacuum columns were of stainless steel, to prevent corrosion. Controls permitted the change of fuel to vary according to the needs of the heaters. The system required 30,000 pounds of fuel per hour, 20,300 gallons of cooling water per minute, and 1,700 kilowatts of electric power.

The yields per barrel of crude oil varied as follows, according to the feedstock:

	West Texas	*Kuwait*	*Wafra-W. Texas*
1. Light Ends	0.6%	2.9%	0.7%
2. Straight-run	11.7	8.3	8.3
3. Inter. Naphtha	17.0	15.0	7.5
4. Heavy Naphtha	2.0	4.0	3.0
5. Distillate	13.0	10.0	7.5
6. Light Gas Oil	15.0	10.0	8.5
7. Heavy Gas Oil	31.7	32.8	32.0
8. Residuum	9.0	17.0	32.5

Photo, Tidewater Oil Co.

2. Fluid Coker

The power company stack to the left is 500 feet high.

2. *Fluid Coker.* The coker took heavy residuum from the vacuum tower and processed it into gasolines and gas oils. Most cokers in the United States were delayed cokers, using two reactors alternatively to collect the coke particles that were removed from the feedstock. The fluid coker, however, was designed to operate in a way similar to the fluid catalytic cracker, with hot combustion air heating up the coke in a burner to a temperature at which, when charged to the reactor, would help decompose the feedstock into light components.

The fluid coker could process 42,000 barrels per stream day of vacuum tower bottoms into 1,400 barrels of butane gases, 7,300 barrels of gasoline, 5,000 barrels of light gas oil, 17,900 barrels of heavy gas oil, and 1,600 net tons of coke per day.

The operation included a reactor, which thermally cracked the feedstock into 74 percent gas liquids and 26 percent fluid coke; a scrubber and fractionator which separated the gas liquids; and a burner, which recycled hot coke particles to the reactor and recovered 80 percent of the coke for sale as heavy burner fuel.

The reactor was 135 feet high and 29 feet in diameter and could hold 600 tons of fluid coke. The feedstock, 2.5° A.P.I. with 5.5 percent sulfur content from the vacuum tower, was sprayed on the fluid coke at 950° F., where it cracked to light materials and additional coke. The material rose upward and entered the scrubber through cyclone separators. The scrubber was mounted directly on top of the reactor and carried the total structure up to 250 feet. The fluid coke, formed at the rate of 6 tons per minute, was recycled to the burner, which was mounted next to the reactor.

The coke in the burner was heated by air combustion to 1,125° F. by a 6,870-horsepower blower which furnished 100,000 cubic feet of combustion air per minute. The burner received 50 tons per minute from the reactor and recycled 44 tons per minute of hot coke to it. It used up 400 tons of coke per day to maintain the temperature in the reactor, and released 1,600 tons to the company coke silo and to the nearby electric powerhouse. Coke fines and carbon monoxide passed off the top of the burner to a boiler which generated 426,000 pounds of steam per hour at 750° F.

Photo, Tidewater Oil Co.

3. Fluid Catalytic Cracker

Towers in the foreground are in the gas plant. The Orthoflow converter in the center has a diameter of 60 feet.

3. Fluid Catalytic Cracker. The fluid catalytic cracker was capable of converting 101,800 barrels of gas oil per day into high-octane gasoline and other products. The feedstock consisted of 23.3° A.P.I. gas oil, 58,000 barrels from crude distillation and the fluid coker and 43,800 barrels of 20.0° A.P.I. recycled from the cracking unit itself. The products were 65,000 pounds per hour of propane gases for catalytic polymerization, 7,900 barrels per day of butanes for alkylation, 29,100 barrels of 56.6° gasoline for blending, 18,700 barrels of 24.4° light gas oil for No. 2 fuel oil, 1,600 barrels of 5.0° heavy fuel oil, and 613 tons of coke per day.

The main structure was an Orthoflow converter, consisting of a catalyst regenerator mounted directly on top of a reactor. The combined structure was 170 feet high and the regenerator had a diameter of 60 feet. Oil feedstock was sprayed through nozzles near the bottom of the reactor into a large bed of fluid catalyst material at 900° F. The oil was cracked to product mixture, covering the catalyst particle with coke. The spent catalyst entered a central partitioned section of the reactor through slots, where it was stripped of excess material in steam baffles, and then blown up through stand pipes to enter the regenerator. In the regenerator, combustion air was blown in to burn off the excess coke and then the regenerated catalyst dropped down through valves into the outside section of the reactor, where it met more oil feedstock.

The system required 33 carloads of catalyst in the regenerator and reactor, and the valves controlled catalyst flow between them at the rate of 2 carloads (90 tons) per minute. A separate storage drum could hold 1,800 tons of catalyst during the annual turnaround period, and another drum had a capacity of 500 tons of fresh catalyst. A 3,000-horsepower compressor lifted spent catalyst to the regenerator, and a 11,250-horsepower steam turbine was required to blow combustion air into the regenerator at 162,000 cubic feet per minute. The overall structure weighed 9,500 tons, and was lined with refractory material. A 151-foot high elevator was provided for personnel, which included one leader and three operators per shift, plus a trainee. A separate fractionating tower, 25 feet in diameter, separated the product yields.

Process units of this type used alumina catalyst priced from 12 cents to 17 cents per pound, depending upon whether they were synthetic (12 cent) or high alumina (17 cent). The oil to catalyst ratio was about 3 or 4 barrels of fresh feed to each pound of catalyst.

Photo, Tidewater Oil Co.

4. Alkylation Plant Reactors

4. Gas Plant—Catalytic Polymerization—Alkylation. The gas plant could take 88 million cubic feet of light ends from crude distillation, coker, cracker, desulfurizer, and reformer, and prepare them for further processing in the polymerization and alkylation units. It separated the ethanes, propanes, and butanes; it removed hydrogen sulfide by contact with diethanolamine solution; and it sweetened the products with caustic, antioxidant, and a doctor solution. The gas plant also yielded light gasoline for blending and heavy gasoline for further processing. The gas plant was combined with the catalytic cracker unit in order to centralize services, instrumentation, and piping, since the catalytic cracker provided much of the feedstock and the reboil heat. Furthermore, the gas compressors, totaling 13,000 horsepower, were located together with the cracker blowers, to provide common maintenance.

The catalytic polymerization unit was designed to convert 9,000 barrels per day of C_3 hydrocarbons (propylene and propane) and 6,500 barrels of C_4 hydrocarbons (butylene, butane, and isobutane) into 5,100 barrels of polymer gasoline, 4,800 of propane, and 3,900 butane. It used four catalyst reactor towers operating in parallel, rather than one large tower, to ensure catalyst contact, maintain temperature controls, and allow operating flexibility below full capacity. The gasoline product was 62.4° A.P.I., with a research octane rating of 97, capable of improvement to 100 with addition of tetraethyl lead.

The alkylation unit was designed to alkylate isobutane with butylenes in the presence of sulfuric acid, to produce 5,000 to 6,000 barrels per day of aviation gasoline. Since isobutane was largely a product of the natural gas producers, the extent to which the alkylation unit was used depended upon what price the Delaware refinery had to pay for gas delivery. The alkylation process required two horizontal reactors, which were refrigerated to remove the heat of reaction. A 3,100-horsepower steam turbine compressed the isobutane to obtain vacuum condensation for refrigeration. Alkylation yielded a very high octane product, suitable for aviation gasoline or for upgrading the pool of premium motor fuel.

Photo, Tidewater Oil Co.

5. Desulfurizer, Train 1

5. *Hydrogen Plant—Desulfurization.* Due to the high sulfur content of the crude oils planned for distillation, large quantities of hydrogen gas were required to desulfurize intermediate products by converting the dissolved sulfur to hydrogen sulfide. Although the 45,200-barrel catalytic reformer generated hydrogen at the rate of about 400 cubic feet per barrel of reforming capacity, it was not enough to treat all the products required, and a separate hydrogen plant was required to generate 30 million cubic feet per day. The capital cost of this plant was about $5 million and produced hydrogen of better than 98 percent purity at a cost of about 40 to 50 cents per 1,000 cubic feet, with fuel and utilities accounting for the major operating cost.

Hydrogen could be generated from natural gas, refinery fuel gas, and ethane, propane, or butane streams. The Delaware refinery had no natural gas or ethane stream, and its fuel gas had a high nitrogen content, so it used a propane stream. The propane stream was first purified in a catalytic reactor and a caustic treating tower. Then the propane was heated to 1,500° F. in alloy steel furnaces in the presence of a nickel catalyst which released carbon monoxide and hydrogen. The plant required 4,700 kilowatts, 7 billion B.T.U. and 30 million gallons of cooling water to convert 100,000 gallons per day of propane.

The hydrogen was used to treat 88,000 barrels of intermediate refinery yields, in five separate trains. Train 1 contained 17,900 to 30,000 barrels of naphtha from crude distillation and gasoline from the fluid coker; train 2 contained 9,300 to 10,000 barrels of middle distillate from crude distillation; train 3 contained 7,700 to 9,500 barrels of heavy naphtha from the cat cracker; train 4 contained 11,600 to 13,500 barrels of gas oil from crude distillation; and train 5 contained 16,400 to 25,000 barrels of gas oil from the coker and the cat cracker.

Train 1 can be taken as an example of hydrogen treatment. The naphtha was charged to a series of two reactors where it was mixed with hydrogen, heated, and contacted catalyst of cobalt molybdenum. Then the effluent was cooled and charged to a high-pressure separator where the hydrogen-rich vapor was flashed off, hydrogen sulfide removed, and the gas was compressed for recycling to the system. The hydrocarbons were pumped to a tower which heated the material, removed pentane, and provided the main naphtha feedstock for the catalytic reformer. Train 1 could take 11,100 barrels of naphtha and 6,800 of gasoline or 26,700 naphtha and 3,300 gasoline.

Photo, Tidewater Oil Co.

6. Solvent Extraction Unit Processing Material from the Catalytic Reformers

6. Catalytic Reformer—Solvent Extraction. The catalytic reformer had the capability of converting 30,500 barrels per day of desulfurized naphtha from crude distillation into 94-octane gasoline, with addition of tetraethyl lead. In order to do so, it had to recycle 15,000 barrels of material from the solvent extraction unit. The 45,000-barrel capacity unit was divided into two trains, each containing three fixed-bed catalytic reactors, a heater, three re-heaters, a compressor, a condenser, and a separator. The shell of the cylindrical reactor was more than five inches thick.

Ordinarily, the reactors operated at 914° F. and a pressure of 520 pounds per square inch. Under these conditions, the catalyst was expected to last a year before regeneration. However, a single regenerator was available to service both trains and operating conditions could be increased in severity to yield higher octane gasoline, in which case the catalyst would have to be regenerated at the rate of 95 barrels of feed per pound of catalyst. Regeneration took 1 to 2 days, during which the alternate train could operate.

The solvent extraction unit processed 27,000 barrels per day of material from the catalytic reformer containing less than 60 percent aromatics and converted it to 15,550 barrels containing 82 to 88 percent aromatics. It enabled the catalytic reformer to operate without the high severity that would reduce the yield of high-octane product. The lower octane product of the extraction unit was recycled to the reformer to increase the separation of aromatics. Alternatively, it could be used as a jet fuel component. Due to local transportation limitations, a single large extractor column could not be prefabricated for delivery, so two extractors, connected in parallel, were installed.

7. *Utilities.* The power plant, owned by an independent power company, took 1,273 million British thermal units per hour in fuel, largely fluid coke, from the refinery, and returned to it 764 million B.T.U. per hour in steam and 163 million in electricity, another 156 million being used for condensing water in the powerhouse and 186 million being lost through the stacks. The steam was delivered at a temperature of 750° F. and a pressure of 600 pounds per hour. In this form, it drove the 11,250-horsepower turbine that regenerated catalyst for the cat cracker, and the centrifugal compressors in the gas plant. Another steam level of 175 pounds per square inch and 425° F. was used for quenching and process, and a third level at 40 p.s.i. and 380° F. was used for processing, space heating, and steam tracing (see Exhibit 1).

EXHIBIT 1

	Steam (Lbs./Hr.)			Fuel Gas (Lbs./Hr.)	Cooling Water (Gal./Min.)	Electricity (K.w.)	Employees per Full Week Day*	Catalyst Inventory (Tons)	Approx. Catalyst Cost ($/Lb.)†
	40 P.S.I.	175 P.S.I.	600 P.S.I.						
1. Crude Unit (130,000 B.P.S.D.)‡‡	18,800 Net Make	154,200	0	29,900	20,300	1,680	18	None	--
2. Fluid Coker (42,000 B.P.S.D.)	63,400 Net Take	102,800 Net Make	263,000 Net Make	17,400††	24,700	637	27	None	--
3. Cat Cracker (101,800 B.P.S.D.)	61,300 Net Take	214,600 Net Make	106,200	‡	18,800	915	27	1,250	0.17
4. Gas Plant (88 MM Std. Cu.Ft./Day)	17,500 Net Make	42,300	150,000	None	32,100	1,350		None	--
5. Cat. Polymer (15,800 B.P.S.D.)	0	19,100	31,800	None	5,800	630	21	155	0.26
6. Alkylation (5,000 B.P.S.D.)	92,400	20,200	17,500	None	12,300	622		117 §	0.01
7. Hydrogen Plant (30 MM Std. Cu.Ft./Day)	63,400 Net Take	5,200 Net Take	57,300	17,100	21,200	4,325	27	205‖	0.55 to 2.45
8. Desulfurization (88,000 B.P.S.D.)	54,400 Net Make	64,200	12,400	14,300	16,700	4,110		275	1.51
9. Cat. Reformer (45,200 B.P.S.D.)	4,000 Net Take	41,200 Net Take	111,400	22,600	22,100	2,100	27	137	8.60
10. Extraction Unit (40,300 B.P.S.D.)¶	0	45,900	185,800	8,300	16,600	1,700		None	--
11. Sulfur Plant (341.5 Long Tons/Day)	46,300 Net Make	48,600 Net Make	0	1,700	84	11	4	111	0.06
12. Solutizer Section of Crude Unit	4,700**	0	0	None	515**	69**		None	--

*Includes supervisory personnel and covers full 24-hour day.
† Approximately January, 1956.
‡ 8,400 lbs./hr. of fuel gas or 7,900 lbs./hr. of fuel oil — used only during unit startup
§ Quantity of sulfuric acid in reactors. Additional approximately 1,200 tons fresh and spent acid in total of three storage tanks.
‖ Total four types.
¶ Design capacity of feed prep section is 45,000 B.P.S.D.
**Included in crude unit.
†† CO boiler supplementary fuel.
‡‡ Barrels per steam day.

Source: Tidewater Oil Co.

The Tidewater refinery also needed 240,800 gallons per minute of cooling water to remove some three billion B.T.U. per hour of excess heat from the powerhouse and process units. Since this was as much water consumption as that of a large metropolitan area, it had to install a major pumping facility to take in water from the Delaware River. Nine pumps, each driven by a 2,000-horsepower electric motor, drove the water through two parallel 6½-foot concrete lines. These pumps took one third of the entire electric load, and supplied 45,000 gallons per minute to the powerhouse itself.

The tank farm held 86 tanks, including some of the largest ever built, at 200,000-barrel capacity each. The crude tankage contained eight such tanks, with space for four more. There were 21 smaller tanks for intermediate storage near the process area. Product storage contained 57 tanks, including 6 general service tanks of 200,000 barrels which could be used in event of shutdown of a process unit or to build inventory of a special product. There were also 27 on-plot tanks in the process units and 26 utility tanks for chemicals, catalyst, sulfur, coke, and so on. The refinery recovered 375 short tons of sulfur per day. A total tank capacity for all 139 tanks was about 7,650,000 barrels.

The marine terminal could handle tankers up to 52,800 tons in size. Three large piers were available. Pier 1 unloaded crude through a 30-inch crude pipeline. Pier 2 unloaded crude and loaded 9 products. Pier 3 loaded products only, through 6- to 18-inch lines. The pier crew was kept to a minimum by installing a hose-handling structure which a single operator could control, from a 68-foot high tower.

There were nine control rooms, seven of which served eleven process units, one for utilities, and one for the tank farm and products blending. There were three automatic in-line blending systems—one for gasoline, which normally handled 60,000 to 70,000 barrels per day; one for No. 2 fuel, 30,000 barrels; and one for distillate products such as kerosene, jet fuel, railroad diesel fuel, at 20,000 barrels. Controls were largely pneumatic rather than electronic. Each control room contained a graphic control board and an information system, which included data logger-scanner, tape punch, and trend recorders. The instruments were maintained by a contract organization which provided 40 people, 25 of them technicians.

The turnaround schedule started March 1 and ended in late April. First the cat cracker was shut down for 3 weeks, and with it, the alkylation unit for 2 weeks and the gas plant, polymerizer, and sulfur recovery for one week. Then these units went back on reduced throughput, and the fluid coker went down for 4 weeks, with the crude distillation 3 weeks. Finally the catalytic reformer and the solvent extractor went off for a week, and the plant came back on full throughput again as a whole. Plant maintenance was handled by an outside contractor, who provided about 200 men normally, but increased the number to a peak of 500 during turnaround time.

TERMINOLOGY

Since an oil refinery is, essentially, a kind of chemical processing plant, it is necessary to learn some of the nomenclature for hydrocarbons and processing operations.

Hydrocarbons

The main types of hydrocarbons involved in oil refining are structured as paraffins, naphthenes, olefins, or aromatics.

Paraffins have simple straight-line carbon chains, of the formula C_nH_{2n+2}, with similar properties and increasing boiling points as "n" increases. The nomenclature for C_1 to C_8 paraffins is: methane, ethane, propane, butane, pentane, hexane, heptane, octane.

Naphthenes are cyclo-paraffins of the formula C_nH_{2n}. The carbon atoms are arranged in a ring, and the nomenclature relates to the paraffin system, as cyclopentane, cyclohexane, etc.

Olefins are hydrocarbons with unsaturated links, that is, missing hydrogen atoms. A single unsaturated link is a mono-olefin of the formula C_nH_{2n}, arranged in a straight chain. Nomenclature is ethylene, propylene, butylene etc. Two unsaturated links are di-olefins of the formula C_nH_{2n-2}, with nomenclature butadiene, etc. Olefins are formed in the cracking process.

Aromatics are unsaturated ring hydrocarbons of the formula C_nH_{2n-6}. The most important are the C_6, C_7, C_8, C_9 aromatics, called benzene, toluene, xylene, and naphthalene.

Although the normal structure of paraffins is in a straight line, hydrocarbons can also be branched, thus changing the structure and some of the properties without changing the formula. Branched hydrocarbons are called isomers, and the nomenclature is iso-butane, iso-pentane, etc. Since the larger hydrocarbons can branch in different ways, the particular structure can be defined more carefully by designating the position of the carbon atoms that have the branch. Thus, one type of iso-octane is 2:2:4-trimethylpentane, which has two single-carbon branches on the second carbon, each forming a methyl or CH_3 group, and one methyl branch on the fourth carbon. This particular isomer is the standard for 100-octane gasoline, with normal heptane forming the standard for 0-octane.

Refinery Products

Since refinery products were marketed before precise terminology was developed, some products or feedstocks have rather flexible meanings. Thus, naphthas and gas oils are used to describe the lighter and heavier effluents of crude distillation, though both terms cover a very broad range of boiling points that include many different products. When referring to naphtha, it is often necessary to specify what cut is meant, so that the C_6 and C_7 heart cut for aromatics at 170° to 200° F. is differentiated from the heavy naphthas boiling up to 400° F. Process flow diagrams often contain shorthand to designate certain cuts, such as "C_6+" which means that the material has been de-pentanized, or separated from all hydrocarbons boiling in the C_5 range or lower. A cut may be designated as "gas oil 500/

700°," referring to the boiling point range, or it may be designated as $94RON_3$, which means that the material will make 94-octane number gasoline by the research method of determining octane numbers, after 3 cubic centimeters of tetraethyl lead have been added.

There is also a rather mixed nomenclature system for heating oils, which are used in domestic heating systems, and burning oils or fuel oils, which are used in heavy industrial heating systems. No. 1 heating oil is in the kerosene range, 450° to 640° F. No. 2 heating oil is in the diesel fuel range, 450° to 640° F., and No. 3 is slightly heavier. These form the middle distillates. No. 4 and No. 5 are heavier fuel oils, with different quality specifications. No. 6 fuel oil is known as "Bunker C," a very heavy material for industrial or ship furnaces.

Processing Operations

The unit of measure in the refinery is in barrels, one barrel being the equivalent of 42 gallons. The designation B.P.C.D. means "barrels per calendar day" and B.P.S.D. means "barrels per stream day," which refers to operating days to allow for the turnaround, or annual maintenance downtime period. The A.P.I. gravity system, developed by the American Petroleum Institute is not the same as the specific gravity system, and in fact works in the opposite way, with low A.P.I. gravity referring to heavy crude oils and high A.P.I. gravity to lighter material with lower boiling point, and usually higher market value. Degrees A.P.I. equals 141.5 divided by specific gravity, minus 131.5.

Gravity, Degrees A.P.I.	*Specific Gravity*	*Pounds per Gallon*	*Pounds per Barrel*
18	0.947	7.88	331
20	0.934	7.78	327
22	0.922	7.68	322
24	0.910	7.58	318
26	0.898	7.48	314
28	0.887	7.39	310
30	0.876	7.30	306
32	0.865	7.21	302
34	0.855	7.12	299
36	0.845	7.03	295
38	0.835	6.95	292
40	0.825	6.87	289

Due to the difficulty and expense of making clean fractions, many process units re-cycle some of the effluent, and this material is usually referred to an "cycle oil." The principal effluent of the reformer is "reformate." The fractionating tower product yields are usually referred to as "overhead" for the light gases and "bottoms" for the heavier material. Hydrogen gas is measured in standard cubic feet, the terms S.C.F.B. or C.F.D. referring to cubic feet per barrel or cubic feet per day. In some process units, space velocity and severity are indications of the capacity of the unit. Space velocity is ratio of the oil feed into the reactor (in pounds per hour) to the amount of catalyst in the reactor bed (in pounds). Severity is the catalyst to oil ratio, divided by the space velocity. In other words, high severity operation uses much catalyst and feeds the oil in slowly, generally obtaining higher yields at higher catalyst cost and reduced throughput.

Viscosity is a measure of resistance to flow, in dynes per square centimeter (centipoises). However, it is most easily measured as an index number relative to water. Pour point is 5° F. above the temperature at which the material solidifies. Diesel fuels use a "cetane" number which is analogous to the octane number.

HYDROGEN BALANCE IN THE REFINERY

In recent years, one of the most important trends in the development of oil refinery technology has been the manufacture, conservation, purification, and use of hydrogen.

The great expansion of the catalytic reforming process during the decade of the 1950's led to increased use of the by-product hydrogen to desulfurize various feedstocks. It has also led to various petrochemical opportunities which require hydrogen, such as making ammonia, dealkylating toluene to make benzene, or making cyclohexane from benzene. In more recent years, the process of hydrocracking has developed, which uses large quantities of hydrogen to obtain high-octane gasolines with little yield of heavier products.

Hydrogen can be manufactured from methane gas. A plant costing $1.8 million and using 15 million cubic feet of methane per day would yield 13.5 million cubic feet of hydrogen. The hydrogen from such a plant would cost about 39 cents per thousand cubic feet, though the cost would increase to 70 cents if low-cost methane from natural gas were not available.

Hydrogen is also generated as a by-product

from the catalytic reforming process. In this process, naphtha of research octane number 70 is charged to the reformer and achieves an 87 percent yield of 90-octane reformate, giving off 800 cubic feet of hydrogen per barrel of feed. If the reformer is used to make aromatics such as benzene or toluene, the naphtha feed must be a special cut in the boiling range about 170° to 200° F. This yields about 73 percent raffinate of 85 octane and about 27 percent of a benzene-toluene mix, as well as the by-product hydrogen.

Benzene is a valuable building block to make petrochemicals, and it can be derived from toluene, with the help of a hydrogen feed. The toluene is de-alkylated to yield 80 percent benzene, with 1,780 cubic feet of hydrogen used up in the process per barrel of feed. This process takes a great deal of electric power.

Benzene can be used to make cyclohexane, an intermediate chemical used in the manufacture of nylon. In this process, the benzene yields 117 percent cyclohexane, but 4,500 cubic feet of hydrogen are required per barrel of feed.

In addition to its use in the manufacture of petrochemical building blocks, hydrogen can be used extensively within the refinery to de-sulfurize feedstocks. Light naphthas with less than 1 percent sulfur require only 30 cubic feet of hydrogen per barrel to achieve less than one tenth of 1 percent sulfur purity. Gas oils with more than 1 percent sulfur require almost 300 cubit feet of hydrogen to achieve such purity. The heavy coker distillates require as much as 800 cubic feet per barrel.

Hydrogen can also be used to hydrocrack gas oils, in a process that uses almost 2,000 cubic feet of hydrogen per barrel and large amounts of electricity.

Oil Industry Reference Notes

The oil industry is one of the largest and most important industries in the United States. From supplying 20 percent of the total energy needs in the nation in 1920, crude oil and natural gas accounted for about 70 percent in 1960 (see Exhibit 4a). In addition to many uses as motor and heating fuels, crude oil is refined into many other products, ranging from lubricants to chemical raw materials.

The oil industry is an outstanding example of a vertically integrated industry. A substantial portion of the industry's operations are conducted by large, integrated companies engaged in exploration, producing, refining, transportation, and marketing facilities. By the end of the 1950's, 35 of the most important oil companies had combined total assets of more than $40 billion and net sales of more than $30 billion. Net fixed plant represented about 60 percent of the fixed assets. Crude oil operations were considered so important to the industry that the ratio of expenditures on potential crude oil producing properties to total expenditures increased from about 65 percent in 1946 to about 75 percent in 1960 (see Exhibits 1, 2, and 3).

The United States has for a long time been both the largest producer of crude oil and the largest user of refined products of any country in the world, although it has only about 10 percent of the world's crude oil reserves, 61 percent of which are in the Middle East. In 1951, the United States produced 52 percent of the world's crude oil and consumed 66 percent of its refined products. Due to such factors as the industrialization of Europe and Japan and the development of new oil producing properties in other areas, these ratios declined to 33 percent of the crude oil production and 52 percent of the refined products consumption in 1960.

Between 1946 and 1956, domestic demand for refined products increased about 60 percent, though it leveled off at a little more than 3 billion barrels per year between 1956 and 1960 (see Exhibit 5). In 1962, about 411 million barrels of crude oil were imported, of which 42 percent came from Venezuela, 16 percent from Kuwait and Saudi Arabia, and about 20 percent from Canada. In addition, more than 260 million barrels of residual fuel oil were imported.

The exploration and production of crude oil requires vast sums of money because of the many failures to find oil where it is expected and because of the markedly increased drilling and lifting costs with each additional foot of well depth (Exhibit 4). Since the United States has about 31.6 billion barrels of crude oil reserves, and it is used up at the rate of about 2.6 billion barrels per year, we have about 12 years of reserves on hand. Actually, new discoveries of domestic reserves, combined with imports, have increased our net crude reserves more than 10 billion barrels since 1946. The annual discovery rate, however, which averaged 2.9 billion barrels in the 1946–1950 period and increased to 3.2 billion in the 1951–1955 period, has declined to 2.8 billion barrels in the 1956–1960 period. It has been estimated that 96.4 billion barrels of oil were discovered in the United States in the century up to 1960, of which 64.8 billion barrels have already been used up. Almost 45 billion barrels of the total discoveries and more than half the total century's production can be traced to the period between 1945 and 1960.

During the period since World War II, the product mix of the oil refineries has changed. While gasoline has about doubled in annual volume between 1946 and 1960, residual fuel oil has declined, and the nature of the markets for these and other products has altered considerably. Changes in the quality requirements, and markets, and price levels of products have placed considerable pressure on the refineries to alter their operations to meet these trends. Since oil is a high-volume low-value material with very costly storage requirements due to the need to construct tankage, seasonal and annual changes in product demand are often reflected promptly in changes to the manufacturing plans at the refineries.

EXPLORATION

The first stage in the oil process is that of exploring for new oil reserves. Three types of activities are carried on by the exploration department of an oil company. The first task is to search for prospective oil territory. Prospecting is carried on by geological and geophysical crews as well as by oil scouts. Oil companies often use their own staffs for exploration, but they may rely upon specialized independent concerns for some part of the work.

A second type of exploratory work is the procurement of leases or freeholds on prospective oil properties. Leases are negotiated by "land men." An oil concern may utilize its own land men or independent brokers in carrying out leasing activities. The typical oil and gas lease runs for a stated period of time, usually one to ten years, and the landowner is ordinarily paid a cash bonus at the time a lease is negotiated plus an annual rental of a certain amount per acre.

The final stage in exploratory work is the actual drilling of wildcat or exploratory wells. An oil company sometimes drills exploratory wells with its own drilling rigs and crews, but ordinarily these wells are drilled by independent contractors.

In order to find new oil reserves at the rate of 3 billion barrels each year, the industry spent $6.4 billion in 1953—30 percent for exploration, 38 percent for development, and 32 percent for production. Of the exploration cost ($2.0 billion), 41 percent was lost through dry holes, 57 percent for lease purchases, lease rentals, geological work and so on, and the rest was overhead. Of the development cost ($2.4 billion), 73 percent was for producing wells, 20 percent for equipment, and the rest overhead. Of the production cost ($2.1 billion), 89 percent was for lifting costs.

Exhibit 4d indicates that the success ratio in finding oil has been declining. During the 1920's and 1930's, about 75 percent of all wells were successful. In 1947, the success ratio dropped to 70 percent and between 1953 and 1956 was about 63 percent. However, these figures include a large amount of development drilling around the edges of oil fields that are already producing. For exploratory drilling the success ratio is now only 15 percent. In fact, "wildcat" drilling on an entirely new location is only 11 percent successful, though recent offshore wells in the water off the Texas and Louisiana coast have been about 40 percent successful. A further difficulty is that the finding of major oil fields is a far more difficult proposition than finding small pools. Yet it is the major fields that are the economical producers and have the reserves to warrant the installation of trunk pipelines.

A survey of 20,000 wildcat wells recently indicated that only 42 wildcats are drilled for each million-barrel field, more than 400 for each 25 million-barrel field, and 700 for each 50 million-barrel field. Theoretically, a million-barrel field might produce 100 barrels a day for 25 years. However, it is estimated that only 25 percent of the petroleum stored underground in proved fields in the United States is actually brought to the surface. The ability to produce from proved developed reserves decreases 7 or 8 percent each year, due to loss of pressure and the presence of water in the surrounding sand. To encourage the oil industry to search for new oil, the United States has enacted legislation giving special tax benefits to offset the loss of oil values through depletion.

Joint interest wells arise in many types of situations. In the first place, the acreage in a particular territory may be split up among many different lessees, each of whom may hold, say, 10 or 20 acres. The conservation laws of the state may, however, provide for a minimum well spacing pattern of one well to 40 acres. Under such circumstances, joint interest arrangements are imperative as a means of conducting the exploratory and producing work. Joint interest wells may also arise when two or more companies decide to share the cost of acquiring leases as a means of spreading the expense and risk of an exploratory venture.

Drilling activity in the United States has increased steadily during the years since the end of World War II. The number of wells completed annually has more than doubled since 1945, and at the same time the average depth per well has increased 16 percent. Meanwhile, drilling contractors have boosted their share of the total drilling from 80 to 92 percent.

Increasing costs have been an important factor in this postwar boom. There have been substantial rises in all the component costs of drilling: labor, equipment, and miscellaneous expenses. As a result, the total drilling cost per foot, to the oil company, has risen 50 percent since 1945. Contract drilling costs, however, have not followed this general trend. In 1955 the average cost of having a contractor drill a well was only $4.90 per foot, 2 percent less than the 1945 figure.

PRODUCTION

After an oil field has been discovered, it is the function of the producing branch of the industry to develop the property and produce the oil in an effective manner.

In addition to the high percentage of dry holes, the cost of drilling has been increasing despite the increasing skill of drilling contractors. For every foot of hole drilled in the United States in 1946, 26 barrels of oil were found; in 1955, 14 barrels were found. During the same period, overall drilling costs increased 21 percent. For example, while it cost $18,000 to keep a seismic crew in the field for one month in 1948, it cost $36,000 in 1956. The cost of drilling increasing depths of hole are indicated in Exhibit 4c. It should be noted that the wells over 10,000 feet are considerably more expensive than a 5,000-foot well. As a result, the theoretical cost of adding one barrel to reserves in the ground, which was 57 cents in 1946, increased to $1.28 in 1955.

The average cost to lift oil from the ground in West Texas was about $1.45 per barrel in 1956. This cost may be apportioned very roughly as follows:

Operating cost of lease	36 cents
Tax (except income tax)	35
Intangible write-offs	28
Depreciation of equipment	21
District overhead	9
Administration	9
Engineering	4
Scientific and research	3

The average drilling rig has been able to drill twice as much footage in 1955 as in 1946. However, the cost of the rig itself continues to increase. The original cost of a deep drilling rig in 1948 was $300,000, whereas its replacement in 1956 would cost $500,000. For an offshore rig, the cost is in millions.

Following a discovery, development wells for producing the oil are drilled until the outer limits of the underground reservoir are defined. Other producing activities include the repressuring of oil fields by gas injection or water flooding and maintenance work on oil properties. Development drilling and producing activities are subject to various state regulations and restrictions. The most important restrictions are the conservation and prorationing measures which set forth the amount of oil that a well is allowed to produce.

Prorationing and Conservation Laws

The prorationing laws, which govern the amount of oil that may be produced in many states, have had a profound effect on the economics of the oil industry.

The large crude oil supplies which developed in the late 1920's, together with the waste which accompanied wide-open production of flush fields, created a widespread interest among state, industry, and government agencies in measures for the regulation of crude oil production and eventually led to the enactment of the prorationing laws by the various producing states. These laws were developed only after several years of trial and error and much bitter controversy in the courts and throughout the industry. By 1935, however, most of the major oil producing states had developed some mechanism for controlling crude oil production.

The programs of conservation and prorationing have developed along different lines in the various states and now involve a fairly complicated set of regulations covering the location, spacing, drilling, operation, and abandonment of wells and the maintenance of specified gas-oil and water-oil ratios. In general, however, the prorationing laws of most of the states which have such laws have two fundamental objectives: (1) the prevention of the waste of oil and gas resources, and (2) the protection of the correlative rights of property owners in underground reservoirs.

First, the conservation laws of most of the states contain provisions of some type for preventing production in excess of a field's maximum efficient rate. Wide-open production under the rule of capture frequently left more oil in the ground than was recovered because the principal sources of reservoir energy, water and gas disolved in the oil or associated with it, were dissipated irregularly or at uneconomic rates. In addition, more wells were frequently drilled into a pool than were necessary to produce the oil efficiently or than were desirable in terms of realizing the maximum ultimate recovery. Many of the provisions of the prorationing laws therefore have been designed to regulate the drilling and operation of wells in each pool in accordance with the reservoir characteristics in order that the natural gas-oil and water-oil pressures will not be wasted and the ultimate recovery thereby jeopardized.

A second important group of provisions in the prorationing laws are designed to allocate the production of a field fairly among the various property holders. At the outset, production was frequently allocated among leaseholders on a flat per-well basis or on a per-well basis modified to take into account individual well characteristics such as bottom-hole pressures, gas-oil ratios, sand thicknesses, and production under open-flow conditions. Under these formulas, the production allowed from a particular lease could be raised by drilling more wells on the property. Lease operators therefore promptly began to drill many more wells than were necessary in order to capture as much of the oil in the reservoir as possible. Most of the major producing states later adopted regulations controlling the spacing of wells and in a number of instances embodied acreage factors in their allocation formulas. Moreover, in recent years progress has been made in some of the states toward the operation of oil pools on a unitized basis. Under unit operation the property owners share in the total development cost and output of a field in accordance with a prearranged formula, and competitive drilling and producing in the field are thereby eliminated.

The third major feature of the prorationing laws has been the adjustment of production to market demand at times when production at maximum efficient rates would produce more oil than the market could readily absorb.

TRANSPORTATION

Crude oil and refined products are transported by means of pipelines, tanker, barges, tank trucks, and railroad tank cars. In general, it can be said that transportation costs are an extremely important element in the final delivered cost of oil products to the consumer and are a key factor in determining the competitive position of all firms engaged in the producing, manufacturing, and distribution cycle. Transportation costs, including terminaling charges, may range from 15 to 33 percent of delivered tank wagon prices and frequently represent about 25 percent of delivered tank wagon prices.

Crude oil trunk and products pipelines, under the proper circumstances, can make very substantial cost savings over other forms of transportation. Large diameter pipelines achieve substantial cost savings over small diameter lines when a sufficient volume can be accumulated in one system to warrant their use. An indication of the significance of the cost savings made possible by the use of large-diameter pipelines may be obtained from Exhibit 5 which shows an illustrative example of the tariffs that would have to be charged to earn a return of 7 percent of the investment in pipelines of different sizes, designed for different volumes of throughput.

An indication of the high capital costs required for pipelines may be gained from the following figures for 1,000-mile trunk lines: An 8-inch line with a capacity of about 30,000 barrels per day would have cost in 1948 approximately $20,000,000; a 30-inch line capable of delivering 350,000 barrels per day would have cost about $58,000,000. The capital costs for products lines tend to run somewhat higher than for crude oil lines of similar diameter and capacity.

The pipeline operations of the industry are affected by several important government regulations. The Hepburn Act of 1906, which was later supported by the Supreme Court decision on The Pipe Line Cases in 1914, established the status of the oil pipeline companies operating in interstate commerce as common carriers subject to regulation by the Interstate Commerce Commission. Among other things, the Interstate Commerce Commission requires the pipeline companies to file their rate schedules with the Commission, to maintain just and reasonable rates, and to establish rules and regulations covering minimum tenders and other shipping practices which will assure the availability of pipeline service to all shippers on a fair and equitable basis. Any interested party, or the Interstate Commerce Commission, may at any time challenge the rates and shipping practices of a pipeline company. Hearings are held on such complaints and remedial orders are entered by the commission where required.

In 1940, the Department of Justice brought a suit against many of the pipeline companies charging that the dividends paid to shipper-owners constituted rebates and were thus in violation of the Elkins Act of 1903. The action was settled by the "pipeline consent decree" which was entered on December 23, 1941, and which was signed by most of the major oil companies in the United States. The decree provides that a shipper-owner may not receive from a pipeline company more than its share of a 7 percent return on the Interstate Commerce Commission's valuation of the pipeline properties. Pipeline earnings in excess of 7 percent of the pipeline valuation are required to be held in special accounts in the pipeline companies and may be used for the extension of pipeline properties, but the value of the facilities so added may not be included in the valuation for dividend purposes.

One general effect of the government regulations with respect to pipeline operations has been to bring about, in conjunction with other factors, a gradual reduction in pipeline earnings.

Pipelines, of course, are considerably cheaper for moving oil than are railroad tank cars. For example, moving crude oil from the producing fields in Wyoming to Wood River, a refining center near St. Louis, costs 36 cents per barrel by pipeline and $1.86 by rail; moving the refined products from Wood River to Chicago costs 25 cents by products pipeline and 96 cents by railroad tank car. However, for those refineries that could make use of marine transportation the cost saving was even greater. For example, ocean tanker shipment of crude oil from Houston, Texas, to Philadelphia costs 37 cents per barrel, while rail shipment would cost $3.06 per barrel.

Although the mileage of crude oil pipelines changed little during the 1950's, the pipeline capacity was increased 50 percent during the decade through the use of more powerful pumping stations and through the replacement of old lines with larger diameter pipe. Meanwhile, however, the mileage of refined products lines was more than doubled, while overall capacity tripled. In 1949, products capacity was only 17 percent of crude oil capacity, while a decade later it was 38 percent.

During the 1950's the world tank ship fleet increased 50 percent in number, though the United States' share decreased from 33 to 14 percent of the total. Due to increased size and modern design, the 50 percent increase in number actually achieved more than double the tonnage and a 14 percent increase in average speed. Since Venezuelan oil ports were 1,800 miles from New York harbor and Middle East ports 8,300 miles distant, the increase in speed from 13 to 15 knots could mean a significant decrease in turnaround time. The World War II T-2 type tankers were of 16,500 deadweight tons and carried 140,000 barrels. A 35,000-ton tanker carries 300,000 barrels, and the largest tanker, of over 100,000 tons, carries 900,000 barrels, or about 18 days' supply for a 50,000-barrel refinery.

Although there was excess tanker capacity in normal times, emergencies such as the Korean War or the Suez crisis created severe shortages. For this reason, tanker rates were highly volatile, changing from 25 cents a barrel for crude oil on the Gulf run in 1949 to 78 cents in 1951 or 66 cents in 1956, with depressed prices again in 1954 and 1960.

REFINING

The profitability of an oil refinery depends in great degree on the cost of its crude oil, which has accounted for about 79 percent of the refinery realization in recent years. From the standpoint of the refinery manager, the principal means of protecting refinery margins against a cost-price squeeze are to obtain cheaper crude oils, to adjust the product mix so as to provide a maximum yield of the most valuable products, and to use the most efficient processing units.

Crude Oil

There were three general increases in the price of crude oil since World War II. Between 1948 and 1952 it held at about $2.63 per barrel for the United States average. By 1954 it had advanced 24 cents, and in 1957, another 31 cents, though the price has declined somewhat since then.

However, there is a considerable spread in price at any one time between crude oil from different sources. For example, in 1956, Middle East crude oil was only $1.72 at ports near the wellhead, while Pennsylvania oil was $4.23. These differences are largely due to transportation costs and import quotas, to differences in processing costs necessary to refine different crude oils, and to differences in the product yields that can be obtained from them. However, supply and demand factors also enter the picture, with the result that lower delivery and operating costs and higher yields do not always offset the higher prices. It is therefore very important for the refinery manager to analyze continually his own market potential and operating flexibility in order to determine whether he can improve his position by using other types of crude oils. (See Exhibit 6.)

Product Mix

As the figures in Exhibit 9 indicate, there is a substantial difference in price among the various products than can be obtained at the refinery from processing crude oil. Distillate prices have been about 20 percent lower and residual fuel prices more than 40 percent lower than the price of gasoline. In fact, residual fuel has often sold at a lower price than the price of the crude oil from which it is derived. These differences are further compounded by geographic location and season of the year. For example, residual fuel prices were much weaker in Oklahoma than in Detroit or Toledo where industrial requirements were greater and natural gas was less available. And, as indicated in Exhibit 7, there is greater demand for gasoline in the summer months and for distillate and residual fuel in the winter months, though the degree of seasonality depends in part on the severity of the weather, and hence on the geographic location.

In Exhibits 8 to 10, the trends in product mix during the 1950's can be determined. The increasing importance of gasoline and distillate fuels at the expense of residual fuel oil is very marked. The reasons for these trends can be noted from the increase in motor vehicle registration and central heating oil burners for homes. However, in addition to the quantitative demand, there has also been a marked increase in the qualitative requirements due to the octane race. As noted in Exhibit 11, octane ratings for gasoline have been increasing, particularly in the mid 1950's. This has in turn been caused by the requirements of the new automotive engines, which increased these compression ratios from 7.03 in 1950 to 9.45 a decade later, while the average horsepower ratings of new engines advanced from 111 to 259. These developments have imposed continual pressures on the refinery to find means of improving and expanding the high-value products, at the same time that geographic and seasonal characteristics have imposed these special market patterns.

Process Units

In response to the demands for improved products and product yields, American refiners have invested very large sums in modern process units. Although there are many process methods to choose from and each unit must be adapted to the special needs in size and product mix of the particular refinery, the principal means of meeting the needs of the octane race has been on catalytic cracking and catalytic reforming, supplemented by small amounts of tetraethyl lead additives.

Straight-run gasoline from distillation has an octane rating of 40 to 60, depending on the nature of the crude oil. Tetraethyl lead can increase an octane rating substantially, but can be used in only limited amounts because it forms a lead deposit in the engine. Susceptibility to tetraethyl lead varies with the material, but the limit of improvement is about 15 octane numbers from three cubic centimeters. Tetraethyl lead costs about $2.00 per thousand cubic centimeters, which would work out to about 1.7 cents per barrel of gasoline, that is 0.04 cents per gallon, per octane number. The market value of one octane number improvement from regular to premium gasoline is about 5.0 cents per barrel, that is 0.12 cents per gallon, though susceptibility declines at higher octane numbers and the market for premium gasoline is limited.

The development of catalytic cracking just prior to World War II received a great boost from the wartime demand for high-octane aviation gasoline, and many cracking units were installed at that period with government help. After the war, as noted in Exhibit 11, thermal cracking capacity was cut in half, while catalytic units increased four times. By the 1950's, there was enough catalytic cracking capacity to take care of substantially all the feedstock capable of being cracked.

The operating costs of refineries have increased steadily since 1946, as indicated in Exhibits 12 and 13. In order to obtain more efficient operations to offset these costs, refineries have installed larger processing units, changed to lower-cost fuels, and have used computers to program their operations. Larger and more automated process units have enabled refiners to increase their throughput with a smaller operating force, although the staffs needed to handle the computers themselves have steadily increased. The use of alternate fuels can be studied by considering the heatings equivalent in terms of its cost per million British thermal units. In areas where natural gas is available, this fuel has become more widely used because of its lower cost. Computer programs have been designed to deal with the very complex problem of maximizing product yields according to the input costs and the various product values, as they change seasonally and with market price fluctuations.

The problem of determining the most effective operating program is one of the most interesting challenges with which a refinery must deal. From the point of view of a manufacturing problem, it involves the selection of crude oils, the operation of the many interrelated process units, and the output of many products of different unit value going to different markets. It is complicated by the cost of storage,[1] since oil products must be stored in necessarily limited tankage, by the changing economics of supply and demand, by the impact of new technologies, and by the particular market position and geographic location of each refinery. For example, a refinery can operate with a minimum of capital equipment if it wishes to rely on lower-value products. In order to obtain the high-value products, it can invest in process units to convert the lighter ends, through catalytic reforming and alkylation, or the heavy ends, through coking units. These decisions will depend in part on its potential sources of crude oils and on its market outlets. Thus the manufacturing program depends directly on the overall integration strategy of the company. Exhibits 14 and 15 provide data bearing on the relative profitability of the independent refiner and the fully integrated oil company, though the importance of its crude oil suppliers and market outlets to the manufacturing program must be examined for each company's geographic location.

The most important new process development in the postwar period was the development of catalytic reforming, which yields a high-octane product from naphtha feedstocks, and hence operates from lighter, lower-boiling point feedstock than the cracking units. A catalytic reformer capable of handling 10,000 barrels per day might cost in the range of $2.5 million.

The rapid and widespread adoption of reformers during the 1950's has been of significance beyond the provision of high-octane motor fuels, though this has been by far their most important single function. The catalytic reformer, however, generates hydrogen during its operation and also can be used to make benzene or toluene rather than high-octane gasoline. As a result, it has been one means of access to the petrochemical field, with its products of high unit value, though limited volume demand. Exhibit 16 indicates some of the processes that use hydrogen. They have become increasingly important, both to the refinery desiring to desulfurize lower-cost crude oils and to the preparation of petrochemicals. In recent years, a new process using large amounts of hydrogen to crack gas oil directly to high-octane gasoline has been developed, which has some advantages over the regular catalytic cracking process, since it has a very high yield of gasoline.

Exhibit 16 can be used to evaluate various refinery processes used to make high-octane motor fuel or petrochemicals, and which generate or use hydrogen. Processes #1 and #2 generate hydrogen, while processes #4 to #7 use up hydrogen. In process #1, 15 million cubic feet of methane are used to make 13.5 million feet of hydrogen per day. In process #2, a 10,000-barrel reformer converts naphtha to 8,700 barrels of 90-octane gasoline and yields 8 million feet of hydrogen as a by-product. In process #3, 6,000 barrels of the gasoline product of the reformer is treated with a solvent to yield 1,600 barrels of a petrochemical mixture containing benzene and toluene and 4,400 barrels of lower octane gasoline. In process #4, 1,000 barrels of toluene are converted to 800 barrels of benzene, using 1,780 feet of hydrogen per barrel, or almost 1.8 million feet per day. In process #5, 600 barrels of benzene are coverted to 705 barrels of cyclohexane, a material used to make nylon, using 4,500 feet of hydrogen per barrel or 2.7 million feet per day. As shown in process #6, hydrogen can also be used to desulfurize other feedstocks throughout the refinery, using about 300,000 cubic feet to treat 10,000 barrels of naphtha or almost 4.4 million feet to treat 15,000 barrels of gas oil for

[1] A storage tank may cost from 70 cents to $2.00 per barrel, with lower costs for the larger tanks above 50,000-barrel capacity. A refinery often has 60 to 70 barrels of storage capacity for each daily barrel of throughput. See W. L. Nelson, "Costimating," in the *Oil and Gas Journal*, Dec. 5, 1955.

the catalytic cracker. The hydrocracking process can turn such gas oil almost entirely into fuel, but would require almost 19 million feet of hydrogen per 10,000 barrels of feed, as well as large amounts of electric power. The cost of utilities for all these processes can be determined by multiplying the regional prices by the requirements noted in the exhibit. The methane requirements are given per thousand cubic feet of feedstock, while the others are given per barrel of feed. The electric power would have to be multiplied by 24 to obtain a daily cost, since it is given on an hourly basis. A small process unit of 1,000 barrels capacity would require one operator per shift plus a fraction of a supervisor's time. Laboratory and maintenance charges would be about $120 per day and royalties about $150. Overhead would be 50 percent of the labor cost and taxes, insurance, interest, and amortization would be about 15 percent of the erected cost of the facilities.

1. OIL INDUSTRY

A. Combined Balance Sheet of Major* Oil Companies, 1944-1952

(In Millions of Dollars)

	1944	1945	1946	1947	1948	1949	1950	1951	1952
Current assets	3,544	3,514	3,687	4,325	5,118	5,347	6,229	7,421	8,045
Investments	910	1,009	1,042	1,064	1,266	1,299	1,318	1,295	1,301
Long-term receivables	38	45	50	64	96	98	110	126	169
Special funds	33	32	30	43	35	34	32	33	90
Net plant	5,461	5,388	5,952	7,047	8,456	9,934	10,384	11,370	13,030
Prepaid and deferred	83	70	89	98	121	120	145	172	190
Total Assets	10,069	10,058	10,850	12,641	15,092	16,832	18,218	20,417	22,825
Current liabilities	1,322	1,029	1,227	1,690	2,207	1,909	2,377	3,077	3,118
Long-term debt	1,032	1,028	1,153	1,437	1,758	2,604	2,423	2,466	3,049
Credits and reserves	609	516	468	460	496	501	503	505	529
Minority interests	289	307	324	354	387	463	473	543	620
Preferred stock	178	154	155	176	172	170	151	149	185
Common and surplus	4,342	4,352	4,379	4,575	4,966	5,216	5,342	5,957	6,418
Reinvested earnings	2,297	2,672	3,144	3,949	5,106	5,969	6,949	7,720	8,906
Total Liabilities and Worth	10,069	10,058	10,850	12,641	15,092	16,832	18,218	20,417	22,825

B. Combined Balance Sheet of Major* Oil Companies, 1953-1961

	1953	1954	1955	1956	1957	1958	1959	1960	1961	1962
Current assets	8,921	9,090	9,838	10,922	11,391	11,781	12,273	12,845	13,744	14,323
Investments	1,444	1,257	1,376	1,491	1,678	1,790	2,058	2,151	2,137	2,242
Long-term receivables	191	194	185	262	229	242	300	414	596	685
Special funds	81	45	105	76	76	86	72	70	70	54
Net plant	14,520	10,095	17,345	19,801	22,017	23,794	24,876	25,741	27,339	29,275
Prepaid	214	230	246	310	381	410	423	428	444	559
Total Assets	25,371	20,911	29,095	32,862	35,772	38,103	40,002	41,649	44,330	47,138
Current liabilities	3,582	3,588	3,967	4,523	4,762	4,868	5,178	5,426	5,836	6,538
Long-term debt	3,365	3,382	3,391	4,201	4,454	4,818	4,713	4,761	4,936	5,070
Deferred credits	92	147	179	193	221	211	359	419	580	675
Other reserves	429	459	482	553	630	656	719	720	736	827
Minority reserves	657	479	502	685	729	595	580	563	625	669
Preferred stock	176	232	208	215	214	203	196	190	241	183
Common and surplus	6,546	7,497	8,080	10,092	11,015	11,900	12,386	12,620	12,968	13,181
Reinvested earnings	10,224	11,127	12,286	12,400	13,747	14,852	15,871	16,950	18,408	19,997
Total Liabilities and Worth	25,071	26,911	29,095	32,862	35,772	38,103	40,002	41,649	44,330	47,138

*Due to mergers, the number of companies included has varied between 30 and 35 during this period.

Source: "Financial Analysis of The Petroleum Industry," The Chase Manhattan Bank, July, 1963.

2. OIL INDUSTRY

A. Combined Income Statement of Major* Oil Companies, 1944-1962

(In Millions of Dollars)

	1944	1945	1946	1947	1948	1949	1950	1951	1952
Gross Income	7,226	7,228	7,425	10,334	13,945	13,675	15,268	17,939	19,326
Nonoperating Income	82	98	124	149	220	217	306	368	447
Total Income	7,308	7,326	7,549	10,483	14,165	13,892	15,574	18,307	19,773
Operating Costs	5,244	5,344	5,523	7,607	9,996	10,321	11,266	12,869	14,261
General Taxes	184	182	197	247	319	379	398	449	497
Depreciation	776	976	763	872	1,109	1,224	1,258	1,511	1,837
Interest	34	31	30	33	42	69	72	69	83
Contingencies	58	32	- 2	19	40	17	13	7	23
Total Deductions	6,296	6,565	6,511	8,778	11,506	12,010	13,007	14,905	16,701
Income Taxes	335	124	239	429	697	408	752	1,219	901
Minority Interests	38	37	37	57	86	67	76	93	96
Net Income	639	600	762	1,219	1,876	1,407	1,739	2,090	2,075

B. Combined Income Statements of Major* Oil Companies, 1953-1961

(In Millions of Dollars)

	1953	1954	1955	1956	1957	1958	1959	1960	1961	1962
Gross Income	21,821	22,158	24,291	27,888	30,576	29,455	31,104	32,069	33,784	36,561
Nonoperating Income	440	604	637	581	586	648	712	774	792	912
Total Income	22,261	22,762	24,928	28,469	31,162	30,103	31,816	32,843	34,576	37,473
Operating Costs	16,142	16,632	17,903	20,611	22,920	22,705	23,838	24,380	25,804	28,015
General Taxes	554	579	638	711	782	832	907	1,074	1,176	1,307
Depreciation	2,040	2,180	2,453	2,758	3,081	3,024	3,125	3,198	3,237	3,429
Interest	110	115	119	141	175	191	209	215	227	257
Other Charges	9	1	5	9	7	18	18	20	7	14
Total Deductions	18,855	19,507	21,118	24,230	26,965	26,770	28,097	28,887	30,451	33,022
Income Taxes	1,021	839	1,062	1,139	993	801	968	992	980	1,042
Minority Interests	99	97	80	97	104	69	59	59	64	65
Net Income	2,286	2,319	2,668	3,003	3,100	2,463	2,692	2,905	3,081	3,344

*Due to mergers, the number of companies included has varied between 30 and 35 during this period.

Source: "Financial Analysis of The Petroleum Industry," The Chase Manhattan Bank, July, 1963.

3. OIL INDUSTRY

Summary of Financial Data, 1951-1961
(In Millions of Dollars)

	1951	1952	1953	1954	1955	1956	1957	1958	1959	1960	1961
CAPITAL EXPENDITURES											
Crude Oil and Gas*	2,575	3,125	3,400	3,700	4,050	4,375	4,400	3,575	3,700	3,575	3,400
Gasoline Plants	75	75	125	100	50	100	125	75	150	160	125
Total Production	2,650	3,200	3,525	3,800	4,100	4,475	4,525	3,650	3,850	3,735	3,525
Pipe Lines	250	335	325	275	190	175	275	225	135	190	165
Marine	35	50	100	50	35	50	70	125	125	75	65
Tank Cars and Motor	15	15	25	25	15	20	15	25	15	25	25
Total Transportation	300	400	450	350	240	245	360	375	275	290	255
Refineries	325	470	675	800	835	825	950	725	525	560	685
Marketing	300	280	325	350	375	450	475	400	450	475	525
Others	50	50	50	50	50	55	90	150	175	115	110
TOTAL--ALL DEPARTMENTS	3,625	4,400	5,025	5,350	5,600	6,050	6,400	5,300	5,275	5,175	5,100
GROSS INVESTMENT IN FIXED ASSETS, December 31											
Crude Oil and Gas	15,000	16,975	18,625	21,500	23,100	25,000	27,000	29,400	31,575	33,475	35,300
Gasoline Plants	550	675	775	800	825	1,000	1,100	1,200	1,600	1,725	1,825
Total Production	15,550	17,650	19,400	22,300	23,925	26,000	28,100	30,600	33,175	35,200	37,125
Pipe Lines	2,050	2,425	2,700	2,950	3,050	3,175	3,400	3,525	3,700	3,850	3,950
Marine	1,100	1,025	1,050	1,025	1,000	1,000	1,000	1,050	1,050	1,175	1,150
Tank Cars and Motor	350	350	350	325	350	350	350	375	375	400	425
Total Transportation	3,500	3,800	4,100	4,300	4,400	4,525	4,750	4,950	5,125	5,425	5,525
Refineries	4,750	5,300	5,850	6,400	7,175	7,850	8,750	9,425	9,750	10,150	10,700
Marketing	3,200	3,450	3,700	4,000	4,300	4,700	5,100	5,400	5,600	5,950	6,375
Others	400	500	550	500	600	625	700	825	950	1,075	1,125
TOTAL-ALL DEPARTMENTS	27,350	30,700	33,600	37,500	40,400	43,700	47,400	51,200	54,600	57,800	60,850
GROSS ASSETS EMPLOYED											
Current	8,100	8,600	9,000	9,150	9,700	10,200	10,500	10,900	11,450	11,750	13,750
Fixed	27,400	30,700	33,600	37,500	40,400	43,700	47,400	51,200	54,700	57,800	60,850
Other	500	700	600	550	600	600	600	600	650	650	---
TOTAL	36,000	40,000	43,200	47,200	50,700	54,500	58,500	62,700	66,800	70,200	74,600

*Includes dry holes and lease acquisitions but excludes exploration expenses and lease rentals.

NOTE: Gross refinery account includes $2,050 million for chemical plants.
Expenditures for refineries included $200 million for chemical plants in 1960 and $325 million in 1961.

Source: "Financial Analysis of The Petroleum Industry," The Chase Manhattan Bank, July, 1962.

4. OIL INDUSTRY

4a. United States Annual Energy Supply, 1920-60 (In Trillions of British Thermal Units)

	Coal	Crude Oil	Natural Gas	Water Power	Total
1920	15,504	3,027	855	775	20,161
1925	14,706	4,641	1,315	701	21,363
1930	13,639	6,148	2,175	785	22,747
1935	10,634	5,799	2,088	831	19,352
1940	12,535	7,662	2,908	917	24,022
1945	15,972	10,199	4,362	1,486	32,019
1950	13,913	12,304	6,752	1,601	34,570
1955	11,695	15,957	10,139	1,494	39,285
1960	10,357	17,172	14,125	1,766	43,420

4b. Average Drilling Costs, All U.S. Wells, 1959

Depth Range (Feet)	Number	Average Depth (Feet)	Total Cost per Foot	Average Cost per Well
0- 1,250	6,977	765	$ 7.84	$ 6,000
1,251- 2,500	9,873	1,830	7.74	14,200
2,501- 3,750	11,439	3,115	8.70	31,200
3,751- 5,000	6,578	4,370	8.96	39,200
5,001- 7,500	8,040	6,175	10.70	66,000
7,501-10,000	3,679	8,655	15.00	129,800
10,001-12,500	1,943	11,175	20.29	226,800
12,501-15,000	814	13,480	28.08	378,700
Over 15,000	220	16,115	40.71	656,100
Total	49,563	4,145	$12.90	$ 53,500

4c. Wells Below 15,000 Feet, 1951, 1958, and 1960

	Total Wells	Average Depth (Feet)	Average Drilling Time (Days)	Average Bits per Well	Average Mud Cost	Average Cost per Foot
1951	12	15,822	178	116	$ 54,000	$33.56
1958	197	16,019	130	79	107,000	43.18
1960	242	15,945	105	66	86,000	42.50

4d. Success Ratios for Drilling New-Field Wildcat Wells

	Number		Total Feet Drilled (Millions)			Percent Successful	
	Producers	Dry Holes	Producers	Dry Holes	Wild-cats	Wild-cats	All Exploratory
1945	352	2,685	1.8	11.6	13.4	NA	NA
1950	592	4,698	3.1	19.0	22.1	11.2%	19.5%
1955	918	7,186	5.3	33.7	39.0	11.3	20.8
1960	745	6,575	4.8	31.1	35.9	10.2	18.7

5. OIL INDUSTRY

Tariff Required to Earn 7 Percent Net Return on Investment for Pipelines of Different Sizes, 1948

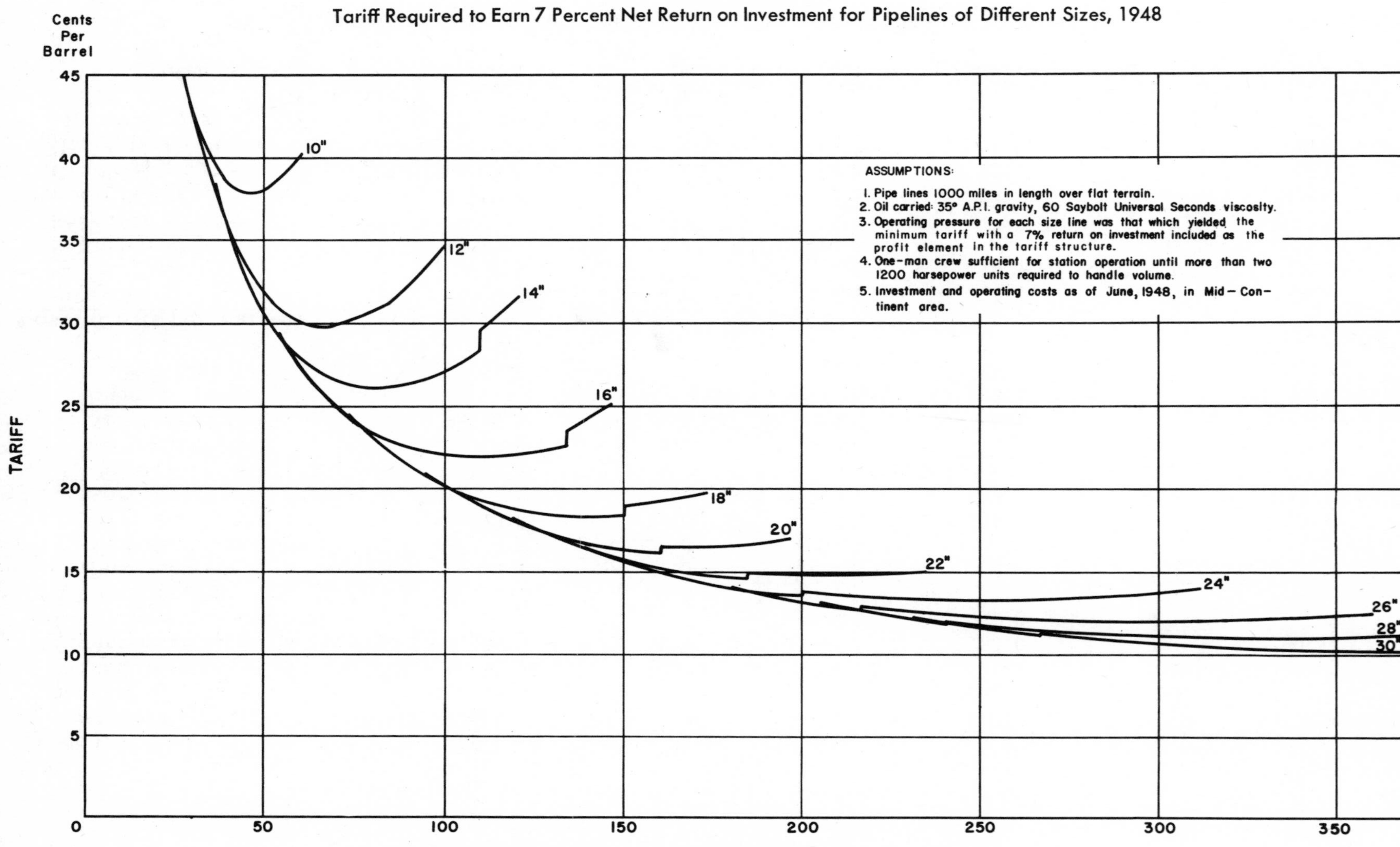
Cents Per Barrel
TARIFF
45
40
35
30
25
20
15
10
5
0
50
100
150
200
250
300
350
THROUGHPUT FOR WHICH DESIGNED (1,000 BARRELS PER DAY)
10"
12"
14"
16"
18"
20"
22"
24"
26"
28"
30"
ASSUMPTIONS:
1. Pipe lines 1000 miles in length over flat terrain.
2. Oil carried: 35° A.P.I. gravity, 60 Saybolt Universal Seconds viscosity.
3. Operating pressure for each size line was that which yielded the minimum tariff with a 7% return on investment included as the profit element in the tariff structure.
4. One-man crew sufficient for station operation until more than two 1200 horsepower units required to handle volume.
5. Investment and operating costs as of June, 1948, in Mid-Continent area.

Source: Standard Oil Company (New Jersey), and F. C. Whiteside, Continental Pipe Line Company

6. OIL INDUSTRY

Refinery Operating Costs for Selected Crude Oils, 1956

Crude Oil	Venezuela	West Texas	Middle East	East Texas	Oklahoma	Pennsylvania
Cost per Barrel	$ 2.23	$ 2.80	$ 1.72	$ 3.25	$ 2.99	$ 4.23
Gravity	16.4	29.7	31.6	38.5	32.0	43.9
Sulfur, percent	2.02	1.49	2.52	0.33	0.82	0.1
Octane of straightrun gasoline	64.0	52.0	41.5	57.0	39.0	46.0
Cracking stock, percent	31.6	33.5	28.4	29.8	18.7	7.9
Yields, percent:						
Unaccounted	2.4	3.0	3.5	3.2	1.6	1.5
Straightrun gasoline	7.8	25.3	27.7	33.2	25.5	35.0
Cracked gasoline	18.6	20.0	17.0	18.3	11.2	4.7
Kerosene				13.6		12.7
Diesel fuel					30.0	
No. 2 distillate	10.8	15.9	13.2	5.1		4.8
No. 3 distillate	5.5	5.9	5.0	5.2	3.3	1.4
Lube				3.3		30.2
Bunker fuel	54.9	29.4	33.6	18.1	28.4	9.7
Costs (Cents per Barrel)						
Investment	4.8	4.8	4.8	4.8	4.8	4.8
General labor	8.5	13.3	12.6	15.5	13.7	17.2
Sulfur penalty	13.4	12.3	16.8		5.0	
Sourness penalty		6.1				
Fuel, power, and water	7.9	12.4	11.6	14.3	12.6	15.8
Cracking	13.5	14.4	12.2	12.8	8.0	3.4
Gasoline upgrading	2.0	13.3	16.9	19.0	8.1	30.8
Miscellaneous	2.5	3.8	3.7	3.3	2.6	3.6
Taxes	5.9	7.1	6.9	7.8	6.5	10.3
Total	58.5	87.5	85.5	77.5	61.3	85.9

Source: W. L. Nelson, "Effect of Gravity on Refinery Operating Costs," The Oil and Gas Journal, November 26, 1956

7. OIL INDUSTRY

Monthly Product Output and Stocks, 1961

	Indiana, Illinois, Kentucky*					
	Daily Output†			Stocks†		
	Gasoline	Distillate	Residual	Gasoline	Distillate	Residual
January	764	367	200	36.4	18.7	5.3
February	765	367	196	38.9	15.9	5.1
March	786	301	157	41.5	15.5	5.2
April	712	255	127	42.3	14.4	5.0
May	693	262	131	38.0	16.1	5.0
June	717	293	112	33.6	18.7	5.3
July	778	313	133	32.6	22.8	5.6
August	808	344	124	32.2	26.9	5.3
September	808	325	134	32.2	29.9	5.7
October	781	330	132	32.0	31.0	6.1
November	782	329	179	31.6	29.9	5.9
December	810	347	213	35.2	23.7	6.0

A. Consumption of Gasoline (In Millions of Gallons)

	Illinois	Indiana	Kentucky	Michigan	Ohio
1953	2,545	1,497	686	2,223	2,619
1954	2,635	1,525	726	2,265	2,709
1955	2,720	1,641	779	2,447	2,913
1956	2,814	1,718	818	2,486	3,071
1957	2,910	1,720	865	2,565	3,129
1958	2,951	1,710	871	2,577	3,121
1959	3,033	1,797	909	2,672	3,252
1960	3,091	1,828	919	2,761	3,263
1961	3,101	1,822	934	2,756	3,259
1962	3,229	1,865	982	2,860	3,390

B. Total Sales of Distillate Fuel Oils (In Millions of Barrels)

	Illinois	Indiana	Kentucky	Michigan	Ohio
1953	29.02	15.17	3.36	22.35	16.54
1954	30.39	16.29	3.29	24.63	18.15
1955	33.37	18.96	4.13	27.40	20.18
1956	35.29	20.44	4.48	29.07	21.94
1957	35.35	20.48	4.55	29.00	22.05
1958	42.87	24.10	4.98	29.39	24.22
1959	43.01	24.50	5.80	28.39	24.85
1960	42.49	25.60	4.83	30.46	23.84
1961	42.47	25.84	4.40	30.38	23.31
1962	NA	NA	NA	NA	NA

C. Total Sales of Residual Fuel Oil (In Millions of Barrels)

	Illinois	Indiana	Kentucky	Michigan	Ohio
1953	20.76	17.64	0.91	14.80	18.70
1954	20.40	14.17	0.94	14.68	18.09
1955	22.13	14.59	1.00	15.39	18.89
1956	22.45	14.96	1.05	16.01	19.26
1957	22.26	14.53	1.04	15.26	18.52
1958	26.78	11.83	0.49	9.34	9.71
1959	23.40	12.91	0.56	13.44	11.03
1960	25.68	12.86	0.31	11.24	11.38
1961	25.75	11.99	0.28	9.90	9.02
1962	NA	NA	NA	NA	NA

*Includes Indiana, Illinois, Kentucky, Tennessee, Michigan, and the western part of Ohio.
†Daily output in thousand barrels/day. Stocks in millions of barrels.

Source: U.S. Bureau of Mines, Monthly Petroleum Statements, 1961, and American Petroleum Institute, Petroleum Facts and Figures, 1959, pp. 246, 308, 324, pp. 157, 190, 198. 1961 and 1962 figures from U.S. Bureau of Mines 1961 Mineral Yearbook and advanced 1962 information.

8. OIL INDUSTRY

Total U.S. Refinery Input and Output, 1946-1961
(Millions of Barrels)

Input: Crude Oils	1946	1947	1948	1949	1950	1951	1952	1953
Domestic	1,646	1,755	1,924	1,790	1,919	2,189	2,235	2,322
Foreign	84	97	124	154	176	182	206	233
Total	1,730	1,852	2,048	1,944	2,095	2,370	2,441	2,555
Natural gas liquids	63	71	76	85	95	99	104	111
Total Input	1,793	1,923	2,125	2,030	2,190	2,470	2,545	2,666
Output: Products								
Gasoline	748	815	896	939	998	1,109	1,141	1,233
Kerosene*	104	110	122	102	119	136	129	123
Distillate fuel oil	288	312	379	341	399	476	518	528
Jet fuel†	--	--	--	--	--	--	21	36
Residual fuel	431	448	480	425	425	469	454	450
Lubricating oil	46	52	51	45	52	61	56	53
Wax	3	4	4	3	4	5	4	5
Coke	11	12	14	17	17	19	18	22
Asphalt	45	49	52	49	58	66	70	72
Still gas	88	86	81	83	84	96	95	102
Road oil	6	7	8	8	7	6	7	7
Other finished products	23	24	31	28	34	40	38	42
Unfinished gasoline (net)	--	--	--	--	--	--	--	--
Other unfinished oil (net)	(1)	(1)	4	(10)	(7)	(11)	(4)	--
Shortage (or average)	1	4	3	--	--	(3)	(3)	(7)
Total Output	1,793	1,923	2,125	2,030	2,190	2,470	2,545	2,666

Input: Crude Oils	1954	1955	1956	1957	1958	1959	1960	1961	1962
Domestic	2,301	2,447	2,563	2,530	2,431	2,566	2,582	2,605	2,676
Foreign	239	283	341	361	345	352	371	382	411
Total	2,540	2,730	2,905	2,890	2,776	2,918	2,953	2,987	3,087
Natural gas liquids	118	126	135	150	151	153	167	169	104
Total Input	2,657	2,857	3,040	3,041	2,927	3,071	3,119	3,156	3,191
Output: Products									
Gasoline	1,233	1,331	1,394	1,417	1,410	1,474	1,508	1,520	1,582
Kerosene*	122	117	123	109	110	111	136	141	157
Distillate fuel oil	542	603	666	669	631	679	667	696	720
Jet fuel†	47	57	66	63	74	93	88	95	296
Residual fuel	417	420	427	416	363	348	332	316	103
Lubricating oil	53	59	59	56	51	56	59	59	61
Wax	5	5	5	5	5	6	6	6	5
Coke	24	28	31	33	38	41	60	75	79
Asphalt	75	83	91	86	89	97	99	102	110
Still gas	103	117	122	126	126	127	129	128	131
Road oil	7	8	8	7	6	6	6	6	7
Other finished products	45	54	64	69	76	90	102	105	32
Unfinished gasoline (net)	--	--	3	(2)	2	(0)	2	(2)	--
Other unfinished oil (net)	(7)	(11)	(4)	(1)	(32)	(26)	(22)	(19)	(28)
Shortage (or average)	(8)	(12)	(16)	(15)	(23)	(32)	(53)	(65)	(64)
Total Output	2,657	2,857	3,040	3,041	2,927	3,071	3,119	3,156	3,191

*Includes commercial jet fuel in 1960 and following years.
†Military jet fuel only, in 1960 and following years.

Source: U.S. Bureau of Mines, Monthly Petroleum Survey.

9. OIL INDUSTRY

Average Wholesale Prices

	Motor Gasoline ¢/Gal.	Kerosene ¢/Gal.	Distillate ¢/Gas	Residual Fuel ¢/Gal.	Average Four Products ¢/Gal.	Average Four Products $/Bbl.	Average Crude Oil $/Bbl.	Refinery Realization $/Bbl.
1946	6.40	5.38	4.84	3.08	5.12	2.15	1.43	0.72
1947	8.45	7.14	6.44	4.48	6.89	2.89	1.97	0.92
1948	10.21	9.62	8.94	5.90	8.70	3.65	2.64	1.01
1949	10.39	8.36	7.34	3.10	7.64	3.21	2.61	0.60
1950	10.77	8.76	7.79	4.10	8.22	3.45	2.62	0.83
1951	11.26	9.31	8.43	4.47	8.70	3.65	2.63	1.02
1952	11.25	9.38	8.40	3.76	8.48	3.56	2.63	0.93
1953	11.79	9.40	8.45	3.59	8.71	3.66	2.77	0.89
1954	11.43	9.55	8.71	3.92	8.68	3.64	2.87	0.77
1955	11.42	9.76	9.02	4.66	8.95	3.76	2.87	0.89
1956	11.55	10.26	9.48	5.34	9.31	3.41	2.89	1.02
1957	12.06	10.64	9.95	6.03	9.86	4.14	3.18	0.96
1958	11.61	9.87	9.12	4.56	9.03	3.79	3.15	0.64
1959	11.57	10.14	9.36	4.70	9.11	3.83	3.09	0.74
1960	11.69	10.01	8.93	4.86	9.14	3.84	3.10	0.74
1961	11.72	10.41	9.31	4.82	9.22	3.87	3.10	0.77

Product Prices Weighted: Okla. 20%, Midwest Grp. 3 25%, W. Penn. 7%, N.Y. 13%, Phila. 4%, Jacksonville, 2%, Boston 2%, Gulf Coast 27%

Four Products Weighted: Gasoline 50%, Kerosene 5%, Distillate 15%, Residual 30%

Crude Price Weighted: Penn. 2%, Illinois 5%, Okla.-Kans. 33%, N.La.-Ark. 5%, East Texas 10%, Texas-New Mex. 15%, Gulf Coast 30%

Average Regional Prices

	Crude Oil (Dollars per Barrel)						Distillate Fuel (Cents per Gallon)		
			Texas						
	Illinois	Michigan	Gulf	East	West	Wyoming	Detroit	Oklahoma	Toledo
1951	2.77	2.72	2.72	2.65	2.50	2.15	10.65¢	8.46¢	10.06¢
1952	2.77	2.72	2.72	2.65	2.50	2.15	10.61	8.10	10.05
1953	2.80	2.75	2.85	2.77	2.62	2.28	10.57	8.23	10.20
1954	2.85	2.80	2.95	2.85	2.70	2.35	10.82	8.69	10.49
1955	2.85	2.80	2.95	2.85	2.70	2.35	11.32	8.90	10.84
1956	2.95	2.90	3.15	3.05	2.80	2.35	11.62	9.35	11.28
1957	3.03	2.95	3.35	3.25	3.01	2.60	12.08	9.80	11.93
1958	3.00	2.94	3.32	3.20	2.99	2.61	11.20	9.11	11.02
1959	2.99	2.94	3.29	3.20	2.85	2.50	10.82	9.45	11.31
1960	2.96	2.91	3.25	3.16	2.85	2.51	10.34	9.19	10.36
1961	2.99	2.92	3.26	3.15	2.86	2.50	10.01	9.38	10.65

Source: Platt's Oil Price Handbook (38th ed., New York: McGraw-Hill, 1962), p. 197, based on Independent Petroleum Association of America.

Source: Crude oil: U.S. Bureau of Mines, Minerals Yearbook, 1961, and previous years. Distillate fuel: Platt's Oil Price Handbook, 38th ed. (New York: McGraw-Hill, 1962), based on prices of #2 fuel.

10. OIL INDUSTRY

U.S. Sales of Distillate and Residual Fuel Oils by Uses, 1946-1961
(In Millions of Barrels)

Distillate

	Vessels	Power Plants	Rail-roads	Oil-Co. Fuel	Industrial	Heating	Military	Other
1946	12.1	10.6	17.6	1.9	21.3	139.6	9.4	27.1
1947	14.5	14.2	23.6	2.2	24.5	178.4	5.2	35.5
1948	14.5	14.9	31.0	3.6	29.9	200.0	9.1	38.9
1949	13.1	12.6	38.6	4.2	26.4	190.4	6.1	37.9
1950	12.9	13.2	48.7	5.7	37.1	220.9	6.6	50.2
1951	14.4	9.6	60.0	7.8	42.6	249.8	8.5	56.4
1952	17.2	8.4	68.0	8.0	42.8	263.4	9.6	61.9
1953	16.9	6.8	75.2	7.8	42.4	267.5	9.6	62.7
1954	15.6	6.1	77.4	7.7	41.6	304.5	8.8	64.6
1955	16.7	5.9	84.7	8.6	43.6	339.2	10.9	71.5
1956	18.5	5.4	89.4	10.1	44.9	359.8	11.3	76.2
1957	20.4	5.3	88.3	10.4	43.5	360.2	12.7	76.3
1958	18.8	5.4	83.7	7.8	37.6	399.2	13.4	87.8
1959	19.3	5.0	87.8	8.6	33.4	401.4	11.4	92.2
1960	18.7	4.7	86.5	8.3	34.3	422.9	10.8	97.1
1961	14.6	4.2	85.2	8.7	31.1	440.6	11.5	95.1

Residual

	Vessels	Power Plants	Rail-roads	Oil-Co. Fuel	Industrial	Heating	Military	Other
1946	88.2	50.9	100.3	58.1	99.0	49.7	35.9	5.0
1947	101.9	61.0	97.5	62.6	115.1	56.4	19.1	6.9
1948	95.8	56.8	89.6	56.6	117.8	58.6	24.7	6.6
1949	89.4	80.1	63.5	51.7	122.6	60.4	22.7	4.6
1950	92.9	93.1	60.9	53.3	148.1	72.7	28.3	4.9
1951	107.0	70.6	55.0	54.1	157.3	76.2	38.1	5.3
1952	110.4	70.5	40.5	54.4	158.4	79.2	37.2	5.7
1953	114.3	85.4	28.5	51.2	166.7	81.8	30.4	6.3
1954	108.8	70.7	16.1	52.2	160.1	78.8	26.9	7.0
1955	115.1	76.0	15.0	53.4	173.0	86.3	28.4	9.8
1956	117.4	74.0	10.6	53.3	177.8	87.6	30.5	10.3
1957	123.7	76.0	7.0	50.2	166.9	81.4	29.5	10.0
1958	106.3	77.0	5.8	46.5	156.2	93.1	37.4	9.7
1959	102.0	82.2	5.6	46.2	167.2	111.9	31.4	7.3
1960	94.1	85.4	5.6	45.1	157.3	125.1	31.7	6.3
1961	87.3	87.9	5.4	44.4	153.8	121.1	36.8	6.4

Source: American Petroleum Institute, Petroleum Facts and Figures, 1961. 1961 figures from U.S. Bureau of Mines, 1961 Minerals Yearbook, Vol. II, pp. 438, 443.

11. OIL INDUSTRY

Refinery Plant Capacity, 1946-1963

	Crude Oil Capacity					Cracking and Reforming Capacity						
	No. of Refineries (January 1)		(MM bbls. Daily)			Cracking (MM bbls. Daily)					Research Octane	
	Operating	Shut-down	Operating	Shut-down	Average Runs	Operating	Shut-down	Thermal	Catalytic	Reforming	Regular	Premium
1946	364	29	5.09	0.23	4.74	1.39	0.11	0.84	0.39	0.27	79.3	84.7
1947	361	38	5.34	0.23	5.07	1.41	0.10	0.81	0.42	0.28	80.2	85.9
1948	352	38	5.83	0.21	5.60	1.56	0.07	0.84	0.50	0.28	80.1	86.1
1949	336	39	6.23	0.21	5.24	1.64	0.08	0.82	0.60	0.29	81.9	88.0
1950	320	47	6.22	0.47	5.74	1.73	0.09	0.78	0.73	0.31	83.5	90.0
1951	325	32	6.70	0.26	6.49	1.81	0.04	0.78	0.78	0.30	82.5	89.7
1952	327	23	7.16	0.17	6.67	1.97	0.05	0.78	0.91	0.33	83.6	90.6
1953	315	28	7.48	0.16	7.00	2.12	0.03	0.80	1.01	0.36	84.2	91.1
1954	308	29	7.78	0.22	6.96	2.19	0.06	0.73	1.11	0.41	85.5	92.9
1955	296	30	8.07	0.35	7.48	2.41	0.13	0.63	1.32	0.59	87.4	95.0
1956	294	24	8.38	0.25	7.94	2.64	0.14	0.59	1.41	0.78	88.8	96.4
1957	298	21	8.81	0.31	7.92	2.95	0.10	0.57	1.53	0.96	89.8	97.6
1958	289	29	8.94	0.47	7.61	3.06	0.15	0.53	1.46	1.22	90.2	98.4
1959	293	22	9.45	0.37	NA	3.28	0.25	0.49	1.55	1.50	91.4	99.1
1960	290	20	9.54	0.36	8.09	3.44	0.26	0.47	1.59	1.63	91.8	99.2
1961	289	22	9.63	0.38	8.18	3.46	0.23	0.45	1.59	1.65	91.9	99.2
1962	287	24	9.79	0.29	8.410	3.50	0.22	0.40	1.65	1.67	93.0	99.7
1963	285	21	9.80	0.30	NA	3.59	0.16	NA	NA	NA	NA	NA

Source: American Petroleum Institute, Petroleum Facts and Figures, 1961, pp. 64, 67, 162. 1962 refinery data from U.S. Bureau of Mines, Petroleum Refineries in the United States (on January 1, 1962). 1963 refinery data from U.S. Bureau of Mines, Monthly Petroleum Statement (March, 1963). 1962 octane figures from National Petroleum News Factbook, 1963 issue.

12. OIL INDUSTRY

Percentage Analysis of Average Operating Costs of U.S. Refineries

	Purchased Fuel	Total Labor	Purchased Power	Chemical Tel. & Supplies	Maint. Nat'ls.	Insurance & Taxes	Royalties or Research	Obsolescence and Improvement	Interest on Capital	Total Cost
1946	6.7	49.2	2.0	9.7	7.4	2.5	1.7	13.7	7.1	100%
1947	8.3	47.7	1.6	10.6	7.0	2.6	1.8	13.5	6.9	100%
1948	9.4	47.5	1.3	11.6	6.2	2.4	1.9	13.0	6.7	100%
1949	6.3	44.5	1.5	12.0	6.4	2.8	2.2	16.9	7.4	100%
1950	6.3	45.6	1.6	13.5	6.3	2.8	2.2	14.3	7.4	100%
1951	6.6	45.8	1.4	13.6	6.1	2.7	2.2	14.4	7.2	100%
1952	6.0	43.9	1.5	14.1	6.2	2.7	2.3	15.8	7.5	100%
1953	5.7	42.7	1.5	14.6	6.1	2.8	2.2	17.0	7.4	100%
1954	4.8	41.1	1.5	15.1	6.1	3.0	2.3	18.2	7.9	100%
1955	4.9	42.0	1.8	16.5	6.2	3.3	2.4	14.1	8.8	100%
1956	5.0	42.3	1.8	17.3	5.6	3.2	2.5	13.6	8.7	100%
1957	5.8	42.4	2.1	16.6	5.2	3.2	2.5	13.6	8.6	100%
1958	4.5	41.8	2.1	17.0	5.3	3.3	2.8	14.2	9.0	100%
1959	4.8	40.7	2.2	17.5	5.3	3.5	3.0	13.7	9.3	100%
1960	5.3	39.6	2.4	18.0	4.7	3.5	3.0	14.0	9.5	100%
1961	5.7	38.7	2.6	16.7	4.8	3.5	3.0	15.5	9.5	100%

Source: Prepared from W. L. Nelson, Process Costimating Series, The Oil and Gas Journal.

13. OIL INDUSTRY

A. Fuel Consumed at U.S. Refineries, 1946-1962

MM B.T.U. per	Fuel Oil 6.29 Barrel	Acid Sludge 4.5 Barrel	Coal 26.0 Short Ton	Natural Gas 1.05 M Cubic Feet	Refinery Gas 1.15 M Cubic Feet	Coke 30.12 Short Ton	Purchased Electricity 3.41 M Kilowatt-Hour	Total B.T.U.
Units	MM Barrels	MM Barrels	MM Short Tons	MMM Cubic Feet	MMM Cubic Feet	MM Short Tons	MMM Kilowatt-Hours	MMMM B.T.U.
1946	38.3	5.2	1.7	331.5	318.2	0.5	2.9	1,131
1947	38.7	5.8	2.3	363.9	324.7	0.7	3.0	1,199
1948	38.7	5.8	2.4	441.5	331.2	0.9	3.0	1,295
1949	44.5	4.3	1.0	442.4	361.7	1.3	3.2	1,336
1950	42.6	4.1	1.1	455.1	370.1	1.5	3.6	1,378
1951	39.9	4.2	1.2	537.8	422.8	1.5	4.0	1,530
1952	40.0	3.6	0.8	536.4	425.8	1.5	4.3	1,527
1953	41.3	2.9	0.7	558.7	477.9	1.8	4.7	1,639
1954	47.4	2.5	0.9	563.3	501.6	1.9	5.4	1,718
1955	42.0	2.2	0.9	625.2	591.2	2.5	6.1	1,895
1956	37.9	1.9	1.1	679.3	653.7	2.7	6.9	2,032
1957	39.6	1.5	0.9	682.3	694.7	4.1	8.6	2,226
1958	44.7	1.1	1.0	681.9	715.2	4.5	8.6	2,298
1959	41.8	.9	1.0	752.2	743.0	5.3	9.4	2,075
1960	41.2	.9	.7	775.1	752.9	9.2	10.4	2,197
1961	40.9	.5	.7	772.0	776.6	10.0	11.2	2,226
1962	41.7	.4	.7	790.0	845.3	10.3	11.4	2,354

Total British thermal units include some liquified petroleum gas and purchased steam, not included in this table. Refinery gas factor declined to 1,050 B.T.U. per cubic foot in 1958, to 997 B.T.U. in 1960, 989 in 1961, and rose to 1,003 in 1962.

Source: U.S. Bureau of Mines, Monthly Petroleum Statement.

B. Employment and Earnings in Refining and All Manufacturing 1946-1962

	Petroleum Refining				All Manufacturing	
	Total Employees (In Thousands)	Plant Workers (In Thousands)	Weekly Hours	Hourly Earnings	Weekly Hours	Hourly Earnings
1946	NA	135	39.9	$1.42	40.3	$1.08
1947	189	142	40.2	1.57	40.4	1.22
1948	197	147	40.3	1.79	40.0	1.33
1949	192	144	40.2	1.87	39.2	1.38
1950	185	136	40.4	1.93	40.5	1.44
1951	199	143	40.7	2.08	40.6	1.56
1952	202	140	40.2	2.20	40.7	1.65
1953	206	142	40.6	2.32	40.5	1.74
1954	204	137	40.6	2.37	39.6	1.78
1955	201	132	40.8	2.46	40.7	1.86
1956	201	131	40.9	2.65	40.4	1.95
1957	199	128	40.9	2.76	39.8	2.05
1958	192	121	40.6	2.83	39.2	2.11
1959	186	118	40.8	2.99	40.3	2.19
1960	178	113	40.8	3.02	39.7	2.26
1961	170	107	40.9	3.16	39.8	2.32
1962	NA	102	41.2	3.18	40.4	2.39

Source: U.S. Bureau of Labor Statistics, Monthly Labor Review. 1962 figures from U.S. Department of Commerce, Survey of Current Business.

14. OIL INDUSTRY

Effect on Gross Margin of Forward Integration by a Crude Oil Producer

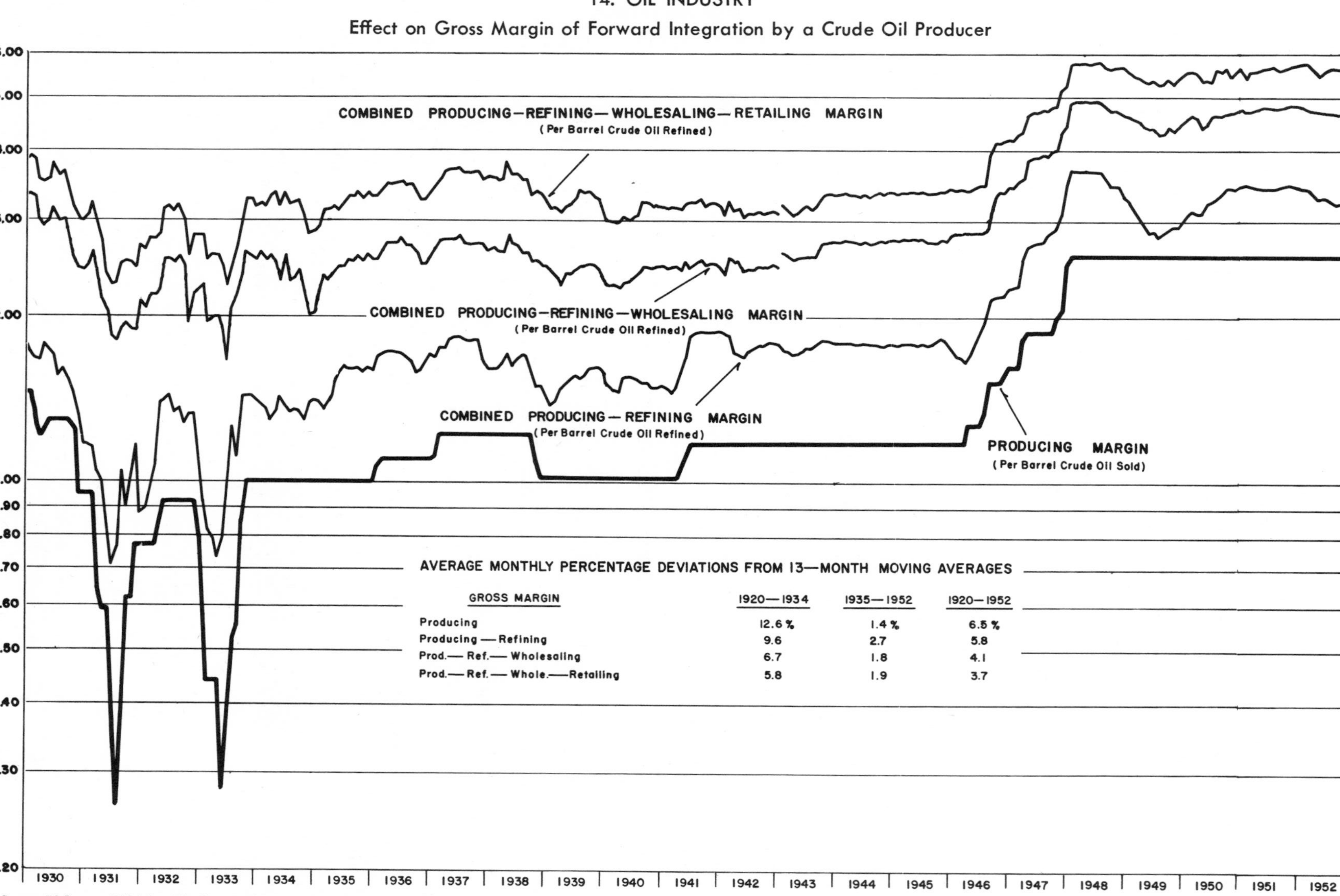

GROSS MARGIN	1920—1934	1935—1952	1920—1952
Producing	12.6 %	1.4 %	6.5 %
Producing — Refining	9.6	2.7	5.8
Prod.— Ref.— Wholesaling	6.7	1.8	4.1
Prod.— Ref.— Whole.— Retailing	5.8	1.9	3.7

Source: *McLean and Haigh, "The Growth of Integrated Oil Companies," Harvard University, 1954.*

15. OIL INDUSTRY

Comparison of Average Level of Return on Investment Earned by Various Types of Oil Companies, 1920–1952

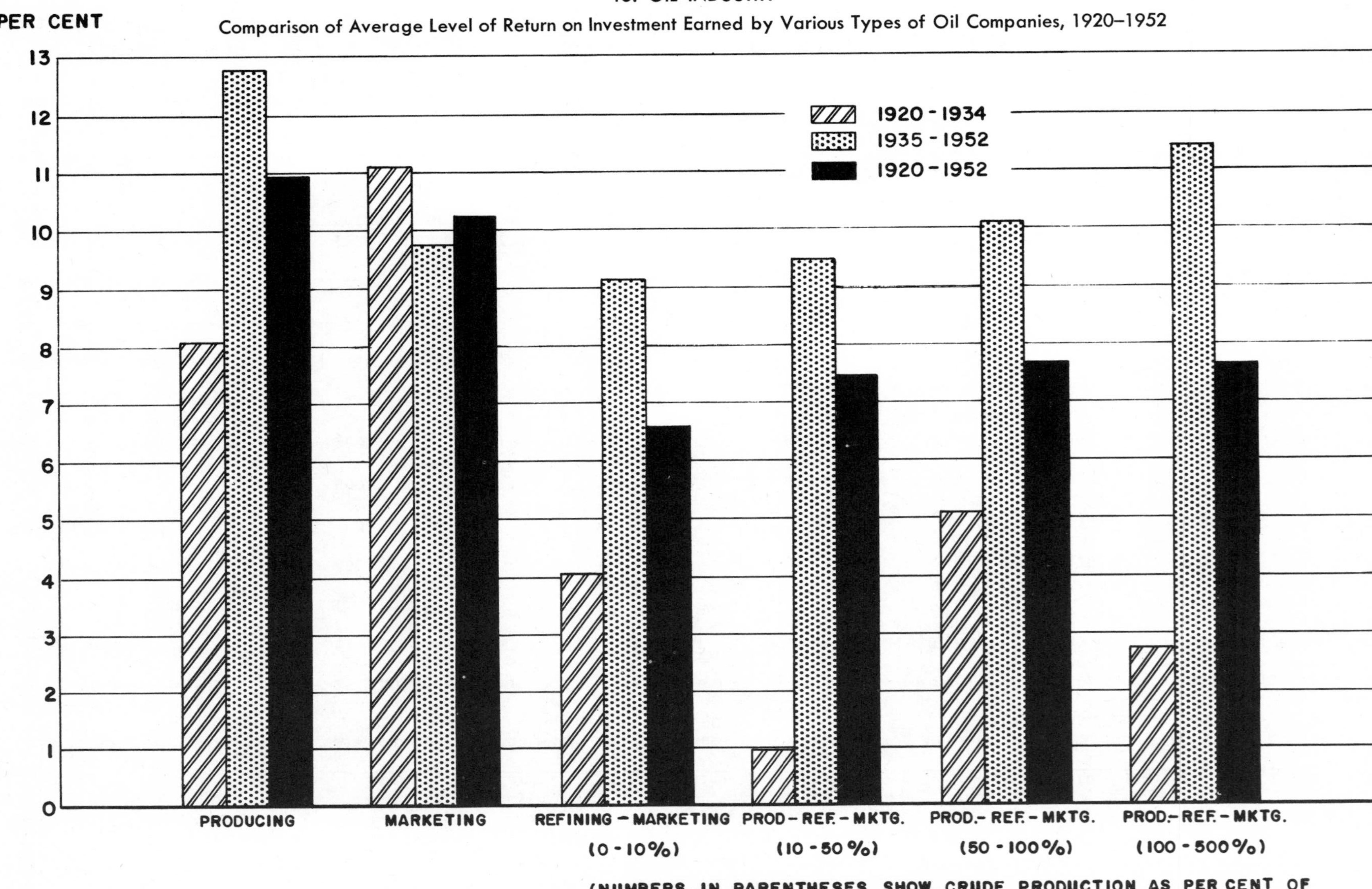

Source: McLean and Haigh, "*The Growth of Integrated Oil Companies*," Harvard University, 1954.

16. OIL INDUSTRY

Hydrogen Process in Oil Refining

	1. Make Hydrogen	2. Catalytic Reform	3. Extract Aromatics	4. De-Alkylate Toluene	5. Make Cyclohexane	6. De-Sulfurize 6a.	6. De-Sulfurize 6b.	7. Hydrocrack
Feed: Material	Methane	Naphtha RON 70	Reformate RON 90	Toluene	Benzene	Naphtha 0.8%S	Gas Oil 1.3%S	Gas Oil
Barrels per day	15 MMCF	10,000	6,000	1,000	600	10,000	15,000	10,000
Investment	$1.8MM	$2.4MM	$1.0MM	$1.5MM	$0.9MM	$0.4MM	$0.6MM	$6.4MM
Utilities (per barrel)	(per MCF)							
Fuel: M B.T.U.	450	448	324	817	380	420	810	338
Steam: Pounds	50	43	122	163	90	30	70	150
Power: Watts	500	790	610	640	520	450	800	7,000
Cool water: Gallons	800	800	1,160	865	820	700	1,300	865
Treatment: (per barrel)								
Catalyst: cents	6.1	3.1	--	10.0	--	0.8	1.2	5.9
Solvent: cents	--	--	3.2	--	--	--	--	--
Hydrogen: SCF	--	--	--	1,780	4,500	30	290	1,875
Product: (per day)	13.5 MMCF of Hydrogen	8MMCF of Hydrogen + 8,700 Reformate (RON 90)	1,600 Benzene-Toluene + 4,400 Raffinate (RON 85)	800 Benzene	705 Cyclohexane	.05S Naphtha	.08S Gas Oil	Gasoline & Distillate

Note: RON means "Research Method Octane Number"
SCF Standard Cubic Feet
MCF Thousand Cubic Feet
MMCF Million Cubic Feet per day

Costs of Utilities (in cents)

	Oklahoma	Michigan
Fuel (MM B.T.U.)	16.1¢	41.0¢
Steam (M Pounds)	30.0	75.0
Power (Kilowatts per Hour)	0.8	1.1
Cooling Water (M Gallons)	1.0	1.1

The Ohio Oil Company (A)

The Ohio Oil Company was attempting to decide whether or not to modernize its principal refinery at Robinson, Illinois in the period 1947–1948. The refinery had a capacity of approximately 15,000 barrels per day. Refinery processes included atmospheric and vacuum distillation, thermal cracking and reforming, gas recovery, and catalytic polymerization. Products included gasoline, kerosene, diesel fuel, distillates, and residual fuel oils. Lubricating oils were not manufactured but were blended and packaged.

Under the modernization plan, refinery capacity would be increased to 27,500 barrels per day through the construction of a new atmospheric-vacuum crude distillation unit. A fluid catalytic cracking unit designed to process 12,400 barrels per day of gas oil would be installed for production of high-octane motor fuel. Other new facilities included a crude desalting unit, a gasoline fractionating column, a nonselective catalytic polymerization unit, a gas-recovery plant, a gasoline treating plant, an ethyl blending building, and various auxiliary facilities.

The management of The Ohio Oil Company planned its refinery renovation during World War II and the immediate postwar period. Early in 1945, a leading refinery engineering and consulting firm submitted a detailed report to the Ohio management proposing a specific modernization program for the Robinson plant. The proposal was accompanied by an economic analysis of the need for new facilities and the forecasted advantages to be derived therefrom. The report was accepted as a useful piece of economic analysis which aided the management in planning the refinery modernization program.

EXCERPTS FROM THE CONSULTANT'S REPORT

Historically, Ohio Oil has always been a "producing" oil company; its reputation, its growth, its financial and industrial success have all come from the producing function of the oil industry. Ohio Oil should continue to be dominantly a producing oil company. Nothing in any reports from this company should be interpreted as recommending any changes in Ohio Oil's basic functions; the primary purpose of these reports is to maintain the overall profitability of the producing operations of Ohio Oil and to increase such overall profitability of Ohio Oil in the postwar period. See Exhibits 1 to 4. A flow diagram of the new refinery is in Exhibit 5.

Size and Location of Refining Facilities

Ohio Oil's management is faced with the problem of determining size and location of any necessary additional postwar refining facilities.

Competent engineering studies seem to indicate:

1. If Robinson's operations remain as they now are, the severity of postwar competition would doubtless terminate Robinson's existence, because of Robinson's physical inability to meet competitors' postwar levels of quality and cost.
2. Maintaining Robinson's postwar crude oil throughput at 14,500 barrels per day with the installation of new fluid catalytic cracking facilities of proportionate size, would undoubtedly enable Robinson to compete, postwar, on the basis of quality, but the higher unit costs for new investment and for overall operation would prevent Robinson from competing on the basis of cost.
3. Increasing Robinson's crude oil operating capacity to, perhaps, 25,000 barrels per day, through addition of new necessary facilities, would enable Robinson to compete continuously on the basis of product quality and of manufacturing cost.
4. The question of expanding Robinson to 25,000 barrels per day, or building a new refinery on the Mississippi River, with a capacity of 25,000 barrels per day, is affected by the following factors:
   (*a*) A completely new refinery on the river would cost approximately $11,500,000.
   (*b*) The replacement value of Robinson's usable equipment and Robinson's utilities would approximate $3,000,000—assumed value for calculating tax and insurance charges was $2,350,000. Their salvage value, if Robinson were dismantled, would probably not equal $500,000; their use at their present location, therefore, would save Ohio Oil approximately $2,500,000.
   (*c*) This proposed saving of $2,500,000

would equal 1 cent per gallon on 6,000,000 barrels of products—approximately one year's gasoline production with Robinson's expanded facilities. It is extremely doubtful that any location on the Mississippi River would provide increased operating flexibility and more economical transportation, to save 1 cent per gallon over the charges for transporting products from Robinson through modern, competitive, efficient transportation facilities.

5. [It was proposed that the gasoline and heating oil output from the Robinson refinery be marketed intensively within a 100-mile radius of terminals on a common carrier pipeline system owned by the Buckeye Pipe Line Company. Deliveries could be made to service stations and homes in this area at costs ranging from 3/4 of one cent to one cent per gallon.] It is doubtful whether any competitor could serve that area more cheaply than Ohio Oil.

Beyond this 100-mile zone, Ohio Oil could develop selected concentrated markets within maximum transportation limits, from Robinson, of 2 cents per gallon. In "less-than-100-mile" zones, Ohio could achieve 10 percent of the potential market; it already has from 10 to 20 percent in areas other than Robinson and Findlay. In "more-than-100-mile" zones, up to the "2 cent limit," Ohio Oil could reasonably expect 5 to 10 percent of total business; many of these latter areas could be economically served by barges from the Ohio River.

[Access to barges would require] construction of a new products pipeline south from Robinson to the Ohio River for barge operation to eastern river markets.

Economic-Engineering Study of Postwar Refining Operations

[The consultant's report recommended that the Robinson refinery install a fluid catalytic cracker and also increase its capacity to 25,000 barrels per day. The cost of the equipment was expected to be $6,850,000, and of plant facilities $1,800,000, making a total investment of $8,650,000. Exhibit 6 compares product yields of the proposed refinery and the existing refinery, together with actual experience in 1945.]

Authorities have estimated that, within a few years following resumption of civilian gasoline production, the level of housebrand (regular) gasoline will rise to 80-octane number, and possibly higher, with premium gasoline following the same trend to about 85 octane.

In this analysis, assumption has been made that refining economics will progressively change during the 5 years following war's end. The basic assumptions of price structure and octane level used in this analysis of postwar operations are quite conservative. Any acceleration in "octane race" or betterment in prices would make more profitably attractive the adoption of this report's recommendations. The basic assumptions are summarized in Exhibit 7.

Economic comparisons of the postwar present and proposed operations are presented in Exhibit 8 for the 76-octane level.

Potential Postwar Earnings of Expanded Refinery Are High

Economic figures developed in this study offer interesting estimates of future refinery operations at Robinson. In the postwar 5-year period, the present operation, with existing facilities, shows a potential "net operating profit" of $6,222,330; the expanded Robinson refinery, can show a potential "net operating profit" of $21,217,450.

"Net operating profit" as defined in this report, includes charges for raw materials, direct operating costs for labor and maintenance, fixed charges for property taxes, insurance, royalties and general refinery overhead; it is exclusive of all sales, general and administrative expenses, and income taxes.

If extra profits resulting from the new facilities, in excess of potential profits to be derived from postwar operation of existing facilities, are applied to amortization of this new investment, then these new facilities will be completely paid for in the first 2.95 years of operation.

After "paying-out" the entire new investment, and after allowing for all potential earnings of existing facilities, Robinson's expanded operation, in 5 years, conservatively will yield an extra operating profit of $6,300,000.

Manufacturing Costs Are Lower for Expanded Operation

New facilities will lower the manufacturing cost of gasoline. Gasoline in Robinson's proposed refinery will have a manufacturing cost 0.3 cent per gallon lower than in Robinson's postwar operation of its present facilities. This superiority arises partly from increased capacity and from the introduction of fluid catalytic cracking.

The "by-products" method of calculation, which is an accounting method widely used in the petroleum industry, has been used in these determinations. For this present purpose of calculating manufacturing cost, a depreciation of 8 percent per year was arbitrarily assumed on the basis of total new investment plus $2,350,000, which has been used as tax value of the usable part of Robinson's existing facilities. The same basis was used to estimate charges for taxes and insurance.

For the present case, a value of $4,000,000 for presently existing facilities was used as basis for taxes and insurance.

Operation of Existing Facilities is Limited

The present case shows that, with existing equipment, Robinson can manufacture gasolines of 76- and 78-octane number using approximately optimum quantities (155 cc/gallon) of tetraethyl lead, and that, with existing equipment in full service, Robinson would be able to produce 80-octane number housebrand gasoline with the permissible limit of 3.0 cc tetraethyl lead per gallon; present facilities cannot exceed this 80-octane number maximum for housebrand gasoline.

With wartime high-octane gasoline processes now available to many refiners, 80-octane housebrand gasoline will doubtless be the accepted standard within 2 years of the war's end; and octane race may accelerate this "80" level to even an earlier date. If so, Robinson's present facilities, as shown by the present case, will be unable to operate, because of their inability to make gasoline of competitive quality at competitive cost.

New Facilities Give Flexibility

New postwar refining operations will require sufficient flexibility to manufacture products of high quality and low cost in varying yield ratios. [The product yields from the Robinson refinery in 1945 are shown in Exhibit 6. The company's sales of refined products in 1945 are given in Exhibit 8.] The flexibility from the new facilities will place Robinson in continued position, during any foreseeable future, to meet any competitive fluctuations in quality and cost as outlined in the following discussion:

Gasoline Flexibility

The new facilities, as proposed, give Robinson adequate flexibility to meet all foreseeable future octane requirements, set by competitors at 80-octane level or above. Installation of fluid catalytic cracking eliminates naphtha reforming, until naphtha reforming becomes cheaper than "leading" to obtain the desired octane level.

These proposed facilities not only assure profitable flexibility in quality, but in quantity also, to yield greater volumes of more profitable products. The proposed refinery produces 29 percent more gasoline than Robinson's present operation through present facilities. Part of this increase is due to purchased natural gasoline; even eliminating all natural gasoline, the proposed refinery would show about 18 to 20 percent greater gasoline production.

The ratio of premium fuel to housebrand fuel has been maintained constant in all cases at 15.7 of total motor gasoline production, assuming 15 to 20 percent postwar premium fuel consumption.

Fuel Oil Flexibility

The inherent flexibility of fluid catalytic cracking is demonstrated by the proposal. The fluid catalytic cracking maintains as constant the present percentage production of distillate and asphalt and yet reduces production of unprofitable fuel oil to 11 percent crude throughput—a reduction of 50 percent below Robinson's postwar operation of its existing facilities.

By producing catalytically cracked furnace oil —with no added investment—fuel oil production can be still further decreased to 4–6 percent of crude throughput—a reduction under present production of 75 percent.

Uneconomical fuel oil is thus converted into profitable gasoline. Fuel oil at 82 to 90 cents per barrel can be considered as replacing crude oil at $1.44 per barrel as charging stock to the fluid catalytic cracking operation, thus eliminating fuel oil as an unprofitable refinery residual product and obtaining profitable, salable gasoline.

Diesel Oil Flexibility

The fluid catalytic cracking unit is designed to include optional cracking of diesel oil. If profitable markets exist for diesel oil, it could be sold as such; if, however, it is more profitable, diesel oil could be included as charging stock to the fluid catalytic cracking units for conversion into gasoline. When diesel or virgin furnace oil is sold, additional capacity of the fluid catalytic cracking unit would be available for the increased recycling of fuel oil to gasoline. Thus, with only slight operating modifications, fluid catalytic cracking gives Robinson flexibility for the profitable manufacture and sale of diesel oil.

SUMMARY OF ECONOMIC ANALYSIS

	Present Refinery (14,546 Barrels/Day)			*Proposed Refinery* (25,000 Barrels/Day)		
Octane number	*76*	*78*	*80*	*76*	*78*	*80*
Annual operating profit (thousands)	$1,200	$1,332	$1,237	$3,933	$4,480	$4,335
Years of operation	1.5	1.0	2.5	1.5	1.0	2.5
Profit at each level (thousands)	$1,800	$1,332	$3,091	$5,900	$4,480	$10,838
Manufacturing cost of gasoline (cents/gallon)	4.50	5.24	5.47	4.27	4.95	5.14
Manufacturing cost including 8% depreciation	—	—	—	4.55	5.23	5.42
Total Profit		$6,222,380			$21,217,450	
Net Investment		—			8,650,000	

1A. THE OHIO OIL COMPANY (A)

Balance Sheets (1943-1947)
(In Millions)

	1943	1944	1945	1946	1947
ASSETS					
Cash	$ 16.2	$ 18.0	$ 20.4	$ 19.3	$ 14.8
U.S. Gov't Notes	8.5	8.6	10.7	16.0	16.2
Accounts Receivable	6.5	7.4	7.1	8.9	16.2
Inventories:					
Crude Oil	$ 1.1	$ 1.4	$ 2.5	$ 4.2	$ 2.3
Refined Products	1.6	2.0	2.5	3.6	6.5
Materials	3.7	3.9	3.8	4.4	5.5
Total Inventories	$ 6.4	$ 7.3	$ 8.8	$ 12.2	$ 14.2
Total Current Assets	$ 37.5	$ 41.4	$ 47.0	$ 56.3	$ 61.4
Other Assets:					
Investments	$ 3.7	$ 3.7	$ 3.7	$ 3.7	$ 3.5
Miscellaneous	1.0	0.8	0.9	1.1	1.5
	$ 4.7	$ 4.4	$ 4.6	$ 4.8	$ 5.1
Property, Plant, and Equipment:					
Leases, plants, equipment, pipe lines	$262.6	$271.6	$273.4	$277.6	$298.4
Less: Depletion and Depreciation	186.4	191.3	193.7	196.6	203.4
	$ 76.2	$ 80.3	$ 79.7	$ 81.0	$ 95.0
Deferred Charges	0.5	0.6	0.6	1.6	2.2
TOTAL ASSETS	$119.0	$126.7	$131.8	$143.8	$163.8
LIABILITIES					
Accounts payable	$ 3.9	$ 4.8	$ 5.1	$ 5.8	$ 9.4
Accrued taxes and interest	0.9	0.9	0.8	1.0	1.2
Federal taxes on income	6.3	5.1	4.0	7.0	10.5
Total Current Liabilities	$ 11.2	$ 10.7	$ 9.9	$ 13.8	$ 21.1
Funded Debt	12.5	11.0	9.5	8.0	3.0
Deferred Liabilities	.2	1.3	1.4	.6	.1
Common stock outstanding	59.2	59.2	59.2	80.0	80.0
Retained Earnings	35.9	44.4	51.8	41.4	59.6
TOTAL LIABILITIES	$119.0	$126.7	$131.8	$143.8	$163.8

1B. THE OHIO OIL COMPANY (A)

Income Statements (1943-1947)
(In Millions)

	1943	1944	1945	1946	1947
Net Sales	$76.4	$81.0	$83.0	$91.9	$130.8
Interest	0.4	0.5	0.5	0.5	0.7
Profit on sales of assets	0.6	0.8	0.6	0.8	0.4
Miscellaneous	0.6	0.7	0.2	0.6	0.5
Reserve for Contingencies	--	--	--	0.2	--
Total Net Sales	$78.0	$82.9	$84.4	$94.0	$132.4
Cost and Expenses:					
Raw Materials	$18.3	$18.9	$20.8	$23.5	$ 36.9
Operating Expense	14.6	16.4	16.5	17.5	34.5
Depletion	2.4	2.8	2.8	1.9	2.2
Depreciation	8.5	8.2	9.3	8.7	8.6
Federal Taxes	5.7	4.3	3.3	6.1	9.6
Other Taxes	3.4	3.2	3.2	3.4	4.2
Canceled Leases	1.5	1.7	2.5	1.6	1.9
Nonproductive Wells	1.0	1.8	2.1	2.1	1.8
Interest	0.2	0.2	0.2	0.2	0.2
Annuities	0.5	--	--	--	3.4
General	7.5	9.2	9.7	10.8	--
Total Costs and Expenses	$63.9	$67.8	$70.4	$75.7	$103.2
Net Income	14.1	15.1	14.0	18.3	29.2
Net Income per Share Common	$ 2.4	$ 2.30	$ 2.13	$ 2.78	$ 4.44

2. THE OHIO OIL COMPANY (A)
Map of Operations, 1950

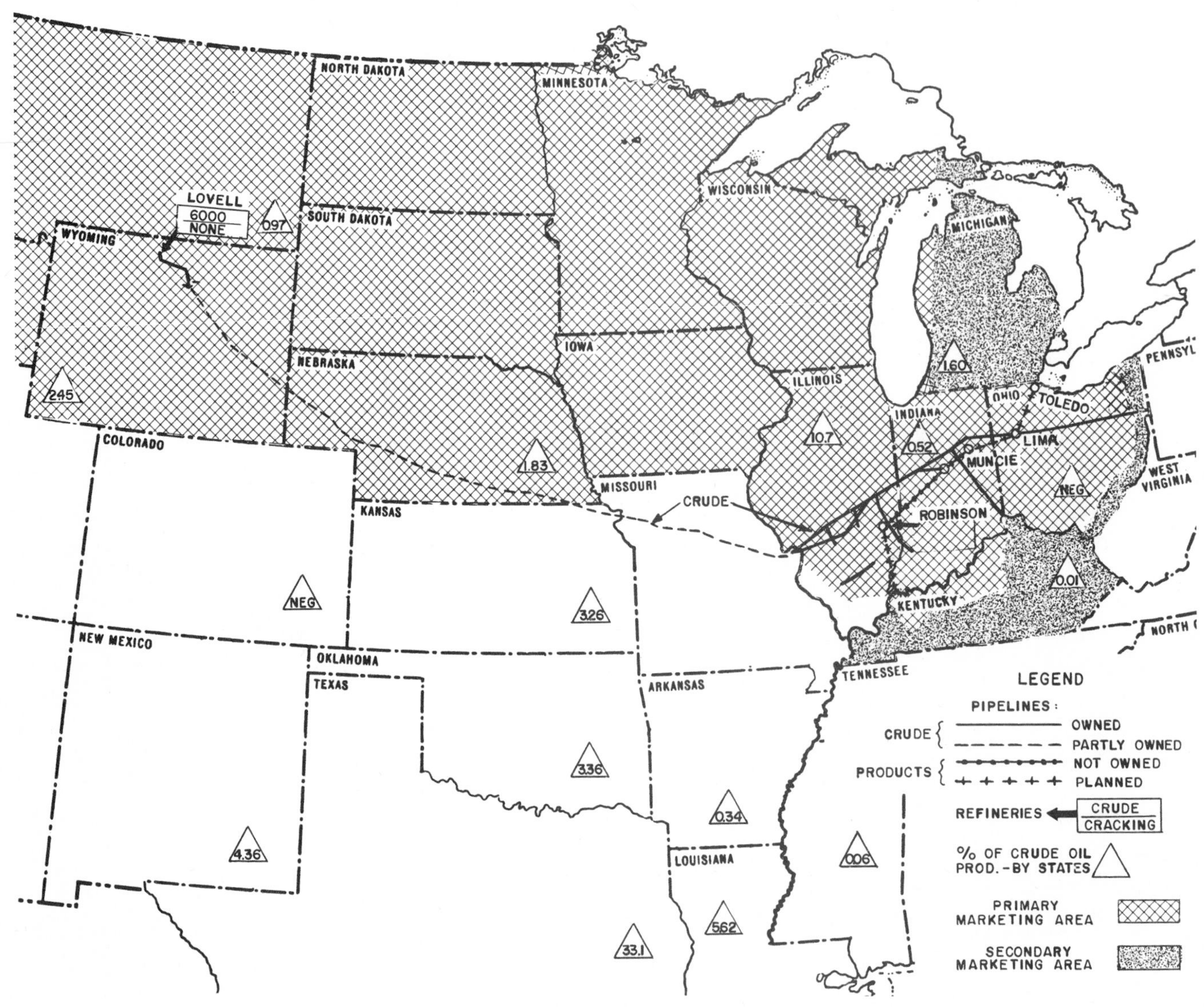

3. THE OHIO OIL COMPANY (A)

Balance of Operations in Selected Years

(In Thousands of Barrels)

	1935	1940	1946
Crude Oil Operations			
Net Domestic Production	18,301	22,625	31,404
Net Purchases (Sales)	(14,072)	(16,815)	(23,157)
Refined Products Operations			
Total new supply refined products in U.S.	5,771	6,713	8,520
Yield of refined products from refineries	5,343	5,886	7,387
Purchases of refined products	428	827	1,133
Crude runs to domestic refineries	5,440	6,982	7,536
Transportation Operations			
Total Crude oil receipts at Refineries	5,430	6,101	7,571
Via company facilities (pipelines)	4,456	5,853	7,088
Via outside facilities	974	248	483
Total products shipments from refineries	5,349	5,820	7,436
Via company facilities (trucks)	0	0	250
Via outside facilities	5,349	5,820	7,186
Marketing Operations			
Total sales refined products	5,332	7,025	8,682
Gasolines	3,475	4,345	4,337
Kerosene and distillate	828	790	1,268
Residual	313	690	1,645
Other	716	1,200	1,432
Gasoline sales by method of sales: total		3,282	4,337
Sales from refineries		307	997
Sales from terminals		0	169
Sales from company operated bulk plants		1,793	1,110
Sales through commission truck drivers		N.A.	433
Sales through commission distributors		N.A.	1,628
Gasoline sales by type customer: total		3,282	4,337
To wholesale resellers		1,489	2,139
Brokers, refiners, cargo sales, export		307	141
Unbranded jobbers		565	662
Branded jobbers		428	678
Tank wagon buyers (peddlers)		189	658
To retail resellers		1,300	1,491
Contract stations		442	310
Dealer operated stations		858	1,181
To final consumers		493	707
Company operated stations		84	36
Industrial, household, and others		409	671

4. THE OHIO OIL COMPANY (A)

Production and Marketing Data, 1937-1950

	1937	1938	1939	1940	1941	1942	1943	1944	1945	1946	1947
Production											
Wells Drilled during Year:											
Oil	233	190	182	212	209	196	117	178	122	90	177
Gas	15	8	5	7	23	5	11	13	16	7	3
Dry Holes	28	18	9	17	39	52	57	57	35	34	41
Exploratory Wells Only:											
Oil							6	8	3	4	5
Gas							1	2	2	2	2
Dry Holes							34	36	24	23	24
Number of Marketing Outlets:											
Wholesale Outlets:		289	283	250	224	228	235	241	275	288	314
Company operated terminals	183	185	182	158	106	94	78	78	88	99	122
Commission distributors	23	24	22	26	27	24	32	28	34	42	29
Branded jobbers		35	40	20	45	43	44	51	62	52	68
Unbranded jobbers		45	39	46	46	67	81	84	91	95	95
Service Stations:	3,066	3,461	3,587	3,122	2,302	1,955	1,334	1,327	1,443	1,749	1,752
Company operated stations	16	15	28	41	62	89	60	11	10	9	5
Dealer operated stations	939	947	1,058	962	729	485	443	485	542	622	653
Contractor stations	2,111	2,499	2,501	2,119	1,511	1,381	831	831	891	1,118	1,094
Monthly Gasoline Sales Volume:											
Wholesale Outlets: (thousand gals.)				54.2						51.6	
Company operated terminals				39.7						45.2	
Commission distributors				146.5						135.7	
Branded jobbers		37.5	45.6	74.8	33.6	33.2	32.0	29.5	33.0	45.7	42.8
Unbranded jobbers		26.5	41.1	43.0	42.2	32.4	24.7	25.6	27.2	24.4	21.5
Service Stations: (thousand gals.)					2.3	2.2	2.5	2.4	2.6	3.1	3.6
Company operated stations					5.2	4.5	6.0	20.5	9.7	14.0	17.5
Dealer operated stations					4.5	5.2	4.5	4.3	4.9	6.6	7.4
Contractor stations					1.1	1.0	1.2	1.0	1.1	1.0	1.2

5. THE OHIO OIL COMPANY (A)

Robinson Refinery Process after Modernization

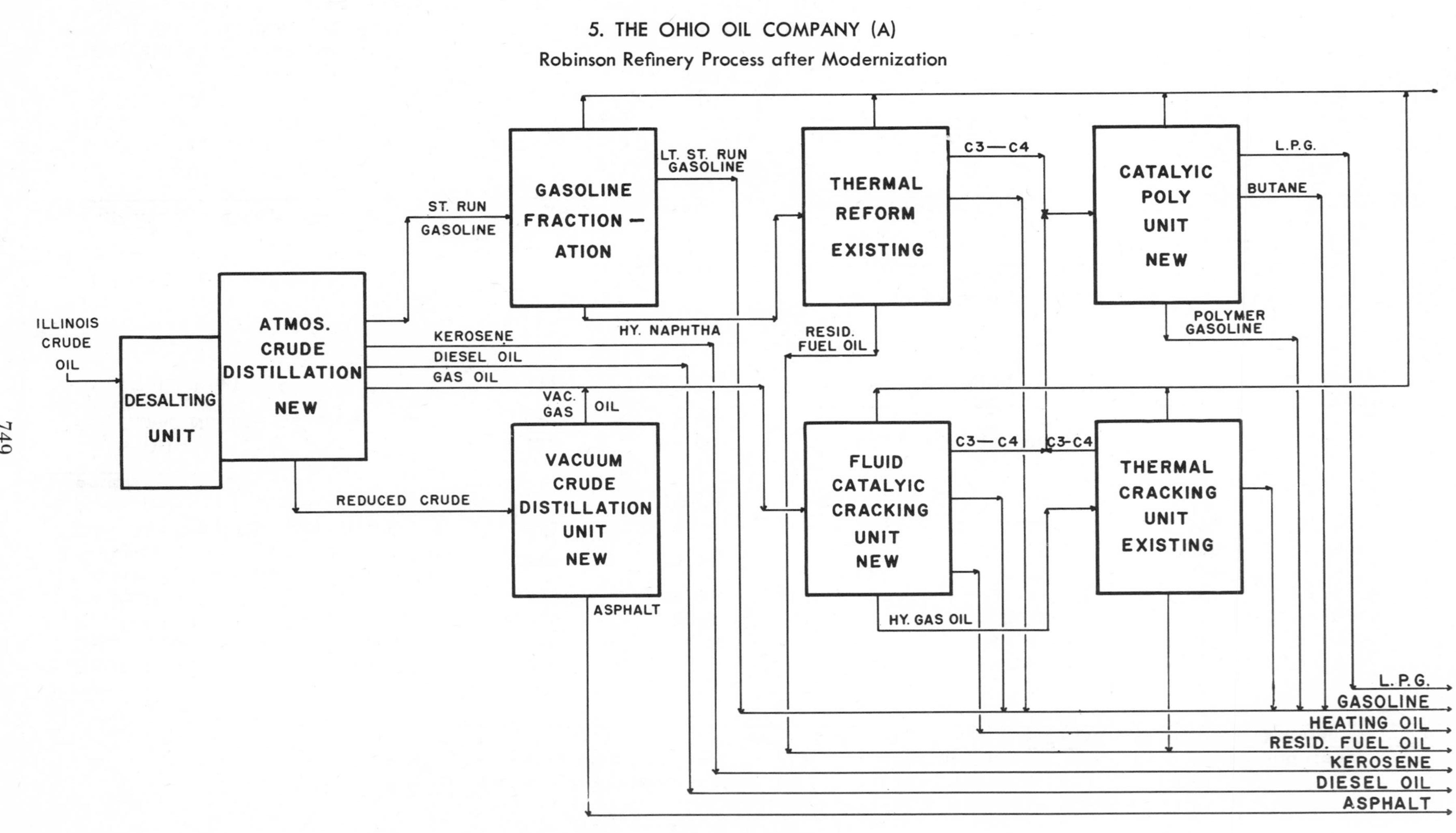

6. THE OHIO OIL COMPANY (A)

Product Yields and Octane Quality

	Actual Experience - 1945 Robinson Refinery		Present Case		Proposed Case	
	B.P.S.D.*	Volume % Crude	B.P.S.D.*	Volume % Crude	B.P.S.D.*	Volume % Crude
Product Yields						
Premium Gasoline (79 octane)	2,275	14.11	1,330	8.31	3,530	12.84
Housebrand Gasoline (74 octane)	6,648	41.22	7,110	44.43	18,986	69.04
Kerosene	1,206	7.48	1,320	8.25	2,270	8.26
Fuel Oil	4,520**	28.03	3,480	21.75	2,905	10.56
Naphtha Cutback Asphalt) Kerosene Cutback Asphalt)	1,684	10.44	920	5.75	1,575	5.73
			920	5.75	1,575	5.73
Fuel Gas (Fuel Oil Equivalent)	531	3.29	1,200	7.50	1,575	5.73
Import						
Crude Oil Run	16,128	100.00	16,000	100.00	27,500	100.00
Purchased Natural Gasoline	649	4.02			4,300	15.64
Total Fuel	16,777	104.02	16,000	100.00	31,800	115.64

Tetraethyl Lead Required (C.C. Per Gallon)

Octane Number (Motor Method)	Actual Experience	Present Case	Proposed Case No Reforming	Proposed Case With Reforming ‡
76	1.55	1.2	1.2	
78	2.1	1.9	1.7	
80	2.9	2.9	2.4	0.6
86	could not make	could not make	could not make	3.0

*Barrels per Stream Day.
**Distillate Fuel Oil, 1,527 B.P.S.D. and Heavy Fuel Oil, 2,993 B.P.S.D.
‡Naphtha reforming process conducted in two Holmes-Manley units from the present refinery.

7. THE OHIO OIL COMPANY (A)

Octane Numbers and Prices Assumed for Five-Year Period

	July 1, 1946 to Dec. 31, 1947	Jan. 1, 1948 to Dec. 31, 1948	Jan. 1, 1949 to June 30, 1951
Number of Years	1.5	1.0	2.5
Octane Numbers			
Regular Gasoline	76	78	80
Premium Gasoline	81	83	85
Prices (f.o.b. Group 3)			
Premium Motor Gasoline (Gal.)	$0.0700	$0.0785	$0.0800
Regular Motor Gasoline (Gal.)	0.0525	0.0610	0.0625
Kerosene (Gal.)	0.0425	0.0450	0.0475
Fuel Oil (Bbl.)	0.82	0.87	0.90
Asphalt (Gal.)	0.0550	0.0500	0.0450
Crude Oil (Bbl.)	1.31	1.44	1.44
Natural Gasoline (Gal.)	0.0475	0.056	0.0575

Sales of Refined Products in 1945

	Barrels	Per Cent Total Sales
Premium Gasoline	928,835	14.90%
Housebrand Gasoline	2,717,201	43.58
Kerosene	476,567	7.64
Fuel Oil*	1,380,016	22.13
Asphalt**	552,509	8.86
Fuel Gas (Fuel Oil Equivalent)***	180,382	2.89
Other Products		
	6,235,510	100.00%

*Distillate fuel oil 288,722 barrels and heavy fuel oil 1,091,294 barrels
**Asphalt 367,176 barrels and cutback asphalt 185,333 barrels
***Burned as Refinery Fuel.

8. THE OHIO OIL COMPANY (A)

Economic Analysis at 76 Octane Level (Regular or Housebrand)

Crude charge		Present Case (14,546 BPCD*)			Proposed Case (25,000 BPCD*)		
Sales Realizations		BPCD	Vol. % on Crude	Dollars	BPCD	Vol. % on Crude	Dollars
Premium motor gasoline	$0.0700/gal.	1,209	8.31	3,554	3,209	12.84	9,434
Housebrand motor gasoline	0.0525/gal.	6,464	44.43	14,253	17,260	69.04	38,058
Kerosene	0.0425/gal.	1,200	8.25	2.142	2,064	8.26	3,684
Fuel oil	0.8200/bbl.	3,164	21.75	2,594	2,641	10.56	2,166
Naphtha cutback asphalt	0.0550/gal.	836	5.75	1,931	1,432	5.73	3,308
Kerosene cutback asphalt	0.0550/gal.	836	5.75	1,931	1,432	5.73	3,308
Fuel gas (fuel oil equiv.)	0.8200/bbl.	1,091	7.50	895	1,432	5.73	1,174
		14,800	101.74	27,300	29,470	117.89	61,132
Stock cost							
Crude	1.31/bbl.	14,546	100.00	19,055	25,000	100.00	32,750
Casinghead	0.0475/gal.	-	-	-	3,909	15.64	7,798
Direct operating cost							
Crude desalting		14,546	-	59	25,000	-	101
Crude topping		14,546	-	559	25,000	-	578
Vacuum flashing		3,509	-	162	7,760	-	267
Asphalt processing		1,450	-	116	2,500	-	92
Fluid catalyst cracking		-	-	-	12,523	-	1,379
Cat. Crkg. Recovery		-	-	-	-	-	311
Thermal reforming and recov.		2,882	-	261	-	-	-
Thermal cracking and recov.		7,050	-	1,072	5,215	-	797
Catalytic polymerization		356	-	155	1,318	-	510
Ethylizing premium gasoline		1,209	-	75	3,209	-	212
Ethylizing regular gasoline		6,464	-	593	17,260	-	1,573
Gasoline finishing		7,673	-	192	20,469	-	512
Direct operating maintenance		-	-	328	-	-	721
Refinery overhead		14,546	-	1,091	25,000	-	1,250
Subtotal costs (ex-royalties, taxes, ins. and dep.)				23,718			48,851
Running Royalties							
Fluid catalyst cracking at 5¢/bbl. fresh feed		-	-	-	12,523		626
Catalytic polymerization at 0.5¢/gal.		356	-	75	1,318		277
Taxes and insurance at 2% of investment				219			603
Total costs as above (ex-depreciation)				$24,012			$50,357
Sales realization less costs/calendar day - as above				3,288			10,775
Net operating profit/calendar year				$1,200,120			$3,932,875

*Barrels per Calendar Day.

Wood River Oil and Refining Company, Inc.

The Wood River Oil and Refining Company, Inc., was organized in January, 1940, primarily for the purpose of constructing and operating a refinery near St. Louis. In June, 1950, the company was engaged in the refining of crude oil, the sale of refined products, and, to a much lesser degree, in the production of crude petroleum. The Rock Island Oil and Refining Company, Inc., a subsidiary acquired in 1946, gathered and transported crude oil by pipeline mainly for use at the refinery.

In June, 1950, the management of Wood River Oil and Refining Company received an offer from the Sinclair Oil Company of $15,500,000 for the refinery at Hartford, Illinois, a small products pipeline in Illinois, and two refined products terminals. Mr. Fred Koch, president of the Wood River Oil and Refining Company, and the other owners were evaluating this proposition in terms of the company's operating history, the future outlook for the company and the industry, and the personal desires of the individual owners.

FOUNDING AND EARLY HISTORY

In 1940, Mr. O. H. Ingram, a graduate of the University of Pennsylvania, decided that he would like to enter the refining business. He was president of the Ingram Products Company which was engaged in certain operations in the textile industry. Mr. Ingram was quite wealthy, having extensive investments in lumber, and textile industries. He was the grandson of a self-made lumberman who had accumulated the family fortune.

Mr. Ingram approached the First National Bank of St. Paul for advice on the project and to obtain funds to finance it. The officers of the bank knew very little about the refining industry, and therefore sought the advice of Mr. I. O'Shaughnessy who had had considerable experience in the petroleum industry. Mr. O'Shaughnessy was president of the Globe Oil and Refining Company which had a shutdown refinery in Blackwell, Oklahoma, as well as large operating refineries at Lemont, Illinois, and McPherson, Kansas. Mr. O'Shaughnessy was convinced that the St. Louis area, readily accessible to river and pipeline transportation, would be an excellent site for a refinery, and he expressed a willingness to become a partner in the venture. Mr. O'Shaughnessy contacted Mr. Fred Koch, a refinery engineer who had always wanted to enter the refining industry but who had never had access to the required capital.

Mr. Koch, a graduate of M.I.T. in chemical engineering, was president of the Winkler-Koch Engineering Company and the Koch Engineering Company, Inc. These were firms of refinery consulting engineers, which had designed and constructed refinery improvements as well as complete refineries in the United States, Europe, and Asia.

The company was incorporated under the laws of the state of Kansas on January 10, 1940, with an authorized capital of $15,000, consisting of 15,000 shares of common stock, $1 par value. The 15,000 shares of common stock were owned roughly as follows:

Mr. O'Shaughnessy	5,000 shares
Mr. Ingram	5,000 shares
Mr. Koch	3,750 to 5,000 shares
Others	0 to 1,250 shares

A bank loan of $1,000,000 and personal notes of the owners aggregating $1,000,000 were relied upon to finance the construction of the new refinery. Mr. Ingram was instrumental in having Mr. Phillip R. Ray, president and chairman of the executive committee of the First Trust Company of St. Paul, placed on the board of directors to render financial advice. Mr. Ray purchased 65 shares of stock for $65. In addition Mr. Ray had an option to purchase 435 additional shares at an undisclosed price, presumably $1 per share.

Construction of a crude oil refinery at Hartford, Illinois, was begun immediately and the refinery was completed in May, 1941, at a cost of approximately $2,000,000. The initial capacity of the plant was approximately 13,000 barrels per day.

The Hartford refinery was designed and constructed by the Winkler-Koch Engineering Company. The engineering fee charged by the Winkler-Koch Engineering Company amounted to only $50,000; the usual fee for such services was 12 to 25 percent of the cost of the refinery.

Operations were difficult during the war period. The crude oil was high priced and of an undesirable quality. Furthermore, product prices were pegged by the government at low figures and excess profits taxes cut deeply into profits which were available. During this period the company was limited to 12,700 barrels per day of crude runs. In 1944 Mr. Koch and Mr. Ingram bought out Mr. O'Shaughnessy's interest in the company.

Immediately after Mr. O'Shaughnessy left the company, the refinery was equipped to run sour or high sulfur crude oil. At that time, the government was making up the crude deficiencies of refineries by shipments of West Texas sour crude. The crude was shipped by tank cars and the government compensated the refiners for the differential in the transportation rate between actual tank car costs and published pipeline tariffs.

On September 16, 1946, a new subsidiary, the Rock Island Oil and Refining Company, Inc., was organized to purchase the 8,000-barrel per day refinery and inventory of the Rock Island Refining Company and also a part of the pipeline gathering system of the Rock Island Oil Company, Inc. These properties were located in and around Duncan, Oklahoma. The Rock Island Oil Company started its crude oil gathering system in 1921. It extended its operations substantially in the early 1930's by purchasing a large portion of the gathering facilities of the Carter Oil Company in the Oklahoma area. At that time the heavy southern Oklahoma crude was often a drug on the market because it yielded very large quantities of heavy fuel oil. When the famous East Texas oil field was discovered, Carter sold its facilities in the southern Oklahoma area at reasonable prices and shifted its attention to the new producing area.

The two Rock Island companies, which had a common management, had been quite successful operations over the years. However, the management believed that the lives of the two companies would be limited unless it built a catalytic cracker and a products pipeline. The Rock Island Refining Company had been shipping to market by tank cars, but competition from the Great Lakes pipeline and river transportation was very severe. Mr. Simmons, owner of the Rock Island properties, sold the refinery and the pipeline gathering system to Wood River and indirectly acquired a 10 percent interest in the latter company. With the purchase of the Rock Island facilities, Wood River expanded its capital structure to 16,667 shares of common stock with a par value of $1 per share. These shares were held by the various owners, roughly as follows:

Mr. Ingram	6,750 shares
Mr. Koch	6,750 shares
Mr. Simmons of Rock Island	1,667 shares
Others	1,500 shares

The management of the Wood River Oil and Refining Company was primarily interested in the gathering system and it originally intended to shut down the Rock Island refinery. However, refinery operations were very profitable in the latter part of 1946.

In 1946, Mr. Ray exercised his option to purchase 435 shares of stock from Mr. Ingram. Mr. Ray was then instrumental in having the company's capital structure reorganized. He argued that it looked strange to have such a large company with a common stock capitalization of only $15,000. Furthermore, he asserted that a stock split would make the company's shares more marketable. On December 19, 1947, the common stock was split on a 30-for-one basis; 500,000 shares were issued in exchange for the 16,667 shares then outstanding. The authorized capital was increased to $3,000,000 consisting of 1,500,000 shares of stock with a stated value of $2 per share. After the stock split, the shares were distributed as follows:

Mr. Ingram	202,500 shares
Mr. Koch	202,500 shares
Mr. Simmons	50,000 shares
Others	45,000 shares

CRUDE OIL SUPPLY

One of the most important problems that confronted the Wood River management throughout the history of the company was that of securing an assured source of crude oil. At the outset the Globe Oil and Refining Company arranged for crude supplies. During the war period government allocations of crude oil resulted in a continuous crude supply of 14,700 barrels per day. Neither of these sources was available in the postwar period.

Mr. Koch stated that contracts with big companies for crude supplies were not too desirable, because if they refused to renew a contract a refiner was out of business. Nevertheless, after the war Wood River contracted with the Zenith

Pipe Line Company[1] for a sizable proportion of its crude requirements. The contract called for the delivery of West Texas and Wyoming crudes, both of which were sour crudes. The company received 11,000 barrels of crude oil per day under this contract. The crude oil was delivered to the Hartford refinery at a total cost that included the posted field price on the date of delivery, plus the published pipeline rates for gathering and transportation, plus 0.5 percent pipeline tender deduction, plus 1.5¢ per barrel marketing charge. The contract had an expiration date of December 31, 1949.

The purchase of the Rock Island properties did much to alleviate the crude supply problem, and this was, in fact, one of the major objectives of the purchase. In September, 1946, Rock Island was gathering approximately 9,000 barrels per day of crude oil from producers connected to its gathering system. Three thousand barrels per day of this total were later lost to the Skelly Oil Company when Skelly built its own gathering system into the area served by the Rock Island system. However, the fact that some very important fields came in on Rock Island's gathering system more than offset the loss of crude oil to the Skelly Oil Company. By 1948, approximately 17,000 barrels of crude oil per day were being gathered in the entire system. Of this amount 14,500 barrels were supplied to the Rock Island refinery at Duncan, Oklahoma, and the Wood River refinery at Hartford, Illinois. The Rock Island refinery ran about 8,000 barrels per day in 1948 and 1949, and its entire requirements were supplied by the gathering system.

In the latter part of 1948 Wood River purchased a one-half interest in a West Texas gathering system. The company had intended to connect this line into the Zenith trunk lines and to pipe crude direct from the field to the refinery at Hartford. When Mr. Koch approached the Zenith management, however, he met with little cooperation. Wood River had no alternative but to sell the pipeline to Zenith. Zenith later agreed to give Wood River more West Texas and Wyoming crude. During the refiners' crisis in 1949, Zenith did not make Wood River adhere to its firm purchase contract, but merely agreed to let the company take what oil it could.

[1] Pipeline subsidiary of a major oil company. Fictitious name used for purposes of disguise.

In 1947 and 1948, when the Wood River Oil and Refining Company was enjoying extremely profitable operations, the management felt it should enter more heavily into the producing business as a means of finding a long-run solution to the crude supply problem. The company spent much of its earnings searching for producing properties and drilling for oil (see Exhibit 2). "The law of probability finally paid off in West Texas in 1949 with some production."

The location of the refinery at Hartford made available the facilities of six common carrier pipelines, Stanolind, Magnolia, Ajax, Sinclair, Sohio, and Shell, and also gave the company access to crude via excellent river and rail transportation routes. The company could obtain crude oil from almost any point in Illinois, Louisiana, Texas, Oklahoma, Kansas, New Mexico, and Wyoming by pipeline.

REFINING

Refining and overhead expenses for the Wood River refinery are shown in Exhibit 7. The average selling price and the yield of products for the Wood River refinery is shown in Exhibit 8. During the war the Wood River refinery had a rated capacity of 15,000 barrels per day. Total expenditures on this refinery for plant and equipment from the end of 1941 to the end of 1944 were $400,000. During the war period octane ratings for gasoline products were specified by the government, and Wood River had no problem in meeting the specifications. In the period 1948 to 1950 the topping capacity of the refinery was increased from 20,000 to 30,000 barrels per day. Expenditures for this expansion were $494,981 in 1948, $473,455 in 1949, and $25,940 in 1950, a total of $994,376 to accomplish the enlargement.

After the war the management felt insecure about the company's refining facilities because the equipment was inadequate to permit the company to keep abreast of competition in the "octane race." In 1946, however, the company could not afford a fluid catalytic cracking unit, capable of handling 6,000 to 7,000 barrels per day of gas oil, which would have been necessary to enable it to keep pace with its competitors. In an effort to increase the quality of its output, the company installed in 1947 and 1948, a

Phillips' cycloversion unit with a charging capacity of 4,000 barrels per day of gas oil at a cost of $1,546,377. Expenditures by years for this unit were: 1947, $1,025,751; 1948, $502,723; 1949, $17,903. The cycloversion unit was designed to perform one or more of several functions; to desulfurize straight-run gasoline, to reform straight-run gasoline, or to crack gas oil.

The Phillips' cycloversion process was less efficient than fluid catalytic cracking and did not produce gasolines of comparable octane ratings. In an effort to rectify these disadvantages, the management decided in the latter part of 1948 to install a 7,500-barrel per day fluid catalytic cracking and vacuum distillation unit. Construction was started immediately and the unit went on steam during February, 1950. The total capital expenditure for the unit was $2,352,519; $85,903 of this amount was spent in 1948, $2,088,766 in 1949, and $177,850 in 1950. The new unit had a guaranteed capacity of 6,000 barrels per day, but the company rated its capacity at 7,500 barrels per day and actually charged 10,000 barrels per day during most of the 1950 operating period.

The company had storage capacity at the refinery for 200,000 barrels of crude oil. The total investment in storage facilities was about $300,000 in December, 1944. By June, 1950, an additional $572,160 had been expended for tankage facilities. In 1949 and 1950, the refinery ran three types of crude oil, southern Oklahoma, Wyoming, and West Texas. The refinery ran up to four consecutive days on each of the three types. Since only four crude storage tanks were available, the refinery schedule was quite inflexible and the length of runs was strictly limited. The length of run on any particular crude was determined primarily by the availability of space in the pipelines from which deliveries were taken. Mr. Read, refinery superintendent, pointed out that while more tankage would have permitted longer runs, it would also have required a larger investment in inventory. Moreover, irregularities in the refinery schedule would still have resulted after the tanks were once filled from the necessity of receiving particular grades of crude at the time they happened to move through the common carrier pipelines. The company's storage facilities for products were also considered inadequate since they did not permit a satisfactory build up of stocks of gasoline or fuel oil to offset the seasonal variations in the demand for these products.

MARKETING ACTIVITIES

The total sales volume of principal products for the period 1941 to May, 1950, is shown in Exhibit 9. As noted previously, when the company was formed in 1940 it took over some of the marketing accounts of the Globe Oil and Refining Company. During the war the company's throughput was restricted by governmental regulation, and product output was allocated to customers at a stipulated scale of prices. In the postwar period, sales by the company were made primarily in the areas surrounding St. Paul, Minnesota; Duncan, Oklahoma; St. Louis, Missouri; and Rockford, Illinois. Sales were also made at eight or nine northern points along the Great Lakes pipeline system.

In 1946 and 1947, the company constructed a 30,000 barrels per day 8-inch products pipeline to service the Rockford market. Products were moved from Hartford to Peru by barge transportation. It was hoped by the management that this products pipeline would permit the company to move products to the Rockford terminal at competitive transportation costs and to develop a substantial market in that area. At a later date, the management planned to extend the pipeline to Madison, Wisconsin, and a right of way was secured for this purpose. Sales in the Rockford area, however, proved disappointing to the management; although burning oil sales were excellent, gasoline sales were very poor. The management attributed the failure of the project to the difficulties involved in getting satisfactory market outlets for gasoline. Total expenditures for the pipeline from 1946 through June, 1950, were $1,878,116.

The St. Louis area was serviced from the Hartford refinery primarily by railroad tank cars and by trucks, although some products were moved by barge. The Duncan area was supplied from the Rock Island refinery as long as it was in operation. After this refinery was shut down in 1949, products were transported to the area from the Hartford refinery.

In the period following World War II, the company sold its products to two large customers and to numerous jobbers. The jobbers, with anywhere from a single station to a chain of 15 to 20 stations, were partially or wholly supplied by the company. The two large customers which accounted for the bulk of the sales volume were the Illinois Farm Bureau and the Mid-Continent Petroleum Corporation. The company sold to these customers at a price somewhat under the low of the *Chicago Journal of Commerce* quoted prices until the shortage of products developed in 1948 at which time the low of the market was charged. Mr. Koch believed that Mid-Continent bought from Wood River for two reasons. First, he believed the management wanted to concentrate on the refining and sale of lube oil but recognized that it was necessary to build up gasoline sales to increase lube oil sales. The Mid-Continent Petroleum Company had insufficient refining capacity and could not accomplish its objectives in the lube oil market without an outside source of supply for gasoline. Second, he believed the management wanted to keep its own refinery output slightly smaller than its sales volume in order to assure capacity operations in times of slack demand.

During 1947 and 1948, petroleum products were in short supply. Therefore, some major companies encouraged distributors to buy Wood River products as a means of augmenting their supplies. The Wood River Oil and Refining Company, itself, purchased a negligible amount of refined products for resale to its accounts. These purchases were largely restricted to those products not refined by the company and were made for the purpose of rounding out the product line.

In the latter part of 1948, market conditions changed drastically and the Wood River Oil and Refining Company was faced with the most pressing problems in its history. In the early part of 1948, the price of fuel oil advanced to a high of $2.50 per barrel. In the latter part of 1948, the bubble burst and fuel oil prices fell throughout the winter to a low of 60 cents per barrel. A very mild winter contributed to this decline. The whole industry was depressed, and there was an oversupply of crude oil, gasoline, and fuel oils. The company's storage tanks at Hartford were filled to capacity with Bunker C fuel oil that could not be moved.

Another factor which influenced the market adversely during this period was the necessity for refiners to sell the low-quality gasoline resulting from recycling operations. Major companies with a large quantity, say 15,000 barrels per day, of recycled gasoline frequently found it necessary to sell part of their output to brokers, who, in turn, sold at cut-rate prices to jobbers. Such sales tended to depress the prices of regular and premium gasolines.

In the latter part of 1948, the Mid-Continent Petroleum Corporation stopped purchasing from Wood River. Mid-Continent had installed a fluid catalytic cracking unit during 1948, and the company was able to supply all the gasoline it needed. At about the same time, the Illinois Farm Bureau also ceased purchasing from Wood River. "We charged them the quoted low for products during the period of shortage in 1947 and 1948," said Mr. Koch. "They felt that they were entitled to a discount off the low price." To supply its needs, the Illinois Farm Bureau purchased a small refinery of its own.

Meanwhile, the distributors of the major companies who had been encouraged to buy from Wood River during the period of shortage, were now called upon to purchase exclusively from the majors. Finally, Wood River's independent jobbers, whom the company had protected during the shortage by supplying them with products without exacting premiums, took their business to other suppliers as soon as they were offered a differential of as little as one-eight of a cent per gallon in price.

After losing its two largest accounts in the latter part of 1948, the company became interested in sales promotion. In 1949, Mr. John Chandler was brought in as advertising manager. Under his leadership a very effective jobber program was initiated. The company designed a trademark and began selling under the Wood River brand name. Numerous cards, pamphlets, and other units of a "sales package" were developed to describe the Wood River sales program to independent jobbers. Mr. Bumgarner, treasurer and secretary of the company, claimed that if the company had started the jobber program before the bottom dropped out of the products market, it would have been much more effective in maintaining its sales volume.

As a further attempt to introduce stability into its marketing activities, the company organized a wholly owned subsidiary to build two company-owned and -operated service stations in the Chicago area in 1949.

PROBLEMS IN 1950

In early 1950, the Wood River owners were considering the capital requirements that they believed would be necessary to place the firm in a sound competitive position for the long run. Securing an adequate supply of crude oil was expected to present continuing financial and operating difficulties. As the postwar history of the company indicated, the development of company-owned crude production involved a considerable element of risk and high capital expenditures.

With the completion of the fluid catalytic cracker in February, 1950, refinery facilities were capable of meeting qualitative standards in the industry. Storage tank facilities at the refinery, however, were considered inadequate. Additional tankage could have been secured at a cost of about $1 per barrel of storage capacity; the increased crude and product inventories, however, would have required a large capital investment.

It was believed that a further requisite for successful operations was assured marketing outlets. It was the consensus of the management group that to get stability of operations 50 percent of the refinery's gasoline output should pass through company-owned and -operated service stations. The management calculated that company-owned and -operated service stations would need a volume of 100,000 gallons a month to operate on a profitable scale. Modern stations of the type contemplated were estimated to cost a total of $65,000 each, $50,000 for buildings and equipment, and $15,000 for land. To market one-half of the refinery gasoline output of 450,000 barrels per month through such stations would have required a total capital expenditure of $6,500,000. The management also believed that the company needed additional products terminals. Prospective sites for new terminals in Chicago and Cincinnati were being considered. These products terminals were expected to cost from $300,000 to $700,000 each.

Mr. Ingram never participated actively in the management of the company. He was extremely interested in water transportation and his interest grew deeper as time progressed. Mr. Ingram was much discouraged by the unprofitable operations in 1949 and was strongly of the opinion that he should not put any additional funds into the company. Mr. Ray, who counseled Mr. Ingram on financial affairs and served on the Wood River board of directors, was 60 years of age in 1950. He owned 15,000 shares of common stock and was most anxious to convert his holdings into liquid assets.

Both Mr. Koch and Mr. Ingram recognized the difficult inheritance tax problem that would arise if one of them should die. Neither could have settled his estate without a forced sale to get the funds necessary to pay the inheritance taxes. Donating the stock to a charitable trust with the owners' heirs named as salaried executors was considered as one possible alternative. Summing up the company's financial status, Mr. Koch said, "during the periods of prosperity substantially all the earnings and continually increasing bank loans were used to get more and more iron and steel. It appears likely that future earnings will have to be used for the same purpose."

During the period of unprofitable operations in 1949, negotiations with the Sinclair Oil Company for the sale of the Wood River refinery were initiated. In November, 1949, the possibility of selling the Wood River refinery and some additional facilities to the Sinclair Oil Company was discussed at a meeting of the board of directors of the Wood River Oil and Refining Company, and the treasurer was asked to prepare pertinent financial and operating data as a basis for negotiations. Earnest negotiations between officials of the two companies commenced in January, 1950. Mr. Koch argued that the products pipeline from Peru to Rockford and the products terminals at these two points should be included with the refinery in any possible deal. If refinery activities at Hartford were discontinued by the Wood River Oil and Refining Company, these additional properties were expected to be of little value to the company. The management of the Sinclair Oil Company was originally interested solely in the refinery properties.

An annual report of the Sinclair Oil Corporation stated in 1950: "Sinclair has been established in the St. Louis distribution area for many years and has a large investment in marketing facilities. . . ." Since the Sinclair company had crude production in the Wyoming area and a crude pipeline into St. Louis, there was a good possibility that it could supply the Wood River refinery with its own crude oil. The Sinclair company had a well-organized distribution system in the Midwest and a well-known brand name, but no refinery between East Chicago and Houston. A map of the Sinclair operations is contained in Exhibit 6.

In June, 1950, the Sinclair Oil Company made a bona fide offer of $15,500,000 for the Wood River refinery at Hartford, the products pipeline extending from Peru to Rockford, and the products terminals at the end points of the line.

1. WOOD RIVER OIL AND REFINING COMPANY, INC.
Balance Sheets
December, 1945 to May 31, 1950

ASSETS	1945	1946	1947	1948	1949	May 31, 1950
Cash	$ 382,092	$ 583,162	$ 832,461	$ 131,593	$ 1,319,318	$ 1,620,846
Notes Receivable	-	-	-	3,000	115,840	79,402
U.S. Gov. Notes	13,637	10,600	-			
Accounts Receivable (Net)	241,993	668,250	2,226,215	2,188,705	2,685,119	3,061,657
Due on Exchange Agreement	244,194	190,541	569,451	1,266,377	135,686	145,283
Due from Assoc. Companies	155,514	173,892	185,541	116,893	68	68,642
Inventories:						
Crude Oil	245,396	161,401	401,160	543,052	276,737	564,265
Refined Products	507,194	536,007	1,614,671	2,907,099	2,448,296	2,468,875
Chemicals	23,844	43,855	54,178	72,683	72,811	82,381
Warehouse Materials	293,720	349,178	565,537	1,021,183	845,801	853,339
In Transit - Crude Oil	418,602	302,541	60,324	13,423	18,616	16,524
Inter. Inventory Profit	-	-	(114,254)	(106,410)	-	102,067
Total Current Assets	$ 2,526,186	$3,019,427	$ 6,395,284	$ 8,157,598	$ 7,918,292	$ 9,063,281
Investments:						
Receivable from Subsid.	81,575	1,255,480	1,169,985	1,255,000	757,325	255,675
Common Stock of Subsid.	7,425	15,000	15,000	120,000	120,000	120,000
Life Insurance Policies	-	-	2,292	10,954	17,939	17,939
Other	-	-	-	5,025	30,643	31,590
Plant, Property, and Equipment						
Refinery Plant and Equipment	2,786,839	3,431,537	5,169,389	6,999,973	9,884,051	10,177,863
Products Pipe Line Property		955,226	1,708,720	1,791,675	1,860,516	1,862,814
Crude Production Property	208,304	207,827	553,008	2,662,346	2,830,156	2,632,158
Crude Pipe Line Property					645	777
Less: Deprec. and Depletion	(1,099,775)	(1,388,274)	(1,788,969)	(2,724,110)	(3,765,195)	(4,228,263)
Prepaid and Deferred	120,482	117,782	108,511	396,823	240,696	236,235
Total Assets	$ 4,631,036	$7,614,005	$13,333,220	$18,675,284	$19,895,068	$20,170,069

LIABILITIES AND CAPITAL	1945	1946	1947	1948	1949	May 31, 1950
Notes Payable to Banks	-	-	-	$ 1,000,000	-	
Accounts Payable	$ 795,137	$ 964,900	$ 2,355,261	2,289,594	$ 2,188,649	$ 2,548,616
Due on Exchange Agreements	182,905	505,050	48,291	143,613	266,190	252,812
Due Subsidiary	-	170,784	499,070	1,149,482	1,792,574	1,858,758
Accrued Expenses	54,537	89,589	101,355	143,743	154,097	145,438
Provision for Taxes	333,341	505,271	1,665,692	1,488,656	199,292	373,669
Current Mortgage Note	114,583	230,417	449,000	468,000	1,300,000	1,300,000
Current Purch. Obligation	6,834	6,834	6,834	11,452	11,453	11,453
Total Current Liabilities	$ 1,487,337	$2,472,845	$ 5,125,503	$ 6,694,540	$ 5,912,255	$ 6,490,746
Long-Term Debt:						
First Mortgage 3 1/2% Notes	829,167	1,898,750	2,831,000	2,363,000	4,550,000	4,008,333
Notes Payable to Stockholders	1,105,000	1,260,649	1,260,649	1,260,649	1,260,649	1,260,649
Property Purchase Obligation	54,672	47,838	41,004	71,117	59,665	52,831
Reserve for Obsolescence	500,000	500,000	-	1,250,000	1,250,000	1,250,000
Capital Stock and Surplus						
Common Stock	15,000	16,667	1,000,000	1,004,000	1,005,000	1,004,200
Earned Surplus	639,860	1,243,066	3,075,064	6,015,978	5,837,499	6,089,318
Paid-In Surplus	-	174,190	-	16,000	20,000	13,792
Total Stock and Surplus	$ 4,631,036	$7,614,005	$13,333,220	$18,675,284	$19,895,068	$20,170,069

2. WOOD RIVER OIL AND REFINING COMPANY, INC.

Income Statements
1945 to May 31, 1950

	1945	1946	1947	1948	1949	5 Mos. to May 31, 1950
Barrels of Products Sold	3,635,395	4,960,159	6,732,278	8,640,602	5,929,452	2,524,076
Gross Operating Income:						
Sales of Refined Products	$ 8,362,911	$11,625,503	$22,977,405	$38,738,144	$22,334,428	$ 9,815,939
Processing Fees	404,178	65,529				268,230
Barge Loading Fees			20,867	2,780	7,754	514
Terminal Fees (Net)			10,372	29,487	20,835	12,702
Barge Revenue (Net)			(8,927)	1,109	(82)	2,269
Pipe Line Revenue			1,076	2,885	2,095	1,319
Miscellaneous (Net)			428	1,005	22,958	8,919
Gross Operating Income	$ 8,767,089	$11,691,032	$23,001,221	$38,775,410	$22,387,988	$10,109,892
Cost of Sales	7,361,295	10,237,190	17,914,676	31,299,060	22,242,549	9,136,204
Gross Profit from Sales	$ 1,405,794	$ 1,453,842	$ 5,086,545	$ 7,476,350	$ 145,439	$ 973,688
Admin. Tank Car. and Selling	318,163	354,467	549,069	650,629	750,542	342,071
Net Profit	$ 1,087,631	$ 1,099,375	$ 4,537,476	$ 6,825,721	$ (605,103)	$ 631,617
Other Income:						
Unloading Charges	72,249	17,723				
Interest Earned	7,907	3,111	624	945	6,684	1,628
Net Profit of Crude Production		149,862	45,399		678,153	45,809
Miscellaneous	15,312	1,845	1,985	19,640	957	1,046
Gross Income	$ 1,183,099	$ 1,271,916	$ 4,585,484	$ 6,846,306	$ 80,691	$ 680,100
Income Charges:						
Net Loss of Crude Production	$ 561,378			$ 1,030,883		
Net Loss of Barge Transpor.	102,733					
Provision for Doubtful Accounts	21,019	$ 29,257	$ 23,498	35,991	$ 25,095	
Provision for Obsolescence				1,250,000		
Interdepartmental Inventory Profit			114,254	(7,844)		$ 102,067
Interest Expense	103,161	116,880	192,601	187,146	293,998	127,507
Other	103,642	187,942	195,475	263,610	67,487	7,923
Total Income Charges	$ 891,933	$ 334,079	$ 525,828	$ 2,759,786	$ 386,580	$ 237,497
Net Income (Loss) before Taxes	$ 291,166	$ 937,837	$ 4,059,656	$ 4,086,520	$ (305,889)	$ 442,603
Federal and State Income Taxes	209,343	330,538	1,482,855	1,305,817	12,924	190,831
Net Income	$ 81,823	$ 607,299	$ 2,576,801	$ 2,780,703	$ (318,813)	$ 251,772

3. WOOD RIVER OIL AND REFINING COMPANY, INC. ROCK ISLAND OIL AND REFINING COMPANY
Balance Sheets, 1947 to May 31, 1950
(In Thousands)

	1947	1948	1949	May 31, 1950
ASSETS				
Cash	$ 844	$ 92	$ 244	$ 139
Notes	36	280	170	123
Accounts Receivable	1,388	1,950	2,065	2,139
Inventories:				
Crude Oil	339	319	179	154
Refined Products	306	628	296	
Chemicals	34	46	25	8
Warehouse Materials	319	590	195	130
Total Current Assets	$3,267	$3,906	$3,155	$2,695
Notes Receivable	7	78		
Refinery	430	609	602	587
Pipe Line	468	878	1,209	1,273
Tank Cars	62	62	65	
Miscellaneous	47	75	73	67
Producing Leaseholds	3	29		
Nonproducing Leaseholds	5	4		
Depreciation and Depletion	(81)	(192)	(329)	(327)
Prepaid Expenses	73	76	40	11
Total Assets	$4,279	$5,525	$4,816	$4,306
LIABILITIES AND CAPITAL				
Accounts Payable	$1,687	$2,110	$2,101	$2,006
Accrued Expenses	25	54	34	25
Provision for Income Taxes	524	471	107	114
Total Current Liabilities	$2,236	$2,636	$2,242	$2,144
Deferred Liability--				
Payable to Wood River	1,155	1,255	755	255
Common Stock	15	15	15	15
Earned Surplus	874	1,618	1,804	1,891
Total Liabilities and Capital	$4,279	$5,525	$4,816	$4,306

4. WOOD RIVER OIL AND REFINING COMPANY, INC. ROCK ISLAND OIL AND REFINING COMPANY
Income Statements, 1947 to May 31, 1950
(In Thousands)

	1947	1948	1949	5 Months Ending May 31, 1950
Number of barrels of refined products sold	2,550	3,049	2,375	
Sale of refined products	$7,693	$11,406	$7,546	
Cost of sales	6,296	9,735	7,499	
Gross profit from sales	$1,397	$ 1,672	$ 46	
Administrative and selling expenses	205	277	204	$ 30
Net profit (loss) from operations	$1,192	$ 1,395	$ (157)	$(30)
Other operating income:				
Pipe line	170	110	271	86
Tank car	7	28	(10)	2
Production	2	29	14	
Net profit from operations	$1,372	$ 1,561	$ 118	$ 57
Other income	11	13	206*	116
Gross income	$1,382	$ 1,575	$ 325	$173
Income charges	54	362	32	52
Net income before taxes	$1,328	$ 1,213	$ 293	$121
Less income taxes	524	471	107	34
Net income for Period	$ 804	$ 742	$ 186	$ 87
Earned surplus, beginning of year	$ 69	$ 874	$1,618	$1,804
Net income for year	804	742	186	87
Surplus credit		3		
Earned Surplus, End of Year	$ 874	$1,618	$1,804	$1,891

*Includes profit of $123 from sale of casing tubing, and line pine in 1949.

5. WOOD RIVER OIL AND REFINING COMPANY, INC.

Location of Wood River with Respect to Outside Pipelines

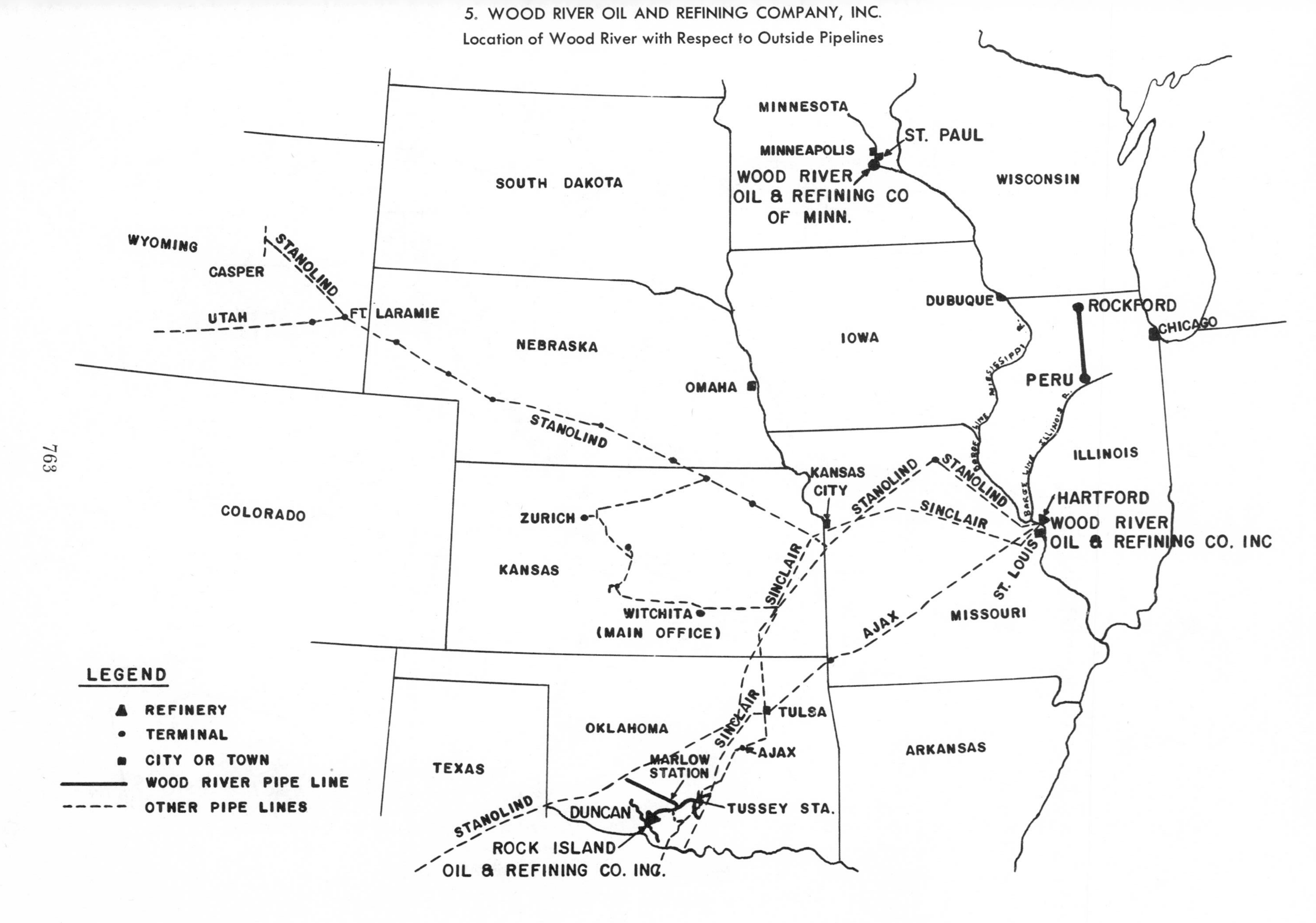

6. WOOD RIVER OIL AND REFINING COMPANY, INC.

Location of Wood River with Respect to Sinclair Oil Company Facilities

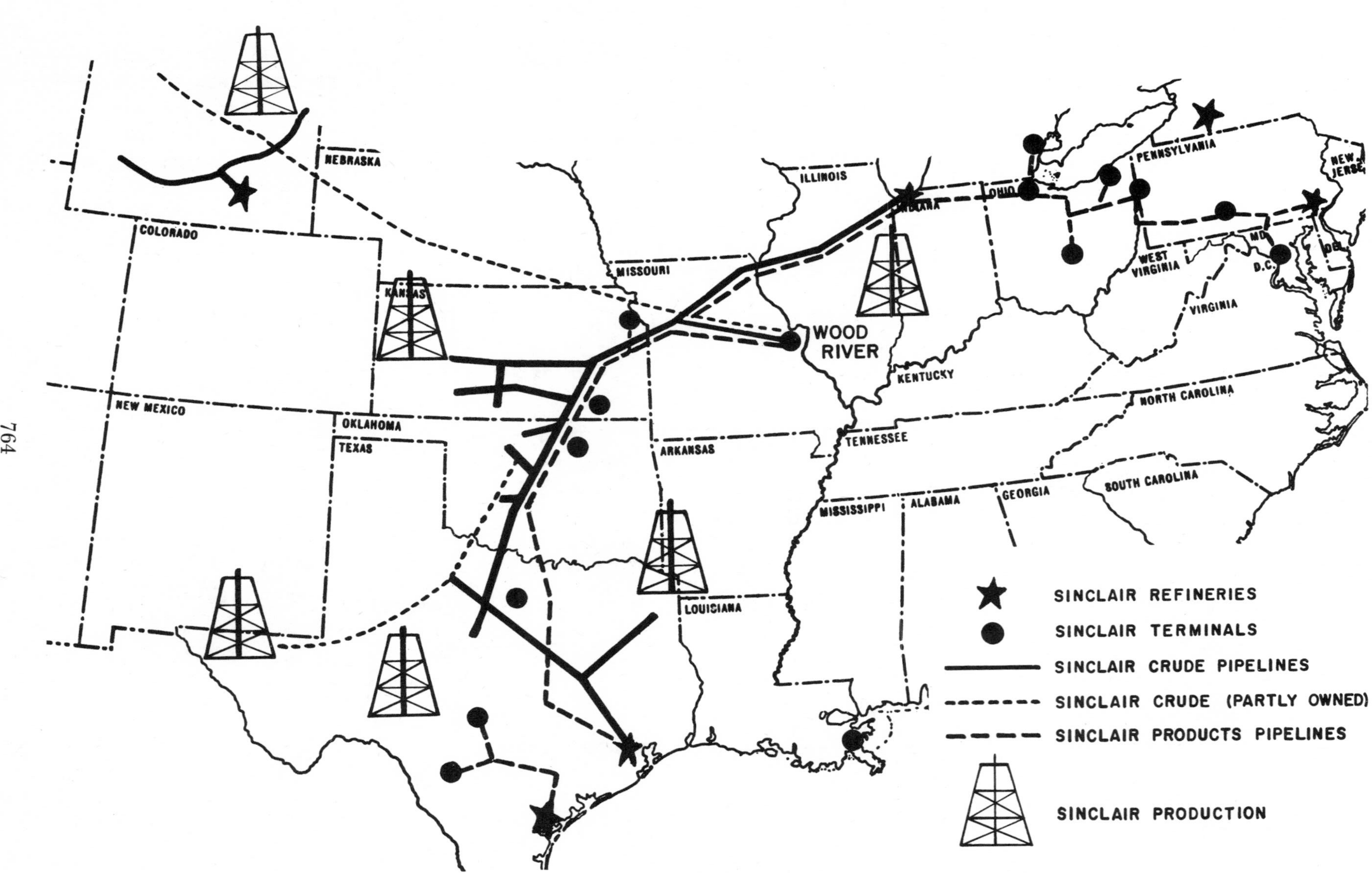

7. WOOD RIVER OIL AND REFINING COMPANY, INC.
Comparative Refining, Administrative Tank Car, and Selling Expense per Barrel of Crude Run

	1944*	1945*	1946*	1947	1948	1949	5/31 1950*
Barrels of crude oil consumed (input)	3,966,926	4,742,131	5,215,459	7,066,045	7,866,731	6,070,479	3,045,117
Refinery Expenses (per bbl. of input):							
Labor and supervision	$0.0739	$0.0666	$0.0705	$0.0662	$0.0716	$0.1064	$0.0981
Fuel, light, and power	0.0003	0.0023	0.0047	0.0041	0.0115	0.0215	0.0197
Maintenance labor	0.0572	0.0591	0.0612	0.0691	0.0669	0.0919	0.0754
Depreciation	0.0574	0.0553	0.0488	0.0498	0.0566	0.0987	0.1016
Treating labor	0.0074	0.0049	0.0056	0.0064	0.0072	0.0080	0.0059
Chemicals	0.0549	0.0814	0.0641	0.0774	0.0768	0.0998	0.1329
Maintenance materials and supplies	0.0587	0.0559	0.0576	0.0652	0.0546	0.0599	0.0491
Automobile expense	0.0015	0.0014	0.0010	0.0012	0.0015	0.0019	0.0013
Insurance	0.0074	0.0139	0.0119	0.0139	0.0209	0.0115	0.0018
Traveling expense	0.0010	0.0006	0.0007	0.0010	0.0013	0.0011	0.0009
Taxes—ad valorem	0.0029	0.0044	0.0030	0.0039	0.0056	0.0092	0.0071
Royalties	0.0069	0.0056	0.0021	0.0016	0.0015	0.0003	0.0148
Sickness and accident insurance					0.0002	0.0025	0.0034
Research						0.0003	0.0026
Total refinery expenses	$0.3295	$0.3514	$0.3312	$0.3598	$0.3762	$0.5130	$0.5246
Administrative expense	0.0615	0.0492	0.0424	0.0497	0.0545	0.0762	0.0693
Tank car rentals		0.0009	0.0074	0.0071	0.0068	0.0169	0.0100
Selling expense	0.0144	0.0170	0.0182	0.0209	0.0214	0.0306	0.0331
Total Expenses	$0.4054	$0.4185	$0.3992	$0.4375	$0.4589	$0.6367	$0.6370

*Total figures for crude oil consumed in these years include crude oil processed as follows: 1944: 285,327; 1945, 1,124,454; 1946, 160,828; 1950, 400,000. See Exhibit 2 for processing fees.

8. WOOD RIVER OIL AND REFINING COMPANY, INC.

Average Selling Price and Per Cent Yield of Products

Products	1944 Average Selling Price (Per Gal.)	1944 Per Cent Yield	1945 Average Selling Price (Per Gal.)	1945 Per Cent Yield	1946 Average Selling Price (Per Gal.)	1946 Per Cent Yield	1947 Average Selling Price (Per Gal.)	1947 Per Cent Yield	1948 Average Selling Price (Per Gal.)	1948 Per Cent Yield	1949 Average Selling Price (Per Gal.)	1949 Per Cent Yield	May 31, 1950 (5 Mos.) Average Selling Price (Per Gal.)	May 31, 1950 (5 Mos.) Per Cent Yield
Finished Gasoline:														
Ethyl stock	$0.0784	7.14	$0.0784	7.62	$0.0765	7.90	$0.10514	6.36	$0.1344	5.07	$0.1249	6.97	$0.12066	12.76
Q stock	0.0703	36.87	0.0696	39.67	0.0691	30.60	0.09820	26.99	0.1265	24.40	0.1155	31.26	0.11212	26.93
U.S. Motor stock	0.0613		0.0615	0.17	0.0663	0.31	0.08603		0.1266	0.03	0.1176			
Cleaner solvent			0.0592		0.0602									
Codimer	0.1865		0.1792											
Unfinished Gasoline:														
Ethyl stock								0.07		0.08		0.12		(.51)
Q stock		(.35)				0.01		(0.01)		(0.06)		0.13		.41
60-70 stock		(.04)		(0.01)		0.01		(0.01)		0.70		0.14		(1.00)
U.S. Motor stock		0.02		0.12		(0.10)				0.13				(.04)
Codimer		0.90		0.47										
Total Gasoline	$0.0741	44.54	$0.0721	48.04	$0.0707	38.73	$0.09948	33.40	$0.1280	30.35	$0.1178	38.62	$0.11460	38.55
Other Refined Products													$0.11360	.01
Kerosene)			($0.0552)	0.24	$0.0600	1.91	$0.08415	2.04	$0.1197	0.77	$0.0966	1.18	0.10044	1.51
Diesel fuel)—	$0.0496	15.03—	(0.0500	0.40					0.1174	0.06	0.0810	0.97	0.08631	1.76
St. run distillate)			(0.0503)	9.71	0.0566	15.37	0.08480	14.68	0.1121	17.12	0.0951	13.96	0.10115	15.16
Cracked distillate	0.0461	4.56	0.0442	8.41	0.0510	8.68	0.08062	10.57	0.1056	8.15	0.0866	5.20	0.09605	8.25
Gas oil			0.0404	4.15			0.07346	3.28	0.0891	7.69	0.0738	1.54		.46
Road oil			0.0342	2.24	0.0735	4.33	0.05782	2.54	0.0792	2.03	0.0613	4.06	0.07273	.93
No. 5 fuel oil	0.0365)—	23.28	0.0341	17.40	0.0417	2.47	0.06175	5.04	0.0784	7.74	0.0562	9.56	0.06605	8.47
No. 6 fuel oil	0.0365)		0.0286	0.85	0.0356	16.43	0.05591	18.31	0.0746	13.95	0.0451	7.32	0.05469	10.41
Uncracked flux	0.0358	3.46			0.0342	4.11	0.04960	2.85	0.0670	4.24	0.0467	6.34	0.04705	5.43
Asphalt					0.0630	0.81	0.06346	1.14	0.0856	1.09	0.0732	1.04	0.08945	.42
Lubricating oil									0.5319		0.6378		0.62239	
Pitch										(0.08)		(0.55)		(.60)
Total Other Refined Products	$0.0417	46.33	$0.0401	43.40	$0.0455	54.11	$0.07003	60.45	$0.0937	62.76	$0.0721	50.62	$0.07828	52.21
Pitch and Still Gas Burned		7.82		6.88		6.11		5.04		5.07)—		10.76		9.24
Loss in Distillation		1.31		1.68		1.05		1.11		0.82)				
Average Price and Total Yield	$0.0574	100.00	$0.0551	100.00	$0.0562	100.00	$0.08126	100.00	$0.1067	100.00	$0.0914	100.00	$0.09321	100.00

*The average prices are not weighted averages of the figures in the columns above. The figure $0.9321, for example,is taken from Exhibit 9 ($9,881,000 ÷ 106,011) and represents an average price for the refined products actually sold. The refinery yields in this exhibit might be different from the mix of products sold because of changes in inventories.

9. WOOD RIVER OIL AND REFINING COMPANY, INC.

Sales of Refined Products, 1941 to May, 1950
(Dollars and Gallons in Thousands)

Year	Refinery	Total Gals.	Total Sales	Gasoline Gals.	Gasoline Sales	Kerosene Gals.	Kerosene Sales	Distillate & Gas Oil Gals.	Distillate & Gas Oil Sales	Fuel Oil Gals.	Fuel Oil Sales	Asphalt Gals.	Asphalt Sales
1941:	Wood River	107,679	$ 5,871	59,157	$ 4,087	10,119	$ 458	11,503	$ 505	26,897	$ 821		
1942:	Wood River	137,433	7,535	70,325	4,850	21,459	1,073	14,558	607	31,088	1,005		
1943:	Wood River	125,682	7,211	64,423	5,538	21,949	1,144	9,766	431	29,543	1,097		
1944:	Wood River	149,953	8,600	72,433	5,370	22,385	1,147	11,757	545	43,376	1,538		
1945:	Wood River	152,686	8,409	71,645	6,162	5,862	324	25,618	1,196	49,560	1,726		
1946:	Wood River	208,327	$11,705	88,396	$ 6,248	5,375	$ 322	51,425	$2,802	61,364	$2,220	1,767	$ 111
	Rock Island	28,065	1,598	15,951	1,108	1,952	101	3,114	144	4,300	122	2,748	123
	Total	236,392	$13,303	104,347	$ 7,356	7,327	$ 423	54,539	$2,946	65,664	$2,342	4,515	$ 234
1947:	Wood River	282,756	$22,977	107,853	$10,729	5,461	$ 460	75,958	$6,308	74,314	$4,421	19,170	$1,059
	Rock Island	107,016	7,760	61,754	5,163	10,319	711	10,886	712	17,442	791	6,615	381
	Total	389,772	$30,737	169,607	$15,892	15,780	$1,171	86,844	$7,020	91,756	$5,212	25,785	$1,440
1948:	Wood River	362,905	$38,738	138,399	$17,711	2,510	$ 300	131,181	$13,911	69,645	$5,259	21,170	$1,556
	Rock Island	128,069	11,500	57,771	6,185	11,180	1,058	28,821	2,388	18,468	986	11,829	882
	Total	490,974	$50,238	196,170	$23,896	13,690	$1,358	160,002	$16,299	88,113	$6,245	32,999	$2,438
1949:	Wood River	303,559	$27,733	127,711	$15,048	2,590	$ 250	88,021	$7,992	82,360	$4,231	2,877	$ 210
	Rock Island	99,757	7,607	42,376	4,256	4,853	401	25,603	1,677	14,063	332	12,862	941
	Total	403,316	$35,340	170,087	$19,304	7,443	$ 651	113,624	$9,669	96,423	$4,563	15,739	$1,151
5 Months 1950:	Wood River	106,011	$ 9,881	43,570	$ 4,993	1,807	$ 181	29,730	$2,921	30,510	$1,750	394	$ 35
	Rock Island	4,335	410	3,810	370	281	23	155	11	44	1	45	4
	Total	110,346	$10,291	47,380	$ 5,363	2,088	$ 204	29,885	$2,932	30,554	$1,751	439	$ 39

Note: 42 gallons equal 1 barrel.

The Ohio Oil Company (B)

In the spring of 1959, executives of The Ohio Oil Company were reviewing their strategy of integration in the industry. Though the company had acquired a refinery at Robinson, Illinois, in 1924, and subsequently expanded and modernized it, it had maintained substantially greater oil production than refining or marketing capacity. The ratio of its oil production to its crude runs to stills had declined from the four-to-one ratio during World War II to a two-and-a-half-to-one ratio during the 1950's. Despite the decline, The Ohio Oil Company still had a markedly different balance of operations than other companies with similar production capacities. For example, the Continental Oil Company was approximately equally balanced in production, refining, and marketing, and the Sinclair Oil Company had about two-and-a-half times as much refining and marketing capacity as its crude oil production. The Ohio Oil Company executives were therefore trying to determine what conditions had made a "crude-heavy" company profitable in the past, and in what way changing conditions of the 1950's might affect the balance of operations.

PRODUCING

The Ohio Oil Company was always known primarily as "a crude producing company." The firm was organized on August 1, 1887, to consolidate the interests of 14 Ohio producers and further to develop and acquire production in the newly discovered Lima fields. The company was the outgrowth of a series of meetings in which a means was sought for bringing some stability to the producing activities of the region. Prices of crude oil were depressed because of the very active development work in the area and because the crude was then undesirable from a refining standpoint. The new company was able to operate profitably on the low-priced crude, however, and expanded its production to 4,000 barrels daily within two years. The success of the company attracted the interest of the Standard Oil Trust, a large refining combination which was then seeking crude oil production, and The Ohio Oil Company was purchased by Standard interests in 1889. From 1889 to 1911, the company served as the primary producing subsidiary of the Standard group and confined its operations to the Ohio, Illinois, and Indiana fields. Under the terms of the Dissolution Decree in 1911, the Ohio Oil Company was re-established as a separate entity.

In its own exploratory work, The Ohio Oil Company sometimes ventured very large sums of money on individual drilling projects. For example, the company lost $7,593,000 in 1950 by drilling two dry holes and one gas well in the Texas Tidelands. The company likewise occasionally tested very deep structures where drilling costs ranged up to or exceeded $1,000,000 for a single well.

In 1951, Mr. O. D. Donnell, the retired president, reviewed the company's oil finding and oil producing activities as follows: "The company had the manpower to do producing work. We were originally the oil producing member of the Standard group and we carried this activity into the future." The management felt that its particular skills and abilities equipped it to do exploratory and producing work most effectively.

The executives of The Ohio Oil Company had no definite figure in mind as to the optimum ratio of crude oil production to refinery runs which the company should seek to maintain in the future (see Exhibits 5 and 6 for past ratios). Generally speaking, however, the executives believed that a ratio of 300 to 400 percent was entirely satisfactory and might well be continued. The executives were of the opinion that the company's most profitable operations were in the producing field and, as noted above, that one of the company's strongest assets was the experience and ability of its personnel in oil-finding activities.

Between 1950 and 1958, sources of the company's crude oil changed as old fields became depleted and new ones were discovered. Texas, which accounted for 33 percent of The Ohio Oil Company's crude oil in 1950 declined to 20 percent in 1958, while Wyoming increased from 23 to 28 percent and Illinois from 10 to 14 percent. Nebraska and Louisiana together contributed 15 percent. Canada which had accounted for only 1/4 of 1 percent in 1950 contributed 5 percent in 1958. Meanwhile, the company had become active in offshore and foreign oil plays.

The largest exploratory and drilling effort

continued to be placed in the United States, despite the increasing importance of foreign ventures. The opening of the Platte pipeline, in which the company held a 25 percent interest, allowd significant quantities of shut-in oil to be brought to Wood River from the company's fields in Wyoming and Nebraska. Extensive waterflooding operations increased the yield from the Illinois fields. Considerable exploratory work was undertaken in Louisiana, Ohio, various Rocky Mountain fields, California, western Canada, and Alaska.

The company's holding in Wyoming consisted largely of sour crude oil, which the company's own refinery at Robinson, Illinois, was not equipped to process. In fact, due to the small number of refineries that could handle such crude oil in the early 1950's, the prices for Wyoming sour crude were lower than for sweeter crudes of the same gravity.

Two situations helped The Ohio Oil Company to dramatize the increasing cost of its exploratory drilling. One was a California well, which the company drilled to a record depth in 1954, at 21,500 feet. After more than three years of drilling under very difficult conditions, it was abandoned as a dry hole. The other was the company's concession in Guatemala, which was located on a mountain top within the jungle interior of the country. Since no roads existed, the field crew was obliged to build its own airstrip and mountain road. Similarly, large costs were experienced in offshore drilling operations, which require extensive facilities of a specialized nature to maintain and supply the drillers.

In order to deal with the higher costs and substantially increased risks of offshore and foreign ventures, the company participated in many jointly shared operations, rather than attempting to shoulder the burden alone. The most important method of entering new fields was through the Conorada group, in which the company shared a one third interest with the Continental and Amerada companies. Through this group, the company drilled many wells in Egypt and Somalia. These holes turned out to be dry, but the group did find oil in Libya. In 1957, the company made a significant step by paying almost $26 million for a 25 percent share in concessions totalling 252,000 acres in Venezuela, mostly offshore. By 1958, offshore drilling in Venezuela had encountered a good oil show.

REFINING

In the early 1950's, The Ohio Oil Company had two refineries, one at Robinson, Illinois, and the other at Lovell, Wyoming. The Robinson plant was acquired in 1924 when The Ohio Oil Company integrated forward for the first time into refining operations through the purchase of one of its crude oil customers, the Lincoln Oil and Refining Company. The precise reasons why this initial venture into refining activities was undertaken by The Ohio Oil Company are not now entirely clear. Some of the executives recall that the move was undertaken primarily as a means of averting loss of an outlet for crude oil at a time when excess stocks were accumulating: others recall that the decision was prompted largely by the attractiveness of the profit opportunities in the refining field. Whatever the original reasons may have been, by the latter 1920's the Robinson refinery had become important to The Ohio Oil Company as a means of disposing of a portion its crude oil output in a seriously oversupplied crude market.

The Robinson plant served as the company's principal source of products supply and was expanded as refining and marketing operations came to play an important part in the operations of The Ohio Oil Company. At the time of purchase, the facilities of the 1,000-barrel per day refinery were technologically obsolete and highly inefficient. The plant was completely rebuilt in 1927 at which time it was enlarged to a capacity of 5,000 barrels per day and thermal cracking facilities were added. From 1927 until after World War II, the capacity of the Robinson plant was gradually increased to 14,500 barrels per day in order to keep pace with the company's growing sales requirements. The enlargement in capacity was accomplished largely through alterations of existing equipment except in 1939, when a 3,000-barrel per day combination unit was moved to the Robinson refinery. After World War II, a fluid catalytic cracker was installed and the capacity was increased to 30,000 barrels per day.

Between 1952 and 1954, The Ohio Oil Company spent almost $15 million to expand and upgrade the Robinson refinery. The increase in capacity from 30,000 to 40,000 barrels per day entailed added power and steam facilities and storage tanks. At the same time, however, special units were installed to increase the octane ratings including enlarged catalytic cracking, polymerization, and a new catalytic reformer. A coking unit was also installed, in order to reduce the yield of residual fuel oil and asphalt and increase the yield of gasoline and heating oil. A contract was later signed to assure delivery of the coke to a single customer, who intended to build a calcining plant adjacent to the refinery. A new quality control laboratory and a computer were installed at Robinson to increase operating efficiency, and an alkylation unit was put in to supply high-octane aviation gasoline. By 1958, a new debutanizer column enabled the Robinson refinery to reach a capacity of 50,000 barrels per day.

As in 1950, the question of using Wyoming crude oil in the Robinson refinery came up for review. However, the Robinson refinery had been designed to handle the sweet light crude of the Illinois fields in which the Ohio company owned large reserves, and additional reserves of similar types of crude were readily available from the mid-continent area slightly further south and west. The Robinson refinery was yielding high ratios of gasoline and heating oil, and sold a relatively small amount of heavy residual fuel, due to the relative lack of industrial markets in the Robinson area.

The Lovell, Wyoming refinery had a crude capacity of 6,000 barrels per day and no cracking facilities. The plant was constructed in 1937 to absorb a portion of the company's crude producing potential in the Wyoming area. It was operated on heavy crudes of 20° to 23° gravity, had a gasoline yield of only about 9 percent, and was used chiefly for the production of asphalts and fuel oils. Products were sold to jobbers, industrial and commercial accounts, and consumers in the company's secondary marketing area in the northwestern and northcentral sections of the country. The capital investment at the Lovell plant was deliberately kept at a low level, and by 1955 it was closed, to enable the company to concentrate effort on its Midwest marketing locations. In the 1930's, the company had also owned three small refineries in Oklahoma and Texas, which had come as part of the acquisition of the Transcontinental Oil Company. However, the Ohio Oil Company had made the acquisitions primarily to obtain the Transcontinental Company's producing properties, and it closed the refineries before World War II.

MARKETING

The Ohio Oil Company first engaged in marketing activities shortly after the purchase of the Lincoln Oil and Refining Company in 1924. The management had intended to market the refinery output entirely to other large companies, but was unable to arrange sales contracts. It began, therefore, to build its own distribution organization and to market under its own brand name, "Marathon."

In 1950, an industry study indicated that The Ohio Oil Company was selling 44.5 percent of its gasoline to wholesale resellers and 55.5 percent to retail resellers or direct to final users. In the same year, the Sinclair Oil Company was selling 34.1 percent to wholesale and Standard Oil of Ohio was selling only 16.2 percent wholesale.[1] In 1952, The Ohio Oil Company had 360 wholesale outlets and 1,877 stations, compared with Standard Oil of Ohio, which had 359 wholesale outlets and 4,612 stations. The Ohio Oil Company's 1,877 stations represented a decline from its high of 3,587 stations in 1939, due largely to the loss of more than a thousand small contractor stations as a result of the World War II manpower mobilization.

During the 1950's, the marketing program of the company was aimed at modernizing its retail stations and increasing their sales volume, as well as to expand the number of stations. Between 1952 and 1954, the company spent almost $20 million to build new service stations and remodel another 140. The refinery modernization program supported this marketing campaign by allowing the company to introduce a new premium grade octane gasoline, the Marathon Mile Maker, and later, a special gasoline for high-compression engines, the Super M.

The management determined the type of distribution method to be employed at a given location largely on the basis of comparative cost and volume considerations. Company-owned and -operated bulk stations were maintained in the

[1] McLean and Haigh, "The Growth of Integrated Oil Companies," p. 442.

metropolitan areas where the volume of business was sufficient to warrant this type of operation. In some towns and rural areas, however, the company was converting some of its company-operated bulk plants to operation by commission agents. It was felt that the "hometown" acceptance and greater incentives of commission agents often led to higher sales volumes than could be secured with salaried employees. Jobber distribution was concentrated primarily in the outlying areas where the company had little long-term prospects of supplying products on a highly economical basis. The company relied heavily upon tank wagon commission distributors to deliver home heating oil from company-operated or commission agent-operated bulk plants. Commission distributors relieved the burden thrust upon bulk plants by the seasonality of the heating oil business.

A few large-volume service stations were operated by the company. Company-operated stations were useful for personnel training purposes and experimentation with merchandizing programs. For its gasoline retailing activities, however, the company was largely dependent upon dealer stations at higher volume locations and contractor stations at the less desirable service station sites.

The management hoped that some day it might be possible to sell all of the company's gasoline on a branded basis, and that 60 to 70 percent of the refinery output might pass through company-owned or -leased facilities.

The primary marketing territory included an area, which was within 75 to 100 miles of the refinery and terminals situated along the Buckeye Pipe Line. It was estimated that gasoline and home heating oil could be moved to outlets in the primary marketing area at a maximum cost of approximately one cent per gallon. Within this area, the company intended to make continued and greater use of deliveries directly from pipeline terminals to large gallonage service stations. Bulk plants would be retained, however, as an intermediate storage point in servicing the large number of farm accounts and smaller service stations throughout the area. In its secondary marketing areas in the Midwest, which lay outside the 75- to 100-mile zone surrounding the pipeline terminals and refinery, the company intended to continue the development of peripheral marketing areas with jobbers, but with no substantial investment in marketing properties. During the 1950's, therefore, a series of terminals were built from Toledo and Columbus in the east, to Griffith, and Chicago, to Mount Vernon and Louisville, on the Ohio River. These terminals, with some new aluminum tank trucks, strengthened the company's marketing territory of Illinois, Indiana, Ohio, Michigan, and Kentucky. Exhibits 7 to 9 contain market information about the company.

TRANSPORTATION

The Ohio Oil Company had begun pipeline operations prior to 1911, at which time the lines were a part of the Standard system, and the company retained and extended its operations in ensuing years. Its wholly owned subsidiary, the Illinois Pipe Line Company of Texas, operated crude gathering and crude trunk lines, and the company had a 25 percent interest in the Platte pipeline for crude oil moving east from Wyoming and a 75 percent interest in the Wabash line, a products line from Robinson and East St. Louis to Chicago. However, The Ohio Oil Company had not carried any of its own crude oil in interstate commerce at the time of the pipeline Consent Decree in 1941, and suit was not brought against it by the Department of Justice under the Elkins Act as it was against many other oil companies. The company subsequently refrained from shipping any of its own oil in interstate commerce. The Ohio Oil Company, therefore, operated under no restraints as to the dividends it could receive from pipeline operations, although like all other companies, it was required to operate its interstate lines as common carriers and to file tariffs with the Interstate Commerce Commission.

In 1958, The Ohio Oil Company's principal crude oil trunk line operations were based on the Platte line, running from the Wyoming fields to Wood River, Illinois, which connected with the company-owned trunk line running from Wood River to northeast Ohio, which was operated as a common carrier.

The Platte pipeline extended 1,080 miles from the producing fields of Wyoming to Wood River, Illinois. The 16, 20-inch pipeline was designed to carry about 110,000 barrels of crude oil per day, and had an estimated cost of approximately $59,000,000. The Platte project was initiated in 1950 by five large, integrated companies. The Ohio Oil Company had a 25 percent interest in the line and was interested in the common carrier line primarily as a means of gaining access to a market outlet for some of its shut-in crude oil producing potential in the Rocky Mountains area.

For product movement from the Robinson refinery, the company used the Buckeye line, which it had built but did not own, and which extended to points in Ohio such as Toledo and Columbus, and up into Detroit and Flint in Michigan, as well as to Mount Vernon on the Ohio River. The Wabash line, in which the company owned a 75 percent interest, ran from Wood River and Robinson up to the Chicago area. This line which had an ultimate capacity of 100,000 barrels per day, was planned to connect with common carriers into Michigan and with water terminals on the Great Lakes.

AURORA PROPOSAL

In reviewing the integration policy of their company in 1959, Ohio Oil executives were faced with a real decision that could have an immediate impact on their long-term strategy. The Aurora Gasoline Company, a principal purchaser of The Ohio Oil Company's sour crude oil from Wyoming, was considering the sale of its assets. The Aurora company had small oil reserves in Michigan, but large refining and marketing capacity, principally in the Detroit area. Therefore, if The Ohio Oil Company decided to acquire Aurora, it would cease to be a crude-heavy company, but would become essentially balanced in production, refining, and marketing. The Ohio Oil Company executives, therefore, had to decide whether it would be better for the company to market crude oil in excess of its own process requirements or to integrate by acquisition to market gasoline and other products.

Balance Sheets

Three Oil Companies, 1959-1958 (In Millions of Dollars)

	1949	1950	1951	1952	1953	1954	1955	1956	1957	1958
The Ohio Oil Company										
1a. Current Assets	$ 73	$ 86	$ 96	$ 93	$ 102	$ 99	$ 109	$ 104	$ 103	$ 111
b. Investments	16	16	18	16	12	9	10	12	12	9
c. Net Plant	121	134	146	169	192	208	220	240	270	274
d. Other	4	5	5	6	7	9	8	10	9	6
e. Total Assets	214	241	265	284	313	325	347	366	394	400
2a. Current Liabilities	$ 21	$ 29	$ 31	$ 30	$ 37	$ 31	$ 32	$ 30	$ 38	$ 33
b. Deferred and Reserves	1	0	0	0	0	0	0	0	0	0
c. Long-Term Debt	0	0	0	0	0	0	0	0	0	0
d. Common Ownership	192	212	234	254	276	294	315	336	356	367
e. Total Liabilities	214	241	265	284	313	325	347	366	394	400
Continental Oil										
1a. Current Assets	$ 98	$ 113	$ 98	$ 112	$ 130	$ 174	$ 169	$ 188	$ 177	$ 193
b. Investments	17	18	19	26	29	33	41	48	98	98
c. Net Plant	153	156	190	218	247	269	290	308	323	324
d. Other	3	5	5	5	3	4	4	5	6	5
e. Total Assets	271	292	312	361	409	480	504	549	604	620
2a. Current Liabilities	$ 41	$ 44	$ 48	$ 50	$ 62	$ 60	$ 63	$ 81	$ 73	$ 72
b. Deferred and Reserves	2	1	0	1	1	2	4	7	9	14
c. Long-Term Debt	1	0	0	32	53	108	108	109	152	147
d. Common Ownership	227	247	264	278	293	310	329	352	370	387
e. Total Liabilities	271	292	312	361	409	480	504	549	604	620
Sinclair Oil										
1a. Current Assets	$ 282	$ 302	$ 321	$ 356	$ 385	$ 383	$ 386	$ 482	$ 454	$ 445
b. Investments	21	20	21	20	19	22	23	76	78	95
c. Net Plant	418	470	531	649	720	762	813	884	918	927
d. Other	3	7	7	10	17	20	28	31	31	33
e. Total Assets	724	799	880	1,035	1,141	1,187	1,250	1,473	1,481	1,500
2a. Current Liabilities	$ 94	$ 127	$ 110	$ 170	$ 145	$ 139	$ 154	$ 170	$ 151	$ 149
b. Deferred and Reserves	10	10	13	14	18	21	18	23	27	31
c. Long-Term Debt	178	177	215	248	335	323	249	355	341	354
d. Common Ownership	442	485	542	603	643	704	829	925	962	966
e. Total Liabilities	724	799	880	1,035	1,141	1,187	1,250	1,473	1,481	1,500

2. THE OHIO OIL COMPANY (B)

Income Statement

Three Oil Companies, 1949-1958 (In Millions of Dollars)

	1949	1950	1951	1952	1953	1954	1955	1956	1957	1958
The Ohio Oil Company										
1a. Net Sales	$166	$192	$209	$223	$242	$ 248	$ 257	$ 275	$ 289	$ 271
b. Other Income	2	5	4	3	2	3	3	3	3	3
2a. Materials and Purchases	$ 55	$ 74	$ 77	$ 87	$ 92	$ 100	$ 94	$ 103	$ 108	$ 105
b. Operate, Sell, and General	45	44	49	55	52	57	60	65	71	73
c. Depreciation and Depletion	12	14	17	16	17	19	22	24	25	25
d. Other Charges and Taxes	22	28	28	29	39	37	43	45	47	39
3. Net Income	$ 34	$ 37	$ 42	$ 39	$ 44	$ 38	$ 41	$ 41	$ 41	$ 32
4. Common Shares Outstanding (in millions)	6.6	6.6	6.6	6.6	6.6	6.6	13.1	13.1	13.1	13.1
Continental Oil										
1a. Net Sales	$315	$348	$380	$397	$477	$ 500	$ 529	$ 576	$ 609	$ 666
b. Other Income	2	4	2	2	3	5	5	5	5	6
2a. Materials and Purchases	$193	$211	$218	$236	$303	$ 318	$ 328	$ 357	$ 389	$ 380
b. Operate, Sell, and General	36	37	44	51	55	49	58	62	67	70
c. Depreciation and Depletion	14	15	17	18	21	23	26	27	30	31
d. Other Charges and Taxes	38	47	62	56	60	73	76	83	81	144
3. Net Income	$ 36	$ 42	$ 41	$ 38	$ 41	$ 42	$ 46	$ 52	$ 47	$ 47
4. Common Shares Outstanding (in millions)	4.8	4.9	9.7	9.7	9.7	9.7	9.8	9.8	19.6	19.7
Sinclair Oil										
1a. Net Sales	$584	$679	$809	$856	$935	$1,021	$1,110	$1,180	$1,251	$1,190
b. Other Income	7	7	7	8	7	7	8	9	17	11
2a-b. Purchases and Expenses	$475	$538	$636	$699	$765	$ 829	$ 896	$ 945	$ 993	$ 963
c. Depreciation and Depletion	30	33	40	46	54	61	68	75	84	89
d. Other Charges and Taxes	32	45	58	33	55	46	73	73	112	100
3. Net Income	$ 54	$ 70	$ 82	$ 86	$ 68	$ 92	$ 81	$ 96	$ 79	$ 49
4. Common Shares Issued (in millions)	12.9	12.9	12.9	12.9	13.0	13.0	14.5	15.5	15.6	15.6

3. THE OHIO OIL COMPANY (B)

Annual Capital Expenditures

Three Oil Companies, 1949-1958 (In Millions of Dollars)

	1949	1950	1951	1952	1953	1954	1955	1956	1957	1958
The Ohio Oil Company										
1a. Domestic Production	13	15	19	23	24	24	27	32	23	23
1b. Foreign Production	--	--	--	--	1	2	3	10	28	2
2. Refining	4	1	1	5	9	5	1	1	2	2
3. Marketing	4	4	4	6	7	6	3	4	4	5
4. Pipeline	2	10	13	12	3	2	2	3	2	2
5. General Property and Research	1	1	1	--	3	3	2	2	4	6
6. Total	24	31	38	46	47	41	39	52	65	39
Continental Oil Company										
1a. Production Leases	6	6	16	10	13	14	20	9	10	14
1b. Production Wells	27	28	50	44	44	58	61	68	76	55
2. Refineries and Petrochem.	11	2	10	16	11	6	2	8	7	2
3. Marketing	3	3	9	11	12	13	11	11	12	4
4a. Pipelines	1	1	1	6	2	2	1	2	1	1
4b. Natural Gasoline	3	1	0	1	1	2	1	2	3	1
5. Other	1	2	3	3	2	5	5	2	3	1
6. Total	53	44	89	91	85	100	101	100	111	79
Sinclair Oil										
1. Oil and Gas Production	34	47	76	77	69	72	93	121	88	75
2. Refineries	14	21	6	25	30	31	35	19	26	21
3. Marketing	19	16	20	19	18	16	18	17	22	13
4a. Pipelines	5	5	13	52	20	8	7	15	17	18
4b. Gas Plants	2	2	1	1	3	2	4	6	3	4
4c. Marine	0	0	2	7	7	2	5	0	0	0
5. Other	0	3	1	1	0	1	4	2	2	1
6. Total	73	95	118	181	147	132	166	180	157	131

Common Stock Prices

	1949	1950	1951	1952	1953	1954	1955	1956	1957	1958
The Ohio Oil Company										
High	33 3/8	46 1/2	57 7/8	60 7/8	57 7/8	70	39	47 1/8	44 7/8	43 1/8
Low	23 1/2	26 1/2	43 1/4	50 1/8	49 7/8	54 1/8	30 1/2*	33 5/8	28 1/2	28 1/2
Continental Oil Company										
High	65 3/8	96	59 3/4	75	62 3/4	75 1/2	105	138	70 1/4	64
Low	47 5/8	55 1/2	48 1/4†	56 1/2	48 3/8	52	70	94	41 1/2‡	38 5/8
Sinclair Oil										
High	24 1/2	34 7/8	46 1/4	48	43 5/8	52 3/8	59 3/4	72 3/4	68 1/2	66 3/8
Low	18 7/8	21 7/8	34 1/4	38 3/4	30 1/2	32 1/8	48 1/2	55 5/8	45 1/2	46 3/8

*2 for 1 split (June 8, 1955).
†100% stock dividend (June 14, 1951).
‡100% stock dividend (February 18, 1957).

4. THE OHIO OIL COMPANY (B)

Gross Plant Account

Three Oil Companies, 1949-58 (In Millions of Dollars)

	1949	1950	1951	1952	1953	1954	1955	1956	1957	1958
The Ohio Oil Company										
1a. Domestic Production	243	258	264	282	301	321	343	367	382	394
1b. Foreign Production	1	1	1	2	3	4	8	17	45	45
2. Refining	26	27	28	30	38	43	44	43	45	47
3. Marketing	18	20	23	28	34	38	39	42	45	48
4. Pipelines	43	51	63	70	63	62	63	66	67	69
5. General	5	4	5	5	7	10	12	14	17	23
6. Total	336	361	384	417	446	477	508	549	602	626
Continental Oil										
1a. Production Leases	50	54	67	74	83	88	98	99	100	105
1b. Production Wells and Equip.	223	241	280	310	342	388	424	462	505	541
2. Refineries and Petrochem.	58	59	69	85	97	103	104	111	117	119
3. Marketing	33	32	41	45	56	57	67	76	87	89
4a. Pipelines	17	15	16	22	21	27	27	29	29	30
4b. Natural Gasoline	19	20	20	20	21	22	23	24	24	25
5. Other	13	18	20	18	20	24	28	27	29	28
6. Total	413	441	513	574	639	710	771	828	892	936
Sinclair Oil										
1. Oil and Gas Production	290	325	383	440	485	526	595	681	733	777
2. Refineries	190	210	215	239	269	298	332	350	372	383
3. Marketing	131	143	160	182	199	210	225	238	248	256
4a. Pipelines	104	108	116	162	170	173	170	177	183	192
4b. Gas Plants	17	19	20	21	24	28	32	37	40	43
4c. Tankers and Marine	28	26	28	35	41	43	24	24	24	25
5a. Research	8	8	8	9	9	9	10	11	11	12
5b. Other	3	6	6	6	6	7	10	11	8	8
6. Total	769	847	937	1,095	1,204	1,294	1,398	1,529	1,620	1,696

5. THE OHIO OIL COMPANY (B)

Producing, Refining, and Marketing Operations, 1927–1950

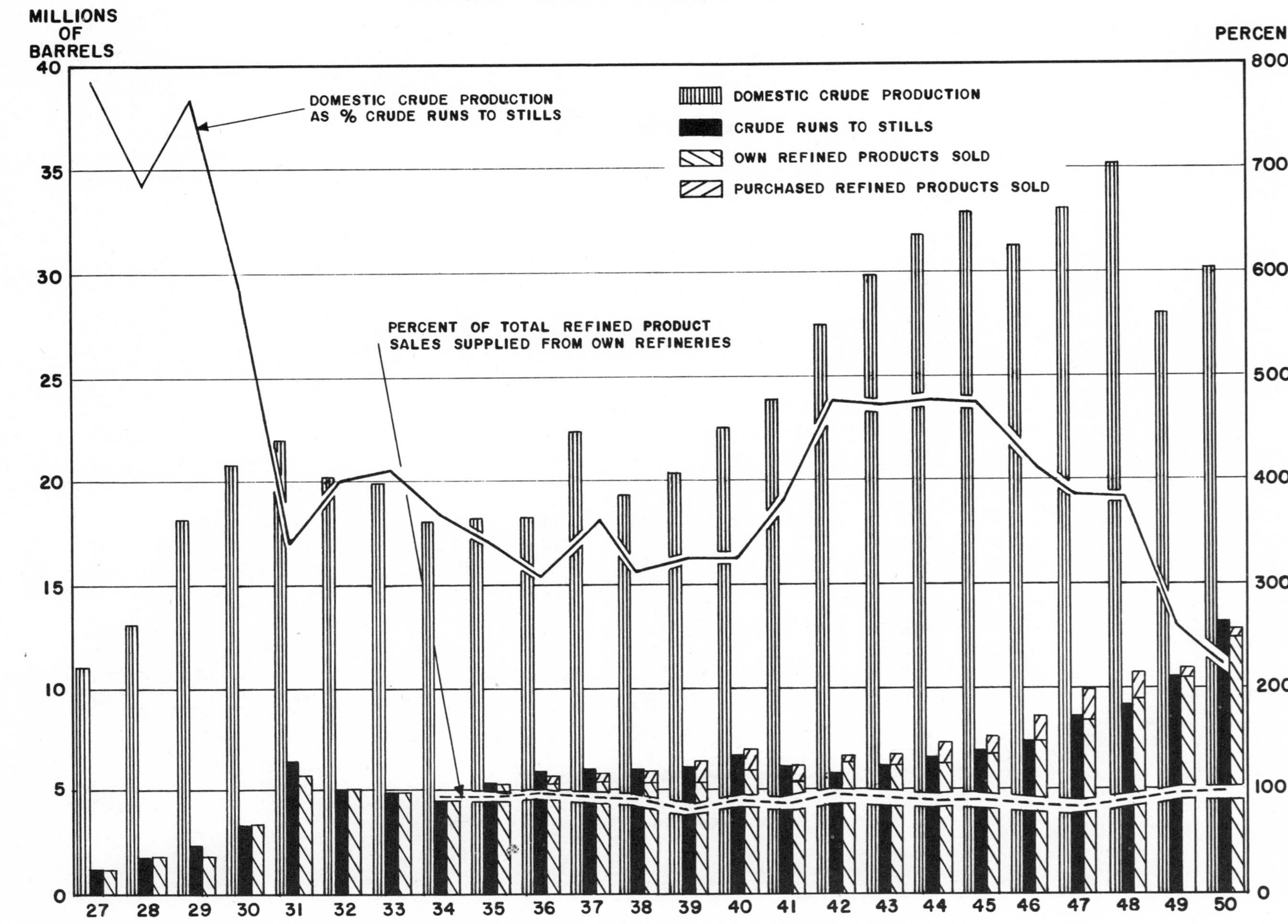

6. THE OHIO OIL COMPANY (B)

Balance of Operations

Three Oil Companies, 1949-1958

	1949	1950	1951	1952	1953	1954	1955	1956	1957	1958
Thousands of Barrels per Day										
(1) Ohio Oil										
Crude Oil Produced	73.3	79.0	88.7	89.0	93.7	90.0	93.3	96.9	95.6	90.1
Crude Oil Refined	29.3	35.7	36.4	37.6	37.7	37.3	42.4	42.4	41.5	41.4
Refined Products Sold	30.1	35.0	36.3	37.9	37.6	36.6	40.8	41.1	41.6	42.7
(2) Continental Oil										
Crude Oil Produced	96.5	104.4	118.4	117.0	123.1	131.2	145.4	154.4	150.0	151.0
Crude Oil Refined	68.1	81.5	89.1	95.3	114.7	126.3	141.2	141.0	147.1	148.6
Refined Products Sold	107.3	110.9	119.7	128.2	145.3	154.5	163.1	172.3	173.3	169.2
(3) Sinclair Oil										
Crude Oil Produced	108.3	112.5	130.0	136.6	142.0	146.4	157.5	166.5	171.6	187.4
Crude Oil Refined	260.6	320.5	371.0	379.7	414.4	413.7	430.6	447.8	443.0	434.1
Refined Products Sold	273.2	318.0	371.0	393.2	415.4	418.6	445.9	445.6	447.9	448.7
Main Sources of Crude Oil										
(1) Ohio Oil										
Wyoming	18.1%	24.6%	23.5%	20.3%	22.8%	25.9%	28.8%	28.9%	27.9%	28.6%
Texas	36.2	33.2	37.3	38.1	33.0	28.9	27.0	25.9	24.4	20.3
Illinois	11.6	10.7	9.4	10.0	10.3	10.3	11.3	11.5	11.5	13.9
Canada	0	0.2	0.3	0.3	0.7	0.7	1.4	2.8	4.4	4.8
(2) Continental Oil										
Wyoming	9.6%	9.9%	17.4%	18.6%	23.7%	27.1%	26.2%	24.1%	22.6%	25.3%
Texas	35.5	34.4	35.1	34.9	33.2	30.3	28.9	26.8	27.7	24.8
Louisiana	7.3	6.5	5.4	5.4	5.7	6.1	5.9	6.6	7.7	8.5
Canada	3.7	3.3	3.3	3.1	3.4	4.4	7.5	10.8	10.7	9.6
(3) Sinclair Oil										
U.S. and Canada	87.3%	89.2%	90.5%	91.0%	89.5%	87.8%	86.3%	84.9%	85.1%	72.7%
Venezuela	12.7	10.8	9.5	9.0	10.5	12.2	13.7	15.1	14.9	27.7

7. THE OHIO OIL COMPANY (B)

Map of the Ohio Oil Facilities

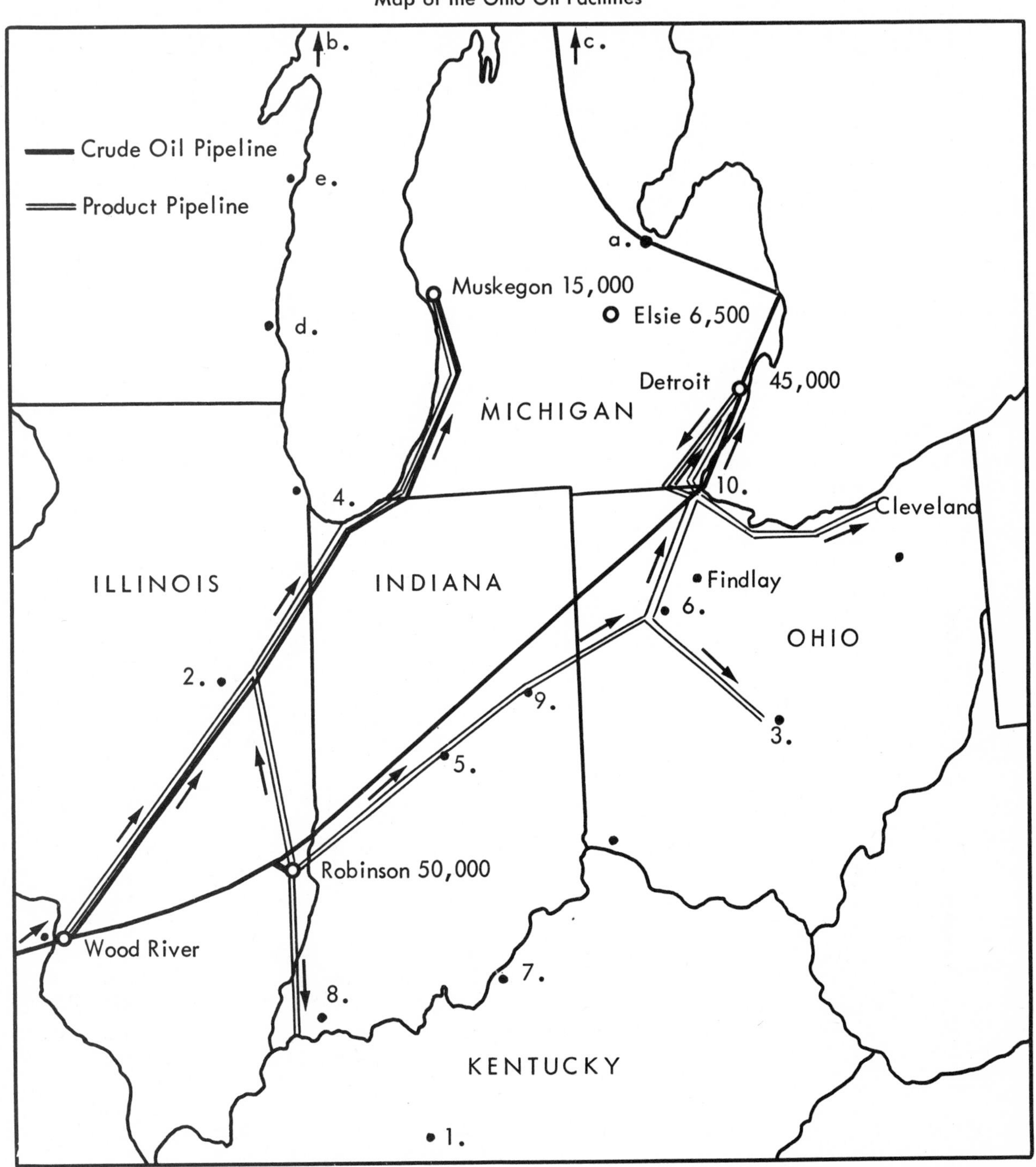

Terminal Points

Aurora Oil	Ohio Oil		Refineries
			Aurora Oil
a. Bay City	1. Bowling Green	6. Lima	Detroit
b. Gladstone	2. Champaign	7. Louisville	Elsie
c. Mackinaw City	3. Columbus	8. Mt. Vernon	Muskegon
d. Milwaukee	4. Griffith	9. Muncie	
e. Two Rivers	5. Indianapolis	10. Toledo	Ohio Oil
			Robinson

8. THE OHIO OIL COMPANY (B)

Consumption and Refined Output of Gasoline in Five Midwest States
(Millions of Barrels)

		1951	1952	1953	1954	1955	1956	1957
Illinois	Consumption	56.6	58.2	60.6	62.7	65.8	67.0	69.3
	Refined	87.1	91.7	97.7	98.4	109.2	105.1	99.4
Indiana	Consumption	31.2	33.2	35.6	36.3	39.1	40.9	41.0
	Refined	66.5	65.2	72.2	68.4	67.6	66.0	68.5
Kentucky	Consumption	14.7	15.6	16.3	17.3	18.5	19.5	20.6
	Refined	13.5	14.7	13.2	11.6	11.0	12.7	14.9
Michigan	Consumption	49.5	50.7	52.9	53.9	58.3	59.2	61.1
	Refined	15.9	16.9	16.9	16.1	17.9	19.5	19.5
Ohio	Consumption	56.0	58.6	62.3	63.6	69.4	73.1	74.5
	Refined	58.1	62.5	66.5	68.2	75.4	79.9	73.6

Share of Gasoline Market in Ohio
(By Companies)

	1952	1953	1954	1955	1956	1957
Standard Ohio	32.7%	32.1%	32.1%	32.2%	31.8%	31.3%
Sun Oil	9.2	8.9	10.1	10.2	10.4	10.2
Gulf Oil	8.1	8.1	8.8	8.4	9.6	9.4
Pure Oil	8.4	8.3	8.0	8.4	7.7	8.2
Shell Oil	7.9	8.3	8.2	8.0	8.1	8.1
Ashland	6.8	7.7	7.2	6.6	6.3	6.5
Sinclair	4.2	4.3	4.4	4.5	4.7	4.9
Texas Oil	4.5	4.3	4.1	4.2	4.2	4.2
Cities Service	3.1	3.3	3.0	3.4	3.7	4.0
Ohio Oil	3.4	3.7	3.7	3.8	3.8	3.8
Socony Mobil	3.8	3.8	3.6	3.5	3.4	3.4
Amoco	2.3	2.1	2.0	2.1	2.0	1.9
Atlantic	1.7	2.1	2.0	1.8	1.7	1.4

Source: Learned and Ellsworth, "Gasoline Pricing in Ohio," Harvard Business School, 1959.

9. THE OHIO OIL COMPANY (B)

Distribution of Gasoline

A. Wholesale and Retail, Two Oil Companies, 1948-1952

	1948	1949	1950	1951	1952
The Ohio Oil Company					
1a. Number of Bulk Plants	96	86	56	59	51
b. Monthly Sales per Plant (thousand gals./month)	46.4	55.6	62.0	70.4	75.9
c. Number of Commission Distributors	47	67	88	94	111
d. Monthly Sales per Distributor	33.1	26.9	40.2	30.8	30.1
2a. Number of Branded Jobbers	93	82	82	78	76
b. Monthly Sales per Jobber	48.8	63.5	67.4	68.9	71.2
c. Number of Unbranded Jobbers	85	90	99	119	122
d. Monthly Sales per Jobber	24.6	19.3	21.4	26.4	26.5
3a. Number of Company Operated Stations	10	10	7	5	7
b. Monthly Sales per Station	9.3	25.2	34.0	40.0	24.8
4a. Number of Dealer Operated Stations	632	664	679	698	763
b. Monthly Sales per Station	8.5	8.6	9.8	10.3	11.0
5a. Number of Contractor Stations	1,011	1,115	1,071	1,085	1,107
b. Monthly Sales per Station	1.7	1.8	1.8	2.1	2.2
Standard Oil Company (Ohio)					
1a. Number of Bulk Plants	176	173	177	176	177
b. Monthly Sales per Plant	NA	NA	NA	NA	NA
c. Number of Commission Distributors	110	108	109	109	110
d. Monthly Sales per Distributor	NA	NA	NA	NA	NA
2a. Number of Branded Jobbers	115	64	71	71	72
b. Monthly Sales per Jobber	91.9	137.3	101.0	86.4	86.3
3a. Number of Company Operated Stations	315	312	325	333	341
b. Monthly Sales per Station	37.2	38.0	40.7	41.8	44.8
4a. Number of Dealer Operated Stations	567	581	595	613	641
b. Monthly Sales per Station	18.0	18.8	20.1	21.1	22.6
5a. Number of Contractor Stations	3,683	3,621	3,660	3,629	3,630
b. Monthly Sales per Station	4.1	4.4	4.8	4.8	5.0

B. Product Mix, 1953-58

Two Oil Companies

	1953	1954	1955	1956	1957	1958
The Ohio Oil Company						
Gasoline	59.5%	61.8%	62.0%	63.2%	65.1%	63.0%
Distillate	24.5	24.5	24.2	24.9	26.5	28.9
Heavy Fuel Oil	13.0	8.1	7.3	5.0	1.4	1.2
Lubricating Oil	0.9	0.9	0.8	0.8	0.8	0.7
Oil	2.1	4.7	5.7	6.1	6.2	6.2
Continental Oil						
Gasoline	57.0%	53.1%	53.1%	51.3%	51.4%	54.0%
Distillate	21.4	27.4	26.1	29.1	29.1	26.5
Heavy Fuel Oil	10.0	8.4	8.7	7.5	7.7	6.5
Lubricating Oil	3.1	2.8	3.1	2.8	2.8	2.7
Other	8.5	8.3	9.0	9.3	9.0	10.3

Source: McLean and Haigh, "The Growth of Integrated Oil Companies," pp. 466, 468.

Aurora Gasoline Company

The Aurora Gasoline Company, an independent refiner and marketer, was the largest refining company in the state of Michigan. It had a 45,000-barrel per day refinery in Detroit, a 14,500-barrel refinery at Muskegon, and a 6,000-barrel refinery at Elsie, Michigan. Its wholly owned subsidiary, the Speedway Petroleum Corporation, had 660 service stations selling under the "Speedway 79" brand name, of which nearly 400 stations were in the Detroit area. The Aurora company had product terminals at Bay City, Mackinaw City, Gladstone, and North Muskegon, in Michigan, at Milwaukee and Two Rivers in Wisconsin, and at East Chicago in Indiana. There were 1,150 employees in 1959.

The Aurora Gasoline Company was formed in 1932 by Messrs. Fisher, Slaughter, and Wenger, as a marketing company. Mr. Fisher, who had recently been graduated from Ohio State University, was the son of the principal owner of Keystone Refining Company, a lubricating oil reclaiming plant in Detroit. When crude oil was discovered in Michigan, the Keystone company installed crude oil distillation units and processed oil under an operations and sales contract for Aurora. Thus, the Aurora company operated Keystone between 1934 and 1957 without actually owning the facilities until the latter year. Meanwhile, the Aurora company built its own downstream facilities at an adjacent site to convert the material to higher value products.

During the 1950's, Aurora company was considerably expanded. It had operated during this period the Elsie refinery, near Bay City Michigan. In 1954, it acquired the Old Dutch refinery at Muskegon. In about 1950, it acquired 50 percent interest in the Speedway Petroleum Corporation, a gasoline marketing company for which Aurora had been principal supplier, and seven years later acquired the rest of the stock. It also acquired the Argo Oil Company, a large distributor of domestic heating oil in the Detroit area. During the 1950's, Aurora also engaged in crude oil exploration activities, and was successful in discovering oil at the Scipio field in Michigan in 1957.

CAPITAL INVESTMENT PROGRAM AT THE DETROIT REFINERY

After World War II, the Aurora management became interested in obtaining greater supplies of low-cost crude oil that would support the expansion of its refining facilities and make full use of its market acceptance. The Ohio Company had substantial production of sour crude oil in Wyoming; the Aurora management became interested due to the price advantage resulting from its high sulfur content. Relatively few refineries were capable of processing this type of crude oil at the time, but the Aurora management decided to run it in large quantities from about 1950. From that time, much of the new capital investment program of the Detroit refinery was geared to provide the capability of handling large amounts of Wyoming sour crude and converting it into high-quality gasoline and heating oils.

The Wyoming sour crude had an A.P.I. gravity of 22°. Its higher sulfur content required more maintenance to offset corrosion, special alloy equipment, and increased use of hydrogen to desulfurize the heavier material. Between 1950 and 1959, therefore, much equipment was installed to maximize the light oil yield from Wyoming crude.

The original 7,500-barrel crude unit was expanded to 15,000-barrel per day capacity and kept full time on sweet crudes from Illinois, later supplemented by the sweet crude discovered at the Scipio field in Michigan. A separate 30,000-barrel crude unit with a large vacuum tower was installed for the Wyoming crude. When running Illinois or Michigan crude, 65 percent could be distilled at atmospheric pressure, 25 percent could be vaporized under vacuum, and 10 percent would be bottoms, while the Wyoming crude ran closer to 45–25–30 percent. The overall balance of crude throughput was maintained at an average of about 18,000 sweet and 22,000 barrels Wyoming sour, by using the No. 2 crude unit for Illinois or Michigan crude two or three days twice a month.

In 1954, Aurora became the first licensee to install a fluid coking unit, to process heavy bottoms from the vacuum unit. The feed was 4,000 barrels per day of 2.5° A.P.I. material, containing 25 to 30 percent carbon residue and

3.8 percent sulfur material. The unit required about 8,500 pounds of steam per hour, 600 kilowatts of electricity, 2,400 gallons per minute of cooling water, and 44 million B.T.U. of fuel per hour. The Wyoming bottoms yielded about 600 barrels of light ends, 720 barrels of heavy naphthas up to 430° F. with about 1.0 percent sulfur, 1,800 barrels of gas oil with about 3.2 percent sulfur and 17° A.P.I., and 150 tons of fluid coke with a 6 percent sulfur content. The naphthas lighter than 300° F. were desulfurized by treatment with hydrogen and charged to the catalytic reformers, while the heavier naphthas from 200° to 500° F. were desulfurized separately. The gas oils were largely used for fuel oil cutter, with the balance treated and used for cat cracker feed.

The fluid catalytic cracker had a capacity of 16,000 barrels of fresh feed per day. It was a modern unit of advanced design installed in 1955, at which time the older catalytic cracker of 1947 was removed and placed on stream at the Muskegon refinery. The cracker handled easily the heavy naphthas and the gas oils from sweet crude oils. The higher sulfur feedstocks were either used for cracker feed directly or were first treated to the limit of the hydrogen gas availability. When running higher sulfur stock, the catalyst inventory in the cracker system was gradually enriched in order to increase the activity of the unit. Although this increased the catalyst consumption, it improved the yield of gasoline. The catalytic cracker was usually operated to the limit of its capacity to handle heavy gas oils.

The Aurora company had pioneered in the installation of catalytic reformers. The first "platformer" in the world had been installed in the Muskegon refinery. In 1951, it installed in the Detroit refinery the first large-scale "platformer," with a capacity of 4,500 barrels per day, later enlarged to 6,500 B.P.D. In 1957, this unit was converted to a "rexformer" by adding a liquid-to-liquid extractor column and a solvent stripper together with the reboilers, washing facilities, and other necessary equipment. With the extraction system, the lower octane material in the platformate could be separated from the higher octane product and recycled to extinction in the reformer reactors. This permitted the reformer to operate at higher space velocity, and lower temperatures and pressures, while yielding a higher octane product. Diethylene glycol was used as a solvent in the liquid extraction column, to catch the desirable aromatics, while rejecting the higher-boiling lower-octane paraffins. The "rexformer" was a pioneer unit of advanced design.

The Detroit refinery also had a polymerization plant which recovered the propanes and propylenes to make gasoline of 100 octane (research method) and an alkylation plant to convert isobutanes and butylenes to 109 octane fuel. Due to the shortage of isobutanes, the Muskegon refinery supplied its yield of this material to the Detroit refinery and the tank truck used for delivery carried some alkylate gasoline in return. A general process flow of the Detroit refinery is given in the exhibits.

EFFECT OF CRUDE OILS ON OPERATIONS

The processing of Wyoming crude oil led the management of the Detroit refinery to pioneer in various methods of handling heavy sour crudes and in the development of technically advanced means to upgrade the material. The use of sour crude coincided with the beginning of the octane race, so the Detroit refinery was obliged to handle more difficult raw material at the same time that the demands for product quality steadily increased. Through its Speedway outlets, the Aurora company was able to remain an octane leader in Michigan throughout the 1950's. It did so by separating the process paths of the Illinois and Wyoming crudes, by using hydrogen to desulfurize feedstock, and by installing equipment that would yield high-grade products and marketable byproducts.

The No. 1 crude unit was maintained on Illinois crude oil, later supplemented by the company's own Michigan crude that had similar properties. The No. 2 crude unit, with its large vacuum unit, was kept predominantly on the heavy Wyoming crude oil. The effluent from No. 1 crude unit provided straight-run kerosenes and middle distillates, naphthas to feed the reformer, and gas oil to feed the catalytic cracker. The bottoms went to a thermal cracker for viscosity improvement and further yield of light products. The main problem was the gas oil and heavy residuum from No. 2 crude unit.

Part of the residuum was processed in the fluid coker to yield coke and sulfur, while the balance of the residuum yielded asphalt and heavy fuel oil as seasonally required.

In order to market the coke and asphalt, the Aurora company serviced special customer needs. The electrode coke had a higher sulfur content than that ordinarily used by United States aluminum companies. However, a Canadian aluminum company equipped itself to use such coke, and become a reliable customer. The Aurora management was also working with Detroit Edison Company to determine the cost and feasibility of using the coke, which had a high B.T.U. content, as a powerhouse fuel. At the same time, a specially heated pipeline was designed to deliver the asphalt to a nearby customer plant in Detroit direct from the refinery.

In order to desulfurize heavy naphthas and gas oils, the refinery made extensive use of the "unifining" process, which used hydrogen gas to treat the feed material. Since the refinery had pioneered in the adoption of catalytic reforming, it generated quantities of hydrogen gas as by-product. At one time, extensive investigations had been made as to the possibility of using this hydrogen to make anhydrous ammonia for fertilizer, and for constructing a hydrogen plant, if necessary, to supplement the supplies of raw material. However, the reformer hydrogen was used instead for extensive desulfurizing by hydrotreating. A naphtha unifiner was installed to pre-treat the reforming naphthas obtained from the various crudes including Wyoming crude, and a second unifiner, was installed to handle gas oils from No. 2 crude and from the fluid coker. Ordinarily, such gas oils required about 450 cubic feet of hydrogen per barrel to be treated. However, when the heaviest gas oils were run in spring and summer to increase the charge to the cracker so as to make additional gasoline rather than heating oil, the hydrogen consumption could run higher if maximum yield from the cracker were to be obtained. The somewhat limited tank farm capacity did not permit excessive seasonal inventories to build up. The naphtha unifiner required about 80 cubic feet of hydrogen per barrel.

There was no doubt that the Wyoming crude required higher maintenance due to corrosion of equipment than the Illinois and Michigan crudes. At first, gunite was blown in as a lining for the towers that handled the Wyoming crude, but gradually, as replacements were made in later years, alloys and stainless steel were used more extensively in heat exchangers and high-temperature locations. After some years of experience, most of the units were placed on a one and a half- to a two-year turnaround schedule, though the fluid coker, which handled the heaviest material, was on a 9- to 12-month schedule.

MARKET SITUATION IN THE SPRING OF 1959

By using the new equipment and process methods, the Aurora management was able to upgrade its products and maintain quality leadership in high-octane motor fuels and heating oils. However, from about 1957, new market trends created new price pressures in the gasoline and heating oil fields.

In about 1957, two products pipelines went into operation from Chicago to Detroit, the Wolverine and the Standard Oil Products lines. These lines ushered in a new period of competition in the Detroit area, in which some of the out-of-state oil corporations strengthened their market outlets in Detroit. A price war ensued and the price of gasoline declined markedly between 1957 and 1959, despite the increase in octane ratings during this period.

During the same period of time, a new natural gas pipeline was laid into Detroit, and large quantities of gas for domestic heating fuels became available. Due to price controls in this regulated industry, the cost per million B.T.U. was lower than the cost for equivalent heating value from middle distillates. As a result, the rate of expansion in the heating oil market declined and price pressures developed as gas heaters were installed in new homes.

In the summer of 1957, a union movement developed at the Detroit refinery, and some of the union leaders insisted on calling a strike for higher wages and stricter work rules, despite the plea of the union headquarters to stop the strike. The Aurora management group was able to operate the refinery itself, at lower throughput, through the rest of the year, and held out against the wage demands. The management believed that the strike did not seriously effect the company's market position, due to the current price situation and excessive product inventories in the area at that time.

In May, 1959, however, the Aurora management was reviewing its competitive situation in view of the increasing cost-price pressures. It received at that time an offer of merger from a larger oil corporation with East Coast affiliations and large supplies of its own crude oil in the middle cost. The corporation believed that the Aurora refinery's ability to process high-sulfur sour crude oil, together with the opening of the St. Lawrence Seaway, would enable it to handle successfully the type of crude oil that the corporation held in reserve at Kuwait.

The Aurora company's long standing ties with its principal supplier of crude oil, The Ohio Oil Company, led to acquisition talks with that company. In discussing the future of the Aurora Gasoline Company, the question arose of the ways its facilities could be used in combination with those of The Ohio Oil Company so as to achieve greater efficiencies for the overall system. Detroit was the only Aurora refinery processing Wyoming sour crude in any significant quantity. The Ohio company sold virtually all of such crude oil to other companies, of which Aurora was a principal customer. Such analysis would help determine the number of shares of The Ohio Oil Company's common stock which might be established as a fair price for the Aurora capital stock.

1. AURORA GASOLINE COMPANY

A. Balance Sheet, March 31, 1959
(In Thousands)

Assets		
Cash		$ 4,098
U.S. Treasury Bills		3,961
Receivables		
Trade	$ 8,979	
Oil Well Development	455	
Officers and Directors	267	
Other	1,180	
	$10,881	
Less: Allowance for Credit Loss	210	10,671
Due from Subsidiary		871
Inventories		
Crude	$ 2,249	
Products	3,409	
Supplies	281	
Drilling Operations	323	6,263
Prepaid		452
Current Assets		$26,316
Investments		
Subsidiaries	$ 6,024	
Other	639	6,663
Plant and Equipment		
Oil Properties	$ 1,289	
Refining	14,109	
Terminals and Pipelines	1,181	
Gasoline Stations	644	
Other	2,712	
	$19,935	
Less Depreciation	10,821	9,115
Deferred Charges		36
Total Assets		$42,130

Liabilities	
Bank Loans	$ 1,250
Purchase Agreements	365
Accounts Payable	
Trade	5,362
Other	2,300
Taxes and Other	1,949
Total Current Liabilities	$11,226
Bank Loans	3,558
Conditional Agreement on Refineries	1,318
Preferred Stock	5,750
Common Stock and Equity	20,157
Total Liabilities	$42,009

B. Income Statements, 1957-1959
(In Thousands) (Year Ended March 31)

	1957	1958	1959
Net Sales	$92,763	$89,359	$74,118
Processing Income	1,562	1,667	1,307
Net Crude Production	332	323	312
Other	631	234	165
	$95,288	$91,583	$75,903
Materials and Operating Expenses	$82,824	$81,601	$69,401
Crude Oil Exploration	626	517	646
Selling, General and Administrative	3,926	4,583	4,432
Interest	196	236	217
Other	850	---	---
	$88,422	$86,937	$74,696
Earnings before Taxes	$ 6,865	$ 4,645	$ 1,207
Federal Tax	3,300	2,380	550
Earnings after Taxes	$ 3,565	$ 2,265	$ 657

2. AURORA GASOLINE COMPANY

Speedway Petroleum Corporation

A. Balance Sheet, April 30, 1959
(In Thousands)

Cash	$1,615		Notes	$ 339
Receivables	3,190		Payables	5,210
Inventories	607		Accruals	633
Other	369			$ 6,182
	$5,782	$ 5,782		
			Dealers' Deposits	234
Investments	243	243		
			Long-Term Debt	570
Plant and Equipment				
Gasoline Stations	3,564		Equity	3,515
Distribution	978			$10,501
Leased Equipment	1,111			
Other	900			
Less Depreciation	2,078	4,476		
Total		$10,501		

B. Income Statements, 1957-1959
(In Thousands, Year Ended April 30)

	1957	1958	1959
Net Sales	$37,528	$28,823	$27,125
Net Gain on Sales of Plant	36	89	2
Other	---	112	129
	$37,564	$29,024	$27,256
Materials and Operating	} $36,876	$25,952	$23,851
Selling, General and Administrative		3,078	3,385
Interest	26	43	47
	$36,902	$29,072	$27,284
Earnings before Tax	662	(48)	(27)
Federal Tax	321	8	(40)
Earnings (Loss)	341	(56)	13

3. AURORA GASOLINE COMPANY

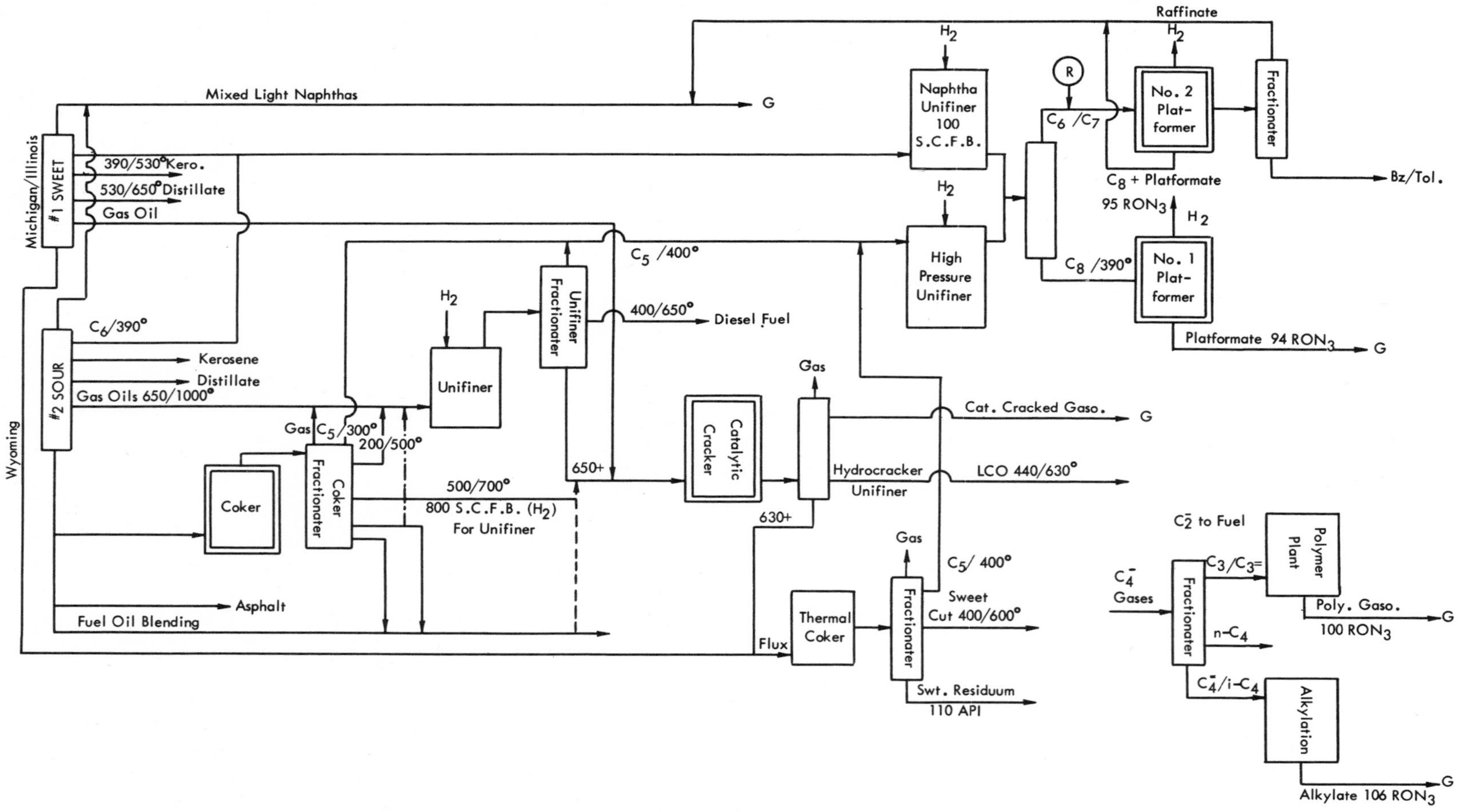

Michigan/Illinois
#1 SWEET
Mixed Light Naphthas
G
Raffinate
390/530° Kero.
530/650° Distillate
Gas Oil
Wyoming
#2 SOUR
C_6/390°
Kerosene
Distillate
Gas Oils 650/1000°
Fuel Oil Blending
Asphalt
Coker
Coker Fractionater
Gas
C_5/300°
200/500°
500/700°
800 S.C.F.B. (H_2) For Unifiner
H_2
Unifiner
Unifiner Fractionater
C_5 /400°
400/650°
Diesel Fuel
650+
Catalytic Cracker
Gas
Hydrocracker Unifiner
630+
Cat. Cracked Gaso.
G
LCO 440/630°
Flux
Thermal Coker
Gas
Fractionater
C_5/ 400°
Sweet Cut 400/600°
Swt. Residuum 110 API
H_2
Naphtha Unifiner 100 S.C.F.B.
H_2
High Pressure Unifiner
R
C_6 /C_7
C_8 /390°
H_2
No. 2 Plat-former
C_8 + Platformate 95 RON_3
H_2
No. 1 Plat-former
Platformate 94 RON_3
G
Fractionater
Bz/Tol.
C_4^- Gases
Fractionater
C_2^- to Fuel
$C_3/C_3=$
Polymer Plant
Poly. Gaso. 100 RON_3
G
n-C_4
C_4^-/i-C_4
Alkylation
Alkylate 106 RON_3
G

4. AURORA GASOLINE COMPANY

A. Crude Oil Costs (Per Barrel)

Crude API°	Wyoming 22°	Oklahoma 36°	Illinois 36°	West Texas 30°	Alberta 37°
In the Field:					
Well head	$2.16	$2.97	$3.00	$2.65	
Gathering	.05	.10	.10	.05	
Cost with 1% Allow.	2.232	3.101	3.131	2.727	
Crude Pipeline Rates to:					
Wood River	34¢	22¢	--	28¢	
Robinson	37	24	5¢	35	
Detroit	49	37	20¢	47	3.2456*
Toledo	47	35	18	45	
Muskegon	54	42	--	--	
Chicago	--	24	12.5	31	
Ponca City	--	10	--	18	

*Total delivered cost.

A. Products Pipeline Rates
(Cents per Barrel of Gasoline[1])

To:	From: Ponca City	Wood River	Robinson	East Chicago	Detroit	Toledo	Gerard, Penn.
Des Moines, Iowa	36.0	--	--	--	--	--	--
Madison, Wis.	55.0	49.0	40.0	24.0	--	--	--
Robinson, Ill.	--	--	--	--	--	--	--
Champaign, Ill.	--	13.5	6.8	--	--	--	--
E. Chicago, Ind.	58.0	25.0	16.0	--	--	32.3	--
Detroit, Mich.	82.3	49.3	28.6	24.3	--	8.8	--
Flint, Mich.	92.1	59.1	38.4	34.1	9.8	18.6	--
Bay City, Mich.	97.1	64.1	43.4	39.1	14.8	21.3	--
Toledo, Mich.	82.3	47.1	28.6	24.3	8.3	--	--
Lima, Ohio	96.6	54.6	23.6	38.6	14.3	7.5	--
Cleveland, Ohio	103.1	59.6	37.5	39.1	20.8	12.5	40.3
Columbus, Ohio	102.6	41.8	28.6	44.6	20.3	14.5	--
Pittsburgh, Pa.	--	--	--	--	--	--	24.3
Buffalo, N.Y.	--	--	--	--	--	--	31.3

B. Product Tanker Rates
(Cents per Barrel of Gasoline)

To:	From: East Chicago	Detroit	Toledo	Cleveland	Sarnia	Buffalo
E. Chicago, Ind.	--	44.4	47.8	52.3	40.4	61.1
Detroit, Mich.	44.4	--	13.9	19.2	13.9	27.0
Bay City, Mich.	39.3	23.2	27.1	34.1	20.0	36.5
Toledo, Ohio	47.8	13.9	--	19.2	17.9	27.1
Cleveland, Ohio	52.3	19.2	18.2	--	23.9	22.4
Sarnia, Ont.	40.4	13.9	17.9	22.3	--	31.8
Buffalo, N.Y.	61.1	27.1	27.1	22.4	31.8	---

[1]Quoted rates are for gasoline or naphtha; kerosene is 10 percent higher; No. 2 heating oil is 17 per cent higher.

5. AURORA GASOLINE COMPANY

Operating Data, May, 1959

A. Yields per thousand barrels of crude oil

Yield:	Michigan	Illinois	Wyoming Crude Fuel	Wyoming Crude Asphalt	Wyoming Crude Coke
Gasoline	467	436	351	329	434
Kerosene	190	170	110	110	110
No. 3 Heating oil	167	198	59	189	260
Fuel Oil	77	101	400	3	64
Butane	9	13	10	9	10
Propane	16	12	9	9	20
Sulfur (tons)	--	--	0.76	0.68	0.775
Loss & Burn	74	70	61	61	102
Asphalt, (tons)	--	--	--	31	--
Coke (tons)	--	--	--	--	37

B. Operating costs (cents per barrel of crude oil)

	Michigan	Illinois	Wyoming Crude Fuel	Wyoming Crude Asphalt	Wyoming Crude Coke
Fixed	21.2¢	21.2¢	27.5¢	27.5¢	33.6¢
Variable	26.0	25.0	28.7	28.7	35.2
Fuel Burn	13.0	12.5	11.0	10.5	17.3
TEL per barrel of gasoline	27.8	26.9	19.5	19.5	31.5

Detroit Market Prices of Products
(Cents per Gallon)

	July, 1958	October, 1958	May, 1959
Regular Gasoline	13.0	13.75	11.3
Premium Gasoline	15.0	14.75	13.3
No. 1 Heating Oil	12.0	12.5	12.0
No. 2	11.0	11.5	11.0
No. 3	11.0	11.5	11.0
No. 4	9.25	9.75	10.00
No. 5	8.75	9.25	9.50
No. 6	8.25	8.75	9.00

Butane	$2.15 per bbl.
Propane	1.34 per bbl.
Sulfur	$30.00 per ton
Asphalt	$20.00 per ton
Fluid Coke	$5.00 per ton

Michigan Crude Delivered to Detroit $3.482 per bbl.

The Ohio Oil Company (C)

On August 1, 1959, the Aurora Gasoline Company was acquired as a wholly owned subsidiary through the exchange of 874,422 newly issued shares of The Ohio Oil Company's common stock for all the capital stock of the Aurora Gasoline Company.

With the resources of The Ohio Oil Company to draw upon, new capital improvement projects at the Detroit refinery were evaluated. The expansion of the refinery's crude distillation capacity above 50,000 barrels per day was accomplished together with the dismantling of the small refinery at Elsie, Michigan. The elimination of the Elsie refinery was made possible by the announcement by a common carrier pipeline company that it would construct a products pipeline from Detroit to Flint, Michigan. The Aurora management took advantage of this move to establish a products terminal at Flint and then make up the loss of Elsie throughput by an expansion of its more modern plant at Detroit.

In 1960, the products pipeline to Flint was extended to Bay City, Michigan, the site of an important chemical plant complex. The expansion at Detroit had already indicated the need for expansion in the refinery to catalytic reforming capacity beyond the 6,000 barrels per day of the existing reformer. The opportunity to move products by pipeline to a chemical plant suggested that the new reformer be combined with extraction facilities to produce chemically pure aromatics.

In addition to its product yields, the new reformer would provide much needed hydrogen for sulfur treating refinery feedstocks. About 50 to 100 cubic feet of hydrogen would be needed to treat each barrel of its own reformer feed, but the rest would be available for other purposes. There was a 12,000-barrel per day unifiner for the heavy naphthas charged to reforming, which used about 150 cubic feet of hydrogen per barrel. There was also a large gas oil unifiner which prepared feedstock for the catalytic cracker. This 8,000-barrel unifiner used at least 450 cubic feet of hydrogen per barrel. It was estimated that 2,000 barrels of additional Wyoming crude oil could be catalytically cracked if hydrogen were available for its pretreatment. The reformer hydrogen would be about 85 percent pure.

PROPOSALS FOR NO. 2 REFORMER AT THE DETROIT REFINERY

The No. 1 reformer had been converted from a "platformer" to a "rexformer" in 1956, by the installation of an extractor column and a solvent stripper. These extraction facilities could form the basis of an aromatics extraction for the No. 2 reformer. About $125,000 would be needed to alter these facilities for aromatics extraction and convert No. 1 unit to a regular "platformer."

The added throughput at the Detroit refinery indicated that about 5,000 barrels of light naphthas, boiling between 170° and 200° F. would be available, with about 6,000 barrels of heavy naphthas, from about 200° to 400° F. for the old reformer. Separate samples were tested of the Wyoming naphthas and the Michigan–Illinois naphthas. The problem of finding aromatics-rich naphthas resolved itself to three steps: first, determining the daily volume of heart cut in the narrow range of 170 to 200 degrees; second, isolating the C_6—C_7—C_8 components in the cut; and third, determining what percent of these hydrocarbons were structured as aromatics or naphthenes that could be converted to aromatics by reforming, rather than being paraffins which were of no use for this purpose. The principal and most valuable product was benzene, the C_6 aromatic. Toluene, the C_7 aromatic, was useful either as a high-octane blending component or a chemical building block. Xylene, the C_8 aromatic, was most useful as an octane component. The yield analysis, as indicated in Exhibit 1B, showed that for each thousand barrels of Wyoming crude, which was running at 30,000 barrels per day, there were 2.94 barrels of C_6 naphthenes and aromatics and 6.62 barrels of C_7 naphthenes and aromatics. For each thousand barrels of Michigan or Illinois crude, running at a combined total of 20,000 barrels per day, the aromatics feed was 8.57 and 8.86 barrels.

In considering the investment in a new reformer, the Aurora management realized that although there was only feedstock for a 5,000-barrel aromatics unit, an operation with double the capacity would cost little more to construct or operate. They therefore asked the Robinson refinery to supply a special heart-cut naphtha to add to the feedstock of the aromatics operation.

The Robinson refinery was processing 50,000 barrels per day. It determined that it could supply all of its #1 light naphtha stock, rich in C_6. It could also supply #2 light naphtha, rich in C_7, from about 27,370 of the 50,000 barrels run daily. The total mixture, with some C_8, could be shipped on the products pipeline from Robinson to Detroit at a rate of 4,000 barrels per day. This would allow the Detroit refinery to build a 9,000-barrel reformer rather than a 5,000-barrel unit. It would, however, require construction of a de-pentanizer tower at Robinson.

Under one plan for the expanded system, the aromatics extraction unit would yield a mixed stream of aromatics at the rate of 1,537 barrels per day, consisting largely of benzene and toluene. Additional extraction towers would have to be built to separate the benzene from the toluene. Furthermore, the hydrogen released from the reformer could be used to convert the toluene into benzene by constructing a de-alkylation unit.

The Aurora refinery, therefore, had many possible alternatives. It could install a 5,000-barrel or a 9,000-barrel reformer. It could operate the reformer for motor fuel or for aromatics. It could supply these aromatics as a mixed stream or as separate products. It could supply the regular yield of aromatics, or it could maximize the benzene by hydro-de-alkylating the toluene. In view of changing market factors in both the oil and chemical industries, the management was anxious to make a capital investment decision that would make the best use of its particular geographic situation and process skills.

1. THE OHIO OIL COMPANY (C)

A. Available Light Naphthas for Aromatics Extraction
(Barrels per Day)

	at Robinson	at Detroit	Paraffin	Naphthene	Aromatic	Total
C_6	2188	1278	71.0%	25.5	3.5	100.0
C_7	1612	1272	57.7%	39.8	2.5	100.0
C_8	200	2450	57.7%	37.6	4.7	100.0
	4000	5000				

B. Aromatics Yield from Available Naphthas
(Barrels of Yield per 1,000 Barrels of Feedstock)

	Robinson		Detroit		
	#1	#2	Wyoming	Mich.-Ill.	Yield
(1) C_6					Benzene
Paraffins	27.31 bbls.	--	11.80 bbls.	30.80 bbls.	0.0
Naphthenes:					
Methylcyclo Pentane	8.25	--	1.40	3.76	47.6%
Cyclo Hexane	4.74	--	1.33	3.76	78.1%
Benzene	1.86	--	0.21	1.05	100.0%
Mixed C_5	1.50	--	0.72	1.35	0.0
					Toluene
(2) C_7					
Paraffins	--	27.93	12.90	25.52	0.0
Naphthenes	--	29.58	5.85	8.41	74.5%
Toluene	--	1.44	0.77	0.45	100.0%
Available Total Run (Barrels per Day)	50,000	27,370	30,000	20,000	
Boiling Points:					
10%	173°F.		169°F.	169°F.	
90%	202°F.		202°F.	200°F.	

2. THE OHIO OIL COMPANY (C)

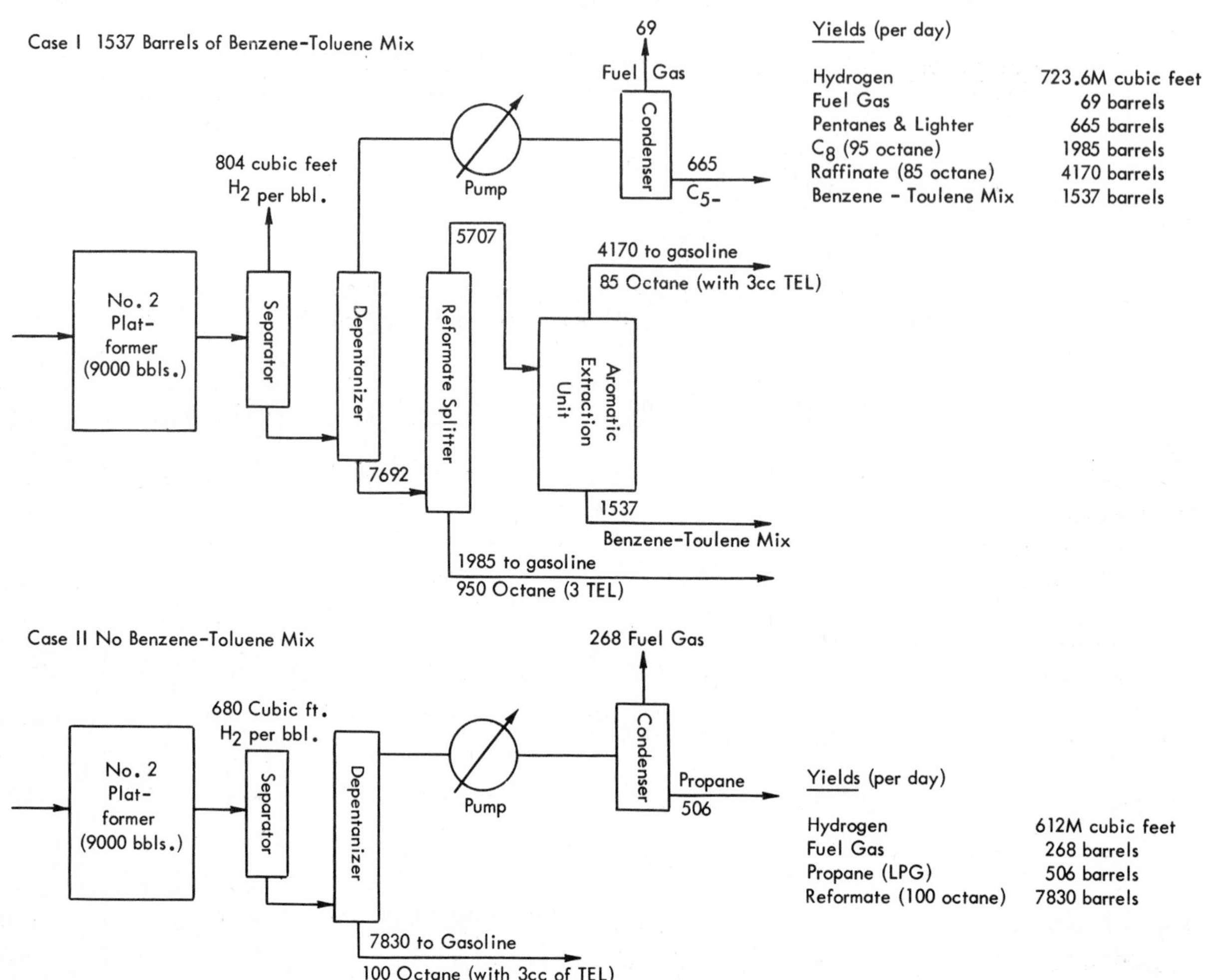

Note: Octane numbers are research method, after addition of 3cc of tetraethyl lead per gallon.

3. THE OHIO OIL COMPANY (C)

A. Yields from No. 2 Reformer on Aromatics Operation

		Dependentanizer		Splitter		Aromatics Extraction	
		O'head	Bottoms	O'head	Bottoms	O'head	Bottoms
C_2 - C_3 Gas		69	---	---	---	---	---
C_3		110	---	---	---	---	---
C_4		315	---	---	---	---	---
C_5		240	50	50	---	---	50
C_6	Paraffin	---	2218	2218	---	---	2218
	Naphthene	---	255	255	---	---	255
	Benzene	---	620	620	---	617	3
C_7	Paraffin	---	1415	1401	14	---	1401
	Naphthene	---	115	114	1	---	114
	Toluene	---	927	918	9	875	43
C_8	Paraffin	---	1139	68	1071	---	68
	Naphthene	---	50	3	47	---	3
	Xylene	---	903	60	843	45	15
		69 + 665	7962	5707	1958	1537	4170

B. Price Factors

	Per Gallon
Light Naphtha (Mixed Wyo. & Michigan crudes at Detroit)	10 cents
Xylene	14
Toluene	19.19
Butane	8.5
Pentane	11.0
85 octane gasoline	9.75
95 octane gasoline	12.0

C. Investment

No. 2 Platformer	$2,415,000
Alter Extraction Plant and Naphtha Unifiner	350,000
Tankage and Offsite	675,000
Engineering	250,000
Depentanizer at Robinson	250,000
	$3,940,000

Continental Oil Company

The Continental Oil Company was a major oil corporation with refineries in Ponca City, Oklahoma; Lake Charles, Louisiana; Wichita Falls, Texas; Billings, Montana; and Denver, Colorado. Between 1952 and 1960, average net crude oil production increased from 105,000 to 196,800 barrels daily. Domestic sales of refined products increased from 52,300 to 118,400 barrels of gasoline daily, from 22,800 to 69,500 barrels of middle distillates, and from 8,400 to 19,600 barrels of heavy fuel oil daily. In addition, the company sold 246 million pounds of petrochemicals and 108 thousand tons of carbon black in 1960.

Between 1952 and 1960, the gross plant accounts increased from $52.8 million in refineries, petrochemical plants and natural gasoline plants and $29.4 million in marketing facilities to $195.3 million in manufacturing and $114.2 in marketing facilities. By 1960, the total gross plant account was over $1,361 million, including $171 million in international operations. The number of employees had increased from 7,300 to 13,200.

The main refinery of the company was in Ponca City, Oklahoma, where it was built up during the 1920's to run the company's sweet mid-continent crude oil. In 1952, the Oklahoma and Kansas crude oil accounted for 21,600 barrels daily out of the company's total crude production of 105,000 barrels, with North Texas crude supplementing the runs. In 1960, Oklahoma and Kansas accounted for 17,100 barrels daily out of the company's 159,200 of domestic and 37,600 barrels of foreign crude oil.

The Ponca City refinery had been an ultramodern plant in the 1920's under the presidency of Mr. Marland. It had the largest tank farm in the world and extensive buildings and recreation facilities. Mr. Marland, who owned a large estate in the city, later served as governor of the state and was a prominent figure in financial circles. After the stockmarket crash of 1929, a period of retrenchment set in during which operating costs were greatly reduced, under the presidency of Mr. Dan Moran. When Mr. L. F. McCollum became president before the end of World War II, a new period of aggressive expansion began, under a gradually extended program of capital investment analysis.

One of the first postwar moves at the Ponca City refinery was to purchase from the Defense Plant Corporation for $3.1 million the thermofor catalytic cracking plant which the company had leased during the war. The plant, with a feedstock charging capacity of 22,500 barrels per day, used a moving bed system for the catalyst pellets, with bucket elevators for the three reactors. The purchase also included a hydrofluoric acid alkylation unit which the government had built to provide facilities for high-octane aviation gasoline. In 1944, the crude capacity of the Ponca City plant was 33,000 barrels per day. However, this was soon increased to 52,000 barrels by the construction of a new crude topping unit, and 15,000 barrels of the company's West Texas crude oil were brought in by a new pipeline system. The refinery also processed 2,000 barrels per day of lubricating oil through the solvent extraction method.

By 1960, the Ponca City refinery had been modernized and expanded to a crude capacity of 70,000 barrels per day. With the construction of the Great Lakes pipeline, in the early 1950's, the refinery served not only the company's traditional southwestern markets, but the midwest and north central states as well. When middle distillate prices declined in 1949, the company's new facilities were flexible enough to enable it to increase the yield of gasoline to 60 percent of crude runs. Exhibit 1 contains a flow chart of the Ponca City refinery.

Between 1950 and 1953, more than $28 million was also invested to increase the capacity of the Lake Charles refinery from 11,000 to 45,000 barrels per day. The new plant contained catalytic cracking facilities, as well as alkylation, polymerization and catalytic reformers with solvent extraction units for aromatics. These expanded facilities coincided with the company's increased interest in offshore drilling operations in the Gulf of Mexico.

During the 1950's, much catalytic reforming capacity was installed. In 1954, the Ponca City refinery converted obsolete equipment into a 4,500-barrel catalytic reformer, and put into operation a 12,500-barrel per day delayed coker. The Billings refinery was outfitted with a catalytic reformer and desulfurizer to handle low-priced high-sulfur crude from Wyoming. In 1956, an 11,000-barrel reformer was installed in

Ponca City which, with the old reformer, enabled it to increase its octane by seven numbers higher than 1951. An 11,000-barrel reformer was also added to the existing 7,000-barrel reformer at Lake Charles in 1959.[1]

The Continental Oil Company owned crude pipelines supplying Ponca City from North Texas, Kansas, and Oklahoma. It owned 50 percent of the Cherokee line which ran products from Ponca City and other Oklahoma points to Wood River and 20 percent of the Platte pipeline running crude from Wyoming to Wood River. The Cherokee line also had a products line from Ponca City to Wood River and then connected to the Wabash to Griffith, Indiana, near Chicago. Continental owned 25 percent of the Wabash and 29 percent of the Great Lakes products line which ran from Ponca City to Iowa, and on to Minnesota and the Dakotas, connecting to Chicago from Des Moines, Iowa.

Since 1951, the company had also made a substantial diversification commitment to the petrochemical field. A petrochemical plant in Baltimore made household detergents and plasticizers from benzene and dodecene, and supplied company plants at Chicago, Illinois; Trainer, Pennsylvania; and Gretna, Louisiana, which made industrial detergents and motor oil additives. Affiliates in the Lake Charles area made ethylene, ethylene glycol, butadiene, and anhydrous ammonia and another affiliate made carbon black. As a result of the expansion of these petrochemical activities and the installation of catalytic reformers during the 1950's, the Ponca City refinery became increasingly involved in the supply and demand for benzene and hydrogen.

The Demand for Benzene, 1951 to 1958

In 1951, the company bought for $1.3 million the outstanding 50 percent interest of its partner in the Sharples-Continental Corporation, which made neolene, a synthetic detergent material. Neolene was manufactured in a plant at Baltimore, Maryland, using benzene and dodecene as raw materials. The dodecyl benzene product was subsequently sulfonated in customer plants to make finished synthetic detergents. In 1952, the company invested $1.7 million to triple the capacity of the Baltimore plant, to acquire sulfonation plants, and to construct an aromatics extraction unit for the new catalytic reformer at the Lake Charles refinery. Between 1952 and 1954, sales of petrochemicals tripled. In 1951, the Baltimore plant had produced 21.7 million pounds of neolene and 10.6 million pounds of by-products.

To meet the increased demand for benzene at the Baltimore plant and to improve octane ratings of motor fuels, a catalytic reformer and aromatics extraction unit was put on stream at the Lake Charles refinery in 1953. However, the Baltimore plant could obtain benzene from the coking ovens of a nearby steel plant, which supplied about 40 percent of its requirements. Another steel company in Colorado offered benzene which could be shipped by tank car to Lake Charles for 6.8 cents per gallon and moved by company tankers, together with the Lake Charles refinery benzene, for 0.94 cents per gallon to Baltimore.

In 1954, the Ponca City refinery completed its first catalytic reformer, which was made over from an old hydroformer and had a rated capacity of 4,500 barrels per day. The aromatics extraction unit, using phenol as a solvent, was converted from a wartime toluene extraction and purification unit that had been purchased from the government in 1948. The reformer could be operated on a blocked-out basis, to run motor fuel and aromatics feeds alternately. It was found that this benzene product could be moved by pipeline and barge to Lake Charles for 3 cents per gallon less than by tank car.

At that time, the new sources of supply put the Lake Charles refinery in an excess position of about 167 barrels per day of the 272 it could process. The Ponca City reformer could produce 103 barrels per day when run for maximum aromatics or 23 barrels per day when run for maximum octane. In 1954, therefore, the company was searching for benzene customers.

By 1956, however, growth in the petrochemicals division caused a reevaluation of the company's benzene requirements. With the detergent demand running between 100 and 125 million pounds per year, between 435 and 550 barrels of benzene per day were needed. Moreover, it was clear that benzene could be used to make other products. For example, 245 barrels per day of benzene could support a 25-million

[1] A 4,500-barrel per day catalytic reformer was added to Denver in 1957, and a 4,000-barrel per day reformer and desulfurizer was added at Wichita Falls in the same year.

pound per year phenol plant; 320 barrels per day could support a 40-million pound styrene plant; 440 barrels could support a 25-million pound caprolactam plant, using cyclohexane to make this type of nylon.

With these market trends in mind, expansion plans were drawn for the catalytic reformers at Lake Charles and Ponca City. In December, 1956, based on crude throughput of 50,500 barrels per day, the Lake Charles refinery could produce 293 barrels of benzene for Baltimore, 637 barrels of a toluene-xylene blending fuel for the Wichita Falls refinery, which needed high-octane material, and 3,000 barrels of aviation gasoline for the motor fuel pool at Lake Charles. By June, 1957, the benzene capacity was increased to 380 barrels per day, yielding motor fuel blending stocks that could be leaded to 95 octane. There was a question as to whether the octane race might require the aromatics extraction unit to be shut down to allow greater high-octane feeds to the motor fuel pool.

To meet these needs, a second catalytic reformer was built at Ponca City for about $2.0 million. When it went on stream in June, 1957, it released the No. 1 reformer for continual aromatics production, which ran 350 barrels per day of benzene.

Between April, 1957 and April, 1958, the benzene situation was under continual review. With benzene requirements at Baltimore about 350 barrels per day in excess of its local purchases from the steel plant, and either the Ponca City and the Lake Charles refineries capable of supplying that amount by itself, outside customers were sought within the market radius of the refineries. However, the principal chemical potential customer reported that test samples of benzene could not be accepted due to poor color tests. In order to market the benzene either purification equipment would have to be installed or price concessions would have to be made, and the long-term availability of adequate volume would have to be assured.

Rough estimates indicated that it would cost $20,000 to install an acid or clay treatment unit and $50,000 to install a segregated 25,000-barrel storage tank to obtain higher color purity. Another 1¢ to 1.25¢ per gallon would be required for purification process costs to obtain nitration grade benzene. Such benzene could be shipped by barge from Lake Charles to a chemical customer in Texas for 0.3¢ per gallon and from Wood River to another chemical customer in St. Louis for 0.4¢ per gallon by tank wagon.

It was determined that Lake Charles could supply an additional 55 barrels of benzene per day by using casinghead gasoline as additional feedstock to the reformer. However, it would cost about $350,000 to install the equipment necessary to handle the casinghead feed.

In determining the cost of making benzene, a formula was developed by which the alternative cost of using the facilities to make motor fuels could be established. Such costs were lower at Ponca City than at Lake Charles, due to the lower capital charges on the equipment and somewhat lower variable processing costs, which were partly offset by the disadvantageous inland geographic location of the Oklahoma refinery.

The Cyclohexane Plant, 1958 to 1960

In April, 1958, a new approach to the benzene situation was outlined in the following proposal:

> The availability of hydrogen and benzene at Ponca City plus the likelihood of using the Cherokee Pipeline to transport cyclohexane to Wood River and thence by barge along the rivers has prompted a more intensive study of benzene sources to supplement our own benzene for the production of 10 to 15 million gallons of cyclohexane per year.
>
> There are seven refineries within 100 miles of Ponca City that are potential benzene producers, but are at a greater location disadvantage to the markets than is Ponca City. We feel these refineries might be able to deliver benzene to us under favorable terms. Alternatively, those refineries within a lower freight limit could supply us with a special naphtha cut which we could process into benzene. Our Wichita Falls refinery can pipe such naphtha to us together with their crude oil, and it could be fractionated out in our existing equipment. The extraction unit at Ponca City would then be expanded by an investment of $300,000 to $400,000.
>
> A cyclohexane plant would cost about $1,200,000. With 9.35 million gallons of benzene from all sources plus the hydrogen from our reformers, we could obtain 11 million gallons of cyclohexane per year.

The construction of a cyclohexane plant would change the benzene situation from an excess to a shortage problem at the Ponca City refinery. It was estimated that for each million gallons per year of cyclohexane, 56 barrels per day of benzene would be required, plus 220 thousand standard cubic feet per day of the hydrogen-rich off-gas from the catalytic reformers. In other words, a 50-million gallon cyclohexane plant would require 2,775 of benzene barrels per day. Since the optimum plant size was nearer 25 million than 15 million gallons, the principal limiting factor would be the availability of benzene, beyond the 350 barrels per day that the Ponca City refinery could currently produce at a crude input of 52,000 barrels per day. In fact, one engineering firm that had been prominent in the development of cyclohexane projects pointed out that the changing economies of benzene were the reason that the firm had become interested in cyclohexane.

The availability of benzene to the Ponca City refinery was somewhat complicated by its inland geographic location. There was a quoted market price for benzene, but these referred to spot purchases of benzene cargoes along the Gulf of Mexico. Benzene available up the Mississippi River was usually 1½ cents per gallon cheaper than Gulf Coast benzene to allow for shipping and handling costs, and benzene inland in Oklahoma was usually another 1½ cents cheaper. The price of benzene had been declining since 1953 when it was 39 cents on the Gulf. The price of cyclohexane was about 37 cents per gallon.

Since there was no established market price for benzene in Oklahoma, prices would have to be negotiated with those refineries that were equipped to supply it. The refineries ordinarily set a value on their benzene by determining what the value would be of running an equivalent amount of naphtha for a maximum yield of motor fuels rather than for aromatics.

Operation of the Aromatics Unit to Feed the Cyclohexane Plant

A decision was made to proceed with the cyclohexane plant, and it was installed on land adjacent to the aromatics extraction unit so that it could be operated from the same control room. Meanwhile, the crude capacity of the Ponca City refinery was expanded to 69,100 barrels per day and the aromatics extraction unit was expanded and improved.

The expansion of the aromatics unit cost $204,800 and was designed to increase its charge capacity as well as to improve its recovery of benzene from 88 to 94 percent. A new feed preparation splitter tower was installed to recover more benzene formers from the heavy naphthas and increase naphtha feed to the No. 1 reformer. The old high-pressure recycle compressor was used to pump hydrogen from the reformers to the cyclohexane unit and a new lower-pressure compressor was installed to maximize the lower benzene production in the reformer. New trays were installed in the fractionating towers of the extraction unit, particularly in T-3 tower, where the phenol solvent was charged. Under the renovation, the crude charge of 69,100 barrels per day could yield 550 barrels of benzene. Exhibits 2 to 4 show the process flow of the reformers in greater detail.

In 1960, the crude capacity of the Ponca City refinery was 69,100 barrels per day. With this throughput, it could produce between 33,000 and 34,000 barrels of gasoline, depending upon the method of operation, plus 7,252 barrels of jet fuel and 1,763 barrels of aviation gasoline. The crude units could supply 8,400 barrels of light naphtha for reforming, boiling below 205° F. They could also supply from 7,699 to 9,359 barrels of heavy naphtha for reforming, boiling above 205° F., the difference of 1,660 barrels depending upon whether the heaviest naphtha was charged to the catalytic reformer or blended to jet fuel.

The light naphtha could be cut into three stocks. The lightest cut, 2,625 barrels of naphtha containing pentanes up to 160° F. boiling point, could be fed directly to gasoline blending as straight-run or casinghead gasoline. The middle cut could either be charged to No. 1 reformer and the aromatics extraction unit or combined directly with the casinghead for the gasoline blending stock. The third cut, 2,259 barrels from 185° to 205° F., was the aviation blending component, which was reformed and fractionated in the aromatics extraction unit to obtain the 1,051 barrels of high-octane material rich in toluene and xylene which could be used for aviation gasoline or to upgrade motor fuel. The heavy naphtha was charged to the No. 2

reformer and the heavy reformate that was produced was an important gasoline blending stock. The charge feed could be supplemented by about 11 percent thermal reformed heavy naphtha.

When No. 1 reformer was operated for benzene and toluene with large quantities of light naphtha, the severity of the operation was lower than when operating it for toluene only. The No. 1 reformer, operated for aromatics, yielded 888 standard cubic feet of gas per barrel which contained 91.5 percent pure hydrogen per barrel of naphtha charge. The gas, which was equivalent of 5.74 barrels of fuel oil equivalent per 100 barrels of charge, could be regarded as fuel to help supply the heat required by the feed preparation unit, the reforming reaction, and the aromatics extraction, or it could be purified and used as feedstock to the cyclohexane unit. No. 2 reformer yielded 800 cubic feet of hydrogen-rich gas per barrel of charge. The No. 1 reformer also yielded 10.1 barrels of fuel oil equivalent of gases containing propanes, butanes, pentanes, and some heavier material, per 100 barrels of naphtha feed. These gases were sent to the gas recovery plant, and some of the material was eventually used for gasoline blending stock.

When operated for aromatics, the catalyst in the reformer did not last as long as when it was on motor fuel operation. The catalyst, with replacement cost of $3.72 per pound, lasted for 70 barrels of charge per pound of catalyst on aromatics operation, and 120 barrels per pound on motor fuel operation. The heavier naphtha had to be desulfurized for the No. 2 reformer, and this catalyst lasted 300 barrels and cost only $1.00 per pound. The reformers required about 6.6 cents per barrel of charge for utilities, such as fuel, cooling water, steam, and electricity to operate the pumps and compressors.

In the aromatics extraction unit, the reformate from No. 1 reformer was fed to T-1 fractionating tower, which passed the bottoms to T-2 tower, where they were separated to a nonaromatic cut which passed overhead and the valuable toluenes left as bottoms to be used as aviation blending component. This separation process would be used whether No. 1 reformer operated for aromatics (on a benzene plus an aviation blend charge) or for an aviation blend charge alone. When operated for benzene, the benzene cut left T-1 tower as overhead and was charged to the T-3 tower, where it was dissolved in phenol. In T-4 and T-5 towers, the solution was distilled, with the benzene passed off overhead and the phenol leaving as bottoms for recirculation. Benzene raffinate was produced overhead from T-3 to be used in gasoline blending or jet fuel blending. Exhibits 5 and 6 contain diagrams of the reformer operations.

In the extraction unit, one man per shift could be eliminated if no benzene were run, though the work force would be the same at the reformers. When running benzene, the costs of extraction were 9.78 cents per barrel of charge for fuel, 0.81 cents for cooling water, 2.48 cents for steam, 0.7 cents for electricity, and 2.97 cents for phenol.

Any change in the reformer operation affected the selection of stocks that could be used to blend automotive and aircraft fuels. For example, there were more than a dozen component stocks to choose from in making gasoline. The objective was to obtain a pool octane number of 93.38 and a Reid vapor pressure of 11. Thus, if two volumes of light casinghead with 76 octane and 23 vapor pressure were increased, some other component such as aviation blending stock (rich in toluene) would be required with 104 octane and 1.5 vapor pressure to balance it. In addition, tetraethyl lead could be used to bring up the octane level, at the rate of about 8.57 cubic centimeters per barrel per octane number, and a cost of 0.2 cents per cubic centimeter. Jet fuels, on the other hand, had no octane requirement, but did have strict vapor pressure, purity, and boiling point specifications, and could use various kinds of naphthas and raffinates, provided that the final blend was satisfactory. Jet fuels for military use were obtained on six-month sealed-bid contracts, and the gain or loss of one of the contracts might well affect the balance of other stocks. However, the Ponca City refinery had more than eight million barrels of storage capacity and could afford to hold stocks for a period of time if it chose to.

In making 550 barrels of benzene, the refinery would also produce 2,699 barrels of benzene raffinate in the extraction unit, plus 185 barrels of thermal reformed material that would otherwise be charged to the No. 2 reformer, plus 147 barrels from the gas recovery plant due to the larger net charge through the reformers, consisting of 66 barrels of isopentane, 37 barrels of normal pentanes, and 44 barrels of hexanes. If no benzene were made, the charge of heavy naphtha to the No. 2 reformer would be increased, yielding an additional 1,568 barrels of reformate and permitting an additional 1,780 barrels of casinghead gasoline to be blended, for a net increase of 769 barrels of gasoline blending stock daily. Exhibits 7, 8, and 9B show the yields, cost factors, and price trends that affected the reforming process.

Availability of Benzene, 1960 to 1962

With 550 barrels per day of benzene, and 2.21 million cubic feet per day of purified hydrogen off-gas from the reformer, the refinery could produce 13.9 million gallons of cyclohexane per year from its own raw materials. However, by the time the cyclohexane plant came on stream in 1960, the increased demand for cyclohexane indicated that by 1962 the company could possibly sell considerably more than the 13.9 million gallons per year. Since the cyclohexane plant had sufficient capacity to meet this demand, its operation depended upon the availability of benzene.

There were four methods open to the Ponca City refinery to increase its supplies of benzene: (1) it could improve its existing facilities to increase the efficiency of the aromatics reforming and extraction units; (2) it could invest in a plant to convert toluene to benzene by using hydrogen gas for de-alkylation of the toluene; (3) it could purchase special cuts of naphthas to increase the throughput in its aromatics plant; (4) it could purchase benzene or benzene concentrate from other refineries.

Improve Existing Facilities: A new extraction, fractionation and isomerization unit would be constructed for $5 million. It was expected to gain 1,500 barrels of benzene per day and would require crude input of 75,000 barrels, full capacity of the No. 1 reformer at 6,500 barrels of naphtha per day, and outside purchase of benzene concentrate from the reformers at other refineries. A 44-percent benzene platformate could be obtained for 20 cents per gallon delivered, to feed the expanded extraction unit.

Install a Unit to De-Alkylate Toluene: Various plans were proposed to convert the toluene to benzene by using hydrogen de-alkylation. Such plans would generate up to 1,000 barrels per day of benzene and would require investments of up to $1.5 million. Such proposals are detailed in the reference notes, Exhibit 16.

Purchase Naphtha Cuts: Seven or eight refineries in the Oklahoma area were contacted with a view to obtaining light naphtha feedstock rich in naphthenes and aromatics. Samples of these stocks were analyzed for their product yields, and the offering prices were compared with the yield values. The three best prospects are detailed in Exhibit 9A. In addition, 450 barrels per day of light naphtha from the Wichita Falls refinery could be moved to Ponca City in the crude pipeline for 5.75 cents per barrel freight cost, to yield 70 barrels of benzene at Ponca City.

Purchase Benzene: Based on the established market in the Gulf Coast area small refiners in the mid-continent area were forced to pay transportation in order to reach the established market. At this point, the company felt that it was impossible to obtain benzene at a competitive price when taking into consideration transportation costs.

1. CONTINENTAL OIL COMPANY

Simplified Flow Chart of Ponca City Refinery

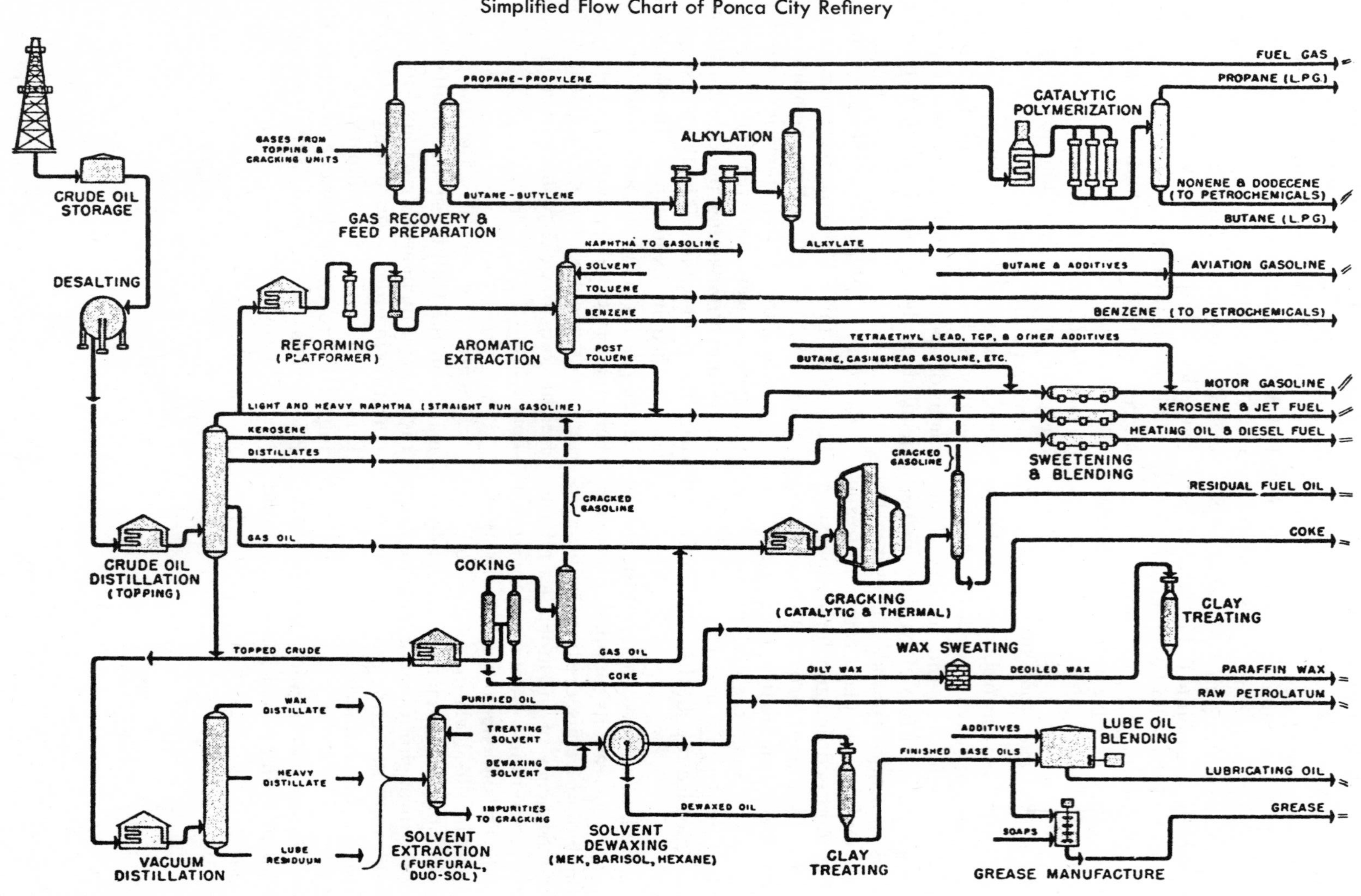

Note: The reforming section contained two units, reformers one and two.

2. CONTINENTAL OIL COMPANY

Catalytic Reformers at Ponca City Refinery

Photo, Continental Oil Co.

2A. Reformer No. 1

Rated capacity of 6,200 B.P.D. This reformer could be operated alternately for motor fuel or aromatics.

Photo, Continental Oil Co.

2B. Reformer No. 2

Rated capacity of 11,000 B.P.D., operated for high-octane motor fuel. Photograph shows the three reactors and the desulfurizer. To the rear is the main furnace

3. CONTINENTAL OIL COMPANY

Catalytic Reforming and Naphtha Desulfurization Unit

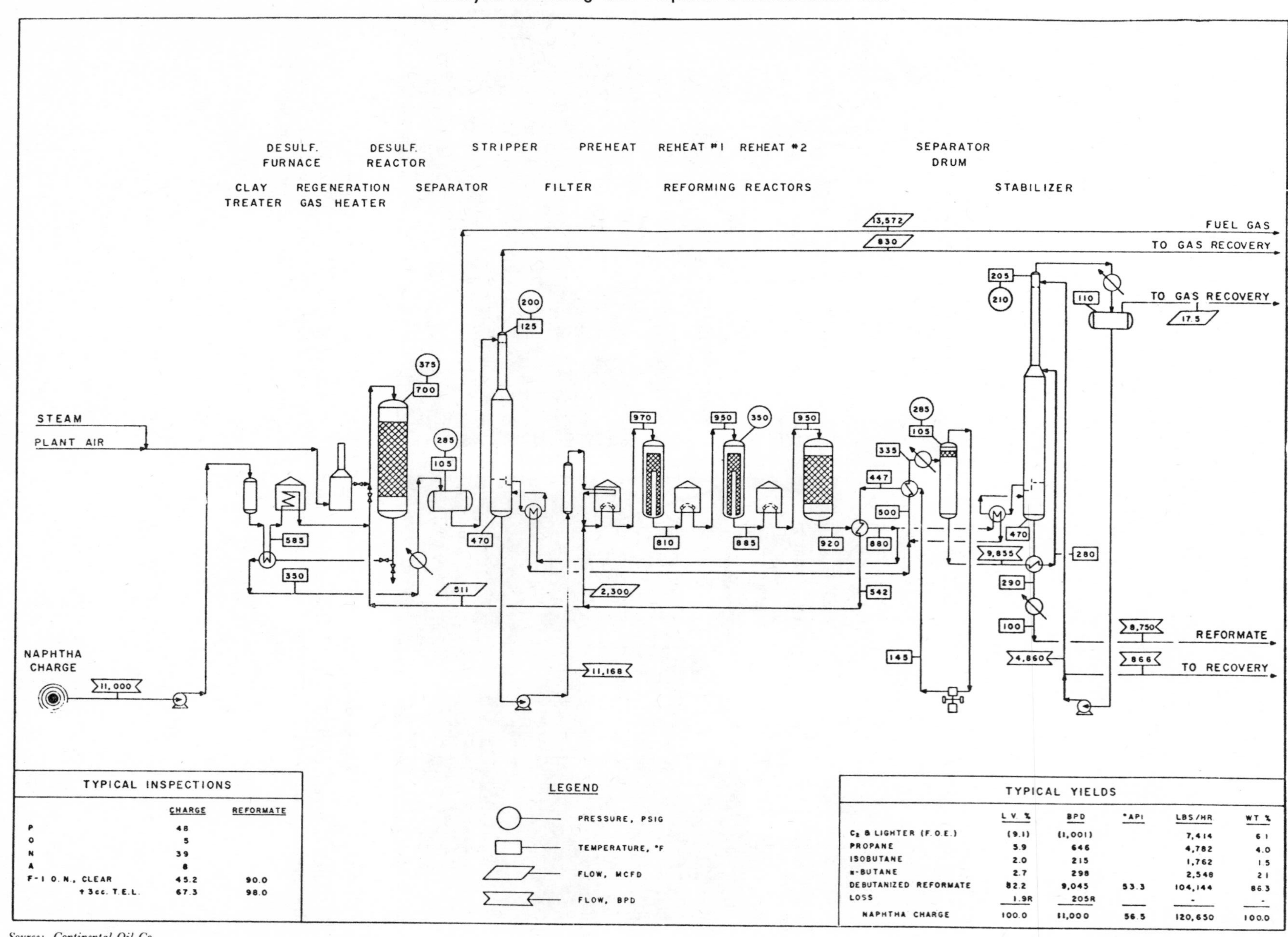

TYPICAL INSPECTIONS

	CHARGE	REFORMATE
P	48	
O	5	
N	39	
A	8	
F-1 O.N., CLEAR	45.2	90.0
+ 3cc. T.E.L.	67.3	98.0

TYPICAL YIELDS

	L.V. %	BPD	°API	LBS/HR	WT %
C_2 & LIGHTER (F.O.E.)	(9.1)	(1,001)		7,414	6.1
PROPANE	5.9	646		4,782	4.0
ISOBUTANE	2.0	215		1,762	1.5
n-BUTANE	2.7	298		2,548	2.1
DEBUTANIZED REFORMATE	82.2	9,045	53.3	104,144	86.3
LOSS	1.9R	205R		-	-
NAPHTHA CHARGE	100.0	11,000	56.5	120,650	100.0

Source: Continental Oil Co.

4. CONTINENTAL OIL COMPANY

Photo, Continental Oil Co.

4A. Aromatics and Cyclohexane Units

To the left are the five, dark towers of the aromatic extraction unit. The central one is the phenol tower. To the right are the lighter fractionating towers of the cyclohexane unit.

Photo, Continental Oil Co.

4B. Reactors for the Cyclohexane Unit

The three main reactors of the cyclohexane unit are in the foreground. Since the process is exothermic, it generates heat which is removed by large fans under the main reactors. The dark towers of the aromatics unit can be seen in the background.

5. CONTINENTAL OIL COMPANY

Process Flow for Aromatics (All Figures in Barrels per Day)

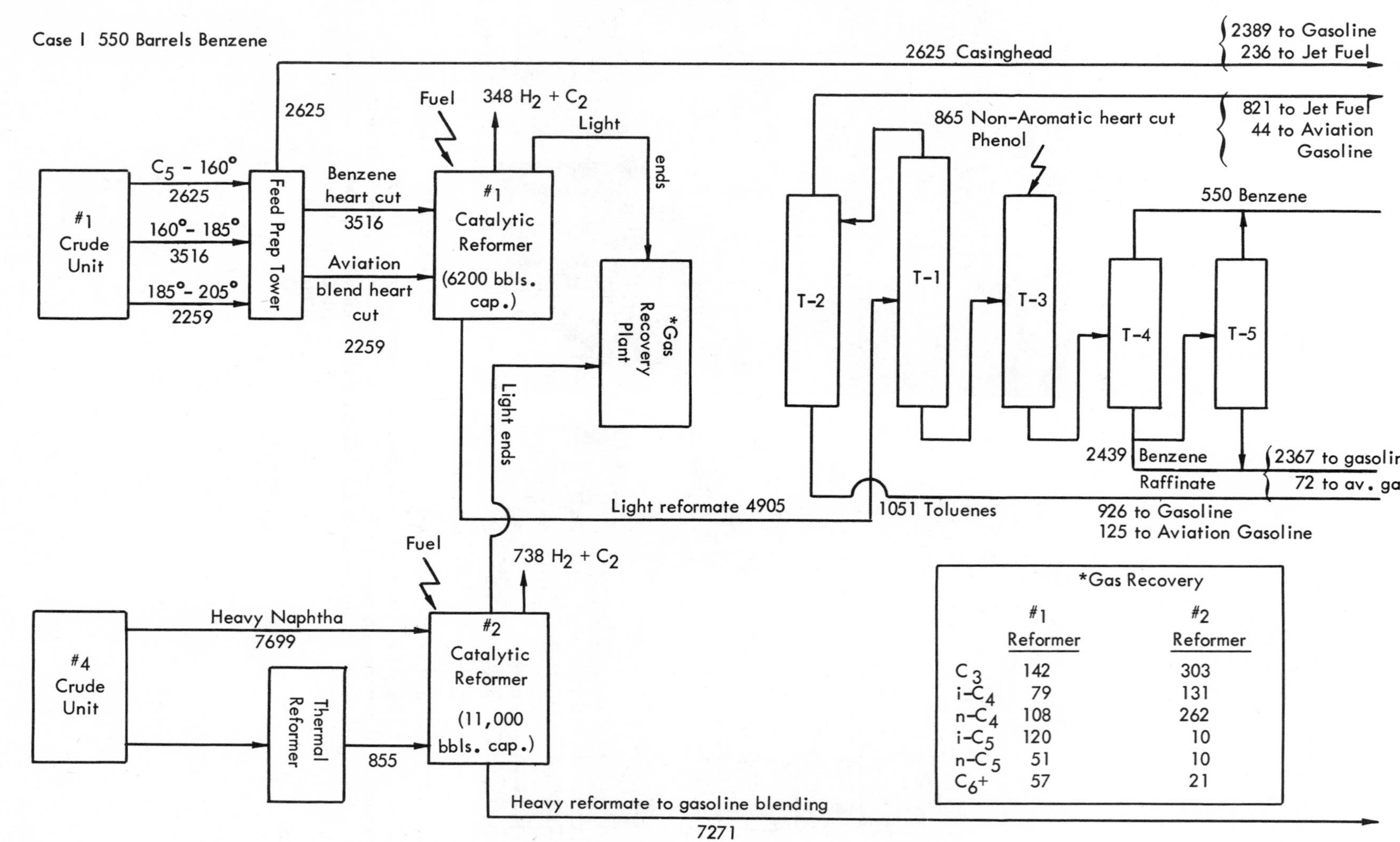

*Gas Recovery

	#1 Reformer	#2 Reformer
C_3	142	303
$i\text{-}C_4$	79	131
$n\text{-}C_4$	108	262
$i\text{-}C_5$	120	10
$n\text{-}C_5$	51	10
C_6^+	57	21

6. CONTINENTAL OIL COMPANY

Process Flow for Motor Fuel (All Figures in Barrels per Day)

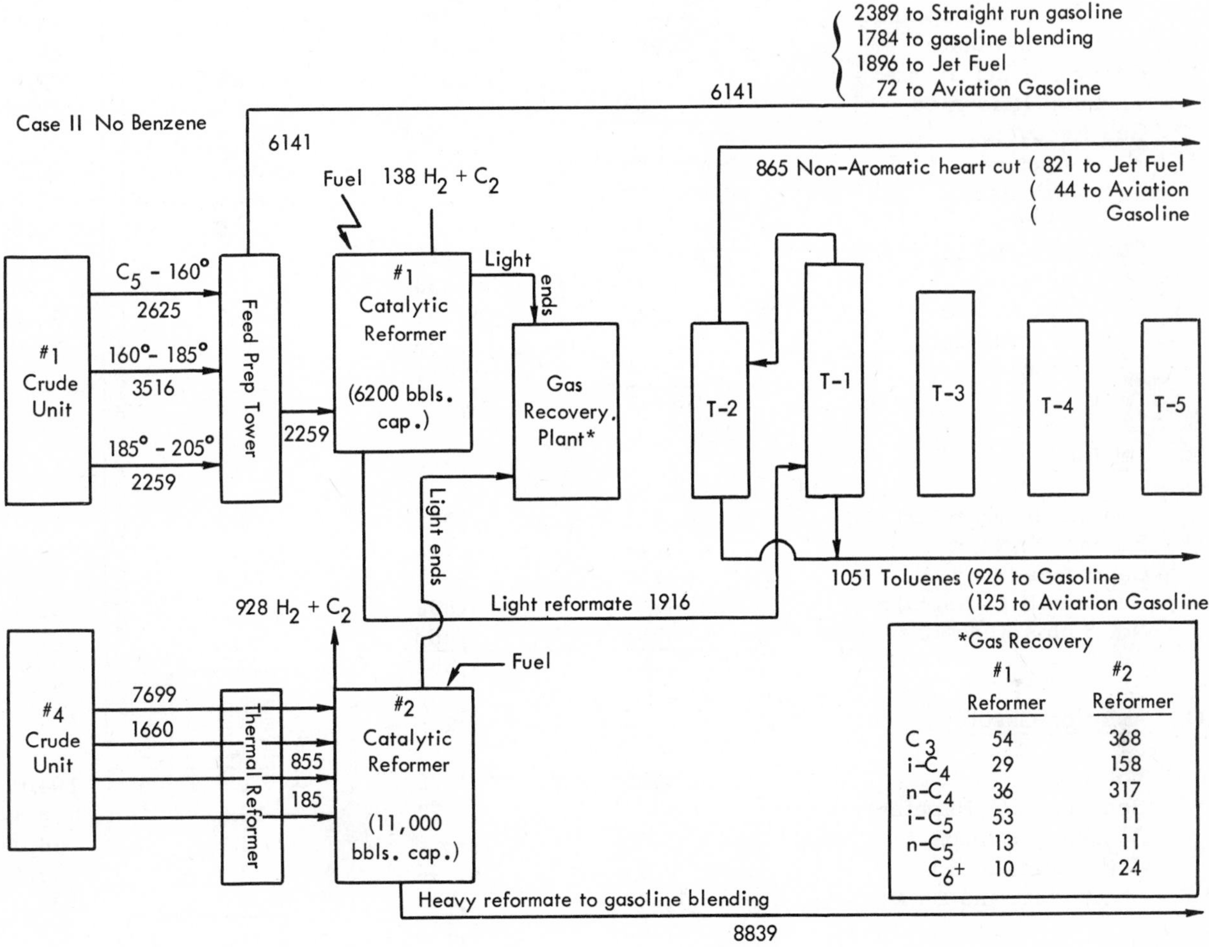

*Gas Recovery

	#1 Reformer	#2 Reformer
C_3	54	368
$i-C_4$	29	158
$n-C_4$	36	317
$i-C_5$	53	11
$n-C_5$	13	11
C_6+	10	24

7. CONTINENTAL OIL COMPANY

Effect of Aromatics Operation on Product Blending

	Aromatics	Motor Fuel	Vapor Pressure	Octane Number
A. Gasoline Blend				
Benzene H.C. Naphtha	---	1,784	16.5	73.8
Benzene Raffinate	2,367	---	6.1	66.0
Heavy Cat Reformate	7,271	8,839	2.5	89.5
Thermal Reformed	185	---	•3.8	67.5
Gas Recovery:				
Isopentane	66	---	25.0	92.0
M-Pentane	37	---	20.0	62.0
Hexanes	44	---	7.0	69.0
Purchased Butanes	---	116	67.0	94.0
Toluenes	926	926	1.5	104.0
Cat Cracked	9,227	9,227	5.2	90.0
Light Alkylate	2,463	2,463	6.4	92.5
Other	10,431	10,431		
	33,017	33,786	11.0	
B. Jet Fuel				
Non-Aromatic Heart Cut	821	821	3.3	48.6
Reform Naphtha	4,712	3,052		
Casinghead	236	---	23.0	76.0
Benzene H.C. Naphtha	---	1,896	16.5	73.8
No. 3 plus Kerosene	1,483	1,483		
	7,252	7,252		
C. Aviation Gasoline				
Toluenes	125	125	1.5	104.0
Benzene H.C. Naphtha	---	72	16.5	73.8
Benzene Raffinate	72	---	6.1	66.0
Non-Aromatic H.C.	44	44	3.3	48.6
Lt Alkylate and Butane	1,522	1,522	8.0	93.0
	1,763	1,763		
D. Other				
Propane	33			
Isobutane	23			
M-Butane	102			
Fuel Gas	43			
Benzene	550			

8. CONTINENTAL OIL COMPANY

Cost Factors in Benzene Production

A. Investment for Benzene Production (In Thousands)

	TOTAL	Benzene Only	Net Invest.	Benzene Factor	Pro Rata Benzene
Cat Reformer Feed Prep.	$ 71.9	$ 57.0	$ 14.9	.609	$ 9.1
No. 1 Cat Reformer	805.2	0	805.2	.609	490.3
Aromatics Extraction	182.5	172.3	10.2	0	0
Tankage, Pumps, Lines	53.2	13.0	40.2	.609	24.5
	$1,112.7	$242.3	$870.4		$523.9

Total Benzene Investment $242,300 + $523,900 = $766,200
Annual Depreciation 6%; Property Insurance 0.15%; Ad Valorem Taxes 1.5%

B. Catalyst and Chemicals Cost

Desulfurizer:
3,516 barrels of benzene heart cut--1,845 No. 2 Reformer increase = 1,671 barrels incremental naphtha

300 barrels per pound of $1.00 per lb. catalyst = $6.20 per calendar day

Reformers:
5,775 barrels for aromatics at 70 barrels per pound = 82.5 lbs. per day

5,775 - 1,671 = 4,104 barrels for motor fuel at 120 barrels per lb. = 34.2 lb./day

Extraction:
Phenol at 14 cents per lb. and 4.7 barrels of feed per lb. for 2,989 barrels = $88.77 per calendar day

C. Utilities Costs

No. 1 Reformer naphtha splitter 2¢ per barrel for 3,200 barrels per day
Catalytic Reforming: 6.6 cents per barrel for 1,671 barrels
maintenance $32,00 per year

Aromatics Extraction:
Fuel 9.78 cents per barrel; cooling water 0.81 cents; steam 2.48 cents; electricity, 0.7 cents; maintenance $47,000 per year

Labor: 1 man per shift saved on aromatics extraction; none on reforming

D. Published Benzene Prices (Gulf Coast)

Per Gallon	Coke	Petroleum
1956	34¢	43¢
1957	34	38
1958	31	32
1959	29	29
1960	32	31

9. CONTINENTAL OIL COMPANY

A. Purchase of Special Naphtha Cuts

Pipeline Rate, from Source to Ponca City--for Naphtha--12¢ per Barrel, Min. 25,000 Barrels

	Source A		Source B		Source C	
	BPD	$/D	BPD	$/D	BPD	$/D
Credits						
Fuel Gas ($1.019/B)	(35)	$ 36	(65)	$ 66	(45)	$ 46
LPG ($2.00/bbl.)	12	24	22	44	16	32
Housebrand gasoline (11¢)	445	2,056	683	3,155	486	2,245
Benzene	122	1,383	86	975	83	941
		$3,499		$4,240		$3,264
Debits						
Value of Naphtha	600	$3,117	800	$3,705	600	$2,878
Motor TEL, Mcc ($2.13/Mcc)	(83)	177	(135.4)	286	(91.4)	195
Op. Expenses 30¢/bbl.	600	180	800	240	600	180
Butane $2.26/bbl.	11	25	4	9	5	11
		$3,499		$4,240		$3,264
Value of Naphtha						
$/bbl.		5.20		4.63		4.79
¢/gal.		12.4		11.0		11.4
Price to us		13.0		11.5		12.0
Volume of Benzene Formers						
MCP		20%		16.5%		
CH		15.1%		2.9%		
BZ		1.7%		1.2%		

B. Price Trends

Gasoline	$4.267 per barrel for 93.38 octane
Tetraethyl Lead	$2.00 per thousand cubic centimeters
L P G Propane	$1.344 per barrel
n - Butane	$2.150 per barrel
Iso - Butane	$3.150 per barrel
Fuel Gas Equivalent	$1.025 per barrel
Phenol	14 cents per pound
Reforming Catalyst	$3.72 per pound
Refinery Wages	$3.75 per hour

APPENDIX A

Assignments

I. Furniture Industry

Process Notes

1. Become familiar with each of the machines used in the Morganton Plant of the Drexel Furniture Company. Which machines require the most setup time? Which operations are the fastest? How does the company relate the fast operations to the slow ones so that an overall balance of output is maintained?
2. Study the floor layouts of the rough mill, finish mill, cabinet assembly, and finishing room. What operations have been mechanized? How is flexibility maintained when a different product design is put through a mechanized operation? How are the mechanized operations related to the individual machine operations? What materials handling equipment could be installed to mechanize additional operations?
3. What is the breakdown of fixed and variable costs in green storage, dry kilns, rough mill, finish mill, cabinet assembly, and finishing room?
4. What would be the effect of establishing a large inventory between finish mill and cabinet assembly? Should the company ship dimension stock from the finish mill and assemble and finish its cabinets at regional plants close to the retail market?

Reference Notes

1. What are the most important problems confronting a furniture manufacturer at the present time? What do you think the manufacturer can do about these problems?
2. How much of the growth of the industry can be attributed to increasing product shipments and how much can be attributed to price increases? Have price changes in the finished product kept pace with changes in the costs of materials and labor?
3. What factors have influenced the profitability of case goods manufacturers during the 1950's.

Assignment for Field Work

1. For the plant which you visit, prepare a one-page sketch representing the general plan of the company's manufacturing operations. The sketch should show the relationship of the manufacturing departments to each other and to the products the company makes.
2. Your observations at the plant should also cover such things as:
   a) The raw materials the company uses.
   b) The approximate sequences of production operations.
   c) The points in the process at which inventories are carried.
   d) The general plan for scheduling work through the plant.
   e) The arrangements for plant supervision.
3. What do you consider to be the least desirable feature of the company's plant layout?

White Furniture Company

1. Examine carefully the exhibit showing the proposed layout for the new finishing room conveyor. What problems do you foresee in the operation of the conveyor if it were to be installed as planned? Can you recommend any changes in the proposed layout?
2. What effect would the new conveyor have on the overall operations of the company? If the conveyor could be operated successfully, with or without changes to the proposed layout, what cost savings or cash income would come to the company?
3. What return would the White company obtain on its investment in the finishing room conveyor if it operated successfully and at peak capacity?

W. F. Whitney Company

1. The case states: "In January, 1949, Mr. Miller found that shipments on many items in the company's line were overdue by as much as two to four months. Meanwhile, excessive inventories were accumulating on other items." To what do you attribute this problem?
2. What recommendations would you make to ensure effective operation of the company in the future?

Mengel Company (A)

1. Assume that at the $12 million sales level, spending $500,000 per year for advertising, the Mengel Company obtains the following cost ratios:

Material	42.8%
Direct labor	14.6
Factory overhead	17.5
Administrative expense	4.1
Selling expense	11.6
	90.6%

   What will its cost structure look like and what will the break-even volume be? Deduct the $500,000 of additional advertising expense from the above cost structure and appraise the result.
2. Summarize your judgment of the program being developed by the Mengel Company and indicate what changes, if any, should be made in it. Be prepared to outline in detail:
   a) The critical factors upon which the success of the venture will hinge.
   b) The effect of those factors on the plant operations.

Mengel Company (B)

Assume that in 1948, the Mengel Company had 24 different patterns of furniture in its line (6 suites with approximately 4 patterns in each suite). Production runs on each pattern averaged 1,000 pieces. The company produced 288,000 pieces per year at an average selling price of $42 per piece. Approximately one eighth of the direct labor time required for any one production run was spent for setup time. Roughly two thirds of the factory overhead was fixed regardless of plant output, and roughly one third varied with the output of the plant.

Assume that by 1954, the Mengel Company found that in order to maintain its sales volume, it was obliged to broaden the product line to 120 patterns (30 suites with 4 patterns each).

1. What impact would these changes have on the company's profitability, assuming 1954 price levels for furniture, materials, and labor? What effect would these changes have on the operating conditions of the rough mill? The finish mill? The assembly floor? The finishing room?
2. As vice-president of manufacturing, you must prepare a memorandum to outline the changes you consider necessary to adapt the Mengel Company's production to the broadened product line. Your memorandum will be used both as an aid to discussion during conference with other senior executives and as a guide to the production supervisor in implementing changes to plant operations.

Devon Furniture Company

1. Assume that, as assistant to Mr. Franklin Price, you are asked "to carry out the recommendations of the consultants." What observations would you make to Mr. Price about the report?
2. What action would you take with regard to patterns 914, 917, 922, and 927?
3. Make recommendations for future action for the Devon company based upon your observations of the company's progress since 1948 and upon your evaluation of the consultants' report.

Drexel Furniture Company

1. On the basis of the information available to the company on May 27, 1957, and assuming no change in production schedules, prepare the following estimates:
   a) Increase in dollar value of physical inventory (on a company-wide basis) from May 27 to July 31, 1957.
   b) Increase in dollar value of unsold inventory (on a company-wide basis) from May 27 to July 31, 1957, and from July 31 to November 30, assuming that the order backlog does not change.
   c) Same as (*b*) allowing for any change in backlog you might expect.

2. As assistant to Mr. Hill, be prepared to give a brief oral résumé of the important issues and alternative courses of action to be considered in the meeting of May 27. Outline the important pros and cons of each alternative.

   Note: A. The terms used by the company were defined as follows: *Physical inventory* included all finished furniture on hand in storage, rubbing, or awaiting shipment.
   Unsold inventory included only those items of finished furniture in storage for which there was no customer order on hand.
   Order backlog includes all orders on hand for which shipment had not been made. This included both orders for items temporarily out of stock and orders for furniture on hand but awaiting shipping arrangements.

   B. In Exhibit 5, the right-hand column headed "stock position" should be read as follows: *Where a percentage figure* is given (e.g., 59%) no significant unsold inventory of pieces in that group was on hand on the date of the stock estimate (either May 17 or May 27). The percentage given indicates the portion of the *scheduled* cut for which orders were on hand on the date of the stock estimate.
   Where a date is given (e.g., 7/4), it indicates the expected date of sale of the last pieces in inventory from lots prior to but not including the scheduled cut. For example, for Plant #1 cuts of group K are scheduled to be ready for shipment on May 21, August 20, and October 18. The May 27 stock position estimates for these three lots indicate that: 70% of the May 21 lot was sold prior to May 27; the May 21 lot would be sold out by July 11 (the date 7/11 on line 10); and the August 20 lot would be sold out on September 19 (9/19 on the next-to-last line).

3. Suggest any appropriate revisions in the existing cutting schedule for Plant #6.
4. What actions will be necessary to implement your recommendations? What are the advantages and disadvantages of the approach you have chosen?

   Note: You may ignore the inventory position and/or sales forecast for any items not already listed on the cutting schedule for Plant #6. You may assume that any style not listed in the column for Plant #6 in Exhibit 7 need not be manufactured in the period ahead.

II. Cotton Textile Industry

Process Notes (First Day)

1. Study the note and try to understand the functions of the different pieces of machinery required.
   a) How can a mill, such as Columbia Weaving, be balanced so that no machines are idle?
   b) In terms of output poundage, where are the *potential* bottlenecks in Columbia as constructions are changed?
   c) What are the major differences, such as skills required or problems faced, between (1) spinning and weaving, and (2) finishing?
   d) How would you expect the components of "cost of goods sold" to differ between (1) spinners, (2) weavers, and (3) finishers?
   e) Given only a limited knowledge of the production processes, what factors have favored and what factors have tended to prevent integration among (1) spinners, (2) weavers, and (3) finishers?
2. Assume that you are operating a textile mill with much the same type of equipment as described for Columbia Weaving. The mill

is operating on a three-shift basis and is balanced to produce combed percale sheeting with the following characteristics:

Warp threads per inch (sley)	100
Filling threads per inch (picks)	100
Width of cloth	39″
Warp yarn count	30's
Filling yarn count	33's
Combed yarn, plain weave	
Loom speed: 180 picks/minute	

What effects would each of the following changes have on the operations and equipment balance of the mill? (In *each* instance, assume that the plant changes from the manufacture of sheeting with the above specifications.)

a) Producing a more expensive 120 x 120 (i.e., sley 120 and picks 120) percale with all other characteristics unchanged?

b) Changing to a 100 x 120 cloth, holding other characteristics constant?

c) Entering the shirting business and producing a 128 x 68 cloth, again with all other characteristics unchanged?

d) Trying the print cloth business with an "80 square":

Warp threads per inch	80
Filling threads per inch	80
Width of cloth	39″
Warp yarn count	31's
Filling yarn count	41's
Carded yarn, plain weave	
Loom speed: 180 picks/minute	

e) Changing from a plain weave to (1) twills, (2) geometric patterns with different colored yarns, and (3) complex figured patterns?

What would be involved in changing from all cotton yarn to: (1) a cotton-rayon or a cotton-polyester (such as Dacron) blend? (2) all rayon staple (filament rayon yarn cut to the staple length of cotton, or any fiber? (3) rayon filament yarn? In changing (1) from undyed to multicolored yarns, (2) from single to plied yarns, (3) from short domestic to long Egyptian staple cotton?

Process Notes (Second Day)

In September, 1962, Mr. Robert H. Danforth, newly hired manufacturing vice-president of the Columbia Weaving Company, was making an analysis for his own use of the company's new print cloth mill. He wanted to be sure he knew (1) such operating characteristics as the labor cost per pound of each operation or the fixed and variable costs; (2) the effects of switching to carded broadcloth $\left[40'' \; \frac{109'' \times 58''}{31's\ W \times 41's}\right]$ from the 80-square print for which the mill was designed $\left[39'' \; \frac{80'' \times 80''}{31's\ W \times 41's}\right]$; (3) the possibility of spinning finer or coarser count yarns; and (4) the possible advantages of installing new Draper X-3 looms or other equipment.

For his study, Mr. Danforth had his assistant pull together the following information: (1) the cost of the mill and equipment (Exhibits 2 and 3); (2) the current operating schedule (Exhibit 4); and (3) the labor costs for each operation (Exhibit 5). In addition, Mr. Danforth knew that 1⅟16-inch middling cotton was used for all the cloths considered and that, while the X-2 looms ran at 190 picks/minute and 80 looms to a fixer or weaver, he could get 212 picks/minute and 130 looms per weaver and 120 per fixer from the X-3. [In September, 1⅟16-inch middling cotton sold for *$.335* per pound, 31's yarn for *$.71* a pound, 41's yarn for *$.83* a pound, the carded broadcloth for *$.2225* a yard, and the print cloth for *$.1775* a yard.]

Assignment for Field Work

1. For the plant you visit, determine how the output of the machines at each stage in the process is affected by a change in the construction of the cloth which the company sells. Does the mill get out of balance easily?
2. To what extent have the business practices of the textile industry been influenced by the character of the manufacturing process?
3. Assume you have just been placed in charge of this mill. Write a memorandum to the president of the company outlining your short- and long-range recommendations for the plant and noting their effect on the corporate strategy.

Reference Notes

1. What are the important characteristics of the Cotton Textile Industry? How have

these developed? What action may a textile weaver, such as Mr. Danforth of Columbia, undertake to correct unfavorable conditions?

2. To what do you attribute the decline in spindle capacity during the past two-three decades? Has the textile industry become more or less efficient?
3. What was the effect of poor years such as 1949, 1954, 1958 on broad woven production, cloth prices, or cotton prices?
4. If you were Mr. Danforth of Columbia, what information could you glean from *each* exhibit? What use would you make of this data?

Textron Incorporated (A)

1. What were the major strategic decisions made by Royal Little since 1923 that determined the kind of company Textron was in 1947? In view of your knowledge of both manufacturing processes and industry trends, were these decisions soundly made?
2. On the basis of the plans for the first quarter of 1947, what balance has the corporation established between the productive capacities at different levels in the integrated structure, such as spinning-weaving, finishing, and cutting and sewing?

What are the advantages and disadvantages of:

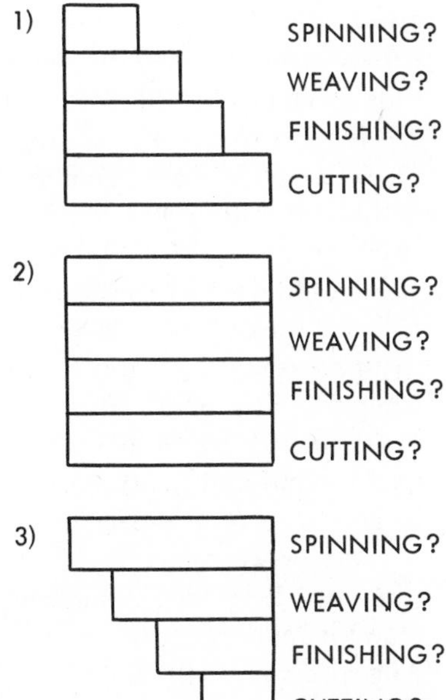

Towards which should Textron work?

Textron Incorporated (B)

1. What is the significance of the Textron company's profit experience in 1949?
2. In what ways were the poor results of 1949 due to inefficiencies within the integrated corporation? In what ways were the results due to the general recession in the textile industry?
3. Do you agree with the 1950 corporate objectives? What resources or skills were needed to capitalize upon the opportunities presented? Did Textron have, or could the company acquire, these skills?

Textron Incorporated (C)

1. Assume you are manufacturing vice-president for Textron in June, 1953. During 1951 and 1952 about 55 percent of the corporate sales and expenses were in cotton and 45 percent in man-made fiber greige goods; of the cotton greige production, 28 percent was Indian Head cloth sold as price goods over-the-counter. Despite the similarity of product line and gross sales, the profit picture changed rapidly over this period. You need to determine some reasonable explanations (such as new plant start-ups or price movements) for these changes and then recommend corrective action.
2. As vice-president for manufacturing for Textron in June, 1953, you are concerned about the product mix for the remainder of the year. The corporation is increasing its production of man-made filament and spun staple fabrics at the expense of cotton staples, such as print cloth, for which most of its cotton mills are balanced.

As requested, your assistant has obtained cost sheets on three fabrics that typify the change. The fabrics are:

Style A, a 43″ $\frac{92 \text{ x } 64}{100/25/3\text{W x } 150/38/2\text{F}}$ acetate chromspun[1]; Style B, a 39″ $\frac{80 \text{ x } 80}{31'\text{sW x } 41'\text{sF}}$ print

[1] 100/25/3 means 100 denier yarn, 25 filaments with three turns or twists. A one denier yarn means that a 450 meter hank of yarn weighs .05 grams.

cloth; and Style C, a 48″ $\frac{66 \times 36}{15'sw \times 20'sF}$ spun acetate suiting (see Exhibit 6).

Background data is available. In terms of specific fabrics, you know that the 80-square print cloth is the bell-weather of the industry and a good indicator of market trends; that the acetate suiting is a heavy staple fabric with a "suggested" (hoped for) sales price of $.32106 per yard, and that the acetate chromspun is the trademark of Tennessee Eastman Company's solution *dyed filament* yarn with a suggested sales price of $.39157 per yard. In terms of industry information, you know the prices of print cloth, the fact that during 1951 and 1952 rayon filament sold at $.78/lb., and rayon staple at $.40 (except $.389 and $.370 in November and December, 1952, respectively), and the information contained in Exhibit 7.

As for the equipment, you know it is all about 1945 vintage except for long-draft spinning and some long-draft roving. The assorted sizes of plain looms average 180 picks per minute while the box looms average 150 p.p.m. For rough calculations, your rule of thumb is that slashing adds 10–12 percent to yarn weight and crimp[2] uses up 8 percent of the filling and 3 percent of the warp yarn. Operating efficiency was 90 percent. New plain looms would cost $1,600 and box looms $4,000 while increasing workloads 35 percent and pickage 15 p.p.m. (box looms were $1,300 in 1945).

You are faced with an Executive Committee meeting in which you'll have to recommend a corporate strategy. In reviewing the above data, you are concerned about the effects on the manufacturing plants and on the corporate strategy of producing any or all of these representative fabrics and of changing from one to another.

Algonquin Mills, Inc.

You are Mr. John Richards, vice-president and mill superintendent, and receive the following memo on Wednesday, February 6, 1957.

February 5, 1957

TO: John Richards
FROM: Thomas Danforth
SUBJ. Production Scheduling

That 35,000 yd./wk. poplin order looks less certain now than it did last week. Poplin prices are down to $.345 a yard, although I think our quality reputation should warrant a premium. In view of time pressure and our urgent need for earnings, I'd appreciate your comments on:

a) Should we take the contract at any lower price, and if so, how much lower?
b) Should we spin the 50's two-ply combed cotton yarn for the poplin ourselves or buy outside? I noted that the New York price yesterday was $1.14 a pound and the market has held firm at that level since the first of the year.
c) If we lose the contract shall we proceed with the proposed operating changes to three-shift operation and/or production schedule #3?
d) For the long-run, on what kind of cloth should we concentrate? Should we stick with polyester blends, go in for poplins, or what?

Salant & Salant, Incorporated

You are Mr. Gold and you have received the following memo:

TO: Mr. M. H. Gold
FROM: Robert S. Salant
RE: Pants Production Schedule

In view of our pants problems this year and the 119,000 dozen sales increase Mr. Reynolds estimates for 1960, I would appreciate receiving a pants production schedule for October 1, 1959–December 31, 1960, together with any comments you think appropriate.

It seems to me that there are several alternative programs. For example, we could fill in the seasonal lows in shirt plants, such as Chester, with pants production and store until needed; we could spread shirt production around and free up a single plant such as Harrissen or Hanover for the extra pants output; or we could buy a plant. Mr. Lipshie says there are no suitable plants available for rent.

Any program will embody many assumptions. For example, Mr. Reynolds estimates

[2] Crimp refers to the extra yardage used up in one yarn going "over and under" another instead of being in a straight line.

that, with the exception of the 24,000 dozen pants for store "A" and 15,000 dozen pairs for store "E," pant sales will approximate the 1959 pattern. I trust you will choose your assumptions carefully and not let them lead us into an inflexible position should events vary markedly from predictions.

[Note that a shirt or pant may be shipped after the sale is billed. Therefore, schedules of *sales, production,* and *shipments* are not necessarily the same. The inventory figures in Exhibit 7 are for the beginning of the month (i.e., October, 1959, will start with 58,000 dozen pants)].

III. Plastics Industry

Process Notes

1. Compare the plant facilities necessary to become a producer of benzene and of styrene monomer with those necessary to make polystyrene molding compound out of purchased monomer, with the plant facilities necessary to mold polystyrene into finished plastic products.
2. Compare and contrast each of the different molding or forming methods to make plastic products. What are the problems in injection molding plastic powders? In casting liquid plastics? In matched die molding reinforced plastics? In hand laying-up reinforced plastics?
3. Should a materials company specialize in one plastic or many? Should a company fabricating plastic products specialize in one process or be prepared to make any kind of plastic product?

Reference Notes

1. What problems does the plastics industry encounter in achieving plastics sales through their substitution for metal in the design of finished products?
2. For what kinds of products are plastics best suited, in contrast to metal products made by sand castings? By die castings? By drop forgings? By stampings? By screw machines?
3. To what extent is the profitability of operations with a plastic such as polystyrene affected by competition from other plastics such as vinyls and polyethylene? What effect do technological changes and competitive materials have on the price of older plastics such as phenolics?

Assignment for Field Work

1. Assume that you are the plant superintendent and that you are making your daily trip through the plant. Make some observations concerning things to be done, things to be investigated, problems to be talked over with people in your organization, and ideas for future contemplation.
2. Find out all you can from discussion with the company officials about:
   a) What constitutes their most troublesome production problems.
   b) The current situation in and future prospects of the plastics industry.

Bell Plastics, Inc.

Assume that you are sitting in conference with Mr. R. E. Bell, Mr. Sheldon, and Mr. Edwin Bell. They have given you the information contained in the case and have asked for:

1. Your appraisal of the company's present program and policies and your suggestions with regard to future plans.
2. Your comments with regard to impending developments in the plastics industry which may have a bearing on the company's position.

Hungerford Plastics Corporation

In August, 1955, the board of directors of the Hungerford Plastics Corporation was considering the proposed plant construction at Morristown. In preparing this recommendation, Mr. Daniel Hungerford, president of the corporation, consulted with Mr. Sandler, manager of the injection molding division. Mr. Sandler stated that, in his opinion, by the end of 1958, sales of injection molded products might be expected to increase 55 percent over the 1955 rate. Mr. Sandler pointed out that it was impractical to attempt to install more than 13 molding machines or to operate for more than 120 hours per week in the present plant at Rockaway.

1. Calculate the return on investment for the new plant based on:
   a) The projected 55 percent sales increase.
   b) No sales increase.
   c) The future sales volume which you would forecast as most probable.
2. Should the new plant be constructed in 1955?

The Victory Plastics Company

1. What level of business will Mr. Beckwith require to break even on his costs?
2. What are his prospects of attaining the sales volume from military and commercial business to support this level?
3. Develop a comprehensive plan to put the company on a firm and profitable basis.

Lunn Laminates, Inc. (A)

1. Prepare a Pro Forma Income Statement for the Lunn plant in Huntington for the period November, 1954, through April, 1955.
2. What should Mr. Lunn do about:
   a) The Ueber Tool Company.
   b) The Ashtabula plant.
   c) Proprietary products.
3. Evaluate the policies and objectives of the Lunn company.

Lunn Laminates, Inc. (B)

1. On January 1, 1962, you have been hired to take charge of all manufacturing for Lunn Laminates, Inc. Mr. Lunn's first request is that you prepare a production schedule for the boat line for the period February 1, 1962, to May 31, 1962. This should include motor whale boats, Ship Shapes, and Sea Winds.
2. Mr. Lunn would also appreciate your recommendations as to the future corporate strategy and supporting plans, especially with respect to product lines, possible alternative raw materials or production processes, the proposed merger with A & S Plastic Company, and the consolidation of manufacturing operations.

Catalin Corporation of America (A)

1. Outline the methods by which the Catalin executives achieved success in establishing their leadership in cast phenolics.
2. What measures should the Catalin company take to ensure continued growth for the future?

Catalin Corporation of America (B)

1. What action should the Catalin company take with regard to its polystyrene plant at

CATALIN CORPORATION (B)

Monthly Production Costs at Varying Levels of Output
(Costs Delivered to Outside Warehouses)*

Manufacturing Expenses	*1,140,000 lbs. 32 men*†	*240,000 lbs. 11 men*	*2,000,000 lbs. 40 men*
Productive and nonproductive labor	$11,662	$ 3,600	$14,600
Maintenance and repair labor	2,528	1,300	3,200
Factory supplies	1,061	200	1,800
Maintenance and repair material	3,272	2,000	4,000
Heat, light and power	6,747	4,100	9,300
Administration and general‡	5,058	5,100	5,100
Research and development‡	1,065	1,000	1,000
Insurance compensation, etc.	1,283	400	1,600
Social Security and unemployment insurance	257	100	300
Depreciation			
Building value $396,000 over 25 years normal	1,320	1,300	1,300
Machinery and equipment $1,000,000 over 15 years normal	5,574	5,600	9,400
Office building portion $50,000 over 25 years normal	89	100	100
Control Laboratory	3,521	3,500	3,500
Shipping bags $151 per M and inward freight plus 2 percent spoilage	4,570	1,600	8,000
	$48,007	$29,900	$63,200
Production (Yield)			
Manufacturing or handling cost per pound	$.0421	$.1245	$.0316
Raw materials including freight	.2406	.2406	.2406
Manufacturing cost F. O. B. Calumet	$.2827	$.3651	$.2722
Shipping cost (Calumet to outside warehouses)	.0030	.0030	.0071
Total cost per pound	$.2857	$.3681	$.2793

* In all cases, the company would also incur the warehousing, local freight, selling, advertising, and general administrative overhead charges set forth in the case text.

† The figures in this column are taken directly from the case.

‡ Out-of-pocket costs incurred as a result of manufacturing operations.

Note: Under the plant leasing agreement referred to in the case text, the company might expect to receive a gross rental of $135,000 per year. All expenses incidental to ownership, including depreciation, would amount to approximately $100,000 per year.

Calumet City? Should it maintain the plant with 32 men, reduce operations to a skeleton crew of 11 men, or attain greater efficiency by expanding operations to 40 men? Should it lease the plant to another company for $135,000 per year? The accompanying exhibit indicates one estimate of production costs under the three alternative levels of production.

2. Suppose that the company could increase the sales of polystyrene within the Midwest territory alone to 2 million pounds per month, without loss of its other sales in the East and far West. Would the potential income be enough to justify a promotional campaign to build up sales in the Chicago area and increase the plant to 40 men?
3. What long-range objective should the Catalin company adopt with respect to its product policies and manufacturing facilities? Include an evaluation of the Calumet plant in your program for the company.

Catalin Corporation of America (C)

1. What action should the Catalin company take with regard to the Calumet City polystyrene plant when the lease expires, on April 1, 1960?
2. What policies should the Catalin company establish with regard to mergers? Should negotiations be reopened with Reichhold Chemicals Incorporated? What advantages or disadvantages would result from such a combination. From a combination with Dow?

IV. Electronics Industry

Process Notes

1. As a plant manager, how would the types of management needed, the production worker skills requirements, and the problems faced differ in plants manufacturing receiving tubes, picture tubes, alloy transistors, or TV sets? What is unique about each process? Which process is the most flexible, requires the most investment, is most subject to technological change?
2. All the jobs described are assembly operations; however, what are the differences in scheduling and supervising girls assembling (*a*) individually, (*b*) in teams, (*c*) on an operator-paced conveyor belt, or (*d*) on a machine-driven belt?
3. Should the same company produce all, some, or only one of the products described above? What factors favor and what discourage integration?
4. You are the transistor plant manager for Consolidated Electric. What does a breakdown of capital investments and labor, material and overhead expenses for the 2N404 tell you about your segment of the electronics industry? Where would you concentrate your industrial engineering personnel? What would be your reaction to seeing the mounting and can sealing job analyses (Exhibits 2-D and 2-E).

Assignment for Field Work

1. Analyze the production processes at the plant which you visit and determine how well suited it would be to a program of plant decentralization. What would be the best basis for dividing the work among the various plants? Would the plant make major savings in unit costs if its size were doubled or tripled?
2. What opportunities are there for increased mechanization and automation. Estimate the investment required and approximate savings at different unit volumes.
3. Assume you have just been made plant manager. Write a memorandum to the president outlining your short- and long-range recommendations for the plant and noting their effect on the corporate strategy.

Reference Notes

1. What are the outstanding characteristics of the electronics industry as a whole? Specifically, how do the various segments (consumer, industrial, military, and replacement parts) differ? How do each react to recessions such as 1958? To price changes? What are the significant trends in each segment?
2. What is required for success? Is the industry one to foster small or large companies? Integrated or nonintegrated ones?
3. As a Consolidated Electric executive, what information can you glean from *each* exhibit? What use would you make of this data?

Sentinel Radio Corporation

1. What is your appraisal of the operating program which the Sentinel Radio Corporation has planned for the remainder of 1954?
2. Assume that by June 30, 1954, it becomes clear that the sales estimates for the remainder of the year can be realized only if the prices at which the company sells to its distributors and private brand customers are reduced about 10 percent. If prices are not reduced, it appears that the number of units sold in each of the two remaining quarters will be about 20 percent below the original estimates.

   Would you recommend that the company *a*) reduce its prices, or *b*) plan to operate at the reduced volume? You may assume that if the latter course is followed, cancellation penalties on contracts for purchased components will be about $100,000.
3. What recommendation would you make concerning the company's plans for the transition period and for its general development in the industry?

Emerson Radio and Phonograph Corporation (A)

1. In the early fall of 1949, the vice-president in charge of sales of the Emerson Radio and Phonograph Corporation estimated that the company would sell 500,000 television sets in 1950. Mr. Israel has asked you, as his assistant, to do the following three things:
   a) To draw up a tentative monthly production schedule.
   b) To outline the problems which will be involved in carrying out the manufacturing program you set up.
   c) To outline briefly the plan you would recommend to meet the problems discussed in (*b*).
2. Mr. Israel has asked for your appraisal of the programs and policies the company has adopted for its television business and your recommendations with regard to changes which should be made in the future. (Note: The plant was running on a one-shift basis in the fall of 1949.)

Emerson Radio and Phonograph Corporation (B)

1. Seven years have passed since your production plans were made for the 1950 season. You now have the task of planning once again the production schedule, this time for the year 1957. You must make your own estimates of how many black-and-white and how many color television sets the Emerson Company will sell in 1957. On the basis of these estimates you must draw up a tentative monthly production schedule for both black-and-white and color sets.
2. Outline the problems involved in carrying out your program for 1957.

National Video Corporation

1. As a man familiar with the economics and processes of the television industry, you have been appointed Special Assistant to Mr. A. J. Cole, president of the National Video Corporation. When you start work at 9:00 A.M. (December 4, 1956), Mr. Cole asks you to help him prepare for a meeting of the executive committee scheduled to start at one o'clock. He has given you a copy of the case and a supplementary memo containing the agenda for his afternoon meeting plus three advisory briefs he has recently received. Prepare data that will be useful to Mr. Cole in bringing his meeting to a decision regarding the various alternatives.
2. Present your opinion, supported by the data you have prepared, regarding each of the four items on the agenda.

Supplement to National Video Case

I. Meeting Agenda—Executive Committee—December 4, 1956
   (1) Authorization of proposed settling belt conveyor and auto dispenser for present belt
   (2) Further development on color television tubes
   (3) Promotion of tubes to replacement market
   (4) Consideration of future policies regarding the company and its place in the electronics industry

II. Recent memoranda to Mr. Cole:
   A. Proposed Settling Belt Conveyor
   It is estimated that installation of the proposed belt would permit saving of from 1,700 to 4,000 man hours of direct labor each month. This is calculated as follows:

1. New belt could screen a maximum of 89,000 bulbs per month. This is based on operation at maximum speed of 20 inches per minute to produce three bulbs per minute of 1,440 units per 8-hour shift. Typical month of 22 working days has 62 productive shifts after allowing for one cleanup shift at end of each week.
2. Probable operating speed will be only 13.3 inches per minute for 90 degree bulbs. This reduces output to 59,500 bulbs per month.
3. Rate of output on merry-go-rounds varies with bulb size. To produce 59,500 bulbs in each size would require the following number of shifts of operation:

186 shifts to produce 59,500 24-inch bulbs (rate 320 per m-g-r per shift)
133 shifts to produce 59,500 21-inch bulbs (rate 448 per m-g-r per shift)
93 shifts to produce 59,500 10 to 17-inch bulbs (640 per m-g-r per shift)

B. Research in Color Tube Development: The engineering department requests authorization to spend a minimum of $100,000 for further research aimed at developing efficient production techniques for latest color tube designs.

C. Market Promotion for Replacement Tube Sales:
It is recommended that a minimum of $75,000 be appropriated for a program of promotion and merchandising designed to increase this company's share of the market for replacement tubes. For the industry as a whole, replacement sales in 1956 accounted for 40 percent of all picture tubes sold. Expenditures by some companies for national consumer magazine and television advertising in 1956 were approximately:

Radio Corporation of America (First Day)

1. You are the vice-president and general manager of the RCA Victor Home Instruments Division on your way to a meeting with Mr. Watts and the other general managers in his group. He wants to review RCA's past growth and frame some concrete recommendations on the future strategy for his area and for the company. As preparation for the discussion, you want to summarize your thoughts in writing and also frame a reply to the following memo that arrived just before you left.

May 23, 1963

FROM: A. M. Glover, Vice-President and Gen. Man., Semi-Conductor and Materials Div.
SUBJ: New Germanium Crystal Growing Furnace

We're thinking of replacing our furnaces at Findlay for $100,000. The new furnaces are so good that we'll have a two-year payback at current volume. The controller's department insists that we get a guarantee from you to buy your current volume of germanium alloy transistors for radios through 1965. As you know, most of these types end up in entertainment devices although some go into computors. With your endorsement, we'll assume our other radio customers will keep on buying. As an unnecessary inducement, we'll cut the price ½ a cent a unit when the furnaces are installed.

Thanks.

Radio Corporation of American (Second Day)

1. It is early June, 1962, and you are production manager of the RCA semiconductor plant with about 1,000 employees producing a variety of germanium and some silicon

Company	*Total Advertising Expenditure*	*Brand Advertising for TV sets*	*Brand Advertising for Picture Tubes*
CBS	$ 2,000,000	$ 600,000	$415,000
General Electric	25,000,000	1,100,000	215,000
Philco	4,350,000	2,500,000	50,000
RCA	7,900,000	1,800,000	266,000
Sylvania	2,600,000	140,000	150,000

Note: Admiral and Motorola each spent more than $500,000 for brand advertising of TV sets, but nothing for TV picture tubes.

transistors for computors and other industrial uses. One of the families going through the alloy area is the 2N404. For purposes of this assignment, you may assume that processes, times, and costs are the same as those given for Consolidated Electric in the Electronics Industry Process Notes; the testing sequence is as summarized in Exhibit 5, and the learning curve for training new operators and retraining old is as shown in Exhibit 4. Sales for the five major selections from 1960 to date are given in Exhibit A below. Standard selection "A" are converted to special customer selections by varying or adding to the testing sequence.

This morning a quarterly sales forecast landed on your desk showing sales of selection E jumping from 12,000 units a month to 47,000 units in September, 1962. Further checking revealed that the extra 35,000 units are part of a potential 100,000-unit order to be delivered evenly from September through November; however, while the sales department was "almost positive" of getting this business, the customer would not give a final "go-ahead" until six weeks before deliveries were to start. Since orders had been spotty for this selection (Exhibit A), the general sales manager promised to try to prevail upon the customer for a July commitment.

The revised forecast poses a production scheduling problem. The original plan was to continue at a 250,000 unit monthly level to meet predicted sales of 120,000 units a month for selection A; 28,000 for selection B; 26,000 for selection C; 65,000 for D; and 12,000 for E. Such a schedule permitted a gradual inventory reduction from the estimated June 30 level of 70,000 units of selection A; 70,000 of selection B; 33,000 of selection C; none of selection D; and 9,000 of selection E. In addition, 14 mounters (plus a 15th for 40 percent of her time) would be kept fully occupied on the 2N404.[1] The new schedule means hiring new help because all available employees are being utilized on other transistors; company policy discourages overtime because of "the excessively high reject rate."

EXHIBIT A

Monthly Sales of 2N4b4, 1960–1962

	Standard Selection A			*Standard Selection B*			*Standard Selection C*		
	1960	*1961*	*1962*	*1960*	*1961*	*1962*	*1960*	*1961*	*1962*
January	57	105	154	—	12	12	—	27	22
February	46	83	98	—	15	26	—	35	—
March	118	118	161	—	8	29	—	20	16
April	11	199	120	—	—	55	—	28	16
May	94	69	377	9	—	12	—	28	16
June	66	75	149(E)	37	—	16(E)	—	—	16(E)
July	69	96	—	11	—	—	—	—	—
August	75	121	—	13	—	—	—	27	—
Sept.	79	87	—	25	—	—	—	2	—
Oct.	52	101	—	12	—	—	28	—	—
Nov.	74	115	—	8	22	—	—	20	—
December	70	81	—	10	46	—	—	11	—
Total	811	1250	1059	113	103	150	28	198	86

	Standard Selection D			*Standard Selection E*		
January	—	—	29	—	—	—
February	—	—	—	—	—	—
March	—	—	13	—	—	—
April	—	—	—	—	—	—
May	—	41	—	—	—	26
June	—	27	27(E)	—	—	24(E)
July	—	27	—	—	—	—
August	—	27	—	—	—	—
Sept.	—	56	—	—	11	—
Oct.	—	121	—	—	3	—
Nov.	—	67	—	—	9	—
Dec.	—	—	—	—	37	—
Total	—	366	66	—	60	50

[1] For 250,000 finished and tested output, some 312,000 units have to go to the mounters. At 7.99 hours per thousand, almost 14.4 mounters are needed on a 2,080 hour year.

Several related problems come to mind. They include:

1. Whether employees will be needed in areas other than mounting (A quick check showed equipment would be no bottleneck).
2. When to hire new help and on what jobs to put them. (Typically, production time was eight weeks and life testing another four.)
3. The effect on overhead of increasing volume. (Overhead averaged $60,000 monthly at the 250,000 unit level. Some $32,000 of manufacturing overhead—consisting of supervision, accounting, standards, and maintenance—was 41 percent fixed, while $15,000 of quality control, the $5,000 of production engineering, and the $8,000 service department's assessment averaged 65 percent fixed.)
4. The wisdom of the company's "avoid overtime" policy.
5. Whether a calculated additional $.02 contribution per unit for the "E" selection was worth it.

Lansing Corporation

1. If you were Mr. Hart, what schedule would you recommend?

V. Steel Industry

Process Notes

1. Why is this equipment so costly? Given the data in the Note, what does each process *per ton of ingot* capacity cost?
2. How can we determine the optimum size of a plant? Is there a bottleneck operation?
3. What are the disadvantages to a company that has the other facilities but does not own iron ore deposits? Ore shipping vessels? Coke ovens? Blast furnaces? Cold-rolling facilities?
4. If a company has only open hearths and hot-rolling mills, should it spend more money to integrate backward into ore deposits, coke ovens, and a blast furnace, or should it spend its available capital to integrate forward into cold-rolling mills and product warehouses? (Assume that the company does not have the available capital to do both.)
5. Are there any advantages in the steel industry to vertical integration (operating at all stages of the manufacturing process from raw material to finished product) that did not exist in the textile or oil industries?
6. From Process Note Exhibits 1 through 3, what can you learn about the comparative advantages and disadvantages of oxygen, open hearths, electric furnaces and cupolas? For example: (1) Which has the higher fixed costs, and why? (2) How do you account for the specific differences in such variable costs as fuel or flux? (3) What is the effect of changing scrap prices on the relative advantages of using these processes? In addition, try to project the range of approximate costs for these processes in 1975.

Assignment for Field Work

1. To what degree can the company you visit use scrap as a raw material? How do price changes in the scrap market affect its operations? (Try to put dollar estimates on your answers.)
2. Would the company do better with oxygen converters, open hearths, or electric furnaces?
3. Assume you were just made manufacturing vice-president. Write a memorandum to the president outlining your recommendations for new or improved facilities and noting their effect on the corporate strategy.

Reference Notes

1. What is the position of the American Steel Industry in the world and American economy? Has the rate of growth in steel kept pace with the economy? Has productivity of labor kept pace with wage increases? Are steel prices too low or too high?
2. From a study of the Steel Industry's balance sheets and income statements, determine the effect of price changes between 1946 and 1962 on the price of steel, cost of labor and the cost of raw materials. Allowing for such price changes, what was the effect of the 1949, 1952, 1954, and 1958 recessions? How much profit and how much cash flow can be expected from a ton of steel each year? How much does it cost to add a ton of steel capacity?
3. If you were a manufacturing executive of Sharon Steel Corporation, what would be your reaction to the shifts in steel distribution shown in Exhibits 13–17? What action would you recommend and why?

4. Suppose you were asked to build an integrated steel mill. Where would you put it, what equipment would you buy, and what would it cost per ton of capacity?
5. As a steel executive, what useful information can you glean from *each* exhibit. What use would you make of this data?

Sharon Steel Corporation

1. In the fall of 1947, the company was operating 10 of the 14 open hearths at the Farrel Works. The price of scrap was about $43 per gross ton (2,240 tons). Would you start up one or more additional open hearths in operation? (Assume that the company would have been able to get about $65 per ton for hot-rolled strip.)
2. Would you start up the 11th furnace if scrap was $25 per gross ton? At what level of scrap prices and of number of furnaces is total gross margin maximized? (Those in quantitative analysis courses might enjoy thinking how a steel company might formulate the problem and design a dynamic program for the blast furnace and open-hearth segment of the process.)
3. Using your knowledge of the steel industry, what suggestions would you make to Mr. Roemer about his corporate strategy? (For example, do you agree with the acquisition of further finishing facilities?)

Armco Steel Corporation (A)

1. What can a detailed analysis of this company's history tell us about its ability to compete in the future?
2. What objectives and policies, especially in the manufacturing area, would you recommend for Armco? With respect to preparing quantitative support for these recommendations, what specific problems would you ask your assistant (with his nimble fingers, calculator, and small imagination) to analyze? Remember the problems have to be presented to him very clearly and the analytical steps specified.

Armco Steel Corporation (B)

1. Prepare payback and return on investment figures for the new open-hearth capacity at Middletown, assuming a scrap price of $25 and a market demand of 120,500 tons per month.

   Assume that the average profit, before depreciation, of $10 per ton on finished sheet given in the case applies only to sheet made from Middletown *open-hearth* ingots at an operating level of 120,000 tons/month. The *total contribution* (before depreciation charges and out-of-pocket fixed costs) on finished sheet made from Middletown open-hearth ingots was $30 per ton at the 120,000-ton operating level.

   Assume that any Ashland ingots not needed at Middletown could in all cases be sold at Ashland with a contribution of about $5.00 per ton being earned.

   Assume that Armco could not buy ingots from outside sources for rolling at Middletown at a price which would permit profitable operations.

   Use the supplement to Armco (B) to check your cost figures.
2. Prepare payback and return on investment figures for the new open-hearth capacity, assuming that the market demand stays at 120,500 tons per month, but that the scrap price increases to $30 per ton; assuming that scrap price stays at $25 per ton, but that market demand drops to 100,500 tons per month; assuming that scrap price increases to $30 and demand drops to 100,500 tons.
3. Would you recommend that the Armco Company invest $12 million for additional steelmaking capacity at Middletown? What long-range considerations as to the future operations of the company would affect your decision?

Supplement to Armco (B)

A. Cost of Open-Hearth Steel at $25 Scrap:

1. Existing open hearths, weighted cost per ton:

60,000 tons at	$39.16 =	$2,349,600
7,900 tons at	39.34 =	310,800
67,900 tons		$2,660,400
	one ton =	$39.18

2. New open hearths, weighted cost per ton:

29,400 tons at	$37.80 =	$1,111,300
3,200 tons at	40.58 =	129,900
32,600 tons		$1,241,200
	one ton =	$38.07

B. Cost of Electric Furnace Steel at $25 Scrap:

Electric furnace steel and open-hearth steel cost the same when scrap is $18.

1. Cost of existing open-hearths ingots with scrap at $18 per ton:

   Amount of scrap required to yield one ton of open-hearth steel:
   .45 ton or scrap (input ratio)
   .875 yield of open hearths = .514 tons of scrap needed for one ton of ingot steel

   Cost of scrap in one ton of ingot steel with scrap at $25
   .514 tons scrap × $25 per ton = $12.90

Cost of scrap in one ton of ingot steel with scrap at $18 .514 tons scrap × $18 per ton =	9.25
Reduction in open-hearth ingot cost when scrap cost moves downward from $25 to $18 per ton ($12.90 − $9.25) =	3.65
Open-hearth ingot cost with scrap $25 =	39.29
Open-hearth ingot cost with scrap at $18 = ($39.29 − $3.65) =	$35.64

2. Electric furnace costs with scrap at $25 per ton:

Electric furnace costs with scrap at $18 =	$35.64
Added costs of scrap at $25: $7 per ton ($25 − $18) increase in cost of input =	7.07
.99 yield of electric furnaces	
	$42.71

C. Incremental Contribution with Scrap at $25 and Volume at 120,500 tons:

Present Contribution:		
Existing open hearths*	72,000 T × $21	= $1,516,000
Electric furnaces†	20,000 T × [$21 − ($42.71 − $39.29)] =	352,000
Ashland ingots‡	11,000 T × [$21 − 4.25] =	184,000
	Present Contribution	$2,052,000
Proposed Contribution:		
Existing open hearths	67,900 T × [$21 + ($39.29 − $39.18)] =	$1,435,000
Electric furnaces	20,000 T × [$21 − ($42.71 − $39.29)] =	352,000
New open hearths	32,600 T × [$21 + ($39.29 − $38.07)] =	725,000
Ashland ingots sold	11,000 T × $5 =	55,000
	Proposed Contribution	$2,567,000
	Less: Present Contribution	2,052,000
	Incremental Contribution	$ 515,000

* The average contribution earned per ton of *finished steel* was $30. Therefore, the average contribution earned per ton of *ingot steel* was $21 ($30 × .7 yield).
Illustration:
120,000 ingot steel yields 84,000 tons finished steel (.7 yield) *Total company* contribution from this steel is identical whether figured at ingot steel level or finished steel level.
Contribution is 84,000 tons (finished) × $30 per ton = $2,520,000
Or contribution is 120,000 tons (ingot) × $21 per ton = $2,520,000

† The contribution earned on electric furnace steel is $21 per ton minus the amount by which the cost of electric furnace steel exceeds the cost of existing open-hearth steel ($42.71 − $39.29).

‡ The contribution earned on steel made from Ashland ingots is $21 per ton minus the amount by which the cost of steel made from Ashland ingots exceeds the cost of existing open-hearth steel (the $4.25 transportation cost from Ashland to Middletown).

McLouth Steel Corporation

Prepare the figures you would need in evaluating the proposals to purchase a battery of coke ovens, a second blast furnace, and additional oxygen inverters. Use the data presented below:

Based upon operations as shown in Exhibits 8 and 9 of the case, McLouth executives estimated that the company would have the profit structure shown below at peak capacity. These figures assume that favorable operating conditions have been attained using the oxygen process. Cost and price levels existing in 1954 have been used.

Net Sales		$152.4
Cost of goods sold		
Materials and electricity	$51.3	
Other process costs	9.1	
Rolling mill costs	52.1	112.5
Gross Margin		$ 39.9
Less:		
Sales and administrative expenses	$ 3.6	
Interest	3.5	7.1
Profit before depreciation		$ 32.8
Depreciation (tax basis)		17.0*
Profit after depreciation		$ 15.8
Taxes		7.9
Net Profit		$ 7.9

* For 1955 to 1959; declines to $4.5 million in 1960.

By December, 1955, McLouth executives were obliged to revise their estimates of the company's profit structure at peak capacity due to the following changes in costs and prices that occurred during 1955:

Increases in Profit:	
Higher selling prices (up 12%)	
12% × $152,400,000	$18,300,000
Decreases in Profit:	
Higher steel scrap pieces	
($47.00 − $31.25) × 1,000,000 tons =	15,750,000
Higher nickel prices	
($3,200* − $1,290) × 6,000 tons =	$11,460,000
Higher ore prices $0.85 × 816,000 tons =	690,000
Higher labor costs =	570,000
	$28,470,000
Net reduction in profit before depreciation and taxes =	$10,170,000

* 30% at $1,290 per ton (64½ cents per pound) and 70% at $4,000 per ton ($2 per pound) = see page 9 of case text.

The cost increases noted above changed the estimate of operating costs at capacity (Exhibit 9) to read as follows:

I. Cost of Pig Iron—Production 41,500 tons per month	
Materials	
Iron ore − 1.84 tons at $ 9.25	$17.05
Scale − .06 tons at 6.00	.36
Coke − .90 tons at 17.14	15.43
Limestone − .40 tons at 1.54	.62
Gross Material Cost	$33.46
Material credits	(1.18)
	$32.28
Cost above materials	6.02
	$38.30*
II. Oxygen Inverter Steel Ingots	
Materials	
Molten Iron − .90 tons at $38.30	$34.47
Steel Scrap − .22 tons at 47.00	10.34
Lime	.42
Less scrap credit − .0225 tons at $47.00	(1.06)
	$44.17
Inverter labor	1.10
Other cost	2.10
Total cost of oxygen metal	$47.37
Cost of alloys	.49
Cost to prepare ingots	1.44
Total Cost of Oxygen Steel Ingots	$49.30†
III. Electric Furnace Steel Ingots	
Materials	
Steel scrap − 1.0375 tons at $47.00	$48.80
Ingot mold scrap − .0250 tons at $47.00	1.18
Ore, alloys, and fluxes	2.55
Less scrap credit − .023 tons at $47.00	(1.08)
Net Material Cost	$51.45
Cost above materials	
Melt labor	3.90
Power	4.75
Electrodes	$ 2.75
Other cost	1.30
Total Cost Electric Furnace Steel Ingots	$64.15

* Cold pig iron could be purchased from outside sources for $42 per ton.
† Cost of oxygen steel ingots would be $53.75 using cold pig iron purchased from outside sources.

Investment Costs of Proposed Facilities

In evaluating various methods of reducing operating costs, McLouth executives considered the advisability of manufacturing their own coke, of adding a second blast furnace, and of replacing some of the electric furnaces with additional oxygen process steel.

The investment cost of a battery of coke ovens with associated facilities to supply two blast furnaces would be $17,000,000.

The investment cost of a second blast furnace, daily capacity 1,350 tons, would be $8,000,000.

The investment cost of three new oxygen inverters capable of producing 500,000 tons of steel ingot plus necessary additions to the oxygen plant would be as follows:

Three additional oxygen inverters	$ 6,000,000
Necessary additions to the oxygen plant	5,000,000
	$11,000,000
Total Investment Cost—Coke Ovens, Blast Furnace, and Oxygen Process	$36,000,000

Summary of Operating Costs and Savings of Proposed Facilities and Costs of Existing Electric Furnaces

Savings from new coke ovens:

800,000 tons of coke at a saving of $3.54 = $2,832,000

Operating costs of new oxygen inverters (replacing electric furnace steel):

Using purchased iron − 500,000 tons × $53.75 = $26,875,000

Using iron from new blast furnace − 500,000 tons × $49.30 = $24,650,000

Operating costs of electric furnaces (would be replaced by oxygen inverter costs) − 500,000 tons × $64.15 = $32,075,000

Monongahela Steel Company (A)

1. You are Mr. Hewitt, vice-president of manufacturing. What analysis of those proposed would you present to the Executive Committee?

Monongahela Steel Company (B)

1. If you were Mr. Hewitt, would you invest in rolling facilities (Plan 1) or basic steel modernization (Plan 2)?

Armco Steel Corporation (C)

1. Develop a capital investment program for the Armco Steel Corporation.

VI. Oil Industry

Process Notes

1. What are the main advantages of the large size of the process units in Tidewater's modern refinery? What limiting factors are

there to decrease the advantages of large size?

2. What is the effect on a refinery of a shift in the type of crude oil from low sulfur to high sulfur? Of an increase in the octane requirements of its gasoline? Of the seasonal shifts from winter fuel oil to summer gasoline demand?
3. The Tidewater refinery in Delaware was designed to process high sulfur crude oil from the Middle East. However, just at the time it went on stream, import quotas restricted the availability of such sources of supply. What effect would this have on the operation of the refinery?

Reference Notes

1. What factors influence the geographic location of a new refinery? The size of the refinery? Its product mix?
2. In what ways have product mix changes affected refinery operating costs during the decade 1952–1961? How has the petrochemical market growth affected refinery operations?
3. In what ways have product price changes affected refinery operating costs? How have they affected new plant investment?

The Ohio Oil Company (A)

Assume that early in 1946, the manufacturing vice-president asked you, as his assistant, to review the consultant's report on the proposed expansion of the Robinson refinery and to report to him on the following subjects:

1. What defects do you see in the economic and market analysis?
2. What recommendations for further analyses should be made, if any, before a decision is reached on the project?

Wood River Oil and Refining Company, Inc.

1. On the basis of the average prices for refined products prevailing during the first five months of 1950, what net profit would have been realized on the refining operation had the plant been operating at its capacity of 30,000 barrels per day?
2. Should the Sinclair offer to purchase the refinery, pipeline, and terminals be accepted at the proposed price?

The Ohio Oil Company (B)

1. Have conditions in the oil industry changed sufficiently between 1946 and 1959 for the Ohio Oil Company to change its long-established policy of being a "crude-heavy" company?
2. In considering the acquisition of a refinery such as Aurora, which would balance the company's crude, refining, and marketing capacities, what kind of facilities would you like the acquisition to have in order for it to be a long-term asset to The Ohio Oil Company?

Aurora Gasoline Company

1. What action should the Aurora Gasoline Company take to deal with the cost-price squeeze?
2. If a merger with The Ohio Oil Company were consummated, in what ways would the combined company change its operations so as to be stronger than the sum of its individual parts?
3. What terms, in cash or common shares, would you consider a fair offer from The Ohio Oil Company?

The Ohio Oil Company (C)

1. Should the Aurora refinery install a new catalytic reformer? If so, should it be operated for motor fuel or for aromatics?
2. Evaluate the various alternatives discussed in the last paragraph of the case? What advantage would the Robinson refinery have of participating in an aromatics project at Aurora?

Continental Oil Company

1. What are the Continental Oil Company's current costs of making benzene?
2. Develop ways of estimating the costs incurred in improving existing facilities; in de-alkylating toluene; in purchasing naphtha cuts; in purchasing benzene.
3. Prepare a benzene program for the Continental Oil Company.

APPENDIX B

Evaluation of Business Figures

Measurement of "Return on Investment" provides a useful yardstick for evaluating over-all business performance. Return on Investment can be calculated in several ways, but basically it is defined as:

$$\frac{\text{Profit}}{\text{Investment}} \times 100.$$

The resulting percentage can be used to compare operating data for different periods in a company's history, or for different companies during the same period of time. The profit component is the reported Net Profit on the income statement (preferably after taxes); the investment component is either Stockholders' Equity (capital stock plus surplus) or Invested Capital (equity + long-term debt). The choice of a base will vary from case to case depending upon the objectives of the analyst. Stockholders are naturally most interested in return on equity capital as a measurement of owners' profits. However, for many purposes, return on invested capital provides a more useful basis of comparison, since it measures the effectiveness of management in using the company's entire capital resources, both owned and borrowed.

To understand the factors which affect Return on Investment it is helpful to redefine it as:

$$\%\ \text{Return} = \frac{\text{Profit}}{\text{Investment}} = \frac{\text{Profit}}{\text{Sales}} \times \frac{\text{Sales}}{\text{Investment}} = \text{Profit Margin} \times \text{Investment Turnover.}$$

A company which has a ratio of sales to invested capital equal to 3, and which earns a profit of 5% after taxes, will have a 15% return on invested capital. If the capital turnover should increase to 3.33 times, while profit margin drops to 3%, this sort of analysis will indicate that the drop to a 10% return was due to a change in profit margin, despite an improvement in utilization of capital investment.

A closer look at income statements and balance sheets can indicate some of the causes underlying changes in profit margin and investment turnover. For example:

Earnings Analysis

By dividing each item on the income statement by the amount of Net Sales and, when possible, by the unit volume of products sold, two useful relationships can be examined. The amount of individual cost, such as materials, labor, manufacturing overhead, and general overhead, per sales dollar can be used to trace changes in the cost structure over the years and possibly to study the relationship between fixed and variable costs. Selling prices and costs *per unit* can be used to isolate price and efficiency changes when the product mix remains relatively constant. When one class of purchased materials represents a great proportion of product cost, as cotton does in the textile industry, it is also useful to consider the changes in margin between the raw material cost and the product selling price.

Cash Flow

The cash flow from earnings is the sum of net profit after taxes plus depreciation and other non-cash charges. Future cash requirements, such as future acquisition of fixed assets or sinking funds and interest charges on long term debt can then be related to the predicted cash flow.

Working Capital

Working capital (the excess of current assets over current liabilities) and the current ratio (the ratio of the two items) are both misleading unless the current assets themselves are evaluated. Accounts receivable can generally be turned into cash far more readily than inventory. It is therefore useful to examine changes in receivables and inventory—that is, to divide Net Sales by the average Inventory and Accounts Receivable.

Plant Value

It should be emphasized that the balance sheet figure for depreciated value of plant is somewhat artificial in that it represents the original cost of plant reduced by the history of annual allowances for depreciation since the date of purchase. It does not represent the "real value" of the plant in terms of its current cost to replace. In recent years the book value of plant has lagged considerably below replacement cost due to a generally inflationary trend in the economy.

Investment

The ratio between stockholders' equity and the total of outside debt and stockholders' equity is a clue to estimating the costs of future capital needs. If the company has a high equity ratio, its future capital resources might come from additional borrowing for which interest payments can be charged off as a *cost* of the business. If the debt is already high, future capital may have to come from a new issue of common stock which dilutes the owners' equity. Since dividends on preferred and common stock are taken from net profits *after taxes,* a 6% preferred stock must earn $12 before taxes to pay $6 for each $100 share. It should be noted that the par value of common stock is of little importance in estimating its book value, which is defined as:

$$\frac{\text{total assets minus total liabilities}}{\text{number of common shares}}$$

It should also be noted that book value may have little relationship to the earning power of the stock or of the price people are willing to pay for it in the stock market.[1]

MAKING DECISIONS IN MANUFACTURING POLICY

To the extent that operations can be judged by comparison of profits with investment, decisions concerning future investment of funds in manufacturing facilities should be made in the light of the expected return on investment. When management decides to modernize or expand all or part of the company's physical plant, it must judge the proposed investment at least in part on the basis of the additional profits that can be earned through increased efficiency, added sales volume, or both. Each investment of corporate funds should achieve a rate of return commensurate with both the risk of the project and the company's average cost of capital.

In examining various proposals for investment, the management must define the alternatives, estimate the investment costs and future savings for each, and forecast their probable useful lives. Often the choice lies between taking some specified action and taking no action at all. When several courses of action are available, the one requiring the least investment can be considered first. The next most expensive alternative can then be explored in terms of the *incremental* investment and savings above those of the least expensive. This is continued for each alternative, in order of increasing magnitude, always asking the question: does the additional saving justify the additional investment?

Two common, though inexact, ratios for comparison of investment alternatives are the payback period and the unadjusted rate of return, defined as follows:

$$\text{Payback Period (Years)} = \frac{\text{Net Initial Investment}}{\text{Annual Savings}}$$

$$\text{Unadjusted Return (Percentage)} = \frac{\text{Profit} \times 100}{\text{Average Investment}} = \frac{\text{Annual Savings minus Amortization}}{\frac{1}{2}\ \text{Initial Investment}} \times 100$$

In many situations these two factors can be helpful yardsticks for evaluating an investment opportunity. For each investment the payback and rate of return can be compared to those predicted for other investment opportunities and to the goals of the company. Thus the ratios can be used to rank investments in order of their value and to weed out those that fail to meet the minimum ratios felt to be appropriate for the company. The following factors should be considered in developing these ratios:

Net Investment. The net investment in each alternative is the amount of cash that must be spent out-of-pocket *now* in order to gain the possibility of added profits *later.* This category could include not only acquisition costs of equipment, land, or buildings, but also the cost of required working capital (receivables and inventories) or even research and development costs, if some technological advance is a prerequisite. It is important to realize that the present book value of the asset being replaced should not be considered at all since these are "sunk costs." However, the cash salvage value or the tax recovery through a capital loss on assets that are being replaced are valid deductions from investment costs since they reduce the amount of the new investment. The *net investment* includes only controllable cash expenditures; that is, costs incurred if management chooses the alternative in

[1] For a more complete evaluation of business figures, see Robert N. Anthony, *Management Accounting: Text and Cases,* Irwin, 1956.

question and which will not be incurred if the alternative is discarded.

Annual Savings. The amount of savings is the added future *cash* saving to be earned. The net cash flow is the relevant consideration, not the accounting definition of earnings. Cash flow can be defined as Net Profit after Taxes plus Depreciation. Cash savings are often derived from two sources: lower operating costs and added cash income from increased sales. The taxable income should first be calculated, subtracting the allowable depreciation charge from cash operating savings. The added income taxes to be paid on the incremental earnings must be deducted. The appropriate tax rate (usually 50%) should be applied to taxable income to calculate the tax payment. The depreciation can then be added back to the net profit after tax.

Economic Life. The life of an investment is the period during which the projected annual cash savings will continue to be realized. The physical life of the asset involved is rarely the factor determining this, and other considerations are usually predominant. For example, the ability of the investment to earn the projected savings ceases when the physical plant is made obsolete by new processes, or when the products can no longer be sold. Economic life is difficult to determine, but it is necessary to have an estimate of the number of years over which the investment is likely to prove effective.

Amortization of Investment. A successful investment should permit recovery of the funds initially invested plus a reasonable rate of profit based on the amount invested. In calculating the rate of return, it is necessary to deduct the amortization of investment from cash income to separate the true "profit" on the investment from the amount set aside to offset the cost of the new facilities. Amortization is not the same as bookkeeping depreciation. Depreciation depends upon tax laws which define the number of years over which new equipment can be written off. Amortization depends only upon the economic life of the investment and is defined as:

$$\frac{\text{Net Initial Investment}}{\text{Years of Economic Life}}$$

The payback period, when compared with economic life, gives a quick, but rough, index of the attractiveness of the investment. Comparing payback periods, however, can be misleading if economic lives differ. For instance, a four-year payback is far more attractive if the economic life is fifteen years than if it is five years. The unadjusted rate of return gives an approximation of the rate of return earned on the invested funds. If the investment includes non-depreciable assets such as land or working capital it is usually desirable to include their total in the average investment but not in the amortization adjustment.

Example

Suppose an investment of \$5,000 will yield \$2,750 in annual lowered costs over an expected life of 10 years.

$$\text{Taxable Income} = \text{Cash Savings minus Depreciation}$$
$$= \$2750 - \frac{\$5000}{20 \text{ yrs}} = \$2500$$
$$\text{Cash Flow} = \text{Taxable Income minus Taxes plus Depreciation}$$
$$= \$2500 - (50\% \times \$2500) + \$250 = \$1500$$
$$\text{Payback} = \frac{\text{Net Investment}}{\text{Cash Flow}} = \frac{\$5000}{\$1500} = 3.3 \text{ years}$$
$$\text{Unadjusted Return} = \frac{\text{Cash Flow minus Amortization}}{\text{Average Investment}}$$
$$= \frac{\$1500 - \$500}{\frac{1}{2}(\$5000)} = \frac{\$1000}{\$2500} = 40\%$$

Note that \$250 is used in the payback calculation because of the 20-year depreciation period, while \$500 is used in the return calculation because of the 10-year economic life.

The unadjusted return is a useful concept, but it fails to take into consideration the important fact that a dollar of savings to be generated some time in the future is worth considerably less than a dollar of savings in cash at the present time. The formula weights future savings equally with present savings, ignoring the value of compound interest over the intervening years and thus making investments look better than they really are. A truer and more flexible system can be used by reducing future savings to their "present value."

The Present Value Concept. When long-run investment opportunities are being considered it is important to consider the true factor that reduces the present value of future earnings. If we have a series of future incomes lasting over the expected life of the equipment the rate of interest that discounts these future incomes to give a total that is the exact equivalent of our out-of-pocket immediate investment is necessarily the rate of return the investment will earn.

In actual practice the numerical task of determining the appropriate rate of discount is not too difficult. Tables are available to show the present value of varying sums of income or outgo in the years in the future. Table A entitled "Present Value of $1" shows rates of interest ranging from 1% to 50% and for periods up to 50 years. What is necessary is to schedule the annual incomes and outgoes over the expected life of the equipment, to apply the discount to each year's income, and to determine the rate of interest that makes the present value of all the future incomes equal to the amount of the initial investment. For example:

Suppose an investment of $5,000 will yield $1,500 annual savings before amortization of investment over an expected life of 10 years. The management will approve a project with a rate of return of 15%, if funds are available in the company.

Using the data of Table A we have the following:

Year	*Annual Savings*	*Present Value of $1 at 15%*	*Present Value of Savings*
1	$1,500	.870	$1,305
2	1,500	.756	1,134
3	1,500	.658	987
4	1,500	.572	858
5	1,500	.497	746
6	1,500	.432	648
7	1,500	.376	564
8	1,500	.327	490
9	1,500	.284	426
10	1,500	.247	370
		5.019	$7,528

Accordingly, we judge that the investment more than meets the test, for the outlay of $5,000 will yield, *at present values* in terms of a 15% rate, something over $7,500. If this present value figure were exactly $5,000 (instead of $7,528) we would say the investment would earn, granted the 10-year life and annual savings of $1,500, exactly 15% per year.

Notice that in the simple problem shown here, each year's saving is the same, so that the figure of $7,528 is really the product of $1,500 times the total of Column 3. Table B gives the subtotals for the entries in Table A, so that in the row for "10 years of life" in Table B and at the "15% rate," we find the "cumulative present value" figure of 5.019 which is the factor which when multiplied by $1,500 gives $7,528. However, this table can only be used if each year's net income is the same.

Also using Table B we can in this simple example approximate the true rate of return. Since the factor from Table B times $1,500 will equal $5,000 at the true rate (for 10 years), we look along the 10-year row for such a factor, which should be, of course, 5,000/1,500 or 3.33 which is equal to the payback period. This we locate as between 26% and 28% and so conclude that rather than making 15% on the investment, the return is somewhat over 26%. Or, by looking elsewhere in Table B for the figure 3.33 we find that if the savings run for only eight years the return will be 25%, and that if the investment becomes obsolete in five years, it still will have earned 15% over and above the principal. The flexibility of the present value approach in these simple situations should be apparent.

Suppose the problem be complicated by the need to replace some element of the new machine after five years at a cost of $4,000. The savings figure in the above tabulation for the fifth year now becomes a loss of $2,500, or, put another way, the 10-year total of $7,528 is reduced by the present value of an extra outlay of $4,000 five years hence, which is computed, at the 15% rate, as 4,000 × .497 or $1,988, to give a net present value of $5,540. We would conclude that even with this need for an additional outlay five years hence the proposed investment meets the company's 15% test.

An important feature of the example is that the present value method allows an additional future investment to be considered as another item in the cash flows that are being discounted. This device can be applied in all problems where the alternatives are many and complex. Sometimes, not only must the savings be estimated, but also the useful life of both the new and the old equipment, for the "savings" will persist only so long as the old machine remains in use. At some future year the "savings" will cease as the present machine is replaced and there appears the capital cost of that future replacement—very probably some years before the end of the estimated life of the investment now being considered.

Effect of New Depreciation Methods

The new depreciation methods permitted by the 1956 tax regulations complicate the process of finding present values by using Tables A and B. Under either the sum-of-the-year's digits method or the declining balance method it is necessary first to calculate the exact depreciation for each year, then work out the yearly operating savings, and finally to use Table A to calculate the present value of the cash flow.[2] In order to simplify and speed these computations, supplementary Tables C and D were prepared. Table C is to be used when the sum-of-the-year's digits method is used for depreciating assets for tax purposes and Table D is for use with the declining balance method.

The revised procedure begins with a calculation of the incremental revenues and costs (except for depreciation and taxes) associated with the new investment. If the difference between the incremental revenues and incremental costs is constant over the life of the investment, only one year's figures must be computed. If the difference between revenues and costs varies, the difference must be calculated for each year. The present value of the resulting figures is then found by using the factors from either Table A or B as described earlier. The result of this calculation yields one figure [or sum] which is the present value of the cash flow before depreciation and taxes.

The depreciation and tax adjustment is then made. First, the present value of the depreciation of the investment is found by (1) selecting the discount factor from the row of Table C or D that corresponds to the discount rate being used by the company in evaluating the investment; (2) multiplying the cost of the equipment by the factor thus selected. For example, if a $5,000 investment is to be depreciated over ten years and the required rate is 10 percent, the $5,000 would be multiplied by 0.7010 if the sum-of-the-digit method was being used, or by 0.6853 if the declining balance method was in effect. The present value of the depreciation would be:

Depreciation Method	*Investment*	*Present Value Factor*	*Present Value of Depreciation*
Sum-of-the-year's-digits	$5,000	0.7010	$3,505
Declining balance	$5,000	0.6853	$3,465

Second, the present value of the depreciation just calculated is subtracted from the present value of the cash flow before depreciation and taxes previously obtained. This step leaves the present value of the taxable income from the investment, which is then reduced by the income tax rate. Finally, the present value of depreciation is added back to the net income after tax to obtain the present value of the after-tax cash flow.

The following example illustrates the calculations under the assumptions that (*a*) the investment cost is $5,000; (*b*) the income from the project before depreciation and taxes is $1,500 for ten years; (*c*) the asset will have a life of ten years; (*d*) the tax rate is 50 percent; and (*e*) 15 percent is the minimum return acceptable to management.

	Sum-of-the Digits Method	*Declining Balance Method*
Present value of $1,500 a year for ten years at 15 percent	$7,528	$7,528
Less: Present value of depreciation of $5,000 asset over ten years at 15 percent (Tables C and D)	3,019	2,938
Taxable income	$4,509	$4,590
Less: Taxes	2,754	2,795
Income after taxes	$2,755	$2,795
Add back: Present value of depreciation	3,019	2,938
Present value of cash flow	$5,774	$5,733
Less: Cost of investment	5,000	5,000
Net present value of investment	$ 774	$ 733

The present value of the investment is greater than zero under either method of depreciation and therefore meets the required rate of return.

If one wishes to approximate the exact return on the investment under these methods, he should proceed to test out various rates by trial and error until he arrives at the one bringing the net present value of the investment closest to zero.

[2] The sum-of-the-year's digits method for depreciating assets operates as follows: the sum of the number of years over which the asset is to be depreciated is found (for ten years, $1+2+3+\cdots+9+10=55$). The cost of the asset is then multiplied by a series of fractions whose denominator is the sum obtained above. The numerator for the first year is the number of years over which the asset will be depreciated. Each year thereafter the numerator is one less. For a $10,000 asset to be depreciated over ten years, the first year's depreciation is ($10,000 × 10/55). The second year's depreciation is ($10,000 × 9/55), and so on to the final year, which is ($10,000 × 1/55).
The declining balance method is easier to operate. The percentage applied for tax purposes is twice the approved straight-line rate. If 10 percent is the usual rate, a company could apply 20 percent to the undepreciated balance of the asset each year in order to obtain a depreciation figure. When the undepreciated value of the asset reaches a negligible amount, it is customary to write it off on a straight-line basis.

TABLE A

Present Value of $1

Years Hence	1%	2%	4%	6%	8%	10%	12%	14%	1·5%	16%	18%	20%	22%	24%	25%	26%	28%	30%	35%	40%	45%	50%
1	0.990	0.980	0.962	0.943	0.926	0.909	0.893	0.877	0.870	0.862	0.847	0.833	0.820	0.806	0.800	0.794	0.781	0.769	0.741	0.714	0.690	0.667
2	0.980	0.961	0.925	0.890	0.857	0.826	0.797	0.769	0.756	0.743	0.718	0.694	0.672	0.650	0.640	0.630	0.610	0.592	0.549	0.510	0.476	0.444
3	0.971	0.942	0.889	0.840	0.794	0.751	0.712	0.675	0.658	0.641	0.609	0.579	0.551	0.524	0.512	0.500	0.477	0.455	0.406	0.364	0.328	0.296
4	0.961	0.924	0.855	0.792	0.735	0.683	0.636	0.592	0.572	0.552	0.516	0.482	0.451	0.423	0.410	0.397	0.373	0.350	0.301	0.260	0.226	0.198
5	0.951	0.906	0.822	0.747	0.681	0.621	0.567	0.519	0.497	0.476	0.437	0.402	0.370	0.341	0.328	0.315	0.291	0.269	0.223	0.186	0.156	0.132
6	0.942	0.888	0.790	0.705	0.630	0.564	0.507	0.456	0.432	0.410	0.370	0.335	0.303	0.275	0.262	0.250	0.227	0.207	0.165	0.133	0.108	0.088
7	0.933	0.871	0.760	0.665	0.583	0.513	0.452	0.400	0.376	0.354	0.314	0.279	0.249	0.222	0.210	0.198	0.178	0.159	0.122	0.095	0.074	0.059
8	0.923	0.853	0.731	0.627	0.540	0.467	0.404	0.351	0.327	0.305	0.266	0.233	0.204	0.179	0.168	0.157	0.139	0.123	0.091	0.068	0.051	0.039
9	0.914	0.837	0.703	0.592	0.500	0.424	0.361	0.308	0.284	0.263	0.225	0.194	0.167	0.144	0.134	0.125	0.108	0.094	0.067	0.048	0.035	0.026
10	0.905	0.820	0.676	0.558	0.463	0.386	0.322	0.270	0.247	0.227	0.191	0.162	0.137	0.116	0.107	0.099	0.085	0.073	0.050	0.035	0.024	0.017
11	0.896	0.804	0.650	0.527	0.429	0.350	0.287	0.237	0.215	0.195	0.162	0.135	0.112	0.094	0.086	0.079	0.066	0.056	0.037	0.025	0.017	0.012
12	0.887	0.788	0.625	0.497	0.397	0.319	0.257	0.208	0.187	0.168	0.137	0.112	0.092	0.076	0.069	0.062	0.052	0.043	0.027	0.018	0.012	0.008
13	0.879	0.773	0.601	0.469	0.368	0.290	0.229	0.182	0.163	0.145	0.116	0.093	0.075	0.061	0.055	0.050	0.040	0.033	0.020	0.013	0.008	0.005
14	0.870	0.758	0.577	0.442	0.340	0.263	0.205	0.160	0.141	0.125	0.099	0.078	0.062	0.049	0.044	0.039	0.032	0.025	0.015	0.009	0.006	0.003
15	0.861	0.743	0.555	0.417	0.315	0.239	0.183	0.140	0.123	0.108	0.084	0.065	0.051	0.040	0.035	0.031	0.025	0.020	0.011	0.006	0.004	0.002
16	0.853	0.728	0.534	0.394	0.292	0.218	0.163	0.123	0.107	0.093	0.071	0.054	0.042	0.032	0.028	0.025	0.019	0.015	0.008	0.005	0.003	0.002
17	0.844	0.714	0.513	0.371	0.270	0.198	0.146	0.108	0.093	0.080	0.060	0.045	0.034	0.026	0.023	0.020	0.015	0.012	0.006	0.003	0.002	0.001
18	0.836	0.700	0.494	0.350	0.250	0.180	0.130	0.095	0.081	0.069	0.051	0.038	0.028	0.021	0.018	0.016	0.012	0.009	0.005	0.002	0.001	0.001
19	0.828	0.686	0.475	0.331	0.232	0.164	0.116	0.083	0.070	0.060	0.043	0.031	0.023	0.017	0.014	0.012	0.009	0.007	0.003	0.002	0.001	
20	0.820	0.673	0.456	0.312	0.215	0.149	0.104	0.073	0.061	0.051	0.037	0.026	0.019	0.014	0.012	0.010	0.007	0.005	0.002	0.001	0.001	
21	0.811	0.660	0.439	0.294	0.199	0.135	0.093	0.064	0.053	0.044	0.031	0.022	0.015	0.011	0.009	0.008	0.006	0.004	0.002	0.001		
22	0·803	0.647	0.422	0.278	0.184	0.123	0.083	0.056	0.046	0.038	0.026	0.018	0.013	0.009	0.007	0.006	0.004	0.003	0.001	0.001		
23	0.795	0.634	0.406	0.262	0.170	0.112	0.074	0.049	0.040	0.033	0.022	0.015	0.010	0.007	0.006	0.005	0.003	0.002	0.001			
24	0.788	0.622	0.390	0.247	0.158	0.102	0.066	0.043	0.035	0.028	0.019	0.013	0.008	0.006	0.005	0.004	0.003	0.002	0.001			
25	0.780	0.610	0.375	0.233	0.146	0.092	0.059	0.038	0.030	0.024	0.016	0.010	0.007	0.005	0.004	0.003	0.002	0.001	0.001			
26	0.772	0.598	0.361	0.220	0.135	0.084	0.053	0.033	0.026	0.021	0.014	0.009	0.006	0.004	0.003	0.002	0.002	0.001				
27	0.764	0.586	0.347	0.207	0.125	0.076	0.047	0.029	0.023	0.018	0.011	0.007	0.005	0.003	0.002	0.002	0.001	0.001				
28	0.757	0.574	0.333	0.196	0.116	0.069	0.042	0.026	0.020	0.016	0.010	0.006	0.004	0.002	0.002	0.002	0.001	0.001				
29	0.749	0.563	0.321	0.185	0.107	0.063	0.037	0.022	0.017	0.014	0.008	0.005	0.003	0.002	0.002	0.001	0.001	0.001				
30	0.742	0.552	0.308	0.174	0.099	0.057	0.033	0.020	0.015	0.012	0.007	0.004	0.003	0.002	0.001	0.001	0.001					
40	0.672	0.453	0.208	0.097	0.046	0.022	0.011	0.005	0.004	0.003	0.001	0.001										
50	0.608	0.372	0.141	0.054	0.021	0.009	0.003	0.001	0.001	0.001												

TABLE B

Present Value of $1 Received Annually for *N* Years

Years (*N*)	1%	2%	4%	6%	8%	10%	12%	14%	15%	16%	18%	20%	22%	24%	25%	26%	28%	30%	35%	40%	45%	50%
1	0.990	0.980	0.962	0.943	0.926	0.909	0.893	0.877	0.870	0.862	0.847	0.833	0.820	0.806	0.800	0.794	0.781	0.769	0.741	0.714	0.690	0.667
2	1.970	1.942	1.886	1.833	1.783	1.736	1.690	1.647	1.626	1.605	1.566	1.528	1.492	1.457	1.440	1.424	1.392	1.361	1.289	1.224	1.165	1.111
3	2.941	2.884	2.775	2.673	2.577	2.487	2.402	2.322	2.283	2.246	2.174	2.106	2.042	1.981	1.952	1.923	1.868	1.816	1.696	1.589	1.493	1.407
4	3.902	3.808	3.630	3.465	3.312	3.170	3.037	2.914	2.855	2.798	2.690	2.589	2.494	2.404	2.362	2.320	2.241	2.166	1.997	1.849	1.720	1.605
5	4.853	4.713	4.452	4.212	3.993	3.791	3.605	3.433	3.352	3.274	3.127	2.991	2.864	2.745	2.689	2.635	2.532	2.436	2.220	2.035	1.876	1.737
6	5.795	5.601	5.242	4.917	4.623	4.355	4.111	3.889	3.784	3.685	3.498	3.326	3.167	3.020	2.951	2.885	2.759	2.643	2.385	2.168	1.983	1.824
7	6.728	6.472	6.002	5.582	5.206	4.868	4.564	4.288	4.160	4.039	3.812	3.605	3.416	3.242	3.161	3.083	2.937	2.802	2.508	2.263	2.057	1.883
8	7.652	7.325	6.733	6.210	5.747	5.335	4.968	4.639	4.487	4.344	4.078	3.837	3.619	3.421	3.329	3.241	3.076	2.925	2.598	2.331	2.108	1.922
9	8.566	8.162	7.435	6.802	6.247	5.759	5.328	4.946	4.772	4.607	4.303	4.031	3.786	3.566	3.463	3.366	3.184	3.019	2.665	2.379	2.144	1.948
10	9.471	8.983	8.111	7.360	6.710	6.145	5.650	5.216	5.019	4.833	4.494	4.192	3.923	3.682	3.571	3.465	3.269	3.092	2.715	2.414	2.168	1.965
11	10.368	9.787	8.760	7.887	7.139	6.495	5.988	5.453	5.234	5.029	4.656	4.327	4.035	3.776	3.656	3.544	3.335	3.147	2.752	2.438	2.185	1.977
12	11.255	10.575	9.385	8.384	7.536	6.814	6.194	5.660	5.421	5.197	4.793	4.439	4.127	3.851	3.725	3.606	3.387	3.190	2.779	2.456	2.196	1.985
13	12.134	11.343	9.986	8.853	7.904	7.103	6.424	5.842	5.583	5.342	4.910	4.533	4.203	3.912	3.780	3.656	3.427	3.223	2.799	2.468	2.204	1.990
14	13.004	12.106	10.563	9.295	8.244	7.367	6.628	6.002	5.724	5.468	5.008	4.611	4.265	3.962	3.824	3.695	3.459	3.249	2.814	2.477	2.210	1.993
15	13.865	12.849	11.118	9.712	8.559	7.606	6.811	6.142	5.847	5.575	5.092	4.675	4.315	4.001	3.859	3.726	3.483	3.268	2.825	2.484	2.214	1.995
16	14.718	13.578	11.652	10.106	8.851	7.824	6.974	6.265	5.954	5.669	5.162	4.730	4.357	4.033	3.887	3.751	3.503	3.283	2.834	2.489	2.216	1.997
17	15.562	14.292	12.166	10.477	9.122	8.022	7.120	6.373	6.047	5.749	5.222	4.775	4.391	4.059	3.910	3.771	3.518	3.295	2.840	2.492	2.218	1.998
18	16.398	14.992	12.659	10.828	9.372	8.201	7.250	6.467	6.128	5.818	5.273	4.812	4.419	4.080	3.928	3.786	3.529	3.304	2.844	2.494	2.219	1.999
19	17.226	15.678	13.134	11.158	9.604	8.365	7.366	6.550	6.198	5.877	5.316	4.844	4.442	4.097	3.942	3.799	3.539	3.311	2.848	2.496	2.220	1.999
20	18.046	16.351	13.590	11.470	9.818	8.514	7.469	6.623	6.259	5.929	5.353	4.870	4.460	4.110	3.954	3.808	3.546	3.316	2.850	2.497	2.221	1.999
21	18.857	17.011	14.029	11.764	10.017	8.649	7.562	6.687	6.312	5.973	5.384	4.891	4.476	4.121	3.963	3.816	3.551	3.320	2.852	2.498	2.221	2.000
22	19.660	17.658	14.451	12.042	10.201	8.772	7.645	6.743	6.359	6.011	5.410	4.909	4.488	4.130	3.970	3.822	3.556	3.323	2.853	2.498	2.222	2.000
23	20.456	18.292	14.857	12.303	10.371	8.883	7.718	6.792	6.399	6.044	5.432	4.925	4.499	4.137	3.976	3.827	3.559	3.325	2.854	2.499	2.222	2.000
24	21.243	18.914	15.247	12.550	10.529	8.985	7.784	6.835	6.434	6.073	5.451	4.937	4.507	4.143	3.981	3.831	3.562	3.327	2.855	2.499	2.222	2.000
25	22.023	19.523	15.622	12.783	10.675	9.077	7.843	6.873	6.464	6.097	5.467	4.948	4.514	4.147	3.985	3.834	3.564	3.329	2.856	2.499	2.222	2.000
26	22.795	20.121	15.983	13.003	10.810	9.161	7.896	6.906	6.491	6.118	5.480	4.956	4.520	4.151	3.988	3.837	3.566	3.330	2.856	2.500	2.222	2.000
27	23.560	20.707	16.330	13.211	10.935	9.237	7.943	6.935	6.514	6.136	5.492	4.964	4.524	4.154	3.990	3.839	3.567	3.331	2.856	2.500	2.222	2.000
28	24.316	21.281	16.663	13.406	11.051	9.307	7.984	6.961	6.534	6.152	5.502	4.970	4.528	4.157	3.992	3.840	3.568	3.331	2.857	2.500	2.222	2.000
29	25.066	21.844	16.984	13.591	11.158	9.370	8.022	6.983	6.551	6.166	5.510	4.975	4.531	4.159	3.994	3.841	3.569	3.332	2.857	2.500	2.222	2.000
30	25.808	22.396	17.292	13.765	11.258	9.427	8.055	7.003	6.566	6.177	5.517	4.979	4.534	4.160	3.995	3.842	3.569	3.332	2.857	2.500	2.222	2.000
40	32.835	27.355	19.793	15.046	11.925	9.779	8.244	7.105	6.642	6.234	5.548	4.997	4.544	4.166	3.999	3.846	3.571	3.333	2.857	2.500	2.222	2.000
50	39.196	31.424	21.482	15.762	12.234	9.915	8.304	7.133	6.661	6.246	5.554	4.999	4.545	4.167	4.000	3.846	3.571	3.333	2.857	2.500	2.222	2.000

TABLE C

The Present Value of the Depreciation of $1 of Assets Depreciated by the Sum-of-the-year's Digits Method over N Years

Years (N)	1%	2%	4%	6%	8%	10%	12%	14%	15%	16%	18%	20%	22%	24%	26%	28%	30%	35%	40%	45%	50%
1......																					
2......																					
3......	0.9836	0.9676	0.9371	0.9083	0.8810	0.8552	0.8308	0.8076	0.7964	0.7855	0.7646	0.7446	0.7256	0.7074	0.6901	0.6735	0.6577	0.6210	0.5880	0.5580	0.5309
4......	0.9803	0.9613	0.9253	0.8915	0.8598	0.8301	0.8022	0.7759	0.7633	0.7511	0.7277	0.7056	0.6847	0.6649	0.6461	0.6282	0.6112	0.5723	0.5377	0.5068	0.4790
5......	0.9771	0.9551	0.9136	0.8751	0.8394	0.8063	0.7751	0.7461	0.7324	0.7190	0.6936	0.6698	0.6474	0.6263	0.6064	0.5876	0.5699	0.5295	0.4941	0.4629	0.4351
6......	0.9739	0.9490	0.9022	0.8593	0.8197	0.7832	0.7494	0.7181	0.7033	0.6891	0.6620	0.6368	0.6132	0.5912	0.5705	0.5511	0.5329	0.4918	0.4562	0.4251	0.3977
7......	0.9704	0.9429	0.8910	0.8438	0.8007	0.7613	0.7251	0.6918	0.6761	0.6610	0.6326	0.6063	0.5819	0.5592	0.5380	0.5182	0.4998	0.4584	0.4230	0.3923	0.3655
8......	0.9676	0.9368	0.8800	0.8288	0.7824	0.7403	0.7019	0.6669	0.6505	0.6348	0.6053	0.5782	0.5531	0.5299	0.5085	0.4885	0.4699	0.4287	0.3937	0.3637	0.3377
9......	0.9644	0.9308	0.8693	0.8142	0.7648	0.7202	0.6799	0.6434	0.6264	0.6102	0.5799	0.5521	0.5266	0.5032	0.4816	0.4616	0.4430	0.4022	0.3678	0.3386	0.3134
10......	0.9613	0.9249	0.8587	0.7800	0.7477	0.7010	0.6591	0.6213	0.6038	0.5871	0.5561	0.5280	0.5022	0.4787	0.4570	0.4371	0.4187	0.3784	0.3448	0.3164	0.2922
11......	0.9581	0.9190	0.8483	0.7861	0.7313	0.6826	0.6392	0.6003	0.5824	0.5655	0.5340	0.5055	0.4797	0.4561	0.4346	0.4148	0.3966	0.3571	0.3243	0.2968	0.2734
12......	0.9550	0.9132	0.8381	0.7727	0.7154	0.6649	0.6203	0.5806	0.5623	0.5451	0.5133	0.4847	0.4588	0.4353	0.4139	0.3944	0.3765	0.3378	0.3059	0.2793	0.2568
13......	0.9519	0.9075	0.8281	0.7596	0.7000	0.6480	0.6022	0.5618	0.5434	0.5259	0.4939	0.4652	0.4394	0.4161	0.3950	0.3757	0.3581	0.3203	0.2893	0.2636	0.2419
14......	0.9489	0.9018	0.8183	0.7468	0.6852	0.6317	0.5851	0.5441	0.5254	0.5079	0.4758	0.4471	0.4214	0.3983	0.3775	0.3585	0.3413	0.3044	0.2743	0.2495	0.2287
15......	0.9458	0.8961	0.8087	0.7344	0.6709	0.6162	0.5687	0.5272	0.5085	0.4909	0.4587	0.4302	0.4047	0.3819	0.3613	0.3428	0.3259	0.2899	0.2608	0.2368	0.2167
16......	0.9427	0.8905	0.7992	0.7223	0.6570	0.6012	0.5531	0.5113	0.4924	0.4748	0.4427	0.4143	0.3891	0.3667	0.3464	0.3282	0.3117	0.2766	0.2484	0.2252	0.2059
17......	0.9397	0.8850	0.7899	0.7105	0.6437	0.5868	0.5381	0.4961	0.4772	0.4596	0.4277	0.3995	0.3746	0.3524	0.3326	0.3147	0.2986	0.2644	0.2371	0.2147	0.1961
18......	0.9367	0.8795	0.7808	0.6991	0.6307	0.6730	0.5239	0.4817	0.4629	0.4452	0.4135	0.3856	0.3610	0.3392	0.3197	0.3022	0.2865	0.2532	0.2267	0.2051	0.1872
19......	0.9337	0.8741	0.7719	0.6879	0.6182	0.5597	0.5103	0.4680	0.4492	0.4317	0.4001	0.3725	0.3483	0.3268	0.3077	0.2906	0.2752	0.2429	0.2172	0.1962	0.1790
20......	0.9307	0.8687	0.7631	0.6770	0.6061	0.5470	0.4972	0.4550	0.4362	0.4188	0.3875	0.3602	0.3364	0.3153	0.2965	0.2798	0.2648	0.2333	0.2084	0.1881	0.1714
21......	0.9277	0.8634	0.7544	0.6664	0.5943	0.5347	0.4848	0.4426	0.4239	0.4066	0.3756	0.3487	0.3251	0.3044	0.2861	0.2698	0.2551	0.2245	0.2002	0.1807	0.1645
22......	0.9248	0.8581	0.7459	0.6560	0.5830	0.5229	0.4728	0.4308	0.4122	0.3950	0.3643	0.3378	0.3146	0.2943	0.2763	0.2604	0.2461	0.2162	0.1927	0.1737	0.1581
23......	0.9218	0.8529	0.7376	0.6459	0.5720	0.5115	0.4614	0.4195	0.4010	0.3840	0.3536	0.3274	0.3047	0.2848	0.2672	0.2516	0.2376	0.2085	0.1857	0.1673	0.1522
24......	0.9189	0.8477	0.7294	0.6361	0.5613	0.5005	0.4504	0.4087	0.3904	0.3735	0.3435	0.3177	0.2953	0.2758	0.2586	0.2433	0.2297	0.2014	0.1792	0.1613	0.1467
25......	0.9160	0.8425	0.7214	0.6265	0.5510	0.4899	0.4399	0.3984	0.3802	0.3635	0.3340	0.3085	0.2865	0.2673	0.2505	0.2356	0.2223	0.1947	0.1731	0.1558	0.1415
26......	0.9130	0.8375	0.7135	0.6171	0.5410	0.4798	0.4298	0.3886	0.3705	0.3540	0.3248	0.2998	0.2782	0.2594	0.2429	0.2283	0.2153	0.1884	0.1674	0.1505	0.1368
27......	0.9102	0.8324	0.7057	0.6080	0.5312	0.4699	0.4201	0.3791	0.3613	0.3450	0.3161	0.2915	0.2703	0.2518	0.2357	0.2214	0.2087	0.1825	0.1620	0.1457	0.1323
28......	0.9073	0.8274	0.6981	0.5991	0.5218	0.4604	0.4108	0.3701	0.3525	0.3363	0.3079	0.2836	0.2628	0.2447	0.2289	0.2149	0.2025	0.1769	0.1570	0.1411	0.1281
29......	0.9044	0.8225	0.6906	0.5904	0.5127	0.4513	0.4019	0.3615	0.3440	0.3281	0.3000	0.2761	0.2557	0.2380	0.2224	0.2088	0.1967	0.1717	0.1523	0.1368	0.1241
30......	0.9016	0.8176	0.6832	0.5819	0.5039	0.4424	0.3933	0.3533	0.3360	0.3202	0.2925	0.2690	0.2489	0.2315	0.2164	0.2030	0.1912	0.1668	0.1479	0.1328	0.1204
40......	0.8738	0.7710	0.6161	0.5072	0.4280	0.3685	0.3227	0.2865	0.2712	0.2574	0.2334	0.2134	0.1965	0.1821	0.1696	0.1587	0.1490	0.1294	0.1143	0.1024	0.0927
50......	0.8474	0.7285	0.5592	0.4476	0 3703	0.3144	0.2725	0.2401	0.2266	0.2145	0.1937	0.1765	0.1620	0.1498	0.1392	0.1301	0.1220	0.1056	0.0931	0.0833	—

Source: Adapted from *Tables for the Analysis of Capital Expenditures*, by H. J. Bracken, Jr., and Charles Christenson. Used by permission.

TABLE D

The Present Value of the Depreciation of $1 of Assets Depreciated by the Declining Balance Method over N Years

Years (N)	1%	2%	4%	6%	8%	10%	12%	14%	15%	16%	18%	20%	22%	24%	26%	28%	30%	35%	40%	45%	50%
1......																					
2......																					
3......	0.9858	0.9719	0.9453	0.9200	0.8960	0.8732	0.8515	0.8308	0.8209	0.8110	0.7922	0.7742	0.7569	0.7404	0.7246	0.7094	0.6949	0.6609	0.6301	0.6019	0.5761
4......	0.9816	0.9638	0.9299	0.8982	0.8684	0.8404	0.8141	0.7893	0.7775	0.7659	0.7438	0.7229	0.7031	0.6842	0.6664	0.6494	0.6332	0.5960	0.5628	0.5330	0.5062
5......	0.9776	0.9561	0.9156	0.8781	0.8433	0.8110	0.7809	0.7528	0.7394	0.7265	0.7019	0.6788	0.6571	0.6367	0.6175	0.5993	0.5821	0.5431	0.5088	0.4785	0.4516
6......	0.9736	0.9484	0.9013	0.8583	0.8188	0.7825	0.7491	0.7182	0.7036	0.6895	0.6630	0.6382	0.6152	0.5937	0.5735	0.5547	0.5370	0.4971	0.4627	0.4325	0.4061
7......	0.9697	0.9410	0.8878	0.8398	0.7961	0.7564	0.7202	0.6870	0.6714	0.6565	0.6284	0.6025	0.5786	0.5564	0.5357	0.5165	0.4985	0.4585	0.4243	0.3948	0.3691
8......	0.9658	0.9335	0.8744	0.8214	0.7740	0.7312	0.6925	0.6574	0.6410	0.6254	0.5963	0.5695	0.5450	0.5224	0.5015	0.4821	0.4642	0.4245	0.3910	0.3623	0.3376
9......	0.9620	0.9263	0.8615	0.8042	0.7533	0.7078	0.6671	0.6305	0.6135	0.5974	0.5674	0.5401	0.5152	0.4924	0.4715	0.4522	0.4344	0.3954	0.3627	0.3350	0.3112
10......	0.9581	0.9191	0.8487	0.7872	0.7331	0.6853	0.6428	0.6050	0.5876	0.5710	0.5405	0.5129	0.4879	0.4651	0.4443	0.4252	0.4077	0.3695	0.3378	0.3111	0.2884
11......	0.9543	0.9120	0.8364	0.7710	0.7141	0.6643	0.6204	0.5816	0.5638	0.5470	0.5162	0.4884	0.4634	0.4408	0.4202	0.4014	0.3842	0.3469	0.3163	0.2906	0.2688
12......	0.9505	0.9050	0.8242	0.7552	0.6957	0.6441	0.5990	0.5594	0.5414	0.5245	0.4934	0.4657	0.4409	0.4185	0.3982	0.3797	0.3629	0.3267	0.2971	0.2724	0.2516
13......	0.9468	0.8981	0.8125	0.7401	0.6783	0.6252	0.5791	0.5390	0.5209	0.5038	0.4727	0.4451	0.4205	0.3984	0.3785	0.3604	0.3440	0.3089	0.2802	0.2565	0.2365
14......	0.9430	0.8912	0.8009	0.7253	0.6614	0.6069	0.5602	0.5197	0.5014	0.4844	0.4534	0.4260	0.4017	0.3799	0.3604	0.3428	0.3268	0.2927	0.2651	0.2423	0.2231
15......	0.9393	0.8845	0.7897	0.7112	0.6454	0.5899	0.5425	0.5017	0.4834	0.4664	0.4356	0.4085	0.3845	0.3632	0.3441	0.3269	0.3113	0.2782	0.2516	0.2296	0.2112
16......	0.9356	0.8778	0.7787	0.6973	0.6299	0.5734	0.5256	0.4847	0.4665	0.4495	0.4190	0.3922	0.3686	0.3477	0.3290	0.3123	0.2971	0.2651	0.2393	0.2182	0.2005
17......	0.9320	0.8712	0.7680	0.6841	0.5152	0.5579	0.5098	0.4689	0.4507	0.4339	0.4036	0.3772	0.3541	0.3336	0.3153	0.2990	0.2842	0.2532	0.2283	0.2079	0.1909
18......	0.9283	0.8647	0.7574	0.6712	0.6009	0.5430	0.4947	0.4539	0.4358	0.4191	0.3892	0.3632	0.3405	0.3204	0.3026	0.2867	0.2724	0.2423	0.2182	0.1985	0.1821
19......	0.9247	0.8583	0.7472	0.6588	0.5874	0.5289	0.4805	0.4397	0.4220	0.4054	0.3757	0.3503	0.3280	0.3084	0.2910	0.2755	0.2615	0.2323	0.2090	0.1899	0.1742
20......	0.9211	0.8519	0.7371	0.6466	0.5742	0.5154	0.4670	0.4265	0.4088	0.3924	0.3633	0.3382	0.3163	0.2971	0.2801	0.2650	0.2515	0.2231	0.2005	0.1821	0.1669
21......	0.9175	0.8457	0.7273	0.6350	0.5617	0.5026	0.4542	0.4140	0.3965	0.3803	0.3516	0.3269	0.3055	0.2867	0.2701	0.2554	0.2422	0.2146	0.1927	0.1749	0.1601
22......	0.9140	0.8394	0.7177	0.6236	0.5495	0.4902	0.4420	0.4022	0.3948	0.3688	0.3405	0.3163	0.2953	0.2770	0.2608	0.2464	0.2336	0.2068	0.1855	0.1682	0.1540
23......	0.9105	0.8333	0.7083	0.6126	0.5379	0.4785	0.4305	0.3910	0.3738	0.3580	0.3302	0.3064	0.2859	0.2679	0.2521	0.2381	0.2256	0.1995	0.1788	0.1621	0.1482
24......	0.9069	0.8272	0.6991	0.6019	0.5267	0.4672	0.4194	0.3803	0.3634	0.3478	0.3205	0.2971	0.2770	0.2594	0.2440	0.2303	0.2181	0.1927	0.1726	0.1564	0.1429
25......	0.9035	0.8212	0.6901	0.5916	0.5159	0.4565	0.4090	0.3703	0.3535	0.3382	0.3113	0.2884	0.2687	0.2515	0.2364	0.2230	0.2111	0.1864	0.1669	0.1510	0.1380
26......	0.8999	0.8153	0.6813	0.5815	0.5055	0.4462	0.3990	0.3607	0.3442	0.3291	0.3026	0.2801	0.2608	0.2440	0.2292	0.2162	0.2046	0.1804	0.1614	0.1460	0.1334
27......	0.8965	0.8095	0.6727	0.5718	0.4955	0.4364	0.3895	0.3516	0.3353	0.3205	0.2944	0.2723	0.2534	0.2369	0.2225	0.2098	0.1984	0.1749	0.1563	0.1414	0.1291
28......	0.8931	0.8037	0.6642	0.5624	0.4858	0.4269	0.3804	0.3430	0.3269	0.3123	0.2867	0.2650	0.2464	0.2303	0.2162	0.2037	0.1927	0.1697	0.1516	0.1370	0.1250
29......	0.8897	0.7980	0.6560	0.5532	0.4765	0.4178	0.3718	0.3348	0.3189	0.3045	0.2793	0.2580	0.2398	0.2240	0.2102	0.1980	0.1872	0.1648	0.1471	0.1329	0.1212
30......	0.8863	0.7923	0.6479	0.5443	0.4675	0.4091	0.3634	0.3269	0.3113	0.2971	0.2723	0.2514	0.2335	0.2181	0.2046	0.1927	0.1821	0.1601	0.1429	0.1291	0.1177
40......	0.8536	0.7392	0.5758	0.4678	0.3928	0.3382	0.2971	0.2649	0.2514	0.2392	0.2180	0.2004	0.1854	0.1726	0.1614	0.1516	0.1429	0.1250	0.1111	0.1000	0.0909
50......	0.8227	0.6918	0.5169	0.4093	0.3383	0.2883	0.2513	0.2229	0.2110	0.2004	0.1820	0.1668	0.1539	0.1429	0.1334	0.1250	0.1177	0.1026	0.0909	0.0816	—

Source: Adapted from *Tables for The Analysis of Capital Expenditures*, by H. J. Bracken, Jr., and Charles Christenson. Used by permission.

APPENDIX C

Reference Sources

I. Periodicals of General Interest for all Six Industries

Barron's, w., \$15, Barron's Publishing Co., 40 New St., New York.

Business Week, w., \$7, McGraw-Hill Pub. Co., 330 W. 42nd St., New York.

Forbes, s-m, \$7.50, B. C. Forbes and Sons Pub. Co., 80 Fifth Ave., New York.

Fortune, m., \$10, Time, Inc., Time and Life Bldg., Rockefeller Plaza, New York.

Harvard Business Review, bi-m., \$10, Harvard Business Review, Soldiers Field, Boston 63, Massachusetts.

Wall Street Journal, 5 times a week, \$24, Dow Jones & Co., Inc., 44 Broad St., New York.

II. Furniture Industry

A. Films

The Bounty of the Forest, color; source: Western Pine Association, Yeon Bldg., Portland 4, Oregon.

Mahogany—Wood of the Ages, color; source: Mahogany Assoc. Inc., 75 E. Wacker Drive, Chicago 1, Ill.

Skilled Hands, color; source: Baker Furniture Inc., Grand Rapids, Mich.

B. Periodicals

Home Furnishings Daily, 5 times a week, \$9, Fairchild Publications, Inc., 7 E. 12th St., New York 3.

National Furniture Review, m., \$3, National Retail Furniture Association, 666 Lake Shore Drive, Chicago, Ill.

C. Specific References

Anderson, I. D. and Duncan, D. J., *Retail Furniture Stores, 1937–1941,* National Retail Furniture Association, 1942.

Anglo-American Council on Productivity, *Productivity Team Report on Furniture,* April 1952.

Bureau of the Census, *Annual Survey of Manufacturers.*

Bureau of Labor Statistics, Bulletin 998, *Occupational Outlook Handbook,* 1950.

Bureau of Labor Statistics, *Handbook of Labor Statistics.*

Bureau of Labor Statistics, *Monthly Labor Review,* "Earnings in the Household Furniture Industry, early 1954."

Chateauneuf, R., "Modern Quality Control," *Industrial Quality Control,* Sept. 1960.

Davis, Kenneth R., *Furniture Marketing,* University of N. Carolina Press, Chapel Hill, N.C., 1957.

Fertig, Arthur & Co., "The Retail Furniture Business," *Annual Reviews, 1931–1944.*

Hjorth, H., *Machine Woodworking,* Bruce Publishing Co., 1937.

Hooper, R., *Modern Furniture Making and Design,* Manual Arts Press, Peoria, Ill., 1939.

Killam, E. R., *Household Furniture, A Statistical Handbook,* Bureau of Foreign and Domestic Commerce, Industrial Series No. 8, June 1944.

Mohr, F. W., "Earnings in Wood Household Furniture," *Monthly Labor Review,* Dec. 1959.

National Association of Furniture Manufacturers, *Annual Experience Report,* 1945.

National Retail Furniture Association, *Annual Furniture Store Operating Report.*

National Retail Furniture Association, *What Is a Furniture Store?* Revised, January 1946.

National Wholesale Furniture Association, *The Facts of Life About Furniture Wholesaling,* 1946.

Printers Ink, "Two Companies Integrate Their Products," Oct. 24, 1958.

Seidman, Frank E., *Retailing Daily,* Jan. 10, 1957, Fairchild Publications, Inc.

Stamey, A. W., *Retailing Daily,* Dec. 18–21, 1956.

III. Textile Industry

A. Films

Bedtime for Jamie, color; source: Association Films, Broad at Elm, Richfield, New Jersey.

Singing Needles, color; source: Singer Sewing Machine Co., Industrial Sales Dept., 149 Broadway, New York 6.

Patterns of Progress, color; source: Burlington Industries, 1430 Broadway, New York 6.

B. Periodicals

Textile Hi-Lights, The American Cotton Manufacturers Institute, Inc., 1501 Johnston Bldg., Charlotte 2, North Carolina.

Textile World, m., $2, McGraw-Hill Pub. Co., 330 W. 42nd St., New York.

C. Specific References

American Wool and Cotton Reporter, Annual Review Statistics and Forecast Number (Second issue in January) and Official Statistics of Textile Corporations (late in July).

Backman, J. and Gainsbrugh, M. R., *Economics of the Textile Industry,* National Industrial Conference Board, 1946.

Bendure, Z. and Pfeiffer, G., *America's Fabrics,* Macmillan Co., 1946.

Business and Defense Services Administration, *Textile Outlook for the Sixties,* 1960.

Howell, L. D., *Changes in American Textile Industry,* U.S. Dept. of Agriculture, Agricultural Marketing Service, Marketing Research Div., Technical Bulletin No. 1210, November 1959.

Journal of Commerce, Annual Textile Number, Southern Mill Number, Worth Street Number, and Annual Raw Cotton Number.

Merrill, G. R.; Macormac, A. R.; and Mauersberger, H. R., *American Cotton Handbook,* American Cotton Handbook Co., 1941.

Surveys and Research Corporation (for the Business and Defense Services Administration), *Comparative Fabric Production Costs in the United States and Four Other Foreign Countries,* U.S. Govt. Printing Office, 1961.

Textile Organon, Annual Review Number (Late in January).

IV. Plastics Industry

A. Films

The Shape of Things to Come, 35 min., color, produced by Films of Industry; source: Boonton Molding Co., Boonton, New Jersey.

The World That Nature Forgot, color; source: Monsanto Chemical Co., 1700 S. Second St., St. Louis, Mo.

Methods of Processing Plastics Materials, Audio Visual Center, University of Michigan, Ann Arbor, Michigan.

B. Periodicals

Modern Plastics, m., $8, Modern Plastics, Inc., 575 Madison Ave., New York, 22.

Chemical Engineering, bi-w., $25, McGraw-Hill, New York.

C. Specific References

Axe-Houghton Economic Studies, *Chemicals, The Fastest Growing Major Industry,* E. W. Axe and Co., New York, 1953.

Clapp, William Howard, and Clark, Donald Sherman, *Engineering Materials and Processes, Metals and Plastics,* International Textbook Co., 2nd. ed., Scranton, 1949.

Cooling, B. F., *World Survey of Plastics,* U.S. Deparment of Commerce, Bus. and Defense Services Admin., Washington, D.C., 1959.

Dearle, D. A., *Plastic Molding and Plant Management,* Chemical Pub. Co., Brooklyn, 1944.

DuMond, Theodore C., *Fabricated Materials and Parts,* Reinhold, New York, 1953.

Kinney, Gilbert F., *Engineering Properties and Applications of Plastics,* Wiley, New York, 1957.

Materials in Design Engineering, pp. 185–226, Reinhold, Mid-Nov. 1960.

Merrill Lynch, Pierce, Fenner and Beane, *Chemicals,* 1951.

Modern Plastics Encyclopedia, annual issues, Modern Plastics, Inc., 575 Madison Ave., New York 22.

Modern Plastics Encyclopedia and Engineer's Handbook, Plastics Catalogue Corp., New York, 1953.

Morris, Joseph L., *Modern Manufacturing Processes,* Prentice-Hall, Englewood Cliffs, N.J., 1955.

Rohm and Haas Co., *Chemicals for Industry,* Rohm & Haas, Philadelphia, 1959.

Simonds, Herbert R., *Source Book of the New Plastics,* Reinhold, New York, 2 vols., 1959 and 1961.

Standard and Poor, Industry Surveys, *Chemicals,* April 29, 1954.

Tarnell Co. Inc., *It's Your Money,* The Dow Chemical Co., 1952.

Tarnell Co., Inc., *The Plastics Molding Industry,* 1956.

The Anglo-American Council on Productivity, *Plastics Moulding,* British Productivity Team, London, 1953.

The First National Bank of Boston, *The Plastics Industry in New England,* 1949.

The Society of the Plastics Industry, Inc., *Plastics, The Story of an Industry,* New York, 1952.

The U.S. President's Materials Policy Commission, *Resources for Freedom,* Washington, 1952, Vol. II.

U.S. Tariff Commission, *Plastics Products,* War Changes in Industry Series, Report No. 28, Washington, 1948.

U.S. Tariff Commission, *Synthetic Organic Chemicals,* Report No. 190, Washington, 1953.

Walsh, John, "Progress of the Plastics Industry" speech dated June 4, 1953, Boston Security Analysts Society.

V. Electronics Industry

A. Films

453 Steps to Electronic Progress through Transistor Quality, color; source: Radio Corporation of America, Sales Department, Needham, Massachusetts.

B. Periodicals

Electronics, $5, McGraw-Hill Pub. Co., 330 W. 42nd St., New York.

Electronic News, $10, Fairchild Publications, Inc., 7 E. 12th St., New York 4.

C. Specific References

Electronics Industries Association (EIA), *Electronic Industries 1962 Yearbook,* 1721 De Sales St., N.W., Washington 6, D.C.

Harris, William B., "The Electronic Business," *Fortune,* April 1957.

Radio Corporation of America, *Thirty Years of Pioneering and Progress in Radio and Television,* New York, 1949.

Small Business Administration, *A Study of Small Business in the Electronics Industry,* 1962.

Television Factbook, Radio News Bureau, Wyatt Building, Washington 5, D.C.

U.S. Department of Commerce, Bureau of Labor Statistics, *Case Study Data on Productivity and Factory Performance, Radio and Television Manufacturing,* February 1952.

VI. Steel Industry

A. Films

Modern Steelmaking, color; source: United States Steel, New York Film Distribution, 71 Broadway, New York 6.

B. Periodicals

Blast Furnace and Steel Plant, $2, Steel Publications, Inc., 624 Grant Bldg., Pittsburgh 30, Pa.

Iron and Steel Engineer, Association of Iron and Steel Engineers, 1010 Empire Bldg., Pittsburgh 22, Pa.

Steel Facts, m., American Iron and Steel Institute, 150 E. 42nd St., New York 17.

Steel, w., $10, Penton Publishing Co., Penton Bldg., Cleveland 13, Ohio.

Iron Age, w., $10, Chilton Co., Inc., Chestnut and 56th Sts., Philadelphia 39, Pa.

Steelways, m, American Iron and Steel Institute, 150 E. 42nd St., New York 17.

C. Specific References

American Iron and Steel Institute (AISA), *Annual Statistical Reports,* 150 East 42nd Street, New York 17.

American Iron and Steel Institute (AISA), *Iron and Steel Works Directory of the United States and Canada, 1960,* 150 East 42nd Street, New York 17.

Barloon, Marvin, "Pricing Policy in the Steel Industry," *The Business History Review,* Boston, Sept. 1954.

Isard and Capron, "The Future Locational Pattern of Iron and Steel Production in the United States," *Journal of Political Economy,* April 1949.

Moore, David D., *Cost Comparisons of the Open Hearth and Electric Furnace,* Battelle Memorial Institute, 1954.

Rueckel, W. C. and Irvin, J. W., "Economic Aspects of the Oxygen Converter," *Iron and Steel Engineer,* March 1955.

Sutch, D. A. and Manley, H. C., "Electric Furnace or Cupola, Basic Oxygen Converter for the Non-Integrated Steel Plant," *Iron and Steel Engineer.*

U.S. Department of Labor, Bureau of Labor Statistics, *Man-Hours per Unit of Output in the Basic Steel Industry,* 1962.

VII. Oil Industry

A. Films

Refinery at Work, 30 min., color; source: Humble Oil and Refinery Co.

Hidden Highways, 42 min., color; source: The Sinclair Pipeline Co., Sinclair Bldg., Independence, Kansas.

Birth of an Oilfield, 30 min., color; source: The Shell Oil Film Library, 160–07 Northern Blvd., Flushing 58, N.Y.

On Stream, reel one, 55 min., color, produced by Cate and McGlone, source: Socony-Mobil Co., New York City.

Highway for Oil, 30 min. color; source: Humble Pipeline Co., Houston 1, Texas.

B. Periodicals

Hydrocarbon Processing, m., $3, Gulf Pub. Co., Houston, Texas.

Oil and Gas Journal, w., $6, Petroleum Publishing Co., 211 S. Cheyenne Ave., Tulsa 1, Okla.

Petroleum Management, m., $4, Petroleum Engineer Pub. Co., Dallas, Texas.

C. Specific References

Cheveney, John E., "Putting Linear Programming to Work," *Oil and Gas Journal,* March 21, 1960.

Coqueron, Frederick G., *Annual Financial Analysis of the Petroleum Industry,* The Chase Manhattan Bank.

De Chazeau, M. G. and Kahn, A. E., *Integration and Competition in the Petroleum Industry,* Yale University Press, New Haven, 1959.

DeGolyer and MacNaughton, *Twentieth Century Petroleum Statistics,* annual, Dallas, Texas.

Grayson, Charles J., *Decisions under Uncertainty,* Harvard Business School, 1960.

Manne, Alan S. *Scheduling of Petroleum Refinery Operations,* Harvard University Press, 1956.

McLean, John G. and Haigh, Robert Wm., *The Growth of Integrated Oil Companies,* Harvard Business School, 1954.

Merrill Lynch, Pierce, Fenner and Beane, *Petroleum,* N.Y.

Nelson, W. L., *Costimating, Oil and Gas Journal,* series.

Petroleum Facts and Figures, American Petroleum Institute, 50 W. 50th St., N.Y. 20.

Pogue, J. E. and Hill, K. E. et al., *Future Growth and Financial Requirements of the World Petroleum Industry,* The Chase Manhattan Bank, New York, 1956.

Primer of Oil and Gas Production, American Petroleum Institute, New York, 1954.

Weinberg, Edgar, and Rothberg, Herman J. *A Case Study of a Modernized Petroleum Refinery,* Bureau of Labor Statistics, Washington, D.C., 1957.

Williamson, H. F. and Daum, A. R., *The American Petroleum Industry,* Northwestern University Press, Evanston, Ill., 1959.

Woodruff, John, *A Primer of Oil Well Drilling,* American Association of Oilwell Drilling Contractors, 1951.

Index of Cases